# Derby County

## The Complete Record 1884-2006

# Derby County

## The Complete Record 1884-2006

Every game, every scorer, every player and every attendance.
Memorable matches, complete history, pen pictures, manager profiles, appearance records

Gerald Mortimer

DB PUBLISHING

First published in Great Britain in 2006 by The Breedon Books Publishing Company Limited Breedon House, 3 The Parker Centre, Derby, DE21 4SZ.

Paperback reprint published in Great Britain in 2012 by The Derby Books Publishing Company Limited, 3 The Parker Centre, Derby, DE21 4SZ.



ISBN 978-1-78091-150-2

# Contents

# Foreword

**By Peter Gadsby**
**Chairman of Derby County**

Everybody with a passing interest in Derby County knows about the 1946 FA Cup win and the two League Championships in 1972 and 1975. There have been great years and bad years. More than most clubs, the Rams have steered an erratic course in the 122 years since they were formed as an offshoot of the County Cricket Club.

I know of nobody more suited to guide supporters through the history and statistics than Gerald Mortimer. His concern for the welfare of the club was apparent during his long service with the *Derby Evening Telegraph.*

It gives me particular pleasure to contribute a few words as chairman of Derby County. We start 2006–07 with a new board and a new manager in Billy Davies, all of us aiming to rebuild this club. It is a great honour to be chairman but I must emphasise that the directors, all local people, are equal partners in the enterprise and were encouraged to launch our project by the remarkable level of support at Pride Park.

That support gives Derby County great potential and our aim is to translate that into achievement. The board, management and playing staff will do our best.

Pride Park
July 2006.

# The History of Derby County

Derby County emerged in 1884, born of financial worries, and began by upsetting established local clubs. It was the beginning of an erratic progress, their periods of glory mixed with frequent crises brought on by an inability to manage their affairs. Derbyshire County Cricket Club, formed in 1871, saw possibilities in the increasing popularity of association football, a game produced in the public schools that was finding a wider audience, especially in the north of England. In March 1884, the first Derbyshire Cup final, between Derby Midland and Staveley, attracted around 7,000 to the County Ground on Nottingham Road, the biggest crowd in the area to watch football. As well as giving players and supporters a winter interest, the cricket club scented extra revenue, and the one thing they could offer at the County Ground was ample space.

Discussions began in the spring before Derbyshire embarked on a disastrous cricket season, in which they lost all 10 of their Championship matches. William Morley, a clerk at the Midland Railway, found other enthusiasts and his father, also William and a cricket committee member, formulated a motion. With the cricket club connection, the proposed name was Derbyshire County, but the Derbyshire FA, formed in 1883, objected. In 1884–85, Derby County had an extensive programme of friendly matches, opening with a 6–0 away defeat by Great Lever on 13 September, and were gathering in players. Derby Midland, run by the railway company, were established and alarmed that George Bakewell, their star winger, was one of the first to join the new club. Darley Abbey allowed Ernest Hickinbottom to play, assuming they would benefit from his extra experience: they did not see much of him after that, as he also played for Derby Midland.

Derby's first-ever home League game against West Bromwich Albion on 15 September 1888.

The Rams, as they were named after the mascot of the Sherwood Foresters, the Nottinghamshire and Derbyshire regiment, secured one of the most important results in their history when, in November 1885, they knocked Aston Villa out of the FA Cup. Villa were already a major force, and the victory enabled Derby to attract better opposition for their friendlies and was probably a factor when, in 1888, the Football League was formed, primarily as a way of guaranteeing regular fixtures. Derby were one of the 12 original members, all from Lancashire and the Midlands, and William McGregor of Aston Villa, the moving spirit, had no idea how his creation would expand and flourish. Derby's first genuine star arrived in 1889 when, astonishingly, they signed John Goodall from Preston North End. Goodall, an England forward, shone in the Preston team that won the League and FA Cup double in 1888–89. It is akin to Derby signing Frank Lampard from Chelsea in 2006.

Goodall accelerated the progress of Steve Bloomer, born in Cradley but reared in Derby, where his father had sought work. Bloomer became one of the great figures of English football, a regular international and a prolific scorer. With him in their side, Derby reached three Cup finals in six seasons but lost them all, most humiliatingly in 1902–03, when Bury won 6–0 at the Crystal Palace ground. It remains the most decisive Cup final victory. By then, Derby were in permanent residence at the Baseball Ground, which was to be their home for 102 years until the move to Pride Park.

The Derby County team which played in the 1898 FA Cup final defeat by Nottingham Forest. Standing at back (left to right): J. Methven, A. Latham (trainer). Standing, middle: J.H. Richardson (honorary secretary), J. Fryer, J. Leiper, J. Reilly (director), H. Newbould (secretary-manager). Seated, second row: J. Cox, A. Goodall, J.Turner. Seated, front row: J. Goodall, S. Bloomer, J. Boag, J. Stevenson, H. McQueen.

Derby County in 1928. Back row (left to right): Barclay, Bowers, Scott, Wilkes, Collin, Prince, Smith, Carr. Second row: Bill Bromage (trainer), Ruddy, Cooke, Cooper, Hampton, Bacon, Stephenson, Davison, McDougall. Seated: W.S.Cooper (secretary), Crooks, Malloch, McIntyre, Whitehouse, George Jobey (manager), Bedford, Ramage, Nicholas, J.C. Robson, Harold Wightman (coach). Front: Fereday, Hope, Robinson, Jessop, Barker, Mann, W. Robson, White.

Rams skipper Tommy Cooper tosses up with ex-Rams striker and Newcastle United's captain Harry Bedford.

Financial constraints forced Bloomer's sale to Middlesbrough in 1906, and the following year Derby County were relegated from Division One for the first time. They did not return until Bloomer, by then 36, rejoined them but, as World War One came and went, Derby shuttled between the Divisions. They were not established as a First Division force until George Jobey became manager in 1925. They won promotion in his first season and stayed up, an attractive team with players, especially centre-forwards, renowned around the country. Other clubs wondered how Derby managed to keep such a glittering array, as they were twice runners-up in Division One without being able to secure a major prize. Their questions were answered in 1941 when a joint Football Association and Football League commission met at the Midland Hotel, Derby. In the days of the maximum wage, Derby paid over the odds and were found guilty of financial irregularities throughout Jobey's period in charge. He was banned from football management and five directors were suspended indefinitely.

Derby were one of the clubs to close down when World War Two began in 1939, but the value of football as a release from the stress of war was widely understood so temporary leagues and cups were formed. Through the efforts of two pre-war players, Jack Nicholas and Jack Webb, Derby began to play again in 1941. They entered the League North in 1942–43 and, like all clubs, were allowed to field guest players who happened to be in the area. Aldershot, a military centre, found they had by far the best team in their history as English internationals looked for a game, and the benefit of the system to Derby was also spectacular. Raich Carter and Peter Doherty, two of the greatest inside-forwards of the

King George VI, escorted by Derby skipper Jack Nicholas, shakes hands with Jack Howe before the 1945–46 FA Cup final. Other players visible in the line are, from the left, Reg Harrison, Vic Woodley, Chick Musson and Raich Carter.

1930s, were posted to an RAF rehabilitation unit at Loughborough and Derby was a convenient venue for them. They provided a wonderful treat for wartime crowds and Ted Magner, manager for a significant spell, was able to push through permanent transfers in December 1945. By then, the war was over and, just in time, they were eligible for the 1945–46 FA Cup. Shortage of time after the end of hostilities, first in Europe, then the Far East, meant that the League did not resume until 1946–47 and the first peacetime FA Cup was, for the only time, played over two legs up to the sixth round. With Carter and Doherty in their side, the Rams were a step ahead of their rivals, especially as they were able to surround them with experienced players of the 1930s and newer talent developed during the war. Magner created the team but left in January, allowing Stuart McMillan to lead the Rams to Wembley success over Charlton Athletic.

This also began one of Derby's nine-year cycles. Although they twice broke the British transfer record, to sign Billy Steel and Johnny Morris as successors to Carter and Doherty, a steady decline set in. Derby were fourth in 1948 and third in 1949, but from there the slide gathered momentum towards relegation in 1953. McMillan did not long survive it and his successor Jack Barker, one of Derby's pre-war greats, could not keep them in the Second Division. Nine years after the great day at Wembley, Derby were contemplating Division Three North and their lowest ebb came in December 1955 when, in the FA Cup, Boston United of the Midland League won 6–1 at the Baseball Ground. Despite that shock – and a home defeat by New Brighton a year later – the Third North offered good entertainment for supporters as Harry Storer moulded a team for promotion in 1957. Attendances were good, Derby twice passed 100 goals and morale was restored. Storer and Tim Ward, who followed him as manager

The Rams in the Third Division North, August 1955. Back row (left to right): Geoff Barrowcliffe, Albert Mays, Reg Ryan, Terry Webster, Martin McDonnell, Keith Savin. Front: Ken Harrison, Jack Parry, Alf Ackerman, Jesse Pye, Tommy Powell.

Rams players before the start of 1968–69. Back row (left to right): Pat Wright, Russ Bostock, Ron Webster, Colin Boulton, Les Green, Tony Rhodes, Barry Butlin, Jim Walker. Seated: Alan Durban, Arthur Stewart, Richie Barker, John O'Hare, Kevin Hector, Alan Hinton. On ground: John Richardson, Peter Daniel, John Robson.

in 1962, were restricted by lack of cash and never looked likely to take the next step, back to the First Division.

Someone special was needed and, in 1967, Derby appointed Brian Clough as manager. Clough brought Peter Taylor as his assistant, and between them they transformed what had become a sleepy Second Division club. They had an eye for players and, in 1969, they surged back into Division One. That was just the start, and although they were banned from the UEFA Cup, after finishing fourth in 1970, because of financial irregularities – a recurrent theme – Derby won their first League Championship in 1971–72. In 1973, they reached the semi-finals of the European Cup but Clough, brash as well as brilliant, made enemies in the boardroom. They struck in October 1973 when Clough and Taylor offered their resignations. These were accepted and, 18 months after the League title, the architects of it were out. The wave of protests around the town could not shift chairman Sam Longson and his prime ally, Jack Kirkland. Dave Mackay, Clough's greatest signing, took over as manager and the Derby board did not deserve their luck. Mackay, with Des Anderson as his assistant, finished third, first and fourth but, like Clough and Taylor, the pair were out 18 months after winning the Championship. They asked for a vote of confidence and when that move failed were sacked. It was a staggering performance by the directors, especially when the new chairman, George Hardy, failed in his attempt to bring Clough and Taylor back from Nottingham Forest. Managers and chairmen came and went and Derby lost their First Division place while finances declined, matching their performances on the field.

Football legend Dave Mackay holds aloft the Second Division Championship trophy, 1968–69.

Derby County pictured in August 1975 with the League Championship trophy: Back row (left to right): Des Anderson (assistant manager), Ron Webster, Peter Daniel, Colin Todd, Colin Boulton, Graham Moseley, Jeff Bourne, Steve Powell, Rod Thomas, Henry Newton, Kevin Hector, Gordon Guthrie (physiotherapist). Front: Francis Lee, Charlie George, Bruce Rioch, Roy McFarland, Dave Mackay (manager), Archie Gemmill, David Nish, Roger Davies, Alan Hinton.

The crisis came in 1983–84, when Derby were in the High Court, facing winding-up petitions from the Inland Revenue and Customs and Excise. At the same time, they were heading for another relegation. Stuart Webb, previously secretary, chief executive and a director, took over as chairman and

Roy McFarland, Stuart Webb and Arthur Cox raise their glasses to celebrate Derby's return to the top flight in 1986–87.

enlisted the help of Robert Maxwell to find the £220,000 needed to have the petition lifted. Maxwell, a millionaire publisher, was chairman of Oxford United and installed one of his sons, Ian, as chairman at the Baseball Ground. Nine years after the second Championship, Derby faced their centenary year in Division Three. They had a new manager in Arthur Cox who, by diligent building and successful work in the transfer market, brought the Rams two successive promotions. As soon as Derby were in the First Division, Robert Maxwell arrived as chairman and, despite fifth position in 1989, the problems began. Maxwell regularly criticised the level of support and seemed surprised that Derby fans did not love him. He authorised the signing of Peter Shilton and Mark Wright soon after he took over but also tried to buy Watford and flirted with Tottenham Hotspur. Cox, utterly frustrated, found himself unable to buy or even borrow players. Maxwell announced his intention to sell the club, but not only rejected an offer from Lionel Pickering, he also banned him from the ground. In 1991, Derby managed to pay off Maxwell, but the cost was another relegation, along with the sale of Wright and Dean Saunders to Liverpool. Maxwell then owned Mirror Group Newspapers and, it was later revealed, raided their pension fund to prop up his empire, hopelessly overstretched by a venture into American publishing. Soon after that, he was lost over the side of his yacht and left his family with unmanageable debts.

A new board, under Brian Fearn, remained strapped for cash until Pickering, previously rejected by Maxwell, assumed control with the majority shareholding but did not immediately take the chair. Only after a bitter extraordinary meeting of shareholders in 1994 did that happen. Pickering's money enabled Cox to buy but, although many of the players maintained their value, Derby found it hard to escape from the second tier. They managed two appearances in the Play-offs, the second under Roy McFarland after Cox stood down with a severe back problem, but the appointment of Jim Smith in 1995 brought a change of fortune. Derby were promoted to what was now the FA Premiership in Smith's first season and, with a move to Pride Park already announced, began to settle at that level, with two top-half finishes. When his coach and assistant Steve McClaren left to join Manchester United in February 1999, there was never again the same certainty of touch. Smith's buying, previously infallible, was more erratic, big fees were laid out simply to stay afloat and, once again, the finances were out of control.

Derby had three managers in 2001–02 – Smith, Colin Todd and John Gregory – so it hardly came as a surprise when they lost their Premiership place. The Co-op Bank, finding it increasingly hard to prise answers from Pickering, suddenly pulled the plug on him in October 2003 with a brief receivership. The new board, with John Sleightholme as chairman, it turned out, paid £3 to buy the club. They had no connection with Derby but proclaimed a business plan based around refinancing, which included selling Pride Park Stadium to the Panama-based ABC Corporation and leasing it back.

Although George Burley, initially brought in as a temporary replacement for Gregory, took Derby to another Play-off in 2005, there was widespread dissatisfaction with the board. Their business plan succeeded only in lifting an already alarming debt past £50 million: they lost an extra £20 million in their 30 months. It is one of the most bizarre and inexplicable episodes even in Derby County's history and there was great relief when a local consortium took over in April 2006. It was led by Peter Gadsby, a property developer who, as vice-chairman under Pickering, was responsible for the creation of Pride Park and the Academy at Moor Farm. The combination of a £25 million investment from six new directors and negotiations with a supportive Co-op Bank reduced the debt to under £10 million. There was much to be tidied after the previous regime, but supporters felt that Derby County now had a chance.

Robbie van der Laan's header has just given Derby County automatic promotion to the Premiership in 1995–96.

# Steve Bloomer Dominates

As Victorian England became Edwardian England and moved towards the hideous destruction of World War One, Steve Bloomer dominated the club. From his debut at the age of 18 in 1892 until his retirement as a 41-year-old, Bloomer was the star. Even when Bloomer spent four years with Middlesbrough, supporters wanted him back, as did the manager, Jimmy Methven. He was in the future when Derby County set off in 1884 with a programme of friendly matches interrupted only by the FA Cup and Derbyshire Cup until they became one of the 12 founder members of the League in 1888. Relations with other clubs became strained as the Rams arrived on the scene, especially so with Derby Midland, the railway company side, but the new organisation prevailed and, in 1891, Midland amalgamated with them. Some talented amateurs helped. Benjamin Spilsbury, born at Findern and educated at Repton School, scored their first goal, against Blackburn Olympic. He can also be considered Derby's first international, as he made his debut against Ireland in 1885 while an undergraduate at Cambridge University. John Chevalier, who twice won the FA Cup with Old Etonians, assisted Derby while on the teaching staff at Repton, and Leonard Gillet, a Cup-winner with Old Carthusians, kept goal in Derby's first Cup tie, a 7–0 defeat by Walsall Town. As curate of St Chad's, the Reverend Llewellyn Gwynne may have assisted the development of the young Bloomer. Gwynne played in a Cup tie and, from 1920 to 1946, was Anglican Bishop in Egypt and the Sudan, Derby County's only bishop, although they can also boast a World War One Victoria Cross, Bernard Vann, and four Test cricketers: William Chatterton, William Storer, Frank Sugg and Arnold Warren.

When the League started, without provoking much media reaction, Derby opened with an away win over Bolton Wanderers. Although their leading scorer, Sandy Higgins, was a Scot engaged from Kilmarnock, they relied largely on local players and finished 10th while Preston North End completed the Double, winning the League without defeat and the Cup without conceding a goal. John Goodall, already an England forward, was one of the stars of the Preston side but was about to join Derby. A paragraph in the *Derby Daily Telegraph* in March 1889 carried the startling news, 'We understand it is now definitely decided that John and Archie Goodall will enter into possession of the Plough, London Street, during the first week in May.' The Plough, in what is now London Road, is long gone but the Goodalls, sons of a regular soldier, are established among Derby's major players. John was already held in high regard for his demeanour (Johnny All-Good) as well as his skill. Although born in London, his football developed around Kilmarnock because of his father's postings. Archie was born in Belfast and played for several clubs, including the Rams in early friendlies, before joining Derby from Aston Villa. He played at centre-half, then an attacking position, was fond of field sports and could be a difficult character. He was also good enough to complete 423 games for Derby and still holds the record for consecutive appearances. Even with the brothers, there were bad days, notably an 11–2 Cup defeat by Everton in 1890, but they helped to attract players of the calibre of Jimmy Methven, who was to serve Derby for 31 years, and Johnny McMillan. Bloomer made his debut on the opening day of 1892–93 and although Derby were well aware of his potential, an early appearance was forced on them by a failure to register three players in time. He was there to stay, soon starting towards his total of 332 goals for the club. He first played for England, in the same team as John Goodall, at the County Ground in March 1895 and his goals at all levels made him the major figure in English football. He remains, surely, the greatest player in Derby's history.

The League formed a Second Division in 1892–93, promotion and relegation decided by Test Matches until 1898. In 1895, Derby needed goals from McMillan and Bloomer to preserve their status

Steve Bloomer takes on the Sheffield United defence during the 1899 FA Cup final.

by beating Notts County at the Leicester Fosse ground, but a year later, their first full season at the Baseball Ground, they were runners-up, four points behind the Champions, Aston Villa. They also reached the Cup semi-final for the first time to begin a sequence of seven last-four appearances in nine seasons. Three times they reached the final but lost 3–1 to Nottingham Forest in 1898, 4–1 to Sheffield United in 1899 and 6–0 to Bury in 1903. So developed the legend of the Gypsies' Curse. The story went that some gypsies, turned off the land when the Baseball Ground was being developed, vowed that Derby would never win a major honour. It made a good newspaper line in 1946 when Jack Nicholas, preparing to lead the Rams at Wembley, crossed palms with silver at a gypsy encampment. As well as moving their home, Derby County became a limited company in 1896 and the prospectus names W.D. Clark as manager. His function was administrative, and the first manager to be concerned with the playing side was Harry Newbould, appointed in 1900. He continued as secretary and for many years the directors had the final say on matters of selection and engaging players. After the third of their Cup finals, Derby had a moderate time in the First Division and money was increasingly tight, to the extent that, in March 1906, they sold Bloomer to Middlesbrough. Supporters were devastated, Bloomer himself was not best pleased and Newbould, seeing what was ahead, became manager of Manchester City at the end of the season.

Jimmy Methven, nearing the end of a magnificent Rams career at right-back, was chosen to succeed Newbould but, with no reliable scorer, his first season in charge ended with relegation. During this season, Bernard Vann played three times as an amateur while teaching at Ashby Grammar School. His playing career did not amount to much, but he earned a Victoria Cross, the highest award for gallantry, in World War One. He was chaplain and history master at Wellingborough School in 1914 and, being in Holy Orders, sought permission from the Bishop of Peterborough to enlist in a combatant unit. He rose to the rank of Lt-Col in the Sherwood Foresters and his conduct earned him a Military Cross and Bar as well as the French Croix de Guerre with Palm Leaves. Bravery at the crossing of the Canal du Nord in September 1918 brought the VC, but he was killed by a sniper the following month, less than five weeks before the Armistice. Donald Bell, of Bradford, was the one professional to be decorated with the VC in the conflict.

Methven had to rebuild the team in Division Two, Derby's first experience outside the elite, but he found a source of goals close to hand by signing Alf Bentley from Alfreton Town. The gap between

A legend returns: Steve Bloomer, then a general assistant at the Baseball Ground, makes a point to (from left to right): Sid Wileman, Sammy Crooks, Dally Duncan, Jack Nicholas, Jack Barker and Jack Bowers.

local sides and League clubs was less pronounced then and, for example, three future England goalkeepers emerged from Ripley Athletic: Horace Bailey, capped while with Leicester Fosse, Harry Maskrey and Ernald Scattergood. Bentley was the first Derby player to hit 30 goals in a League season but promotion was elusive until, in September 1910, Methven brought back Bloomer. The player was delighted and he had partners who could provide goals, notably Horace Barnes and Harry Leonard. Promotion came in 1912, relegation in 1914, another Second Division title in 1915 before League football came to a stop. Methven, a hard worker with an eye for a player, did an excellent job but it would be just as difficult in 1919.

## George Jobey Reigns

Jimmy Methven had to rebuild after World War One. There were some veterans like Jimmy Bagshaw and Jimmy Moore, good enough to win solitary England caps in their 30s. Two wingers in their early 20s went on to play for England, Alf Quantrill and George Thornewell, while the old warrior Jack Atkin still had a couple of seasons in him. Methven was beginning to feel the strain, especially as his sight was fading, and after a narrow escape from relegation in the first post-war season, by winning four of their last five games, the Rams went down again in 1921. Methven had one more year before giving way and, despite rumours that the former Newcastle United and England defender Colin Veitch was to take over, Derby appointed Cecil Potter, at various times a player, secretary and manager at

Hartlepools United. Potter was close but not quite there in his three years at the Baseball Ground. Derby reached the FA Cup semi-final at Stamford Bridge in 1923 but were two down after nine minutes and West Ham United went on to compete in the first Wembley final. The following year, Derby needed to beat Leicester City 5–0 in their final game to pip Bury for the second promotion place on goal average. They managed four but Bury went up by 0.015 of a goal. Had goal difference been the decider, Derby would have been promoted but that did not come until 1976.

Derby persuaded George Jobey back into football in 1925. Once a League Champion and Cup finalist with Newcastle, Jobey steered Wolverhampton Wanderers out of Division Three North in 1924, then went into the hotel business. Jobey imposed firm discipline on Derby and won promotion in his first season, something only Jim Smith emulated at the Baseball Ground 70 years later. Under Jobey, the Rams embarked on their longest continuous spell in the First Division and were in the top half in 10 of his 13 active seasons. Their transfer activity was ceaseless, and, although many players came and went without much impact, the policy was justified by some sensational bargains. Sammy Crooks was signed from Durham City for £300, Jack Barker from Denaby United for £275 and Jack Bowers from Scunthorpe and Lindsey United for £150. All played for England, Crooks on 27 occasions, behind only Arsenal and England captain Eddie Hapgood in the years between the wars. They and others were leading figures in English football: Barker and right-back Tommy Cooper captained England, the first Derby players to do so since John Goodall and Steve Bloomer. Above all, Derby entertained, four times reaching or passing 90 goals in the First Division. They also conceded too regularly and, despite being runners-up in 1930 and 1936, never took the final step to the title. Crooks said in later years: "We were too much about attack to win the League. Other clubs were better

Derby County's playing staff at the start of the 1930–31 season. Back row (left to right): J. Smith, J.C. Robson, F. Jessop, J. Barker, J. Nicholas, J. Bowers, W. Robson, J. Webb, A. White. Middle row: Laurie Edwards (trainer), G. Collin, F. Eckersley, T. Cooper, G. Stephenson, J. Kirby, T. Davidson, H. Wilkes, T. Ruddy, Bill Bromage (assistant trainer). Seated: N. Robson, W. Carr, J. Randall, H. Bedford, George Jobey (manager), J. McIntyre, G. Malloch, P. Ramage, A. Scott. On ground: S. Crooks, D. Fereday, R. Barclay, S. Reid.

at keeping games tight." Their best chance was in 1938–39, before World War Two halted competitive football. Derby were top for 15 weeks, from October to early February, but instead of reaching out they suddenly lost three consecutive home games. They faltered badly, losing nine of the last 14 to finish sixth, and the £9,500 signing of centre-forward Dave McCulloch from Brentford was held to have failed. It was hard on McCulloch, who scored 16 times in his 31 League games, but contemporary opinion says he abandoned the marauding style that brought him success at Griffin Park and became too intricate.

It was, though, a typical Jobey signing. He loved centre-forwards, accepting the obvious truth that success is impossible without a regular supply of goals, and had some of the best in the land at Derby. Harry Bedford, who cost £3,250 from Blackpool in September 1925, was the first and his 27 goals helped to set up promotion. Bedford equalled Derby's League record with 30 goals and his successor Jack Bowers, the bargain from Scunthorpe, promptly shattered it with 37 in 1930–31. Bowers was fearless, prepared to go in where there was every chance of being hurt if there was a sniff of a goal: he collected 183 in 220 League and Cup games – so put a contemporary price on that record. When Bowers was injured, Jobey went for Hughie Gallacher, one of the all-time greats with Scotland, Newcastle and Chelsea. Gallacher was brilliant but could also be a handful. Jobey managed him astutely and continued his line of scorers with Dai Astley, Ronnie Dix and McCulloch.

There were other rocks in his team, such as George Collin, the phenomenally consistent Jack Nicholas and, on the opposite wing to Crooks, the elegant Scot Douglas 'Dally' Duncan. Jobey turned Derby into one of the big clubs but the prizes that would have cemented his reputation eluded him and, in 1939, World War Two began. Happily for the Rams, the Cup resumed in 1945 but the League was delayed until 1946, although there was much good football seen in the wartime Leagues, not least at the Baseball Ground. Derby and Jobey faced a major hurdle in August 1941, when they were called before a joint Football Association and Football League commission. The question of how the Rams managed to keep their star players was about to be answered. The maximum wage was still in force and a successful challenge to the system was 20 years away. Curiously, allegations were put forward by Jobey, who supplied details in support of them. 'The commission found that various payments in excess of those allowed under the transfer, bonus and signing-on regulations of the Football League had been made by the Derby County club over a period of 12 seasons.' Jobey and five directors, Messrs Bendle Moore, Pattison, Ann, Robshaw and Jackson, were suspended *sine die*. Another director, A. Green, was suspended for three years, the secretary, W.S. Moore, was severely censured and the club was fined £500. Jobey's suspension was lifted in 1945 but he was not the same force when he managed Mansfield Town. The fine seems small for an offence striking at the heart of League regulations, but a similar penalty was imposed on Leicester City and the commission may have been mindful that several other clubs were guilty in the same areas.

## FA Cup and the Third Division North

George Jobey's influence lived on in the 1946 Cup triumph. Of the 18 players involved, Jobey signed 11 as professionals and another, Leon Leuty, was on Derby's books as an amateur. Much of the credit for constructing the team goes to Ted Magner, manager for a short but significant period, at the end of which he handed over to Stuart McMillan. First of all, Derby had to start again. All round the League, players' contracts were cancelled on the outbreak of World War Two and Derby ceased to operate after the aborted 1939–40 season was three games old. Two former players, Jack Nicholas and

Jack Webb, were responsible for the Rams resuming operations with a handful of friendly matches in 1941–42. Tommy Powell, from Bemrose School, made his debut as a 16-year-old in the first of them, against an RAF XI. The following season, Derby were in the League North, with a regular programme of fixtures. War service meant players were spread around the country or abroad, so guests were allowed and two of Derby's greatest players emerged from this system. Peter Doherty, who won the Championship with Manchester City in 1936–37, first appeared against Nottingham Forest in August 1944. Raich Carter, who helped Sunderland to the Championship and the Cup, joined him at the beginning of November. They were acknowledged as the top inside-forwards of the 1930s in their contrasting styles. Carter, already silver-haired, was imperious on the field, a deadly finisher who, as England football and cricket international Willie Watson once said, seemed to carry his own space around with him. While Carter ran the show, Doherty was tireless in his movement, a dribbler, a runner, a finisher, starting moves and ending them with a few touches in between, something like Alfredo di Stefano in his great days with Real Madrid. Other players adored them and why not? They gave Derby extra class, as they would have done to any team, and in 1944–45 the Rams pulled off a wartime double. They won the second period of the League North and demolished Aston Villa in the Midland Cup final. Carter's hat-trick saw them through at Villa Park and, in the second leg, Doherty scored five in a 6–0 win that gave Derby a 9–0 aggregate. They came together because they were working at an RAF rehabilitation unit in Loughborough and provided Derby followers with sumptuous football.

It was soon time for Ted Magner, appointed manager in March 1944, to take action. The Allied victories in Europe, then the Far East, came too late for the League to resume in 1945–46 but there was a Cup, played for the only time over two legs. There were no guests for that: in order to take part, players had to be registered, so Derby entered negotiations with Sunderland and Manchester City. Carter and Doherty were signed for £6,000 each but time almost ran out on the Carter deal. He and secretary Jack Catterall missed their train connection at York and hired a taxi to take them to Sunderland. The forms were completed with an hour to spare before the third-round deadline. Luton Town were beaten comfortably and a fine second-leg win at The Hawthorns saw to West Bromwich Albion. Carter and Doherty shared nine of the goals as Brighton & Hove Albion were beaten 10–1 on aggregate, paving the way for a mighty clash with Aston Villa. Before the quarter-final, regular goalkeeper Frank Boulton was injured in a clash with Swansea Town's aggressive centre-forward Trevor Ford. Poor Boulton was out for the remainder of the Cup run and, although Billy Townsend played in both legs against Villa, Derby were not happy so, in March, signed England's pre-war goalkeeper Vic Woodley, then 36. Woodley was in the Southern League with Bath City and not Cup-tied, although Derby had also to negotiate with his former club, Chelsea. If there was to be a fairy-tale end to Woodley's career, there was no such luck for Sammy Crooks, injured in the second leg against Villa. The unluckiest of them all was Jack Parr, left-back in every tie until he broke his right arm at Luton four weeks before the final. Fortunately for Derby, Jack Howe returned in March from war service in India and, after standing in for Leon Leuty in the semi-final replay, took Parr's place at Wembley. Tim Ward, who played in the first tie at Luton, had little chance of making the final because he spent so long playing exhibition matches for the British Army on the Rhine (BAOR). He was home in time for the final but only as a spectator, as Stuart McMillan, who succeeded Magner when the Cup run was under way, understandably kept faith with wing-halves Jim Bullions and Chick Musson.

Birmingham, managed by Harry Storer, were tough opponents in the semi-final. The first game at Hillsborough was featureless but, for the replay, 80,407 piled into Maine Road, Manchester. It was 0–0

Rams skipper Jack Nicholas receives the FA Cup from Queen Elizabeth and the King.

after 90 minutes only because Woodley made a great save from Harold Bodle and Derby went ahead when Doherty slid in Duncan's centre as Ted Duckhouse came in to challenge. They collided and the unfortunate Duckhouse was carried off with a broken leg. Derby cashed in against 10 men, won 4–0 and were off to Wembley for the first time. There were two things to be done. Nicholas was taken to a gypsy encampment to lift the legendary curse, a newspaper stunt but one which may have relieved the players. More urgently, the directors had to find better seats for the players' wives. They were originally placed in the open, cheaper seats at the mercy of the weather, and senior players delivered an ultimatum: upgrade or there will be no match. It was resolved, as was Reg Harrison's position on the right. Crooks, returning from a scouting trip, had a puncture and kicked the tyre in frustration, causing his injured knee to click back into place. He could have played but McMillan decided he was short of match fitness, so Crooks devoted all his energy and good humour into preparing Harrison for the big day. It belonged to Derby, especially in extra-time. Bert Turner scored for both sides and the ball burst as Jack Stamps was in the act of shooting. The Rams won 4–1, the first major trophy in their history, with directors suspended in 1941 relishing the day, H.T. Ann as president and Ben Robshaw as chairman. Robshaw gave genuine leadership and Derby twice broke the British transfer record, for Billy Steel and Johnny Morris, before the chairman again fell foul of the football authorities.

The problem this time lay with Jack Cattarall, secretary from March 1945 to July 1946. Derby dismissed him when they discovered he was an undischarged bankrupt, then found financial irregularities from his time in office. The Football League auditors hit upon this and, in 1949, summoned another joint commission with the FA, at which the main accusation was a failure to apply the PAYE tax system to the whole of players' wages, to accrued shares of benefit and to payments on a Czechoslovakian tour undertaken as Cup holders. Derby paid excessive wages on the tour and, while directors admitted the club's guilt, they denied instructing Cattarall. Robshaw's 1941 suspension told against him and he was suspended *sine die* for a second time, having taken the blame for lack of supervision. Robshaw left football for good and Catterall, after a series of fraudulent acts in other fields, committed suicide in 1954. Ossie Jackson, one of those punished in 1941, replaced Robshaw as chairman and it was not good news for the Rams. Jackson, more austere and remote than the hearty Robshaw, oversaw a steady decline as, not for the last time, Derby showed themselves totally incapable of handling success. The first blunder was a refusal to allow Doherty to take over the Arboretum Hotel, leaving the Irishman bitterly resentful that they should doubt his commitment. He moved to Huddersfield Town when, in truth, he wanted to end his career at Derby but at least the club aimed high for a replacement in 1947, paying Morton a record £15,500 for Steel soon after his stunning display for Great Britain against the Rest of Europe at Hampden Park. Steel was a fine player but was given special treatment, thus upsetting other stars when they discovered what was happening. Carter and Leuty were especially annoyed and even such a courteous man as Ward said in later years: "Billy Steel started the downhill run at Derby County and I don't mean that because of his playing ability." Gifted though Steel was, others doubted his dedication to the club: "Billy only played when Billy felt like it," said Ward, "and it became more and more so after his first season with us." Carter left for Hull City, who offered him a way into a management career, in March 1948, and a year later Derby spent big again, a record £24,500 to Manchester United for Morris. Derby were fourth and third in those two seasons but, from there, the slide was in progress. The Cup winners either retired or moved, Harrison outlasting them all, and replacements were not of the same quality.

The Rams were relegated in 1953, ending their longest period as a First Division club, and Stuart

The Rams' 1948 FA Cup semi-final team who lost to Manchester United at Hillsborough. Back row (left to right): Stuart McMillan (manager), Tim Ward, Bert Mozley, Leon Leuty, Jock Wallace, Jack Howe, Chick Musson, Jack Poole (trainer). Front row: Reg Harrison, Raich Carter, Jack Stamps, Billy Steel, Angus Morrison.

McMillan did not survive an uncertain start the next season. His replacement, Jack Barker, was one of Derby's great players in the 1930s but had a wretched time as a manager and was sacked after a second relegation in 1955. Derby needed someone to impose discipline and restore shattered morale. They found him in another former player, Harry Storer, whose priority was to sign an effective captain, Paddy Ryan from West Bromwich Albion. The darkest playing day in Derby's history was at hand when, in December 1955, Boston United of the Midland League beat them 6–1 at the Baseball Ground. Harrison, one of the Wembley winners, and Geoff Hazledine, who scored a hat-trick, were among six ex-Rams in the Boston side. Despite one of the biggest Cup shocks in history, Storer fashioned two exhilarating seasons in Division Three North as the goals flowed and the crowds returned. Tommy Powell showed the skill as a creator not often seen at this level and, in 1956–57, Ray Straw, a miner from Ilkeston, equalled the club record set by Jack Bowers with 37 League goals. Derby, second in 1956 behind Grimsby Town, went up as Champions in 1957 but that was as far as Storer was able to take them. Geoff Barrowcliffe and Jack Parry were on their way past 500 appearances, major careers in any context, and occasional signings caught the imagination. Bill Curry added a swagger at centre-forward and ex-England goalkeeper Reg Matthews was always exciting but, whatever the manager's ambitions, the club lacked drive. Storer improved the financial situation and the directors intended to keep it that way, content to potter along as a safe Second Division club.

There was no change in the atmosphere when the conscientious Tim Ward took over as manager in 1962 and was soon as frustrated as Storer had been. Ward found a tremendous bargain in Eddie

Ray Straw hammers in a shot against Northern League amateurs Crook Town in a first-round FA Cup replay at the Baseball Ground in November 1955.

Thomas and later admitted this acted against him as the board expected stars on the cheap. He signed Alan Durban from Cardiff City and suddenly shook supporters in September 1966 with the capture of Kevin Hector who, at 21, had scored 113 League goals for Bradford. Hector cost £38,000 and Derby simply did not contemplate fees like that. The forward was an instant success and there were plenty of people at the Baseball Ground ready to claim the credit. That belonged to Ward but it did not save him and, at the end of the season, he was told his contract would not be renewed. The Rams needed a revolution and it was on the way.

## Championships and Chaos

The group of Derby directors who travelled to the Scotch Corner Hotel in May 1967 were bemused as they returned home. They thought the purpose of the trip was to interview Brian Clough as manager in succession to Tim Ward but came away feeling he had interviewed them. As indeed he had. The chairman, Sam Longson, was keenest to engage Clough, having been tipped off about him by Len Shackleton, the former Sunderland and England inside-forward who was then a football journalist in the North East. Clough was with Hartlepools United after his career as a prolific scorer for Middlesbrough and Sunderland was ended by a severe knee injury. He managed to create publicity even for the North East's traditional poor relations and, having persuaded Peter Taylor to work with him there, told the Derby board they were engaging a partnership. Clough kept this until negotiations were settled but it proved to be an inspired move. Taylor, a Nottingham man and a goalkeeper who worked under Harry Storer at Coventry, was Burton Albion's manager before he went to Hartlepools and had a clear vision of Derby's potential as a football town. Until they fell out so spectacularly in the 1980s, it was a

Rams chairman Sam Longson welcomes Brian Clough and Peter Taylor to the Baseball Ground in June 1967.

wonderful partnership and they immediately began to blow away the cobwebs at the Baseball Ground. The first three signings were John O'Hare, Roy McFarland and Alan Hinton who, for a joint outlay of £75,000, helped to take the club to heights that had never even been contemplated. Results in the first season were disappointing, and Derby finished one place lower than in Tim Ward's final year, but supporters sensed something good was happening.

Interest was heightened by a run to the semi-finals of the League Cup, even now Derby's only impact on the competition, before they lost to Leeds United. As Clough and Taylor were to demonstrate even more convincingly with Nottingham Forest, they always understood the value of the League Cup. More ingredients were required to turn progress into success and the major capture of the summer stretched belief for supporters. Dave Mackay, a great player in a wonderful Tottenham Hotspur team, was coming to the end of his time at White Hart Lane and appeared all set to rejoin Heart of Midlothian, his first club. Clough nipped in and, after haggling over terms, persuaded him to join the Rams. Mackay was 33, older than his new manager, and there was a different role for him. The all-action midfield player in the Spurs Double team was to sit in the back four, direct operations and teach the younger members how to play. Mackay's skill and infectious personality equipped him for this so perfectly that he ended the season as joint Footballer of the Year with another veteran, Tony Book of Manchester City. Even with Mackay in the team, the start was poor, three points from the first five games. In the last of these, at home to Hull City, Willie Carlin made his debut after moving from Sheffield United for £60,000, then a Rams record. Carlin's combative nature and strength in midfield did the trick. The remainder of the season was a joy as Derby surged away at the top, ending with a

Reg Matthews is beaten by Johnny Giles's penalty to give Leeds United a 1–0 win in the first leg of the League Cup semi-final at the Baseball Ground in January 1968.

club record nine consecutive victories. After 16 years, Derby were back where supporters believed they belonged and, equally important, the team was ready for the First Division. There were no newcomers as Derby were unbeaten for the first 11 games, including a memorable 5–0 victory over Spurs in front of a record 41,826. The football in that first season up was wonderfully entertaining and uninhibited as players, precisely aware of their individual responsibilities, fully explored their potential. Clough and Taylor began their habit of a major signing in February by taking Terry Hennessey from Nottingham Forest, Derby's first £100,000 player. Fourth place in 1970 qualified Derby for the UEFA Cup, or so they thought. Administrative problems again caught them and a joint FA and League commission found them guilty of 'gross negligence', a verdict accompanied by a fine of £10,000 and a ban from playing in Europe for one year. The 1969 accounts reported an unexplained gap of £3,000 in season-ticket income and the sudden rise of the club was not matched by increased efficiency in the office. In addition, Derby were paying Mackay, outside the terms of his contract, for contributions to the programme. They brought in a new secretary, Stuart Webb from Preston North End, to clear the mess and, in a number of ways, he was to play a considerable part in the Derby story, but losing the European place was a savage blow to the players who earned it. Instead, they played in and won the pre-season Watney Cup, beating Manchester United in the final. Towards the end of an unremarkable season came the big February capture, this time the brilliant young defender Colin Todd from Sunderland for £170,000. It was a great show of faith in Derby's future at a time when the town was rocked by the collapse of Rolls-Royce.

Mackay's job was done and he left in 1971, fulfilling a personal ambition by playing in all 42 League games for the first time. The stage was set for the greatest season in Derby's history as they gathered in three trophies, the League Championship, the Texaco Cup and the Central League. Clough and Taylor took every competition seriously. The Texaco Cup, involving teams from England, Scotland and Northern Ireland, was an entertaining sideshow. It created far more interest than some of its successors, such as the Anglo-Italian Cup, and Derby's home gates were always above 20,000 as, in

The masses of people who turned out to see Derby County parade their trophies in season 1971–72.

two-leg ties, they beat Dundee United, Stoke, Newcastle and, in the final, Airdrieonians. The reserve team provided tremendous entertainment and a good supply of goals, especially from Roger Davies, then the record signing from a non-League club, and Jeff Bourne. The big prize was the League title, for which Derby had been striving since 1888. The Rams had been runners-up three times but even George Jobey's talented team never came really close to top place. In 1971–72, Derby had a balanced team in which every player knew his job. If any of them failed to perform, there were sharp reminders from the management and Clough was savage after Derby caved in against Leeds United two days after Christmas. It had the desired effect. Derby lost only three of their last 19 games and did enough to hold off Leeds and Liverpool. It was not a big squad and Clough never believed in change for the sake of it. Only 16 players were used and three of those made only 10 appearances, including substitutions, between them. Only occasionally did they sweep away the opposition, four against Stoke and Nottingham Forest at home, four against Sheffield United on a heady day at Bramall Lane. An Easter victory over Leeds was crucial but Manchester City set them back with a 2–0 victory at Maine Road at the end of April. That was one of Rodney Marsh's good days, but Malcolm Allison upset City's balance by signing such an individualistic talent. City's programme was over after that game but the Rams had one more, against Liverpool at the Baseball Ground. Steve Powell, aged 16, stood in brilliantly for the injured Ron Webster and John McGovern drove in the only goal of the game. Then Derby had to wait until after the Cup final. Clough was with his family in the Isles of Scilly, Taylor with the players in Majorca when two games that affected the destination of the title were played. A draw was enough to put Leeds top but Wolves fought like tigers to beat them at Molineux: Liverpool had to win but were held 0–0 by Arsenal at Highbury. The Rams were Champions and if a party erupted in Majorca, there was an even bigger one in the streets of Derby. 'Lucky' said their rivals, but Clough was entitled to point out that the League is won over 42 games.

The European Cup was launched when Derby were in Division Three North and now they were in it as England's representatives. After beating a testy and niggling Zeljeznicar Sarajevo, Derby were drawn against Benfica, the Portuguese Champions featuring Eusebio. The Rams were majestic at the Baseball Ground, 3–0 up at half-time, the lead they took to Lisbon. There, they had to do some defending but goalkeeper Colin Boulton and Terry Hennessey were outstanding. Spartak Trnava won in Czechoslovakia but were sunk by Kevin Hector's two goals in the return to put Derby in the last four. Juventus pulled every trick and the two who needed to be cautioned to miss the second leg, Roy McFarland and Archie Gemmill, were duly punished. Hector's goal gave hope but Roger Davies was sent off in the second leg and Alan Hinton missed a penalty, killing dreams of overturning a 3–1 deficit. The quest was over and the end was approaching for Clough and Taylor. The chairman, Sam Longson, began to resent the publicity accorded to Clough and a comparatively recent director, Jack Kirkland, was firmly behind him. Clough milked the acclaim and was much in demand on television, the chosen ground for Longson's attempt to curtail him. It came to a head in October 1973, when Clough and Taylor offered their resignations. The board accepted them and the vast majority of supporters reacted with outrage. A protest movement was formed, public meetings held and a Derby MP, the greatly respected Phillip Whitehead, spoke on Clough's behalf. The situation should have been resolved in private but there were two stubborn opponents and the board had the security of the Bass

36,472 saw Derby win 2–0 with Kevin Hector scoring to level the aggregate against Czech Champions Spartak Trnava at the Baseball Ground in the European Cup quarter-final.

Brewery shares, which always went with the government in power. Bobby Robson was approached but preferred the tranquillity of Ipswich Town, so the board looked towards Nottingham Forest and Dave Mackay. Even Mackay, revered as a player so recently, found it hard in company with his assistant, Des Anderson. The players threatened to go on strike, although they pulled back from that extreme. It was not that they were opposed to Mackay: they simply wanted Clough back.

Mackay was never one to duck a challenge and knew he had a good squad but he had to persuade them to concentrate on football, as well as swinging the crowd behind him. Clough and Taylor joined Brighton & Hove Albion but moves to restore them rumbled on. It was hard work for Mackay, with six League games without victory and a League Cup exit at Sunderland before they won at Newcastle. He was not helped when Longson was heard to say at West Ham: "I could manage this lot". Given all the circumstances, it was a considerable feat to lead Derby to third place and he made a significant signing in February 1974 when Bruce Rioch arrived from Aston Villa for £200,000 to add goals from midfield. Before the new season, Mackay paid Manchester City £100,000 for Francis Lee, appreciating his bustling aggression, and better was to come in 1974–75 as Derby won a second Championship. As Brian Clough was to say: "David Mackay was never given the credit he deserved". Half the First Division led the table over a strange season, starting with Carlisle United, and when Derby lost at Luton just before Christmas, a title was the last thing on their minds. Only three more games were lost as Derby timed their run to perfection and they had a brilliant Easter. Roger Davies scored all five against Luton at the Baseball Ground, Burnley were hammered 5–2 at Turf Moor and Manchester City lost a tight game. Again, Derby were not on the field when they were crowned. Instead, they were enjoying their Awards night, at which Peter Daniel, who stood in marvellously after Roy McFarland was injured while playing for England, was named Player of the Year. News of Ipswich Town's draw with Manchester City at Maine Road, meaning Bobby Robson's side could not catch Derby, lifted the celebrations to new heights. Several players were still limp when they ended the season with a 0–0 draw against relegated Carlisle. Mackay had little pedigree as a manager from Swindon or Forest but the board backed character and Mackay provided it. During the summer, he broke a holiday in Scotland to sign Charlie George from Arsenal for £100,000. George, who played wonderful football in his first season, made his competitive debut in a 2–0 Charity Shield victory over West Ham, Derby's first appearance at Wembley since 1946. He was, too, the hero of one of the greatest Baseball Ground nights when Real Madrid were beaten 4–1. George's hat-trick included two penalties and he added another goal in Madrid, although the Rams lost 5–1 to go out on aggregate. Even so, it was a good season. Derby finished fourth and reached the FA Cup semi-final, but the inspiration left them when George suffered a shoulder injury against Stoke City in March. Until that moment, talk of a League and Cup double was not far-fetched, but Derby's days at the top ended on an April day at Hillsborough, when Manchester United secured their Wembley place.

Mackay's record should have insulated him against a bad start to 1976–77. They failed to win any of their first eight League games, ending that run with an 8–2 demolition of Tottenham Hotspur. They also registered a club record victory, 12–0 against Finn Harps in the UEFA Cup, but when Mackay, concerned by rumours, sought a vote of confidence in November 1976, the board would not give it. He and Anderson were sacked, to be replaced, initially on a temporary basis, by reserve-team coach Colin Murphy. Although Murphy brought in Dario Gradi, who later worked miracles in a long spell with Crewe Alexandra, only subsequent events made sense of the decision. George Hardy, who replaced Sam Longson as chairman, wanted Brian Clough and Peter Taylor back at Derby. Directors were confident and there was a rush on tickets for a fifth-round FA Cup tie against Blackburn Rovers.

The Rams team bus makes its way back to the Council House to celebrate another title in 1975 under manager Dave Mackay.

In February, Clough and Taylor announced they were staying with Nottingham Forest. The board turned again to Murphy, who did well to keep Derby up before being scurvily treated the following September. He watched his team in action against Leeds while knowing that Tommy Docherty was driving to Derby to replace him. It was an undignified performance and Docherty's ceaseless changes

One of British football's most famous punch-ups, against Leeds United in November 1975, when tempers boiled over. Norman Hunter later clobbered Francis Lee, who retaliated as both men were sent off.

Derby County in 1980–81. Back row (left to right): Colin Addison (manager), Richie Norman (coach), Barry Powell, Steve Buckley, Roger Jones, Steve Cherry, Aiden McCaffery, Steve Emery, John Newman (assistant manager), Gordon Guthrie (physiotherapist). Middle: Paul Emson, Steve Powell, Roy McFarland, Keith Osgood, Dave Swindlehurst, Alan Biley. Front: Jon Clark, Steve Carter, Kevin Wilson, Gerry Daly.

weakened the club. Too many good players left and only Steve Buckley among the signings built a significant Derby career.

Just as Hardy was wondering how to effect a change, Docherty left for a second spell at Queen's Park Rangers and Colin Addison, with John Newman as his assistant, took over. Hardy appointed Addison but, at the pre-season photograph, Richard Moore was in the chairman's seat. It was not the ideal start and while Derby struggled on the field, there was turmoil off it, police having entered the club in summer 1979 to investigate allegations of corruption. After being suspended, secretary Stuart Webb resigned to concentrate on his travel business. After a long and costly investigation, the police decided there would be no prosecution, but the Rams were in a sharp decline. They lost their First Division place in 1980, Addison was sacked in January 1982 and, reluctantly, Newman agreed to hold the fort, although he knew he was on a loser. Chairmen changed as regularly as managers and snooker impresario Mike Watterson took control. By then, Peter Taylor had retired from football and Clough was incensed when Watterson appointed him as Derby manager. Roy McFarland, player-manager of Bradford City, returned as Taylor's assistant, sparking a League fine for an illegal approach. Taylor performed a miracle to keep Derby in the Second Division on the back of an unbeaten run of 15 matches and, for good measure, eliminated Clough's Nottingham Forest from the FA Cup.

But Derby were on borrowed time as the financial situation reached crisis point, highlighted when they were unable to pay Telford United their share of a Cup gate. Webb, appointed as a director by Watterson, set about acquiring shares and striving to find investors. There was time pressure, too, because the Inland Revenue and Customs and Excise issued winding-up petitions against the club: payments of tax and VAT were hopelessly behind. Webb cottoned on to Robert Maxwell who, as owner of Oxford United, realised the publicity value of football. He also appeared to have colossal wealth at his disposal. The directors raised funds themselves, Maxwell helped and, in April 1984, the £220,000 necessary to lift the petition was passed over in the gentlemen's lavatory at the High Court in London. Derby were safe and another phase began.

## Ups, Downs and the Mystery Board

As soon as Derby were clear of the High Court, they ended Peter Taylor's stint as manager. Roy McFarland was in temporary charge for the last nine games but the situation was too far gone and Derby faced their centenary season in the Third Division – nine years after the second Championship win. Robert Maxwell installed one of his sons, Ian, as chairman and the arrangement worked well for three years, giving what was then the financial stability of the Maxwell empire while keeping the owner at arm's length. Despite having just taken Newcastle United into the First Division, Arthur Cox fell out because they were prevaricating over his contract and Stuart Webb was able to engage him as manager. He was to be the longest serving at Derby since George Jobey, although, the appointment having been made, Robert Maxwell said he wanted Jim Smith. It was the first of many battles. There was no sudden influx of money and Cox began to build around free transfers like Rob Hindmarch, Charlie Palmer and Eric Steele. They served him well and there was a regular scorer in Bobby Davison, Taylor's most successful signing. The sale of Kevin Wilson to Ipswich Town raised important funds which went towards lifting the standard with Trevor Christie, Gary Micklewhite and Geraint Williams so, although the Rams finished an uninspiring seventh, a team was taking shape. They further strengthened in the summer with Jeff Chandler, Steve McClaren, Ross MacLaren and Mark Wallington and a promotion challenge began. It was a long season – 60 competitive matches – and when McClaren was injured, Derby signed John Gregory from Queen's Park Rangers to add midfield quality. The Rams sealed third place and promotion on Cup final eve when they beat Rotherham United on a tense night at the Baseball Ground.

Thousands of spectators rushed on to the pitch during a game against Fulham, but there were still 78 seconds to play. Bobby Davison scored the goal against Fulham which ensured Derby's Second Division survival on the last day of 1982–83. Fulham wanted the game replayed but the League refused.

Stuart Webb chairs his first Derby County board meeting in April 1984. From left to right are: Colin McKerrow, John Kirkland, Stuart Webb, Chris Charlton, Fred Fern, Bill Hart and Trevor East.

The first step was taken and the second followed more quickly than anyone expected. It was much the same side, although Michael Forsyth took over from Steve Buckley and Phil Gee, signed from Gresley Rovers, emerged as a swift, free-running and uncomplicated partner for Davison. Oldham won at the Baseball Ground on the opening day of the season, but nobody else managed it and Derby won the Second Division title, six points clear of Portsmouth. Cox, who added Nigel Callaghan from Watford in February, was in his pomp, with McFarland as his assistant. He had a tightly-knit group of players who knew their jobs and respected each other, producing a balanced unit. The trouble was that, with First Division football back, Robert Maxwell felt it was time to take the chair, so he installed another son, Kevin, to run Oxford. The start was encouraging: Peter Shilton, the world's top goalkeeper, was signed from Southampton, as was England defender Mark Wright. Their contribution to negotiating the tricky first season after promotion was immense and, after that, there was another infusion of class with Paul Goddard and Trevor Hebberd. In October 1988, Dean Saunders became Derby's first £1 million signing although, as he came from Oxford, the cheque merely moved around Maxwell's capacious pockets. Saunders, full of life and with a smile on his face, was an instant hit and the Rams finished fifth in 1988–89. It would have been Third Division to Europe in three years except that, after the Heysel disaster, there was no Europe for English clubs. Cox had performed miracles but, if Derby were to advance, that was the time to strengthen. Already, though, Robert Maxwell was drawing away from Derby. His criticism of Derby attendances, coupled with his brief and infrequent appearances, failed to endear him to supporters and he could not understand why he was not loved. He was at war with the League, blocked when he tried to add Watford to his portfolio of clubs, then

Stuart Webb with Ian Maxwell, who took over as chairman.

Sitting with Robert Maxwell at a press conference at the Baseball Ground after he assumed the chair following the Rams' promotion.

lending money to Tottenham Hotspur. Cox and Webb found it increasingly difficult to deal with the owner and, far from developing, Derby struggled to make sense of the regime. When Maxwell announced the club was for sale, they were in limbo, unable to trade, unable even to bring in players on loan. Derby still had some major players but, when injuries bit, there was no depth to the squad and relegation in 1991 was hardly a surprise. The Rams paid off Maxwell in 1991 but the price was losing Wright and Saunders to Liverpool. The new board, under Brian Fearn as chairman, had no significant money to invest and it came as a relief to them when Lionel Pickering bought a majority shareholding and invested £12 million in the form of a loan. Pickering, an Ashbourne man, made his fortune by founding and running a free newspaper, the *Derby Trader*. He earlier tried to deal with Maxwell and was banned from the ground although, by then, he had more ready cash available than the owner, who was overstretching himself in the United States publishing business. The fees escalated on players such as Marco Gabbiadini, Paul Simpson, Tommy Johnson, Paul Kitson and Craig Short, but there was no instant success. They were beaten by Blackburn Rovers in the 1992 Play-offs and, after Cox was laid low with back trouble, beaten by Leicester City at Wembley in the 1994 Play-offs under Roy McFarland. Fearn was removed from the board following a bitter dispute with Pickering and, in 1995, McFarland was told his contract would not be renewed.

Some unlikely and, indeed, alarming names were mentioned as possible managers before Jim Smith took the job, happily giving up his post with the League Managers' Association to return to the mainstream. It was in his favour that many of Cox's signings retained their value and Smith was able to capture useful players in part-exchange. Incoming fees covered the cost of Croatian defender Igor Stimac who, after an alarming debut in a 5–1 defeat at Tranmere, gave character to the side as they embarked on 20 games without defeat. By the time that run ended at Sunderland, Derby were almost up and even more important than Stimac was the presence of Steve McClaren as coach and assistant to Smith. Before promotion was assured, Derby announced their intention to move to Pride Park and they settled nerves by beating Crystal Palace in the decisive game, the second goal headed in by their splendid captain, Robbie van der Laan. They were in the Premiership for the first time and gave the Baseball Ground a fitting farewell after 102 years as they negotiated the first season up, helped by the

Chairman and owner of Derby County, Lionel Pickering, acknowledges the applause of grateful Rams fans as their team rejoin the elite of British football.

inspired short-term signing of Paul McGrath from Aston Villa. There was delightful football in the first two years at Pride Park with foreign stars like Aljosa Asanovic, Francesco Baiano, Stefano Eranio, Jacob Laursen, Mart Poom and Paulo Wanchope demonstrating their skill. The Rams finished ninth and eighth, enough to suggest they were settled, but in February 1999 McClaren joined Sir Alex Ferguson at Old Trafford and it was never the same again. From the start of the following season, Derby battled to retain their status and, although Smith produced the occasional rabbit from the hat, like the languidly brilliant Taribo West, his certainty in the market deserted him. Craig Burley, the fitful Giorgi Kinkladze, Lee Morris and Branko Strupar, both cruelly restricted by injuries, cost £3 million each within the space of six months. While all helped to keep the Rams afloat, the only one to bring in a fee when he left was Morris, a trifling £120,000 from Leicester, so the finances were veering out of control. On a unilateral decision, Pickering extended Smith's contract but the paradox was that, having stayed too long, Smith was dismissed too soon, seven games into the 2001–02 season. Pickering wanted to keep Smith as director of football but Colin Todd, brought in by Smith as assistant, did not want his former boss around the training ground. Todd, one of Derby's greatest defenders, survived for only 15 Premiership matches and John Gregory replaced him in January 2002. Three managers in a season was a recipe for disaster but Derby had a way out when they beat Bolton, also in trouble, at the Reebok Stadium. While Bolton recovered, Derby crumpled feebly and lost the next seven games, a spell that inevitably ended in relegation. Worse was to follow as an offer by Peter Gadsby and John Kirkland, who left the board to facilitate talks, was spurned and Pickering put temporary faith in Bryan Richardson, a former Coventry City chairman who arrived with a notional £30 million bond. In March 2003, Gregory was suspended for, it was alleged, 'gross misconduct', and after George Burley was installed on a temporary basis, was dismissed, a decision that later landed Derby County with a seven-figure out-of-court settlement. Burley's appointment was confirmed but, in October 2003, Pickering was removed from the chair as the club suffered a brief and curiously artificial receivership. The shares were wiped out so Pickering and other major investors were heavily out of pocket. Dealing with Pickering could be difficult, as other directors found, but in the light of his financial contribution, it was a monstrous decision by the Co-op Bank, especially as a new board was instantly installed. Their names, John Sleightholme as chairman, Jeremy Keith and Steve Harding, meant nothing in Derby, so they were inevitably viewed with suspicion, especially as it cost them only a token £3 to acquire the club. Burley's first battle was to prevent another relegation and, after accomplishing that, the Rams reached the Play-offs in 2004–05, losing to Preston North End in the semi-finals. Burley then left, alleging interference from Murdo Mackay, a former football agent who appeared with the new board as director of football. Action was required in 2003, with the debt well above £30 million, and refinancing schemes included selling Pride Park Stadium to the mysterious, Panama-based ABC Corporation. They had to pay rent of around £1 million a year to play there which, to those who put everything into building Pride Park, was an affront.

Derby were going nowhere, unless it was towards extinction. Phil Brown, Burley's successor, lost his way and Terry Westley, the Academy manager, was called in for yet another relegation battle, which he did well to win. Happily, a group of local businessmen, with Gadsby as the focal point, emerged to take over the club at the end of April 2006, although Keith, backed by London venture capital company SISU, fought to retain control. By then, the debt was in the £50 millions, so the board's business plan failed spectacularly. Just when you thought Derby County had lost the capacity to surprise, they went through one of the most inexplicable periods in their history. Tough negotiating with the Co-op Bank enabled the local board to achieve instant financial stability and recover the ground. Then they faced a big job to reshape a club that had been in turmoil for more than six years.

The final League game of 2004–05 after the Rams beat Preston North End 3–1, which gave George Burley's team a Play-off against the same opponents. Neither were to gain promotion that season.

## 1898

# Nottingham Forest 3 Derby County 1

### At Crystal Palace, 16 April.

Derby County's dressing room was restless before the players embarked on their first Cup Final because Archie Goodall was missing. The centre-half, scenting a profit, speculated heavily on tickets for Crystal Palace and, worryingly close to the kick-off, was still outside trying to dispose of them. As Derby were to be reminded a year later, life with Archie Goodall was never entirely straightforward.

By virtue of a more difficult route to the Final, Derby were installed as favourites. They beat Aston Villa, Wolverhampton Wanderers, thanks to an heroic display by goalkeeper Jack Fryer at Molineux,

Nottingham Forest's first goal against the Rams in the 1898 FA Cup final at the Crystal Palace.

Liverpool 5–1, in a replay at Anfield Road, and Everton. In contrast, Nottingham Forest squeezed past Southampton in the last two minutes of their semi-final. And, five days earlier, the Rams beat Forest 5–0 in a League match at the Baseball Ground. However, Derby would have been unwise to place too much reliance on the Easter Monday result as only five of Forest's final team were involved, and Derby had another League game on the Tuesday. *The Graphic* reported that Forest played "with far more dash and vigour than their more talented opponents." Arthur Capes, once of Burton Wanderers, gave Forest the lead after 19 minutes, converting Willie Wragg's free-kick. Derby also made good use of a free-kick, Steve Bloomer heading in when Joe Leiper hit the ball into the penalty area, but Capes restored Forest's lead before half-time.

Despite a reshuffle caused by injury to Wragg, Forest held the lead as goalkeeper Dan Allsop, a former Derby Junction player, stopped everything. Skipper John McPherson made sure he would collect the Cup with a third goal eight minutes from the end, having won the ball in a dangerous area. Frank Forman who, with his brother Fred, played a handful of games for Derby at the start of his career, was picked out for praise in contemporary reports. The brothers played together for England, so the Rams missed out on their talent.

**NOTTINGHAM FOREST:** Allsop, Ritchie, Scott, Frank Forman, McPherson, Wragg, McInnes, Richards, L. Benbow, Arthur Capes, Spouncer.
**DERBY COUNTY:** Fryer, Methven, Leiper, Cox, A. Goodall, Turner, J. Goodall, Bloomer, Boag, Stevenson, McQueen.
*Referee:* J. Lewis (Blackburn).
*Attendance:* 62,017.
*Receipts:* £2,312

## 1899
# Sheffield United 4 Derby County 1
### At Crystal Palace, 15 April.

Archie Goodall was involved in more controversy a year after his attempt to sell surplus tickets. He refused to go to Buxton for special training before the semi-final against Stoke, saying that he had private business and his fitness was never in question. Unimpressed by this response, Derby County's directors suspended Goodall and the situation was not resolved until the following September. The inexperienced Robert Paterson, who played only 21 senior games for the Rams, took over.

Derby began well and led at half-time through John Boag, the Scottish centre-forward who was one of three to appear in all the early finals. It would have been 2–0 had Steve Bloomer not wasted a clear chance. *Sporting Sketches* reported that Sheffield United's play had 'stubbornness in an enhanced degree,' and they turned the game around in the space of 10 second-half minutes with goals from Walter Bennett, Billy Beers and Jack Almond. This burst coincided with an ankle injury to Johnny May, the outstanding Scottish wing-half, causing the Rams to rearrange their team.

England wing-half Ernest 'Nudger' Needham was just the man to exploit the weakness – 'the life

Two views of the 1899 FA Cup final at the Crystal Palace between the Rams and Sheffield United.

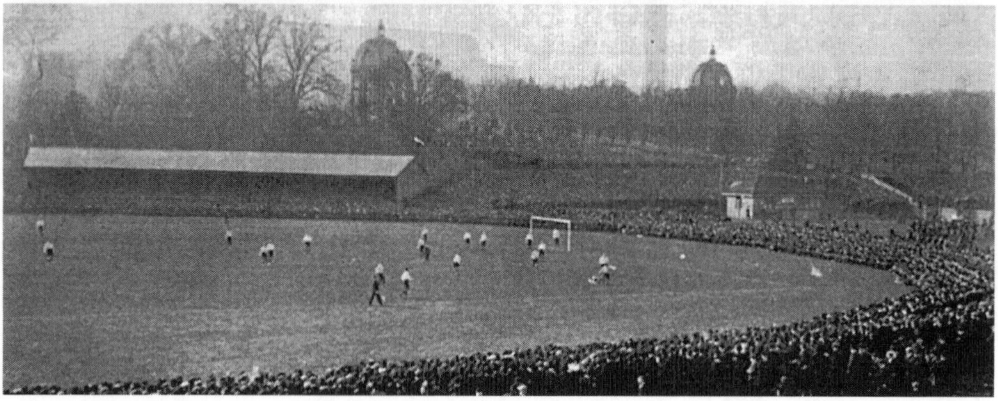

and soul of the side' it was reported. Needham won 16 caps for England and played first-class cricket for Derbyshire from 1901 to 1912. Sheffield United's massive goalkeeper Billy Foulke, whose weight zoomed past 20 stone when he was later signed by Chelsea, also represented Derbyshire at cricket in 1900.

A late goal by Fred Priest settled any doubts and *Sporting Sketches* delivered a verdict. 'Although it was a keen and in the first half very exciting encounter, the play was by no means of a high order.' Some of the blame lay in a sodden pitch and there was an alarming comment on the facilities when a spectator fell 30ft from a tree and suffered severe concussion.

**SHEFFIELD UNITED:** Foulke, Thickett, Boyle, Johnson, Morren, Needham, Bennett, Beers, Hedley, Almond, Priest.
**DERBY COUNTY:** Fryer, Methven, Staley, Cox, Paterson, May, Arkesden, Bloomer, Boag, McDonald, Allen.
*Referee:* A.Scragg (Crewe).
*Attendance:* 73,833.
*Receipts:* £2,747.

## 1903
# Bury 6 Derby County 0
### At Crystal Palace, 18 April.

To Derby County's embarrassment, this result has survived for more than 100 years as the most resounding defeat in an FA Cup Final. Nor has it been under threat. The decision to include Jack Fryer in goal, only five days after he suffered a groin injury at Middlesbrough, rebounded. The *Athletic News* was unequivocal: Derby were 'sorely handicapped by being badly served in goal, for Fryer ought never to have played, owing to an accident on Easter Monday from which he had not recovered.'

Who made the decision, the directors, manager Harry Newbould or Fryer himself?

The Rams used three goalkeepers, as Charlie Morris and Jimmy Methven also took turns, and their trials reduced the credit given to Bury. "Briefly and candidly," said the *Daily Chronicle*, "the Cup Final was a fiasco." The *Daily Telegraph* was also cutting: "The Derby players, on their form of Saturday, had no chance whatever."

An ankle injury kept Steve Bloomer out and while this was obviously a major blow, problems at the other end torpedoed Derby. Even so, they were only 1–0 down at the interval but contemporary opinion, perhaps influenced by hindsight, suggested it was surprising that it took 20 minutes for Bury captain George Ross to open the scoring. Then the roof fell in. Fryer was injured as he came out to challenge, and Charlie Sagar scored the second. While Fryer was being treated, Morris was beaten by Joe Leeming. Fryer came back but, after Willie Wood scored past him, broke down completely. Jack Plant scored past Morris, Bury's fourth goal in a 12-minute spell, and Leeming put in the sixth. Methven then went in goal but without informing the referee who, in an act of mercy, waited until the final whistle before informing Derby's skipper that he should have awarded a penalty every time hands were used. It was a nightmare.

A rare Derby attack on the Shakers' goal as Bury won by a record 6–0 scoreline.

**BURY:** Monteith, Lindsey, McEwen, Johnstone, Thorpe, Ross, Richards, Wood, Sagar, Leeming, Plant.
**DERBY COUNTY:** Fryer, Methven, Morris, Warren, A. Goodall, May, Warrington, York, Boag, Richards, Davis.
*Referee:* J. Adams (Birmingham).
*Attendance:* 63,102.
*Receipts:* £2,470.

1946

# Derby County 4 Charlton Athletic 1

**(after extra-time)**

At Wembley, 27 April.

The key decisions were taken the previous December when, under Ted Magner, Derby turned Raich Carter and Peter Doherty from wartime guests into permanent signings. Carter won the Championship and the Cup with Sunderland, Doherty was in Manchester City's Championship side, and, in any era, they were great inside-forwards. The Rams almost had an unfair advantage as the first Cup after World War Two was decided, uniquely, by two-leg ties up to the sixth round.

It was, inevitably, the Veterans' final. Seven of Derby's team and six from Charlton Athletic played League football before the war, with Charlton centre-half John Oakes being the oldest at 40. Derby captain Jack Nicholas visited a gypsy encampment before the final to lay the famous curse that had supposedly existed since land was cleared for the Baseball Ground in 1895.

More seriously, senior players threatened there would be no match unless their wives were given adequate and covered seats: under pressure, Derby managed to find enough.

Bert Turner scored for both sides, although Doherty always disputed that, the ball burst and, in extra-time, Derby ran away with the game in what was reckoned to be among the best of finals. Derby missed chances to take control in the first half, and Charlton were more positive after the interval, but no goals came for 85 minutes. Then Bert Turner, trying to deal with Dally Duncan's low centre, turned the ball past Sam Bartram. A minute later, Turner hammered in a free-kick that glanced off Doherty

Getting in before Dally Duncan, Peter Doherty puts the Rams 2–1 ahead.

Jack Stamps scores in extra-time.

to put Vic Woodley on the wrong foot. Jack Stamps might have settled it, but his shot died as the ball burst and Bartram, thinking quickly, threw the lump of leather as far away as possible.

It was all Derby in extra-time as Stamps came into his own. From his centre, parried by Bartram, Doherty pushed Duncan out of the way to score, Stamps added two more and Nicholas became the first Derby captain to lift a major trophy.

**DERBY COUNTY:** Woodley, Nicholas, Howe, Bullions, Leuty, Musson, Harrison, Carter, Stamps, Doherty, Duncan.
**CHARLTON ATHLETIC:** Bartram, Phipps, Shreeve, H. Turner, Oakes, Johnson, Fell, Brown, A. Turner, Welsh, Duffy.
*Referee:* E.D. Smith (Whitehaven).
*Attendance:* 98,215.
*Receipts:* £43,378.

# Other Wembley visits

From its opening in 1923 until 1951, Wembley staged a maximum of two football matches annually, the FA Cup final and, in alternate years, England v Scotland. Later, England made more use of the facility and the number of domestic competitions increased. Especially when Play-offs were introduced, the number of players who trod the Wembley turf swelled until the lengthy reconstruction process began. Derby County returned for the first time since their Cup triumph when they contested the FA Charity Shield in 1975. After that, they played in an Anglo-Italian Cup final and a Play-off.

When they won the Championship in 1971–72, Derby declined to play in the Charity Shield but three years later they faced FA Cup winners West Ham United after again winning the Championship. Charlie George, signed from Arsenal in the summer, became the only player to make a competitive debut for Derby at Wembley. In scorching heat, 59,000 saw the Rams register an untroubled 2–0 victory with goals from Kevin Hector and Roy McFarland. The Anglo-Italian Cup never attracted significant support, although attendances in England were significantly better than those attracted by Italian Serie B clubs. Derby went all the way in 1992–93 and beat Brentford on away goals in the semi-final to fix a Wembley date. Their opponents were US Cremonese who, in December, won at the Baseball Ground in the group stage. They were, by some distance, the most impressive side Derby faced in the competition and, despite a goal from Marco Gabbiadini and a penalty save by Martin Taylor, deservedly repeated their earlier 3–1 victory on 27 March in front of 37,024.

Just over a year later, on 30 May 1994, Derby had more serious business at Wembley, a First Division Play-off final against Leicester City, losers there in the two previous seasons. After their unpleasant semi-final against Millwall, Roy McFarland's team started as if they would sweep away Leicester.

They had chances before Tommy Johnson opened the scoring, but Leicester plugged away and Steve Walsh equalised after Iwan Roberts flattened Martin Taylor. John Harkes, who was soon to report to the United States team for the World Cup finals, could have scored a late winner but dragged his shot wide. Instead, Simon Grayson, who was earlier fortunate to escape with a caution after fouling Johnson from behind, provided an opening for Ian Ormondroyd and Walsh nudged in the winner.

It was third-time lucky for Leicester, and the Rams had to wait another two years before earning a Premiership place.

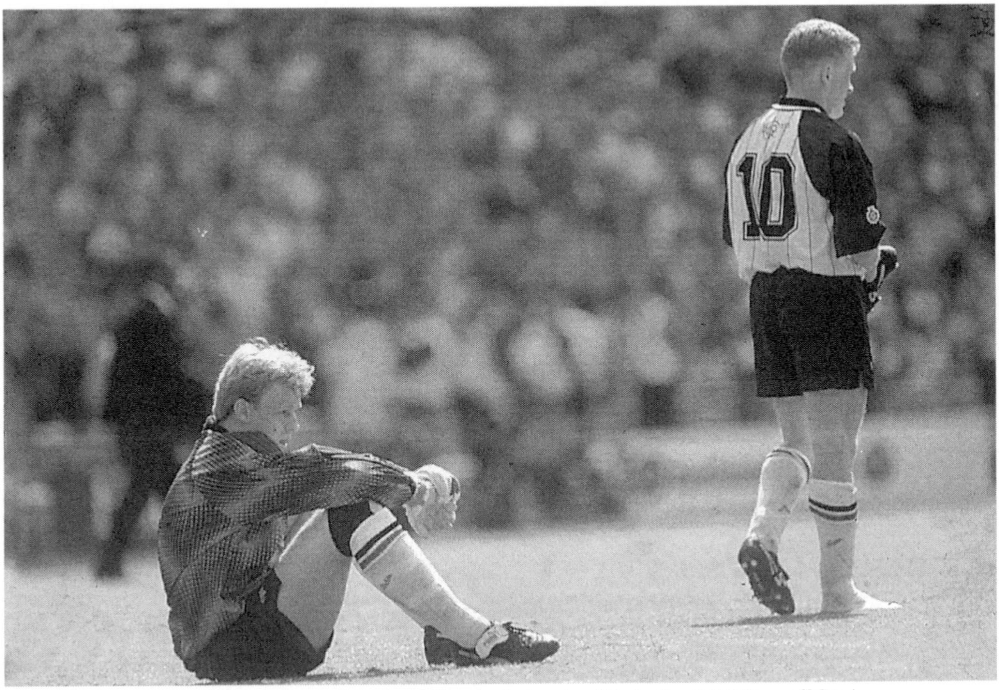

Martin Taylor and Mark Pembridge after the defeat by Leicester City in the 1994 Play-off final.

# Homes of Derby County

As they were formed as an offshoot of Derbyshire County Cricket Club, it was natural for Derby County to set out at the County Ground on Nottingham Road. They moved to the Baseball Ground in 1895 and spent 102 years, either as tenants or owners, in that stadium crammed between a foundry and houses. They had two offers of sites elsewhere in Derby before, in 1997, they moved into regenerated land at Pride Park. Each of their three grounds staged a full England international.

## The County Ground

There was an opportunity in Derby to construct the first and largest sports complex in England but, at the end of the 19th century, nobody grasped such a concept. From 1888, four years after Derby County's formation, until 1895, when they moved, the vast spaces of the playing fields next to Nottingham Road staged county cricket, although Derbyshire did not regain their first-class status until 1894, League football and horse racing. Cricket remains, although the playing area was moved in 1955 to take advantage of the racing grandstand built in 1910, and racing, with the famous straight mile, lasted until 1939. If there was ample room, facilities were less impressive: Steve Bloomer once summed them up as 'plenty of fresh air and cold water'. Those who have watched cricket on bleak days know all too well how the wind, with little to obstruct it, can penetrate. The cricket ground had a pavilion facing Nottingham Road, a straight thoroughfare before the construction of the present giant roundabout. Derby County's committee used a balcony at the back of the pavilion on match days. A stand was built and was sound enough to become part of the Baseball Ground facilities when the move took place.

Perhaps because of Derby's geographical situation, there were a number of representative matches

Pictured in front of the football pavilion steps at the County Ground. Cricket facilities are on the other side of the pavilion.

at the County Ground. The 1886 FA Cup final replay, in which Blackburn Rovers beat West Bromwich Albion 2–0, attracted a crowd of 12,000 to the County Ground and there were semi-finals or replays in 1885, 1886, 1890, 1892, 1895, 1899 and 1901. In March 1895, England beat Ireland 9–0 at the County Ground. Bloomer, making his international debut, and his mentor John Goodall each scored twice but it was close to the end as a football venue. The Rams opened 1895–96 at the Baseball Ground and were there to stay.

Conflicts between the Derby Recreation Company, who leased the County Ground and racecourse from Derby Corporation, and the football club became increasingly irksome and two League games, in March and September 1892, were played at the Baseball Ground because dates clashed. The final straw was the enforced cancellation of an Easter game against the Corinthians in 1895. Fixtures against the Corinthians, powers of the amateur game, were treasured, not only because of the standard of football but also because of the guarantee of a good attendance. There was a race meeting later that week, so football had to take a back seat. The committee called a public meeting at the Derwent Hotel in April 1895 and unanimously recommended a move to the Baseball Ground. It was the end of Derby County's first stage and the chance to create a spectacular sporting facility at the County Ground was missed comprehensively.

### England at the County Ground

County Ground, 9 March 1895
England 9 Ireland 0
Bloomer 2, Goodall 2, Becton 2, Bassett, Howell, Torrans (og)
ENGLAND: Sutcliffe (Bolton); Crabtree (Burnley), Holmes (Preston), Howell (Sheffield Utd), Crawshaw (Sheffield Wed), Turner (Stoke), Bassett (West Brom), Bloomer, Goodall (Derby County), Becton (Preston), Schofield (Stoke).
IRELAND: T. Gordon; H. Gordon, S. Torrans (Linfield), McKie (Cliftonville), Milne (Linfield), Burnett, Morrison (Glentoran), Gaffikin (Linfield Athletic), Stanfield (Distillery), Sherrard (Cliftonville), Jordan (Linfield).

## The Baseball Ground

Francis Ley laid out a sports ground in the 1880s in order that employees at his Vulcan Works foundry should have recreational facilities. After a visit to the United States in 1889, Ley introduced baseball to the area, hence the name of the ground, but like other imported sports, it struggled to gain a firm footing. Derby County won the English Cup at baseball in 1897, with Steve Bloomer at second base. Ley, later Sir Francis, had already spent £7,000 to improve the Baseball Ground and added another £500 to extend the football pitch and transfer stands from the County Ground. There were fears that attendances would suffer but there was almost a captive audience with so many from the foundry and the railway works living on the doorstep. The first home match as full tenants, on 14 September 1895, brought a 2–0 victory over Sunderland, both goals scored by Bloomer, and an attendance estimated at 10,000. The Rams were on the way to their best finish so far, runners-up in Division One.

The Football Association recognised Derby's standing in the game, although they were then in Division Two, with an international against Ireland in February 1911. There were no Derby players involved but Rams followers had the chance to see one of their former favourites, Ben Warren of

The Baseball Ground pictured in April 1921. The Osmaston End is a cinder bank. The Popular Side is uncovered, the Normanton End is covered terracing and the Main Stand will soon be demolished to make way for the 'A', 'B' and 'C' Stands.

Chelsea, as England won 2–1. Soon after moving, Derby expressed an ambition to buy the Baseball Ground but had an opportunity to move again in 1923. It was a new conception, a stadium funded by the Corporation in return for an annual rent of £500. The site was the Municipal Sports Ground on Osmaston Park Road, described at the time as being in the wilds of Allenton. Housing developments soon made it distinctly urban. The club broke off the talks and, in July 1924, bought the freehold of the Baseball Ground from Sir Francis Ley for £10,000. When they were promoted under George Jobey in 1925–26, an ambitious development plan was set in motion and Derby engaged the services of Archibald Leitch, the foremost designer of football grounds.

Work began immediately on a new main stand, known as B Pavilion, with a frontage on Shaftesbury Crescent. The dressing rooms and offices were moved under it so that, for the first time at the Baseball Ground, players emerged from the side rather than an end.

The Popular side came next. The terracing was deepened towards the front, with gangways going across, and a roof was built later, with a higher step in the centre. The roof offered advertising space, for many years proclaiming the virtues of Offiler's Ales. When that brewery closed, there was a message asserting, to general disbelief, that the Bus Station café offered 'the best feed in town'. With Jobey as manager, Derby were an attractive side, even if major prizes continued to elude them. The demand for increased accommodation was answered in 1933 by the construction of the double-decker stand at the Osmaston End, although it did not fill the entire width. The north-eastern section, known as Catcher's Corner from the baseball days, remained uncovered. There was a small hut and a

Ley's foundry is in the background as Arsenal's Cliff Bastin has just scored at the Baseball Ground, but the Rams were already 3–0 ahead and went on to win 4–2 in October 1930.

platform, in front of which half-time scores were displayed. The Normanton End stand, similar in design, opened in 1935 so, in less than a decade, the capacity increased from around 20,000 to 38,000. The Osmaston End was damaged in January 1941, during a German air-raid, and remained out of commission as the Rams made their way towards the 1946 FA Cup final, although not entirely unoccupied as supporters were prepared to take risks.

Once that was repaired, the Baseball Ground had the look familiar to post-war generations but there was another chance for the Rams to have a new home. Maxwell Ayrton, who had been involved

The Osmaston Stand pictured in January 1941 after Derby suffered its heaviest air-raid of the war.

in the construction of Wembley Stadium, submitted an attractive design for the Municipal Sports Ground site, but the directors again elected to stay where they were. Apart from the installation of floodlights, set low on the corners of the end stands in 1953, nothing changed significantly at the Baseball Ground until 1969. As in 1926, Derby took advantage of promotion, this time under Brian Clough and Peter Taylor, to increase capacity. A fourth stand was squeezed in above the Pop Side, backing against Ley's Malleable Castings. Derby obtained enough land from their neighbours to make the construction feasible, naming it the Ley Stand in recognition, but so cramped was the site that access to the seats was possible only with walkways above the terracing. Priority was given to supporters prepared to buy seats for two years, and such was the enthusiasm generated by the Clough era that there was no problem in finding buyers. For the first time, Derby could cope with 40,000 crowds and, for a time, had one of the few grounds with seating and standing accommodation on all four sides. Entry into the European Cup in 1972 compelled the installation of new floodlights to match UEFA specifications. This development was a considerable relief to Press photographers, who had struggled through the gloom of outmoded lights for years.

The 1970s were the best days of the Baseball Ground. After Derby County's second League title, in 1974–75, the team and the club's finances deteriorated. So did their home. In a period of crowd trouble throughout the game, fences around the pitch came and, after the Hillsborough disaster, went. The Taylor Report pushed clubs towards seating throughout but the confines of the Baseball Ground made conversion difficult. Seats bolted on terracing are not the same as areas designed for seating and there were misjudgements, such as siting a family area at the Osmaston End directly below visiting supporters. For local residents, Derby's home matches became a regular ordeal because crowd

This publicity photograph of chairman Sam Longson shows him taking the Osmaston End penalty spot after the decision to resurface the pitch in 1975.

violence was in fashion. By the time Derby left in 1997, capacity was under 18,000. Land was available for a new stadium when the City of Derby earned £37.5 million from the City Challenge Awards, a scheme for regenerating urban areas. Derby was a candidate to stage the Millennium celebrations, although clearly outsiders despite excellent road, rail and air communications. That prize was destined for London, but those who praised easy access to Greenwich had clearly never laboured to reach a Charlton Athletic midweek match. Pride Park was based on the former Chaddesden Sidings and a gas plant. The soil had to be decontaminated and, in August 1993, the Derby board voted to move. A wildly optimistic scheme by a company called Stadivarios failed to advance the project, so the plans were scrapped in January 1995 in favour of staying at the Baseball Ground. Designs were conceived for a massive redevelopment that would have left only the Ley Stand, its name now changed for sponsorship purposes, in use. For all that many hearts cherished the Baseball Ground, it would have been a completely different arena, while retaining the difficulties of access for a car-based support. Pride Park needed a central attraction and Peter Gadsby, a property developer who was then the club's vice-chairman, was restless about the decision, finally seeing the chance to acquire land on favourable terms.

The announcement was made at the Baseball Ground on 21 February 1996, just before the Derby and Luton Town teams emerged. At the third time of asking, Derby were to move and caught the tide

Derby County and Arsenal players observe a minute's silence before the final League game at the Baseball Ground. Spectators were asked to remember players and supporters who had joined together over the past century to create the Baseball Ground's unique atmosphere.

with a successful team, heading for promotion under Jim Smith. The first Premiership season was at the Baseball Ground while the new stadium took shape, Arsenal the final opponents on 11 May 1997. Even then, the Baseball Ground was not finished, as reserve matches continued there. The site was not cleared until 2004 and, when the stands went, the overriding impression was the smallness of the area. Did Juventus and Real Madrid really play European Cup matches in that tiny space? The Baseball Ground was renowned for its atmosphere, best savoured for a night match when the sparks flew at the foundry and the fumes gave a special tang. It was also famous for an awful pitch, in part a consequence of the playing area being below street level and creating drainage problems. After the second Championship, the pitch was dug up, with earth from the centre circle sold in plastic bubbles attached to a commemorative card, but the surface was never ideal. When England played Scotland at Under-23 level in February 1972, Scotland manager Tommy Docherty likened the surface to a farmyard. One regime saw sand as the answer, but it was like playing on a dry beach and the more usual mud was preferable. It was home to generations of Derby supporters, a typical product of football's development in the Victorian age. Derby County, like so many other clubs, realised it was time to move on.

Thousands spill on to the Baseball Ground pitch after the final whistle signalled the end of an era.

## England at the Baseball Ground

Baseball Ground, 11 February 1911
England 2 Ireland 1
Shepherd, Evans. McAuley
ENGLAND: Williamson (Middlesbrough); Crompton (Blackburn), Pennington (West Brom), Warren (Chelsea), Wedlock (Bristol City), Sturgess (Sheffield Utd), Simpson (Blackburn), Fleming (Swindon), Shepherd (Newcastle), Woodger (Oldham), Evans (Sheffield Utd).
IRELAND: W. Scott (Everton); Burnison (Distillery), McCann (Belfast Celtic), Harris (Everton), Connor (Belfast Celtic), Hampton (Bradford City), Lacey (Everton), Hannon, McDonnell (Bohemians), McAuley (Huddersfield), Thompson (Bradford City).

# Pride Park

It was one thing to make an announcement that Derby County would relocate. Finding the money to make the dream come true was altogether more difficult, especially with potential investors wary of the methane gas present in the soil. At this time, Lionel Pickering's board was at its most effective, as a common aim focussed attention, and the target of £16.9 million was raised. It was also a good time for stadium development and, having looked at many, Derby settled on a model, Middlesbrough's Riverside Stadium. Middlesbrough moved to their new ground from Ayresome Park in 1995. It was built on the site of what had been Yorkshire Tube Works and, in common with Derby's proposals, was part of an urban regeneration scheme. The first stage was a detached main stand facing a horseshoe running unbroken round the other three sides and Derby planned along those lines. The corners could be filled in later and Pride Park's capacity increased if necessary by raising the horseshoe roof

Derby County's new stadium at Pride Park under construction in January 1997.

The Queen meets Derby County chairman and owner Lionel Pickering when opening the Rams' new stadium.

Derby saw details at the Riverside that could be improved, but were grateful to Middlesbrough for their help and encouragement. They engaged the same architects, the Miller Partnership, and the construction was in the hands of Taylor Woodrow. After decontamination, the first piles were driven into the ground in September 1996 and the site soon became a major attraction for supporters wanting to see their new home take shape. Derby encouraged this with a visitor centre, including computer-generated images that simulated a tour of the stadium about to take shape. At the same time, Derby were playing out their final season at the Baseball Ground, with Premiership survival the basic aim. To this end, they were assisted by the inspired short-term signing of Republic of Ireland defender Paul McGrath from Aston Villa. Even after seeing the virtual reality images, it was hard to relate to the future, especially in November 1995 when Pickering laid the foundation stone. It was a foul day, cold, wet and windy, and those who watched felt they were in the middle of nowhere: mounds of earth, rubble, temporary roads. Stand in the same spot now and it becomes clear how central the stadium is to the Pride Park development.

The winter weather was not kind to the contractors but extra urgency was provided by the news that the stadium was to be opened by Her Majesty the Queen and the Duke of Edinburgh on 18 July 1997. That was a wonderful day for all who worked so hard to realise a dream, Derby's directors as well as the builders and the 30,000 who attended. By then, the south-west corner, between the main stand and the horseshoe, was filled in. Such was the interest from potential corporate clients that Pickering pressed his board to go the whole way, thus raising the overall cost to £22 million. Even five years later, it was impossible to build a major stadium for that amount of money. Work was in progress on the remaining corner on opening day and, seeing that it was incomplete, the Duke of Edinburgh asked Ross Walters, Taylor Woodrow's contract manager, about it. "Haven't you been paid yet?" was his mischievous question. Following such a memorable opening, all was in hand for football to start and the Rams played their pre-season friendly against the Italians Sampdoria as the overture. The first Premiership match there was against Wimbledon on Wednesday 13 August – and the lights failed. Derby were playing well, 2–1 up and heading for victory. Ashley Ward, who scored Derby's last senior goal at the Baseball Ground, opened their account at Pride Park but, after 56 minutes, there was a sudden and complete darkness.

Electricians set about trying to rectify the fault, but Uriah Rennie, the referee, had to set a time limit and Wimbledon manager Joe Kinnear, sensing a way out, made sure his players were inside the dressing room. Three minutes after Rennie abandoned the game, the lights were back on, but only briefly. Poor Ward lost his unique niche in Rams history and the fault, caused by slight overloading, was eventually identified, by which time the Wimbledon players were back in London.

That was the only major problem with the facilities. Pride Park delivered everything that was promised and gained international recognition. In November 1999, England played an Under-21 game against France at Pride Park and chief executive Keith Loring was determined to break the attendance record for games at this level. He succeeded and Germany were Under-21 visitors in October 2000, helping to prove that Derby could stage a full international. The chance was there because Wembley was being redeveloped, at a considerably higher cost than Pride Park, and England toured the provinces. The policy was popular with supporters, while players found the atmosphere more immediate. Mexico, England's opponents in May 2001, were well beaten and Chris Powell was

The lights have failed at Pride Park in the Rams' first home Premiership game, causing the match to be abandoned with Derby leading. Jim Smith (front) was keener to continue than Wimbledon manager Joe Kinnear.

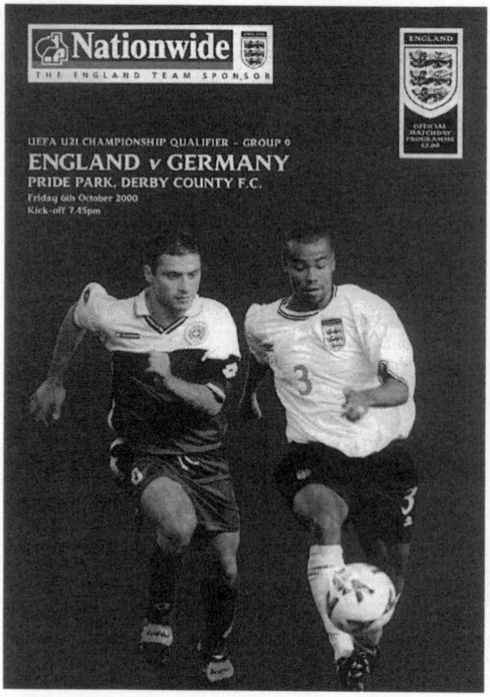


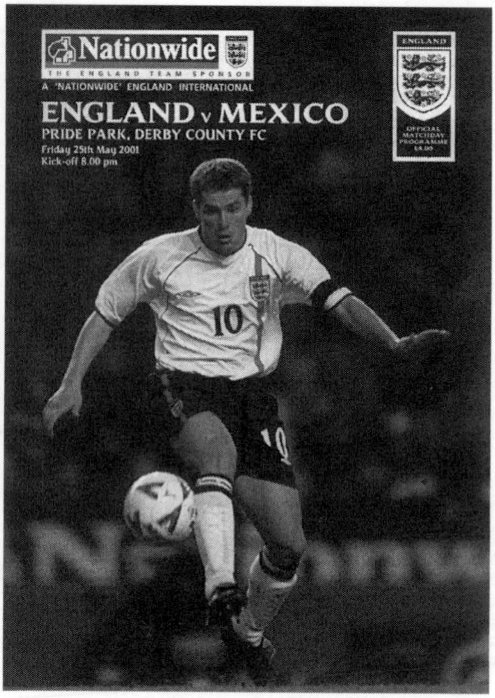


International football comes to Pride Park.

one of the substitutes on his return to Pride Park as Derby County staged the international efficiently.

The quality of the venue is, in all probability, a factor in the continued high level of attendances after the Rams were relegated from the Premiership in 2002, although they became lodgers as a result of the board changing in 2003. In order to redistribute their alarming debts, the new board, with John Sleightholme as chairman, sold the ground to the ABC Corporation, based in Panama. From that time, the Rams paid around £1 million annually to play in the stadium they had built, another cause of dissatisfaction with the regime.

## England at Pride Park

Pride Park, 25 May 2001.

England 4 Mexico 0

Scholes, Fowler, Beckham, Sheringham

Attendance: 33,597

ENGLAND: Martyn (Leeds) [James (Aston Villa)], P.Neville (Manchester U), A. Cole (Arsenal) [Powell (Charlton)], Gerrard (Liverpool) [Carrick (West Ham)], Keown (Arsenal) [Southgate (Aston Villa)], Ferdinand (Leeds) [Carragher (Liverpool)], Beckham (Manchester U) [J. Cole (West Ham)], Scholes (Manchester U) [Butt (Manchester U)], Fowler (Liverpool) [Sheringham (Manchester U)], Owen (Liverpool) [Smith (Leeds)], Heskey (Liverpool) [Mills (Leeds)].

MEXICO: Sanchez, Beltran [Davino], Suarez, Oteo, Chavez [Pardo], V. Ruiz [Osomo], Rodriguez [Perez], Coyote [Rangel], M. Ruiz, de Nigris, Abundis.

# Top 100 players:

## ASTLEY David John

*Forward*

*Born: Dowlais, 11 October 1909. Died: Birchington, Kent, 7 November 1989.*
*Career: Dowlais Welfare. Amateur, Merthyr Town, July 1927: professional August 1927. Charlton Athletic January 1928. Aston Villa June 1931. Derby County November 1936. Blackpool January 1939. Retired during the war. Coach, Internazionale Milan. Coach, Sampdoria. Coach, Djurgardens 1950 to 1954. Coach, Sandvikens, 1954 to 1956.*

■ Few footballers before Johnny Morris enjoyed such a start to a career with Derby as Welsh international Dai Astley, who scored 16 goals in his first 14 League appearances and four in three FA Cup ties. Astley came to the Baseball Ground in November

1936 and in his first 30 matches for the Rams he scored 29 goals, including three hat-tricks. He was a centre-forward who had both punch and craft, yet another of the Rams' forward line of the late 1930s who could both make and score goals. Charlton wanted to re-sign him when he was ready to leave Villa but Astley had a philosophy of 'never going back' and the Rams side attracted him because it contained so many fine internationals. He was at home at both centre-forward and inside-left and did not want to leave the club when George Jobey told him that he was on offer. Astley won two of his 13 Welsh caps while with Derby and boosted his tally to 12 international goals.

---

## ATKIN John Thomas

*Full-back*

*Born: Newhall, 1882. Died: Midway, 15 December 1961.*
*Career: Newhall Swifts. Derby County May 1907.*
***Division Two Champions 1911–12, 1914–15 (captain).***

■ When Jimmy Methven went to sign him from Newhall Swifts in 1907, Jack Atkin would not agree unless Derby took his brother, Harry, as well. Methven agreed and the brothers shared the 15s per week wages. In Atkin's final season with the Swifts they reached the last qualifying round of the FA Cup before losing 2–1 to Second Division Glossop, a team which included the former Rams star Johnny McMillan. Atkin often trained at Newhall with another native of the village, Ben Warren, who was a Rams international.

Atkin gave the Rams many years of loyal service, including being ever-present in 1919–20 when, at the age of 34 and after wartime army service, he helped Derby stave off relegation with his first goal in 13 years – a header against Everton that started a remarkable run in which the Rams won enough points to stay in Division One. The following season Atkin scored four goals in successive matches – two penalties followed by two own-goals. In 1921–22, the Rams skipper played his last game, a 'far from convincing performance' in the 6–1 FA Cup defeat at Villa Park. Atkin was unlucky not to win an England cap, but the great Bob Crompton of Blackburn monopolised the international right-back position. His only representative honour was for an FA team against Cambridge University in 1920 in the same side as Puddefoot of West Ham United and the great Spurs left wing of Bliss and Dimmock. His total of 308 League appearances puts him in Derby's top 20.

---

## BAGSHAW John James

*Wing-half*

*Born: Derby, 25 December 1885.*
*Died: Nottingham, 25 August 1966.*
*Career: Fletcher's Athletic. Graham Street Prims. Derby County October 1906. Notts County February 1920. Watford May 1921. Ilkeston United August 1922. Grantham July 1924.*
***Division Two Champions 1911–12, 1914–15.***

■ Jimmy Bagshaw was born in Russell Street, Derby, close to the Baseball Ground, on Christmas Day 1885, when the Rams still played at the County Ground. His first club was Graham Street Prims and he also had a few games for his works side, Fletcher's

Athletic, before becoming a full-time professional with the Rams, making his debut in their 2–0 win at Sunderland. After being a reserve for England against Scotland in 1918, he played in the Victory international against Wales and was later capped against Ireland. By then, Bagshaw was the Rams' longest-serving player and in 1920 he moved to Notts County, for whom he had guested during the war. He returned to the East Midlands after a spell with Watford, later working for Raleigh Industries in Nottingham and scouting for both Forest and County.

---

## BARBOUR Thomas Parkhill

*Wing-half/full-back*

*Born: Largs, 13 November 1887.*
*Died: Marlpool, 29 August 1967.*
*Career: Kilbirnie. Derby County July 1908. Darlington July 1921. Burton All Saints 1922.*
***Division Two Champions 1911–12, 1914–15.***

■ Manager Jimmy Methven had to move fast when he secured Tommy Barbour from the Ayrshire junior club Kilbirnie in 1908. George Morrell, manager of Woolwich Arsenal, had reached agreement with the club but Methven completed negotiations through Tommy's brother. Either at wing-half, the position for which he was signed, or full-back, Barbour gave Derby excellent value for 13 years, broken by World War One. He served with the Derbyshire Yeomanry at Gallipoli, in Egypt and on the Italian front. While in Egypt, he played against Tewfik Abdallah, who represented the Egyptian Army, and told the Rams of his talent. He and Jack Atkin, both well over 30, helped to keep Derby

in Division One when peacetime football resumed. Barbour was in the first Football League team ever fielded by Darlington but left them in 1922 because he was not allowed to train in Derby, where he was a publican. Later licensee of the Jolly Colliers in Heanor.

---

## BARKER John William

*Centre-half*

*Born: Denaby, 27 February 1907.*
*Died: Derby, 20 January 1982.*
*Career: Denaby Rovers. Denaby United 1926. Derby County April 1928. Manager, Bradford City, May 1946. Manager, Dundalk, January 1947. Coach, Oldham Athletic, November 1948 to January 1949. Manager, Derby County, November 1953 to April 1955.*
***Division One runners-up 1929–30, 1935–36 (captain).***

■ Jack Barker was one of the giants in the fine team George Jobey created in the 1930s, a centre-half who was commanding, hard and physically imposing. He was also a throwback to another era. Despite the 1925 change in the offside law that gave birth to the stopper centre-half, Barker always had an eye on attack. He could do it by accurate long passing but also joined in when the Rams were going forward. Full-backs Tommy Cooper and George Collin believed he attacked too much and Sammy Crooks felt that was true of the whole team. "That was why we came close, rather than winning the League or the Cup," Crooks said in later days. All acknowledged that Barker was a magnificent footballer and he

played 11 times for England, captaining them in his final appearance, against Wales at Ninian Park in 1936. There might have been more caps but some selectors considered he was too rough. It was not an accusation that worried him, a tough ex-miner who had survived a pit disaster. When he was on the way to play Scotland at Hampden Park for the first time, Barker was asked by Ivan Sharpe, journalist and former Derby player, if he was worried about the Hampden Roar. "I told him I had heard far worse than that, the roar of a pit falling in," Barker said. His footballer philosophy was simple: "I followed the ball and played as I knew how." Sadly, his brief period as Derby's manager was a failure and he resented taking orders from directors.

---

## BARNES Horace

*Forward*

*Born: Wadsley Bridge, 3 January 1890. Died: Manchester, 12 September 1961.*
*Career: Wadsley Bridge. Derby County October 1908. Manchester City May 1914. Preston North End November 1924. Oldham Athletic November 1925. Ashton National August 1927 to cs 1931.*
***Division Two Champions 1911–12.***

■ Horace Barnes burst on the Derby County scene after being signed from Wadsley Bridge. An outing in the Reserves was so impressive that he was instantly drafted into the first team and scored on his debut at Blackpool. He was inside-left for the rest of the 1908–09 season and, inevitably, the combination with Alf Bentley and Fred Bevan, joined by Jimmy Beauchop the following season as Bevan moved on, came to be known as the Busy Bees. Barnes had a fierce shot in his left foot, which helped to bring him 78 goals in 167 appearances for the Rams. He developed steadily and was leading scorer in 1913–14 with 24 League goals in 37 games, scoring in each of the first six fixtures to equal a club record, but the Rams were relegated. Barnes stayed in the First Division, signing for Manchester City after a transfer which also involved Arsenal, Newcastle, Liverpool and Sheffield Wednesday. He was engaged to a Manchester girl. The fee of £2,500 equalled the record and it brought the usual debate about inflationary fees, and Leslie Knighton, an Arsenal manager,

wrote in his book *Behind the Scenes in Big Football*: 'Men argued with each other in pubs up and down England, not about the menace of the Kaiser's steel-helmeted hordes, but about the price paid for Horace Barnes.' The closeness of World War One made the transfer a risk but Barnes, who formed a fine partnership with Tommy Browell, repaid City with 125 goals in 235 senior games, including their first at Maine Road. He played in a Victory international against Wales and represented the Football League twice, against the Irish League and the Scottish League, while with City. He ended with a flourish, 240 goals in four seasons for Ashton National.

## BARROWCLIFFE Geoffrey

*Full-back*

*Born: Ilkeston, 18 October 1931.*
*Career: Heanor Athletic 1949. Ilkeston Town August 1950. Derby County October 1950. Boston United July 1966. Heanor Town July 1969. Moorgreen Colliery January 1970. Long Eaton United September 1973: manager August 1974. Manager, Kimberley Town, November 1977 to 1981. Coach, Radford, August 1987: manager January 1988. Assistant manager, Rolls-Royce, cs 1990. Manager, Sandiacre Town, July 1996.*
***Division Three North Champions 1956–57.***

■ The displays of a young full-back playing for Ilkeston Town in the Central Alliance quickly brought scouts to the Manor Ground in 1950. Wolves were among the clubs interested in signing the teenage miner called Geoff Barrowcliffe, but Derby County, closer to home, won the race and so began one of the greatest careers in the Rams' history. Barrowcliffe started as a part-time professional, training in the evenings after a day down the pit. In September 1951 he was rewarded with a first-team debut against Stoke. Barrowcliffe played at left-back in those early days but after the departure of Bert Mozley and a brief tenure by Roy Patrick, right-back became his position. Unlucky to play in a Rams team heading in the wrong direction, Barrowcliffe was one of the best footballing full-backs in England and Reg Ryan, his skipper in Derby's Third Division North days, was convinced that England caps would have come had he been with a more fashionable and successful club. Barrowcliffe was not the hardest tackler but his ball

control and distribution were immaculate. He played a few games at centre-forward and, in the 1955 Christmas holiday, turned out on the left wing. The crowd jeered when it was announced as a team change, but after only a few minutes he laid on a goal for Jesse Pye. Barrowcliffe was a high-scoring full-back, many of his 39 goals coming from powerfully-struck penalties as he became one of only seven to pass 500 appearances for Derby County.

---

## BAUCHOP James Rae

*Inside-forward*

*Born: Sauchie, 24 May 1886. Died: Bradford, 13 June 1948.*
*Career: Sauchie May 1902. Alloa Athletic May 1904. Glasgow Celtic January 1906. Norwich City May 1907. Crystal Palace March 1908. Derby County May 1909. Tottenham Hotspur May 1913. Bradford December 1913. Doncaster Rovers June 1922. Lincoln City May 1923. Trainer, Bradford, 1924.*
***Division Two Champions 1911–12.***

■ Jimmy Methven first tried to sign Jimmy Bauchop from Celtic, where he was understudy to Scottish international Jimmy Quinn, in 1907. The Derby manager was outbid by Norwich City but did not return empty-handed, taking Ted Garry from the Glasgow giants. Methven had to wait a couple of years before tracking down his man but was well-rewarded when Bauchop scored goals consistently. One of

the most important was at Oakwell, when the Rams clinched the Division Two title in 1912 and found 20,000 delighted fans waiting for them as their train pulled into Derby. Although he played centre-forward on occasions, Bauchop was happiest at inside-left where he had three major wing partners – Jack Davis, Davie Donald and Ivan Sharpe. He was always a potential scorer, whatever the state of the game, one of the reasons why he was called the 'catch of the season' when he arrived from Crystal Palace. He hit 72 goals in 135 games for the Rams, helped Bradford into Division One in 1914 and only World War One interrupted 20 seasons in the game.

## BEDFORD Henry

*Centre-forward*

*Born: Calow, 15 October 1899. Died: Derby, 24 June 1976. Career: Grassmoor Ivanhoe. Nottingham Forest August 1919. Blackpool March 1921. Derby County September 1925. Newcastle United December 1930. Sunderland January 1932. Bradford May 1932. Chesterfield June 1933. Player-coach, Heanor Town, August 1934. Trainer, Newcastle United, October 1937. Manager, Heanor Town, March 1955 to May 1956.*

***Division Two promotion 1925–26. Division One runners-up 1929–30.***

■ George Jobey, manager of Derby County from 1925 to 1941, signed a succession of great centre-forwards. Harry Bedford, who had scored 112 League goals for Blackpool and was the League's leading scorer in 1922–23 and 1923–24, was the first, the one against whom others would be judged. Bedford set a high standard, 142 League goals for the Rams in 203 games, another ten in 15 FA Cup ties. He was leading scorer in each of his five full seasons and in 1929–30 equalled Alf Bentley's club record

of 30 League goals. Three times, he scored four in a game: three on ten occasions. Jobey appreciated courage and Bedford had plenty of that to go with his dash and energy. As Jack Bowers began to emerge, Bedford played at inside-right before a swift and surprising transfer to Newcastle. Sammy Crooks said he was one of the best partners he ever had. Bedford played twice for England while he was at Blackpool and scored four goals for the Football League against the Irish League. By the time his League career ended with Chesterfield, Bedford had scored 308 goals in 485 games and it is tempting to speculate on his value in today's transfer market. He settled in Derby and was Derbyshire County Cricket Club's masseur for a time. From 1941 to 1964, he served with the Rolls-Royce Fire Service. Bedford cost Derby £3,500, helped them to promotion in his first season and was instrumental in establishing them as a First Division force before he moved to Newcastle for £4,000.

---

## BENTLEY Alfred

*Centre-forward*

*Born: Alfreton, September 1886. Died: Derby, 15 April 1940. Career: Alfreton Town. Derby County December 1906. Bolton Wanderers May 1911. West Bromwich Albion June 1913. Burton All Saints cs 1922. Alfreton Town 1923.*

■ One of Jimmy Methven's first signings as manager, after his distinguished playing career, was a 5ft 5½in centre-forward from Alfreton Town, Alf Bentley. Snobby, as he was known, was a bustler but he had quick feet when the ball came to him near goal. Methven paid £50 and was prepared to go higher because Alfreton secretary Ernie Davis tipped off Methven's predecessor Harry Newbould, then with Manchester City. The Rams were relegated at the end of Bentley's

first season, so most of his goals were scored in the Second Division, including successive club records of 27 in the League in 1907–08, including four against Barnsley and Leeds City, and 30 in 1909–10, when he hit three hat-tricks. He equalled another club record, set by John Goodall, that season when he scored in six consecutive League games, one of eight players to do it for Derby. Bentley moved to Bolton before the Rams recovered their First Division status but his greatest success was to win a League Championship medal with West Bromwich Albion in 1919–20, when he scored 15 in 24 appearances. He finished his playing career with Alfreton and was in the team beaten 8–2 by Port Vale in an FA Cup qualifying match in December 1924.

## BLOOMER Stephen

*Inside-right*

*Born: Cradley, 20 January 1874. Died: Derby, 16 April 1938. Career: Derby Swifts. Derby Midland March 1891. Amateur, Derby County, June 1891: professional April 1892. One game for Tutbury Hawthorn April 1892. Middlesbrough March 1906. Derby County September 1910. Coach, Berlin Britannia, July 1914. Interned in Ruhleben, November 1914 to March 1918. Coach, Blauw Wit Amsterdam, May 1918. Derby County Reserves, player-coach, August 1919: retired from playing January 1920: first-team coach August 1921. Coach, Grenadier Guards, Montreal, May 1922 (summer engagement). Coach, Real Irun, October 1923 to April 1925.*

***Division One runners-up 1895–96. FA Cup finalists 1897–98, 1898–99. Division Two Champions 1911–12 (captain).***

■ Steve Bloomer moved to Derby as a child, learned his football at St James' School and played with Derby Swifts in the Derbyshire Minor League, scoring 14 goals for them in one match. That form brought him to the Rams' attention and in his first game in a Derby shirt, against Darley Dale, he scored four times. Bloomer made his League debut at Stoke in September 1892 and soon established himself as a favourite with the crowd. Pale-faced, almost ill-looking, Bloomer's appearance belied his worth to the side. He scored goals from all angles, plundering them from close range and launching rockets from 25 yards. He was Derby's leading scorer in all matches for 14 seasons and won the first of 23 England caps in 1895, scoring twice in a 9–0 win over the Irish at Derby. Bloomer took his fair share of digging elbows and clogging feet, but nothing could stop this peerless footballer whose rapier shot was matched by exquisite, defence-splitting passes. Some critics said that he played too much for himself and colleagues dreaded a Bloomer stare when the ball was not put to his feet. Yet Bloomer was a legend. One writer said of him: 'He is as crafty as an Oriental and as slippery as an eel and is much given to dealing out electric shocks to goalkeepers at the end of a sinuous run'. In 1906 he went to Middlesbrough, rejoining Derby to a hero's welcome in 1910 and skippering the Rams to promotion. In 1914 he went to coach in Germany where he was interned during World War One. After the war he played with and coached the Rams, at reserve and first-team level, then enjoyed a successful spell with Real Irun in Spain, winning the King's Cup, before returning to the Baseball Ground as a general assistant. In failing health, Bloomer was sent on a cruise, but in April 1938, three weeks after returning home, Derby County's greatest player was dead.

## BOULTON Colin Donald

*Goalkeeper*

*Born: Cheltenham, 12 September 1945.*
*Career: Charlton Kings. Gloucestershire Police. Derby County August 1964. Southampton, loan, September 1976. Tulsa Roughnecks March 1978. Los Angeles Aztecs July 1979. Lincoln City July 1980.*
***Division One Champions 1971–72, 1974–75.***

■ Only one man played in all 84 games of Derby County's two League Championship seasons, goalkeeper Colin Boulton. He made more appearances than any other goalkeeper in the club's history, beating the record set by Reg Matthews. Two sequences of consecutive appearances, 131 and 115, were interrupted only by a two-match suspension. Boulton was a police cadet in his native Cheltenham when Tim Ward signed him in 1964. He was understudy to Matthews and it came as a setback when Brian Clough signed Les Green from

Rochdale in 1968. Not until Green lost form at the end of 1970 was Boulton recalled, but this time he made the most of it. His handling was high-class, greater experience taught him to deal with crosses and, above all, he was consistent, giving away remarkably few soft goals. In 1971–72, he kept a clean sheet in 23 League games as well as six Cup ties of various kinds. For a time Dave Mackay preferred Graham Moseley, but recalled Boulton shortly before he was sacked as manager. Tommy Docherty ended Boulton's career but, to the day he left, Boulton was, by some way, the best goalkeeper on the books. Following an unhappy time with Los Angeles Aztecs, Boulton played under Colin Murphy for Lincoln City but, after four games, a severe injury at Crewe ended his career.

## BOWERS John William Anslow

*Centre-forward*

*Born: Low Santon, near Scunthorpe, 22 February 1908. Died: Lichfield, 4 July 1970.*
*Career: Appleby Works. Scunthorpe United December 1927. Derby County May 1928. Leicester City November 1936. Coach, Notts County Colts, August 1943. Assistant trainer, Derby County, September 1945: physiotherapist.*
***Division One runners-up 1929–30, 1935–36.***

■ There has never been a braver centre-forward on Derby County's books than Jack Bowers, who scored on his debut in the 2–1 win over Bolton at the Baseball Ground on 2 February 1929. A week later, as the Rams crushed Portsmouth 5–1 at Fratton Park, the young centre-forward hurled himself at a Crooks centre and scored a goal 'worthy of Steve Bloomer at his best'. Bowers went on to score the first of his 16 hat-tricks that afternoon and thereafter became as well-known a Rams star as the great Steve. His courage at diving head first through a forest of legs became legendary and, in 1930–31, he smashed the Rams' scoring record with 37 League goals in only 33 matches. He holds a double share of the club record,

twice scoring in six consecutive League games, but his sequence in January and February 1931 sets him apart – 2 v Birmingham, 3 v Sheffield United, 2 v Manchester City, 3 v Grimsby, 4 v Portsmouth and 1 v Arsenal. The centre-forward hit 15 in six matches and Derby contrived to lose three of them. Bowers was the First Division's leading scorer twice and in 1933 played for the Football League. Three England caps soon followed. In September 1934 he badly injured a knee against Spurs and his recovery was slow, although in 1935–36 his 30 goals for the Reserves helped Derby to the Central League Championship. George Jobey brought the great Hughie Gallacher as a short-term replacement. In September 1936, Derby were losing 4–1 at home to Manchester United. Then Bowers struck with four goals in an amazing 15-minute spell to give his side a spectacular victory. Two months later he was sold to Leicester City and scored 33 goals in 27 games to shoot them to the Division Two title. For his two clubs, Bowers scored 239 League and FA Cup goals in 304 appearances.

## BUCKLEY Steven

*Left-back*

*Born: Brinsley, 16 October 1953. Career: Ilkeston Town June 1970. Redfern Athletic (Sunday football) February 1972. Burton Albion May 1973. Luton Town April 1974. Derby County January 1978. Lincoln City August 1986. Boston United November 1988. Eastwood Town, loan, October 1990. Manager, Shepshed Charterhouse, February to May 1991. Assistant manager, Boston United, July 1991.*

*Assistant-manager, Kettering Town, July 1992. Manager, Corby Town, September 1994.*
***Division Three promotion 1985–86.***

■ Had Derby County been sufficiently alert, they could have snapped up Steve Buckley from Ilkeston Town or Burton Albion long before they paid Luton Town £163,000 for him. Of all Tommy Docherty's signings, Buckley was the only long-term success and was undisputed first choice at left-back for more than eight years. He became the only player in the club's history to complete two separate centuries of consecutive League appearances. Burton signed Buckley as a forward and then manager Ken Gutteridge converted him to left-back, although his attacking instincts produced some spectacular goals for the Rams. He was a favourite at the Baseball Ground, one of the more consistent players in a period of decline and ever-present in four of his eight complete League seasons. He broke a leg in his 200th League appearance for Derby, against Charlton in 1983, and was obscurely transfer-listed by Peter Taylor the following season, when he was still recovering. Arthur Cox took him off the list and, in helping to re-establish the club, Buckley's Derby career ended on a high note with promotion from the Third Division. Elder brother Alan was a forward with Nottingham Forest, Walsall and Birmingham City. His management career took in Walsall, Grimsby Town in two spells, West Bromwich Albion, Lincoln City and Rochdale.

## CARLIN William

*Midfield*

*Born: Liverpool, 6 October 1940. Career: Juniors, Liverpool: professional May 1958. Halifax Town August 1962. Carlisle United October 1964. Sheffield United September 1967. Derby County August 1968. Leicester City October 1970. Notts County September 1971. Cardiff City November 1973.*
***Division Two Champions 1968–69.***

■ Before Willie Carlin joined Derby in August 1968, the Rams had played four League games and failed to win one. After Carlin's £60,000 move – then a Rams record payment – Derby went 13 matches undefeated and by the end of the season had romped away with the Second Division title. Carlin's authority, competitiveness and skill in midfield were big factors in the Rams' promotion. After playing one League game for Liverpool, the 5ft 4in Carlin went to Halifax and he says that the experience almost cost him his career. He was in Carlisle United's Third Division promotion team of 1964–65 and it was from Brunton Park that

Brian Clough and Peter Taylor first tried to sign him. Carlin, still playing well, was shattered when the Rams sold him but he had two more promotions up his sleeve, as Second Division Champions with Leicester City in 1970–71 and from the Third Division with Notts County two years later. After retiring, Carlin went into business as a newsagent and later lived for a time in Majorca.

---

## CARTER Horatio Stratton

*Inside-forward*

*Born: Sunderland, 21 December 1913. Died: Willerby, 9 October 1994.*

*Career: Amateur, Sunderland, November 1930: professional, November 1931. Derby County December 1945. Hull City, player/assistant manager, March 1948: player-manager May 1948. Resigned as manager September 1951. Retired as player April 1952. Cork Athletic January to May 1953. Manager, Leeds United, May 1953 to June 1958. Manager, Mansfield Town, February 1960. Manager, Middlesbrough, January 1963 to February 1966.*

***FA Cup winners 1945–46.***

■ By the time he was 24, Raich Carter had won every honour

then open to an English footballer – First Division Championship medal, FA Cup-winners' medal, as captain, and full England caps. Carter was a brilliant schoolboy international. He signed for Sunderland and made his debut in 1932; by 1937 he was at the top of English football. Carter joined the fire service on the outbreak of war and then transferred to the RAF. He gained permission to guest for Derby because his wife was living in the town with her parents. At the time Carter was posted at Innsworth Lane, Gloucester, but on visits to Derby he met the CO of RAF Loughborough and gained a posting there to help rehabilitate injured airmen. At Loughborough, Carter teamed up with Peter Doherty and week after week Rams fans enjoyed the spectacle of two of the greatest inside-forwards of all time running opposing defences ragged. Like Doherty with Manchester City, Carter was unsettled by Sunderland's attitude and in December 1945, a midnight taxi dash resulted in him being transferred officially in time for that season's FA Cup competition. It cost Derby £6,000 to sign him – "Sunderland were silly to let me go for that," Carter said later – and it was money amazingly well spent. Carter and Doherty helped Derby to Wembley and both scored freely. Carter was the only player with Cup-winners' medals before and after World War Two, during which he shone in a fine England side, scoring 18 goals in 17 appearances. Like Stanley Matthews and Tommy Lawton, he won full caps on both sides of the war. Unlike Doherty, Carter stayed at Derby until 1948 when the Rams were beaten by Manchester United in the FA Cup semi-final. Over 35,000 fans turned up to see his last game in a Rams shirt, against Blackpool at the Baseball Ground and, inevitably, he scored. Carter moved to Hull and helped them to the Third Division North title as player-manager. He made a short comeback with Cork Athletic, adding an FA of Ireland Cup-winners' medal to his collection. Carter took Leeds United back to the First Division in 1956 and was heading for further promotion, from the Fourth Division, when he left Mansfield Town to join Middlesbrough. He failed at Middlesbrough, for the only time in his career, but is remembered as a great player in Sunderland, Derby and Hull.

---

## COLLIN George

*Left-back*

*Born: Oxhill, 13 September 1905. Died: Derby, 1 February 1989.*

*Career: Juniors, West Ham United. West Stanley. Arsenal February*

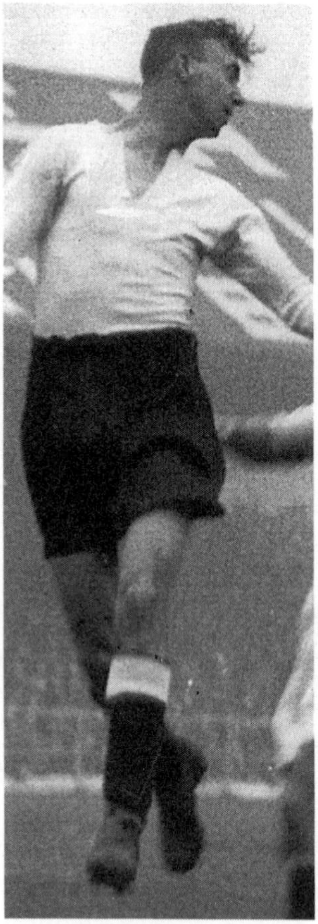

*1924. Bournemouth and Boscombe Athletic August 1925. West Stanley August 1927. Derby County November 1927. Sunderland June 1936. Port Vale June 1938. Burton Town August 1939.*
***Division One runners-up 1929–30, 1935–36.***

■ George Collin was one of those safe, yet unspectacular players who served his club well for a number of years in more than 300 League games, but who never caught the eyes of the international selectors. He played alongside the brilliant Tommy Cooper, who inevitably stole the limelight. A native of the North-East, Collin first played for Arsenal before failing to agree terms with the Highbury club. He followed his manager, Leslie Knighton, to Bournemouth where he broke a leg and returned to play with West Stanley in the North-Eastern League. When Jobey signed him in November 1927, he had to deal with two clubs. On his Rams debut, one critic wrote. 'Derby have found a class back. He is cool and discriminate.' From then until his final season, Collin was rarely out of the side. After signing Jack Howe, George Jobey felt safe in allowing Collin to join Sunderland. It was at Roker Park in December 1933 that Collin had been sent off, one of only three Derby players punished in this way in League games between the wars. Bill Paterson and Albert Fairclough were the others.

---

## COOPER Thomas

*Right-back*

*Born: Fenton, 9 April 1904. Died: Aldeburgh, 25 June 1940.*
*Career: Longton. Trentham. Port Vale August 1924. Derby County March 1926. Liverpool December 1934.*
***Division Two promotion 1925–26. Division One runners-up 1929–30.***

■ It was a fine performance for Port Vale against the Rams which induced George Jobey to pay £2,500 for snowy-haired full-back Tommy Cooper in March 1926. Cooper went on to become one of the best English full-backs of his day and his polished football made him stand out among his contemporaries. His tackling and distribution soon brought him to the attention of the England selectors and he won 15 caps, all of them with Derby. Cooper would have won many more, but

for the injuries which saw him lose cartilages from both knees. Cooper took over the Rams captaincy from Johnny McIntyre in November 1931 and he skippered the side until he moved to Liverpool for £8,000. He became captain of Liverpool and led England four times, against Scotland, Hungary and Czechoslovakia in 1933–34 and Wales the following season. He scored only one goal for the Rams – against Middlesbrough at the Baseball Ground in February 1932 – but as a defender he had few peers, although goalkeeper Harry Wilkes felt he had a weakness in not being very strong in the air. Tommy Cooper met a tragic end. In June 1940, he was killed in a motorcycle accident in Suffolk while serving with the King's (Liverpool) Regiment.

---

## COX John Davies

*Right-half*

*Born: Spondon, 1870. Died: Toronto, June 1957.*
*Career: Spondon. Long Eaton Rangers. Derby County cs 1891.*

*Division One runners-up 1895–96. FA Cup finalists 1897–98, 1898–99.*

■ Jack Cox's prowess at the game was noted at a very early age. Cox signed for his local club before he had left school and his form at half-back brought him to the notice of Long Eaton Rangers, then one of the leading Midlands clubs and a team which appeared in the FA Cup competition proper. The Rams soon heard about Cox and he made his first-team debut in the last match of 1890–91, signing during the summer. Cox was a wing-half who played accurate passes through to his forwards and, in addition, could tackle hard and was good in the air. All these qualities led to him playing for England against Ireland in Belfast in March 1892. In November 1899, Cox was a member of the first FA touring team to Germany. All four games were won, with 38 goals scored and four conceded. Cox played in three and refereed the other. He was known to the other Rams players as the 'squire of Spondon'. After leaving the Rams in 1899. Cox emigrated to Canada, where he went into business as a painter and decorator, although he returned to England to fight in World World One.

## CROOKS Samuel Dickinson

*Outside-right*

*Born: Bearpark, 16 January 1908. Died: Belper, 3 February 1981. Career: Bearpark Colliery. Brandon Juniors. Tow Law Town. Durham City June 1926. Derby County April 1927. Chief scout, Derby County, February 1946 to August 1949. Player-manager, Retford Town, December 1949. Secretary-manager, Shrewsbury Town, May 1950 to July 1954. Gresley Rovers, player, December 1954: player-manager, January 1955 to May 1957. Manager, Burton Albion, May to November 1957. Manager Gresley Rovers June 1958. Manager-coach, Heanor Town, April 1959. Chief scout, Derby County, June 1960 to May 1967.*
***Division One runners-up 1929–30, 1935–36.***

■ A place in Derby's 1946 FA Cup-winning team would have crowned Sammy Crooks' brilliant career but he was not regarded as fit enough to play. He felt that he might have got through the game but it was entirely typical of the man that his comments after the Cup had come to Derby for the first time were in praise of his young deputy, Harrison. 'Reg, didn't let me down,' was Sammy's theme. George Jobey signed Crooks from Durham City, then in Division Three North, for £300. "I stepped off a coal lorry one Thursday and Jobey met me," Crooks recalled. "He told me not to say anything because he knew five other clubs planned to watch me on the Saturday and he wanted me to put one over on them." It was clear that Derby had another star because Crooks, despite his frail appearance, had pace, a bundle of tricks and a sharp football brain. He was England's outside-right on 26 occasions and played four times for the Football League in an era when there was competition from the likes of Joe Hulme (Arsenal), Albert Geldard (Everton) and, of course, the Stoke City wizard Stanley Matthews. Only Arsenal full-back Eddie Hapgood played more times for England between the wars. Crooks scored more than 100 goals for Derby and his name is still linked with that of left-winger Dally Duncan. "We didn't hit passes from wing to wing," said Crooks. "I would find Dally from midfield and go up to inside-right for the return. We had a great side but the accent was too much on attack for us to win trophies." Even Arsenal could not prise Crooks, Players' Union chairman for 14 years, away from Derby and after the war he served them as chief scout. He was secretary-manager of Shrewsbury Town when they entered the League in 1950. "I was the worst secretary in the world," he once said but they loved him at Gay Meadow. Crooks was a vintage winger whose affection for Derby lasted until he died, without a enemy in the world.

## CURRY William Morton

*Centre-forward*

*Born: Newcastle, 12 October 1935. Died: Mansfield, 20 August 1990. Career: Juniors, Newcastle United: professional October 1953. Brighton & Hove Albion July 1959. Derby County September 1960. Mansfield Town February 1965. Chesterfield January 1968. Boston FC, loan, October 1968. Trainer, Worksop Town June 1969. Manager, Boston FC, February 1971 to May 1976. Manager, Sutton Town, May 1977 to May 1980.*

■ When Harry Storer brought Bill Curry to the Baseball Ground in 1960, the fee of £12,000 was not only the biggest that the Rams had paid for some time. Curry was also one of the most colourful players to appear in a Derby shirt for many years. He had a swagger to his play and his style, coupled

with the fact that he was leading scorer in each of his first three seasons, made him a favourite with the fans. Curry won an England Under-23 cap while with Newcastle United and gave good value to his clubs, with 178 League goals in 394 games.

## DALY Gerard Anthony

*Midfield*

*Born: Dublin, 30 April 1954. Career: Bohemians. Manchester United April 1973. Derby County March 1977. New England Tea Men, loan, May 1978 and May 1979. Coventry City August 1980. Leicester City, loan, January 1983. Birmingham City August 1984. Shrewsbury Town October 1985. Stoke City March 1987. Doncaster Rovers July 1988. Player-coach, Telford United, December 1989: manager August 1990 to September 1993.*

■ Gerry Daly was one of the brightest stars in Tommy Docherty's young Manchester United team which reached the FA Cup final in 1976, beating Derby in the semi-final at Hillsborough. Colin Murphy signed him for £175,000 and Daly made an immediate impact, helping to lift the Rams from the

bottom of Division One to a position of safety. At his best, he was a delightful player, quick-footed and inventive with a gift for finding scoring positions. Daly had fallen out with Docherty at Old Trafford and was unhappy when Docherty succeeded Murphy at the Baseball Ground. A transfer request followed and, although this was subsequently withdrawn, the peace was uneasy. Daly spent two summers in the North American Soccer League before Colin Addison sold him to Coventry City for £300,000. Having helped Manchester United to the Second Division Championships in 1974–75. Daly won another promotion with Birmingham City ten years later. He made 14 of his 46 Republic of Ireland appearances while with Derby.

## DANIEL Peter Aylmer

*Defender*

*Born: Ripley, 22 December 1946.*
*Career: Apprentice, Derby County: professional December 1964. Vancouver Whitecaps, loan, April 1978. Vancouver Whitecaps February 1979. Burton Albion February 1980. Belper Town October 1980.*
***Division Two Champions 1968–69. Division One Champions 1974–75.***

■ Peter Daniel was a safe but unspectacular player whose consistent efforts were mostly overshadowed by colleagues of international status. But, for Daniel, there came a glorious season of triumph when he helped Derby County to their second League Championship in 1974–75. Daniel was signed by Tim Ward in August 1963 as an apprentice, one of a number of youngsters whose career began

under Ward and who went on to greater deeds. Daniel made steady progress and survived Clough's purge to become a valued member of the Reserves, especially in the 1971–72 Central League title team. At senior level, he filled in at full-back whenever one of the established stars was injured or on international duty. Daniel always gave a solid performance but never threatened to establish a regular place. He was always the bridesmaid until an injury to Roy McFarland in an international match in May 1974. Daniel did not play a single game when Derby first won the title in 1971–72. Now he stepped into Dave Mackay's side, took the vacant number-five shirt, played brilliantly as the Rams marched towards their second Championship in four seasons and was voted Player of the Year by supporters.

## DAVIES Roger

*Centre-forward*

*Born: Wolverhampton, 25 October 1950.*
*Career: Bridgnorth Town. Worcester City August 1971. Derby County September 1971. Preston North End, loan, August 1972. Club Brugge KV July 1976. Leicester City December 1977. Tulsa Roughnecks March 1979. Derby County September 1979. Seattle Sounders March 1980. Fort Lauderdale Strikers April 1983. Burnley October 1983. Gresley Rovers November 1983. Darlington November 1983. Gresley Rovers February 1984: player-manager, July 1984 to January 1985. Player-manager, Stapenhill, November 1985. Manager, Rolls-Royce, 1990.*
***Division One Champions 1974–75.***

■ Roger Davies joined Derby from Southern League Worcester City in September 1971 for £12,000, then a record for a non-League player, although he made his League debut when on loan with Preston. After returning, Davies, who had been in the Central League-winning team in 1971–72, began to force his way in. He scored a spectacular hat-trick in the great FA Cup replay recovery at Tottenham and was sent-off in the European Cup semi-final against Juventus after reacting to provocation. Davies earned an England Under-23 cap and was a regular member of the 1974–75 Championship-winning side. That season he scored all five

goals against Luton at Derby. In August 1976, Davies signed for Brugge for £135,000, helping them to a Belgian League and Cup double, and then joined Leicester. Between two spells in the North American Soccer League, Davies returned to the Baseball Ground but could do nothing to stave off relegation from Division One.

---

## DAVISON Robert

*Centre-forward*

*Born: South Shields, 17 July 1959.*
*Career: Seaham Red Star. Huddersfield Town July 1980. Halifax Town August 1981. Derby County December 1982. Leeds United November 1987. Derby County, loan, September 1991. Sheffield United, loan, March 1992. Leicester City August 1992. Sheffield United, loan, September 1993: permanent November 1993. Rotherham United October 1994. Hull City, loan, November 1995. Halifax Town July 1996. Guiseley, loan, November 1996: player-coach June 1997: manager February 1998. Youth coach, Bradford City, August 2003: assistant manager June 2004.*
***Division Three promotion 1985–86. Division Two Champions 1986–87.***

■ When Peter Taylor returned to the Baseball Ground as manager in November 1982, his first and best cash signing was Bobby Davison, for £80,000. He immediately became Derby's likeliest source of goals and was leading scorer for five consecutive seasons. After starting with three appearances as substitute, Davison soon became a popular hero with the crowd because of his speed, enthusiasm and, above all, his goals. He gave the Rams a

taste of his skill in 1982–83 by scoring three times for Halifax Town in the two legs of a Milk Cup tie and Roy McFarland had wanted to sign him for Bradford City when he was still manager there. Davison flourished under Arthur Cox. He scored 26 League and Cup goals in 1982–83, Derby's best since Ray Straw hit 37 in 1956–57, and was the spearhead as the Rams won two promotions in successive seasons. Oxford United, for a totally unrealistic fee, and Watford tried to take Davison into Division One during the Second Division Championship season but he saw Derby back to the top flight before joining Leeds United in a £350,000 deal. He gave Derby brilliant service and fully deserved his high standing with supporters. He confirmed that when he returned on loan to transform Derby's 1991–92 Second Division season with eight goals in ten games, including his 100th for the club. He stands 10th in Derby's all-time list of scorers and showed his durability with 105 consecutive League games between September 1983 and December 1985.

---

## DOHERTY Peter Dermont

*Inside-forward*

*Born: Magherafelt, 5 June 1913.*
*Died: Fleetwood, 6 April 1990.*
*Career: Station United (Coleraine). Amateur, Coleraine. Glentoran June 1930. Blackpool November 1933. Manchester City February 1936. Derby County December 1945. Huddersfield Town December 1946. Player-manager, Doncaster Rovers, June 1949: retired as player 1953: manager to January 1958. Manager, Bristol City, January 1958 to March 1960. Manager, Northern Ireland, October 1951 to February 1962. Notts County, joint adviser with Andy Beattie, December 1965. Chief scout, Aston Villa July 1968. Assistant manager, Preston North End, October 1970 to January 1973. Assistant manager, Sunderland.*
***FA Cup winners 1945–46.***

■ They used to say that Peter Doherty, the flame-haired Irishman who danced his brilliant way through English football with Blackpool and Manchester City in the 1930s, was a discontented footballer. Doherty was not pompous or petulant, sulky or ill-mannered. Indeed, it would be impossible to meet a more gentle and courteous man. Doherty's discontent was with the system – he was a football trade unionist ahead of his time – and it manifested itself in the need to be more exciting and innovative than any other player. The former Coleraine junior bus conductor who became an Irish national hero was already a famous star

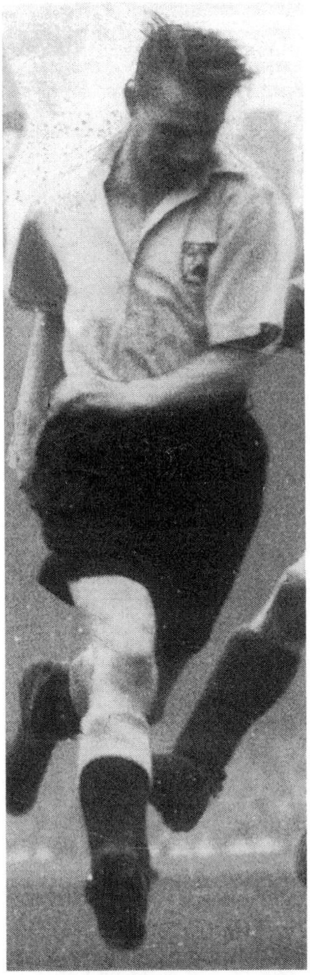

when he joined Derby in World War Two as a guest player. Doherty was a member of the Manchester City team that won the League Championship in 1937. His style of play involved constant movement. One minute he would be back helping out in his own penalty area, the next he would be weaving through the opposition's 18-yard box. In September 1944, Doherty scored all Ireland's four goals against the Combined Services. Raich Carter matched him and the Services won 8–4. Doherty went one better as he helped the Rams win the Midland Cup in 1945, scoring five times when they beat Aston Villa in the second leg of the final at Derby. Less than a year later Manchester City had let him go for £6,000 and he was scoring at Wembley as the Rams won the FA Cup. Doherty played a handful of games when the Football League started up again in 1946. He wanted to take over the Arboretum Hotel, near the Baseball Ground, but the Derby directors refused permission and told him that they thought it might affect his game. Doherty said: "If they thought that, then they didn't know me. I had no option but to leave, though it almost broke my heart because I loved Derby." Doherty was listed in the Huddersfield programme as their new player on Boxing Day 1946 but the deal had not quite gone through and he played one more game for the Rams, bowing out in style with two goals in the 5–1 win over Everton. After Huddersfield he led Doncaster Rovers to the Third Division North title in 1949–50 and managed Northern Ireland when they reached the World Cup quarter-finals in Sweden in 1958.

## DUNCAN Douglas

*Outside-left*

*Born: Aberdeen, 14 October 1909. Died: Brighton, 2 January 1990. Career: Aberdeen Richmond. Hull City August 1928. Derby County March 1932. Player-coach, Luton Town, October 1946: player-manager June 1947: retired as player April 1948. Manager, Blackburn Rovers, October 1958 to July 1960.*

***Division One runners-up 1935–36. FA Cup winners 1945–46.***

■ Derby County knew that they were getting a goalscoring winger when they signed Douglas 'Dally' Duncan from Hull City in 1932. The Aberdonian had averaged more than a goal every three games for the Tigers. It cost the Rams £2,000 to bring him to Derby but he repaid the fee many times over. Duncan took over from Georgie Mee on the Rams left wing and was soon seen by the Scottish selectors as the natural successor to the legendary Alan Morton. He scored seven times in his 14 appearances for Scotland, including both goals in a 2–0 victory over England at Hampden Park in April 1935. His friendly rivalry with Sammy Crooks over who would be Derby's top-scoring winger was good for Derby County and in the late 1930s the Rams' goals from the wings helped them to become one of the best teams in the land. Duncan worked at the Derby Carriage and Wagon works during World War Two and, aged 36, helped the Rams to win the FA Cup in 1946. He joined Luton Town and, as manager, steered them into Division One for the first time in

1955. Duncan moved to Blackburn and took them to the 1960 FA Cup final but his time at Ewood Park soon ended unhappily. He was asked to resign, refused and was sacked only weeks after leading out his team at Wembley.

## DURBAN William Alan

*Inside-forward/midfield*

*Born: Port Talbot, 7 July 1941. Career: Juniors, Cardiff City: professional September 1958. Derby County July 1963. Player-assistant manager, Shrewsbury Town, September 1973: acting manager December 1973: player-manager, February 1974. Manager, Stoke City, February 1978. Manager, Sunderland, June 1981 to March 1984. Manager, Cardiff City, September 1984 to May 1986. Chief Scout, Derby County October 1993: assistant manager, August 1994 to May 1995. Chief scout, Sunderland June 1995. Assistant manager, Stoke City September 1997: acting manager, March to May 1998.*

*Division Two Champions 1968–69. Division One Champions 1971–72.*

■ Alan Durban was 22 when Tim Ward signed him from Cardiff City for £10,000 in July 1963. It was money well spent, for Durban was one of the few to survive and play a significant part in the Clough era. He had two distinct phases at Derby, the first as a goalscoring inside-forward and the second as an intelligent midfield payer. In his first role, he formed a productive partnership with Eddie Thomas which brought them 24 goals each in 1964–65 after Thomas had arrived from Swansea Town. Durban went on to score more than 100 goals for Derby, including four hat-tricks, but his best days were in midfield. He had no great pace, nor was he a particularly good tackler but he had a wonderful feel for the flow of the game and a delicate touch. Perhaps his greatest attribute was an ability to find space in crowded penalty areas, arriving late to score a large percentage of his goals from close range. He earned 27 Welsh caps before joining Shrewsbury Town, where he became player-manager and steered them out of the Fourth Division in 1974–75. Durban played more than 550 League games (on all 92 grounds) before he retired. He became manager of Stoke City in February 1978, and was involved in another promotion success in 1978–79, third place in Division Two. After an unhappy spell with Cardiff he became manager of the Telford Tennis Centre but returned to football with Derby, helping Roy McFarland after back trouble ended Arthur Cox's time as manager.

## ERANIO Stefano

*Midfield*

*Born: Genoa, 29 December 1966. Career: Genoa August 1984. Milan August 1992. Derby County July 1997.*

■ Stefano Eranio brought style to Derby County, on and off the field, when he joined them at the end of his contract with Milan. Eranio played in Italy for 13 seasons but not in Serie A until 1989, when his first club, Genoa, won promotion. He made his debut for them as a teenager in 1984 and adapted to the top division so well that reigning Champions Milan signed him in 1992. He was involved in three titles during his five seasons and twice went on as substitute in European Cup final defeats. On the first occasion, when Olympique Marseille won in 1993, Eranio took over from Marco Van Basten, whom he rates as the best player he ever saw. "Van Basten was from another planet," he said. Eranio won 20 caps for Italy but injury kept him out of

the 1994 World Cup finals in the United States. His arrival in Derby coincided with the opening of Pride Park and was a great coup by Jim Smith. Whether playing as a wing-back or in midfield, Eranio was a joy to watch, with his instant control, passes which made it easy for the receiver and ability to score goals. He had a setback in November 1999, a broken leg as the result of a tackle from behind by Liverpool defender Sami Hyypia at Anfield, but came back strongly. Eranio planned to retire at the end of 2000–01 and was given an emotional farewell by a full house at Pride Park. He returned before the following season as a favour to Smith but an injury kept him out of the side. When Smith lost his job, Eranio was close to fitness but promptly left the club, so distressed was he at the decision.

## FORSYTH Michael Eric

*Left-back*

*Born: Liverpool, 20 March 1966.*
*Career: Apprentice, West Bromwich Albion: professional November 1983. Northampton Town, loan, March 1986. Derby County March 1986. Notts County February 1995, Hereford United, loan, September 1996. Wycombe Wanderers December 1996. Burton Albion October 1999. Gresley Rovers, loan, March 2001. Reserve-team coach, Wycombe Wanderers, July 2001.*
***Division Two Champions 1986–87.***

■ For six seasons, Michael Forsyth was one of Derby's consistent players, in the bad times as well as the good. He stepped into the left-back vacancy created when Steve Buckley left after the 1986 Third Division promotion and went on to play for England

Under-21 and England 'B'. Forsyth was a Youth international with West Bromwich Albion, and cost the Rams £26,000 when they beat the 1986 transfer deadline. He had just gone on loan to Northampton Town but was recalled to the Hawthorns, without playing for them, when Derby's bid came in. For the remainder of that season, Forsyth played as a central defender, his recognised position, in the Central League Championship team. He was given first chance to replace Buckley and, as he said: "Started on a trial and error basis." He adapted to the position well enough to be voted Player of the Year in 1987–88 and only suspensions, plus an occasional injury, kept him out. He made 124 consecutive appearances between April 1988 and January 1991. When Blades partnered Forsyth, the Rams had outstanding heading ability at full-back. With his strength in the tackle and absolute determination, Forsyth became an established First Division defender although the Rams always hoped for more from him in the other half of the field. After a memorable equaliser against Liverpool and another goal in an important victory at Coventry in March 1988, Forsyth did not score again until October 1991, in a League Cup tie at Oldham. He succeeded Geraint Williams as captain in 1992 but relinquished the position. After leaving Wycombe, he beame oart of Jenson Button's Formula One motor racing back-up team.

## GABBIADINI Marco

*Centre-forward*

*Born: Nottingham, 20 January 1968.*
*Career: Apprentice, York City: professional September 1985. Sunderland September 1987. Crystal Palace October 1991. Derby County January 1992. Birmingham City, loan, October 1996. Oxford United, loan, January 1997. Panionios August 1997. Stoke City December 1997. York City February 1998. Darlington July 1998. Northampton Town June 2000. Hartlepool United July 2003.*
***Division One promotion 1995–96.***

■ Arthur Cox, backed by Lionel Pickering's massive investment, began to form a new strike force when he signed Marco Gabbiadini for £1-million. Paul Simpson, Paul Kitson and Tommy Johnson followed within weeks. Gabbiadini emerged as a teenager at York and followed manager Denis Smith to Sunderland for £80,000. He was a big hit at Roker Park, averaging 20 goals a season as well as winning England Under-21 and 'B' caps. Crystal Palace signed him for £1.8-million but his four months at Selhurst Park were

extremely unhappy. Although he scored the winner at Portsmouth on his debut for the Rams, Gabbiadini needed a few weeks to rid himself of the Palace experience but went on to score 68 goals before he was released in 1997. He was important in Derby's promotion under Jim Smith, with Dean Sturridge as his partner and Ron Willems behind them. On some days, Gabbiadini looked a world-beater and on others his control deserted him but he always had enthusiasm. He continued to score goals, passing 200 in the League while with Northampton, but a knee injury forced his retirement in January 2004.

## GALLACHER Hugh Kilpatrick

*Centre-forward*

*Born: Bellshill, 2 February 1903. Died: Low Fell, Gateshead, 11 June 1957.*
*Career: Bellshill Athletic March 1920. Queen of the South December 1920. Airdrieonians May 1921. Newcastle United December 1925. Chelsea May 1930. Derby County November 1934. Notts County September 1936. Grimsby Town January 1938. Gateshead June 1938.*
***Division One runners-up 1935–36.***

■ In 1934, Derby manager George Jobey, confronted with a serious injury to centre-forward Jack Bowers, paid £2,750 for Chelsea's Scottish international Hughie Gallacher. Jobey knew that he was buying more than one of the greatest centre-forwards who ever lived and that Gallacher had a reputation off the field. Married at 17, and divorced at 23, his debts were so high that Derby had to settle them as part of the transfer deal. His Derby debut, against Birmingham in November 1934, was watched by nearly 20,000 fans, who turned up at the Baseball Ground despite driving rain. He scored within six minutes and, in December 1934, hit all five against Blackburn Rovers at Ewood Park. A member of the famous Wembley Wizards team that beat England 5–1 in 1928, Gallacher won a Scottish Cup medal at Airdrie and captained Newcastle United to the 1926–27 League Championship, the season

in which he set a club record of 36 goals in 38 League games. When he returned after a £10,000 move to Chelsea, there were 68,386 in St James' Park to smash Newcastle's attendance record. He died in June 1957, throwing himself in front of the Edinburgh-York express train while facing a charge of cruelty to his son.

## GEMMILL Archibald

*Midfield*

*Born: Paisley, 24 March 1947.*
*Career: Drumchapel Amateurs. St Mirren 1964. Preston North End June 1967. Derby County September 1970. Nottingham Forest September 1977. Birmingham City August 1979. Jacksonville Tea Men March 1982. Wigan Athletic September 1982. Derby County November 1982. Released May 1984. Coach, Nottingham Forest, August 1985 to May 1994: registered as player January 1986. Joint manager (with John McGovern), Rotherham United, September 1994 to September 1996.*
***Division One Champions 1971–72, 1974–75 (captain).***

■ Archie Gemmill cost Derby County £66,000 when he was signed from Preston to take over from Willie Carlin in midfield. So keen was Brian Clough to complete the deal that he stayed overnight in the Gemmills' house. Pace was the first important ingredient Gemmill added but he soon developed into one of the finest midfield players in Britain. He began running every August and did not stop until the following May, urging the rest of the team, competing in every area of the field and using his speed as the ace. After a stunning UEFA Cup performance against Atlético

Madrid in Spain, their Argentine manager, Juan Carlos Lorenzo, embraced an embarrassed Gemmill shouting "Magnifico". Gemmill made 40 appearances for the 1971–72 Champions, and, in the absence of Roy McFarland, was an inspirational captain when the title returned to Derby three years later. He won a third Championship medal in 1977–78, after joining Nottingham Forest in what was for Derby a disastrous exchange deal that brought in goalkeeper John Middleton and £25,000. He played 43 games for Scotland, 22 of them while with Derby, including six as captain, and gained a League Cup-winners' medal with Forest but was disappointed to be left out of Forest's 1979 European Cup final team. He was the first signing after Peter Taylor's appointment as manager and did more than most in a successful fight against relegation. In 1983–84, Taylor fell out with Gemmill and although McFarland restored him to the team, his career ended sadly with relegation to Division Three. He was on Clough's coaching staff and, after two years as joint manager of Rotherham United, returned to Derby as overseas scout under Jim Smith.

---

## GEORGE Charles Frederick

*Forward/midfield*

*Born: Islington, 10 October 1950.*
*Career: Apprentice, Arsenal: professional February 1968. Derby County July 1975. St George's Budapest, NSW, loan, May 1977. Minnesota Kicks, loan, May 1978. Southampton December 1978. Nottingham Forest, loan, January 1980. Bulova, Hong Kong, September 1981. AFC Bournemouth March 1982. Derby County March 1982.*

■ Dave Mackay interrupted a holiday in Scotland and flew to London when, in July 1975, he heard that Charlie George might be available, although Tottenham Hotspur were favourites. Mackay wanted to add even more skill to his League Champions and was exceptionally pleased with himself when he captured George, a member of Arsenal's 1970–71 double side, for £100,000. George made his competitive debut at Wembley in the Charity Shield and had a brilliant first season. His shooting was deadly, his passing both exquisite and startling in its vision. Until he dislocated a shoulder against Stoke at the Baseball Ground in March 1976, Derby had a realistic chance of the double. George was the first Midlands Player of the Year but was upset when Mackay was sacked in November 1976. He never again reached the same heights, although one England appearance was poor reward for his skill. He had knee problems when Tommy Docherty sold him to Southampton for £400,000 in December 1978. John Newman brought him back to Derby in March 1982, a short-term move that helped Derby to stay up for another season, but they could not meet his terms for a longer stay. George had trials with Dundee United and Coventry City without proving fit enough for a contract but no returning former player is ever given a more passionate welcome at Derby.

## GOODALL Archibald Lee

*Centre-half*

*Born: Belfast, 19 June 1864. Died: London N10, 29 November 1929.*
*Career: Liverpool Stanley. Preston North End. Aston Villa October 1888. Derby County May 1889. Plymouth Argyle May 1903. Glossop January 1904. Wolverhampton Wanderers October 1905.*
***Division One runners-up 1895–96. FA Cup finalists 1897–98, 1902–03.***

■ Born in Ireland and raised in Scotland, Archie Goodall was as rumbustious as his brother John was gentle. He played for several clubs, including the Rams, before 1888 and when the Football League was formed he played for Preston and Aston Villa. His move from Preston to Villa was the first transfer during a season to be approved by the League. *Athletic News* reported: 'Goodall's arrival at Perry Barr led to a good deal of bickering.' Derby had a first taste of his cussedness when he tried to back out of the move to them. Primarily a centre-half in the days when that position was not that of a stopper, Archie scored over 50 goals for Derby. He was one of the greatest characters ever to play for the club, causing alarm before the 1898 Cup final because he was outside trying to unload tickets on which he had speculated, and once refusing to play extra-time in a United Counties League Cup final because he said that his contract ended after 90 minutes. He was suspended before the 1899 FA Cup final against Sheffield United, for 'insubordination and inattention to training' but the ban was lifted in time for him to play at Crystal Palace. He asked to

be left out 'in consequence of the many mischievous and idle rumours' that had circulated since the dispute, so the inexperienced Bob Paterson was included. Goodall was still chuntering at the start of 1899–1900 and missed the first four matches before re-signing. He toured Europe and America with a strongman act, 'walking' around a giant metal hoop, and was a great follower of country sports. He was an Ireland regular and his records of consecutive appearances for Derby, 167 in all matches and 151 in the League, survived into the new millennium.

## GOODALL John

*Forward*

*Born: Westminster, 19 June 1863. Died: Watford, 20 May 1942.*
*Career: Kilmarnock Athletic 1880. Great Lever 1883. Preston North End August 1885. Derby County May 1889. New Brighton Tower October 1899. Glossop February 1901. Player-manager, Watford, May 1903: manager-trainer June 1909. Player-manager, Racing Club de Rubaix, France, June 1910. Player-manager, Mardy, May 1912 to cs 1913.*
***Division One runners-up 1895–96 (captain). FA Cup finalists 1897–98 (captain).***

■ Derby County had good reason to remember John Goodall. He scored five goals for Great Lever in the Rams' first match in 1884. Derby never forgot him and after he played in the 1888–89 Preston double-winning side, signed Goodall in time for the League's second season. It was a sensational capture, considering his status in the Preston and England teams, and Goodall, one of the great footballers of his time, did not disappoint Derby supporters. It is possible that Preston would not have enjoyed such sweeping success, Champions without losing a game and Cup winners without conceding a goal, had Derby's attempt to sign Goodall, along with brother Archie, in May 1888 been successful. Although the two were dissimilar players, Goodall taught Steve Bloomer much about the game. He knew just when to pass or shoot and his great strength was to bring out the best in those around him. Though born in England – he played 14 times for

his country – Goodall was raised in the Scottish school of soccer and was a pioneer of scientific football and the passing game. Such was his exemplary character, he was known as Johnny All-Good and twice captained England in the days when the honour usually went to an amateur. He also played cricket for Derbyshire and Hertfordshire.

## HALL Benjamin

*Centre-half*

*Born: Ecclesfield, 6 March 1879.*
*Died: Leicester, 1963.*
*Career: Grimsby Town January 1900. Derby County August 1903. Leicester Fosse August 1911. Hyde 1912. South Shields 1913. Coach, Grimsby Town. Coach, Heywood United. Trainer, Huddersfield Town, 1919. Manager, Bristol Rovers, July 1920 to May 1921. Manager, Loughborough Corinthians May 1929.*

■ When Archie Goodall left the Rams for Plymouth in 1903 the club knew that they needed to sign a first-class centre-half to fill the gap left by the Irish international. They turned to Grimsby Town's Ben Hall and

brought to the Baseball Ground one of the most skilful half-backs in the Football League. In the days when a centre-half was the key man, linking defence with attack, Hall's immaculate ball control and delightful passing were vital. Grimsby had dropped into Division Two and Hall wanted to continue in the top flight, which made Derby's task of signing him easier. He stayed at Derby when they, too, were relegated. He relied on skill rather than brawn and was considered a gentlemanly player in 269 appearances with the Rams. A good cricketer, Hall was popular with both players and spectators. He returned to play some wartime games for Derby in 1915–16, along with his brother Ellis. Hall was manager of Bristol Rovers when they entered the League in 1920 and later scouted for Southend United.

## HARRISON Reginald Frederick

*Outside-right*

*Born: Derby, 22 May 1923.*
*Career: Derby Corinthians. Derby County March 1944. Boston United July 1955. Player-coach, Long Eaton United May 1957: player-manager, January 1958. Coach, Wilmorton and Alvaston, May 1962. Player-coach, Alfreton Town, July 1962. Manager, Crewton, July 1966. Coach, Belper Town, June 1970.*
***FA Cup winners 1945–46.***

■ Little Reg Harrison could hardly have expected an FA Cup-winners' medal so early in his career. A hard-running outside-right who scored his fair share of goals – 59 in 281 senior appearances – Harrison returned to the Rams team for the semi-final matches against Birmingham

when Sammy Crooks was injured. Crooks was not risked at Wembley, although he had managed a League South game earlier, and manager Stuart McMillan had no worries in handing over the number seven shirt to Harrison. The player has always paid tribute to the help he received from Crooks and from Raich Carter, who took the baby-faced winger into his charge. After war service with the Royal Artillery, Harrison proved himself as highly skilled as well as enthusiastic player. He was of First Division quality but stayed while the club declined. Harrison was in the Boston United team that won 6–1 at the Baseball Ground to provide an FA Cup humiliation and later did an immense amount for junior football in Derby.

## HECTOR Kevin James

*Forward*

*Born: Leeds, 2 November 1944.*
*Career: Juniors, Bradford: professional July 1962. Derby County September 1966. Vancouver Whitecaps January 1978. Boston United, loan, September 1978. Burton Albion, loan,*

*November 1979. Burton Albion September 1980. Derby County October 1980. Gresley Rovers September 1982. Shepshed Charterhouse October 1982. Burton Albion December 1982. Gresley Rovers September 1983. Belper Town July 1984. Eastwood Town August 1987. Heanor Town July 1988.*
***Division Two Champions 1968–69. Division One Champions 1971–72, 1974–75.***

■ Kevin Hector had scored 113 League goals in 176 games for Bradford when Tim Ward astonished supporters by signing him for £38,000. Derby, pottering along unambitiously in the Second Division, were not expected to play fees of that size but Hector was an instant success. He was christened the King by supporters and retained the nickname, even when he became one fine player among many in the great days of the early 1970s. He did more than survive the advent of Brian Clough and Peter Taylor; he was an integral part of the teams which won the Second Division and two League Championships. He was gifted with pace and a marvellous balance, so the goals flowed regularly. Between 1970 and 1972, he played in 105 consecutive League games: from August 1967 to December 1974, he missed only four of 314 League games, an astonishing record for a striker. Sir Alf Ramsey should have given him an earlier England run and his debut, against Poland in October 1973, was farcical, a couple of minutes as substitute to try and get England through to the World Cup finals. He nearly did it too, being denied only by a Polish kneecap on the goal-line. His only other cap was also as substitute. Tommy Docherty sold Hector to Vancouver Whitecaps and he spent the English seasons playing for Boston United and Burton Albion before Colin Addison brought him back in October 1980. By the time he bowed out, with a goal against Watford in a match Derby had to win to ensure their Second Division place, Hector had made more appearances than any other player in Derby's history and scored 201 goals, a total surpassed only by Steve Bloomer. He gave supporters immense pleasure through his style, his goals and his manner on and off the field. He was still a winner in Belper Town's Northern Counties (East) League Championship team of 1984–85.

## HINDMARCH Robert

*Centre-half*

*Born: Stannington, 17 April 1961.*
*Died: Philadelphia, 5 November 2002.*
*Career: Apprentice, Sunderland: professional April 1978. Portsmouth, loan, December 1983. Derby County July 1984. Wolverhampton Wanderers June 1990. Gillingham August 1993. Telford United. Player-manager, Cork City, 1995. Cannes 1996.*
***Division Three promotion 1985–86 (captain). Division Two Champions 1986–87 (captain).***

■ Rob Hindmarch had been captain of Sunderland as a teenager but was allowed to leave Roker Park on a free transfer. Arthur Cox moved in quickly, saying: "I would have signed Rob had I still been manager of

Newcastle United in the First Division." Hindmarch was a magnificent capture. He was appointed captain in 1985 and led Derby brilliantly in their two promotions. Although not blessed with pace, he was tremendous in the air, solid on the ground and had moral as well as physical strength. When Mark Wright was signed, Hindmarch was left out after one game as his partner and was not recalled for almost six months. With Hindmarch back in, the Rams began to move towards safety and Wright clearly appreciated his presence. At the end of the season, Cox spoke of Hindmarch as the backbone of the club: 'A man's man'. The mystery was that no other club had come in with an offer the Rams could not refuse while Hindmarch was playing in the Central League. When his contract was up, Hindmarch joined Wolverhampton Wanderers for £300,000 but he was right out of the picture in his second season at Molineux and did not make a senior appearances. He was running soccer schools in the United States when his many friends were shocked to hear of his death, from motor neurone disease, at the age of 41.

## HINTON Alan Thomas

*Outside-right*

*Born: Wednesbury, 6 October 1942.*
*Career: Juniors, Wolverhampton Wanderers: professional October 1959. Nottingham Forest January 1964. Derby County September 1967. Borrowash Victoria August 1976. Dallas Tornado March 1977. Player-assistant coach, Vancouver Whitecaps, October 1977. Head coach, Tulsa Roughnecks, October 1978 to August 1979. Head coach, Seattle Sounders, November 1979 to January 1983. Head coach, Vancouver Whitecaps, April to October 1984. Head coach, Tacoma Stars, January 1986 to December 1989.*
***Division Two Champions 1968–69. Division One Champions 1971–72, 1974–75.***

■ Alan Hinton had won three England caps, one with Wolverhampton Wanderers and two with Nottingham Forest, before Brian Clough and Peter Taylor signed him from the City Ground for £30,000 in September 1967. Some Forest committee men were heard to suggest that Derby would be asking for their money back but they were absolutely wrong. Hinton's ability to cross the ball from any position and with either foot amounted almost to genius. His explosive goals were a bonus. He was Derby's creator-in-chief as they won the Second and First Division titles in the space of four years as well as their acknowledged artist from free-kicks and corners. He had a short run in the 1974–75 Championship success, giving Derby a different shape at a time when they were beginning to lose their way, but played little in the next season after the death of his son Matthew. He went into the North American Soccer League and set a new record for 'assists' in 1978, laying on 30 goals to beat the mark previously shared by Pelé and George Best. He was a successful coach, going indoors after the collapse of the NASL. As Peter Taylor predicted, he was fully appreciated at Derby only after he had left.

## HOWE John Robert

*Left-back*

*Born: West Hartlepool, 7 October 1915. Died: Hartlepool, 5 April 1987.*
*Career: Hartlepools United June 1934. Derby County March 1936. Huddersfield Town October 1949. Player-manager, King's Lynn, July 1951: manager to May 1953: player to May 1955. (Appointed player-manager Long Sutton United in August 1955 but did not take it up). Wisbech Town August 1955.*
***Division One runners-up 1935–36. FA Cup winners 1945–46.***

■ Jack Howe was one of the best two-footed full-backs in Britain. Standing six-feet tall. Howe could

kick a ball equally hard and accurately with either foot. Another George Jobey capture from the North-East, Howe made his debut as Derby were finishing eight points behind Champions Sunderland and was a regular until the war when he joined the Cameron Highlanders and guested for Hearts, Falkirk, Aberdeen and St Mirren. He played for the Scottish League against the British Army and, after service in India, he was demobbed in time to earn an FA Cup-winners' medal, playing centre-half in the semi-final replay and left-back at Wembley. Howe never shirked a tackle, was totally dominant and took over the captaincy when Raich Carter went to Hull in 1948. When Howe won the first of his three England caps, in a memorable 4–0 victory over Italy in Turin, it was considered long overdue. Howe, among Derby's greatest defenders, was one of the first professional sportsmen to wear contact lenses. He was over 40 before he ended his career with Wisbech Town.

## JOHNSON Thomas

*Forward*

*Born: Newcastle upon Tyne, 15 January 1971.*
*Career: Trainee, Notts County: professional January 1989. Derby County, loan and permanent, March 1992. Aston Villa January 1995. Glasgow Celtic March 1997. Everton, loan, September 1999. Sheffield Wednesday September 2001. Kilmarnock December 2001. Gillingham August 2002. Sheffield United February 2005. Scunthorpe United June 2005. Tamworth, loan, February 2006: permanent May 2006.*

■ Derby County's transfer record, £1.3-million for Paul Kitson, was only ten days old when Tommy Johnson's signing beat it. He made his debut on loan and the deal was completed the following week for £1,375,000. Johnson was developed by Notts County and made his debut as a 17-year-old before helping them to successive promotions from Third Division to First, both times through the Play-offs. He scored in the two Wembley finals. An England Under-21 international with both clubs, Johnson's speed made him a constant threat. He has phases when he missed good chances, often created by himself, but never stopped going in for the next opportunity. That honesty, coupled with a friendly approach, made him popular at the Baseball Ground and, after a joint move with Gary Charles, Villa Park. At that time, sales were forced on Roy McFarland. Johnson was sparingly used by Celtic following a £2.4-million move but achieved a good striking rate for them.

## KEEN Errington Ridley Liddell

*Left-half*

*Born: Walker-on-Tyne, 4 September 1910. Died: Fulham, July 1984.*
*Career: Nun's Moor. Newcastle United September 1927. Derby County December 1930. Chelmsford City May 1938. Player-manager, Hereford United, July 1939. Leeds United December 1945. Bacup Borough July 1946. Hull City, trial, 1946. Coached in Hong Kong. Coach, IFK Norrkoping, 1949.*
***Division One runners-up 1935–36.***

■ Blond haired wing-half 'Ike' Keen played only one game for his first club Newcastle United. It was against the Rams and, two months later, he signed for Derby, George Jobey having seen enough to convince him that Keen, a powerful half-back, would do a useful job at the Baseball Ground. He quickly established himself as a fine player and in December 1932 won the first of his four

England caps. Keen was one of four Rams stars – Crooks, Barker and Cooper were the others – to play for England against The Rest in a trial match in March 1933. In March 1936 Keen earned a £650 benefit cheque but the business in which he invested it foundered and he found himself in Derby Bankruptcy Court. Keen was a fine attacking wing-half, but his defensive qualities were often questioned and against Leicester, in January 1938, he gave away a goal when trying to dribble his way out of trouble only a dozen yards from his goal line. Shortly afterwards Tim Ward took his place and Keen went into the Southern League.

## LAURSEN Jacob

*Defender*

*Born: Vejle, 6 October 1971.*
*Career: Vejle Boldklub August 1990. Silkeborg IF August 1992. Derby County July 1996. FC Copenhagen August 2000. Leicester City January 2002. Wolverhampton Wanderers, loan, March 2002. AGF Aarhus, loan, April 2002. Rapid Vienna November 2002. Vejle Boldklub September 2003.*

■ A Danish international and League Champion with Silkeborg in 1993–94, Jacob Laursen agreed to join Derby County before he was involved in the 1996 European Championship finals. Jim Smith signed him for the Premiership and, after starting disconcertingly with an own-goal against Leeds United, Laursen proved a major acquisition. He was a great professional, as immaculate and courteous off the field as he was determined on it.

He set a high standard of defensive diligence, at his best when man-marking, and wanted to play every minute of a season. If Laursen was absent, everybody knew the injury was severe. Supporters appreciated his honesty and voted him Player of the Year for 1998–99. It was a surprise and a disappointment when he left and although he won another Danish title, with FC Copenhagen in 2000–01, his career tailed off after that. He will always be remembered with respect and affection at Derby as one of the main planks in the prosperous Premiership years.

## LEE Francis Henry

*Forward*

*Born: Westhoughton, 29 April 1944.*
*Career: Juniors, Bolton Wanderers: professional May 1961. Manchester City October 1967. Derby County August 1974. Chairman, Manchester City, January 1994 to March 1998.*
***Division One Champions 1974–75.***

■ An inspired signing by Dave Mackay, Francis Lee created a lasting impact at the Baseball Ground. When he retired to look after his waste paper conversion business in Bolton, he left a host of friends as well as the feeling that he could have had at least one more season. After joining Manchester City, Lee won League, FA Cup, League Cup and European Cup Winners' Cup medals in the space of three glorious seasons as well as 27 England caps. Mackay paid City £100,000 in August 1974, rightly thinking that Lee could score goals and, as important, give a good side extra aggression. Lee, full of bustle in

opposing penalty areas, promptly added another League Championship medal to his collection. His second season was marred by a brawl with Norman Hunter in the League match against Leeds United at Derby. Lee, sent off for allowing his lip to be cut by Hunter's fist, attacked the Leeds man on the way to the tunnel and was later suspended for four weeks. He went out with a typical flourish, scoring twice against Ipswich Town at Portman Road in the last two minutes of his 500th and final League game in April 1976. He became a racehorse trainer and was involved in a takeover of Manchester City. He was chairman of his old club until coming under heavy criticism as City faced their second relegation in three seasons.

---

## LEONARD Henry Doxford

*Centre-forward*

*Born: Sunderland, 1886. Died: Derby, 3 November 1951.*

*Career: Sunderland West End. Newcastle United November 1907. Grimsby Town May 1908. Middlesbrough March 1911. Derby County October 1911. Manchester United September 1920. Heanor Town June 1921.*

***Division Two Champions 1911–12, 1914–15.***

■ Harry Leonard was a high-scoring centre-forward who led the Rams' line with gusto before World War One. He was signed in 1911 to replace Alf Bentley and, coupled with Steve Bloomer in a second spell at the Baseball Ground, made Derby a potent attacking force. He scored 17 League goals in the Second Division Championship side, including four against Fulham, in his first winter. Two years later he missed three months of the season through injury when the Rams were relegated, but 12 months on he was celebrating promotion once more. Leonard ended 1914–15 second-highest scorer and continued to find the net regularly in wartime games. He was still at the Baseball Ground when League soccer resumed in 1919 but was by then a veteran and landlord of the Albert Vaults, Brook Street. Leonard went to Manchester United in 1920, leaving Derby with 73 goals in 150 League and Cup appearances.

## LEUTY Leon Harry

*Centre-half*

*Born: Meole Brace, 23 October 1920. Died Nottingham, 19 December 1955.*

*Career: Amateur, Derby County, 1936. Notts County wartime guest. Derby Corinthians. Rolls-Royce. Amateur, Derby County, August 1943: professional May 1944. Bradford March 1950. Notts County September 1950.*

***FA Cup winners 1945–46.***

■ No less a centre-forward than Tommy Lawton once nominated Leon Leuty as the most difficult centre-half he had faced. In the late 1940s Leuty established his reputation as a calm, confident defender who possessed more footballing skill than most First Division stoppers, although he never won a full England cap. He was unlucky to play at the same time as Stoke's Neil Franklin, one of England's greats until he went to Bogota to break free of the maximum wage. Leuty, an impressive member of the 1946

FA Cup-winning team, captained England 'B' while at Derby and appeared in the unofficial Bolton Disaster Fund international against Scotland at Maine Road, Manchester. Like other senior players, he became unsettled by the arrival of Billy Steel and moved to Bradford for £20,000, then to Notts County for £25,000 six months later. He was still a young man when he died of leukaemia but he was unchallenged as Derby's best post-war centre-half until the emergence of Roy **McF**arland.

## McFARLAND Roy Leslie

*Centre-half*

*Born: Liverpool, 5 April 1948.*
*Career: Edge Hill Boys Club. Tranmere Rovers July 1966. Derby County August 1967. Player-manager, Bradford City, May 1981. Assistant manager, Derby County, November 1982: registered as player August 1983: caretaker manager, April 1984: assistant manager, June 1984: manager, October 1993 to April 1995. Joint manager (with Colin Todd), Bolton Wanderers, June 1995 to January 1996. Manager, Cambridge United, November 1996 to February 2001. Manager, Torquay United, July 2001 to April 2002. Manager, Chesterfield, May 2003.*
***Division Two Champions 1968–69. Division One Champions 1971–72 (captain), 1974–75.***

■ Brian Clough and Peter Taylor had seen Roy McFarland playing for Tranmere Rovers when they were in charge of Hartlepool and made him their second signing at Derby. He was then 19 and had been snatched from under the noses of Liverpool, the team he supported. For less than £25,000, Clough and Taylor bought a player who, they felt sure, would develop into the best centre-half in England. With Dave Mackay alongside him to speed up his maturing process in 1968–69, McFarland was a key-figure in the team that romped away with the Second Division title. He made his England debut in Malta in February 1971 and led Derby to the 1971–72 League Championship. McFarland had the football world at his feet, although he suffered a black week in 1973 when Clough and Taylor resigned and England were knocked out of the World Cup in the qualifying stages because they were unable to beat Poland at Wembley. It was also at Wembley, in May 1974, that McFarland sustained the severe

Achilles tendon injury which was to keep him out of all but the last four games in the 1974–75 Championship triumph. He was able to regain his England place briefly and his 28 appearances constituted a record for a Rams player, passing Alan Durban's 27 for Wales but later overtaken by Peter Shilton and others. Sadly for McFarland, the best part of his playing career came first and, in a declining side, he was increasingly susceptible to injuries. He became player-manager of Bradford City, and promptly led them to promotion from Division Four in 1981–82 before returning to Derby in controversial circumstances. Derby were fined for an illegal approach. He played a few matches when he was Taylor's assistant in the first part of the sad 1983–84 season. At his peak, he was one of Derby's all-time greats, skilful, consistent and ruthless; a superb professional and one of England's best post-war defenders. McFarland was caretaker manager after Taylor's dismissal and worked successfully with Arthur Cox as Derby rose back through the divisions. He became manager in his own right when back trouble forced Cox's resignation but the days of lavish spending were over.

## McGOVERN John Prescott

*Midfield*

*Born: Montrose, 28 October 1949.*
*Career: Apprentice, Hartlepools United: professional May 1967. Derby County September 1968. Leeds United August 1974. Nottingham Forest February 1975. Player-manager, Bolton Wanderers, June 1982 to January 1985. Horwich RMI February 1985. Assistant manager, Chorley, December 1989: manager March*

*1990. Assistant manager Plymouth Argyle March 1992. Joint manager (with Archie Gemmill), Rotherham United, September 1994 to September 1996. Manager, Woking, June 1997 to September 1998. Assistant manager, Hull City, November 1998 to April 2000. Manager, Ilkeston Town, October 2000 to March 2001.*
***Division Two Champions 1968–69. Division One Champions 1971–72.***

■ John McGovern's headmaster was reluctant to allow him to join Hartlepools United from a rugby-playing grammar school. Even then, however, McGovern was his own man, showing the strength of character which he needed to sustain him through a career in which success was never matched by whole-hearted appreciation from the stands and terraces. His total dedication to the team effort tended to mask skill and a lovely touch on the ball but, above all others, Brian Clough and Peter Taylor appreciated his value. He followed Clough from Hartlepools to Derby for £7,500, then to Leeds and Nottingham Forest, whom he captained to two European Cups successes as he reached his peak. McGovern looked frail, but he was as tough physically as he was mentally. He oiled the midfield wheels in Derby's first League Championship and, after sharing Clough's unhappy experiences at Leeds, led Forest to their first Championship in 1977–78. He was self-effacing, closing down the opposition's key man and keeping his own side ticking by pushing around simple passes. He was an intelligent player, accepting his own limitations and devoting himself to the needs of the team, an approach he continued as manager of Bolton Wanderers before he fell victim to internal politics. He played briefly for Horwich RMI while waiting for another job in the League but it was seven years, including a period living in the Canaries, before Peter Shilton took him to Plymouth.

## McGRATH Paul

*Central defender*

*Born: Ealing, 4 December 1959.*
*Career: St Patrick's Athletic. Manchester United April 1982. Aston Villa August 1989. Derby County October 1996. Sheffield United August 1997. Director of Football, Waterford, February 2004.*

■ One of the most gifted defenders of the 1980s and early 1990s, Paul McGrath was an inspired short-term signing for Derby County in their first Premiership season. He cost £100,000 at the age of 36 plus the same again when the Rams stayed up in their final season at the Baseball Ground. By the time he arrived at Derby with a history of knee trouble, McGrath did little

training beyond a gentle trundle round Raynesway but Jim Smith wanted his skill, knowledge and, above all, presence among his three centre-halves. Other Derby players regarded McGrath with awe and he had unquestioned respect from opponents. He was quietly spoken, almost shy, and did a wonderful job. He helped Manchester United, under Ron Atkinson, to win the FA Cup in 1985. When Alex Ferguson decided McGrath's lifestyle did not suit him, Atkinson paid £400,000 to sign him for Aston Villa. The return was 323 appearances, with League Cup-winners' medals in 1994 and 1996. A World Cup veteran, McGrath won the last of his 83 Republic of Ireland caps while with Derby. He played only 26 times for Derby but ranks among their finest players.

## McINTYRE John McMutrie

*Right-half*

*Born: Glasgow, 19 October 1898. Died: Derby, 7 June 1974.*

*Career: Perthshire (Glasgow Junior League). Stenhousemuir 1918. Derby County June 1921. Chesterfield December 1931. Derby County 'A' team coach/scout, 1944: assistant manager, November 1953: scout to May 1960.*

***Division Two promotion 1925–26. Division One runners-up 1929–30 (captain).***

■ Johnny McIntyre cost the Rams no more than a £10 signing-on fee when he came from Stenhousemuir as an inside-forward. Seldom has a football club spent a tenner more wisely and McIntyre settled down to become a key member of the Rams side for more than a decade. He made his debut against Blackpool on 27 August 1921 and scored in the Rams' 4–2 defeat at Bloomfield Road. He was also tried at outside-left, but eventually found his true position at right-half. There he became a regular, although injury dogged his career and but for that ill-luck he would have played many more than his 369 games. McIntyre was a player of polish, precision and determination, unchallenged in his position until Jack Nicholas took over. He became assistant manager when Harry Storer was appointed.

## MACKAY David Craig

*Wing-half*

*Born: Edinburgh, 14 November 1934.*

*Career: Slateford Athletic. Newtongrange Star. Heart of Midlothian April 1952. Tottenham Hotspur March 1959. Derby County July 1968. Swindon Town May 1971: player-manager, November 1971. Manager, Nottingham Forest, November 1972. Manager, Derby County, October 1973 to November 1976. Manager, Walsall, March 1977. Manager, Al-Arabi, Kuwait, August 1978. Manager, Alba Shabab, Dubai, 1986. Manager, Doncaster Rovers, December 1987 to March 1989. General manager, Birmingham City, April 1989 to January 1991. Coach, Zamalek, Egypt, September 1991. National Youth Coach, Qatar, 1993 to 1996.*

***Division Two Champions 1968–69 (captain).***

■ For three unforgettable seasons. Dave Mackay conducted a master class at the Baseball Ground. He was already a legend in two countries before he joined Derby County. In five seasons with Heart of Midlothian, Mackay earned Scottish League, Cup and League Cup-winners' medals before Bill Nicholson signed him for Tottenham Hotspur. With them, he was in the first team of the 20th century to win the

League and FA Cup double in 1960–61, helped to retain the FA Cup the next year and led Spurs to a third FA Cup victory in 1967 after twice breaking his left leg. When Brian Clough announced that he had signed Mackay for £5,000, many Derby people could not grasp it fully until they had seen him in a Rams shirt. Clough later called that: "The best day's work of my life." Mackay, the inspiration of Tottenham's midfield, was to patrol at the back, tell the young players where to go and what to do, tidy up the loose ends, and, most important, lead. At the time he was the highest paid player in the League and was worth every penny because he was a natural captain as well as a great player. He was supremely skilful, a lovely kicker of the ball however it came to him, and he inspired Derby. They raced away with the Second Division Championship in 1968–69 and Mackay was joint Footballer of the Year with Manchester City's Tony Book. He then proved that, in his mid-30s, he remained a force in the First Division. He finished at Derby in 1970–71 with a full house of 42 League appearances for the first time in his career. Only one mystery persists – why he played for Scotland on only 22 occasions. He would have been a top player in any era and returned as manager to lead the Rams to their second Championship.

## McMINN Kevin Clifton

*Midfield*

*Born: Castle Douglas, 28 September 1962.*
*Career: Glenafton Athletic. Queen of the South November 1982. Glasgow Rangers October 1984. Seville January 1987. Derby County February 1988. Birmingham City July 1993. Burnley, loan, March 1994: permanent April 1994. Joondalup City (Western Australia) March 1996 to March 1997. Assistant manager, Southport, February 2000. Assistant manager, Oxford United, May to December 2001. Assistant manager, Chester, January to July 2002. Assistant manager, Mickleover Sports, April to May 2004.*

■ Arthur Cox chased Ted McMinn for five years before signing him for £300,000 from Seville and was rewarded by seeing him become one of Derby's most popular players. McMinn was close to the Scotland side when, in November 1989, he severely damaged knee ligaments in a victory over Tottenham Hotspur at White Hart Lane. It was 14 months before he played again but, after a tentative return in the 1990–91 relegation season, McMinn was back to his colourful best the following season and was voted Derby's Player of the Year. Tall for a winger, McMinn loved to take on opponents, although his scoring record was poor. Cox first chased McMinn, then with Queen of the South, when he was manager of Newcastle United but Rangers had more appeal. After joining Derby, Cox had two more tries and, on the second occasion, McMinn followed his Rangers manager Jock Wallace, son of a former Derby goalkeeper, to Spain. The persistent Cox at last landed his man in February 1988 and ended a depressing period in which Robert Maxwell, squabbling with the League over his proposed purchase of Watford, put a block on transfers. In 2005, McMinn had part of a leg amputated after a mysterious infection. A testimonial was staged in 2006.

## MASKREY Harry Mart

*Goalkeeper*

*Born: Unstone, nr Dronfield, 8 October 1880. Died: Derby, 21 April 1927.*
*Career: Ripley Athletic 1898. Derby County December 1902. Bradford City October 1909. Ripley Town and Athletic May 1911. Stalybridge Celtic September 1911. Mansfield Mechanics July 1913. British Cellulose FC. Derby County September 1920. Burton All Saints August 1921.*

■ Derbyshire has a long tradition of producing top class goalkeepers. Robinson and Fryer began it for the Rams, along with Sheffield United's 'Fatty' Foulke: it went down the years to Ernald Scattergood of Derby, Sam Hardy of Liverpool and Villa, and, more recently, West Brom's John Osborne and Bob Wilson of Arsenal. Harry Maskrey is most worthy of a place in that gallery. Soon after he succeeded Jack Fryer he was described as having 'all the collier's contempt for hard knocks.' Maskrey, while not as tall as the man he replaced, was still quite a size. His reach was over 6ft 7in from finger-tip to finger-tip of his outstretched arms, a physique that helped him into the Grenadier Guards in World War One. Maskrey spent only a short time in the Reserves before establishing himself as the regular first-team goalkeeper and was remarkably assured. He played for the Football League against the Irish League and was capped by England against Ireland in Belfast

in February 1908. He was playing for British Cellulose in the midweek Works League when he returned to Derby County in an emergency in 1920, passing 200 League appearances for them in the process. Maskrey collapsed and died at his pub, The New Inn in Russell Street, Derby.

## MATTHEWS Reginald Derrick

*Goalkeeper*

*Born: Coventry, 20 December 1932. Died: Coventry, 6 October 2001. Career: Modern Machine Tools FC. Juniors, Coventry City: professional May 1950. Chelsea November 1956. Derby County October 1961. Player-manager, Rugby Town, August 1968 to May 1969.*

■ Reg Matthews was a natural goalkeeper. His lightning reflexes, athleticism and immense courage allied themselves to great ability and sound positional sense to make him, for a decade, one of the best in Britain. Harry Storer signed him for his local club, Coventry City, and after break for National Service, Matthews became one of the outstanding young goalkeepers of the age. It was no surprise when he won five England caps although he was still a Third Division player, and in 1956 Chelsea paid £20,000 for him, at the time a record fee for a 'keeper. Harry Storer signed him for a second time, paying £6,300 to bring him to Derby. His acrobatic saves and courage in hurling himself at forwards' feet were loved by the supporters and he set a club record, later beaten by Colin Boulton, with 246 appearances in goal. Matthews totally dominated his own penalty area and fellow defenders had to be as wary as opposing forwards.

For one season Matthews was a major factor in keeping the Rams in Division Two.

## MAY John

*Wing-half*

*Born: Cambusnethan, 5 August 1880. Died: July 1933. Career: Paisley. Wishaw Thistle. Abercorn. Derby County May 1898. Glasgow Rangers May 1904. Morton August 1910.*
***FA Cup finalists 1898–99, 1902–03.***

■ "Johnny May was one of the finest half-backs who ever kicked a ball," said Steve Bloomer about the Scotsman whose injury was a key factor in the Rams losing the 1899 FA Cup final to Sheffield United. May fell heavily after colliding with Bennett and despite showing great pluck in continuing for a while, eventually had to retire. The subsequent need to reorganise the team, together with some missed chances by May's great admirer, Bloomer, cost the Rams the game. After joining Derby, May quickly developed into one of the best half-backs in

the Football League and, not long after he signed, the *Derby Daily Telegraph* described him as 'a fine tackler and not deficient in making a game for his forwards. He has been a great acquisition to the Derby club and, depending as he does on purely scientific methods, is a very instructive player to watch.' May played in another final for the Rams, the thrashing of 1903, and then moved to Glasgow Rangers where he won five Scottish caps and captained his country. May ran a chain of billiard halls in Falkirk and Glasgow, one of them managed by John Boag.

## MAYS Albert Edward

*Wing-half*

*Born: Ynyshir, 18 April 1929. Died: Derby, 5 July 1973.*
*Career: Allenton Juniors. Juniors, Derby County, July 1943: professional, May 1946. Chesterfield July 1960. Burton Albion June 1961.*
***Division Three North Champions 1956–57.***

■ Born in the Rhondda, the son of a former Wrexham and Wales footballer, Albert Mays was in fact a product of local Derby football, his father working on the maintenance staff at Derby Police

Station when Albert was a youngster. He made his League debut in 1949–50 and established a place at wing-half. Mays, who was also an accomplished snooker player and cricketer, had a strong shot and scored some of his goals from free-kicks. He was not always as effective in the tackle as he might have been, although when he was going forward in attack, he showed some delightful touches. Mays was also something of a character – he once offered his shirt to a Popular Side barracker – and he was the man the crowd either loved or hated. He would have been ideal in later tactical formations as a creative midfield player and if a bad back-pass in a 1959 FA Cup tie against Preston North End was to haunt him, he was one of the key men in Harry Storer's Third Division North Championship team. Mays missed only one match in that season and represented the Third North against the Third South in October 1956. He later managed the Regent Billiard Hall in Derby and was a licensee when he died.

## METHVEN James

*Right-back*

*Born: Ceres, 7 December 1868. Died: Derby, 25 March 1953.*
*Career: Leith. Heart of Midlothian. St Bernard's 1886. Derby County May 1891: manager August 1906 to June 1922.*
***Division One runners-up 1895–96. FA Cup finalists. 1897–98, 1898–99 (captain), 1902–03 (captain).***

■ Jimmy Methven was unchallenged at right-back for Derby County for 15 years after joining them from Edinburgh St Bernard's. Methven, who also played a few games for Leith and Hearts, was reserve for Scotland against England in 1890. He had turned down a contract with Burton Swifts because it included a hotel managership which his wife did not want, and it was a former St Bernards' teammate, Johnny McMillan, who persuaded him to join Derby. Methven was ever-present in five seasons and with Boag and Fryer played in all three of Derby's early FA Cup finals. Towards the end of his career he had slowed considerably

but even on his last appearance, after becoming Derby manager in 1906, he still showed his cool, confident style. He was, according to one writer 'one of the wonders of the football world', continuing his service to the Rams with 16 years as manager.

## MICKLEWHITE Gary

*Midfield*

*Born: Southwark, 21 March 1961.*
*Career: Apprentice, Manchester United: professional March 1978. Queen's Park Rangers July 1979. Derby County, February 1985. Gillingham July 1993: player-coach March 1995. Slough Town August 1996. Youth development officer, Queen's Park Rangers, October 1996. Assistant manager, Wycombe Wanderers, August 1998 to February 1999.*
***Division Three promotion 1985–86. Division Two Champions 1986–87.***

■ The sale of Kevin Wilson to Ipswich Town in January 1985 financed two significant purchases by Arthur Cox, Trevor Christie from Nottingham Forest and, for £92,500, Gary Micklewhite from Queen's Park Rangers. Micklewhite was signed for Rangers by Tommy Docherty and played for them in the 1982 FA Cup final, a substitute in the first game and as a starter in the replay. He was in their Second Division Championship team a year later but Derby's ambition and potential persuaded him to take what he felt was a temporary drop into the Third Division. In a run of 112 consecutive League games, he was an essential part of two promotions, covering the ground tirelessly on the right and scoring his share of goals. Two major operations, on an Achilles tendon

in September 1987 and knee ligaments in December 1989, set back his career but he returned both times. After Derby's big transfer splash in 1992, Micklewhite was made available but continued to play his part, often as substitute, in a promotion bid that foundered at the Play-off stage. For eight years with the Rams he was an excellent player and a model professional.

## MOORE James

*Inside-forward*

*Born: Handsworth, 11 May 1889.*
*Died: 1972.*
*Career: Quebec Albion. Cradley Heath. Glossop May 1911. Derby County October 1913. Chesterfield March 1926. Mansfield Town November 1927. Worcester City March 1929.*
***Division Two Champions 1914–15. Division Two promotion 1925–26.***

■ 'Gentleman' Jim Moore joined Derby County as a centre-forward from Glossop but it was as an inside-forward that he made his mark, for it was there he could show his dribbling powers to their best advantage. It cost Derby £1,500 to bring Moore to the Baseball Ground and although World War One soon intervened, the club had full value. Moore skippered the side that reached the FA Cup semi-final in 1923 and although he was on the losing side that day, could look back to a fine scoring feat not long before. On Christmas Day 1922, Moore scored the first five as Derby hammered Crystal Palace 6–0 at the Baseball Ground. Moore shrugged it off modestly: "The ball just came to me at the right time." The arrival of Harry Storer cut down his appearances and then, having just regained his place, he had the misfortune to

suffer a knee injury that required an operation. Moore, who won one England cap, was the only survivor of the 1914–15 Second Division Championship team to appear in the promotion 11 years later, although in only two matches. He had guested for Chesterfield in World War One and when he returned to Saltergate at the age of 36 was still good enough to score 21 goals in 41 League games.

## MORRIS Charles Richard

*Left-back*

*Born: Oswestry, 29 August 1880. Died: Chirk Bank, 18 January 1952.*
*Career: Chirk. Derby County April 1900. Huddersfield Town August 1910. Wrexham May 1911.*
***FA Cup finalists 1902–03.***

■ Charlie Morris worked down a Welsh mine for eight years and played football for Chirk, winning three Welsh caps before signing for the Rams to replace Joe Blackett, whose form had been affected by poor health. Morris made his debut against Blackburn Rovers and it was soon obvious that the Rams had made an

important capture. He became one of the finest defenders to represent Derby and was a regular choice for Wales during his ten years at the Baseball Ground, winning 21 of his 27 caps. His brothers John and Robert were also capped by Wales. After the 1903 FA Cup final disaster, Morris went from strength to strength and Derby appointed him skipper in succession to Archie Goodall. Morris was one of the best players in British football in the early 1900s, a brilliant international full-back and a First Division star. It was written of him: 'Morris not only knows the game from A to Z but he is also a model footballer'. In the close season of 1910 he moved to Huddersfield, who had just been elected to Division Two, and played in the first Football League team they fielded. Morris is the only player to have been asked to replace the goalkeeper in both an FA Cup final and an international. He took over from Fryer at the Crystal Palace in 1903 and in March 1908 stood in for the injured Roose against England, although Wales were allowed to call upon regular goalkeeper Davies of Bolton for the second half. From 1910 to 1916 he was cricket professional to the Duke of Westminster's XI at Eaton Hall. He was a Methodist lay preacher in Chirk.

## MORRIS John

*Inside-right*

*Born: Radcliffe, 27 September 1923.*
*Career: Mujacs FC. Amateur, Manchester United, August 1939: professional March 1941. Derby County March 1949. Leicester City October 1952. Player-manager, Corby Town, May 1958. Kettering Town June 1961. Manager, Great Harwood, cs 1964. Manager, Oswestry Town, October 1967 to January 1969.*

■ Derby County broke the British transfer record for the second time in less than two years when they paid £24,500 to bring Manchester United inside-forward Johnny Morris to the Baseball Ground. Twenty-one months after the record signing of Billy Steel, the Rams bought Morris to form, with the Scotsman, a new 'Carter-Doherty' duo. Morris made a brilliant start at the Baseball Ground, with 13

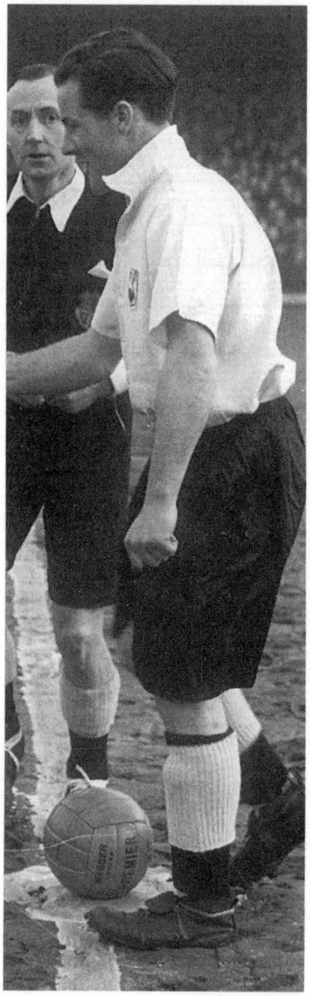

goals in 13 games to earn an England place, but it was impossible to emulate Carter and Doherty. After active service with the Royal Armoured Corps, Morris was in Manchester United's 1948 FA Cup winning team against Blackpool and played for the Football League but was a player Matt Busby confessed he could never understand. Liverpool were the favourites to sign him until Stuart McMillan stepped in with a record cheque. Morris was a fine dribbler who was difficult to dispossess and he combined artistry with power in front of goal. He won his three England caps at Derby before leaving a declining team to move to Leicester for £21,500. He played more than 200 games and helped the Filbert Street club to two Second Division Championships, in 1953–54 and 1956–57. Morris and Steel were highly talented players but, for the supporters, nothing could dim the memory of the 1946 FA Cup final pairing.

## MOZLEY Bert

*Right-back*

*Born: Derby, 23 September 1923.*
*Career: Derby Boys. Shelton United. Nottingham Forest, amateur, 1944. Derby County, amateur, May 1945: professional, October 1945.*

■ Bert Mozley was that rarity, a Derby-born player who went on to the full England side. Jimmy Bagshaw and Jack Cox, from Spondon, achieved it before World War One: Ray Parry won caps as a Bolton Wanderers player. Mozley went about his business in such an unflappable manner that he always appeared to have plenty in reserve, yet throughout the late 1940s and into the 1950s he had

few equals as a First Division right-back of international class. His League debut came in the first post-war season and in 1949–50 he won three England caps before losing his place through injury. Mozley was unlucky that his replacement was Tottenham's Alf Ramsey, who established himself as an England regular. The Rams' dressing-room jester, Mozley was always organising practical jokes. He was also a skilled defender who delighted in coming forward to try speculative shots, although they brought him only two goals in 321 first-team appearances. With Tim Ward he went on the FA Canadian tour in 1950 and four years later emigrated to country, taking over an hotel. He played for Western Canada All Stars against a touring Russian side in Winnipeg.

## MURPHY Lionel

*Outside-left*

*Born: Hovingham Spa, 15 September 1895. Died: Derby, 27 October 1968.*
*Career: Melton Mowbray. Derby County February 1922. Bolton Wanderers January 1928. Mansfield Town September 1929. Norwich City May 1931. Luton Town October 1934. Southport February 1935.*
***Division Two promotion 1925–26.***

■ When Alf Quantrill left for Preston in the close season of 1921, Derby County struggled hard to fill the vacant outside-left spot until Lionel 'Spud' Murphy, a former army footballer, made the position his own soon after signing. A few days after joining the Rams, Murphy made his League debut against Clapton Orient and midway through the following season one local journalist wrote: 'Spud Murphy, the Derby County left winger, is a genius. All his work is done without effort, and yet the results he gets with one touch of the ball often equal the results secured by other players after they have expounded pounds of energy. That marks a true-born player, but we must hope that the Melton lad won't play to the gallery. A hint in time might save him from a terrible complaint which shall be nameless.' Presumably Murphy

took the hint. He missed only four matches when the Rams won promotion in 1925–26 and scored 12 goals, starring at inside-left towards the end of the season when Georgie Mee came from Blackpool Murphy moved to Bolton in part-exchange for another outside-left, Albert Picken.

---

## MUSSON Walter Urban

*Left-half*

*Born: Kilburn, 8 October 1920. Died: Loughborough, 22 April 1955.*
*Career: Holbrook St Michael's. Amateur, Derby County, March 1936: professional, October 1937. Player-manager, Brush Sports, June 1954.*
***FA Cup winners 1945–46.***

■ 'Is Chick playing today?' asked more than a few nervous opposing forwards in the late 1940s. The rugged little wing-half, who was known all his playing days by that misleading nickname, certainly knew how to 'put himself about' and few, if any, opposing forwards relished a visit to the Baseball Ground when he was in the side. Musson was one of the band of local youngsters who helped restart Derby County in 1942 after the closure for war. Musson could play on either flank but it was as a left-half that he forced his way into the team and he was a key member of the 1946 Cup winning side. His ferocious tackling was well-known on the First Division circuit but under Peter Doherty's tuition Musson developed his skills and the primarily defensive wing-half became a useful supporter of the attack, although he never scored a goal for the Rams. Musson played for the Football League against the

Irish League in April 1950, and missed only five games in the first five post-war seasons. Sadly, like Leuty, Musson died in his mid-30s.

---

## NEWTON Henry Albert

*Midfield*

*Born: Nottingham, 18 February 1944.*
*Career: Juniors, Nottingham Forest: professional June 1961. Everton October 1970. Derby County September 1973. Walsall July 1977.*
***Division One Champions 1974–75.***

■ Henry Newton took a roundabout route to Derby from Nottingham Forest, where he made 315 senior appearances and won four England Under-23 caps. Because of the success of Alan Hinton and the £100,000 move of Terry Hennessey, not to mention Derby's later attempt to sign Ian Moore, Forest became increasingly reluctant to do business with Brian Clough and Peter Taylor. So

Newton went to Everton and Clough and Taylor had to wait almost three years before they got their man for £100,000. It was their last major signing, for they left Derby the following month. Along with others players, Newton was upset by the turn of events but his reward came in 1974–75, when he won a League Championship medal. He was a player of great courage and one of the fiercest tacklers in the game. Newton's versatility enabled him to play in midfield, the centre of defence and at left-back. He had to battle against injuries and his move to Walsall in May 1977 was a prelude to retirement. Arthritis caught up with him and in 1984, when he was running a sub-Post Office in Derby, he underwent a hip operation.

---

## NICHOLAS John Thomas

*Right-half/right-back*

*Born: Derby, 26 November 1910. Died: Nottingham, 4 February 1977.*
*Career: Juniors, Swansea Town. Derby County December 1927. Acting player-manager 1942 to*

*March 1944. Retired 1947. Chief scout, Derby County.*
***Division One runners-up 1929–30, 1935–36. FA Cup winners 1945–46 (captain).***

■ Jack Nicholas spent a lifetime with Derby County, first as a supremely consistent player. Son of a Rams defender, Nicholas was born in Derby but soon moved to Wales, where he won schoolboy international honours, when his father was transferred. Swansea Town wanted to sign him but Nicholas chose the Rams. Known as 'Owd Nick' on the Popular Side, Nicholas set out in September 1931 on a run of 328 out of a possible 331 League games to the end of 1938–39, adding another three in the first post-war season. He took over from Johnny McIntyre at right-half, played occasionally at centre-half and full-back and in 1938 became Jack Howe's regular partner at right-back. Nicholas, along with Jack Webb, was largely responsible for starting the Rams up again in 1942 and his reward was to lead the club to Wembley four years later. Nicholas was a fearsome and rugged defender and a hard man – there were stories of him taking cold showers even on freezing days. Even as formidable a player as Stan Cullis, the Wolverhampton Wanderers and England centre-half, winced when he recalled Nicholas waiting, with his foot cocked, for over-ambitious opponents. In Derby's first 120 years, he was unique, the only Rams skipper to lift the FA Cup.

---

## NISH David John

*Left-back*

*Born: Burton upon Trent, 26 September 1947.*
*Career: Measham. Amateur, Leicester City: professional July 1966. Derby County August 1972. Tulsa Roughnecks February 1979. Seattle Sounders March 1980. Shepshed Charterhouse April 1982. Player-manager, Gresley Rovers, June 1982 to July 1984: chairman, cs 1985 to August 1987. Youth coach, Middlesbrough, July 1988: reserve-team coach March 1989: first-team coach April 1990 to March 1991. Youth development officer, Leicester City, July 1991. Chief scout, Derby County, July 2002 to June 2003.*
***Division One Champions 1974–75.***

■ Derby County were reigning Champions when, in August 1972, they broke the British record transfer fee for the third time

since the war, signing David Nish for £225,000 from Leicester City to follow Billy Steel and Johnny Morris, their big signings of the 1940s. Nish captained Leicester in the 1969 FA Cup final defeat by Manchester City at the age of 21 and was one of the most elegant defenders ever seen at Derby. He was geared to attack and had the delicate touch of a skilful inside-forward. Nish relished the arrival of Charlie George and could always find his runs on the Derby left. His brief international career of five games was then over. A perforated ulcer, requiring immediate surgery, put him out of an England tour to Eastern Europe and he was not picked again. His effectiveness was gradually curtailed by three operations on his right knee, the result of an injury sustained when scoring against Sheffield United at Derby in December 1975. He joined Alan Hinton in the North American Soccer League and even at the end of his career, remained upset that what he thought was an equaliser in the 1976 FA Cup semi-final against Manchester

United had been disallowed because other players were offside. "I had worked out exactly how I would beat their offside trap," he said, "and I was annoyed that the referee penalised others who were coming back." Nish worked at Middlesbrough with Bruce Rioch and Colin Todd before returning to Leicester. He was briefly chief scout under John Gregory but the club was unduly eager to expunge traces of that regime.

---

## O'HARE John

*Centre-forward*

*Born: Renton, 24 September 1946.*
*Career: Drumchapel Amateurs. Juniors, Sunderland: professional October 1963. Derby County August 1967. Leeds United August 1974. Nottingham Forest February 1975. Dallas Tornado, loan, April 1977 and May 1978. Belper Town August 1981. Carriage and Wagon 1982. Manager, Ockbrook. Manager, Stanton, March 1988.*
***Division Two Champions 1968–69. Division One Champions 1971–72.***

■ When Brian Clough took over a manager, he was soon in touch

with Sunderland over a centre-forward he had coached in the Youth team. John O'Hare became Clough's first signing, for £20,000, and was an immediate fixture in the team, missing only four League games in his first five seasons. In that time he made 13 appearances for Scotland. O'Hare was a steady rather than prolific scorer. He had no great pace, nor was he a battering ram, so supporters regarded him with certain reservations. They soon began to realise, however, that he was absolutely essential to Derby's style. He had marvellous ball control, could accept and hold passes under intense pressure from behind and was totally unselfish. As Alan Durban said: "Anybody in defence or midfield knew that he would be available. You only had to glance up to find him and if Solly was given the ball, it was his. It would not fizz back past you and put the defence under pressure." Solly was his universal nickname. A move to Leeds United didn't work but O'Hare was involved in a Second Division promotion, another League Championship and a League Cup victory with Nottingham Forest, ending his senior career by going on as substitute in their second European Cup triumph against Hamburg in Madrid.

---

## PARRY Jack

*Inside-forward/wing-half*

*Born: Derby, 29 July 1931.*
*Career: Juniors, Derby County: professional, July 1948. Boston United June 1967.*
***Division Three North Champions 1956–57.***

■ Jack Parry came from a Derby football family. One brother, Ray,

played for Bolton and England, while another, Glyn, was on Derby County's staff and Cyril played for Notts County. Jack played for Derby Boys and signed for the Rams when Raich Carter and Billy Steel were there. He was still at the Baseball Ground 20 years later, having set a club record of 517 appearances which survived until Kevin Hector overtook it. Like Geoff Barrowcliffe and Albert Mays, Parry might have made a bigger name in football had he moved to a more successful club. He was a lively inside-forward and had a brilliant year when the Rams found themselves in the Third Division North in 1955–56. He scored 24 goals in 34 League games but his season was ended by injury in the key clash with Grimsby Town, watched by 33,330 at the Baseball Ground. Ray de Gruchy's challenge left Parry with a back injury, limiting his contribution to the Third North Championship the following season. In the Second Division he established himself at wing-half and was club captain. He lost his place in 1965–66 and was unable to regain a regular position, spending a final season with Boston United. Parry's wit made him a popular member of the dressing-room and once Ralph Hann was treating him in a match. Fearing concussion, Hann asked him where he was. "I'm at Wembley," said Parry. "We're beating Brazil 2–0 – and I've scored both."

## POOM Mart

*Goalkeeper*

*Born: Tallinn, 3 February 1972.*
*Career: Flora Tallinn. FC Wil (Switzerland) August 1993. Portsmouth August 1994. Flora Tallinn May 1996. Derby County March 1997. Sunderland, loan, November 2002: permanent January 2003. Arsenal, loan, August 2005: permanent January 2006.*

■ Although injuries meant that Mart Poom was unable to renew his work permit with Portsmouth, Jim Smith never forgot the goalkeeper's presence and dedicated attitude. A brilliant performance for Estonia in a 0–0 draw with Scotland hastened Smith's decision to bring Poom back to England, especially when he was worried about Russell Hoult's inconsistency, and Derby supporters quickly took to their £500,000 signing. Poom made his debut in a sensational victory over Manchester United at Old Trafford and went on from there, often having to be dragged off the training ground. At 6ft 4ins, Poom is an imposing figure but also has tremendous agility and the confidence to dominate the whole penalty area. He was Derby's Player of the Year in 1999–2000 and picked up the Estonian equivalent on a regular basis while heading for 100 caps. When Derby lurched into financial crisis, Poom was expected to leave in summer 2002, with Everton the favourites

to sign him, but chairman Lionel Pickering was involved in fruitless discussions with Bryan Richardson and by the time players were sold, the transfer market had collapsed. Poom joined Sunderland and made a spectacular return to Pride Park in September 2003. After a moving reception from supporters, he went up for a late corner and saved a point with a soaring, unstoppable header. And still Derby people cheered a fine goalkeeper and a fine man.

## POWELL Darryl Anthony

*Midfield*

*Born: Lambeth, 15 November 1971.*
*Career: Trainee, Portsmouth: professional December 1988. Derby County July 1995. Birmingham City September 2002. Sheffield Wednesday January 2003. Colorado Rapid May 2003. Nottingham Forest February 2005.*
***Division One promotion 1995–96.***

■ Enthusiasm made Darryl Powell a valuable player at the Baseball Ground and Pride Park for seven seasons, during which he became the 71st and, to the end of 2005–06, last player to reach 200 senior appearances for the club. Although born in London, Powell was educated at St John's College, Southsea, and developed at Portsmouth, where Jim Smith was his fourth manager. At one stage, Smith planned an exchange with Port Vale to take Robbie van der Laan to Fratton Park but finished with both at Derby. Powell had limitations in his control and passing but was always a competitor and played 37 times when the Rams won promotion to the Premiership for the first time. He was less sure of a place when Derby were up but always forced his way back into contention. He also timed his entry into the Jamaican side, qualifying by parentage. Jamaica had already reached the World Cup finals when he made his debut as a substitute against Wales

in March 1998. Powell went to France with them and played twice, although sent off against Argentina. Derby missed him when his contract ended because he had to capacity to lift players around him. Powell gave a good return for £750,000.

---

## POWELL Stephen

*Midfield/central defender*

*Born: Derby, 20 September 1955.*
*Career: Apprentice, Derby County: professional November 1972. Arcadia Shepherds, loan, May 1977. Tulsa Roughnecks, loan, May 1979. Player-coach, Shepshed Charterhouse, June 1986: player-manager, March 1987. Assistant coach, Albany Capitals, April 1988. Shepshed Charterhouse 1988: caretaker player-manager December 1988. Player-manager Burton Albion, February 1990 to April 1991. Manager, Belper Town, June 1991.*
***Division One Champions 1971–72, 1974–75.***

■ Steve Powell was 16 years and 30 days old when he made a remarkable debut against Stoke City in a Texaco Cup tie at the Baseball Ground in October 1971. His father, Tommy, had been a distinguished Rams player. Steve, educated at Bemrose School like his father, was captain of England Boys and, in 1973, led the England Youth team to victory in the UEFA tournament in Florence. Even more amazingly mature than his debut was Powell's performance in the final League match of 1971–72 against Liverpool. He played at right-back in the victory that gave Derby their first Championship. He was playing European football in his teens and, during those early seasons, England caps seemed inevitable. He was equally happy in midfield or defence but, as his career developed, he suffered a great deal from injuries. The most serious brought about an operation on damaged knee ligaments in 1981–82. He also had back and pelvic trouble and, in 1982–83, a broken jaw. Some of his problems seemed to have stemmed from a summer with Tulsa Roughnecks in 1979 but Powell battled against injuries as he always competed on the field. He turned from a schoolboy star into a fine League professional who, despite playing in a declining side, was totally dedicated to Derby County. Experience and knowledge of the game enable him to overcome a lack of pace, but this international honours stopped at an Under-23 appearance against Scotland in 1974–75. He and his father appeared in 826 senior games between them for Derby.

---

## POWELL Thomas

*Inside-forward/Winger*

*Born: Derby, 12 April 1925. Died: Derby, 7 September 1998.*
*Career: Derby Corinthians. Derby County April 1942. Northcliffe United. Player-manager, Redfern Athletic, November 1965 to October 1966. Manager, Northcliffe United to August 1984.*
***Division Three North Champions 1956–57.***

■ Tommy Powell first played on the Baseball Ground in the 1930s for the Firs Estate Junior School in a local schools Cup final. He went on to Bemrose School and on Christmas Day 1941 played for the Rams as a 16-year-old against an RAF team, Derby's first match since re-forming after the outbreak of war. The *Derby Evening Telegraph* reported: 'Tom, a big lad with a long stride, need not be too downhearted if he felt out of it before the course was run ...he did get at least one chance to show that he had a fine shot in his gun...' Powell was a great success in wartime soccer. He was called up and played in the BAOR side, his National Service preventing him making League debut until 1948. Although not obviously strong, Powell had immaculate ball control, and perhaps his two best years came when the Rams were in Division Three North. Seldom had the Third Division seen such skill and when Derby won promotion, Powell had the perfect understanding with Ray Straw, able to drop the ball in from all angles to exploit the centre-forward's strength in the air. Powell's deceptive body swerve and complete mastery of the ball made him vital to the side. In 1953 Derby and Hull agreed on a fee of £10,000 but Powell did not want to leave his native town. In his younger days many considered him unlucky not to have won an England cap. He retired in 1961, but made a brief comeback the

following season until an injury against Portsmouth in a League Cup replay at the Baseball Ground ended his career for good. For many years, he worked in the accounts department of the *Derby Evening Telegraph*.

---

## RICHARDS George Henry

*Wing-half/inside-forward*

*Born: Bulwell, 10 May 1880. Died: Derby, 1 November 1959.*
*Career: Castle Donington Juniors. Whitwick White Cross. Derby County April 1902.*
***FA Cup finalists 1902–03. Division Two Champions 1911–12.***

■ George Richards, a basketmaker by trade, spent most of his life in Castle Donington His early Derby days saw him playing inside-left to George Davis, a partnership as close off the field as it was successful on it. Jimmy Methven once said: "They were partners in the noble game of nap, in which they had phenomenal luck. They are said to have set up a library with their winnings." Richards became even better when he moved to left-half and played for England against Austria in Vienna in June 1909. It was a reward for some brilliant performances by the noted ball-juggler, known as 'Corkscrew'. He was reserve for England against Scotland in 1910 and later that year toured South Africa with an FA side, appearing in two

unofficial internationals. Injured for much of the following season, Richards fought back before retiring in 1914. During World War One he guested for Queen's Park Rangers and Chelsea.

---

## RIOCH Bruce David

*Midfield*

*Born: Aldershot, 6 September 1947.*
*Career: Apprentice, Luton Town: professional September 1964. Aston Villa July 1969. Derby County February 1974. Everton December 1976. Derby County November 1977. Birmingham City, loan, December 1978. Sheffield United, loan, March 1979. Seattle Sounders March 1980. Player-coach, Torquay United, October 1980 (alternating with Seattle). Manager, Torquay United, July 1982 to January 1984. Coach, Seattle Sounders, July 1985. Assistant manager, Middlesbrough, January 1986: manager, February 1986 to March 1990. Manager, Millwall, April 1990 to March 1992. Manager, Bolton Wanderers, May 1992. Manager, Arsenal, June 1995 to August 1996. Assistant manager, Queen's Park Rangers, September 1996 to November 1997. Manager, Norwich City, July 1998 to March 2000. Manager, Wigan Athletic, June 2000 to February 2001. Head coach, OB Odense, June 2005.*
***Division One Champions 1974–75.***

■ Dave Mackay bought Bruce Rioch from Aston Villa for £200,000 because he wanted more scoring power in midfield. The choice paid off in 1974–75 when Rioch, leading scorer with 15 League goals, was vital to Derby's second Championship success. In March of that season he scored one of his most memorable goals with a surging run from near the halfway line against Newcastle United at St James' Park. The following season he hit a thunderous free-kick in the FA Cup sixth-round tie against Newcastle at the Baseball Ground. As an attacking player he had pace, power and a magnificent shot, qualities which took Rioch – with his Scottish parentage – into the Scotland side. He won 18 of his 24 caps while with Derby and captained his country in the 1978 World Cup in Argentina. In October 1976, Rioch scored four goals against Spurs at Derby but two months later Colin Murphy sold him to Everton for £180,000. Within a year Tommy Docherty had bought him back to form a midfield trio with Gerry Daly and Don Masson. "Come and see my three Van Goghs," said Docherty but the promised artistry did not materialise. Rioch's second spell was unhappy. He was sent off twice in 1977–78 and had rows

with Docherty and his successor, Colin Addison. Rioch won medals with Luton Town, Fourth Division Champions in 1967–68, and Aston Villa, Third Division winners in 1971–72. He also found success as a manager, taking Middlesbrough from liquidation to promotion from the Third Division in 1986–87 and to the First Division in 1988. He gained another promotion with Bolton Wanderers and was in charge when they reached the League Cup final in 1995. As manager of Arsenal, he signed Dennis Bergkamp but was eased out after a year to make way for Arsene Wenger.

---

## ROBINSON John William

*Goalkeeper*

*Born: Derby, 22 April 1870. Died: Derby, 28 October 1931.*
*Career: Derby Midland. Lincoln City January 1889. Derby County June 1891. New Brighton Tower August 1897. Southampton May 1898. Plymouth Argyle April 1903. Millwall November 1905. Exeter City December 1905. Green Waves (Plymouth) October 1906. Exeter City November 1908. Stoke May 1909. Rochester (New York) October 1912.*
***Division One runners-up 1895–96.***

■ Jack Robinson, an agile and daring goalkeeper, had spent six excellent seasons with Derby County and broken into the England team when, in August 1897, he rocked the club by joining New Brighton Tower. An FA commission, held in Manchester on 11 August, ruled that the registration was invalid as the club was not affiliated. Only after New Brighton joined the FA via the Cheshire FA did the transfer go through and a tart contemporary report gave the opinion: 'If Robinson thinks he can enhance his reputation by joining a mushroom organisation like the New Brighton club, whose purse may not always be so heavy

as at present, he has done well to leave Derby.' It did not do Robinson any harm, for he retained his England place and, a year later, joined Southampton. At The Dell he took his total of England caps to 11, played in two FA Cup final defeats, by Bury in 1900 and Sheffield United in 1902, and was involved in three Southern League Championships – in 1898–99, 1900–01 and 1902–03. Robinson, who was reported to the FA for allegedly trying to poach Steve Bloomer for Southampton, may have been a wayward character. For four years, however, he was indisputably the best goalkeeper in England.

---

## ROBSON John Dixon

*Left-back*

*Born: Consett, 15 July 1950. Died: Sutton Coldfield, 12 May 2004.*
*Career: Birtley YC. Derby County October 1967. Aston Villa December 1972.*
***Division Two Champions 1968–69. Division One Champions 1971–72.***

■ It was said that Peter Taylor earned his salary for that year simply by signing John Robson from North-East junior football in October 1967. Taylor had spotted the 17-year-old playing for Birtley Youth Club and knew at once that he must have him at Derby. The following season Robson was an ever-present member of the side that stormed away with the Second Division Championship and he missed only one game as the Rams won the First Division title for the first time three years later. Robson was not a physically commanding full-back but he rarely gave an inch to opposing forwards and was far from out of place in a defence that

included Roy McFarland and Colin Todd. But Brian Clough wanted Leicester City's classy David Nish and as soon as the player was eligible for the later stages of the 1972–73 European Cup, Clough allowed Robson to join Aston Villa for £90,000 – then a record incoming fee for Derby. It was a happy move for the England Under-23 defender and he played in the Villa team that won promotion in 1975 and took the League Cup in 1975 and 1977. Sadly, Robson's career was ended in 1978 by multiple sclerosis.

---

## RYAN Reginald Alphonsus

*Wing-half/inside-forward*

*Born: Dublin, 30 October 1925. Died: Birmingham, 13 February 1997.*
*Career: Nuneaton Borough. Amateur, Coventry City, March 1943. West Bromwich Albion April 1945. Derby County July 1955. Coventry City September 1958: pools organiser, November 1960. West Bromwich Albion, pools organiser, December 1961: chief scout, September 1962 to October 1976.*
***Division Three North Champions 1956–57 (captain).***

■ When Harry Storer took over the Rams in 1955, his priority was to sign West Brom's international inside-forward Reg Ryan for £3,000. Ryan starred in Albion's 1954 FA Cup final victory over Preston North End and was the very man to carry Storer's work on to the field. Ryan, who played Gaelic football for his school, appeared 16 times for the Republic of Ireland – once while with Derby – and once for Northern Ireland before southern players were barred from the Home International Championship. Ryan's first job was to instill some spirit back into a Derby side that had sunk to rock bottom. Soon he welded a happy family and he was the link between Storer and the players. In three seasons he missed only three matches – two because of injury and one through international duty – and his part in the Rams' promotion drive of 1956–57 cannot be overestimated. On the return to Division Two, Ryan was leading scorer and looked equally at home at wing-half. In 1955, he played for the Third Division North team against the Third South.

## SAUNDERS Dean Nicholas

*Striker*

*Born: Swansea, 21 June 1964.*
*Career: Apprentice, Swansea City: professional June 1982. Cardiff City, loan, March 1985. Brighton & Hove Albion August 1985. Oxford United March 1987. Derby County October 1988. Liverpool July 1991. Aston Villa September 1992. Galatasaray July 1995. Nottingham Forest July 1996. Sheffield United December 1997. SL Benfica December 1998. Bradford City August 1999. Coach, Blackburn Rovers, 2001. Coach, Newcastle United, September 2004 to February 2006.*

■ Little more than three years after being given a free transfer by Swansea manager John Bond, Dean Saunders became Derby's first £1-million signing. The transfer was between two clubs owned by Robert Maxwell, so the money did not travel far, but it cost Oxford manager Mark Lawrenson his job, because he made his objections public. Saunders, who made his debut for Wales when he was at Brighton, not only scored goals regularly but excited Derby supporters by his speed, flair and sheer love of playing. And he was consistent, 130 consecutive appearances. When he joined Paul Goddard in attack, Derby surged to fifth place

in the First Division in 1988–89 but, because of Maxwell's policies, were unable to develop the team. Saunders was leading scorer in each of his three seasons before joining Liverpool for a then British domestic record of £2.9-million. The main benefit from the transfer of Saunders and Mark Wright was that Derby were able to buy out Maxwell's shares. Saunders was in Liverpool's 1992 FA Cup winning team but, despite that and his goals, did not look as happy at Anfield as he had at Derby. The spark returned after a £2.3-million move to Aston Villa and he scored twice in the 1993–94 League Cup final victory over Manchester United. Villa also had their money back when Saunders went to Galatasaray and Nottingham Forest paid £1.5-million for him a year later. At his best, and Derby saw plenty of that, Saunders was a devastating forward and took his total of Welsh caps to 75, with 22 goals putting him fourth in the all-time list. His father Roy played for Liverpool and Swansea.

## SHILTON Peter Leslie

*Goalkeeper*

*Born: Leicester, 18 September 1949. Career: Apprentice, Leicester City: professional September 1966. Stoke City November 1974. Nottingham Forest September 1977. Southampton August 1982. Derby County July 1987. Player-manager, Plymouth Argyle, March 1992 to January 1995. Wimbledon February 1995. Bolton Wanderers March 1995. Coventry City July 1995. West Ham United January 1996. Leyton Orient November 1996.*

■ Peter Shilton was the best goalkeeper in the country, perhaps the world, when he became Derby County's first major signing in Robert Maxwell's time as chairman. When Mark Wright followed from Southampton, it was assumed that Arthur Cox was to be given the money to build a top-class team quickly but it did not turn out like that. Shilton had been an England player for almost 17 years when he joined Derby. He made his debut for Leicester at the age of 16 and was so good as a teenager that one of England's greatest goalkeepers, Gordon Banks, was allowed to move to Stoke City. Shilton succeeded Banks again at Stoke but his greatest days in club football were with Nottingham

Forest. Brian Clough and Peter Taylor had wanted him at Derby in the early 1970s. With Shilton in goal, Forest won their first League title, a League Cup and two European Cups. Mark Wallington, who had taken over from Shilton at Leicester, gave way to him at Derby 13 years later and, in November 1987, Shilton marked his 800th League appearance with a fantastic display against Newcastle United at St James' Park. Eight days later he played in his 1,000th competitive club match and broke Terry Paine's record of 824 League appearances in April 1988, at Watford. He had equalled it against Southampton, not only the club from which he joined Derby but also the one for which Paine played most of his career. Shilton set a world record with 125 caps before bowing out of international football after the 1990 World Cup. Unfortunately, Maxwell's promise to build a great team in front of Shilton was not fulfilled and he suffered relegation before becoming player-manager of Plymouth Argyle. He was not a success in that role and, at the age of 45, returned as a player with a series of short contracts. Leyton Orient enabled him to fulfil an ambition of playing 1,000 League games when, on 22 December 1996, he was greeted by a fanfare from the band of the Coldstream Guards before facing Brighton & Hove Albion – and keeping a clean sheet. The final League game of a great career came a month later.

---

## SIMPSON Paul David

*Winger*

*Born: Carlisle, 26 July 1966.*
*Career: Apprentice, Manchester City: professional August 1983.*

*Oxford United October 1988. Derby County February 1992. Sheffield United, loan, December 1996. Wolverhampton Wanderers, loan, October 1997: permanent November 1997. Walsall, loan, September 1998 and December 1998. Blackpool August 2000. Rochdale March 2002: player-manager May 2002 to May 2003. Carlisle United August 2003: caretaker manager August 2003: player-manager October 2003. Manager, Preston North End, June 2006.*
***Division One promotion 1995–96.***

■ An England Youth international, Paul Simpson made his debut for Manchester City as a 16-year-old and earned five Under-21 caps. Oxford United were able to sign him with some of the cash received when Dean Saunders joined Derby. His scoring record from the left wing, 50 goals in 167 games for Oxford, attracted Arthur Cox, who made his move when Oxford were struggling for cash after the collapse of the Maxwell empire. There was an immediate return for the Rams, four goals in his first five games. Simpson's immaculate left foot was always a danger from corners and free-kicks, as well as in open play. He was a bargain at £500,000 and scored three hat-tricks for the Rams. A penalty at Oldham, ensured a priceless victory in the 1995–96 promotion campaign but he reckoned an earlier penalty, to save a home point against Watford, was more testing to his nerves. His career extended for more than 20 years, with well over 700 matches, and he was still scoring goals as a player-manager in tough jobs at Rochdale and Carlisle. He was close to rescuing Carlisle from a woeful start in 2003–04 but they lost their League place. Under Simpson they won the Conference Play-offs a year later and immediately mounted another promotion campaign.

---

## STAMPS John David

*Centre-forward*

*Born: Thrybergh, 2 December 1918. Died: Winshill, Burton upon Trent, 19 November 1991.*
*Career: Silverwood Colliery. Mansfield Town October 1937. New Brighton August 1938. Derby County January 1939. Shrewsbury Town December 1953. Burton Albion August 1954: player-coach, June 1955: general assistant (coaching and scouting), June 1956: re-signed as a player, October 1956: assistant manager, May 1957: temporary manager, November 1957: manager, February 1958 to October 1959.*
***FA Cup winners 1945–46.***

■ 'A rare battler' was how the 1946 FA Cup final programme summed up Derby County centre-forward Jack Stamps. It was a sound judgement, for Stamps was one of the bravest players to wear the Rams colours, but it undersold his considerable skill. Stamps was given a free transfer by Mansfield and snapped up by New Brighton, then a Third Division North club. His goalscoring exploits soon had the scouts hurrying to Cheshire

and George Jobey won the race to sign him for £1,500. Like so many players of his time, Stamps lost his best years to the war – he was one of the last members of the British Expeditionary Force to be evacuated from Dunkirk in 1940 – but in 1946 he scored two goals at Wembley as the Rams lifted the FA Cup. For the rest of his life he carried the medal everywhere. Stamps was originally an inside-forward and no less an expert than Raich Carter was quick to extol his virtues as a fine footballing forward. But it is as a big, burly centre-forward that most fans choose to remember him and it was from that position that he scored the majority of his 100 League goals for Derby, playing between Doherty and Carter, and later between Morris and Steel. One memory is of him losing teeth in a collision with Burnley defender Tommy Cummings on Easter Monday 1949 and heading the winner against Birmingham five days later. Those who played alongside, and against him, will testify to his courage. Stamps, who became totally blind, was elected an honorary vice-president of Derby County in January 1983.

---

## STEEL William

*Inside-left*

*Born: Denny, 1 May 1923. Died: Los Angeles, 13 May 1982.*
*Career: Dunipace Thistle 1937. Bo'ness Cadora 1938. Leicester City groundstaff January 1939. Amateur, St Mirren, cs 1939. Morton May 1940. Derby County June 1947. Dundee September 1950. Los Angeles Danes (officially transferred) January 1956. Hollywood.*

■ Derby paid a British record fee of £15,500 for blond-haired Billy Steel in June 1947 after he had made overnight headlines with an electrifying display for Great Britain against the Rest of Europe at Hampden Park the previous month. Although he had played only a handful of League games for Morton and one international for Scotland, Steel fitted in well with the other forwards, Stanley Matthews, Wilf Mannion, Tommy Lawton and Billy Liddell, and scored the most spectacular of Britain's six goals. Although he had many fine games for Derby with his terrific left-foot shot and brilliant ball control, Steel was difficult to play with and was a law unto himself. His teammates felt that he reserved his best for Scotland or games in London. They resented his status and the fact that he had other 'jobs' which increased his earnings in the days of the maximum wage. His pleasant smile also masked an intolerant side to his character. Eventually Dundee paid a Scottish record of £23,000 for Steel, whom many former Rams players of his era still hold partly responsible for the decline of the 1950s. Steel helped Dundee to two League Cup final victories and a Scottish Cup final before emigrating to America in August 1954, taking up a position in advertising in California.

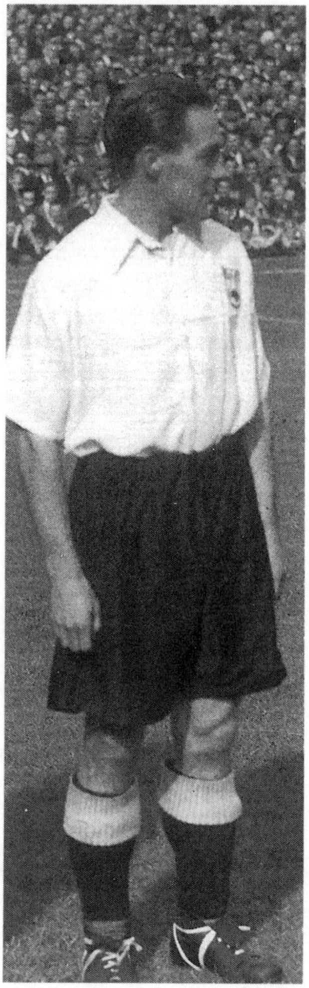

## STIMAC Igor

*Defender*

*Born: Metkovic, 6 September 1967.*
*Career: Hajduk Split. Dinamo Vinkovci 1985. Hajduk Split 1987. Cibalia Vinkovci August 1990. Cadiz August 1992. Hajduk Split August 1994. Derby County October 1995. West Ham United September 1999. Hajduk Split July 2001. Coach, April 2005.*
***Division One promotion 1995–96.***

■ Perhaps the most influential of all Jim Smith's signings, Igor Stimac brought a new dimension to Derby County. He was a regular member of the increasingly successful Croatia team when a fee of £1.57-million brought him from Hajduk Split. If Stimac was alarmed by what he saw on his debut, a 5–1 defeat by Tranmere Rovers at Prenton Park, he did not show it. The defensive formation changed after that and Derby embarked on an unbeaten run of 20 League games, putting them well on the way to the Premiership. Stimac had an unshakeable faith in his considerable ability and his confidence affected those around him. Especially in the First Division, it often appeared to intimidate opponents. When he arrived at Derby, Stimac spoke little English but, within a matter of weeks, became fluent. Although he did not believe he should play unless fully fit, Stimac could always point to the results when he was there. He had presence, style and class, a magnificent player. He was one of five current Derby players at the 1998 World Cup finals in France where, to his pride, Croatia were third. After a brief spell with West Ham United, Stimac returned to Split to attend to his many business interests. He became Hajduk's sporting director but, in 2004, was suspended for six months after being charged with hitting a linesman at half-time in an away game against Rijeka.

## STORER Harry

*Wing-half/inside-forward*

*Born: Liverpool, 2 February 1898.*
*Died: Derby, 1 September 1967.*
*Career: Ripley Town. Eastwood. Amateur, Notts County, one match in November 1918. Amateur, Grimsby Town, February 1919: professional, April 1919. Derby County March 1921. Burnley February 1929. Manager, Coventry City, June 1931. Manager, Birmingham City, May 1945. Manager, Coventry City, November 1948 to November 1953. Manager, Derby County, July 1955 to May 1962.*
***Division Two promotion 1925–26.***

■ Uniquely, Harry Storer played nine matches in a County Championship winning team while in office as a Football League manager. Although he was born in Liverpool and came to the Rams from Grimsby Town for £4,500, Storer had fine Derbyshire connections. His father, also

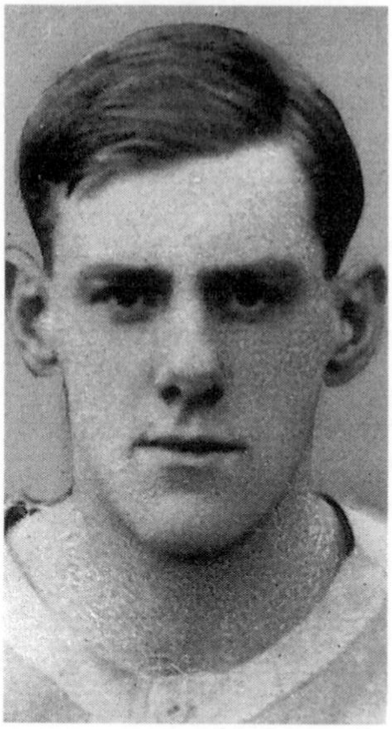

Harry, was born in Ripley and played in goal for Derby Midland, Woolwich Arsenal and Liverpool, as well as cricket for Derbyshire. Uncle William was a Rams forward and a Derbyshire and England cricketer. Harry junior also played for Derbyshire from 1920 to 1936, scoring 13,513 runs (average 27.63) with 18 centuries and taking over 200 wickets. He was one of Derbyshire's finest opening batsmen and a member of the 1936 Championship team. His partnership of 322 with Joe Bowden against Essex at the County Ground in 1929 lasted out the Millennium as Derbyshire's first-wicket record. His career with the Rams was just as distinguished. Although he played most of his games in the half-back line, he had one outstanding season at inside-forward when he scored 24 League goals in 1923–24, including four when the Rams beat Bristol City 8–0 at Ashton Gate. At the end of that season he won the first of his two caps, at inside-left against France in Paris. Storer was a hard player and a tough manager. He was firm with his players and successful: the Division Three South title with Coventry in 1935–36, the Second Division Championship with Birmingham in 1947–48 and the Third North success with the Rams in 1956–57.

---

## STRAW Raymond

*Centre-forward*

*Born: Ilkeston, 22 May 1933. Died: Ilkeston, 12 May 2001.*
*Career: Ilkeston MW. Ilkeston Town August 1951. Derby County October 1951. Coventry City November 1957. Mansfield Town August 1961. Lockheed Leamington July 1963.*
***Division Three North Champions 1956–57.***

■ There have been few more placid characters to play for Derby County than Ray Straw, the former Ilkeston miner who equalled Jack Bowers' record of 37 League goals in a season. Straw's tally came in the Third Division North promotion season and a large proportion of them were headed in from Tommy Powell's centres. His training in the days of Harry Storer's management consisted mainly of heading in centres from Powell and Woodhead, the two wingers. It paid Straw twice over. Before the 1956–57 season began, his brother had offered him half-a-crown a goal and ten shilling for every hat-trick (he bagged three). Straw joined the Rams when they were still in Division One. He played in the top flight, making his debut in a 1–1 home draw with Chelsea in the last game of 1951–52, but did not establish himself until Derby had been relegated twice, when he became the key man in attack. He injured his ankle during the 1957 close season tour of Holland and

by the time he regained full fitness and form, Storer had sold him to Coventry. Straw, known in his playing days as 'Toffee' because of his passion for sweets, enjoyed two more promotions, from the Fourth Division with Coventry in 1958–59, thereby appearing in all six divisions of the Football League, and Mansfield Town in 1962–63. The goals still flowed, 85 in 151 games for Coventry and 14 in 49 for Mansfield.

---

## THOMAS Roderick John

*Right-back*

*Born: Glyncorrwg, 11 January 1947.*
*Career: Gloucester City. Swindon Town July 1964. Derby County November 1973. Cardiff City November 1977. Gloucester City February 1982. Newport County March 1982. Barry Town. Director of football Derby County, April to November 2003.*
***Division One Champions 1974–75.***

■ Dave Mackay went back to Swindon Town, where he started his managerial career, for his first signing after taking over at Derby. Rod Thomas, already established in the Wales team, cost Derby

£80,000. The first to react was Ron Webster who, presented with a threat to his position, asked Mackay where he stood. Mackay assured him that he would remain in the team while his form justified selection. Thomas had to wait until an injury to Webster let him in and, during the second half of the 1974–75 Championship-winning season, was at last able to show his quality. He was deceptively quick and a long leg would often stretch around an opponent who thought he had escaped. He played in the Swindon team that beat Arsenal in the 1969 League Cup final as well as finishing runners-up in the Third Division and won 50 Welsh caps, 19 of them with Derby. Thomas and Francis Lee were joint owners of a racehorse. His brief appointment as Derby's Director of football offered a title but no authority and was a pointless gesture in the late days of Lionel Pickering's time as chairman.

## THORNEWELL George

*Outside-right*

*Born: Romiley, 8 July 1898. Died: Derby, 6 March 1986.*
*Career: Rolls-Royce. Derby County May 1919. Blackburn Rovers December 1927. Chesterfield August 1929. Newark Town August 1932.*
***Division Two promotion 1925–26.***

■ Nippy little George Thornewell was a regular fixture in the Rams' team in the years following World War One. The youngest of eight children, Thornewell moved to Derby after his father died. He became an apprentice at Rolls-Royce and during World War One trained as a pilot. When peace was restored, he went back to Royces and played with the Rams in the 1919 Midland Victory League. Later that year the former schoolboy star was making his First Division debut against Manchester United at the Baseball Ground. Thereafter Thornewell was the Rams' regular outside-right, making 295 appearances before Sammy Crooks took over, and played for England four times, twice each against Sweden and France. Thornewell, a cheeky winger who liked to hug the touchline, helped Derby to promotion in 1925–26. He moved to Blackburn and a few months later, in the 1928 FA Cup final victory over Huddersfield Town, was involved in a first-minute goal. Later he helped Chesterfield to the Third Division North title in 1930–31, played briefly with Newark Town and for many years kept a pub at Duffield, at the same time playing an active role on the committee of the Derby County Supporters' Association.

## TODD Colin

*Central defender/midfield*

*Born: Chester-le-Street, 12 December 1948.*
*Career: Apprentice, Sunderland: professional February 1966. Derby County February 1971. Everton September 1978. Birmingham City September 1979. Nottingham Forest August 1982. Oxford United February 1984. Vancouver Whitecaps May 1984. Luton Town October 1984. Manager, Whitley Bay, 1985. Youth coach, Middlesbrough, May 1986: assistant manager September 1986: manager March 1990 to June 1991. Assistant manager, Bradford City, January 1992. Assistant manager, Bolton Wanderers, June 1992: joint manager June 1995: manager January 1996 to September 1999. Manager, Swindon Town, May 2000. Assistant manager, Derby County, November 2000: manager October 2001 to January 2002. Assistant manager, Bradford City, November 2003: manager June 2004.*
***Division One Champions 1971–72, 1974–75.***

■ "We're not signing Colin Todd. We can't afford him," said Brian Clough in answer to reporters' persistent questions one day in February 1971. Clough promptly got into his car and, 24 hours later, produced Todd to those same reporters. Derby paid Sunderland £170,000 for one of the most promising young players in the country and Clough, once Sunderland's youth coach, knew he had a cast-iron certainty. Todd, paired with Roy McFarland, was a central defender with the capacity both to excite and produce ripples of appreciative applause. He was devastatingly fast and strong in the tackle. He made the game so easy, because all he did was to catch opponents, take the ball off them and give it to one of his own players. He played 40 games in the 1971–72 Championship side but 1974–75 was his greatest season. Peter Daniel stood in admirably for the injured McFarland and Todd made scarcely an error. Deservedly he was elected as the Professional Footballers' Association Player of the Year. He could easily have won more than 27 England caps and there was great resentment when Tommy Docherty sold him to Everton for £300,000 in September 1978. Todd helped Birmingham City to promotion

from the Second Division in 1980 and gave Oxford United a vital thrust towards the Third Division title in 1984. He became Bruce Rioch's assistant at Middlesbrough before being manager for 15 months and they were together again with Bolton Wanderers. He returned to Derby as Jim Smith's assistant and was briefly manager in what developed into a disastrous season.

---

## UPTON Frank

*Wing-half/full-back*

*Born: Ainsley Hill, 18 October 1934.*

*Career: Nuneaton Borough. Northampton Town March 1953. Derby County June 1954. Chelsea August 1961. Derby County September 1965. Notts County September 1966. Worcester City July 1967. Player-manager, Workington, January to July 1968. Coach, Northampton Town, October 1969. Coach, Aston Villa, January 1970. Assistant manager/coach, Chelsea, August 1977: temporary manager, December 1978. Coach, Randers Freja, February 1979 to February 1980. Coach, Dundee, August 1980. Coach, Al Arabi, 1981. Youth coach, Wolverhampton Wanderers, October 1982. Coach, Bedworth United, October 1984. Assistant manager/coach, Coventry City, December 1984 to April 1986. Coach, IBK Keflavik, May 1987. Chief scout/youth development, Aston Villa. Caretaker manager, Burton Albion, January to February 1990. Youth development officer, Northwich Victoria, April 1990. Coach, Sabah (Malaysia), May 1990. YTS officer, Cheltenham Town to November 1990. National coach, India, January 1994 to June 1995. Chief Scout, Aston Villa, 1998.*

***Division Three North Champions 1956–57.***

■ Bone-crunching tackles and rocket-powered shots were the trade mark of Frank 'The Tank' Upton. After 17 League appearances for Northampton Town, Upton's first Derby career lasted six years. He was just the sort of forceful, determined player to capture Harry Storer's eye, although he played only a handful of games when the Rams won promotion in 1956–57. Later he gained a regular place until Storer sold him to Chelsea. Upton was a success at Stamford Bridge, playing some of his 74 League matches at centre-forward, helping them to promotion from the Second Division in 1962–63 and picking up a League Cup-winners' tankard in 1964–65. Tim Ward re-signed him for Derby and a year later he was off again, making the short trip to Meadow Lane. As a coach, he earned a good

reputation for working with young players, including an FA Youth Cup success with Villa, but had ups and downs, winning an industrial tribunal for wrongful dismissal by Wolves and becoming a globe-trotter in search of football.

## VAN DER LAAN Robertus Petrus

*Midfield*

*Born: Schiedam, 5 September 1968.*
*Career: Wageningen. Port Vale February 1991. Derby County August 1995. Wolverhampton Wanderers, loan, October 1996. Barnsley July 1998.*
***Division One promotion 1995–96 (captain).***

■ The extrovert Dutchman was the ideal leader when Derby won promotion in 1995–96 and Jim Smith was too ready to jettison

Robbie van der Laan when they were in the Premiership. When Smith was manager of Portsmouth, he tried to sign van der Laan with Darryl Powell offered in part-exchange. Instead he brought both to Derby, with van der Laan part of a deal that took striker Lee Mills to Port Vale. John Rudge spotted van der Laan in Dutch football, one of many shrewd captures on behalf of Vale. At Derby, van der Laan had the knack of bringing out the best in players around him, reminding supporters of Rob Hindmarch in the promotions under Arthur Cox. A loan to Wolverhampton Wanderers suggested van der Laan was on his way out but, when he returned, he did much to see Derby through the difficult first season in the Premiership with his midfield drive and enthusiasm. Injuries cut short his career after he joined Barnsley.

## WARD Timothy Victor

*Wing-half*

*Born: Cheltenham, 17 October 1917. Died: Barton-under-Needwood, 28 January 1993.*
*Career: Cheltenham Town August 1935. Derby County April 1937. Barnsley March 1951. Manager, Exeter City, March 1953 (for eight days while still registered with Barnsley). Manager, Barnsley, March 1953. Manager, Grimsby Town, February 1960. Manager, Derby County, June 1962 to May 1967. Manager, Carlisle United, June 1967 to September 1968.*

■ A part-timer with his local club, Cheltenham Town, Tim Ward was spotted by Jackie Whitehouse and in his first trial match for Derby County 'A', scored with his first kick. George Jobey paid Cheltenham £100 and Ward became a full-time professional. In January 1938 he took over at left-half in the League side, displacing England international Errington Keen. Ward was the regular number six until the outbreak of war. Although he played in the first game of the

1945–46 FA Cup run, at Luton, Ward was in Germany with the BAOR side for most of the season. As a result he had no chance of displacing Bullions and Musson, but looked back philosophically. "So many of my friends were killed in the war," he said, "and I regarded myself lucky to emerge from it, rather than unlucky to miss Wembley." Later that year Arsenal offered £10,000 for him but Derby found him a place at right-half and in that position he went on to win two England caps and skipper the Rams. In the late 1940s, Ward had few superiors as a stylish wing-half and in 1950 went on the FA tour of Canada. His sudden sale to Barnsley shook not only supporters but Ward himself although he later returned to Derby as manager.

## WARREN Benjamin

*Wing-half/inside-forward*

*Born: Newhall, 1879. Died: Newhall, 15 January 1917.*
*Career: Newhall Town. Newhall Swifts. Derby County May 1899. Chelsea August 1908.*
***FA Cup finalists 1902–03.***

■ For five years Ben Warren was probably the finest wing-half in the League and as late as 1972, his

13 caps held fourth place in the list of Derby County's England internationals. Warren rose to national fame, yet his death at the age of 38 was tragic. He was essentially a right-half, a position in which he played 19 consecutive games for England with his two clubs, but he was also an effective inside-forward. In 1902, he scored eight FA Cup goals, including a hat-trick against Lincoln. Warren was a courageous player who allied a fierce tackle to perfect ball control and abundant hard work. After Derby were relegated in 1907 he stayed another season before resuming his First Division career with Chelsea. He found it a wrench to leave the Baseball Ground and every Saturday night caught the first available train back to his South Derbyshire home. After his enforced retirement in February 1912, Chelsea played a testimonial for him. Warren was certified insane and spent a period in Derbyshire Lunatic Asylum. It was a terrible end for a great player.

## WEBSTER Ronald

*Right-back/wing-half*

*Born: Belper, 21 June 1943.*
*Career: Juniors, Derby County: professional, June 1960. Minnesota Kicks, loan, April 1976. Minnesota Kicks April 1978. Youth coach, Derby County, August 1978 to November 1982.*
***Division Two Champions 1968–69. Division One Champions 1971–72, 1974–75.***

■ Ron Webster was the one local man in Derby County's League Championship teams. First as a player then as youth coach, he served under eight managers at the Baseball Ground. Harry Storer was in the manager's office when the young Webster went to ask why he was not in the first team and his promise brightened considerably in what was then, under Tim Ward, an average Second Division team. Bigger clubs saw Webster's potential but he stayed at Derby and, under Brian Cough and Peter Taylor, became the regular right-back in the surge towards the top. He was not a flamboyant player and tended to shun publicity. Because he had been around for a long time, managers as well as Press observers often underestimated him but his hallmarks were utter reliability and dedicated professionalism. He was a top-class defender and his rare goals in the 1970s – one in each of the Championship seasons – assumed a prophetic significance. Dave Mackay bought Rod Thomas to play right-back but Webster, characteristically, made the Welsh international wait. Only when Webster was injured did he lose his place. When he turned to coaching, he had made more senior appearances then any other player in the Rams' history. Kevin Hector subsequently took the record off him but Webster was a popular and effective youth coach until he became a victim of Peter Taylor's reorganisation.

## WHITEHOUSE John Charles

*Inside-forward*

*Born: Smethwick, 4 March 1897.*
*Died: Halesowen, 3 January 1948.*
*Career: Blackheath Town. Redditch. Birmingham August 1916. Derby County May 1923. Sheffield Wednesday February 1929. Bournemouth and Boscombe Athletic August 1930. Folkestone Town May 1933. Player-manager, Worcester City, June 1934 to May 1936.*
***Division Two promotion 1925–26.***

■ Jackie Whitehouse, who had guested for Derby County and Chelsea during World War One, was a vital signing from Birmingham. The following season he helped Derby to become Division Two's leading scorers – one more goal and they would have been promoted – and with Storer and Galloway formed a prolific inside trio. Had injury not prevented him from playing in the final two League games, thus robbing him of an ever-

present record, the Rams might have found the goal they needed for promotion, because he scored 86 in his 200 senior appearances for the Rams. Whitehouse could create as well as score and was equally comfortable at centre or inside-forward. When Derby did win promotion he proved himself a First Division player and scored four when the Rams beat Sheffield Wednesday 8–0 in March 1927. Perhaps Wednesday remembered that when they signed him a little under two years later. In the late 1930s, he was a Derby County scout, with Tim Ward to his credit.

---

## WILLIAMS David Geraint

*Midfield*

*Born; Cwn-Parc, 5 January 1962.*
*Career: Apprentice, Bristol Rovers: professional January 1980. Derby County March 1985. Ipswich Town July 1992. Colchester United July 1998: player-coach 1999: assistant manager; acting manager January to February 2003: Manager July 2006.*
***Division Three promotion 1985–86. Division Two Champions 1986–87.***

■ Arthur Cox pursued Geraint Williams for five months before Bristol Rovers agreed to sell him for £43,500 on the eve of the 1985 transfer deadline. He had won two Welsh Under-21 caps at Eastville and proved an excellent signing for the Rams. Through two promotions, Williams took each division in his stride and his midfield industry was essential to Derby. Although his goals were rare, he had a sharp eye for danger, often popping up as back man, and his most fruitful partnership was with John Gregory. The blend was right and Williams won 11 caps for Wales.

When the Rams were relegated in 1990–91, Williams had an almost impossible burden, trying to keep the midfield afloat virtually on his own. Supporters voted him Player of the Year after the Second Division Championship and he bounced back in style as captain in 1991–92. After 332 senior appearances for the Rams, Ipswich Town signed Williams for £650,000 on a four-year contract, John Lyall seeing him as a man who could help cement their Premier League status. As it turned out, Lyall left in 1994 and Ipswich went down the following year but Williams gave them good service, with 267 appearances, before passing 650 in the League when he joined Colchester.

---

## WRIGHT Mark

*Centre-half*

*Born: Dorchester-on-Thames, 1 August 1963.*
*Career: Apprentice, Oxford United: professional August 1980. Southampton March 1982. Derby County August 1987. Liverpool July 1991. Manager, Southport, December 1999. Manager, Oxford United, May to November 2001. Manager, Chester City, January 2002 to August 2004. Manager, Peterborough United, May 2005 to January 2006. Manager, Chester City, February 2006.*

■ The early days of Robert Maxwell's chairmanship were full of optimism. Peter Shilton was signed from Southampton and when Arthur Cox returned to The Dell for England centre-half Mark Wright, it was felt that a formidable team was taking shape. Wright cost £760,000, shattering the club record of £410,000 which had stood for more than seven years since the signing of David Swindlehurst. The Rams would probably not have survived their first season back in Division One without Wright and Shilton. The centre-

half continued to grow in stature and, although he fell out with England manager Bobby Robson after the 1988 European Championship finals, returned splendidly for the 1990 World Cup in Italy. He captained England against USSR in 1990–91. Wright was twice voted Derby's Player of the Year but was also sent off three times while he was with the club. A move became inevitable in 1991, when the Rams were desperate to raise cash to pay off Maxwell, and it was no great surprise when Wright moved to Liverpool for £2.3-million. As captain, Wright led Liverpool to victory in the 1992 FA Cup final but missed the European Championships in Sweden because of a tendon injury. His retirement in 1998 was hastened by injuries and his first venture into League management, with Oxford United, was cut short by a charge arising from a dispute with referee Joe Ross. He responded by leading Chester City to the Conference title in 2003–04 but left abruptly as controversy studded his career.

---

## YOUNG George Raymond

*Centre-half*

*Born: Derby, 14 March 1934.*
*Career: Juniors, Derby County: professional March 1951. Heanor Town September 1966. Burton Albion May 1967.*
***Division Three North Champions 1956–57.***

■ When Ray Young joined Derby in 1949, after a successful schoolboy career in which he played for England Boys, there were high hopes that this skilful and intelligent centre-half would develop into another Leon Leuty. Young was nursed through Colts and Reserves before making his League debut at Doncaster in 1954. It was felt that he would make the number-five spot his own, yet he did not until his career was almost over. When he was playing well, Young looked international class. He seemed to have time on his hands and strolled around the back with consummate ease. But then he would become too casual and his lack of pace could be exposed. There were those who felt that he was too 'philosophical' in his approach to the game. He lost many appearances to the more physical approach of Martin McDonnell and, later, Les Moore. Nevertheless, Young gave a touch of style to Derby County, flourishing more under Tim Ward than Harry Storer.

# The Managers

## Harry Newbould

### 1900–1906

*FA Cup finalists 1903.*

W.D. Clark was named as manager when Derby County became a limited company in 1896 but Harry Newbould was the first to be concerned with team affairs. He was appointed in 1900, having already served as secretary, a duty he continued to perform along with his managerial post. Newbould was well-known in the Midlands as a fine sprinter and that speed helped him as a right-winger with Derby St Luke's when they were a leading local club.

A qualified accountant, Newbould was appointed assistant secretary in 1896. He was promoted to secretary and when Derby decided to appoint a manager, they looked no further than Newbould. He was not solely responsible for selecting the team but during his reign many fine players arrived at Derby, including Ben Warren, Charlie Morris, George Richards, Harry Maskrey and Ben Hall.

Newbould was popular with players, directors and supporters and though one of his last pieces of business was to sell Steve

Bloomer to Middlesbrough, the instruction certainly came from the board. The loss of Bloomer cast a shadow over the Rams' battle to stay up and the following year they were relegated. Newbould was not at Derby County to see it. In July 1906 he was appointed secretary-manager of Manchester City and it was reported that the Derby directors were both 'surprised and disappointed'. After Tom Maley created a fine team, City became involved in charges of bribery and illegal payments. A change was essential. Later Newbould became a prominent figure in the forerunner of today's PFA, as secretary of the Players' Union. He died in 1929.

## Jimmy Methven

### 1906–1922

*Division Two Champions 1911–12, 1914–15.*

WHEN Jimmy Methven was appointed Rams manager on 7 August 1906, he continued an association with the club he joined as a player in the close season of 1891. Methven's appointment was the first of its kind in Derby's history as the previous manager was also secretary. Methven was uncluttered by such administrative chores, yet his control over Derby's playing affairs was limited by the board of directors. Throughout his period as Derby manager, from 1906 to 1922, with a break during World War One when he worked at Rolls-Royce, there was always a 'selection committee'. Similarly, players were

bought 'by the Derby directors', though presumably on Methven's recommendations. His son Alfred clearly remembered his father coming home in the small hours of the morning after long scouting trips.

Methven was unable to prevent Derby, without Bloomer, from being relegated in his first season as manager and the following years were fraught with financial problems, meaning there was little money to buy new players. Immediately after World War One his efforts were described as 'unsparing in difficult days of financial crisis'.

In 1922 Methven, suffering from glaucoma, was admitted to hospital for what turned out to be an unsuccessful eye operation. As manager, he faded from the scene and in June of that year, his job was advertised. An association of 31 years, during which he was totally committed as player and the manager, makes him a major figure in Derby County's history.

## Cecil Potter

### 1922–1925

WHEN 33-year-old Cecil Potter was offered the Derby manager's job in July 1922, the Rams had just finished 12th in Division Two, their lowest position so far. Although Potter never achieved promotion for Derby, he built the basis of a side good enough to win back a place in Division One the season after he left. Cecil Bertram Potter was born in West Hoathly, Sussex, the son of a Congregationalist minister. He signed for Norwich City after a trial in 1911 and was their joint top-scorer in 1914–15. After military service – and a few wartime games for Spurs – Potter went to Hull, then to Hartlepools United as secretary, player and manager in 1920.

When Methven retired at Derby, rumours swept the town that the famous Newcastle United and England player Colin Veitch was to become the Rams manager. In fact Veitch never applied for the job and on 4 July 1922, Derby announced that, after interviewing four candidates, Potter was their man.

Potter brought with him from Hartlepools two players, full-back Tommy Crilly and centre-half Harry Thoms. Although his first season saw the Rams finish 14th in Division Two, their lowest position until then, Potter developed a side that narrowly missed promotion in 1924 and 1925 and went within 90 minutes of the first Wembley FA Cup final. In 1923, as the Empire Stadium rose in North London, Derby lost to West Ham United in the semi-final at Stamford Bridge.

Potter took Derby close to promotion before leaving in 1925. He had originally intended to take a dairy business in Sussex but, a week after leaving the Baseball Ground, he was approached by Huddersfield Town, who had already won two successive League Championships. Herbert Chapman, who built that team, was lured away by the potential of Arsenal. In his only full season at Leeds Road, Potter completed the Championship hat-trick, the first to be achieved. Chapman set about creating an Arsenal team to emulate it in the 1930s but did not live to complete the hat-trick. Potter managed Norwich from December 1926 until January 1929 before failing to survive the humiliation of being knocked out of the FA Cup, 5–0 by the amateur Corinthians. He died in October 1975.

---

## George Jobey

### 1925–1941

***Division Two promotion 1925–66. Division One runners-up 1929–30, 1935–36. Central League Champions 1935–36.***

AFTER Brian Clough and Dave Mackay, George Jobey ranks as the most successful manager in Derby County's history. His 16-year reign at the Baseball Ground, from August 1925 into World War Two, was the Rams' most consistently successful period in Division One, notwithstanding the two Championships of the 1970s.

Jobey was born at Heddon on Tyneside and played with Newcastle United, Arsenal, scoring the Gunners' first goal at Highbury, Bradford and Leicester City. He was in Newcastle's 1909 Championship side and played in the 1911 FA Cup final. Jobey appeared for Hamilton Academical during World War One, became player-manager of Northampton Town in May 1920 and manager of Wolverhampton Wanderers in 1922. After Wolves won the Third Division North in 1923–24, Jobey went into the hotel business until Derby tempted him back into football.

He reinforced Potter's side, notably with Harry Bedford, and won promotion in his first season. Thereafter, his shrewdness in the transfer market served Derby well and although he was not afraid to back judgement with cash, three of his greatest signings, Jack Barker, Jack Bowers and Sammy

Crooks, cost the Rams next to nothing. He signed some of the greatest players in Derby's history among a large number he introduced to the Baseball Ground: not all were successful. He had the imagination to go for Hughie Gallacher when Bowers was injured and proved that he had the character to tame a player like the difficult Scotsman. Rams players would tremble before him and those who played for him winced at the thought of his waspish tongue.

Tim Ward recalled how Jobey would rarely attend training, but when he did he was quite likely to order two or three players straight off for a haircut. Ward, prompted by other players, ran into Jobey at his fiercest by asking for first-team money to match his status, then found out next pay-day that he had been awarded his rise. Though, with the exception of the irrepressible Sammy Crooks, they feared him, they were all Jobey's men to the end, Crooks included.

George Jobey presented the Derby public with an impressive array of talent throughout the 1930s and people sometimes wondered how he managed it. In 1941 they had their question partly answered. A joint FA and League Commission, sitting at the Midland Hotel, Derby, found that between 1925 and 1938 the Rams had paid illegal bonuses and inducements, balancing their books with some inventive entries.

Jobey was suspended permanently from all football, five directors received *sine-die* suspensions and the club was fined £500. Although Jobey's suspension was lifted in 1945, it was not until 1952 that he made a managerial comeback with Mansfield, only to be sacked for 'lack of interest'. Jobey died at his home in Bangor Street, Chaddesden, in May 1962, aged 76. With him went a significant part of Derby County's history.

## Ted Magner

### 1944–1946

*Football League North Champions, Midland Cup winners 1944–45.*

TED Magner managed the Rams for a brief but significant period during World War Two. When he took over in March 1944, the vagaries of wartime soccer were still dominant. When he left 22 months later, he had persuaded both Raich Carter and Peter Doherty to sign officially and the Rams were poised to win the FA Cup for the first time.

A native of Newcastle, Magner signed for Gainsborough Trinity, then a Second Division club, at the age of 17, and his second League appearance was against Derby County. Magner also played for Everton against the Rams in an FA Cup match at the Baseball Ground in 1911, when

Bloomer scored twice in Derby's 5–0 win. From Goodison Park, Magner moved to St Mirren and scored five goals against Queen's Park to set a Scottish League Division One record.

During World War One Magner served in the Northumberland Fusiliers, during which time he contracted malaria, and when peace was restored worked as a coach in Amsterdam and elsewhere on the Continent before returning to become a tutor on FA coaching refresher courses at Leeds and Loughborough.

In 1938 he was appointed assistant manager of Huddersfield and when Clem Stephenson left in 1941–42, Magner stepped up. He left Leeds Road in 1943 and a year later was at Derby. From an ever-shifting parade of players Magner fashioned a team which did the double, the Football League North Championship and Midland Cup, in 1944–45. The following year the FA Cup proper resumed and Magner was instrumental in Carter and Doherty committing themselves to Derby County on a permanent basis.

"Ted Magner was an outstanding manager and if he had not left Derby, then I would have stayed," Doherty said. "His man-management was superb and he had an immense knowledge of the game. He would take us out on to the pitch and hit the crossbar from the 18-yard line six times out of six, just to show us that he could play".

Magner saw the Rams to the fourth round before going back to work abroad in January 1946. Had he stayed, and lived, he may have prevented the decline of the 1950s and become a great Derby manager. It cannot be proved. In 1948 illness prevented him from taking up a Continental appointment and in July of that year he died at his home in Sunny Hill Avenue, Derby, being buried in Nottingham Road Cemetery.

## Stuart McMillan

### 1946–1953

*FA Cup winners 1946.*

STUART McMillan stands unique among Derby managers in that he was in charge when the Rams won the FA Cup. The son of Johnny McMillan, a star in Steve Bloomer's day, Stuart McMillan was a fine all-round sportsman, though he played only one League game for Derby at the start of a long career. He also played four first-class cricket matches for Derbyshire, golf for Derbyshire and billiards for Derby Institutes.

McMillan took over the Nag's Head, Mickleover, scouted for the Rams and often drove officials to matches. In 1942 he was appointed adviser to the club and when Ted Magner left, McMillan inherited his Wembley-bound team.

Although he twice broke the British transfer record for Derby, buying first Billy Steel and then Johnny Morris, he never enjoyed the same success in the transfer market as George Jobey experienced and to which he had contributed as a scout. The signing of Steel actually worked against him when several senior players became unsettled and left. While personally fond of McMillan, Morris was far from impressed by his grasp of the game.

Ageing stars were not replaced by men of the same calibre and McMillan did not survive the Rams sailing perilously close to Division Three. In November 1953, he was replaced by Jack Barker and went to the Station Hotel, Ashbourne, where he died in September 1963. Raich Carter was one of the mourners at the funeral of this quiet and essentially modest man.

## Jack Barker

### 1953–1955

WITH Derby County slipping towards the Third Division in 1953–54 the Rams board turned to their former England international centre-half Jack Barker. Barker arrested the slide that season but the following campaign, despite paying around £40,000 for new players, Derby dropped out of the Second Division for the first time. Signings like Bury's little Scottish winger Stewart Imlach, former Wolves and England centre-forward Jesse Pye, Celtic goalkeeper George Hunter, and the Hull City pair, Alf Ackerman and Ken Harrison, failed to keep Derby up.

Barker had previously

managed Bradford City and Dundalk, and coached Oldham, but his experiences as manager at the Baseball Ground left him bitter, as he revealed in 1981. "It was a rotten experience," he said. "I wouldn't be a manager again for £10,000 a week. The trouble is that the people you are working for know nothing about the game." His reign was as depressing as that of any Rams manager.

## Harry Storer

### 1955–1962

*Division Three North Champions 1956–57.*

FORMER Derby County and England player Harry Storer faced a daunting task when he took over from Jack Barker in 1955. Derby had never previously sunk as low as the Third Division North and the club was bereft of the spirit that gave it such a fine Division One side in the 1930s and 1940s. In the 1920s, Storer was respected as a hard, as well as skilful wing-half or inside-forward, an unselfish and intelligent player who gave his absolute all for the team. As a manager Storer was equally firm and dedicated. He took Coventry City up to the Second Division in 1936 and Birmingham to the First in 1948. Two years earlier he had won the Football League South title for the Blues and pushed the Rams hard in the FA Cup semi-final.

Storer's first signing as Derby manager was Reg Ryan. The former West Brom schemer said:. "I chose the manager as well as the club. I'd always admired Harry Storer. He had a sharp tongue, a heart of gold and a fantastic knowledge of the game."

Storer took the Rams to promotion in his second season and by the time he retired in 1962, had reduced the club's overdraft from £60,000 to around £23,000. He had not, however, pushed the Rams towards another promotion. His biggest signing was Bill Curry who came for £12,000. The former Brighton and Newcastle centre-forward gave the Rams a touch of flair. Storer had much time for the likes of Frank Upton, Glyn Davies and Martin McDonnell, all ferocious defenders: and admiration, too, for the delightful skills of Tommy Powell who, during the Third Division days, would be told by Storer, "Go out and play where you like."

There are plenty of Harry Storer tales, like the time Joe Mercer asked him about the six players who, Mercer claimed, had been clogging during a match against Sheffield United. Storer's reply was typical: "Give me the names." When Mercer said he did not want to land them in trouble, Storer came back with: "They're not the ones to worry. It's the other five I'm after."

At the end of 1961–62, Storer retired, saying that it was time to make way for a younger man, although he did not particularly want to go. He had a special place in Derby: 274 games and 63 goals for the Rams, followed by a spell as manager that revived the club. Uniquely, he helped Derbyshire to win the County Championship in 1936 while a Football League manager, with Coventry. Storer tried to sign a young Brian Clough for Derby and knew Peter Taylor from Coventry but did not live to see the impact they made at the Baseball Ground.

## Tim Ward

### 1962–1967

WHEN Tim Ward succeeded Harry Storer as Derby manager in June 1962, he was still remembered as a classy wing-half, good enough to play twice for England. His sudden move to Barnsley in March 1951 surprised supporters as much as it did Ward.

He played only 33 League games for Barnsley and, in March 1953, was named as Exeter City's new manager. It was an extraordinary episode. Ward travelled with Exeter for a Third Division South match against Ipswich Town at Portman Road on 7 March but Barnsley had never released him. He was recalled to Oakwell on 12 March and appointed manager of Barnsley on 30 March. They were relegated in his first season but Ward brought them back as Third Division North Champions in 1954–55. Barnsley slipped back to the Third Division in 1959 but Ward was comfortably established at Oakwell until Grimsby Town appointed him in January 1960.

Everything was completed rapidly as Ward was preferred to Raich Carter, his former colleague at Derby, and ex-Newcastle United captain Joe Harvey. He enjoyed another promotion at Blundell Park, from the Third Division in 1961–62, before Derby came in for him. They were always close to Ward's heart and remained so in later years, when he ran the ex-Rams football side and was instrumental in the formation of the Former Players' Association in 1991, becoming the first chairman.

Ward's five years as manager of Derby were not happy because he was so hampered by lack of cash and a parochial attitude in

the boardroom. He made some important signings, Alan Durban from Cardiff City and, to the surprise of supporters, Kevin Hector from Bradford for almost £40,000. Ward had to work for months before he persuaded the directors to make a record investment and Hector was so successful that some of the board promptly tried to claim the credit. Colin Boulton and Peter Daniel, who were to play important parts in League Championship teams, came in as youngsters but one of his most succesful captures, Eddie Thomas from Swansea Town, worked against him.

When told his contract would not be renewed, Ward said: "The job has been the toughest I have ever had and the shortage of money has been frustrating. The trouble with this club is that you can't put a threepenny stamp on a letter without consulting the board personally. I was told that money was available but I could never get an answer when I asked how much.

"Perhaps the worst thing I ever did was to sign Eddie Thomas for £3,500, because he proved a marvellous bargain and after that I was expected to sign other players as cheaply." Ward was even more upset by the dismissal of two other former Derby players, chief scout Sammy Crooks and trainer Ralph Hann. Ward spent 15 months with Carlisle United, his last post in management.

## Brian Clough and Peter Taylor

### 1967–1973

***Division Two Champions 1968–69. Division One Champions 1971–72. European Cup semi-finalists 1972–73. Texaco Cup winners 1971–72. Central League Champions 1971–72.***

BRIAN Clough and Peter Taylor transformed Derby County. When they arrived from Hartlepools United in July 1967, on the strong recommendation of Len Shackleton, Derby were pottering along aimlessly in the Second Division. Their first season brought no improvement in results but the buying attracted a public starved of success.

The first three in were John O'Hare, Roy McFarland and Alan Hinton at a combined cost of less than £75,000 and when Dave Mackay and Willie Carlin were added in 1968–69, Derby County took off. They won the Second Division in a canter, the team was ready for the First Division and the signings became more ambitious and exciting. Terry Hennessey was Derby's first £100,000 player, Archie Gemmill and Colin Todd arrived and David Nish was a British record deal at £225,000. When Nish was signed Derby were reigning Champions, having won the League in 1971–72 for the first time in their history. In 1972–73, they reached the semi-finals of the European Cup.

There was a great hunger for success in Clough, perhaps because his career was cut short by a knee injury. He was born in Middlesbrough on 21 March 1935 and, after working as clerk at ICI, became a professional at Ayresome Park in May 1952. It was more than three years before he made his debut but he began to score so regularly from centre-forward that it became impossible to leave him out. He hit 204 goals in 222 senior games for 'Boro, winning two England caps. While he was there, he formed a close friendship with Taylor but Clough moved to Sunderland for £45.000 in July 1961. He added another 63 goals in 74 games but severly damaged knee ligaments in a collision with Bury goalkeeper Chris Harker on Boxing Day 1962. After a spell as Sunderland's youth coach, Clough became manager of Hartlepool United in October 1965 and persuaded

Taylor to become his assistant. Clough and Taylor formed a partnership in every sense of the word, their talents and their moods complementing each other. They did not buy many players after their initial clear-out but they bought brilliantly and the new prosperity at the Baseball Ground was given tangible form by the building of the Ley Stand after promotion had been earned. Seats were sold out for two seasons even before it had been completed.

Clough, controversial but always interesting, became a target for newspapers and television and, because he was not afraid to stir a few things, worried League and FA officials as well as his chairman, Sam Longson. There were constant suggestions that Clough and Taylor would move to another club and the party they threw after the final match of 1971–72 had originally been intended as a farewell before they left to take over Coventry City. Disputes between board and management became more bitter

until, in October 1973, Clough and Taylor resigned.

They had come to a confrontation with Longson and another director, Jack Kirkland, and decided they must go. The players were as upset as the vast majority of the supporters but not even the formation of a protest movement could change events. Clough and Taylor went to Brighton then, while Taylor stayed, Clough had a brief and unhappy spell with Leeds United. They rejoined forces at Nottingham Forest and were even more spectacularly successful than at Derby; a first Championship for Forest, two League Cup victories, a third final and two European Cup triumphs.

On his own, Clough continued to produce teams that illustrated the best aspects of the game. He was rewarded with League Cup final victories in 1989 and 1990, followed by an FA Cup final appearance in 1991. Sadly, his retirement in 1993 coincided with relegation.

The Executive Stand at the City Ground mirrored their talent as surely as the Ley Stand. As a partnership they were magnificent and it was infinitely sad that their parting in 1982 was so acrimonious. Derby has never known anybody like them: nor has Nottingham. Following Clough's death in September 2004, the A52 linking Derby and Nottingham was named Brian Clough Way.

## Dave Mackay

### 1973–1976

*Division One Champions 1974–75.*

DAVE Mackay walked into a situation unique in football when, in October 1973, he left Nottingham Forest with his assistant Des Anderson to manage Derby County. It was the best of jobs, because there was a talented team awaiting him, and the worst of jobs because the Baseball Ground was in turmoil following the departure of Brian Clough and Peter Taylor. Mackay, a hero as a player at Derby, had to fight for acceptance because the players wanted Clough and Taylor back but gradually won his way through.

After six weeks without a victory under Mackay, Derby revived to finish third and qualify for the UEFA Cup. Mackay bought Rod Thomas and Bruce Rioch and, before the start of the following season, the 30-year-old Francis Lee from Manchester City.

Derby were Champions again in 1974–75, a magnificent achievement by Mackay and Anderson, and a year later, with Charlie George in the side and Leighton James becoming their first £300,000 player, finished fourth and reached the semi-finals of the FA Cup. Derby were beaten at Hillsborough by Tommy Docherty's young Manchester United side and, disappointing though that performance was, few realised that the great days had come to a full stop in one afternoon. The following season began badly and there was increasing criticism from the boardroom of Mackay's free-wheeling style.

In November 1976 Mackay sought a vote of confidence and when the directors felt they could not give this, he and Anderson were sacked. It was an astonishing decision because they were at least entitled to be given time. Mackay had a brief spell with Walsall, then went to work in Kuwait. After a year in Dubai, Mackay returned to English football with Doncaster Rovers in December 1987. He joined Birmingham City before again finding further success abroad with the Egyptian club, Zamalek.

It seemed that the worst thing that a manager could do at the Baseball Ground was to win the Championship and nothing that has happened since has in any way diminished Mackay's stature and achievements. Third, first and fourth in his three seasons: those credentials should have impressed even Derby's board.

## Colin Murphy

### 1976–1977

COLIN Murphy, who had been reserve-team coach under Dave Mackay with Nottingham Forest and Derby County, became Derby's manager in November 1976, at first on a temporary basis. Born in Croydon on 21 January 1944, he never played League football, although he was with Crystal Palace as well as Cork Hibernian, Wimbledon and Hastings United.

He brought in Dario Gradi as his assistant but the early season struggles continued and only five of the first 23 League matches had been won when, in February 1977, chairman George Hardy and the board invited Brian Clough and Peter Taylor to leave Nottingham Forest and return to Derby.

Murphy had, it seemed, merely been keeping the seat warm but when Clough and Taylor shattered Derby's plans by deciding to stay with Forest, Murphy was asked to continue in office.

Murphy invested more than £300,000 in Derek Hales and, in March 1977, bought Gerry Daly from Manchester United for £175,000. Daly watched Derby go to the foot of the First Division when they lost to West Bromwich Albion at The Hawthorns and Sam Longson, by then president, called publicly for Dave Mackay to return. It was humiliating for Murphy but he stuck at it and steered Derby clear of the relegation zone. The 1977–78 season was only six matches old when Murphy had to watch a draw against Leeds United knowing that Tommy Docherty was on the way to the Baseball Ground to succeed him. It had been an extraordinary ten months for Murphy and the shameful final day in office reflected no credit on Derby County. After working with Jimmy Sirrel at Notts County, Murphy became manager of Lincoln City. He returned to Sincil Bank after two spells with Stockport County and a year in Saudi Arabia to guide Lincoln out of the GM Vauxhall Conference. He worked with David Pleat as youth coach at Leicester and assistant manager at Luton, before succeeding David Webb as manager of Southend United in May 1992. Murphy's subsequent travels included a spell in Vietnam as national coach and a League One promotion with Hull City as assistant to Peter Taylor, who had succeeded him at Southend.

## Tommy Docherty

### 1977–1979

CHANGES were needed to a Derby County squad which had lost its impetus but Tommy Docherty's 20 months of buying and selling seriously diminished the quality of the players at the Baseball Ground.

Docherty, born in Glasgow on 24 April 1928, was a rugged wing-half with Celtic, Preston North End and Arsenal, winning 25 caps for Scotland. With him in the side, Preston won the Second Division in 1950–51, were twice First Division runners-up and reached the 1954 FA Cup final. One of his

teammates at Deepdale was former Derby forward Angus Morrison.

Docherty joined Chelsea as player-coach, became manager in January 1962 and created a fine young team. He was equally likely to break up teams and managed Rotherham United, Queen's Park Rangers, Aston Villa and Oporto. He was briefly assistant manager at Hull, then Scotland's team manager from September 1971 to December 1972.

After a hectic career, Docherty appeared to have found the right niche with Manchester United but, after winning the FA Cup with an exciting team in 1977, he lost his job as the result of an affair with the physiotherapist's wife. Docherty and his assistant, Frank Blunstone, were still very much tuned in to United in their first season. In the second, Docherty was in and out of court, suffering a major setback with the collapse of his libel action against Willie Morgan and Granada Television. Docherty kept Derby in the First Division but the departure of players such as Colin Boulton, Colin Todd, Archie Gemmill, Kevin Hector, Charlie George and Leighton James upset supporters. Of all Docherty's purchases, only Steve Buckley proved a long-term investment and the midfield trio of Gerry Daly, already there when Colin Murphy left, Don Masson and Bruce Rioch flopped despite the manager's description of them as three Van Goghs.

In May 1979 Docherty resigned to become manager of Queen's Park Rangers for a second time, leaving Derby still paying for players who were of limited use to them. He also managed Sydney Olympic, twice, Preston North End, Wolverhampton Wanderers and Altrincham before concentrating on radio work and after-dinner speaking.

## Colin Addison

### 1979–1982

GEORGE Hardy was chairman when Colin Addison was appointed as manager. By the time Derby lined up for the pre-season photograph, Richard Moore had taken the chair. It was an unsettling start for Addison, especially when coupled with a police investigation, begun during the summer of 1979 into previous affairs at the Baseball Ground.

Addison, born in Taunton on 18 May 1940, was a goalscoring inside-forward with York City, Nottingham Forest, Arsenal and Sheffield United before joining Hereford United as player-manager. He saw them into the Football League and, after working with Durban City, had a good year with Newport County. He came to Derby from West Bromwich Albion, where he

worked under Ron Atkinson, and appointed John Newman as his assistant.

The Derby job was hard, for the club had been in decline for three years, and despite paying more than £1-million for Barry Powell, Alan Biley and David Swindlehurst, Derby's first £400,000 player, Addison's first season ended in relegation. Derby were also beginning to lose control of their finances. They were never good enough to challenge for promotion in 1980–81 and, with the downward trend continuing, Addison was sacked in January 1982, rejoining Newport. In 1986–87, he took Celta Vigo to promotion from the Spanish Second Division, then rejoined Atkinson at West Bromwich. They went together to Atletico Madrid, where Addison succeeded Atkinson in January 1989. He also managed Cadiz, had another spell with Hereford and coached Al Arabi in Kuwait. He was still full of enthusiasm in his 60s, unfortunate not to keep Scarborough in the League but able to revive Forest Green Rovers in the Conference.

## John Newman

### 1982

AFTER proving himself in the lower divisions with Exeter City and Grimsby Town, John Newman joined Derby County as Colin Addison's assistant and succeeded him in January 1982, although only on a temporary, untitled basis until March. During that time the directors talked about appointing a managing director, rather hoping that Brian Clough would be interested. It was typical of the atmosphere in which Newman had to work and, at a time when Derby changed chairmen as often as managers, he had little chance of success, as he was well aware.

Newman was born in Hereford on 13 December 1933 and began his career with Birmingham City, where he was in the Second Division Championship team of 1954–55 and played in the 1956 FA Cup final as deputy for Roy Warhurst. He moved to Leicester City in search of more regular first-team football and spent almost eight years with Plymouth Argyle before joining Exeter City where, in April 1969, he was appointed player-manager, succeeding Frank Broome. He left a promotion-bound team to take over at Grimsby in January 1977 and moved to Derby after a Fourth Division promotion at Blundell Park.

His immediate task after taking over from Addison was to keep Derby in the Second Division. He brought back Charlie George, signed Brian Attley and John McAlle and achieved his objective. When Mike Watterson took over the club, it was obvious that Newman's days were numbered. He was dismissed in November 1982 and, typically for that time, the sacking was handled without dignity or compassion.

Newman managed Hereford United from March 1983 to October 1987, briefly assisted Bobby Saxton at York, was assistant to John Barnwell at Notts County and worked with George Foster as chief scout at Mansfield. In later years, he was a sounding board for his friend John Barton, manager of Worcester City. His nine months in charge at the Baseball Ground must have seemed like a lifetime.

## Peter Taylor

### 1982–1984

PETER Taylor had been in retirement for six months when new chairman Mike Watterson brought him back to the Baseball Ground. Taylor engaged Roy McFarland and Mick Jones from Bradford City and thereby involved the club in a costly controversy. The Rams were fined £10,000 by the Football League for illegally inducing McFarland to break his contract at Valley Parade and were then ordered to pay £55,000 in compensation.

Taylor, facing a desperate fight against relegation, restored Archie Gemmill to Derby and paid substantial fees for Bobby Davison, Paul Futcher and Paul Hooks. A run of 15 League games without defeat was a fine achievement and victory over Fulham in the final game ensured

safety. Even then, with thousands of spectators around the touchline in the closing minutes, there was more controversy.

The summer signings of John Robertson and Bobby Campbell seemed to point Derby towards better days but they never recovered from a dreadful start and the financial crisis came to a head with the Inland Revenue issuing a winding-up petition. When Derby cleared themselves in the High Court, they parted company with Taylor in April 1984. Taylor's second season was disastrous and Derby were as good as down when he left, despite an FA Cup run to the sixth round.

His greatest days were with Brian Clough, first with Derby, then with Nottingham Forest. Taylor was born in Nottingham on 2 July 1928 and was on Forest's books as an amateur goalkeeper before joining Coventry City in May 1946. He was deeply influenced by Harry Storer's methods and personality before, in August 1955, he joined Middlesbrough, there becoming a close friend of Clough. He was briefly with Port Vale before entering management with Burton Albion and steering them to the Southern League Cup in 1963–64 with a team including Richie Barker.

Taylor, a private man happiest with his family, died in Majorca in October 1990. His funeral in the Nottinghamshire village of Widmerpool was packed with the kind of class players he loved.

## Roy McFarland

### 1984 and 1993–1995

AFTER Peter Taylor's departure, Roy McFarland had nine games in which to save Derby County from relegation. By playing a settled side, he improved results but could not make up an alarming deficit in such a short time. Although McFarland was on a short list of four at the end of 1983–84, it was clear that the Rams would look outside the club but he stayed as Arthur Cox's assistant. They worked well together as Derby surged from the Third Division to fifth in the top flight in the space of four seasons.

When Cox succumbed to back trouble, McFarland took the job, at first on a temporary basis but as manager in his own right in October 1993. He engaged the experienced Alan Durban, another of Derby's 1971–72 Champions, as his assistant but the big spending days were over. McFarland steered Derby to the Play-off finals in 1994, past a frightening second leg at Millwall, and they were unfortunate to lose to Leicester City at Wembley. After that, Derby began to sell. Paul Kitson's transfer to Newcastle United caused a rift between chairman Brian Fearn and owner Lionel Pickering: Gary Charles and Tommy Johnson moved to Aston Villa on the eve of an FA Cup third round tie against Everton at Goodison Park. Once Pickering became chairman, it was increasingly clear that McFarland's contract would not be renewed at the end of 1994–95. He was appointed manager of Bolton Wanderers but, at a televised Press conference, discovered he was joint manager with Colin Todd. McFarland did well as manager of Cambridge United, making significant money on transfers, and Torquay United before taking over at Chesterfield.

## Arthur Cox

### 1984–1993

*Division Three promotion 1985–86. Division Two Champions 1986–87. Central League Champions 1985–86.*

ARTHUR Cox had just clinched promotion to the First Division with an exciting Newcastle United team, featuring Kevin Keegan, Peter Beardsley, Chris Waddle and Terry McDermott, when he left on a point of principle over contract negotiations. He was appointed by Derby County in May 1984 as their ninth manager in less than 11 years, a statistic that helps to explain why they celebrated their Centenary in the Third Division.

He became Derby's longest-serving manager since George Jobey. Cox was born in Southam on 14 December 1939 and joined Coventry City as a junior. When his playing career was ended by a broken leg at the age of 18, he turned to coaching. He was Coventry's Youth coach as a teenager and subsequently worked at Walsall, Aston Villa with Tommy Docherty, Halifax Town and Preston North End. He was Bob Stokoe's assistant when Sunderland won the FA Cup in 1973 and, after a brief spell in Turkey with Galatasaray, entered League management at Chesterfield in October 1976.

Cox took them close to promotion and, astonishingly for

Saltergate, was the biggest spender on transfer-deadline day, 1980. Newcastle appointed him the following September and, to the delight of Geordie fans, he restored skill and a flourish to the club. When he returned with Derby, the standing ovation he received was intensely moving. He started from scratch at the Baseball Ground, although the Maxwell takeover was completed in August 1984, with Ian as chairman while Robert stayed with Oxford United, bringing stability but not unlimited funds. Rob Hindmarch, Charlie Palmer and Eric Steele were outstandingly successful free transfers: the sale of Kevin Wilson to Ipswich Town helped to fund investment in Trevor Christie, Gary Micklewhite and Geraint Williams.

After a year of building, Derby scrapped their way out of Division Three in 1985–86 and sailed away with the Second Division 12 months later. At this point, Robert Maxwell became chairman, keen to make a mark. Peter Shilton and Mark Wright were signed from Southampton as Derby's horizons were extended and in 1988, Dean Saunders became Derby's first £1-million player. Derby finished fifth, their peak under Cox, but Maxwell was reluctant or perhaps, as revelations after his death suggested, unable to build. The Rams still had major players, but not enough round them, when they were relegated in 1990–91. It was a bitter blow to Cox but he soon became a free spender when, after Maxwell was paid off at the expense of Wright and Saunders, Lionel Pickering invested in the club. Good players were signed but the blend was elusive and a Play-off in 1991–92 was the nearest they came to promotion.

In 1993, Cox was struck by severe back trouble, which led to his resignation. After that, he worked with Kevin Keegan on behalf of Newcastle, Fulham, England and Manchester City, still enthusiastic, still driven until he retired in June 2004.

---

## Jim Smith

### 1995–2001

***Division One promotion 1995–96. Premiership Reserve League (South) Champions 1999–2000, 2000–01.***

THERE were some unlikely names touted for the Derby County job in 1995, Barry Fry and Osvaldo Ardiles being the most alarming. Brian Horton was interviewed twice before Derby appointed the experienced Jim Smith. Their reward was an immediate promotion to the Premiership when the board expected little more than a season of regrouping. Born in Sheffield on 17 October 1940, Smith played as a wing-half in the lower divisions, for Aldershot, Halifax Town and Lincoln City before he became player-manager of Boston United in June 1969.

He moved to Colchester United in a similar capacity in October 1972 to begin a long League career that took in Blackburn Rovers, Birmingham City, Oxford United, Newcastle United, Middlesbrough as coach and Portsmouth before he arrived at the Baseball Ground. His most spectacular success was at Oxford, Third and Second Division Championships in successive seasons, 1983–84 and 1984–85, before he left because of difficulties in dealing with the chairman, Robert Maxwell. After being sacked by Portsmouth who, curiously, wanted Terry Fenwick as manager, Smith joined the League Managers' Association in an administrative capacity until welcoming Derby's approach.

Smith immediately made an important appointment, taking former Derby player Steve McClaren from Oxford as his coach, and had an initial advantage because highly-rated players Mark Pembridge, Craig Short and Paul Williams were determined to leave. Shrewd part-exchange deals brought in Sean Flynn and Gary Rowett, Smith

returned to Portsmouth for Darryl Powell and signed Robbie van der Laan, a player who could lift those around him, from Port Vale. Summer sales funded the purchase of Igor Stimac, the imposing and supremely confident Croatian defender, from Hajduk Split so, with Dean Sturridge promoted into a regular scorer, Derby were in business, embarking on an unbeaten run of 20 matches. Victory over Crystal Palace in the final home game clinched a Premiership place.

Smith exploited the European market, bringing in Aljosa Asanovic and Jacob Laursen, but the most important capture for the difficult first season in the Premiership was the short-term signing from Aston Villa of the legendary Republic of Ireland defender Paul McGrath. When Derby moved to Pride Park, they finished ninth and eighth with a glittering team. They appeared to have established themselves but Sir Alex Ferguson was attracted by McClaren's work when he sought a successor to Brian Kidd as Manchester United coach. The ideal management team was split when McClaren moved to Old Trafford in February 1999 and despite engaging such respected coaches as Ray Harford and Malcolm Crosby, Smith was never again as comfortable.

His buying became less successful, although Taribo West's short-term contract in 2000–01 was a typical coup, and it became a struggle to stay in the Premiership. Smith knew 2001–02 would be difficult but it was absurd to unseat him in October, seven League games into the season. He rejected an offer to become Director of Football, because Colin Todd did not want him around the training ground. Instead, he joined Coventry City as assistant manager, then worked with Harry Redknapp at Portsmouth and Southampton. In March 2006, he began a second spell as Oxford manager under new owners. He is remembered with affection at Derby.

## Colin Todd

### 2001–2002

THERE was a reminder of Derby's great days when Colin Todd returned as assistant manager in November 2000 because, beyond dispute, he was one of their greatest players, a defensive pillar of two Championship teams. He worked with Bruce Rioch at Middlesbrough and Bolton Wanderers, later managing both in his own right. When Derby approached him, Todd had been manager of Swindon Town for six months. Understandably, Swindon were upset by Derby's move and suspended Todd before an agreement was reached.

The partnership with Jim Smith began promisingly, as the Rams retained their Premiership place in 2000–01, but went wrong the following season. Smith was upset by the fact that Todd did not want him as an active Director of football, so the parting had a touch of bitterness. Todd was then

to find he had little time to make an impression and his major transfer business flopped. Having persuaded Leeds United to part with £7-million for Seth Johnson, a deal set in motion by Smith, Todd used the windfall to bring in three players from France, Pierre Ducrocq on a long loan, Francois Grenet and Luciano Zavagno.

Soon after a dispiriting FA Cup home defeat by Bristol Rovers, Todd was sacked. He was in charge for only 15 Premiership matches and Derby could not have it both ways. Either they were wrong to appoint him or wrong to dismiss him in January 2002. The final phase of Lionel Pickering's chairmanship was pointing the club towards disaster, sadly as he went in with such good intentions. Todd was out of the game until November 2003, when he became Bradford City's assistant manager under Bryan Robson, succeeding him the following year.

## John Gregory

### 2002–2003

AN influential player for Derby in Arthur Cox's two promotion teams, John Gregory appeared to have the personality to revive the club when, in January 2002, he became the third manager in a troubled season. Cox was annoyed when Gregory left for a coaching job with Portsmouth, where he eventually succeeded Alan Ball as manager. The appointment lasted for a year before Gregory was dismissed in January 1990.

Feeling he had much to learn, Gregory accepted coaching positions with Leicester City and Aston Villa before taking over as manager of Wycombe Wanderers in October 1996. He did well there

but it was still a surprise when he took the Villa job in February 1998. At one stage with Villa, Gregory was touted as a future England manager but his relationship with chairman Doug Ellis became strained and he resigned, arriving at Derby within a matter of days. He immediately signed two players from Newcastle United, Warren Barton and Rob Lee, and Derby had a road to survival when they beat Bolton Wanderers at the Reebok Stadium in March 2002.

While Bolton recovered, Derby subsided and, with the financial situation already chaotic, found it no easier in Division One. In March 2003, Gregory was suspended, the club making unspecified and unproven allegations of 'gross misconduct'. It was a shabby, shambolic episode and his dismissal was as inevitable as a claim for damages. After Lionel Pickering's departure as chairman, the new board agreed an out-of-court settlement with Gregory in April 2004.

## George Burley

### 2003–2005

WITHIN two years of being named Manager of the Year for his achievements with Ipswich Town, George Burley accepted an 'interim' job with Derby County

in March 2003. The appointment was ratified the following summer and in two full seasons at Pride Park, Burley survived a relegation battle before steering Derby to the Championship Play-offs. It was significant progress but Burley left in May 2005, alleging interference by the director of football, Murdo Mackay. Accusations about Burley's conduct were also aired as the incident caused further frustration for supporters. He found far more meddling by chairman Vladimir Romanov as he led Heart of Midlothian to the top of the Scottish League, then replaced Harry Redknapp at Southampton. Born in Cumnock on 3 June 1956, Burley made 394 League appearances for Ipswich, was in their 1978 FA Cup winning side and earned 11 caps for Scotland. He returned as manager in December 1994 and, after several near misses, gained promotion to the Premiership through the Play-offs in 2000. It became better still when Ipswich finished fifth the following season, earning a UEFA Cup place, but it was only brief success. After Ipswich were relegated, Burley was dismissed in October 2002, his compensation severely cut by 'temporary administration'. Having patched up with loans and free transfers in his first full season at Derby, Burley began to build around Inigo Idiakez and Grzegorz Rasiak. Injuries to both those key players hampered them in the Play-off defeat by Preston North End.

## Phil Brown

### 2005–2006

AFTER 788 senior appearances and coaching experience under Sam Allardyce, Phil Brown felt, at the age of 46, that he was ready for management when Derby County appointed him in June 2005. He was born in South Shields on 30 May 1959 and built an impressive career as a full-back in the lower Divisions with Hartlepool United, Halifax Town, Bolton Wanderers and Blackpool. He turned towards coaching under Allardyce at Blackpool and they enjoyed considerable success together at Bolton. Brown needed a wise head with him as assistant. Instead

Dean Holdsworth, untried in the role, was appointed and they were feeling their way together. In addition, the financial troubles at Pride Park made it an extremely difficult job. Hard though Brown worked, the playing side was in constant flux, with too many ineffective loan players introduced. After a 6–1 defeat by Coventry and an FA Cup exit at Colchester, an upset Brown was sacked in January 2006, only seven months into his first management post.

## Terry Westley

### 2006

DERBY County were fortunate to have Terry Westley on the premises to act as caretaker manager from the end of January 2006. Westley, born in Ipswich on 18 September 1959, already had wide experience when the Rams appointed him Academy manager in May 2002, including nine months as Luton Town manager

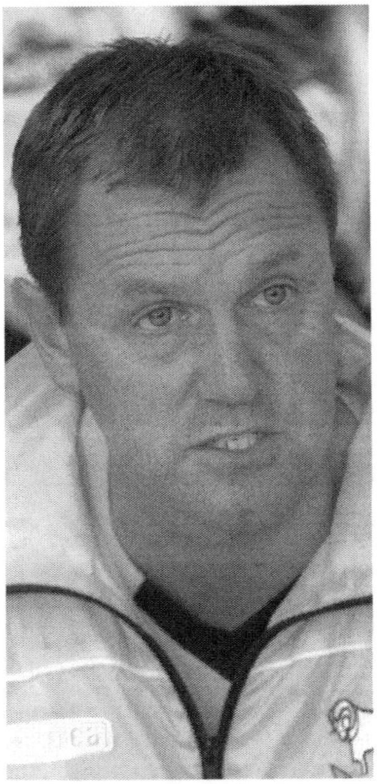

in 1995. He was a junior at Ipswich Town but played no League football, setting out as manager of Diss Town in 1980. From 1984, he worked with young players, for Ipswich, Luton, before he stepped up, and Charlton Athletic. He was assistant manager with Rushden and Diamonds before his move to work at Derby's new Moor Farm facility. His success with the Academy is measurable in the development of players like Lee Camp, Tom Huddlestone, Lee Holmes, Lewin Nyatanga and Giles Barnes. His task as caretaker was clear, to keep the Rams in the Championship against a background of takeover talks. His teams played with a renewed sense of purpose and there was a consistent logic about his selections. It was a professional performance by Westley, but, in July, he left to become Birmingham City's Academy director.

## Billy Davies

### 2006–

WHEN the new board, with Peter Gadsby as chairman, took control, they identified Billy Davies as the manager they wanted. After agreement was reached with Preston North End, Davies took over at Pride Park in June. William McIntosh Davies was born in Glasgow on 31 May 1964 and began his senior career with Rangers. He played for two Swedish clubs, Jonkoping and IF Elfsborg, before returning to Scotland with St Mirren in 1987. Following a brief spell with Leicester City, he played for Dunfermline Athletic and Motherwell. At the age of 34, he was appointed as Motherwell's manager and made an impact in England with two successful seasons at Deepdale, taking Preston to the Championship Play-offs both times.

# A-Z of Players

### ABBOTT Shirley Wray
*Wing-half*
*Born: Alfreton, 19 February 1889. Died: Portsmouth, 26 September 1947.*
*Career: Alfreton Town. Derby County June 1911. Portsmouth June 1913. Queen's Park Rangers May 1923. Chesterfield September 1924: trainer, May 1928 to May 1939.*
***Division Two Champions 1911–12.***

### ABBOTT William Lee
*Winger*
*Career: Riddings. Derby County February 1894. Poolsbrook United May 1895. Riddings July 1896. Chesterfield August 1897. Riddings January 1898. Clowne Rovers October 1898. Walgrave October 1900. Market Harborough September 1901.*

### ABDALLAH Tewfik
*Inside-forward*
*Born: Cairo, 23 June 1897.*
*Career: International Sporting Club, Cairo. Derby County September 1920. Cowdenbeath May 1922. Bridgend Town August 1923. Hartlepools United March 1924. Providence Clamdiggers September 1924. Fall River Marksmen January 1927. Hartford August 1927. New York Nationals October 1927. Fall River Marksmen February 1928. Montreal Carsteel.*

### ABLETT Gary Ian
*Midfield/defender*
*Born: Liverpool, 19 November 1965.*
*Career: Apprentice, Liverpool: professional November 1983. Derby County, loan, January 1985. Hull City, loan, September 1986. Everton January 1992. Sheffield United, loan, March 1996. Birmingham City July 1996. Wycombe Wanderers, loan, December 1999. Blackpool January 2000.*

### ACKERMAN Alfred Albert Eric
*Centre-forward*
*Born: Daspoort, Pretoria, 5 January 1929. Died: Dunnottar, Transvaal, 10 July 1988.*
*Career: Pretoria Municipal. Clyde cs 1947. Hull City July 1950. Norwich City August 1951. Hull City October 1953. Derby County March 1955. Carlisle United November 1956. Millwall January 1959. Player-manager, Dartford, July 1961 to June 1966. Manager, Gravesend and Northfleet, November 1968 to February 1974.*
***Division Three North Champions 1956–57.***

### ADDISON Miles Vivien Esifi
*Central defender*
*Born: Waltham Forest, 7 January 1989.*
*Career: Academy, Derby County.*

### ADLINGTON Terence
*Goalkeeper*
*Born: Blackwell, 21 November 1935. Died: Nottingham, April 1994.*
*Career: Stonebroom YC. Blackwell CW. Amateur, Derby County, December 1955: professional October 1956. Torquay United June 1962. Baltimore Bays April 1967. Dallas Tornado August 1968. Boston United January 1969 (transfer never completed). Player-manager, Dover Town, March 1969: manager to May 1975. Manager, Maidstone United, May 1975 to February 1977.*
***Division Three North Champions 1956–57.***

### AINSWORTH Charles
*Outside-left*
*Born: Ashbourne, 1885. Died: 1955.*
*Career: Queen's Park Rangers 1907. Derby County August 1908. Grimsby Town August 1909.*

### AINSWORTH Fred
*Inside-forward*
*Born: Loughborough, 29 June 1894.*

*Died: Redcar, 5 January 1981.*
*Career: Loughborough. Derby County August 1919. Ashington.*

**AINSWORTH Lionel Glenn Robert**
*Forward*
*Born: Nottingham, 1 October 1987.*
*Career: Academy, Derby County: professional August 2005. AFC Bournemouth, loan, August 2006.*

**ALDERMAN Albert Edward**
*Wing/inside-forward*
*Born: Alvaston, Derby, 30 October 1907. Died: Frimley, 6 June 1990.*
*Career: Alvaston House. Derby County March 1927. Burnley August 1934.*
***Division One runners-up 1929–30.***

**ALLAN John**
*Winger/inside-forward*
*Born: Glasgow.*
*Career: Glasgow Thistle. Derby County August 1893. Notts County December 1894. Heanor Town, September 1898.*

**ALLEN Henry**
*Outside-left*
*Born: Spondon. Died: Bulawayo, September 1939.*
*Career: Alvaston. Derby County October 1898. Leicester Fosse December 1899. Alvaston and Boulton 1900. Derby County March 1901.*
***FA Cup finalists 1898–99.***

**ALTON Thomas William**
*Right-back*
*Born: Chesterfield, 1917. Died: Bolsover, 9 August 1964.*
*Career: New Tupton Ivanhoe. Derby County November 1936.*

**ANTONIO George Rowlands**
*Inside-forward*
*Born: Whitchurch, 20 October 1914. Died: Oswestry, 2 July 1997.*
*Career: Oswestry Town. Stoke City February 1936. Derby County March 1947. Doncaster Rovers October 1948. Mansfield Town October 1949. Player-manager, Oswestry Town, July 1951. Player-coach, Wellington Town, July 1954: player-manager January 1955 to May 1957. Player-manager, Stafford Rangers, September 1957. Player-coach, Oswestry Town, July 1958: player-manager June 1959 to June 1962.*

**ARKESDEN Thomas Arthur**
*Inside-forward/winger*
*Born: Warwick, July 1878. Died: Hulme, 25 June 1922.*
*Career: Burton Wanderers January 1896. Derby County January 1898. Burton United July 1901. Manchester United February 1903. Gainsborough Trinity July 1907.*
***FA Cup finalists 1898–99.***

**ARMSTRONG Arthur Singleton**
*Outside-right*
*Born: Southwell, 1887. Died: Wolverhampton, 13 August 1962.*
*Career: Ripley Athletic. Bakewell. Derby County October 1906. Heanor United November 1908. Brighton & Hove Albion June 1909. Pontypridd. Loughborough Corinthians. Heanor Town August 1910.*

**ASANOVIC Aljosa**
*Midfield*
*Born: Split, 14 December 1965.*
*Career: Hajduk Split. Metz 1990. Cannes 1991. Montpellier 1992. Hajduk Split 1994. Valladolid 1995. Hajduk Split 1996. Derby County June 1996. Napoli January 1998. Panathinaikos 1998. Rapid Vienna 2000.*

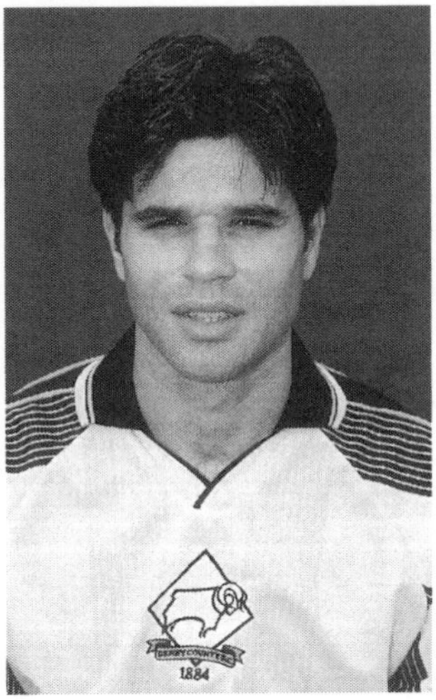

**ASHBEE Ian Michael**
*Midfield*
*Born: Birmingham, 6 September 1975.*
*Career: Trainee, Derby County: professional November 1994. IR (Iceland), loan, July 1996. Cambridge United December 1996. Hull City July 2002.*

**ATTLEY Brian Robert**
*Full-back*
*Born: Cardiff, 27 August 1955.*
*Career: Apprentice, Cardiff City: professional August 1973. Swansea City February 1979. Derby County February 1982. Oxford United, loan, March 1983. Gresley Rovers July 1984. Stapenhill March 1986.*

**BACON Arthur**
*Forward*
*Born: Birdholme, 1905. Died: Derby, 27 July 1942.*
*Career: New Tupton BB. New Tupton Ivanhoe. Chesterfield, trial, September 1923. Derby County October 1923. Manchester City December 1928. Reading June 1929. Chesterfield June 1932. Coventry City June 1933. Retired with an eye injury but returned with Burton Town, March 1937.*
***Division Two promotion 1925–26.***

**BAIANO Francesco**
*Forward*
*Born: Naples, 24 February 1968.*
*Career: Napoli 1984. Empoli, loan, 1986. Parma, loan, 1987. Empoli, loan, 1988. Avellino, loan, 1989. Foggia 1990. Fiorentina 1992. Derby County August 1997. Ternana November 1999. Pistoiese 2000. Sangiovannese 2002.*

**BAILEY Anthony David**
*Defender*
*Born: Burton upon Trent, 23 September 1946.*
*Career: Burton Albion June 1966. Derby County February 1970. Oldham Athletic, loan, January 1974: permanent March 1974. Bury December 1974. Mossley November 1980.*
***Division One Champions 1971–72.***

**BAILEY Horace Peter**
*Goalkeeper*
*Born: Derby, 3 July 1881. Died: Biggleswade, 1 August 1960.*
*Career: Derby County Reserves September 1899. Crich 1901. Ripley Athletic December 1902. Leicester Imperial 1905. Leicester Fosse January 1907. Derby County April 1910. Stoke, loan, November 1910. Birmingham February 1911.*

**BAILEY Leslie Albert**
*Centre-half*
*Born: Worksop, 2 October 1916. Died: Worksop, 27 June 1980.*
*Career: Manton Colliery. Gainsborough Trinity. Bradford May 1936. Derby County March 1937.*

**BAKER John**
*Full-back*
*Career: Derby County November 1890.*

**BAKER William Edward**
*Left winger*
*Born: Woolwich, 11 May 1892. Died: Plymouth, 8 March 1980.*
*Career: Plumstead. Northfleet. Queen's Park Rangers. Dartford. Woolwich Arsenal, trial. Derby County May 1914. Plymouth Argyle July 1921.*
***Division Two Champions 1914–15.***

**BAKEWELL George**
*Right-winger*
*Born: Derby, 1864.*
*Career: Derby Midland. Derby County 1884. Notts County July 1891.*

**BALKWILL Alexander**
*Centre-forward*
*Born: Scotland, 1878.*
*Career: Alvaston. Derby County July 1900. Ripley Town August 1901. Derby County October 1901.*

**BANOVIC Vjekoslav**
*Goalkeeper*
*Born: Bihac, Yugoslavia, 12 November 1956.*
*Career: Adelaide Croatia 1972. Toronto Metros 1977. Melbourne Croatia. Heidelburg United. Derby County September 1980. Melbourne Croatia 1984.*

**BARCLAY Robert**
*Inside-forward*
*Born: Scotswood, 27 October 1906. Died: Huddersfield, 13 July 1969.*
*Career: Scotswood United Church. Bell's Close Juniors, Allendale. Scotswood. Derby County February 1927. Sheffield United June 1931. Huddersfield Town March 1937. Hurst FC May 1946.*
***Division One runners-up 1929–30.***

**BARKER Frederick Charles**
*Inside-forward*
*Died: Derby, 25 November 1904.*
*Career: Derby County March 1903.*

**BARKER Richard Joseph**
*Forward*
*Born: Derby, 23 November 1939.*
*Career: Morris Sports. Burton Albion October 1960. Loughborough United May 1962. Matlock Town July 1963. Burton*

*Albion November 1963. Primo Hamilton (Canada), loan, April 1965. Derby County October 1967. Notts County December 1968. Peterborough United September 1971. Coach, Enderby Town, August 1973. Coach, Shrewsbury Town, February 1974: manager, February 1978. Assistant manager, Wolverhampton Wanderers, November 1978. Manager, Stoke City, June 1981 to December 1983. Manager, Notts County, November 1984 to April 1985. Manager, Ethnikos, 1985. Manager Zamalek (Egypt), 1986. Chief coach, Luton Town, August 1988. Assistant manager, Sheffield Wednesday, February 1989: development director 1995 to May 1996. Chief scout, West Bromwich Albion, September 1997: caretaker manager December 1997. Assistant manager, Halifax Town, October 2000 to August 2001.*
***Division Two Champions 1968–69.***

### BARNES Giles Gordon
*Midfield*
*Born: Barking, 5 August 1988.*
*Career: Academy, Derby County: professional August 2005.*

### BARNES James
*Outside-left*
*Born: Earlsdon, 21 July 1900.*
*Career: Harkford. Derby County August 1921. Rochdale cs 1923.*

### BARTLETT Paul John
*Outside-left*
*Born: Grimsby, 17 January 1960.*
*Career: Apprentice, Derby County: professional December 1977. Boston United December 1980. Kettering Town cs 1983.*

### BARTON John Stanley
*Full-back*
*Born: Birmingham, 24 October 1953.*
*Career: Boldmere St Michael's July 1972. Paget Rangers July 1973. Sutton Coldfield Town February 1974. Stourbridge July 1974. Worcester City June 1976. Everton December 1978. Derby County March 1982. Player/assistant manager, Kidderminster Harriers, August 1984. Tamworth December 1990. Assistant manager, Nuneaton Borough, July 1991: manager, November 1992 to March 1994. Manager, Burton Albion, April 1994 to September 1998. Manager, Worcester City, November 1999 to January 2005.*

### BARTON Warren Dean
*Defender*
*Born: Islington, 19 March 1969.*
*Career: Apprentice, Leyton Orient. Leytonstone and Ilford (became Redbridge Forest) cs 1987. Maidstone United July 1989. Wimbledon June 1990. Newcastle United June 1995. Derby County February 2002. Queen's Park Rangers October 2003. Player-coach, Wimbledon, February 2004. Daganham and Redbridge August 2004.*

### BAYLISS Hervey Hugo Robert
*Forward*
*Born: Burton upon Trent, 17 April 1895. Died: Burton upon Trent, 1943.*
*Career: Overseal Swifts. Burton All Saints. Gresley Rovers 1919. Derby County February 1921. Gresley Rovers June 1921.*

### BECK Mikkel Venge
*Forward*
*Born: Aarhus, 4 May 1973.*
*Career: Kolding. B1909 Copenhagen 1992. Fortuna Koln August 1993. Middlesbrough September 1996. Derby County March 1999. Nottingham Forest, loan, November 1999. Queen's Park Rangers, loan, February 2000. AaB Aalborg, loan, April 2000. Lille OSC July 2000. AaB Aalborg, loan, March 2002.*

### BELL Colin
*Half-back*
*Born: Horsley, 24 March 1926. Died: Heanor, 21 July 2004.*
*Career: Holbrook MW. Amateur, Derby County, May 1945: professional September 1946. Gresley Rovers June 1955. Long Eaton United July 1957.*

### BELL David
*Right-back/wing-half*
*Born: Gorebridge, Lothian, 24 December 1909. Died: Monkseaton, April 1986.*
*Career: Musselburgh Bruntonians. Wallyford Bluebell. Newcastle United May 1930. Derby County June 1934. Ipswich Town October 1938.*

### BELLHOUSE E.W.
*Centre-half*
*Career: Derby County 1888.*

### BENFIELD Thomas Charles
*Inside-forward*
*Born: Leicester, 1889. Died: France, 10 November 1918.*
*Career: Amateur, Leicester Fosse, February 1907: professional July*

*1910. Derby County June 1914.*
***Division Two Champions 1914–15.***

**BESTWICK T. Harold**
*Goalkeeper*
*Died: Long Eaton, July 1946.*
*Career: Long Eaton Rangers. Derby County 1886.*

**BETTS Arthur Charles**
*Left-back*
*Born: Scunthorpe, 2 January 1886.*
*Died: Scunthorpe, 1967.*
*Career: North Lindsey. Gainsborough Trinity May 1905. Watford May 1907. Gainsborough Trinity May 1910. Newcastle United July 1911. Derby County October 1911. Hull City May 1914. Scunthorpe United June 1920. Player-coach, Normanby Park Steelworks, May 1923. Coach, Lysaghts Sports.*
***Division Two Champions 1911–12.***

**BEVAN Frederick Edward Walter**
*Centre-forward*
*Born: Poplar, 27 February 1879.*
*Died: Poplar, 10 December 1935.*
*Career: Millwall St John's. Millwall Athletic August 1899. Manchester City May 1901. Reading April 1903. Queen's Park Rangers June 1904. Bury May 1906. Fulham August 1907. Derby County October 1907. Clapton Orient November 1909. Chatham 1914. Coach, Clapton Orient, 1920 to 1923.*

**BIGGINS Stephen James**
*Forward*
*Born: Lichfield, 20 June 1954.*
*Career: Hednesford Town. Shrewsbury Town December 1977. Oxford United July 1982. Derby County October 1984. Wolverhampton Wanderers, loan, March 1985. Port Vale, loan, March 1986. Trelleborgs FF (Sweden) July 1986. Exeter City October 1986. Telford United March 1987. Worcester City March 1989. Ludlow. Willenhall Town, loan, April 1991.*

**BILEY Alan Paul**
*Centre-forward*
*Born: Leighton Buzzard, 26 February 1957.*
*Career: Apprentice, Luton Town. Professional, Cambridge United, July 1975. Derby County January 1980. Everton July 1981. Stoke City,*

*loan, March 1982. Portsmouth August 1982. Brighton & Hove Albion March 1985. New York Express July 1986. Cambridge United, loan, November 1986. Panionios (Greece) July 1987. Player/assistant manager, Waterford, 1987. Dulwich Hamlet. Whyteleafe. Welton Rovers November 1989. Fisher Athletic. Management or coaching posts: Ely City. Potton United. Diss Town. Spalding United. Barton Rovers. Wooton Blue Cross 2003. Kettering Town January 2004. Spalding United 2005.*

**BIRD Donald William Carlton**
*Outside-left*
*Born: Llandrindod Wells, 5 January 1908. Died: 1987.*
*Career: Llandrindod Wells. Cardiff City May 1929. Bury May 1931. Torquay United June 1932. Derby County June 1934. Sheffield United December 1935. Southend United October 1936.*
***Division One runners-up 1935–36.***

**BIRDSALL George**
*Outside-left/left-back*
*Born: Saxton, 30 September 1891.*
*Career: Brompton (Northallerton league). War service. Harpenden Town 1919. Derby County March 1921. Levensden.*

**BISGAARD Morten**
*Midfield*
*Born: Randers 25 June 1974.*

*Career: OB Odense 1993. Udinese 1998. FC Copenhagen 2001. Derby County August 2004.*

**BLACKETT Joseph**
*Left-back*
*Born: Newcastle upon Tyne, 20 June 1875.*
*Career: Newcastle United. Gateshead. Loughborough Town June 1896. Wolverhampton Wanderers May 1897. Derby County July 1900. Sunderland April 1901. Middlesbrough October 1901. Luton Town May 1905. Leicester Fosse July 1906. Player-manager, Rochdale, June 1909. Barrow August 1912. Trainer, Reading, 1913.*

**BLACKSTOCK Dexter Anthony**
*Forward*
*Born Oxford: 20 May 1986.*

*Career: Academy, Oxford United. Academy, Southampton: professional May 2004. Plymouth Argyle, loan, February 2005. Derby County, loan, October 2005.*

**BLADES Paul Andrew**
*Central defender/right-back*
*Born: Peterborough, 5 January 1965.*
*Career: Apprentice, Derby County: professional December 1982. Norwich City July 1990. Wolverhampton Wanderers, loan, August 1992: permanent October 1992. Rotherham United July 1995. Hednesford Town July 1997. Player/assistant manager Gresley Rovers March 1999. Manager, Stapenhill, May 2004.*
***Division Three promotion 1985–86. Division Two Champions 1986–87.***

**BLATSIS Con**
*Defender*
*Born: Melbourne, Australia, 6 July 1977.*
*Career: South Melbourne August 1999. Derby County August 2000. Sheffield Wednesday, loan, December 2000. Colchester United March 2002. Kocaelispor (Turkey), September 2002. St Patrick's Athletic March 2004.*

**BLESSINGTON James**
*Outside/inside-right*
*Born: Linlithgow, 28 February 1874. Died: Newton Abbot, 18 April 1939.*
*Career: Hibernian 1889. Leith Hibernian 1891. Leith Athletic 1891. St Bernard's, loan, August 1892. Glasgow Celtic August 1892. Preston North End February 1898. Derby County June 1899. Bristol City November 1899. Luton Town August 1900. Leicester Fosse May 1903: team manager January 1907 to April 1909. Cliftonville August 1909: trainer July 1911. Coach, Belfast Celtic, 1913. Manager, Abertillery Town, June 1921.*

**BLOCKLEY Jeffrey Paul**
*Centre-half*
*Born: Leicester, 12 September 1949.*
*Career: Apprentice, Coventry City: professional June 1967. Arsenal October 1972. Leicester City January 1975. Derby County, loan, February 1978. Notts County June 1978. Player-coach, Enderby Town, August 1980. Gloucester City June 1981. Manager, Leicester United, July 1983. Manager, Shepshed Charterhouse, May 1984 to May 1985. Manager, Hinckley Athletic, April to May 1989.*

**BLOOMER Phillip**
*Left-back*
*Born: Cradley, 1875. Died: Derby, 5 June 1896.*
*Career: Derby County May 1895.*
***Division One runners-up 1895–96.***

**BLORE Vincent**
*Goalkeeper*
*Born: Uttoxeter, 25 February 1907. Died: Ewell, 16 January 1997.*
*Career: Uttoxeter Amateurs. Burton Town. Aston Villa August 1932. Derby County August 1933. West Ham United July 1935. Crystal Palace October 1936. Exeter City October 1938.*

**BOAG John M.**
*Centre-forward*
*Born: Glasgow, 6 April 1874. Died: Clydebank, 7 February 1954.*
*Career: Cowlairs. Ashfield. East Stirlingshire. Derby County May 1896. Brentford May 1904.*
***FA Cup finalists 1897–98, 1898–99, 1902–03.***

**BODEN Christopher Desmond**
*Defender*
*Born: Wolverhampton, 13 October 1973.*
*Career: Trainee, Aston Villa: professional December 1991. Barnsley, loan, October 1993. Derby County March 1995. Shrewsbury Town, loan, January 1996. Hereford United August 1998.*
***Division One promotion 1995–96.***

**BOERTIEN Paul**
*Defender*
*Born: Haltwhistle, 20 January 1979.*
*Career: Trainee, Carlisle United: professional May 1997. Derby County March 1999. Crewe Alexandra, loan, February 2000. Notts County, loan, January 2004.*

**BOHINEN Lars**
*Midfield*
*Born: Vadso, 8 September 1969.*
*Career: Valerenga IF January 1988. Viking FK Stavanger January 1990. Young Boys Berne August 1990. Nottingham Forest November 1993. Blackburn Rovers October 1995. Derby County March 1998. Lyngby January 2001. Farum BK 2001. Valerenga IF August 2002.*

**BOLDER Adam Peter**
*Midfield*
*Born: Hull, 25 October 1980.*
*Career: Trainee, Hull City: professional July 1999. Derby County April 2000.*

**BORBOKIS Vassilios**
*Defender*
*Born: Serres, 10 February 1969.*
*Career: Apollon. AEK Athens 1993. Sheffield United July 1997. Derby County March 1999. PAOK Salonika December 1999. AEK Athens July 2002.*

**BOSWORTH Samuel**
*Outside-right*
*Career: Long Eaton Rangers July 1895. Loughborough Town September 1898. Derby County December 1898. Sheffield Wednesday March 1899. Whitwick White Cross October 1901. Ilkeston United.*

**BOULTON Frank Preece**
*Goalkeeper*
*Born: Yate, 12 August 1917. Died: Swindon, June 1987.*
*Career: Bristol City November 1934. Bath City July 1936. Arsenal*

*October 1936. Derby County August 1938. Swindon Town August 1946. Crystal Palace October 1950. Bedford Town March 1951.*

**BOURNE Jeffrey Albert**
*Forward*
*Born: Linton, 19 June 1948.*
*Career: Linton United. Derby County January 1969. Dallas Tornado, loan, April 1976. Crystal Palace March 1977. Dallas Tornado March 1978. Atlanta Chiefs March 1979. Sheffield United September 1979. Atlanta Chiefs March 1980. Seattle Sounders July 1980. Wichita Wings 1982. Coach, Gresley Rovers, 1986 to June 1987.*
***Division One Champions 1974–75.***

**BOWDEN Oswald**
*Inside-forward*
*Born: Byker, 7 September 1912. Died: Newcastle upon Tyne, 20 May 1977.*
*Career: Newcastle United Swifts. Amateur, Newcastle United, October 1929. Derby County May 1930. Nottingham Forest June 1935. Brighton & Hove Albion June 1937. Southampton June 1938.*

**BOWER T.**
*Half-back*
*Career: Derby County 1886.*

**BOWERS John Anslow**
*Forward*
*Born: Leicester, 14 November 1939.*
*Career: Derby Corinthians. Derby County February 1957. Notts County June 1966.*

**BOWLER George Henry**
*Wing-half*
*Born: Newhall, 23 January 1890. Died: Bethnal Green, 1948.*
*Career: Gresley Rovers. Derby County May 1911. Tottenham Hotspur June 1913. Luton Town July 1919.*

**BOXLEY Harold H.**
*Wing-half*
*Born: Stourbridge, 1894.*
*Career: Stourbridge. Shrewsbury Town. Wellington Town May 1914. Derby County May 1919. Bristol Rovers August 1920. Bournemouth and Boscombe Athletic 1923. Darlaston October 1925, Oswestry Town cs 1926. Stourbridge.*

**BOYD James Murray**
*Outside-right*
*Born: Glasgow, 29 April 1907. Died: Bournemouth, 22 March 1991.*
*Career: Petershill. Edinburgh St Bernard's October 1924. Newcastle United May 1925. Derby County May 1935. Bury January 1937. Dundee September 1937. Grimsby Town June 1938.*
***Division One runners-up 1935–36.***

**BRADBURY John Jackson Longstaff**
*Outside-right*
*Born: South Bank, 1878.*
*Career: Stockport County. Lincoln City January 1896. Ashton North End September 1896. Blackburn Rovers August 1897. Ashton North End November 1897. Derby County May 1899. Barnsley June 1900. Bristol City June 1901. New Brompton May 1902. Millwall May 1904. Carlisle United cs 1906. Penrith 1908.*

**BRADBURY Lee Michael**
*Forward*
*Born: Cowes, 3 July 1975.*
*Career: Cowes. Portsmouth August 1995. Exeter City, loan, December 1995. Manchester City August 1997. Crystal Palace October 1998. Birmingham City, loan, March 1999. Portsmouth October 1999. Sheffield Wednesday, loan, December 2002 and March 2003. Derby County, loan, August 2003 and November 2003. Walsall March 2004. Oxford United July 2004. Southend United January 2006.*

**BRAGSTAD Bjorn Otto**
*Defender*
*Born: Trondheim, 5 January 1971.*
*Career: Utleira 1988. Rosenborg BK August 1989. Derby County August 2000. Birmingham City, loan, September 2001. SW Bregenz January 2003.*

**BRAND Robert**
*Inside-left*
*Career: Queen of the South Wanderers. Accrington September 1888. Sunderland Albion 1889. Accrington February 1890. Derby County November 1890.*

**BRIDGE-WILKINSON Marc**
*Midfield*
*Born: Nuneaton, 16 March 1979.*
*Career: Trainee, Derby County: professional March 1997. Carlisle United, loan, March 1999. Port Vale July 2000. Stockport County August 2004. Bradford City, loan, February 2005: permanent March 2005.*

**BRINTON John Victor**
*Outside-left*
*Born: Avonmouth, 11 July 1916.*
*Died: Leigh, Bristol, 22 February 1997.*
*Career: Avonmouth. Bristol City August 1935. Newport County July 1937. Derby County January 1938. Stockport County July 1946. Leyton Orient August 1948. Streets FC July 1949.*

**BRISCOE Robert Dean**
*Midfield*
*Born: Derby, 4 September 1969.*
*Career: Trainee, Derby County: professional September 1987. Gresley Rovers August 1992. Burton Albion March 1993. Sandiacre Town May 1995. Mickleover Sports. Heanor Town. Borrowash Victoria 1997. Player/assistant manager, Mickleover Sports, cs 1998. Long Eaton United August 2002. Borrowash Victoria December 2004.*

**BROLLY Michael Joseph**
*Midfield*
*Born: Galston, 6 October 1954.*
*Career: Kilmarnock Star. Chelsea October 1971. Bristol City June 1974. Grimsby Town September 1976. Derby County August 1982. Scunthorpe United August 1983. Scarborough July 1986. Goole Town, loan, January 1987: permanent March 1987. Boston United February 1988. Holbeach United February 1989.*

**BROMAGE Enos**
*Goalkeeper*
*Born: Mickleover, 1864.*
*Career: Derby Junction. Derby County March 1889. Derby Junction.*

**BROMAGE Enos**
*Outside-left*
*Born: Mickleover, 22 October 1898.*
*Died: Derby, 7 April 1978.*
*Career: Stapleford Town. Sheffield United 1922. Derby County November 1923. Gillingham August 1927. West Bromwich Albion March 1928. Nottingham Forest October 1929. Chester. Wellington Town.*
***Division Two promotion 1925–26.***

**BROMAGE Henry**
*Goalkeeper*
*Born: Derby.*
*Career: Derby Constitutional. Derby County April 1896. Burton United July 1903. Leeds City August 1905. Doncaster Rovers 1911. Bentley Colliery.*

**BROOKS George**
*Wing-half*
*Born: Radcliffe. Died: France, 11 November 1918.*
*Career: Longfield. Manchester City January 1911. Bury April 1912. South Shields. Derby County June 1914.*
***Division Two Champions 1914–15.***

**BROOKS Joseph T.**
*Outside-right*
*Career: Melbourne Town. Derby County March 1894. Heanor Town September 1895. Melbourne Town February 1896.*

**BROOME Frank Henry**
*Forward*
*Born: Berkhamstead, 11 June 1915.*
*Died: Exeter, 5 September 1994.*
*Career: Boxmoor United. Berkhamstead Town. Aston Villa November 1934. Derby County September 1946. Notts County*

*October 1949. Brentford July 1953. Crewe Alexandra October 1953. Shelbourne February 1955. Assistant trainer, Notts County, August 1955: acting manager, January to May 1957: assistant manager to December 1957. Manager, Exeter City, January 1958. Manager, Southend United, May to December 1960. Manager-coach, Bankstown (NSW) July 1961. Manager-coach, Corinthians (Sydney) October 1962. Manager, Exeter City, May 1967 to February 1969.*

**BROWN Gordon**

*Inside-forward*

*Born: Ellesmere Port, 30 June 1933.*

*Career: Juniors, Wolverhampton Wanderers: professional September 1951. Ellesmere Port Town December 1951. Scunthorpe United December 1952. Derby County January 1957. Southampton March 1960. Barrow July 1961. Southport January 1964.*

***Division Three North Champions 1956–57.***

**BROWN Harold Thomas**

*Goalkeeper*

*Born: Kingsbury, 9 April 1924. Died: Abingdon, June 1982.*

*Career: Queen's Park Rangers April 1941. Notts County April 1946. Derby County October 1949. Queen's Park Rangers August 1951. Plymouth Argyle August 1956. Exeter City September 1958.*

**BUCHANAN John**

*Forward*

*Born: Underwood, near Stirling, 9 June 1928. Died: Bradford, December 2000.*

*Career: Kilsyth Rangers. Clyde 1946. Derby County February 1955. Bradford November 1957. Retired May 1963 and worked as Bradford pools promoter. Team manager, Bradford, May 1964 to March 1967.*

***Division Three North Champions 1956–57.***

**BUCKLEY Franklin Charles**

*Centre-half*

*Born: Urmston, 9 November 1882. Died: Walsall, 22 December 1964.*

*Career: Aston Villa April 1903. Brighton & Hove Albion May 1905. Manchester United June 1906. Manchester City September 1907. Birmingham July 1909. Derby County May 1911. Bradford City May 1914. Retired during World War One but made one appearance for Norwich City in September 1919. Secretary-manager, Norwich City, March 1919 to July 1920. Manager, Blackpool, July 1923. Manager, Wolverhampton Wanderers, May 1927. Manager, Notts County, March 1944 to January 1946. Manager, Hull City, May 1946 to April 1948. Manager, Leeds United, May 1948. Manager, Walsall, April 1953 to June 1955.*

***Division Two Champions 1911–12.***

**BULLIONS James Law**

*Wing-half*

*Born: Dennyloanhead, 12 March 1924.*

*Career: Clowne 1940. Amateur, Chesterfield, December 1942. Derby County October 1944. Leeds*

*United November 1947. Shrewsbury Town September 1950. Worksop Town August 1955. Gresley Rovers August 1956. Sutton Town December 1956. Matlock Town October 1958. Alfreton Town, August 1960: player-manager September 1960: manager to September 1968.*

***FA Cup winners 1945–46.***

**BUNYAN Charles**

*Goalkeeper*

*Born: Brimington. Died: Ixelles, Belgium, 3 August 1922.*

*Career: Old Horns (Chesterfield). Spital Olympic. Chesterfield Town 1886. Hyde United 1887. Sheffield United. Derby County 1890. Chesterfield Town August 1892. Sheffield United February 1894. Derby County March 1894. Ilkeston Town July 1895. Walsall November 1896. New Brompton June 1898. Newcastle United January 1901. Ripley Athletic March 1903. Canadian football*

*1905. Grassmoor Red Rose August 1906. Player-coach, Brimington Athletic, August 1908. Coach, Racing Club Brussels, 1910. Swedish Olympic Council 1912.*

**BURLEY Craig William**

*Midfield*

*Born: Irvine, 24 September 1971.*

*Career: Trainee, Chelsea: professional September 1989. Glasgow Celtic July 1997. Derby County December 1999. Dundee September 2003. Preston North End January 2004. Walsall March 2004.*

**BURNS Kenneth**

*Central defender*

*Born: Glasgow, 23 September 1953.*

*Career: Glasgow Rangers. Apprentice, Birmingham City: professional July 1971. Nottingham Forest July 1977. Leeds United October 1981. Derby County, loan, March 1983 and February 1984: permanent March 1984. Notts County, loan, February 1985. Barnsley August 1985. IF Elfsborg March 1986. Sutton Town August 1986: joint manager, March 1987. Stafford Rangers July 1987. Grantham Town October 1988. Gainsborough Trinity 1989. Ilkeston Town July 1989. Oakham*

*United. Assistant manager, Telford United, July 1993.*

**BURRIDGE John**

*Goalkeeper*

*Born: Workington, 3 December 1951.*

*Career: Apprentice, Workington: professional January 1970. Blackpool, loan, April 1971: permanent May 1971. Aston Villa September 1975. Southend United, loan, January 1978. Crystal Palace March 1978. Queen's Park Rangers December 1980. Wolverhampton Wanderers, loan, August 1982: permanent September 1982. Derby County, loan, September 1984. Sheffield United October 1984. Southampton August 1987. Newcastle United October 1989. Hibernian August 1991. Newcastle United August 1993 (part-time player and goalkeeping coach). Scarborough October 1993. Lincoln City December 1993. Enfield February 1994. Aberdeen March 1994. Barrow September 1994. Dumbarton October 1994. Falkirk November 1994. Manchester City December 1994. Notts County August 1995. Witton Albion October 1995. Darlington November 1995. Grimsby Town December 1995. Gateshead January 1996. Northampton Town January 1996. Durham City March 1996. Queen of the South March 1996. Purfleet March 1996. Blyth Spartans August 1996. Scarborough December 1996. Player-manager, Blyth Spartans, March 1997.*

**BURTON Deon John**

*Forward*

*Born: Reading, 25 October 1976.*

*Career: Trainee, Portsmouth: professional February 1994. Cardiff City, loan, December 1996. Derby County August 1997. Barnsley, loan, December 1998. Stoke City, loan, February 2002. Portsmouth, loan, August 2002. Portsmouth December 2002. Walsall, loan, September 2003. Swindon Town, loan, October 2003. Brentford August 2004. Rotherham United July 2005. Sheffield Wednesday January 2006.*

**BURTON John Henry**

*Inside-forward*

*Born: Derby, 13 August 1874. Died: Derby, 13 May 1949.*

*Career: Derby St Andrew's. Derby County October 1896. Chatham June 1899. Tottenham Hotspur March 1901. Preston North End October 1906.*

**BURTON Noah**

*Forward*

*Born: Basford, 18 December 1896. Died: Nottingham, 16 July 1956.*

*Career: Bulwell St Albans. Ilkeston United August 1915. Derby County December 1915. Nottingham Forest June 1921.*

**BUTLIN Barry Desmond**

*Centre-forward*

*Born: Rosliston, 9 November 1949.*

*Career: Juniors, Derby County: professional January 1967. Notts County, loan, January 1969. Luton Town November 1972. Nottingham Forest October 1974. Brighton & Hove Albion, loan, September 1975. Reading, loan, January 1977. Peterborough United August 1977. Sheffield United August 1979.*

**BUTTERWORTH Charles E.**

*Outside-right*

*Career: Derby Midland. Derby County June 1891. Loughborough Town August 1892. Long Eaton Rangers. Heanor Town by 1896.*

**BUXTON Ian Ray**

*Centre-forward*

*Born: Cromford, 17 April 1938.*

*Career: Matlock Town January 1958. Derby County March 1959.*

*Luton Town September 1967. Notts County July 1969. Port Vale December 1969.*

**CALDWELL Gary**
*Defender*
*Born: Stirling, 12 April 1982.*
*Career: Trainee, Newcastle United: professional April 1999. Darlington, loan, November 2001. Hibernian, loan, January 2002. Coventry City, loan, July 2002. Derby County, loan, August 2003. Hibernian January 2004. Glasgow Celtic June 2006.*

**CALLAGHAN Nigel Ian**
*Outside-left/right*
*Born: Singapore, 12 September 1962.*

*Career: Apprentice, Watford: professional July 1980. Derby County February 1987. Aston Villa February 1989. Derby County, loan, September 1990. Watford, loan, March 1991. Huddersfield Town, loan, January 1992. Stafford Rangers March 1992. Millwall Reserves (non contract) January 1993. Berkhamstead Town February 1993. Walton and Hersham October 1993. Berkhamstead Town December 1993. Hellenic, South Africa, player-coach February to March 1994. Borrowash Victoria February 1995. Beaconsfield Sycob October 1995.*
***Division Two Champions 1986–87.***

**CALLAN William**
*Inside-forward*
*Born: Glasgow, 10 June 1900.*
*Career: Shawland Thistle. Pollock. Derby County May 1921.*

**CALLENDER Reginald Henry**
*Outside-left*
*Born: Stockton-on-Tees, 1892.*
*Died: September 1915.*
*Career: Stockton School. St John's College, Cambridge. One match for Glossop, 1912–13. Amateur, Derby County, March 1914.*

**CAMP Lee Michael John**
*Goalkeeper*
*Born: Derby, 22 August 1984.*

*Career: Academy, Derby County: professional July 2002. Burton Albion, loan, January 2003. Queen's Park Rangers, loan, March 2004.*

**CAMPBELL Robert McFaul**
*Centre-forward*
*Born: Belfast, 13 September 1956.*
*Career: Apprentice, Aston Villa: professional January 1974. Halifax Town, loan, February 1975. Huddersfield Town April 1975. Sheffield United, loan, July 1977: permanent August 1977. Vancouver Whitecaps May 1978. Huddersfield Town September 1978. Halifax Town October 1978. Brisbane City May 1979. Bradford City December 1979. Derby County August 1983. Bradford City, loan and permanent, November 1983. Wigan Athletic October 1986. Guiseley July 1988.*

**CARBON Matthew Phillip**
*Defender*
*Born: Nottingham, 8 June 1975.*
*Career: Trainee, Lincoln City: professional April 1993. Derby County March 1996. West Bromwich Albion January 1998. Walsall July 2001. Lincoln City, loan, October 2003. Barnsley July 2004.*
***Division One promotion, 1995–96.***

**CARBONARI Horacio Angel**
*Central defender*
*Born: Rosario, 2 May 1973.*
*Career: Rosario Central August 1993. Derby County July 1998. Coventry City, loan, March 2002. Rosario Central February 2003.*

**CARBONE Benito**
*Forward*
*Born: Bagnara Calabra, 14 August 1971.*
*Career: Torino August 1988. Reggina July 1990. Casertana July 1991. Ascoli July 1992. Torino July 1993. Napoli July 1994. Internazionale Milan August 1995. Sheffield Wednesday October 1996. Aston Villa October 1999. Bradford City August 2000. Derby County, loan, October 2001. Middlesbrough, loan, February 2002. Como July 2002. Parma November 2003.*

**CARGILL David Anderson**
*Outside-left*
*Born: Arbroath, 21 July 1936.*
*Career: Juniors, Burnley: professional July 1953. Sheffield Wednesday September 1956. Derby*

*County April 1958. Lincoln City December 1960. Arbroath February 1962.*

**CARR William Paterson**
*Full-back*
*Born: Cambois, 6 November 1901.*
*Died: Derby, April 1990.*
*Career: Seaton Delaval. Derby County February 1924. Queen's Park Rangers August 1935. Barrow July 1937.*
***Division Two promotion 1925–26. Division One runners-up 1929–30.***

**CARRUTHERS Eric**
*Forward*
*Born: Edinburgh, 22 February 1953.*
*Career: Heart of Midlothian. Derby County March 1975. Arcadia Shepherds 1978.*

**CARSLEY Lee Kevin**
*Midfield*
*Born: Birmingham, 28 February 1974.*
*Career: Trainee, Derby County: professional July 1992. Blackburn Rovers March 1999. Coventry City December 2000. Everton February 2002.*
***Division One promotion 1995–96.***

**CARTER Stephen Charles**
*Outside-right*
*Born: Great Yarmouth, 23 April 1953.*
*Career: Apprentice, Manchester City: professional August 1970. Notts County February 1972. Derby County August 1978. Notts County September 1981. AFC Bournemouth March 1982. Torquay United July 1984. Lymington 1985.*

**CASKEY William Thomas**
*Centre-forward*
*Born: Belfast, 12 October 1953.*
*Career: Glentoran September 1974. Tulsa Roughnecks, loan, March 1978. Derby County September 1978. Tulsa Roughnecks December 1979. Dallas Sidekicks 1985. Glentoran July 1986: assistant manager cs 1993 to May 1994. Dundela cs 1994.*

**CHADWICK Nicholas Gerald**
*Forward*
*Born: Market Drayton, 26 October 1982.*
*Career: Trainee, Everton: professional October 1999. Derby County, loan, February 2003. Millwall, loan, November 2003 and March 2004. Plymouth Argyle February 2005.*

**CHALK Martyn Peter Glyn**
*Winger*
*Born: Swindon, 30 August 1969.*
*Career: Grimsby Amateurs. Louth United August 1989. Derby County January 1990. Stockport County June 1994. Wrexham February 1996. Rhyl August 2002. Caernarfon Town June 2004.*

**CHALMERS Bruce**
*Half-back*
*Born: Whifflet, nr Coatbridge, 1868.*
*Career: Albion Rovers. Derby County 1890. Sheffield Wednesday December 1892.*

**CHANDLER Albert**
*Right-back*
*Born: Carlisle, 15 January 1897.*
*Died: Carlisle, 28 January 1963.*
*Career: Carlisle schools. Army football. Derby County August 1919. Newcastle United June 1925. Sheffield United October 1926. Mansfield Town cs 1929. Northfleet November 1929. Manchester Central February 1930. Holme Head (Carlisle district) cs 1930. Queen of the South cs 1931.*

**CHANDLER Jeffrey George**
*Outside-left*
*Born: Hammersmith, 19 June 1959.*
*Career: Apprentice, Blackpool: professional August 1976. Leeds United September 1979. Bolton Wanderers October 1981. Derby County July 1985. Mansfield Town, loan, November 1986. Bolton Wanderers July 1987. Cardiff City November 1989.*
***Division Three promotion 1985–86. Division Two Champions 1986–87.***

**CHARLES Gary Andrew**
*Right-back*
*Born, Newham, 19 April 1970.*
*Career: Trainee, Nottingham Forest: professional November 1987. Leicester City, loan, March 1989. Derby County July 1993. Aston Villa January 1995. SL Benfica January 1999. West Ham United October 1999. Birmingham City, loan, September 2000.*

**CHATTERTON William**
*Inside-forward*
*Born: Birch Vale, 27 December 1861. Died: Hyde, 19 March 1913.*

**CHERRY Steven Reginald**
*Goalkeeper*
*Born: Nottingham, 5 August 1960.*
*Career: Apprentice, Derby County: professional March 1978. Port Vale,*

*loan, November 1980. Walsall August 1984. Plymouth Argyle, loan, October 1986: permanent November 1986. Chesterfield, loan, December 1988 and January 1989. Notts County February 1989. Watford July 1995. Plymouth Argyle, loan, February 1996: permanent May 1996. Rotherham United August 1996. Kettering Town February 1997. Rushden and Diamonds March 1997. Stalybridge Celtic January 1998. Notts County March 1998. Mansfield Town July 1998. Oldham Athletic March 1999. Lincoln United 2002. Kidsgrove Athletic December 2003. Belper Town October 2004. Spalding United March 2005. Coach, Notts County, July 2006.*

**CHESTERS Colin Wayne**
*Centre-forward*
*Born: Crewe, 21 November 1959.*
*Career: Apprentice, Derby County: professional November 1977. Waterford, loan, January 1979. Crewe Alexandra September 1979. Northwich Victoria August 1982. Altrincham August 1984. Weymouth March 1986.*

**CHIEDOZIE John Okey**
*Winger/centre-forward*
*Born: Owerri, Nigeria, 18 April 1960.*
*Career: Apprentice, Orient: professional April 1977. Notts County August 1981. Tottenham Hotspur August 1984. Derby County August 1988. Notts County January 1990. Chesterfield March 1990. Bashley October 1991. Banks of Barking October 1991. Bashley cs 1992.*

**CHOLERTON William**
*Left-back*
*Born: Derby, 1 January 1949.*
*Career: Derby Boys. Apprentice, Derby County: professional December 1966. Mansfield Town August 1968. Rugby Town September 1968. Belper Town October 1969.*

**CHRISTIE Malcolm Neil**
*Forward*
*Born: Stamford, 11 April 1979.*

*Career: Market Deeping Rangers. Nuneaton Borough March 1998. Derby County November 1998. Middlesbrough January 2003.*

**CHRISTIE Trevor John**
*Forward*
*Born: Cresswell, Northumberland, 28 February 1959.*
*Career: Apprentice, Leicester City: professional December 1976. Notts County June 1979. Nottingham Forest July 1984. Derby County February 1985. Manchester City August 1986. Walsall October 1986. Mansfield Town March 1989. Kettering Town August 1991. VS Rugby March 1992. Player-coach, Hucknall Town, November 1992. Arnold Town March 1995.*
***Division Three promotion 1985–86.***

**CLAMP Edward**
*Goalkeeper*
*Born: Burton, 13 November 1922.*
*Died: Swadlincote, 2 June 1990.*
*Career: John Knowles. Moira United. Gresley Rovers. Derby County November 1947. Oldham Athletic July 1949. Buxton August 1950.*

**CLARK Benjamin**
*Wing-half*
*Born: North Shields, 14 April 1933.*
*Career: North Shields. Sunderland August 1950. Yeovil Town, loan, October 1952. Derby County May 1954. Barrow February 1959.*
***Division Three North Champions 1956–57.***

**CLARK Jonathan**
*Midfield*
*Born: Swansea, 12 November 1958.*
*Career: Apprentice, Manchester United: professional November 1975. Derby County September 1978. Preston North End August 1981: caretaker manager, March to June 1986. Bury December 1986. Carlisle United August 1987. Morecambe February 1989. Rhyl August 1989.*

**CLAYTON John**
*Forward*
*Born: Elgin, 20 August 1961.*
*Career: Apprentice, Derby County: professional December 1978. Bulova, Hong Kong, August 1982. Chesterfield June 1983. Tranmere Rovers July 1984. Plymouth Argyle August 1985. Fortuna Sittard (Holland) July 1988. FC Volendam (Holland) 1990. Burnley August 1992.*

**CLEAVER Frederick Louis**
*Centre-forward*
*Born: Ashbourne, 22 April 1885.*
*Career: Ashbourne Town. Derby County February 1906. Preston North End May 1907. Watford August 1908. Redditch cs 1910. Atherstone.*

**CLEEVELY Nigel Robert**
*Outside-left*
*Born: Cheltenham, 23 December 1945.*

Career: Juniors, Derby County: professional July 1964. Burton Albion February 1968. Ilkeston Town June 1970. Redfern Athletic August 1971.

**CLIFTON G.**
*Half-back*
Career: Long Eaton Rangers. Derby County 1886. Long Eaton Rangers January 1889.

**COLEMAN Simon**
*Centre-half*
Born: Worksop, 13 March 1968.
Career: Apprentice, Mansfield Town: professional July 1985.

Middlesbrough September 1989. Derby County August 1991. Sheffield Wednesday, loan, November 1993: permanent January 1994. Bolton Wanderers October 1994. Wolverhampton Wanderers, loan, September 1997. Southend United February 1998. Rochdale July 2000. Ilkeston Town August 2002. Hyde United 2002.

**COMYN Andrew John**
*Central defender*
Born: Wakefield, 2 August 1968.
Career: Juniors, Manchester United: professional August 1986. Birmingham University. Alvechurch. Aston Villa August 1989. Derby County August 1991. Plymouth Argyle August 1993. West Bromwich Albion March 1996. Hednesford Town cs 1996. Halesowen Town 2000.

**CONWELL Anthony**
*Full-back*
Born: Bradford, 17 January 1932.
Career: Bradford junior football. Juniors, Sheffield Wednesday: professional February 1949. Huddersfield Town July 1955. Derby County June 1959. Doncaster Rovers July 1962.

**COOKE John Alfred**
*Outside-left*
Born: Sutton-in-Ashfield.
Career: Mansfield. Derby County March 1899.

**COOP Michael Anthony**
*Right-back*
Born: Grimsby, 10 July 1948.
Career: Apprentice, Coventry City: professional January 1966. York City, loan, November 1974. Detroit Express, loan, May 1979. Derby County July 1981. Contract cancelled January 1982. AP Leamington December 1983. Coventry City coaching staff May 1986 to cs 1990. Manager, Jaguar-Daimler, April 1993 to March 1994.

**COOPER G.F.**
*Half-back*
Career: Derby County 1885.

**COOPER Kevin Lee**
*Midfield*
Born: Kilburn, 8 February 1975.
Career: Trainee, Derby County: professional July 1993. Stockport County, loan, March 1997. Stockport County August 1997. Wimbledon March 2001. Wolverhampton Wanderers March 2002. Sunderland, loan, January 2004. Norwich City, loan, March 2004. Cardiff City July 2005.
**Division One promotion 1995–96.**

**COOPER Lewis**
*Forward*
Born: Belper, 1864. Died: Derby, 12 February 1937.
Career: Darley Dale. Derby County. Grimsby Town. Derby County June 1888.

**CORISH Robert**
*Left-back*
Born: Liverpool, 13 September 1958.
Career: Apprentice, Derby County, professional August 1976. Fort Lauderdale Strikers November 1978.

**COSTA Candido Alves Moreira da**
*Midfield*
Born: San Joao da Madeira, 30 April 1981.
Career: Benfica. Salgueiros 1999.

Porto 2000. Vitoria Setubal, loan, December 2002. Derby County, loan, August 2003. Sporting Braga July 2004.

**COWANS Gordon Sidney**
*Midfield*
Born: Cornforth, 27 October 1958.
Career: Apprentice, Aston Villa: professional September 1976. Bari July 1985. Aston Villa July 1988. Blackburn Rovers November 1991. Aston Villa July 1993. Derby

*County February 1994. Wolverhampton Wanderers December 1994. Sheffield United December 1995. Bradford City June 1996. Stockport County March 1997. Player-coach, Burnley, August 1997. Coach, Aston Villa, 1998.*

**COWELL William**
*Goalkeeper*
*Born: Acomb, near Hexham, 7 December 1902.*
*Career: Newburn. Mickley. Newburn. Amateur, Huddersfield Town, October 1921: professional January 1922. Hartlepools United September 1924. Derby County May 1926. Grimsby Town February 1927. Millwall June 1928. Carlisle United September 1929.*

**CRAWFORD Andrew**
*Forward*
*Born: Filey, 30 January 1959.*
*Career: Filey Town. Apprentice, Derby County: professional January 1978. Manawatu (New Zealand), loan, May 1979. Blackburn Rovers October 1979. AFC Bournemouth November 1981. Cardiff City August 1983. Middlesbrough October 1983.*

*Stockport County December 1984. Torquay United February 1985. Tennyson 1985. Edgehill. Poole Town August 1988. Bournemouth Sports 1989. Swanage Town and Herston 1991. AFC Lymington 1992. Filey Town 1993. Bridlington Town November 1993. Pickering Town 1994.*

**CRAWFORD James**
*Outside-right*
*Born: Leith, 1877.*
*Career: Abercorn. Reading cs 1897. Sunderland May 1898. Derby County May 1900. Middlesbrough November 1901.*

**CRESSWELL Peter Frank**
*Outside-right*
*Born: Chesterfield, 9 November 1935.*
*Career: Heanor Town. Amateur, Derby County, October 1953: professional April 1954. Peterborough United August 1957. Heanor Town September 1959. Sutton Town January 1962. Matlock Town July 1962. Long Eaton United July 1963. Crewton cs 1965.*
***Division Three North Champions 1956–57.***

**CRILLY Thomas**
*Left-back*
*Born: Stockton, 20 July 1895. Died: Derby, 18 January 1960.*
*Career: Stockton. Hartlepools United January 1920. Derby County August 1922. Crystal Palace May 1928. Northampton Town July 1933. Player-manager, Scunthorpe and Lindsey United, May 1935 to April 1937.*
***Division Two promotion 1925–26.***

**CROPPER William**
*Centre-forward*
*Born: Brimington, 27 December 1862. Died: Grimsby, 13 January 1889.*
*Career: Chesterfield Spital. Derby County 1886. Staveley October 1888.*

**CROSS Steven Charles**
*Midfield*
*Born: Wolverhampton, 22 December 1959.*
*Career: Apprentice, Shrewsbury Town: professional December 1977. Derby County June 1986. Bristol Rovers September 1991: player-coach May 1992: reserve-team manager: caretaker manager March 1993: assistant manager March 1993. Mangotsfield United July 1996. Bath City November 1996.*
***Division Two Champions 1986–87.***

**CROWSHAW Allan Alfred**
*Outside-left*
*Born: Willenhall, 12 December 1932.*
*Career: Bloxwich Wesley. West Bromwich Albion May 1950. Derby County June 1956. Millwall May 1958. Sittingbourne July 1960.*
***Division Three North Champions 1956–57.***

**CRUMP Frederick**
*Centre-forward*
*Born: Stourbridge, 1880.*
*Career: Stourbridge. Derby County June 1899. Glossop May 1900. Northampton Town 1902. Stalybridge Rovers 1903. Stockport County August 1905. Brighton & Hove Albion August 1908. Portsmouth. Walsall August 1909. Darlaston cs 1910.*

**CULLEN Michael Joseph**
*Inside-forward*
*Born: Glasgow, 3 July 1931.*
*Career: Douglasdale Juniors. Luton Town August 1949. Grimsby Town June 1958. Derby County November 1962. Wellington Town February 1965. Burton Albion February 1966.*

**CURRAN Edward**
*Outside-right*
*Born: Kinsley, 20 March 1955.*
*Career: Kinsley. Doncaster Rovers July 1973. Nottingham Forest August 1975. Bury, loan, October 1977. Derby County November 1977. Southampton August 1978. Sheffield Wednesday March 1979. Sheffield United August 1982. Everton, loan, December 1982. Everton September 1983. Huddersfield Town July 1985. Panionios (Greece) July 1986. Hull City October 1986. Sunderland November 1986. Grantham September 1987. Grimsby Town November 1987. Chesterfield March 1988. Goole Town August 1988: coach, March 1989: manager, November 1989 to March 1992. Manager, Mossley, November to December 1992.*

**CUSHLOW Richard**
*Centre-half*
*Born: Shotton, 15 June 1920. Died: Chesterfield, June 2002.*
*Career: Murton Colliery. Chesterfield May 1946. Sheffield United December 1947. Derby County March 1948. Crystal Palace February 1951.*

**DAFT T.**
*Forward*
*Career: Derby Midland. Derby County 1890.*

**DAILLY Christian Eduard**
*Defender*
*Born: Dundee, 23 October 1973.*
*Career: Juniors, Dundee United: professional August 1990. Derby County August 1996. Blackburn Rovers August 1998. West Ham United January 2001.*

**DAINO Daniele**
*Defender*
*Born: Alessandria, 8 September 1979.*
*Career: Milan August 1996. Napoli, loan, August 1998. Perugia, loan, August 1999. Derby County, loan, August 2001. Ancona August 2003. Bologna 2004.*

**DALZIEL Ian**
*Defender/midfield*
*Born: South Shields, 24 October 1962.*
*Career: Apprentice, Derby County: professional October 1979. Hereford United May 1983. Carlisle United July 1988. Gateshead September 1993.*

**DARWIN George Hedworth**
*Inside-forward*
*Born: Chester-le-Street, 16 May 1932.*
*Career: Wimblesworth Juniors. Huddersfield Town May 1950. Mansfield Town November 1953. Derby County May 1957. Rotherham United October 1960. Barrow July 1961. Boston United cs 1964.*

**DAVIDSON Jonathan Stewart**
*Defender*
*Born: Werrington, 1 March 1970.*
*Career: Trainee, Derby County: professional July 1988. Preston North End July 1992. Chesterfield, loan, March 1993. Telford United March 1994. Dagenham and Redbridge October 1995. Ilkeston Town December 1995. Nuneaton Borough cs 1996. Shepshed Dynamo October 1996.*

**DAVIES Andrew John**
*Central defender*
*Born: Stockton, 17 December 1984.*
*Career: Academy, Middlesbrough: professional July 2002. Queen's Park Rangers, loan, January 2005. Derby County, loan, July 2005.*

**DAVIES Frank**
*Goalkeeper*
*Born: Birkenhead.*
*Career: Birkenhead. Derby County May 1902. Glossop June 1904. Manchester City June 1906.*

**DAVIES Glyn**
*Defender*
*Born: Swansea, 31 May 1932.*
*Career: Juniors, Derby County: amateur May 1949: professional July 1949. Swansea Town July 1962. Player-manager, Yeovil Town, January 1964. Manager, Swansea Town, June 1965 to October 1966. Player-coach, Pembroke United, December 1966 to May 1967.*
***Division Three North Champions 1956–57.***

**DAVIES William**
*Forward*
*Born: Derby, 27 September 1975.*
*Career: Trainee, Derby County: professional July 1994. Buxton, loan, December 1995. Bangor (Northen Ireland), loan, February 1996. IR (Iceland), loan, July 1996. Cobh Ramblers December 1996. Gresley Rovers 1997. Matlock Town August 1998. Hendon July 2004. Chesham United August 2004. Belper Town October 2005.*

**DAVIS George Henry**
*Outside-left*
*Born: Alfreton, 5 June 1881. Died: Wimbledon, 28 April 1969.*
*Career: Alfreton Town 1896. Derby County December 1899. Alfreton Town May 1908.*
***FA Cup finalists 1902–03.***

**DAVIS John William**
*Wing-forward*
*Born: Ironville, 10 April 1882.*
*Died: Ripley, 29 October 1963.*
*Career: Somercotes. Derby County April 1905. Ilkeston United September 1910. Eastwood Rangers July 1912. Sutton Junction December 1912. Ilkeston United August 1919.*

**DAVISON Thomas Reay**
*Centre-half*
*Born: West Stanley, 3 October 1901.*
*Died: Derby, 1 January 1971.*
*Career: Tanfield Lea Juniors. Durham City August 1920 Wolverhampton Wanderers June 1923. Derby County July 1925. Sheffield Wednesday February 1931. Coventry City July 1932. Player-coach, Rhyl Athletic, July 1935. Bath City August 1936.*
***Division Two promotion 1925–26. Division One runners-up 1929–30.***

**DAYKIN Reginald Brian**
*Wing-half*
*Born: Long Eaton, 4 August 1937.*
*Career: Ericsson Telephones. Long Eaton Town 1954. Derby County November 1955. Notts County July 1962. Corinthians, Sydney, May 1963. Player-coach, Adamstown Rosebuds (Newcastle, New South Wales), January 1964. Belper Town January 1966. Lockheed Leamington May 1966. Player-manager, Long Eaton West Park. Player-manager, Long Eaton Albion 1969. Manager, Long Eaton United, December 1972. Assistant manager Brighton & Hove Albion, August 1974.*

**DEACY Eamonn Stephen**
*Full-back*
*Born: Galway, 1 October 1958.*
*Career: Galway Rovers. Limerick November 1976. Galway Rovers June 1977. Aston Villa March 1979. Derby County, loan, October 1983. Galway United 1984.*

**DELAP Rory John**
*Defender/midfield*
*Born: Sutton Coldfield, 6 July 1976.*
*Career: Trainee, Carlisle United: professional July 1994. Derby County February 1998. Southampton July 2001. Sunderland January 2006.*

**DEVINE Stephen Bernard**
*Midfield*
*Born: Strabane, 11 December 1964.*
*Career: Apprentice, Wolverhampton Wanderers: professional December 1982. Derby County March 1983. Stockport County August 1985. Hereford United October 1985. Corby Town August 1993. Hednesford Town June 1994. Gresley Rovers March 1997. Coach, Hednesford Town September 1997.*

**DEVONSHIRE William James**
*Outside-left*
*Career: Lewisham Park. Catford South End. Amateur, Derby County, October 1914: professional December 1914.*
***Division Two Champions 1914–15.***

**DICHIO Daniele Salvatore Ernest**
*Forward*
*Born: Hammersmith, 9 July 1968.*
*Career: Trainee, Queen's Park Rangers: professional May 1993. Welling United, loan, February 1994. Barnet, loan, March 1994. Sampdoria July 1997. Lecce, loan, September 1997. Sunderland January 1998. West Bromwich Albion, loan, August 2001: permanent November 2001. Derby County, loan, October 2003. Millwall, loan, January 2004: permanent February 2004. Preston North End July 2005.*

**DILLY Thomas**
*Wing-forward*
*Born: Arbroath, November 1882.*
*Died: 1960.*
*Career: Forfar County. Arbroath. Heart of Midlothian. Everton July 1902. West Bromwich Albion March 1906. Derby County October 1907. Bradford June 1908. Walsall August 1909. Shrewsbury Town cs 1910. Worcester City. Kidderminster Harriers. Cadbury Works 1938. Retired 1939.*

**DIX Ronald William**
*Inside-forward*
*Born: Bristol, 5 September 1912.*
*Died: Bristol, 2 April 1998.*
*Career: Juniors, Bristol Rovers:*

*professional September 1929. Blackburn Rovers May 1932. Aston Villa May 1933. Derby County February 1937. Tottenham Hotspur June 1939. Reading November 1947.*

**DOBBS Arthur**
*Centre-forward*
*Career: St Roth, Glasgow. Derby County November 1933.*

**DOCHERTY James**
*Wing-half*
*Born: Pollokshaws.*
*Career: Pollokshaw. Clyde. Hibernian. Derby County cs 1893. Luton Town May 1895. Cowes May 1898.*

**DOCKERY George**
*Goalkeeper*
*Career: Third Lanark. Derby County August 1893.*

**DONAGHY Edward**
*Left-half*
*Born: Grangetown, 8 January 1900.*
*Career: Grangetown. Middlesbrough February 1922. Bradford City May 1923. Derby County May 1926. Gillingham July 1927. French football June 1928.*

**DONALD David Morgan**
*Outside-left*
*Born: Coatbridge, 21 July 1885. Died: Derby, 19 January 1932.*
*Career: Albion Rovers July 1905. Bradford June 1908. Derby County March 1910. Chesterfield June 1912. Watford June 1913. Queen's Park Rangers cs 1914. Hamilton Academical July 1922.*
***Division Two Champions 1911–12.***

**DORIGO Anthony Robert**
*Left-back*
*Born: Melbourne, Australia, 31 December 1965.*
*Career: Apprentice, Aston Villa: professional July 1983. Chelsea July 1987. Leeds United June 1991. Torino July 1997. Derby County October 1998. Stoke City July 2000.*

**DOYLE Nathan Luke Robert**
*Midfield*

*Born: Derby, 12 January 1987.*
*Career: Academy, Derby County: professional January 2004. Notts County, loan, February 2006. Bradford City, loan, August 2006.*

**DRAPER Derek**
*Midfield*
*Born: Swansea, 11 May 1943.*
*Career: Juniors, Swansea Town: professional May 1962. Derby County April 1966. Bradford September 1967. Chester January 1969.*

**DUCROCQ Pierre**
*Midfield*
*Born: Pontoise, 18 December 1976.*
*Career: Juniors, Paris Saint-Germain: professional August 1994. Laval, loan, August 1996. Derby County, loan, October 2001. Le Havre July 2002.*

**DUNCAN John Pearson**
*Forward*
*Born: Lochee, 22 February 1949.*
*Career: Dundee April 1966. Tottenham Hotspur October 1974. Derby County September 1978. Player-manager, Scunthorpe United, June 1981: manager to February 1983. Manager, Hartlepool United, April 1983. Manager, Chesterfield, June 1983. Manager, Ipswich Town, June 1987 to May 1990. Manager, Chesterfield February 1993 to April 2000.*

**DUNN George**
*Inside-forward*
*Career: Derby County 1890. Ilkeston Town.*

**DUNN James**
*Inside-forward*
*Born: Edinburgh, 25 November 1923.*
*Career: St Teresa's, Liverpool. Amateur, Wolverhampton Wanderers, 1941: professional, November 1942. Derby County November 1952. Worcester City July 1955. Runcorn June 1957 to May 1959. Trainer/coach, West Bromwich Albion, 1965 to July 1971.*

**EADIE William Phillips**
*Centre-half*
*Born: Greenock.*
*Career: Morton. Manchester City August 1906. Derby County June 1914.*
***Division Two Champions 1914–15.***

**EDWARDS John W.**
*Inside-forward*
*Career: Carr Vale, Bolsover. Derby County January 1909.*

**EDWARDS Robert Owen**
*Defender*
*Born: Telford, 25 December 1982.*
*Career: Trainee, Aston Villa: professional January 2000. Crystal Palace, loan, November 2003. Derby County, loan, January 2004. Wolverhampton Wanderers July 2004.*

**EDWORTHY Marc**
*Right-back*
*Born: Barnstaple, 24 December 1972.*
*Career: Trainee, Plymouth Argyle: professional March 1991. Crystal Palace June 1995. Coventry City August 1998. Wolverhampton Wanderers August 2002. Norwich City August 2003. Derby County July 2005.*

**EGGLESTON Thomas**
*Wing-half*
*Born: Consett, 21 February 1920. Died: Wetherby, January 2004.*
*Career: Amateur, Derby County, December 1936: professional February 1937. Leicester City July 1946. Watford February 1948. Trainer, Brentford, September 1954. Trainer, Watford, May 1957. Coach, Sheffield Wednesday, October 1958. Coach, Everton, June 1961. Manager, Mansfield Town, August 1967. Manager, Ethnikos (Greece), July 1970. Manager, Panahaiki (Greece), 1971. Youth coach, Everton, February 1972: assistant manager May 1972 to June 1973: acting manager April 1973. Physiotherapist, Plymouth Argyle. Physiotherapist, Ipswich Town, December 1978 to retirement.*

**EKINS Frederick George**
*Forward*
*Born: New Brompton, 27 September 1871.*
*Career: New Brompton Rovers. Chatham. Derby County October 1891. Burton Swifts August 1893. Luton Town May 1895.*

**EL HAMDAOUI Mounir**
*Forward*
*Born: Rotterdam, 14 July 1984.*
*Career: Excelsior, Rotterdam, 2001. Tottenham Hotspur January 2005. Derby County, loans, September 2005 and January 2006. Willem II July 2006.*

**ELLIOTT Steven William**
*Defender*
*Born: Derby, 29 October 1978.*
*Career: Trainee, Derby County: professional March 1997. Blackpool, loan, November 2003: permanent February 2004. Bristol Rovers July 2004.*

**EMERY Stephen Roger**
*Midfield/full-back*
*Born: Ledbury, 7 February 1956.*
*Career: Apprentice, Hereford United: professional February 1974. Derby County September 1979. Newport County March 1983. Hereford United June 1983. Wrexham August 1985. Gloucester City February 1987. Westfields April 1987: manager.*

**EMSON Paul David**
*Outside-left*
*Born: Lincoln, 22 October 1958.*
*Career: Athletico FC, Grimsby Sunday League. Brigg Town cs 1978. Derby County September 1978. Grimsby Town August 1983. Wrexham July 1986. Darlington August 1988. Kettering Town March 1991. Gateshead October 1991.*

**EVANS George**
*Centre-forward*
*Born: Sutton-in-Ashfield, 1865. Died: 1930.*
*Career: Derby Midland/St Luke's. Derby County 1884. West Bromwich Albion May 1889. Brierley Hill Alliance 1890. Oldbury Town. Oldbury St John's.*

**EVANS William**
*Outside-left*
*Died: Chesterfield, 9 November 1963.*
*Career: Clay Cross Zingari. Chesterfield Town October 1904. Clay Cross Zingari October 1905. Clay Cross Works July 1906. Derby County October 1907. Clay Cross Works October 1907.*

**EVATT Ian Ross**
*Defender/midfield*
*Born: Coventry, 19 November 1981.*
*Career: Trainee, Derby County: professional December 1998. Northampton Town, loan, August 2001. Chesterfield August 2003. Queen's Park Rangers June 2005. Blackpool, loan, August 2006.*

**EXHAM Percy George**
*Left-half*
*Born: Cork, 16 June 1859. Died: Repton, 7 October 1922.*

**FABIAN Aubrey Howard**
*Inside-forward*
*Born: Barnet, 20 March 1909. Died: Cranbrook, 6 September 1984.*
*Career: Casuals, Corinthians and Corinthian-Casuals 1928 to 1946. Cambridge University 1929 to 1931. Derby County December 1931 to May 1933. Sutton United. Fulham December 1934 to February 1935.*

**FADIGA Khalilou**
*Midfield*
*Born: Dakar, Senegal, 30 December 1974.*
*Career: Paris Saint-Germain. Royal Standard Liege 1994. KFC Lommelse SK 1995. Club Brugge KV 1997. AJ Auxerre 2000. Internazionale Milan 2003. Bolton Wanderers October 2004. Derby County, loan, September 2005.*

**FAGAN Fionan**
*Wing-forward*
*Born: Dublin, 7 June 1930.*
*Career: Transport. Hull City March 1951. Manchester City December 1953. Derby County March 1960. Player-manager, Altrincham, June 1961: manager to April 1962: player to May 1963. Ashton United September 1963. Northwich Victoria.*

**FAIRCLOUGH Albert**
*Centre-forward*
*Born: St Helens, 4 October 1891. Died: Stockport, 5 November 1958.*
*Career: Windle Villa. Eccles Borough. Manchester City April 1913. Southend United May 1920. Bristol City March 1921. Derby*

County July 1924. Gillingham February 1927.
***Division Two promotion 1925–26.***

**FAZACKERLEY Stanley Nicholas**
*Forward*
*Born: Preston, 3 October 1891. Died: Sheffield, 20 June 1946.*
*Career: Lane Ends United. Amateur, Preston North End, August 1909: professional September 1909. Charlestown, Boston League, USA, 1910. Accrington Stanley. Hull City April 1912. Sheffield United March 1913. Everton November 1920. Wolverhampton Wanderers November 1922. Kidderminster Harriers, while on Wolves' transfer list, March 1925. Derby County August 1925.*
***Division Two promotion 1925–26.***

**FELLOWS Percy James**
*Outside-left*
*Born: Dudley, 1984.*
*Career: Dudley. Derby County January 1914.*

**FEREDAY David Thomas**
*Outside-right*
*Born: Walsall Wood, 6 July 1908. Died: Walsall, November 1995.*
*Career: Walsall Wood. Walsall August 1927. Derby County February 1928. West Ham United May 1931. Yeovil and Petters United.*
***Division One runners-up 1929–30.***

**FERGUSON Archibald**
*Full-back*
*Career: Heart of Midlothian. Derby County June 1888. Preston North End 1891. Ardwick July 1894. Baltimore October 1894.*

**FERGUSON Robert Burnitt**
*Left-back*
*Born: Dudley, Northumberland, 8 January 1938.*
*Career: Dudley Welfare. Newcastle United May 1955. Derby County October 1962. Cardiff City December 1965. Player-manager, Barry Town, December 1968. Player-manager, Newport County, July 1969. dismissed as manager November 1970: player to May 1971. Coach, Ipswich Town, July 1971: manager July 1982 to May 1987. Manager Al-Arabi (Kuwait), June 1987. Assistant manager, Birmingham City, June 1989 to January 1991. Coach, Colchester United, April 1991. Coach, Sunderland, June 1992 to May 1993.*

**FEUER Anthony Ian**
*Goalkeeper*
*Born: Las Vegas, 20 May 1971.*
*Career: Club Brugge KV. Los Angeles Salsa 1993. West Ham United March 1994. Peterborough United, loan, February 1995. Luton Town, loan, September 1995: permanent December 1995. New England Revolution March 1998. Rushden and Diamonds, loan, December 1998. Colorado Rapids February 1999. Cardiff City January 2000. West Ham United February 2000. Wimbledon June 2000. Derby County, loan, October 2001. Tranmere Rovers August 2002. Wolverhampton Wanderers September 2002.*

**FIFE**
*Goalkeeper*
*Career: Derby County 1889.*

**FINDLAY John Williamson**
*Goalkeeper*
*Born: Blairgowrie, 13 July 1954.*
*Career: Apprentice, Aston Villa: professional June 1972. Luton Town November 1978. Barnsley, loan, September 1983. Derby County, loan, January 1984. Swindon Town July 1985. Peterborough United January 1986. Portsmouth January 1986. Coventry City August 1986.*

**FINDLAY Thomas**
*Full-back*
*Born: Port Glasgow, 1899.*
*Career: Port Glasgow Athletic. Derby County March 1922. Merthyr Town May 1925. Brechin City 1926.*

**FISHER William**
*Inside-forward*
*Born: 1873.*
*Career: Dalry. Kilmarnock, June 1895. Derby County May 1896. Burton Swifts October 1897. Bristol Eastville Rovers May 1898.*

**FLANDERS Frederick**
*Left-back*
*Born: Derby, 1 January 1894. Died: Birmingham, 1967.*
*Career: Derby Boys. Shelton United. Derby County May 1910. Ilkeston Town cs 1912. Newport County August 1913. Mansfield Town October 1920. Newport County cs 1921. Hartlepools United June 1922. Nuneaton Town cs 1923.*

**FLETCHER Frederick**
*Outside-left*
*Born: Ripley, 1877.*

*Career: Derby County August 1892. Notts County November 1894. Worcester Rovers October 1895.*

**FLETCHER Thomas**
*Forward*
*Born: Heanor, 15 June 1881. Died: Derby, 29 September 1954.*
*Career: Hill's Ivanhoe. Derby Nomads. Leicester Fosse April 1902. Derby Nomads. Derby County November 1904.*

**FLOWERS Jack**
*Half-back*
*Career: Darley Abbey. Derby Midland. Derby County 1885.*

**FLYNN Sean Michael**
*Midfield*
*Born: Birmingham, 13 March 1968.*
*Career: Halesowen Town. Coventry City December 1991. Derby County August 1995. Stoke City, loan, March 1997. West Bromwich Albion August 1997. Tranmere Rovers July 2000. Kidderminster Harriers August 2002. Evesham United September 2003.*
***Division One promotion, 1995–96.***

**FOLETTI Patrick**
*Goalkeeper*
*Born: Sorengo, 27 May 1974.*
*Career: Mendrisia. Grasshopper Zurich. FC Shaffhausen. Luzern August 1999. Derby County February 2002. Luzern May 2002. St Kriens July 2002.*

**FORD David**
*Goalkeeper*
*Born: Belper, 1878. Died: Derby, November 1914.*
*Career: Derby County July 1898. Chesterfield October 1899.*

**FORDHAM Norman Mills**
*Centre-forward*
*Born: Willesborough, Kent, 5 December 1890.*
*Career: Ashford. Derby County February 1914.*
***Division Two Champions 1914–15.***

**FORMAN Frank**
*Half-back*
*Born: Aston on Trent, 23 May 1875. Died: West Bridgford, 4 December 1961.*
*Career: Aston on Trent. Beeston Town. Derby County March 1894. Nottingham Forest December 1894.*

**FORMAN Frederick Ralph**
*Outside-left*
*Born: Aston on Trent, 8 November 1873. Died: Skegness, 14 June 1910.*
*Career: Beeston Town. Derby County January 1892. Nottingham Forest 1894.*

**FOSTER George Walter**
*Centre-half*
*Born: Plymouth, 26 September 1956.*
*Career: Apprentice, Plymouth Argyle: professional September 1974. Torquay United, loan, October 1976. Exeter City, loan, December 1981. Derby County June 1982. Mansfield Town August 1983: player-manager February 1989 to September 1993. Burton Albion September 1993. Player-manager, Telford United, October 1993 to June 1995. Coach, Doncaster Rovers, July 1995 to August 1996. Community officer, Chesterfield, 1996. Academy coach, Birmingham City, 1998. Coach, Lincoln City, February 2000: assistant manager to February 2001. Chief scout, Wolverhampton Wanderers, April 2001.*

**FOX Walter Cyril**
*Goalkeeper*
*Born: Derby, 3 April 1901. Died: Derby, 1972.*
*Career: Matlock Town. Alfreton Town. Amateur, Derby County, August 1925: professional, September 1925.*
***Division Two promotion 1925–26.***

**FRAIL Martin Joseph**
*Goalkeeper*
*Born: Burslem, 1869. Died: Hanley, 4 September 1939.*
*Career: Burslem Port Vale December 1891. Gorton Villa October 1894. Glossop North End April 1895. Derby County June 1896. Chatham June 1898. Middlesbrough May 1900. Luton Town May 1902. Brentford May 1903. Stalybridge Rovers December 1903. Middlesbrough May 1904. Stockport County November 1905. Glossop March 1906.*

**FRANCIS Kevin Michael Derek**
*Centre-forward*
*Born: Birmingham, 6 December 1967.*
*Career: Redditch United April 1988. Mile Oak Rovers July 1988. Derby County February 1989. Stockport County February 1991. Birmingham City January 1995. Oxford United February 1998. Stockport County March 2000. Castleton Gabriels. Exeter City November 2000. Hull City December 2000. Hednesford Town July 2001.*

**FRANCIS Percy Ollivant**
*Outside/inside-right*
*Born: Derby, 1875. Died: Derby, 21 June 1947.*
*Career: Amateur. Registered with Derby County 1893.*
***Division One runners-up 1895–96.***

**FRITH Robert William**
*Defender*
*Born: Hassop, 1892. Died: Sheffield, 1 January 1939.*
*Career: Sheffield United April 1909. Derby County December 1910. Luton Town July 1913. South Shields July 1919. Rotherham County March 1920. Mansfield Town September 1921. Mid Rhondda cs 1923. Rochdale cs 1924.*

**FRYER John Spencer**
*Goalkeeper*
*Born: Cromford, 1877. Died: Westminster, 22 December 1933.*
*Career: Abbey Rovers. Cromford. Clay Cross Town August 1895. Derby County September 1897. Fulham May 1903: coach 1911.*
***FA Cup finalists 1897–98, 1898–99, 1902–03.***

**FUERTES Esteban Oscar**
*Centre-forward*

*Born: Corronel Dorido, 26 December 1972.*
*Career: Platense 1995. Racing Club de Buenos Aires 1996. Colon de Santa Fe 1997. Derby County August 1999. Colon de Santa Fe, loan, February 2000. Racing Club Lens June 2000. CD Tenerife, loan, 2001. River Plate, loan, August 2002.*

**FULTON William**
*Inside-forward*
*Born: Alva 1877.*
*Career: Alva Albion Rangers. Trial for Preston North End 1897. Sunderland May 1898. Bristol City June 1900. Derby County May 1901. Alloa Athletic June 1902.*

**FUTCHER Paul**
*Central defender*
*Born: Chester, 25 September 1956.*
*Career: Apprentice, Chester: professional January 1974. Luton Town June 1974. Manchester City June 1978. Oldham Athletic August 1980. Derby County January 1983. Barnsley March 1984. Halifax Town July 1990. Grimsby Town, loan, January 1991: permanent February 1991. Player-manager, Darlington, March to April 1995. Dundalk 1995. Droylesden 1995. Player-manager, Gresley Rovers, November 1995. Manager, Southport, June 1997 to November 1999. Manager, Stalybridge Celtic, July 2001 to March 2002. Manager, Ashton United, March 2005.*

**GALLOWAY Septimus Randolph**
*Centre-forward*
*Born: Sunderland, 22 December 1896. Died: Mapperley, 10 April 1964.*
*Career: Army, boy musician. Yorkshire Regiment in World War One. Sunderland Tramways. Derby County October 1922. Nottingham Forest November 1924. Luton Town June 1927. Coventry City January 1928. Tottenham Hotspur August 1928. Grantham Town September 1929. Coach, Sporting Lisbon. Coach, Penarol. Coach, Gillingham.*

**GAMBLE Francis**
*Forward*
*Born: Liverpool, 21 August 1961.*
*Career: Burscough. Derby County, loan, March 1981: permanent May 1981. Barrow November 1982. Rochdale December 1984. Morecambe March 1986. Northwich Victoria, loan, October 1987. Southport November 1987. Rhyl October 1989.*

**GARDEN Henry Whitworth**
*Centre-half*
*Born: Curragh Camp, Dublin, 1869.*
*Career: Derby Midland. Derby County June 1891. Long Eaton Rangers 1893.*

**GARDNER William**
*Centre-forward*
*Born: Langley Moor, 7 June 1893.*
*Career: Bishop Auckland. Derby County August 1920. Spennymoor United November 1921. Queen's Park Rangers March 1923. Ashington July 1923. Grimsby Town October 1925. Darlington September 1927. Torquay United June 1928. York City July 1929. Crewe Alexandra July 1931. Rochdale September 1932.*

**GARNER Andrew**
*Forward*
*Born: Stonebroom, 8 March 1966.*
*Career: Apprentice, Derby County: professional December 1983. Blackpool August 1988. Gresley Rovers August 1994: player/assistant manager July 1997. Burton Albion September 1997: coach.*
***Division Three promotion***

***1985–86. Division Two Champions 1986–87.***

**GARRY Edward**
*Inside-forward/wing-half*
*Born: Renton, 7 March 1885. Died: Derby, 28 May 1955.*
*Career: Dumbarton Hibs. Galston. Glasgow Celtic January 1905. Ayr United, loan, September 1905. Stenhousemuir, loan, February 1907. Derby County May 1907. Bradford May 1913. Dumbarton during World War One. Coached in Spain.*
***Division Two Champions 1911–12.***

**GEE Phillip John**
*Striker*
*Born: Pelsall, 19 December 1964.*
*Career: Riley Sports. Gresley Rovers July 1985. Derby County September 1985. Leicester City March 1992. Plymouth Argyle, loan, January 1995. Hednesford Town January 1997. Shepshed Dynamo March 1997.*
***Division Three promotion 1985–86. Division Two Champions 1986–87.***

**GIBSON Aidan Michael**
*Outside-left*
*Born: Clayton, 17 May 1963.*
*Career: Apprentice, Derby County: professional May 1981. Exeter City July 1982. Stourbridge August 1983. Willenhall Town.*

**GILCHRIST Leonard**
*Inside-forward*
*Born: Burton upon Trent, 1881.*
*Career: Burton United February 1903. Derby County May 1904.*

**GILL James**
*Inside-forward*
*Born: Sheffield, 9 November 1894.*
*Career: Sheffield Wednesday June 1913. Cardiff City July 1920. Blackpool October 1925. Derby County February 1926. Crystal Palace May 1928.*
***Division Two promotion 1925–26.***

**GILLET Leonard Francis**
*Goalkeeper*
*Born: Borrowash, 21 January 1861. Died: Harbertonford, 23 November 1915.*
*Career: Oxford University. Old Carthusians. Notts County. Derby County November 1884.*

**GODDARD Paul**
*Centre-forward*
*Born: Harlington, 12 October 1959.*
*Career: Apprentice, Queen's Park*

*Rangers: professional July 1977. West Ham United August 1980. Newcastle United November 1986. Derby County August 1988. Millwall December 1989. Ipswich Town January 1991: joint first-team coach May 1994: caretaker manager December 1994. Coach, West Ham United, July 2001 to January 2004.*

**GOLBY Joseph Allen**
*Centre-half*
*Born: Burton upon Trent 1897.*
*Career: Burton All Saints. Derby County August 1922. Halifax Town July 1926.*

**GOODCHILD George**
*Outside-right*
*Born: Ryhope, 1875.*
*Career: Ryhope Colliery. Sunderland June 1894. Derby County June 1896. Nottingham Forest March 1897. Burton Swfits October 1897. Jarrow July 1899. South Shields Athletic July 1901. Ashington July 1904.*

**GORHAM C.**
*Half-back*
*Career: Derby County 1884.*

**GOULOOZE Richard**
*Midfield*
*Born: Heemskerk, 16 November 1967.*
*Career: Juniors, Ajax Amsterdam. AZ Alkmaar 1986. SC Heerenveen 1989. Derby County September 1992. Cambuur-Leeuwarden June 1994. New England Revolution January 1998. NEC Nijmegen June 1999. FC Lisse 2003.*

**GRAHAM Daniel Anthony William**
*Centre-forward*
*Born: Gateshead, 12 August 1985.*
*Career: Academy, Middlesbrough: professional March 2004. Darlington, loan, March 2004. Derby County, loan, November 2005. Leeds United, loan, March 2006. Blackpool, loan, August 2006.*

**GRANT Alexander Frank**
*Goalkeeper*
*Born: Peasedown St John, 11 August 1916.*
*Career: Doncaster Rovers (mid-week League). Amateur, Sheffield United. Amateur, Bury, April 1937:*

*professional, August 1937. Aldershot May 1938. Leicester City December 1941. Derby County November 1946. Newport County November 1948. Leeds United August 1949. York City March 1950. Worksop Town July 1950. Corby Town July 1953.*

**GRANT Lee Anderson**

*Goalkeeper*

*Born: Hemel Hempstead, 27 January 1983.*

*Career: Academy, Derby County: professional February 2001. Burnley, loan, November 2005. Oldham Athletic, loan, January 2006.*

**GREEN Joseph James**

*Goalkeeper*

*Born: Derby, 1871.*

*Career: Derby Bedford Rangers. Derby County January 1894. Belper Town.*

**GREEN Leslie**

*Goalkeeper*

*Born: Atherstone, 17 October 1941.*

*Career: Atherstone Town. Hull City August 1960. Nuneaton Borough*

*July 1962. Burton Albion June 1965. Hartlepools United November 1965. Rochdale April 1967. Derby County May 1968. Durban City August 1971. Commercial manager, Nuneaton Borough, 1989: manager September 1989 to January 1991. Manager, Hinckley Town, April 1991. Manager, Tamworth, March 1994.* ***Division Two Champions 1968–69.***

**GREEN Robert Edward**

*Inside-forward*

*Born: Tewkesbury. Died: Cheltenham.*

*Career: Amateur, Bournemouth and Boscombe Athletic, February 1929: professional, March 1929. Derby County May 1931. Manchester United June 1933. Stockport County July 1934. Cheltenham Town June 1936.*

**GREENWOOD Roy Thornton**

*Forward*

*Born: Leeds, 26 September 1952.*

*Career: Apprentice, Hull City: professional October 1970. Sunderland January 1976. Derby County January 1979. Swindon Town February 1980. Huddersfield Town August 1982. Tranmere Rovers, loan, November 1983. Scarborough June 1984. North Ferriby United June 1985.*

**GREGORY John Charles**

*Midfield*

*Born: Scunthorpe, 11 May 1954.*

*Career: Apprentice, Northampton Town: professional May 1972. Aston Villa June 1977. Brighton & Hove Albion July 1979. Queen's Park Rangers June 1981. Derby County November 1985. Coach, Portsmouth, August 1988: manager January 1989 to January 1990. Playing registration, Derby County to Portsmouth, July 1989.*

*Plymouth Argyle January 1990: temporary manager February 1990. Bolton Wanderers March 1990. Coach, Leicester City, June 1991. Coach, Aston Villa, November 1994. Manager, Wycombe Wanderers, October 1996. Manager, Aston Villa, February 1998. Manager, Derby County, January 2002 to May 2003.* ***Division Three promotion 1985–86. Division Two Champions 1986–87.***

**GRENET Francois**

*Defender*

*Born: Bordeaux, 8 March 1975.*

*Career: Trainee, Girondins de Bordeaux: professional August*

*1992. Derby County November 2001. Stade Rennais, loan, August 2002: permanent February 2003.*

**GRIMES William John**
*Outside-right*
*Born: Ickleford, 27 March 1886. Died: Arlesey, 6 January 1936.*
*Career: St John's, Hitchin. Hitchin Town. Watford May 1906. Glossop May 1907. Bradford City December 1908. Derby County March 1910. Luton Town July 1919.*
***Division Two Champions 1911–12, 1914–15.***

**GROVES Arthur**
*Inside-forward*
*Born: Killamarsh, 27 September 1907. Died: Derby, 27 September 1979.*
*Career: Langwith Colliery. Halifax Town, May 1927. Blackburn Rovers January 1929. Derby County July 1933. Portsmouth January 1936. Stockport County June 1939. Atherstone Town July 1945. Player-coach, Heanor Athletic, November 1946.*
***Division One runners-up 1935–36.***

**GUDJONSSON Thordur**
*Midfield*
*Born: Akranes, 14 October 1973.*
*Career: KA Akranes 1990. IA Akranes 1991. Vfl Bochum 1994. KRC Genk August 1997. UD Las Palmas August 2000. Derby County, loan, March 2001. Preston North End, loan, February 2002. Vfl Bochum July 2002. Stoke City January 2005. IA Akranes November 2005.*

**GWYNNE Revd Llewellyn Henry**
*Centre-forward*
*Born: Kilvey, near Swansea. Died: Epping, 3 December 1957.*
*Career: Derby County 1888.*

**HADDOW David**
*Goalkeeper*
*Born: Dalserf, Lanarkshire, 12 June 1869.*
*Career: Coatbridge junior football. Albion Rovers 1888. Derby County August 1890. Albion Rovers January 1891. Glasgow Rangers cs 1891. Motherwell June 1895. Burnley December 1895. New Brighton Tower August 1898. Retired 1899. Returned with Tottenham Hotspur November 1899.*

**HAGAN James**
*Inside-forward*
*Born: Washington, 21 January 1918. Died: Sheffield, 27 February 1998.*
*Career: Amateur, Liverpool, January 1932. Amateur, Derby*

*County, May 1933: professional January 1935. Sheffield United November 1938. Manager, Peterborough United, August 1958 to October 1962. Manager, West Bromwich Albion, April 1963 to May 1967. Coach, Benfica, March 1970 to September 1973. Coached in Kuwait 1973 to 1975. Coach, Sporting Lisbon, 1976. Coach, Oporto, 1976. Coach, Boavista.*
***Division One runners-up 1935–36.***

**HAIG James**
*Wing-half*
*Born: Rothesay, 1876.*
*Career: Rothesay Royal Victoria. St Mirren. Derby County May 1898. Kilbarchan 1899. Chesterfield November 1900.*

**HAJTO Tomasz**
*Central defender*
*Born: Krakow: 11 October 1972.*
*Career: Hutnik Krakow 1990. Gornik Zabrze 1993. MSV Duisburg 1997. FC Schalke 04 2000. Southampton July 2005. Derby County January 2006.*

**HALES Derek David**
*Centre-forward*
*Born: Lower Halstow, 15 December 1951.*
*Career: Juniors, Gillingham. Faversham Town. Dartford October 1971. Luton Town March 1972. Charlton Athletic, loan, July 1973: permanent October 1973. Derby County December 1976. West Ham United September 1977. Charlton Athletic July 1978. Gillingham March 1985.*

**HALEY William Thomas**
*Inside/Centre-forward*
*Born: Woolwich, 16 February 1904. Died: Rochester, 20 January 1960.*
*Career: Bostall Heath. Charlton Athletic May 1924. Derby County February 1925. Dartford, loan, July 1927. Fulham June 1928. Queen's Park Rangers May 1931. Dartford cs 1932. Sheppey United August 1935.*
***Division Two promotion 1925–26.***

**HALFORD David**
*Outside-left*
*Born: Crossley Green, 19 October 1915.*

*Career: Rowntrees FC. Amateur, Scarborough, August 1932: professional October 1932. Derby County December 1932. Bolton Wanderers June 1936. Oldham Athletic June 1938.*

### HALL Ian William

*Midfield*

*Born: Sutton Scarsdale, 27 December 1939.*

*Career: Amateur, Wolverhampton Wanderers. Amateur, Derby County, August 1958: professional*

*September 1959. Mansfield Town September 1962. Tamworth August 1968. Burton Albion March 1972. Derbyshire Amateurs. Tamworth September 1974.*

### HALLIGAN William

*Forward*

*Born: Athlone, 18 February 1886. Died: 1950.*

*Career: Belfast Celtic. Belfast Distillery. Leeds City May 1909. Derby County February 1910. Wolverhampton Wanderers June 1911. Hull City May 1913. Preston North End July 1919. Oldham Athletic January 1920. Nelson August 1921.*

### HAMILTON John

*Forward*

*Born: Ayr, 1872.*

*Career: Ayr United. Wolverhampton Wanderers. Derby County November 1894. Ilkeston Town May 1895.*

### HAMPTON John William

*Goalkeeper*

*Born: Wolverhampton, 1901.*

*Career: Wellington Town. Oakengates Town. Wolverhampton Wanderers May 1920. Derby County June 1927. Preston North End May 1930. Dundalk June 1931.*

***Division One runners-up 1929–30.***

### HANDLEY George

*Outside-right*

*Born: Burton-on-the-Wolds, 1868.*

*Career: Loughborough Town. Notts County December 1895. Coalville Town September 1897. Derby County November 1897. Northampton Town August 1899. Newark Town.*

### HANN Ralph

*Wing-half*

*Born: Whitburn, 4 July 1911. Died: Derby, 17 July 1990.*

*Career: Marsden Colliery. Amateur, Sunderland, April 1929: professional January 1930. Newcastle United August 1930. Derby County March 1932. Trainer, Crystal Palace, September 1946: registered as player, April 1947. Trainer-masseur, Luton Town, July 1947. Head trainer, Derby County, November 1953 to May 1967.*

***Division One runners-up 1935–36.***

### HANNAY John

*Outside-right*

*Born: Newcastle.*

*Career: Newcastle District. Derby County October 1920.*

### HANNIGAN John Leckie

*Forward*

*Born: Glasgow, 17 February 1933.*

*Career: Morton. Sunderland July 1955. Derby County May 1958. Bradford June 1961. Weymouth July 1964. Bath City July 1968.*

### HARBEY Graham Keith

*Left-back/midfield*

*Born: Chesterfield, 29 August 1964.*

*Career: Apprentice, Derby County: professional August 1982. Ipswich Town July 1987. West Bromwich Albion, loan, November 1989: permanent December 1989. Stoke City July 1992. Gresley Rovers August 1994. Burton Albion.*

***Division Three promotion 1985–86. Division Two Champions 1986–87.***

### HARBOUR Henry

*Wing-half*

*Career: Everton. Borrowed by Derby to complete the team against Everton, October 1888.*

### HARDCASTLE Douglas Scott

*Inside-forward*

*Born: Worksop, 1886.*

*Career: Worksop Town. Derby County May 1905. Worksop Town August 1907.*

### HARDMAN John Andrew

*Half-back*

*Born: Miles Platting, 1889. Died: France, February 1917.*

*Career: Longfield. Amateur, Oldham Athletic, December 1910: professional March 1911. Pontypridd August 1912. Derby County August 1913. Bristol Rovers October 1914.*

***Division Two Champions 1914–15.***

### HARDY Arthur

*Inside-forward*

*Career: Derby Midland. Derby County June 1891. Heanor Town cs 1893.*

### HARDY John James

*Centre-half*

*Born: Sunderland, 10 February*

*1899. Died: Sunderland, January 1932.*
*Career: Sunderland Celtic. South Shields August 1921. Derby County August 1924. Grimsby Town July 1925. Oldham Athletic January 1927. South Shields October 1927. Scarborough Town August 1930. West Stanley December 1930. Clapton Orient September 1931.*

**HARFORD Michael Gordon**
*Centre-forward*
*Born: Sunderland, 12 February 1959.*
*Career: Lambton Star BC. Lincoln City July 1977. Newcastle United December 1980. Bristol City August 1981. Newcastle United March 1982. Birmingham City March 1982. Luton Town December 1984. Derby County January 1990. Luton Town September 1991. Chelsea August 1992. Sunderland March 1993. Coventry City July 1993. Wimbledon August 1994: coach 1997. Coach, Luton Town, May 2001 to May 2003: reinstated as Director of football/first-team coach August 2003. Coach, Nottingham Forest, November 2004: acting-manager December 2004. Assistant manager, Swindon Town, February 2005. Manager, Rotherham United, April to December 2005.*

**HARKES John Andrew**
*Defender/midfield*
*Born: Kearny, New Jersey, 8 March 1967.*
*Career: University of Virginia. Sheffield Wednesday October 1990. Derby County August 1993. United States Soccer Federation October 1995. West Ham United, loan, October 1995. Washington DC United March 1996. Nottingham Forest, loan, January 1999. New England Revolution March 1999. Columbus Crew May 2001.*
***Division One promotion 1995–96.***

**HARPER Kevin Patrick**
*Forward*
*Born: Oldham, 15 January 1976.*
*Career: Hutchison Vale BC. Hibernian August 1992. Derby County September 1998. Walsall,*

*loan, December 1999. Portsmouth March 2000. Norwich City, loan, September 2003. Leicester City, loan, September 2004. Stoke City February 2005.*

**HARRISON Kenneth**
*Outside-right*
*Born: Stockton, 20 January 1926.*
*Career: Billingham Synthonia and army football. Hull City April 1947. Derby County March 1955. Goole Town July 1956.*

**HARRISON Thomas William**
*Goalkeeper*
*Career: South Normanton Town August 1899. Stanton Hill Town September 1899. South Normanton Town March 1901. Ripley Athletic November 1901. Derby County December 1901. Pinxton September 1902.*

**HART John Leslie**
*Centre-forward*
*Born: Bolsover, 21 November 1904. Died: Sheffield, 2 January 1974.*
*Career: New Hucknall Colliery. Bolsover Colliery. Worksop Town cs 1924. Chesterfield March 1925. Mansfield Town September 1925. Derby County January 1926. Newark Town June 1927. Ebbw Vale August 1928.*
***Division Two promotion 1925–26.***

**HARVEY John Arthur H.**
*Half-back*
*Career: Partick Thistle. Derby County July 1894. Ilkeston Town March 1895. Abercorn January 1896.*

**HASLAM Harry B.**
*Outside-left*
*Career: Gresley Rovers. Belper Town January 1897. Derby County March 1901. Belper Town August 1902.*

**HAVENHAND Keith**
*Inside-forward*
*Born: Dronfield, 11 September 1937.*
*Career: Juniors, Chesterfield: professional September 1954. Derby County October 1961. Oxford United December 1963. King's Lynn June 1965.*

**HAWDEN Kenneth**
*Centre-forward*
*Born: Huddersfield, 16 September 1931.*
*Career: Ashenhurst SC, Huddersfield. Derby County April 1953. Matlock Town August 1954. Belper Town October 1954. Sutton Town February 1955. Gresley Rovers August 1958.*

**HAYWARD Steve Lee**
*Midfield*
*Born: Pelsall, 8 September 1971.*
*Career: Trainee, Derby County: professional September 1988. Carlisle United March 1995. Fulham June 1997. Barnsley January 2001.*

**HAYWOOD Frederick**
*Centre-forward*
*Career: Mexborough Town. Derby County April 1907.*

**HAZLEDINE Donald**
*Inside-forward*
*Born: Arnold, 10 July 1929.*
*Career: Notts Regent. Derby County August 1951. Northampton Town June 1954. Boston United July 1955. Skegness Town July 1961. Holbeach United July 1962. Bourne Town August 1965. Coach, Boston United Reserves, July 1966: joint coach with brother Geoff, August 1966.*

**HAZLEDINE Geoffrey**
*Forward*
*Born: Arnold, 27 December 1932.*
*Died: Mansfield, 21 December 2002.*
*Career: Ransome and Marles. Derby County July 1952. Boston United September 1954. Southport July 1957. Skegness Town July 1958. Loughborough United July 1960: player-manager designate June 1962: player-manager May 1963 to May 1965. Bourne Town September 1965. Joint coach, Boston United Reserves, August 1966.*

**HEBBERD Trevor Neal**
*Midfield*
*Born: Winchester, 19 June 1958.*
*Career: Apprentice, Southampton: professional July 1976. Washington Diplomats, loan, March 1981. Bolton Wanderers, loan, September 1981. Leicester City, loan, November 1981. Oxford United March 1982. Derby County August 1988. Portsmouth October 1991. Chesterfield November 1991. Lincoln City July 1994. Grantham Town August 1995.*

**HENNESSEY William Terence**
*Central defender/midfield*

*Born: Llay, 1 September 1942.*
*Career: Juniors, Birmingham City: professional September 1959. Nottingham Forest November 1965. Derby County February 1970. Manager, Tamworth, April to November 1974. Advisory coach, Kimberley Town, September 1976: temporary manager, November 1977. Assistant coach, Tulsa Roughnecks, 1978. Shepshed Charterhouse August 1978 to October 1980. Assistant coach, Tulsa Roughnecks, November 1980: chief coach 1981 to 1983. Assistant coach, Vancouver Whitecaps. Manager, Heidelberg, 1987 to 1988.*
***Division One Champions 1971–72.***

**HICKINBOTTOM Ernest Thomas**
*Half-back*
*Born: Darley Abbey, Derby, 1865.*
*Died: Derby, 2 September 1939.*
*Career: Darley Abbey, Derby Midland. Derby County September 1888.*

**HICKLING William**
*Full-back*
*Career: Somercotes United April 1902. Derby County April 1903. Tottenham Hotspur May 1905. Middlesbrough April 1906. Mansfield Mechanics cs 1908. Ilkeston United cs 1909.*

**HIGGINBOTHAM Daniel John**
*Defender*
*Born: Manchester, 29 December 1978.*

*Career: Trainee, Manchester United: professional July 1997. Royal Antwerp, loan, September 1998. Derby County July 2000. Southampton, loan, January 2003: permanent May 2003. Stoke City August 2006.*

**HIGGINS Alexander F.**
*Centre-forward*
*Born: Kilmarnock, 7 November 1863. Died: 17 April 1920.*
*Career: Kilmarnock 1882. Derby County July 1888. Nottingham Forest July 1890.*

**HILL Andrew Robert**
*Centre-forward*
*Born: Ilkeston, 10 November 1960.*
*Career: Kimberley Town. Derby County June 1981. Carlisle United September 1983. Boston United January 1987. Shepshed Charterhouse July 1987. Hinckley Athletic November 1987.*

**HILL Gordon Alec**
*Outside-left*
*Born: Sunbury, 1 April 1954.*
*Career: Staines Town. Slough Town. Southall. Millwall January 1973. Chicago Sting, loan, April 1975. Manchester United November 1975. Derby County April 1978. Queen's Park Rangers November 1979. Montreal Manic January 1981. Chicago Sting May 1982. HJK Helsinki. Twente Enschede. Northwich Victoria September 1986: caretaker manager, December 1986. Stafford Rangers August 1987. Northwich Victoria January 1988: player-manager May 1988: player-coach to October 1988. Radcliffe Borough March 1990.*

**HINCHCLIFFE Thomas**
*Inside-forward*
*Born: Denaby, 6 December 1913.*
*Died: Rushcliffe, 1978.*
*Career: Denaby United August 1933. Grimsby Town October 1933. Huddersfield Town February 1938. Derby County November 1938. Nottingham Forest May 1946. Gainsborough Trinity September 1946. Denaby United August 1948.*

**HIND F.**
*Full-back*
*Career: Derby Junction. Derby County. Derby Junction.*

**HODGE Stephen Brian**
*Midfield*
*Born: Nottingham, 25 October 1962.*
*Career: Apprentice, Nottingham Forest: professional October 1980. Aston Villa August 1985. Tottenham Hotspur December 1986. Nottingham Forest August 1988. Leeds United July 1991. Derby County, loan, August 1994. Queen's Park Rangers October 1994. Watford December 1995. Hong Kong. Leyton Orient August 1997.*

**HODGES Glyn Peter**
*Midfield*
*Born: Streatham, 30 April 1963.*
*Career: Apprentice, Wimbledon: professional February 1981. Newcastle United July 1987. Watford October 1987. Crystal Palace July 1990. Sheffield United, loan, January 1991: permanent April 1991. Derby County February 1996. Sin Tao, Hong Kong, August 1996. Hull City August 1997. Nottingham Forest February 1998. Scarborough January 1999. Coach, Barnsley: acting manager October 2002 to June 2003. Coach, Wales Under-21, March 2004.*
***Division One promotion 1995–96.***

**HODGKINSON William H.**
*Centre-forward*
*Career: Hinckley Town. Derby County March 1901. Hinckley Town July 1902. Derby County May 1903. Plymouth Argyle May 1904.*

**HODGSON William**
*Outside-left*
*Born: Govan, 9 July 1935.*
*Career: Dunoon Athletic. St Johnstone cs 1954. Guildford City, loan, September 1956. Sheffield United May 1957. Leicester City September 1963. Derby County June 1965. Player-coach, Rotherham United, September 1967. Player-coach, York City, December 1967: temporary manager August to October 1968. Coach, Sheffield United, July 1970. Hamilton Academical 1971. Manager, Irvine Victoria.*

**HOFFMAN Ernest Henry**
*Goalkeeper*
*Born: South Shields, 16 July 1892.*
*Died: South Shields, 20 January 1959.*
*Career: Hebburn Argyle. Amateur, South Shields, 1914. Tottenham Hotspur, one match during World War One. Amateur, South Shields 1919: professional May 1920. Derby County April 1923. Ashington August 1923. Darlington August 1924. Wood Skinner's FC October 1925. York City September 1929. Manager, Jarrow.*

**HOLDSWORTH Dean Christopher**
*Forward*
*Born: Walthamstow, 8 November 1968.*
*Career: Apprentice, Watford: professional November 1986. Carlisle United, loan, February 1988. Port Vale, loan, March 1988. Swansea City, loan, August 1988. Brentford, loan, October 1988. Brentford September 1989. Wimbledon, loan, July 1992: permanent August 1992. Bolton Wanderers October 1997. Coventry City, loan, November 2002: permanent December 2002. Rushden and Diamonds March 2003. Wimbledon July 2003. Player/coach,*

*Havant and Waterlooville, June 2004. Player/assistant manager, Derby County, August 2005. Weymouth February 2006.*

### HOLMES Lee Daniel

*Outside-left*
*Born: Mansfield, 2 April 1987.*
*Career: Academy, Derby County:*

*professional May 2004. Swindon Town, loan, December 2004. Bradford City, loan, August 2006.*

### HOLMES Samuel

*Inside-forward*
*Career: Crich. Derby County, November 1889.*

### HOLYOAKE James Ernest

*Full-back*
*Career: Derby County January 1900. Ripley Town September 1902. Ripley Athletic 1908.*

### HOOKS Paul

*Midfield*
*Born: Wallsend, 30 May 1959.*
*Career: Apprentice, Notts County: professional July 1977. Derby County March 1983. Mansfield Town, non-contract, August 1985. Boston United August 1985. Cotgrave Miners' Welfare 1987.*

### HOPE John

*Inside-forward*
*Born: Bishop Auckland, 10 June 1905. Died: Bishop Auckland, 1982.*
*Career: Crook Town. Derby County January 1927. Bury February 1930. Falkirk October 1932.*
***Division One runners-up 1929–30.***

### HOPEWELL W.

*Centre-half*
*Career: Grimsby Town. Derby County September 1888. Grimsby Town December 1888.*

### HOPKINS William

*Full-back*
*Career: Derby Junction. Derby County 1890. Ardwick cs 1891.*

### HOPKINSON Michael Edward

*Midfield/full-back*
*Born: Ambergate, 24 February 1942.*
*Career: West End Boys Club. Juniors, Derby County: professional, July 1959. Mansfield Town July 1968. Port Vale July 1970. Boston United June 1971. Coach, Belper Town, November 1973: manager, January to September 1974. Coach, Burton Albion: assistant manager, November 1978.*

### HOULT Russell

*Goalkeeper*
*Born: Ashby-de-la-Zouch, 22 November 1972.*
*Career: Trainee, Leicester City: professional March 1991. Lincoln City, loan, August 1991. Cheltenham Town, loan, December 1991. Blackpool, loan, March 1992. Kettering Town, loan, July 1993. Bolton Wanderers, loan, November 1993. Lincoln City, loan, August 1994. Derby County, loan, February 1995. Derby County June 1995. Portsmouth, loan, January 2000: permanent March 2000. West Bromwich Albion January 2001. Nottingham Forest, loan, September 2005.*
***Division One promotion 1995–96.***

### HOUNSFIELD Reginald Edward

*Outside-right*
*Born: Sheffield, 14 August 1882.*
*Career: Sheffield FC. Sheffield Wednesday March 1902. Derby County October 1903.*

### HOWARD Frank

*Centre-half*
*Born: Hardingstone, 12 March 1878.*
*Career: Northampton Town. Derby County April 1899. Ripley Town.*

### HOWARD Frederick Julian

*Inside-forward*
*Born: Long Eaton.*
*Career: Stapleford Brookhill. Long Eaton. Derby County May 1919. Gillingham July 1920. Ayr United June 1922. Long Eaton.*

### HUDDLESTONE Thomas Andrew

*Midfield/Central defender*
*Born: Nottingham, 28 December 1986.*
*Career: Academy, Derby County: professional February 2004. Tottenham Hotspur July 2005. Wolverhampton Wanderers, loan, October 2005.*

**HUGHES Alan**
*Outside-right*
*Born: South Shields, 1909.*
*Career: Wigan Athletic. Chesterfield May 1933. Derby County September 1934. Everton, trial, June 1935. Fleetwood June 1935. South Liverpool May 1936. Wigan Athletic July 1937. South Liverpool January 1938. Fleetwood cs 1938.*

**HUGHES Gordon**
*Outside-right*
*Born: Washington, 19 June 1936.*
*Career: Tow Law Town. Newcastle United August 1956. Derby County August 1963. Lincoln City March 1968. Boston United March 1971.*

**HUGHES William**
*Forward*
*Born: Coatbridge, 30 December 1948.*
*Career: Coatbridge Juniors. Juniors, Sunderland: professional February 1966. Derby County, loan, August 1977: permanent September 1977. Leicester City December 1977. Carlisle United, loan, September 1979. San Jose Earthquakes April 1980. Enderby Town July 1980.*

**HUNT Archibald**
*Centre-forward*
*Career: Bulwell United December 1901. Whitwick White Cross. Derby County August 1904. Walsall September 1906. Mansfield Wesley September 1908. Walsall December 1908.*

**HUNT David**
*Defender/midfield*
*Born: Leicester, 17 April 1959.*
*Career: Apprentice, Derby County: professional April 1977. Notts County March 1978. Aston Villa July 1987. Mansfield Town June 1989. Burton Albion August 1991. Leicester United September 1991.*

**HUNT John**
*Wing-half*
*Career: Alvaston and Boulton September 1899. Derby Hill's Ivanhoe August 1900. Derby County March 1902. Ripley Athletic August 1902. Three games for Glossop in 1903–04. Derby County August 1905.*

**HUNT Jonathan Richard**
*Midfield*
*Born: Camden, 2 November 1971.*
*Career: Trainee, Barnet: professional January 1990. Southend United July 1993. Birmingham City September 1994. Derby County May 1997. Sheffield United, loan, August 1998. Ipswich Town, loan, October 1998. Sheffield United March 1999. Cambridge United, loan, March 2000. Wimbledon September 2000.*

**HUNT Lewis James**
*Defender*
*Born: Birmingham, 25 August 1982.*
*Career: Trainee, Derby County: professional February 2001. Southend United, loan, October 2003: permanent July 2004.*

**HUNT Ralph Arthur Robert**
*Centre-forward*
*Born: Portsmouth, 14 August 1933.*
*Died: Grantham, 17 December 1964.*
*Career: Gloucester City 1949. Juniors, Portsmouth: professional August 1950. Bournemouth and Boscombe Athletic February 1954. Norwich City July 1955. Derby County August 1958. Grimsby Town August 1959. Swindon Town July 1961. Port Vale December 1961. Newport County July 1962. Chesterfield July 1964.*

**HUNTER George Irwin**
*Goalkeeper*
*Born: Troon, 29 August 1930. Died: Nottingham, 10 May 1990.*
*Career: Neilston Juniors 1947. Glasgow Celtic December 1949. Derby County June 1954. Exeter City August 1955. Yiewsley July 1960. Darlington June 1961. Weymouth July 1962. Burton Albion July 1963. Lincoln City September 1965. Matlock Town August to September 1966.*

**HURST William**
*Forward*
*Born: Newcastle upon Tyne.*
*Career: Walker Celtic. Derby County September 1922. Queen's Park Rangers August 1923.*

**HUTCHINSON F.**
*Wing-half*
*Career: Derby County 1886.*

**HUTCHINSON James Barry**
*Inside-forward*
*Born: Sheffield, 27 January 1936.*
*Died: Rotherham, 12 July 2005.*
*Career: Amateur, Bolton Wanderers. Professional, Chesterfield, April 1953. Derby County July 1960. Weymouth July 1964. Lincoln City July 1965. Darlington February 1966. Halifax Town November 1966. Rochdale July 1967. Bangor City August 1968. Hyde United September 1968.*

**HUTCHISON Duncan**
*Inside-forward*
*Born: Kelty, Fife, 3 March 1903.*
*Died: Dundee, December 1972.*
*Career: Rosewell (Edinburgh). Dunfermline Athletic. Dundee United cs 1927. Newcastle United August 1929. Derby County March 1932. Hull City July 1934. Dundee United June 1935.*

**IDIAKEZ Inigo [Inigo Idiakez Barkaiztegui]**
*Midfield*
*Born: San Sebastian, 8 November 1973.*

Inigo Idiakez

*Career: Real Sociedad 1994. Real Oviedo 2002. Rayo Vallecano 2003. Derby County July 2004.*

**IMLACH James John Stewart**

*Outside-left*

*Born: Lossiemouth, 6 January 1932. Died: Formby, 3 October 2001.*

*Career: Lossiemouth United. Lossiemouth. Bury May 1952. Derby County May 1954. Nottingham Forest July 1955. Luton Town June 1960. Coventry City October 1960. Crystal Palace June 1962. Dover January 1965. Chelmsford City February 1965. Player-coach, Crystal Palace, February 1966. Youth coach, Notts County, March 1967. Assistant coach, Everton, May 1969: first-team trainer, July 1972 to January 1976. Coach, Blackpool, June 1976 to August 1977. Coach, Bury, June 1978 to October 1979.*

**JACKSON James Herbert**

*Centre-forward*

*Born: Bollington, 27 December 1897. Died: Macclesfield, 23 December 1964.*

*Career: Bollington Cross. Macclesfield Town. Amateur, Derby County December 1920: professional December 1921. Bollington Cross 1922. Norwich City June 1923.*

**JACKSON John**

*Midfield*

*Born: Camden, 15 August 1982.*

*Career: Trainee, Tottenham Hotspur: professional March 2000. Swindon Town, loan, September 2002. Colchester United, loan, March 2003. Coventry City, loan, November 2003. Watford, loan, December 2004. Derby County, loan, September 2005. Colchester United June 2006.*

**JACKSON Richard**

*Right-back*

*Born: Whitby, 18 April 1980.*

*Career: Trainee, Scarborough: professional March 1998. Derby County March 1999.*

**JAMES Leighton**
*Outside-left*
*Born: Llwchwyr, 16 February 1953.*
*Career: Apprentice, Burnley: professional February 1970. Derby County November 1975. Queen's Park Rangers October 1977. Burnley September 1978 Swansea City May 1980. Sunderland January 1983. Bury August 1984. Newport County August 1985. Burnley August 1986: youth coach, June 1987 to May 1989. Youth coach, Bradford City, February 1990: acting-manager November to December 1991. Manager, Gainsborough Trinity, October 1993. Manager, Morecambe, January 1994. Manager, Netherfield, June 1994. Manager, Ilkeston Town, October 1995 to February 1996. Manager, Accrington Stanley, October 1997. Manager, Llanelli, March 1998 to 2000. Coach, Garden Village. Manager, Llanelli, 2003. Academy director, Port Talbot 2004.*

**JARDINE Robert J.**
*Inside-left*
*Born: Glasgow. Died: Nottingham, 30 July 1941.*
*Career: Notts County 1888. Heanor Town June 1889. Derby County October 1889. Nottingham Forest 1889. Heanor Town.*

**JEFFRIES Alfred**
*Outside-right*
*Born: Bishop Auckland, 22 September 1915. Died: Nottingham, 28 January 2004.*
*Career: Willington. Norwich City August 1934. Bradford City May 1935. Derby County February 1937. Sheffield United June 1939. Basingstoke Town 1945.*

**JESSOP Frederick Samuel**
*Half-back*
*Born: Barrow Hill, 7 February 1907. Died: 1979.*
*Career: Barrow Hill. Staveley Works. Amateur, Derby County, January 1926: professional, March 1926. Sheffield United December 1937. Atherstone Town 1945.*
***Division One runners-up 1935–36.***

**JOHN Stern**
*Centre-forward*
*Born: Tunapuna, Trinidad, 30 October 1976.*
*Career: Columbus Crew. Nottingham Forest November 1999. Birmingham City February 2002. Coventry City September 2004. Derby County, loan, September 2005.*

**JOHNSON Michael Owen**
*Central defender*
*Born: Nottingham, 4 July 1973.*
*Career: Trainee, Notts County: professional July 1991. Birmingham City September 1995. Derby County August 2003.*

**JOHNSON Seth Art Maurice**
*Midfield*
*Born: Birmingham, 12 March 1979.*
*Career: Trainee, Crewe Alexandra: professional July 1996. Derby County May 1999. Leeds United October 2001. Derby County August 2005.*

**JOHNSTON John Murray**
*Centre-forward*
*Born: Durham, 1905.*
*Career: Seaton Delaval. Derby County December 1923. Rotherham County May 1924.*

**JONES Norman Edward**
*Inside-right*
*Born: Liverpool.*
*Career: Walker Celtic 1919. Derby County May 1922. Gillingham June 1923.*

**JONES Roger**
*Goalkeeper*
*Born: Upton-upon-Severn, 8 November 1946.*
*Career: Apprentice, Portsmouth: professional November 1964. Bournemouth and Boscombe*

*Athletic May 1965. Blackburn Rovers January 1970. Newcastle United March 1976. Stoke City February 1977. Derby County July 1980. Birmingham City, loan, February 1982. York City July 1982. Coach, Sunderland, November 1988 to May 1993.*

**JONES Verdun Aubrey**
*Inside-forward*
*Born: Edmonton, 22 June 1916. Died: Ware, January 1987.*
*Career: Aston Villa September 1936. Derby County November 1937. Southend United May 1948.*

**JUNIOR [Jose Luis Guimaraes Sanibio]**
*Forward*
*Born: Fortaleza, Brazil, 20 July 1976.*
*Career: Union Espanola. Cordoba. Aleanzea. KSK Beveren. Treze (Brazil). KSK Beveren, loan, 2000. AJ Ajaccio, loan, 2001. Walsall August 2002. Derby County August 2003. Rotherham United, loan, October 2004. OB Odense October 2005.*

**KAKU Blessing**
*Midfield*
*Born: Ughelli, Nigeria, 5 March 1978.*
*Career: Steel Pioneers 1994. Sharks 1996. SV Braunau 1997. RWD Molenbeek 1998. KRC Haralbeke 1999. KRC Genk 2000. Hapoel Beer Sheva 2002. MS Ashdod 2003. Bolton Wanderers August 2004. Derby County, loan, November 2004.*

**KAVANAGH Jason Colin**
*Defender*
*Born: Birmingham, 23 November 1971.*
*Career: Schoolboy, Birmingham City. FA School of Excellence. Trainee, Derby County, June 1988: professional December 1988. Wycombe Wanderers, loan and permanent, November 1996. Stoke City March 1999. Cambridge United December 1999. Burton Albion July 2000. Mickleover Sports December 2002.*
***Division One promotion 1995–96.***

**KEAY Walter**
*Inside-forward/wing-forward*
*Born: Whiteinch, August 1871. Died: Winchester, 16 January 1943.*
*Career: Partick Thistle. Darlington. Derby County July 1893. Southampton St Mary's May 1895.*

**KEETLEY Frank**
*Forward*
*Born: Derby, 23 March 1901. Died: Worcester, 13 January 1968.*
*Career: Victoria Ironworks. Derby County February 1921. Doncaster Rovers June 1926. Bradford City November 1929. Lincoln City May 1931. Margate July 1933. Worcester City July 1934: player-manager May 1935 to May 1936.*
***Division Two promotion 1925–26.***

**KELHAM Harold J.**
*Wing-half*
*Career: Derby County April 1907.*

**KELLY Daniel**
*Outside-right*
*Born: Blantyre, 25 June 1904.*
*Career: Hamilton Academical. Derby County February 1927. Torquay United June 1928. York City July 1930. Doncaster Rovers June 1932. Dundalk cs 1935.*

**KENNA Jeffrey Jude**
*Defender*
*Born: Dublin, 27 August 1970.*
*Career: Trainee, Southampton: professional April 1989. Blackburn Rovers March 1995. Tranmere Rovers, loan, March 2001. Wigan Athletic, loan, November 2001. Birmingham City, loan, December 2001: permanent February 2002. Derby County March 2004. Kidderminster Harriers August 2006.*

**KENNEDY Peter Henry James**
*Left-back*
*Born: Lurgan, 10 September 1973.*
*Career: Glentoran. Glenavon July 1992. Portadown 1995. Notts County August 1996. Watford July 1997. Wigan Athletic July 2001. Derby County, loan, October 2003. Peterborough United August 2004. Portadown May 2006.*

**KIDD James**
*Goalkeeper*
*Born: Darlington.*
*Career: Spennymoor United. Blackpool July 1910. Bolton Wanderers March 1915. Derby County September 1919. Fleetwood.*

**KIFFORD John**
*Full-back*
*Born: Paisley, 1878.*
*Career: Paisley FC. Abercorn. Derby County June 1898. Bristol Rovers July 1900. West Bromwich Albion June 1901. Millwall Athletic May 1905. Player-manager, Carlisle United, cs 1906. Coventry City June 1907.*

**KING Francis Oliver**
*Goalkeeper*
*Born: Alnwick, 13 March 1917. Died: 8 May 2003.*
*Career: Blyth Spartans. Everton October 1933. Derby County May 1937. Assistant trainer, Leicester City, 1954. Trainer, Luton Town, 1958 to 1964.*

**KING Jeffrey**
*Midfield*
*Born: Fauldhouse, 9 November 1953.*
*Career: Fauldhouse United. Albion Rovers December 1972. Derby County April 1974. Notts County, loan, January 1976. Portsmouth, loan, March 1976. Walsall November 1977. Sheffield Wednesday August 1979. Sheffield United January 1982. Chesterfield October 1983. Stafford Rangers November 1983. Altrincham February 1984. Burton Albion August 1984. Kettering Town 1984. Torquay United August 1985.*

**KING W. George**
*Outside-right*
*Career: Derby County January 1906.*

**KINKLADZE Georgiou**
*Midfield*
*Born: Tbilisi, Georgia, 6 November 1973.*

*Career: Mretebi Tbilisi 1989. Dinamo Tbilisi August 1992. Saarbrucken, loan, January 1994. Boca Juniors, loan, 1994. Manchester City August 1995. Ajax Amsterdam May 1998. Derby County, loan, November 1999: permanent April 2000. Anorthosis Famagusta September 2004. FC Rubin Kazan, Russia, August 2005.*

**KINSEY George**
*Left-half*
*Born: Burton upon Trent, 20 June 1866. Died: Aston, January 1911.*
*Career: Burton Crusaders 1883. Burton Swifts 1885. Mitchell St George's 1888. Wolverhampton Wanderers August 1891. Aston Villa June 1894. Derby County May 1895. Notts County March 1897. Eastville Rovers May 1897. Burton Swifts December 1900. Gresley Rovers August 1901. Burton Early Closing September 1902. Reinstated as amateur August 1904.*
***Division One runners-up 1895–96.***

**KIRBY John**
*Goalkeeper*
*Born: Overseal, 30 September 1910. Died: Derby, 15 June 1960.*

*Career: Newhall United. Derby County April 1929. Player-manager, Folkestone Town, August 1938 to August 1939.*
***Division One runners-up 1929–30, 1935–36.***

**KITSON Paul**
*Forward*
*Born: Murton, 9 January 1971.*
*Career: Trainee Leicester City: professional December 1988. VS Rugby, loan, March 1988. Derby County March 1992. Newcastle*

*United September 1994. West Ham United February 1997. Charlton Athletic, loan, March 2000. Crystal Palace, loan, September 2000. Brighton & Hove Albion August 2002. Rushden and Diamonds September 2003.*

**KNOWLES Frederick Edmund**
*Centre-half*
*Born: Derby, 21 June 1901. Died: Salisbury, 9 February 1991.*
*Career: YMCA Derby. Derby County November 1921.*

**KNOX J.**
*Inside-right*
*Career: Bakewell. Derby County 1885.*

**KONJIC Muhamed**
*Central defender*
*Born: Brijesnica Velika, Bosnia, 14 May 1970.*

*Career: Sloboda Tuzla 1991. Croatia Belisce 1992. Croatia Zagreb 1993. FC Zurich 1996. AS Monaco 1997. Coventry City February 1999. Derby County May 2004.*

**KOZLUK Robert**
*Right-back*

*Born: Sutton-in-Ashfield, 5 August 1977.*
*Career: Trainee, Derby County: professional February 1996. Sheffield United March 1999. Huddersfield Town, loan, September 2000. Preston North End, loan, January 2005.*

**KUHL Martin**
*Midfield*
*Born: Frimley, 10 January 1965.*
*Career: Apprentice, Birmingham City: professional January 1983. Sheffield United March 1987. Watford February 1988. Portsmouth September 1988. Derby County September 1992. Notts County, loan, September 1994. Bristol City December 1994. Hong Kong 1997. Farnborough Town August 1999. Weymouth August 2002. Coach, Aldershot Town.*

**LABARTHE TOME Albert Gianfranco**
*Forward*
*Born: Lima, 20 September 1984.*
*Career: Cantolao. Sport Boys. Huddersfield Town January 2003. Derby County August 2003.*

**LAMB Samuel**
*Outside-left*
*Born: Alfreton, 1886. Died: Willesden, 1960.*
*Career: Alfreton Town. Amateur, Derby County, 1904: professional October 1905. Alfreton Town cs 1907. Sutton Town December 1907. Plymouth Argyle May 1909. Swindon Town May 1910. Millwall Athletic April 1913. Rotherham County August 1919. Caerphilly July 1920.*

**LAMPH Thomas**
*Wing-half*
*Born: Gateshead, 1893. Died: Leeds, 24 February 1926.*
*Career: Pelaw United. Spennymoor. Leeds City May 1914. Manchester City October 1919. Derby County March 1920. Leeds United February 1921.*

**LANE Moses Alexander Edmund**
*Centre-forward*
*Born: Willenhall, 17 February 1895. Died: Cannock, 14 July 1949.*
*Career: Willenhall Pickwick. Willenhall Town August 1920. Birmingham April 1922. Derby County June 1924. Wellington Town May 1925. Worcester City October 1926. Walsall June 1927. Brierley Hill Alliance.*

**LANE Sean Brendon**
*Outside-left*
*Born: Bristol, 16 January 1964.*
*Career: Apprentice, Hereford United: professional March 1981. Derby County May 1983. Australia cs 1984.*

**LANGAN David Francis**
*Right-back*
*Born: Dublin, 15 February 1957.*
*Career: Apprentice, Derby County: professional February 1975. Birmingham City July 1980.*

*Oxford United August 1984. Leicester City, loan, October 1987. AFC Bournemouth, loan, November 1987: permanent December 1987. Peterborough United August 1988. Ramsey Town 1989. Holbeach United August 1989. Nuneaton Borough September 1989. Rothwell Town August 1990. Mirlees Blackstone 1990.*

**LANGLAND Albert Edward**
*Inside-forward*
*Career: Derby County 1889.*

**LATHAM Arthur**
*Right-back*
*Died: Derby, 8 November 1929.*
*Career: St Luke's. Derby Midland. Derby County 1886: trainer 1891. Trainer, Norwich City, 1919 to June 1920.*

**LAUNDERS Brian Terence**
*Midfield*
*Born: Dublin, 8 January 1976.*
*Career: Cherry Orchard. Crystal Palace August 1993. Oldham*

*Athletic, loan, March 1996. Crewe Alexandra August 1996. BV Veendam cs 1997. Derby County September 1998. Colchester United, loan, March 1999: permanent July 1999. Crystal Palace October 1999. Sheffield United November 1999.*

**LAW Cecil Richard**
*Outside-left*
*Born: Salisbury, Rhodesia, 10 March 1930.*
*Career: Alexandra FC, Salisbury. Derby County August 1951. Bury May 1954.*

**LAWRENCE George Harold**
*Goalkeeper*
*Born: Basford, 10 March 1889.*
*Died: Derby, 1 March 1959.*
*Career: Manners Rangers. Ilkeston United September 1909. Derby County May 1910. Bristol City September 1924. Lincoln City August 1925. Ilkeston United November 1926.*
***Division Two Champions 1914–15.***

**LAWRENCE Samuel Eaton**
*Wing-half*
*Career: Burton Wanderers. Derby County October 1886.*

**LEACH Samuel**
*Left-back*
*Career: Derby County May 1897. Heanor Town 1898.*

**LECKIE Charles T.**
*Half-back*
*Born: Alva 1876.*
*Career: Dundee. Derby County December 1898.*

**LEE John**
*Centre-forward*
*Born: Sileby, 4 November 1920.*
*Died: Loughborough, 15 January 1995.*
*Career: Quorn Methodists. Amateur, Leicester City, December 1940: professional, February 1941. Derby County June 1950. Coventry City November 1954.*

**LEE Robert Martin**
*Midfield*
*Born: Plaistow, 1 February 1966.*
*Career: Hornchurch. Charlton*

*Athletic July 1983. Newcastle United September 1992. Derby County February 2002. West Ham United August 2003. Oldham Athletic November 2004. Wycombe Wanderers March 2005.*

**LEES John**
*Inside-forward*
*Career: Sawley Rangers. Derby County August 1887.*

**LEIGH Alfred Sidney**
*Centre-forward*
*Born: Shardlow, August 1893.*
*Died: Nottingham, 1958.*
*Career: Osmaston. Derby County June 1914. Bristol Rovers July 1920.*

**LEIPER Joseph**
*Left-back*
*Born: Partick, 1873.*
*Career: Minerva. Partick Thistle. Derby County August 1892. Grimsby Town July 1900. Chesterfield July 1902. Partick Thistle May 1903. Motherwell September 1903. Hull City August 1904. Aberdare Athletic October 1904. Belper Town September 1905.*
***Division One runners-up 1895–96. FA Cup finalists 1897–98.***

**LEONARD John**
*Outside-right*
*Career: St Mirren. Derby County May 1897. Notts County March 1898. Badminster June 1898. Bristol Eastville Rovers May 1899.*

**LEWIS Alan Trevor**
*Left-back*
*Born: Oxford, 19 August 1954.*
*Career: Apprentice, Derby County: professional May 1972. Peterborough United, loan, March 1974. Brighton & Hove Albion, loan, January 1975: permanent March 1975. Sheffield Wednesday, loan, May 1977. Reading July 1977. Witney Town July 1982.*

**LEWIS Michael**
*Midfield*
*Born: Birmingham, 15 February 1965.*
*Career: Apprentice, West Bromwich Albion: professional February 1982. Derby County November 1984. Oxford United August 1988: reserve-team coach July 1996: acting manager October 1999 to February 2000. Coach, Doncaster Rovers, 2002.*
***Division Three promotion 1985–86.***

**LEWIS Wilfred Leslie**
*Inside-right*
*Born: Swansea, 1 July 1903. Died: Swansea, 1976.*
*Career: Baldwins Welfare. Swansea Amateurs. Swansea Town March 1924. Huddersfield Town November 1928. Derby County April 1931. Yeovil and Petters United July 1932. Bath City December 1933. Altrincham July 1934. Cardiff City August 1934. Haverfordwest August 1936.*

**LIEVESLEY Wilfred**
*Inside-forward*
*Born: Staveley, 6 October 1902. Died: Staveley, 21 February 1979.*
*Career: Staveley Old Boys. Derby County May 1920. Manchester United October 1922. Exeter City August 1923. Wigan Borough May 1928. Cardiff City May 1929.*

**LILLIS Mark Anthony**
*Forward/midfield*
*Born: Manchester, 17 January 1960.*
*Career: Manchester Boys. Schoolboy, Manchester City. Huddersfield Town July 1978. Manchester City June 1985. Derby County August 1986. Aston Villa September 1987. Scunthorpe United September 1989. Stockport County September 1991. Witton Albion August 1992. Macclesfield Town cs 1993. Coach, Huddersfield Town. Assistant manager Scunthorpe United 1996. Manager, Halifax Town, June 1999 to September 2000. Coach, Derby County, February 2002 to June 2003. Part-time coach, Northern Ireland, March to October 2003. Assistant manager, Stockport County, October 2003. Acting assistant manager, Morecambe, December 2005: permanent May 2006.*
***Division Two Champions 1986–87.***

**LINACRE James Henry**
*Goalkeeper*
*Born: Aston on Trent, 26 March 1881. Died: Nottingham, 11 May 1957.*
*Career: Loughborough GS. Aston on Trent. Draycott Mills. Derby County December 1898. Nottingham Forest August 1899.*

**LISBIE Kevin Anthony**
*Centre-forward*
*Born: Hackney, 17 October 1978.*
*Career: Trainee, Charlton Athletic: professional May 1996. Gillingham, loan, March 1999. Reading, loan, November 1999. Queen's Park Rangers, loan, December 2000. Norwich City, loan, September 2005. Derby County, loan, February 2006.*

**LITTLE Thomas**
*Inside/outside-left*
*Born: Dumfries, April 1872.*
*Career: Derby County December 1892. Manchester City June 1894. Baltimore October 1894. Manchester City November 1894. Ashton North End November 1895. Wellingborough August 1896. Luton Town August 1897. Swindon Town May 1898. Barnsley August 1899. Dumfries March 1900.*

**LLOYD Arthur**
*Centre-half*
*Career: Ripley Athletic. Derby County November 1902. Aston Villa. Wolverhampton Wanderers April 1907. Brighton & Hove Albion May 1908. Gresley Rovers.*

**LLOYD George Henry**
*Half-back*
*Born: Derby 1877.*
*Career: Derby County December 1900. New Brompton July 1903.*

**LONG James**
*Forward*
*Born: 1881.*
*Career: Clyde. Grimsby Town February 1902. Reading May 1904. Derby County May 1906.*

**LOVATT John**
*Right-back*
*Born: Middlesbrough, 21 January 1962.*
*Career: Apprentice, Derby County: professional January 1980. Whitby Town August 1983. Guisborough Town.*

**LOWELL Eric James**
*Inside forward*
*Born: Cheadle, 8 March 1935.*
*Career: Juniors, Derby County:*

*professional March 1952. Stoke City May 1955. Stafford Rangers September 1956.*

**LUNTLEY Walter**
*Goalkeeper*
*Born: Croydon, 12 January 1856.*
*Career: Nottingham Forest 1878. Derby County 1885.*

**LYLE Robert Chalmers**
*Centre-half*
*Career: Partick Thistle. Derby County May 1910.*

**LYONS James**
*Inside-right*
*Born: Hednesford, 27 September 1897. Died: Lichfield, 1970.*
*Career: Hednesford Town. Derby County January 1920. Wrexham July 1925.*

**McALLE John Edward**
*Central defender*
*Born: Liverpool, 31 January 1950.*
*Career: Apprentice, Wolverhampton Wanderers: professional February 1967. Sheffield United August 1981. Derby County, loan, February 1982: permanent April 1982. Harrisons August 1984.*

**McALLISTER Alexander**
*Centre-half*
*Born: Kilmarnock. Died: France, February 1918.*
*Career: Kilmarnock. Sunderland December 1896. Derby County June 1904. Oldham Athletic June 1905. Spennymoor United July 1909.*

**McANDREW Robert**
*Left-back*
*Born: Derby, 6 April 1943.*
*Career: Derby Boys. Amateur, Derby County, June 1958: professional, April 1960. Lockheed Leamington June 1965. Ilkeston Town September 1965. Loughborough United May 1970.*

**McCAFFERY Aiden**
*Central defender*
*Born: Jarrow, 30 August 1957.*
*Career: Apprentice, Newcastle United: professional January 1975. Derby County August 1978. Bristol Rovers August 1980. Bristol City February 1982. Bristol Rovers March 1982. Torquay United, loan, March 1985. Exeter City July 1985. Hartlepool United February 1987. Whitley Bay cs 1987. Player-coach, Carlisle United, January 1988: youth coach May 1990: acting manager March 1991: manager April 1991 to September 1992.*

**McCANN John**
*Outside-left*
*Born: Govan, 23 July 1934.*
*Career: Bridgeton Waverley. Barnsley December 1955. Bristol City May 1959. Huddersfield Town October 1960. Derby County September 1962. Darlington August 1964. Chesterfield October 1964. Skegness Town August 1966. Lockheed Leamington June 1967.*

**McCLAREN Stephen**
*Midfield*
*Born: Fulford, 3 May 1961.*

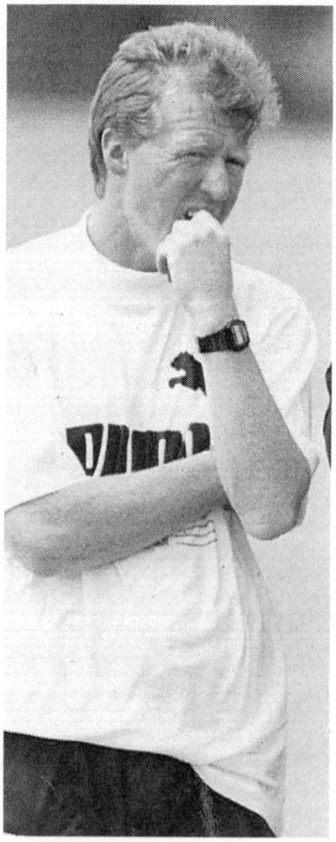

*Career: Apprentice, Hull City: professional April 1979. Derby County August 1985. Lincoln City, loan, February 1987. Bristol City February 1988. Oxford United August 1989: coach, 1992. Coach, Derby County, June 1995. Assistant manager, Manchester United, February 1999. Manager, Middlesbrough, June 2001. Assistant coach, England, from November 2000. Manager, England, August 2006.*
***Division Three promotion 1985–86.***

**McCORD Brian John**
*Midfield*
*Born: Derby, 24 August 1969.*
*Career: Apprentice, Derby County: professional June 1987. Barnsley, loan, November 1989. Barnsley March 1990. Mansfield Town, loan, August 1992. Stockport County December 1992. Telford United 1998.*

**McCORMICK Henry**
*Outside-left*
*Born: Coleraine, 10 January 1924.*
*Career: Coleraine. Derby County November 1946. Everton July 1948. Coleraine September 1949.*

**McCULLOCH David**
*Centre-forward*
*Born: Hamilton, 5 October 1911. Died: Hamilton, May 1979.*
*Career: Hamilton Amateurs. Shotts United. Third Lanark May 1932. Heart of Midlothian June 1934. Brentford November 1935. Derby County October 1938. Leicester City July 1946. Bath City December 1946. Player-coach, Waterford, August 1949. Player-manager, Alloa Athletic July 1951 to August 1952.*

**MacDONALD William James**
*Inside-left*
*Born: Inverness, 1877.*
*Career: Dundee. Derby County December 1898. Dundee June 1900. Stoke 1901. Dundee 1902.*
***FA Cup finalists 1898–99.***

**McDONNELL Martin Henry**
*Centre-half*
*Born: Newton-le-Willows, 27 April 1924. Died: Coventry, 13 April 1988.*
*Career: Haydock C and B. Everton August 1942. Earlestown. Southport August 1946. Birmingham City May 1947. Coventry City October 1949. Derby County July 1955. Crewe Alexandra July 1958.*
***Division Three North Champions 1956–57.***

**MacDOUGALL Alexander Lindsay**
*Right-half*
*Born: Motherwell, 1904.*
*Career: Wishaw Juniors. Wolverhampton Wanderers February 1925. Derby County August 1928.*

**McGILL James**
*Inside-forward*
*Born: Kilsyth, 10 March 1926.*
*Career: Maryhill Harp. Bury December 1945. Derby County March 1947. Kilmarnock October 1949. Berwick Rangers January 1951. Queen of the South 1953. Berwick Rangers, loan, 1954–55. Heart of Midlothian, loan, 1954–55. Cowdenbeath 1959.*

**McINDOE Michael**
*Outside-left*
*Born: Edinburgh, 2 December 1979.*
*Career: Trainee, Luton Town: professional April 1998. Hereford United July 2000. Yeovil Town February 2001. Doncaster Rovers August 2003. Derby County, loan, March 2006. Barnsley July 2006.*

**McKELLAR David**
*Goalkeeper*
*Born: Ardrossan, 22 May 1956.*
*Career: Apprentice, Ipswich Town: professional March 1974. Colchester United, loan, September 1974. Peterborough United, loan, December 1975. Ardrossan Winton Rovers 1976. Derby County March 1978. Brentford, loan, September 1980: permanent October 1980. Hong Kong FC April 1983. Carlisle United August 1983. Hibernian August 1985. Manchester City, loan, December 1985. Newcastle United, loan, February 1986. Hamilton Academical July 1986. Dunfermline Athletic January 1988. Hartlepool United, loan, August 1988. Carlisle United, loan, October 1988: permanent November 1988. Kilmarnock March 1990. Glasgow Rangers August 1991.*

**MACKEN Anthony**
*Midfield*
*Born: Dublin, 30 July 1950.*
*Career: Home Farm. Glentoran May 1968. Waterford September 1972. Derby County August 1974. Portsmouth, loan, November 1975 and February 1976. Washington Diplomats, loan, April 1976 and May 1977. Dallas Tornado, loan, July 1977. Walsall October 1977. Drogheda United August 1982: player-manager January 1983 to April 1985. Manager, Belgrave, 1987. Assistant manager, Shamrock Rovers.*

**McLACHLAN James**
*Inside-forward*
*Career: Vale of Leven. Derby County cs 1890. Notts County September 1893. Derby County September 1894. Ilkeston Town May 1895.*

**McLACHLAN Stephen**
*Wing-half*
*Born: Kirkudbright, 19 September 1918. Died: Kirkcudbright, July 1990.*
*Career: Dalbeatie. Derby County March 1938. Kilmarnock June 1953.*

**McLAREN Hugh**
*Outside-left*
*Born: Hamilton, 24 June 1926. Died: Derby, 8 December 1965.*
*Career: Blantyre Celtic. Kilmarnock August 1947. Derby County October 1949. Nottingham Forest January 1954. Walsall July 1955. Burton Albion July 1956. Gresley Rovers June 1957.*

**MacLAREN Ross**
*Defender*
*Born: Edinburgh, 14 April 1962.*
*Career: Juniors, Glasgow Rangers. Shrewsbury Town August 1980. Derby County July 1985. Swindon Town August 1988: coach to September 1998. Chief scout, Aston Villa, 1998. Coach, Derby County, February 2002 to May 2003. Youth coach, Southend United, July 2004.*

*Assistant manager, Notts County, July 2005 to May 2006.*
***Division Three promotion 1985–86. Division Two Champions 1986–87.***

### McLAVERTY Bernard
*Half-back*
*Born: Chester Moor, 15 March 1898. Died: Duffield, 24 December 1952.*
*Career: Chester Moor. Leadgate Park. Durham City December 1919. Derby County May 1920. Norwich City January 1928. Heanor Town December 1932.*
***Division Two promotion 1925–26.***

### McLEAN Thomas
*Left-back*
*Born: Alexandria, August 1866. Died: Nottingham, 27 November 1936.*
*Career: Vale of Leven. Notts County 1888. Derby County August 1892. Notts County September 1893: assistant trainer 1908 to 1929.*

### McLEOD Izale Michael
*Forward*
*Born: Perry Bar, 15 October 1984.*
*Career: Trainee, Derby County:*

*professional February 2003. Sheffield United, loan, March 2004. Milton Keynes Dons August 2004.*

### McMILLAN John Stuart
*Inside-left*
*Born: Port Glasgow, 16 February 1871. Died: Derby, 4 November 1941.*
*Career: Port Glasgow Athletic. St Bernard's cs 1890. Derby County December 1890. Leicester Fosse May 1896. Small Heath January 1901. Bradford City July 1903. Glossop May 1906: trainer 1908. Trainer, Birmingham, August 1909. Manager, Gillingham, July 1920 to August 1923.*
***Division One runners-up 1895–96.***

### McMILLAN Stuart Thomas
*Outside-right*
*Born: Leicester, 17 September 1896. Died: Ashbourne, 27 September 1963.*
*Career: Derby County December 1914. War service with Derbyshire Yeomanry. Chelsea cs 1919. Gillingham March 1921. Wolverhampton Wanderers June 1922. Bradford City May 1924. Nottingham Forest June 1927. Clapton Orient August 1928. Manager, Derby County, January 1946 to November 1953.*
***Division Two Champions 1914–15.***

### MACONNACHIE Alexander
*Forward*
*Career: Ashfield. Derby County May 1897. Notts County March 1898. Third Lanark June 1901. Ripley Athletic August 1902. Newton Rovers 1903. Ilkeston United September 1905. Alfreton Town. Tibshelf cs 1908.*

### McQUEEN Hugh
*Outside-left*
*Born: Harthill, 1 October 1873. Died: Norwich, 8 April 1944.*
*Career: Leith Athletic 1890.*

*Liverpool October 1892. Derby County July 1895. Queen's Park Rangers May 1901. Gainsborough Trinity July 1902. Player-trainer, Fulham, October 1903. Kilmarnock September 1904. Hibernian January 1905. Assistant trainer, Norwich City, cs 1905.*
***Division One runners-up 1895–96. FA Cup finalists 1897–98.***

**McQUILLAN Dennis**
*Outside-right*
*Born: Derby, 16 March 1934.*
*Career: Juniors, Derby County: professional March 1951. Aldershot July 1956. Luton Town March 1957. Banbury Spencer July 1957. Long Eaton United June 1958: joint player-manager (with Reg Harrison), April 1960 to August 1961.*

**MAKIN Christopher Gregory**
*Left-back*
*Born: Manchester, 8 May 1973.*
*Career: Trainee, Oldham Athletic: professional November 1991. Wigan Athletic, loan, August 1992. Olympique Marseille August 1996. Sunderland August 1997. Ipswich Town March 2001. Leicester City August 2004. Derby County February 2005. Reading August 2005.*

**MALLOCH Gavin Cooper**
*Left-half*
*Born: Glasgow, 18 July 1905. Died: Glasgow, 10 December 1974.*
*Career: Benburb. Derby County January 1927. Sheffield Wednesday December 1931. Millwall August 1936. Barrow August 1937. Greenock Morton 1938.*
***Division One runners-up 1929–30.***

**MANEL [Manuel Martinez Fernandez]**
*Centre-forward*
*Born: Barcelona, 3 November 1973.*
*Career: Sabadell 1993. CD Logrones 1995. RCD Espanyol 2000. Sporting Gijon, loan, 2001 and 2002. Derby County January 2004.*

**MANN Herbert Henry**
*Outside-left*
*Born: Nuneaton, 30 December 1907. Died: Derby, 1976.*
*Career: Griff Colliery. Derby County February 1926. Grantham August 1929. Manchester United May 1931. Ripley Town November 1933.*

**MARSHALL Joseph**
*Goalkeeper*
*Born: Mosbrough, 25 July 1862. Died: Derby, 15 January 1913.*
*Career: Staveley. Derby County 1887. Derby Junction March 1889.*

**MARTIN Blakey**
*Right-half*
*Born: Halifax, 1891. Died: Bradford, 30 September 1960.*
*Career: Castleford 1913. Glossop July 1914. Derby County August 1919. Southend United August 1920. Llanelly June 1922.*

**MARTIN Lilian**
*Right-back*
*Born: Valreas, 28 May 1971.*
*Career: USL Dunkerque. AS Monaco 1996. Olympique Marseille August 1999. Derby County November 2000. Olympique Marseille July 2001. Hibernian February 2002.*

**MARTIN Robert**
*Left-back*
*Born: Kilwinning, 16 May 1929.*
*Career: Kilwinning Rangers. Birmingham City March 1950. Derby County March 1956. Chesterfield July 1960. Burton Albion July 1961. Long Eaton United July 1963.*
***Division Three North Champions 1956–57.***

**MASSON Donald Sandison**
*Midfield*
*Born: Banchory, 26 August 1946.*
*Career: Apprentice, Middlesbrough: professional September 1963. Notts County September 1968. Queen's Park Rangers December 1974. Derby County October 1977. Notts County August*

*1978. Minnesota Kicks May 1981. Notts County September 1981. Bulova, Hong Kong, April 1982. Player-manager, Kettering Town, April to October 1983. Player-manager, Los Angeles Kickers, March 1987.*

**MATTHEWS William**
*Wing-half*
*Born: Derby, 1882. Died: Melbourne, 1 May 1916.*
*Career: Nottingham Forest September 1899. Ripley Athletic October 1901. Aston Villa October 1903. Notts County December 1906. Derby County July 1912. Newport County August 1913.*

**MAWENE Youl**
*Central defender*
*Born: Caen, 16 July 1979.*
*Career: Apprentice, RC Lens:*

*professional. Derby County August 2000. Preston North End August 2004.*

**MAY Hugh**
*Centre-forward*
*Born: Dykehead, 13 October 1882. Died: 1944.*
*Career: Abercorn. Paisley. Wishaw United. Glasgow Rangers December 1901. Derby County July 1902. Fulham May 1903.*

**MAYCROFT D.**
*Centre-half*
*Career: Melbourne Town. Derby County.*

**MEE George Wilfred**
*Outside-left*
*Born: Bulwell, 12 April 1900. Died: Poulton-le-Fylde, 9 July 1978.*
*Career: Highbury Vale United. Notts County August 1919. Blackpool July 1920. Derby County February 1926. Burnley September 1932. Mansfield Town July 1933. Great Harwood November 1934. Accrington Stanley October 1935. Reserve-team trainer-coach, Rochdale, July 1938. Player-coach, Accrington Stanley, January to May 1939.*
***Division Two promotion 1925–26. Division One runners-up 1929–30.***

**MERCER John Thompson**
*Outside-right*
*Born: Belfast, 1879. Died: January 1947.*
*Career: Belview. Ligoniel. 81st North Lancashire Regiment. Preston North End. 8th Belfast Boys' Brigade. Linfield Swifts. Distillery. Brighton United May 1899. Leicester Fosse February 1900. Linfield cs 1900. Distillery March 1903. Derby County October 1903. Director, Glentoran. Director, Distillery.*

**METCALFE Ronald**
*Outside-left*
*Born: South Shields, 8 December 1947.*
*Career: Marsden Colliery Juniors. Derby County January 1965. Burton Albion November 1967.*

**METHVEN James junior**
*Inside-forward*
*Born: Edinburgh, 11 October 1890. Died: Derby, 20 March 1964.*
*Career: Everton Reserves. Ilkeston United November 1912. Derby County, amateur, March 1914. Cardiff City August 1914.*

**MIDDLETON Francis**
*Outside-left*
*Born: Whitwick, 1881.*
*Career: Whitwick White Cross. Derby County November 1901. Leicester Fosse August 1906.*

**MIDDLETON John**
*Goalkeeper*
*Born: Lincoln, 24 December 1956.*
*Career: Apprentice, Nottingham Forest: professional November 1974. Derby County September 1977.*

**MIDDLETON Raymond**
*Goalkeeper*
*Born: Boldon, 6 September 1919. Died: Boston, 12 April 1977.*
*Career: Washington Chemical Works. Boldon CW. North Shields. Amateur, Chesterfield, August 1937: professional, October 1937. Derby County June 1951. Player-manager, Boston United, April 1954. Manager, Hartlepools United, May 1957 to October 1959. Manager, Boston United, June 1960 to May 1961: director February 1963: secretary 1972.*

**MILARVIE Robert**
*Outside-left*
*Born: Pollokshields. Died: Gorton, November 1912.*
*Career: Pollokshields. Hibernian. Stoke October 1888. Port Vale June 1889. Derby County September 1889. Newton Heath July 1890. Ardwick cs 1891.*

**MILLER David**
*Centre-half*
*Born: Middlesbrough, 21 January 1921. Died: Doncaster, June 1989.*
*Career: Middlesbrough September 1938. Wolverhampton Wanderers August 1945. Derby County April 1947. Doncaster Rovers January 1948. Aldershot March 1954. Boston United July 1954.*

**MILLER John**
*Centre-forward*
*Born: Dumbarton.*
*Career: Clyde. Derby County June 1895. Bolton Wanderers November 1897.*
***Division One runners-up 1895–96.***

**MILLIN Alfred**
*Outside-left*
*Born: Rotherham, 18 December 1933.*
*Career: Juniors, Derby County: professional August 1951. Brush*

*Sports August 1956. Gresley Rovers June 1957. Heanor Town June 1958. Gresley Rovers August 1959.*

**MILLS Gary Roland**
*Midfield*
*Born: Northampton, 11 November 1961.*
*Career: Apprentice, Nottingham Forest: professional November 1978. Seattle Sounders March 1982. Derby County, loan, October 1982. Seattle Sounders April 1983. Nottingham Forest December 1983. Notts County August 1987. Leicester City March 1989. Notts County September 1994. Player-manager, Grantham Town, September 1996 to May 1998. Gresley Rovers August 1998. Manager, King's Lynn September 1998. Boston United November 2000. Manager, Tamworth, January 2001. Coach, Coventry City, May 2002. Manager, Notts County, January to November 2004. Manager, Alfreton Town, May 2005.*

**MILLS Pablo Simeon**
*Central defender*
*Born: Birmingham: 27 May 1984.*
*Career: Trainee, Derby County: professional July 2002. Milton Keynes Dons, loan, August 2005. Walsall, loan, February 2006. Rotherham United July 2006.*

**MILLS Rowan Lee**
*Forward*
*Born: Mexborough, 10 July 1970.*
*Career: Stocksbridge Park Steels. Wolverhampton Wanderers December 1992. Derby County, loan, February 1995: permanent March 1995. Port Vale August 1995. Bradford City August 1998. Manchester City, loan, March 2000. Portsmouth August 2000. Coventry City, loan, November 2001: permanent January 2002. Stoke City, loan, January 2003: permanent February 2003. Telford United July 2003. Hereford United.*

**MILLS Samuel**
*Outside-right*
*Born: Derby, 1871.*
*Career: Derby Midland, Derby County June 1891. Leicester Fosse 1893. Loughborough Town 1894. Woolwich Arsenal June 1895. Heanor Town November 1896.*

**MINNEY George**
*Centre-forward*
*Career: Hertfordshire junior football. Derby County 1920.*

**MITCHELL Harry**
*Outside-right*
*Born: Barrow Hill, Staveley.*
*Career: Barrow Hill. Derby County May 1905.*

**MITCHELL James Donald**
*Goalkeeper*
*Born: Ilkeston, 1 July 1937.*
*Career: Horsley Woodhouse MW. Ilkeston Town 1955. Amateur, Derby County, May 1958: professional October 1958. Ilkeston Town June 1961. Matlock Town November 1965.*

**MONEY Richard**
*Central defender*
*Born: Lowestoft, 13 October 1955.*
*Career: Lowestoft Town. Scunthorpe United July 1973. Fulham December 1977. Liverpool May 1980. Derby County, loan, December 1981. Luton Town, loan, March 1982: permanent April 1982. Portsmouth August 1983. Scunthorpe United October 1985: acting manager February 1987: youth development officer. Youth coach, Aston Villa, September 1989. Manager, Scunthorpe United, January 1993 to March 1994. Coach, Nottingham Forest, June 1994. Assistant manager, Manchester City, January 1997. Head of Coventry City Academy, May 1998 to June 2002. Coach, AIK Stockholm, January 2003 to April 2004. Coach, Vasteras SK, May 2004. Manager, Newcastle Jets (Australia), October 2004. Manager, Walsall, May 2006.*

**MONKS Isaac**
*Centre-half*
*Career: Derby County 1887.*

**MOONEY Thomas John**
*Forward*
*Born: Billingham 11 August 1971.*
*Career: Trainee, Aston Villa: professional November 1989. Scarborough August 1990. Southend United July 1993. Watford, loan, March 1994: permanent July 1994. Birmingham City July 2001. Stoke City, loan, September 2002. Sheffield United, loan, January 2003. Derby County, loan, March 2003. Swindon Town July 2003. Oxford United July 2004. Wycombe Wanderers June 2005.*

**MOORE Darren Mark**
*Central defender*
*Born: Birmingham, 22 April 1974.*
*Career: Trainee, Torquay United: professional November 1992. Doncaster Rovers July 1995. Bradford City June 1997. Portsmouth November 1999. West Bromwich Albion September 2001. Derby County January 2006.*

**MOORE John**
*Forward*
*Born: Wellington, Shropshire.*
*Career: Burton United 1904. Derby County January 1905. Oldham Athletic September 1907. Watford July 1909.*

**MOORE John Leslie**
*Centre-half*
*Born: Sheffield, 7 July 1933. Died: Sheffield, 1992.*
*Career: Sheffield FC. Worksop Town August 1957. Derby County October 1957. Boston FC July 1965. Lincoln City October 1965.*

*Lockheed Leamington July 1967. Buxton August 1968: player-manager May to November 1970. Manager, Worksop Town, June 1972 to July 1973.*

**MOORE Ralph**
*Inside-forward*
*Born: Derby.*
*Career: Crewton United. Derby County June 1919.*

**MOORE William C.**
*Full-back*
*Career: Graham Street Prims. Derby County October 1906. Stockport County August 1909. Ilkeston United March 1911.*

**MORAN John**
*Inside-forward*
*Born: Cleland, 9 March 1933.*
*Career: Coltness United. Derby County November 1954. St Mirren August 1955.*

**MORELAND Victor**
*Defender/midfield*
*Born: Belfast, 15 June 1957.*
*Career: Glentoran. Tulsa Roughnecks, loan, March 1978. Derby County September 1978. Tulsa Roughnecks March 1980. Dallas Sidekicks. Wichita Wings.*

**MORLEY Haydn Arthur**
*Full-back*
*Born: Derby, 26 November 1860. Died: Hathersage, 15 May 1953.*
*Career: Derby Midland. Derby County 1884. Notts County 1886. Nottingham Forest September 1888. Derby County February 1889. Sheffield Wednesday 1889. Loughborough February 1892.*

**MORRIS Lee**
*Forward*
*Born: Driffield, 30 April 1980.*
*Career: Trainee, Sheffield United: professional December 1997. Derby County October 1999. Huddersfield Town, loan, March 2001. Leicester City February 2004. Yeovil Town August 2006.*

**MORRISON Angus Cameron**
*Forward*
*Born: Dingwall, 26 April 1924.*

*Died: Derby, 18 December 2002.*
*Career: Ross County. Derby County October 1944. Preston North End November 1948. Millwall October 1957. Player-manager, Nuneaton Borough, June 1958 to January 1961. Player-manager, Belper Town, April 1961 to April 1964. Coach, Ripley MW, September 1966: manager, August 1967. Manager, Belper Town, January 1970 to December 1973.*

**MORTON William Henry**
*Wing-half*
*Born: Ilkeston, 16 December 1896.*
*Career: West Hallam. Ilkeston St John's. War service. Ilkeston United August 1919. Derby County August 1920. Newcastle United September 1921. Lincoln City August 1922. Wigan Borough June 1923. Trainer, Ollerton Colliery, 1929.*

**MOSELEY Graham**
*Goalkeeper*
*Born: Urmston, 16 November 1953.*
*Career: Apprentice, Blackburn Rovers: professional September 1971. Derby County September 1971. Aston Villa, loan, August 1974. Walsall, loan, October 1977. Brighton & Hove Albion November 1977. Ipswich Town, loan, March 1984. Cardiff City August 1986.*

**MURRAY Adam David**
*Midfield*
*Born: Solihull, 30 September 1981.*
*Career: Trainee, Derby County: professional October 1998. Mansfield Town, loan, February 2002. Kidderminster Harriers, loan, August 2003. Solihull Borough November 2003. Burton Albion November 2003. Notts County November 2003. Kidderminster Harriers January 2004. Mansfield Town July 2004. Carlisle United March 2005.*

**MURRAY William**
*Inside-forward*
*Born: South Church, Bishop Auckland, 1898.*
*Career: Eildon Lane. Bishop Auckland 1919. Derby County August 1920. Middlesbrough July 1921. Heart of Midlothian June 1923. Dunfermline Athletic November 1934.*

**MYNARD Leslie Daniel**
*Wing-forward*
*Born: Bewdley, 19 December 1925.*
*Career: Bewdley. Amateur, Wolverhampton Wanderers, 1942–43: professional, May 1945. Derby County July 1949. Scunthorpe United August 1952. Worcester City July 1953. Halesowen 1954. Bromsgrove Rovers 1955. Kidderminster Harriers 1957.*

**NAPIER Charles Edward**
*Inside-forward*
*Born: Bainsford, Falkirk, 8 October 1910. Died: Falkirk, 5 September 1973.*

*Career: Alva Albion Rangers. Glasgow Celtic October 1928. Maryhill Hibernian, loan, 1928. Derby County June 1935. Sheffield Wednesday March 1938. Falkirk September 1945. Stenhousemuir September 1946. Scout, Luton Town, August 1948. Coach, Bonnybridge Juniors, January 1955.*
***Division One runners-up 1935–36.***

**NASH R.**
*Forward*
*Career: Derby County 1885.*

**NEAL Richard Marshall**
*Wing-forward*
*Born: Rotherham, 14 January 1906. Died: Fence, 26 December 1986.*
*Career: Dinnington Main. Amateur, Blackpool, January 1926: professional, February 1926. Derby County May 1931. Southampton February 1932. Bristol City May 1937. Accrington Stanley June 1938.*

**NEEDHAM George Wright**
*Wing-half*
*Born: Staveley, 28 April 1894. Died: Banbury, 30 March 1967.*
*Career: Luton Town. Staveley. Derby County August 1919. Gillingham July 1920. Northampton Town February 1924. Worksop Town.*

**NEEDHAM Thomas**
*Forward*
*Career: Derby County 1888.*

**NELSON Edward**
*Wing-half*
*Born: Bishop Auckland, 21 April 1907. Died: West Auckland, 1972.*
*Career: Crook Town. Derby County January 1927. Doncaster Rovers June 1928.*

**NELSON James**
*Outside-left*
*Career: Derby County 1890.*

**NEVE Edwin**
*Outside-left*
*Born: Prescot, 3 May 1885. Died: Prescot, August 1920.*
*Career: St Helens Recreational. Hull City May 1906. Derby County August 1912. Nottingham Forest July 1914. Chesterfield April 1916.*

**NEWBERY Peter John**
*Centre-forward*
*Born: Derby, 4 March 1938.*
*Career: Derby Boys. Amateur, Derby County, May 1953: professional, March 1955. Burton Albion July 1961. Lockheed Leamington July 1962. Derbyshire Amateurs 1964. Long Eaton United August to October 1966.*

**NICHOLAS William Joseph**
*Right-back*
*Born: Staines.*
*Career: Staines. Derby County April 1905. Swansea Town August 1912.*

**NICHOLSON Shane Michael**
*Left-back*
*Born: Newark, 3 June 1970.*

*Career: Trainee, Lincoln City: professional July 1988. Derby County April 1992. West Bromwich Albion, loan, February 1996: permanent March 1996. Chesterfield August 1998. Stockport County June 1999. Sheffield United July 2001. Tranmere Rovers July 2002. Chesterfield July 2004.*
***Division One promotion 1995–96.***

**NICHOLLS H.**
*Centre-half*
*Career: Derby County 1885.*

**NIELSON Norman Fred**
*Centre-half*
*Born: Johannesburg, 6 December 1928. Died: Derby, 20 January 2002.*

*Career: Arcadia Pretoria. Charlton Athletic July 1949. Derby County September 1951. Bury May 1954. Hull City April 1957. Corby Town July 1958. Gresley Rovers August 1959. Hinckley Athletic November 1959. Long Eaton United May 1960. Wilmorton 1966. Ripley MW July 1967.*

**NIMNI Avi**
*Midfield*
*Born: Tel Aviv, 26 April 1972.*
*Career: Maccabi Tel Aviv. Atletico Madrid 1997. Maccabi Tel Aviv August 1998. Derby County, loan, November 1999. Beitar Jerusalem November 2003. Maccabi Tel Aviv August 2005.*

**NYATANGA Lewin John**
*Central defender*
*Born: Burton upon Trent, 18*

*August 1988.*
*Career: Academy, Derby County: professional August 2005.*

**OAKDEN Harry**
*Outside-right*
*Born: Derby 1877.*
*Career: Alvaston and Boulton. Derby County November 1898. Distillery 1899. Brighton United cs 1900. Swindon Town September 1901.*

**OAKES Andrew Mark**
*Goalkeeper*
*Born: Northwich, 11 January 1977.*
*Career: Trainee, Burnley. Macclesfield Town August 1996. Winsford United August 1998. Hull City December 1998. Derby County June 1999. Port Vale, loan, August 1999. Bolton Wanderers, loan, August 2004. Walsall March 2005. Swansea City August 2006.*

**O'BRIEN Michael Terence**
*Centre-half*
*Born: Kilcock, 10 August 1893. Died: Uxbridge, 21 September 1940.*
*Career: Walker Celtic. Wallsend. Blyth Spartans. Newcastle East End. Glasgow Celtic. Brentford December 1914. Alloa Athletic March 1919. Norwich City August 1919. South Shields December 1919. Queen's Park Rangers May 1920. Leicester City March 1922. Hull City June 1924. Brooklyn Wanderers May 1926. Derby County December 1926. Walsall June 1928. Norwich City May 1929. Watford June 1931. Manager, Queen's Park Rangers, May 1933 to April 1935. Assistant manager, Brentford, November 1935. Manager, Ipswich Town, May 1936 to August 1937.*

**O'BRIEN Raymond Christopher**
*Left-back*
*Born: Dublin, 21 May 1951.*
*Career: Shelbourne. Manchester United May 1973. Notts County March 1974. Derby County, loan, September 1983. Boston United July 1984: caretaker manager, November 1985: manager, January 1986. Manager, Corby Town, November 1987. Manager, Arnold Town, August 1991 to January 1994.*

**OLIVER James Henry Kenneth**
*Centre-half*
*Born: Loughborough, 10 August 1924. Died: Derby, 13 May 1994.*
*Career: Brush Sports. Sunderland August 1946. Derby County September 1949. Exeter City January 1958.*
***Division Three North Champions 1956–57.***

**OLIVER Joseph Allen**
*Outside-left*
*Born: Blyth, 8 September 1924.*

*Career: Crofton CW. Derby County October 1946. Stockport County August 1950. Gateshead July 1954.*

**OLNEY Benjamin Albert**
*Goalkeeper*
*Born: Holborn, 30 March 1899.*
*Died: Derby, 23 September 1943.*
*Career: Fairleys Athletic. Aston Park Rangers. Stourbridge September 1920. Derby County*

*April 1921. Aston Villa December 1927. Bilston United July 1930: player-manager May 1931. Walsall August 1931. Shrewsbury Town August 1932. Moor Green.*
***Division Two promotion 1925–26.***

**O'NEIL Brian**
*Defender/midfield*
*Born: Paisley, 6 September 1972.*
*Career: Celtic BC. Glasgow Celtic November 1989. Porirua Viard United (New Zealand), loan, summer 1991. Nottingham Forest, loan, March 1997. Aberdeen July 1997. Vfl Wolfsburg July 1998. Derby County November 2000. Preston North End January 2003.*

**O'RIORDAN Donald Joseph**
*Defender/midfield*
*Born: Dublin, 14 May 1957.*
*Career: Apprentice, Derby County: professional July 1975. Doncaster Rovers, loan, January 1978. Tulsa Roughnecks February 1978. Preston North End October 1978. Tulsa Roughnecks, loan, May 1979. Carlisle United August 1983. Middlesbrough August 1985. Player-coach, Grimsby Town, August 1986: player/assistant-manager, July 1987. Notts County July 1988. Mansfield Town, loan, September 1989. Player-coach, Torquay United, February 1993: player-manager, May 1993 to October 1995. Player-coach, Scarborough, December 1995 to March 1996. Gloucester City 1996. Dorchester Town, loan, September 1996. Manager, Galway United, July 1997.*

**ORMONDROYD Ian**
*Forward*
*Born: Bradford, 22 September 1964.*
*Career: Manningham Mills. Thackley. Bradford City September 1985. Oldham Athletic, loan, March 1987. Aston Villa February 1989. Derby County, loan, September 1991: permanent December 1991. Leicester City March 1992. Hull City, loan, January 1995. Bradford City July 1995. Oldham Athletic September 1996. Scunthorpe United September 1997.*

**O'ROURKE John**
*Centre-forward*
*Career: Willington Athletic. Derby County January 1901.*

**OSGOOD Keith**
*Central defender*
*Born: Isleworth, 8 May 1955.*
*Career: Apprentice, Tottenham Hotspur: professional May 1972. Coventry City January 1978. Derby County October 1979. Orient December 1981. HJK Helsinki May 1984. Cambridge United November 1984. Burton Albion February 1986. Stapenhill March 1986. Orgryte May 1987.*

**OSMAN Leon**
*Midfield*
*Born: Billinge, 17 May 1981.*
*Career: Trainee, Everton: professional August 1998. Carlisle United, loan, October 2002. Derby County, loan, January 2004.*

**OSMAN Rex Charles Herbert**
*Wing-half*
*Born: Derby, 4 April 1932. Died: Ipswich, 9 June 2005.*
*Career: Juniors and Derby County office staff: professional, July 1949. Boston United July 1956. Ilkeston Town August 1957. Gresley Rovers September 1959: player-coach, November 1959.*

**OXFORD Kenneth**
*Goalkeeper*
*Born: Oldham, 14 November 1929.*
*Died: Nottingham, 6 August 1993.*
*Career: Ardwick LC. Manchester City November 1947. Derby County December 1948. Chesterfield June 1950. Norwich City July 1951. Derby County December 1957. Doncaster Rovers July 1964. Port Vale March 1965. Boston United November 1965 to June 1967: reserve-team coach, 1968.*

Boston FC October 1968: caretaker manager April 1969: manager May 1969: general manager, May 1970.

**PALMER Charles Anthony**
*Right-back*
*Born: Aylesbury, 10 July 1963.*
*Career: Apprentice, Watford: professional July 1981. Derby County July 1984. Hull City February 1987. Notts County, loan, February 1989: permanent March 1989. Walsall July 1994. Burton Albion July 1996. Moor Green, loan, December 1997. Assistant manager, Hinckley United.*
***Division Three promotion 1985–86.***

**PALMER Desmond Frederick**
*Forward*
*Born: Swansea, 23 September 1931.*
*Career: Juniors, Swansea Town: professional April 1950. Liverpool March 1959. Johannesburg Ramblers 1960. Derby County June 1961. Wellington Town July 1962. Slavia Melbourne 1963. Yugal, Sydney, 1964. Player-manager, Llanelli, 1965.*

**PARKER Paul Andrew**
*Right-back*
*Born: West Ham, 4 April 1964.*
*Career: Apprentice, Fulham: professional April 1982. Queen's Park Rangers June 1987. Manchester United August 1991. Derby County August 1996. Sheffield United November 1996. Fulham January 1997. Golden Club, Hong Kong, February 1997. Chelsea March 1997. Heybridge Swifts October 1997. Farnborough Town December 1997. Director of football, Ashford Town, January 1998. Assistant manager, Chelmsford City: manager June 2001 to May 2003.*

**PARKIN Albert Geoffrey**
*Centre-forward*
*Born: Mansfield, 11 April 1928.*
*Career: Juniors, Derby County: professional May 1946. Ilkeston Town November 1952.*

**PARKIN Frederick W.**
*Goalkeeper*
*Career: Folkestone Town. Derby County May 1936. Notts County 1939. Lincoln City August 1945. Scarborough cs 1946.*

**PARNELL Gresham Frederick**
*Outside-right*
*Born: Sutton-in-Ashfield, 1886.*
*Career: Skegby United. Pinxton. Derby County December 1903. Leeds City August 1905. Exeter City May 1908. Preston North End May 1909. Exeter City July 1910. Sutton Junction June 1912. Mansfield Town November 1913.*

**PARR Jack**
*Left-back*
*Born: Derby, 21 November 1920.*
*Died: Derby, 28 March 1985.*
*Career: Little Eaton St Peter's. Amateur, Derby County, December 1937: professional March 1938. Shrewsbury Town July 1953.*

*Gresley Rovers August 1956. Burton Albion June 1957. Gresley Rovers November 1957. Belper Town May 1958: player-coach May 1959.*

**PARRY Anthony John**
*Midfield*
*Born: Burton upon Trent, 8 September 1945.*
*Career: Amateur, Burton Albion 1963: professional May 1964. Hartlepools United November 1965. Derby County January 1972. Mansfield Town, loan, January 1974. Gresley Rovers August 1976. Local football. Gresley Rovers August 1981.*

**PATERSON Robert**
*Centre-half*
*Born: Glasgow.*
*Career: Clyde. Derby County October 1897. Coventry City.*
***FA Cup finalists 1898–99.***

**PATERSON William**
*Centre-forward*
*Born: Hill O'Beath, 5 March 1897.*
*Died: Cowdenbeath, 1970.*
*Career: Cowdenbeath 1914. Derby County January 1921. Cowdenbeath June 1924. Armadale, loan, 1925. Coventry City August 1925. Springfield 1926. Fall River 1926. New Bedford 1927. Providence 1928. New Bedford 1930. Brooklyn 1930. Fall River 1931.*

**PATON Thomas H.**
*Centre-forward*
*Born: Larkhall.*
*Career: Glasgow Rangers. Derby County May 1904. Sheffield United March 1906. St Mirren cs 1907.*

**PATRICK Roy**
*Right-back*
*Born: Overseal, 4 December 1935.*
*Died: Renfrew, 26 March 1998.*
*Career: Juniors, Derby County: professional December 1952. Nottingham Forest May 1959. Southampton June 1961. Exeter City March 1963. Burton Albion August 1965.*

**PATTERSON Mark**
*Defender*
*Born: Leeds, 13 September 1968.*
*Career: Trainee, Carlisle United: professional August 1986. Derby County November 1987. Plymouth Argyle July 1993. Gillingham October 1997. Dover Athletic December 2002.*

**PATTISON John William**
*Outside-left*
*Born: Durham, 10 April 1897.*
*Died: Bristol, 11 April 1970.*
*Career: Leadgate Park. Framwellgate Moor. Durham City January 1920. Newcastle United April 1920. Durham City November 1920. Derby County July 1921. Bristol Rovers September 1922. Leadgate Park June 1924. South Shields January 1925. Durham City August 1925. South Shields October 1925. Torquay United August 1926. Taunton United August 1928. Grays Thurrock United cs 1929. Dunston United September 1929. Amateur, Durham City, December 1929. Amateur, Bath City, 1930. Frenchay United December 1932. Glastonbury September 1933. Warminster Town November 1936*

**PAUL David Dryburgh**
*Goalkeeper*
*Born: Kircaldy, 19 February 1936.*
*Career: Juniors, Derby County: professional February 1953. Boston United July 1956. Matlock Town July 1961. Belper Town September 1963. Matlock Town September 1964. Crewton May 1967.*

**PAUL John**
*Wing-forward*
*Career: Hibernian. Derby County November 1894. Bristol Rovers May 1898.*
***Division One runners-up 1895–96.***

**PAYNE Frank Ernest**
*Goalkeeper*
*Born: Ipswich, 18 March 1926.*
*Died: Ipswich, January 2001.*
*Career: Ollerton Colliery. Derby County December 1947. Hull City August 1948. Lincoln City August 1949. Kippax Legionaires September 1950. Swillington Welfare July 1951. Farsley Celtic October 1956.*

**PEART John George**
*Centre-forward*
*Born: South Shields, 3 October 1888. Died: Paddington, 3 September 1948.*
*Career: South Shields Adelaide 1905. Sheffield United May 1907. Stoke June 1910. Newcastle United March 1912. Notts County February 1913. Birmingham November 1919. Derby County January 1920. Player-manager, Ebbw Vale, August 1920. Port Vale January 1922. Norwich City July 1922. Player-manager, Rochdale, March 1923: retired as player May 1924, manager to July 1930. Manager, Bradford City, July 1930 to March 1935. Manager, Fulham May 1935 until his death.*

**PEART Ronald**
*Centre-forward*
*Born: Brandon, 8 March 1920.*
*Died: 1999.*
*Career: Langley Moor. Hartlepools United September 1938. Derby County May 1939. York City June 1948. Spennymoor United 1949.*

**PEMBRIDGE Mark Anthony**
*Midfield*
*Born: Merthyr Tydfil, 29 November 1970.*

*Career: Trainee, Luton Town: professional July 1989. Derby County June 1992. Sheffield Wednesday July 1995. SL Benfica July 1998. Everton August 1999. Fulham September 2003.*

**PENNEY David Mark**
*Forward*
*Born: Wakefield, 17 August 1964.*
*Career: Pontefract Collieries. Derby County September 1985. Oxford United June 1989. Swansea City, loan, March 1991 and March 1994: permanent June 1994. Cardiff City July 1997. Doncaster Rovers August*

*1998: manager March 2002.*
***Division Two Champions 1986–87.***

**PESCHISOLIDO Paolo Pasquale**
*Forward*
*Born: Scarborough, Canada, 25 May 1971.*

*Career: Toronto Blizzard. Birmingham City November 1992. Stoke City August 1994. Birmingham City March 1996. West Bromwich Albion July 1996. Fulham October 1997. Queen's Park Rangers, loan, November 2000. Sheffield United, loan, January 2001. Norwich City, loan, March 2001. Sheffield United July 2001. Derby County March 2004.*

**PHILBIN John**
*Inside-forward*
*Born: Jarrow, 6 September 1913.*
*Died: Torbay, 1973.*
*Career: Washington Colliery. Derby County December 1933. Torquay United May 1936. Brighton & Hove Albion June 1938.*

**PHILLIPS Justin Lee**
*Centre-half*
*Born: Derby, 17 December 1971.*
*Career: Trainee, Derby County: professional July 1990. Cork City, loan, November 1993.*

**PICKERING Nicholas**
*Midfield*
*Born: Newcastle upon Tyne, 4 August 1963.*

*Career: Apprentice, Sunderland: professional August 1981. Coventry City January 1986. Derby County August 1988. Darlington October 1991. Burnley, loan and permanent, March 1993.*

**PITMAN Reuben John**
*Goalkeeper*
*Career: Derby County 1888.*

**PLACE Charles Arthur**
*Outside-left*
*Born: Ilkeston, 26 November 1937.*
*Career: Juniors, Derby County: professional November 1954. Ilkeston Town July 1956. Bourne Town November 1958. Stamford June 1959. Long Eaton United July 1960.*

**PLACKETT Henry**
*Forward*
*Born: Breaston, 1869.*
*Career: Long Eaton Midland. Derby County 1888. Nottingham Forest April 1889.*

**PLACKETT Lawrence**
*Forward*
*Born: Breaston, 1869.*
*Career: Long Eaton Alexandra. Derby County 1886. Nottingham Forest cs 1889.*

**PLACKETT Sydney**
*Left-half*
*Born: Sawley, 21 September 1898.*
*Died: Whitwick, near Coalville, May 1950.*
*Career: Sawley United Church. Service in World War One. Sawley Discharged Soldiers' Federation March 1919. Derby County January 1921. Notts County February 1927.*
***Division Two promotion 1925–26.***

**PLUMMER Calvin Anthony**
*Outside-right*
*Born: Nottingham, 14 February 1963.*
*Career: Apprentice, Nottingham Forest: professional February 1981. Chesterfield, loan, December 1982: permanent January 1983. Derby County August 1983. Barnsley March 1984. Amateur, Nottingham Forest, October 1986: contract, December 1986. Lahden Reipas (Finland) May 1987. Nottingham Forest October 1987. Derry City, loan, March 1988. Plymouth Argyle, loan, September 1988: permanent October 1988. Chesterfield July 1989. Gainsborough Trinity September 1991. Shepshed Albion July 1992. Corby Town January 1993. Nuneaton Borough July 1994. Birstall United September 1995. Grantham cs 1996. Arnold Town, loan, November 1996. Shepshed Dynamo July 1997. Kirby Muxloe November 1997.*

**POOLE Kevin**
*Goalkeeper*
*Born: Bromsgrove, 21 July 1963.*
*Career: Apprentice, Aston Villa:*

*professional June 1981. Northampton Town, loan, November 1984. Middlesbrough August 1987. Hartlepool United, loan, March 1991. Leicester City July 1991. Birmingham City August 1997. Bolton Wanderers October 2001. Player/coach, Derby County, July 2005.*

**POPPITT John**

*Right-back*

*Born: West Sleekburn, 20 January 1923.*

*Career: West Sleekburn. Derby County May 1945. Queen's Park Rangers September 1950. Chelmsford City July 1954. Burton Albion June 1955. Banbury Spencer May 1957. Corby Town June 1958. Long Eaton United January 1960. Player-coach, Matlock Town, May 1965 to May 1967.*

**POWELL Barry Ivor**

*Midfield*

*Born: Kenilworth, 29 January 1954.*

*Career: Apprentice, Wolverhampton Wanderers: professional January 1972. Portland Timbers April 1975. Coventry City September 1975. Derby County October 1979. Portland Timbers, temporary transfer, April 1981. Bulova, Hong Kong, August 1982. Burnley July 1984. Swansea City February 1985. South China FC, Hong Kong, July 1986. Wolverhampton Wanderers November 1986: youth coach, August 1987. Community officer, Coventry City, June 1991. Manager, Aberystwyth Town 1998 to 2001. Assistant manager, Hednesford Town, November 2001. Assistant manager, Stafford Rangers, August 2002. Manager, Hednesford Town, May 2003 to May 2004. Coach, Redditch United, 2004 to October 2005.*

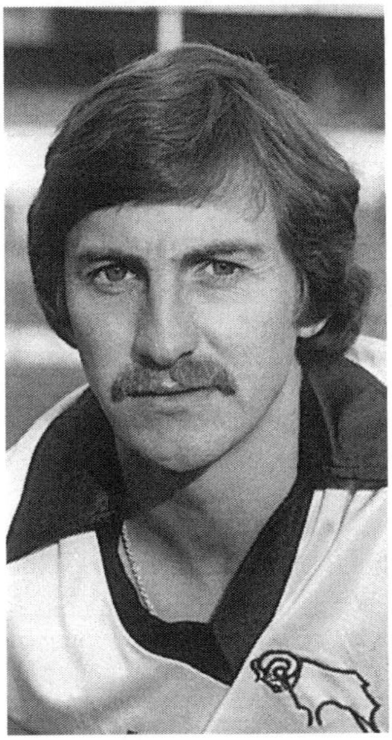

**POWELL Christopher George Robin**

*Left-back*

*Born: Lambeth, 8 September 1969.*

*Career: Trainee, Crystal Palace: professional December 1987. Aldershot, loan, January 1990. Southend United August 1990. Derby County January 1996. Charlton Athletic July 1998. West Ham United, loan, September 2004: permanent December 2004. Charlton Athletic July 2005. Watford July 2006.*

***Division One promotion 1995–96.***

**POWELL Kenneth**

*Outside-left*

*Born: Mansfield, 2 March 1920. Died: 1976.*

*Career: Mansfield CWS. Derby County May 1939. Southport June 1947.*

**PRATLEY Richard George**

*Centre-half*

*Born: Banbury, 12 January 1963.*

*Career: Banbury United. Derby County July 1983. Scunthorpe United, loan, March 1984. Shrewsbury Town February 1988: youth coach 1991.*

***Division Three promotion 1985–86. Division Two Champions 1986–87.***

**PREECE David William**

*Midfield*

*Born: Bridgnorth, 28 May 1963.*

*Career: Apprentice, Walsall: professional July 1980. Luton Town December 1984. Derby County August 1995. Birmingham City, loan, November 1995. Swindon Town, loan, March 1996. Cambridge United September 1996. Coach, Torquay United, August 2001 to April 2002: registered as player October 2001. Assistant manager, Telford United, May 2003 to May 2004.*

***Division One promotion 1995–96.***

**PRIOR Spencer Justin**

*Central defender*

*Born: Rochford, 22 April 1971.*

*Career: Trainee, Southend United: professional May 1989. Norwich City June 1993. Leicester City August 1996. Derby County August 1998. Manchester City March 2000. Cardiff City July 2001. Southend United August 2004.*

**PUMFORD George Leslie**

*Centre-forward*

*Born: Ruabon, 23 April 1902. Died: Heywood, 1972.*

*Career: Manchester North. Derby County January 1925. Walsall July 1926.*

**PYE Jesse**
*Centre-forward*
*Born: Treeton, 22 December 1919.*

*Died: Blackpool, 20 February 1984.*
*Career: Treeton. Sheffield United December 1938. Notts County August 1945. Wolverhampton Wanderers May 1946. Luton Town July 1952. Derby County October 1954. Wisbech Town July 1957: player-manager March 1960: manager to December 1966.*
***Division Three North Champions 1956–57.***

**PYNEGAR Algernon**
*Inside-forward*
*Born: Heanor, 1883. Died: Ilkeston, 23 June 1948.*
*Career: Marlpool. Derby County August 1904. Grimsby Town August 1905. Heanor United.*

**QUANTRILL Alfred Edward**
*Outside-left*
*Born: Punjab, 22 January 1897. Died: Trefriw, 19 April 1968.*
*Career: Boston Swifts. Derby County August 1914. Preston North End July 1921. Chorley August 1924. Bradford September 1924. Nottingham Forest May 1930.*
***Division Two Champions 1914–15.***

**QUY Andrew John**
*Goalkeeper*
*Born: Harlow, 4 July 1976.*
*Career: Trainee, Tottenham Hotspur. Derby County July 1994. Stalybridge Celtic, loan, September 1995. Grimsby Town October 1996. Stevenage Borough August 1997. Kettering Town September 1997. Hereford United October 1997. Halesowen Town August 2000. Belper Town June 2001.*

**RAHMBERG Marino**
*Forward*
*Born: Orebro, 7 August 1974.*
*Career: Forward Orebro. Lyngby, loan, 1995. Degerfors August 1995. Derby County, loan, January 1997. AIK Stockholm 1998. Raufoss IL (Norway) 1999. IFK Goteborg August 2002.*

**RAISBECK William**
*Wing-half*
*Born: Wallacetown, 1876.*
*Career: Larkhall Thistle. Hibernian July 1896. Clyde September 1896. Sunderland December 1896. Royal Albert September 1897. Clyde October 1897. Sunderland August 1898. Derby County May 1901. New Brompton July 1902. Reading June 1904.*

**RAMAGE Alan**
*Centre-half*
*Born: Guisborough, 29 November 1957.*

*Career: Apprentice, Middlesbrough: professional December 1975. Derby County July 1980.*

**RAMAGE Craig Darren**
*Midfield*
*Born: Derby, 30 March 1970.*
*Career: Trainee, Derby County: professional July 1988. Wigan Athletic, loan, February 1989. Watford February 1994. Peterborough United, loan, February 1997. Bradford City June 1997. Notts County August 1999.*

**RAMAGE Peter Martin Fairgrieve**
*Inside-left*
*Born: Bonnyrigg, 26 March 1908. Died: Ballyclare, 17 December 1982.*
*Career: Tranant Juniors. Newtongrange Star. Coventry City June 1927. Derby County August 1928. Chesterfield August 1937. Chelmsford City May 1939. Atherstone Town July 1945. Ilkeston Town September 1947 to October 1948.*
***Division One runners-up 1929–30, 1935–36.***

**RAMSELL Ernest Arthur**
*Wing-half*
*Born: Stanton, near Burton upon Trent 1883. Died: Newhall, 24 December 1954.*
*Career: Stanton. Derby County January 1906.*

**RANCE Charles Stanley**
*Centre-half*
*Born: Bow, 28 February 1889. Died: Chichester, 29 December 1966.*
*Career: Clapton 1904. Tottenham Hotspur July 1910. Derby County March 1921. Queen's Park Rangers September 1922. Coached in Holland. Secretary-manager, Guildford City, April 1925 to June 1927. Coach, Wood Green, May 1930.*

**RANDALL James**
*Outside-left*
*Born: Guide Post, Northumberland, 12 December 1904. Died: Northumberland, July 1995.*
*Career: Ashington Colliery Welfare. Sleekburn Albion. Bedlington United. Ashington June 1925. Bradford City October 1928. Derby County May 1930. Bristol City May 1935. Ashington July 1936.*

**RANSFORD James**
*Centre-forward*
*Born: Blackwell.*
*Career: Blackwell. Ripley Athletic February 1904. Blackwell 1905. Alfreton Town August 1906. Derby County September 1906. Alfreton Town cs 1907.*

**RASIAK Grzegorz**
*Centre-forward*
*Born: Szczecin, 12 January 1979.*
*Career: Olimpia Poznan. SKS13 Poznan. MSP Szamotuly. Warta Poznan. GKS Belchatow. Odra Wodzislaw. Dyskobolia Grodzisk Wilekopolski 2001. (AC Siena July 2004: never registered). Derby County September 2004. Tottenham Hotspur August 2005. Southampton, loan, February 2006: permanent May 2006.*

**RATCLIFFE Emor**
*Left-back*
*Born: Hyde, 1880.*
*Career: Loughborough Corinthians. Derby County May 1902. Middlesbrough March 1906.*

**RATCLIFFE Kevin**
*Central defender*
*Born: Mancot, 12 November 1960.*
*Career: Apprentice, Everton: professional November 1978. Dundee, loan, August 1992. Cardiff City January 1993. Nottingham Forest October 1993. Derby County January 1994. Player-coach, Chester City, July 1994: player-manager April 1995: retired as player July 1997: manager to August 1999. Manager, Shrewsbury Town, November 1999 to April 2003.*

**RAVANELLI Fabrizio**
*Forward*
*Born: Perugia, 11 December 1968.*
*Career: Perugia August 1986. Avellino August 1989. Casertana, loan, September 1989. Reggiana August 1990. Juventus August 1992. Middlesbrough August 1996. Olympique Marseille October 1997. Lazio January 2000. Derby County August 2001. Dundee September 2003. Perugia January 2004.*

**RAYBOULD Samuel**
*Outside-right*
*Born: Poolsbrook, 1875.*
*Career: Poolsbrook United. Staveley Colliery. Chesterfield Town (trial) February 1894. Ilkeston Town March 1894. Derby County April 1894. Ilkeston Town January 1895. Poolsbrook United October 1897. Ilkeston Town February 1898. Bolsover Colliery May 1899. New Brighton Tower October 1899. Liverpool January 1900. Sunderland May 1907. Woolwich Arsenal May 1908. Chesterfield Town September 1909. Sutton Town August 1911. Barlborough United cs 1913.*

**READER Richard**
*Outside-right*
*Born: Derby, 8 November 1890. Died: Miami, September 1974.*
*Career: Belper Town. Ripley Town and Athletic. Leicester Fosse October 1912. Ripley Town and Athletic January 1913. Derby County December 1913. Bristol City June 1914. Luton Town June 1922*

.

**REDFERN William Joseph**
*Inside-forward*
*Born: Connah's Quay, 15 October 1910. Died: Deeside, Flintshire, September 1988.*

*Career: Hollywell Arcadians 1931. Bangor City 1933. Newry Town. Luton Town July 1937. Derby County August 1939. Wrexham during World War Two.*

**REICH Marco**
*Midfield*
*Born: Meisenheim, 30 December 1977.*

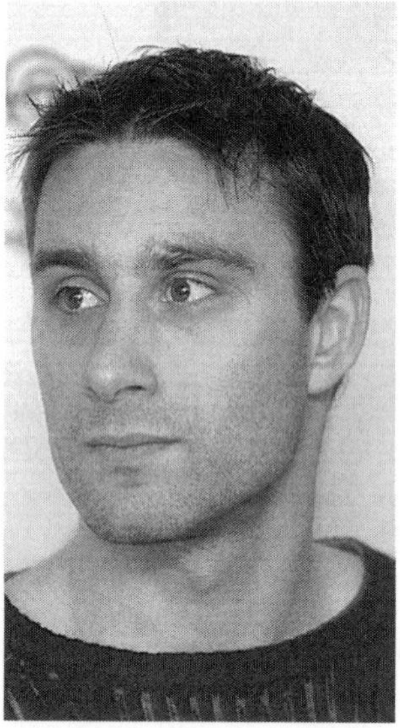

*Career: Viktoria Merxheim. Juniors, 1.FC Kaiserslautern: professional August 1996. 1.FC Koln July 2001. SV Werder Bremen June 2002. Derby County January 2004. Crystal Palace September 2005.*

**REID Anthony James**
*Midfield*
*Born: Nottingham, 9 May 1963.*
*Career: Apprentice, Derby County: professional May 1980. Scunthorpe United, loan, February 1983. Newport County March 1983. Chesterfield July 1985. Stafford Rangers December 1987. Burton Albion September 1988. Matlock Town October 1988. Stafford Rangers cs 1989. Sutton Town February 1990. Arnold Town February 1990.*

**REID Sidney Edward**
*Left-back*
*Born: Belfast, 20 June 1908.*
*Career: Cliftonville Strollers. Belfast Distillery. Derby County December 1929. Reading June 1936.*
***Division One runners-up 1935–36.***

**REVELL Charles**
*Defender*
*Born: Belvedere, 5 June 1919. Died: Sidcup, 11 December 1999.*
*Career: Callenders Athletic. Tottenham Hotspur January 1937. Northfleet July 1937. Charlton Athletic May 1939. Derby County March 1951. Player-manager, Eynesbury Rovers, June 1952. Manager, Edgware Town, July 1955. Player-coach, Canterbury City Reserves, August 1957. Manager, Erith and Belvedere, June 1958. Coach, Crystal Palace.*

**RHODES John Anthony**
*Centre-half*
*Born: Dover, 17 September 1946.*
*Career: Juniors, Derby County: professional October 1963. Halifax Town November 1970. Southport August 1976. Burton Albion September 1977.*

**RICHARDS Frederick**
*Inside-forward*
*Career: Burton Wanderers. Derby County December 1898. Sheffield Wednesday February 1899. Burton Wanderers August 1899. Woodville Excelsior. Trent Rovers January 1903.*

**RICHARDS John Peter**
*Centre-forward*
*Born: Warrington, 9 November 1950.*
*Career: Apprentice, Wolverhampton Wanderers: professional July 1969. Derby County, loan, November 1982. Maritimo Funchal*

*(Portugal) August 1983. Director, Wolverhampton Wanderers, December 1994: managing director November 1997 to June 2000.*

**RICHARDS Wayne**
*Left-back*
*Born: Scunthorpe, 10 May 1961.*
*Career: Normanby Parr Works, Scunthorpe. Apprentice, Derby County: professional May 1979. Matlock Town August 1982. Heanor Town November 1982.*

**RICHARDSON John**
*Right-back*
*Born: Worksop, 20 April 1945.*
*Career: Apprentice, Derby County: professional April 1962. Notts County July 1971. King's Lynn July 1973.*
***Division Two Champions 1968–69.***

**RICHARDSON Paul Andrew**
*Midfield*
*Born: Hucknall, 7 November 1962.*
*Career: Rolls-Royce, Hucknall. Eastwood Town February 1983. Nuneaton Borough August 1983. Derby County August 1984. Retired from League football on medical advice. Kettering Town August 1986. Eastwood Town, loan,*

October 1988. Boston United, loan, September 1990. Barnet October 1990. Boston United August 1991. Redbridge Forest November 1991. Kidderminster Harriers, loan, January 1993. Rushden and Diamonds August 1993.

**RICHMOND John Frederick**
*Wing-half*
*Born: Derby, 17 September 1938.*
*Career: Derby Boys. Derby Corinthians. Derby County January 1956. Chelmsford City June 1963.*

**RIDDELL Frank**
*Inside-forward*
*Career: Derby County 1908. Bristol Rovers 1909.*

**RIDDELL Frederick William**
*Inside-forward*
*Born: Newhall, 1887. Died: Nottingham, 16 October 1959.*
*Career: Newhall Swifts. Derby County May 1907. Watford August 1908. Norwich City May 1909.*

**RIGGOTT Christopher Mark**
*Centre-half*
*Born: Derby, 1 September 1980.*
*Career: Trainee, Derby County: professional October 1998. Middlesbrough, loan, January 2003: permanent May 2003.*

**RITCHIE Archibald**
*Left-back*
*Born: Stenhousemuir, 11 May 1894. Died: Guildford, 24 November 1973..*
*Career: Stenhousemuir. Dumbarton July 1914. Glasgow Rangers April 1919. Derby County June 1920. Player-manager, Guildford City July 1927.*
***Division Two promotion 1925–26.***

**RITCHIE Duncan**
*Outside-left*
*Career: Dumbarton. Raith Rovers cs 1911. Sheffield United November 1911. Derby County July 1913.*

**RITCHIE Paul Simon**
*Central defender*
*Born: Kirkaldy, 21 August 1975.*
*Career: Links United. Heart of Midlothian July 1992. Bolton Wanderers December 1999. Glasgow Rangers February 2000. Manchester City August 2000. Portsmouth, loan, September 2002. Derby County, loan, March 2003. Walsall August 2003. Dundee United July 2004.*

**RITCHIE William**
*Inside-right*
*Born: Carlisle, 1897. Died: Carlisle.*
*Career: Amateur, Derby County, August 1919: professional November 1919. Millwall May 1923. Ashington July 1924. Barrow June 1925. Montreal Scottish 1926. New Bedford 1926. J and P Coats 1927. Boston Bears 1928.*

**ROBERTS Edward**
*Inside-forward*
*Born: Chesterfield, 2 November 1916. Died: 1970.*
*Career: Glapwell Colliery. Derby County April 1934. Coventry City March 1937. King's Lynn August 1952. Banbury Spencer September 1952. Bedworth Town January 1954. Coach, Coventry City, July 1959 to November 1961.*
***Division One runners-up 1935–36.***

**ROBERTS William**
*Right-back*
*Died: Nottingham, c.1937.*

**ROBERTSON John Neilson**
*Outside-left*
*Born: Uddingston, 20 January 1953.*
*Career: Drumchapel Amateurs. Apprentice, Nottingham Forest:*

*professional May 1970. Derby County June 1983. Nottingham Forest August 1985. Corby Town August 1986. Stamford March 1987. Assistant manager, Grantham, August 1987. Assistant manager, Shepshed Charterhouse, June to September 1989. Manager, Grantham, February 1990 to March 1992. Scout, Wycombe Wanderers, January 1994. Chief scout, Norwich City, June 1995. Management staff, Leicester City, December 1995: assistant manager August 1996. Assistant manager, Glasgow Celtic, August 2000 to May 2005. Assistant manager, Aston Villa, August 2006.*

**ROBINSON Arnold**
*Outside-left*
*Career: Alfreton Town. Tibshelf Colliery. Derby County May 1909. Tibshelf Colliery September 1910.*

**ROBINSON Marvin Leon St Clair**
*Centre-forward*
*Born: Crewe, 11 April 1980.*
*Career: Trainee, Derby County: professional July 1998. Stoke City, loan, September 2000. Tranmere Rovers, loan, November 2002. Chesterfield September 2003. Notts County September 2004. Rushden and Diamonds November 2004. Walsall December 2004. Stockport County March 2005. Lincoln City August 2005. Macclesfield Town June 2006.*

**ROBINSON Thomas Charles**
*Wing-half*
*Born: Burton upon Trent, 2 October 1903. Died: Surrey.*
*Career: Derby County December 1926. Bury April 1930. Torquay United cs 1932.*
***Division One runners-up 1929–30.***

**ROBINSON William**
*Forward*
*Career: Walsall. Lincoln City May 1908. Walsall December 1908. Derby County May 1909. Walsall cs 1910.*

**ROBSON John Cecil**
*Outside-left*
*Born: Birtley, 24 March 1906. Died: Ashbourne, 20 October 1966.*
*Career: Birtley. Hull City April 1923. Reading August 1925. Derby County June 1928. Southend United June 1932. Chester August 1933. Rochdale November 1933. Oldham Athletic June 1934.*
***Division One runners-up 1929–30.***

**ROBSON James W.**
*Centre-half*
*Born: Cambois, 16 August 1900.*
*Career: Seaton Delaval. Derby County January 1922. Durham City September 1924.*

**ROBSON Norman**
*Inside-forward*
*Born: Ryton-on-Tyne, 1908.*
*Career: West Stanley. Preston North End June 1926. Derby County May 1930. Bradford City March 1933. Wigan Athletic September 1934.*

**ROBSON William**
*Left-back*
*Born: Castletown, 1906. Died: Oxford, 11 August 1960.*
*Career: Hylton Colliery. Derby County January 1927. West Ham United May 1933. Reading June 1934: coach 1938. Coach, Newbury Town, 1946. Assistant trainer, Reading, August 1948.*
***Division One runners-up 1929–30.***

**ROBY Donald**
*Outside-right*
*Born: Billinge, 15 November 1933.*
*Career: Juniors, Notts County: professional February 1951. Derby County August 1961. Burton Albion June 1965. Loughborough United July 1967.*

**ROSE Charles H.**
*Inside-forward*
*Born: Derby 1872*
*Career: Derby Midland. Derby County June 1891. Loughborough Town August 1895. Ilkeston United September 1904.*

**ROSE Walter**
*Wing-half*
*Born: Borrowash, 1870. Died: Draycott, February 1953.*
*Career: Derby Midland. Derby County June 1891. Loughborough Town 1893. Ilkeston Town June 1897. Ilkeston United September 1904.*

**ROULSTONE Frank**
*Left-back*
*Career: Sawley Rangers. Derby County.*

**ROULSTONE Walter**
*Left-back*
*Died: Castle Donington, 20 February 1953.*

*Career: Sawley Rangers. Derby County 1887. Heanor Town September 1895. Castle Donington Town October 1897. Heanor Town. Castle Donington Town December 1898.*

**ROUND Stephen John**
*Full-back*
*Born: Derby, 9 November 1970.*
*Career: Trainee, Derby County: professional July 1989. Nuneaton Borough March 1996. Coach, Derby County, March 1996. Coach, Middlesbrough, June 2001: assistant manager October 2005: head coach June 2006.*

**ROWE George William**
*Left-back*
*Born: Boosbeck, Cleveland, 1899.*
*Died: Derby, 8 November 1966.*
*Career: Loftus (Cleveland League). Hartlepools United December 1921. Derby County June 1923. Norwich City May 1927. Chesterfield September 1928. Chester January 1930.*
***Division Two promotion 1925–26.***

**ROWE Valentine Norman**
*Right-back*
*Born: Shouldham, 14 February 1926. Died: 1988.*
*Career: King's Lynn. Derby County December 1949. Walsall August 1952.*

**ROWETT Gary**
*Defender*
*Born: Bromsgrove, 6 March 1974.*
*Career: Trainee, Cambridge United: professional September 1991. Everton May 1994. Blackpool, loan, January 1995. Derby County July 1995. Birmingham City August 1998. Leicester City July 2000. Charlton Athletic May 2002. Burton Albion November 2005.*
***Division One promotion 1995–96.***

**RUDDY Thomas**
*Centre-forward*
*Born: Stockton-on-Tees, 1 March 1902. Died: Stockton-on-Tees, 11 November 1979.*
*Career: Stockton Shamrock. Amateur, Darlington, November 1921: professional, February 1922. Derby County May 1928. Chesterfield December 1931. Southampton September 1932. Spennymoor United July 1934. Linfield January 1935.*
***Division One runners-up 1929–30.***

**RUSSELL John**
*Inside-forward*
*Career: Derby County December 1898.*

**RUTHERFORD James B.**
*Inside-forward*
*Died: South Africa, June 1902.*
*Career: St Mirren. Derby County August 1898. Darwen January 1899.*

**RYAN Gerard Joseph**
*Outside-left*
*Born: Dublin, 4 October 1955.*
*Career: Bohemians. Derby County September 1977. Brighton & Hove Albion September 1978: assistant manager, January 1994 to November 1995: caretaker manager November 1995.*

**SAGE Melvyn**
*Right-back*
*Born: Gillingham, 24 March 1964.*
*Career: Apprentice, Gillingham: professional March 1982. Derby County August 1986.*
***Division Two Champions 1986–87.***

**SAUNDERS Samuel**
*Left-half*
*Career: Alfreton Town. Derby County April 1904. Sutton Town December 1909.*

**SAVIN Keith Anthony**
*Left-back*
*Born: Oxford, 5 June 1929. Died: Leicester, 18 December 1992.*
*Career: Oxford City. Derby County May 1950. Mansfield Town May 1957. Nuneaton Borough July 1959. Bourne Town March 1960. Nuneaton Borough.*

**SAWYER Thomas**
*Inside-forward*
*Career: Derby County August 1894. Macclesfield Town February 1895. Stockport County April 1896. Newton Heath November 1900.*

**SAXTON Robert**
*Centre-half*
*Born: Bagby, 6 September 1943.*
*Career: Denaby United. Derby County February 1962. Plymouth Argyle February 1968. Exeter City September 1975: player-manager, January 1977. Manager, Plymouth Argyle, January 1979. Manager, Blackburn Rovers, May 1981 to December 1986. Adviser, Preston North End, January 1987. Manager, York City, June 1987. Assistant manager, Blackpool, September 1988. Assistant manager, Newcastle United, December 1988 (caretaker manager March 1991) to April 1991. Chief scout, Manchester City, October 1991. Coach, Blackpool, July 1994 to April 1995. Coach, Sunderland, June 1995 to October 2002: assistant manager July 2006.*

**SCARBOROUGH Brian**
*Outside-left*
*Born: Ironville, 11 December 1941.*
*Career: Juniors, Derby County: professional January 1959. Burton Albion July 1961. Heanor Town June 1962. Bourne Town August 1963.*

**SCATTERGOOD Ernald Oak**
*Goalkeeper*
*Born: Riddings, 29 May 1887.*
*Died: Worksop, 2 July 1932.*
*Career: Riddings. Ripley Athletic February 1906. Derby County August 1907. Bradford October 1914. Alfreton Town cs 1925.*
***Division Two Champions 1911–12, 1914–15.***

**SCATTERGOOD Kenneth**
*Goalkeeper*
*Born: Riddings, 6 April 1912. Died: Chesterfield, June 1988.*
*Career: Wolverhampton Wanderers November 1931. Bristol City August 1933. Stoke City May 1934. Derby County July 1935.*

**SCHNOOR Stefan**
*Left-back*
*Born: Neumunster, 18 April 1971.*

*Career: Neumunster. Hamburger SV 1991. Derby County July 1998. Vfl Wolfsburg November 2000.*

**SCOTT Archibald Teasdale**
*Half-back*
*Born: Airdrie, 27 July 1905. Died: Gosport, 2 May 1990.*
*Career: Bellshill Athletic. Gartsherrie. Airdrieonians August 1925. Derby County April 1927. Brentford July 1934. Trainer, Reading, 1947.*
***Division One runners-up 1929–30.***

**SCOTT Kenneth**
*Outside-right*
*Born: Maltby, 13 August 1931.*
*Career: Denaby United. Derby County August 1950. Denaby United March 1952. Mansfield Town July 1952.*

**SEAL Christopher E.**
*Left-back*
*Career: Hyson Green. Derby County May 1905. Mansfield Woodhouse November 1908. Basford United 1910.*

**SELVEY Scotch**
*Wing-half*
*Born: Derby, 1 November 1863. Died: Derby, 19 March 1947.*
*Career: Derby St Luke's. Derby Midland. Derby County 1888.*

**SELVEY Walter**
*Inside-forward*
*Born: Derby.*
*Career: Derby Midland. Derby County 1888. Derby Junction.*

**SHANKS Thomas**
*Inside-left*
*Born: New Ross, County Wexford, 1880.*
*Career: Wexford. Derby West End. Derby County April 1898. Brentford October 1901. Woolwich Arsenal January 1903. Brentford May 1904. Leicester Fosse October 1906. Leyton cs 1909. Clapton Orient 1911. York City 1912.*

**SHARMAN Donald William**
*Goalkeeper*
*Born: Rothwell, 2 February 1932.*
*Career: Juniors, Derby County: professional February 1949. Ilkeston Town September 1951. Gresley Rovers June 1955. Bradford City June 1956. Burton Albion July 1958. Long Eaton United August 1959. Wilmorton and Alvaston. Long Eaton Reprobates. Loughborough United January 1996.*

**SHARPE Ivan Gordon**
*Outside-left*
*Born: St Albans, 15 June 1889. Died: Southport, 9 February 1968.*

*Career: St Albans Abbey. Watford October 1907. Glossop August 1908. Derby County October 1911. Leeds City June 1913. One match for Leeds United in 1920.*
***Division Two Champions 1911–12.***

**SHEPHERD George**
*Forward*
*Career: Rocester. Derby County September 1919.*

**SHERIDAN Frank Michael**
*Midfield/central defender*
*Born: Stepney, 9 December 1961.*
*Career: Apprentice, Derby County: professional July 1978. Torquay United June 1982. Teignmouth 1984.*

**SHINER Albert James**
*Centre-forward*
*Born: Isle of Wight, 1899. Died: Ryde, 19 April 1961.*
*Career: Seaview FC (Isle of Wight). Derby County September 1920.*

**SHIRTCLIFFE Edward**
*Outside-right*
*Career: Derby County October 1901. Ripley Town September 1902.*

**SHORT Jonathan Craig**
*Central defender*
*Born: Bridlington, 25 June 1968.*
*Career: Pickering Town. Scarborough October 1987. Notts County July 1989. Derby County September 1992. Everton July 1995. Blackburn Rovers August 1999. Sheffield United June 2005.*

**SIMS John**
*Forward*
*Born: Belper, 14 August 1952.*
*Career: Apprentice, Derby County: professional August 1970. Luton Town, loan, November 1973. Oxford United, loan, September 1974. Colchester United, loan, January 1975. Notts County December 1975. Exeter City December 1978. Plymouth Argyle October 1979. Torquay United August 1983. Exeter City February 1984. Player-coach, Torquay United, November 1984: manager, August to September 1985. Saltash United 1985. Player-manager, Waldon Athletic.*

**SKIVINGTON Glenn**
*Midfield*
*Born: Barrow, 19 January 1962.*
*Career: Barrow 1979. Derby County July 1980. Halifax Town, loan, March 1983. Southend United August 1983. Barrow March 1984.*

**SMITH Albert**
*Wing-half*
*Born: Nottingham, 23 July 1869.*
*Died: 18 April 1921.*
*Career: Notts Rangers. Long Eaton Rangers. Derby County 1884. Nottingham Forest February 1889. Notts County February 1890. Blackburn Rovers November 1891. Nottingham Forest 1892.*

**SMITH Frederick**
*Left-back*
*Born: Buxton.*
*Career: Buxton 1904. Stockport County September 1906. Derby County September 1909. Macclesfield Town 1910. Southampton May 1913.*

**SMITH Frederick Edward**
*Centre-forward*
*Born: Draycott, 7 May 1926.*
*Career: Draycott. Derby County June 1947. Sheffield United March 1948. Manchester City May 1952. Grimsby Town September 1952. Bradford City July 1954. Frickley Colliery December 1954.*

**SMITH Herbert**
*Left-back*
*Born: Witney, 22 November 1879.*
*Died: Oxford, 6 January 1951.*
*Career: Reading 1900 to 1909 as amateur. Also played for Oxford City, Witney, Richmond, Stoke, Derby County, Oxfordshire.*

**SMITH J.**
*Centre-half*
*Career: Derby County December 1888.*

**SMITH John William**
*Goalkeeper*
*Born: Beeston.*
*Career: Long Eaton St Helen's. Derby County November 1903. Newark Town March 1908. Nottingham Forest May 1909. Ilkeston United July 1911.*

**SMITH Joshua**
*Right-back*
*Born: Sutton upon Trent.*
*Career: Worksop North End. Sheffield United April 1907. South Shields cs 1913. Derby County August 1914. Division Two Champions 1914–15.*

**SMITH Michael John**
*Centre-half*
*Born: Quarndon, 22 September 1935.*
*Career: Juniors, Derby County: professional October 1952. Bradford City June 1961. Crewton Sports August 1967. Lockheed Leamington September 1967.*

**SMITH Sydney Joseph**
*Centre-forward*
*Born: Aston, Birmingham, 11 July 1895.*
*Career: Aston Manor. War Service. Aston Park Rangers. Stourbridge July 1920. Cradley Heath St Luke's March 1921. Derby County August 1921. Norwich City June 1923. Gillingham July 1924.*

**SMITH Thomas William**
*Midfield*
*Born: Hemel Hempstead, 22 May 1980.*

*Career: Trainee, Watford: professional October 1997. Sunderland September 2003. Derby County July 2004.*

**SMITH Valentine**
*Outside-right*
*Born: Sandiacre, 14 February 1903.*

*Career: Newark Town. Derby County October 1925. Newark Town cs 1927.*
***Division Two promotion 1925–26.***

**SOAR Thomas Albert**
*Outside-right*
*Born: Heanor, 20 May 1881.*
*Career: Heanor St Mary's. Nottingham Forest March 1900. Alfreton Town June 1900. Newark Town December 1901. Derby County January 1903. Fulham May 1903. Watford May 1906.*

**SOLIS Mauricio [Mauricio Solis Mora]**
*Midfield*
*Born: San Jose, Costa Rica, 13 December 1972.*
*Career: CS Herediano August 1995. Derby County March 1997. Comunicaciones, Guatemala cs 1998. San Jose Earthquakes June 1999. LD Alajuelense January 2000. OFI Iraklion June 2002. Irapuato 2004. Communicaciones 2005.*

**SPILSBURY Benjamin Ward**
*Inside-forward*
*Born: Findern, 1 August 1864.*
*Died: Vancouver, 15 August 1938.*
*Career: Cambridge University 1884 to 1887. Corinthians 1885 to 1888. Derby County 1884 to 1889.*

**SPOONER Stephen Alan**
*Midfield*
*Born: Sutton, London, 25 January 1961.*
*Career: Apprentice, Derby County: professional December 1978. Halifax Town, loan, December 1981: permanent February 1982. Chesterfield July 1983. Hereford United July 1986. York City July 1988. Rotherham United July 1990. Mansfield Town March 1991. Blackpool February 1993. Chesterfield October 1993. Rushden and Diamonds November 1994. Burton Albion June 1996. Coach, Rushden and Diamonds, October 2000 to March 2004. Manager, Notts County School of Excellence, May 2004.*

**SPRINGHTORPE James A.**
*Outside-right*
*Career: Draycott. Derby County October 1907. Draycott 1907.*

**STALEY Jonathon**
*Left-back*
*Born: Newhall, 1868.*
*Career: Derby Midland. Derby County June 1891. Ripley Athletic October 1901.*
***Division One runners-up 1895–96. FA Cup finalists 1898–99.***

**STALLARD Mark**
*Striker*
*Born: Derby, 24 October 1974.*
*Career: Trainee, Derby County: professional October 1991. Fulham, loan, September 1994. Bradford City, loan and permanent, January 1996. Preston North End, loan, February 1997. Wycombe Wanderers March 1997. Notts County March 1999. Barnsley January 2004. Chesterfield, loan, September 2004. Notts County, loan, February 2005. Shrewsbury Town July 2005. Lincoln City July 2006.*
***Division One promotion 1995–96.***

**STAPLETON Francis Anthony**
*Striker*
*Born: Dublin, 10 July 1956.*
*Career: St Martin's. Bolton Athletic (Dublin). Apprentice, Arsenal: professional September 1973. Manchester United August 1981. Ajax Amsterdam July 1987. Derby County, loan, March 1988. Le Havre AC October 1988. Blackburn Rovers July 1989. Aldershot September 1991. Player-coach, Huddersfield Town, October 1991. Player-manager, Bradford City, December 1991. Brighton & Hove Albion November 1994. Coach, Queen's Park Rangers, November 1994 to February 1995. Coach, New England Revolution, January to September 1996.*

**STEEL William Gilbert**
*Left-back*
*Born: Blantyre, 6 February 1908.*
*Career: Bridgton Waverley. St Johnstone September 1926. Liverpool September 1931. Birmingham March 1935. Derby County February 1939. Trainer, Airdrieonians, April 1950: manager April 1954. Manager, Third Lanark, January 1963 to June 1964.*

**STEELE Eric Graham**
*Goalkeeper*
*Born: Wallsend, 14 May 1954.*
*Career: Amateur, Newcastle United: professional, July 1972. Peterborough United, loan,*

*December 1973: permanent July 1974. Brighton & Hove Albion February 1977. Watford October 1979. Cardiff City, loan, March 1983. Derby County July 1984. Southend United July 1987.*

*Mansfield Town, loan, March 1988. Notts County October 1988. Wolverhampton Wanderers March 1989. Coach, Derby County, July 1992. Coach, Aston Villa, July 2001.*
***Division Three promotion 1985–86. Division Two Champions 1986–87.***

**STEPHENSON George Robert**
*Outside-right*
*Born: Derby, 19 November 1942.*
*Career: Derwent Sports. Juniors, Derby County: professional September 1960. Shrewsbury Town June 1964. Rochdale July 1965. Lockheed Leamington July 1967. Worcester City October 1967. Buxton August 1968.*

**STEPHENSON George Ternent**
*Inside-forward*
*Born: New Delaval, 3 September 1900. Died: Derby, 18 August 1971.*

*Career: New Delaval Villa. Leeds City August 1919. Aston Villa October 1919. Stourbridge, loan, August 1920 to May 1921. Derby County November 1927. Sheffield Wednesday February 1931. Preston North End July 1933. Charlton Athletic May 1934: chief scout 1939. Manager, Huddersfield Town, August 1947 to March 1952.*
***Division One runners-up 1929–30.***

**STEVENSON James**
*Inside-left*
*Born: Paisley, 1876. Killed in World War One.*
*Career: Clyde 1894. Derby County January 1895. Newcastle United October 1898. Bristol City cs 1900. Clyde cs 1901. Grimsby Town September 1901. Leicester Fosse January 1902. Clyde October 1902.*
***Division One runners-up 1895–96. FA Cup finalists 1897–98.***

**STEWART Arthur**
*Midfield*
*Born: Ballymena, 13 January 1942.*
*Career: Ballymena 1957. Glentoran August 1961. Derby County*

*December 1967. Ballymena August 1970: player-manager August 1971 to March 1976. New Jersey Americans April 1976. Bangor October 1976. Cliftonville January 1977. Manager, Glentoran, May 1977. Coach, New Jersey Americans, January 1979. Manager, Ballyclare Comrades, 1981.*
***Division Two Champions 1968–69.***

**STEWART F. Harry**
*Outside-left*
*Career: Dundee. Derby County March 1900. Blackburn Rovers September 1900.*

**STOCKILL Reginald Robert**
*Inside-forward*
*Born: York, 23 November 1913. Died: York, 24 December 1995.*
*Career: York City August 1929. Scarborough February 1931. Arsenal May 1931. Derby County September 1934. Luton Town August 1939.*
***Division One runners-up 1935–36.***

**STOKOE James**
*Inside-forward*
*Born: Jarrow, 12 July 1898. Died: South Shields, 1970.*
*Career: Jarrow. Swindon Town June 1920. Derby County August 1922. Durham City June 1923.*

**STORER William**
*Forward*
*Born: Butterley, 25 January 1867. Died: Derby, 28 February 1912.*
*Career: Derby Midland. Derby County June 1891. Loughborough Town August 1893. Glossop North End May 1895.*

**STREETE Floyd Anthony**
*Defender*
*Born: Lionell Town, Clarendon, Jamaica, 5 May 1959.*

*Career: Rivet Sports. Cambridge United July 1976. FC Utrecht cs 1983. SC Cambuur 1983–84. Derby County September 1984. Wolverhampton Wanders October 1985. Reading July 1990. Leighton Town 1992.*
***Division Three promotion 1985–86.***

**STRUPAR Branko**
*Forward*
*Born: Zagreb, 9 February 1970.*
*Career: Spansko Zagreb. KRC Genk August 1994. Derby County December 1999. Dinamo Zagreb October 2003.*

**STURRIDGE Dean Constantine**
*Forward*
*Born: Birmingham, 27 July 1973.*
*Career: Trainee, Derby County: professional July 1991. Torquay*

*United, loan, December 1994. Leicester City January 2001. Wolverhampton Wanderers, loan, November 2001: permanent December 2001. Sheffield United, loan, January 2004. Queen's Park Rangers March 2005. Kidderminster Harriers June 2006.*
***Division One promotion 1995–96.***

**SUGG Frank Howe**
*Centre-forward*
*Born: Ilkeston, 11 January 1862.*
*Died: Liverpool, 29 May 1933.*
*Career: Derby County 1884. Burnley 1886. Everton 1888. Burnley 1889.*

**SUMMERS John Lawrence**
*Outside-right*
*Born: Chorlton, 8 February 1915.*
*Died: Southampton, 12 April 1991.*
*Career: Manchester North End 1931. Burnley February 1932. Fleetwood, loan, 1932. Preston North End 1932. Tunbridge Wells Rangers June 1933. Leicester City May 1934. Derby County May 1935. Southampton October 1936.*
***Division One runners-up 1935–36.***

**SUTTON Stephen John**
*Goalkeeper*
*Born: Hartington, 16 April 1961.*
*Career: Apprentice, Nottingham Forest: professional April 1979. Mansfield Town, loan, March 1981. Derby County, loan, January 1985. Coventry City, loan, February 1991. Luton Town, loan, November 1991. Derby County March 1992. Reading, loan, January 1996. Birmingham City August 1996. Notts County 1997. Grantham Town November 1997.*
***Division One promotion 1995–96.***

**SUTTON Wayne Frank**
*Midfield*
*Born: Derby, 1 October 1975.*
*Career: Trainee, Derby County: professional October 1992. Hereford United, loan, September 1996. Woking October 1997. Burton Albion November 1998. Hinckley United September 1999. Mickleover Sports August 2000.*
***Division One promotion 1995–96.***

**SVENSSON Mathias**
*Forward*
*Born: Boras, 24 September 1974.*
*Career: IF Elfsborg. Portsmouth December 1996. Tirol Innsbruck July 1998. Crystal Palace September 1998. Charlton Athletic January 2000. Derby County, loan, August 2003. Norwich City December 2003. IF Elfsborg June 2005.*

**SWALLOW Raymond**
*Forward*
*Born: Southwark, 15 June 1935.*
*Career: Tooting and Mitcham United. Juniors, Arsenal; professional December 1952. Derby County September 1958. Poole Town August 1964.*

**SWINDLEHURST David**
*Striker/midfield*
*Born: Edgware, 6 January 1956.*
*Career: Apprentice, Crystal Palace: professional January 1973. Derby County, loan, February 1980: permanent April 1980. West Ham United March 1983. Sunderland August 1985. Anorthosis (Cyprus) July 1987. Wimbledon March 1988. Colchester United June 1988. Peterborough United, loan, December 1988. Manager, Bromley, June 1989 to January 1990, remaining as a*

*director. Manager, Haywards Heath, 1991. Assistant manager, Crawley Town, August 2003 to September 2005.*

**SYLVESTER Thomas**
*Right-back*
*Career: Derby County October 1907. Mansfield Town September 1910.*

**TAFT Douglas**
*Centre-forward*
*Born: Leicester, 9 March 1926. Died: Derby, 29 September 1987.*
*Career: Army football. Derby County November 1947. Wolverhampton Wanderers July 1949. Chelmsford City August 1950. Bedford Town May 1952. Peterborough United June 1953. Kettering Town June 1955. Rugby Town July 1956. Player-manager, Hinckley Athletic, June 1957. Long Eaton United February 1959.*

**TALBOT Jason Christopher**
*Left-back*
*Born: Irlam, 30 September 1985.*
*Career: Academy, Bolton Wanderers: professional September 2004. Derby County, loan, September 2004. Mansfield Town, loan, November 2004. Mansfield Town June 2005. Port Vale, loan, January 2006: permanent May 2006.*

**TATE Geoffrey Michael**
*Outside-right*
*Born: Leicester, 16 December 1937.*
*Career: Juniors, Derby County. Juniors, Leicester City. Professional, Derby County, August 1955. Rugby Town July 1958. Burton Albion June 1961. Loughborough United November 1961.*

**TAYLOR Ian Kenneth**
*Midfield*
*Born: Birmingham, 4 June 1968.*
*Career: Moor Green August 1991.*

*Port Vale July 1992. Sheffield Wednesday July 1994. Aston Villa December 1994. Derby County July 2003. Northampton Town July 2005.*

**TAYLOR Kevin**
*Midfield*
*Born: Wakefield, 22 January 1961.*
*Career: Apprentice, Sheffield Wednesday: professional October 1978. Derby County July 1984. Crystal Palace March 1985. Scunthorpe United October 1987. Frickley Athletic 1991. Farsley Celtic. Pontefract Collieries.*

**TAYLOR Martin James**
*Goalkeeper*
*Born: Tamworth, 9 December 1966.*
*Career: Mile Oak Rovers. Derby County July 1986. Carlisle United, loan, September 1987. Scunthorpe United, loan, December 1987. Crewe Alexandra, loan, September 1996. Wycombe Wanderers, loan, March 1997. Wycombe Wanderers June 1997. Barnsley, loan, March 2003. Coach, Telford United, July 2003 to May 2004. Player-coach, Burton Albion, July 2004.*

**TAYLOR Robert Craig**
*Outside-left*
*Born: 4 January 1897.*
*Career: Seaton Delaval. Derby County January 1922.*

**THIRLWELL Paul**
*Midfield*
*Born: Washington, 13 February 1979.*

*Trainee, Sunderland: professional April 1997. Swindon Town, loan, September 1999. Sheffield United July 2004. Derby County, loan and permanent, August 2005.*

**THOMAS Andrew Mark**
*Forward*
*Born: Oxford, 16 December 1962.*
*Career: Apprentice, Oxford United: professional December 1980. Fulham, loan, December 1982. Derby County, loan, March 1983. Newcastle United September 1986. Bradford City June 1988. Plymouth Argyle July 1989. Thame United 1992. Oxford City cs 1993: manager to 1996. Manager, Chesham United, 1997.*

**THOMAS Edward**
*Forward*
*Born: Newton-le-Willows, 23 October 1933. Died: Derby, 12 November 2003.*
*Career: Juniors, Everton: professional October 1951. Blackburn Rovers February 1960. Swansea*

*Town July 1962. Derby County August 1964. Orient September 1967. Nuneaton Borough, loan, February 1968. Heanor Town August 1968.*

### THOMAS Michael Reginald

*Midfield*

*Born: Mochdre, 7 July 1954.*

*Career: Amateur, Wrexham: apprentice: professional May 1972. Manchester United November 1978. Everton August 1981. Brighton & Hove Albion November 1981. Stoke City August 1982. Chelsea January 1984. West Bromwich Albion September 1985. Derby County, loan, March 1986. Wichita Wings August 1986. Shrewsbury Town August 1988. Leeds United June 1989. Stoke City, loan, March 1990. Stoke City August 1990. Wrexham July 1991. Conway United July to August 1993. Inter Cardiff August 1994. Porthmadog, caretaker manager, January 1995. Director of football, Rhyl, 2000.*

***Division Three promotion 1985–86.***

### THOME Emerson Augusto

*Central defender*

*Born: Porto Alegre, Brazil, 30 March 1972.*

*Career: SL Benfica. Sheffield Wednesday March 1998. Chelsea December 1999, Sunderland September 2000. Bolton Wanderers August 2003. Wigan Athletic August 2004. Derby County, loan, October 2005.*

### THOMPSON Cyril Alfred

*Centre-forward*

*Born: Southend, 18 December 1918. Died: Folkestone, 5 April 1972.*

*Career: Southend United July 1945. Derby County July 1948. Brighton & Hove Albion March 1950. Watford March 1951. Folkestone Town July 1953: later trainer.*

### THOMPSON George Alexander

*Outside-right*

*Born: South Shields, 23 March 1883.*

*Career: South Shields Bertram 1904–05. South Shields Adelaide 1905. North Shields. Sheffield United October 1906. Derby County September 1908. Newcastle United 1911. Manager, Luton Town, February to October 1925.*

### THOMPSON George Harry

*Inside-forward*

*Career: Ticknall. Derby County December 1920.*

### THOMPSON James

*Wing-half*

*Career: Derby County February 1898.*

### THOMPSON Peter

*Centre-forward*

*Born: Blackhall, 16 February 1936.*

*Career: Blackhall CW. Amateur, Wrexham, November 1955. Professional, Hartlepools United, July 1957. Derby County November 1958. Bournemouth and Boscombe Athletic January 1962. Hartlepools United September 1963. Boston United August 1966.*

### THOMS Harry James

*Centre-half*

*Born: Stockton, 19 November 1896.*

*Died: Newcastle upon Tyne, December 1970.*

*Career: Greatham. Service in World War One. Amateur, Hartlepools United, December 1919: professional January 1920. Derby County August 1922. Crystal Palace May 1928. Glentoran February 1930.*

***Division Two promotion 1925–26 (captain).***

### TINKLER Alfred

*Inside-forward*

*Born: Manchester, 1887. Died: Croydon, 1950.*

*Career: Derby County January 1909. Heanor United 1910. Ilkeston United May 1911. Birmingham December 1911. Burton United 1915.*

### TODD Thomas Bell

*Centre-forward*

*Born: Stonehouse, 1 June 1926.*

*Career: Burnbank Athletic. Motherwell 1944. Airdrieonians. Stonehouse Violet. Hamilton Academical January 1951. Crewe Alexandra August 1955. Derby County November 1955. Rochdale May 1956.*

### TOOTLE James

*Full-back*

*Born: Skelmersdale, 22 April 1899. Died: Westhead, 18 November 1947.*

*Career: Skelmersdale United. Southport May 1922. Derby County December 1924. Chester. Skelmersdale United.*

***Division Two promotion 1925–26.***

### TOWIE Thomas

*Wing-forward*

*Career: Dumbarton Union. Preston North End August 1891. Renton. Glasgow Celtic, loan, October 1892. Derby County August 1893. Renton August 1995. Rossendale January 1896.*

**TOWNSEND William**
*Goalkeeper*
*Born: Bedworth, 27 December 1922. Died: Thornton Cleveleys, 21 December 1988.*
*Career: Nuneaton Borough. Amateur, Derby County May 1939: professional September 1942. Burton Albion July 1953. Banbury Spencer June 1957. Burton Albion September 1959: player-manager, October 1959: secretary-manager, May to October 1962.*

**TRAVIS Henry**
*Centre-forward*
*Born: Manchester, 26 December 1911.*
*Career: Manchester City October 1931. Oldham Athletic June 1932. Accrington Stanley July 1933. Leeds United June 1934. Bradford City June 1935. Derby County February 1937. Tranmere Rovers November 1938. Kidderminster Harriers July 1939.*

**TREMELLING Elijah Solomon**
*Centre-forward*
*Born: Newhall, 1885.*
*Career: Newhall Swifts. Derby County November 1905. Burton United 1909. Ilkeston United November 1909. Gresley Rovers 1911. Bradford City March 1913. Mansfield Town 1915. Gresley Rovers cs 1921.*

**TROLLOPE Paul Jonathan**
*Midfield*
*Born: Swindon, 3 June 1972.*
*Career: Trainee, Swindon Town: professional December 1989. Torquay United, loan, March 1992: permanent July 1992. Derby County, loan, December 1994: permanent January 1995. Grimsby Town, loan, August 1996. Crystal Palace, loan, October 1996. Fulham November 1997. Coventry City*

*March 2002. Northampton Town July 2002. Bristol Rovers July 2004: player-coach August 2005: acting manager September 2005: chief coach November 2005.*
***Division One promotion 1995–96.***

**TRUEMAN Ronald**
*Outside-right*
*Career: Macclesfield Town. Derby County May 1908. Sutton Town May 1910. Macclesfield Town 1911. Sutton Town July 1912.*

**TUDGAY Marcus**
*Forward*
*Born: Shoreham, 3 February 1983.*
*Career: Trainee, Derby County: professional July 2002. Sheffield Wednesday, loan and permanent, January 2006.*

**TURNER Arthur Dowcra**
*Outside-right*
*Born: Farnborough, June 1877. Died: Farnborough, 4 April 1925.*
*Career: Aldershot North End 1892. South Farnborough. Camberley St Michael's. Southampton May 1899. Derby County May 1902. Newcastle United January 1903. Tottenham Hotspur February 1904. Southampton May 1904. Bristol City, one match loan, February 1905.*

**TURNER James Albert**
*Left-half*
*Born: Black Bull, Staffordshire 1866. Died: Stoke, 9 April 1904.*
*Career: Black Lane, Radcliffe. Bolton Wanderers July 1888. Stoke September 1894. Derby County June 1896. Stoke August 1898.*
***FA Cup finalists 1897–98.***

**TWIGG Gary**
*Forward*
*Born: Glasgow, 19 March 1984.*
*Career: Trainee, Derby County: professional March 2001. Burton Albion, loan, September 2003. Bristol Rovers, loan, March 2004. Airdrie United July 2005.*

**UDALL William Edward Gisbourne**
*Right-back*
*Born: Atherstone, 28 May 1910. Died: Tamworth, 3 January 1978.*
*Career: Atherstone Town. Leicester City November 1931. Derby County May 1934. Manager, Atherstone Town, July 1945.*
***Division One runners-up 1935–36.***

**VALAKARI Simo Johannes**
*Midfield*
*Born: Helsinki, 28 April 1973.*
*Career: Kaba. FinnPa April 1995. Motherwell February 1997. Derby County July 2000. Dallas Burn March 2004.*

**VANN Bernard William**
*Centre-forward*
*Born: Rushden, 9 July 1887. Died:*

*Ramicourt, Belgium, 3 October 1918.*
*Career: Northampton Town 1905. Burton United February 1907. Derby County March 1907. Leicester Fosse June 1907.*

**VARNEY Herbert**
*Outside-right*
*Born: Belper, 2 February 1885. Died: 1952.*
*Career: Belper Town. Derby County April 1902. Belper Town cs 1903. West Bromwich Albion October 1905. Mansfield Mechanics August 1906. Belper Town May 1907.*

**VINCENT Jamie Roy**
*Left-back*
*Born: Wimbledon, 18 June 1975.*
*Career: Trainee, Crystal Palace:*

*professional July 1993. AFC Bournemouth, loan, November 1994. AFC Bournemouth August 1996. Huddersfield Town March 1999. Portsmouth February 2001. Walsall, loan, October 2003. Derby County January 2004. Millwall, loan, August 2005. Yeovil Town January 2006. Millwall, loan, March 2006. Swindon Town July 2006.*

**WALKER Colin**
*Wing-half*
*Born: Long Eaton, 7 July 1929.*
*Career: Juniors, Derby County: professional October 1946. Gresley Rovers February 1955.*

**WALKER James Henry**
*Wing-half*
*Born: Wirksworth, 1890. Died: West Bromwich, 14 April 1934.*
*Career: Clay Cross. Derby County May 1910. Notts County June 1920. Fulham March 1921. Aberdare Athletic May 1923. Bournemouth and Boscombe Athletic March 1924. Chesterfield June 1924. Amateur, Derby County, May 1925.*
***Division Two Champions 1911–12, 1914–15.***

**WALKER James McIntyre**
*Midfield*
*Born: Northwich, 10 June 1947.*
*Career: Northwich Victoria. Derby County February 1968. Hartlepool, loan, March 1970. Brighton & Hove Albion September 1974. Peterborough United, loan, October 1975: permanent February 1976. Chester November 1976. Coach, Al-Arabi 1983. Physiotherapist, Blackburn Rovers 1985. Physiotherapist, Aston Villa July 1987 to November 2003. Assistant manager, Walsall, June 2004 to February 2005.*
***Division Two Champions 1968–69. Division One Champions 1971–72.***

**WALKER John Allsop**
*Half-back*
*Born: Plumtree, 30 November 1871.*
*Career: Oxford Universeity. Derby Junction. Derby County 1889 Notts County October 1891.*

**WALLACE John Martin**
*Goalkeeper*
*Born: Deantown, 13 April 1911. Died: 1978.*
*Career: Wallyford Bluebell. Raith Rovers December 1930. Blackpool February 1934. Derby County February 1948. Leith Athletic August 1948.*

**WALLER Philip**
*Wing-half*
*Born: Leeds, 12 April 1943.*
*Career: Juniors, Derby County: professional May 1961. Mansfield Town March 1968. Player-manager, Ilkeston Town, June 1972.*

*Boston United January 1973. Matlock Town August 1974. Burton Albion October 1974. Player-coach, Belper Town, July 1975 to September 1976. Kimberley Town November 1976. Manager, Burton Albion, March 1977 to November 1978.*

**WALLINGTON Francis Mark**
*Goalkeeper*
*Born: Sleaford, 17 September 1952.*
*Career: Walsall October 1971. Leicester City March 1972. Derby County July 1985 Lincoln City*

*August 1988: player-coach July 1990. Assistant manager, Grantham Town, January 1995.*
***Division Three promotion 1985–86. Division Two Champions 1986–87.***

**WALSH Wilfred**
*Outside-right*
*Born: Pentelottyn, 29 July 1917. Died: Hednesford, 23 December 1977.*
*Career: Amateur, Arsenal, May 1935: professional May 1936. Margate (Arsenal nursery) May 1936. Derby County June 1939. Walsall March 1947. Hednesford Town cs 1948. Player-manager, Redditch Town, 1949. Player-manager, Hednesford Town, 1952: manager August 1955.*

**WALTON David Lee**
*Central defender*
*Born: Bedlington, 10 April 1973.*
*Career: Ashington. Sheffield United March 1992. Shrewsbury Town November 1993. Crewe Alexandra October 1997. Derby County July 2003. Stockport County, loan, February 2004. Shrewsbury Town August 2004.*

**WALTON Gordon**
*Right-back*
*Career: Sevenoaks. Derby County April 1906.*

**WALTON John**
*Left-half*
*Born: Chester-le-Street.*
*Career: West Stanley. Derby County November 1920. Walsall August 1922.*

**WANCHOPE Paulo [Paulo Cesar Wanchope Watson]**
*Centre-forward*
*Born: Heredia, 31 July 1976.*
*Career: CS Herediano August 1995. Derby County March 1997. West Ham United July 1999. Manchester City August 2000. Malaga CF August 2004. Al Gharafa (Qatar) July 2005. CS Herediano January 2006. Rosario Central July 2006.*

**WARD Ashley Stewart**
*Centre-forward*
*Born: Manchester, 24 November 1970.*
*Career: Trainee, Manchester City: professional August 1989. Wrexham, loan, January 1991. Leicester City July 1991. Blackpool, loan, November 1992. Crewe Alexandra December 1992. Norwich City December 1994. Derby County March 1996. Barnsley September 1997. Blackburn Rovers December 1998. Bradford City August 2000. Sheffield United August 2003.*
***Division One promotion 1995–96.***

**WARD Charles**
*Outside-left*
*Career: Derby Midland. Derby County 1884.*

**WARMBY Harry**
*Half-back*
*Career: Derby St Luke's. Derby County 1884.*

**WARREN Arnold R.**
*Outside-right*
*Born: Codnor, 2 April 1875. Died: Codnor, 3 September 1951.*
*Career: Heanor Town May 1895. Ripley Athletic. Glossop November 1899. Ripley Town December 1899. Derby County November 1901. Brentford July 1902. Ripley Town April 1903.*

**WARRINGTON Joseph**
*Forward*
*Born: Macclesfield.*
*Career: Derby Wanderers. Derby County April 1901. Brentford May 1904. Portsmouth May 1905. New Brompton May 1906. Macclesfield Town April 1907. Chesterfield Town October 1907.*
***FA Cup finalists 1902–03.***

**WASSALL Darren Paul James**
*Centre-half*
*Born: Edgbaston, 27 June 1968.*
*Career: Apprentice, Nottingham Forest: professional June 1986. Hereford United, loan, October 1987. Bury, loan, March 1989. Derby County June 1992. Manchester City, loan, September 1996. Birmingham City, loan, March 1997: permanent May 1997. Burton Albion August 2000.*
***Division One promotion 1995–96.***

**WATERHOUSE Frank**
*Right-half*
*Born: Oldbury, July 1889. Died: Smethwick, 1967.*
*Career: Langley St Michael's. Langley St Michael's Guild.*

*Langley Green. Wednesbury Old Athletic. West Bromwich Albion February 1908. Derby County March 1920. Dudley Town.*

**WATSON Alexander Francis**
*Centre-half*
*Born: Liverpool, 5 April 1968.*
*Career: Apprentice Liverpool: professional May 1985. Derby County, loan, August 1990. AFC Bournemouth January 1991. Gillingham, loan, September 1995. Torquay United November 1995: player-coach. Exeter City July 2001.*

**WATSON David Vernon**
*Centre-half*
*Born: Stapleford, 5 October 1946.*
*Career: Stapleford Old Boys. Notts County January 1967. Rotherham United January 1968. Sunderland December 1970. Manchester City June 1975. SV Werder Bremen June 1979. Southampton October 1979. Stoke City January 1982. Vancouver Whitecaps April 1983. Derby County September 1983. Fort Lauderdale Sun May 1984. Player-coach, Notts County, September 1984. Kettering Town August 1985.*

**WAUGH Robert**
*Left-back*
*Born: Newcastle upon Tyne.*
*Career: Newcastle Bentonians. Newcastle United January 1908. Derby County August 1912. Jarrow September 1919.*
***Division Two Champions 1914–15.***

**WEBB David James**
*Central defender*
*Born: East Ham, 9 April 1946.*
*Career: Amateur, West Ham United. Leyton Orient May 1963. Southampton March 1966. Chelsea February 1968. Queen's Park Rangers July 1974. Leicester City September 1977. Derby County*

*December 1978. Player-coach, AFC Bournemouth, May 1980: manager, December 1980 to December 1982. Manager, Torquay United, February 1984 to August 1985: managing director to June 1986. Manager, Southend United, June 1986 to March 1987: general manager, December 1988 to May 1992. Manager, Chelsea, February 1993. Manager, Brentford, May 1993: chief executive August to November 1997. Manager, Yeovil Town, March 2000. Manager, Southend United, October 2000 to October 2001: caretaker manager November 2003.*

**WEBB George H.**
*Half-back*
*Born: Birmingham, c.1900.*
*Career: Aston Villa 1918. Nuneaton Town (remaining registered with Villa) 1918. Derby County June 1921. Bristol Rovers October 1922.*

**WEBB John Armstrong**
*Full-back*
*Born: Sunderland, 19 May 1908.*
*Died: Derby, 12 January 1984.*
*Career: Southwick. Derby County May 1927. Newport County June 1937. Ilkeston Town September 1947. Trainer, Wilmorton and Alvaston August 1958.*
***Division One runners-up 1929–30, 1935–36.***

**WEBSTER Simon Paul**
*Central defender*
*Born: Earl Shilton, 20 January 1964.*
*Career: Apprentice, Tottenham Hotspur: professional December 1981. Barnet, loan, December 1982. Exeter City, loans, November 1983 and January 1984. Norwich City, loan, January 1985. Huddersfield Town, loan, February 1985: permanent March 1985. Sheffield United March 1988. Charlton Athletic, loan and permanent, August 1990. West Ham United June 1993. Oldham Athletic, loan, March 1995. Derby County, loan, August 1995.*
***Division One promotion 1995–96.***

**WEBSTER Terence Charles**
*Goalkeeper*
*Born: Doncaster, 9 July 1930.*
*Career: Intake YC, Sheffield. Doncaster Rovers June 1948. Derby*

*County October 1948. Skegness Town July 1958 to July 1961.*
***Division Three North Champions 1956–57.***

**WEST Taribo**
*Central defender*
*Born: Port Harcourt, 26 March 1974.*

*Career: Port Harcourt Sharks. Enugu Rangers. Julius Berger 1993. AJ Auxerre 1993. Internazionale August 1997. Milan January 2000. Derby County November 2000. 1.FC Kaiserslautern November 2001. Partizan Belgrade January 2003. Al Arabi 2004. Plymouth Argyle July 2005.*

**WHEATCROFT Frederick George**
*Centre-forward*
*Born: Alfreton, 1882. Died: Bourlon Wood, France, 26 November 1917.*
*Career: Alfreton Town. Derby County May 1903. Swindon Town January 1905. Fulham March 1906. Derby County (one game in April 1906). Derby County, professional, February 1907. Reading May 1908. Swindon Town May 1909.*

**WHEATLEY Steven Peter**
*Outside-right*
*Born: Hinckley, 26 December 1929.*
*Career: Hinckley United. Derby County December 1950. Boston United July 1954. Chesterfield July 1955. Boston United September 1955.*

**WHEELER William**
*Outside-left*
*Born: Chesham.*
*Career: Chesham. Amateur, Watford: professional May 1910. Derby County April 1911. Watford December 1911. Peterborough.*

**WHELAN Noel David**
*Forward*
*Born: Leeds, 30 December 1974.*

*Career: Trainee, Leeds United: professional March 1993. Coventry City December 1995. Middlesbrough August 2000. Crystal Palace, loan, March 2003. Millwall August 2003. Derby County January 2004. Aberdeen August 2004. Boston United June 2005. Livingstone March 2006. Dunfermline Athletic July 2006.*

**WHITE Alfred**
*Centre-forward*
*Born: Spennymoor, 1910. Died: Spennymoor.*
*Career: Spennymoor United. Derby County November 1927. Bournemouth and Boscombe Athletic October 1931. Wrexham May 1936. Spennymoor United July 1937.*

**WHITE William**
*Goalkeeper*
*Born: Clackmannan, 25 September 1932.*
*Career: Alva Albion Rangers. Motherwell July 1952. Accrington Stanley August 1953. Mansfield Town May 1954. Derby County August 1955. Mansfield Town September 1955. Bacup Borough cs 1956.*

**WHITTAKER Walter**
*Goalkeeper*
*Born: Manchester, 20 September 1878. Died: Swansea, 2 June 1917.*
*Career: Molyneaux (Manchester League). Buxton September 1894. Molyneaux December 1894. Newton Heath February 1896. Fairfield May 1896. Grimsby Town May 1897. Reading May 1898. Blackburn Rovers February 1900. Grimsby Town December 1901. Derby County April 1903. Brentford May 1904. Reading May 1906. Clapton Orient July 1907. Exeter City May 1910. Player-manager, Swansea Town, July 1912 to April 1914. Manager, Llanelli, June to November 1914.*

**WHITTINGHAM Peter Michael**
*Left-back/midfield*
*Born: Nuneaton, 8 September 1984.*
*Career: Academy, Aston Villa: professional November 2002. Burnley, loan, February 2005. Derby County, loan, September 2005.*

**WHYMARK Trevor John**
*Forward*
*Born: Burston, 4 May 1950.*
*Career: Diss Town. Ipswich Town May 1969. Vancouver Whitecaps*

*November 1978. Sparta Rotterdam, loan, September 1979. Derby County, loan December 1979. Grimsby Town December 1980. Southend United January 1984. Peterborough United August 1985. Diss Town September 1985. Colchester United November 1985.*

**WICKS Stephen John**
*Centre-half*
*Born: Reading, 3 October 1956.*
*Career: Apprentice, Chelsea: professional June 1974. Derby County January 1979. Queen's Park Rangers September 1979. Crystal Palace June 1981. Queen's Park Rangers March 1982. Chelsea July 1986. Coach, Tampa Bay Rowdies, August 1988. Assistant manager, Portsmouth, January to July 1989. Wycombe Wanderers August 1989. Manager, Crawley Town, May to December 1992. Manager, Scarborough, October 1993 to August 1994. Head coach, Lincoln City, September to October 1995. Chief scout, Newcastle United, November 1995 to January 1996.*

**WIGHTMAN Harold**
*Centre-half/full-back*
*Born: Sutton-in-Ashfield, 19 June 1894. Died: Nottingham, 5 April 1945.*
*Career: Sutton Town. Eastwood Rangers January 1913. Chesterfield Town May 1913. Nottingham Forest (wartime football) September 1915. Derby County May 1919: assistant manager 1928. Player-coach, Chesterfield, May 1929. Team manager/coach, Notts County, May 1930. Manager, Luton Town June 1931 to October 1935. Chief scout, Derby County, November 1935. Manager, Mansfield Town, January 1936. Manager, Nottingham Forest, May 1936 to March 1939.*
***Division Two promotion 1925–26.***

**WIGNALL Frank**
*Forward*
*Born: Blackrod, 21 August 1939.*
*Career: Horwich RMI. Everton, May 1958. Nottingham Forest June*

*1963. Wolverhampton Wanderers March 1968. Derby County February 1969. Mansfield Town November 1971. Player-manager, King's Lynn, July 1973. Burton Albion August 1974. National coach, Qatar, October 1974. Manager, Shepshed Charterhouse, July 1981 to March 1983.*
***Division Two Champions 1968–69. Division One Champions 1971–72.***

**WILCOX George Edwin**
*Right-back*
*Born: Treeton, 23 August 1917. Died: Rotherham, October 1991.*
*Career: Denaby United. Derby County October 1936. Rotherham United July 1948.*

**WILEMAN Sydney**
*Inside-forward*
*Born: Coalville, 26 April 1910. Died: Coalville, 26 June 1985.*
*Career: Hugglescote Weslyans. Gresley Rovers. Derby County April 1931. Port Vale June 1938. Hinckley United August 1939.*

**WILKES Harry Theodore**
*Goalkeeper*
*Born: Sedgeley, 24 June 1907. Died: Derby, 5 April 1984.*
*Career: Sedgeley Congregationals. Wellington Town. Derby County February 1927. Sheffield United March 1934. Rhyl Athletic October 1935. Heanor Town August 1936.*
***Division One runners-up 1929–30.***

**WILKINS Raymond John Hamilton**
*Centre-forward*
*Born: Albert Village, 16 August 1928.*
*Career: Loughborough College. Moira United. Derby County January 1950. Boston United July 1954. Wrexham May 1957: later third-team coach. Oswestry Town June 1960. Macclesfield Town February 1962. Gresley Rovers September 1962. Wilmorton and Alvaston February 1963. Manager, Crewton, October 1964 to July 1966.*

**WILLEMS Hendrick Andries Ronald**
*Forward*
*Born: Epe, 20 September 1966.*
*Career: PEC Zwolle 1983. Twente*

*Enschede 1985. Ajax Amsterdam 1988. Grasshopper Zurich 1993. Derby County July 1995.*
***Division One promotion 1995–96.***

**WILLIAMS Paul Darren**
*Midfield*
*Born: Burton upon Trent, 26 March 1971.*
*Career: Trainee, Derby County: professional July 1989. Lincoln City, loan, November 1989. Coventry City August 1995. Southampton, loan and permanent, October 2001. Stoke City August 2003.*

**WILLIAMS Peter John**
*Outside-left*
*Born: Nottingham, 21 October 1931.*
*Career: South Normanton. Derby County August 1952. Boston United July 1954. Chesterfield July 1955. Boston United February 1956. King's Lynn December 1956. Arnold St Mary's 1959. Ransom and Marles.*

**WILLIAMSON Albert**
*Right-half*
*Born: Sawley 1866.*
*Career: Sawley Rangers. Derby County 1884. Notts County July 1891. Nottingham Forest.*

**WILLIAMSON Michael**
*Outside-left*
*Born: Ashbourne, 30 May 1942.*
*Career: Ashbourne Town. Derby County August 1961. Gillingham July 1964. Ramsgate Athletic July 1967. Canterbury City January 1973. Sheppey United June 1973. Ramsgate Athletic July 1975: manager.*

**WILSON Albert**
*Outside-left*
*Born: Rotherham, 28 January 1915. Died: Rotherham, 20 July 1998.*
*Career: Rotherham YMCA. Rawmarsh Welfare. Stafford Rangers. Derby County May 1936. Mansfield Town July 1938. Crystal Palace January 1939. Rotherham United June 1946. Grimsby Town July 1947. Boston United June 1948.*

**WILSON Angus**
*Outside-right*
*Career: Derby County May 1898. Darwen January 1899.*

**WILSON Cyril Kershaw**
*Inside-forward*
*Born: Basford, 1904.*
*Career: Amateur, West Bromwich Albion. Amateur, Derby County, March 1923. Worcester City 1923.*

**WILSON Ian William**
*Inside-forward*
*Born: Aberdeen, 27 March 1958.*
*Career: Juniors, Aberdeen. Juniors, Dundee. Elgin City. Leicester City April 1979. Everton September 1987. Besiktas August 1989. Derby County, loan, February 1991. Bury August 1991. Wigan Athletic August 1992. Peterhead November 1992: manager. Coach, Nagoya Grampus Eight (Japan), February 1994. Coach, Bursaspor (Turkey), May 1996. Manager, Peterhead, November 1997 to December 2003.*

**WILSON James**
*Inside-forward*
*Born: Seaham Harbour, c.1916.*
*Career: Seaham Colliery. Lincoln City July 1937. Derby County June 1939. Linfield.*

**WILSON Kevin James**
*Centre-forward*
*Born: Banbury, 18 April 1961.*
*Career: Ruscote Sports. Banbury United 1978. Derby County December 1979. Ipswich Town January 1985. Chelsea June 1987. Notts County March 1992. Bradford City, loan, January 1994.*

*Player-coach, Walsall, August 1994. Player/assistant manager, Northampton Town, July 1997: joint caretaker manager October 1999: manager November 1999 to September 2001. Manager, Bedford Town, October 2002. Manager, Aylesbury United, October 2003. Manager, Kettering Town, December 2003 to November 2005: December 2005. Manager, Hucknall Town, February 2006.*

**WOMACK Albert Roy**

*Outside-left*

*Born: Denaby, 20 September 1934.*

*Career: Denaby United. Derby County October 1957. Southampton May 1959. Workington July 1960. Denaby United cs 1961. Sutton Town March 1962. Goole Town July 1962. Bourne Town June 1964.*

**WOMBWELL Richard**

*Forward*

*Born: Nottingham, 1877.*

*Career: Bulwell. Ilkeston Town December 1898. Derby County May 1899. Bristol City August 1902. Manchester United March 1905. Heart of Midlothian January 1907. Brighton & Hove Albion June 1907. Blackburn Rovers February 1908. Ilkeston United August 1910.*

**WOOD Alfred Josiah Edward**

*Centre-half/wing-half*

*Born: Smallthorne, near Burslem, June 1876. Died: April 1919.*

*Career: Smallthorne Albion. Burslem Port Vale December 1892. Stoke October 1895. Aston Villa March 1901. Derby County May 1905. Bradford May 1907.*

**WOOD John**

*Inside-forward*

*Born: West Kirby.*

*Career: Port Sunlight. Southern United 1905. Derby County March 1906. Manchester City June 1907. Plymouth Argyle July 1909. Huddersfield Town July 1910. Aberdeen July 1911.*

**WOODHEAD Dennis**

*Outside-left*

*Born: Sheffield, 12 June 1925. Died: Sheffield, 26 July 1995.*

*Career: Hillsborough Boys' Club. Amateur, Sheffield Wednesday,*

*June 1942: professional, April 1945. Chesterfield September 1955. Derby County January 1956. Southport February 1959. Derby County March 1959. Frickley Colliery July 1959. Worksop Town July 1960. Manager, Retford Town, April 1964 to March 1967.*

***Division Three North Champions 1956–57.***

**WOODLEY Victor Robert**

*Goalkeeper*

*Born: Cippenham, 26 February 1910. Died: Bradford-on-Avon, 23 October 1978.*

*Career: Cippenham. Windsor and Eton. Chelsea May 1931. Bath City December 1945. Derby County*

*March 1946. Bath City May 1947: player-manager to December 1949.*

***FA Cup winners 1945–46.***

**WOOLLEY Albert**

*Outside-left*

*Born: Hockley, June 1870. Died: Manchester 1896.*

*Career: Park Mills. Aston Villa August 1892. Derby County January 1895.*

**WRACK Darren**

*Midfield*

*Born: Cleethorpes, 5 May 1976.*

*Career: Trainee, Derby County: professional July 1994. Grimsby Town July 1996. Shrewsbury Town, loan, February 1997. Walsall August 1998.*

***Division One promotion 1995–96.***

**WRIGHT Alan Geoffrey**
*Left-back*
*Born: Ashton-under-Lyne, 28 September 1971.*
*Career: Trainee, Blackpool: professional April 1989. Blackburn Rovers October 1991. Aston Villa March 1995. Middlesbrough August 2003. Sheffield United October 2003. Derby County, loan, February 2006.*

**WRIGHT Henry Edward**
*Goalkeeper*
*Born: Tottenham, 3 June 1909. Died: King's Lynn, April 1994.*
*Career: Harwich and Parkeston. Amateur, Charlton Athletic, June 1932: professional December 1932. Aldershot May 1936. Derby County September 1937. Colchester United July 1946. Guildford City. Coach in Norway. Manager-coach, St Albans City, May 1951. Trainer, Walsall, December 1952. Trainer, Luton Town, January 1954 to September 1956. Trainer, Everton, October 1956. Coach in Lebanon. Coach National Institute of Sport, Patiala, 1961 to 1965.*

**WRIGHT Horace Duncan**
*Outside-right*
*Born: Ilkeston, 1892.*
*Career: Bulwell White Star. Ilkeston United August 1910. Derby County September 1910. Portsmouth August 1912. Coventry City September 1919. Exeter City 1920. Aberaman Athletic. Abertillary May 1921. Sutton Town December 1921.*
***Division Two Champions 1911–12.***

**WRIGHT Levi George**
*Half-back*
*Born: Oxford, 15 January 1862. Died: Derby, 11 January 1953.*
*Career: Derby Midland. Derby County. Derby Junction.*

**WRIGHT Patrick Daniel Joseph**
*Full-back*
*Born: Oldbury, 17 November 1940.*
*Career: Springfield BC. Birmingham City November 1959. Shrewsbury Town September 1962. Derby County October 1967. Southend United, loan, March 1970. Player-coach, Rotherham United, September 1970. Coach, Portsmouth July 1971 to April 1976: player-manager of nursery club Waterlooville, 1971. National coach, Zambia, September 1976. National coach, Saudi Arabia, 1978: youth team manager 1979. Coach, United Arab Emirates, 1979. Coach, Al Nasr, Dubai, 1980 to 1984.*

**WYER Peter William**
*Inside-right*
*Born: Coventry, 10 February 1937.*
*Career: Coventry City October 1955. Derby County June 1956. Coventry City July 1958. Rugby Town July 1959. Nuneaton Borough.*
***Division Three North Champions 1956–57.***

**YATES Dean Richard**
*Central defender*
*Born: Leicester, 26 October 1967.*
*Career: Apprentice, Notts County: professional June 1985. Derby*

*County January 1995. Watford July 1998.*
***Division One promotion 1995–96.***

**YORK Charles H.**
*Forward*
*Born: Edinburgh, 1882.*
*Career: Reading April 1901. Derby County April 1902. Sunderland January 1904. Heart of Midlothian May 1904. Southampton December 1904. Sheppey United March 1906. South Farnborough October 1906.*
*FA Cup finalists **1902–03.***

**ZAVAGNO Luciano**
*Left-back*
*Born: Rosario, 6 August 1987.*
*Career: Union de Santa Fe. RC Strasbourg August 1997. ES Troyes AC July 1999. Derby County October 2001. Ancona January 2004.*

# Against Other League clubs

Derby County have played 98 clubs in the Football League and FA Premiership since 1888–89. Below is the Rams' record against each club. Some clubs changed their names (eg Small Heath became Birmingham then Birmingham City) and some clubs modified their titles (eg Leicester Fosse became Leicester City). In all cases the current name used by each club covers all games under previous names.

| | | | | *HOME* | | | | | *AWAY* | | |
|---|---|---|---|---|---|---|---|---|---|---|---|
| | P | W | D | L | F | A | W | D | L | F | A |
| Accrington | 10 | 1 | 2 | 2 | 10 | 10 | 1 | 1 | 3 | 7 | 17 |
| Accrington Stanley | 4 | 1 | 1 | 0 | 8 | 4 | 0 | 1 | 1 | 0 | 2 |
| AFC Bournemouth | 4 | 1 | 0 | 1 | 5 | 3 | 0 | 1 | 1 | 1 | 2 |
| Arsenal | 96 | 25 | 10 | 13 | 89 | 57 | 12 | 10 | 26 | 51 | 84 |
| Aston Villa | 116 | 28 | 11 | 19 | 98 | 77 | 9 | 10 | 39 | 61 | 143 |
| Barnsley | 46 | 14 | 5 | 4 | 45 | 17 | 8 | 4 | 11 | 23 | 35 |
| Barrow | 4 | 1 | 1 | 0 | 5 | 4 | 1 | 1 | 0 | 4 | 3 |
| Birmingham City | 88 | 22 | 16 | 6 | 87 | 45 | 12 | 10 | 22 | 64 | 82 |
| Blackburn Rovers | 102 | 21 | 18 | 12 | 103 | 67 | 11 | 10 | 30 | 62 | 110 |
| Blackpool | 54 | 16 | 8 | 3 | 57 | 26 | 5 | 7 | 15 | 30 | 50 |
| Bolton Wanderers | 112 | 37 | 11 | 8 | 131 | 61 | 20 | 6 | 30 | 76 | 110 |
| Bradford Park Avenue | 18 | 6 | 1 | 2 | 21 | 9 | 3 | 1 | 5 | 13 | 18 |
| Bradford City | 34 | 8 | 4 | 5 | 26 | 15 | 6 | 6 | 5 | 23 | 23 |
| Brentford | 18 | 5 | 1 | 3 | 17 | 14 | 3 | 3 | 3 | 16 | 21 |
| Brighton & Hove Albion | 22 | 7 | 1 | 3 | 22 | 11 | 4 | 1 | 6 | 11 | 16 |
| Bristol City | 46 | 18 | 1 | 4 | 57 | 22 | 8 | 8 | 7 | 33 | 29 |
| Bristol Rovers | 24 | 7 | 3 | 2 | 18 | 11 | 3 | 3 | 6 | 17 | 24 |
| Burnley | 82 | 25 | 8 | 8 | 86 | 43 | 13 | 8 | 20 | 53 | 74 |
| Bury | 58 | 22 | 4 | 3 | 70 | 30 | 5 | 9 | 15 | 29 | 54 |
| Cambridge United | 14 | 3 | 3 | 1 | 5 | 5 | 4 | 2 | 1 | 8 | 5 |
| Cardiff City | 42 | 8 | 5 | 8 | 38 | 34 | 3 | 6 | 12 | 21 | 32 |
| Carlisle United | 18 | 3 | 2 | 4 | 13 | 13 | 2 | 3 | 4 | 10 | 13 |
| Charlton Athletic | 72 | 14 | 10 | 12 | 65 | 53 | 14 | 7 | 15 | 54 | 60 |
| Chelsea | 92 | 24 | 10 | 12 | 84 | 56 | 11 | 15 | 20 | 53 | 73 |
| Chester | 4 | 2 | 0 | 0 | 6 | 1 | 1 | 1 | 0 | 7 | 4 |
| Chesterfield | 10 | 2 | 3 | 0 | 11 | 2 | 2 | 1 | 2 | 8 | 7 |
| Coventry City | 62 | 18 | 7 | 6 | 51 | 29 | 7 | 8 | 16 | 31 | 52 |
| Crewe Alexandra | 10 | 2 | 2 | 1 | 14 | 8 | 2 | 1 | 2 | 9 | 9 |
| Crystal Palace | 52 | 17 | 5 | 4 | 57 | 20 | 8 | 8 | 10 | 22 | 33 |
| Darlington | 8 | 1 | 2 | 1 | 8 | 6 | 0 | 1 | 3 | 2 | 7 |
| Darwen | 4 | 2 | 0 | 0 | 9 | 1 | 1 | 0 | 1 | 3 | 4 |
| Doncaster Rovers | 10 | 4 | 1 | 0 | 12 | 2 | 3 | 0 | 2 | 9 | 6 |
| Everton | 124 | 30 | 9 | 23 | 113 | 100 | 12 | 12 | 38 | 60 | 137 |
| Fulham | 44 | 13 | 6 | 3 | 52 | 27 | 4 | 8 | 10 | 24 | 38 |
| Gainsborough Trinity | 10 | 4 | 1 | 0 | 20 | 4 | 2 | 3 | 0 | 9 | 4 |
| Gateshead | 14 | 5 | 1 | 1 | 18 | 7 | 1 | 2 | 4 | 9 | 13 |
| Gillingham | 10 | 4 | 1 | 0 | 8 | 2 | 2 | 1 | 2 | 6 | 5 |
| Glossop | 14 | 6 | 1 | 0 | 20 | 4 | 2 | 3 | 2 | 12 | 13 |

| | | HOME | | | | | AWAY | | | | |
|---|---|---|---|---|---|---|---|---|---|---|---|
| | P | W | D | L | F | A | W | D | L | F | A |
| Grimsby Town | 66 | 20 | 7 | 6 | 72 | 40 | 12 | 8 | 13 | 43 | 48 |
| Halifax Town | 4 | 2 | 0 | 0 | 10 | 1 | 0 | 1 | 1 | 2 | 3 |
| Hartlepool United | 4 | 2 | 0 | 0 | 5 | 2 | 0 | 0 | 2 | 1 | 4 |
| Huddersfield Town | 80 | 27 | 9 | 4 | 87 | 49 | 5 | 13 | 22 | 29 | 69 |
| Hull City | 42 | 10 | 5 | 6 | 44 | 25 | 2 | 9 | 10 | 17 | 36 |
| Ipswich Town | 58 | 13 | 9 | 7 | 48 | 38 | 7 | 7 | 15 | 34 | 50 |
| Leeds City | 12 | 4 | 1 | 1 | 20 | 8 | 3 | 0 | 3 | 15 | 15 |
| Leeds United | 88 | 17 | 13 | 14 | 73 | 61 | 6 | 10 | 28 | 34 | 77 |
| Leicester City | 86 | 25 | 7 | 11 | 78 | 47 | 14 | 16 | 13 | 52 | 58 |
| Leyton Orient | 44 | 14 | 3 | 5 | 38 | 18 | 6 | 4 | 12 | 20 | 31 |
| Lincoln City | 24 | 12 | 0 | 0 | 38 | 4 | 5 | 4 | 3 | 19 | 19 |
| Liverpool | 124 | 26 | 13 | 23 | 102 | 104 | 6 | 15 | 41 | 53 | 136 |
| Luton Town | 34 | 7 | 7 | 3 | 25 | 14 | 4 | 2 | 11 | 16 | 27 |
| Manchester City | 90 | 24 | 10 | 11 | 86 | 49 | 8 | 9 | 28 | 45 | 92 |
| Manchester United | 88 | 16 | 17 | 11 | 91 | 69 | 11 | 10 | 23 | 44 | 83 |
| Mansfield Town | 4 | 2 | 0 | 0 | 8 | 0 | 1 | 1 | 0 | 3 | 2 |
| Middlesbrough | 116 | 29 | 13 | 16 | 110 | 89 | 14 | 13 | 31 | 68 | 122 |
| Millwall | 32 | 6 | 4 | 6 | 23 | 21 | 4 | 4 | 8 | 13 | 22 |
| Nelson | 2 | 1 | 0 | 0 | 6 | 0 | 0 | 0 | 1 | 1 | 2 |
| Newcastle United | 106 | 21 | 14 | 18 | 76 | 72 | 13 | 13 | 27 | 56 | 87 |
| Newport County | 4 | 0 | 2 | 0 | 4 | 4 | 1 | 1 | 0 | 4 | 2 |
| Northampton Town | 6 | 1 | 2 | 0 | 6 | 5 | 2 | 1 | 0 | 5 | 2 |
| Norwich City | 50 | 8 | 11 | 6 | 29 | 27 | 5 | 3 | 17 | 25 | 46 |
| Nottingham Forest | 72 | 14 | 8 | 14 | 58 | 47 | 10 | 10 | 16 | 53 | 69 |
| Notts County | 54 | 14 | 9 | 4 | 48 | 25 | 8 | 9 | 10 | 35 | 39 |
| Oldham Athletic | 40 | 12 | 5 | 3 | 34 | 21 | 5 | 7 | 8 | 19 | 29 |
| Oxford United | 10 | 2 | 1 | 2 | 6 | 5 | 2 | 1 | 2 | 3 | 4 |
| Peterborough United | 4 | 1 | 0 | 1 | 4 | 3 | 0 | 1 | 1 | 2 | 3 |
| Plymouth Argyle | 34 | 11 | 3 | 3 | 34 | 22 | 7 | 5 | 5 | 28 | 23 |
| Portsmouth | 78 | 25 | 5 | 9 | 74 | 35 | 9 | 9 | 21 | 49 | 78 |
| Port Vale | 18 | 7 | 1 | 1 | 23 | 7 | 2 | 2 | 5 | 7 | 13 |
| Preston North End | 90 | 27 | 6 | 12 | 79 | 47 | 7 | 8 | 30 | 38 | 96 |
| Queen's Park Rangers | 32 | 8 | 3 | 5 | 29 | 20 | 4 | 8 | 4 | 15 | 21 |
| Reading | 18 | 5 | 2 | 2 | 21 | 10 | 1 | 1 | 7 | 5 | 17 |
| Rochdale | 4 | 2 | 0 | 0 | 5 | 0 | 1 | 0 | 1 | 6 | 3 |
| Rotherham United | 44 | 12 | 6 | 4 | 46 | 28 | 4 | 8 | 10 | 23 | 37 |
| Scunthorpe United | 16 | 4 | 3 | 1 | 24 | 14 | 3 | 1 | 4 | 15 | 14 |
| Sheffield United | 94 | 30 | 6 | 11 | 99 | 56 | 11 | 8 | 28 | 55 | 82 |
| Sheffield Wednesday | 100 | 27 | 13 | 10 | 111 | 63 | 10 | 15 | 25 | 59 | 82 |
| Shrewsbury Town | 10 | 2 | 2 | 1 | 8 | 6 | 1 | 1 | 3 | 3 | 9 |
| Southampton | 56 | 15 | 10 | 3 | 59 | 30 | 7 | 8 | 13 | 33 | 53 |
| Southend United | 10 | 2 | 0 | 3 | 6 | 7 | 1 | 1 | 3 | 5 | 7 |
| Southport | 4 | 2 | 0 | 0 | 4 | 0 | 1 | 0 | 1 | 7 | 5 |
| Stockport County | 24 | 11 | 0 | 1 | 31 | 4 | 0 | 3 | 9 | 10 | 24 |
| Stoke City | 122 | 36 | 16 | 9 | 136 | 60 | 12 | 21 | 28 | 72 | 99 |

| | | HOME | | | | | AWAY | | | | |
|---|---|---|---|---|---|---|---|---|---|---|---|
| | P | W | D | L | F | A | W | D | L | F | A |
| Sunderland | 124 | 34 | 14 | 14 | 124 | 75 | 12 | 11 | 39 | 55 | 123 |
| Swansea City | 30 | 8 | 1 | 6 | 37 | 25 | 3 | 1 | 11 | 21 | 36 |
| Swindon Town | 10 | 5 | 0 | 0 | 14 | 4 | 2 | 2 | 1 | 9 | 8 |
| Tottenham Hotspur | 62 | 17 | 9 | 5 | 70 | 36 | 7 | 8 | 16 | 30 | 51 |
| Tranmere Rovers | 14 | 4 | 1 | 2 | 20 | 5 | 2 | 0 | 5 | 8 | 18 |
| Walsall | 12 | 3 | 1 | 2 | 10 | 7 | 2 | 2 | 2 | 7 | 7 |
| Watford | 26 | 5 | 5 | 3 | 23 | 17 | 2 | 7 | 4 | 15 | 22 |
| West Bromwich Albion | 96 | 28 | 13 | 7 | 110 | 59 | 9 | 14 | 25 | 49 | 83 |
| West Ham United | 64 | 16 | 8 | 8 | 54 | 33 | 6 | 15 | 11 | 35 | 52 |
| Wigan Athletic | 8 | 1 | 3 | 0 | 6 | 5 | 1 | 0 | 3 | 3 | 7 |
| Wimbledon | 20 | 4 | 4 | 2 | 17 | 10 | 1 | 4 | 5 | 9 | 16 |
| Wolverhampton W | 128 | 35 | 11 | 18 | 148 | 101 | 19 | 17 | 28 | 81 | 123 |
| Workington | 4 | 0 | 1 | 1 | 4 | 5 | 1 | 0 | 1 | 4 | 2 |
| Wrexham | 8 | 3 | 0 | 1 | 5 | 2 | 1 | 2 | 1 | 6 | 6 |
| York City | 8 | 4 | 0 | 0 | 7 | 3 | 1 | 2 | 1 | 5 | 4 |
| TOTALS | 4,264 | 1,150 | 492 | 490 | 4,226 | 2,544 | 509 | 538 | 1,085 | 2,409 | 3,810 |

# In the Football League

| | | HOME | | | | | AWAY | | | | | | |
|---|---|---|---|---|---|---|---|---|---|---|---|---|---|
| | *P* | *W* | *D* | *L* | *F* | *A* | *W* | *D* | *L* | *F* | *A* | *Pts* | *Pos* |
| **FOOTBALL LEAGUE** | | | | | | | | | | | | | |
| 1888-89 | 22 | 5 | 1 | 5 | 22 | 20 | 2 | 1 | 8 | 19 | 41 | 16 | 10th |
| 1889-90 | 22 | 8 | 2 | 1 | 32 | 13 | 1 | 1 | 9 | 11 | 42 | 21 | 7th |
| 1890-91 | 22 | 6 | 1 | 4 | 38 | 28 | 1 | 0 | 10 | 9 | 53 | 15 | 11th |
| 1891-92 | 26 | 6 | 3 | 4 | 28 | 18 | 4 | 1 | 8 | 18 | 34 | 24 | 10th |
| **FIRST DIVISION** | | | | | | | | | | | | | |
| 1892-93 | 30 | 5 | 6 | 4 | 30 | 28 | 4 | 3 | 8 | 22 | 36 | 27 | 13th |
| 1893-94 | 30 | 9 | 2 | 4 | 47 | 32 | 7 | 2 | 6 | 26 | 30 | 36 | 3rd |
| 1894-95 | 30 | 4 | 5 | 6 | 23 | 23 | 3 | 4 | 8 | 22 | 45 | 23 | 15th |
| 1895-96 | 30 | 12 | 2 | 1 | 42 | 13 | 5 | 5 | 5 | 26 | 22 | 41 | 2nd |
| 1896-97 | 30 | 10 | 2 | 3 | 45 | 22 | 6 | 2 | 7 | 25 | 28 | 36 | 3rd |
| 1897-98 | 30 | 10 | 3 | 2 | 40 | 19 | 1 | 3 | 11 | 17 | 42 | 28 | 10th |
| 1898-99 | 34 | 11 | 5 | 1 | 46 | 19 | 1 | 6 | 10 | 16 | 38 | 35 | 9th |
| 1899-1900 | 34 | 11 | 2 | 4 | 32 | 15 | 3 | 6 | 8 | 13 | 28 | 36 | 6th |
| 1900-01 | 34 | 10 | 4 | 3 | 43 | 18 | 2 | 3 | 12 | 12 | 24 | 31 | 12th |
| 1901-02 | 34 | 11 | 5 | 1 | 26 | 10 | 2 | 4 | 11 | 13 | 31 | 35 | 6th |
| 1902-03 | 34 | 13 | 2 | 2 | 34 | 11 | 3 | 1 | 13 | 16 | 36 | 35 | 9th |
| 1903-04 | 34 | 7 | 3 | 7 | 41 | 33 | 2 | 7 | 8 | 17 | 27 | 28 | 14th |
| 1904-05 | 34 | 9 | 4 | 4 | 29 | 19 | 3 | 4 | 10 | 8 | 29 | 32 | 11th |
| 1905-06 | 38 | 10 | 5 | 4 | 27 | 16 | 4 | 2 | 13 | 12 | 42 | 35 | 15th |
| 1906-07 | 38 | 8 | 6 | 5 | 29 | 19 | 1 | 3 | 15 | 12 | 40 | 27 | 19th |
| **SECOND DIVISION** | | | | | | | | | | | | | |
| 1907-08 | 38 | 15 | 1 | 3 | 50 | 13 | 6 | 3 | 10 | 27 | 32 | 46 | 6th |
| 1908-09 | 38 | 13 | 5 | 1 | 38 | 11 | 3 | 6 | 10 | 17 | 30 | 43 | 5th |
| 1909-10 | 38 | 15 | 2 | 2 | 46 | 15 | 7 | 7 | 5 | 26 | 32 | 53 | 4th |
| 1910-11 | 38 | 11 | 5 | 3 | 48 | 24 | 6 | 3 | 10 | 25 | 28 | 42 | 6th |
| 1911-12 | 38 | 15 | 2 | 2 | 55 | 13 | 8 | 6 | 5 | 19 | 15 | 54 | 1st |
| **FIRST DIVISION** | | | | | | | | | | | | | |
| 1912-13 | 38 | 10 | 2 | 7 | 40 | 29 | 7 | 6 | 6 | 29 | 37 | 42 | 7th |
| 1913-14 | 38 | 6 | 5 | 8 | 34 | 32 | 2 | 6 | 11 | 21 | 39 | 27 | 20th |
| **SECOND DIVISION** | | | | | | | | | | | | | |
| 1914-15 | 38 | 14 | 3 | 2 | 40 | 11 | 9 | 4 | 6 | 31 | 22 | 53 | 1st |
| **FIRST DIVISION** | | | | | | | | | | | | | |
| 1919-20 | 42 | 12 | 5 | 4 | 36 | 18 | 1 | 7 | 13 | 11 | 39 | 38 | 18th |
| 1920-21 | 42 | 3 | 12 | 6 | 21 | 23 | 2 | 4 | 15 | 11 | 35 | 26 | 21st |
| **SECOND DIVISION** | | | | | | | | | | | | | |
| 1921-22 | 42 | 11 | 3 | 7 | 34 | 22 | 4 | 6 | 11 | 26 | 42 | 39 | 12th |
| 1922-23 | 42 | 9 | 5 | 7 | 25 | 16 | 5 | 6 | 10 | 21 | 34 | 39 | 14th |
| 1923-24 | 42 | 15 | 4 | 2 | 52 | 15 | 6 | 5 | 10 | 23 | 27 | 51 | 3rd |
| 1924-25 | 42 | 15 | 3 | 3 | 49 | 15 | 7 | 8 | 6 | 22 | 21 | 55 | 3rd |
| 1925-26 | 42 | 17 | 2 | 2 | 57 | 17 | 8 | 5 | 8 | 20 | 25 | 57 | 2nd |

## FIRST DIVISION

| | | HOME | | | | | AWAY | | | | | | |
|---|---|---|---|---|---|---|---|---|---|---|---|---|---|
| | *P* | *W* | *D* | *L* | *F* | *A* | *W* | *D* | *L* | *F* | *A* | *Pts* | *Pos* |
| 1926-27 | 42 | 14 | 4 | 3 | 60 | 28 | 3 | 3 | 15 | 26 | 45 | 41 | 12th |
| 1927-28 | 42 | 12 | 4 | 5 | 59 | 30 | 5 | 6 | 10 | 37 | 53 | 44 | 4th |
| 1928-29 | 42 | 12 | 5 | 4 | 56 | 24 | 6 | 5 | 10 | 30 | 47 | 46 | 6th |
| 1929-30 | 42 | 16 | 4 | 1 | 61 | 32 | 5 | 4 | 12 | 29 | 50 | 50 | 2nd |
| 1930-31 | 42 | 12 | 6 | 3 | 56 | 31 | 6 | 4 | 11 | 38 | 48 | 46 | 6th |
| 1931-32 | 42 | 13 | 5 | 3 | 51 | 25 | 1 | 5 | 15 | 20 | 50 | 38 | 15th |
| 1932-33 | 42 | 11 | 8 | 2 | 49 | 25 | 4 | 6 | 11 | 27 | 44 | 44 | 7th |
| 1933-34 | 42 | 11 | 8 | 2 | 45 | 22 | 6 | 3 | 12 | 23 | 32 | 45 | 4th |
| 1934-35 | 42 | 10 | 4 | 7 | 44 | 28 | 8 | 5 | 8 | 37 | 38 | 45 | 6th |
| 1935-36 | 42 | 13 | 5 | 3 | 43 | 23 | 5 | 7 | 9 | 18 | 29 | 48 | 2nd |
| 1936-37 | 42 | 13 | 3 | 5 | 58 | 39 | 8 | 4 | 9 | 38 | 51 | 49 | 4th |
| 1937-38 | 42 | 10 | 5 | 6 | 42 | 36 | 5 | 5 | 11 | 24 | 51 | 40 | 13th |
| 1938-39 | 42 | 12 | 3 | 6 | 39 | 22 | 7 | 5 | 9 | 27 | 33 | 46 | 6th |
| 1946-47 | 42 | 13 | 2 | 6 | 44 | 28 | 5 | 3 | 13 | 29 | 51 | 41 | 14th |
| 1947-48 | 42 | 11 | 6 | 4 | 38 | 24 | 8 | 6 | 7 | 39 | 33 | 50 | 4th |
| 1948-49 | 42 | 17 | 2 | 2 | 48 | 22 | 5 | 7 | 9 | 26 | 33 | 53 | 3rd |
| 1949-50 | 42 | 11 | 5 | 5 | 46 | 26 | 6 | 5 | 10 | 23 | 35 | 44 | 11th |
| 1950-51 | 42 | 10 | 5 | 6 | 53 | 33 | 6 | 3 | 12 | 28 | 42 | 40 | 11th |
| 1951-52 | 42 | 10 | 4 | 7 | 43 | 37 | 5 | 3 | 13 | 20 | 43 | 37 | 17th |
| 1952-53 | 42 | 9 | 6 | 6 | 41 | 29 | 2 | 4 | 15 | 18 | 45 | 32 | 22nd |

## SECOND DIVISION

| | | | | | | | | | | | | | |
|---|---|---|---|---|---|---|---|---|---|---|---|---|---|
| 1953-54 | 42 | 9 | 5 | 7 | 38 | 35 | 3 | 6 | 12 | 26 | 47 | 35 | 18th |
| 1954-55 | 42 | 6 | 6 | 9 | 39 | 34 | 1 | 3 | 17 | 14 | 48 | 23 | 22nd |

## THIRD DIVISION NORTH

| | | | | | | | | | | | | | |
|---|---|---|---|---|---|---|---|---|---|---|---|---|---|
| 1955-56 | 46 | 18 | 4 | 1 | 67 | 23 | 10 | 3 | 10 | 43 | 32 | 63 | 2nd |
| 1956-57 | 46 | 18 | 3 | 2 | 69 | 18 | 8 | 8 | 7 | 42 | 35 | 63 | 1st |

## SECOND DIVISION

| | | | | | | | | | | | | | |
|---|---|---|---|---|---|---|---|---|---|---|---|---|---|
| 1957-58 | 42 | 11 | 3 | 7 | 37 | 36 | 3 | 5 | 13 | 23 | 45 | 36 | 16th |
| 1958-59 | 42 | 15 | 1 | 5 | 46 | 29 | 5 | 7 | 9 | 28 | 42 | 48 | 7th |
| 1959-60 | 42 | 9 | 4 | 8 | 31 | 28 | 5 | 3 | 13 | 30 | 49 | 35 | 18th |
| 1960-61 | 42 | 9 | 6 | 6 | 46 | 35 | 6 | 4 | 11 | 34 | 45 | 40 | 12th |
| 1961-62 | 42 | 10 | 7 | 4 | 42 | 27 | 4 | 4 | 13 | 26 | 48 | 39 | 16th |
| 1962-63 | 42 | 10 | 5 | 6 | 40 | 29 | 2 | 7 | 12 | 21 | 43 | 36 | 18th |
| 1963-64 | 42 | 10 | 6 | 5 | 34 | 27 | 4 | 5 | 12 | 22 | 40 | 39 | 13th |
| 1964-65 | 42 | 11 | 5 | 5 | 48 | 35 | 5 | 6 | 10 | 36 | 44 | 43 | 9th |
| 1965-66 | 42 | 13 | 2 | 6 | 48 | 31 | 3 | 9 | 9 | 23 | 37 | 43 | 8th |
| 1966-67 | 42 | 8 | 6 | 7 | 40 | 32 | 4 | 6 | 11 | 28 | 40 | 36 | 17th |
| 1967-68 | 42 | 8 | 5 | 8 | 40 | 35 | 5 | 5 | 11 | 31 | 43 | 36 | 18th |
| 1968-69 | 42 | 16 | 4 | 1 | 43 | 16 | 10 | 7 | 4 | 22 | 16 | 63 | 1st |

## FIRST DIVISION

| | | | | | | | | | | | | | |
|---|---|---|---|---|---|---|---|---|---|---|---|---|---|
| 1969-70 | 42 | 15 | 3 | 3 | 45 | 14 | 7 | 6 | 8 | 19 | 23 | 53 | 4th |
| 1970-71 | 42 | 9 | 5 | 7 | 32 | 26 | 7 | 5 | 9 | 24 | 28 | 42 | 9th |
| 1971-72 | 42 | 16 | 4 | 1 | 43 | 10 | 8 | 6 | 7 | 26 | 23 | 58 | 1st |
| 1972-73 | 42 | 15 | 3 | 3 | 43 | 18 | 4 | 5 | 12 | 13 | 36 | 46 | 7th |
| 1973-74 | 42 | 13 | 7 | 1 | 40 | 16 | 4 | 7 | 10 | 12 | 26 | 48 | 3rd |

| | | HOME | | | | | AWAY | | | | | | |
|---|---|---|---|---|---|---|---|---|---|---|---|---|---|
| | *P* | *W* | *D* | *L* | *F* | *A* | *W* | *D* | *L* | *F* | *A* | *Pts* | *Pos* |
| 1974-75 | 42 | 14 | 4 | 3 | 41 | 18 | 7 | 7 | 7 | 26 | 31 | 53 | 1st |
| 1975-76 | 42 | 15 | 3 | 3 | 45 | 30 | 6 | 8 | 7 | 30 | 28 | 53 | 4th |
| 1976-77 | 42 | 9 | 9 | 3 | 36 | 18 | 0 | 10 | 11 | 14 | 37 | 37 | 15th |
| 1977-78 | 42 | 10 | 7 | 4 | 37 | 24 | 4 | 6 | 11 | 17 | 35 | 41 | 12th |
| 1978-79 | 42 | 8 | 5 | 8 | 25 | 25 | 2 | 6 | 13 | 19 | 46 | 31 | 19th |
| 1979-80 | 42 | 9 | 4 | 8 | 36 | 29 | 2 | 4 | 15 | 11 | 38 | 30 | 21st |
| **SECOND DIVISION** | | | | | | | | | | | | | |
| 1980-81 | 42 | 9 | 8 | 4 | 34 | 26 | 6 | 7 | 8 | 23 | 26 | 45 | 6th |
| 1981-82 | 42 | 9 | 8 | 4 | 32 | 23 | 3 | 4 | 14 | 21 | 45 | 48 | 16th |
| 1982-83 | 42 | 7 | 10 | 4 | 27 | 24 | 3 | 9 | 9 | 22 | 34 | 49 | 13th |
| 1983-84 | 42 | 9 | 5 | 7 | 26 | 26 | 2 | 4 | 15 | 10 | 46 | 42 | 20th |
| **THIRD DIVISION** | | | | | | | | | | | | | |
| 1984-85 | 46 | 14 | 7 | 2 | 40 | 20 | 5 | 6 | 12 | 25 | 34 | 70 | 7th |
| 1985-86 | 46 | 13 | 7 | 3 | 45 | 20 | 10 | 8 | 5 | 35 | 21 | 84 | 3rd |
| **SECOND DIVISION** | | | | | | | | | | | | | |
| 1986-87 | 42 | 14 | 6 | 1 | 42 | 18 | 11 | 3 | 7 | 22 | 20 | 84 | 1st |
| **FIRST DIVISION** | | | | | | | | | | | | | |
| 1987-88 | 40 | 6 | 7 | 7 | 18 | 17 | 4 | 6 | 10 | 17 | 28 | 43 | 15th |
| 1988-89 | 38 | 9 | 3 | 7 | 23 | 18 | 8 | 4 | 7 | 17 | 20 | 58 | 5th |
| 1989-90 | 38 | 9 | 1 | 9 | 29 | 21 | 4 | 6 | 9 | 14 | 19 | 46 | 16th |
| 1990-91 | 38 | 3 | 8 | 8 | 25 | 36 | 2 | 1 | 16 | 12 | 39 | 24 | 20th |
| **SECOND DIVISION: FIRST DIVISION from 1992** | | | | | | | | | | | | | |
| 1991-92 | 46 | 11 | 4 | 8 | 35 | 24 | 12 | 5 | 6 | 34 | 27 | 78 | 3rd |
| 1992-93 | 46 | 11 | 2 | 10 | 40 | 33 | 8 | 7 | 8 | 28 | 24 | 66 | 8th |
| 1993-94 | 46 | 15 | 3 | 5 | 44 | 25 | 5 | 8 | 10 | 29 | 43 | 71 | 6th |
| 1994-95 | 46 | 12 | 6 | 5 | 44 | 23 | 6 | 6 | 11 | 22 | 28 | 66 | 9th |
| 1995-96 | 46 | 14 | 8 | 1 | 48 | 22 | 7 | 8 | 8 | 23 | 29 | 79 | 2nd |
| **FA PREMIERSHIP** | | | | | | | | | | | | | |
| 1996-97 | 38 | 8 | 6 | 5 | 25 | 22 | 3 | 7 | 9 | 20 | 36 | 46 | 12th |
| 1997-98 | 38 | 12 | 3 | 4 | 33 | 18 | 4 | 4 | 11 | 19 | 31 | 55 | 9th |
| 1998-99 | 38 | 8 | 7 | 4 | 22 | 19 | 5 | 6 | 8 | 18 | 26 | 52 | 8th |
| 1999-2000 | 38 | 6 | 3 | 10 | 22 | 25 | 3 | 8 | 8 | 22 | 32 | 38 | 16th |
| 2000-01 | 38 | 8 | 7 | 4 | 23 | 24 | 2 | 5 | 12 | 14 | 35 | 42 | 17th |
| 2001-02 | 38 | 5 | 4 | 10 | 20 | 26 | 3 | 2 | 14 | 13 | 37 | 30 | 19th |
| **FIRST DIVISION: CHAMPIONSHIP from 2004** | | | | | | | | | | | | | |
| 2002-03 | 46 | 9 | 5 | 9 | 33 | 32 | 6 | 2 | 15 | 22 | 42 | 52 | 18th |
| 2003-04 | 46 | 11 | 5 | 7 | 39 | 33 | 2 | 8 | 13 | 14 | 34 | 52 | 20th |
| 2004-05 | 46 | 10 | 7 | 6 | 38 | 30 | 12 | 3 | 8 | 33 | 30 | 76 | 4th |
| 2005-06 | 46 | 8 | 10 | 5 | 33 | 27 | 2 | 10 | 11 | 20 | 40 | 50 | 20th |

# 1884-88

## Pre-Football League FA Cup Matches

### 1884-85

| | | | | | | | | |
|---|---|---|---|---|---|---|---|---|
| 1 | Nov | 8 | (h) | Walsall T | L | 0-7 | | 1,5 |

Appearanc
Go

### 1885-86

| | | | | | | | | |
|---|---|---|---|---|---|---|---|---|
| 1 | Oct | 24 | (h) | Birmingham St G | W | 3-0 | Smith, Spilsbury, Evans | 2,0 |
| 2 | Nov | 14 | (h) | Aston Villa | W | 2-0 | Smith, Evans | 5,0 |
| 3 | Dec | 12 | (a) | Small Heath A | L | 2-4 | Evans 2 | 3,0 |

Appearanc
Go

### 1886-87

| | | | | | | | | |
|---|---|---|---|---|---|---|---|---|
| 1 | Oct | 30 | (a) | Aston Unity | W | 4-1 | Evans 2, L.Cooper, Knox | 2,5 |
| 2 | Nov | 20 | (h) | Mitchell St G | L | 1-2 | Bakewell | 2,0 |

Appearanc
Go

### 1887-88

| | | | | | | | | |
|---|---|---|---|---|---|---|---|---|
| 1 | Oct | 15 | (a) | Staveley | W | 2-1 | Monks 2 | 1,5 |
| 2 | Nov | 5 | (h) | Ecclesfield | W | 6-0 | Spilsbury 3, Williamson, Bakewell, Needham | 2,0 |
| 3 | | 26 | (h) | Owlerton | W | 6-2 | Spilsbury 3, Needham 2, Nash | 2,0 |
| 4 | | | | Bye | | | | |
| 5 | Jan | 7 | (a) | Crewe A | L | 0-1 | | 4,0 |

Appearanc
Go

| Gillet L | Evans G | Morley H | Gorham C | Maycroft D | Exham P | Bakewell G | Chatterton W | Sugg F | Smith A | Ward C | Luntley W | Williamson A | Cooper GF | Nicholls H | Warmby H | Spilsbury B | Nash R | Flowers J | Cooper L | Bestwick T | Latham A | Clifton G | Hutchinson F | Knox J | Plackett L | Bower T | Cropper W | Lawrence S | Roulstone W | Monks I | Needham T | Gwynne Rev L | |
|---|---|---|---|---|---|---|---|---|---|---|---|---|---|---|---|---|---|---|---|---|---|---|---|---|---|---|---|---|---|---|---|---|---|
| 1 | 2 | 3 | 4 | 5 | 6 | 7 | 8 | 9 | 10 | 11 | | | | | | | | | | | | | | | | | | | | | | | 1 |
| 1 | 1 | 1 | 1 | 1 | 1 | 1 | 1 | 1 | 1 | 1 | | | | | | | | | | | | | | | | | | | | | | | |
| | | | | | | | | | | | | | | | | | | | | | | | | | | | | | | | | | |
| | | | | | | | | | | | | | | | | | | | | | | | | | | | | | | | | | |
| | 9 | 2 | | | | 7 | | | 10 | | 1 | 3 | 4 | 5 | 6 | 8 | 11 | | | | | | | | | | | | | | | | 1 |
| | 9 | 2 | | | | 7 | | | 10 | | 1 | 3 | 4 | | 6 | 8 | | 5 | 11 | | | | | | | | | | | | | | 2 |
| | 9 | 2 | | | | 7 | | | 10 | | 1 | 3 | 5 | | 4 | 8 | | 6 | 11 | | | | | | | | | | | | | | 3 |
| | 3 | 3 | | | | 3 | | | 3 | | 3 | 3 | 3 | 1 | 3 | 3 | 1 | 2 | 2 | | | | | | | | | | | | | | |
| | 4 | | | | | | | | 2 | | | | | | | 1 | | | | | | | | | | | | | | | | | |
| | | | | | | | | | | | | | | | | | | | | | | | | | | | | | | | | | |
| | 9 | | | | | 7 | | | | | | 4 | | | 3 | | | | 10 | 1 | 2 | 5 | 6 | 8 | 11 | | | | | | | | 1 |
| | | | | | | 7 | | | | | | 3 | | | 6 | | | | 10 | 1 | 2 | 5 | | 8 | 11 | 4 | 9 | | | | | | 2 |
| | 1 | | | | | 2 | | | | | | 2 | | | 2 | | | | 2 | 2 | 2 | 2 | 1 | 2 | 2 | 1 | 1 | | | | | | |
| | 2 | | | | | 1 | | | | | | | | | | | | | 1 | | | | | 1 | | | | | | | | | |
| | | | | | | | | | | | | | | | | | | | | | | | | | | | | | | | | | |
| | | | | | | 7 | | | | | | 4 | | | 5 | 8 | | | | 1 | 2 | | | | 11 | | | 3 | 6 | 9 | 10 | | 1 |
| | | | | | | 7 | | | | | | 4 | | | 5 | 8 | 9 | | | 1 | 2 | | | | 11 | | | 3 | 6 | | 10 | | 2 |
| | | | | | | 7 | | | | | | 4 | | | 5 | 8 | 9 | | | 1 | | | | | 11 | | | 3 | 6 | 2 | 10 | | 3 |
| | | | | | | | | | | | | | | | | | | | | | | | | | | | | | | | | | 4 |
| | | | | | | 7 | | | | | | 4 | | | 5 | 8 | | | | 1 | 2 | | | | 11 | | | 3 | 6 | | 10 | 9 | 5 |
| | | | | | | 4 | | | | | | 4 | | | 4 | 4 | 2 | | | 4 | 3 | | | | 4 | | | 4 | 4 | 2 | 4 | 1 | |
| | | | | | | 1 | | | | | | 1 | | | | 6 | 1 | | | | | | | | | | | | | 2 | 3 | | |

# 1888-89

| | P | W | D | L | F | A | Pts |
|---|---|---|---|---|---|---|---|
| Preston N.E. | 22 | 18 | 4 | 0 | 74 | 15 | 40 |
| Aston Villa | 22 | 12 | 5 | 5 | 61 | 43 | 29 |
| Wolves | 22 | 12 | 4 | 6 | 50 | 37 | 28 |
| Blackburn R | 22 | 10 | 6 | 6 | 66 | 45 | 26 |
| Bolton W | 22 | 10 | 2 | 10 | 63 | 59 | 22 |
| W.B.A. | 22 | 10 | 2 | 10 | 40 | 46 | 22 |
| Accrington | 22 | 6 | 8 | 8 | 48 | 48 | 20 |
| Everton | 22 | 9 | 2 | 11 | 35 | 46 | 20 |
| Burnley | 22 | 7 | 3 | 12 | 42 | 62 | 17 |
| Derby Co | 22 | 7 | 2 | 13 | 41 | 61 | 16 |
| Notts Co | 22 | 5 | 2 | 15 | 40 | 73 | 12 |
| Stoke | 22 | 4 | 4 | 14 | 26 | 51 | 12 |

Leading scorer: Sandy Higgins, League 11, all matches 12.

League ever-present: Lawrence Plackett.

- Between 29 September and 8 December, Derby lost eight consecutive League matches. Although this was equalled in 1965 and 1987–88, they have never suffered a worse sequence.
- Sandy Higgins became the first Derby player to score four goals in a League match, against Aston Villa at the County Ground on 9 March.
- Derby had only 10 men for the match against Everton on 27 October. They borrowed Henry Harbour, an Everton reserve, for the fixture at Anfield Road, Everton's home until 1892.
- Harbour was one of 29 players used by the Rams and one of eight who made only a single appearance.

## Football League

| Match No. | Date | | Venue | Opponents | Result | | Scorers | Attend |
|---|---|---|---|---|---|---|---|---|
| 1 | Sep | 8 | (a) | Bolton W | W | 6-3 | Bakewell 2, Cooper 2, L.Plackett 2 | 3,0 |
| 2 | | 15 | (h) | West Brom A | L | 1-2 | H.Plackett | 3,0 |
| 3 | | 22 | (h) | Accrington | D | 1-1 | Higgins | 2,0 |
| 4 | | 29 | (h) | Preston NE | L | 2-3 | H.Plackett, Wright | 5,0 |
| 5 | Oct | 6 | (a) | West Brom A | L | 0-5 | | 1,5 |
| 6 | | 13 | (a) | Accrington | L | 2-6 | Higgins, L.Plackett | 3,0 |
| 7 | | 20 | (h) | Everton | L | 2-4 | Bakewell, Chatterton | 3,0 |
| 8 | | 27 | (a) | Everton | L | 2-6 | L.Plackett, Needham | 3,0 |
| 9 | Nov | 3 | (a) | Wolves | L | 1-4 | Lees | 2,0 |
| 10 | | 24 | (h) | Blackburn R | L | 0-2 | | 3,0 |
| 11 | Dec | 8 | (a) | Preston NE | L | 0-5 | | 5,0 |
| 12 | | 22 | (h) | Notts C | W | 3-2 | Bakewell, Higgins, unknown | 2,5 |
| 13 | | 26 | (h) | Bolton W | L | 2-3 | Higgins 2 | 3,5 |
| 14 | | 29 | (a) | Aston Villa | L | 2-4 | Bakewell, Spilsbury | 4,0 |
| 15 | Jan | 12 | (h) | Wolves | W | 3-0 | L.Plackett, Higgins, Cooper | 1,5 |
| 16 | | 19 | (a) | Burnley | L | 0-1 | | 3,0 |
| 17 | | 26 | (h) | Stoke | W | 2-1 | L.Plackett, Cooper | 3,0 |
| 18 | Mar | 2 | (h) | Burnley | W | 1-0 | Cooper | 3,0 |
| 19 | | 9 | (h) | Aston Villa | W | 5-2 | Higgins 4, Cooper | 2,5 |
| 20 | | 16 | (a) | Notts C | W | 5-3 | Cooper 2, Bakewell, Higgins, Lees | 3,0 |
| 21 | Apr | 6 | (a) | Stoke | D | 1-1 | L.Plackett | 4,0 |
| 22 | | 15 | (a) | Blackburn R | L | 0-3 | | 4,0 |

FINAL LEAGUE POSITION: 10th in Football League

Appearanc

Go

## FA Cup

| | | | | | | | | |
|---|---|---|---|---|---|---|---|---|
| 1 | Feb | 2 | (h) | Derby Junction | W | 1-0 | Higgins | 4,0 |
| 2 | | 16 | (a) | Aston Villa | L | 3-5 | Cooper 2, L.Plackett | 2,0 |

Appearanc

Go

| Marshall J | Latham A | Ferguson A | Williamson A | Monks I | Roulstone W | Bakewell G | Cooper L | Higgins A | Plackett H | Plackett L | Selvey W | Wright L | Needham T | Roulstone F | Hopewell W | Chatterton W | Bestwick T | Harbour H | Selvey S | Lees J | Smith J | Clifton G | Hickinbottom E | Spilsbury B | Bellhouse E | Pitman R | Morley H | Bromage E | |
|---|---|---|---|---|---|---|---|---|---|---|---|---|---|---|---|---|---|---|---|---|---|---|---|---|---|---|---|---|---|
| 1 | 2 | 3 | 4 | 5 | 6 | 7 | 8 | 9 | 10 | 11 | | | | | | | | | | | | | | | | | | | 1 |
| 1 | 2 | 3 | 4 | 5 | 6 | 7 | 8 | 9 | 10 | 11 | | | | | | | | | | | | | | | | | | | 2 |
| 1 | 2 | 3 | 4 | 5 | 6 | | 7 | 9 | 10 | 11 | 8 | | | | | | | | | | | | | | | | | | 3 |
| 1 | 2 | 3 | 4 | | 6 | 7 | 8 | 9 | 10 | 11 | | 5 | | | | | | | | | | | | | | | | | 4 |
| 1 | 2 | 3 | 4 | | 6 | | 8 | 9 | 10 | 11 | | 5 | 7 | | | | | | | | | | | | | | | | 5 |
| 1 | 2 | | 4 | | 6 | 7 | | 9 | 10 | 11 | | | | 3 | 5 | 8 | | | | | | | | | | | | | 6 |
| | 2 | | 4 | | 6 | 7 | | 9 | 10 | 11 | | 3 | | | 5 | 8 | 1 | | | | | | | | | | | | 7 |
| | | | 2 | | 3 | | | 9 | 10 | 11 | | | 7 | | 5 | 8 | | 4 | 6 | | | | | | | | | | 8 |
| 1 | 2 | 3 | 4 | | 6 | 7 | | 8 | | 10 | | | 11 | | 5 | | | | | 9 | | | | | | | | | 9 |
| 1 | 2 | 3 | 4 | | 6 | 7 | | 8 | 10 | 11 | | 9 | | | 5 | | | | | | | | | | | | | | 10 |
| 1 | 2 | 3 | | | 6 | 4 | | 8 | 9 | 10 | | | 11 | | | 7 | | | | | 5 | | | | | | | | 11 |
| 1 | 2 | 3 | 4 | | 6 | 7 | 11 | 8 | 9 | 10 | | | | | | | | | | | 5 | | | | | | | | 12 |
| 1 | 2 | 3 | | | 6 | 7 | | 8 | 9 | 10 | | | 8 | | | | | | | | | 4 | 5 | | | | | | 13 |
| 1 | 2 | 3 | 4 | | 6 | 7 | 11 | | 9 | 10 | | | | | | | | | | | 5 | | | 8 | | | | | 14 |
| 1 | 2 | 3 | 4 | | 6 | 7 | 11 | 9 | | 10 | | | 8 | | | | | | | | | | | | 5 | | | | 15 |
| 1 | 2 | 3 | | | 6 | | 11 | 9 | | 10 | | | 8 | | | 7 | | | | | 4 | | | | 5 | | | | 16 |
| 1 | 2 | 3 | 4 | | 6 | 7 | 11 | 9 | | 10 | | | 8 | | | | | | | | 5 | | | | | | | | 17 |
| | 2 | | 4 | | 6 | 7 | 11 | 9 | | 10 | | | 8 | | | | | | | | 5 | | | | | 1 | 3 | | 18 |
| | 2 | | 4 | | 6 | | 11 | 9 | 7 | 10 | | | | | | | | | | 8 | 5 | | | | | 1 | 3 | | 19 |
| | | | 2 | | 6 | 7 | 11 | 9 | 4 | 10 | | | | | | | | | | 8 | 5 | | | | | 1 | 3 | | 20 |
| | 2 | 6 | 4 | | | | 11 | 9 | 7 | 10 | | | | | | | | | | 8 | 5 | | | | | | 3 | 1 | 21 |
| | 2 | 3 | 4 | | 6 | 7 | 11 | 9 | | 10 | | | | | | | | | | 8 | 5 | | | | | | | 1 | 22 |
| 6 | 20 | 16 | 19 | 3 | 21 | 16 | 15 | 21 | 16 | 22 | 1 | 4 | 9 | 1 | 5 | 5 | 1 | 1 | 1 | 5 | 10 | 1 | 1 | 1 | 2 | 3 | 4 | 2 | |
| | | | | | | 6 | 8 | 11 | 2 | 7 | | 1 | 1 | | | 1 | | | | 2 | | | | 1 | | | | | |

1 goal unknown

| Marshall J | Latham A | Ferguson A | Williamson A | Monks I | Roulstone W | Bakewell G | Cooper L | Higgins A | Plackett H | Plackett L | Selvey W | Wright L | Needham T | Roulstone F | Hopewell W | Chatterton W | Bestwick T | Harbour H | Selvey S | Lees J | Smith J | Clifton G | Hickinbottom E | Spilsbury B | Bellhouse E | Pitman R | Morley H | Bromage E | |
|---|---|---|---|---|---|---|---|---|---|---|---|---|---|---|---|---|---|---|---|---|---|---|---|---|---|---|---|---|---|
| | 2 | | 4 | 5 | 6 | 7 | 11 | 9 | | 10 | | | | | | | | | | | | | | 8 | | 1 | 3 | | 1 |
| | 5 | 2 | 4 | | 6 | 7 | 11 | 9 | | 10 | | | 8 | | | | | | | | | | | | | 1 | 3 | | 2 |
| | 2 | 1 | 2 | 1 | 2 | 2 | 2 | 2 | | 2 | | | 1 | | | | | | | | | | | 1 | | 2 | 2 | | |
| | | | | | | | 2 | 1 | | 1 | | | | | | | | | | | | | | | | | | | |

# 1889-90

| | P | W | D | L | F | A | Pts |
|---|---|---|---|---|---|---|---|
| Preston N.E. | 22 | 15 | 3 | 4 | 71 | 30 | 33 |
| Everton | 22 | 14 | 3 | 5 | 65 | 40 | 31 |
| Blackburn R | 22 | 12 | 3 | 7 | 78 | 41 | 27 |
| Wolves | 22 | 10 | 5 | 7 | 51 | 38 | 25 |
| W.B.A. | 22 | 11 | 3 | 8 | 47 | 50 | 25 |
| Accrington | 22 | 9 | 6 | 7 | 53 | 56 | 24 |
| Derby Co | 22 | 9 | 3 | 10 | 43 | 55 | 21 |
| Aston Villa | 22 | 7 | 5 | 10 | 43 | 51 | 19 |
| Bolton W | 22 | 9 | 1 | 12 | 54 | 65 | 19 |
| Notts Co | 22 | 6 | 5 | 11 | 43 | 51 | 17 |
| Burnley | 22 | 4 | 5 | 13 | 36 | 65 | 13 |
| Stoke | 22 | 3 | 4 | 15 | 27 | 69 | 10 |

Leading scorer: Sandy Higgins, League/all matches 14.
League ever-present: Walter Roulstone.

- Derby completed one of the most astonishing transfers in their history in May when John Goodall was signed. Already an England international, Goodall starred for Preston North End when they won the League and Cup in 1888–89. His brother Archie also joined the Rams.
- Sandy Higgins beat his scoring record from the previous season with five goals on 28 December. Aston Villa were again on the receiving end.
- Higgins was the first of seven players to claim five or more goals in a game for Derby.
- Everton beat Derby 11–2 in the first round of the Cup at Anfield Road on 18 January. It remains the heaviest defeat in Derby's history.
- John Goodall was picked to keep goal against Wolves on 25 January.

## Football League

| Match No. | Date | | Venue | Opponents | Result | | Scorers | Attend |
|---|---|---|---|---|---|---|---|---|
| 1 | Sep | 7 | (a) | Stoke | D | 1-1 | Cooper | 4, |
| 2 | | 14 | (h) | West Brom A | W | 3-1 | J.Goodall, Cooper, Higgins | 4,0 |
| 3 | | 21 | (a) | Blackburn R | L | 2-4 | J.Goodall 2 | 5, |
| 4 | | 28 | (h) | Notts C | W | 2-0 | J.Goodall 2 | 3,0 |
| 5 | Oct | 5 | (h) | Everton | D | 2-2 | Cooper 2 | 2,5 |
| 6 | | 12 | (a) | Aston Villa | L | 1-7 | Needham | 5,0 |
| 7 | | 19 | (h) | Preston NE | W | 2-1 | Cooper, Jardine | 4,5 |
| 8 | | 26 | (h) | Stoke | W | 2-0 | Cooper, Higgins | 3,0 |
| 9 | Nov | 9 | (a) | West Brom A | W | 3-2 | Higgins, Milarvie, Needham | 1,5 |
| 10 | | 16 | (a) | Accrington | L | 1-6 | Higgins | 3,0 |
| 11 | | 23 | (h) | Wolves | D | 3-3 | Higgins 2, Cooper | 3,5 |
| 12 | | 30 | (a) | Bolton W | L | 1-7 | Opp og | 3,0 |
| 13 | Dec | 21 | (a) | Notts C | L | 1-3 | A.Goodall | 3,0 |
| 14 | | 26 | (h) | Bolton W | W | 3-2 | A.Goodall, Milarvie, Holmes | 4,5 |
| 15 | | 28 | (h) | Aston Villa | W | 5-0 | Higgins 5 | 5,0 |
| 16 | Jan | 4 | (h) | Burnley | W | 4-1 | Higgins, Cooper, Milarvie, Holmes | 3,0 |
| 17 | | 11 | (a) | Preston NE | L | 0-5 | | 5,0 |
| 18 | | 25 | (a) | Wolves | L | 1-2 | Higgins | 2,0 |
| 19 | Feb | 8 | (h) | Blackburn R | W | 4-0 | Roulstone, Higgins, Milarvie, Holmes | 5,0 |
| 20 | | 15 | (h) | Accrington | L | 2-3 | A.Goodall, Latham | 1,5 |
| 21 | Mar | 8 | (a) | Burnley | L | 0-2 | | 2,0 |
| 22 | | 15 | (a) | Everton | L | 0-3 | | 12,0 |

FINAL LEAGUE POSITION: 7th in the Football League

Appearanc
Go

## FA Cup

| | | | | | | | | |
|---|---|---|---|---|---|---|---|---|
| 1 | Jan | 18 | (a) | Everton | L | 2-11 | J.Goodall 2 | 10,0 |

Appearanc
Go

Derby County fielded 10 men at Preston on 11 January when Archie Goodall refused to travel because of his wife's illness.

| Bromage E | Latham A | Ferguson A | Williamson A | Smith J | Roulstone W | Higgins A | Lees J | Goodall J | Goodall A | Cooper L | Bakewell G | Langland A | Walker J | Needham T | Jardine R | Milarvie R | Pitman R | Holmes S | Fife | Bunyan C | Hind F | |
|---|---|---|---|---|---|---|---|---|---|---|---|---|---|---|---|---|---|---|---|---|---|---|
| 1 | 2 | 3 | 4 | 5 | 6 | 7 | 8 | 9 | 10 | 11 | | | | | | | | | | | | 1 |
| 1 | 2 | 3 | 4 | | 6 | 8 | 10 | 9 | 5 | 11 | 7 | | | | | | | | | | | 2 |
| 1 | 2 | 3 | 4 | | 6 | 8 | | 9 | 5 | 11 | 7 | 10 | | | | | | | | | | 3 |
| 1 | 2 | 3 | 4 | | 6 | 8 | | 9 | 5 | 11 | 7 | | 10 | | | | | | | | | 4 |
| 1 | 2 | 3 | 4 | | 6 | 8 | | 9 | 5 | 11 | 7 | | | 10 | | | | | | | | 5 |
| 1 | 2 | 3 | 4 | | 6 | 8 | | 9 | 5 | 11 | 7 | | | 10 | | | | | | | | 6 |
| 1 | 2 | 3 | 4 | | 6 | 8 | | 9 | 5 | 11 | 7 | | | | 10 | | | | | | | 7 |
| 1 | 2 | 3 | 4 | | 6 | 8 | 11 | 9 | 5 | 10 | 7 | | | | | | | | | | | 8 |
| 1 | 2 | 3 | 4 | | 6 | 8 | | 9 | 5 | 10 | | | | 7 | | 11 | | | | | | 9 |
| 1 | 2 | 3 | 4 | | 6 | 8 | | 9 | 5 | 10 | | | | 7 | | 11 | | | | | | 10 |
| 1 | 2 | 3 | 4 | | 6 | 8 | | 9 | 5 | 10 | | | | 7 | | 11 | | | | | | 11 |
| 1 | 2 | 3 | 4 | | 6 | 8 | | 9 | 5 | 10 | | | | 7 | | 11 | 1 | | | | | 12 |
| | 2 | 3 | 4 | | 6 | 8 | | 9 | 5 | 10 | 7 | | | | | 11 | 1 | | | | | 13 |
| 1 | 2 | 3 | 4 | | 6 | 8 | | | 9 | | 7 | | 5 | | | 11 | | 10 | | | | 14 |
| 1 | 2 | 3 | 4 | | 6 | 9 | 8 | | 5 | | 7 | | | | | 11 | | 10 | | | | 15 |
| 1 | 2 | | 4 | 5 | 6 | 9 | | | 3 | 8 | 7 | | | | | 11 | | 10 | | | | 16 |
| 1 | 2 | 3 | 4 | | 6 | | 9 | | | 8 | 7 | | | | | 11 | | 10 | | | | 17 |
| | 2 | 3 | 4 | | 6 | 9 | | 1 | 5 | 8 | 7 | | | | | 11 | | 10 | | | | 18 |
| | 2 | 3 | 4 | | 6 | 9 | | | 5 | 8 | 7 | | | | | 11 | | 10 | 1 | | | 19 |
| | 2 | 3 | | | 6 | 9 | | | 5 | 8 | 7 | 4 | | | | 11 | | 10 | 1 | | | 20 |
| | | 3 | 4 | | 6 | 8 | | 9 | 5 | 7 | | | | | | 11 | | 10 | | 1 | 2 | 21 |
| | 2 | 3 | 4 | | 6 | 9 | | | 5 | 8 | 7 | | | | | 11 | | 10 | | 1 | | 22 |
| 5 | 21 | 21 | 21 | 2 | 22 | 21 | 5 | 15 | 21 | 20 | 16 | 2 | 2 | 6 | 1 | 14 | 2 | 9 | 2 | 2 | 1 | |
| | 1 | | | | 1 | 14 | | 5 | 3 | 8 | | | | 2 | 1 | 4 | | 3 | | | | |

1 own-goal

| | | | | | | | | | | | | | | | | | | | | | | |
|---|---|---|---|---|---|---|---|---|---|---|---|---|---|---|---|---|---|---|---|---|---|---|
| 1 | 2 | 3 | 4 | | 6 | 8 | | 9 | 5 | 10 | 7 | | | | | 11 | | | | | | 1 |
| 1 | 1 | 1 | 1 | | 1 | 1 | | 1 | 1 | 1 | 1 | | | | | 1 | | | | | | |
| | | | | | | | | 2 | | | | | | | | | | | | | | |

# 1890-91

| | P | W | D | L | F | A | Pts |
|---|---|---|---|---|---|---|---|
| Everton | 22 | 14 | 1 | 7 | 63 | 29 | 29 |
| Preston NE | 22 | 12 | 3 | 7 | 44 | 23 | 27 |
| Notts Co | 22 | 11 | 4 | 7 | 52 | 35 | 26 |
| Wolves | 22 | 12 | 2 | 8 | 39 | 50 | 26 |
| Bolton W | 22 | 12 | 1 | 9 | 47 | 34 | 25 |
| Blackburn R | 22 | 11 | 2 | 9 | 52 | 43 | 24 |
| Sunderland * | 22 | 10 | 5 | 7 | 51 | 31 | 23 |
| Burnley | 22 | 9 | 3 | 10 | 52 | 63 | 21 |
| Aston Villa | 22 | 7 | 4 | 11 | 45 | 58 | 18 |
| Accrington | 22 | 6 | 4 | 12 | 28 | 50 | 16 |
| Derby Co | 22 | 7 | 1 | 14 | 47 | 81 | 15 |
| WBA | 22 | 5 | 2 | 15 | 34 | 57 | 12 |

*Sunderland deducted two points for unapproved registration

Leading scorer: John Goodall, League 13, all matches 14.

League ever-present: Archie Goodall, James McLachlan, Walter Roulstone.

- On an extraordinary opening day at the County Ground, Derby beat Blackburn Rovers 8–5.
- Derby's defence was never safe, conceding 81 goals in 22 League games. Not until 1927–28 did they let in more, 83 in 42 matches. David Haddow, later a Scottish international with Rangers, kept goal 16 times after joining Derby from Albion Rovers and was beaten 69 times. He returned to Albion.
- His successor, Charles Bunyan, had kept goal for Hyde United when Preston beat them 26–0 in an 1887 Cup tie.
- Johnny McMillan equalled Sandy Higgins' record with five goals against Wolves at the County Ground on 10 January. Derby won 9–0, the first of three occasions on which they have scored nine in a League game.
- A week earlier, the Rams lost 8–0 at Blackburn.
- John Goodall became the first Derby professional to win an England cap when he played against Wales at Sunderland's Newcastle Road ground on 7 March.

## Football League

| Match No. | Date | | Venue | Opponents | Result | | Scorers | Atten |
|---|---|---|---|---|---|---|---|---|
| 1 | Sep | 6 | (h) | Blackburn R | W | 8-5 | J.Goodall 3, Nelson 2, A.Goodall, Chalmers, McLachlan | 4 |
| 2 | | 13 | (a) | Bolton W | L | 1-3 | J.Goodall | 7 |
| 3 | | 20 | (h) | Preston NE | L | 1-3 | McLachlan | 5, |
| 4 | | 27 | (a) | Notts C | L | 1-2 | Holmes | 7 |
| 5 | Oct | 4 | (a) | Everton | L | 0-7 | | 12 |
| 6 | | 11 | (a) | Wolves | L | 1-5 | McLachlan | 3 |
| 7 | | 18 | (h) | Aston Villa | W | 5-4 | J.Goodall 3, Bakewell, Holmes | 3 |
| 8 | | 25 | (a) | Aston Villa | L | 0-4 | | 3 |
| 9 | Nov | 8 | (a) | Accrington | L | 0-4 | | 2 |
| 10 | | 15 | (a) | Burnley | L | 1-6 | Unknown | 6, |
| 11 | | 22 | (h) | West Brom A | W | 3-1 | J.Goodall 2, Cooper | 2, |
| 12 | | 29 | (a) | West Brom A | W | 4-3 | Cooper 2, Bakewell, J.Goodall | |
| 13 | Dec | 6 | (h) | Accrington | L | 1-2 | Bakewell | 2, |
| 14 | | 13 | (h) | Everton | L | 2-6 | J.Goodall, Holmes | 4, |
| 15 | | 20 | (a) | Preston NE | L | 0-6 | | 3, |
| 16 | | 26 | (h) | Bolton W | D | 1-1 | Cooper | 2, |
| 17 | | 27 | (h) | Notts C | W | 3-1 | Cooper 2, McLachlan | 5, |
| 18 | Jan | 3 | (a) | Blackburn R | L | 0-8 | | 3, |
| 19 | | 10 | (h) | Wolves | W | 9-0 | McMillan 5, Holmes 2, Roulstone, J.Goodall | 3, |
| 20 | | 24 | (h) | Burnley | L | 2-4 | Cooper, McLachlan | 2, |
| 21 | Feb | 7 | (h) | Sunderland | W | 3-1 | McLachlan, J.Goodall, McMillan | 3, |
| 22 | Mar | 21 | (a) | Sunderland | L | 1-5 | McLachlan | 3, |

FINAL LEAGUE POSITION: 11th in the Football League

Appearan

Gc

## FA Cup

| | | | | | | | | |
|---|---|---|---|---|---|---|---|---|
| 1 | Jan | 17 | (a) | Royal Arsenal | W | 2-1 | Cooper, McMillan | 8, |
| 2 | | 31 | (h) | Sheffield W | L | 2-3 | Bakewell, J.Goodall | 7, |

Appearan

Gc

| | Haddow D | Hopkins W | Latham A | Chalmers B | Goodall A | Roulstone W | Bakewell G | McLachlan J | Goodall J | Holmes S | Nelson J | Cooper L | Ferguson A | Williamson A | Walker J | Daft T | Roberts W | Brand R | Baker J | McMillan J | Bunyan C | Cox J | Dunn G |
|---|---|---|---|---|---|---|---|---|---|---|---|---|---|---|---|---|---|---|---|---|---|---|---|
| 1 | 1 | 2 | 3 | 4 | 5 | 6 | 7 | 8 | 9 | 10 | 11 | | | | | | | | | | | | |
| 2 | 1 | 2 | 3 | 4 | 5 | 6 | 7 | 8 | 9 | | 11 | 10 | | | | | | | | | | | |
| 3 | 1 | 2 | | 4 | 5 | 6 | 7 | 8 | 9 | 10 | 11 | | 3 | | | | | | | | | | |
| 4 | 1 | 11 | 2 | 4 | 5 | 6 | 7 | 8 | 9 | 10 | | | 3 | | | | | | | | | | |
| 5 | 1 | 2 | 3 | 4 | 5 | 6 | 7 | 8 | 9 | 10 | | 11 | | | | | | | | | | | |
| 6 | 1 | 2 | | | 11 | 6 | | 7 | 9 | 10 | | | 3 | 4 | 5 | 8 | | | | | | | |
| 7 | 1 | 3 | | 4 | 2 | 6 | 7 | 8 | 9 | 10 | 11 | | | | 5 | | | | | | | | |
| 8 | 1 | 3 | 2 | 4 | 5 | 6 | | 8 | 9 | 10 | | 11 | | | | 7 | | | | | | | |
| 9 | 1 | | | 5 | 9 | 6 | 7 | 8 | | 10 | | 11 | 3 | | 4 | | 2 | | | | | | |
| 10 | 1 | | 2 | 4 | 9 | 6 | | 7 | 8 | 10 | | 11 | 3 | | 5 | | | | | | | | |
| 11 | 1 | | | 4 | 5 | 6 | 7 | 8 | 9 | | | 11 | 3 | | | | 2 | 10 | | | | | |
| 12 | 1 | | | 4 | 5 | 6 | 7 | 8 | 9 | | | 11 | 3 | | | | | 10 | 2 | | | | |
| 13 | 1 | | | 4 | 5 | 6 | 7 | 8 | 9 | | | | 3 | | | | | 10 | 2 | 11 | | | |
| 14 | 1 | | | 4 | 5 | 6 | 7 | 8 | 9 | 11 | | | 3 | | | | | | 2 | 10 | | | |
| 15 | 1 | | | 4 | 5 | 6 | 7 | 8 | 9 | | | 10 | 3 | | | | | | 2 | 11 | | | |
| 16 | | | | 5 | 3 | 6 | 7 | 8 | 9 | | | 10 | 2 | | 4 | | | | | 11 | 1 | | |
| 17 | | | | 5 | 3 | 6 | 7 | 8 | 9 | | | 10 | 2 | | 4 | | | | | 11 | 1 | | |
| 18 | 1 | | | 5 | 3 | 6 | 7 | 8 | | | | 10 | | | 4 | 9 | | | 2 | 11 | | | |
| 19 | | | | 5 | 3 | 6 | 7 | 8 | 9 | 10 | | | | | 4 | | 2 | | | 11 | 1 | | |
| 20 | | | | 5 | 3 | 6 | 7 | 8 | 9 | | | 10 | | | 4 | | | | 2 | 11 | 1 | | |
| 21 | | | | 4 | 5 | 6 | | 7 | 9 | 10 | | 8 | | | | | 2 | | 3 | 11 | 1 | | |
| 22 | | | | | 5 | 6 | | 7 | 9 | | | 8 | | | | | 2 | | 3 | 11 | 1 | 4 | 10 |
| | 6 | 8 | 6 | 20 | 22 | 22 | 17 | 22 | 20 | 12 | 4 | 14 | 12 | 1 | 9 | 3 | 5 | 3 | 8 | 10 | 6 | 1 | 1 |
| | | | | 1 | 1 | 1 | 3 | 7 | 13 | 5 | 2 | 7 | | | | | | | | 6 | | | |

1 goal unknown

| | Haddow D | Hopkins W | Latham A | Chalmers B | Goodall A | Roulstone W | Bakewell G | McLachlan J | Goodall J | Holmes S | Nelson J | Cooper L | Ferguson A | Williamson A | Walker J | Daft T | Roberts W | Brand R | Baker J | McMillan J | Bunyan C | Cox J | Dunn G |
|---|---|---|---|---|---|---|---|---|---|---|---|---|---|---|---|---|---|---|---|---|---|---|---|
| 1 | | | | 5 | 3 | 6 | 7 | 8 | 9 | | | 10 | | | 4 | | | | 2 | 11 | 1 | | |
| 2 | | | | 5 | 3 | 6 | 7 | 8 | 9 | 10 | | | | | 4 | | | | 2 | 11 | 1 | | |
| | | | | 2 | 2 | 2 | 2 | 2 | 2 | 1 | | 1 | | | 2 | | | | 2 | 2 | 2 | | |
| | | | | | | | 1 | | 1 | | | 1 | | | | | | | | 1 | | | |

# 1891-92

| | P | W | D | L | F | A | Pts |
|---|---|---|---|---|---|---|---|
| Sunderland | 26 | 21 | 0 | 5 | 93 | 36 | 42 |
| Preston NE | 26 | 18 | 1 | 7 | 61 | 31 | 37 |
| Bolton W | 26 | 17 | 2 | 7 | 51 | 37 | 36 |
| Aston Villa | 26 | 15 | 0 | 11 | 89 | 56 | 30 |
| Everton | 26 | 12 | 4 | 10 | 49 | 49 | 28 |
| Wolves | 26 | 11 | 4 | 11 | 59 | 46 | 26 |
| Burnley | 26 | 11 | 4 | 11 | 49 | 45 | 26 |
| Notts Co | 26 | 11 | 4 | 11 | 55 | 51 | 26 |
| Blackburn R | 26 | 10 | 6 | 10 | 58 | 65 | 26 |
| Derby Co | 26 | 10 | 4 | 12 | 46 | 52 | 24 |
| Accrington | 26 | 8 | 4 | 14 | 40 | 78 | 20 |
| WBA | 26 | 6 | 6 | 14 | 51 | 58 | 18 |
| Stoke | 26 | 5 | 4 | 17 | 38 | 61 | 14 |
| Darwen | 26 | 4 | 3 | 19 | 38 | 112 | 11 |

Leading scorer: John Goodall, League/all matches 15.

League ever-present: Jimmy Methven.

- Jimmy Methven, signed from the Edinburgh club St Bernard's, made his debut at Stoke on 5 September. It was the first of 511 appearances and, with 16 years as manager, he was a vital part of Derby County until 1922, a spell of 31 years.
- William Storer also appeared for the first time on the opening day. A Derbyshire and England wicketkeeper, he is one of four Test cricketers to appear for the Rams. William Chatterton and Frank Sugg preceded him, Arnold Warren came later.
- On 19 March, Derby used the Baseball Ground for the first time and lost to Sunderland. Clashes with race meetings became a more frequent problem at the County Ground.

## Football League

| Match No. | Date | | Venue | Opponents | Result | | Scorers | Attenda |
|---|---|---|---|---|---|---|---|---|
| 1 | Sep | 5 | (a) | Stoke | L | 1-2 | J.Goodall | 3,0 |
| 2 | | 12 | (h) | Accrington | W | 3-1 | McMillan 2, J.Goodall | 3,5 |
| 3 | | 19 | (h) | Notts C | W | 3-0 | J.Goodall, McMillan, Whitelaw (og) | 8,0 |
| 4 | | 26 | (a) | Wolves | W | 3-1 | J.Goodall 3 | 3,0 |
| 5 | Oct | 3 | (h) | Aston Villa | W | 4-2 | Storer 2, Mills, J.Goodall | 6,5 |
| 6 | | 17 | (h) | Stoke | D | 3-3 | A.Goodall, J.Goodall, McLachlan | 5,0 |
| 7 | | 24 | (h) | Everton | L | 0-3 | | 7,0 |
| 8 | | 31 | (h) | Wolves | W | 2-1 | Storer, Hardy | 5,5 |
| 9 | Nov | 14 | (a) | Sunderland | L | 1-7 | J.Goodall | 5,0 |
| 10 | | 21 | (h) | Darwen | W | 7-0 | McMillan 2, McLachlan 2, Cox, Mills, Ekins | 5,0 |
| 11 | | 28 | (a) | Darwen | L | 0-2 | | 1,0 |
| 12 | Dec | 5 | (h) | Preston NE | L | 1-2 | McMillan | 8,0 |
| 13 | | 12 | (a) | West Brom A | L | 2-4 | J.Goodall, Mills | 2,0 |
| 14 | | 19 | (h) | Burnley | L | 0-1 | | 4,0 |
| 15 | | 26 | (h) | Bolton W | W | 3-2 | Storer 2, McLachlan | 5,0 |
| 16 | Jan | 1 | (a) | Bolton W | L | 1-3 | A.Goodall | 8,0 |
| 17 | | 2 | (a) | Blackburn R | W | 2-0 | Ekins, Storer | 2,0 |
| 18 | | 9 | (a) | Aston Villa | L | 0-6 | | 10,0 |
| 19 | Feb | 6 | (h) | West Brom A | D | 1-1 | J.Goodall | 3,0 |
| 20 | | 20 | (a) | Notts C | L | 1-2 | McLachlan | 3,0 |
| 21 | Mar | 5 | (a) | Preston NE | L | 0-3 | | 5,0 |
| 22 | | 19 | (h*) | Sunderland | L | 0-1 | | 6,0 |
| 23 | | 26 | (h) | Blackburn R | D | 1-1 | McMillan | 5,0 |
| 24 | Apr | 2 | (a) | Accrington | D | 1-1 | Mills | 2,0 |
| 25 | | 15 | (a) | Everton | W | 2-1 | J.Goodall 2 | 12,0 |
| 26 | | 16 | (a) | Burnley | W | 4-2 | J.Goodall 2 (1 pen), McLachlan, Mills | 6,0 |

FINAL LEAGUE POSITION: 10th in the Football League — Appearanc

* Played at the Baseball Ground not the County Ground. — Goa

## FA Cup

| | | | | | | | | |
|---|---|---|---|---|---|---|---|---|
| 1 | Jan | 16 | (a) | Blackburn R | L | 1-4 | Storer | 10,0 |

Appearanc

Goa

| Robinson J | Methven J | Staley J | Cox J | Goodall A | Roulstone W | McLachlan J | Storer W | Goodall J | Hardy A | McMillan J | Hickinbottom E | Mills S | Ekins F | Rose W | Butterworth C | Bunyan C | Cooper L | Rose C | |
|---|---|---|---|---|---|---|---|---|---|---|---|---|---|---|---|---|---|---|---|
| 1 | 2 | 3 | 4 | 5 | 6 | 7 | 8 | 9 | 10 | 11 | | | | | | | | | 1 |
| 1 | 2 | 3 | 4 | | 6 | 8 | 10 | 9 | | 11 | 5 | 7 | | | | | | | 2 |
| 1 | 2 | 3 | 4 | | 6 | 8 | 10 | 9 | | 11 | 5 | 7 | | | | | | | 3 |
| 1 | 2 | 3 | 4 | | 6 | 8 | 10 | 9 | | 11 | 5 | 7 | | | | | | | 4 |
| 1 | 2 | 3 | 4 | | 6 | 8 | 10 | 9 | | 11 | 5 | 7 | | | | | | | 5 |
| 1 | 2 | 3 | 4 | 11 | 6 | 8 | 10 | 9 | | | 5 | 7 | | | | | | | 6 |
| 1 | 2 | 3 | 4 | 5 | 6 | 8 | 10 | 9 | | 11 | | 7 | | | | | | | 7 |
| 1 | 2 | 3 | 4 | 5 | 6 | 8 | 9 | | 10 | 11 | | 7 | | | | | | | 8 |
| 1 | 2 | | 4 | 3 | 6 | 8 | 11 | 9 | | 10 | 5 | 7 | | | | | | | 9 |
| 1 | 2 | | 4 | 5 | 6 | 8 | 3 | 9 | | 11 | | 7 | 10 | | | | | | 10 |
| 1 | 2 | 3 | 4 | 5 | 6 | 8 | | 9 | | 11 | | 7 | 10 | | | | | | 11 |
| 1 | 2 | 3 | 4 | 5 | 6 | 8 | | 9 | | 11 | | 7 | 10 | | | | | | 12 |
| 1 | 2 | 3 | 4 | 5 | 6 | 8 | | 9 | | 11 | | 7 | 10 | | | | | | 13 |
| 1 | 2 | 3 | 4 | 5 | 6 | 8 | 11 | 9 | | | | 7 | 10 | | | | | | 14 |
| 1 | 2 | 3 | 4 | 5 | 6 | 8 | 11 | 9 | | | 10 | 7 | | | | | | | 15 |
| 1 | 2 | 3 | 4 | 9 | 6 | 8 | 11 | | | | 5 | 7 | 10 | | | | | | 16 |
| 1 | 2 | 3 | 4 | 9 | 6 | 8 | 11 | | | | 5 | 7 | 10 | | | | | | 17 |
| 1 | 2 | 3 | 4 | 9 | 6 | | 11 | 7 | | | 5 | 8 | 10 | | | | | | 18 |
| 1 | 2 | 3 | | 5 | | 8 | | 9 | | 11 | 6 | 7 | 10 | 4 | | | | | 19 |
| 1 | 2 | 3 | | 5 | 6 | 8 | 9 | 11 | | | | | 10 | 4 | 7 | | | | 20 |
| 1 | 2 | 3 | | 5 | | 8 | | 9 | | 11 | 6 | 7 | 10 | 4 | | | | | 21 |
| 1 | 2 | 3 | 4 | 5 | | | 7 | 9 | | 11 | 6 | 8 | 10 | | | | | | 22 |
| | 2 | 3 | 4 | 5 | | 8 | | 9 | | 11 | 6 | 7 | | | | 1 | 10 | | 23 |
| 1 | 2 | 3 | 4 | 9 | 6 | 8 | | | | 11 | 5 | 7 | 10 | | | | | | 24 |
| 1 | 2 | 3 | 4 | 5 | 6 | 8 | | 9 | | 11 | | 7 | 10 | | | | | | 25 |
| 1 | 2 | 3 | 4 | 5 | 6 | 8 | | 9 | | 11 | | 7 | | | | | | 10 | 26 |
| 5 | 26 | 24 | 23 | 22 | 22 | 24 | 17 | 22 | 2 | 19 | 15 | 24 | 14 | 3 | 1 | 1 | 1 | 1 | |
| | | | 1 | 2 | | 6 | 6 | 15 | 1 | 7 | | 5 | 2 | | | | | | |

1 own-goal

| | | | | | | | | | | | | | |
|---|---|---|---|---|---|---|---|---|---|---|---|---|---|
| 1 | 2 | 3 | 4 | 5 | 6 | 8 | 10 | 9 | | 11 | | 7 | 1 |
| 1 | 1 | 1 | 1 | 1 | 1 | 1 | 1 | 1 | | 1 | | 1 | |
| | | | | | | | 1 | | | | | | |

# 1892-93

| | P | W | D | L | F | A | Pts |
|---|---|---|---|---|---|---|---|
| Sunderland | 30 | 22 | 4 | 4 | 100 | 36 | 48 |
| Preston NE | 30 | 17 | 3 | 10 | 57 | 39 | 37 |
| Everton | 30 | 16 | 4 | 10 | 74 | 51 | 36 |
| Aston Villa | 30 | 16 | 3 | 11 | 73 | 62 | 35 |
| Bolton W | 30 | 13 | 6 | 11 | 56 | 55 | 32 |
| Burnley | 30 | 13 | 4 | 13 | 51 | 44 | 30 |
| Stoke | 30 | 12 | 5 | 13 | 58 | 48 | 29 |
| WBA | 30 | 12 | 5 | 13 | 58 | 69 | 29 |
| Blackburn R | 30 | 8 | 13 | 9 | 47 | 56 | 29 |
| Nottingham F | 30 | 10 | 8 | 12 | 48 | 52 | 28 |
| Wolves | 30 | 12 | 4 | 14 | 47 | 68 | 28 |
| Sheffield W | 30 | 12 | 3 | 15 | 55 | 65 | 27 |
| Derby Co | 30 | 9 | 9 | 12 | 52 | 64 | 27 |
| Notts Co | 30 | 10 | 4 | 16 | 53 | 61 | 24 |
| Accrington | 30 | 6 | 11 | 13 | 57 | 81 | 23 |
| Newton Heath | 30 | 6 | 6 | 18 | 50 | 85 | 18 |

Leading scorer: John Goodall, League 13, all matches 14.
League ever-present: Jack Robinson.

- Steve Bloomer made his debut at the age of 18 in the opening game at Stoke.
- Derby had failed to register three players, Ernest Hickinbottom, James McLachlan and Sam Mills, in time for the first match, hastening Bloomer's promotion.
- Bloomer held his place and scored the first of his 332 goals for the club, a penalty against West Bromwich Albion, on 24 September.
- Archie Goodall played his first game of the season on 1 October. He was embarking on Derby's record runs of consecutive appearances, in the League and all matches. His next absence was on 2 October 1897.
- On 19 October, Walter Roulstone became the first Derby player to appear in 100 League and Cup games.
- Derby appeared at the Baseball Ground for the second time on 12 November, beating Burnley to earn one of only nine victories in a poor season.

## Division One

| Match No. | Date | | Venue | Opponents | Result | | Scorers | Attend |
|---|---|---|---|---|---|---|---|---|
| 1 | Sep | 3 | (a) | Stoke | W | 3-1 | McMillan 2, J.Goodall | 5, |
| 2 | | 10 | (h) | Preston NE | L | 1-2 | McLachlan | 10, |
| 3 | | 17 | (a) | Notts C | D | 1-1 | Ekins | 12, |
| 4 | | 24 | (h) | West Brom A | D | 1-1 | Bloomer (pen) | 8, |
| 5 | Oct | 1 | (h) | Nottingham F | L | 2-3 | A.Goodall, Bloomer | 8, |
| 6 | | 8 | (a) | Burnley | L | 1-2 | J.Goodall | 5, |
| 7 | | 19 | (h) | Notts C | L | 4-5 | Storer 2, McMillan, J.Goodall | 5, |
| 8 | | 22 | (h) | Blackburn R | W | 3-0 | A.Goodall, Mills, McMillan | 5, |
| 9 | | 29 | (a) | Aston Villa | L | 1-6 | J.Goodall | 5, |
| 10 | Nov | 5 | (h) | Everton | L | 1-6 | J.Goodall | 5, |
| 11 | | 12 | (h*) | Burnley | W | 1-0 | A.Goodall | 5, |
| 12 | | 26 | (h) | Wolves | D | 2-2 | Bloomer 2 | 2, |
| 13 | Dec | 3 | (h) | Accrington | D | 3-3 | Mills, McLachlan, Roulstone | 2, |
| 14 | | 10 | (a) | Sheffield W | D | 3-3 | J.Goodall 2, A.Goodall | 5, |
| 15 | | 17 | (h) | Aston Villa | W | 2-1 | Bloomer, Roulstone | 4, |
| 16 | | 24 | (h) | Stoke | W | 1-0 | J.Goodall | 8, |
| 17 | | 26 | (h) | Bolton W | D | 1-1 | J.Goodall | 7, |
| 18 | | 31 | (a) | Newton Heath | L | 1-7 | Clements (og) | 3, |
| 19 | Jan | 2 | (a) | Bolton W | W | 3-0 | J.Goodall 3 | 5, |
| 20 | | 7 | (a) | Blackburn R | D | 2-2 | Bloomer 2 | 5, |
| 21 | | 28 | (a) | Nottingham F | L | 0-1 | | 12, |
| 22 | Feb | 11 | (h) | Newton Heath | W | 5-1 | Bloomer, J.Goodall, A.Goodall, McMillan, Little | 5, |
| 23 | | 25 | (a) | Wolves | L | 1-2 | Storer | 5, |
| 24 | Mar | 11 | (a) | Sunderland | L | 1-3 | Storer | 4, |
| 25 | | 25 | (h) | Sheffield W | D | 2-2 | Forman, Bloomer | 6, |
| 26 | | 31 | (a) | Accrington | W | 3-0 | Forman 2, Bloomer | 2, |
| 27 | Apr | 1 | (a) | West Brom A | L | 1-3 | A.Goodall | 5, |
| 28 | | 8 | (h) | Sunderland | D | 1-1 | Bloomer | 8, |
| 29 | | 15 | (a) | Everton | L | 0-5 | | 12, |
| 30 | | 17 | (a) | Preston NE | W | 1-0 | McMillan | 4, |

FINAL LEAGUE POSITION: 13th in Division One — Appearan
*Played at the Baseball Ground, not the County Ground. — Go

## FA Cup

| | | | | | | | | |
|---|---|---|---|---|---|---|---|---|
| 1 | Jan | 21 | (a) | Sheffield W | L | 2-3* | J.Goodall, Bloomer | 20, |
| R | | 30 | (h) | Sheffield W | W | 1-0 | J.Goodall | 15, |
| R | Feb | 2 | (a) | Sheffield W | L | 2-4 | J.Goodall, Little | 10, |

*after extra-time — Appearan
Go

The clubs had already met in Sheffield, when J.Goodall and Bloomer scored in Derby's 3-2 defeat, after which the Rams successfully protested; and at Derby, when J.Goodall scored the only goal of the game before Wednesday protested successfully. As both protests concerned the eligibility of players, it seems logical that only appearances and goals in the third meeting should count in the records.

| Robinson J | Methven J | Staley J | Cox J | Garden H | Roulstone W | Ekins F | Bloomer S | Goodall J. | Rose C | McMillan J | Hickinbottom E | Mills S | McLachlan J | Goodall A | Rose W | Storer W | McLean T | Leiper J | Little T | Forman FR | Hardy A | |
|---|---|---|---|---|---|---|---|---|---|---|---|---|---|---|---|---|---|---|---|---|---|---|
| 1 | 2 | 3 | 4 | 5 | 6 | 7 | 8 | 9 | 10 | 11 | | | | | | | | | | | | 1 |
| 1 | 2 | 3 | 4 | | 6 | | 10 | 9 | | 11 | 5 | 7 | 8 | | | | | | | | | 2 |
| 1 | 2 | 3 | 4 | | 6 | 7 | 10 | | 9 | 11 | 5 | | 8 | | | | | | | | | 3 |
| 1 | 2 | 3 | 4 | | 6 | | 10 | | 9 | 11 | 5 | 7 | 8 | | | | | | | | | 4 |
| 1 | 2 | 3 | 4 | | 6 | 7 | 11 | 9 | | 10 | | | 8 | 5 | | | | | | | | 5 |
| 1 | 2 | 3 | | | 6 | | 10 | 8 | | 11 | 5 | 7 | | 9 | 4 | | | | | | | 6 |
| 1 | 2 | 3 | 4 | | 6 | | 10 | 8 | | 11 | | 7 | | 5 | | 9 | | | | | | 7 |
| 1 | 2 | 3 | 4 | | 6 | | 10 | 8 | | 11 | | 7 | | 5 | | 9 | | | | | | 8 |
| 1 | 2 | | | | 6 | | 10 | 8 | | 11 | | 7 | | 5 | 4 | 9 | 3 | | | | | 9 |
| 1 | | | 4 | | 6 | | 10 | 8 | | 11 | | 7 | | 5 | | 9 | 3 | 2 | | | | 10 |
| 1 | 2 | | 4 | | 6 | | 10 | 8 | | | 5 | 7 | | 9 | | 11 | | 3 | | | | 11 |
| 1 | 2 | | 4 | | 6 | | 10 | 9 | | 11 | | 7 | 8 | 5 | | | | 3 | | | | 12 |
| 1 | 2 | | 4 | | 6 | | 10 | 9 | | 11 | | 7 | 8 | 5 | | | | 3 | | | | 13 |
| 1 | 2 | | | | 6 | | 11 | 9 | | 10 | 4 | 7 | 8 | 5 | | | | 3 | | | | 14 |
| 1 | 2 | | | | 6 | | 8 | 9 | | 11 | 4 | 7 | | 5 | | | | 3 | 10 | | | 15 |
| 1 | 2 | 3 | | | 6 | | 8 | 9 | | 10 | 4 | 7 | | 5 | | | | | 11 | | | 16 |
| 1 | 2 | 3 | | | 6 | | 8 | 9 | | 11 | 4 | 7 | | 5 | | | | | 10 | | | 17 |
| 1 | 2 | 3 | | | 6 | | 8 | 9 | | 11 | 4 | 7 | | 5 | | | | | 10 | | | 18 |
| 1 | 2 | | | | 6 | | 8 | 9 | | 11 | 4 | 7 | | 5 | | | | 3 | 10 | | | 19 |
| 1 | 2 | | 4 | | 6 | 7 | 8 | | 10 | 11 | 5 | | | 9 | | | | 3 | | | | 20 |
| 1 | 2 | | | | 6 | | 8 | 9 | | 10 | 4 | 7 | | 5 | | | | 3 | 11 | | | 21 |
| 1 | 2 | | | | 6 | | 8 | 9 | | 10 | 4 | 7 | | 5 | | | | 3 | 11 | | | 22 |
| 1 | 2 | | | | 6 | | | 9 | | 10 | 4 | 7 | | 5 | | 8 | | 3 | 11 | | | 23 |
| 1 | 2 | | | | 6 | | | 9 | | 10 | 4 | 7 | | 5 | | 8 | | 3 | 11 | | | 24 |
| 1 | 2 | | 4 | | 6 | | 7 | 9 | | 11 | | | | 5 | | 10 | | 3 | | 8 | | 25 |
| 1 | 2 | | 4 | | | | 8 | 9 | | 10 | 6 | | | 5 | | | | 3 | 11 | 7 | | 26 |
| 1 | 2 | | 4 | | 6 | | 8 | | | 11 | 5 | | | 9 | | | | 3 | | 7 | 10 | 27 |
| 1 | 2 | | 4 | | | | 7 | 9 | | 11 | 6 | | | 5 | | | | 3 | 10 | 8 | | 28 |
| 1 | 2 | | 4 | | | | 8 | 9 | | 10 | 6 | | 7 | 5 | | | | 3 | 11 | | | 29 |
| 1 | 2 | | 4 | | | | 9 | | | 10 | 6 | 7 | 8 | 5 | | | | 3 | 11 | | | 30 |
| 30 | 29 | 11 | 18 | 1 | 26 | 4 | 28 | 25 | 4 | 29 | 21 | 21 | 9 | 26 | 2 | 8 | 2 | 18 | 13 | 4 | 1 | |
| | | | | | 2 | 1 | 11 | 13 | | 6 | | 2 | 2 | 6 | | 4 | | | 1 | 3 | | |

1 own-goal

| | | | | | | | | | | | | | | | | | | | | | | |
|---|---|---|---|---|---|---|---|---|---|---|---|---|---|---|---|---|---|---|---|---|---|---|
| 1 | 2 | | | | 6 | | 8 | 9 | | 10 | 4 | 7 | | 5 | | | | 3 | 11 | | | 1 |
| 1 | 2 | | | | 6 | | 8 | 9 | | 10 | 4 | 7 | | 5 | | | | 3 | 11 | | | R |
| 1 | 2 | | | | 6 | | | 9 | | 10 | 4 | 7 | | 5 | | 8 | | 3 | 11 | | | R |
| 1 | 1 | | | | 1 | | | 1 | | 1 | 1 | 1 | | 1 | | 1 | | 1 | 1 | | | |
| | | | | | | | | 1 | | | | | | | | | | | 1 | | | |

# 1893-94

| | P | W | D | L | F | A | Pts |
|---|---|---|---|---|---|---|---|
| Aston Villa | 30 | 19 | 6 | 5 | 84 | 42 | 44 |
| Sunderland | 30 | 17 | 4 | 9 | 72 | 44 | 38 |
| Derby Co | 30 | 16 | 4 | 10 | 73 | 62 | 36 |
| Blackburn R | 30 | 16 | 2 | 12 | 69 | 53 | 34 |
| Burnley | 30 | 15 | 4 | 11 | 61 | 51 | 34 |
| Everton | 30 | 15 | 3 | 12 | 90 | 57 | 33 |
| Nottingham F | 30 | 14 | 4 | 12 | 57 | 48 | 32 |
| WBA | 30 | 14 | 4 | 12 | 66 | 59 | 32 |
| Wolves | 30 | 14 | 3 | 13 | 52 | 63 | 31 |
| Sheffield U | 30 | 13 | 5 | 12 | 47 | 61 | 31 |
| Stoke | 30 | 13 | 3 | 14 | 65 | 79 | 29 |
| Sheffield W | 30 | 9 | 8 | 13 | 48 | 57 | 26 |
| Bolton W | 30 | 10 | 4 | 16 | 38 | 52 | 24 |
| Preston NE | 30 | 10 | 3 | 17 | 44 | 56 | 23 |
| Darwen | 30 | 7 | 5 | 18 | 37 | 83 | 19 |
| Newton Heath | 30 | 6 | 2 | 22 | 36 | 72 | 14 |

Leading scorers: Steve Bloomer, League 19. Johnny McMillan, all matches 21.
League ever-present: John Allan, Archie Goodall, Johnny McMillan, Jimmy Methven.

- Steve Bloomer was Derby's leading League scorer for the first time and went on to occupy that position for 13 consecutive seasons. In the next 12 of them, he also led the way in all matches.
- Johnny McMillan was the first Derby player to pass 20 League and Cup goals in a season.
- Four players appeared in every League game. Only twice more has that occurred in Derby's history, in 1895–96 and 1938–39.
- Derby won 16 League games, their best so far, achieved their highest position, third, and scored 73 goals, the most until they were in the Second Division in 1907–08.

## Division One

| Match No. | Date | | Venue | Opponents | Result | | Scorers | Attenda |
|---|---|---|---|---|---|---|---|---|
| 1 | Sep | 2 | (a) | Preston NE | L | 0-1 | | 4,0 |
| 2 | | 4 | (a) | Sheffield U | W | 2-1 | Bloomer, McMillan | 6,0 |
| 3 | | 9 | (h) | Everton | W | 7-3 | Bloomer 2, McMillan 2, A.Goodall, Allan, Keay | 8,0 |
| 4 | | 16 | (h) | West Brom A | L | 2-3 | Bloomer, Keay | 6,6 |
| 5 | | 23 | (a) | Stoke | L | 1-3 | J.Goodall | 5,0 |
| 6 | | 30 | (a) | Aston Villa | D | 1-1 | J.Goodall | 12,0 |
| 7 | Oct | 7 | (h) | Newton Heath | W | 2-0 | McMillan, Clements (og) | 6,0 |
| 8 | | 14 | (a) | Sheffield W | L | 0-4 | | 8,0 |
| 9 | | 21 | (h) | Sheffield W | D | 3-3 | Bloomer 2, McMillan | 6,0 |
| 10 | | 28 | (a) | Sunderland | L | 0-5 | | 6,0 |
| 11 | Nov | 4 | (h) | Sheffield U | W | 2-1 | Bloomer, J.Goodall | 7,0 |
| 12 | | 11 | (a) | Everton | W | 2-1 | Bloomer 2 | 15,0 |
| 13 | | 18 | (h) | Darwen | W | 2-1 | Bloomer, Towie | 7 |
| 14 | Dec | 2 | (h) | Aston Villa | L | 0-3 | | 7,0 |
| 15 | | 9 | (h) | Nottingham F | L | 3-4 | A.Goodall, Bloomer, McMillan | 6,5 |
| 16 | | 23 | (h) | Stoke | W | 5-2 | Bloomer 2, J.Goodall, Allan, A.Goodall | 7,5 |
| 17 | | 26 | (h) | Bolton W | W | 6-1 | McMillan 3, J.Goodall 2, A.Goodall | 10,5 |
| 18 | | 30 | (a) | Nottingham F | L | 2-4 | Bloomer, J.Goodall | 8,0 |
| 19 | Jan | 1 | (a) | Bolton W | D | 1-1 | A.Goodall | 7,0 |
| 20 | | 6 | (h) | Preston NE | W | 2-1 | Bloomer, McMillan | 3,0 |
| 21 | | 20 | (a) | Wolves | W | 4-2 | Allan 2, Bloomer, McMillan | 4,0 |
| 22 | Feb | 3 | (h) | Wolves | W | 4-1 | Allan 2, Bloomer, McMillan | 6,0 |
| 23 | Mar | 7 | (h) | Sunderland | L | 1-4 | J.Goodall | 2,5 |
| 24 | | 10 | (a) | Burnley | L | 1-3 | Allan | 5,0 |
| 25 | | 17 | (a) | Newton Heath | W | 6-2 | McMillan 3, Francis 2, Abbott | 7,0 |
| 26 | | 23 | (a) | Blackburn R | W | 2-0 | Francis, J.Goodall | 7,0 |
| 27 | | 24 | (a) | West Brom A | W | 1-0 | Francis | 3,0 |
| 28 | | 31 | (h) | Blackburn R | W | 5-2 | Bloomer 2, Cox, J.Goodall, Francis | 4,0 |
| 29 | Apr | 2 | (h) | Burnley | D | 3-3 | J.Goodall, Allan, McMillan | 2,1 |
| 30 | | 14 | (a) | Darwen | W | 3-2 | McMillan 2, J.Goodall | 3,0 |

FINAL LEAGUE POSITION: 3rd in Division One

Appearanc
Goa

## FA Cup

| | | | | | | | | |
|---|---|---|---|---|---|---|---|---|
| 1 | Jan | 27 | (h) | Darwen | W | 2-0 | J.Goodall, McMillan | 7,5 |
| 2 | Feb | 10 | (a) | Leicester F | D | 0-0* | | 12,0 |
| R | | 17 | (h) | Leicester F | W | 3-0 | Allan, McMillan, Francis | 4,0 |
| 3 | | 24 | (h) | Blackburn R | L | 1-4 | McMillan | 15,5 |

* after extra-time

Appearanc
Goa

**United Counties League – Division Two**

| | | | | | | |
|---|---|---|---|---|---|---|
| 1 | Jan | 13 | (h) | Notts C | W | 8-1 |
| 2 | Feb | 12 | (a) | Sheffield U | W | 2-0 |
| 3 | Mar | 3 | (h) | Sheffield W | D | 1-1 |
| 4 | | 26 | (a) | Notts C | W | 4-0 |
| 5 | Apr | 7 | (a) | Sheffield U | L | 2-5 |
| 6 | | 12 | (a) | Nottingham F | W | 3-0 |
| 7 | | 21 | (h) | Sheffield U | W | 2-0 |
| 8 | | 25 | (h) | Nottingham F | D | 0-0 |

*Championship decider*

| | | | | | | |
|---|---|---|---|---|---|---|
| 9 | Apr | 30 | (h) | West Brom A | D | 1-1 |

(For replay see 1894-5)

**United Counties League**

The League was formed, based on West and East Midlands divisions, to give extra competitive football but lasted only two seasons because of the increasing importance of promotion and relegation.

**Second Division table**

| | P | W | D | L | F | A | Pts |
|---|---|---|---|---|---|---|---|
| Derby County | 8 | 5 | 2 | 1 | 22 | 7 | 12 |
| Nottingham F | 8 | 4 | 3 | 1 | 15 | 10 | 11 |
| Sheffield W | 8 | 2 | 3 | 3 | 15 | 15 | 7 |
| Sheffield U | 7 | 1 | 3 | 3 | 4 | 8 | 5 |
| Notts County | 7 | 1 | 1 | 5 | 6 | 22 | 3 |

**Appearances (including championship decider):** Allan 9, Cox 9, A.Goodall 9, McMillan 9, Leiper 8, Methven 8, Robinson 8, Docherty 7, Bloomer 6, Francis 6, J.Goodall 6, Keay 4, Staley 4, Hickinbottom 2, Abbott 1, Dockery 1, F. Forman 1, Raybould 1.

**Goalscorers (including championship decider):** A.Goodall 8, McMillan 6, Allan 3, Francis 3, J.Goodall 2, Cox 1.

| Match | Robinson J | Methven J | Leiper J | Cox J | Goodall A | Docherty J | Towie T | Bloomer S | Goodall J | Allan J | McMillan J | Keay W | Little T | Dockery G | Staley J | Roulstone W | Hickinbottom E | Francis P | Abbott W |
|---|---|---|---|---|---|---|---|---|---|---|---|---|---|---|---|---|---|---|---|
| 1 | 1 | 2 | 3 | 4 | 5 | 6 | 7 | 8 | 9 | 10 | 11 | | | | | | | | |
| 2 | 1 | 2 | 3 | 4 | 5 | 6 | | 8 | 9 | 10 | 11 | 7 | | | | | | | |
| 3 | 1 | 2 | 3 | 4 | 5 | 6 | | 8 | 9 | 10 | 11 | 7 | | | | | | | |
| 4 | 1 | 2 | 3 | 4 | 5 | 6 | | 8 | 9 | 10 | 11 | 7 | | | | | | | |
| 5 | 1 | 2 | 3 | 4 | 5 | 6 | | 8 | 9 | 10 | 11 | 7 | | | | | | | |
| 6 | 1 | 2 | 3 | 4 | 5 | 6 | | 8 | 9 | 7 | 10 | | 11 | | | | | | |
| 7 | 1 | 2 | 3 | 4 | 5 | 6 | | 8 | 9 | 7 | 10 | | 11 | | | | | | |
| 8 | 1 | 2 | 3 | 4 | 5 | 6 | | 8 | 9 | 7 | 10 | | 11 | | | | | | |
| 9 | 1 | 2 | 3 | 4 | 5 | 6 | 11 | 7 | 8 | 9 | 10 | | | | | | | | |
| 10 | 1 | 2 | 3 | 4 | 5 | 6 | 11 | 7 | 8 | 9 | 10 | | | | | | | | |
| 11 | | 2 | | 4 | 5 | | 11 | 8 | 9 | 7 | 10 | | | 1 | 3 | 6 | | | |
| 12 | | 2 | | | 5 | | 11 | 8 | 9 | 7 | 10 | | | 1 | 3 | 6 | 4 | | |
| 13 | | 2 | | | 5 | | 11 | 8 | 9 | 7 | 10 | | | 1 | 3 | 6 | 4 | | |
| 14 | | 2 | | | 5 | | 11 | 8 | 9 | 7 | 10 | | | 1 | 3 | 6 | 4 | | |
| 15 | | 2 | | | 5 | 6 | 11 | 8 | 9 | 7 | 10 | | | 1 | 3 | | 4 | | |
| 16 | 1 | 2 | 3 | 4 | 5 | | | 8 | 9 | 7 | 10 | 11 | | | | | 6 | | |
| 17 | 1 | 2 | 3 | 4 | 5 | | | 8 | 9 | 7 | 10 | 11 | | | | | 6 | | |
| 18 | 1 | 2 | 3 | 4 | 5 | | | 8 | 9 | 7 | 10 | 11 | | | | | 6 | | |
| 19 | 1 | 2 | 3 | 4 | 9 | | | 8 | | 7 | 10 | 11 | | | 6 | | 5 | | |
| 20 | 1 | 2 | 3 | 4 | 5 | | | 8 | 9 | 7 | 10 | 11 | | | | | 6 | | |
| 21 | 1 | 2 | 3 | 4 | 5 | | | 8 | 9 | 7 | 10 | 11 | | | | | 6 | | |
| 22 | 1 | 2 | 3 | 4 | 5 | | | 8 | 9 | 7 | 10 | 11 | | | | | 6 | | |
| 23 | 1 | 2 | 3 | 4 | 5 | | | | 9 | 7 | 10 | 11 | | | | | 6 | 8 | |
| 24 | 1 | 2 | 3 | 4 | 5 | 6 | | | 9 | 7 | 10 | | | | | | | 8 | 11 |
| 25 | 1 | 2 | | | 5 | 6 | | | 9 | 7 | 10 | | | | 3 | | 4 | 8 | 11 |
| 26 | 1 | 2 | 3 | 4 | 5 | 6 | | | 9 | 7 | 10 | | | | | | | 8 | 11 |
| 27 | 1 | 2 | 3 | 4 | 5 | 6 | | | 9 | 7 | 10 | | | | | | | 8 | 11 |
| 28 | 1 | 2 | 3 | 4 | 5 | 6 | | 11 | 9 | 7 | 10 | | | | | | | 8 | |
| 29 | 1 | 2 | 3 | 4 | 5 | 6 | | 11 | 9 | 7 | 10 | | | | | | | 8 | |
| 30 | 1 | 2 | 3 | 4 | 5 | 6 | | 11 | 9 | 7 | 10 | | | | | | | 8 | |
| | 25 | 30 | 24 | 25 | 30 | 18 | 8 | 25 | 29 | 30 | 30 | 12 | 3 | 5 | 7 | 4 | 13 | 8 | 4 |
| | | | | 1 | 5 | | 1 | 19 | 12 | 8 | 18 | 2 | | | | | | 5 | 1 |

1 own-goal

| Match | Robinson J | Methven J | Leiper J | Cox J | Goodall A | Docherty J | Towie T | Bloomer S | Goodall J | Allan J | McMillan J | Keay W | Little T | Dockery G | Staley J | Roulstone W | Hickinbottom E | Francis P | Abbott W |
|---|---|---|---|---|---|---|---|---|---|---|---|---|---|---|---|---|---|---|---|
| 1 | 1 | 2 | 3 | 4 | 5 | | | 8 | 9 | 7 | 10 | 11 | | | | | 6 | | |
| 2 | 1 | 2 | 3 | 4 | 5 | | | 8 | 9 | 7 | 10 | 11 | | | | | 6 | | |
| R | 1 | 2 | 3 | 4 | 5 | 6 | | | 9 | 7 | 10 | 11 | | | | | | 8 | |
| 3 | 1 | 2 | 3 | 4 | 5 | 6 | | | 9 | 7 | 10 | 11 | | | | | | 8 | |
| | 4 | 4 | 4 | 4 | 4 | 2 | | 2 | 4 | 4 | 4 | 4 | | | | | 2 | 2 | |
| | | | | | | | | | 1 | 1 | 3 | | | | | | | 1 | |

# 1894-95

| | P | W | D | L | F | A | Pts |
|---|---|---|---|---|---|---|---|
| Sunderland | 30 | 21 | 5 | 4 | 80 | 37 | 47 |
| Everton | 30 | 18 | 6 | 6 | 82 | 50 | 42 |
| Aston Villa | 30 | 17 | 5 | 8 | 82 | 43 | 39 |
| Preston NE | 30 | 15 | 5 | 10 | 62 | 46 | 35 |
| Blackburn R | 30 | 11 | 10 | 9 | 59 | 49 | 32 |
| Sheffield U | 30 | 14 | 4 | 12 | 57 | 55 | 32 |
| Nottingham F | 30 | 13 | 5 | 12 | 50 | 56 | 31 |
| Sheffield W | 30 | 12 | 4 | 14 | 50 | 55 | 28 |
| Burnley | 30 | 11 | 4 | 15 | 44 | 56 | 26 |
| Bolton W | 30 | 9 | 7 | 14 | 61 | 62 | 25 |
| Wolves | 30 | 9 | 7 | 14 | 43 | 63 | 25 |
| Small Heath | 30 | 9 | 7 | 14 | 50 | 74 | 25 |
| WBA | 30 | 10 | 4 | 16 | 51 | 66 | 24 |
| Stoke | 30 | 9 | 6 | 15 | 50 | 67 | 24 |
| Derby Co | 30 | 7 | 9 | 14 | 45 | 68 | 23 |
| Liverpool | 30 | 7 | 8 | 15 | 51 | 70 | 22 |

Leading scorer: Steve Bloomer, League 10, all matches 11.

League ever-present: Archie Goodall, Jimmy Methven.

- Opening day horror, Derby's heaviest League defeat.
- Steve Bloomer won his first England cap against Ireland at the County Ground, Derby, on 9 March. He and John Goodall scored two each in a 9–0 victory.
- From 1892–93, when the Second Division was formed, Test matches decided promotion and relegation. Bottom three and top three clubs met at neutral venues in single games.
- In 1894–95, Derby County (15th) met Notts County (second in Division Two) at Walnut Street, Leicester, later known as Filbert Street.
- The system lasted for six seasons, until 1898–99. After that, promotion and relegation were automatic until the Play-offs were introduced in 1986–87.

## Division One

| Match No. | Date | | Venue | Opponents | Result | | Scorers | Attendan |
|---|---|---|---|---|---|---|---|---|
| 1 | Sep | 1 | (a) | Sunderland | L | 0-8 | | 7,50 |
| 2 | | 8 | (h) | Nottingham F | W | 4-2 | McMillan 2, Bloomer, Raybould | 6,0C |
| 3 | | 15 | (h) | Sheffield W | L | 1-2 | Raybould | 6,0C |
| 4 | | 22 | (h) | Aston Villa | L | 0-2 | | 8,0C |
| 5 | | 29 | (a) | Burnley | L | 0-2 | | 6,0C |
| 6 | Oct | 13 | (h) | Sunderland | L | 1-2 | McMillan | 7,5C |
| 7 | | 20 | (a) | West Brom A | D | 2-2 | J.Goodall, Keay | 3,0C |
| 8 | | 27 | (h) | West Brom A | D | 1-1 | Keay | 2,0C |
| 9 | Nov | 3 | (a) | Nottingham F | L | 1-2 | A.Goodall | 8,0C |
| 10 | | 17 | (a) | Preston NE | L | 2-3 | A.Goodall, Keay | 6,0C |
| 11 | | 24 | (h) | Preston NE | W | 2-1 | Cox, McLachlan | 6,0C |
| 12 | Dec | 8 | (a) | Wolves | D | 2-2 | A.Goodall, Keay | 5,0C |
| 13 | | 12 | (h) | Burnley | L | 0-2 | | 1,75 |
| 14 | | 15 | (h) | Sheffield U | W | 4-1 | Paul 2, Bloomer, A.Goodall | 2,0C |
| 15 | | 25 | (a) | Sheffield U | W | 4-1 | Hamilton 2, McLachlan, Bloomer | 3,0C |
| 16 | | 26 | (h) | Bolton W | D | 2-2 | Bloomer 2 | 6,0C |
| 17 | | 29 | (a) | Sheffield W | D | 1-1 | Bloomer | 3,0C |
| 18 | Jan | 1 | (a) | Bolton W | L | 0-6 | | 8,0C |
| 19 | | 5 | (a) | Aston Villa | L | 0-4 | | 4,0C |
| 20 | | 9 | (h) | Liverpool | L | 0-1 | | 6,0C |
| 21 | | 12 | (h) | Everton | D | 2-2 | A.Goodall, Keay | 1,5C |
| 22 | | 19 | (h) | Stoke | D | 1-1 | Francis | 4,0C |
| 23 | | 26 | (h) | Wolves | L | 1-3 | Woolley | 6,0C |
| 24 | Mar | 2 | (a) | Liverpool | L | 1-5 | A.Goodall | 12,0C |
| 25 | | 16 | (a) | Small Heath | W | 5-3 | J.Goodall 2, McMillan, Bloomer, Woolley | 5,0C |
| 26 | | 23 | (a) | Stoke | L | 1-4 | Bloomer | 4,0C |
| 27 | | 30 | (h) | Small Heath | W | 4-1 | Paul 2, McMillan, Woolley | 2,0C |
| 28 | Apr | 6 | (h) | Blackburn R | D | 0-0 | | 1,5C |
| 29 | | 12 | (a) | Blackburn R | D | 0-0 | | 5,0C |
| 30 | | 13 | (a) | Everton | W | 3-2 | Bloomer 2, J.Goodall | 10,0C |

FINAL LEAGUE POSITION: 15th in Division One – To play Test Match against Notts County. Appearanc

Goa

## Test Match

| | | | | | | | | |
|---|---|---|---|---|---|---|---|---|
| | Apr | 27 | (n*) | Notts C | W | 2-1 | Bloomer, McMillan | 8,0C |

*Played at Walnut Street (later Filbert Street), Leicester. Appearanc

Goa

## FA Cup

| | | | | | | | | |
|---|---|---|---|---|---|---|---|---|
| 1 | Feb | 2 | (a) | Aston Villa | L | 1-2 | J.Goodall | 6,0 |

Appearanc

Goa

**United Counties League**

*1893-94 Championship decider, replay*

| | | | | | | |
|---|---|---|---|---|---|---|
| 1 | Oct | 6 | (h) | West Brom A | W | 2-1 |

*1894-95 competition*

| | | | | | | |
|---|---|---|---|---|---|---|
| 2 | Nov | 10 | (a) | Sheffield U | W | 5-4 |
| 3 | Feb | 16 | (h) | Leicester F | D | 2-2 |
| 4 | Mar | 9 | (a) | Nottingham F | L | 0-2 |
| 5 | Apr | 1 | (a) | Leicester F | W | 4-1 |
| 6 | | 16 | (h) | Nottingham F | W | 3-0 |

| | P | W | D | L | F | A | Pts |
|---|---|---|---|---|---|---|---|
| Nottingham F | 8 | 5 | 1 | 2 | 16 | 7 | 11 |
| Derby County | 5 | 3 | 1 | 1 | 14 | 9 | 7 |
| Sheffield W | 4 | 2 | 2 | 0 | 8 | 3 | 6 |
| Sheffield U | 6 | 2 | 2 | 2 | 11 | 14 | 6 |
| Leicester F | 7 | 2 | 2 | 3 | 10 | 14 | 6 |
| Notts County | 6 | 0 | 0 | 6 | 3 | 15 | 0 |

**Appearances (including 1893-94 championship replay):** Methven 6, Bloomer 5, Cox 5, J. Goodall 5, Leiper 5, A.Goodall 4, McMillan 4, Robinson 4, Forester 3, Hamilton 3, Woolley 3, Docherty 2, F. Forman 2, Francis 2, Green 2, Paul 2, Staley 2, Alder 1, Brooks 1, Fletcher 1, Harvey 1, Keay 1, McLachlan 1, Stevenson 1.

**Goalscorers (including 1893-94 championship replay):** Bloomer 4, Hamilton 4, A.Goodall 3, McMillan 2, Cox 1, J.Goodall 1, Paul 1.

| Robinson J | Methven J | Staley J | Cox J | Goodall A | Docherty J | Allan J | Fletcher F | Goodall J | McMillan J | Bloomer S | Leiper J | Forman F | Raybould S | Keay W | Harvey W | McLachlan J | Hamilton J | Roulstone W | Francis P | Paul J | Green J | Sawyer T | Brooks J | Stevenson J | Woolley A | |
|---|---|---|---|---|---|---|---|---|---|---|---|---|---|---|---|---|---|---|---|---|---|---|---|---|---|---|
| | 2 | 3 | 4 | 5 | 6 | 7 | 8 | 9 | 10 | 11 | | | | | | | | | | | | | | | | 1 |
| | 2 | | 4 | 5 | | 8 | | 9 | 10 | 11 | 3 | 6 | 7 | | | | | | | | | | | | | 2 |
| | 2 | | 4 | 5 | | 8 | | 9 | 10 | 11 | 3 | 6 | 7 | | | | | | | | | | | | | 3 |
| | 2 | | 4 | 5 | | | | 9 | 10 | 8 | 3 | 6 | 7 | 11 | | | | | | | | | | | | 4 |
| | 2 | | 4 | 5 | | | 11 | 9 | 10 | 8 | 3 | 6 | 7 | | | | | | | | | | | | | 5 |
| | 2 | | 4 | 5 | | 7 | 11 | 9 | 10 | 8 | 3 | 6 | | | | | | | | | | | | | | 6 |
| | 2 | | 4 | 5 | 6 | 7 | | 9 | 10 | 8 | 3 | | | 11 | | | | | | | | | | | | 7 |
| | 2 | | 4 | 5 | 6 | 7 | | 9 | 10 | 8 | 3 | | | 11 | | | | | | | | | | | | 8 |
| | 2 | | 4 | 8 | 6 | | | 9 | 10 | 11 | 3 | 5 | 7 | | | | | | | | | | | | | 9 |
| | 2 | | | 9 | 6 | | | 10 | | 8 | 3 | 5 | | 11 | 4 | 7 | | | | | | | | | | 10 |
| | 2 | | 4 | 9 | 6 | | | 10 | | 8 | 3 | 5 | | | | 7 | 11 | | | | | | | | | 11 |
| | 2 | | 4 | 9 | 6 | | | 10 | | 8 | 3 | | | 11 | 5 | 7 | | | | | | | | | | 12 |
| | 2 | | 4 | 9 | | | | | | 8 | 3 | | | 10 | 5 | | | 6 | 7 | 11 | | | | | | 13 |
| | 2 | | 4 | 5 | 6 | | | | | 8 | 3 | | | 10 | | 7 | 9 | | | 11 | | | | | | 14 |
| | 2 | | 4 | 5 | 6 | | | | | 8 | 3 | | | 10 | | 7 | 9 | | | 11 | | | | | | 15 |
| | 2 | | 4 | 5 | 6 | | | | | 8 | 3 | | | 10 | | 7 | 9 | | | 11 | | | | | | 16 |
| | 2 | | 4 | 5 | 6 | | | | | 7 | 3 | | | | | 10 | 9 | | | 11 | 1 | 8 | | | | 17 |
| | 2 | | 4 | 5 | 6 | | | | 10 | 8 | 3 | | | | | 7 | 9 | | | 11 | 1 | | | | | 18 |
| | 2 | 3 | 4 | 5 | 6 | | | | | 7 | | | | | | | 9 | | | 11 | 1 | 8 | 10 | | | 19 |
| | 2 | | 4 | 5 | | | | | 10 | 9 | 3 | | | | 6 | | 8 | | | 11 | 1 | | 7 | | | 20 |
| | 2 | | 4 | 5 | | | | | 10 | 9 | 3 | | | 11 | 6 | | 8 | | | | | | 7 | | | 21 |
| | 2 | | 4 | 5 | 6 | | | | 10 | 9 | 3 | | | 11 | | | | | 7 | | 1 | | | 8 | | 22 |
| | 2 | | 4 | 5 | 6 | | | 9 | | 8 | 3 | | | 10 | | | | | 7 | | 1 | | | | 11 | 23 |
| | 2 | | 4 | 5 | 6 | | | 7 | | 9 | 3 | | | | | | 8 | | | 10 | 1 | | | | 11 | 24 |
| | 2 | 6 | 4 | 5 | | | | 9 | 10 | 8 | 3 | | | | | | | | 7 | | | | | | 11 | 25 |
| | 2 | 6 | 4 | 5 | | | | 9 | 10 | 8 | 3 | | | | | | | | 7 | | | | | | 11 | 26 |
| | 2 | 6 | 4 | 5 | | | | 9 | 10 | 8 | 3 | | | | | | | | | 7 | | | | | 11 | 27 |
| | 2 | | 4 | 5 | 6 | | | | 10 | | 3 | | | | | | 9 | | 7 | 8 | | | | | 11 | 28 |
| 1 | 2 | 6 | 4 | 5 | | | | 9 | 10 | 8 | 3 | | | | | | | | 7 | 11 | | | | | | 29 |
| 1 | 2 | 6 | 4 | 5 | | | | 9 | 10 | 8 | 3 | | | | | | 7 | | | 11 | | | | | | 30 |
| 23 | 30 | 7 | 29 | 30 | 17 | 6 | 3 | 19 | 19 | 29 | 28 | 8 | 5 | 12 | 5 | 8 | 12 | 1 | 7 | 13 | 7 | 2 | 3 | 1 | 6 | |
| | | | 1 | 6 | | | | 4 | 5 | 10 | | | 2 | 5 | | 2 | 2 | | 1 | 4 | | | | | 3 | |

| | | | | | | | | | | | | | | | | | | | | | | | | | | |
|---|---|---|---|---|---|---|---|---|---|---|---|---|---|---|---|---|---|---|---|---|---|---|---|---|---|---|
| 1 | 2 | 6 | 4 | 5 | | | | 9 | 10 | 8 | 3 | | | | | | | | 7 | 11 | | | | | | |
| 1 | 1 | 1 | 1 | 1 | | | | 1 | 1 | 1 | 1 | | | | | | | | 1 | 1 | | | | | | |
| | | | | | | | | | 1 | 1 | | | | | | | | | | | | | | | | |

| | | | | | | | | | | | | | | | | | | | | | | | | | | |
|---|---|---|---|---|---|---|---|---|---|---|---|---|---|---|---|---|---|---|---|---|---|---|---|---|---|---|
| 1 | 2 | | 4 | 5 | 6 | | | 8 | 10 | 9 | 3 | | | 11 | | | | | 7 | | | | | | | 1 |
| 1 | 1 | | 1 | 1 | 1 | | | 1 | 1 | 1 | 1 | | | 1 | | | | | 1 | | | | | | | |
| | | | | | | | | 1 | | | | | | | | | | | | | | | | | | |

# 1895-96

| | P | W | D | L | F | A | Pts |
|---|---|---|---|---|---|---|---|
| Aston Villa | 30 | 20 | 5 | 5 | 78 | 45 | 45 |
| Derby Co | 30 | 17 | 7 | 6 | 68 | 35 | 41 |
| Everton | 30 | 16 | 7 | 7 | 66 | 43 | 39 |
| Bolton W | 30 | 16 | 5 | 9 | 49 | 37 | 37 |
| Sunderland | 30 | 15 | 7 | 8 | 52 | 41 | 37 |
| Stoke | 30 | 15 | 0 | 15 | 56 | 47 | 30 |
| Sheffield W | 30 | 12 | 5 | 13 | 44 | 53 | 29 |
| Blackburn R | 30 | 12 | 5 | 13 | 40 | 50 | 29 |
| Preston NE | 30 | 11 | 6 | 13 | 44 | 48 | 28 |
| Burnley | 30 | 10 | 7 | 13 | 48 | 44 | 27 |
| Bury | 30 | 12 | 3 | 15 | 50 | 54 | 27 |
| Sheffield U | 30 | 10 | 6 | 14 | 40 | 50 | 26 |
| Nottingham F | 30 | 11 | 3 | 16 | 42 | 57 | 25 |
| Wolves | 30 | 10 | 1 | 19 | 61 | 65 | 21 |
| Small Heath | 30 | 8 | 4 | 18 | 39 | 79 | 20 |
| WBA | 30 | 6 | 7 | 17 | 30 | 59 | 19 |

Leading scorer: Steve Bloomer, League 22, all matches 27.
League ever-present: Archie Goodall, George Kinsey, Johnny Miller, Jack Robinson.

- The Baseball Ground was now Derby's permanent home. They stayed until 1997, when Pride Park opened.
- Steve Bloomer became the first Derby player to score more than 20 League goals in a season.
- After scraping clear of relegation through the Test matches a year earlier, Derby were second, their best position so far. They did not equal it in the top Division until 1929–30.
- Derby's first appearance in the FA Cup semi-finals began a remarkable sequence. They were in the last four in seven out of nine seasons, during which time they reached – and lost – three finals.
- The Rams had four ever-presents for the second time and used only 16 players in the League.

## Division One

| Match No. | Date | | Venue | Opponents | Result | | Scorers | Attend |
|---|---|---|---|---|---|---|---|---|
| 1 | Sep | 7 | (a) | Stoke | L | 1-2 | S.Bloomer | 10, |
| 2 | | 14 | (h) | Sunderland | W | 2-0 | S.Bloomer 2 | 10, |
| 3 | | 21 | (a) | Aston Villa | L | 1-4 | McQueen | 12, |
| 4 | | 28 | (h) | Sheffield W | W | 3-1 | A.Goodall, S.Bloomer, McMillan | 10, |
| 5 | Oct | 5 | (a) | Nottingham F | W | 5-2 | S.Bloomer 3, McQueen, Stevenson | 12, |
| 6 | | 12 | (h) | Stoke | W | 2-1 | S.Bloomer, Miller | 10, |
| 7 | | 19 | (h) | Bury | W | 2-1 | Miller, Stevenson | 8, |
| 8 | | 26 | (h) | Wolves | W | 5-2 | S.Bloomer 3, Stevenson 2 | 8, |
| 9 | Nov | 2 | (a) | Sunderland | D | 2-2 | J.Goodall (pen), Stevenson | 15, |
| 10 | | 9 | (h) | Burnley | W | 5-1 | McQueen 2, A.Goodall (pen), Miller, S.Bloomer | 6, |
| 11 | | 16 | (a) | Wolves | L | 0-2 | | 2, |
| 12 | | 23 | (a) | Bury | W | 2-1 | S.Bloomer, Stevenson | 7, |
| 13 | | 30 | (h) | Small Heath | W | 8-0 | Miller 2, Paul 2, Stevenson 2, McQueen, S.Bloomer | 8, |
| 14 | Dec | 7 | (h) | Nottingham F | W | 4-0 | S.Bloomer 3, Miller | 6, |
| 15 | | 14 | (h) | West Brom A | W | 4-1 | S.Bloomer 2, Miller 2 | 7, |
| 16 | | 21 | (a) | Sheffield U | D | 1-1 | Stevenson | 7, |
| 17 | | 26 | (h) | Bolton W | W | 2-1 | Miller, Stevenson | 12, |
| 18 | | 28 | (a) | Sheffield W | W | 4-0 | Stevenson 2, Miller, Crawshaw (og) | 17, |
| 19 | Jan | 1 | (a) | Bolton W | L | 1-2 | Miller | 18, |
| 20 | | 4 | (a) | Small Heath | W | 3-1 | A.Goodall, Cox, McQueen | 10, |
| 21 | | 18 | (a) | West Brom A | D | 0-0 | | 10, |
| 22 | Feb | 8 | (h) | Aston Villa | D | 2-2 | S.Bloomer, Stevenson | 15, |
| 23 | | 22 | (a) | Blackburn R | W | 2-0 | S.Bloomer 2 | 12, |
| 24 | Mar | 4 | (h) | Preston NE | W | 1-0 | Miller | 4, |
| 25 | | 14 | (h) | Sheffield U | L | 0-2 | | 7,0 |
| 26 | | 28 | (a) | Preston NE | L | 0-1 | | 6, |
| 27 | Apr | 3 | (a) | Everton | D | 2-2 | McMillan, Stevenson | 25,0 |
| 28 | | 4 | (a) | Burnley | D | 2-2 | Paul, unknown | 6, |
| 29 | | 7 | (h) | Everton | W | 2-1 | McMillan, Paul | 7,0 |
| 30 | | 11 | (h) | Blackburn R | D | 0-0 | | 6, |

FINAL LEAGUE POSITION: 2nd in Division One

Appearanc
Go

## FA Cup

| | | | | | | | | |
|---|---|---|---|---|---|---|---|---|
| 1 | Feb | 1 | (h) | Aston Villa | W | 4-2 | Bloomer 2, Miller 2 | 20,0 |
| 2 | | 15 | (a) | Newton Heath | D | 1-1 | Bloomer | 20, |
| R | | 19 | (h) | Newton Heath | W | 5-1 | Miller 3, Bloomer, McQueen | 6,0 |
| 3 | | 29 | (h) | West Brom A | W | 1-0 | A.Goodall | 13, |
| SF | Mar | 21 | (n*) | Wolves | L | 1-2 | Bloomer | 35,0 |

*Played at Perry Barr, Birmingham

Appearanc
Go

| Robinson J | Methven J | Leiper J | Cox J | Goodall A | Kinsey G | Goodall J | Bloomer S | Miller J | McMillan J | McQueen H | Staley J | Bloomer P | Stevenson J | Francis P | Paul J | |
|---|---|---|---|---|---|---|---|---|---|---|---|---|---|---|---|---|
| 1 | 2 | 3 | 4 | 5 | 6 | 7 | 8 | 9 | 10 | 11 | | | | | | 1 |
| 1 | 2 | 3 | 4 | 5 | 6 | 7 | 8 | 9 | 10 | 11 | | | | | | 2 |
| 1 | 2 | | 4 | 5 | 6 | 7 | 8 | 9 | 10 | 11 | 3 | | | | | 3 |
| 1 | 2 | | 4 | 5 | 6 | 7 | 8 | 9 | 10 | 11 | | 3 | | | | 4 |
| 1 | 2 | | 4 | 5 | 6 | 7 | 8 | 9 | | 11 | 3 | | 10 | | | 5 |
| 1 | 2 | 3 | 4 | 5 | 6 | 7 | 8 | 9 | | 11 | | | 10 | | | 6 |
| 1 | 2 | 3 | 4 | 5 | 6 | 7 | 8 | 9 | | 11 | | | 10 | | | 7 |
| 1 | 2 | 3 | | 5 | 6 | 7 | 8 | 9 | | 11 | | | 10 | 4 | | 8 |
| 1 | 2 | 3 | | 5 | 6 | 7 | 8 | 9 | | 11 | 4 | | 10 | | | 9 |
| 1 | 2 | 3 | | 5 | 6 | 7 | 8 | 9 | | 11 | 4 | | 10 | | | 10 |
| 1 | 2 | 3 | | 5 | 6 | 7 | 8 | 9 | | 11 | 4 | | 10 | | | 11 |
| 1 | 2 | 3 | | 5 | 6 | 7 | 8 | 9 | | 11 | 4 | | 10 | | | 12 |
| 1 | | 2 | 4 | 5 | 6 | | 8 | 9 | | 11 | 3 | | 10 | | 7 | 13 |
| 1 | 2 | 3 | 4 | 5 | 6 | 7 | 8 | 9 | | 11 | | | 10 | | | 14 |
| 1 | 2 | 3 | 4 | 5 | 6 | 7 | 8 | 9 | | 11 | | | 10 | | | 15 |
| 1 | 2 | 3 | 4 | 5 | 6 | 7 | 8 | 9 | | 11 | | | 10 | | | 16 |
| 1 | 2 | 3 | 4 | 5 | 6 | 7 | 8 | 9 | | 11 | | | 10 | | | 17 |
| 1 | 2 | 3 | 4 | 5 | 6 | 7 | 8 | 9 | | 11 | | | 10 | | | 18 |
| 1 | 2 | 3 | 4 | 5 | 6 | 7 | 8 | 9 | | 11 | | | 10 | | | 19 |
| 1 | 2 | 3 | 4 | 5 | 6 | 7 | 8 | 9 | | 11 | | | 10 | | | 20 |
| 1 | 2 | 3 | 4 | 5 | 6 | 7 | 8 | 9 | | 11 | | | 10 | | | 21 |
| 1 | 2 | 3 | 4 | 5 | 6 | 7 | 8 | 9 | | 11 | | | 10 | | | 22 |
| 1 | 2 | | | 5 | 6 | 4 | 8 | 9 | | 11 | 3 | | 10 | | 7 | 23 |
| 1 | 2 | 3 | | 5 | 6 | 10 | 8 | 9 | 11 | | 4 | | | | 7 | 24 |
| 1 | 2 | 3 | 4 | 5 | 6 | 7 | 8 | 9 | | 11 | | | 10 | | | 25 |
| 1 | 2 | 3 | 4 | 5 | 6 | 8 | | 9 | | 11 | | | 10 | | 7 | 26 |
| 1 | 2 | 3 | 4 | 5 | 6 | | | 8 | 9 | 11 | | | 10 | | 7 | 27 |
| 1 | 2 | 3 | | 5 | 6 | | | 8 | 9 | 11 | 4 | | 10 | | 7 | 28 |
| 1 | | 3 | 4 | 5 | 6 | | | 8 | 9 | 11 | 2 | | 10 | | 7 | 29 |
| 1 | | 3 | 4 | 5 | 6 | | | 8 | 9 | 11 | 2 | | 10 | | 7 | 30 |
| 30 | 27 | 26 | 22 | 30 | 30 | 25 | 25 | 30 | 9 | 29 | 12 | 1 | 25 | 1 | 8 | |
| | | | 1 | 3 | | 1 | 22 | 12 | 3 | 6 | | | 14 | | 4 | |

1 own-goal, 1 untraced

| Robinson J | Methven J | Leiper J | Cox J | Goodall A | Kinsey G | Goodall J | Bloomer S | Miller J | McMillan J | McQueen H | Staley J | Bloomer P | Stevenson J | Francis P | Paul J | |
|---|---|---|---|---|---|---|---|---|---|---|---|---|---|---|---|---|
| 1 | 2 | 3 | 4 | 5 | 6 | 7 | 8 | 9 | | 11 | | | 10 | | | 1 |
| 1 | 2 | 3 | 4 | 5 | 6 | 7 | 8 | 9 | | 11 | | | 10 | | | 2 |
| 1 | 2 | 3 | 4 | 5 | 6 | 7 | 8 | 9 | | 11 | | | 10 | | | R |
| 1 | 2 | 3 | | 5 | 6 | 7 | 8 | 9 | | 11 | 4 | | 10 | | | 3 |
| 1 | 2 | 3 | 4 | 5 | 6 | 7 | 8 | 9 | | 11 | | | 10 | | | SF |
| 5 | 5 | 5 | 4 | 5 | 5 | 5 | 5 | 5 | | 5 | 1 | | 5 | | | |
| | | | | 1 | | | 5 | 5 | | 1 | | | | | | |

# 1896-97

| | P | W | D | L | F | A | Pts |
|---|---|---|---|---|---|---|---|
| Aston Villa | 30 | 21 | 5 | 4 | 73 | 38 | 47 |
| Sheffield U | 30 | 13 | 10 | 7 | 42 | 29 | 36 |
| Derby Co | 30 | 16 | 4 | 10 | 70 | 50 | 36 |
| Preston NE | 30 | 11 | 12 | 7 | 55 | 40 | 34 |
| Liverpool | 30 | 12 | 9 | 9 | 46 | 38 | 33 |
| Sheffield W | 30 | 10 | 11 | 9 | 42 | 37 | 31 |
| Everton | 30 | 14 | 3 | 13 | 62 | 57 | 31 |
| Bolton W | 30 | 12 | 6 | 12 | 40 | 43 | 30 |
| Bury | 30 | 10 | 10 | 10 | 39 | 44 | 30 |
| Wolves | 30 | 11 | 6 | 13 | 45 | 41 | 28 |
| Nottingham F | 30 | 9 | 8 | 13 | 44 | 49 | 26 |
| WBA | 30 | 10 | 6 | 14 | 33 | 56 | 26 |
| Stoke | 30 | 11 | 3 | 16 | 48 | 59 | 25 |
| Blackburn R | 30 | 11 | 3 | 16 | 35 | 62 | 25 |
| Sunderland | 30 | 7 | 9 | 14 | 34 | 47 | 23 |
| Burnley | 30 | 6 | 7 | 17 | 43 | 61 | 19 |

Leading scorer: Steve Bloomer, League 24, all matches 31.
League ever-present: Archie Goodall, Hugh McQueen, Jack Robinson.

- Steve Bloomer beat his year-old scoring record and became the first Derby player to pass 30 League and Cup goals in a season, including four against Wolves on 19 September.
- On 12 September, Archie Goodall became the first Derby player to complete 200 appearances.
- Jimmy Stevenson scored four against Blackburn Rovers on 21 November.
- Derby's record FA Cup victory, 8–1 against Barnsley St Peter's.

## Division One

| Match No. | Date | | Venue | Opponents | Result | | Scorers | Attend |
|---|---|---|---|---|---|---|---|---|
| 1 | Sep | 1 | (a) | Wolves | L | 0-1 | | 5, |
| 2 | | 5 | (h) | Nottingham F | D | 1-1 | Stevenson | 5, |
| 3 | | 12 | (a) | Liverpool | L | 0-2 | | 20, |
| 4 | | 19 | (h) | Wolves | W | 4-3 | Bloomer 4 | 5, |
| 5 | | 26 | (h) | Bury | W | 7-2 | Bloomer 3, McQueen 2, J.Goodall, Stevenson | 5, |
| 6 | Oct | 10 | (h) | Sheffield U | L | 1-3 | Miller | 6, |
| 7 | | 17 | (h) | Aston Villa | L | 1-3 | McQueen | 8, |
| 8 | | 24 | (a) | Aston Villa | L | 1-2 | Bloomer | 7, |
| 9 | | 31 | (a) | Sheffield U | D | 2-2 | A.Goodall, Stevenson | 9, |
| 10 | Nov | 7 | (h) | Stoke | W | 5-1 | J.Goodall, Cox, Stevenson, Miller, Turner | 6, |
| 11 | | 14 | (h) | Burnley | W | 3-2 | Bloomer, Miller, Stevenson | 6, |
| 12 | | 18 | (a) | Nottingham F | W | 2-1 | Bloomer, Stevenson | 5, |
| 13 | | 21 | (h) | Blackburn R | W | 6-0 | Stevenson 4, A.Goodall, Bloomer | 7, |
| 14 | | 28 | (a) | Sheffield W | L | 0-2 | | 10, |
| 15 | Dec | 5 | (a) | Stoke | D | 2-2 | Bloomer, Stevenson | 2, |
| 16 | | 19 | (h) | Liverpool | W | 3-2 | Bloomer, Miller, Stevenson | 10, |
| 17 | | 25 | (h) | West Brom A | W | 8-1 | Bloomer 3, A.Goodall 2, McQueen 2, Miller | 12, |
| 18 | | 26 | (h) | Bolton W | W | 1-0 | Fisher | 19, |
| 19 | Jan | 2 | (a) | Sunderland | W | 2-1 | Bloomer, Fisher | 10, |
| 20 | | 9 | (h) | Sheffield W | W | 2-1 | Fisher, A.Goodall | 5, |
| 21 | | 16 | (a) | Blackburn R | L | 2-5 | Miller, A.Goodall (pen) | 6, |
| 22 | | 23 | (h) | Sunderland | W | 1-0 | Bloomer | 7, |
| 23 | Feb | 6 | (a) | West Brom A | W | 4-1 | A.Goodall 2, J.Goodall, Bloomer | 6, |
| 24 | Mar | 6 | (a) | Bolton W | W | 3-1 | Bloomer, Paul, Fisher | 12, |
| 25 | | 27 | (h) | Preston NE | D | 2-2 | Bloomer, Stevenson | 5, |
| 26 | Apr | 5 | (a) | Burnley | W | 3-2 | Bloomer 2, Fisher | 3, |
| 27 | | 10 | (a) | Bury | L | 0-1 | | 4, |
| 28 | | 16 | (a) | Everton | L | 2-5 | A.Goodall, Miller | 25, |
| 29 | | 19 | (a) | Preston NE | W | 2-0 | Bloomer, Stevenson | 6, |
| 30 | | 20 | (h) | Everton | L | 0-1 | | 14, |

FINAL LEAGUE POSITION: 3rd in Division One

Appearan
Gc

## FA Cup

| | | | | | | | | |
|---|---|---|---|---|---|---|---|---|
| 1 | Jan | 30 | (h) | Barnsley St Peter's | W | 8-1 | Bloomer 3, Fisher 2, A.Goodall, J.Goodall, McQueen | 8, |
| 2 | Feb | 13 | (h) | Bolton W | W | 4-1 | Bloomer 3, Fisher | 13,7 |
| 3 | | 27 | (h) | Newton Heath | W | 2-0 | Bloomer, McQueen | 11,2 |
| SF | Mar | 20 | (n*) | Everton | L | 2-3 | A.Goodall, J.Goodall | 25,0 |

*Played at the Victoria Ground, Stoke-on-Trent.

Appearan
Go

| Robinson J | Methven J | Leiper J | Turner J | Goodall A | Kinsey G | Goodchild G | Bloomer S | Miller J | Stevenson J | McQueen H | Cox J | Goodall J | Paul J | Fisher W | Staley J | Boag J | |
|---|---|---|---|---|---|---|---|---|---|---|---|---|---|---|---|---|---|
| 1 | 2 | 3 | 4 | 5 | 6 | 7 | 8 | 9 | 10 | 11 | | | | | | | 1 |
| 1 | 2 | 3 | | 5 | 6 | | 8 | 9 | 10 | 11 | 4 | 7 | | | | | 2 |
| 1 | 2 | 3 | | 5 | 6 | | 8 | 9 | 10 | 11 | 4 | 7 | | | | | 3 |
| 1 | 2 | 3 | | 5 | 6 | | 8 | 9 | 10 | 11 | 4 | 7 | | | | | 4 |
| 1 | 2 | 3 | | 5 | 6 | | 8 | 9 | 10 | 11 | 4 | 7 | | | | | 5 |
| 1 | 2 | 3 | 6 | 5 | | | 8 | 9 | 10 | 11 | 4 | | 7 | | | | 6 |
| 1 | 2 | | 5 | 3 | 6 | 7 | 8 | 9 | 10 | 11 | 4 | | | | | | 7 |
| 1 | 2 | 3 | 6 | 5 | | | 8 | 9 | 10 | 11 | 4 | 7 | | | | | 8 |
| 1 | 2 | 3 | 6 | 5 | | | 8 | 9 | 10 | 11 | 4 | 7 | | | | | 9 |
| 1 | 2 | 3 | 6 | 5 | | | | 9 | 10 | 11 | 4 | 7 | | 8 | | | 10 |
| 1 | 2 | 3 | 6 | 5 | | | 8 | 9 | 10 | 11 | 4 | 7 | | | | | 11 |
| 1 | 2 | 3 | 6 | 5 | | | 8 | 9 | 10 | 11 | 4 | 7 | | | | | 12 |
| 1 | 2 | 3 | 6 | 5 | | | 8 | 9 | 10 | 11 | 4 | 7 | | | | | 13 |
| 1 | 2 | 3 | 6 | 5 | | | 8 | 9 | 10 | 11 | 4 | 7 | | | | | 14 |
| 1 | 2 | 3 | 6 | 5 | | | 8 | 9 | 10 | 11 | 4 | 7 | | | | | 15 |
| 1 | 2 | 3 | 6 | 5 | | | 8 | 9 | 10 | 11 | 4 | 7 | | | | | 16 |
| 1 | 2 | 3 | 6 | 5 | | | 8 | 9 | | 11 | 4 | | 7 | 10 | | | 17 |
| 1 | 2 | 3 | 6 | 5 | | | 8 | 9 | | 11 | 4 | | 7 | 10 | | | 18 |
| 1 | 2 | 3 | 6 | 5 | | | 8 | 9 | | 11 | 4 | | 7 | 10 | | | 19 |
| 1 | 2 | 3 | 6 | 5 | | | 8 | 9 | | 11 | 4 | 7 | | 10 | | | 20 |
| 1 | 2 | 3 | 6 | 5 | | | 8 | 9 | | 11 | 4 | 7 | | 10 | | | 21 |
| 1 | 2 | 3 | 6 | 5 | | | 8 | 9 | | 11 | 4 | 7 | | 10 | | | 22 |
| 1 | 2 | 3 | 6 | 5 | | | 8 | 9 | | 11 | 4 | 7 | | 10 | | | 23 |
| 1 | | 3 | 6 | 5 | | | 8 | | | 11 | 4 | | 7 | 10 | 2 | 9 | 24 |
| 1 | 2 | | 6 | 5 | | | 8 | 9 | 10 | 11 | 4 | 7 | | | 3 | | 25 |
| 1 | 2 | | 6 | 5 | | | 8 | 9 | | 11 | 4 | 7 | | 10 | 3 | | 26 |
| 1 | 2 | | 6 | 5 | | | 8 | 9 | | 11 | 4 | 7 | | 10 | 3 | | 27 |
| 1 | 2 | 6 | | 5 | | | 8 | 9 | 10 | 11 | 4 | 7 | | | 3 | | 28 |
| 1 | 2 | 3 | 6 | 5 | | | 8 | | 10 | 11 | 4 | 7 | | | | 9 | 29 |
| 1 | 2 | | 6 | 5 | | | 8 | 9 | 10 | 11 | 4 | 7 | | | 3 | | 30 |
| 30 | 29 | 25 | 25 | 30 | 6 | 2 | 29 | 28 | 20 | 30 | 29 | 23 | 5 | 11 | 6 | 2 | |
| | | | 1 | 9 | | | 24 | 7 | 14 | 5 | 1 | 3 | 1 | 5 | | | |

| | | | | | | | | | | | | | | | | | |
|---|---|---|---|---|---|---|---|---|---|---|---|---|---|---|---|---|---|
| 1 | 2 | 3 | 6 | 5 | | | 8 | 9 | | 11 | 4 | 7 | | 10 | | | 1 |
| 1 | 2 | | 6 | 5 | | | 8 | 9 | | 11 | 4 | 7 | | 10 | 3 | | 2 |
| 1 | 2 | 3 | 6 | 5 | | | 8 | 9 | | 11 | 4 | 7 | | 10 | | | 3 |
| 1 | 2 | 3 | 6 | 5 | | | 8 | 9 | | 11 | 4 | 7 | | 10 | | | SF |
| 4 | 4 | 3 | 4 | 4 | | | 4 | 4 | | 4 | 4 | 4 | | 4 | 1 | | |
| | | | | 2 | | | 7 | | | 2 | | 2 | | 3 | | | |

# 1897-98

| | P | W | D | L | F | A | Pts |
|---|---|---|---|---|---|---|---|
| Sheffield U | 30 | 17 | 8 | 5 | 56 | 31 | 42 |
| Sunderland | 30 | 16 | 5 | 9 | 43 | 30 | 37 |
| Wolves | 30 | 14 | 7 | 9 | 57 | 41 | 35 |
| Everton | 30 | 13 | 9 | 8 | 48 | 39 | 35 |
| Sheffield W | 30 | 15 | 3 | 12 | 51 | 42 | 33 |
| Aston Villa | 30 | 14 | 5 | 11 | 61 | 51 | 33 |
| WBA | 30 | 11 | 10 | 9 | 44 | 45 | 32 |
| Nottingham F | 30 | 11 | 9 | 10 | 47 | 49 | 31 |
| Liverpool | 30 | 11 | 6 | 13 | 48 | 45 | 28 |
| Derby Co | 30 | 11 | 6 | 13 | 57 | 61 | 28 |
| Bolton W | 30 | 11 | 4 | 15 | 28 | 41 | 26 |
| Preston NE | 30 | 8 | 8 | 14 | 35 | 43 | 24 |
| Notts Co | 30 | 8 | 8 | 14 | 36 | 46 | 24 |
| Bury | 30 | 8 | 8 | 14 | 39 | 51 | 24 |
| Blackburn R | 30 | 7 | 10 | 13 | 39 | 54 | 24 |
| Stoke | 30 | 8 | 8 | 14 | 35 | 55 | 24 |

Leading scorer: Steve Bloomer, League 15, all matches 20.
League ever-present: Hugh McQueen.

- Steve Bloomer's first goal of the season, against Blackburn Rovers on 4 September, was his 100th for Derby. He reached this mark in 151 appearances, 138 League, 12 FA Cup and one Test match.
- Bloomer's 100th League goal came on 11 April, the second in his hat-trick against Nottingham Forest.
- Five days later, Forest beat Derby in the FA Cup Final at Crystal Palace.
- On 2 October, Archie Goodall missed his first game for five years. He made 167 consecutive appearances, 151 in the League. These runs remain club records.

## Division One

| Match No. | Date | | Venue | Opponents | Result | | Scorers | Attend |
|---|---|---|---|---|---|---|---|---|
| 1 | Sep | 1 | (a) | Sheffield U | L | 1-2 | J.Goodall (pen) | 2, |
| 2 | | 4 | (h) | Blackburn R | W | 3-1 | Bloomer, Boag, J.Goodall | 7, |
| 3 | | 11 | (h) | Everton | W | 5-1 | Bloomer 2, Boag 2, J.Goodall | 12, |
| 4 | | 18 | (h) | West Brom A | W | 3-2 | Bloomer 2, A.Goodall | 6, |
| 5 | | 25 | (a) | Notts C | D | 1-1 | McQueen | 12, |
| 6 | Oct | 2 | (a) | Stoke | L | 1-2 | Maconnachie | 10, |
| 7 | | 9 | (a) | Sunderland | L | 1-2 | J.Goodall | 10, |
| 8 | | 16 | (h) | Bury | D | 2-2 | McQueen, Miller | 7, |
| 9 | | 23 | (a) | Liverpool | L | 2-4 | Bloomer, Maconnachie | 12, |
| 10 | | 30 | (a) | Nottingham F | W | 4-3 | Maconnachie 2, A.Goodall, Bloomer | 10, |
| 11 | Nov | 6 | (h) | Stoke | W | 4-1 | J.Goodall 3, A.Goodall | 8, |
| 12 | | 13 | (h) | Sheffield U | D | 1-1 | Maconnachie | 10, |
| 13 | | 20 | (a) | West Brom A | L | 1-3 | Stevenson | 10,5 |
| 14 | | 27 | (a) | Blackburn R | D | 1-1 | Maconnachie | 6, |
| 15 | Dec | 4 | (a) | Wolves | L | 0-2 | | 4, |
| 16 | | 11 | (h) | Sunderland | D | 2-2 | J.Goodall, Stevenson | 7, |
| 17 | | 25 | (h) | Notts C | L | 1-2 | Bloomer | 11, |
| 18 | | 27 | (h) | Bolton W | W | 1-0 | Bloomer | 15, |
| 19 | Jan | 1 | (a) | Bolton W | D | 3-3 | Bloomer 3 | 10, |
| 20 | | 8 | (h) | Wolves | W | 3-2 | Handley, Maconnachie, Eccles (og) | 6, |
| 21 | | 15 | (a) | Sheffield W | L | 1-3 | A.Goodall | 8, |
| 22 | | 22 | (h) | Aston Villa | W | 3-1 | Maconnachie 2, McQueen | 12, |
| 23 | Feb | 19 | (h) | Sheffield W | L | 1-2 | Leonard | 8,0 |
| 24 | Mar | 5 | (a) | Aston Villa | L | 1-4 | Boag | 12, |
| 25 | | 12 | (h) | Preston NE | W | 3-1 | Cox, Stevenson, J.Goodall | 5,0 |
| 26 | | 29 | (a) | Bury | L | 0-4 | | 3, |
| 27 | Apr | 8 | (a) | Everton | L | 0-3 | | 30,0 |
| 28 | | 9 | (a) | Preston NE | L | 0-5 | | 10, |
| 29 | | 11 | (h) | Nottingham F | W | 5-0 | Bloomer 3, Boag, Turner | 12,0 |
| 30 | | 12 | (h) | Liverpool | W | 3-1 | Boag 2, Burton | 4,0 |

FINAL LEAGUE POSITION: 10th in Division One

Appearanc
Go

## FA Cup

| | | | | | | | | |
|---|---|---|---|---|---|---|---|---|
| 1 | Jan | 29 | (h) | Aston Villa | W | 1-0 | McQueen | 12,0 |
| 2 | Feb | 12 | (a) | Wolves | W | 1-0 | Leonard | 20,0 |
| 3 | | 26 | (h) | Liverpool | D | 1-1 | Stevenson | 15,0 |
| R | Mar | 2 | (a) | Liverpool | W | 5-1 | Boag 3, Bloomer 2 | 10,0 |
| SF | | 19 | (n*) | Everton | W | 3-1 | Bloomer 2, J.Goodall | 30,0 |
| F | Apr | 16 | (n†) | Nottingham F | L | 1-3 | Bloomer | 62,0 |

*Played at the Molineux Grounds, Wolverhampton. †Played at the Crystal Palace.

Appearanc
Go

| | Trail J | Methven J | Leiper J | Cox J | Goodall A | Staley J | Goodall J | Bloomer S | Boag J | Maconnachie A | McQueen H | Turner J | Miller J | Stevenson J | Fryer J | Paterson R | Handley G | Burton J | Paul J | Leonard J | Leach S | Thompson J |
|---|---|---|---|---|---|---|---|---|---|---|---|---|---|---|---|---|---|---|---|---|---|---|
| 1 | | 2 | 3 | 4 | 5 | 6 | 7 | 8 | 9 | 10 | 11 | | | | | | | | | | | |
| 2 | | 2 | 3 | 4 | 5 | 6 | 7 | 8 | 9 | 10 | 11 | | | | | | | | | | | |
| 3 | | 2 | 3 | 4 | 5 | | 7 | 8 | 9 | 10 | 11 | 6 | | | | | | | | | | |
| 4 | | 2 | | 4 | 5 | 3 | 7 | 8 | 9 | 10 | 11 | 6 | | | | | | | | | | |
| 5 | | 2 | 3 | 4 | 5 | | 7 | 8 | 9 | 10 | 11 | 6 | | | | | | | | | | |
| 6 | | 2 | 3 | 4 | | | 7 | 8 | 9 | 10 | 11 | 6 | 5 | | | | | | | | | |
| 7 | | 2 | 3 | 4 | | | 7 | 8 | 9 | 10 | 11 | 6 | 5 | | | | | | | | | |
| 8 | | 2 | 3 | 4 | 5 | | 7 | 8 | | | 11 | 6 | 9 | 10 | | | | | | | | |
| 9 | | 2 | 3 | 4 | 5 | | 9 | 8 | | 7 | 11 | 6 | | 10 | 1 | | | | | | | |
| 10 | | 2 | 3 | 4 | 5 | | 9 | 8 | | 7 | 11 | 6 | | 10 | 1 | | | | | | | |
| 11 | | 2 | 3 | 4 | 5 | | 9 | | | 7 | 11 | 6 | 8 | 10 | 1 | | | | | | | |
| 12 | | 2 | | 4 | 5 | 3 | 9 | 8 | | 7 | 11 | 6 | | 10 | 1 | | | | | | | |
| 13 | | 2 | 3 | 4 | 5 | | 9 | 8 | | 7 | 11 | 6 | | 10 | 1 | | | | | | | |
| 14 | | 2 | 3 | 4 | 9 | | | 8 | | 7 | 11 | 6 | | 10 | 1 | 5 | | | | | | |
| 15 | | 2 | 3 | 4 | 9 | | | 8 | | 7 | 11 | 6 | | 10 | 1 | 5 | | | | | | |
| 16 | | 2 | 3 | 4 | 5 | | 9 | 8 | | 7 | 11 | 6 | | 10 | 1 | | | | | | | |
| 17 | | 2 | | 4 | 5 | 3 | 9 | 8 | | 7 | 11 | 6 | | 10 | 1 | | | | | | | |
| 18 | | 2 | | 4 | 5 | 3 | | 8 | | 9 | 11 | 6 | | 10 | 1 | | 7 | | | | | |
| 19 | | | | 4 | 2 | 3 | | 8 | | 9 | 11 | 6 | | 10 | 1 | 5 | 7 | | | | | |
| 20 | | 2 | | 4 | 5 | 3 | | | | 9 | 11 | 6 | | 10 | 1 | | 7 | 8 | | | | |
| 21 | | 2 | 3 | 4 | 5 | | | | | 9 | 11 | | | 10 | 1 | 6 | 7 | | 8 | | | |
| 22 | | 2 | 3 | 4 | 5 | | 8 | | | 9 | 11 | 6 | | 10 | 1 | | 7 | | | | | |
| 23 | 1 | 2 | 3 | 4 | 5 | | | 8 | | 9 | 11 | 6 | | 10 | | | | | | 7 | | |
| 24 | | | | 4 | 5 | 2 | 7 | | 9 | 8 | 11 | | | 10 | 1 | | | | | | 3 | 6 |
| 25 | | 2 | 3 | 4 | 5 | | 7 | 8 | 9 | | 11 | 6 | | 10 | 1 | | | | | | | |
| 26 | 1 | 2 | 3 | | 5 | | | | 9 | | 11 | 4 | | 10 | | 6 | 7 | | 8 | | | |
| 27 | | 2 | 3 | | 5 | | | 8 | 9 | | 11 | 4 | | 10 | 1 | 6 | 7 | | | | | |
| 28 | | | 3 | 4 | 9 | 2 | | | 8 | | 11 | 6 | | 10 | 1 | 5 | 7 | | | | | |
| 29 | | 2 | 3 | 4 | 5 | | 7 | 8 | 9 | | 11 | 6 | | 10 | 1 | | | | | | | |
| 30 | | 2 | | 4 | 5 | 3 | | 7 | 9 | | 11 | 6 | | 10 | 1 | | | 8 | | | | |
| Apps | 0 | 27 | 22 | 28 | 28 | 11 | 19 | 23 | 14 | 23 | 30 | 26 | 4 | 23 | 20 | 7 | 8 | 2 | 2 | 1 | 1 | 1 |
| Goals | | | | 1 | 4 | | 9 | 15 | 7 | 9 | 3 | 1 | 1 | 3 | | | 1 | 1 | | 1 | | |

1 own-goal

| | Trail J | Methven J | Leiper J | Cox J | Goodall A | Staley J | Goodall J | Bloomer S | Boag J | Maconnachie A | McQueen H | Turner J | Miller J | Stevenson J | Fryer J | Paterson R | Handley G | Burton J | Paul J | Leonard J | Leach S | Thompson J |
|---|---|---|---|---|---|---|---|---|---|---|---|---|---|---|---|---|---|---|---|---|---|---|
| 1 | | 2 | 3 | 4 | 5 | | 8 | | | 9 | 11 | 6 | | 10 | 1 | | | | 7 | | | |
| 2 | | 2 | 3 | 4 | 5 | | 8 | | | 9 | 11 | 6 | | 10 | 1 | | | | | 7 | | |
| 3 | | | 3 | 4 | 5 | 2 | 8 | | | 9 | 11 | 6 | | 10 | 1 | | | | | 7 | | |
| R | | | 3 | 4 | 5 | 2 | 7 | 8 | 9 | | 11 | 6 | | 10 | 1 | | | | | | | |
| SF | | 2 | 3 | 4 | 5 | | 7 | 8 | 9 | | 11 | 6 | | 10 | 1 | | | | | | | |
| F | | 2 | 3 | 4 | 5 | | 7 | 8 | 9 | | 11 | 6 | | 10 | 1 | | | | | | | |
| Apps | | 4 | 6 | 6 | 6 | 2 | 6 | 3 | 3 | 3 | 6 | 6 | | 6 | 6 | | | | 1 | 2 | | |
| Goals | | | | | | | 1 | 5 | 3 | | 1 | | | 1 | | | | | | 1 | | |

# 1898-99

| | P | W | D | L | F | A | Pts |
|---|---|---|---|---|---|---|---|
| Aston Villa | 34 | 19 | 7 | 8 | 76 | 40 | 45 |
| Liverpool | 34 | 19 | 5 | 10 | 49 | 33 | 43 |
| Burnley | 34 | 15 | 9 | 10 | 45 | 47 | 39 |
| Everton | 34 | 15 | 8 | 11 | 48 | 41 | 38 |
| Notts Co | 34 | 12 | 13 | 9 | 47 | 51 | 37 |
| Blackburn R | 34 | 14 | 8 | 12 | 60 | 52 | 36 |
| Sunderland | 34 | 15 | 6 | 13 | 41 | 41 | 36 |
| Wolves | 34 | 14 | 7 | 13 | 54 | 48 | 35 |
| Derby Co | 34 | 12 | 11 | 11 | 62 | 57 | 35 |
| Bury | 34 | 14 | 7 | 13 | 48 | 49 | 35 |
| Nottingham F | 34 | 11 | 11 | 12 | 42 | 42 | 33 |
| Stoke | 34 | 13 | 7 | 14 | 47 | 52 | 33 |
| Newcastle U | 34 | 11 | 8 | 15 | 49 | 48 | 30 |
| WBA | 34 | 12 | 6 | 16 | 42 | 57 | 30 |
| Preston NE | 34 | 10 | 9 | 15 | 44 | 47 | 29 |
| Sheffield U | 34 | 9 | 11 | 14 | 45 | 51 | 29 |
| Bolton W | 34 | 9 | 7 | 18 | 37 | 51 | 25 |
| Sheffield W | 34 | 8 | 8 | 18 | 32 | 61 | 24 |

Leading scorer: Steve Bloomer, League 24, all matches 30.

- Steve Bloomer set a club record that still stands when he scored six goals against Sheffield Wednesday on 21 January. He matched his club record 24 League goals, set two years earlier.
- Derby won 9–0, equalling their record League victory against Wolves in January 1891.
- The only higher score in their history is 12–0 against Finn Harps in the UEFA Cup in September 1976.
- Archie Goodall became the first Derby player to represent Ireland, against Wales in Belfast on 4 March.
- For the second successive season, Derby were beaten FA Cup finalists. Sheffield United won 4–1.

## Division One

| Match No. | Date | | Venue | Opponents | Result | | Scorers | Attendan |
|---|---|---|---|---|---|---|---|---|
| 1 | Sep | 1 | (a) | Stoke | D | 0-0 | | 5,00 |
| 2 | | 3 | (h) | Bury | L | 1-2 | Boag | 7,00 |
| 3 | | 10 | (a) | West Brom A | D | 1-1 | Bloomer | 7,50 |
| 4 | | 17 | (h) | Blackburn R | D | 0-0 | | 8,50 |
| 5 | | 24 | (a) | Sheffield W | L | 1-3 | Burton | 11,00 |
| 6 | Oct | 1 | (h) | Sunderland | W | 4-2 | Shanks 2, Burton, Handley | 6,00 |
| 7 | | 8 | (a) | Wolves | D | 2-2 | Bloomer 2 | 6,00 |
| 8 | | 15 | (h) | Everton | D | 5-5 | Arkesden 2, Bloomer 2 (1 pen), McQueen | 7,00 |
| 9 | | 22 | (a) | Notts C | D | 2-2 | Bloomer (pen), Shanks | 15,00 |
| 10 | | 29 | (h) | Stoke | D | 1-1 | Arkesden | 8,00 |
| 11 | Nov | 5 | (a) | Aston Villa | L | 1-7 | Arkesden | 20,00 |
| 12 | | 12 | (h) | Burnley | W | 2-1 | Arkesden, Allen | 8,00 |
| 13 | | 19 | (a) | Sheffield U | L | 1-2 | May | 8,00 |
| 14 | | 26 | (h) | Newcastle U | W | 3-1 | Bloomer 2, Arkesden | 7,00 |
| 15 | Dec | 3 | (a) | Preston NE | L | 1-3 | Bloomer | 4,00 |
| 16 | | 10 | (h) | Liverpool | W | 1-0 | Bloomer | 6,00 |
| 17 | | 17 | (a) | Nottingham F | D | 3-3 | Cox, Bloomer, Rutherford | 8,00 |
| 18 | | 26 | (h) | Bolton W | D | 1-1 | Bosworth | 8,00 |
| 19 | | 31 | (a) | Bury | D | 0-0 | | 5,0 |
| 20 | Jan | 2 | (a) | Sunderland | L | 0-1 | | 15,00 |
| 21 | | 7 | (h) | West Brom A | W | 4-1 | Boag 2, Allen, MacDonald | 6,00 |
| 22 | | 14 | (a) | Blackburn R | L | 0-3 | | 6,00 |
| 23 | | 21 | (h) | Sheffield W | W | 9-0 | Bloomer 6, MacDonald, Oakden, Earp (og) | 5,00 |
| 24 | Feb | 4 | (h) | Wolves | W | 6-2 | Boag 2, Oakden, MacDonald, A.Goodall, Bloomer | 8,00 |
| 25 | | 18 | (h) | Notts C | W | 4-2 | Oakden 2, J.Goodall (pen), Bull (og) | 8,00 |
| 26 | Mar | 4 | (h) | Aston Villa | D | 1-1 | Bloomer | 10,00 |
| 27 | | 11 | (a) | Burnley | L | 1-2 | Bloomer | 7,00 |
| 28 | | 25 | (a) | Newcastle U | L | 0-2 | | 15,00 |
| 29 | | 31 | (a) | Bolton W | L | 1-2 | Oakden | 8,00 |
| 30 | Apr | 1 | (h) | Preston NE | W | 1-0 | Boag | 7,00 |
| 31 | | 3 | (a) | Everton | W | 2-1 | Bloomer, Allen | 20,0 |
| 32 | | 8 | (a) | Liverpool | L | 0-4 | | 12,00 |
| 33 | | 20 | (h) | Nottingham F | W | 2-0 | Bloomer 2 | 3,0 |
| 34 | | 22 | (h) | Sheffield U | W | 1-0 | Bloomer | 10,00 |

FINAL LEAGUE POSITION: 9th in Division One

Appearanc

Goa

## FA Cup

| | | | | | | | | |
|---|---|---|---|---|---|---|---|---|
| 1 | Jan | 28 | (a) | W Arsenal | W | 6-0 | Bloomer 2, Boag 2, MacDonald, Allen | 25,0 |
| 2 | Feb | 11 | (h) | Wolves | W | 2-1 | Allen, MacDonald | 19,00 |
| 3 | | 25 | (a) | Southampton | W | 2-1 | Bloomer, MacDonald | 20,0 |
| SF | Mar | 18 | (n*) | Stoke | W | 3-1 | Bloomer 3 | 24,5 |
| F | Apr | 15 | (n†) | Sheffield U | L | 1-4 | Boag | 73,8 |

*Played at the Molineux Grounds, Wolverhampton. †Played at the Crystal Palace.

Appearanc

Goa

| Fryer J | Methven J | Leiper J | Cox J | Paterson R | May J | Goodall J | Bloomer S | Boag J | Stevenson J | McQueen H | Ford D | Staley J | Goodall A | Burton J | Shanks T | Handley G | Arkesden T | Kifford J | Wilson A | Allen H | Haig J | Richards F | Bosworth S | Rutherford J | MacDonald W | Oakden H | Leckie C | Linacre H | Russell J | Cooke J | |
|---|---|---|---|---|---|---|---|---|---|---|---|---|---|---|---|---|---|---|---|---|---|---|---|---|---|---|---|---|---|---|---|
| 1 | 2 | 3 | 4 | 5 | 6 | 7 | 8 | 9 | 10 | 11 | | | | | | | | | | | | | | | | | | | | | 1 |
| 1 | 2 | 3 | 4 | 5 | 6 | 7 | 8 | 9 | 10 | 11 | | | | | | | | | | | | | | | | | | | | | 2 |
| | 2 | | 4 | | 6 | 7 | 8 | 9 | 10 | 11 | 1 | 3 | 5 | | | | | | | | | | | | | | | | | | 3 |
| | 2 | | 4 | | 6 | 7 | 8 | 9 | 10 | 11 | 1 | 3 | 5 | | | | | | | | | | | | | | | | | | 4 |
| | 2 | | 4 | | 6 | 7 | | 9 | | 11 | 1 | 3 | 5 | 8 | 10 | | | | | | | | | | | | | | | | 5 |
| | 2 | | 4 | | 6 | | 9 | | | 11 | 1 | 3 | 5 | 8 | 10 | 7 | | | | | | | | | | | | | | | 6 |
| | 2 | | 4 | | 6 | | 9 | | | 11 | 1 | 3 | 5 | 8 | | 7 | 10 | | | | | | | | | | | | | | 7 |
| | 2 | | 4 | | 6 | 8 | 9 | | | 11 | 1 | | 5 | | | 7 | 10 | 3 | | | | | | | | | | | | | 8 |
| 1 | 2 | | 4 | | 6 | | 9 | | | 11 | | 3 | 5 | | 8 | 7 | 10 | | | | | | | | | | | | | | 9 |
| 1 | 2 | | 4 | | 6 | | 9 | | | 11 | | 3 | 5 | | 8 | 7 | 10 | | | | | | | | | | | | | | 10 |
| 1 | 2 | | 4 | | 6 | | | 9 | | 11 | | 3 | 5 | | 8 | 7 | 10 | | | | | | | | | | | | | | 11 |
| 1 | 2 | | 4 | | 6 | | 9 | | | | | 3 | 5 | 8 | | | 10 | | 7 | 11 | | | | | | | | | | | 12 |
| 1 | 2 | | 4 | | 6 | 7 | 9 | | | 11 | | 3 | 5 | 8 | | | 10 | | | | | | | | | | | | | | 13 |
| 1 | | | 4 | 5 | 6 | 7 | 9 | | | 11 | | 3 | 2 | 8 | | | 10 | | | | | | | | | | | | | | 14 |
| 1 | | 3 | | 5 | 6 | 7 | 9 | | | 11 | | 2 | | 8 | | | 10 | | | | 4 | | | | | | | | | | 15 |
| 1 | 2 | | 4 | | 6 | 7 | 9 | | | | | 3 | 5 | | | | 10 | | | 11 | | 8 | | | | | | | | | 16 |
| 1 | 2 | | 4 | | 6 | | 9 | | | | | 3 | 5 | | | | | | | 11 | | 8 | 7 | 10 | | | | | | | 17 |
| 1 | 2 | | 4 | | 6 | | 8 | | | 11 | | 3 | 5 | 9 | | | | | | | | | 7 | | 10 | | | | | | 18 |
| 1 | 2 | | 4 | | 6 | 9 | 8 | 5 | | 11 | | 3 | | | | | | | | | | | | | 10 | 7 | | | | | 19 |
| 1 | 2 | | 4 | | 6 | 7 | 8 | 9 | | 11 | | 3 | 5 | | | | | | | | | | | | 10 | | | | | | 20 |
| 1 | 2 | | 4 | | 6 | | 8 | 9 | | | | 3 | 5 | | | | | | | 11 | | | | | 10 | 7 | | | | | 21 |
| 1 | 2 | | 4 | | 6 | | 8 | 9 | | | | 3 | 5 | | | | | | | 11 | | | | | 10 | 7 | | | | | 22 |
| 1 | 2 | | 4 | | 6 | | 8 | 9 | | | | 3 | 5 | | | | | | | 11 | | | | | 10 | 7 | | | | | 23 |
| 1 | 2 | | 4 | | | | 8 | 9 | | | | 3 | 5 | | | | | | | 11 | | | | | 10 | 7 | 6 | | | | 24 |
| | 2 | | 4 | | 6 | 8 | | 9 | | | | 3 | 5 | | | | | | | 11 | | | | | 10 | 7 | | 1 | | | 25 |
| 1 | 2 | | 4 | 5 | 6 | | 8 | 9 | | | | 3 | | | | | | | | 11 | | | | | 10 | 7 | | | | | 26 |
| 1 | 2 | | 4 | | 6 | | 8 | | | | | 3 | 5 | | | | 10 | | | 11 | | | | | 9 | 7 | | | | | 27 |
| 1 | 2 | | | 5 | 6 | | 8 | 9 | | 11 | | 3 | | | | 7 | | | | | 4 | | | | 10 | | | | | | 28 |
| 1 | 2 | | 4 | | 6 | | | 9 | | | | 3 | 5 | | | | 11 | | | | | | | | 10 | 7 | | | 8 | | 29 |
| 1 | 2 | | 4 | | 6 | | | 9 | | | | 3 | 5 | | | | 7 | | | 11 | | | | | 10 | | | | 8 | | 30 |
| 1 | 2 | | | | 6 | | 8 | 9 | | | | 3 | 5 | | | | 7 | | | 11 | 4 | | | | 10 | | | | | | 31 |
| | 2 | | 4 | | 6 | 8 | | 9 | | | | | 5 | | | | 7 | | | 11 | | | | | 10 | | 3 | 1 | | | 32 |
| 1 | | | 4 | 5 | | | 8 | 9 | | | | 3 | | | | | 7 | 2 | | | | | | | 10 | | 6 | | | 11 | 33 |
| 1 | 2 | | 4 | 5 | | | 8 | 9 | | | | 3 | | | 10 | | 7 | | | 11 | | | | | | | 6 | | | | 34 |
| 26 | 31 | 3 | 31 | 8 | 31 | 14 | 28 | 21 | 4 | 18 | 6 | 30 | 26 | 8 | 6 | 7 | 17 | 2 | 1 | 14 | 3 | 2 | 2 | 1 | 16 | 9 | 4 | 2 | 2 | 1 | |
| | | | 1 | | 1 | 1 | 24 | 6 | | 1 | | | 1 | 2 | 3 | 1 | 6 | | | 3 | | | 1 | 1 | 3 | 5 | | | | | |

2 own-goals

| Fryer J | Methven J | Leiper J | Cox J | Paterson R | May J | Goodall J | Bloomer S | Boag J | Stevenson J | McQueen H | Ford D | Staley J | Goodall A | Burton J | Shanks T | Handley G | Arkesden T | Kifford J | Wilson A | Allen H | Haig J | Richards F | Bosworth S | Rutherford J | MacDonald W | Oakden H | Leckie C | Linacre H | Russell J | Cooke J | |
|---|---|---|---|---|---|---|---|---|---|---|---|---|---|---|---|---|---|---|---|---|---|---|---|---|---|---|---|---|---|---|---|
| 1 | 2 | | 4 | | 6 | | 8 | 9 | | | | 3 | 5 | | | | | | | 11 | | | | | 10 | 7 | | | | | 1 |
| 1 | 2 | | 4 | | 6 | | 8 | 9 | | | | 3 | 5 | | | | | | | 11 | | | | | 10 | 7 | | | | | 2 |
| 1 | 2 | | 4 | | 6 | | 8 | 9 | | | | 3 | 5 | | | | | | | 11 | | | | | 10 | 7 | | | | | 3 |
| 1 | 2 | | 4 | 5 | 6 | 7 | 8 | 9 | | | | 3 | | | | | | | | 11 | | | | | 10 | | | | | | SF |
| 1 | 2 | | 4 | 5 | 6 | | 8 | 9 | | | | 3 | | | | | 7 | | | 11 | | | | | 10 | | | | | | F |
| 5 | 5 | | 5 | 2 | 5 | 1 | 5 | 5 | | | | 5 | 3 | | | | 1 | | | 5 | | | | | 5 | 3 | | | | | |
| | | | | | | | 6 | 3 | | | | | | | | | | | | 2 | | | | | 3 | | | | | | |

# 1899-1900

| | P | W | D | L | F | A | Pts |
|---|---|---|---|---|---|---|---|
| Aston Villa | 34 | 22 | 6 | 6 | 77 | 35 | 50 |
| Sheffield U | 34 | 18 | 12 | 4 | 63 | 33 | 48 |
| Sunderland | 34 | 19 | 3 | 12 | 50 | 35 | 41 |
| Wolves | 34 | 15 | 9 | 10 | 48 | 37 | 39 |
| Newcastle U | 34 | 13 | 10 | 11 | 53 | 43 | 36 |
| Derby Co | 34 | 14 | 8 | 12 | 45 | 43 | 36 |
| Manchester C | 34 | 13 | 8 | 13 | 50 | 44 | 34 |
| Nottingham F | 34 | 13 | 8 | 13 | 56 | 55 | 34 |
| Stoke | 34 | 13 | 8 | 13 | 37 | 45 | 34 |
| Liverpool | 34 | 14 | 5 | 15 | 49 | 45 | 33 |
| Everton | 34 | 13 | 7 | 14 | 47 | 49 | 33 |
| Bury | 34 | 13 | 6 | 15 | 40 | 44 | 32 |
| WBA | 34 | 11 | 8 | 15 | 43 | 51 | 30 |
| Blackburn R | 34 | 13 | 4 | 17 | 49 | 61 | 30 |
| Notts Co | 34 | 9 | 11 | 14 | 46 | 60 | 29 |
| Preston NE | 34 | 12 | 4 | 18 | 38 | 48 | 28 |
| Burnley | 34 | 11 | 5 | 18 | 34 | 54 | 27 |
| Glossop | 34 | 4 | 10 | 20 | 31 | 74 | 18 |

Leading scorer: Steve Bloomer, League/all matches 19.
League ever-present: Johnny May, Jimmy Methven.

- Archie Goodall continued to lead the way in appearances, playing his 300th game on 11 November.
- Derby made their worst start to a League season, losing the first four games without managing to score a goal. They also lost the first four in 1965–66.
- Ben Warren, signed from Newhall Swifts, made his debut on 17 March. He was soon recognised as one of the best wing-halves in the country.

## Division One

| Match No. | Date | | Venue | Opponents | Result | | Scorers | Attend |
|---|---|---|---|---|---|---|---|---|
| 1 | Sep | 2 | (h) | Notts C | L | 0-1 | | 15, |
| 2 | | 9 | (a) | Manchester C | L | 0-4 | | 20, |
| 3 | | 16 | (h) | Sheffield U | L | 0-1 | | 10, |
| 4 | | 23 | (a) | Newcastle U | L | 0-2 | | 19, |
| 5 | | 30 | (h) | Aston Villa | W | 2-0 | Bloomer, Arkesden | 12, |
| 6 | Oct | 7 | (a) | Liverpool | W | 2-0 | Bloomer 2 | 12, |
| 7 | | 14 | (h) | Burnley | W | 4-1 | Arkesden 3, Bloomer | 10, |
| 8 | | 21 | (a) | Preston NE | D | 0-0 | | 7, |
| 9 | | 28 | (h) | Nottingham F | D | 2-2 | Bloomer, Wombwell | 12, |
| 10 | Nov | 11 | (h) | Stoke | W | 2-0 | Shanks, Wombwell | 7, |
| 11 | | 25 | (h) | West Brom A | W | 4-1 | Bloomer 2, Cooke 2 | 9, |
| 12 | Dec | 2 | (a) | Everton | L | 0-3 | | 15, |
| 13 | | 9 | (h) | Blackburn R | L | 0-2 | | 8, |
| 14 | | 16 | (h) | Wolves | L | 0-2 | | 5, |
| 15 | | 23 | (a) | Bury | D | 1-1 | Bloomer | 3, |
| 16 | | 25 | (h) | Liverpool | W | 3-2 | MacDonald, Bloomer, Crump | 11, |
| 17 | | 26 | (h) | Glossop | W | 4-1 | Bloomer 2, Arkesden 2 | 12, |
| 18 | | 30 | (a) | Notts C | D | 0-0 | | 8, |
| 19 | Jan | 6 | (h) | Manchester C | D | 0-0 | | 5, |
| 20 | | 13 | (a) | Sheffield U | D | 1-1 | Boag | 12, |
| 21 | | 20 | (h) | Newcastle U | W | 2-1 | Bloomer, Boag | 8, |
| 22 | Feb | 3 | (a) | Aston Villa | L | 2-3 | Bloomer, Boag | 6, |
| 23 | | 17 | (a) | Burnley | W | 2-1 | Bloomer, Arkesden | 5,0 |
| 24 | Mar | 3 | (a) | Nottingham F | L | 1-4 | Bloomer | 10, |
| 25 | | 17 | (a) | Stoke | D | 1-1 | Bradbury | 4,0 |
| 26 | | 21 | (a) | Sunderland | L | 0-2 | | 13, |
| 27 | | 24 | (h) | Sunderland | W | 2-0 | Wombwell 2 | 5,0 |
| 28 | | 31 | (a) | West Brom A | D | 0-0 | | 5, |
| 29 | Apr | 4 | (h) | Preston NE | W | 2-0 | Bloomer, Shanks | 3,0 |
| 30 | | 7 | (h) | Everton | W | 2-1 | Shanks, Stewart | 4, |
| 31 | | 13 | (a) | Glossop | W | 3-1 | May, Bloomer, Wombwell | 2,0 |
| 32 | | 14 | (a) | Blackburn R | L | 0-2 | | 9, |
| 33 | | 21 | (a) | Wolves | L | 0-3 | | 5,0 |
| 34 | | 28 | (h) | Bury | W | 3-0 | Bloomer 2, Shanks | 5, |

FINAL LEAGUE POSITION: 6th in Division One

Appearanc
Go

## FA Cup

| Match No. | Date | | Venue | Opponents | Result | | Scorers | Attend |
|---|---|---|---|---|---|---|---|---|
| 1 | Jan | 27 | (h) | Sunderland | D | 2-2 | A.Goodall (pen), Boag | 15,0 |
| R | | 31 | (a) | Sunderland | L | 0-3 | | 5,0 |

Appearanc
Go

| Match | Fryer J | Methven J | Staley J | Cox J | Paterson R | May J | Bradbury J | Bloomer S | Crump F | Shanks T | Allen H | Wombwell R | McQueen H | Blessington J | Arkesden T | Cooke J | Leiper J | Leckie C | Goodall A | Boag J | Howard E | MacDonald W | Bromage H | Kifford J | Warren B | Stewart H |
|---|---|---|---|---|---|---|---|---|---|---|---|---|---|---|---|---|---|---|---|---|---|---|---|---|---|---|
| 1 | 1 | 2 | 3 | 4 | 5 | 6 | 7 | 8 | 9 | 10 | 11 | | | | | | | | | | | | | | | |
| 2 | 1 | 2 | 3 | 4 | 5 | 6 | 7 | 8 | 9 | | | 10 | 11 | | | | | | | | | | | | | |
| 3 | 1 | 2 | 3 | 4 | 5 | 6 | | 9 | | | | 7 | | 8 | 10 | 11 | | | | | | | | | | |
| 4 | 1 | 2 | 3 | 4 | 5 | 6 | | 9 | | | | 7 | | 8 | 10 | 11 | | | | | | | | | | |
| 5 | 1 | 2 | | | | 6 | | 8 | | | | 7 | | | 10 | 11 | 3 | 4 | 5 | 9 | | | | | | |
| 6 | 1 | 2 | | | | 6 | | 8 | | | | 7 | | | 10 | 11 | 3 | 4 | 5 | 9 | | | | | | |
| 7 | 1 | 2 | | | | 6 | | 8 | | | | 7 | | | 10 | 11 | 3 | 4 | 5 | 9 | | | | | | |
| 8 | 1 | 2 | | | | 6 | | 8 | | | | 7 | | | 10 | 11 | 3 | 4 | 5 | 9 | | | | | | |
| 9 | 1 | 2 | | | | 6 | | 8 | | | | 7 | | | 10 | 11 | 3 | 4 | 5 | 9 | | | | | | |
| 10 | 1 | 2 | | | | 6 | | | | 8 | | 7 | | | 10 | 11 | 3 | 4 | 5 | 9 | | | | | | |
| 11 | 1 | 2 | 3 | | | 6 | | 8 | | | | 7 | | | 10 | 11 | | 4 | 5 | 9 | | | | | | |
| 12 | 1 | 2 | | | | 6 | | 8 | | | | 7 | | | 10 | 11 | 3 | 4 | 5 | 9 | | | | | | |
| 13 | 1 | 2 | 3 | | | 6 | | 8 | | 11 | | 7 | | | 10 | | | 4 | 5 | 9 | | | | | | |
| 14 | 1 | 2 | | | | 6 | | 8 | | | | 7 | 11 | | 10 | | 3 | 4 | | 9 | 5 | | | | | |
| 15 | 1 | 2 | | 4 | | 6 | | 8 | | | | 7 | 11 | | | | 3 | 5 | | 9 | | 10 | | | | |
| 16 | 1 | 2 | | 4 | | 6 | | 8 | 9 | | | 7 | 11 | | | | 3 | 5 | | | | 10 | | | | |
| 17 | | 2 | | | | 6 | | 8 | 9 | | | | 11 | | 7 | | 3 | 4 | 5 | | | 10 | 1 | | | |
| 18 | 1 | 2 | 3 | | | 6 | | 8 | 9 | | | | 11 | | 7 | | | 4 | 5 | | | 10 | | | | |
| 19 | 1 | 2 | 3 | | | 6 | | | 8 | | | | 11 | | 7 | | | 4 | 5 | 9 | | 10 | | | | |
| 20 | 1 | 2 | 3 | | | 6 | | | | | | 8 | 11 | | 7 | | | 4 | 5 | 9 | | 10 | | | | |
| 21 | 1 | 2 | 3 | | | 6 | 7 | 8 | | | | | 11 | | | | | 4 | 5 | 9 | | 10 | | | | |
| 22 | 1 | 2 | | | | 6 | | 8 | | 10 | | 7 | 11 | | | | | 4 | 5 | 9 | | | | 3 | | |
| 23 | 1 | 2 | 3 | | | 6 | | 8 | | | | 7 | 11 | | 10 | | | 4 | 5 | 9 | | | | | | |
| 24 | 1 | 2 | 3 | | | 6 | | 8 | | | | 7 | 11 | | 10 | | | 4 | 5 | 9 | | | | | | |
| 25 | 1 | 2 | 3 | | | 6 | 7 | 8 | | 10 | | 9 | 11 | | | | | 5 | | | | | | | 4 | |
| 26 | 1 | 2 | 3 | | | 6 | 7 | 8 | | 10 | | 9 | 11 | | | | | 4 | 5 | | | | | | | |
| 27 | 1 | 2 | | | | 6 | 7 | | | 10 | | 8 | 11 | | | | | 4 | 5 | 9 | | | | 3 | | |
| 28 | 1 | 2 | 3 | | | 6 | 7 | | | 10 | | 8 | 11 | | | | | 4 | 5 | 9 | | | | | | |
| 29 | 1 | 2 | | | | 6 | | 8 | | 10 | | 7 | 11 | | | | | 4 | 5 | 9 | | | | 3 | | |
| 30 | 1 | 2 | | | | 6 | | | | 10 | | 8 | | | 7 | | | 5 | 3 | 9 | | | | | 4 | 11 |
| 31 | 1 | 2 | 3 | | | 6 | | 8 | | | | 10 | 11 | | 7 | | | 5 | | 9 | | | | | 4 | |
| 32 | 1 | 2 | 3 | | | 6 | | 8 | | | | 10 | 11 | | 7 | | | 5 | | 9 | | | | | 4 | |
| 33 | 1 | 2 | | | | 6 | | 8 | | 10 | | 7 | | | | | | 5 | | 9 | | | | 3 | 4 | 11 |
| 34 | 1 | 2 | 3 | | | 6 | | 8 | | 10 | | 9 | 11 | | 7 | | | 5 | | | | | | | 4 | |
| | 33 | 34 | 18 | 6 | 4 | 34 | 7 | 28 | 6 | 12 | 1 | 29 | 20 | 2 | 22 | 10 | 11 | 30 | 22 | 24 | 1 | 7 | 1 | 4 | 6 | 2 |
| | | | | | | 1 | 1 | 19 | 1 | 4 | | 5 | | | 7 | 2 | | | | 3 | | 1 | | | | 1 |

| Round | Fryer J | Methven J | Staley J | Cox J | Paterson R | May J | Bradbury J | Bloomer S | Crump F | Shanks T | Allen H | Wombwell R | McQueen H | Blessington J | Arkesden T | Cooke J | Leiper J | Leckie C | Goodall A | Boag J | Howard E | MacDonald W | Bromage H | Kifford J | Warren B | Stewart H |
|---|---|---|---|---|---|---|---|---|---|---|---|---|---|---|---|---|---|---|---|---|---|---|---|---|---|---|
| 1 | 1 | 2 | 3 | | | 6 | | 8 | | | | 7 | 11 | | | | | 4 | 5 | 9 | | 10 | | | | |
| R | 1 | 2 | 3 | | | 6 | | 8 | | 10 | | 7 | 11 | | | | | 4 | 5 | 9 | | | | | | |
| | 2 | 2 | 2 | | | 2 | | 2 | | 1 | | 2 | 2 | | | | | 2 | 2 | 2 | | 1 | | | | |
| | | | | | | | | | | | | | | | | | | | 1 | 1 | | | | | | |

# 1900-01

| | P | W | D | L | F | A | Pts |
|---|---|---|---|---|---|---|---|
| Liverpool | 34 | 19 | 7 | 8 | 59 | 35 | 45 |
| Sunderland | 34 | 15 | 13 | 6 | 57 | 26 | 43 |
| Notts Co | 34 | 18 | 4 | 12 | 54 | 46 | 40 |
| Nottingham F | 34 | 16 | 7 | 11 | 53 | 36 | 39 |
| Bury | 34 | 16 | 7 | 11 | 53 | 37 | 39 |
| Newcastle U | 34 | 14 | 10 | 10 | 42 | 37 | 38 |
| Everton | 34 | 16 | 5 | 13 | 55 | 42 | 37 |
| Sheffield W | 34 | 13 | 10 | 11 | 52 | 42 | 36 |
| Blackburn R | 34 | 12 | 9 | 13 | 39 | 47 | 33 |
| Bolton W | 34 | 13 | 7 | 14 | 39 | 55 | 33 |
| Manchester C | 34 | 13 | 6 | 15 | 48 | 58 | 32 |
| Derby Co | 34 | 12 | 7 | 15 | 55 | 42 | 31 |
| Wolves | 34 | 9 | 13 | 12 | 39 | 55 | 31 |
| Sheffield U | 34 | 12 | 7 | 15 | 35 | 52 | 31 |
| Aston Villa | 34 | 10 | 10 | 14 | 45 | 51 | 30 |
| Stoke | 34 | 11 | 5 | 18 | 46 | 57 | 27 |
| Preston NE | 34 | 9 | 7 | 18 | 49 | 75 | 25 |
| WBA | 34 | 7 | 8 | 19 | 35 | 62 | 22 |

Manager: Harry Newbould.
Leading scorer: Steve Bloomer, League/all matches 24.
League ever-present: Dicky Wombwell.

- Harry Newbould was the first manager of Derby to be concerned with team affairs, although directors retained the final say. Newbould also continued as secretary.
- Charlie Morris, capped three times before he left Chirk, became the first Derby player to represent Wales, against Scotland at Wrexham.
- Jimmy Methven made his 300th appearance for the Rams in the 4–0 home win over Sheffield United on 20 October.

## Division One

| Match No. | Date | | Venue | Opponents | Result | | Scorers | Attend |
|---|---|---|---|---|---|---|---|---|
| 1 | Sep | 1 | (a) | Bolton W | W | 1-0 | Bloomer | 10, |
| 2 | | 3 | (a) | West Brom A | D | 1-1 | Bloomer | 5, |
| 3 | | 8 | (h) | Notts C | W | 2-1 | Bloomer 2 | 10, |
| 4 | | 15 | (a) | Preston NE | L | 2-3 | Bloomer 2 | 7, |
| 5 | | 22 | (h) | Wolves | L | 4-5 | Boag, McQueen, May, Goodall (pen) | 9, |
| 6 | | 29 | (a) | Aston Villa | L | 1-2 | Bloomer | 20, |
| 7 | Oct | 6 | (h) | Liverpool | L | 2-3 | Boag, Goodall (pen) | 8, |
| 8 | | 13 | (a) | Newcastle U | L | 1-2 | Bloomer | 15, |
| 9 | | 20 | (h) | Sheffield U | W | 4-0 | Bloomer 3, May | 10, |
| 10 | | 27 | (a) | Manchester C | L | 0-2 | | 20, |
| 11 | Nov | 3 | (h) | Bury | W | 5-2 | Boag 2, Bloomer 2, Wombwell | 8, |
| 12 | | 10 | (a) | Nottingham F | L | 0-1 | | 17, |
| 13 | | 17 | (h) | Blackburn R | W | 4-0 | Bloomer 2 (1 pen), Crawford, Wombwell | 7, |
| 14 | | 24 | (a) | Stoke | W | 1-0 | McQueen | 4, |
| 15 | Dec | 1 | (h) | West Brom A | W | 4-0 | Davis, Bloomer, Boag, Wombwell | 6, |
| 16 | | 8 | (a) | Everton | L | 0-2 | | 14, |
| 17 | | 22 | (a) | Sheffield W | L | 1-2 | Shanks | 6, |
| 18 | | 25 | (a) | Liverpool | D | 0-0 | | 17, |
| 19 | | 26 | (h) | Sunderland | D | 1-1 | McQueen | 18, |
| 20 | | 29 | (h) | Bolton W | W | 4-2 | Bloomer 2 (1 pen), Blackett, Wombwell | 8, |
| 21 | Jan | 1 | (a) | Sunderland | L | 1-2 | Wombwell | 20, |
| 22 | | 5 | (a) | Notts C | L | 1-2 | Shanks | 12, |
| 23 | | 12 | (h) | Preston NE | D | 0-0 | | 5, |
| 24 | | 19 | (a) | Wolves | D | 0-0 | | 4, |
| 25 | Feb | 16 | (h) | Newcastle U | D | 1-1 | Bloomer | 7, |
| 26 | Mar | 2 | (h) | Manchester C | W | 2-0 | Bloomer 2 | 5, |
| 27 | | 9 | (a) | Bury | L | 1-2 | Bloomer | 8, |
| 28 | | 11 | (a) | Sheffield U | L | 1-2 | Wombwell | 7, |
| 29 | | 16 | (h) | Nottingham F | D | 0-0 | | 12, |
| 30 | | 23 | (a) | Blackburn R | L | 0-1 | | 8, |
| 31 | | 30 | (h) | Stoke | W | 4-1 | May 2, Wombwell, Arkesden | 5, |
| 32 | Apr | 13 | (h) | Everton | L | 0-1 | | 4, |
| 33 | | 22 | (h) | Aston Villa | W | 3-0 | Bloomer, Wombwell, Davis | 6, |
| 34 | | 27 | (h) | Sheffield W | W | 3-1 | Bloomer, Wombwell, Davis | 4, |

FINAL LEAGUE POSITION: 12th in Division One

Appearan
Go

## FA Cup

| | | | | | | | |
|---|---|---|---|---|---|---|---|
| 1 | Feb | 9 | (a) | Bolton W | L | 0-1 | 14, |

Appearan
Go

| Match | rryer J | Methven J | Blackett J | May J | Goodall A | Leckie C | Crawford J | Bloomer S | Wombwell R | Shanks T | McQueen H | Arkesden T | Boag J | Bromage H | Morris C | Davis G | Warren B | Staley J | O'Rourke J | Haslam H |
|---|---|---|---|---|---|---|---|---|---|---|---|---|---|---|---|---|---|---|---|---|
| 1 | [illegible] | 2 | 3 | 4 | 5 | 6 | 7 | 8 | 9 | 10 | 11 | | | | | | | | | |
| 2 | [illegible] | 2 | 3 | 4 | 5 | 6 | 7 | 8 | 9 | | 11 | 10 | | | | | | | | |
| 3 | [illegible] | 2 | 3 | 4 | 5 | 6 | 7 | 8 | 9 | | 11 | 10 | | | | | | | | |
| 4 | [illegible] | 2 | 3 | 4 | 5 | 6 | 7 | 8 | 9 | 10 | 11 | | | | | | | | | |
| 5 | [illegible] | 2 | 3 | 4 | 5 | 6 | 7 | 8 | 10 | | 11 | | 9 | | | | | | | |
| 6 | [illegible] | 2 | 3 | 4 | 5 | 6 | 7 | 8 | 10 | | 11 | | 9 | 1 | | | | | | |
| 7 | [illegible] | 2 | 3 | 4 | 5 | 6 | 7 | 8 | 10 | | 11 | | 9 | 1 | | | | | | |
| 8 | [illegible] | 2 | 3 | 4 | 5 | 6 | 7 | 8 | 10 | | 11 | | 9 | 1 | | | | | | |
| 9 | [illegible] | 2 | 3 | 4 | 5 | 6 | 7 | 8 | 10 | | 11 | | 9 | | | | | | | |
| 10 | [illegible] | 2 | 3 | 4 | | 6 | 7 | 8 | 10 | | 11 | | 9 | | 5 | | | | | |
| 11 | [illegible] | 2 | 3 | 4 | 5 | 6 | 7 | 8 | 10 | | 11 | | 9 | | | | | | | |
| 12 | [illegible] | 2 | 3 | 4 | 5 | 6 | 7 | | 8 | 10 | 11 | | 9 | | | | | | | |
| 13 | [illegible] | 2 | | 4 | 5 | 6 | 7 | 8 | 10 | | 11 | | 9 | | 3 | | | | | |
| 14 | [illegible] | 2 | | 4 | 5 | 6 | 7 | 8 | 10 | | 11 | | 9 | | 3 | | | | | |
| 15 | [illegible] | 2 | | 4 | 5 | 6 | | 8 | 10 | | 11 | | 9 | | 3 | 7 | | | | |
| 16 | [illegible] | 2 | | | 5 | 6 | 7 | 8 | 10 | | 11 | | 9 | | 3 | | 4 | | | |
| 17 | 1 | 2 | | 4 | 5 | 6 | 7 | | 8 | 10 | 11 | | 9 | | 3 | | | | | |
| 18 | 1 | 2 | | | 5 | 6 | 7 | 8 | 10 | | 11 | | 9 | | 3 | | 4 | | | |
| 19 | 1 | 2 | | 6 | 5 | | 7 | 8 | 10 | | 11 | | 9 | | 3 | | 4 | | | |
| 20 | 1 | 2 | 9 | 6 | 5 | | | 7 | 8 | 10 | 11 | | | | 3 | | 4 | | | |
| 21 | 1 | 2 | 9 | 6 | 5 | | | 7 | 8 | 10 | 11 | | | | 3 | | 4 | | | |
| 22 | 1 | 2 | 9 | 6 | 5 | | 7 | | 8 | 10 | 11 | | | | | | 4 | 3 | | |
| 23 | 1 | 2 | | 4 | 5 | 6 | 7 | | 10 | | | 8 | 9 | | 3 | 11 | | | | |
| 24 | [illegible] | | 2 | 4 | 5 | 6 | 7 | | 10 | 11 | | 8 | 9 | | 3 | | | | | |
| 25 | 1 | 2 | | 4 | 5 | 6 | 7 | 8 | 10 | 11 | | | | | 3 | | | | 9 | |
| 26 | 1 | 2 | | 6 | 5 | | 7 | 8 | 10 | | | 11 | | | | | 4 | 3 | 9 | |
| 27 | 1 | 2 | | 6 | | | 7 | 8 | 10 | | | 11 | 5 | | 3 | | 4 | | 9 | |
| 28 | 1 | 2 | | 6 | 5 | | 7 | 8 | 10 | | | 11 | | | 3 | | 4 | | 9 | |
| 29 | 1 | 2 | | | 5 | 6 | 7 | 8 | 10 | | | | | | 3 | | 4 | | 9 | 11 |
| 30 | 1 | 2 | 3 | | 5 | 6 | 7 | 8 | 10 | | | 11 | 9 | | | | 4 | | | |
| 31 | 1 | 2 | | 4 | 5 | 6 | 7 | | 10 | | | 8 | 9 | | 3 | | | | | 11 |
| 32 | 1 | 2 | | 4 | 5 | 6 | 7 | | 10 | | 11 | 8 | 9 | | 3 | | | | | |
| 33 | 1 | 2 | | 4 | 5 | 6 | 7 | 8 | 9 | | | 10 | | | 3 | 11 | | | | |
| 34 | 1 | 2 | | | 5 | 6 | 7 | 8 | 9 | | | | 10 | | 3 | 11 | 4 | | | |
| | 1 | 33 | 17 | 29 | 32 | 27 | 31 | 27 | 34 | 9 | 23 | 11 | 22 | 3 | 20 | 4 | 12 | 2 | 5 | 2 |
| | [illegible] | | 1 | 4 | 2 | | 1 | 24 | 9 | 2 | 3 | 1 | 5 | | | 3 | | | | |

| Match | rryer J | Methven J | Blackett J | May J | Goodall A | Leckie C | Crawford J | Bloomer S | Wombwell R | Shanks T | McQueen H | Arkesden T | Boag J | Bromage H | Morris C | Davis G | Warren B | Staley J | O'Rourke J | Haslam H |
|---|---|---|---|---|---|---|---|---|---|---|---|---|---|---|---|---|---|---|---|---|
| 1 | 1 | 2 | | 4 | 5 | 6 | 7 | 8 | 10 | | 11 | | 9 | | 3 | | | | | |
| | 1 | 1 | | 1 | 1 | 1 | 1 | 1 | 1 | | 1 | | 1 | | 1 | | | | | |

# 1901-02

| | P | W | D | L | F | A | Pts |
|---|---|---|---|---|---|---|---|
| Sunderland | 34 | 19 | 6 | 9 | 50 | 35 | 44 |
| Everton | 34 | 17 | 7 | 10 | 53 | 35 | 41 |
| Newcastle U | 34 | 14 | 9 | 11 | 48 | 34 | 37 |
| Blackburn R | 34 | 15 | 6 | 13 | 52 | 48 | 36 |
| Nottingham F | 34 | 13 | 9 | 12 | 43 | 43 | 35 |
| Derby Co | 34 | 13 | 9 | 12 | 39 | 41 | 35 |
| Bury | 34 | 13 | 8 | 13 | 44 | 38 | 34 |
| Aston Villa | 34 | 13 | 8 | 13 | 42 | 40 | 34 |
| Sheffield W | 34 | 13 | 8 | 13 | 48 | 52 | 34 |
| Sheffield U | 34 | 13 | 7 | 14 | 53 | 48 | 33 |
| Liverpool | 34 | 10 | 12 | 12 | 42 | 38 | 32 |
| Bolton W | 34 | 12 | 8 | 14 | 51 | 56 | 32 |
| Notts Co | 34 | 14 | 4 | 16 | 51 | 57 | 32 |
| Wolves | 34 | 13 | 6 | 15 | 46 | 57 | 32 |
| Grimsby T | 34 | 13 | 6 | 15 | 44 | 60 | 32 |
| Stoke | 34 | 11 | 9 | 14 | 45 | 55 | 31 |
| Small Heath | 34 | 11 | 8 | 15 | 47 | 45 | 30 |
| Manchester C | 34 | 11 | 6 | 17 | 42 | 58 | 28 |

Manager: Harry Newbould.
Leading scorer: Steve Bloomer, League 15, all matches 18.

- Steve Bloomer scored his 200th goal for the Rams on 30 November, his second against Everton in his 279th appearance.
- Only one other player in Derby's history has reached 200 goals and 80 years passed before Kevin Hector achieved it.
- Arnold Warren was a Derbyshire fast bowler from 1897 to 1920. He became the last of Derby County's Test cricketers when he played against Australia at Headingley in 1905. Despite taking five for 57 in the first innings, he was not picked again.
- Having played his last game as a full-back in November 1890, Arthur Latham, the trainer, was forced to keep goal at Blackburn on 19 April because Tom Harrison missed his train.

## Division One

| Match No. | Date | | Venue | Opponents | Result | | Scorers | Attend |
|---|---|---|---|---|---|---|---|---|
| 1 | Sep | 3 | (a) | Grimsby T | D | 1-1 | Fulton | 8,0 |
| 2 | | 7 | (h) | Notts C | W | 2-0 | Bloomer, Wombwell | 10,0 |
| 3 | | 14 | (a) | Bolton W | L | 1-2 | Davis | 10,0 |
| 4 | | 21 | (h) | Manchester C | W | 2-0 | Bloomer 2 | 10,0 |
| 5 | | 28 | (a) | Wolves | D | 0-0 | | 8,0 |
| 6 | Oct | 5 | (h) | Liverpool | D | 1-1 | Davis | 10,0 |
| 7 | | 12 | (a) | Newcastle U | W | 1-0 | B.Warren | 16,0 |
| 8 | | 19 | (h) | Aston Villa | W | 1-0 | Bloomer | 15,0 |
| 9 | | 26 | (a) | Sheffield U | L | 0-3 | | 12,0 |
| 10 | Nov | 2 | (h) | Nottingham F | D | 1-1 | Bloomer | 13,0 |
| 11 | | 9 | (a) | Bury | L | 0-2 | | 5,0 |
| 12 | | 16 | (h) | Blackburn R | D | 1-1 | Bloomer | 6,0 |
| 13 | | 23 | (a) | Stoke | D | 1-1 | B.Warren | 8,0 |
| 14 | | 30 | (h) | Everton | W | 3-1 | Bloomer 2, A.Warren | 12,0 |
| 15 | Dec | 25 | (h) | Wolves | W | 3-1 | Bloomer, B.Warren, May | 13,0 |
| 16 | | 26 | (h) | Newcastle U | W | 1-0 | Bloomer | 20,0 |
| 17 | Jan | 1 | (a) | Sunderland | L | 0-1 | | 20,0 |
| 18 | | 4 | (a) | Notts C | L | 2-3 | A.Warren, Wombwell | 6,0 |
| 19 | | 11 | (h) | Bolton W | L | 1-2 | Bloomer | 10,0 |
| 20 | | 18 | (a) | Manchester C | D | 0-0 | | 20,0 |
| 21 | Feb | 15 | (a) | Aston Villa | L | 2-3 | Goodall (pen), Boag | 15,0 |
| 22 | Mar | 1 | (a) | Nottingham F | L | 1-3 | Bloomer | 8,0 |
| 23 | | 8 | (h) | Bury | W | 1-0 | Lindsay (og) | 7,0 |
| 24 | | 17 | (a) | Sheffield W | L | 0-2 | | 3,0 |
| 25 | | 22 | (h) | Stoke | W | 1-0 | Balkwill | 7,0 |
| 26 | | 29 | (a) | Everton | L | 0-2 | | 12,0 |
| 27 | | 31 | (h) | Small Heath | D | 0-0 | | 6,0 |
| 28 | Apr | 1 | (h) | Grimsby T | W | 2-0 | Bloomer 2 | 7,0 |
| 29 | | 5 | (h) | Sunderland | W | 1-0 | B.Warren | 2,0 |
| 30 | | 12 | (a) | Small Heath | L | 1-5 | Goodall | 5,0 |
| 31 | | 14 | (a) | Liverpool | W | 2-0 | Wombwell, Middleton | 12,0 |
| 32 | | 19 | (a) | Blackburn R | L | 1-3 | May | 2,0 |
| 33 | | 26 | (h) | Sheffield W | D | 2-2 | Bloomer, May | 5,0 |
| 34 | | 28 | (h) | Sheffield U | W | 3-1 | Boag 2, Middleton | 5,0 |

FINAL LEAGUE POSITION: 6th in Division One

Appearanc
Go

## FA Cup

| | | | | | | | | |
|---|---|---|---|---|---|---|---|---|
| 1 | Feb | 1 | (a) | Blackburn R | W | 2-0 | B.Warren 2 | 15,0 |
| 2 | | 8 | (a) | Lincoln C | W | 3-1 | B.Warren 3 | 8,9 |
| 3 | | 22 | (a) | Portsmouth | D | 0-0 | | 22,5 |
| R | | 27 | (h) | Portsmouth | W | 6-3 | Bloomer 3, B.Warren 2, Boag | 17,8 |
| SF | Mar | 15 | (n#) | Sheffield U | D | 1-1 | B.Warren | 33,6 |
| R | | 20 | (n†) | Sheffield U | D | 1-1* | Wombwell | 17,5 |
| 2R | | 27 | (n‡) | Sheffield U | L | 0-1 | | 15,0 |

*after extra-time. #Played at The Hawthorns, West Bromwich. †Played at the Molineux Grounds, Wolverhampton. ‡Played at the City Ground, Nottingham.

Appearanc
Go

| Fryer J | Methven J | Morris C | May J | Leckie C | Warren B | Crawford J | Bloomer S | Wombwell R | Fulton W | Haslam H | Goodall A | Davis G | Balkwill A | Boag J | Bromage H | Raisbeck W | Lloyd G | Middleton F | Warren A | Warrington J | Holyoake E | Hunt J | Shirtcliffe E | Harrison T | Latham A | Varney H | Richards G | |
|---|---|---|---|---|---|---|---|---|---|---|---|---|---|---|---|---|---|---|---|---|---|---|---|---|---|---|---|---|
| 1 | 2 | 3 | 4 | 5 | 6 | 7 | 8 | 9 | 10 | 11 | | | | | | | | | | | | | | | | | | 1 |
| 1 | 2 | 3 | 4 | 6 | | 7 | 8 | 9 | 10 | | 5 | 11 | | | | | | | | | | | | | | | | 2 |
| 1 | 2 | 3 | 4 | 6 | | 7 | 8 | 9 | 10 | | 5 | 11 | | | | | | | | | | | | | | | | 3 |
| 1 | 2 | 3 | 4 | 6 | | 7 | 8 | 9 | 10 | | 5 | 11 | | | | | | | | | | | | | | | | 4 |
| 1 | 2 | 3 | 4 | 6 | | 7 | 8 | 9 | 10 | | 5 | 11 | | | | | | | | | | | | | | | | 5 |
| 1 | 2 | 3 | 4 | 6 | | 7 | 8 | 9 | 10 | | 5 | 11 | | | | | | | | | | | | | | | | 6 |
| 1 | 2 | 3 | 4 | 6 | 10 | 7 | 8 | 11 | | | 5 | | 9 | | | | | | | | | | | | | | | 7 |
| 1 | 2 | 3 | 4 | 6 | 10 | 7 | 8 | 11 | | | 5 | | 9 | | | | | | | | | | | | | | | 8 |
| 1 | 2 | 3 | 4 | 6 | 5 | 7 | 8 | 11 | 10 | | | | 9 | | | | | | | | | | | | | | | 9 |
| 1 | 2 | 3 | 4 | 6 | 10 | 7 | 8 | 11 | | | 5 | | 9 | | | | | | | | | | | | | | | 10 |
| | 2 | 3 | | 6 | 10 | 7 | | 11 | | | 5 | | 9 | 8 | 1 | 4 | | | | | | | | | | | | 11 |
| 1 | 2 | 3 | 6 | | 10 | | 8 | 7 | | | 5 | | 9 | | | | 4 | 11 | | | | | | | | | | 12 |
| 1 | 2 | 3 | 4 | 6 | 10 | | 8 | | | | 5 | | | 9 | | | | 11 | 7 | | | | | | | | | 13 |
| 1 | 2 | 3 | 4 | 6 | 10 | | 8 | | | | 5 | | | 9 | | | | 11 | 7 | | | | | | | | | 14 |
| 1 | 2 | 3 | 4 | 6 | 10 | | 8 | | | | 5 | | | 9 | | | | 11 | 7 | | | | | | | | | 15 |
| 1 | 2 | 3 | 4 | 6 | 10 | | 8 | | | | 5 | | | 9 | | | | 11 | 7 | | | | | | | | | 16 |
| 1 | 2 | 3 | 4 | 6 | 10 | | 8 | | | | 5 | | | 9 | | | | 11 | 7 | | | | | | | | | 17 |
| 1 | 2 | 3 | 4 | 6 | 10 | | | 8 | | | 5 | | | 9 | | | | 11 | 7 | | | | | | | | | 18 |
| 1 | 2 | 3 | | 6 | 10 | | 8 | | | 4 | 5 | 11 | | 9 | | | | | 7 | | | | | | | | | 19 |
| 1 | 2 | | 4 | 3 | 10 | | 8 | | | | 5 | | | 9 | | 6 | | 11 | 7 | | | | | | | | | 20 |
| 1 | 2 | 3 | 10 | 4 | | | 8 | 7 | | | 5 | 11 | | 9 | | 6 | | | | | | | | | | | | 21 |
| 1 | 2 | 3 | | 6 | | | 8 | 7 | | 4 | | | | 9 | | | 5 | 11 | | 10 | | | | | | | | 22 |
| 1 | 2 | 3 | | 6 | 10 | | | 7 | | | 5 | | | 9 | | | 4 | 11 | | 8 | | | | | | | | 23 |
| 1 | 2 | | | | | | 8 | 7 | 10 | 6 | 5 | | | 9 | | | 4 | 11 | | | 3 | | | | | | | 24 |
| 1 | | 3 | | 2 | | | | 7 | 8 | 4 | 5 | | 9 | 6 | | | | 11 | | 10 | | | | | | | | 25 |
| 1 | 2 | 3 | | 6 | | | 8 | | 10 | | 5 | | | 9 | | | | 11 | | | | 4 | 7 | | | | | 26 |
| 1 | 2 | 3 | | 6 | 10 | | 8 | 7 | | | 5 | | | 9 | | | | 11 | | | | 4 | | | | | | 27 |
| 1 | | 3 | | 2 | 10 | | 8 | | | 6 | 5 | 11 | 9 | | | | | | | | | 4 | 7 | | | | | 28 |
| 1 | 2 | 3 | 4 | 6 | 10 | | | | 8 | | 5 | 11 | 9 | | | | | | | | | | 7 | | | | | 29 |
| 1 | 2 | 3 | 4 | 6 | 10 | | 8 | | | | 5 | 11 | 9 | | | | | | | | | | 7 | | | | | 30 |
| | 2 | 3 | 4 | 6 | | | 8 | 7 | 10 | | 5 | | | 9 | | | | 11 | | | | | | 1 | | | | 31 |
| | 2 | 3 | 4 | 6 | | | 8 | 7 | 10 | | | | 9 | | | | 5 | 11 | | | | | | | 1 | | | 32 |
| 1 | 2 | 3 | 4 | 6 | 9 | | 8 | | | | 5 | | | | | | | 11 | | | | | | | | 7 | 10 | 33 |
| 1 | 2 | 3 | 4 | 6 | 10 | | 8 | 7 | | | 5 | | | 9 | | | | 11 | | | | | | | | | | 34 |
| 31 | 32 | 32 | 25 | 32 | 22 | 11 | 29 | 22 | 13 | 6 | 30 | 10 | 11 | 18 | 1 | 3 | 5 | 18 | 8 | 3 | 1 | 3 | 4 | 1 | 1 | 1 | 1 | |
| | | | 3 | | 4 | | 15 | 3 | 1 | | 2 | 2 | 1 | 3 | | | | 2 | 2 | | | | | | | | | |

1 own-goal

| Fryer J | Methven J | Morris C | May J | Leckie C | Warren B | Crawford J | Bloomer S | Wombwell R | Fulton W | Haslam H | Goodall A | Davis G | Balkwill A | Boag J | Bromage H | Raisbeck W | Lloyd G | Middleton F | Warren A | Warrington J | |
|---|---|---|---|---|---|---|---|---|---|---|---|---|---|---|---|---|---|---|---|---|---|
| 1 | 2 | 3 | 4 | 6 | 10 | | 8 | 7 | | | 5 | 11 | | 9 | | | | | | | 1 |
| 1 | 2 | 3 | 4 | 6 | 10 | | 8 | 7 | | | 5 | 11 | | 9 | | | | | | | 2 |
| 1 | 2 | 3 | | 6 | 10 | | 8 | 7 | | | 5 | 11 | | 9 | | 4 | | | | | 3 |
| 1 | 2 | 3 | | 6 | 10 | | 8 | 7 | | | 5 | 11 | | 9 | | 4 | | | | | R |
| 1 | 2 | 3 | | 6 | 10 | | 8 | 7 | | | 5 | 11 | | 9 | | 4 | | | | | SF |
| 1 | 2 | 3 | | 6 | 10 | | 8 | 7 | | | 5 | 11 | | 9 | | | 4 | | | | R |
| 1 | 2 | 3 | | 6 | 4 | | 8 | 7 | | | 5 | 11 | | 9 | | | | | | 10 | 2R |
| 7 | 7 | 7 | 2 | 7 | 7 | | 7 | 7 | | | 7 | 7 | | 7 | | 3 | 1 | | | 1 | |
| | | | | | 8 | | 3 | 1 | | | | | | 1 | | | | | | | |

# 1902-03

| | P | W | D | L | F | A | Pts |
|---|---|---|---|---|---|---|---|
| Sheffield W | 34 | 19 | 4 | 11 | 54 | 36 | 42 |
| Aston Villa | 34 | 19 | 3 | 12 | 61 | 40 | 41 |
| Sunderland | 34 | 16 | 9 | 9 | 51 | 36 | 41 |
| Sheffield U | 34 | 17 | 5 | 12 | 58 | 44 | 39 |
| Liverpool | 34 | 17 | 4 | 13 | 68 | 49 | 38 |
| Stoke | 34 | 15 | 7 | 12 | 46 | 38 | 37 |
| WBA | 34 | 16 | 4 | 14 | 54 | 53 | 36 |
| Bury | 34 | 16 | 3 | 15 | 54 | 43 | 35 |
| Derby Co | 34 | 16 | 3 | 15 | 50 | 47 | 35 |
| Nottingham F | 34 | 14 | 7 | 13 | 49 | 47 | 35 |
| Wolves | 34 | 14 | 5 | 15 | 48 | 57 | 33 |
| Everton | 34 | 13 | 6 | 15 | 45 | 47 | 32 |
| Middlesbrough | 34 | 14 | 4 | 16 | 41 | 50 | 32 |
| Newcastle U | 34 | 14 | 4 | 16 | 41 | 51 | 32 |
| Notts Co | 34 | 12 | 7 | 15 | 41 | 49 | 31 |
| Blackburn R | 34 | 12 | 5 | 17 | 44 | 63 | 29 |
| Grimsby T | 34 | 8 | 9 | 17 | 43 | 62 | 25 |
| Bolton W | 34 | 8 | 3 | 23 | 37 | 73 | 19 |

Manager: Harry Newbould.
Leading scorer: Steve Bloomer, League 12, all matches 13.
League ever-present: Jimmy Methven.

- Bury's 6–0 victory over Derby at Crystal Palace remains the most one-sided FA Cup Final in history.
- Steve Bloomer missed the match through injury but goalkeeper Jack Fryer was declared fit despite a strained groin. Fryer had a bad time and twice went off, Charlie Morris and, later, Jimmy Methven replacing him.
- Fryer, Methven and John Boag played in all three of Derby's early Cup finals.
- Archie Goodall played his 400th game for the Rams on 15 November. Eight players in Derby's history exceeded Goodall's final total of 423 appearances.

## Division One

| Match No. | Date | | Venue | Opponents | Result | | Scorers | Attend |
|---|---|---|---|---|---|---|---|---|
| 1 | Sep | 1 | (a) | Wolves | L | 0-3 | | 6, |
| 2 | | 6 | (a) | Aston Villa | D | 0-0 | | 20, |
| 3 | | 13 | (h) | Notts C | W | 4-1 | J.May, Bloomer, Goodall, Montgomery (og) | 12, |
| 4 | | 20 | (a) | Nottingham F | W | 3-2 | Bloomer 2, York | 20, |
| 5 | | 27 | (h) | Bolton W | W | 5-0 | Bloomer 3, York, Warren | 12, |
| 6 | Oct | 4 | (a) | Bury | L | 0-1 | | 8, |
| 7 | | 11 | (h) | Middlesbrough | W | 3-2 | J.May 2, Goodall | 10, |
| 8 | | 18 | (a) | Blackburn R | W | 4-2 | Richards 2, Lloyd, Warrington | 6, |
| 9 | | 25 | (h) | Newcastle U | D | 0-0 | | 12, |
| 10 | Nov | 1 | (h) | Sunderland | W | 5-2 | Goodall, Turner, Bloomer, Warren, Richards | 10, |
| 11 | | 8 | (h) | Wolves | W | 3-1 | Leckie, Bloomer, Richards | 8, |
| 12 | | 15 | (a) | Stoke | L | 0-2 | | 10, |
| 13 | | 22 | (h) | Liverpool | W | 2-1 | Goodall, Richards | 10, |
| 14 | | 29 | (a) | Everton | L | 1-2 | Richards | 12, |
| 15 | Dec | 6 | (h) | Sheffield U | W | 1-0 | Bloomer | 10, |
| 16 | | 13 | (a) | Sheffield W | W | 1-0 | York | 14, |
| 17 | | 20 | (a) | Grimsby T | L | 1-4 | York | 5, |
| 18 | | 27 | (h) | West Bom A | W | 1-0 | Bloomer | 25, |
| 19 | Jan | 1 | (a) | Sunderland | L | 0-2 | | 20, |
| 20 | | 3 | (h) | Aston Villa | W | 2-0 | York, Noon (og) | 12, |
| 21 | | 10 | (a) | Notts C | L | 1-2 | Bull (og) | 16,0 |
| 22 | | 17 | (h) | Nottingham F | L | 0-1 | | 10, |
| 23 | | 24 | (a) | Bolton W | L | 0-2 | | 12,0 |
| 24 | | 31 | (h) | Bury | W | 2-0 | Bloomer, Richards | 8, |
| 25 | Feb | 14 | (h) | Blackburn R | W | 1-0 | Bloomer (pen) | 8,0 |
| 26 | Mar | 14 | (h) | Stoke | W | 2-0 | Boag, Warrington | 6, |
| 27 | | 23 | (a) | Liverpool | L | 1-3 | J.May | 12,5 |
| 28 | | 28 | (h) | Everton | L | 0-1 | | 5, |
| 29 | | 30 | (a) | Sheffield U | L | 2-3 | Warren, Richards | 2,0 |
| 30 | Apr | 10 | (a) | Newcastle U | L | 1-2 | Boag | 25, |
| 31 | | 11 | (h) | Sheffield W | W | 1-0 | Richards | 10,0 |
| 32 | | 13 | (a) | Middlesbrough | L | 1-3 | Davis | 12, |
| 33 | | 22 | (h) | Grimsby T | D | 2-2 | Warrington, York | 5 |
| 34 | | 25 | (a) | West Brom A | L | 0-3 | | 5, |

FINAL LEAGUE POSITION: 9th in Division One

Appearanc
Go

## FA Cup

| | | | | | | | | |
|---|---|---|---|---|---|---|---|---|
| 1 | Feb | 7 | (h) | Small Heath | W | 2-1 | Boag, Warrington | 15,0 |
| 2 | | 21 | (h) | Blackburn R | W | 2-0 | Bloomer, Warrington | 15,0 |
| 3 | Mar | 7 | (h) | Stoke | W | 3-0 | Warren, Davis, Warrington | 16,0 |
| SF | | 21 | (n*) | Millwall | W | 3-0 | Warren, Boag, Richards | 40,5 |
| F | Apr | 18 | (n†) | Bury | L | 0-6 | | 63,1 |

*Played at Villa Park, Birmingham. †Played at the Crystal Palace.

Appearanc
Go

| …ryer J | Methven J | Morris C | May J | Goodall A | Leckie C | Turner A | Bloomer S | York C | Warren B | Middleton F | Boag J | Lloyd G | Warrington J | Richards G | May H | Davis G | Soar A | Ratcliffe E | Varney H | Maskrey H | Davies F | Match |
|---|---|---|---|---|---|---|---|---|---|---|---|---|---|---|---|---|---|---|---|---|---|---|
| | 2 | 3 | 4 | 5 | 6 | 7 | 8 | 9 | 10 | 11 | | | | | | | | | | | | 1 |
| | 2 | 3 | 4 | 5 | 6 | 7 | 8 | 9 | 10 | 11 | | | | | | | | | | | | 2 |
| | 2 | 3 | 4 | 5 | 6 | 7 | 8 | 9 | 10 | 11 | | | | | | | | | | | | 3 |
| | 2 | 3 | 4 | 5 | 6 | 7 | 8 | 9 | 10 | 11 | | | | | | | | | | | | 4 |
| | 2 | 3 | 4 | 5 | 6 | 7 | 8 | 9 | 10 | 11 | | | | | | | | | | | | 5 |
| | 2 | 3 | 4 | 5 | 6 | 7 | 8 | 9 | 10 | 11 | | | | | | | | | | | | 6 |
| | 2 | 3 | 4 | 5 | 6 | 7 | | 8 | 10 | 11 | 9 | | | | | | | | | | | 7 |
| | 2 | 3 | | 5 | | 7 | 8 | | 6 | 11 | | 4 | 9 | 10 | | | | | | | | 8 |
| | 2 | 3 | | 5 | 6 | 7 | 8 | | 4 | 11 | | | | 10 | 9 | | | | | | | 9 |
| | 2 | 3 | | 5 | 6 | 7 | 8 | | 4 | | | | | 10 | 9 | 11 | | | | | | 10 |
| | 2 | 3 | | 5 | 6 | 7 | 8 | | 4 | | | | | 10 | 9 | 11 | | | | | | 11 |
| | 2 | 3 | | 5 | 6 | 7 | 8 | | 4 | | | | | 10 | 9 | 11 | | | | | | 12 |
| | 2 | 3 | 6 | 5 | | 7 | 8 | | 4 | | | | | 10 | 9 | 11 | | | | | | 13 |
| | 2 | 3 | 6 | 5 | | 7 | 8 | | 4 | 11 | | | | 10 | 9 | | | | | | | 14 |
| | 2 | 3 | 6 | 5 | | 7 | 8 | 9 | 4 | 11 | | | | 10 | | | | | | | | 15 |
| | 2 | 3 | 6 | 5 | | 7 | 8 | 9 | 4 | 11 | | | | 10 | | | | | | | | 16 |
| | 2 | 3 | 6 | 5 | | 7 | 8 | 9 | 4 | 11 | | | | 10 | | | | | | | | 17 |
| | 2 | 3 | 6 | 5 | | 7 | 8 | 9 | 4 | 11 | | | | 10 | | | | | | | | 18 |
| | 2 | 3 | 6 | 5 | | 7 | 8 | 9 | 4 | 11 | | | | 10 | | | | | | | | 19 |
| | 2 | 3 | 6 | 5 | | 7 | 8 | 9 | | 11 | | 4 | | 10 | | | | | | | | 20 |
| | 2 | 3 | 6 | 5 | | | 8 | | 4 | 11 | | | | 9 | | 10 | 7 | | | | | 21 |
| | 2 | 3 | | 5 | 4 | 7 | 8 | | 6 | | | | 9 | 10 | | 11 | | | | | | 22 |
| | 2 | 3 | 7 | 5 | 6 | | | 9 | 4 | | | | 8 | 10 | | 11 | | | | | | 23 |
| | 2 | 3 | 9 | 5 | 6 | | 8 | | 4 | 11 | | | 7 | 10 | | | | | | | | 24 |
| | 2 | 3 | 6 | | 5 | | 8 | | 4 | | 9 | | 7 | 10 | | 11 | | | | | | 25 |
| | 2 | 3 | 6 | 5 | | | | 8 | 4 | | 9 | | 7 | 10 | | 11 | | | | | | 26 |
| | 2 | 3 | 6 | 5 | | | | 8 | 4 | 11 | 9 | | | 10 | | | 7 | | | | | 27 |
| | 2 | | 6 | | | | | | 4 | | 9 | 5 | 8 | 10 | | 11 | | 3 | 7 | | | 28 |
| | 2 | 3 | 6 | 5 | | | | 8 | 4 | | 9 | | 7 | 10 | | 11 | | | | | | 29 |
| 1 | 2 | 3 | 6 | 5 | | | 8 | 11 | 4 | | 9 | | 7 | 10 | | | | | | | | 30 |
| | 2 | 3 | 6 | 5 | | | | 8 | 4 | | 9 | | 7 | 10 | | 11 | | | | | | 31 |
| 1 | 2 | 3 | | | 6 | | | 8 | 4 | | 9 | 5 | 7 | 10 | | 11 | | | | | | 32 |
| | 2 | 3 | 6 | 5 | | | | 8 | 4 | | 9 | | 7 | 10 | | 11 | | | | 1 | | 33 |
| | 2 | 3 | 6 | 5 | | | | 8 | | | 9 | 4 | 7 | 10 | | 11 | | | | | 1 | 34 |
| 2 | 34 | 33 | 27 | 31 | 16 | 21 | 24 | 22 | 32 | 19 | 11 | 5 | 13 | 27 | 6 | 15 | 2 | 1 | 1 | 1 | 1 | App |
| | | | 4 | 4 | 1 | 1 | 12 | 6 | 3 | | 2 | 1 | 3 | 9 | | 1 | | | | | | Gls |

3 own-goals

| …ryer J | Methven J | Morris C | May J | Goodall A | Leckie C | Turner A | Bloomer S | York C | Warren B | Middleton F | Boag J | Lloyd G | Warrington J | Richards G | May H | Davis G | Round |
|---|---|---|---|---|---|---|---|---|---|---|---|---|---|---|---|---|---|
| 1 | 2 | 3 | 6 | | | | 8 | | 4 | | 9 | 5 | 7 | 10 | | 11 | 1 |
| 1 | 2 | 3 | 6 | 5 | | | 8 | | 4 | | 9 | | 7 | 10 | | 11 | 2 |
| 1 | 2 | 3 | 6 | 5 | | | | 8 | 4 | | 9 | | 7 | 10 | | 11 | 3 |
| 1 | 2 | 3 | 6 | 5 | | | | 8 | 4 | | 9 | | 7 | 10 | | 11 | SF |
| 1 | 2 | 3 | 6 | 5 | | | | 8 | 4 | | 9 | | 7 | 10 | | 11 | F |
| 5 | 5 | 5 | 5 | 4 | | | 2 | 3 | 5 | | 5 | 1 | 5 | 5 | | 5 | App |
| | | | | | | | 1 | | 2 | | 2 | | 3 | 1 | | 1 | Gls |

# 1903-04

| | P | W | D | L | F | A | Pts |
|---|---|---|---|---|---|---|---|
| Sheffield W | 34 | 20 | 7 | 7 | 48 | 28 | 47 |
| Manchester C | 34 | 19 | 6 | 9 | 71 | 45 | 44 |
| Everton | 34 | 19 | 5 | 10 | 59 | 32 | 43 |
| Newcastle U | 34 | 18 | 6 | 10 | 58 | 45 | 42 |
| Aston Villa | 34 | 17 | 7 | 10 | 70 | 48 | 41 |
| Sunderland | 34 | 17 | 5 | 12 | 63 | 49 | 39 |
| Sheffield U | 34 | 15 | 8 | 11 | 62 | 57 | 38 |
| Wolves | 34 | 14 | 8 | 12 | 44 | 66 | 36 |
| Nottingham F | 34 | 11 | 9 | 14 | 57 | 57 | 31 |
| Middlesbrough | 34 | 9 | 12 | 13 | 46 | 47 | 30 |
| Small Heath | 34 | 11 | 8 | 15 | 39 | 52 | 30 |
| Bury | 34 | 7 | 15 | 12 | 40 | 53 | 29 |
| Notts Co | 34 | 12 | 5 | 17 | 37 | 61 | 29 |
| Derby Co | 34 | 9 | 10 | 15 | 58 | 60 | 28 |
| Blackburn R | 34 | 11 | 6 | 17 | 48 | 60 | 28 |
| Stoke | 34 | 10 | 7 | 17 | 54 | 57 | 27 |
| Liverpool | 34 | 9 | 8 | 17 | 49 | 62 | 26 |
| WBA | 34 | 7 | 10 | 17 | 36 | 60 | 24 |

Manager: Harry Newbould.
Leading scorer: Steve Bloomer, League 20, all matches 25.

- Steve Bloomer scored his 200th League goal for Derby on 14 November, in a 6–2 home defeat by Nottingham Forest. Nobody else in Derby's history has achieved this.
- Derby's most regular wingers, Toby Mercer and George Davis, played against each other at international level when England beat Ireland 3–1 in Belfast.
- Mercer encountered another Rams opponent, Charlie Morris, when Ireland beat Wales 1–0 in Bangor.
- The Rams recorded their highest victory over Sunderland, 7–2 at the Baseball Ground on 28 November.

## Division One

| Match No. | Date | | Venue | Opponents | Result | | Scorers | Attend |
|---|---|---|---|---|---|---|---|---|
| 1 | Sep | 1 | (h) | Small Heath | W | 4-1 | Richards 2, Bloomer, Warren | 7, |
| 2 | | 5 | (h) | Wolves | W | 2-1 | Davis 2 | 10, |
| 3 | | 12 | (a) | Manchester C | L | 1-2 | Hodgkinson | 28, |
| 4 | | 19 | (h) | Notts C | L | 0-1 | | 12, |
| 5 | | 26 | (a) | Sheffield U | L | 2-3 | Davis 2 | 20, |
| 6 | Oct | 3 | (h) | Newcastle U | L | 1-3 | Richards | 11, |
| 7 | | 10 | (a) | Aston Villa | L | 0-3 | | 20, |
| 8 | | 17 | (h) | Middlesbrough | D | 2-2 | Bloomer, Warren | 7, |
| 9 | | 24 | (a) | Liverpool | L | 1-3 | Richards | 13, |
| 10 | | 31 | (h) | Bury | D | 2-2 | Bloomer, Boag | 8, |
| 11 | Nov | 7 | (a) | Blackburn R | L | 1-2 | Bloomer | 10, |
| 12 | | 14 | (h) | Nottingham F | L | 2-6 | Hall, Bloomer | 7, |
| 13 | | 21 | (a) | Sheffield W | L | 0-1 | | 5, |
| 14 | | 28 | (h) | Sunderland | W | 7-2 | Hodgkinson 3, Bloomer 2 (1 pen), Hall, Richards | 5, |
| 15 | Dec | 14 | (a) | West Brom A | D | 0-0 | | 5, |
| 16 | | 19 | (a) | Everton | W | 1-0 | Richards | 10, |
| 17 | | 25 | (h) | Liverpool | W | 2-0 | Hodgkinson, Richards | 12, |
| 18 | | 26 | (h) | Stoke | W | 5-0 | Bloomer 3, Hodgkinson, Mercer | 18, |
| 19 | | 28 | (h) | Aston Villa | D | 2-2 | Hodgkinson 2 | 22, |
| 20 | Jan | 2 | (a) | Wolves | D | 2-2 | Bloomer, Warrington | 7, |
| 21 | | 9 | (h) | Manchester C | L | 2-3 | Bloomer, Richards | 10, |
| 22 | | 16 | (a) | Notts C | D | 2-2 | Bloomer, Warrington | 14, |
| 23 | | 23 | (h) | Sheffield U | L | 3-5 | Bloomer 2, Warrington | 12, |
| 24 | | 30 | (a) | Newcastle U | D | 0-0 | | 16, |
| 25 | Feb | 13 | (a) | Middlesbrough | D | 0-0 | | 10, |
| 26 | | 27 | (a) | Bury | D | 2-2 | Warrington, Hodgkinson | 4, |
| 27 | Mar | 12 | (a) | Nottingham F | L | 1-5 | Barker | 10, |
| 28 | | 26 | (a) | Sunderland | W | 3-0 | May 2, Bloomer | 6, |
| 29 | Apr | 2 | (h) | West Brom A | W | 4-2 | May 2, Bloomer, Richards | 7, |
| 30 | | 9 | (a) | Small Heath | L | 0-1 | | 7, |
| 31 | | 11 | (h) | Blackburn R | W | 3-0 | Bloomer 2, Richards | 4, |
| 32 | | 16 | (h) | Everton | L | 0-1 | | 6, |
| 33 | | 23 | (a) | Stoke | D | 1-1 | Bloomer | 7, |
| 34 | | 30 | (h) | Sheffield W | L | 0-2 | | 5, |

FINAL LEAGUE POSITION: 14th in Division One

Appearanc
Go

## FA Cup

| | | | | | | | | |
|---|---|---|---|---|---|---|---|---|
| 1 | Feb | 6 | (a) | Portsmouth | W | 5-2 | Bloomer 2, Warren, Richards, Davis | 18, |
| 2 | | 20 | (h) | Wolves | D | 2-2 | Warren 2 | 17, |
| R | | 24 | (a) | Wolves | D | 2-2‡ | Bloomer, Richards | 16, |
| 2R | | 29 | (n*) | Wolves | W | 1-0 | Bloomer | 21, |
| 3 | Mar | 5 | (h) | Blackburn R | W | 2-1 | Warrington, Bloomer | 14, |
| SF | | 19 | (n†) | Bolton W | L | 0-1 | | 20, |

*Played at Villa Park, Birmingham. †Played at the Molineux Grounds, Wolverhampton.
‡after extra-time

Appearanc
Go

| Whittaker W | Methven J | Morris C | Warren B | Hall B | May J | Warrington J | Bloomer S | Hodgkinson W | Richards G | Davis G | Leckie C | Middleton F | York C | Boag J | Mercer J | Hickling W | Maskrey H | Smith J | Lloyd A | Parnell G | Barker F | Ratcliffe E | Wheatcroft F | |
|---|---|---|---|---|---|---|---|---|---|---|---|---|---|---|---|---|---|---|---|---|---|---|---|---|
| | 2 | 3 | 4 | 5 | 6 | 7 | 8 | 9 | 10 | 11 | | | | | | | | | | | | | | 1 |
| | 2 | 3 | 4 | 5 | 6 | 7 | 8 | 9 | 10 | 11 | | | | | | | | | | | | | | 2 |
| | 2 | 3 | 4 | 5 | 6 | 7 | 8 | 9 | 10 | 11 | | | | | | | | | | | | | | 3 |
| | 2 | 3 | 4 | 5 | 6 | 7 | 8 | 9 | 10 | 11 | | | | | | | | | | | | | | 4 |
| | 2 | 3 | 4 | 5 | 9 | 7 | 8 | | 10 | 11 | 6 | | | | | | | | | | | | | 5 |
| | 2 | 3 | 4 | 5 | 9 | 7 | 8 | | 10 | 11 | 6 | | | | | | | | | | | | | 6 |
| | 2 | 3 | 5 | | 4 | | | | 10 | 11 | 6 | 7 | 8 | 9 | | | | | | | | | | 7 |
| | 2 | 3 | 6 | | 5 | | 8 | | 10 | 11 | 4 | | 7 | 9 | | | | | | | | | | 8 |
| | 2 | 3 | 4 | 5 | 6 | | 8 | | 10 | 11 | | | | 9 | 7 | | | | | | | | | 9 |
| | 2 | 3 | 4 | 5 | 6 | | 8 | | 10 | 11 | | | | 9 | 7 | | | | | | | | | 10 |
| | | 3 | | 5 | 4 | 10 | 8 | | 6 | 11 | | | | 9 | 7 | 2 | | | | | | | | 11 |
| | | 3 | 4 | 5 | 6 | | 8 | 9 | 10 | 11 | | | | | 7 | 2 | | | | | | | | 12 |
| | 2 | 3 | 4 | 5 | 6 | | 8 | 9 | 10 | 11 | | | | | 7 | | 1 | | | | | | | 13 |
| | 2 | 3 | 4 | 5 | 6 | | 8 | 9 | 10 | 11 | | | | | 7 | | 1 | | | | | | | 14 |
| | 2 | 3 | 4 | 5 | 6 | | 8 | 9 | 10 | 11 | | | | | 7 | | 1 | | | | | | | 15 |
| | 2 | 3 | 9 | 5 | 6 | | 8 | | 10 | 11 | 4 | | | | 7 | | 1 | | | | | | | 16 |
| | 2 | 3 | 4 | 5 | 6 | | 8 | 9 | 10 | 11 | | | | | 7 | | 1 | | | | | | | 17 |
| | 2 | 3 | 4 | 5 | 6 | | 8 | 9 | 10 | 11 | | | | | 7 | | 1 | | | | | | | 18 |
| | 2 | 3 | 4 | 5 | 6 | | 8 | 9 | 10 | 11 | | | | | 7 | | 1 | | | | | | | 19 |
| | 2 | 3 | 4 | 5 | 6 | 10 | 8 | 9 | | 11 | | | | | 7 | | 1 | | | | | | | 20 |
| | 2 | 3 | 4 | 5 | 6 | | 8 | 9 | 10 | 11 | | | | | 7 | | 1 | | | | | | | 21 |
| | 2 | | 4 | 5 | 6 | 10 | 8 | 9 | | 11 | 3 | | | | 7 | | 1 | | | | | | | 22 |
| | 2 | 3 | 4 | 5 | 6 | 9 | 8 | | 10 | 11 | | | | | 7 | | 1 | | | | | | | 23 |
| | 2 | 3 | 4 | 5 | 6 | | 8 | 9 | 10 | 11 | | | | | 7 | | 1 | | | | | | | 24 |
| | 2 | 3 | 9 | 5 | 6 | 8 | | | 10 | 11 | 4 | | | | 7 | | 1 | | | | | | | 25 |
| | 2 | 3 | 4 | | 6 | 8 | | 9 | 10 | 11 | | | | | 7 | | | 1 | 5 | | | | | 26 |
| | 2 | 3 | 4 | 5 | 6 | 9 | | | 10 | | | 11 | | | | | 1 | | | 7 | 8 | | | 27 |
| | 2 | | 4 | 9 | 6 | | 8 | | 10 | | | 11 | | | 7 | 3 | 1 | | | | | 5 | | 28 |
| | 2 | | 4 | 5 | 9 | | 8 | | 10 | | | 11 | | | 7 | 3 | 1 | | | | | 6 | | 29 |
| | 2 | | 4 | 5 | 9 | | | | 10 | 11 | | | | | 7 | 3 | 1 | | | | 8 | 6 | | 30 |
| | 2 | | 4 | 5 | 9 | | 8 | | 10 | 11 | 6 | | | | 7 | 3 | 1 | | | | | | | 31 |
| | 2 | | 4 | 5 | | | 8 | | 10 | | 6 | 11 | | | 7 | 3 | 1 | | | | | | 9 | 32 |
| | 2 | | 4 | 5 | 9 | | 8 | | 10 | | 6 | 11 | | | 7 | 3 | 1 | | | | | | | 33 |
| | 2 | | 4 | 5 | 9 | | 8 | | 10 | 11 | 6 | | | | | 3 | 1 | | | 7 | | | | 34 |
| 2 | 32 | 26 | 33 | 31 | 33 | 13 | 29 | 16 | 32 | 29 | 11 | 6 | 2 | 5 | 24 | 9 | 21 | 1 | 1 | 2 | 2 | 3 | 1 | |
| | | | 2 | 2 | 4 | 4 | 20 | 9 | 10 | 4 | | | | 1 | 1 | | | | | | 1 | | | |

| Whittaker W | Methven J | Morris C | Warren B | Hall B | May J | Warrington J | Bloomer S | Hodgkinson W | Richards G | Davis G | Leckie C | Middleton F | York C | Boag J | Mercer J | Hickling W | Maskrey H | Smith J | Lloyd A | Parnell G | Barker F | Ratcliffe E | Wheatcroft F | |
|---|---|---|---|---|---|---|---|---|---|---|---|---|---|---|---|---|---|---|---|---|---|---|---|---|
| | 2 | 3 | 9 | 5 | 6 | | 8 | | 10 | 11 | 4 | | | | 7 | | 1 | | | | | | | 1 |
| | 2 | 3 | 9 | 5 | 6 | | 8 | | 10 | 11 | 4 | | | | 7 | | 1 | | | | | | | 2 |
| | 2 | 3 | 9 | 5 | 6 | | 8 | | 10 | 11 | 4 | | | | 7 | | 1 | | | | | | | R |
| | 2 | 3 | 4 | 5 | 6 | 9 | 8 | | 10 | | | 11 | | | 7 | | 1 | | | | | | | 2R |
| | 2 | 3 | 4 | 5 | 6 | 9 | 8 | | 10 | 11 | | | | | 7 | | 1 | | | | | | | 3 |
| | 2 | 3 | 4 | 5 | 6 | 9 | 8 | | 10 | 11 | | | | | 7 | | 1 | | | | | | | SF |
| | 6 | 6 | 6 | 6 | 6 | 3 | 6 | | 6 | 5 | 3 | 1 | | | 6 | | 6 | | | | | | | |
| | | | 3 | | | 1 | 5 | | 2 | 1 | | | | | | | | | | | | | | |

# 1904-05

| | P | W | D | L | F | A | Pts |
|---|---|---|---|---|---|---|---|
| Newcastle U | 34 | 23 | 2 | 9 | 72 | 33 | 48 |
| Everton | 34 | 21 | 5 | 8 | 63 | 36 | 47 |
| Manchester C | 34 | 20 | 6 | 8 | 66 | 37 | 46 |
| Aston Villa | 34 | 19 | 4 | 11 | 63 | 43 | 42 |
| Sunderland | 34 | 16 | 8 | 10 | 60 | 44 | 40 |
| Sheffield U | 34 | 19 | 2 | 13 | 64 | 56 | 40 |
| Small Heath | 34 | 17 | 5 | 12 | 54 | 38 | 39 |
| Preston NE | 34 | 13 | 10 | 11 | 42 | 37 | 36 |
| Sheffield W | 34 | 14 | 5 | 15 | 61 | 57 | 33 |
| Woolwich A | 34 | 12 | 9 | 13 | 36 | 40 | 33 |
| Derby Co | 34 | 12 | 8 | 14 | 37 | 48 | 32 |
| Stoke | 34 | 13 | 4 | 17 | 40 | 58 | 30 |
| Blackburn R | 34 | 11 | 5 | 18 | 40 | 51 | 27 |
| Wolves | 34 | 11 | 4 | 19 | 47 | 73 | 26 |
| Middlesbrough | 34 | 9 | 8 | 17 | 36 | 56 | 26 |
| Nottingham F | 34 | 9 | 7 | 18 | 40 | 61 | 25 |
| Bury | 34 | 10 | 4 | 20 | 47 | 67 | 24 |
| Notts Co | 34 | 5 | 8 | 21 | 36 | 69 | 18 |

Manager: Harry Newbould.
Leading scorer: Steve Bloomer, League/all matches 13.
League ever-present: Ben Warren.

- Derby scored only 37 goals, their lowest to this date although they played fewer games in the first 10 seasons. They did not have a worse return until 1920–21.
- Fred Barker scored the winner against Nottingham Forest at the City Ground on 29 October. It was his last game for Derby and, within a month, he was dead.
- Reginald Hounsfield, educated at Repton School, played as an amateur. He was rated as one of Derby's fastest players but was unavailable if fixtures clashed with the Old Reptonians' commitments in the Arthur Dunn Cup.

## Division One

| Match No. | Date | | Venue | Opponents | Result | | Scorers | Attend |
|---|---|---|---|---|---|---|---|---|
| 1 | Sep | 1 | (a) | Stoke | W | 2-1 | Bloomer, Richards | 10, |
| 2 | | 3 | (a) | Sheffield U | L | 1-3 | Warren | 15,0 |
| 3 | | 10 | (h) | Newcastle U | D | 1-1 | Middleton | 10, |
| 4 | | 17 | (a) | Preston NE | L | 0-2 | | 12,0 |
| 5 | | 24 | (h) | Middlesbrough | W | 4-2 | Bloomer 2, Richards, Hounsfield | 8,0 |
| 6 | Oct | 1 | (a) | Wolves | L | 0-2 | | 8,0 |
| 7 | | 8 | (h) | Bury | W | 3-2 | Bloomer, Hounsfield, Hunt | 9, |
| 8 | | 15 | (a) | Aston Villa | W | 2-0 | Bloomer 2 | 22,0 |
| 9 | | 22 | (h) | Blackburn R | D | 1-1 | Hounsfield | 12, |
| 10 | | 29 | (a) | Nottingham F | W | 1-0 | Barker | 15,0 |
| 11 | Nov | 5 | (h) | Sheffield W | W | 1-0 | Richards | 14, |
| 12 | | 12 | (a) | Sunderland | L | 0-3 | | 16,0 |
| 13 | | 19 | (h) | W Arsenal | D | 0-0 | | 12, |
| 14 | | 26 | (h) | Stoke | W | 3-0 | Bloomer, Paton, Hounsfield | 6,5 |
| 15 | Dec | 3 | (a) | Everton | D | 0-0 | | 15, |
| 16 | | 10 | (h) | Small Heath | W | 3-0 | Bloomer 2, Fletcher | 6,0 |
| 17 | | 17 | (a) | Manchester C | L | 0-6 | | 20,0 |
| 18 | | 24 | (h) | Notts C | D | 1-1 | Bloomer | 8,0 |
| 19 | | 26 | (a) | Bury | L | 0-2 | | 9,0 |
| 20 | | 27 | (h) | Everton | L | 1-2 | Wheatcroft | 15,0 |
| 21 | | 31 | (h) | Sheffield U | L | 2-3 | Wheatcroft 2 | 15,0 |
| 22 | Jan | 2 | (a) | Blackburn R | L | 1-3 | Richards | 6,0 |
| 23 | | 7 | (a) | Newcastle U | L | 0-2 | | 20,0 |
| 24 | | 14 | (h) | Preston NE | W | 3-1 | Bloomer 2 (1 pen), Fletcher | 7,0 |
| 25 | | 21 | (a) | Middlesbrough | L | 0-2 | | 12,0 |
| 26 | | 28 | (h) | Wolves | W | 2-1 | Bloomer, Fletcher | 7,0 |
| 27 | Feb | 11 | (h) | Aston Villa | L | 0-2 | | 7,0 |
| 28 | | 18 | (a) | Notts C | D | 0-0 | | 8,0 |
| 29 | | 25 | (h) | Nottingham F | W | 3-2 | G.Davis, Hall, Fletcher | 5,0 |
| 30 | Mar | 4 | (h) | Manchester C | L | 0-1 | | 5,0 |
| 31 | | 11 | (h) | Sunderland | W | 1-0 | G.Davis | 5,0 |
| 32 | | 18 | (a) | W Arsenal | D | 0-0 | | 5,0 |
| 33 | Apr | 3 | (a) | Sheffield W | D | 1-1 | Fletcher | 2,0 |
| 34 | | 8 | (a) | Small Heath | L | 0-2 | | 12,0 |

FINAL LEAGUE POSITION: 11th in Division One

Appearanc
Go

## FA Cup

| | | | | | | | |
|---|---|---|---|---|---|---|---|
| 1 | Feb | 4 | (h) | Preston NE | L | 0-2 | 14,0 |

Appearanc
Go

| Maskrey H | Methven J | Morris C | Warren B | McAllister A | Leckie C | Parnell G | Bloomer S | Paton T | Richards G | Davis G | Ratcliffe E | Gilchrist L | Middleton F | Hounsfield R | Hall B | Hunt A | Barker F | Smith J | Fletcher T | Mercer J | Pynegar A | Wheatcroft F | Moore J | Saunders S | Davis J | |
|---|---|---|---|---|---|---|---|---|---|---|---|---|---|---|---|---|---|---|---|---|---|---|---|---|---|---|
| 1 | 2 | 3 | 4 | 5 | 6 | 7 | 8 | 9 | 10 | 11 | | | | | | | | | | | | | | | | 1 |
| | | 3 | 4 | 5 | 6 | 7 | 8 | 9 | 10 | 11 | 2 | | | | | | | | | | | | | | | 2 |
| 1 | 2 | 3 | 4 | 5 | 6 | 7 | 8 | 9 | | | | 10 | 11 | | | | | | | | | | | | | 3 |
| 1 | 2 | 3 | 9 | 5 | 6 | | 8 | | 4 | | | 10 | 11 | 7 | | | | | | | | | | | | 4 |
| 1 | 2 | 3 | 4 | | 6 | | 8 | | 10 | 11 | | | | 7 | 5 | 9 | | | | | | | | | | 5 |
| 1 | 2 | 3 | 4 | | 6 | | 8 | | | 11 | | 10 | | 7 | 5 | 9 | | | | | | | | | | 6 |
| 1 | 2 | 3 | 4 | 6 | | | 8 | | | | | | 11 | 7 | 5 | 9 | 10 | | | | | | | | | 7 |
| 1 | 2 | 3 | 4 | 6 | | | 8 | | 10 | | | | 11 | 7 | 5 | 9 | | 1 | | | | | | | | 8 |
| 1 | 2 | 3 | 4 | 6 | | | | 8 | 10 | | | | 11 | 7 | 5 | 9 | | | | | | | | | | 9 |
| 1 | 2 | 3 | 4 | 5 | | | 8 | | 6 | | | | 11 | 7 | | 9 | 10 | | | | | | | | | 10 |
| 1 | 2 | 3 | 4 | 6 | | | 8 | | 10 | | | | 11 | 7 | 5 | 9 | | | | | | | | | | 11 |
| 1 | 2 | 3 | 4 | 6 | | | 8 | | 10 | | | | 11 | 7 | 5 | 9 | | | | | | | | | | 12 |
| 1 | 2 | 3 | 4 | 6 | | | 8 | 9 | 10 | | | | 11 | 7 | 5 | | | | | | | | | | | 13 |
| 1 | 2 | 3 | 4 | 5 | | | 8 | 9 | 6 | | | 10 | | 7 | | | | | 11 | | | | | | | 14 |
| 1 | 2 | 3 | 4 | 5 | | | 8 | 9 | 6 | 11 | | 10 | | 7 | | | | | | | | | | | | 15 |
| 1 | 2 | 3 | 4 | 5 | | | 8 | 9 | 6 | | | 10 | | 7 | | | | | 11 | | | | | | | 16 |
| 1 | 2 | 3 | 4 | 5 | | | | 9 | 6 | | | 10 | | | | | | | 11 | 7 | 8 | | | | | 17 |
| 1 | 2 | 3 | 4 | 5 | | | 8 | | 6 | 11 | | 10 | | | | 9 | | | | 7 | | | | | | 18 |
| 1 | 2 | 3 | 4 | 5 | | 7 | 8 | | | 11 | 6 | | | | | 9 | | | 10 | | | | | | | 19 |
| 1 | | 3 | 4 | 5 | | 7 | 8 | | 6 | 11 | 2 | | | | | | | | 10 | | | 9 | | | | 20 |
| 1 | | 3 | 4 | 5 | | 7 | 8 | | 6 | 11 | 2 | | | | | | | | 10 | | | 9 | | | | 21 |
| 1 | | 3 | 4 | 6 | | 7 | | | 10 | 11 | 2 | | | | 5 | | | | 8 | | | 9 | | | | 22 |
| 1 | | 3 | 4 | 6 | | | 8 | 9 | 10 | | 2 | | | 7 | 5 | | | | | | | | 11 | | | 23 |
| 1 | 2 | 3 | 4 | | | | 8 | 9 | 6 | | | | | 7 | 5 | | | | 10 | | | | 11 | | | 24 |
| 1 | 2 | 3 | 4 | | | | 8 | 9 | 6 | | | 7 | | | 5 | | | | 10 | | | | 11 | | | 25 |
| 1 | 2 | 3 | 4 | | | | 8 | 9 | 6 | 11 | | | | 7 | 5 | | | | 10 | | | | | | | 26 |
| 1 | 2 | 3 | 4 | 5 | | | 8 | 9 | 10 | | 6 | | | 7 | | | | | 11 | | | | | | | 27 |
| 1 | 2 | 3 | 4 | 5 | | | 8 | | 10 | 11 | | | | | | 9 | | | 7 | | | | | 6 | | 28 |
| 1 | 2 | 3 | 4 | | | | | | 10 | 11 | | | | 7 | 5 | 9 | | | 8 | | | | | 6 | | 29 |
| 1 | 2 | 3 | 4 | | | | 8 | | 10 | 11 | | | | 7 | 5 | | | | 9 | | | | | 6 | | 30 |
| 1 | | 3 | 4 | | | | | | 10 | 11 | 2 | 8 | | 7 | 5 | | | | 9 | | | | | 6 | | 31 |
| 1 | | 3 | 4 | | | | 8 | | 10 | 11 | 2 | 7 | | | 5 | | | | 9 | | | | | 6 | | 32 |
| 1 | 2 | 3 | 4 | | | | 8 | | 10 | 11 | | | | 7 | 5 | | | | 9 | | | | | 6 | | 33 |
| 1 | 2 | | 4 | 5 | | | 8 | | | 11 | 3 | | | | | | | | 9 | | | | 10 | 6 | 7 | 34 |
| 3 | 27 | 33 | 34 | 24 | 6 | 7 | 29 | 14 | 29 | 18 | 10 | 11 | 9 | 21 | 18 | 12 | 2 | 1 | 18 | 2 | 1 | 3 | 4 | 7 | 1 | |
| | | | 1 | | | | 13 | 1 | 4 | 2 | | | 1 | 4 | 1 | 1 | 1 | | 5 | | | 3 | | | | |

| | | | | | | | | | | | | | | | | | | | | |
|---|---|---|---|---|---|---|---|---|---|---|---|---|---|---|---|---|---|---|---|---|
| 1 | 2 | 3 | 4 | | | | 8 | 9 | 6 | | | | 11 | 7 | 5 | | | | 10 | 1 |
| 1 | 1 | 1 | 1 | | | | 1 | 1 | 1 | | | | 1 | 1 | 1 | | | | 1 | |
| | | | | | | | | | | | | | | | | | | | | |

# 1905-06

| | P | W | D | L | F | A | Pts |
|---|---|---|---|---|---|---|---|
| Liverpool | 38 | 23 | 5 | 10 | 79 | 46 | 51 |
| Preston NE | 38 | 17 | 13 | 8 | 54 | 39 | 47 |
| Sheffield W | 38 | 18 | 8 | 12 | 63 | 52 | 44 |
| Newcastle U | 38 | 18 | 7 | 13 | 74 | 48 | 43 |
| Manchester C | 38 | 19 | 5 | 14 | 73 | 54 | 43 |
| Bolton W | 38 | 17 | 7 | 14 | 81 | 67 | 41 |
| Birmingham | 38 | 17 | 7 | 14 | 65 | 59 | 41 |
| Aston Villa | 38 | 17 | 6 | 15 | 72 | 56 | 40 |
| Blackburn R | 38 | 16 | 8 | 14 | 54 | 52 | 40 |
| Stoke | 38 | 16 | 7 | 15 | 54 | 55 | 39 |
| Everton | 38 | 15 | 7 | 16 | 70 | 66 | 37 |
| Woolwich A | 38 | 15 | 7 | 16 | 62 | 64 | 37 |
| Sheffield U | 38 | 15 | 6 | 17 | 57 | 62 | 36 |
| Sunderland | 38 | 15 | 5 | 18 | 61 | 70 | 35 |
| Derby Co | 38 | 14 | 7 | 17 | 39 | 58 | 35 |
| Notts Co | 38 | 11 | 12 | 15 | 55 | 71 | 34 |
| Bury | 38 | 11 | 10 | 17 | 57 | 74 | 32 |
| Middlesbrough | 38 | 10 | 11 | 17 | 56 | 71 | 31 |
| Nottingham F | 38 | 13 | 5 | 20 | 58 | 79 | 31 |
| Wolves | 38 | 8 | 7 | 23 | 58 | 99 | 23 |

Manager: Harry Newbould.
Leading scorer: Steve Bloomer, League/all matches 12.

- The unthinkable. At a time of financial crisis, Steve Bloomer was sold to Middlesbrough. Because there was a cap on fees, Emor (Jack) Ratcliffe, a reserve full-back, was part of the deal to give Derby a more realistic return.
- Derby won their first five games. That remains their best start to a League season.
- Ben Warren made his England debut against Ireland in Belfast in February, the first of 19 consecutive appearances with Derby and Chelsea.
- In July 1906, Harry Newbould became secretary-manager of Manchester City. Derby's directors said they were surprised and disappointed about his departure.

## Division One

| Match No. | Date | | Venue | Opponents | Result | | Scorers | Attenc |
|---|---|---|---|---|---|---|---|---|
| 1 | Sep | 2 | (h) | Bury | W | 3-1 | Warren, J.Davis, Paton | 8, |
| 2 | | 9 | (a) | Middlesbrough | W | 1-0 | Richards | 8, |
| 3 | | 16 | (h) | Preston NE | W | 3-0 | Bloomer 3 | 9, |
| 4 | | 23 | (a) | Newcastle U | W | 1-0 | Richards | 31, |
| 5 | | 30 | (h) | Aston Villa | W | 1-0 | J.Davis | 8, |
| 6 | Oct | 7 | (a) | Liverpool | L | 1-4 | Warren | 20, |
| 7 | | 14 | (h) | Sheffield U | W | 1-0 | J.Davis | 10, |
| 8 | | 21 | (a) | Notts C | L | 0-1 | | 14, |
| 9 | | 28 | (h) | Stoke | W | 1-0 | Paton | 10, |
| 10 | Nov | 4 | (a) | Bolton W | L | 0-5 | | 20, |
| 11 | | 11 | (h) | W Arsenal | W | 5-1 | Bloomer 3, Richards, Fletcher | 8, |
| 12 | | 18 | (a) | Blackburn R | L | 0-3 | | 10, |
| 13 | | 25 | (h) | Sunderland | W | 1-0 | Richards | 7, |
| 14 | Dec | 2 | (a) | Birmingham | L | 1-3 | Fletcher | 18, |
| 15 | | 9 | (h) | Everton | D | 0-0 | | 10, |
| 16 | | 16 | (h) | Wolves | W | 2-0 | Bloomer 2 | 7, |
| 17 | | 23 | (a) | Sheffield W | L | 0-1 | | 12, |
| 18 | | 25 | (h) | Manchester C | L | 1-2 | Bloomer (pen) | 14, |
| 19 | | 26 | (h) | Nottingham F | D | 2-2 | Fletcher, Wheatcroft | 15, |
| 20 | | 30 | (a) | Bury | W | 2-0 | Bloomer, Warren | 8, |
| 21 | Jan | 6 | (h) | Middlesbrough | D | 1-1 | Bloomer | 3, |
| 22 | | 20 | (a) | Preston NE | L | 1-3 | Lamb | 6, |
| 23 | | 27 | (h) | Newcastle U | W | 2-1 | Bloomer, Paton | 7, |
| 24 | Feb | 10 | (h) | Liverpool | L | 0-3 | | 3, |
| 25 | | 17 | (a) | Sheffield U | L | 0-1 | | 15, |
| 26 | | 24 | (h) | Notts C | D | 1-1 | A.Wood | 6, |
| 27 | Mar | 3 | (a) | Stoke | D | 2-2 | A.Wood, Richards | 10, |
| 28 | | 10 | (h) | Bolton W | L | 0-1 | | 7, |
| 29 | | 17 | (a) | W Arsenal | L | 0-1 | | 20, |
| 30 | | 24 | (h) | Blackburn R | L | 1-2 | Cleaver | 3, |
| 31 | | 31 | (a) | Sunderland | L | 0-2 | | 10, |
| 32 | Apr | 7 | (h) | Birmingham | D | 0-0 | | 5, |
| 33 | | 13 | (a) | Manchester C | W | 2-1 | J.Wood, Hardcastle | 15, |
| 34 | | 14 | (a) | Everton | L | 1-2 | Cleaver | 12, |
| 35 | | 16 | (a) | Aston Villa | L | 0-6 | | 9, |
| 36 | | 17 | (a) | Nottingham F | D | 0-0 | | 12, |
| 37 | | 21 | (a) | Wolves | L | 0-7 | | 8, |
| 38 | | 28 | (h) | Sheffield W | W | 2-1 | Cleaver, J.Wood | 4, |

FINAL LEAGUE POSITION: 15th in Division One

Appearan
Gc

## FA Cup

| | | | | | | | | |
|---|---|---|---|---|---|---|---|---|
| 1 | Jan | 13 | (h) | Kettering T | W | 4-0 | J.Davis, Hall, Warren (pen), Fletcher | 6, |
| 2 | Feb | 3 | (h) | Newcastle U | D | 0-0 | | 18, |
| R | | 7 | (a) | Newcastle U | L | 1-2 | Orr (og) | 28, |

Appearan
Gc

| Maskrey H | Methven J | Morris C | Warren B | Wood A | Saunders S | Davis J | Bloomer S | Paton T | Richards G | Middleton F | Hall B | Smith J | Nicholas J | Lamb S | Seal C | Fletcher T | Ratcliffe E | Hunt J | Wheatcroft F | Hunt A | Hounsfield R | Hardcastle D | Mitchell H | Ramsell E | Cleaver F | Wood J | King J | Moore J | Davis G | Walton G | Tremelling S | |
|---|---|---|---|---|---|---|---|---|---|---|---|---|---|---|---|---|---|---|---|---|---|---|---|---|---|---|---|---|---|---|---|---|
| | 2 | 3 | 4 | 5 | 6 | 7 | 8 | 9 | 10 | 11 | | | | | | | | | | | | | | | | | | | | | | 1 |
| | 2 | 3 | 4 | 6 | | 7 | 8 | 9 | 10 | 11 | 5 | | | | | | | | | | | | | | | | | | | | | 2 |
| | 2 | 3 | 4 | 6 | | 7 | 8 | 9 | 10 | 11 | 5 | | | | | | | | | | | | | | | | | | | | | 3 |
| | 2 | 3 | 4 | 6 | | 7 | 8 | 9 | 10 | 11 | 5 | | | | | | | | | | | | | | | | | | | | | 4 |
| | 2 | 3 | 4 | 6 | | 7 | 8 | 9 | 10 | 11 | 5 | | | | | | | | | | | | | | | | | | | | | 5 |
| | 2 | 3 | 4 | 6 | | 7 | 8 | 9 | 10 | 11 | 5 | | | | | | | | | | | | | | | | | | | | | 6 |
| | | 3 | 4 | 6 | | 7 | 8 | 9 | 10 | 11 | 5 | 1 | 2 | | | | | | | | | | | | | | | | | | | 7 |
| | 2 | | 4 | 6 | | 7 | 8 | 9 | 10 | 11 | 5 | | 3 | | | | | | | | | | | | | | | | | | | 8 |
| | 2 | 3 | 4 | 6 | | 7 | 8 | 9 | 10 | | 5 | | | 11 | | | | | | | | | | | | | | | | | | 9 |
| | 2 | | 4 | 6 | | 7 | 8 | 9 | 10 | | 5 | | | 11 | 3 | | | | | | | | | | | | | | | | | 10 |
| | 2 | 3 | 4 | 6 | | 7 | 8 | | 10 | | 5 | | | 11 | | 9 | | | | | | | | | | | | | | | | 11 |
| | 2 | | 4 | 6 | | 7 | 8 | 9 | 10 | | 5 | | | 11 | | | 3 | | | | | | | | | | | | | | | 12 |
| | 2 | | 4 | 6 | | 7 | | 8 | 10 | | 5 | | 3 | 11 | | 9 | | | | | | | | | | | | | | | | 13 |
| | 2 | | 4 | | | 7 | 8 | 10 | 6 | | 5 | | 3 | 11 | | 9 | | | | | | | | | | | | | | | | 14 |
| | 2 | 3 | 4 | 6 | | 7 | 8 | | 10 | 11 | 5 | | | | | 9 | | | | | | | | | | | | | | | | 15 |
| | 2 | 3 | 4 | 6 | | 7 | 8 | | 10 | | 5 | | | 11 | | 9 | | | | | | | | | | | | | | | | 16 |
| | 2 | 3 | 4 | 6 | | 7 | 8 | 9 | | | 5 | | | 11 | | 10 | | | | | | | | | | | | | | | | 17 |
| | 2 | 3 | 4 | | | 7 | 8 | 9 | 10 | | 5 | | | 11 | | | | 6 | | | | | | | | | | | | | | 18 |
| | 2 | 3 | 4 | 6 | | 7 | | 10 | | 11 | 5 | | | | | 9 | | | 8 | | | | | | | | | | | | | 19 |
| | 2 | 3 | 4 | 6 | | 7 | 8 | | 10 | 11 | 5 | | | | | | | | | 9 | | | | | | | | | | | | 20 |
| | 2 | 3 | 4 | 6 | | 7 | 8 | | 10 | | 5 | 1 | | 11 | | | | | | 9 | | | | | | | | | | | | 21 |
| | 2 | 3 | 4 | 6 | | | 8 | | 10 | | 5 | | | 11 | | 9 | | | | | 7 | | | | | | | | | | | 22 |
| | 2 | 3 | 4 | 6 | | | 8 | 9 | 10 | 11 | 5 | | | | | | | | | | 7 | | | | | | | | | | | 23 |
| | | 3 | 4 | 6 | | | 8 | 9 | | | 5 | | | 11 | | | 2 | | | | | 10 | 7 | | | | | | | | | 24 |
| | 2 | 3 | | 6 | | | | 8 | 10 | | 5 | | | 11 | | 7 | | 4 | | 9 | | | | | | | | | | | | 25 |
| | 2 | 3 | | 6 | | | | 8 | 10 | | 5 | | | 11 | | 7 | | | | | | | | 4 | 9 | | | | | | | 26 |
| | 2 | | 4 | 6 | | | | 8 | 10 | | 5 | | 3 | 11 | | 7 | | | | | | | | | 9 | | | | | | | 27 |
| | 2 | 3 | 4 | 6 | | | 8 | | | | 5 | | | 11 | | 7 | | | | | | | | | 9 | 10 | | | | | | 28 |
| | 2 | | 4 | 6 | | | | | | | 5 | 1 | 3 | 11 | | | | | | | | | | | 9 | 10 | 7 | 8 | | | | 29 |
| | 2 | | | 6 | | | | | 10 | | 5 | 1 | 3 | 11 | | 7 | | | | | | | | 4 | 8 | 9 | | | | | | 30 |
| | 2 | | 4 | 6 | | 7 | | | 10 | | 5 | | 3 | 11 | | 8 | | | | | | | | | | 9 | | | | | | 31 |
| | 2 | | | 6 | | 7 | | | 10 | | 5 | | 3 | 11 | | | | | | | | | | 4 | 8 | 9 | | | | | | 32 |
| | 2 | 3 | 9 | 6 | | 7 | | | 4 | 11 | 5 | | | | | | | | | | | 10 | | | | 8 | | | | | | 33 |
| | 2 | | 9 | | | 7 | | | 6 | | 5 | | 3 | 11 | | | | | | | | | | 4 | 10 | 8 | | | | | | 34 |
| | 2 | | 9 | 6 | | 7 | | | | | 5 | | 3 | | | | | | | | | | | 4 | 10 | 8 | | | 11 | | | 35 |
| | | | 2 | 6 | | 7 | | | 4 | | 5 | 1 | 3 | 11 | | | | | 9 | | | 10 | | | | 8 | | | | | | 36 |
| | | | 4 | | | 7 | | | 6 | | 5 | 1 | 3 | 11 | | | | | | | | 10 | | | | 8 | | | | 2 | 9 | 37 |
| | 2 | | 4 | 5 | | 7 | | | 6 | | | | 3 | 11 | | | | | | | | 10 | | | 9 | 8 | | | | | | 38 |
| 2 | 34 | 23 | 34 | 34 | 1 | 29 | 23 | 21 | 32 | 13 | 36 | 6 | 14 | 24 | 1 | 14 | 2 | 2 | 2 | 3 | 2 | 5 | 1 | 5 | 9 | 11 | 1 | 1 | 1 | 1 | 1 | |
| | | | 3 | 2 | | 3 | 12 | 3 | 5 | | | | | 1 | | 3 | | | 1 | | | 1 | | | 3 | 2 | | | | | | |

| Maskrey H | Methven J | Morris C | Warren B | Wood A | Saunders S | Davis J | Bloomer S | Paton T | Richards G | Middleton F | Hall B | Smith J | Nicholas J | Lamb S | Seal C | Fletcher T | Ratcliffe E | Hunt J | Wheatcroft F | Hunt A | Hounsfield R | Hardcastle D | Mitchell H | Ramsell E | Cleaver F | Wood J | King J | Moore J | Davis G | Walton G | Tremelling S | |
|---|---|---|---|---|---|---|---|---|---|---|---|---|---|---|---|---|---|---|---|---|---|---|---|---|---|---|---|---|---|---|---|---|
| | 2 | 3 | 4 | 6 | | 7 | 8 | | 10 | | 5 | 1 | | 11 | | 9 | | | | | | | | | | | | | | | | 1 |
| | 2 | 3 | 4 | 6 | | | 8 | 9 | 10 | 11 | 5 | | | | | | | | | | 7 | | | | | | | | | | | 2 |
| | 2 | 3 | 4 | 6 | | | 8 | 9 | | | 5 | | | 11 | | | | | | | 7 | 10 | | | | | | | | | | R |
| 2 | 3 | 3 | 3 | 3 | | 1 | 3 | 2 | 2 | 1 | 3 | 1 | | 2 | | 1 | | | | | 2 | 1 | | | | | | | | | | |
| | | | 1 | | | 1 | | | | | 1 | | | | | 1 | | | | | | | | | | | | | | | | |

1 own-goal

# 1906-07

| | P | W | D | L | F | A | Pts |
|---|---|---|---|---|---|---|---|
| Newcastle U | 38 | 22 | 7 | 9 | 74 | 46 | 51 |
| Bristol C | 38 | 20 | 8 | 10 | 66 | 47 | 48 |
| Everton | 38 | 20 | 5 | 13 | 70 | 46 | 45 |
| Sheffield U | 38 | 17 | 11 | 10 | 57 | 55 | 45 |
| Aston Villa | 38 | 19 | 6 | 13 | 78 | 52 | 44 |
| Bolton W | 38 | 18 | 8 | 12 | 59 | 47 | 44 |
| Woolwich A | 38 | 20 | 4 | 14 | 66 | 59 | 44 |
| Manchester U | 38 | 17 | 8 | 13 | 53 | 56 | 42 |
| Birmingham | 38 | 15 | 8 | 15 | 52 | 52 | 38 |
| Sunderland | 38 | 14 | 9 | 15 | 65 | 66 | 37 |
| Middlesbrough | 38 | 15 | 6 | 17 | 56 | 63 | 36 |
| Blackburn R | 38 | 14 | 7 | 17 | 56 | 59 | 35 |
| Sheffield W | 38 | 12 | 11 | 15 | 49 | 60 | 35 |
| Preston NE | 38 | 14 | 7 | 17 | 44 | 57 | 35 |
| Liverpool | 38 | 13 | 7 | 18 | 64 | 65 | 33 |
| Bury | 38 | 13 | 6 | 19 | 58 | 68 | 32 |
| Manchester C | 38 | 10 | 12 | 16 | 53 | 77 | 32 |
| Notts Co | 38 | 8 | 15 | 15 | 46 | 50 | 31 |
| Derby Co | 38 | 9 | 9 | 20 | 41 | 59 | 27 |
| Stoke | 38 | 8 | 10 | 20 | 41 | 64 | 26 |

Manager: Jimmy Methven.
Leading scorer: George Davis, Jimmy Long, League 8. Jimmy Long, all matches 9.

- Jimmy Methven, appointed as manager in August 1906, made the last of his 511 appearances for the Rams against Manchester City on 26 January. Only five have played more times for Derby.
- Methven could not prevent Derby from losing their Division One status for the first time. They did not regain it until Steve Bloomer was back at the Baseball Ground.
- Herbert Smith joined the list of internationals because he was on a social visit to Derbyshire cricketer Bertie Lawton at Cromford Hall and agreed to assist the Rams on 1 April. Smith had four full caps as well as 17 at amateur level and was an Olympic gold medallist with the Great Britain football team in the London games of 1908.

## Division One

| Match No. | Date | | Venue | Opponents | Result | | Scorers | Atten |
|---|---|---|---|---|---|---|---|---|
| 1 | Sep | 1 | (a) | Sheffield U | L | 0-2 | | 8, |
| 2 | | 3 | (h) | Manchester U | D | 2-2 | Morris, Warren (pen) | 5, |
| 3 | | 8 | (h) | Bury | W | 2-1 | G.Davis, Long | 5, |
| 4 | | 15 | (a) | Bolton W | L | 0-1 | | 16, |
| 5 | | 22 | (h) | Manchester C | D | 2-2 | G.Davis, Richards | 6, |
| 6 | | 29 | (a) | Manchester U | D | 1-1 | Long | 25, |
| 7 | Oct | 6 | (h) | Middlesbrough | W | 1-0 | Ransford | 10, |
| 8 | | 13 | (a) | Stoke | L | 1-2 | J.Wood | 5, |
| 9 | | 20 | (h) | Preston NE | W | 3-0 | J.Wood, Warren (pen), Ransford | 7, |
| 10 | | 27 | (a) | Blackburn R | L | 1-5 | Ransford | 15, |
| 11 | Nov | 3 | (h) | Newcastle U | D | 0-0 | | 9, |
| 12 | | 10 | (a) | Sunderland | W | 2-0 | J.Davis, J.Wood | 10, |
| 13 | | 17 | (h) | Aston Villa | L | 0-1 | | 7, |
| 14 | | 24 | (a) | Birmingham | L | 1-2 | J.Davis | 10, |
| 15 | Dec | 1 | (h) | Liverpool | L | 0-1 | | 8, |
| 16 | | 8 | (a) | Everton | L | 0-2 | | 10, |
| 17 | | 15 | (a) | Bristol C | L | 0-3 | | 10, |
| 18 | | 22 | (h) | W Arsenal | D | 0-0 | | 7, |
| 19 | | 24 | (h) | Notts C | W | 3-0 | Warren (pen), Long, G.Davis | 8, |
| 20 | | 25 | (a) | Sheffield W | D | 1-1 | J.Wood | 22, |
| 21 | | 29 | (h) | Sheffield U | W | 3-0 | Bentley 2, J.Wood | 7, |
| 22 | Jan | 1 | (a) | Newcastle U | L | 0-2 | | 30, |
| 23 | | 5 | (a) | Bury | L | 0-1 | | 11, |
| 24 | | 19 | (h) | Bolton W | L | 0-1 | | 5, |
| 25 | | 26 | (a) | Manchester C | D | 2-2 | J.Davis, Long | 15, |
| 26 | Feb | 9 | (a) | Middlesbrough | L | 1-4 | G.Davis | 10, |
| 27 | | 16 | (h) | Stoke | W | 2-1 | G.Davis 2 | 7, |
| 28 | Mar | 2 | (h) | Blackburn R | L | 2-3 | G.Davis, Long | 10, |
| 29 | | 9 | (a) | Preston NE | L | 0-1 | | 8, |
| 30 | | 16 | (h) | Sunderland | D | 1-1 | Hall | 6, |
| 31 | | 23 | (a) | Aston Villa | L | 0-2 | | 16, |
| 32 | | 29 | (a) | Notts C | L | 0-4 | | 20, |
| 33 | | 30 | (h) | Birmingham | D | 1-1 | Wheatcroft | 5, |
| 34 | Apr | 1 | (h) | Sheffield W | W | 1-0 | Wheatcroft | 10, |
| 35 | | 6 | (a) | Liverpool | L | 0-2 | | 7, |
| 36 | | 13 | (h) | Everton | W | 5-2 | Bentley 2, Long 2, J.Davis | 4, |
| 37 | | 20 | (h) | Bristol C | L | 1-3 | Armstrong | 6, |
| 38 | | 27 | (a) | W Arsenal | L | 2-3 | G.Davis, Long | 2, |

FINAL LEAGUE POSITION: 19th in Division One – Relegated

Appearan
Go

## FA Cup

| | | | | | | | | |
|---|---|---|---|---|---|---|---|---|
| 1 | Jan | 12 | (h) | Chesterfield | D | 1-1 | Ransford | 13, |
| R | | 21 | (n*) | Chesterfield | W | 4-0 | Long, A.Wood, Bentley, Morris | 13, |
| 2 | Feb | 2 | (h) | Lincoln C | W | 1-0 | Bentley | 14, |
| 3 | | 23 | (a) | West Brom A | L | 0-2 | | 35, |

*Played at Trent Bridge, Nottingham.

Appearan
Go

First round replay at Chesterfield on 16 January was abandoned seven minutes from the end of extra-time because of bad light. Derby led 2–1 through Long and Ransford before what was then record crowd for the Chesterfield ground,14,000. Because the game had lasted at least 90 minutes, the FA ruled that the replay should be on a neutral ground.

Derby team at Chesterfield: Maskrey; Nicholas, Morris, Warren, Hall, A.Wood, J.Davis, Long, Ransford, Bentley, G.Davis.

| Maskrey H | Nicholas J | Morris C | Warren B | Hall B | Wood A | Davis J | Wood J | Long J | Richards G | Davis G | Fletcher T | Cleaver F | Ransford J | Methven J | Bagshaw J | Wheatcroft F | Bentley A | Lamb S | Moore W | Vann B | Smith H | Smith J | Armstrong A | Haywood F | |
|---|---|---|---|---|---|---|---|---|---|---|---|---|---|---|---|---|---|---|---|---|---|---|---|---|---|
| | 2 | 3 | 4 | 5 | 6 | 7 | 8 | 9 | 10 | 11 | | | | | | | | | | | | | | | 1 |
| | 2 | 3 | 4 | 5 | 6 | 7 | 8 | 9 | 10 | 11 | | | | | | | | | | | | | | | 2 |
| | 2 | 3 | 4 | 5 | 6 | 7 | 8 | 10 | | 11 | 9 | | | | | | | | | | | | | | 3 |
| | 2 | 3 | 4 | 5 | 6 | 7 | | 8 | 10 | 11 | | 9 | | | | | | | | | | | | | 4 |
| | 2 | 3 | 4 | 5 | 6 | 7 | 8 | 9 | 10 | 11 | | | | | | | | | | | | | | | 5 |
| | 2 | 3 | 4 | 5 | 6 | 7 | | 8 | 10 | 11 | | | 9 | | | | | | | | | | | | 6 |
| | | 3 | 4 | 5 | 6 | 7 | | 8 | 10 | 11 | | | 9 | 2 | | | | | | | | | | | 7 |
| | | 3 | | 5 | 6 | 7 | 10 | 8 | 4 | 11 | | | 9 | 2 | | | | | | | | | | | 8 |
| | 2 | 3 | 4 | | 5 | 7 | 10 | 8 | 6 | 11 | | | 9 | | | | | | | | | | | | 9 |
| | 2 | 3 | 4 | | 5 | 7 | 10 | 8 | 6 | 11 | | | 9 | | | | | | | | | | | | 10 |
| | 2 | 3 | 4 | | 5 | 7 | 10 | 8 | 6 | 11 | | | 9 | | | | | | | | | | | | 11 |
| | 2 | 3 | 4 | | 5 | 7 | 10 | 8 | | 11 | | | 9 | | 6 | | | | | | | | | | 12 |
| | 2 | 3 | 4 | | 5 | 7 | 10 | 8 | | 11 | | | 9 | | 6 | | | | | | | | | | 13 |
| | 2 | 3 | 4 | 5 | | 7 | 10 | 8 | | 11 | | | 9 | | 6 | | | | | | | | | | 14 |
| | 2 | 3 | 4 | 5 | 6 | 7 | 10 | 8 | | 11 | | | 9 | | | | | | | | | | | | 15 |
| | 2 | 3 | 4 | 5 | 6 | 7 | 10 | 8 | | 11 | | | 9 | | | | | | | | | | | | 16 |
| | 2 | 3 | 4 | 5 | 6 | 7 | 10 | 8 | | 11 | | | | | 4 | | | | | | | | | | 17 |
| | 2 | 3 | 4 | 5 | | 7 | 8 | | | | | | | | 6 | 9 | 10 | 11 | | | | | | | 18 |
| | 2 | 3 | 4 | 5 | | 7 | 8 | 9 | | 11 | | | | | 6 | 10 | | | | | | | | | 19 |
| | 2 | 3 | 4 | 5 | | 7 | 8 | 9 | | 11 | | | | | 6 | | 10 | | | | | | | | 20 |
| | 2 | 3 | 4 | 5 | | 7 | 8 | | | 11 | | | | | 6 | 10 | 9 | | | | | | | | 21 |
| | 2 | 3 | 4 | 5 | | 7 | 8 | | | 11 | | | | | 6 | 10 | 9 | | | | | | | | 22 |
| | 2 | 3 | 4 | 5 | | 7 | 8 | | | 11 | | | 9 | | 6 | | 10 | | | | | | | | 23 |
| | 2 | 3 | 4 | 5 | | 7 | 8 | 10 | | | | | 9 | | 6 | | | 11 | | | | | | | 24 |
| | 3 | | 4 | 5 | 6 | 7 | | 8 | | | | | | 2 | 10 | | 9 | 11 | | | | | | | 25 |
| | 2 | 3 | 4 | 5 | 6 | 7 | 8 | 10 | | 11 | | | | | | | 9 | | | | | | | | 26 |
| | 2 | 3 | | 5 | 4 | 7 | | 8 | | 11 | | | 9 | | 6 | 10 | | | | | | | | | 27 |
| | 2 | 3 | | 5 | 4 | 7 | | 8 | | 11 | | 9 | | | 6 | 10 | | | | | | | | | 28 |
| | 2 | 3 | 4 | 5 | 6 | 7 | 8 | 9 | | 11 | | | | | | 10 | | | | | | | | | 29 |
| | 2 | 3 | 4 | 5 | 6 | 7 | 8 | | | 11 | | | 9 | | | 10 | | | | | | | | | 30 |
| | 2 | | 4 | 5 | 6 | 7 | 8 | 10 | | 11 | | | | | | | | | 3 | 9 | | | | | 31 |
| | 2 | | 4 | 5 | 6 | 7 | 8 | | | 11 | | | | | | 10 | | | 3 | 9 | | | | | 32 |
| | 2 | | 4 | 5 | | 7 | | 8 | | | | | | | 6 | 10 | | 11 | 3 | 9 | | | | | 33 |
| | 2 | | 4 | | 5 | 7 | | 8 | | | | | | | 6 | 10 | 9 | 11 | | | 3 | | | | 34 |
| | 2 | | | 5 | 4 | 7 | | 8 | | | | | | | 6 | 10 | 9 | 11 | 3 | | | | | | 35 |
| | 2 | | 4 | 5 | | 7 | | 8 | | 11 | | | | | 6 | 10 | 9 | | 3 | | | | | | 36 |
| | 2 | | 4 | 5 | | | | 8 | | 11 | | | | | 6 | 10 | 9 | | 3 | | | 1 | 7 | | 37 |
| | 2 | | 4 | 5 | | | | 8 | 10 | 11 | | | | | 6 | | | | 3 | | | | 7 | 9 | 38 |
| 7 | 36 | 29 | 34 | 32 | 26 | 36 | 26 | 32 | 11 | 32 | 1 | 2 | 15 | 3 | 20 | 14 | 11 | 6 | 7 | 3 | 1 | 1 | 2 | 1 | |
| | | 1 | 3 | 1 | | 4 | 5 | 8 | 1 | 8 | | | 3 | | | 2 | 4 | | | | | | 1 | | |

| Maskrey H | Nicholas J | Morris C | Warren B | Hall B | Wood A | Davis J | Wood J | Long J | Richards G | Davis G | Fletcher T | Cleaver F | Ransford J | Methven J | Bagshaw J | Wheatcroft F | Bentley A | Lamb S | |
|---|---|---|---|---|---|---|---|---|---|---|---|---|---|---|---|---|---|---|---|
| 1 | 3 | | 4 | 5 | | 7 | 8 | | | 11 | | | 9 | 2 | 6 | | 10 | | 1 |
| 1 | 2 | 3 | 4 | 5 | 6 | 7 | | 8 | | 11 | | 9 | | | | | 10 | | R |
| 1 | | 3 | 4 | 5 | 6 | 7 | 8 | 9 | | | | | | 2 | | | 10 | 11 | 2 |
| 1 | 2 | 3 | 4 | 5 | 6 | 7 | 10 | 8 | | 11 | | | 9 | | | | | | 3 |
| 4 | 3 | 3 | 4 | 4 | 3 | 4 | 3 | 3 | | 3 | | 1 | 2 | 2 | 1 | | 3 | 1 | |
| | | 1 | | | 1 | | | 1 | | | | | 1 | | | | 2 | | |

# 1907-08

| | P | W | D | L | F | A | Pts |
|---|---|---|---|---|---|---|---|
| Bradford C | 38 | 24 | 6 | 8 | 90 | 42 | 54 |
| Leicester F | 38 | 21 | 10 | 7 | 72 | 47 | 52 |
| Oldham A | 38 | 22 | 6 | 10 | 76 | 42 | 50 |
| Fulham | 38 | 22 | 5 | 11 | 82 | 49 | 49 |
| W.B.A. | 38 | 19 | 9 | 10 | 61 | 39 | 47 |
| Derby Co | 38 | 21 | 4 | 13 | 77 | 45 | 46 |
| Burnley | 38 | 20 | 6 | 12 | 67 | 50 | 46 |
| Hull C | 38 | 21 | 4 | 13 | 73 | 62 | 46 |
| Wolves | 38 | 15 | 7 | 16 | 50 | 45 | 37 |
| Stoke | 38 | 16 | 5 | 17 | 57 | 52 | 37 |
| Gainsborough T | 38 | 14 | 7 | 17 | 47 | 71 | 35 |
| Leeds C | 38 | 12 | 8 | 18 | 53 | 65 | 32 |
| Stockport Co | 38 | 12 | 8 | 18 | 48 | 67 | 32 |
| Clapton O | 38 | 11 | 10 | 17 | 40 | 65 | 32 |
| Blackpool | 38 | 11 | 9 | 18 | 51 | 58 | 31 |
| Barnsley | 38 | 12 | 6 | 20 | 54 | 68 | 30 |
| Glossop | 38 | 11 | 8 | 19 | 54 | 74 | 30 |
| Grimsby T | 38 | 11 | 8 | 19 | 43 | 71 | 30 |
| Chesterfield | 38 | 6 | 11 | 21 | 46 | 92 | 23 |
| Lincoln C | 38 | 9 | 3 | 26 | 46 | 83 | 21 |

Manager: Jimmy Methven.
Leading scorer: Alf Bentley, League 27, all matches 28.

- Alf Bentley set a new Rams record with 27 League goals, three ahead of the 24 Steve Bloomer achieved in three separate seasons. Bentley twice scored four in a game.
- Ted Garry, signed from Celtic in May 1907, is the only player in Derby's history to score a hat-trick on his debut, against Lincoln City at the Baseball Ground. It was his only hat-trick for the Rams but he moved to wing-half in the second part of his stay.
- Harry Maskrey played for England against Ireland in Belfast in February, the first of three former Ripley Athletic goalkeepers with Derby connections to be capped. He was followed by Horace Bailey, with Leicester Fosse at the time, and Ernald Scattergood.
- Bailey also won an Olympic gold medal with the Great Britain football side at the 1908 London games.

## Division Two

| Match No. | Date | | Venue | Opponents | Result | | Scorers | Attend |
|---|---|---|---|---|---|---|---|---|
| 1 | Sep | 2 | (h) | Lincoln C | W | 4-0 | Garry 3, Wheatcroft | 6, |
| 2 | | 7 | (h) | Fulham | L | 0-1 | | 7, |
| 3 | | 14 | (a) | Barnsley | W | 4-2 | Bentley 4 | 3, |
| 4 | | 28 | (a) | Burnley | D | 2-2 | Bentley, Long | 10, |
| 5 | Oct | 5 | (h) | Oldham A | W | 1-0 | Warren | 10, |
| 6 | | 12 | (a) | Clapton O | L | 0-1 | | 8, |
| 7 | | 19 | (h) | Leeds C | W | 6-1 | Bentley 4 (1 pen), Dilly, Garry | 6, |
| 8 | | 26 | (a) | Wolves | D | 2-2 | Bentley 2 | 6, |
| 9 | Nov | 2 | (h) | Gainsborough T | W | 5-2 | Bentley 2, Bevan 2, Garry | 6, |
| 10 | | 9 | (a) | Stockport C | L | 1-2 | Bevan | 4, |
| 11 | | 16 | (h) | Glossop | W | 2-0 | Bentley (pen), Bevan | 6, |
| 12 | | 23 | (a) | Leicester F | W | 3-1 | Bevan, Long, G.Davis | 18, |
| 13 | | 30 | (h) | Blackpool | W | 2-1 | Long 2 | 9, |
| 14 | Dec | 7 | (a) | Stoke | W | 3-0 | Long 2, Warren | 5, |
| 15 | | 14 | (h) | West Brom A | W | 2-0 | Bentley, Richards | 9,5 |
| 16 | | 21 | (a) | Bradford C | L | 1-3 | Bentley | 20, |
| 17 | | 24 | (h) | Barnsley | W | 3-0 | Bevan 2, Hall | 2, |
| 18 | | 25 | (h) | Grimsby T | W | 4-0 | Bevan, Bentley, G.Davis, Garry | 11, |
| 19 | | 26 | (h) | Chesterfield | D | 0-0 | | 18, |
| 20 | | 28 | (h) | Hull C | W | 4-1 | Bentley 2 (1 pen), Dilly, Bevan | 12, |
| 21 | Jan | 4 | (a) | Fulham | D | 0-0 | | 20, |
| 22 | | 18 | (a) | Chesterfield | W | 2-0 | Riddell, Wheatcroft | 10,0 |
| 23 | | 25 | (h) | Burnley | W | 1-0 | Bevan | 10, |
| 24 | Feb | 8 | (h) | Clapton O | W | 4-0 | Bentley 2, G.Davis, Long | 10, |
| 25 | | 15 | (a) | Leeds C | L | 1-5 | Bevan | 10,0 |
| 26 | | 22 | (h) | Leicester F | L | 1-2 | Bentley | 6, |
| 27 | | 29 | (a) | Gainsborough T | W | 4-1 | Bentley 2, Long, G.Davis | 2,0 |
| 28 | Mar | 7 | (h) | Stockport C | W | 3-0 | Garry 2, Warren | 10, |
| 29 | | 14 | (a) | Glossop | W | 3-2 | Bevan 2, Garry | 3,0 |
| 30 | | 28 | (a) | Blackpool | L | 0-1 | | 4, |
| 31 | | 30 | (a) | Oldham A | L | 1-3 | Bentley | 7,0 |
| 32 | Apr | 4 | (h) | Stoke | W | 3-0 | G.Davis 2, Long | 8, |
| 33 | | 8 | (h) | Wolves | W | 3-2 | Bentley 2, Long | 8,0 |
| 34 | | 11 | (a) | West Brom A | L | 0-1 | | 10, |
| 35 | | 17 | (a) | Lincoln C | L | 0-1 | | 6,0 |
| 36 | | 18 | (h) | Bradford C | L | 2-3 | G.Davis, J.Davis | 15, |
| 37 | | 20 | (a) | Grimsby T | L | 0-1 | | 6,0 |
| 38 | | 25 | (a) | Hull C | L | 0-4 | | 2, |

FINAL LEAGUE POSITION: 6th in Division Two

Appearanc
Go

## FA Cup

| | | | | | | | | |
|---|---|---|---|---|---|---|---|---|
| 1 | Jan | 11 | (a) | Liverpool | L | 2-4 | Bentley (pen), Bevan | 10,0 |

Appearanc
Go

| Maskrey H | Nicholas J | Morris C | Warren B | Hall B | Bagshaw J | Armstrong A | Garry E | Wheatcroft F | Richards G | Davis G | Atkin J | Davis J | Long J | Bentley A | Springthorpe J | Evans W | Dilly T | Bevan F | Moore W | Tremelling S | Scattergood E | Riddell FW | |
|---|---|---|---|---|---|---|---|---|---|---|---|---|---|---|---|---|---|---|---|---|---|---|---|
| 1 | 2 | 3 | 4 | 5 | 6 | 7 | 8 | 9 | 10 | 11 | | | | | | | | | | | | | 1 |
| 1 | 2 | 3 | 4 | 5 | 6 | 7 | 8 | 9 | 10 | 11 | | | | | | | | | | | | | 2 |
| 1 | | 3 | 4 | 5 | | | 8 | | 6 | 11 | 2 | 7 | 9 | 10 | | | | | | | | | 3 |
| 1 | | 3 | 4 | 5 | | | 8 | | 6 | 11 | 2 | 7 | 9 | 10 | | | | | | | | | 4 |
| 1 | 2 | 3 | 4 | 5 | | | 8 | | 6 | 11 | | 7 | 9 | 10 | | | | | | | | | 5 |
| 1 | | 3 | 4 | 5 | | | 8 | | 6 | | 2 | | 9 | 10 | 7 | 11 | | | | | | | 6 |
| 1 | | 3 | 4 | 5 | | | 8 | | 6 | | 2 | | 9 | 10 | 7 | | 11 | | | | | | 7 |
| 1 | 2 | 3 | 4 | 5 | | | 8 | | 6 | | | 7 | 9 | 10 | | | 11 | | | | | | 8 |
| 1 | 2 | 3 | 4 | 5 | | | 8 | | 6 | | | 7 | | 10 | | | 11 | 9 | | | | | 9 |
| 1 | 2 | 3 | 4 | 5 | | | 8 | | 6 | | | 7 | | 10 | | | 11 | 9 | | | | | 10 |
| 1 | 2 | 3 | 4 | 5 | | | 8 | | 6 | 11 | | 7 | | 10 | | | | 9 | | | | | 11 |
| 1 | 2 | 3 | 4 | 5 | | | 8 | | 6 | 11 | | | 9 | 10 | | | | 7 | | | | | 12 |
| 1 | 2 | 3 | 4 | 5 | | | 8 | | 6 | 11 | | | 9 | 10 | | | | 7 | | | | | 13 |
| 1 | 2 | 3 | 4 | 5 | | | 8 | | 6 | 11 | | | 9 | 10 | | | | 7 | | | | | 14 |
| 1 | 2 | 3 | 4 | 5 | | | 8 | | 6 | 11 | | | 9 | 10 | | | | 7 | | | | | 15 |
| 1 | 2 | 3 | 4 | 5 | | | 8 | | 6 | 11 | | | 9 | 10 | | | | 7 | | | | | 16 |
| 1 | 2 | 3 | 4 | 5 | | | 8 | | | | | | 9 | 10 | | | 11 | 7 | 6 | | | | 17 |
| 1 | 2 | 3 | 4 | 5 | | | 8 | | 6 | 11 | | | 7 | 10 | | | | 9 | | | | | 18 |
| 1 | 2 | 3 | 4 | | | | 8 | | 6 | 11 | | | 7 | 10 | | | | 9 | | 5 | | | 19 |
| | 2 | 3 | 4 | | 5 | | | | 6 | | | 7 | | 10 | | | 11 | 9 | | | 1 | 8 | 20 |
| 1 | 2 | 3 | 4 | 5 | | | 8 | | 6 | | | | 7 | 10 | | | 11 | 9 | | | | | 21 |
| 1 | 2 | 3 | 4 | 5 | | | | 10 | 6 | | | 7 | 9 | 11 | | | | | | | | 8 | 22 |
| | | 3 | 4 | 5 | | | | | 6 | | 2 | 7 | | 10 | | | 11 | 9 | | | 1 | 8 | 23 |
| 1 | 2 | 3 | 4 | 5 | | | | | 6 | 11 | | 7 | 8 | 10 | | | | 9 | | | | | 24 |
| | 2 | 3 | | 5 | 4 | | | | 6 | 11 | | 7 | 8 | 10 | | | | 9 | | | 1 | | 25 |
| 1 | 2 | 3 | 4 | 5 | | | 8 | | 6 | 11 | | 7 | | 10 | | | | 9 | | | | | 26 |
| 1 | 2 | 3 | | 5 | 6 | | 8 | | | 11 | 4 | | 9 | 10 | | | | 7 | | | | | 27 |
| 1 | 2 | | 4 | 5 | | | 8 | | 6 | 11 | | | 9 | 10 | | | | 7 | 3 | | | | 28 |
| 1 | 2 | 3 | 4 | 5 | | | 8 | | 6 | | | | 9 | 10 | | | 11 | 7 | | | | | 29 |
| 1 | 2 | 3 | 4 | 5 | | | 8 | | 6 | 11 | | | 9 | 10 | | | | 7 | | | | | 30 |
| 1 | | 3 | 4 | 5 | | | 8 | | 6 | 11 | 2 | | 9 | 10 | | | | 7 | | | | | 31 |
| 1 | | 3 | | 4 | 5 | | 8 | | 6 | 11 | 2 | | 9 | 10 | | | | 7 | | | | | 32 |
| 1 | | 3 | 4 | 5 | | | 8 | | 6 | 11 | 2 | | 9 | 10 | | | | 7 | | | | | 33 |
| 1 | | 3 | 4 | 5 | | | 8 | | 6 | 11 | 2 | | 9 | 10 | | | | 7 | | | | | 34 |
| 1 | | 3 | 4 | 5 | | | | | 6 | | 2 | 11 | 9 | 10 | | | 7 | 8 | | | | | 35 |
| 1 | | 3 | 4 | 5 | 6 | | | 10 | | 11 | 2 | 7 | 8 | | | | | 9 | | | | | 36 |
| 1 | | 3 | 4 | 5 | | | | | 6 | 11 | 2 | 7 | 8 | 10 | | | | 9 | | | | | 37 |
| 1 | | 3 | 4 | 5 | | | 8 | 10 | 6 | | 2 | 7 | | 11 | | | | 9 | | | | | 38 |
| 35 | 25 | 37 | 35 | 36 | 7 | 2 | 30 | 5 | 35 | 25 | 14 | 17 | 29 | 35 | 2 | 1 | 10 | 29 | 2 | 1 | 3 | 3 | |
| | | | 3 | 1 | | | 9 | 2 | 1 | 7 | | 1 | 10 | 27 | | | 2 | 13 | | | | 1 | |

| Maskrey H | Nicholas J | Morris C | Warren B | Hall B | Bagshaw J | Armstrong A | Garry E | Wheatcroft F | Richards G | Davis G | Atkin J | Davis J | Long J | Bentley A | Springthorpe J | Evans W | Dilly T | Bevan F | Moore W | Tremelling S | Scattergood E | Riddell FW | |
|---|---|---|---|---|---|---|---|---|---|---|---|---|---|---|---|---|---|---|---|---|---|---|---|
| 1 | 2 | 3 | 4 | 5 | | | | | 6 | 11 | | 7 | 8 | 10 | | | | 9 | | | | | 1 |
| 1 | 1 | 1 | 1 | 1 | | | | | 1 | 1 | | 1 | 1 | 1 | | | | 1 | | | | | |
| | | | | | | | | | | | | | | 1 | | | | 1 | | | | | |

# 1908-09

| | P | W | D | L | F | A | Pts |
|---|---|---|---|---|---|---|---|
| Bolton W | 38 | 24 | 4 | 10 | 59 | 28 | 52 |
| Tottenham H | 38 | 20 | 11 | 7 | 67 | 32 | 51 |
| W.B.A. | 38 | 19 | 13 | 6 | 56 | 27 | 51 |
| Hull C | 38 | 19 | 6 | 13 | 63 | 39 | 44 |
| Derby Co | 38 | 16 | 11 | 11 | 55 | 41 | 43 |
| Oldham A | 38 | 17 | 6 | 15 | 55 | 43 | 40 |
| Wolves | 38 | 14 | 11 | 13 | 56 | 48 | 39 |
| Glossop | 38 | 15 | 8 | 15 | 57 | 53 | 38 |
| Gainsborough T | 38 | 15 | 8 | 15 | 49 | 70 | 38 |
| Fulham | 38 | 13 | 11 | 14 | 58 | 48 | 37 |
| Birmingham | 38 | 14 | 9 | 15 | 58 | 61 | 37 |
| Leeds C | 38 | 14 | 7 | 17 | 43 | 53 | 35 |
| Grimsby T | 38 | 14 | 7 | 17 | 41 | 54 | 35 |
| Burnley | 38 | 13 | 7 | 18 | 51 | 58 | 33 |
| Clapton O | 38 | 12 | 9 | 17 | 37 | 49 | 33 |
| Bradford P.A. | 38 | 13 | 6 | 19 | 51 | 59 | 32 |
| Barnsley | 38 | 11 | 10 | 17 | 48 | 57 | 32 |
| Stockport Co | 38 | 14 | 3 | 21 | 39 | 71 | 31 |
| Chesterfield | 38 | 11 | 8 | 19 | 37 | 67 | 30 |
| Blackpool | 38 | 9 | 11 | 18 | 46 | 68 | 29 |

Manager: Jimmy Methven.
Leading scorer: Alf Bentley, League 24, all matches 32.

- Alf Bentley lifted the bar again with 32 League and Cup goals, beating Steve Bloomer's 31 in 1896–97. Bentley's record survived for 22 years.
- For the second successive season, Bentley scored four in a home match against Leeds City.
- Horace Barnes, signed from Wadsley Bridge, was so impressive in his first game for the Reserves that he was instantly promoted and scored on his senior debut at Blackpool.

## Division Two

| Match No. | Date | | Venue | Opponents | Result | | Scorers | Atten |
|---|---|---|---|---|---|---|---|---|
| 1 | Sep | 5 | (a) | Oldham A | D | 1-1 | Bentley | 20, |
| 2 | | 7 | (a) | Burnley | L | 0-2 | | 12, |
| 3 | | 12 | (h) | Clapton O | W | 1-0 | Hall | 6, |
| 4 | | 16 | (h) | Wolves | W | 2-1 | Bevan, Bentley | 2, |
| 5 | | 19 | (a) | Leeds C | W | 5-2 | Bentley 4, Hall | 20, |
| 6 | | 26 | (h) | Barnsley | D | 0-0 | | 7, |
| 7 | Oct | 3 | (a) | Tottenham H | D | 0-0 | | 25, |
| 8 | | 10 | (h) | Hull C | D | 0-0 | | 6, |
| 9 | | 17 | (h) | Bolton W | W | 1-0 | Bentley | 7, |
| 10 | | 21 | (a) | Gainsborough T | D | 0-0 | | 6, |
| 11 | | 24 | (a) | Blackpool | D | 2-2 | Barnes, Crewdson (og) | 6, |
| 12 | | 31 | (h) | Chesterfield | D | 1-1 | Bentley | 9, |
| 13 | Nov | 7 | (a) | Glossop | L | 1-3 | Thompson | 2, |
| 14 | | 14 | (h) | Stockport C | W | 5-0 | Bentley 3, Barnes, Hall | 5, |
| 15 | | 21 | (a) | West Brom A | L | 0-2 | | 18, |
| 16 | | 28 | (h) | Birmingham | L | 1-2 | Barnes | 8, |
| 17 | Dec | 12 | (h) | Grimsby T | W | 2-1 | Bentley 2 | 6, |
| 18 | | 19 | (a) | Fulham | W | 2-1 | Thompson 2 | 16, |
| 19 | | 25 | (a) | Wolves | D | 1-1 | Bentley | 15, |
| 20 | | 26 | (h) | Burnley | W | 1-0 | Ogden (og) | 12, |
| 21 | | 28 | (h) | Bradford PA | W | 3-1 | Barnes, Bentley, Thompson | 10, |
| 22 | Jan | 2 | (h) | Oldham A | W | 1-0 | Bentley | 10, |
| 23 | | 9 | (a) | Clapton O | L | 0-2 | | 8, |
| 24 | | 23 | (h) | Leeds C | W | 5-1 | Bentley 2 (1 pen), Barnes 2, Richards | 7, |
| 25 | | 30 | (a) | Barnsley | L | 0-1 | | 3, |
| 26 | Feb | 13 | (a) | Hull C | L | 0-4 | | 7, |
| 27 | | 27 | (h) | Blackpool | D | 1-1 | Edwards | 3, |
| 28 | Mar | 17 | (a) | Chesterfield | W | 4-2 | Bevan 2, Garry, Richards | 5, |
| 29 | | 20 | (a) | Stockport C | L | 0-1 | | 1,5 |
| 30 | Apr | 3 | (a) | Birmingham | D | 1-1 | Bentley (pen) | 4, |
| 31 | | 9 | (a) | Bradford PA | L | 0-2 | | 12, |
| 32 | | 10 | (h) | Gainsborough T | W | 5-0 | Bentley 2 (1 pen), Hall, Bevan, Barnes | 6, |
| 33 | | 17 | (a) | Grimsby T | L | 0-2 | | 4, |
| 34 | | 21 | (h) | Glossop | W | 4-0 | Garry 2, Bentley (pen), Barnes | 2, |
| 35 | | 24 | (h) | Fulham | W | 2-1 | Bentley, Barnes | 5, |
| 36 | | 26 | (h) | West Brom A | W | 2-1 | Garry, Barnes | 6, |
| 37 | | 28 | (h) | Tottenham H | D | 1-1 | Bentley | 6, |
| 38 | | 30 | (a) | Bolton W | L | 0-1 | | 31, |

FINAL LEAGUE POSITION: 5th in Division Two

Appearan
Gc

## FA Cup

| | | | | | | | | |
|---|---|---|---|---|---|---|---|---|
| 1 | Jan | 16 | (a) | Northampton T | D | 1-1 | Bentley | 20, |
| R | | 20 | (h) | Northampton T | W | 4-2 | Bentley 2, Davis, Thompson | 12, |
| 2 | Feb | 6 | (a) | Leicester F | W | 2-0 | Bentley (pen), Trueman | 20, |
| 3 | | 20 | (h) | Plymouth A | W | 1-0 | Bentley | 22,5 |
| 4 | Mar | 6 | (h) | Nottingham F | W | 3-0 | Bentley 3 | 16, |
| SF | | 27 | (n*) | Bristol C | D | 1-1 | Garry | 34, |
| R | | 31 | (n†) | Bristol C | L | 1-2 | Davis | 27,6 |

*Played at Stamford Bridge, Chelsea. †Played at St Andrew's, Birmingham.

Appearan
Go

| Maskrey H | Nicholas J | Morris C | Atkin J | Hall B | Richards G | Trueman R | Garry E | Bevan F | Bentley A | Ainsworth C | Davis J | Bagshaw J | Thompson G | Barbour T | Riddell F | Sylvester T | Barnes H | Scattergood E | Edwards J | Moore W | Kelham H | |
|---|---|---|---|---|---|---|---|---|---|---|---|---|---|---|---|---|---|---|---|---|---|---|
| | 2 | 3 | 4 | 5 | 6 | 7 | 8 | 9 | 10 | 11 | | | | | | | | | | | | 1 |
| | 2 | 3 | 4 | 5 | 6 | 7 | 8 | 9 | 10 | 11 | | | | | | | | | | | | 2 |
| | 2 | 3 | 4 | 5 | 6 | 7 | 8 | 9 | 10 | 11 | | | | | | | | | | | | 3 |
| | 2 | 3 | 4 | 5 | 6 | | 8 | 9 | 10 | 11 | 7 | | | | | | | | | | | 4 |
| | 2 | 3 | 4 | 5 | 6 | | 8 | 9 | 10 | 11 | 7 | | | | | | | | | | | 5 |
| | 2 | 3 | 4 | 5 | | | 8 | 9 | 10 | | 11 | 6 | 7 | | | | | | | | | 6 |
| | 2 | 3 | | 5 | 6 | 7 | 8 | 9 | 10 | | 11 | | | 4 | | | | | | | | 7 |
| | 2 | 3 | | 5 | 6 | | 10 | | 9 | | 11 | | 7 | 4 | 8 | | | | | | | 8 |
| | 2 | 3 | | 5 | 6 | | | 9 | 10 | 11 | 7 | | | 4 | 8 | | | | | | | 9 |
| | 2 | 3 | | 5 | 6 | | 8 | 9 | 10 | 11 | 7 | | | 4 | | | | | | | | 10 |
| | | 3 | | 5 | 6 | | | 8 | 9 | | 11 | | 7 | 4 | | 2 | 10 | | | | | 11 |
| 1 | 2 | 3 | | 5 | 6 | | | 9 | 8 | | 11 | | 7 | 4 | | | 10 | 1 | | | | 12 |
| 1 | 2 | 3 | | 5 | 6 | | | 9 | 8 | | 11 | | 7 | 4 | | | 10 | | | | | 13 |
| 1 | 2 | 3 | | 5 | 6 | | | | 9 | | 11 | 8 | 7 | 4 | | | 10 | | | | | 14 |
| 1 | 2 | 3 | | 5 | 6 | | 8 | | 9 | | 11 | | 7 | 4 | | | 10 | | | | | 15 |
| 1 | 2 | 3 | | 5 | | | 8 | | 9 | | 11 | 6 | 7 | 4 | | | 10 | | | | | 16 |
| 1 | 2 | 3 | | 5 | | | | 8 | 9 | | 11 | 6 | 7 | 4 | | | 10 | | | | | 17 |
| 1 | 2 | 3 | | 5 | 6 | | 8 | | 9 | | 11 | | 7 | 4 | | | 10 | | | | | 18 |
| 1 | 2 | 3 | | 5 | 6 | | 8 | | 9 | | 11 | | 7 | 4 | | | 10 | | | | | 19 |
| 1 | 2 | 3 | | 5 | 10 | | 8 | | 9 | | 11 | 6 | 7 | 4 | | | | | | | | 20 |
| 1 | 2 | 3 | | 5 | 6 | | 8 | | 9 | | 11 | | 7 | 4 | | | 10 | | | | | 21 |
| 1 | 2 | 3 | | 5 | 6 | | 8 | | 9 | | 11 | | 7 | 4 | | | 10 | | | | | 22 |
| 1 | 2 | 3 | | 5 | 6 | | | | 9 | | 11 | | 7 | 4 | 8 | | 10 | | | | | 23 |
| 1 | 2 | 3 | | 5 | 6 | 8 | | | 9 | | 11 | | 7 | 4 | | | 10 | | | | | 24 |
| 1 | 2 | 3 | | 5 | 6 | 8 | | | 9 | 11 | | | 7 | 4 | | | 10 | | | | | 25 |
| 1 | | 3 | | 5 | 6 | | | | 9 | | 11 | | 7 | 4 | | 2 | 10 | | 8 | | | 26 |
| 1 | 2 | 3 | | 5 | 6 | 8 | | 9 | | | 11 | | 7 | 4 | | | | | 10 | | | 27 |
| | | | 3 | | 6 | | 8 | 10 | 9 | | 11 | 5 | 7 | 4 | | | | 1 | | 2 | | 28 |
| 1 | | | 2 | 5 | 6 | | | 8 | 9 | | 11 | 4 | 7 | | | | 10 | | | 3 | | 29 |
| | 2 | | 3 | 5 | | | | 8 | 9 | | 11 | 4 | 7 | | | | 10 | 1 | | | 6 | 30 |
| 1 | 2 | 3 | | 5 | 6 | | 8 | 7 | 9 | | 11 | | | 4 | | | 10 | | | | | 31 |
| 1 | | 3 | 2 | 5 | 6 | | | 7 | 9 | | 11 | 4 | | 8 | | | 10 | | | | | 32 |
| 1 | 2 | 3 | | 5 | 6 | | | 8 | 9 | | 11 | | 7 | 4 | | | 10 | | | | | 33 |
| 1 | | 3 | 2 | 5 | 6 | 7 | 8 | | 9 | | 11 | | | 4 | | | 10 | | | | | 34 |
| 1 | | 3 | 2 | 5 | | 7 | 8 | | 9 | | 11 | 6 | | 4 | | | 10 | | | | | 35 |
| 1 | 2 | 3 | | 5 | | 7 | 8 | | 9 | | 11 | 6 | | 4 | | | 10 | | | | | 36 |
| 1 | | 3 | 2 | 5 | | 7 | 8 | | 9 | | 11 | 6 | | 4 | | | 10 | | | | | 37 |
| | | 3 | 2 | 5 | | 7 | 9 | 8 | | | 11 | 6 | | 4 | | | 10 | 1 | | | | 38 |
| 4 | 29 | 35 | 14 | 37 | 30 | 12 | 23 | 21 | 36 | 8 | 34 | 13 | 23 | 30 | 3 | 2 | 25 | 4 | 2 | 2 | 1 | |
| | | | | 4 | 2 | | 4 | 4 | 24 | | | | 4 | | | | 10 | | 1 | | | |

2 own-goals

| | | | | | | | | | | | | | | | | | | | | | | |
|---|---|---|---|---|---|---|---|---|---|---|---|---|---|---|---|---|---|---|---|---|---|---|
| 1 | 2 | 3 | | 5 | 6 | | 8 | | 9 | | 11 | | 7 | 4 | | | 10 | | | | | 1 |
| 1 | 2 | 3 | | 5 | 6 | 8 | | | 9 | | 11 | | 7 | 4 | | | 10 | | | | | R |
| 1 | 2 | 3 | | 5 | 6 | 8 | | | 9 | | 11 | | 7 | 4 | | | 10 | | | | | 2 |
| 1 | 2 | 3 | | 5 | 6 | 8 | | | 9 | | 11 | | 7 | 4 | | | 10 | | | | | 3 |
| | 2 | 3 | | | 6 | | 8 | | 9 | | 11 | 5 | 7 | 4 | | | 10 | 1 | | | | 4 |
| 1 | 2 | 3 | | 5 | 6 | | 8 | | 9 | | 11 | | 7 | 4 | | | 10 | | | | | SF |
| 1 | 2 | 3 | | 5 | 6 | | 8 | | 9 | | 11 | | 7 | 4 | | | 10 | | | | | R |
| 6 | 7 | 7 | | 6 | 7 | 3 | 4 | | 7 | | 7 | 1 | 7 | 7 | | | 7 | 1 | | | | |
| | | | | | | 1 | 1 | | 8 | | 2 | | 1 | | | | | | | | | |

# 1909-10

| | P | W | D | L | F | A | Pts |
|---|---|---|---|---|---|---|---|
| Manchester C | 38 | 23 | 8 | 7 | 81 | 40 | 54 |
| Oldham A | 38 | 23 | 7 | 8 | 79 | 39 | 53 |
| Hull C | 38 | 23 | 7 | 8 | 80 | 46 | 53 |
| Derby Co | 38 | 22 | 9 | 7 | 72 | 47 | 53 |
| Leicester F | 38 | 20 | 4 | 14 | 79 | 58 | 44 |
| Glossop | 38 | 18 | 7 | 13 | 64 | 57 | 43 |
| Fulham | 38 | 14 | 13 | 11 | 51 | 43 | 41 |
| Wolves | 38 | 17 | 6 | 15 | 64 | 63 | 40 |
| Barnsley | 38 | 16 | 7 | 15 | 62 | 59 | 39 |
| Bradford P.A. | 38 | 17 | 4 | 17 | 64 | 59 | 38 |
| W.B.A. | 38 | 16 | 5 | 17 | 58 | 56 | 37 |
| Blackpool | 38 | 14 | 8 | 16 | 50 | 52 | 36 |
| Stockport Co | 38 | 13 | 8 | 17 | 50 | 47 | 34 |
| Burnley | 38 | 14 | 6 | 18 | 62 | 61 | 34 |
| Lincoln C | 38 | 10 | 11 | 17 | 42 | 69 | 31 |
| Clapton O | 38 | 12 | 6 | 20 | 37 | 60 | 30 |
| Leeds C | 38 | 10 | 7 | 21 | 46 | 80 | 27 |
| Gainsborough T | 38 | 10 | 6 | 22 | 33 | 75 | 26 |
| Grimsby T | 38 | 9 | 6 | 23 | 50 | 77 | 24 |
| Birmingham | 38 | 8 | 7 | 23 | 42 | 78 | 23 |

Manager: Jimmy Methven.
Leading scorer: Alf Bentley, League 30, all matches 31.
League ever-present: Jimmy Bauchop, Alf Bentley.

- Alf Bentley became the first Derby player to score 30 League goals in a season. In his Rams career, Bentley scored 112 goals in 168 appearances, an average of one every 1.5 games.
- Bentley, Jimmy Bauchop and Horace Barnes – Derby's Busy Bs as they were called at the time – shared 59 of the 72 League goals.
- One more point would have earned Derby promotion. In the key game on 26 April, they lost 4–0 to Oldham Athletic, who were second on goal average.

## Division Two

| Match No. | Date | | Venue | Opponents | Result | | Scorers | Attend |
|---|---|---|---|---|---|---|---|---|
| 1 | Sep | 1 | (h) | Gainsbrough T | D | 2-2 | Bentley, Bauchop | 5, |
| 2 | | 4 | (h) | Burnley | W | 5-2 | Bauchop 3, Barnes, Richards | 5, |
| 3 | | 11 | (a) | Leeds C | L | 1-2 | Barnes | 12, |
| 4 | | 18 | (h) | Wolves | W | 5-0 | Bauchop 2, Bentley 2, Garry | 6, |
| 5 | | 25 | (a) | Gainsborough T | W | 4-2 | Bentley 3, Garry | 2, |
| 6 | Oct | 2 | (h) | Grimsby T | W | 6-0 | Bentley 3 (1 pen), Bauchop 2, Garry | 8, |
| 7 | | 9 | (a) | Manchester C | L | 1-2 | Barnes | 20, |
| 8 | | 16 | (h) | Leicester F | L | 0-1 | | 12, |
| 9 | | 23 | (a) | Lincoln C | W | 3-2 | Barnes 2, Bentley | 6, |
| 10 | | 30 | (h) | Clapton O | W | 1-0 | Bauchop | 6, |
| 11 | Nov | 6 | (a) | Blackpool | D | 1-1 | Bentley | 5, |
| 12 | | 13 | (h) | Hull C | W | 4-0 | Bauchop 2, Bentley, Thompson | 8, |
| 13 | | 20 | (a) | Bradford PA | W | 2-1 | Bentley (pen), Bauchop | 14, |
| 14 | | 27 | (a) | Stockport C | D | 1-1 | Bentley | 4, |
| 15 | Dec | 4 | (h) | Glossop | W | 2-1 | Bentley 2 | 8, |
| 16 | | 11 | (a) | Birmingham | W | 3-1 | Barnes 2, Bentley | 5, |
| 17 | | 18 | (h) | West Brom A | W | 2-1 | Bauchop, Davis | 9, |
| 18 | | 25 | (h) | Barnsley | W | 2-1 | Hall, Bentley | 15, |
| 19 | | 28 | (a) | Barnsley | L | 1-5 | Bentley | 10, |
| 20 | Jan | 1 | (h) | Fulham | W | 3-1 | Barnes, Bauchop, Bentley | 7, |
| 21 | | 8 | (a) | Burnley | W | 2-1 | Bentley, Bauchop | 8, |
| 22 | | 22 | (h) | Leeds C | W | 1-0 | Bauchop | 7, |
| 23 | | 29 | (a) | Wolves | W | 3-2 | Bentley 2, Bauchop | 8, |
| 24 | Feb | 12 | (a) | Grimsby T | D | 1-1 | Bagshaw | 3, |
| 25 | | 26 | (a) | Leicester F | L | 0-6 | | 18, |
| 26 | Mar | 5 | (h) | Lincoln C | W | 2-0 | Bagshaw, Bauchop | 8, |
| 27 | | 12 | (a) | Clapton O | W | 2-0 | Bentley 2 | 5,0 |
| 28 | | 16 | (h) | Manchester C | W | 3-1 | Bentley 3 | 7, |
| 29 | | 19 | (h) | Blackpool | W | 2-1 | Bagshaw, Halligan | 11, |
| 30 | | 25 | (a) | Fulham | D | 0-0 | | 9, |
| 31 | | 26 | (a) | Hull C | D | 0-0 | | 8,0 |
| 32 | | 28 | (h) | Oldham A | D | 1-1 | Bauchop | 10, |
| 33 | Apr | 2 | (h) | Bradford PA | L | 1-2 | Bauchop | 7,0 |
| 34 | | 9 | (h) | Stockport C | W | 1-0 | Halligan | 7, |
| 35 | | 23 | (h) | Birmingham | W | 3-1 | Bauchop, Bentley, Halligan | 5,0 |
| 36 | | 26 | (a) | Oldham A | L | 0-4 | | 4, |
| 37 | | 28 | (a) | Glossop | D | 1-1 | Bentley | 2,0 |
| 38 | | 30 | (a) | West Brom A | D | 0-0 | | 6, |

FINAL LEAGUE POSITION: 4th in Division Two

Appearan
Go

## FA Cup

| | | | | | | | | |
|---|---|---|---|---|---|---|---|---|
| 1 | Jan | 15 | (h) | Millwall | W | 5-0 | Hall 2, Bentley, Davis, Barnes | 9,5 |
| 2 | Feb | 5 | (a) | Aston Villa | L | 1-6 | Bauchop | 30, |

Appearan
Go

| askrey H | Nicholas J | Morris C | Barbour T | Hall B | Richards G | Trueman R | Bentley A | Bauchop J | Barnes H | Davis J | Scattergood E | Atkin J | Bevan F | Garry E | Thompson G | Bagshaw J | Robinson W | Smith F | Robinson A | Tinkler A | Halligan W | Grimes W | Donald D | Bailey H | |
|---|---|---|---|---|---|---|---|---|---|---|---|---|---|---|---|---|---|---|---|---|---|---|---|---|---|
| | 2 | 3 | 4 | 5 | 6 | 7 | 8 | 9 | 10 | 11 | | | | | | | | | | | | | | | 1 |
| | 2 | 3 | 4 | 5 | 6 | 7 | 8 | 9 | 10 | 11 | | | | | | | | | | | | | | | 2 |
| | 2 | 3 | 4 | 5 | 6 | 7 | 8 | 9 | 10 | 11 | | | | | | | | | | | | | | | 3 |
| | 2 | | 4 | 5 | 6 | | 9 | 10 | 11 | | 1 | 3 | 7 | 8 | | | | | | | | | | | 4 |
| | 2 | | 4 | 5 | 6 | | 9 | 10 | 11 | | 1 | 3 | | 8 | 7 | | | | | | | | | | 5 |
| | 2 | | 4 | 5 | 6 | | 9 | 10 | 11 | | | 3 | | 8 | 7 | | | | | | | | | | 6 |
| | 2 | | 4 | 5 | 6 | | 9 | 10 | 11 | | 1 | 3 | | 8 | 7 | | | | | | | | | | 7 |
| | 2 | | 4 | 5 | 6 | | 9 | 10 | 11 | | 1 | 3 | | 8 | 7 | | | | | | | | | | 8 |
| | 2 | | 4 | | 6 | | 9 | 10 | 8 | 11 | 1 | 3 | | | 7 | 5 | | | | | | | | | 9 |
| | 5 | 3 | | | 6 | | 9 | 10 | 8 | 11 | 1 | 2 | | | 7 | 4 | | | | | | | | | 10 |
| | | 3 | | 5 | 6 | | 9 | 10 | | 11 | 1 | 2 | | | 7 | 4 | 8 | | | | | | | | 11 |
| | | | | 5 | 6 | | 9 | 10 | 8 | 11 | 1 | 2 | | | 7 | 4 | | 3 | | | | | | | 12 |
| | 3 | | | 5 | 6 | | 9 | 10 | 8 | 11 | 1 | 2 | | | 7 | 4 | | | | | | | | | 13 |
| | 2 | | | 5 | 6 | | 9 | 10 | 8 | 11 | 1 | 3 | | | 7 | 4 | | | | | | | | | 14 |
| | 2 | | | 5 | 6 | | 9 | 10 | 8 | 11 | 1 | 3 | | | 7 | 4 | | | | | | | | | 15 |
| | 2 | | | 5 | 6 | | 9 | 10 | 8 | | 1 | 3 | | | 7 | 4 | | | 11 | | | | | | 16 |
| | 2 | | | 5 | 6 | | 9 | 10 | 8 | 11 | 1 | 3 | | | 7 | 4 | | | | | | | | | 17 |
| | 2 | | | 5 | 6 | | 9 | 10 | 8 | 11 | 1 | 3 | | | 7 | 4 | | | | | | | | | 18 |
| | | 3 | 4 | 5 | | 8 | 9 | 10 | | 11 | 1 | 2 | | | 7 | 6 | | | | | | | | | 19 |
| | 2 | | 4 | 5 | | | 9 | 10 | 8 | 11 | 1 | 3 | | | 7 | 6 | | | | | | | | | 20 |
| | 2 | | 4 | 5 | | | 9 | 10 | 8 | 11 | 1 | 3 | | | 7 | 6 | | | | | | | | | 21 |
| | 2 | | 7 | 5 | 6 | | 9 | 10 | 8 | 11 | 1 | 3 | | | | 4 | | | | | | | | | 22 |
| | 2 | | | 5 | 6 | | 9 | 10 | | 11 | 1 | 3 | | 8 | | 4 | 7 | | | | | | | | 23 |
| | | 3 | | 5 | 6 | | 9 | 10 | | 11 | 1 | 2 | | | 7 | 4 | | | | 8 | | | | | 24 |
| | | 3 | | 5 | 6 | | 9 | 10 | | 11 | 1 | 2 | | | | 4 | 7 | | | | 8 | | | | 25 |
| | 2 | | | 5 | 6 | | 9 | 10 | | 11 | 1 | 3 | | | | 4 | | | | 7 | 8 | | | | 26 |
| | 2 | | 4 | 5 | 6 | | 9 | 10 | | | 1 | 3 | | | | | | | | | 8 | 7 | 11 | | 27 |
| | 2 | | | 5 | 6 | | 9 | 10 | | | 1 | 3 | | | | 4 | | | | | 8 | 7 | 11 | | 28 |
| | 2 | | | 5 | 6 | | 9 | 10 | | | 1 | 3 | | | | 4 | | | | | 8 | 7 | 11 | | 29 |
| | | | 4 | 5 | | | 9 | 10 | | | 1 | 2 | | | | 6 | | 3 | | | 8 | 7 | 11 | | 30 |
| | | | 4 | 5 | | | 9 | 10 | | | 1 | 2 | | | | 6 | | 3 | | | 8 | 7 | 11 | | 31 |
| | | | 4 | 5 | | | 9 | 10 | | | 1 | 2 | | | | 6 | | 3 | | | 8 | 7 | 11 | | 32 |
| | | | | 5 | 6 | | 9 | 10 | | | 1 | 2 | | | | 4 | | 3 | | | 8 | 7 | 11 | | 33 |
| | | | 3 | 5 | 6 | | 9 | 10 | | | 1 | 2 | | | | 4 | | | | | 8 | 7 | 11 | | 34 |
| | | | 2 | 5 | 6 | | 9 | 10 | | | 1 | 3 | | | | 4 | | | | | 8 | 7 | 11 | | 35 |
| | | | 2 | 5 | 6 | | 9 | 10 | | | | 3 | | | | 4 | | | | | 8 | 7 | 11 | 1 | 36 |
| | | | 2 | 5 | 6 | | 9 | 10 | | | | 3 | | 4 | 7 | | | | | | 8 | | 11 | 1 | 37 |
| | | | 2 | 5 | 6 | | 9 | 10 | | 11 | | 3 | | | 7 | 4 | | | | | 8 | | | 1 | 38 |
| 4 | 24 | 8 | 22 | 36 | 32 | 4 | 38 | 38 | 20 | 21 | 31 | 35 | 1 | 7 | 20 | 28 | 3 | 5 | 1 | 2 | 14 | 10 | 11 | 3 | |
| | | | | 1 | 1 | | 30 | 21 | 8 | 1 | | | | 3 | 1 | 3 | | | | | 3 | | | | |

| askrey H | Nicholas J | Morris C | Barbour T | Hall B | Richards G | Trueman R | Bentley A | Bauchop J | Barnes H | Davis J | Scattergood E | Atkin J | Bevan F | Garry E | Thompson G | Bagshaw J | |
|---|---|---|---|---|---|---|---|---|---|---|---|---|---|---|---|---|---|
| | 2 | 3 | | 5 | 6 | | 9 | 10 | 8 | 11 | 1 | | | | 7 | 4 | 1 |
| | 2 | | 6 | 5 | | | 9 | 10 | | 11 | 1 | 3 | | 8 | 7 | 4 | 2 |
| | 2 | 1 | 1 | 2 | 1 | | 2 | 2 | 1 | 2 | 2 | 1 | | 1 | 2 | 2 | |
| | | | | 2 | | | 1 | 1 | 1 | 1 | | | | | | | |

# 1910-11

| | P | W | D | L | F | A | Pts |
|---|---|---|---|---|---|---|---|
| W.B.A. | 38 | 22 | 9 | 7 | 67 | 41 | 53 |
| Bolton W | 38 | 21 | 9 | 8 | 69 | 40 | 51 |
| Chelsea | 38 | 20 | 9 | 9 | 71 | 35 | 49 |
| Clapton O | 38 | 19 | 7 | 12 | 44 | 35 | 45 |
| Hull C | 38 | 14 | 16 | 8 | 55 | 39 | 44 |
| Derby Co | 38 | 17 | 8 | 13 | 73 | 52 | 42 |
| Blackpool | 38 | 16 | 10 | 12 | 49 | 38 | 42 |
| Burnley | 38 | 13 | 15 | 10 | 45 | 45 | 41 |
| Wolves | 38 | 15 | 8 | 15 | 51 | 52 | 38 |
| Fulham | 38 | 15 | 7 | 16 | 52 | 48 | 37 |
| Leeds C | 38 | 15 | 7 | 16 | 58 | 56 | 37 |
| Bradford P.A. | 38 | 14 | 9 | 15 | 53 | 55 | 37 |
| Huddersfield T | 38 | 13 | 8 | 17 | 57 | 58 | 34 |
| Glossop | 38 | 13 | 8 | 17 | 48 | 62 | 34 |
| Leicester F | 38 | 14 | 5 | 19 | 52 | 62 | 33 |
| Birmingham | 38 | 12 | 8 | 18 | 42 | 64 | 32 |
| Stockport Co | 38 | 11 | 8 | 19 | 47 | 79 | 30 |
| Gainsborough T | 38 | 9 | 11 | 18 | 37 | 55 | 29 |
| Barnsley | 38 | 7 | 14 | 17 | 52 | 62 | 28 |
| Lincoln C | 38 | 7 | 10 | 21 | 28 | 72 | 24 |

Manager: Jimmy Methven.
Leading scorer: Steve Bloomer, League 20, all matches 24.

- After scoring 62 goals in 130 League and Cup games for Middlesbrough, Steve Bloomer was as delighted to be back at Derby as supporters were to see him at the age of 35.
- The attendance was double that for the previous home game when Bloomer returned against Lincoln City and scored twice, one a penalty, in a 5–0 victory.
- Bloomer resumed his usual place as leading scorer, having taken over penalty duties from Alf Bentley. Even so, Derby fell well short of their promotion target.

## Division Two

| Match No. | Date | | Venue | Opponents | Result | | Scorers | Atten |
|---|---|---|---|---|---|---|---|---|
| 1 | Sep | 3 | (h) | Chelsea | L | 1-4 | Bentley (pen) | 12, |
| 2 | | 5 | (a) | Wolves | W | 2-1 | Bentley, Wright | 8, |
| 3 | | 10 | (a) | Clapton O | L | 0-1 | | 10, |
| 4 | | 17 | (h) | Blackpool | D | 1-1 | Bentley | 6, |
| 5 | | 24 | (a) | Glossop | D | 2-2 | Halligan 2 | 4, |
| 6 | Oct | 1 | (h) | Lincoln C | W | 5-0 | Bloomer 2 (1 pen), Bauchop 2, Barnes | 12, |
| 7 | | 8 | (h) | Huddersfield T | D | 1-1 | Bauchop | 12, |
| 8 | | 15 | (h) | Birmingham | W | 1-0 | Barnes | 10, |
| 9 | | 22 | (a) | West Brom A | D | 1-1 | Barnes | 18, |
| 10 | | 29 | (h) | Hull C | L | 2-3 | Garry, Halligan | 9, |
| 11 | Nov | 5 | (a) | Fulham | L | 1-3 | Bloomer | 12, |
| 12 | | 12 | (h) | Bradford PA | W | 4-2 | Bloomer 2, Bauchop, Bentley | 6, |
| 13 | | 19 | (a) | Burnley | L | 1-2 | Barnes | 8, |
| 14 | | 26 | (h) | Gainsborough T | W | 4-0 | Barnes 2, Bentley, Bloomer | 4, |
| 15 | Dec | 3 | (a) | Leeds C | L | 2-3 | Barnes, Bentley | 10, |
| 16 | | 10 | (h) | Stockport C | W | 4-1 | Bloomer 2 (1 pen), Bauchop 2 | 3, |
| 17 | | 17 | (h) | Bolton W | D | 2-2 | Bentley 2 | 5, |
| 18 | | 24 | (a) | Barnsley | W | 2-0 | Bentley, Bauchop | 5, |
| 19 | | 26 | (h) | Leicester F | W | 3-0 | Bloomer 2, Hall | 20, |
| 20 | | 27 | (h) | Wolves | W | 2-0 | Bauchop, Halligan | 18, |
| 21 | | 31 | (a) | Chelsea | L | 2-3 | Barnes 2 | 20, |
| 22 | Jan | 7 | (h) | Clapton O | W | 3-1 | Bloomer, Bauchop, Garry | 8, |
| 23 | | 21 | (a) | Blackpool | W | 1-0 | Bauchop | 5, |
| 24 | | 28 | (h) | Glossop | W | 2-1 | Bloomer, Bauchop | 7, |
| 25 | Feb | 8 | (a) | Lincoln C | W | 2-0 | Bentley, Halligan | 1,5 |
| 26 | | 11 | (a) | Huddersfield T | W | 3-0 | Bentley 2, Bloomer | 8, |
| 27 | | 18 | (a) | Birmingham | L | 0-2 | | 15, |
| 28 | Mar | 1 | (h) | West Brom A | L | 1-3 | Bentley | 7, |
| 29 | | 4 | (a) | Hull C | L | 0-2 | | 5, |
| 30 | | 15 | (h) | Fulham | D | 2-2 | Bauchop 2 | 2, |
| 31 | | 18 | (a) | Bradford PA | L | 1-2 | Bloomer | 7, |
| 32 | | 25 | (h) | Burnley | W | 3-0 | Bloomer 2 (1 pen), Bauchop | 3,5 |
| 33 | Apr | 1 | (a) | Gainsborough T | D | 0-0 | | 4, |
| 34 | | 8 | (h) | Leeds C | D | 2-2 | Barnes, Donald | 5, |
| 35 | | 15 | (a) | Stockport C | L | 2-3 | Bloomer, Bauchop | 5, |
| 36 | | 17 | (a) | Leicester F | W | 2-1 | Bloomer 2 | 12, |
| 37 | | 22 | (a) | Bolton W | L | 1-2 | Bauchop | 5, |
| 38 | | 29 | (h) | Barnsley | W | 5-1 | Bauchop 3, Bloomer, Bentley | 4, |

FINAL LEAGUE POSITION: 6th in Division Two

Appearan
Go

## FA Cup

| | | | | | | | | |
|---|---|---|---|---|---|---|---|---|
| 1 | Jan | 14 | (h) | Plymouth A | W | 2-1 | Bloomer, Barnes | 16, |
| 2 | Feb | 4 | (h) | West Brom A | W | 2-0 | Bauchop, Bloomer | 18, |
| 3 | | 25 | (h) | Everton | W | 5-0 | Bloomer 2 (1 pen), Bentley, Barnes, Bauchop | 22, |
| 4 | Mar | 13 | (a) | Newcastle U | L | 0-4 | | 59, |

Appearan
Go

| Scattergood E | Barbour T | Atkin J | Bagshaw J | Hall B | Richards G | Wright H | Barnes H | Bentley A | Bauchop J | Donald D | Garry E | Lyle R | Lawrence G | Halligan W | Grimes W | Bloomer S | Flanders F | Nicholas J | Thompson G | Frith R | Wheeler W | |
|---|---|---|---|---|---|---|---|---|---|---|---|---|---|---|---|---|---|---|---|---|---|---|
| | 2 | 3 | 4 | 5 | 6 | 7 | 8 | 9 | 10 | 11 | | | | | | | | | | | | 1 |
| | 2 | 3 | 6 | | | 7 | 8 | 9 | 10 | 11 | 4 | 5 | | | | | | | | | | 2 |
| | 2 | 3 | 6 | | | 7 | 8 | 9 | 10 | 11 | 4 | 5 | | | | | | | | | | 3 |
| | 2 | 3 | 6 | | | | 8 | 9 | 10 | 11 | 4 | 5 | 1 | 7 | | | | | | | | 4 |
| | 2 | 3 | 6 | 5 | | 7 | 10 | 9 | | 11 | 4 | | 1 | 8 | | | | | | | | 5 |
| | 2 | 3 | 6 | 5 | | | 10 | | 9 | 11 | 4 | | | | 7 | 8 | | | | | | 6 |
| | 2 | 3 | 6 | 5 | | | 10 | | 9 | 11 | 4 | | | | 7 | 8 | | | | | | 7 |
| | 2 | | 6 | 5 | | | 10 | | 9 | 11 | 4 | | | | 7 | 8 | 3 | | | | | 8 |
| | 2 | 3 | 6 | 5 | | | 10 | | | 11 | 4 | | | 9 | 7 | 8 | | | | | | 9 |
| | 6 | 3 | | 5 | | | 10 | 9 | | 11 | 4 | | | 8 | 7 | | | 2 | | | | 10 |
| | 2 | 3 | | 5 | | | 10 | 9 | 6 | 11 | 4 | | | | 7 | 8 | | | | | | 11 |
| | 2 | 3 | 5 | | | 7 | 10 | 9 | 6 | 11 | 4 | | | | | 8 | | | | | | 12 |
| | 2 | 3 | 5 | | | 7 | 10 | 9 | 6 | 11 | 4 | | | | | 8 | | | | | | 13 |
| | 2 | 3 | 6 | 5 | | 7 | 10 | 9 | | 11 | 4 | | | | | 8 | | | | | | 14 |
| | 2 | 3 | 6 | | | 7 | 10 | 9 | 11 | | 4 | 5 | | | | 8 | | | | | | 15 |
| | 2 | 3 | 6 | | | | | 9 | 10 | 11 | 4 | 5 | | | 7 | 8 | | | | | | 16 |
| | 2 | 3 | 6 | | | | | 9 | 10 | 11 | 4 | 5 | | | 7 | 8 | | | | | | 17 |
| | 2 | 3 | 6 | | | 7 | | 9 | 10 | 11 | 4 | 5 | | | | 8 | | | | | | 18 |
| | 2 | 3 | 6 | 5 | | 7 | | 9 | 10 | 11 | 4 | | | | | 8 | | | | | | 19 |
| | 2 | 3 | 6 | 5 | | | | | 10 | 11 | 4 | | | 9 | 7 | 8 | | | | | | 20 |
| | 2 | 3 | 6 | 5 | | 7 | 10 | | 9 | 11 | 4 | | | | | 8 | | | | | | 21 |
| | 2 | 3 | 6 | 5 | | 7 | 11 | 9 | 10 | | 4 | | | | | 8 | | | | | | 22 |
| | 5 | 2 | 6 | | | | | 9 | 10 | 11 | 4 | | | | 7 | 8 | 3 | | | | | 23 |
| | 5 | 2 | 6 | | | | 10 | | 9 | 11 | 4 | | | | 7 | 8 | 3 | | | | | 24 |
| | 5 | 2 | 6 | | | | | 9 | 10 | 11 | 4 | | | 8 | 7 | | 3 | | | | | 25 |
| | 6 | 2 | | 5 | | | 11 | 9 | 10 | | 4 | | | | 7 | 8 | 3 | | | | | 26 |
| | 5 | 2 | 6 | | | | 11 | 9 | 10 | | 4 | | | | 7 | 8 | 3 | | | | | 27 |
| | 5 | 2 | 6 | | | | 8 | 9 | 10 | 11 | 4 | | | | 7 | | | 3 | | | | 28 |
| | 3 | 2 | 4 | 5 | 6 | | | 9 | 10 | 11 | | | | 8 | 7 | | | | | | | 29 |
| | | 2 | 5 | | 6 | | 11 | 9 | 10 | | 4 | | | | 7 | 8 | 3 | | | | | 30 |
| | 4 | 2 | 6 | 5 | | | | 9 | 10 | 11 | | | | | 7 | 8 | 3 | | | | | 31 |
| | 5 | 2 | 6 | | | | 11 | 9 | 10 | | 4 | | | | | 8 | 3 | | 7 | | | 32 |
| | 5 | 2 | 6 | | | | 11 | 9 | 10 | | 4 | | | | | 8 | 3 | | 7 | | | 33 |
| | 5 | 2 | 6 | | | | 10 | 9 | | 11 | 4 | | | | | 8 | 3 | | 7 | | | 34 |
| | 2 | | 6 | 5 | | | 10 | 11 | 9 | | 4 | | | | 7 | 8 | 3 | | | | | 35 |
| | 2 | | 6 | 5 | | | 11 | 9 | 10 | | 4 | | | | 7 | 8 | 3 | | | | | 36 |
| | 3 | 2 | 6 | 5 | | | 11 | 9 | 10 | | 4 | | | 8 | 7 | | | | | | | 37 |
| | 3 | 2 | 6 | | | | | 9 | 10 | | 4 | | | | 7 | 8 | | | | 5 | 11 | 38 |
| 6 | 37 | 35 | 35 | 19 | 3 | 12 | 28 | 31 | 33 | 27 | 35 | 7 | 2 | 8 | 22 | 28 | 13 | 2 | 3 | 1 | 1 | |
| | | | | 1 | | 1 | 10 | 14 | 19 | 1 | 2 | | | 5 | | 20 | | | | | | |

| | | | | | | | | | | | | | | | | | | |
|---|---|---|---|---|---|---|---|---|---|---|---|---|---|---|---|---|---|---|
| | 2 | 3 | 6 | 5 | | 7 | 11 | 9 | 10 | | 4 | | | | | 8 | | 1 |
| | 5 | 2 | 6 | | | | 11 | 9 | 10 | | 4 | | | | 7 | 8 | 3 | 2 |
| | 5 | 2 | 6 | | | | 11 | 9 | 10 | | 4 | | | | 7 | 8 | 3 | 3 |
| 1 | 5 | 2 | 6 | | | | 11 | 9 | 10 | | 4 | | | | 7 | 8 | 3 | 4 |
| 4 | 4 | 4 | 4 | 1 | | 1 | 4 | 4 | 4 | | 4 | | | | 3 | 4 | 3 | |
| | | | | | | | 2 | 1 | 2 | | | | | | | 4 | | |

# 1911-12

| | P | W | D | L | F | A | Pts |
|---|---|---|---|---|---|---|---|
| Derby Co | 38 | 23 | 8 | 7 | 74 | 28 | 54 |
| Chelsea | 38 | 24 | 6 | 8 | 64 | 34 | 54 |
| Burnley | 38 | 22 | 8 | 8 | 77 | 41 | 52 |
| Clapton O | 38 | 21 | 3 | 14 | 61 | 44 | 45 |
| Wolves | 38 | 16 | 10 | 12 | 57 | 33 | 42 |
| Barnsley | 38 | 15 | 12 | 11 | 45 | 42 | 42 |
| Hull C | 38 | 17 | 8 | 13 | 54 | 51 | 42 |
| Fulham | 38 | 16 | 7 | 15 | 66 | 58 | 39 |
| Grimsby T | 38 | 15 | 9 | 14 | 48 | 55 | 39 |
| Leicester F | 38 | 15 | 7 | 16 | 49 | 66 | 37 |
| Bradford P.A. | 38 | 13 | 9 | 16 | 44 | 45 | 35 |
| Birmingham | 38 | 14 | 6 | 18 | 55 | 59 | 34 |
| Bristol C | 38 | 14 | 6 | 18 | 41 | 60 | 34 |
| Blackpool | 38 | 13 | 8 | 17 | 32 | 52 | 34 |
| Nottingham F | 38 | 13 | 7 | 18 | 46 | 48 | 33 |
| Stockport Co | 38 | 11 | 11 | 16 | 47 | 54 | 33 |
| Huddersfield T | 38 | 13 | 6 | 19 | 50 | 64 | 32 |
| Glossop | 38 | 8 | 12 | 18 | 42 | 56 | 28 |
| Leeds C | 38 | 10 | 8 | 20 | 50 | 78 | 28 |
| Gainsborough T | 38 | 5 | 13 | 20 | 30 | 64 | 23 |

Manager: Jimmy Methven.
Leading scorer: Steve Bloomer, League 18, all matches 19.
League ever-present: Ernald Scattergood.

- Steve Bloomer's 300th goal for Derby was the second of two penalties against Huddersfield Town on 23 September.
- He was given powerful support by Jimmy Bauchop and Harry Leonard. These three scored 51 of Derby's 74 goals as they won the Second Division title ahead of Chelsea on goal average.
- Derby clinched first place on the final day by winning at Barnsley while Chelsea were beating Blackpool.
- Journalist and outside-left Ivan Sharpe, later editor of the *Athletic News*, won an Olympic gold medal with the Great Britain football team at the 1912 Stockholm games.

## Division Two

| Match No. | Date | | Venue | Opponents | Result | | Scorers | Atten |
|---|---|---|---|---|---|---|---|---|
| 1 | Sep | 2 | (a) | Clapton O | L | 0-3 | | 16 |
| 2 | | 9 | (h) | Bristol C | W | 3-0 | Barnes 2, Donald | 8 |
| 3 | | 11 | (a) | Chelsea | L | 0-1 | | 20 |
| 4 | | 16 | (a) | Birmingham | W | 4-0 | Barnes 2, Bauchop, Bloomer (pen) | 8 |
| 5 | | 23 | (h) | Huddersfield T | W | 4-2 | Bloomer 2 (2 pens), Grimes, Walker | 10 |
| 6 | | 30 | (a) | Blackpool | L | 0-1 | | 4, |
| 7 | Oct | 7 | (h) | Glossop | W | 5-0 | Bauchop 3, Bloomer, Barnes | 10 |
| 8 | | 14 | (a) | Hull C | D | 0-0 | | 14 |
| 9 | | 21 | (h) | Barnsley | D | 0-0 | | 9 |
| 10 | | 28 | (a) | Bradford PA | W | 1-0 | Bauchop | 20 |
| 11 | Nov | 4 | (h) | Fulham | W | 6-1 | Leonard 4, Bauchop, Bloomer | 12 |
| 12 | | 25 | (h) | Leeds C | W | 5-2 | Sharpe 2, Bauchop, Bloomer, Grimes | 12 |
| 13 | Dec | 2 | (a) | Wolves | W | 1-0 | Leonard | 20, |
| 14 | | 6 | (h) | Burnley | W | 2-0 | Bloomer, Leonard | 12, |
| 15 | | 9 | (h) | Leicester F | W | 5-0 | Bloomer 2, Leonard 2, Wright | 12, |
| 16 | | 16 | (a) | Gainsborough T | D | 1-1 | Sharpe | 1, |
| 17 | | 23 | (a) | Grimsby T | W | 3-0 | Bloomer 2, Bauchop | 7, |
| 18 | | 25 | (h) | Grimsby T | W | 2-1 | Bloomer, Bauchop | 15, |
| 19 | | 26 | (a) | Nottingham F | W | 3-1 | Bloomer, Bauchop, Leonard | 33, |
| 20 | | 30 | (h) | Clapton O | W | 5-1 | Bauchop 3, Bloomer, Leonard | 15, |
| 21 | Jan | 1 | (a) | Stockport C | L | 0-4 | | 10, |
| 22 | | 6 | (a) | Bristol C | D | 1-1 | Leonard | 4, |
| 23 | | 27 | (a) | Huddersfield T | D | 0-0 | | 8, |
| 24 | Feb | 10 | (a) | Glossop | L | 1-3 | Bloomer (pen) | 3, |
| 25 | | 17 | (h) | Hull C | L | 2-3 | Bloomer 2 | 8, |
| 26 | | 21 | (h) | Birmingham | L | 0-1 | | 5, |
| 27 | | 24 | (h) | Blackpool | W | 5-1 | Barnes 3, Sharpe 2 | 5, |
| 28 | Mar | 2 | (h) | Bradford PA | W | 1-0 | Bauchop | 7, |
| 29 | | 16 | (a) | Burnley | D | 0-0 | | 30, |
| 30 | | 23 | (h) | Stockport C | W | 2-0 | Barnes, Grimes | 5, |
| 31 | | 30 | (a) | Leeds C | W | 1-0 | Sharpe | 4, |
| 32 | Apr | 6 | (h) | Wolves | D | 1-1 | Grimes | 12, |
| 33 | | 8 | (h) | Chelsea | W | 2-0 | Leonard 2 | 18, |
| 34 | | 9 | (h) | Nottingham F | W | 1-0 | Leonard | 14, |
| 35 | | 13 | (a) | Leicester F | W | 1-0 | Bloomer | 15, |
| 36 | | 15 | (a) | Fulham | D | 0-0 | | 10, |
| 37 | | 20 | (h) | Gainsborough T | W | 4-0 | Leonard 3, Bauchop | 12, |
| 38 | | 22 | (a) | Barnsley | W | 2-0 | Buckley, Bauchop | 4, |

FINAL LEAGUE POSITION: 1st in Division Two - Promoted

Appearan

Gc

## FA Cup

| | | | | | | | | |
|---|---|---|---|---|---|---|---|---|
| 1 | Jan | 13 | (h) | Newcastle U | W | 3-0 | Bauchop, Richards, Leonard | 21, |
| 2 | Feb | 3 | (h) | Blackburn R | L | 1-2 | Bloomer (pen) | 22, |

Appearan

Gc

| Scattergood E | Atkin J | Barbour T | Garry E | Buckley F | Bagshaw J | Grimes W | Bloomer S | Bauchop J | Walker H | Donald D | Richards G | Barnes H | Sharpe I | Betts C | Leonard H | Wright H | Abbott S | |
|---|---|---|---|---|---|---|---|---|---|---|---|---|---|---|---|---|---|---|
| | 2 | 3 | 4 | 5 | 6 | 7 | 8 | 9 | 10 | 11 | | | | | | | | 1 |
| | 2 | 3 | 4 | | 5 | 7 | 8 | 9 | | 11 | 6 | 10 | | | | | | 2 |
| | 2 | 3 | 4 | | 5 | 7 | 8 | 9 | | 11 | 6 | 10 | | | | | | 3 |
| | 2 | 3 | 4 | | 5 | 7 | 8 | 9 | | 11 | 6 | 10 | | | | | | 4 |
| | 2 | 3 | | 5 | 4 | 7 | 8 | 9 | 10 | 11 | 6 | | | | | | | 5 |
| | 2 | 3 | | 5 | 4 | 7 | 8 | 9 | 10 | 11 | 6 | | | | | | | 6 |
| | 2 | 3 | | 5 | 4 | 7 | 8 | 10 | | | 6 | 9 | 11 | | | | | 7 |
| | 2 | 3 | | 5 | 4 | 7 | 8 | 10 | | | 6 | 9 | 11 | | | | | 8 |
| | 2 | | 4 | | 5 | 7 | 8 | | | | 6 | 10 | 11 | 3 | 9 | | | 9 |
| | 2 | | | 5 | 4 | 7 | | 10 | | | 6 | 8 | 11 | 3 | 9 | | | 10 |
| | | 2 | | 5 | 4 | 7 | 8 | 10 | | | 6 | | 11 | 3 | 9 | | | 11 |
| | 2 | | | 5 | 4 | 7 | 8 | 10 | | | 6 | | 11 | 3 | 9 | | | 12 |
| | 2 | | | 5 | 4 | 7 | 8 | 10 | | | 6 | | 11 | 3 | 9 | | | 13 |
| | 2 | | | 5 | 4 | 7 | 8 | 10 | | | 6 | | 11 | 3 | 9 | | | 14 |
| | 2 | | | 5 | 4 | | 8 | 10 | | | 6 | | 11 | 3 | 9 | 7 | | 15 |
| | 2 | 3 | 4 | 5 | 6 | | 8 | 10 | | | | | 11 | | 9 | 7 | | 16 |
| | 2 | | | 5 | 4 | 7 | 8 | 10 | | | 6 | | 11 | 3 | 9 | | | 17 |
| | 2 | | 6 | 5 | 4 | 7 | 8 | 10 | | | | | 11 | 3 | 9 | | | 18 |
| | 2 | | | 5 | 4 | 7 | 8 | 10 | | | 6 | | 11 | 3 | 9 | | | 19 |
| | 2 | | 6 | 5 | 4 | 7 | 8 | 10 | | | | | 11 | 3 | 9 | | | 20 |
| | 2 | | 6 | 5 | 4 | 7 | 8 | 10 | | | | | 11 | 3 | 9 | | | 21 |
| | 2 | | 4 | | 5 | 7 | 8 | 10 | | 11 | 6 | | | 3 | 9 | | | 22 |
| | 2 | | | 5 | 4 | 7 | 8 | 10 | | | | | 11 | 3 | 9 | | 6 | 23 |
| | 2 | | 6 | 5 | 4 | | 8 | 10 | | | | | 11 | 3 | 9 | 7 | | 24 |
| | 2 | | 6 | 5 | 4 | 7 | 8 | 10 | | | | | 11 | 3 | 9 | | | 25 |
| | 2 | 5 | 4 | | | 7 | 8 | | | | 6 | 10 | 11 | 3 | 9 | | | 26 |
| 1 | 2 | 3 | 4 | | 5 | 7 | 8 | 10 | | | 6 | 9 | 11 | | | | | 27 |
| 1 | 2 | 4 | 6 | | 5 | 7 | 8 | 10 | | | | 9 | 11 | 3 | | | | 28 |
| 1 | 2 | | 4 | 5 | | 7 | 8 | | | | 6 | 10 | 11 | 3 | 9 | | | 29 |
| 1 | 2 | 4 | 6 | | 5 | 7 | 8 | | | | | 10 | 11 | 3 | 9 | | | 30 |
| 1 | | 2 | 6 | 5 | 4 | 7 | | 10 | | | | 8 | 11 | 3 | 9 | | | 31 |
| 1 | | 2 | | 5 | 4 | 7 | 8 | 10 | | | 6 | 9 | 11 | 3 | | | | 32 |
| 1 | 2 | 4 | 6 | 5 | | 7 | 8 | | | | | 10 | 11 | 3 | 9 | | | 33 |
| 1 | 2 | 4 | | 5 | 6 | 7 | 8 | | | | | 10 | 11 | 3 | 9 | | | 34 |
| 1 | 2 | 4 | 6 | 5 | | 7 | 8 | | | | | 10 | 11 | 3 | 9 | | | 35 |
| 1 | 2 | 4 | | 5 | 6 | 7 | 8 | 10 | | | | | 11 | 3 | 9 | | | 36 |
| 1 | 2 | 4 | 6 | | 5 | 7 | 8 | 10 | | | | 11 | | 3 | 9 | | | 37 |
| 1 | 2 | 3 | 4 | 5 | | 7 | 8 | 10 | | | 6 | 11 | | | 9 | | | 38 |
| 8 | 35 | 22 | 22 | 28 | 33 | 35 | 36 | 31 | 3 | 7 | 22 | 19 | 29 | 27 | 27 | 3 | 1 | |
| | | | | 1 | | 4 | 18 | 16 | 1 | 1 | | 9 | 6 | | 17 | 1 | | |

| | | | | | | | | | | | | | | | | | | |
|---|---|---|---|---|---|---|---|---|---|---|---|---|---|---|---|---|---|---|
| 1 | 2 | | | 5 | 4 | 7 | 8 | 10 | | | 6 | | 11 | 3 | 9 | | | 1 |
| 1 | 2 | | | 5 | 4 | 7 | 8 | 10 | | | 6 | | 11 | 3 | 9 | | | 2 |
| 2 | 2 | | | 2 | 2 | 2 | 2 | 2 | | | 2 | | 2 | 2 | 2 | | | |
| | | | | | | | 1 | 1 | | | 1 | | | | 1 | | | |

# 1912-13

| | P | W | D | L | F | A | Pts |
|---|---|---|---|---|---|---|---|
| Sunderland | 38 | 25 | 4 | 9 | 86 | 43 | 54 |
| Aston Villa | 38 | 19 | 12 | 7 | 86 | 52 | 50 |
| Sheffield W | 38 | 21 | 7 | 10 | 75 | 55 | 49 |
| Manchester U | 38 | 19 | 8 | 11 | 69 | 43 | 46 |
| Blackburn R | 38 | 16 | 13 | 9 | 79 | 43 | 45 |
| Manchester C | 38 | 18 | 8 | 12 | 53 | 37 | 44 |
| Derby Co | 38 | 17 | 8 | 13 | 69 | 66 | 42 |
| Bolton W | 38 | 16 | 10 | 12 | 62 | 63 | 42 |
| Oldham A | 38 | 14 | 14 | 10 | 50 | 55 | 42 |
| WBA | 38 | 13 | 12 | 13 | 57 | 50 | 38 |
| Everton | 38 | 15 | 7 | 16 | 48 | 54 | 37 |
| Liverpool | 38 | 16 | 5 | 17 | 61 | 71 | 37 |
| Bradford C | 38 | 12 | 11 | 15 | 50 | 60 | 35 |
| Newcastle U | 38 | 13 | 8 | 17 | 47 | 47 | 34 |
| Sheffield U | 38 | 14 | 6 | 18 | 56 | 70 | 34 |
| Middlesbrough | 38 | 11 | 10 | 17 | 55 | 69 | 32 |
| Tottenham H | 38 | 12 | 6 | 20 | 45 | 72 | 30 |
| Chelsea | 38 | 11 | 6 | 21 | 51 | 73 | 28 |
| Notts Co | 38 | 7 | 9 | 22 | 28 | 56 | 23 |
| Woolwich A | 38 | 3 | 12 | 23 | 26 | 74 | 18 |

Manager: Jimmy Methven.
Leading scorer: Harry Leonard, League/all matches 15.
League ever-present: Jack Atkin.

- Harry Leonard, playing the most consistent football in a career that produced 105 League goals for four clubs, was Derby's leading scorer.
- That had been Steve Bloomer's prerogative since 1894, apart from the four seasons he spent with Middlesbrough.
- A penalty in the final game of the season brought Ernald Scattergood the first of his three goals for Derby. He remains the only goalkeeper to score for the club.
- Scattergood won his one England cap in a 4–3 victory over Wales at Ashton Gate, Bristol, in March.

## Division One

| Match No. | Date | | Venue | Opponents | Result | | Scorers | Atten |
|---|---|---|---|---|---|---|---|---|
| 1 | Sep | 7 | (h) | Blackburn R | D | 1-1 | Barnes | 7, |
| 2 | | 14 | (a) | Sunderland | W | 2-0 | Barnes, Leonard | 12, |
| 3 | | 18 | (h) | Everton | L | 1-4 | Leonard | 15, |
| 4 | | 21 | (a) | Tottenham H | W | 2-1 | Bloomer, Leonard | 30, |
| 5 | | 28 | (h) | Middlesbrough | L | 0-2 | | 12, |
| 6 | Oct | 5 | (a) | Notts C | W | 1-0 | Bloomer | 30, |
| 7 | | 12 | (h) | Manchester U | W | 2-1 | Bloomer, Leonard | 16, |
| 8 | | 19 | (a) | Aston Villa | L | 1-5 | Bauchop | 37, |
| 9 | | 26 | (h) | Liverpool | W | 4-2 | Bloomer 3, Leonard | 6, |
| 10 | Nov | 2 | (a) | Bolton W | D | 1-1 | Sharpe | 20, |
| 11 | | 9 | (h) | Sheffield U | W | 5-1 | Bloomer 3, Bauchop, Sharpe | 11, |
| 12 | | 16 | (a) | Newcastle U | W | 4-2 | Bauchop 2, Bagshaw, Sharpe | 25, |
| 13 | | 23 | (h) | Oldham A | L | 1-2 | Leonard | 12, |
| 14 | | 30 | (a) | Chelsea | L | 1-3 | Leonard | 30, |
| 15 | Dec | 7 | (h) | W Arsenal | W | 4-1 | Buckley, Grimes, Bloomer, Leonard | 10, |
| 16 | | 14 | (a) | Bradford C | W | 3-2 | Bloomer, Barnes, Neve | 15, |
| 17 | | 21 | (h) | Manchester C | W | 2-0 | Bauchop, Barnes | 12, |
| 18 | | 25 | (h) | West Brom A | L | 1-2 | Leonard | 20, |
| 19 | | 26 | (a) | West Brom A | D | 0-0 | | 25, |
| 20 | | 28 | (a) | Blackburn R | W | 1-0 | Walker | 15, |
| 21 | Jan | 1 | (a) | Sheffield W | D | 3-3 | Leonard 2, Barnes | 40, |
| 22 | | 18 | (h) | Tottenham H | W | 5-0 | Bauchop 3, Bloomer 2 | 10, |
| 23 | | 25 | (a) | Middlesbrough | L | 1-4 | Bauchop | 15, |
| 24 | Feb | 8 | (h) | Notts C | W | 1-0 | Barnes | 12, |
| 25 | | 15 | (a) | Manchester U | L | 0-4 | | 30, |
| 26 | | 26 | (h) | Sunderland | L | 0-3 | | 6, |
| 27 | Mar | 1 | (a) | Liverpool | L | 1-2 | Barnes | 15, |
| 28 | | 8 | (h) | Bolton W | D | 3-3 | Bauchop 2, Bagshaw | 10, |
| 29 | | 12 | (h) | Aston Villa | L | 0-1 | | 6, |
| 30 | | 15 | (a) | Sheffield U | L | 1-4 | Sharpe | 10, |
| 31 | | 21 | (a) | Everton | D | 2-2 | Leonard, Barnes | 25, |
| 32 | | 22 | (h) | Newcastle U | W | 2-1 | Leonard, Barnes | 6, |
| 33 | | 24 | (h) | Sheffield W | L | 1-4 | Grimes | 12, |
| 34 | Apr | 5 | (h) | Chelsea | W | 3-1 | Grimes, Barnes, Sharpe | 10, |
| 35 | | 12 | (a) | W Arsenal | W | 2-1 | Barnes 2 | 4, |
| 36 | | 15 | (a) | Oldham A | D | 2-2 | Bauchop, Barnes | 3, |
| 37 | | 19 | (h) | Bradford C | W | 4-0 | Leonard 2, Sharpe, Barbour | 7, |
| 38 | | 26 | (a) | Manchester C | D | 1-1 | Scattergood (pen) | 12, |

FINAL LEAGUE POSITION: 7th in Division One

Appearan
Go

## FA Cup

| | | | | | | | | |
|---|---|---|---|---|---|---|---|---|
| 1 | Jan | 15 | (h) | Aston Villa | L | 1-3 | Bloomer | 15, |

Appearan
Go

| Scattergood E | Atkin J | Betts C | Barbour T | Buckley F | Richards G | Grimes W | Bloomer S | Leonard H | Barnes H | Sharpe I | Garry E | Neve E | Bagshaw J | Bauchop J | Matthews W | Waugh R | Lawrence G | Walker H | Bowler G | |
|---|---|---|---|---|---|---|---|---|---|---|---|---|---|---|---|---|---|---|---|---|
| | 2 | 3 | 4 | 5 | 6 | 7 | 8 | 9 | 10 | 11 | | | | | | | | | | 1 |
| | 2 | 3 | 4 | 5 | 6 | 7 | 8 | 9 | 10 | 11 | | | | | | | | | | 2 |
| | 2 | 3 | 4 | 5 | | 7 | 8 | 9 | 10 | 11 | 6 | | | | | | | | | 3 |
| | 2 | 3 | 4 | 5 | | 7 | 8 | 9 | 10 | | 6 | 11 | | | | | | | | 4 |
| | 2 | 3 | 4 | 5 | 6 | 7 | 8 | 9 | 10 | | | 11 | | | | | | | | 5 |
| | 2 | 3 | 4 | | 6 | 7 | 8 | 9 | 10 | | | 11 | 5 | | | | | | | 6 |
| | 2 | 3 | 4 | 5 | 6 | 7 | 8 | 9 | | | | 11 | | 10 | | | | | | 7 |
| | 2 | | 3 | 5 | | 7 | 8 | 9 | | | | 11 | 6 | 10 | 4 | | | | | 8 |
| | 2 | 3 | 4 | 5 | | 7 | 8 | 9 | | 11 | | | 6 | 10 | | | | | | 9 |
| | 2 | 3 | 4 | 5 | | 7 | 8 | 9 | | 11 | | | 6 | 10 | | | | | | 10 |
| | 2 | 3 | 4 | 5 | | 7 | 8 | 9 | | 11 | | | 6 | 10 | | | | | | 11 |
| | 2 | 3 | 4 | 5 | | 7 | 8 | 9 | | 11 | | | 6 | 10 | | | | | | 12 |
| | 2 | 3 | 4 | | 6 | 7 | 8 | 9 | | 11 | | | 5 | 10 | | | | | | 13 |
| | 2 | 3 | 4 | 5 | 6 | 7 | | 9 | 8 | 11 | | | | 10 | | | | | | 14 |
| | 2 | | 4 | 5 | | 7 | 8 | 9 | | | | 11 | 6 | 10 | | 3 | | | | 15 |
| | 2 | | 4 | | 6 | 7 | 8 | 9 | 10 | | | 11 | 5 | | | 3 | | | | 16 |
| | 2 | 3 | 4 | 5 | | 7 | 8 | | 10 | | | 11 | 6 | 9 | | | | | | 17 |
| | 2 | | 4 | 5 | | 7 | 8 | 9 | | | | 11 | 6 | 10 | | 3 | | | | 18 |
| | 2 | | | 5 | 6 | | 8 | 9 | 10 | 7 | | 11 | 4 | | | 3 | 1 | | | 19 |
| | 2 | 3 | 4 | 5 | | | | 9 | 10 | 7 | | 11 | 6 | | | | 1 | 8 | | 20 |
| | 2 | 3 | 4 | 5 | 6 | | 8 | 9 | 10 | 7 | | 11 | | | | | 1 | | | 21 |
| | 2 | 3 | | | 6 | | 8 | 9 | | 7 | 4 | 11 | 5 | 10 | | | | | | 22 |
| | 2 | 3 | 4 | 5 | | | 8 | 9 | | 7 | | 11 | 6 | 10 | | | | | | 23 |
| | 2 | 3 | 4 | | 6 | 7 | 8 | | 10 | | | 11 | 5 | 9 | | | | | | 24 |
| | 2 | 3 | 4 | | 6 | 7 | 8 | 9 | 10 | | | 11 | 5 | | | | | | | 25 |
| | 2 | 3 | | | 6 | 7 | 8 | 9 | 10 | | | 11 | 5 | | | | | | 4 | 26 |
| | 2 | 3 | 4 | 5 | | 7 | | | 10 | 11 | | | 6 | 9 | | | | 8 | | 27 |
| | 2 | 3 | 4 | 5 | | 7 | | | 10 | 11 | | | 6 | 9 | | | | 8 | | 28 |
| | 2 | 3 | 4 | 5 | | 7 | 8 | 9 | | 11 | | | 6 | 10 | | | | | | 29 |
| | 2 | 3 | 4 | 5 | | 7 | 8 | 9 | | 11 | | | 6 | 10 | | | 1 | | | 30 |
| | 2 | 3 | 4 | 5 | | 7 | | 9 | 8 | 11 | | | 6 | 10 | | | | | | 31 |
| | 2 | 3 | 4 | 5 | | 7 | | 9 | 8 | 11 | | | 6 | 10 | | | | | | 32 |
| | 2 | 3 | 4 | 5 | | 7 | | 9 | 8 | 11 | | | 6 | 10 | | | | | | 33 |
| | 2 | 3 | 4 | | 6 | 7 | 8 | 9 | 10 | 11 | | | 5 | | | | | | | 34 |
| | 2 | 3 | 4 | 5 | | 7 | | | 10 | 11 | | | 6 | 9 | | | | 8 | | 35 |
| | 2 | 3 | 4 | 5 | | | 8 | | 10 | | | 11 | 6 | 9 | | | | 7 | | 36 |
| | 2 | 3 | 4 | | 6 | 7 | 8 | 9 | | 11 | | | 5 | 10 | | | | | | 37 |
| | 2 | 3 | 4 | 5 | 6 | 7 | | 9 | 10 | 11 | | | | | | | | 8 | | 38 |
| 4 | 38 | 33 | 35 | 29 | 17 | 32 | 29 | 32 | 24 | 25 | 3 | 18 | 29 | 24 | 1 | 4 | 4 | 6 | 1 | |
| | | | 1 | 1 | | 3 | 13 | 15 | 13 | 6 | | 1 | 2 | 12 | | | | 1 | | |

| | | | | | | | | | | | | | | | |
|---|---|---|---|---|---|---|---|---|---|---|---|---|---|---|---|
| 1 | 2 | 3 | 4 | 5 | | | 8 | 9 | | 7 | | 11 | 6 | 10 | 1 |
| 1 | 1 | 1 | 1 | 1 | | | 1 | 1 | | 1 | | 1 | 1 | 1 | |
| | | | | | | | 1 | | | | | | | | |

# 1913-14

| | P | W | D | L | F | A | Pts |
|---|---|---|---|---|---|---|---|
| Blackburn R | 38 | 20 | 11 | 7 | 78 | 42 | 51 |
| Aston Villa | 38 | 19 | 6 | 13 | 65 | 50 | 44 |
| Middlesbrough | 38 | 19 | 5 | 14 | 77 | 60 | 43 |
| Oldham A | 38 | 17 | 9 | 12 | 55 | 45 | 43 |
| WBA | 38 | 15 | 13 | 10 | 46 | 42 | 43 |
| Bolton W | 38 | 16 | 10 | 12 | 65 | 52 | 42 |
| Sunderland | 38 | 17 | 6 | 15 | 63 | 52 | 40 |
| Chelsea | 38 | 16 | 7 | 15 | 46 | 55 | 39 |
| Bradford C | 38 | 12 | 14 | 12 | 40 | 40 | 38 |
| Sheffield U | 38 | 16 | 5 | 17 | 63 | 60 | 37 |
| Newcastle U | 38 | 13 | 11 | 14 | 39 | 48 | 37 |
| Burnley | 38 | 12 | 12 | 14 | 61 | 53 | 36 |
| Manchester C | 38 | 14 | 8 | 16 | 51 | 53 | 36 |
| Manchester U | 38 | 15 | 6 | 17 | 52 | 62 | 36 |
| Everton | 38 | 12 | 11 | 15 | 46 | 55 | 35 |
| Liverpool | 38 | 14 | 7 | 17 | 46 | 62 | 35 |
| Tottenham H | 38 | 12 | 10 | 16 | 50 | 62 | 34 |
| Sheffield W | 38 | 13 | 8 | 17 | 53 | 70 | 34 |
| Preston NE | 38 | 12 | 6 | 20 | 52 | 69 | 30 |
| Derby Co | 38 | 8 | 11 | 19 | 55 | 71 | 27 |

Manager: Jimmy Methven.
Leading scorer: Horace Barnes, League 24, all matches 25.

- Steve Bloomer, aged 40, scored his 332nd and last goal for Derby on 6 September. He remains 131 ahead of his nearest challenger, Kevin Hector.
- Bloomer scored a goal, on average, every 1.58 games. He made the last of his 525 appearances in a Cup defeat at Burnley on 31 January. Only Kevin Hector, Ron Webster and Roy McFarland have overtaken him.
- Derby were in an erratic period, two promotions and two relegations in the six seasons around World War One.

## Division One

| Match No. | Date | | Venue | Opponents | Result | | Scorers | Atten |
|---|---|---|---|---|---|---|---|---|
| 1 | Sep | 1 | (h) | Liverpool | D | 1-1 | Barnes | 7, |
| 2 | | 6 | (h) | Sheffield U | L | 3-5 | Bloomer 2, Barnes | 12, |
| 3 | | 10 | (h) | Middlesbrough | D | 2-2 | Barnes, Grimes | 6, |
| 4 | | 13 | (a) | Tottenham H | D | 1-1 | Barnes | 40, |
| 5 | | 20 | (a) | Manchester C | W | 2-1 | Barnes, Leonard | 30, |
| 6 | | 27 | (h) | Bradford C | W | 3-1 | Barnes 2, Scattergood (pen) | 12, |
| 7 | Oct | 4 | (a) | Blackburn R | L | 1-3 | Leonard | 30, |
| 8 | | 11 | (h) | Sunderland | D | 1-1 | Buckley | 12, |
| 9 | | 18 | (a) | Everton | L | 0-5 | | 30, |
| 10 | | 25 | (h) | West Brom A | L | 1-2 | Walker | 12, |
| 11 | Nov | 1 | (a) | Sheffield W | W | 3-1 | Leonard, Barnes, Moore | 20, |
| 12 | | 8 | (h) | Bolton W | D | 3-3 | Barnes 2, Moore | 12, |
| 13 | | 15 | (a) | Chelsea | L | 1-2 | Walker | 35, |
| 14 | | 22 | (h) | Oldham A | L | 1-2 | Barnes | 12, |
| 15 | | 29 | (a) | Manchester U | D | 3-3 | Moore 2, Leonard | 20, |
| 16 | Dec | 6 | (h) | Burnley | W | 3-1 | Leonard 2, Barnes | 12, |
| 17 | | 13 | (a) | Preston NE | L | 0-2 | | 12, |
| 18 | | 20 | (h) | Newcastle U | W | 2-0 | Moore, Leonard | 12, |
| 19 | | 25 | (h) | Aston Villa | L | 0-2 | | 9, |
| 20 | | 27 | (a) | Sheffield U | D | 2-2 | Leonard, Barnes | 12, |
| 21 | Jan | 1 | (a) | Middlesbrough | L | 2-3 | Barnes 2 | 18, |
| 22 | | 3 | (h) | Tottenham H | W | 4-0 | Barbour, Barnes, Moore, Cartwright (og) | 11, |
| 23 | | 17 | (h) | Manchester C | L | 2-4 | Barnes, Moore | 10, |
| 24 | | 24 | (a) | Bradford C | D | 0-0 | | 15, |
| 25 | Feb | 7 | (h) | Blackburn R | L | 2-3 | Moore, Barnes | 10, |
| 26 | | 14 | (a) | Sunderland | L | 0-1 | | 15, |
| 27 | | 21 | (h) | Everton | W | 1-0 | Fordham | 10, |
| 28 | | 28 | (a) | West Brom A | L | 1-2 | Fellows | 15, |
| 29 | Mar | 11 | (h) | Sheffield W | D | 1-1 | Moore | 10, |
| 30 | | 14 | (a) | Bolton W | L | 1-3 | Moore | 18, |
| 31 | | 21 | (h) | Chelsea | L | 0-1 | | 10, |
| 32 | | 28 | (a) | Oldham A | D | 0-0 | | 6, |
| 33 | Apr | 4 | (h) | Manchester U | W | 4-2 | Barnes 2, Leonard, Scattergood (pen) | 5, |
| 34 | | 10 | (a) | Liverpool | L | 0-1 | | 40, |
| 35 | | 11 | (a) | Burnley | L | 1-5 | Barnes | 18, |
| 36 | | 13 | (a) | Aston Villa | L | 2-3 | Barnes 2 | 20, |
| 37 | | 18 | (h) | Preston NE | L | 0-1 | | 4, |
| 38 | | 25 | (a) | Newcastle U | D | 1-1 | Barnes | 15, |

FINAL LEAGUE POSITION: 20th in Division One – Relegated

Appearan
Go

## FA Cup

| | | | | | | | | |
|---|---|---|---|---|---|---|---|---|
| 1 | Jan | 10 | (h) | Northampton T | W | 1-0 | Moore | 12, |
| 2 | | 31 | (a) | Burnley | L | 2-3 | Barnes, Waugh | 30, |

Appearan
Go

| …attergood E | Atkin J | Betts C | Barbour T | Buckley F | Bagshaw J | Grimes W | Bloomer S | Leonard H | Barnes H | Neve E | Waugh R | Richards G | Walker H | Ritchie D | Hardman J | Moore J | Lawrence G | Fordham N | Fellows P | Methven J | Callender R | Reader R | |
|---|---|---|---|---|---|---|---|---|---|---|---|---|---|---|---|---|---|---|---|---|---|---|---|
| | 2 | 3 | 4 | 5 | 6 | 7 | 8 | 9 | 10 | 11 | | | | | | | | | | | | | 1 |
| | 2 | | 4 | 5 | 6 | 7 | 8 | 9 | 10 | 11 | 3 | | | | | | | | | | | | 2 |
| | 2 | | 3 | 5 | 4 | 7 | | 9 | 10 | 11 | | 6 | 8 | | | | | | | | | | 3 |
| | 2 | | 3 | 5 | 4 | 7 | | 9 | 10 | | | 6 | 8 | 11 | | | | | | | | | 4 |
| | 2 | | 3 | | 4 | 7 | | 9 | 10 | | | 6 | 8 | 11 | 5 | | | | | | | | 5 |
| | 2 | | 3 | 5 | 4 | 7 | | 9 | 10 | 11 | | | 8 | | 6 | | | | | | | | 6 |
| | 2 | | 3 | 5 | 4 | 7 | | 9 | 10 | 11 | | 6 | 8 | | | | | | | | | | 7 |
| | 2 | | 3 | 5 | 4 | 7 | | 9 | 10 | 11 | | 6 | 8 | | | | | | | | | | 8 |
| | 2 | | 3 | 5 | 4 | 7 | 8 | 9 | | 11 | | 6 | 10 | | | | | | | | | | 9 |
| | 2 | 3 | 4 | 5 | | 7 | | 9 | 10 | 11 | | | 8 | | 6 | | | | | | | | 10 |
| | 2 | | 3 | 5 | 4 | 7 | | 9 | 10 | 11 | | | | | 6 | 8 | | | | | | | 11 |
| | 2 | | 3 | 5 | 4 | 7 | 8 | | 10 | 11 | | | | | 6 | 9 | | | | | | | 12 |
| | 2 | | 3 | 5 | | 7 | | | 10 | 11 | | 6 | 9 | | 4 | 8 | | | | | | | 13 |
| | 2 | 3 | | 5 | | 7 | | | 10 | 11 | | 6 | 9 | | 4 | 8 | 1 | | | | | | 14 |
| | 2 | | 3 | 5 | 4 | 7 | | 9 | 10 | 11 | | | | | 6 | 8 | | | | | | | 15 |
| | 2 | | 3 | 5 | 4 | 7 | | 9 | 10 | 11 | | 6 | | | | 8 | | | | | | | 16 |
| | 2 | | 3 | 5 | 4 | 7 | | 9 | 10 | 11 | | 6 | | | | 8 | 1 | | | | | | 17 |
| | 2 | | 3 | 5 | 4 | 7 | | 9 | 10 | 11 | | 6 | | | | 8 | 1 | | | | | | 18 |
| | 2 | | 3 | 5 | 4 | 7 | | 9 | 10 | 11 | | 6 | | | | 8 | 1 | | | | | | 19 |
| | | | 3 | 5 | 4 | 7 | | 9 | 10 | 11 | 2 | | | | 6 | 8 | 1 | | | | | | 20 |
| | 2 | 3 | 4 | 5 | | 7 | | 9 | 10 | 11 | | | | | 6 | 8 | 1 | | | | | | 21 |
| | 2 | 3 | 4 | 5 | 6 | 7 | | | 10 | 11 | | | 8 | | | 9 | 1 | | | | | | 22 |
| | 2 | | 3 | 5 | 4 | 7 | | | 10 | 11 | | | 8 | | 6 | 9 | 1 | | | | | | 23 |
| | 2 | | 4 | 5 | 6 | 7 | 9 | | 10 | 11 | 3 | | | | | 8 | 1 | | | | | | 24 |
| | 2 | 3 | 4 | 5 | | 7 | | | 10 | 11 | | 6 | | | | 8 | | 9 | | | | | 25 |
| | 2 | 3 | 4 | | | 7 | | | 10 | 11 | | | 6 | | 5 | 8 | | 9 | | | | | 26 |
| | 2 | | 4 | 5 | | 7 | | | 10 | | 3 | | 6 | | | 8 | | 9 | 11 | | | | 27 |
| | 2 | | 4 | 5 | | 7 | | | 10 | | 3 | | 6 | | | 8 | | 9 | 11 | | | | 28 |
| | 2 | | 4 | 5 | | 7 | | | 10 | 11 | 3 | | 6 | | | 8 | | 9 | | | | | 29 |
| | | 3 | 4 | 5 | 6 | 7 | | | 10 | 11 | 2 | | | | | 9 | | | | 8 | | | 30 |
| | 2 | | 4 | 5 | 6 | 7 | | | 10 | | 3 | | | | | 8 | | 9 | | | 11 | | 31 |
| | 2 | | 4 | 5 | | | | 9 | 10 | | 3 | | 6 | | | 8 | | | | | 11 | 7 | 32 |
| | 2 | | 4 | 5 | | | | 9 | 10 | 11 | 3 | | 6 | | | 8 | | | | | | 7 | 33 |
| | 2 | | 4 | 5 | | | | 9 | 10 | | 3 | | 6 | | | 8 | | | | | 11 | 7 | 34 |
| | 2 | | 4 | 5 | 6 | | | 9 | 10 | | 3 | | | | | 8 | | | | | 11 | 7 | 35 |
| | | 3 | 4 | | 6 | 7 | | 9 | 10 | | 2 | | 8 | | 5 | | | | | | 11 | | 36 |
| | | 3 | 2 | 5 | 6 | 7 | | 9 | 10 | 11 | | | 4 | | | 8 | | | | | | | 37 |
| | | 3 | 4 | 5 | 6 | 7 | | | 10 | 11 | 2 | | 8 | | | 9 | | | | | | | 38 |
| 9 | 33 | 11 | 37 | 35 | 26 | 34 | 5 | 24 | 37 | 29 | 14 | 13 | 22 | 2 | 13 | 27 | 9 | 6 | 2 | 1 | 5 | 4 | |
| | | | 1 | 1 | | 1 | 2 | 9 | 24 | | | | 2 | | | 10 | | 1 | 1 | | | | |

1 own-goal

| …attergood E | Atkin J | Betts C | Barbour T | Buckley F | Bagshaw J | Grimes W | Bloomer S | Leonard H | Barnes H | Neve E | Waugh R | Richards G | Walker H | Ritchie D | Hardman J | Moore J | Lawrence G | Fordham N | Fellows P | Methven J | Callender R | Reader R | |
|---|---|---|---|---|---|---|---|---|---|---|---|---|---|---|---|---|---|---|---|---|---|---|---|
| | 2 | | 3 | 5 | 4 | 7 | | 9 | 10 | 11 | | | | | 6 | 8 | 1 | | | | | | 1 |
| | 2 | | 4 | 5 | 6 | 7 | 9 | | 10 | | 3 | | 11 | | | 8 | 1 | | | | | | 2 |
| | 2 | | 2 | 2 | 2 | 2 | 1 | 1 | 2 | 1 | 1 | | 1 | | 1 | 2 | 2 | | | | | | |
| | | | | | | | | | 1 | | 1 | | | | | 1 | | | | | | | |

# 1914-15

| | P | W | D | L | F | A | Pts |
|---|---|---|---|---|---|---|---|
| Derby Co | 38 | 23 | 7 | 8 | 71 | 33 | 53 |
| Preston N.E. | 38 | 20 | 10 | 8 | 61 | 42 | 50 |
| Barnsley | 38 | 22 | 3 | 13 | 51 | 51 | 47 |
| Wolves | 38 | 19 | 7 | 12 | 77 | 52 | 45 |
| Arsenal | 38 | 19 | 5 | 14 | 69 | 41 | 43 |
| Birmingham | 38 | 17 | 9 | 12 | 62 | 39 | 43 |
| Hull C | 38 | 19 | 5 | 14 | 65 | 54 | 43 |
| Huddersfield T | 38 | 17 | 8 | 13 | 61 | 42 | 42 |
| Clapton O | 38 | 16 | 9 | 13 | 50 | 48 | 41 |
| Blackpool | 38 | 17 | 5 | 16 | 58 | 57 | 39 |
| Bury | 38 | 15 | 8 | 15 | 61 | 56 | 38 |
| Fulham | 38 | 15 | 7 | 16 | 53 | 47 | 37 |
| Bristol C | 38 | 15 | 7 | 16 | 62 | 56 | 37 |
| Stockport Co | 38 | 15 | 7 | 16 | 54 | 60 | 37 |
| Leeds C | 38 | 14 | 4 | 20 | 65 | 64 | 32 |
| Lincoln C | 38 | 11 | 9 | 18 | 46 | 65 | 31 |
| Grimsby T | 38 | 11 | 9 | 18 | 48 | 76 | 31 |
| Nottingham F | 38 | 10 | 9 | 19 | 43 | 77 | 29 |
| Leicester F | 38 | 10 | 4 | 24 | 47 | 88 | 24 |
| Glossop | 38 | 6 | 6 | 26 | 31 | 87 | 18 |

Manager: Jimmy Methven.
Leading scorer: Jimmy Moore, League/all matches 22.
League ever-present: Tommy Benfield, Jimmy Moore.

- Tommy Benfield, signed from Leicester Fosse, had a great first season, an ever-present with 15 goals in the Second Division Championship side. It was to be his last appearance in peacetime football. Benfield was a regular soldier before signing for Fosse and rejoined the Leicestershire Regiment. He was a sergeant when he was killed in France in 1918.
- Stuart McMillan made his single Derby appearance on 2 January. He gained greater fame as the FA Cup-winning manager in 1946.

## Division Two

| Match No. | Date | | Venue | Opponents | Result | | Scorers | Atter |
|---|---|---|---|---|---|---|---|---|
| 1 | Sep | 2 | (h) | Barnsley | W | 7-0 | Fordham 3, Moore 2, Baker, Bethune (og) | 2 |
| 2 | | 5 | (a) | Glossop | D | 1-1 | Benfield | |
| 3 | | 12 | (h) | Wolves | W | 3-1 | Benfield 2, Fordham | 5 |
| 4 | | 19 | (a) | Fulham | L | 0-2 | | 14 |
| 5 | | 26 | (h) | Stockport C | W | 1-0 | Benfield | 5 |
| 6 | Oct | 3 | (a) | Hull C | L | 0-1 | | 6 |
| 7 | | 10 | (h) | Leeds C | L | 1-2 | Baker | 6 |
| 8 | | 17 | (a) | Clapton O | W | 1-0 | Moore | 10 |
| 9 | | 24 | (h) | Arsenal | W | 4-0 | Benfield 2, Moore, Leonard | 8 |
| 10 | | 31 | (h) | Blackpool | W | 5-0 | Leonard 2, Moore 2, Devonshire | 4 |
| 11 | Nov | 7 | (a) | Lincoln C | D | 0-0 | | 5 |
| 12 | | 14 | (h) | Birmingham | W | 1-0 | Leonard | 5 |
| 13 | | 21 | (a) | Grimsby T | W | 2-1 | Leonard, Benfield | 8 |
| 14 | | 28 | (h) | Huddersfield T | W | 1-0 | Leonard (pen) | 7, |
| 15 | Dec | 5 | (a) | Bristol C | W | 3-2 | Leonard, Moore, Benfield | 6 |
| 16 | | 12 | (h) | Bury | W | 2-1 | Benfield, Moore | 6 |
| 17 | | 19 | (a) | Preston NE | W | 3-1 | Leonard, Grimes, Benfield | 8 |
| 18 | | 25 | (a) | Nottingham F | D | 2-2 | Leonard (pen), Moore | 15 |
| 19 | | 26 | (h) | Nottingham F | W | 1-0 | Leonard | 14, |
| 20 | | 28 | (a) | Leicester F | W | 6-0 | Leonard 2, Moore 2, Benfield 2 | 5 |
| 21 | Jan | 2 | (h) | Glossop | D | 1-1 | Leonard (pen) | 7, |
| 22 | | 16 | (a) | Wolves | W | 1-0 | Baker | 6, |
| 23 | | 23 | (h) | Fulham | D | 1-1 | Benfield | 6, |
| 24 | | 30 | (a) | Stockport C | L | 2-3 | Leonard, Moore | 8, |
| 25 | Feb | 6 | (h) | Hull C | W | 4-1 | Moore 3, Leonard | 5, |
| 26 | | 13 | (a) | Leeds C | W | 5-3 | Leonard 2, Moore 2, Baker | 5, |
| 27 | | 20 | (h) | Clapton O | L | 0-3 | | 6, |
| 28 | | 27 | (a) | Arsenal | W | 2-1 | Benfield, Moore | 18, |
| 29 | Mar | 6 | (a) | Blackpool | L | 1-2 | Grimes | 5, |
| 30 | | 13 | (h) | Lincoln C | W | 3-0 | Moore 2, Baker | 7, |
| 31 | | 20 | (a) | Birmingham | W | 2-0 | Moore, Leonard | 30, |
| 32 | | 27 | (h) | Grimsby T | D | 1-1 | Benfield | 6, |
| 33 | Apr | 2 | (a) | Barnsley | L | 0-1 | | 10, |
| 34 | | 3 | (a) | Huddersfield T | D | 0-0 | | 6, |
| 35 | | 5 | (h) | Leicester F | W | 1-0 | Baker | 10, |
| 36 | | 10 | (h) | Bristol C | W | 1-0 | Moore | 7, |
| 37 | | 17 | (a) | Bury | L | 0-2 | | 6, |
| 38 | | 24 | (h) | Preston NE | W | 2-0 | Grimes, Leonard | 12, |

FINAL LEAGUE POSITION: 1st in Division Two - Promoted

Appearan
Go

## FA Cup

| | | | | | | | | |
|---|---|---|---|---|---|---|---|---|
| 1 | Jan | 9 | (h) | Leeds C | L | 1-2 | Fordham | 9, |

Appearan
Go

| Scattergood E | Smith J | Waugh R | Bagshaw J | Eadie W | Brooks G | Barbour T | Benfield T | Fordham N | Moore J | Baker W | Hardman J | Grimes W | Walker H | Devonshire W | Leonard H | Lawrence G | Atkin J | Quantrill A | McMillan S | |
|---|---|---|---|---|---|---|---|---|---|---|---|---|---|---|---|---|---|---|---|---|
| | 2 | 3 | 4 | 5 | 6 | 7 | 8 | 9 | 10 | 11 | | | | | | | | | | 1 |
| | 2 | 3 | 4 | | 6 | 7 | 8 | 9 | 10 | 11 | 5 | | | | | | | | | 2 |
| | 2 | 3 | 5 | | 6 | 4 | 8 | 9 | 10 | 11 | | 7 | | | | | | | | 3 |
| | 2 | 3 | 4 | 5 | 6 | | 8 | 9 | 10 | 11 | | 7 | | | | | | | | 4 |
| | 2 | | 5 | | 6 | 3 | 8 | 9 | 10 | 11 | | 7 | 4 | | | | | | | 5 |
| | 2 | | 4 | 5 | 6 | 3 | 8 | 9 | 10 | 11 | | 7 | | | | | | | | 6 |
| | | 3 | 4 | 5 | 6 | 2 | 8 | | 10 | 11 | | | | 7 | 9 | | | | | 7 |
| | | | | 5 | 6 | 3 | 8 | | 10 | 11 | | | 4 | 7 | 9 | 1 | 2 | | | 8 |
| | | | | 5 | 6 | 3 | 8 | | 10 | 11 | | | 4 | 7 | 9 | 1 | 2 | | | 9 |
| | | | | 5 | 6 | 3 | 8 | | 10 | 11 | | | 4 | 7 | 9 | 1 | 2 | | | 10 |
| | | 3 | | 5 | 6 | 4 | 8 | | 10 | 11 | | | | 7 | 9 | 1 | 2 | | | 11 |
| | | 3 | | 5 | 6 | 4 | 8 | | 10 | 11 | | | | 7 | 9 | 1 | 2 | | | 12 |
| | | 3 | | 5 | 6 | 4 | 8 | | 10 | 11 | | 7 | | | 9 | 1 | 2 | | | 13 |
| | | | | 5 | 6 | 3 | 8 | | 10 | 11 | | 7 | 4 | | 9 | 1 | 2 | | | 14 |
| | | | | 5 | 6 | 3 | 8 | | 10 | 11 | | 7 | 4 | | 9 | 1 | 2 | | | 15 |
| | | | | 5 | 6 | 3 | 8 | | 10 | 11 | | | 4 | 7 | 9 | 1 | 2 | | | 16 |
| | | | 6 | 5 | | 3 | 8 | | 10 | 11 | | 7 | 4 | | 9 | 1 | 2 | | | 17 |
| | | | 6 | 5 | | 3 | 8 | | 10 | 11 | | 7 | 4 | | 9 | 1 | 2 | | | 18 |
| | | | 5 | | 6 | 3 | 8 | | 10 | | | 7 | 4 | | 9 | 1 | 2 | 11 | | 19 |
| | | | | 5 | 6 | 3 | 8 | | 10 | | | 7 | 4 | | 9 | 1 | 2 | 11 | | 20 |
| | | | | 5 | 6 | 3 | 8 | | 10 | | | | 4 | | 9 | 1 | 2 | 11 | 7 | 21 |
| | | | 5 | | 6 | 3 | 8 | | 10 | 11 | | 7 | 4 | | 9 | 1 | 2 | | | 22 |
| | | | | 5 | 6 | 3 | 8 | | 10 | 11 | | 7 | 4 | | 9 | 1 | 2 | | | 23 |
| | | | 4 | 5 | 6 | 3 | 8 | | 10 | 11 | | 7 | | | 9 | 1 | 2 | | | 24 |
| | | 3 | 6 | 5 | | 4 | 8 | | 10 | 11 | | 7 | | | 9 | 1 | 2 | | | 25 |
| | | | 6 | 5 | | 3 | 8 | | 10 | 11 | | 7 | 4 | | 9 | 1 | 2 | | | 26 |
| | | | 6 | 5 | | 3 | 8 | | 10 | 11 | | 7 | 4 | | 9 | 1 | 2 | | | 27 |
| | | | | 5 | 6 | 3 | 8 | | 10 | 11 | | 7 | 4 | | 9 | 1 | 2 | | | 28 |
| | | | | 5 | 6 | 3 | 8 | | 10 | 11 | | 7 | 4 | | 9 | 1 | 2 | | | 29 |
| | | | | 5 | 6 | 3 | 8 | | 10 | 11 | | 7 | 4 | | 9 | 1 | 2 | | | 30 |
| | | | | 5 | 6 | 3 | 8 | | 10 | 11 | | 7 | 4 | | 9 | 1 | 2 | | | 31 |
| | | | | 5 | 6 | 3 | 8 | | 10 | 11 | | 7 | 4 | | 9 | 1 | 2 | | | 32 |
| | | | | 5 | 6 | 3 | 8 | | 10 | 11 | | 7 | 4 | | 9 | 1 | 2 | | | 33 |
| | | 2 | | 5 | 6 | 3 | 8 | | 10 | 11 | | 7 | 4 | | 9 | 1 | | | | 34 |
| | | | | 5 | 6 | 3 | 8 | | 10 | 11 | | 7 | 4 | | 9 | 1 | 2 | | | 35 |
| | | | 5 | | 6 | 3 | 8 | | 10 | 11 | | 7 | 4 | | 9 | 1 | 2 | | | 36 |
| | | | 4 | | 6 | 3 | 8 | 5 | 10 | 11 | | 7 | | | 9 | 1 | 2 | | | 37 |
| | | | | 5 | 6 | 3 | 8 | | 10 | 11 | | 7 | 4 | | 9 | 1 | 2 | | | 38 |
| | 6 | 10 | 17 | 31 | 33 | 37 | 38 | 7 | 38 | 35 | 1 | 28 | 26 | 7 | 32 | 31 | 30 | 3 | 1 | |
| | | | | | | | 15 | 4 | 22 | 6 | | 3 | | 1 | 19 | | | | | |

1 own-goal

| | | | | | | | | | | | | | | | | | | | | |
|---|---|---|---|---|---|---|---|---|---|---|---|---|---|---|---|---|---|---|---|---|
| | | | 5 | | 6 | 3 | 8 | 9 | 10 | | | 7 | 4 | | | 1 | 2 | 11 | | 1 |
| | | | 1 | | 1 | 1 | 1 | 1 | 1 | | | 1 | 1 | | | 1 | 1 | 1 | | |
| | | | | | | | | 1 | | | | | | | | | | | | |

# 1919-20

| | P | W | D | L | F | A | Pts |
|---|---|---|---|---|---|---|---|
| WBA | 42 | 28 | 4 | 10 | 104 | 47 | 60 |
| Burnley | 42 | 21 | 9 | 12 | 65 | 59 | 51 |
| Chelsea | 42 | 22 | 5 | 15 | 56 | 51 | 49 |
| Liverpool | 42 | 19 | 10 | 13 | 59 | 44 | 48 |
| Sunderland | 42 | 22 | 4 | 16 | 72 | 59 | 48 |
| Bolton W | 42 | 19 | 9 | 14 | 72 | 65 | 47 |
| Manchester C | 42 | 18 | 9 | 15 | 71 | 62 | 45 |
| Newcastle U | 42 | 17 | 9 | 16 | 44 | 39 | 43 |
| Aston Villa | 42 | 18 | 6 | 18 | 75 | 73 | 42 |
| Arsenal | 42 | 15 | 12 | 15 | 56 | 58 | 42 |
| Bradford PA | 42 | 15 | 12 | 15 | 60 | 63 | 42 |
| Manchester U | 42 | 13 | 14 | 15 | 54 | 50 | 40 |
| Middlesbrough | 42 | 15 | 10 | 17 | 61 | 65 | 40 |
| Sheffield U | 42 | 16 | 8 | 18 | 59 | 69 | 40 |
| Bradford C | 42 | 14 | 11 | 17 | 54 | 63 | 39 |
| Everton | 42 | 12 | 14 | 16 | 69 | 68 | 38 |
| Oldham A | 42 | 15 | 8 | 19 | 49 | 52 | 38 |
| Derby Co | 42 | 13 | 12 | 17 | 47 | 57 | 38 |
| Preston NE | 42 | 14 | 10 | 18 | 57 | 73 | 38 |
| Blackburn R | 42 | 13 | 11 | 18 | 64 | 77 | 37 |
| Notts Co | 42 | 12 | 12 | 18 | 56 | 74 | 36 |
| Sheffield W | 42 | 7 | 9 | 26 | 28 | 64 | 23 |

Manager: Jimmy Methven.
Leading scorers: Noah Burton, Harry Leonard, League 12: Noah Burton, all matches 13.
League ever-present: Jack Atkin, George Thornewell, Harry Wightman.

- Jimmy Bagshaw was capped in England's first international after World War One, a 1–1 draw with Ireland in Belfast. He was 34 at the time and, although he had played in a Victory International against Wales, it was his only cap.
- In a moderate season for Derby, outside-left Alf Quantrill also won England honours.
- A late revival kept the Rams clear of relegation. They dropped only one point in their last five games to clamber out of trouble, if only for another year.

## Division One

| Match No. | Date | Venue | Opponents | Result | | Scorers | Atten… |
|---|---|---|---|---|---|---|---|
| 1 | Aug 30 | (h) | Manchester U | D | 1-1 | Leonard | 12 |
| 2 | Sep 1 | (a) | Aston Villa | D | 2-2 | Leonard, Burton | 20 |
| 3 | 6 | (a) | Manchester U | W | 2-0 | J.Moore 2 | 15 |
| 4 | 8 | (h) | Aston Villa | W | 1-0 | Ritchie | 14 |
| 5 | 13 | (h) | Bradford C | W | 3-0 | Leonard 2, Bagshaw | 12 |
| 6 | 20 | (a) | Bradford C | L | 1-3 | Wightman | 12 |
| 7 | 24 | (a) | Newcastle U | D | 0-0 | | 20 |
| 8 | 27 | (h) | Bolton W | L | 1-2 | Leonard | 15 |
| 9 | Oct 4 | (a) | Bolton W | L | 0-3 | | 30 |
| 10 | 11 | (h) | Notts C | W | 3-1 | Burton 2 (1 pen), Quantrill | 15 |
| 11 | 18 | (a) | Notts C | D | 2-2 | Baker, Wightman | 26 |
| 12 | 25 | (h) | Oldham A | D | 1-1 | Leonard | 10 |
| 13 | Nov 1 | (a) | Oldham A | L | 0-3 | | 8 |
| 14 | 8 | (h) | Sheffield W | W | 2-1 | Leonard 2 | 9 |
| 15 | 15 | (a) | Sheffield W | L | 0-2 | | 9 |
| 16 | 22 | (a) | Manchester C | L | 1-3 | Burton (pen) | 20 |
| 17 | 29 | (h) | Manchester C | D | 0-0 | | 8 |
| 18 | Dec 6 | (a) | Blackburn R | L | 0-2 | | 25 |
| 19 | 13 | (h) | Blackburn R | D | 0-0 | | 10 |
| 20 | 20 | (h) | West Brom A | L | 0-4 | | 14 |
| 21 | 25 | (h) | Arsenal | W | 2-1 | Burton 2 | 12 |
| 22 | 26 | (a) | Arsenal | L | 0-1 | | 25 |
| 23 | 27 | (a) | West Brom A | L | 0-3 | | 34 |
| 24 | Jan 3 | (h) | Sunderland | W | 3-1 | Quantrill, Leonard, Thornewell | 10 |
| 25 | 17 | (a) | Sunderland | L | 1-2 | Lyons | 20 |
| 26 | 24 | (h) | Sheffield U | W | 5-1 | Lyons 2, Wightman (pen), Thornewell, Barbour | 14 |
| 27 | Feb 7 | (h) | Middlesbrough | L | 1-2 | J.Moore | 16 |
| 28 | 9 | (a) | Sheffield U | D | 0-0 | | 12 |
| 29 | 14 | (a) | Middlesbrough | L | 0-2 | | 20 |
| 30 | 21 | (h) | Burnley | L | 0-2 | | 12 |
| 31 | 28 | (a) | Burnley | L | 0-2 | | 20 |
| 32 | Mar 6 | (a) | Preston NE | D | 1-1 | Burton | 12 |
| 33 | 13 | (h) | Preston NE | W | 2-0 | Lyons, Peart | 12 |
| 34 | 20 | (a) | Bradford PA | D | 1-1 | Burton | 15 |
| 35 | 27 | (h) | Bradford PA | D | 0-0 | | 14 |
| 36 | Apr 2 | (a) | Everton | L | 0-4 | | 30 |
| 37 | 3 | (a) | Liverpool | L | 0-3 | | 35 |
| 38 | 5 | (h) | Everton | W | 2-1 | Atkin, Lyons | 18 |
| 39 | 10 | (h) | Liverpool | W | 3-0 | Burton 2, Leonard (pen) | 10 |
| 40 | 17 | (a) | Chelsea | D | 0-0 | | 40 |
| 41 | 24 | (h) | Chelsea | W | 5-0 | Burton 2, Lyons, Leonard, Thornewell | 21 |
| 42 | May 1 | (h) | Newcastle U | W | 1-0 | Leonard | 21 |

FINAL LEAGUE POSITION: 18th in Division One

Appearan…
G…

## FA Cup

| | | | | | | | |
|---|---|---|---|---|---|---|---|
| 1 | Jan 10 | (a) | Blackpool | D | 0-0 | | 10 |
| R | 14 | (h) | Blackpool | L | 1-4 | Burton | 20 |

Appearan…
G…

| Lawrence G | Atkin J | Barbour T | Bagshaw J | Wightman H | Martin B | Thornewell G | Moore J | Leonard H | Burton N | Baker W | Walker H | Ritchie W | Quantrill A | Kidd J | Howard F | Moore R | Leigh S | Boxley H | Ainsworth F | Needham G | Chandler A | Lyons J | Peart J | Shepherd G | Lampht T | Waterhouse F | |
|---|---|---|---|---|---|---|---|---|---|---|---|---|---|---|---|---|---|---|---|---|---|---|---|---|---|---|---|
| | 2 | 3 | 4 | 5 | 6 | 7 | 8 | 9 | 10 | 11 | | | | | | | | | | | | | | | | | 1 |
| | 2 | 3 | 4 | 5 | 6 | 7 | 8 | 9 | 10 | 11 | | | | | | | | | | | | | | | | | 2 |
| | 2 | 3 | 6 | 5 | | 7 | 8 | 9 | 10 | 11 | 4 | | | | | | | | | | | | | | | | 3 |
| | 2 | 3 | 4 | 5 | | 7 | | 9 | 10 | | 6 | 8 | 11 | | | | | | | | | | | | | | 4 |
| | 2 | 3 | 4 | 5 | | 7 | | 9 | 10 | | 6 | 8 | 11 | | | | | | | | | | | | | | 5 |
| | 2 | 3 | 4 | 5 | | 7 | | 9 | 10 | 11 | 6 | | 8 | | | | | | | | | | | | | | 6 |
| | 2 | 3 | 4 | 5 | | 7 | | 9 | 10 | | 6 | | 11 | 1 | 8 | | | | | | | | | | | | 7 |
| | 2 | 3 | 4 | 5 | | 7 | 8 | 9 | 10 | | 6 | | 11 | 1 | | | | | | | | | | | | | 8 |
| | 2 | 3 | 4 | 5 | | 7 | 8 | 9 | | | 6 | | 11 | | 10 | | | | | | | | | | | | 9 |
| | 2 | 3 | 4 | 5 | 6 | 7 | 8 | 9 | 10 | | | | 11 | | | | | | | | | | | | | | 10 |
| | 2 | 3 | | 5 | 6 | 7 | 8 | 9 | 10 | 11 | 4 | | | | | | | | | | | | | | | | 11 |
| | 2 | 3 | | 5 | | 7 | 8 | 9 | 6 | | 4 | | 11 | | | 10 | | | | | | | | | | | 12 |
| | 2 | 3 | 4 | 5 | | 7 | 10 | | 6 | | | | 11 | | 8 | | 9 | | | | | | | | | | 13 |
| | 2 | 3 | 4 | 5 | | 7 | | 9 | 10 | | 6 | | 11 | | 8 | | | | | | | | | | | | 14 |
| | 2 | 3 | 4 | 5 | | 7 | | 9 | 10 | | 6 | | 11 | | 8 | | | | | | | | | | | | 15 |
| | 2 | 3 | 4 | 5 | | 7 | 8 | 9 | 10 | | 6 | | 11 | | | | | | | | | | | | | | 16 |
| | 2 | 3 | | 5 | | 7 | | 9 | 10 | | 6 | 8 | 11 | | | | | 4 | | | | | | | | | 17 |
| | 2 | 3 | | 5 | | 7 | | | 10 | | 6 | 8 | 11 | | | | 9 | 4 | | | | | | | | | 18 |
| | 2 | 3 | 6 | 5 | | 7 | | | 9 | | 8 | | 11 | | | | | 4 | 10 | | | | | | | | 19 |
| | 2 | 3 | 6 | 5 | | 7 | | | 10 | | 8 | | 11 | | | | | 4 | | 9 | | | | | | | 20 |
| | 2 | 6 | | 5 | | 7 | | 9 | 10 | | 8 | | 11 | | | | | 4 | | | 3 | | | | | | 21 |
| | 2 | | 6 | 5 | | 7 | | 9 | 10 | | 8 | | 11 | | | | | 4 | | | 3 | | | | | | 22 |
| | 2 | | 4 | 5 | | 7 | | | 9 | 11 | 10 | | 8 | | | | | | | 6 | 3 | | | | | | 23 |
| | 2 | 4 | | 5 | | 7 | 8 | 9 | 10 | | 6 | | 11 | | | | | | | | 3 | | | | | | 24 |
| | 2 | 4 | | 5 | | 7 | 10 | 9 | | | 6 | | 11 | | | | | | | | 3 | 8 | | | | | 25 |
| | 2 | 4 | | 5 | | 7 | 10 | | | | 6 | | 11 | | | | | | | | 3 | 8 | 9 | | | | 26 |
| | 2 | 4 | | 5 | | 7 | 10 | | | | 6 | | 11 | | | | | | | | 3 | 8 | 9 | | | | 27 |
| | 2 | | | 5 | | 7 | 11 | | 10 | | 4 | | | | | | | | | 6 | 3 | 8 | 9 | | | | 28 |
| | 2 | 3 | | 5 | | 7 | 10 | | | | 4 | | 11 | | | | | | | 6 | | 8 | 9 | | | | 29 |
| | 2 | 3 | | 5 | | 7 | | 9 | | | | | 11 | 1 | | | | 4 | | 6 | | 8 | 10 | | | | 30 |
| | 2 | 3 | | 5 | | 7 | | | | | 4 | | 11 | 1 | | | | | | | 6 | 8 | 9 | 10 | | | 31 |
| | 2 | 3 | | 5 | 6 | 7 | | | 10 | | 4 | | 11 | 1 | | | | | | | | 8 | 9 | | | | 32 |
| | 2 | 3 | | 5 | 6 | 7 | | | 10 | | | | 11 | 1 | | | | | | | | 8 | 9 | | 4 | | 33 |
| | 2 | 3 | | 5 | | 7 | | | 10 | | | | 11 | 1 | | | | | | | | 8 | 9 | | 6 | 4 | 34 |
| | 2 | 3 | | 5 | | 7 | | 9 | 10 | | | | 11 | 1 | | | | | | | | 8 | | | 6 | 4 | 35 |
| | 2 | 3 | | 5 | | 7 | | 9 | 10 | | | | 11 | 1 | | | | | | | | 8 | | | 6 | 4 | 36 |
| | 2 | 3 | | 5 | | 7 | | 9 | 10 | | | | 11 | 1 | | | | | | | | 8 | | | 6 | 4 | 37 |
| | 2 | 3 | | 5 | | 7 | | 9 | 10 | | | | 11 | | | | | | | | | 8 | | | 6 | 4 | 38 |
| | 2 | | | 5 | | 7 | 11 | 9 | 10 | | | | | | | | | | | | 3 | 8 | | | 6 | 4 | 39 |
| | 2 | | | 5 | | 7 | | 9 | 10 | | | | 11 | | | | | | | | 3 | 8 | | | 6 | 4 | 40 |
| | 2 | 3 | | 5 | | 7 | | 9 | 10 | | | | 11 | | | | | | | | | 8 | | | 6 | 4 | 41 |
| | 2 | 3 | | 5 | | 7 | | 9 | 10 | | | | 11 | | | | | | | | | 8 | | | 6 | 4 | 42 |
| 2 | 42 | 37 | 18 | 42 | 6 | 42 | 17 | 29 | 35 | 6 | 27 | 4 | 36 | 10 | 5 | 1 | 2 | 7 | 1 | 5 | 11 | 18 | 9 | 1 | 10 | 9 | |
| | 1 | 1 | 1 | 3 | | 3 | 3 | 12 | 12 | 1 | | 1 | 2 | | | | | | | | | 6 | 1 | | | | |

| | | | | | | | | | | | | | | | | | | | | | | | | | | | |
|---|---|---|---|---|---|---|---|---|---|---|---|---|---|---|---|---|---|---|---|---|---|---|---|---|---|---|---|
| | 2 | 4 | | 5 | | 7 | 8 | 9 | 10 | | 6 | | 11 | | | | | | | | 3 | | | | | | 1 |
| 1 | 2 | 4 | | 5 | | 7 | 8 | 9 | 10 | | 6 | | 11 | | | | | | | | 3 | | | | | | R |
| 2 | 2 | 2 | | 2 | | 2 | 2 | 2 | 2 | | 2 | | 2 | | | | | | | | 2 | | | | | | |
| | | | | | | | | | 1 | | | | | | | | | | | | | | | | | | |

# 1920-21

| | P | W | D | L | F | A | Pts |
|---|---|---|---|---|---|---|---|
| Burnley | 42 | 23 | 13 | 6 | 79 | 36 | 59 |
| Manchester C | 42 | 24 | 6 | 12 | 70 | 50 | 54 |
| Bolton W | 42 | 19 | 14 | 9 | 77 | 53 | 52 |
| Liverpool | 42 | 18 | 15 | 9 | 63 | 35 | 51 |
| Newcastle U | 42 | 20 | 10 | 12 | 66 | 45 | 50 |
| Tottenham H | 42 | 19 | 9 | 14 | 70 | 48 | 47 |
| Everton | 42 | 17 | 13 | 12 | 66 | 55 | 47 |
| Middlesbrough | 42 | 17 | 12 | 13 | 53 | 53 | 46 |
| Arsenal | 42 | 15 | 14 | 13 | 59 | 63 | 44 |
| Aston Villa | 42 | 18 | 7 | 17 | 63 | 70 | 43 |
| Blackburn R | 42 | 13 | 15 | 14 | 57 | 59 | 41 |
| Sunderland | 42 | 14 | 13 | 15 | 57 | 60 | 41 |
| Manchester U | 42 | 15 | 10 | 17 | 64 | 68 | 40 |
| WBA | 42 | 13 | 14 | 15 | 54 | 58 | 40 |
| Bradford C | 42 | 12 | 15 | 15 | 61 | 63 | 39 |
| Preston NE | 42 | 15 | 9 | 18 | 61 | 65 | 39 |
| Huddersfield T | 42 | 15 | 9 | 18 | 42 | 49 | 39 |
| Chelsea | 42 | 13 | 13 | 16 | 48 | 58 | 39 |
| Oldham A | 42 | 9 | 15 | 18 | 49 | 86 | 33 |
| Sheffield U | 42 | 6 | 18 | 18 | 42 | 68 | 30 |
| Derby Co | 42 | 5 | 16 | 21 | 32 | 58 | 26 |
| Bradford PA | 42 | 8 | 8 | 26 | 43 | 76 | 24 |

Manager: Jimmy Methven.
Leading scorer: Bill Paterson, League/all matches 8.

- Derby equalled their record of 1905–06 by using 32 players in League matches. Not until 2001–02 did they field more.
- They set an unwelcome club record with only 32 goals, their thinnest ever scoring season.
- More than 11 years after joining Bradford City from Derby, Harry Maskrey returned for five matches in a goalkeeping emergency. He was 40 and playing for British Cellulose in the midweek Works League.
- Tewfik Abdallah, spotted by Tommy Barbour when he was serving in the Near East, became the second Egyptian to appear in League football. Hassan Hegazi, an amateur with Dulwich Hamlet, played once for Fulham in 1911–12.

## Division One

| Match No. | Date | | Venue | Opponents | Result | | Scorers | Atten |
|---|---|---|---|---|---|---|---|---|
| 1 | Aug | 28 | (h) | Chelsea | D | 0-0 | | 21, |
| 2 | | 30 | (h) | Tottenham H | D | 2-2 | Burton, Lyons | 18 |
| 3 | Sep | 4 | (a) | Chelsea | D | 1-1 | Burton | 42, |
| 4 | | 6 | (a) | Tottenham H | L | 0-2 | | 26, |
| 5 | | 11 | (h) | Everton | L | 2-4 | Quantrill, Gardner | 17, |
| 6 | | 18 | (a) | Everton | L | 1-3 | Murray | 35 |
| 7 | | 25 | (h) | West Brom A | D | 1-1 | Quantrill | 16 |
| 8 | Oct | 2 | (a) | West Brom A | L | 0-3 | | 25 |
| 9 | | 9 | (h) | Manchester C | W | 3-0 | Burton, Murray, Abdallah | 18 |
| 10 | | 16 | (a) | Manchester C | D | 0-0 | | 35 |
| 11 | | 23 | (h) | Arsenal | D | 1-1 | Thornewell | 19, |
| 12 | | 30 | (a) | Arsenal | L | 0-2 | | 45, |
| 13 | Nov | 6 | (h) | Bolton W | D | 0-0 | | 15, |
| 14 | | 13 | (a) | Bolton W | L | 0-1 | | 25, |
| 15 | | 20 | (a) | Middlesbrough | L | 0-1 | | 30, |
| 16 | | 27 | (h) | Middlesbrough | L | 0-1 | | 12, |
| 17 | Dec | 4 | (a) | Blackburn R | L | 0-2 | | 25, |
| 18 | | 11 | (h) | Blackburn R | L | 0-1 | | 14, |
| 19 | | 18 | (a) | Huddersfield T | L | 0-2 | | 12, |
| 20 | | 25 | (a) | Bradford C | D | 2-2 | Thornewell, Burton | 28, |
| 21 | | 27 | (h) | Bradford C | D | 1-1 | Atkin (pen) | 23, |
| 22 | Jan | 1 | (h) | Huddersfield T | W | 2-1 | Atkin (pen), Thornewell | 12, |
| 23 | | 15 | (a) | Preston NE | L | 1-2 | Quantrill | 17, |
| 24 | | 22 | (h) | Preston NE | D | 1-1 | Paterson | 16, |
| 25 | Feb | 5 | (h) | Oldham A | D | 3-3 | Paterson 2, Moore | 15, |
| 26 | | 12 | (a) | Burnley | L | 1-2 | Paterson | 30, |
| 27 | | 14 | (a) | Oldham A | L | 1-2 | Morton | 21, |
| 28 | | 23 | (h) | Burnley | D | 0-0 | | 16, |
| 29 | | 26 | (a) | Sheffield U | W | 1-0 | Paterson | 35, |
| 30 | Mar | 5 | (h) | Sheffield U | D | 1-1 | Paterson | 16, |
| 31 | | 12 | (a) | Bradford PA | L | 1-2 | Murray | 16, |
| 32 | | 19 | (h) | Bradford PA | W | 1-0 | Paterson | 16, |
| 33 | | 25 | (a) | Sunderland | L | 0-3 | | 20, |
| 34 | | 26 | (h) | Newcastle U | L | 0-1 | | 20, |
| 35 | | 28 | (h) | Sunderland | L | 0-1 | | 16, |
| 36 | Apr | 2 | (a) | Newcastle U | W | 1-0 | Lyons | 30, |
| 37 | | 9 | (h) | Liverpool | D | 0-0 | | 10, |
| 38 | | 16 | (a) | Liverpool | D | 1-1 | Storer | 30, |
| 39 | | 23 | (h) | Aston Villa | L | 2-3 | Moore, Paterson | 14, |
| 40 | | 30 | (a) | Aston Villa | L | 0-1 | | 20, |
| 41 | May | 2 | (h) | Manchester U | D | 1-1 | Ritchie (pen) | 8, |
| 42 | | 7 | (a) | Manchester U | L | 0-3 | | 10, |

FINAL LEAGUE POSITION: 21st in Division One – Relegated

Appearan

G

## FA Cup

| | | | | | | | | |
|---|---|---|---|---|---|---|---|---|
| 1 | Jan | 8 | (h) | Middlesbrough | W | 2-0 | Murray, Burton | 23, |
| 2 | | 29 | (h) | Wolves | D | 1-1 | Thornewell | 25, |
| R | Feb | 3 | (a) | Wolves | L | 0-1 | | 39, |

Appearan

G

| Kidd J | Atkin J | Ritchie A | Waterhouse F | Wightman H | McLaverty B | Thornewell G | Burton N | Lyons J | Murray W | Quantrill A | Gardner W | Maskrey H | Barbour T | Lievesley W | Shiner A | Lawrence G | Moore J | Lamph T | Abdallah T | Baker W | Morton W | Shepherd G | Chandler A | Paterson W | Thompson H | Bayliss R | Storer H | Rance C | Olney B | Hannay J | Minney G | |
|---|---|---|---|---|---|---|---|---|---|---|---|---|---|---|---|---|---|---|---|---|---|---|---|---|---|---|---|---|---|---|---|---|
| | 2 | 3 | 4 | 5 | 6 | 7 | 8 | 9 | 10 | 11 | | | | | | | | | | | | | | | | | | | | | | 1 |
| | 2 | 3 | 4 | 5 | 6 | 7 | 10 | 8 | | 11 | 9 | | | | | | | | | | | | | | | | | | | | | 2 |
| | 2 | 3 | 4 | | 5 | 7 | 8 | | 10 | 11 | 9 | 1 | 6 | | | | | | | | | | | | | | | | | | | 3 |
| | 2 | 3 | 4 | | 5 | 7 | | | 10 | 11 | 9 | 1 | 6 | 8 | | | | | | | | | | | | | | | | | | 4 |
| | 2 | 3 | 4 | 5 | 6 | 7 | 10 | 8 | | 11 | 9 | 1 | | | | | | | | | | | | | | | | | | | | 5 |
| | 2 | 3 | 4 | 5 | 6 | 7 | | 8 | 10 | 11 | | | | | 9 | | | | | | | | | | | | | | | | | 6 |
| | 2 | 3 | 4 | 5 | 6 | 7 | | 9 | 10 | 11 | | | | | | 1 | 8 | | | | | | | | | | | | | | | 7 |
| | 2 | 3 | 4 | 5 | | | 8 | 9 | 10 | 11 | | | | | | 1 | 7 | 6 | | | | | | | | | | | | | | 8 |
| | 2 | 3 | 4 | 5 | | 7 | 9 | | 10 | 11 | | | | | | 1 | | 6 | 8 | | | | | | | | | | | | | 9 |
| | 2 | 3 | 4 | 5 | | 7 | 9 | | | 11 | | | | | | 1 | 10 | 6 | 8 | | | | | | | | | | | | | 10 |
| | 2 | | 4 | 5 | | 7 | 9 | | | | | | 3 | | | 1 | 10 | 6 | 8 | 11 | | | | | | | | | | | | 11 |
| | 2 | | 4 | 5 | | 7 | 9 | | 10 | 11 | | | 3 | | | 1 | | | 8 | | 6 | | | | | | | | | | | 12 |
| | 2 | | 4 | 5 | | 7 | 9 | | 10 | 11 | | | 3 | | | 1 | | | 8 | | 6 | | | | | | | | | | | 13 |
| | 2 | 5 | | 9 | 4 | 7 | | 8 | 10 | | | | 3 | | | 1 | | | | 11 | 6 | | | | | | | | | | | 14 |
| | 2 | 4 | | 5 | | 7 | 9 | 8 | 10 | 11 | | | 3 | | | 1 | | | | | 6 | | | | | | | | | | | 15 |
| | | 3 | 4 | 2 | 5 | 7 | 9 | 8 | 10 | 11 | | 1 | | | | | | | | | 6 | | | | | | | | | | | 16 |
| | 2 | 3 | | 5 | 4 | 7 | | 8 | 10 | | | 1 | | | | | 9 | 6 | | | | 11 | | | | | | | | | | 17 |
| | 2 | 6 | 4 | | 5 | 7 | | | | 11 | | | 3 | | | 1 | 10 | | 8 | | | | 9 | | | | | | | | | 18 |
| | 2 | 6 | | 5 | 4 | 7 | 9 | | | 11 | | | 3 | | | 1 | 10 | | 8 | | | | | | | | | | | | | 19 |
| | 2 | 6 | | 5 | 4 | 7 | 8 | | 10 | 11 | | | 3 | | | 1 | 9 | | | | | | | | | | | | | | | 20 |
| | 2 | 6 | | 5 | 4 | 7 | 8 | | 10 | 11 | | | 3 | | | 1 | 9 | | | | | | | | | | | | | | | 21 |
| | 2 | 6 | 4 | 5 | | 7 | 8 | | 10 | 11 | | | 3 | | | 1 | 9 | | | | | | | | | | | | | | | 22 |
| | 2 | 6 | 4 | 5 | | 7 | 8 | | | 11 | 10 | | 3 | | | 1 | 9 | | | | | | | | | | | | | | | 23 |
| | 2 | 6 | | 5 | | 7 | 4 | | 10 | 11 | | | 3 | | | 1 | 8 | | | | | | | 9 | | | | | | | | 24 |
| | 2 | 6 | | | | 7 | | | 10 | | | | 3 | | | 1 | 11 | 4 | | | 5 | | | 9 | 8 | | | | | | | 25 |
| | 2 | 6 | | 5 | | 7 | | | 10 | | | | 3 | | | 1 | 11 | | | | 4 | | | 9 | 8 | | | | | | | 26 |
| | 2 | 6 | | 5 | | 7 | | | 10 | | | | | | | 1 | 11 | | | | 4 | | 3 | 9 | 8 | | | | | | | 27 |
| 1 | 2 | 3 | | 5 | 6 | 7 | | | 10 | | | | | | | | 11 | | | | 4 | | | 9 | 8 | | | | | | | 28 |
| 1 | 2 | 3 | | 5 | 6 | 7 | | | 10 | | | | | | | | 8 | | | | 4 | | | 9 | | 11 | | | | | | 29 |
| 1 | 2 | 3 | | 5 | 6 | 7 | 8 | | 10 | 11 | | | | | | | | | | | 4 | | | 9 | | | | | | | | 30 |
| 1 | 2 | 3 | | 5 | 4 | 7 | | | 10 | 11 | | | | | | | 8 | | | | | | | 9 | | | 6 | | | | | 31 |
| | 2 | 3 | | | | 7 | | | 10 | 11 | | | | | | 1 | 8 | | | | 4 | | | 9 | | | 6 | 5 | | | | 32 |
| | 2 | 3 | | | | 7 | | | 10 | 11 | | | | | | 1 | 8 | | | | 4 | | | 9 | | | 6 | 5 | | | | 33 |
| | | 3 | | | 4 | 7 | | | 10 | 11 | | | | | | 1 | 8 | | | | 2 | | | 9 | | | 6 | 5 | | | | 34 |
| | | 3 | | 5 | | 7 | 10 | 8 | | 11 | | | | | | 1 | | | | | 4 | | 2 | 9 | | | 6 | | | | | 35 |
| | | 3 | | | | 7 | | 8 | 11 | | | | | | | 1 | 10 | | | | 4 | | 2 | 9 | | | 6 | 5 | | | | 36 |
| | | 3 | | | | 7 | | 8 | | 11 | | | | | | 1 | 10 | | | | 4 | | 2 | 9 | | | 6 | 5 | | | | 37 |
| | | 3 | | | | | | | 7 | 11 | | | | | | 1 | 10 | | 8 | | 4 | | 2 | 9 | | | 6 | 5 | | | | 38 |
| | | 3 | | | | | | | 7 | 11 | | | | | | 1 | 10 | | 8 | | 4 | | 2 | 9 | | | 6 | 5 | | | | 39 |
| | | 3 | | | | 7 | | | 10 | 11 | | | | | | 1 | | | 8 | | 4 | | 2 | 9 | | | 6 | 5 | | | | 40 |
| | | 3 | | | | | 10 | | | 11 | | | | | | | | | 8 | | 4 | | 2 | | | | 6 | 5 | 1 | 7 | 9 | 41 |
| | | 3 | | | | | | | | 7 | | | | | | | 10 | | 8 | 11 | 4 | | 2 | | | | 6 | 5 | 1 | | 9 | 42 |
| 7 | 32 | 39 | 17 | 28 | 19 | 37 | 21 | 13 | 31 | 33 | 5 | 5 | 16 | 1 | 1 | 28 | 26 | 6 | 12 | 3 | 22 | 1 | 10 | 17 | 4 | 1 | 12 | 10 | 2 | 1 | 2 | |
| | 2 | 1 | | | | 3 | 4 | 2 | 3 | 3 | 1 | | | | | | 2 | | 1 | | 1 | | | 8 | | | 1 | | | | | |

| Kidd J | Atkin J | Ritchie A | Waterhouse F | Wightman H | McLaverty B | Thornewell G | Burton N | Lyons J | Murray W | Quantrill A | Gardner W | Maskrey H | Barbour T | Lievesley W | Shiner A | Lawrence G | Moore J | Lamph T | Abdallah T | Baker W | Morton W | Shepherd G | Chandler A | Paterson W | Thompson H | Bayliss R | Storer H | Rance C | Olney B | Hannay J | Minney G | |
|---|---|---|---|---|---|---|---|---|---|---|---|---|---|---|---|---|---|---|---|---|---|---|---|---|---|---|---|---|---|---|---|---|
| | 2 | 6 | 4 | 5 | | 7 | 8 | | 10 | 11 | | | 3 | | | 1 | 9 | | | | | | | | | | | | | | | 1 |
| | 2 | 6 | 4 | 5 | | 7 | 8 | | 10 | | | | 3 | | | 1 | 11 | | | | | | | 9 | | | | | | | | 2 |
| | 2 | 6 | | | | 7 | 8 | | 10 | | | | 3 | | | 1 | 11 | 4 | | | 5 | | | 9 | | | | | | | | R |
| | 3 | 3 | 2 | 2 | | 3 | 3 | | 3 | 1 | | | 3 | | | 3 | 3 | 1 | | | 1 | | | 2 | | | | | | | | |
| | | | | | | 1 | 1 | | 1 | | | | | | | | | | | | | | | | | | | | | | | |

# 1921-22

| | P | W | D | L | F | A | Pts |
|---|---|---|---|---|---|---|---|
| Nottingham F | 42 | 22 | 12 | 8 | 51 | 30 | 56 |
| Stoke | 42 | 18 | 16 | 8 | 60 | 44 | 52 |
| Barnsley | 42 | 22 | 8 | 12 | 67 | 52 | 52 |
| West Ham U | 42 | 20 | 8 | 14 | 52 | 39 | 48 |
| Hull C | 42 | 19 | 10 | 13 | 51 | 41 | 48 |
| South Shields | 42 | 17 | 12 | 13 | 43 | 38 | 46 |
| Fulham | 42 | 18 | 9 | 15 | 57 | 38 | 45 |
| Leeds U | 42 | 16 | 13 | 13 | 48 | 38 | 45 |
| Leicester C | 42 | 14 | 17 | 11 | 39 | 34 | 45 |
| Sheffield W | 42 | 15 | 14 | 13 | 47 | 50 | 44 |
| Bury | 42 | 15 | 10 | 17 | 54 | 55 | 40 |
| Derby Co | 42 | 15 | 9 | 18 | 60 | 64 | 39 |
| Notts Co | 42 | 12 | 15 | 15 | 47 | 51 | 39 |
| Crystal Palace | 42 | 13 | 13 | 16 | 45 | 51 | 39 |
| Clapton O | 42 | 15 | 9 | 18 | 43 | 50 | 39 |
| Rotherham C | 42 | 14 | 11 | 17 | 32 | 43 | 39 |
| Wolves | 42 | 13 | 11 | 18 | 44 | 49 | 37 |
| Port Vale | 42 | 14 | 8 | 20 | 43 | 57 | 36 |
| Blackpool | 42 | 15 | 5 | 22 | 44 | 57 | 35 |
| Coventry C | 42 | 12 | 10 | 20 | 51 | 60 | 34 |
| Bradford P.A. | 42 | 12 | 9 | 21 | 46 | 62 | 33 |
| Bristol C | 42 | 12 | 9 | 21 | 37 | 58 | 33 |

Manager: Jimmy Methven.
Leading scorer: Jimmy Moore, League 16, all matches 17.
League ever-present: Albert Chandler.

- After 31 years, as player and then manager, Jimmy Methven left Derby County. He was 53, suffering from glaucoma and underwent an unsuccessful eye operation.
- It was a subdued end, Derby finishing in the lowest League position they occupied to that date.
- Jimmy Lyons, once suspended by Derby for 'insubordination', scored all four goals in the home victory over Rotherham County in April.

## Division Two

| Match No. | Date | | Venue | Opponents | Result | | Scorers | Atten |
|---|---|---|---|---|---|---|---|---|
| 1 | Aug | 27 | (a) | Blackpool | L | 2-4 | McIntyre, Moore | 16, |
| 2 | | 29 | (h) | Sheffield W | L | 0-1 | | 12, |
| 3 | Sep | 3 | (h) | Blackpool | W | 1-0 | Pattison | 10, |
| 4 | | 5 | (a) | Sheffield W | D | 1-1 | Moore | 15, |
| 5 | | 10 | (h) | Bristol C | W | 5-1 | Paterson 3, Moore, Thornewell | 12, |
| 6 | | 17 | (a) | Bristol C | W | 2-1 | Moore 2 | 13, |
| 7 | | 24 | (h) | Nottingham F | L | 1-2 | Paterson | 22, |
| 8 | Oct | 1 | (a) | Nottingham F | L | 0-3 | | 28, |
| 9 | | 8 | (h) | Wolves | L | 2-3 | Moore 2 | 10, |
| 10 | | 15 | (a) | Wolves | W | 3-0 | Thornewell, Paterson, Keetley | 15, |
| 11 | | 22 | (a) | Barnsley | L | 1-2 | Wightman | 10, |
| 12 | | 29 | (h) | Barnsley | W | 1-0 | Moore | 11, |
| 13 | Nov | 5 | (h) | Coventry C | W | 1-0 | Wightman (pen) | 10, |
| 14 | | 17 | (a) | Coventry C | W | 2-1 | Paterson, Keetley | 8, |
| 15 | | 19 | (h) | Bury | W | 1-0 | Paterson | 8, |
| 16 | | 26 | (a) | Bury | L | 0-2 | | 10, |
| 17 | Dec | 3 | (h) | Leicester C | L | 0-1 | | 10, |
| 18 | | 10 | (a) | Leicester C | D | 1-1 | Moore | 20, |
| 19 | | 17 | (a) | West Ham U | L | 1-3 | Moore | 20, |
| 20 | | 24 | (h) | West Ham U | W | 3-1 | Moore, Keetley, Jackson | 12, |
| 21 | | 26 | (a) | Port Vale | D | 1-1 | Pattison | 11, |
| 22 | | 27 | (h) | Port Vale | W | 3-2 | Jackson, Lyons, Moore | 19, |
| 23 | | 31 | (h) | Fulham | D | 1-1 | Jackson | 12, |
| 24 | Jan | 14 | (a) | Fulham | D | 2-2 | Keetley, Lyons | 18, |
| 25 | | 21 | (a) | Bradford PA | L | 1-5 | Lyons | 7, |
| 26 | Feb | 4 | (a) | Clapton O | L | 2-3 | Lyons, Moore | 7, |
| 27 | | 11 | (h) | Clapton O | W | 3-0 | Moore, Lyons, Jackson | 10, |
| 28 | | 18 | (h) | Bradford PA | L | 1-3 | Murphy | 10, |
| 29 | | 25 | (h) | Stoke | L | 2-4 | Lyons, Knowles | 10, |
| 30 | Mar | 4 | (a) | Leeds U | L | 1-2 | Murphy | 12, |
| 31 | | 6 | (a) | Stoke | D | 1-1 | Paterson | 12, |
| 32 | | 11 | (h) | Leeds U | W | 2-0 | Paterson, Wightman (pen) | 9, |
| 33 | | 18 | (h) | Hull C | D | 0-0 | | 9, |
| 34 | | 25 | (a) | Hull C | D | 1-1 | Paterson | 8, |
| 35 | Apr | 1 | (h) | Notts C | D | 1-1 | Storer | 12, |
| 36 | | 8 | (a) | Notts C | W | 2-1 | Storer, Paterson | 6, |
| 37 | | 14 | (a) | South Shields | L | 1-3 | Lyons | 6, |
| 38 | | 15 | (h) | Crystal P | W | 2-0 | Moore 2 | 9, |
| 39 | | 17 | (h) | South Shields | L | 0-2 | | 12, |
| 40 | | 22 | (a) | Crystal P | L | 1-3 | Lyons | 6, |
| 41 | | 29 | (h) | Rotherham C | W | 4-0 | Lyons 4 | 7, |
| 42 | May | 6 | (a) | Rotherham C | L | 0-2 | | 8, |

FINAL LEAGUE POSITION: 12th in Division Two

Appearan
Gc

## FA Cup

| | | | | | | | | |
|---|---|---|---|---|---|---|---|---|
| 1 | Jan | 7 | (a) | Aston Villa | L | 1-6 | Moore | 41, |

Appearan
Go

| dd J | Chandler A | Ritchie A | Morton W | Rance C | Storer H | Thornewell G | McIntyre J | Paterson W | Moore J | Barnes J | Webb G | Lawrence G | McLaverty B | Pattison J | Abdallah T | Wightman H | Keetley F | Birdsall G | Walton J | Lyons J | Jackson J | Olney B | Taylor R | Murphy L | Robson JW | Knowles F | Callan W | Plackett S | Atkin J | |
|---|---|---|---|---|---|---|---|---|---|---|---|---|---|---|---|---|---|---|---|---|---|---|---|---|---|---|---|---|---|---|
| | 2 | 3 | 4 | 5 | 6 | 7 | 8 | 9 | 10 | 11 | | | | | | | | | | | | | | | | | | | | 1 |
| | 2 | 3 | 4 | 5 | | 7 | 8 | 9 | 10 | 11 | 6 | | | | | | | | | | | | | | | | | | | 2 |
| | 2 | 3 | | 5 | 6 | 7 | 8 | 9 | 10 | | | 1 | 4 | 11 | | | | | | | | | | | | | | | | 3 |
| | 2 | 3 | | 5 | 6 | 7 | 8 | 9 | 10 | | | 1 | 4 | 11 | | | | | | | | | | | | | | | | 4 |
| | 2 | 3 | | 5 | 6 | 7 | | 9 | 10 | | | 1 | 4 | 11 | 8 | | | | | | | | | | | | | | | 5 |
| | 2 | 3 | | 5 | 6 | 7 | | 9 | 10 | | | 1 | 4 | 11 | 8 | | | | | | | | | | | | | | | 6 |
| | 2 | 3 | | 5 | 6 | 7 | | 9 | 10 | 11 | | 1 | 4 | | 8 | | | | | | | | | | | | | | | 7 |
| | 2 | 3 | | | 6 | 7 | | 9 | 10 | | | 1 | 4 | 11 | | 5 | 8 | | | | | | | | | | | | | 8 |
| | 2 | 3 | | 5 | 6 | 7 | | 9 | 10 | | | 1 | 4 | 11 | | | 8 | | | | | | | | | | | | | 9 |
| | 2 | 3 | | | 6 | 7 | | 9 | 10 | | | 1 | 4 | 11 | | 5 | 8 | | | | | | | | | | | | | 10 |
| | 2 | 3 | | | 6 | 7 | | 9 | 10 | | | 1 | 4 | 11 | | 5 | 8 | | | | | | | | | | | | | 11 |
| | 2 | 3 | | | 6 | 7 | | 9 | 10 | | | | 4 | 11 | | 5 | 8 | | | | | | | | | | | | | 12 |
| | 2 | 3 | | | 6 | 7 | | 9 | 10 | | | 1 | 4 | 11 | | 5 | 8 | | | | | | | | | | | | | 13 |
| | 2 | 3 | | | 6 | 7 | | 9 | 10 | | | 1 | 4 | | | 5 | 8 | 11 | | | | | | | | | | | | 14 |
| | 2 | 3 | | | 6 | 7 | 10 | 9 | | | | 1 | 4 | | | 5 | 8 | 11 | | | | | | | | | | | | 15 |
| | 2 | 3 | | | 6 | 7 | 11 | 9 | 10 | | | 1 | 4 | | | 5 | 8 | | | | | | | | | | | | | 16 |
| | 2 | 3 | | | 9 | 7 | | | 10 | | | 1 | 4 | 11 | | 5 | 8 | | 6 | | | | | | | | | | | 17 |
| | 2 | 3 | | | 6 | 11 | 8 | 9 | 10 | | | 1 | 4 | | | 5 | 7 | | | | | | | | | | | | | 18 |
| | 2 | 3 | | | 6 | 11 | 8 | 9 | 10 | | | 1 | 4 | | | 5 | 7 | | | | | | | | | | | | | 19 |
| | 2 | | | | 3 | | | | 10 | | | 1 | 4 | 11 | | 5 | 7 | | 6 | 8 | 9 | | | | | | | | | 20 |
| | 2 | | | | 3 | | | | 10 | | | 1 | 4 | 11 | | 5 | 7 | | 6 | 8 | 9 | | | | | | | | | 21 |
| | 2 | | | | 3 | | 4 | | 10 | | | 1 | 5 | 11 | | | 7 | | 6 | 8 | 9 | | | | | | | | | 22 |
| | 2 | | | | 3 | | | | 10 | | 11 | 1 | 4 | | | 5 | 7 | | 6 | 8 | 9 | | | | | | | | | 23 |
| | 2 | | | 5 | 6 | | 4 | | 10 | | | | | 11 | | | 7 | 3 | | 8 | 9 | 1 | | | | | | | | 24 |
| | 2 | | | 5 | 6 | | 4 | | 10 | | | | | | | | 7 | 3 | | 8 | 9 | 1 | 11 | | | | | | | 25 |
| | 2 | | | | 6 | | 4 | | 10 | | | 1 | | | | 5 | 7 | 3 | | 8 | 9 | | 11 | | | | | | | 26 |
| | 2 | | | | 6 | | 4 | | 10 | | | 1 | | | | 5 | 7 | 3 | | 8 | 9 | | | 11 | | | | | | 27 |
| | 2 | | | | 6 | | 4 | | 10 | | | 1 | | | | 5 | 7 | 3 | | 8 | 9 | | | 11 | | | | | | 28 |
| | 2 | | | | 3 | | 4 | | | | | | | | | | 7 | | 6 | 8 | 10 | 1 | | 11 | 5 | 9 | | | | 29 |
| | 2 | | | | 3 | | 4 | 10 | | | | | | | | | 7 | | 6 | 8 | | 1 | | 11 | 5 | 9 | | | | 30 |
| | 2 | 3 | | | 6 | 7 | 4 | 9 | | | | | | | | | | | | 8 | 10 | 1 | | 11 | 5 | | | | | 31 |
| | 2 | 3 | | | 6 | | 4 | 9 | | | | | | | | 5 | 7 | | | 8 | 10 | 1 | | 11 | | | | | | 32 |
| | 2 | 3 | | | 6 | | 4 | 9 | | | | | | | | 5 | 7 | | | 8 | 10 | 1 | | 11 | | | | | | 33 |
| | 2 | 3 | | | 6 | 7 | 4 | 9 | | | | | | | | 5 | | | | 8 | | 1 | | 11 | | | 10 | | | 34 |
| | 2 | 3 | | | 10 | | 4 | 9 | | | | | 6 | | | 5 | | | | 8 | | 1 | | 11 | | 7 | | | | 35 |
| | 2 | 3 | | | 10 | | 4 | 9 | | | | | 6 | | | 5 | 7 | | | 8 | | 1 | | 11 | | | | | | 36 |
| | 2 | 3 | | | 10 | | 4 | | 9 | | | | 6 | | | 5 | 7 | | | 8 | | 1 | | 11 | | | | | | 37 |
| | 2 | 3 | | | 10 | | 4 | | 9 | | | | 6 | | | 5 | 7 | | | 8 | | 1 | | 11 | | | | | | 38 |
| | 2 | 3 | | | 10 | | 4 | | 9 | | | | | | | 5 | 7 | | | 8 | | 1 | | 11 | | | | 6 | | 39 |
| | 2 | | | 5 | 10 | | 4 | | 9 | | | | | | | | 7 | 3 | | 8 | | 1 | | 11 | | | | 6 | | 40 |
| | 2 | 3 | | 5 | 6 | 7 | | 9 | | 10 | | | 4 | | | | | | | 8 | | 1 | | 11 | | | | | | 41 |
| | 2 | 3 | | 5 | | 7 | 4 | 9 | 10 | | | | 6 | | | | | | | 8 | | 1 | | 11 | | | | | | 42 |
| 3 | 42 | 30 | 2 | 13 | 40 | 23 | 27 | 27 | 32 | 4 | 2 | 23 | 27 | 15 | 3 | 25 | 30 | 8 | 7 | 23 | 13 | 16 | 2 | 16 | 3 | 3 | 1 | 2 | | |
| | | | | | 2 | 2 | 1 | 11 | 16 | | | | | 2 | | 3 | 4 | | | 12 | 4 | | | 2 | | 1 | | | | |

| dd J | Chandler A | Ritchie A | Morton W | Rance C | Storer H | Thornewell G | McIntyre J | Paterson W | Moore J | Barnes J | Webb G | Lawrence G | McLaverty B | Pattison J | Abdallah T | Wightman H | Keetley F | Birdsall G | Walton J | Lyons J | Jackson J | Olney B | Taylor R | Murphy L | Robson JW | Knowles F | Callan W | Plackett S | Atkin J | |
|---|---|---|---|---|---|---|---|---|---|---|---|---|---|---|---|---|---|---|---|---|---|---|---|---|---|---|---|---|---|---|
| 1 | 3 | | | | 4 | 11 | | | 10 | | | | 5 | | | | 7 | | 6 | 8 | 9 | | | | | | | | 2 | 1 |
| 1 | 1 | | | | 1 | 1 | | | 1 | | | | 1 | | | | 1 | | 1 | 1 | 1 | | | | | | | | 1 | |
| | | | | | | | | | 1 | | | | | | | | | | | | | | | | | | | | | |

# 1922-23

| | P | W | D | L | F | A | Pts |
|---|---|---|---|---|---|---|---|
| Notts Co | 42 | 23 | 7 | 12 | 46 | 34 | 53 |
| West Ham U | 42 | 20 | 11 | 11 | 63 | 38 | 51 |
| Leicester C | 42 | 21 | 9 | 12 | 65 | 44 | 51 |
| Manchester U | 42 | 17 | 14 | 11 | 51 | 36 | 48 |
| Blackpool | 42 | 18 | 11 | 13 | 60 | 43 | 47 |
| Bury | 42 | 18 | 11 | 13 | 55 | 46 | 47 |
| Leeds U | 42 | 18 | 11 | 13 | 43 | 36 | 47 |
| Sheffield W | 42 | 17 | 12 | 13 | 54 | 47 | 46 |
| Barnsley | 42 | 17 | 11 | 14 | 62 | 51 | 45 |
| Fulham | 42 | 16 | 12 | 14 | 43 | 32 | 44 |
| Southampton | 42 | 14 | 14 | 14 | 40 | 40 | 42 |
| Hull C | 42 | 14 | 14 | 14 | 43 | 45 | 42 |
| South Shields | 42 | 15 | 10 | 17 | 35 | 44 | 40 |
| Derby Co | 42 | 14 | 11 | 17 | 46 | 50 | 39 |
| Bradford C | 42 | 12 | 13 | 17 | 41 | 45 | 37 |
| Crystal Palace | 42 | 13 | 11 | 18 | 54 | 62 | 37 |
| Port Vale | 42 | 14 | 9 | 19 | 39 | 51 | 37 |
| Coventry C | 42 | 15 | 7 | 20 | 46 | 63 | 37 |
| Clapton O | 42 | 12 | 12 | 18 | 40 | 50 | 36 |
| Stockport Co | 42 | 14 | 8 | 20 | 43 | 58 | 36 |
| Rotherham C | 42 | 13 | 9 | 20 | 44 | 63 | 35 |
| Wolves | 42 | 9 | 9 | 24 | 42 | 77 | 27 |

Manager: Cecil Potter.
Leading scorers: Jimmy Lyons, Jimmy Moore, League 11. Jimmy Moore, all matches 16.
League ever-present: Tom Crilly.

- Cecil Potter, secretary, player and manager at Hartlepools United, was appointed to succeed Jimmy Methven in July. He brought with him two Hartlepools defenders, Tom Crilly and Harry Thoms, who, between them, made 406 appearances for the Rams.
- Derby slipped a further two places down the Second Division but a new team began to take shape.
- Potter was able to play the same team through five FA Cup ties as Derby fell just short of the first Wembley final. They were well beaten by West Ham United, also from the Second Division, in the semi-final at Stamford Bridge.
- Like Jimmy Bagshaw three seasons earlier, Jimmy Moore was in the veteran stage when he won his only England cap. He scored all five goals against Crystal Palace on Christmas Day and was 34 when he played against Sweden in Stockholm, a match in which George Thornewell also appeared.

## Division Two

| Match No. | Date | | Venue | Opponents | Result | | Scorers | Atten |
|---|---|---|---|---|---|---|---|---|
| 1 | Aug | 26 | (a) | Wolves | W | 1-0 | Moore | 18 |
| 2 | | 28 | (a) | West Ham U | D | 0-0 | | 12 |
| 3 | Sep | 2 | (h) | Wolves | D | 1-1 | Paterson | 12 |
| 4 | | 4 | (h) | West Ham U | W | 2-1 | Moore 2 | 11 |
| 5 | | 9 | (a) | Sheffield W | D | 0-0 | | 20 |
| 6 | | 16 | (h) | Sheffield W | D | 1-1 | Paterson | 12 |
| 7 | | 23 | (a) | Barnsley | L | 0-5 | | 13 |
| 8 | | 30 | (h) | Barnsley | L | 0-1 | | 13 |
| 9 | Oct | 7 | (a) | Blackpool | L | 2-3 | Storer, Wightman (pen) | 12 |
| 10 | | 14 | (h) | Blackpool | W | 1-0 | Keetley | 10 |
| 11 | | 21 | (a) | Coventry C | L | 0-1 | | 17 |
| 12 | | 28 | (h) | Coventry C | W | 4-0 | Paterson 2, Wightman (pen), Lyons | 9 |
| 13 | Nov | 4 | (a) | South Shields | L | 1-3 | Storer | 7, |
| 14 | | 11 | (h) | South Shields | W | 1-0 | Paterson | 9, |
| 15 | | 18 | (h) | Bradford C | L | 0-2 | | 9, |
| 16 | | 25 | (a) | Bradford C | D | 0-0 | | 10, |
| 17 | Dec | 2 | (h) | Southampton | L | 0-2 | | 10, |
| 18 | | 9 | (a) | Southampton | W | 4-0 | Lyons 2, Galloway 2 | 15, |
| 19 | | 16 | (h) | Leicester C | W | 2-0 | Galloway 2 | 14, |
| 20 | | 23 | (a) | Leicester C | W | 1-0 | Murphy | 20, |
| 21 | | 25 | (h) | Crystal P | W | 6-0 | Moore 5, Lyons | 17, |
| 22 | | 26 | (a) | Crystal P | D | 2-2 | Moore, Galloway | 10, |
| 23 | | 30 | (h) | Notts C | D | 0-0 | | 22, |
| 24 | Jan | 6 | (a) | Notts C | W | 2-1 | Lyons 2 | 24, |
| 25 | | 20 | (h) | Fulham | W | 2-0 | Lyons (pen), Murphy | 11, |
| 26 | | 27 | (a) | Fulham | L | 1-3 | Lyons | 16, |
| 27 | Feb | 10 | (h) | Port Vale | L | 1-2 | Lyons (pen) | 10, |
| 28 | | 17 | (a) | Manchester U | D | 0-0 | | 20, |
| 29 | | 26 | (a) | Port Vale | W | 3-2 | Stokoe, Murphy, Lyons | 5, |
| 30 | Mar | 3 | (a) | Bury | L | 1-4 | Thornewell | 10, |
| 31 | | 14 | (h) | Manchester U | D | 1-1 | Moore | 12, |
| 32 | | 17 | (h) | Rotherham C | W | 1-0 | Lyons | 12, |
| 33 | | 26 | (a) | Rotherham C | L | 0-3 | | 7, |
| 34 | | 30 | (h) | Hull C | L | 0-2 | | 10, |
| 35 | | 31 | (h) | Clapton O | D | 0-0 | | 8, |
| 36 | Apr | 2 | (a) | Hull C | L | 2-4 | Thornewell, Keetley | 15, |
| 37 | | 7 | (a) | Clapton O | D | 0-0 | | 15, |
| 38 | | 11 | (h) | Bury | W | 1-0 | Galloway | 4, |
| 39 | | 14 | (h) | Stockport C | L | 1-2 | Moore | 7, |
| 40 | | 21 | (a) | Stockport C | L | 1-2 | Galloway | 12, |
| 41 | | 28 | (h) | Leeds U | L | 0-1 | | 5, |
| 42 | May | 5 | (a) | Leeds U | L | 0-1 | | 4, |

FINAL LEAGUE POSITION: 14th in Division Two

Appearan
Go

## FA Cup

| | | | | | | | | |
|---|---|---|---|---|---|---|---|---|
| 1 | Jan | 13 | (h) | Blackpool | W | 2-0 | Moore, Lyons | 22, |
| 2 | Feb | 3 | (a) | Bristol C | W | 3-0 | Moore 2, Lyons (pen) | 32, |
| 3 | | 24 | (h) | Sheffield W | W | 1-0 | Moore | 16, |
| 4 | Mar | 10 | (a) | Tottenham H | W | 1-0 | Galloway | 50, |
| SF | | 24 | (n*) | West Ham U | L | 2-5 | Moore, Henderson (og) | 50, |

*Played at Stamford Bridge, Chelsea.

Appearan
Go

| ney B | Chandler A | Crilly T | McIntyre J | Wightman H | Storer H | Thornewell G | Lyons J | Paterson W | Moore J | Murpy L | Keetley F | Thoms H | Stokoe J | McLaverty B | Smith S | Hurst W | Lawrence G | Jones N | Galloway R | Plackett S | Ritchie A | Wilson C | Findlay T | Golby A | Hoffman E | |
|---|---|---|---|---|---|---|---|---|---|---|---|---|---|---|---|---|---|---|---|---|---|---|---|---|---|---|
| | 2 | 3 | 4 | 5 | 6 | 7 | 8 | 9 | 10 | 11 | | | | | | | | | | | | | | | | 1 |
| | 2 | 3 | 4 | 5 | 6 | | 8 | 9 | 10 | 11 | 7 | | | | | | | | | | | | | | | 2 |
| | 2 | 3 | 4 | 5 | 6 | 7 | 8 | 9 | 10 | 11 | | | | | | | | | | | | | | | | 3 |
| | 2 | 3 | 4 | | 6 | 7 | | 9 | 10 | 11 | | 5 | 8 | | | | | | | | | | | | | 4 |
| | 2 | 3 | 4 | 5 | 6 | 7 | | 9 | 10 | 11 | | | 8 | | | | | | | | | | | | | 5 |
| | 2 | 3 | 4 | 5 | 6 | 7 | | 9 | 10 | 11 | | | 8 | | | | | | | | | | | | | 6 |
| | 2 | 3 | | 5 | 6 | 7 | | 9 | 10 | 11 | | 4 | 8 | | | | | | | | | | | | | 7 |
| | 2 | 3 | | 5 | 6 | 7 | | | | 11 | 8 | | 10 | 4 | 9 | | | | | | | | | | | 8 |
| | 2 | 3 | 4 | 5 | 10 | 7 | | | | 11 | 8 | | | 6 | | 9 | | | | | | | | | | 9 |
| | 2 | 3 | 4 | 5 | 10 | | | 7 | 9 | 11 | 8 | | | 6 | | | 1 | | | | | | | | | 10 |
| | 2 | 3 | 4 | 5 | 9 | | 8 | | 10 | 11 | 7 | | | 6 | | | 1 | | | | | | | | | 11 |
| | 2 | 3 | 4 | 5 | 10 | | 8 | 9 | | 11 | 7 | | | 6 | | | 1 | | | | | | | | | 12 |
| | 2 | 3 | 4 | 5 | 10 | | 8 | 9 | | 11 | 7 | | | 6 | | | 1 | | | | | | | | | 13 |
| | 2 | 3 | 4 | 5 | | | 8 | 9 | 10 | 11 | 7 | | | 6 | | | 1 | | | | | | | | | 14 |
| | 2 | 3 | 4 | 5 | | 7 | 8 | 9 | 10 | 11 | | | | 6 | | | 1 | | | | | | | | | 15 |
| | 2 | 3 | 4 | | 10 | | | 9 | | 11 | 7 | 5 | | 6 | | | 1 | 8 | | | | | | | | 16 |
| | 2 | 3 | 4 | | 10 | | | 7 | | 11 | | 5 | | 6 | | | | 8 | 9 | | | | | | | 17 |
| | 2 | 3 | 4 | 5 | | 11 | 8 | 7 | 10 | | | | | | | | | | 9 | 6 | | | | | | 18 |
| | 2 | 3 | 4 | | | 11 | 8 | 7 | 10 | | | 5 | | | | | | | 9 | 6 | | | | | | 19 |
| | 2 | 3 | 4 | | | | 8 | 7 | 10 | 11 | | 5 | | | | | | | 9 | 6 | | | | | | 20 |
| | 2 | 3 | 4 | | | 7 | 8 | | 10 | 11 | | 5 | | | | | | | 9 | 6 | | | | | | 21 |
| | 2 | 3 | 4 | | | 7 | 8 | | 10 | 11 | | 5 | | | | | | | 9 | 6 | | | | | | 22 |
| | 2 | 3 | 4 | | | 7 | 8 | | 10 | 11 | | 5 | | | | | | | 9 | 6 | | | | | | 23 |
| | 2 | 3 | 4 | | | 7 | 8 | | 10 | 11 | | 5 | | | | | | | 9 | 6 | | | | | | 24 |
| | 2 | 3 | 4 | | | 7 | 8 | | 10 | 11 | | 5 | | | | | | | 9 | 6 | | | | | | 25 |
| | 2 | 3 | 4 | | | 7 | 8 | | 10 | 11 | | 5 | | | | | | | 9 | 6 | | | | | | 26 |
| | 2 | 3 | 4 | | | 7 | 8 | | 10 | 11 | | 5 | | | | | | | 9 | 6 | | | | | | 27 |
| | 2 | 3 | 4 | | | 7 | 8 | | 10 | 11 | | 5 | | | | | | | 9 | 6 | | | | | | 28 |
| | 2 | 3 | 4 | | | 7 | 8 | | | 11 | | 5 | 10 | | | | | | 9 | 6 | | | | | | 29 |
| | | 3 | 4 | | | 7 | 8 | | 10 | 11 | | 5 | | | | | | | 9 | 6 | 2 | | | | | 30 |
| | 2 | 3 | 4 | | | 7 | 8 | | 10 | 11 | | 5 | | | | | | | 9 | 6 | | | | | | 31 |
| | 2 | 3 | 4 | | | 7 | 8 | | 10 | 11 | | 5 | | | | | | | 9 | 6 | | | | | | 32 |
| | 2 | 3 | 4 | | | 7 | 8 | | 10 | 11 | | 5 | | | | | | | 9 | 6 | | | | | | 33 |
| | 2 | 3 | 4 | 5 | | 11 | 8 | | 9 | | 7 | | | | | | | | | 6 | | 10 | | | | 34 |
| | 2 | 3 | 4 | 5 | | 7 | | 9 | 10 | 11 | 8 | | | | | | | | | 6 | | | | | | 35 |
| | 2 | 3 | 4 | | 6 | 7 | | 9 | 10 | 11 | 8 | 5 | | | | | | | | | | | | | | 36 |
| | | 2 | 4 | | 6 | 7 | 8 | 9 | 10 | 11 | | 5 | | | | | | | | | | | 3 | | | 37 |
| | | 2 | 4 | | 6 | 7 | | | 10 | 11 | | 5 | 8 | | | | | | 9 | | | | 3 | | | 38 |
| | | 2 | 4 | | 6 | 7 | | | 10 | 11 | | 5 | 8 | | | | | | 9 | | | | 3 | | | 39 |
| | 2 | 3 | 4 | | | 7 | | | 10 | 11 | | 5 | | | | 8 | | | 9 | 6 | | | | | | 40 |
| | 2 | 3 | 4 | 5 | | 7 | | | 10 | 11 | | | | | | 8 | | | 9 | 6 | | | | | | 41 |
| | | 3 | 4 | 2 | | 7 | | | 10 | 11 | | | | | | | | 8 | 9 | 6 | | | | 5 | 1 | 42 |
| 4 | 37 | 42 | 40 | 19 | 19 | 33 | 26 | 20 | 35 | 39 | 12 | 24 | 8 | 10 | 1 | 3 | 7 | 3 | 22 | 21 | 1 | 1 | 3 | 1 | 1 | |
| | | | | 2 | 2 | 2 | 11 | 5 | 11 | 3 | 2 | | 1 | | | | | | 7 | | | | | | | |

| | | | | | | | | | | | | | | | | | | | | | | | | | | |
|---|---|---|---|---|---|---|---|---|---|---|---|---|---|---|---|---|---|---|---|---|---|---|---|---|---|---|
| 1 | 2 | 3 | 4 | | | 7 | 8 | | 10 | 11 | | 5 | | | | | | | 9 | 6 | | | | | | 1 |
| 1 | 2 | 3 | 4 | | | 7 | 8 | | 10 | 11 | | 5 | | | | | | | 9 | 6 | | | | | | 2 |
| | 2 | 3 | 4 | | | 7 | 8 | | 10 | 11 | | 5 | | | | | | | 9 | 6 | | | | | | 3 |
| | 2 | 3 | 4 | | | 7 | 8 | | 10 | 11 | | 5 | | | | | | | 9 | 6 | | | | | | 4 |
| | 2 | 3 | 4 | | | 7 | 8 | | 10 | 11 | | 5 | | | | | | | 9 | 6 | | | | | | SF |
| 5 | 5 | 5 | 5 | | | 5 | 5 | | 5 | 5 | | 5 | | | | | | | 5 | 5 | | | | | | |
| | | | | | | | 2 | | 5 | | | | | | | | | | 1 | | | | | | | |

1 own-goal

# 1923-24

| | P | W | D | L | F | A | Pts |
|---|---|---|---|---|---|---|---|
| Leeds U | 42 | 21 | 12 | 9 | 61 | 35 | 54 |
| Bury | 42 | 21 | 9 | 12 | 63 | 35 | 51 |
| Derby Co | 42 | 21 | 9 | 12 | 75 | 42 | 51 |
| Blackpool | 42 | 18 | 13 | 11 | 72 | 47 | 49 |
| Southampton | 42 | 17 | 14 | 11 | 52 | 31 | 48 |
| Stoke | 42 | 14 | 18 | 10 | 44 | 42 | 46 |
| Oldham A | 42 | 14 | 17 | 11 | 45 | 52 | 45 |
| Sheffield W | 42 | 16 | 12 | 14 | 54 | 51 | 44 |
| South Shields | 42 | 17 | 10 | 15 | 49 | 50 | 44 |
| Clapton O | 42 | 14 | 15 | 13 | 40 | 36 | 43 |
| Barnsley | 42 | 16 | 11 | 15 | 57 | 61 | 43 |
| Leicester C | 42 | 17 | 8 | 17 | 64 | 54 | 42 |
| Stockport Co | 42 | 13 | 16 | 13 | 44 | 52 | 42 |
| Manchester U | 42 | 13 | 14 | 15 | 52 | 44 | 40 |
| Crystal Palace | 42 | 13 | 13 | 16 | 53 | 65 | 39 |
| Port Vale | 42 | 13 | 12 | 17 | 50 | 66 | 38 |
| Hull C | 42 | 10 | 17 | 15 | 46 | 51 | 37 |
| Bradford C | 42 | 11 | 15 | 16 | 35 | 48 | 37 |
| Coventry C | 42 | 11 | 13 | 18 | 52 | 68 | 35 |
| Fulham | 42 | 10 | 14 | 18 | 45 | 56 | 34 |
| Nelson | 42 | 10 | 13 | 19 | 40 | 74 | 33 |
| Bristol C | 42 | 7 | 15 | 20 | 32 | 65 | 29 |

Manager: Cecil Potter.
Leading scorer: Harry Storer, League 24, all matches 27.

- For five seasons after World War One, clubs met each other on successive Saturdays and there was an extraordinary reversal in September. Seven days after losing 3–2 to Bristol City at the Baseball Ground, Derby beat them 8–0 at Ashton Gate, the most decisive away win in their history.
- Harry Storer scored four goals against Bristol City and repeated that against Nelson on Boxing Day. His fine form brought him a first England cap, against France.
- Derby were a goal away from returning to the First Division. They needed to beat Leicester City 5–0 in their final game but had to settle for 4–0, so Bury pipped them on goal average – by 0.015 of a goal.

## Division Two

| Match No. | Date | | Venue | Opponents | Result | | Scorers | Atter |
|---|---|---|---|---|---|---|---|---|
| 1 | Aug | 25 | (h) | Stockport C | W | 4-1 | Galloway 2, Storer, Whitehouse | 13 |
| 2 | | 27 | (a) | Oldham A | L | 0-2 | | 10 |
| 3 | Sep | 1 | (a) | Stockport C | D | 0-0 | | 13 |
| 4 | | 3 | (h) | Oldham A | W | 2-1 | Whitehouse, Storer | 12 |
| 5 | | 8 | (h) | Clapton O | W | 1-0 | Thoms | 12 |
| 6 | | 15 | (a) | Clapton O | L | 0-2 | | 19 |
| 7 | | 22 | (h) | Bristol C | L | 2-3 | Galloway, Storer | 12 |
| 8 | | 29 | (a) | Bristol C | W | 8-0 | Storer 4, Galloway 2, Thornewell, Plackett | 20 |
| 9 | Oct | 6 | (a) | Hull C | W | 1-0 | Storer | 9, |
| 10 | | 13 | (h) | Hull C | W | 4-1 | Murphy, Storer, Galloway, Whitehouse | 14 |
| 11 | | 20 | (a) | Southampton | D | 0-0 | | 12 |
| 12 | | 27 | (h) | Southampton | W | 1-0 | Storer | 14 |
| 13 | Nov | 3 | (a) | Stoke | D | 1-1 | Murphy | 15 |
| 14 | | 10 | (h) | Stoke | D | 1-1 | Brittleton (og) | 17 |
| 15 | | 17 | (a) | Fulham | L | 2-3 | Whitehouse, Storer | 16, |
| 16 | | 24 | (h) | Fulham | D | 3-3 | Murphy, Storer, McIntyre | 14, |
| 17 | Dec | 1 | (h) | Crystal P | W | 5-0 | Whitehouse 2, Galloway 2, Murphy | 11, |
| 18 | | 8 | (a) | Crystal P | W | 1-0 | Galloway | 10, |
| 19 | | 15 | (h) | Blackpool | W | 2-0 | Storer, Whitehouse | 15, |
| 20 | | 22 | (a) | Blackpool | L | 0-4 | | 12, |
| 21 | | 25 | (a) | Nelson | L | 1-2 | Galloway | 10, |
| 22 | | 26 | (h) | Nelson | W | 6-0 | Storer 4, Whitehouse 2 | 19, |
| 23 | | 29 | (h) | Sheffield W | D | 1-1 | Whitehouse | 16, |
| 24 | Jan | 5 | (a) | Sheffield W | L | 0-1 | | 25, |
| 25 | | 19 | (h) | South Shields | W | 6-1 | Storer 3, Plackett, Galloway, Murphy | 13, |
| 26 | | 26 | (a) | South Shields | L | 2-3 | Whitehouse, Storer | 6, |
| 27 | Feb | 9 | (a) | Bury | L | 0-1 | | 8, |
| 28 | | 16 | (h) | Manchester U | W | 3-0 | Whitehouse 2 (1 pen), Galloway | 12, |
| 29 | | 23 | (a) | Manchester U | D | 0-0 | | 25, |
| 30 | | 27 | (h) | Bury | L | 0-2 | | 7, |
| 31 | Mar | 1 | (h) | Barnsley | W | 2-1 | Whitehouse, Murphy | 8, |
| 32 | | 8 | (a) | Barnsley | W | 3-1 | Plackett, Galloway, Murphy | 12, |
| 33 | | 15 | (a) | Bradford C | W | 2-1 | Galloway, Keetley | 10, |
| 34 | | 22 | (h) | Bradford C | D | 0-0 | | 11, |
| 35 | | 29 | (a) | Port Vale | L | 0-2 | | 8, |
| 36 | Apr | 5 | (h) | Port Vale | W | 2-0 | Galloway, Bromage | 9, |
| 37 | | 12 | (a) | Leeds U | D | 1-1 | Storer | 20, |
| 38 | | 19 | (h) | Leeds U | W | 2-0 | Storer, Whitehouse (pen) | 21, |
| 39 | | 21 | (h) | Coventry C | W | 1-0 | Whitehouse | 15, |
| 40 | | 22 | (a) | Coventry C | W | 1-0 | Galloway | 16, |
| 41 | | 26 | (a) | Leicester C | L | 0-3 | | 16, |
| 42 | May | 3 | (h) | Leicester C | W | 4-0 | Moore 2, Storer, Galloway | 20, |

FINAL LEAGUE POSITION: 3rd in Division Two

Appearan
Go

## FA Cup

| | | | | | | | | |
|---|---|---|---|---|---|---|---|---|
| 1 | Jan | 12 | (h) | Bury | W | 2-1 | Murphy, Whitehouse | 20, |
| 2 | Feb | 2 | (h) | Newcastle U | D | 2-2 | Storer 2 | 27, |
| R | | 6 | (a) | Newcastle U | D | 2-2* | Galloway, Mooney (og) | 50, |
| 2R | | 11 | (n‡) | Newcastle U | D | 2-2* | Galloway, Thornewell | 17, |
| 3R | | 13 | (a) | Newcastle U | L | 3-5 | Galloway 2, Storer | 32, |

‡Played at Burnden Park, Bolton.

*after extra-time

Appearan
Go

| iney B | Chandler A | Crilly T | McIntyre J | Thoms H | Plackett S | Thornewell G | Whitehouse J | Galloway R | Storer H | Murphy L | Moore J | McLaverty B | Keetley F | Lawrence G | Paterson W | Wightman H | Johnston J | Ritchie A | Findlay T | Bromage E | |
|---|---|---|---|---|---|---|---|---|---|---|---|---|---|---|---|---|---|---|---|---|---|
| | 2 | 3 | 4 | 5 | 6 | 7 | 8 | 9 | 10 | 11 | | | | | | | | | | | 1 |
| | 2 | 3 | 4 | 5 | 6 | 7 | 8 | 9 | 10 | 11 | | | | | | | | | | | 2 |
| | 2 | 3 | 4 | 5 | 6 | 7 | 8 | 9 | 10 | 11 | | | | | | | | | | | 3 |
| | 2 | 3 | 4 | 5 | 6 | 7 | 8 | 9 | 10 | 11 | | | | | | | | | | | 4 |
| | 2 | 3 | 4 | 5 | 6 | 7 | 8 | 9 | 10 | 11 | | | | | | | | | | | 5 |
| | 2 | 3 | 4 | 5 | 6 | 7 | 8 | | 9 | 11 | 10 | | | | | | | | | | 6 |
| | 2 | 3 | | 5 | 6 | 7 | 8 | 9 | 10 | 11 | | 4 | | | | | | | | | 7 |
| | 2 | 3 | 4 | 5 | 6 | 7 | 8 | 9 | 10 | 11 | | | | | | | | | | | 8 |
| | 2 | 3 | 4 | 5 | 6 | 7 | 8 | 9 | 10 | 11 | | | | | | | | | | | 9 |
| | 2 | 3 | 4 | 5 | 6 | 7 | 8 | 9 | 10 | 11 | | | | | | | | | | | 10 |
| | 2 | 3 | 4 | 5 | 6 | 7 | 8 | 9 | 10 | 11 | | | | | | | | | | | 11 |
| | 2 | 3 | 4 | 5 | 6 | 7 | 8 | 9 | 10 | 11 | | | | | | | | | | | 12 |
| | 2 | 3 | 4 | 5 | 6 | 7 | 8 | 9 | 10 | 11 | | | | | | | | | | | 13 |
| | 2 | 3 | 4 | 5 | 6 | 7 | 8 | 9 | 10 | 11 | | | | | | | | | | | 14 |
| | 2 | 3 | 4 | 5 | 6 | | 8 | 9 | 10 | 11 | | | 7 | | | | | | | | 15 |
| | 2 | 3 | 4 | 5 | 6 | | 8 | 9 | 10 | 11 | | | 7 | 1 | | | | | | | 16 |
| | 2 | 3 | 4 | 5 | 6 | | 8 | 9 | 10 | 11 | | | | | 7 | | | | | | 17 |
| | 2 | 3 | 4 | | 6 | | 8 | 9 | | 11 | 10 | | | | 7 | 5 | | | | | 18 |
| | 2 | 3 | 4 | 5 | 6 | 7 | 8 | 9 | 10 | 11 | | | | | | | | | | | 19 |
| | 2 | 3 | 4 | 5 | 6 | 7 | 8 | 9 | 10 | 11 | | | | | | | | | | | 20 |
| | 2 | 3 | 4 | | 6 | 7 | 8 | 9 | 10 | 11 | | | | | | 5 | | | | | 21 |
| | 2 | 3 | 4 | | 6 | 7 | 8 | 9 | 10 | 11 | | | | | | 5 | | | | | 22 |
| | 2 | 3 | 4 | | 6 | 7 | 8 | | 10 | 11 | 9 | | | | | 5 | | | | | 23 |
| | 2 | 3 | 4 | | 6 | 7 | 8 | | 10 | 11 | | | | | | 5 | 9 | | | | 24 |
| | 2 | | 4 | 5 | 6 | 7 | 8 | 9 | 10 | 11 | | | | | | | | 3 | | | 25 |
| | 2 | | 4 | 5 | 6 | 7 | 8 | 9 | 10 | 11 | | | | | | | | 3 | | | 26 |
| | | 3 | | | 6 | 7 | 8 | 9 | | 11 | 10 | 4 | | | | 5 | | | 2 | | 27 |
| | 2 | 3 | 4 | 5 | 6 | 7 | 8 | 9 | 10 | 11 | | | | | | | | | | | 28 |
| | 2 | 3 | 4 | 5 | 6 | 7 | 8 | 9 | 10 | 11 | | | | | | | | | | | 29 |
| | 2 | 3 | 4 | 5 | 6 | 7 | 8 | 9 | 10 | 11 | | | | | | | | | | | 30 |
| | 2 | 3 | 4 | 5 | 6 | 7 | 8 | 9 | 10 | 11 | | | | | | | | | | | 31 |
| | | 3 | 4 | 5 | 6 | 7 | 10 | 9 | | 11 | | | 8 | | | 2 | | | | | 32 |
| | | 3 | 4 | 5 | 6 | 7 | 10 | 9 | | 11 | | | 8 | | | 2 | | | | | 33 |
| | | 3 | 4 | 5 | 6 | 7 | 10 | 9 | | 11 | | | 8 | | | 2 | | | | | 34 |
| | | 3 | 4 | 5 | 6 | 7 | 8 | 9 | 10 | 11 | | | | | | 2 | | | | | 35 |
| | | 3 | | 5 | 6 | 7 | 8 | 9 | 10 | | | 4 | | | | 2 | | | | 11 | 36 |
| | | 3 | | 5 | 6 | 7 | 8 | 9 | 10 | | | 4 | | | | 2 | | | | 11 | 37 |
| | | 3 | | 5 | 6 | 7 | 8 | 9 | 10 | 11 | | 4 | | | | 2 | | | | | 38 |
| | | 3 | | 5 | 6 | 7 | 8 | 9 | 10 | 11 | | 4 | | | | 2 | | | | | 39 |
| | | 3 | 4 | 5 | | 7 | 8 | 9 | 10 | 11 | | 6 | | | | 2 | | | | | 40 |
| | | 3 | | 5 | 6 | 7 | | 9 | 10 | 11 | | 4 | 8 | | | 2 | | | | | 41 |
| | 2 | 3 | 4 | 5 | | 7 | | 9 | 10 | 11 | 8 | | | | | 6 | | | | | 42 |
| 1 | 31 | 40 | 35 | 36 | 40 | 38 | 40 | 39 | 37 | 40 | 5 | 8 | 6 | 1 | 2 | 17 | 1 | 2 | 1 | 2 | |
| | | | 1 | 1 | 3 | 1 | 16 | 17 | 24 | 7 | 2 | | 1 | | | | | | | 1 | |

1 own-goal

| | | | | | | | | | | | | | | | | | | | | | |
|---|---|---|---|---|---|---|---|---|---|---|---|---|---|---|---|---|---|---|---|---|---|
| | 2 | 3 | 4 | | 6 | 7 | 8 | 9 | 10 | 11 | | | | | | 5 | | | | | 1 |
| | 2 | 3 | 4 | 5 | 6 | 7 | 8 | 9 | 10 | 11 | | | | | | | | | | | 2 |
| | 2 | 3 | 4 | 5 | 6 | 7 | 8 | 9 | 10 | 11 | | | | | | | | | | | R |
| | 2 | 3 | 4 | 5 | 6 | 7 | 8 | 9 | 10 | 11 | | | | | | | | | | | 2R |
| | 2 | 3 | 4 | 5 | 6 | | 8 | 9 | 10 | 11 | | | 7 | | | | | | | | 3R |
| 5 | 5 | 5 | 5 | 4 | 5 | 4 | 5 | 5 | 5 | 5 | | | 1 | | | 1 | | | | | |
| | | | | | | 1 | 1 | 4 | 3 | 1 | | | | | | | | | | | |

1 own-goal

# 1924-25

| | P | W | D | L | F | A | Pts |
|---|---|---|---|---|---|---|---|
| Leicester C | 42 | 24 | 11 | 7 | 90 | 32 | 59 |
| Manchester U | 42 | 23 | 11 | 8 | 57 | 23 | 57 |
| Derby Co | 42 | 22 | 11 | 9 | 71 | 36 | 55 |
| Portsmouth | 42 | 15 | 18 | 9 | 58 | 50 | 48 |
| Chelsea | 42 | 16 | 15 | 11 | 51 | 37 | 47 |
| Wolves | 42 | 20 | 6 | 16 | 55 | 51 | 46 |
| Southampton | 42 | 13 | 18 | 11 | 40 | 36 | 44 |
| Port Vale | 42 | 17 | 8 | 17 | 48 | 56 | 42 |
| South Shields | 42 | 12 | 17 | 13 | 42 | 38 | 41 |
| Hull C | 42 | 15 | 11 | 16 | 50 | 49 | 41 |
| Clapton O | 42 | 14 | 12 | 16 | 42 | 42 | 40 |
| Fulham | 42 | 15 | 10 | 17 | 41 | 56 | 40 |
| Middlesbrough | 42 | 10 | 19 | 13 | 36 | 44 | 39 |
| Sheffield W | 42 | 15 | 8 | 19 | 50 | 56 | 38 |
| Barnsley | 42 | 13 | 12 | 17 | 46 | 59 | 38 |
| Bradford C | 42 | 13 | 12 | 17 | 37 | 50 | 38 |
| Blackpool | 42 | 14 | 9 | 19 | 65 | 61 | 37 |
| Oldham A | 42 | 13 | 11 | 18 | 35 | 51 | 37 |
| Stockport Co | 42 | 13 | 11 | 18 | 37 | 57 | 37 |
| Stoke | 42 | 12 | 11 | 19 | 34 | 46 | 35 |
| Crystal Palace | 42 | 12 | 10 | 20 | 38 | 54 | 34 |
| Coventry C | 42 | 11 | 9 | 22 | 45 | 84 | 31 |

Manager: Cecil Potter.
Leading scorer: Albert Fairclough, League/all matches 22.
League ever-present: Johnny McIntyre, Lionel Murphy, Ben Olney.

- Derby County owned the Baseball Ground after a £10,000 purchase from Sir Francis Ley in July 1924.
- A feeble finish cost Derby promotion. They won only two of their last 11 games, four of which were lost, and again finished third, two points behind Manchester United.
- Cecil Potter left after three seasons, intending to take a dairy business in his native Sussex. Instead, he became the only Derby manager to win a League Championship for another 47 years, until another manager came from Hartlepool.
- Potter did it with Huddersfield Town, who won two successive titles under Herbert Chapman. Arsenal lured Chapman away, Huddersfield approached Potter and he completed the first Championship hat-trick in League history.

## Division Two

| Match No. | Date | Venue | Opponents | Result | | Scorers | Atten |
|---|---|---|---|---|---|---|---|
| 1 | Aug 30 | (h) | Hull C | W | 4-0 | Whitehouse 3 (1 pen), Storer | 20, |
| 2 | Sep 1 | (a) | Sheffield W | W | 1-0 | Storer | 35, |
| 3 | 6 | (a) | Portsmouth | D | 1-1 | Murphy | 27, |
| 4 | 8 | (h) | Sheffield W | W | 2-1 | Storer, Fairclough | 20, |
| 5 | 13 | (h) | Fulham | W | 5-1 | Fairclough 4, Storer | 17, |
| 6 | 15 | (a) | Blackpool | L | 1-5 | Storer | 16, |
| 7 | 20 | (a) | Wolves | W | 4-0 | Fairclough 2, Murphy, Storer | 27, |
| 8 | 27 | (h) | Barnsley | D | 1-1 | McIntyre | 18, |
| 9 | Oct 4 | (a) | Middlesbrough | W | 3-1 | Fairclough 2, Storer | 24, |
| 10 | 11 | (h) | Port Vale | W | 4-1 | Murphy 2, Storer, Whitehouse | 19, |
| 11 | 18 | (a) | Bradford C | W | 3-0 | Fairclough, Murphy, Whitehouse | 12, |
| 12 | 25 | (h) | Clapton O | W | 3-0 | Fairclough 2, Murphy | 15, |
| 13 | Nov 1 | (a) | Crystal P | L | 0-2 | | 10, |
| 14 | 8 | (h) | Southampton | W | 3-0 | Storer, Galloway, Whitehouse | 16, |
| 15 | 15 | (a) | Chelsea | D | 1-1 | Murphy | 35, |
| 16 | 22 | (h) | Stockport C | W | 2-0 | Fairclough 2 | 15, |
| 17 | 29 | (a) | Manchester U | D | 1-1 | Fairclough | 59, |
| 18 | Dec 6 | (h) | Leicester C | L | 0-3 | | 25, |
| 19 | 13 | (a) | Stoke | D | 1-1 | Moore | 10, |
| 20 | 20 | (h) | Coventry C | W | 5-1 | Fairclough 2 (1 pen), Moore, Murphy, Whitehouse | 11, |
| 21 | 25 | (a) | Oldham A | W | 1-0 | Whitehouse | 18, |
| 22 | 26 | (h) | Oldham A | W | 1-0 | Fairclough (pen) | 26, |
| 23 | 27 | (a) | Hull C | D | 1-1 | Murphy | 12, |
| 24 | Jan 3 | (h) | Portsmouth | W | 6-1 | Fairclough 3, Moore 2, Whitehouse | 14, |
| 25 | 17 | (a) | Fulham | W | 2-0 | Moore, Whitehouse | 25, |
| 26 | 24 | (h) | Wolves | L | 0-1 | | 15, |
| 27 | Feb 7 | (h) | Middlesbrough | W | 3-1 | McIntyre, Whitehouse, Moore | 14, |
| 28 | 14 | (a) | Port Vale | L | 1-2 | Thornewell | 15, |
| 29 | 25 | (h) | Bradford C | W | 2-0 | Fairclough (pen), Whitehouse | 6, |
| 30 | 28 | (a) | Clapton O | W | 1-0 | Thornewell | 25, |
| 31 | Mar 7 | (h) | Crystal P | W | 3-0 | Whitehouse, Moore, Strang (og) | 15, |
| 32 | 9 | (a) | Barnsley | L | 0-3 | | 8, |
| 33 | 14 | (a) | Southampton | L | 0-2 | | 13, |
| 34 | 21 | (h) | Chelsea | W | 1-0 | Storer | 16, |
| 35 | 28 | (a) | Stockport C | D | 0-0 | | 19, |
| 36 | Apr 4 | (h) | Manchester U | W | 1-0 | Wightman | 24, |
| 37 | 10 | (a) | South Shields | L | 0-1 | | 20, |
| 38 | 11 | (a) | Leicester C | D | 0-0 | | 30, |
| 39 | 13 | (h) | South Shields | D | 0-0 | | 17, |
| 40 | 18 | (h) | Stoke | L | 1-2 | Murphy | 15, |
| 41 | 25 | (a) | Coventry C | D | 0-0 | | 10, |
| 42 | May 2 | (h) | Blackpool | D | 2-2 | Moore, Storer | 7, |

FINAL LEAGUE POSITION: 3rd in Division Two

Appearan
Goa

## FA Cup

| | | | | | | |
|---|---|---|---|---|---|---|
| 1 | Jan 10 | (h) | Bradford C | L | 0-1 | 20, |

Appearan
Go

| Olney B | Chandler A | Crilly T | McIntyre J | Thoms H | Plackett S | Thornewell G | Whitehouse J | Galloway R | Storer H | Murphy L | Fairclough A | McLaverty B | Moore J | Wightman H | Keetley F | Hardy J | Pumford G | Haley W | Tootle J | Lane M | |
|---|---|---|---|---|---|---|---|---|---|---|---|---|---|---|---|---|---|---|---|---|---|
| 1 | 2 | 3 | 4 | 5 | 6 | 7 | 8 | 9 | 10 | 11 | | | | | | | | | | | 1 |
| 1 | 2 | 3 | 4 | 5 | 6 | 7 | 8 | 9 | 10 | 11 | | | | | | | | | | | 2 |
| 1 | 2 | 3 | 4 | 5 | 6 | 7 | 8 | | 10 | 11 | 9 | | | | | | | | | | 3 |
| 1 | 2 | 3 | 4 | 5 | | 7 | 8 | | 10 | 11 | 9 | 6 | | | | | | | | | 4 |
| 1 | 2 | 3 | 4 | 5 | | 7 | | | 10 | 11 | 9 | 6 | 8 | | | | | | | | 5 |
| 1 | 2 | 3 | 4 | 5 | | 7 | | | 10 | 11 | 9 | 6 | 8 | | | | | | | | 6 |
| 1 | | 3 | 4 | 5 | 6 | | 8 | | 10 | 11 | 9 | | | 2 | 7 | | | | | | 7 |
| 1 | | 3 | 4 | 5 | 6 | | 8 | | 10 | 11 | 9 | | | 2 | 7 | | | | | | 8 |
| 1 | 2 | 3 | 4 | 5 | 6 | | 8 | | 10 | 11 | 9 | | | | 7 | | | | | | 9 |
| 1 | 2 | | 4 | 5 | | | 8 | | 10 | 11 | 9 | 6 | | 3 | 7 | | | | | | 10 |
| 1 | 2 | 3 | 4 | 5 | | | 8 | | 10 | 11 | 9 | 6 | | | 7 | | | | | | 11 |
| 1 | 2 | 3 | 4 | 5 | | | 8 | | 10 | 11 | 9 | 6 | | | 7 | | | | | | 12 |
| 1 | | 3 | 4 | 5 | | | 8 | 9 | 10 | 11 | | 6 | | 2 | 7 | | | | | | 13 |
| 1 | 2 | 3 | 4 | 5 | | | 8 | 9 | 10 | 11 | | 6 | | | 7 | | | | | | 14 |
| 1 | 2 | 3 | 4 | 5 | | | 8 | 9 | 10 | 11 | | 6 | | | 7 | | | | | | 15 |
| 1 | 2 | 3 | 4 | 5 | 6 | | 8 | | 10 | 11 | 9 | | | | 7 | | | | | | 16 |
| 1 | 2 | | 4 | | | | 8 | | 10 | 11 | 9 | 6 | | 3 | 7 | 5 | | | | | 17 |
| 1 | 2 | | 4 | | 6 | 7 | 8 | | 10 | 11 | 9 | | | 3 | | 5 | | | | | 18 |
| 1 | 2 | 3 | 4 | | | | 8 | | 6 | 11 | 9 | | 10 | 5 | 7 | | | | | | 19 |
| 1 | 2 | 3 | 4 | | 6 | | 8 | | | 11 | 9 | | 10 | 5 | 7 | | | | | | 20 |
| 1 | 2 | 3 | 4 | 5 | 6 | | 8 | | | 11 | 9 | | 10 | | 7 | | | | | | 21 |
| 1 | 2 | 3 | 4 | 5 | 6 | | 8 | | | 11 | 9 | | 10 | | 7 | | | | | | 22 |
| 1 | 2 | 3 | 4 | | 6 | | 8 | | | 11 | 9 | | 10 | 5 | 7 | | | | | | 23 |
| 1 | 2 | 3 | 4 | 5 | 6 | | 8 | | | 11 | 9 | | 10 | | 7 | | | | | | 24 |
| 1 | 2 | 3 | 4 | | | 7 | 8 | | | 11 | | 6 | 10 | 5 | | | 9 | | | | 25 |
| 1 | 2 | 3 | 4 | 5 | | 7 | 8 | | | 11 | 9 | 6 | 10 | | | | | | | | 26 |
| 1 | 2 | 3 | 4 | 5 | | 7 | 8 | | | 11 | 9 | 6 | 10 | | | | | | | | 27 |
| 1 | 2 | 3 | 4 | | 6 | 7 | 8 | | | 11 | 9 | | 10 | 5 | | | | | | | 28 |
| 1 | 2 | 3 | 4 | 5 | | 7 | 8 | | | 11 | 9 | 6 | 10 | | | | | | | | 29 |
| 1 | 2 | 3 | 4 | 5 | 6 | 7 | 9 | | | 11 | | | 10 | | | | | 8 | | | 30 |
| 1 | 2 | 3 | 4 | | | 7 | 8 | | | 11 | 9 | 6 | 10 | 5 | | | | | | | 31 |
| 1 | 2 | 3 | 4 | | | 7 | 9 | | | 11 | | 6 | 10 | | 8 | 5 | | | | | 32 |
| 1 | | 3 | 4 | 5 | | 7 | 10 | | | 11 | 9 | 6 | 8 | | | | | | 2 | | 33 |
| 1 | 2 | 3 | 4 | | 6 | 7 | 8 | | 10 | 11 | 9 | | | 5 | | | | | | | 34 |
| 1 | 2 | 3 | 4 | | 6 | 7 | 8 | | | 11 | 9 | | 10 | 5 | | | | | | | 35 |
| 1 | 2 | 3 | 4 | | 6 | 7 | 10 | | | 11 | 9 | | | 5 | 8 | | | | | | 36 |
| 1 | 2 | | 4 | 5 | | | 8 | | | 11 | 9 | 6 | 10 | | 7 | | | | 3 | | 37 |
| 1 | 2 | 3 | 4 | | 6 | 7 | 8 | | 10 | 11 | 9 | | | 5 | | | | | | | 38 |
| 1 | 2 | 3 | 4 | | 6 | 7 | 8 | | 10 | 11 | 9 | | | 5 | | | | | | | 39 |
| 1 | 2 | | 4 | 5 | 6 | 7 | 8 | | | 11 | | | 10 | | | | 9 | | 3 | | 40 |
| 1 | 2 | 3 | 4 | | 6 | 7 | 8 | | 10 | 11 | 9 | | | 5 | | | | | | | 41 |
| 1 | 2 | | 4 | | 6 | 7 | 9 | | 10 | 11 | | | 8 | 5 | | | | | 3 | | 42 |
| 2 | 38 | 36 | 42 | 26 | 23 | 24 | 40 | 5 | 24 | 42 | 32 | 18 | 21 | 19 | 20 | 3 | 2 | 1 | 4 | | |
| | | | 2 | | | 2 | 13 | 1 | 11 | 10 | 22 | | 8 | 1 | | | | | | | |

1 own-goal

| | | | | | | | | | | | | | | | | | | | | | |
|---|---|---|---|---|---|---|---|---|---|---|---|---|---|---|---|---|---|---|---|---|---|
| 1 | 2 | 3 | 4 | 5 | 6 | | 8 | | | 11 | | | 10 | | 7 | | | | | 9 | 1 |
| 1 | 1 | 1 | 1 | 1 | 1 | | 1 | | | 1 | | | 1 | | 1 | | | | | 1 | |
| | | | | | | | | | | | | | | | | | | | | | |

# 1925-26

| | P | W | D | L | F | A | Pts |
|---|---|---|---|---|---|---|---|
| Sheffield W | 42 | 27 | 6 | 9 | 88 | 48 | 60 |
| Derby Co | 42 | 25 | 7 | 10 | 77 | 42 | 57 |
| Chelsea | 42 | 19 | 14 | 9 | 76 | 49 | 52 |
| Wolves | 42 | 21 | 7 | 14 | 84 | 60 | 49 |
| Swansea T | 42 | 19 | 11 | 12 | 77 | 57 | 49 |
| Blackpool | 42 | 17 | 11 | 14 | 76 | 69 | 45 |
| Oldham A | 42 | 18 | 8 | 16 | 74 | 62 | 44 |
| Port Vale | 42 | 19 | 6 | 17 | 79 | 69 | 44 |
| South Shields | 42 | 18 | 8 | 16 | 74 | 65 | 44 |
| Middlesbrough | 42 | 21 | 2 | 19 | 77 | 68 | 44 |
| Portsmouth | 42 | 17 | 10 | 15 | 79 | 74 | 44 |
| Preston N.E. | 42 | 18 | 7 | 17 | 71 | 84 | 43 |
| Hull C | 42 | 16 | 9 | 17 | 63 | 61 | 41 |
| Southampton | 42 | 15 | 8 | 19 | 63 | 63 | 38 |
| Darlington | 42 | 14 | 10 | 18 | 72 | 77 | 38 |
| Bradford C | 42 | 13 | 10 | 19 | 47 | 66 | 36 |
| Nottingham F | 42 | 14 | 8 | 20 | 51 | 73 | 36 |
| Barnsley | 42 | 12 | 12 | 18 | 58 | 84 | 36 |
| Fulham | 42 | 11 | 12 | 19 | 46 | 77 | 34 |
| Clapton O | 42 | 12 | 9 | 21 | 50 | 65 | 33 |
| Stoke C | 42 | 12 | 8 | 22 | 54 | 77 | 32 |
| Stockport Co | 42 | 8 | 9 | 25 | 51 | 97 | 25 |

Manager: George Jobey.
Leading scorer: Harry Bedford, League 27, all matches 28.
League ever-present: Syd Plackett.

- After guiding Wolves to the Third Division North title, George Jobey went into the hotel business. Derby tempted him back into football and he spent 16 years at the Baseball Ground.
- Jobey always wanted talented centre-forwards, so Harry Bedford set the trend. Bedford was twice the League's leading scorer with Blackpool and played two games for England while he was at Bloomfield Road.
- As Derby neared promotion, Jobey signed two more from Blackpool, Jimmy Gill and George Mee. The Rams were in the First Division for the remainder of Jobey's period in office.
- From 1925–26, the Football League recorded precise attendances. Until then, figures given are usually estimates, with crowds not divulged by clubs.

## Division Two

| Match No. | | Date | Venue | Opponents | Result | | Scorers | Atter |
|---|---|---|---|---|---|---|---|---|
| 1 | Aug | 29 | (a) | Hull C | D | 0-0 | | 11 |
| 2 | | 31 | (h) | Clapton O | W | 3-1 | Fazackerley 2, Thornewell | 13 |
| 3 | Sep | 5 | (h) | Darlington | L | 0-2 | | 13 |
| 4 | | 12 | (a) | Blackpool | W | 2-1 | Fairclough 2 | 14 |
| 5 | | 19 | (h) | Southampton | D | 2-2 | Whitehouse (pen), Murphy | 5 |
| 6 | | 24 | (a) | Clapton O | W | 1-0 | Storer | 7 |
| 7 | | 26 | (a) | Nottingham F | W | 2-1 | Thoms, Murphy | 19 |
| 8 | Oct | 3 | (h) | Swansea T | W | 5-0 | Bedford 3, Storer, Whitehouse | 16 |
| 9 | | 10 | (h) | Bradford C | D | 0-0 | | 17, |
| 10 | | 17 | (a) | Sheffield W | W | 4-1 | Bedford 2, Murphy, Whitehouse | 31, |
| 11 | | 24 | (h) | Stoke C | W | 7-3 | Bedford 3, Storer 2, Whitehouse, Murphy | 16 |
| 12 | | 31 | (a) | Portsmouth | D | 2-2 | Storer, Bedford | 16, |
| 13 | Nov | 7 | (h) | Wolves | W | 2-0 | Bedford 2 (1 pen) | 9 |
| 14 | | 14 | (a) | Fulham | D | 1-1 | Bedford | 12 |
| 15 | | 21 | (h) | South Shields | W | 2-0 | Thornewell, Whitehouse | 13, |
| 16 | | 28 | (a) | Preston NE | L | 1-2 | Murphy | 19 |
| 17 | Dec | 5 | (h) | Middlesbrough | W | 2-0 | Haley, Thornewell | 14, |
| 18 | | 14 | (a) | Oldham A | L | 0-2 | | 9, |
| 19 | | 19 | (h) | Stockport C | W | 4-0 | Murphy 2, Storer, Bedford | 11, |
| 20 | | 25 | (a) | Port Vale | W | 1-0 | Bedford | 15, |
| 21 | | 26 | (h) | Port Vale | W | 2-0 | Bedford, Storer | 23, |
| 22 | | 28 | (h) | Chelsea | W | 4-2 | Bedford 2, Storer, Thoms | 25, |
| 23 | Jan | 2 | (h) | Hull C | W | 3-1 | Bedford 2, Murphy | 12, |
| 24 | | 16 | (a) | Darlington | L | 0-3 | | 8, |
| 25 | | 23 | (h) | Blackpool | W | 5-2 | Hart (pen), Bromage, Keetley, Storer, Thornewell | 14, |
| 26 | Feb | 6 | (h) | Nottingham F | W | 2-0 | Hart, Murphy | 19, |
| 27 | | 10 | (a) | Southampton | L | 1-2 | Moore | 7, |
| 28 | | 13 | (a) | Swansea T | L | 0-2 | | 21, |
| 29 | | 20 | (a) | Bradford C | D | 0-0 | | 15, |
| 30 | | 27 | (h) | Sheffield W | W | 4-1 | Bedford 3, Murphy | 26, |
| 31 | Mar | 6 | (a) | Stoke C | W | 1-0 | Gill | 14, |
| 32 | | 13 | (h) | Portsmouth | L | 0-2 | | 18, |
| 33 | | 20 | (a) | Wolves | L | 0-2 | | 19, |
| 34 | | 27 | (h) | Fulham | W | 3-1 | Bacon 2, Gill | 13, |
| 35 | Apr | 3 | (a) | South Shields | D | 0-0 | | 7, |
| 36 | | 5 | (a) | Barnsley | W | 1-0 | Murphy | 16, |
| 37 | | 6 | (h) | Barnsley | W | 4-0 | Bedford 2, Murphy, Thornewell | 17, |
| 38 | | 10 | (h) | Preston NE | W | 2-0 | Gill, Thornewell | 17, |
| 39 | | 17 | (a) | Middlesbrough | W | 2-1 | Bedford, Thornewell | 9, |
| 40 | | 24 | (h) | Oldham A | W | 1-0 | Bedford | 20, |
| 41 | | 26 | (a) | Chelsea | L | 1-2 | Bedford | 9, |
| 42 | May | 1 | (a) | Stockport C | L | 0-3 | | 3, |

FINAL LEAGUE POSITION: 2nd in Division Two – Promoted

Appearan
Go

## FA Cup

| | | | | | | | | |
|---|---|---|---|---|---|---|---|---|
| 3 | Jan | 9 | (h) | Portsmouth | D | 0-0 | | 18, |
| R | | 13 | (a) | Portsmouth | D | 1-1* | Bedford | 25, |
| 2R | | 18 | (n‡) | Portsmouth | W | 2-0 | Thornewell, Bromage | 11, |
| 4 | | 30 | (a) | Southend U | L | 1-4 | Murphy | 14, |

‡Played at Filbert Street, Leicester
*after extra time

Appearan
Go

| Match | ney B | Tootle J | Crilly T | McIntyre J | Thoms H | Plackett S | Thornewell G | Whitehouse J | Fairclough A | Storer H | Murphy L | Fazackerley S | Wightman H | Keetley F | Bedford H | Fox W | Ritchie A | Haley W | Bromage E | Hart J | Smith V | Davison T | Moore J | Carr W | Rowe G | Gill J | Cooper T | Bacon A | Mee G | McLaverty B |
|---|---|---|---|---|---|---|---|---|---|---|---|---|---|---|---|---|---|---|---|---|---|---|---|---|---|---|---|---|---|---|
| 1 | | 2 | 3 | 4 | 5 | 6 | 7 | 8 | 9 | 10 | 11 | | | | | | | | | | | | | | | | | | | |
| 2 | | 2 | 3 | 4 | 5 | 6 | 7 | 8 | | 10 | 11 | 9 | | | | | | | | | | | | | | | | | | |
| 3 | | 2 | 3 | 4 | 5 | 6 | 7 | 8 | | 10 | 11 | 9 | | | | | | | | | | | | | | | | | | |
| 4 | | | 3 | 4 | 5 | 6 | 7 | 8 | 9 | 10 | 11 | | 2 | | | | | | | | | | | | | | | | | |
| 5 | | | 3 | 4 | 5 | 6 | 7 | 9 | | 10 | 11 | 8 | 2 | | | | | | | | | | | | | | | | | |
| 6 | | | 3 | 4 | 5 | 6 | 7 | 8 | | 10 | 11 | | 2 | 9 | | | | | | | | | | | | | | | | |
| 7 | | | 3 | 4 | 5 | 6 | 7 | 8 | | 10 | 11 | | 2 | | 9 | | | | | | | | | | | | | | | |
| 8 | | | 3 | 4 | 5 | 6 | 7 | 8 | | 10 | 11 | | 2 | | 9 | | | | | | | | | | | | | | | |
| 9 | | | 3 | 4 | 5 | 6 | 7 | 8 | | 10 | 11 | | 2 | | 9 | | | | | | | | | | | | | | | |
| 10 | | | 3 | 4 | 5 | 6 | 7 | 8 | | 10 | 11 | | 2 | | 9 | | | | | | | | | | | | | | | |
| 11 | | | 3 | 4 | 5 | 6 | 7 | 8 | | 10 | 11 | | 2 | | 9 | | | | | | | | | | | | | | | |
| 12 | | | 3 | 4 | 5 | 6 | 7 | 8 | | 10 | 11 | | 2 | | 9 | | | | | | | | | | | | | | | |
| 13 | | | 3 | 4 | 5 | 6 | 7 | 8 | | 10 | 11 | | 2 | | 9 | | | | | | | | | | | | | | | |
| 14 | | | 3 | 4 | 5 | 6 | 7 | 8 | | 10 | 11 | | 2 | | 9 | | | | | | | | | | | | | | | |
| 15 | | | 2 | 4 | 5 | 6 | 7 | 8 | | 10 | 11 | | | | 9 | 1 | 3 | | | | | | | | | | | | | |
| 16 | | | 2 | 4 | 5 | 6 | 7 | 8 | | 10 | 11 | | | | 9 | | 3 | | | | | | | | | | | | | |
| 17 | | | 2 | 4 | 5 | 6 | 7 | | | 10 | 11 | | | | 9 | | 3 | 8 | | | | | | | | | | | | |
| 18 | | | 2 | 4 | 5 | 6 | 7 | | | 10 | 11 | | | | 9 | | 3 | 8 | | | | | | | | | | | | |
| 19 | | | 2 | 4 | 5 | 6 | 7 | | | 10 | 11 | | | | 9 | | 3 | 8 | | | | | | | | | | | | |
| 20 | | | | 4 | 5 | 6 | 7 | | | 10 | 11 | | 2 | | 9 | | 3 | 8 | | | | | | | | | | | | |
| 21 | | | | 4 | 5 | 6 | 7 | 8 | | 10 | 11 | | 2 | | 9 | | 3 | | | | | | | | | | | | | |
| 22 | | | | 4 | 5 | 6 | 7 | 8 | | 10 | 11 | | 2 | | 9 | | 3 | | | | | | | | | | | | | |
| 23 | | | | 4 | 5 | 6 | 7 | 8 | | 10 | 11 | | 2 | | 9 | | 3 | | | | | | | | | | | | | |
| 24 | | | 3 | 4 | 5 | 6 | 11 | | | 10 | | | 2 | 7 | 9 | | | 8 | | | | | | | | | | | | |
| 25 | | | | 4 | 5 | 6 | 7 | | | 10 | | | 2 | 8 | | | 3 | | 11 | 9 | | | | | | | | | | |
| 26 | | | | 4 | 5 | 6 | | | | 10 | 11 | | 2 | 8 | | | 3 | | | 9 | 7 | | | | | | | | | |
| 27 | | | 3 | 4 | | 6 | 7 | | | 10 | 11 | | 2 | 8 | | | | | | | | 5 | 9 | | | | | | | |
| 28 | | | | 4 | 5 | 6 | 7 | | | 10 | 11 | | | | | | | 9 | | | | | 8 | 2 | 3 | | | | | |
| 29 | | | 2 | 4 | 5 | 6 | | | | 10 | 11 | | | | 9 | | 3 | 8 | | | 7 | | | | | | | | | |
| 30 | | | 3 | 4 | 5 | 6 | 7 | | | 10 | 11 | | 2 | 8 | 9 | | | | | | | | | | | | | | | |
| 31 | | | 3 | 4 | 5 | 6 | 7 | | | | 11 | | 2 | 8 | 9 | | | | | | | | | | | 10 | | | | |
| 32 | | | 3 | 4 | | 6 | 7 | | | | 11 | | 5 | 8 | | | | | | 9 | | | | | | 10 | 2 | | | |
| 33 | | | 3 | 4 | 5 | 6 | 7 | | | | 11 | | | | 9 | | | | | | | | | | | 8 | 2 | 10 | | |
| 34 | | | 3 | 4 | 5 | 6 | 7 | | | | | | | | 9 | | | | | | | | | | | 8 | 2 | 10 | 11 | |
| 35 | | | | 4 | 5 | 6 | 7 | | | | | | | | 9 | | 3 | | | | | | | | | 8 | 2 | 10 | 11 | |
| 36 | | | 3 | 4 | 5 | 6 | 7 | | | | 10 | | 2 | | 9 | | | | | | | | | | | 8 | | | 11 | |
| 37 | | | 3 | 4 | 5 | 6 | 7 | | | | 10 | | 2 | | 9 | | | | | | | | | | | 8 | | | 11 | |
| 38 | | | 3 | | 5 | 6 | 7 | | | | 10 | | 2 | | 9 | | | | | | | | | | | 8 | | | 11 | 4 |
| 39 | | | 3 | | 5 | 6 | 7 | | | | 10 | | 2 | | 9 | | | | | | | | | | | 8 | | | 11 | 4 |
| 40 | | | 3 | | 5 | 6 | 7 | | | | 10 | | 2 | | 9 | | | | | | | | | | | 8 | | | 11 | 4 |
| 41 | | | 3 | | 5 | 6 | 7 | | | | 10 | | 2 | | 9 | | | | | | | | | | | 8 | | | 11 | 4 |
| 42 | | | | 4 | 5 | 6 | 7 | | | | 10 | | | | 9 | | 3 | | | | | | | | | 8 | 2 | | 11 | |
| Total | 1 | 3 | 33 | 38 | 40 | 42 | 40 | 19 | 2 | 30 | 38 | 3 | 28 | 8 | 31 | 1 | 14 | 7 | 1 | 3 | 2 | 1 | 2 | 1 | 1 | 12 | 5 | 3 | 9 | 4 |
| Goals | | | | | 2 | | 7 | 5 | 2 | 9 | 12 | 2 | | 1 | 27 | | | 1 | 1 | 2 | | | 1 | | | 3 | | 2 | | |

| Round | ney B | Tootle J | Crilly T | McIntyre J | Thoms H | Plackett S | Thornewell G | Whitehouse J | Fairclough A | Storer H | Murphy L | Fazackerley S | Wightman H | Keetley F | Bedford H | Fox W | Ritchie A | Haley W | Bromage E | Hart J | Smith V | Davison T | Moore J | Carr W | Rowe G | Gill J | Cooper T | Bacon A | Mee G | McLaverty B |
|---|---|---|---|---|---|---|---|---|---|---|---|---|---|---|---|---|---|---|---|---|---|---|---|---|---|---|---|---|---|---|
| 3 | | | 3 | 4 | 5 | 6 | 7 | | | 10 | | | 2 | | 9 | | | 8 | 11 | | | | | | | | | | | |
| R | | | | 4 | 5 | 6 | 11 | | | 10 | | | 2 | 7 | 9 | | 3 | 8 | | | | | | | | | | | | |
| 2R | | | | 4 | 5 | 6 | 7 | | | 10 | | | 2 | 8 | 9 | | 3 | | 11 | | | | | | | | | | | |
| 4 | | | | 4 | 5 | 6 | 7 | | | 10 | 11 | | 2 | 8 | 9 | | 3 | | | | | | | | | | | | | |
| Total | 4 | | 1 | 4 | 4 | 4 | 4 | | | 4 | 1 | | 4 | 3 | 4 | | 3 | 2 | 2 | | | | | | | | | | | |
| Goals | | | | | | | 1 | | | | 1 | | | | 1 | | | | 1 | | | | | | | | | | | |

# 1926-27

| | P | W | D | L | F | A | Pts |
|---|---|---|---|---|---|---|---|
| Newcastle U | 42 | 25 | 6 | 11 | 96 | 58 | 56 |
| Huddersfield T | 42 | 17 | 17 | 8 | 76 | 60 | 51 |
| Sunderland | 42 | 21 | 7 | 14 | 98 | 70 | 49 |
| Bolton W | 42 | 19 | 10 | 13 | 84 | 62 | 48 |
| Burnley | 42 | 19 | 9 | 14 | 91 | 80 | 47 |
| West Ham U | 42 | 19 | 8 | 15 | 86 | 70 | 46 |
| Leicester C | 42 | 17 | 12 | 13 | 85 | 70 | 46 |
| Sheffield U | 42 | 17 | 10 | 15 | 74 | 86 | 44 |
| Liverpool | 42 | 18 | 7 | 17 | 69 | 61 | 43 |
| Aston Villa | 42 | 18 | 7 | 17 | 81 | 83 | 43 |
| Arsenal | 42 | 17 | 9 | 16 | 77 | 86 | 43 |
| Derby Co | 42 | 17 | 7 | 18 | 86 | 73 | 41 |
| Tottenham H | 42 | 16 | 9 | 17 | 76 | 78 | 41 |
| Cardiff C | 42 | 16 | 9 | 17 | 55 | 65 | 41 |
| Manchester U | 42 | 13 | 14 | 15 | 52 | 64 | 40 |
| Sheffield W | 42 | 15 | 9 | 18 | 75 | 92 | 39 |
| Birmingham | 42 | 17 | 4 | 21 | 64 | 73 | 38 |
| Blackburn R | 42 | 15 | 8 | 19 | 77 | 96 | 38 |
| Bury | 42 | 12 | 12 | 18 | 68 | 77 | 36 |
| Everton | 42 | 12 | 10 | 20 | 64 | 90 | 34 |
| Leeds U | 42 | 11 | 8 | 23 | 69 | 88 | 30 |
| WBA | 42 | 11 | 8 | 23 | 65 | 86 | 30 |

Manager: George Jobey.
Leading scorers: Harry Bedford, Jimmy Gill, League 22. Harry Bedford, all matches 26.
League ever-present: Harry Thoms.

- The main stand, on Shaftesbury Crescent, was opened in September and lasted until Derby left the Baseball Ground. They recorded the first 30,000 attendance, 30,557 against Bolton Wanderers on 27 December.
- Harry Bedford scored four goals against Bradford City in the FA Cup and Jackie Whitehouse did it in the League when Sheffield Wednesday were beaten 8–0 in March. Bedford and Jack Stamps are the only two to do it in the FA Cup.
- Derby scored 86 League goals, their most prolific season so far. The record did not survive for long and in the 14 peacetime seasons under Jobey, the Rams averaged fractionally under 80 goals. They conceded, on average, 70.

## Division One

| Match No. | Date | Venue | Opponents | Result | | Scorers | Attendan |
|---|---|---|---|---|---|---|---|
| 1 | Aug 28 | (a) | Arsenal | L | 1-2 | Storer | 32,99 |
| 2 | Sep 4 | (h) | Liverpool | W | 2-1 | Gill, Bedford | 21,46 |
| 3 | 11 | (a) | Leeds U | L | 0-1 | | 17,41 |
| 4 | 13 | (a) | Sheffield U | L | 0-1 | | 19,60 |
| 5 | 18 | (h) | Newcastle U | D | 1-1 | Storer | 26,30 |
| 6 | 25 | (a) | Burnley | L | 0-1 | | 17,67 |
| 7 | 27 | (h) | Sheffield U | W | 1-0 | Storer | 17,45 |
| 8 | Oct 2 | (h) | Cardiff C | W | 6-3 | Storer 2, Bedford 2 (1 pen), Gill, Murphy | 21,2 |
| 9 | 9 | (a) | Aston Villa | L | 1-3 | Gill | 22,38 |
| 10 | 16 | (a) | Birmingham | L | 0-1 | | 23,14 |
| 11 | 23 | (h) | Tottenham H | W | 4-1 | Bedford 2, Gill, McLaverty | 20,32 |
| 12 | 30 | (a) | Sheffield W | L | 1-2 | Murphy | 29,80 |
| 13 | Nov 6 | (h) | Leicester C | W | 4-1 | Bedford 2, Gill 2 | 22,23 |
| 14 | 13 | (a) | Everton | L | 2-3 | Thornewell, Hart | 29,9 |
| 15 | 20 | (h) | Blackburn R | L | 4-5 | Gill 2, Bedford, Storer | 12,7 |
| 16 | 27 | (a) | Huddersfield T | L | 2-4 | Bedford, Gill | 16,7 |
| 17 | Dec 4 | (h) | Sunderland | W | 4-2 | Mee 2, Gill, Storer | 18,9 |
| 18 | 11 | (a) | West Brom A | L | 1-3 | Mee | 19,9 |
| 19 | 18 | (h) | Bury | W | 2-0 | Fairclough, Gill | 15,0 |
| 20 | 25 | (a) | Bolton W | L | 1-3 | Gill | 31,5 |
| 21 | 27 | (h) | Bolton W | W | 2-0 | Gill, Fairclough | 30,5 |
| 22 | 28 | (h) | West Ham U | W | 3-0 | Gill 2, Whitehouse | 21,8 |
| 23 | Jan 1 | (a) | West Ham U | W | 2-1 | Murphy 2 | 20,8 |
| 24 | 15 | (h) | Arsenal | L | 0-2 | | 21,8 |
| 25 | 22 | (a) | Liverpool | L | 2-3 | Whitehouse, Bedford | 20,6 |
| 26 | Feb 5 | (a) | Newcastle U | L | 0-3 | | 30,8 |
| 27 | 12 | (h) | Burnley | W | 4-1 | Bedford 3, Gill | 14,0 |
| 28 | 19 | (h) | Leeds U | W | 1-0 | Murphy | 14,5 |
| 29 | 26 | (h) | Aston Villa | L | 2-3 | Murphy, Whitehouse | 22,3 |
| 30 | Mar 5 | (h) | Birmingham | W | 4-1 | Murphy 2, Whitehouse 2 | 15,1 |
| 31 | 12 | (a) | Tottenham H | L | 2-3 | Bedford, Thoms | 26,5 |
| 32 | 16 | (a) | Cardiff C | L | 0-2 | | 10,0 |
| 33 | 19 | (h) | Sheffield W | W | 8-0 | Whitehouse 4, Bedford 3 (1 pen), Gill | 19,3 |
| 34 | 26 | (a) | Leicester C | D | 1-1 | Whitehouse | 25,3 |
| 35 | Apr 2 | (h) | Everton | D | 0-0 | | 18,0 |
| 36 | 9 | (a) | Blackburn R | D | 4-4 | Murphy 2, Whitehouse, Thornewell | 10,7 |
| 37 | 15 | (a) | Manchester U | D | 2-2 | Bedford, Whitehouse | 31,1 |
| 38 | 16 | (h) | Huddersfield T | D | 4-4 | Gill 2, Storer, Whitehouse | 24,6 |
| 39 | 18 | (h) | Manchester U | D | 2-2 | Thornewell, Gill | 17,3 |
| 40 | 23 | (a) | Sunderland | W | 2-1 | Bedford 2 | 15,0 |
| 41 | 30 | (h) | West Brom A | W | 2-1 | Gill, Bedford | 11,8 |
| 42 | May 7 | (a) | Bury | W | 2-1 | Gill, Bedford (pen) | 9,4 |

FINAL LEAGUE POSITION: 12th in Division One

Appearan
Go

## FA Cup

| | | | | | | | |
|---|---|---|---|---|---|---|---|
| 3 | Jan 8 | (a) | Bradford C | W | 6-2 | Bedford 4, Whitehouse, Murphy | 20,2 |
| 4 | 29 | (h) | Millwall | L | 0-2 | | 25,7 |

Appearan
Go

| …ney B | Cooper T | Crilly T | McIntyre J | Thoms H | Plackett S | Thornewell G | Gill J | Bedford H | Storer H | Murphy L | Whitehouse J | Smith V | Wightman H | McLaverty B | Donaghy E | Mee G | Bromage E | Hart J | Cowell W | Ritchie A | Carr W | Fairclough A | Bacon A | Kelly D | Haley W | Nelson E | O'Brien M | Hope J | |
|---|---|---|---|---|---|---|---|---|---|---|---|---|---|---|---|---|---|---|---|---|---|---|---|---|---|---|---|---|---|
| | 2 | 3 | 4 | 5 | 6 | 7 | 8 | 9 | 10 | 11 | | | | | | | | | | | | | | | | | | | 1 |
| | 2 | 3 | 4 | 5 | 6 | 7 | 8 | 9 | 10 | 11 | | | | | | | | | | | | | | | | | | | 2 |
| | 2 | 3 | 4 | 5 | 6 | 7 | 8 | | 10 | 11 | 9 | | | | | | | | | | | | | | | | | | 3 |
| | 2 | 3 | 4 | 5 | 6 | 7 | 8 | | 10 | 11 | 9 | | | | | | | | | | | | | | | | | | 4 |
| | 2 | 3 | 4 | 5 | 6 | | 8 | 9 | 10 | 11 | | 7 | | | | | | | | | | | | | | | | | 5 |
| | 2 | 3 | 4 | 5 | 6 | | 8 | 9 | 10 | 11 | | 7 | | | | | | | | | | | | | | | | | 6 |
| | 2 | 3 | 4 | 5 | 6 | | 7 | 9 | 10 | 11 | 8 | | | | | | | | | | | | | | | | | | 7 |
| | 2 | 3 | 4 | 5 | 6 | | 7 | 9 | 10 | 11 | 8 | | | | | | | | | | | | | | | | | | 8 |
| | | 3 | 4 | 5 | 6 | | 7 | 9 | 10 | 11 | 8 | | 2 | | | | | | | | | | | | | | | | 9 |
| | 2 | 3 | | 5 | | | 7 | 9 | | 10 | 8 | | | 4 | 6 | 11 | | | | | | | | | | | | | 10 |
| | 2 | 3 | | 5 | | 7 | 8 | 9 | 10 | 11 | | | | 4 | 6 | | | | | | | | | | | | | | 11 |
| | 2 | 3 | 4 | 5 | | 7 | 8 | 9 | | 11 | | | | 6 | | | 10 | | | | | | | | | | | | 12 |
| | 2 | 3 | | 5 | | 7 | 8 | 9 | | 10 | | | | 4 | 6 | 11 | | | | | | | | | | | | | 13 |
| | 2 | 3 | | 5 | | 7 | 8 | | | 10 | | | | 4 | 6 | 11 | | 9 | | | | | | | | | | | 14 |
| | 2 | | | 5 | | 7 | 8 | 9 | 10 | | | | | 4 | 6 | 11 | | | 1 | 3 | | | | | | | | | 15 |
| | 2 | | 4 | 5 | 6 | 7 | 8 | 9 | 10 | | | | | | | 11 | | | | | 3 | | | | | | | | 16 |
| | 2 | 3 | 4 | 5 | | 7 | 8 | 9 | 10 | | | | | 6 | | 11 | | | | | | | | | | | | | 17 |
| | 2 | 3 | 4 | 5 | | 7 | 8 | 9 | 10 | | | | | 6 | | 11 | | | | | | | | | | | | | 18 |
| | 2 | 3 | 4 | 5 | | 7 | 8 | | 10 | | | | | 6 | | 11 | | | | | | 9 | | | | | | | 19 |
| | 2 | 3 | 4 | 5 | | 7 | 8 | | 10 | | | | | 6 | | 11 | | | | | | 9 | | | | | | | 20 |
| | 2 | 3 | 4 | 5 | | 7 | 8 | | 10 | | | | | 6 | | 11 | | | | | | 9 | | | | | | | 21 |
| | | 3 | 4 | 5 | 6 | 7 | 8 | 9 | | 11 | 10 | | | | | | | | | | 2 | | | | | | | | 22 |
| | | 3 | 4 | 5 | | 7 | 8 | 9 | | 11 | 10 | | | 6 | | | | | | | 2 | | | | | | | | 23 |
| | | 3 | 4 | 5 | | 7 | 8 | 9 | | 11 | 10 | | | 6 | | | | | | | 2 | | | | | | | | 24 |
| | | 3 | 4 | 5 | | 7 | 8 | 9 | | 11 | 10 | | | 6 | | | | | | | 2 | | | | | | | | 25 |
| | | 3 | 4 | 5 | 6 | | | 9 | | 11 | | | | | | | | | | | 2 | | 10 | 7 | 8 | | | | 26 |
| | | 3 | | 5 | | | 8 | 9 | 10 | 11 | | | | | 6 | | | | | | 2 | | | 7 | | 4 | | | 27 |
| | | 3 | 4 | 5 | | 7 | 8 | | 9 | 11 | 10 | | | 6 | | | | | | | 2 | | | | | | | | 28 |
| | | 3 | 4 | 5 | | | 8 | | 9 | 11 | 10 | | | 6 | | | | | | | 2 | | | 7 | | | | | 29 |
| | | 3 | 4 | 5 | | 7 | 8 | 9 | | 11 | 10 | | | 6 | | | | | | | 2 | | | | | | | | 30 |
| | | 3 | 4 | 5 | | 7 | 8 | 9 | | 11 | 10 | | | 6 | | | | | | | 2 | | | | | | | | 31 |
| | 2 | | | 5 | | 7 | | | 9 | 11 | 10 | | | | | | | | | | 3 | | | | | 4 | 6 | 8 | 32 |
| | | 3 | | 5 | | 7 | 8 | 9 | 6 | 11 | 10 | | | 4 | | | | | | | 2 | | | | | | | | 33 |
| | | 3 | | 5 | | 7 | 8 | 9 | 6 | 11 | 10 | | | 4 | | | | | | | 2 | | | | | | | | 34 |
| | | 3 | | 5 | | 7 | 8 | 9 | 6 | 11 | 10 | | | 4 | | | | | | | 2 | | | | | | | | 35 |
| | | 3 | | 5 | | 7 | 8 | 9 | 6 | 11 | 10 | | | 4 | | | | | | | 2 | | | | | | | | 36 |
| | | 3 | | 5 | | 7 | 8 | 9 | 6 | 11 | 10 | | | 4 | | | | | | | 2 | | | | | | | | 37 |
| | | 3 | | 5 | | 7 | 8 | 9 | 6 | 11 | 10 | | | 4 | | | | | | | 2 | | | | | | | | 38 |
| | 2 | 3 | 4 | 5 | | 7 | 8 | 9 | 6 | 11 | 10 | | | | | | | | | | | | | | | | | | 39 |
| | 2 | 3 | 4 | 5 | | 7 | 10 | 9 | 6 | 11 | | | | | | | | | | | | | | | | | | 8 | 40 |
| | 2 | 3 | 4 | 5 | | 7 | 10 | 9 | | 11 | | | | 6 | | | | | | | | | | | | | | 8 | 41 |
| | 2 | | 4 | 5 | | | 8 | 9 | | | 10 | | | 6 | | 11 | | | | | 3 | | | 7 | | | | | 42 |
| 1 | 25 | 38 | 29 | 42 | 12 | 32 | 40 | 33 | 29 | 34 | 23 | 2 | 1 | 26 | 6 | 11 | 1 | 1 | 1 | 1 | 19 | 3 | 1 | 4 | 1 | 2 | 1 | 3 | |
| | | | | 1 | | 3 | 22 | 22 | 8 | 10 | 13 | | | 1 | | 3 | | 1 | | | | 2 | | | | | | | |

| …ney B | Cooper T | Crilly T | McIntyre J | Thoms H | Plackett S | Thornewell G | Gill J | Bedford H | Storer H | Murphy L | Whitehouse J | Smith V | Wightman H | McLaverty B | Donaghy E | Mee G | Bromage E | Hart J | Cowell W | Ritchie A | Carr W | Fairclough A | Bacon A | Kelly D | Haley W | Nelson E | O'Brien M | Hope J | |
|---|---|---|---|---|---|---|---|---|---|---|---|---|---|---|---|---|---|---|---|---|---|---|---|---|---|---|---|---|---|
| | | 3 | 4 | 5 | | | 8 | 9 | | 11 | 10 | | | 6 | | | | | | | 2 | | 7 | | | | | | 3 |
| | | 3 | 4 | 5 | 6 | 7 | | 9 | 10 | 11 | 8 | | | | | | | | | | 2 | | | | | | | | 4 |
| 2 | | 2 | 2 | 2 | 1 | 1 | 1 | 2 | 1 | 2 | 2 | | | 1 | | | | | | | 2 | | 1 | | | | | | |
| | | | | | | | | 4 | | 1 | 1 | | | | | | | | | | | | | | | | | | |

# 1927-28

| | P | W | D | L | F | A | Pts |
|---|---|---|---|---|---|---|---|
| Everton | 42 | 20 | 13 | 9 | 102 | 66 | 53 |
| Huddersfield T | 42 | 22 | 7 | 13 | 91 | 68 | 51 |
| Leicester C | 42 | 18 | 12 | 12 | 96 | 72 | 48 |
| Derby Co | 42 | 17 | 10 | 15 | 96 | 83 | 44 |
| Bury | 42 | 20 | 4 | 18 | 80 | 80 | 44 |
| Cardiff C | 42 | 17 | 10 | 15 | 70 | 80 | 44 |
| Bolton W | 42 | 16 | 11 | 15 | 81 | 66 | 43 |
| Aston Villa | 42 | 17 | 9 | 16 | 78 | 73 | 43 |
| Newcastle U | 42 | 15 | 13 | 14 | 79 | 81 | 43 |
| Arsenal | 42 | 13 | 15 | 14 | 82 | 86 | 41 |
| Birmingham | 42 | 13 | 15 | 14 | 70 | 75 | 41 |
| Blackburn R | 42 | 16 | 9 | 17 | 66 | 78 | 41 |
| Sheffield U | 42 | 15 | 10 | 17 | 79 | 86 | 40 |
| Sheffield W | 42 | 13 | 13 | 16 | 81 | 78 | 39 |
| Sunderland | 42 | 15 | 9 | 18 | 74 | 76 | 39 |
| Liverpool | 42 | 13 | 13 | 16 | 84 | 87 | 39 |
| West Ham U | 42 | 14 | 11 | 17 | 81 | 88 | 39 |
| Manchester U | 42 | 16 | 7 | 19 | 72 | 80 | 39 |
| Burnley | 42 | 16 | 7 | 19 | 82 | 98 | 39 |
| Portsmouth | 42 | 16 | 7 | 19 | 66 | 90 | 39 |
| Tottenham H | 42 | 15 | 8 | 19 | 74 | 86 | 38 |
| Middlesbrough | 42 | 11 | 15 | 16 | 81 | 88 | 37 |

Manager: George Jobey.
Leading scorer: Harry Bedford, League 27, all matches 28.

- Harry Bedford scored four times in the 7–1 defeat of Cardiff City at the end of March as Derby beat the previous season's record with 96 goals. They equalled it in 1936–37 and this remains their highest in the top flight.
- Sammy Crooks, one of Derby's greatest players, made his debut against Leicester City in September. Crooks attracted Derby's attention when playing for Durham City in the Third Division North and George Jobey met him off his coal lorry to clinch the signing.
- George Stephenson, one of the players auctioned when Leeds City were expelled from the League in 1919, scored in six consecutive matches in November and December. Three players had previously done this for Derby: John Goodall (1891–92), Alf Bentley (1909–19) and Horace Barnes (1913–14).

## Division One

| Match No. | Date | | Venue | Opponents | Result | | Scorers | Attendan |
|---|---|---|---|---|---|---|---|---|
| 1 | Aug | 27 | (h) | West Ham U | L | 2-3 | Bedford, Whitehouse | 18,53 |
| 2 | Sep | 3 | (a) | Portsmouth | D | 2-2 | Bedford, Whitehouse | 23,48 |
| 3 | | 5 | (h) | Newcastle U | D | 1-1 | Gill | 20,82 |
| 4 | | 10 | (h) | Leicester C | W | 2-1 | Gill, Whitehouse | 26,00 |
| 5 | | 14 | (a) | Newcastle U | L | 3-4 | Bedford 3 | 36,96 |
| 6 | | 17 | (a) | Liverpool | L | 2-5 | Bedford 2 | 34,33 |
| 7 | | 24 | (h) | Arsenal | W | 4-0 | Gill, Whitehouse, Murphy, Crooks | 16,53 |
| 8 | Oct | 1 | (a) | Burnley | L | 2-4 | Gill, Whitehouse | 11,91 |
| 9 | | 8 | (h) | Bury | W | 5-2 | Crooks 2, Murphy, Bedford, McIntyre | 15,53 |
| 10 | | 15 | (a) | Sheffield U | L | 0-1 | | 24,86 |
| 11 | | 22 | (a) | Manchester U | L | 0-5 | | 18,39 |
| 12 | | 29 | (h) | Tottenham H | D | 1-1 | Hope | 15,76 |
| 13 | Nov | 5 | (a) | Huddersfield T | L | 1-2 | Bedford | 7,09 |
| 14 | | 12 | (h) | Everton | L | 0-3 | | 21,59 |
| 15 | | 19 | (a) | Cardiff C | D | 4-4 | Stephenson 2, Crooks, Bedford | 6,6 |
| 16 | | 26 | (h) | Sheffield W | L | 4-6 | Whitehouse 2, Mee, Stephenson | 16,06 |
| 17 | Dec | 10 | (h) | Blackburn R | W | 6-0 | Bedford 2 (1 pen), Stephenson 2, Crooks, Whitehouse | 10,61 |
| 18 | | 17 | (a) | Middlesbrough | D | 3-3 | Stephenson, Crooks, Whitehouse | 15,22 |
| 19 | | 24 | (h) | Birmingham | W | 4-1 | Stephenson, Mee, Crooks, Bedford | 8,53 |
| 20 | | 26 | (h) | Aston Villa | W | 5-0 | Bedford 2, Whitehouse 2, Stephenson | 23,3 |
| 21 | | 27 | (a) | Aston Villa | W | 1-0 | McIntyre | 43,22 |
| 22 | | 31 | (a) | West Ham U | D | 2-2 | Bedford, Stephenson | 17,76 |
| 23 | Jan | 2 | (a) | Bolton W | W | 3-1 | Whitehouse 2, Stephenson | 23,5 |
| 24 | | 7 | (h) | Portsmouth | D | 2-2 | Stephenson 2 | 18,6 |
| 25 | | 21 | (a) | Leicester C | L | 0-4 | | 36,0 |
| 26 | Feb | 4 | (a) | Arsenal | W | 4-3 | Gill 3, Crooks | 21,4 |
| 27 | | 11 | (h) | Burnley | L | 3-4 | Gill 2, Storer | 8,5 |
| 28 | | 15 | (h) | Liverpool | L | 2-3 | Gill, Bedford | 9,0 |
| 29 | | 18 | (a) | Bury | L | 0-3 | | 11,4 |
| 30 | | 25 | (h) | Sheffield U | W | 2-1 | Bedford, Whitehouse | 14,2 |
| 31 | Mar | 10 | (a) | Tottenham H | W | 2-1 | Bedford, Whitehouse | 22,4 |
| 32 | | 17 | (h) | Huddersfield T | D | 0-0 | | 24,6 |
| 33 | | 24 | (a) | Everton | D | 2-2 | Bedford, Storer | 28,5 |
| 34 | | 28 | (h) | Manchester U | W | 5-0 | Bedford 2, Stephenson 2, Whitehouse | 8,3 |
| 35 | | 31 | (h) | Cardiff C | W | 7-1 | Bedford 4, Whitehouse 2, Crooks | 15,5 |
| 36 | Apr | 6 | (a) | Sunderland | W | 1-0 | Bedford | 27,4 |
| 37 | | 7 | (a) | Sheffield W | D | 2-2 | McIntyre, Stephenson | 28,5 |
| 38 | | 9 | (h) | Sunderland | W | 1-0 | Stephenson | 24,2 |
| 39 | | 14 | (h) | Bolton W | W | 1-0 | Whitehouse | 12,3 |
| 40 | | 26 | (a) | Blackburn R | L | 2-3 | Whitehouse, Crooks | 21,4 |
| 41 | | 28 | (h) | Middlesbrough | W | 2-1 | Whitehouse, Bacon | 12,0 |
| 42 | May | 5 | (a) | Birmingham | L | 1-2 | Stephenson | 16,4 |

FINAL LEAGUE POSITION: 4th in Division One

Appearan
Go

## FA Cup

| | | | | | | | | |
|---|---|---|---|---|---|---|---|---|
| 3 | Jan | 14 | (a) | Millwall | W | 2-1 | Stephenson, Bedford | 38,8 |
| 4 | | 28 | (h) | Nottingham F | D | 0-0 | | 22,5 |
| 5 | Feb | 1 | (a) | Nottingham F | L | 0-2 | | 35,6 |

Appearan
Go

| Olney B | Cooper T | Crilly T | McIntyre J | O'Brien M | McLaverty B | Thornewell G | Gill J | Bedford H | Whitehouse J | Murphy L | Davison T | Storer H | Crooks S | Scott A | Thoms H | Hope J | Wilkes H | Carr W | Wightman H | Malloch G | Bacon A | Mee G | Stephenson G | Collin G | Robinson T | White A | Hampton J | Kelly D | Robson W | |
|---|---|---|---|---|---|---|---|---|---|---|---|---|---|---|---|---|---|---|---|---|---|---|---|---|---|---|---|---|---|---|
| 1 | 2 | 3 | 4 | 5 | 6 | 7 | 8 | 9 | 10 | 11 | | | | | | | | | | | | | | | | | | | | 1 |
| 1 | 2 | 3 | 4 | | | 7 | 8 | 9 | 10 | 11 | 5 | 6 | | | | | | | | | | | | | | | | | | 2 |
| 1 | 2 | 3 | 4 | | 5 | 7 | 8 | 9 | 10 | 11 | | 6 | | | | | | | | | | | | | | | | | | 3 |
| 1 | 2 | 3 | 4 | | 5 | | 8 | 9 | 10 | 11 | | 6 | 7 | | | | | | | | | | | | | | | | | 4 |
| 1 | 2 | 3 | | | | | | 9 | 10 | 11 | | 6 | 7 | 4 | 5 | 8 | | | | | | | | | | | | | | 5 |
| 1 | 2 | 3 | 4 | | | | 8 | 9 | 10 | 11 | | 6 | 7 | | 5 | | | | | | | | | | | | | | | 6 |
| | 2 | 3 | 4 | | | | 8 | 9 | 10 | 11 | | 6 | 7 | | 5 | | 1 | | | | | | | | | | | | | 7 |
| | 2 | 3 | 4 | | | | 8 | 9 | 10 | 11 | 5 | 6 | 7 | | | | 1 | | | | | | | | | | | | | 8 |
| | 2 | | 4 | | | | 8 | 9 | 10 | 11 | 5 | 6 | 7 | | | | 1 | 3 | | | | | | | | | | | | 9 |
| | 2 | | 4 | | | 7 | | 9 | 10 | 11 | 5 | 6 | | | | 8 | 1 | 3 | | | | | | | | | | | | 10 |
| | | | 4 | | | 7 | | | 10 | 11 | 5 | | | | | 8 | 1 | 3 | 2 | 6 | 9 | | | | | | | | | 11 |
| | 2 | | 4 | | | 7 | | | 10 | 11 | | 6 | | | 5 | 8 | 1 | 3 | | | 9 | | | | | | | | | 12 |
| | 2 | | 4 | | | | | 9 | 10 | | | 6 | 7 | | 5 | 8 | 1 | 3 | | | | 11 | | | | | | | | 13 |
| | 2 | | 4 | | | | | 9 | 8 | | | 6 | 7 | | 5 | | 1 | 3 | | | | 11 | 10 | | | | | | | 14 |
| | | | 4 | | | | | 9 | 8 | | | 6 | 7 | | 5 | | 1 | 2 | | | | 11 | 10 | 3 | | | | | | 15 |
| | | | 4 | | | | | 9 | 8 | | | 6 | 7 | | 5 | | 1 | 2 | | | | 11 | 10 | 3 | | | | | | 16 |
| | | | | | | | | 9 | 8 | | 5 | 6 | 7 | 4 | | | 1 | 2 | | | | 11 | 10 | 3 | | | | | | 17 |
| | | | | | | | | 9 | 8 | | 5 | 6 | 7 | 4 | | | 1 | 2 | | | | 11 | 10 | 3 | | | | | | 18 |
| | | | | | | | | 9 | 8 | | 5 | 6 | 7 | 4 | | | 1 | 2 | | | | 11 | 10 | 3 | | | | | | 19 |
| | | | | | | | | 9 | 8 | | 5 | 6 | 7 | | | | 1 | 2 | | | | 11 | 10 | 3 | 4 | | | | | 20 |
| | | | 4 | 5 | | | | 9 | 8 | | | 6 | | | | | 1 | 2 | | | 7 | 11 | 10 | 3 | | | | | | 21 |
| | | | | | | | | 9 | 8 | | 5 | 6 | 7 | | | | 1 | 2 | | | | 11 | 10 | 3 | 4 | | | | | 22 |
| | | | | | | | | 9 | 8 | | 5 | 6 | 7 | | | | 1 | 2 | | | | 11 | 10 | 3 | 4 | | | | | 23 |
| | | | | | | | | 9 | 8 | | 5 | 6 | 7 | 4 | | | 1 | 2 | | | | 11 | 10 | 3 | | | | | | 24 |
| | | | | | | | | | 8 | | 5 | 6 | 7 | 4 | | | 1 | 2 | | | | 11 | 10 | 3 | | 9 | | | | 25 |
| | | | | | | | 8 | 9 | | | 5 | 6 | 7 | 4 | | | 1 | 2 | | | | 11 | 10 | 3 | | | | | | 26 |
| | | | | | | | 8 | 9 | | | 5 | 6 | 7 | 4 | | | 1 | 2 | | | | 11 | 10 | 3 | | | | | | 27 |
| | | | | | | | 8 | 9 | | | 5 | 6 | 7 | 4 | | | 1 | 2 | | | | 11 | 10 | 3 | | | | | | 28 |
| | | | 4 | | | | 8 | 9 | | | 5 | 6 | 7 | | | | | 2 | | | | 11 | 10 | 3 | | | 1 | | | 29 |
| | | | 4 | | | | | 9 | 8 | | 5 | | 7 | | | | 1 | 2 | | 6 | | 11 | 10 | 3 | | | | | | 30 |
| | | | 4 | | | | | 9 | 8 | | 5 | 6 | 7 | | | | 1 | 2 | | | | 11 | 10 | 3 | | | | | | 31 |
| | | | 4 | | | | | 9 | 8 | | 5 | 6 | 7 | | | | 1 | 2 | | | | 11 | 10 | 3 | | | | | | 32 |
| | | | 4 | | | | | 9 | 8 | | 5 | 6 | 7 | | | | 1 | 2 | | | | 11 | 10 | 3 | | | | | | 33 |
| | | | 4 | | | | | 9 | 8 | | 5 | 6 | 7 | | | | 1 | 2 | | | | 11 | 10 | 3 | | | | | | 34 |
| | | | 4 | | | | | 9 | 8 | | 5 | 6 | 7 | | | | 1 | 2 | | | | 11 | 10 | 3 | | | | | | 35 |
| | | | 4 | | | | | 9 | 8 | | 5 | 6 | 7 | | | | | 2 | | | | 11 | 10 | 3 | | | 1 | | | 36 |
| | | | 4 | | | | 8 | 9 | | | | 6 | | | 5 | | | 2 | | | | 11 | 10 | 3 | | | 1 | 7 | | 37 |
| | | | 4 | | | | | 9 | 8 | | | | 7 | | 5 | | | 2 | | 6 | | 11 | 10 | 3 | | | 1 | | | 38 |
| | | | 4 | | | | | 9 | 8 | | | | 7 | | 5 | | | 2 | | 6 | | 11 | 10 | 3 | | | 1 | | | 39 |
| | | | 4 | | | | | 9 | 8 | | 5 | 6 | 7 | | | | | 2 | | | | 11 | 10 | 3 | | | 1 | | | 40 |
| | | | 4 | | | | | | 8 | | 5 | 10 | 7 | | | | | 2 | | 6 | 9 | 11 | | 3 | | | 1 | | | 41 |
| | | | 4 | | | | | 9 | 8 | | 5 | | 7 | | | | | 2 | | 6 | | 11 | 10 | 3 | | | 1 | | | 42 |
| 6 | 13 | 8 | 30 | 2 | 3 | 6 | 13 | 38 | 37 | 12 | 27 | 36 | 34 | 9 | 11 | 5 | 28 | 34 | 1 | 6 | 4 | 30 | 28 | 28 | 3 | 1 | 8 | 1 | | |
| | | | 3 | | | | 10 | 27 | 21 | 2 | | 2 | 10 | | | 1 | | | | | 1 | 2 | 17 | | | | | | | |

| Olney B | Cooper T | Crilly T | McIntyre J | O'Brien M | McLaverty B | Thornewell G | Gill J | Bedford H | Whitehouse J | Murphy L | Davison T | Storer H | Crooks S | Scott A | Thoms H | Hope J | Wilkes H | Carr W | Wightman H | Malloch G | Bacon A | Mee G | Stephenson G | Collin G | Robinson T | White A | Hampton J | Kelly D | Robson W | |
|---|---|---|---|---|---|---|---|---|---|---|---|---|---|---|---|---|---|---|---|---|---|---|---|---|---|---|---|---|---|---|
| | | | | | | | | 9 | 8 | | 5 | 6 | 7 | 4 | | | 1 | 2 | | | | 11 | 10 | | | | | | 3 | 3 |
| | | | | 5 | | | | 9 | 8 | | | 6 | 7 | 4 | | | 1 | 2 | | | | 11 | 10 | | | | | | 3 | 4 |
| | | | | 5 | | | | 9 | 8 | | | 6 | 7 | 4 | | | 1 | 2 | | | | 11 | 10 | | | | | | 3 | 5 |
| | | | | 2 | | | | 3 | 3 | | 1 | 3 | 3 | 3 | | | 3 | 3 | | | | 3 | 3 | | | | | | 3 | |
| | | | | | | | | 1 | | | | | | | | | | | | | | | 1 | | | | | | | |

# 1928-29

| | P | W | D | L | F | A | Pts |
|---|---|---|---|---|---|---|---|
| Sheffield W | 42 | 21 | 10 | 11 | 86 | 62 | 52 |
| Leicester C | 42 | 21 | 9 | 12 | 96 | 67 | 51 |
| Aston Villa | 42 | 23 | 4 | 15 | 98 | 81 | 50 |
| Sunderland | 42 | 20 | 7 | 15 | 93 | 75 | 47 |
| Liverpool | 42 | 17 | 12 | 13 | 90 | 64 | 46 |
| Derby Co | 42 | 18 | 10 | 14 | 86 | 71 | 46 |
| Blackburn R | 42 | 17 | 11 | 14 | 72 | 63 | 45 |
| Manchester C | 42 | 18 | 9 | 15 | 95 | 86 | 45 |
| Arsenal | 42 | 16 | 13 | 13 | 77 | 72 | 45 |
| Newcastle U | 42 | 19 | 6 | 17 | 70 | 72 | 44 |
| Sheffield U | 42 | 15 | 11 | 16 | 86 | 85 | 41 |
| Manchester U | 42 | 14 | 13 | 15 | 66 | 76 | 41 |
| Leeds U | 42 | 16 | 9 | 17 | 71 | 84 | 41 |
| Bolton W | 42 | 14 | 12 | 16 | 73 | 80 | 40 |
| Birmingham | 42 | 15 | 10 | 17 | 68 | 77 | 40 |
| Huddersfield T | 42 | 14 | 11 | 17 | 70 | 61 | 39 |
| West Ham U | 42 | 15 | 9 | 18 | 86 | 96 | 39 |
| Everton | 42 | 17 | 4 | 21 | 63 | 75 | 38 |
| Burnley | 42 | 15 | 8 | 19 | 81 | 103 | 38 |
| Portsmouth | 42 | 15 | 6 | 21 | 56 | 80 | 36 |
| Bury | 42 | 12 | 7 | 23 | 62 | 99 | 31 |
| Cardiff C | 42 | 8 | 13 | 21 | 43 | 59 | 29 |

Manager: George Jobey.
Leading scorer: Harry Bedford, League 27, all matches 30.

- Holiday football saw the Baseball Ground attendance record raised: 30,651 for Huddersfield Town's Boxing Day visit.
- Harry Bedford scored four goals in a match for the third time as a Rams player, against West Ham United on 8 December.
- His successor at centre-forward, Jack Bowers, scored on his debut in February and hit a hat-trick at Portsmouth in his second game. George Jobey nursed him along and Bowers was not a regular choice until 1930–31.

## Division One

| Match No. | Date | | Venue | Opponents | Result | | Scorers | Attendan |
|---|---|---|---|---|---|---|---|---|
| 1 | Aug | 25 | (h) | Blackburn R | W | 5-1 | Whitehouse 2, Bedford, Ramage, Crooks | 19,43 |
| 2 | | 29 | (a) | Arsenal | W | 3-1 | Crooks, Bedford, Mee | 20,06 |
| 3 | Sep | 1 | (a) | Sunderland | L | 0-4 | | 37,13 |
| 4 | | 8 | (h) | Cardiff C | W | 2-0 | Whitehouse, Mee | 20,46 |
| 5 | | 15 | (h) | Sheffield W | W | 6-0 | Stephenson 3, Bedford 2, Whitehouse | 22,76 |
| 6 | | 22 | (a) | Bolton W | L | 0-3 | | 20,40 |
| 7 | | 26 | (h) | Arsenal | D | 0-0 | | 16,75 |
| 8 | | 29 | (h) | Portsmouth | W | 1-0 | Whitehouse | 16,76 |
| 9 | Oct | 6 | (a) | Birmingham | W | 4-1 | Bedford 2, Whitehouse 2 | 27,02 |
| 10 | | 13 | (h) | Manchester C | D | 1-1 | Crooks | 25,05 |
| 11 | | 20 | (a) | Sheffield U | L | 1-2 | Bedford | 29,76 |
| 12 | | 27 | (h) | Burnley | W | 4-0 | Bedford 3, Storer | 13,09 |
| 13 | Nov | 3 | (a) | Aston Villa | W | 3-2 | Bedford, J.C.Robson, Bowen (og) | 43,08 |
| 14 | | 10 | (h) | Leicester C | W | 5-2 | Whitehouse 2, McIntyre, Stephenson, J.C.Robson | 24,67 |
| 15 | | 17 | (a) | Manchester U | W | 1-0 | Bedford | 26,12 |
| 16 | | 24 | (h) | Leeds U | L | 3-4 | Whitehouse 2, Stephenson | 16,60 |
| 17 | Dec | 1 | (a) | Liverpool | L | 0-3 | | 28,71 |
| 18 | | 8 | (h) | West Ham U | W | 6-0 | Bedford 4, Whitehouse, Davison (pen) | 15,28 |
| 19 | | 15 | (a) | Newcastle U | L | 1-4 | Ruddy | 27,54 |
| 20 | | 22 | (h) | Bury | W | 3-1 | Bedford, Stephenson, J.C.Robson | 11,97 |
| 21 | | 25 | (a) | Huddersfield T | D | 0-0 | | 11,5 |
| 22 | | 26 | (h) | Huddersfield T | L | 1-2 | J.C.Robson | 30,65 |
| 23 | | 29 | (a) | Blackburn R | L | 1-3 | Fereday | 22,5 |
| 24 | Jan | 1 | (a) | Everton | L | 0-4 | | 37,2 |
| 25 | | 5 | (h) | Sunderland | D | 0-0 | | 12,4 |
| 26 | | 19 | (a) | Cardiff C | L | 0-3 | | 14,6 |
| 27 | Feb | 2 | (h) | Bolton W | W | 2-1 | Bedford, Bowers | 9,3 |
| 28 | | 9 | (a) | Portsmouth | W | 5-1 | Bowers 3, Crooks, Whitehouse | 15,8 |
| 29 | | 16 | (h) | Birmingham | D | 2-2 | Whitehouse, Bedford | 12,5 |
| 30 | | 18 | (a) | Sheffield W | L | 0-5 | | 16,0 |
| 31 | | 23 | (a) | Manchester C | W | 3-2 | Stephenson 2, Crooks | 27,9 |
| 32 | Mar | 2 | (h) | Sheffield U | D | 2-2 | Bedford 2 | 12,7 |
| 33 | | 9 | (a) | Burnley | D | 2-2 | Mee, Bowers | 19,9 |
| 34 | | 16 | (h) | Aston Villa | W | 1-0 | Barclay | 18,8 |
| 35 | | 23 | (a) | Leicester C | L | 0-1 | | 23,6 |
| 36 | | 30 | (h) | Manchester U | W | 6-1 | Ruddy 2, Stephenson 2, Bedford 2 | 14,3 |
| 37 | Apr | 2 | (h) | Everton | W | 3-0 | Ruddy, Stephenson, Bedford | 15,8 |
| 38 | | 6 | (a) | Leeds U | D | 1-1 | Ruddy | 19,9 |
| 39 | | 13 | (h) | Liverpool | L | 2-5 | Bedford 2 | 11,3 |
| 40 | | 20 | (a) | West Ham U | D | 2-2 | Ramage, Crooks | 15,0 |
| 41 | | 27 | (h) | Newcastle U | L | 1-2 | Bedford | 13,2 |
| 42 | May | 4 | (a) | Bury | D | 3-3 | Mee 2, Barclay | 5,3 |

FINAL LEAGUE POSITION: 6th in Division One

Appearanc
Go

## FA Cup

| | | | | | | | | |
|---|---|---|---|---|---|---|---|---|
| 3 | Jan | 12 | (h) | Notts C | W | 4-3 | Bedford 2, Whitehouse 2 | 21,3 |
| 4 | | 26 | (a) | Blackburn R | D | 1-1 | Bedford | 45,4 |
| R | | 30 | (h) | Blackburn R | L | 0-3 | | 28,5 |

Appearanc
Go

| Wilkes H | Cooper T | Collin G | McIntyre J | Davison T | Storer H | Crooks S | Whitehouse J | Bedford H | Ramage P | Mee G | Carr W | Stephenson G | Ruddy T | Hampton J | Robson JC | Fereday D | Barclay R | Barker J | MacDougall A | Nicholas J | Alderman A | Scott A | Robinson T | Mann H | Bowers J | Malloch G | Robson W | |
|---|---|---|---|---|---|---|---|---|---|---|---|---|---|---|---|---|---|---|---|---|---|---|---|---|---|---|---|---|
| | 2 | 3 | 4 | 5 | 6 | 7 | 8 | 9 | 10 | 11 | | | | | | | | | | | | | | | | | | 1 |
| | 2 | 3 | 4 | 5 | 6 | 7 | 8 | 9 | 10 | 11 | | | | | | | | | | | | | | | | | | 2 |
| | 2 | 3 | 4 | 5 | 6 | 7 | 8 | 9 | 10 | 11 | | | | | | | | | | | | | | | | | | 3 |
| | 2 | 3 | 4 | 5 | 6 | 7 | 8 | 9 | 10 | 11 | | | | | | | | | | | | | | | | | | 4 |
| | | 3 | 4 | 5 | 6 | 7 | 8 | 9 | | 11 | 2 | 10 | | | | | | | | | | | | | | | | 5 |
| | | 3 | 4 | 5 | 6 | 7 | 8 | 9 | | 11 | 2 | 10 | | | | | | | | | | | | | | | | 6 |
| | 2 | 3 | 4 | 5 | 6 | 7 | | 8 | | 11 | | 10 | 9 | | | | | | | | | | | | | | | 7 |
| | 2 | 3 | 4 | 5 | 6 | 7 | 8 | 9 | | 11 | | 10 | | 1 | | | | | | | | | | | | | | 8 |
| | 2 | 3 | 4 | 5 | 6 | 7 | 8 | 9 | | | | 10 | | | 11 | | | | | | | | | | | | | 9 |
| | 2 | 3 | 4 | 5 | 6 | 7 | 8 | 9 | | | | 10 | | | 11 | | | | | | | | | | | | | 10 |
| | 2 | 3 | 4 | 5 | 6 | 7 | 8 | 9 | | | | 10 | | | 11 | | | | | | | | | | | | | 11 |
| | | 3 | 4 | 5 | 6 | 7 | 8 | 9 | | | 2 | 10 | | | 11 | | | | | | | | | | | | | 12 |
| | 2 | 3 | 4 | 5 | 6 | 7 | 8 | 9 | | | | 10 | | | 11 | | | | | | | | | | | | | 13 |
| | 2 | 3 | 4 | 5 | 6 | | 8 | 9 | | | | 10 | | | 11 | 7 | | | | | | | | | | | | 14 |
| | | 3 | 4 | 5 | 6 | | 8 | 9 | | | 2 | 10 | | | 11 | 7 | | | | | | | | | | | | 15 |
| | | 3 | 4 | 5 | 6 | 7 | 8 | 9 | | | 2 | 10 | | | 11 | | | | | | | | | | | | | 16 |
| | | 3 | 4 | 5 | 6 | 7 | 8 | 9 | | | 2 | 10 | | | 11 | | | | | | | | | | | | | 17 |
| | 2 | 3 | 4 | 5 | 6 | | 8 | 9 | | | | 10 | | | 11 | 7 | | | | | | | | | | | | 18 |
| | 2 | 3 | 4 | 5 | 6 | 7 | | | | | | 10 | 9 | | 11 | | 8 | | | | | | | | | | | 19 |
| | 2 | 3 | 4 | | 6 | | 8 | 9 | | | | 10 | | | 11 | 7 | | 5 | | | | | | | | | | 20 |
| | 2 | 3 | | | 6 | | | 9 | | | | 10 | | | 11 | 7 | 8 | 5 | 4 | | | | | | | | | 21 |
| | 2 | 3 | | 5 | 6 | 7 | 8 | 9 | | | | 10 | | | 11 | | | | 4 | | | | | | | | | 22 |
| | 2 | 3 | | | 6 | | 8 | 9 | | | | 10 | | | 11 | 7 | | 5 | | 4 | | | | | | | | 23 |
| | 2 | 3 | | | 6 | | 8 | 9 | | | | 10 | | | 11 | | | 5 | | 4 | 7 | | | | | | | 24 |
| | 2 | 3 | | 5 | 6 | | 8 | 9 | | | | 10 | | | 11 | 7 | | | | | | 4 | | | | | | 25 |
| | 2 | 3 | | | 6 | | 8 | 9 | | | | 10 | | | 11 | 7 | | 5 | | | | 4 | | | | | | 26 |
| | 2 | 3 | | | 6 | 7 | 8 | 10 | | | | | | | | | | 5 | | | | | 4 | 11 | 9 | | | 27 |
| | 2 | 3 | | | 6 | 7 | 8 | 10 | | | | | | | | | | 5 | | | | 4 | | 11 | 9 | | | 28 |
| | | 3 | 4 | | 6 | 7 | 8 | 10 | | | 2 | | | | | | | 5 | | | | | | 11 | 9 | | | 29 |
| | | 3 | 4 | | 6 | 7 | 8 | 10 | | | 2 | | | | | | | 5 | | | | | | 11 | 9 | | | 30 |
| | | 3 | 4 | | | 7 | | 9 | | | 2 | 10 | | | 11 | | 8 | 5 | | | | | | | | 6 | | 31 |
| | | 3 | 4 | | | 7 | | 9 | | 11 | 2 | 10 | | | | | 8 | 5 | | | | | | | | 6 | | 32 |
| | | 3 | 4 | | | 7 | | 10 | | 11 | 2 | | | | | | 8 | 5 | | | | | | | 9 | 6 | | 33 |
| | | 3 | 4 | | | 7 | | 9 | | 11 | 2 | 10 | | | | | 8 | 5 | | | | | | | | 6 | | 34 |
| | 2 | 3 | 4 | | | | | 9 | | 11 | | 10 | | | | 7 | 8 | 5 | | | | | | | | 6 | | 35 |
| | 2 | 3 | 4 | | | | | 8 | | 11 | | 10 | 9 | | 7 | | | 5 | | | | | | | | 6 | | 36 |
| | 2 | 3 | 4 | | | 7 | | 8 | | 11 | | 10 | 9 | | | | | 5 | | | | | | | | 6 | | 37 |
| | 2 | 3 | 4 | | | | | 8 | | 11 | | 10 | 9 | | 7 | | | 5 | | | | | | | | 6 | | 38 |
| | | 3 | 4 | | | | | 8 | | 11 | 2 | 10 | | | | 7 | | 5 | | | | | | | 9 | 6 | | 39 |
| | 2 | | 4 | 5 | | 7 | | 9 | 10 | 11 | | 8 | | | | | | | | | | | | | | 6 | 3 | 40 |
| | 2 | | 4 | | | 7 | | 9 | 10 | 11 | | 8 | | | | | | 5 | | | | | | | | 6 | 3 | 41 |
| | | | 4 | | | 7 | | 9 | 10 | 11 | 2 | | | | | | 8 | 5 | | | | | | | | 6 | 3 | 42 |
| 1 | 28 | 39 | 34 | 22 | 30 | 29 | 27 | 41 | 7 | 19 | 14 | 32 | 5 | 1 | 21 | 10 | 8 | 20 | 2 | 2 | 1 | 3 | 1 | 4 | 6 | 12 | 3 | |
| | | | 1 | 1 | 1 | 6 | 14 | 27 | 2 | 5 | | 11 | 5 | | 4 | 1 | 2 | | | | | | | | 5 | | | |

1 own-goal

| Wilkes H | Cooper T | Collin G | McIntyre J | Davison T | Storer H | Crooks S | Whitehouse J | Bedford H | Ramage P | Mee G | Carr W | Stephenson G | Ruddy T | Hampton J | Robson JC | Fereday D | Barclay R | Barker J | MacDougall A | Nicholas J | Alderman A | Scott A | Robinson T | Mann H | Bowers J | Malloch G | Robson W | |
|---|---|---|---|---|---|---|---|---|---|---|---|---|---|---|---|---|---|---|---|---|---|---|---|---|---|---|---|---|
| | 2 | 3 | | 5 | 6 | | 8 | 9 | | | | 10 | | | 11 | 7 | | | | | | 4 | | | | | | 3 |
| | 2 | 3 | | | 6 | 7 | 8 | 9 | | | | 10 | | | | | | 5 | | | | | 4 | 11 | | | | 4 |
| | 2 | 3 | | | 6 | 7 | 8 | 9 | | | | 10 | | | | | | 5 | | | | | 4 | 11 | | | | R |
| 3 | 3 | 3 | | 1 | 3 | 2 | 3 | 3 | | | | 3 | | | 1 | 1 | | 2 | | | | 1 | 2 | 2 | | | | |
| | | | | | | | 2 | 3 | | | | | | | | | | | | | | | | | | | | |

# 1929-30

| | P | W | D | L | F | A | Pts |
|---|---|---|---|---|---|---|---|
| Sheffield W | 42 | 26 | 8 | 8 | 105 | 57 | 60 |
| Derby Co | 42 | 21 | 8 | 13 | 90 | 82 | 50 |
| Manchester C | 42 | 19 | 9 | 14 | 91 | 81 | 47 |
| Aston Villa | 42 | 21 | 5 | 16 | 92 | 83 | 47 |
| Leeds U | 42 | 20 | 6 | 16 | 79 | 63 | 46 |
| Blackburn R | 42 | 19 | 7 | 16 | 99 | 93 | 45 |
| West Ham U | 42 | 19 | 5 | 18 | 86 | 79 | 43 |
| Leicester C | 42 | 17 | 9 | 16 | 86 | 90 | 43 |
| Sunderland | 42 | 18 | 7 | 17 | 76 | 80 | 43 |
| Huddersfield T | 42 | 17 | 9 | 16 | 63 | 69 | 43 |
| Birmingham | 42 | 16 | 9 | 17 | 67 | 62 | 41 |
| Liverpool | 42 | 16 | 9 | 17 | 63 | 79 | 41 |
| Portsmouth | 42 | 15 | 10 | 17 | 66 | 62 | 40 |
| Arsenal | 42 | 14 | 11 | 17 | 78 | 66 | 39 |
| Bolton W | 42 | 15 | 9 | 18 | 74 | 74 | 39 |
| Middlesbrough | 42 | 16 | 6 | 20 | 82 | 84 | 38 |
| Manchester U | 42 | 15 | 8 | 19 | 67 | 88 | 38 |
| Grimsby T | 42 | 15 | 7 | 20 | 73 | 89 | 37 |
| Newcastle U | 42 | 15 | 7 | 20 | 71 | 92 | 37 |
| Sheffield U | 42 | 15 | 6 | 21 | 91 | 96 | 36 |
| Burnley | 42 | 14 | 8 | 20 | 79 | 97 | 36 |
| Everton | 42 | 12 | 11 | 19 | 80 | 92 | 35 |

Manager: George Jobey.
Leading scorer: Harry Bedford, League 30, all matches 31.
League ever-present: Harry Bedford.

- Sammy Crooks won his first cap in England's 5–2 victory over Scotland at Wembley. Between the wars, his 26 appearances were exceeded only by Arsenal full-back Eddie Hapgood.
- Harry Bedford equalled Alf Bentley's 20-year-old club record by scoring 30 League goals. The only two to pass them are Jack Bowers and Ray Straw.
- Derby were runners-up in the First Division, 10 points behind Sheffield Wednesday, for only the second time, equalling their position in 1895–96.
- George Stephenson scored four times in the 5–4 defeat of Grimsby Town on 14 December. His son Bob later played 14 times for the Rams but won more lasting fame as a county cricketer.

## Division One

| Match No. | Date | | Venue | Opponents | Result | | Scorers | Attendan |
|---|---|---|---|---|---|---|---|---|
| 1 | Aug | 31 | (h) | Sunderland | W | 3-0 | Barclay 2, Bedford | 13,9 |
| 2 | Sep | 4 | (h) | Aston Villa | W | 4-0 | Stephenson 2, Bedford, Barclay | 21,9 |
| 3 | | 7 | (a) | Bolton W | W | 2-1 | Bedford, Stephenson | 20,9 |
| 4 | | 9 | (a) | Aston Villa | D | 2-2 | Bedford, Davison | 23,5 |
| 5 | | 14 | (h) | Everton | W | 2-1 | Bedford, Fereday | 22,2 |
| 6 | | 21 | (a) | West Ham U | L | 0-2 | | 26,6 |
| 7 | | 25 | (h) | Burnley | L | 1-3 | Davison | 14,4 |
| 8 | | 28 | (a) | Manchester C | L | 0-3 | | 42,0 |
| 9 | Oct | 5 | (h) | Portsmotuh | W | 3-2 | Stephenson 2, Bedford | 13,3 |
| 10 | | 12 | (a) | Arsenal | D | 1-1 | Ramage | 42,4 |
| 11 | | 19 | (h) | Liverpool | D | 2-2 | Ramage, Bedford | 15,6 |
| 12 | | 26 | (a) | Middlesbrough | L | 0-4 | | 18,4 |
| 13 | Nov | 2 | (h) | Blackburn R | W | 4-3 | Bedford 2, Barclay, Ramage | 12,1 |
| 14 | | 9 | (a) | Manchester U | L | 2-3 | Mee, Bedford | 15,1 |
| 15 | | 16 | (h) | Sheffield U | W | 2-1 | Mee, Davison | 11,6 |
| 16 | | 23 | (a) | Huddersfield T | W | 1-0 | Ramage | 11,4 |
| 17 | | 30 | (h) | Birmingham | W | 3-1 | Bedford, Stephenson, Crooks | 13,5 |
| 18 | Dec | 7 | (a) | Leicester C | D | 0-0 | | 25,3 |
| 19 | | 14 | (h) | Grimsby T | W | 5-4 | Stephenson 4, Bedford | 13,8 |
| 20 | | 21 | (a) | Newcastle U | W | 3-2 | Bedford 2, Crooks | 16,9 |
| 21 | | 25 | (a) | Leeds U | L | 1-2 | Crooks | 25,3 |
| 22 | | 26 | (h) | Leeds U | W | 3-0 | Bedford 3 | 30,3 |
| 23 | | 28 | (a) | Sunderland | L | 1-3 | Stephenson | 23,6 |
| 24 | Jan | 4 | (h) | Bolton W | W | 2-1 | Bedford, Crooks | 16,5 |
| 25 | | 18 | (a) | Everton | L | 0-4 | | 35,4 |
| 26 | Feb | 1 | (h) | Manchester C | W | 4-2 | Bedford 2, Crooks, Bowers | 18,4 |
| 27 | | 5 | (h) | West Ham U | W | 4-3 | Hope, Stephenson, J.C.Robson, Crooks | 10,7 |
| 28 | | 8 | (a) | Portsmouth | L | 1-3 | Bowers | 17,7 |
| 29 | | 19 | (h) | Arsenal | W | 4-1 | Bowers, Stephenson, Bedford, Crooks | 11,1 |
| 30 | | 22 | (a) | Liverpool | D | 2-2 | Crooks, Barclay | 22,7 |
| 31 | Mar | 1 | (h) | Middlesbrough | W | 3-1 | Barclay 2, Bedford | 15,7 |
| 32 | | 8 | (a) | Blackburn R | W | 3-0 | Mee, Stephenson, Bedford (pen) | 21,1 |
| 33 | | 15 | (h) | Manchester U | D | 1-1 | Crooks | 9,1 |
| 34 | | 22 | (a) | Sheffield U | L | 0-2 | | 32,4 |
| 35 | | 29 | (h) | Huddersfield T | D | 2-2 | Barclay, Bedford | 16,3 |
| 36 | Apr | 5 | (a) | Birmingham | W | 4-2 | Bedford 3, Barclay | 13,6 |
| 37 | | 12 | (h) | Leicester C | D | 2-2 | Bedford, Davison | 19,0 |
| 38 | | 19 | (a) | Grimsby T | L | 1-2 | Barclay | 14,8 |
| 39 | | 21 | (h) | Sheffield W | W | 4-1 | Barclay 3, J.C.Robson | 25,4 |
| 40 | | 22 | (a) | Sheffield W | L | 3-6 | Barclay, Bedford, J.C.Robson | 41,2 |
| 41 | | 26 | (h) | Newcastle U | W | 3-1 | J.C.Robson 2, Ruddy | 9,9 |
| 42 | May | 3 | (a) | Burnley | L | 2-6 | Bedford, Crooks | 18,3 |

FINAL LEAGUE POSITION: 2nd in Division One

Appearanc
Go

## FA Cup

| | | | | | | | | |
|---|---|---|---|---|---|---|---|---|
| 3 | Jan | 11 | (h) | Bristol C | W | 5-1 | Stephenson 2, Barclay 2, Bedford | 22,5 |
| 4 | | 25 | (h) | Bradford PA | D | 1-1 | Barclay | 26, |
| R | | 29 | (a) | Bradford PA | L | 1-2 | Ramage | 29,7 |

Appearanc
Go

| Wilkes H | Carr W | Collin G | McIntyre J | Davison T | Malloch G | Crooks S | Barclay R | Bedford H | Stephenson G | Mee G | Fereday D | Robson W | Alderman A | Scott A | Ruddy T | Cooper T | Robinson T | Barker J | Ramage P | Webb J | Nicholas J | Bowers J | Hope J | Robson JC | Hampton J | Kirby J | |
|---|---|---|---|---|---|---|---|---|---|---|---|---|---|---|---|---|---|---|---|---|---|---|---|---|---|---|---|
| 1 | 2 | 3 | 4 | 5 | 6 | 7 | 8 | 9 | 10 | 11 | | | | | | | | | | | | | | | | | 1 |
| 1 | 2 | 3 | 4 | 5 | 6 | | 8 | 9 | 10 | 11 | 7 | | | | | | | | | | | | | | | | 2 |
| 1 | 2 | | 4 | 5 | 6 | | 8 | 9 | 10 | 11 | 7 | 3 | | | | | | | | | | | | | | | 3 |
| 1 | 2 | | 4 | 5 | 6 | | 8 | 9 | 10 | 11 | 7 | 3 | | | | | | | | | | | | | | | 4 |
| 1 | 2 | | 4 | 5 | 6 | | 8 | 9 | 10 | 11 | 7 | 3 | | | | | | | | | | | | | | | 5 |
| 1 | 2 | | 4 | 5 | 6 | | 8 | 9 | 10 | 11 | | 3 | 7 | | | | | | | | | | | | | | 6 |
| 1 | | 2 | | 5 | 6 | | 8 | 10 | | 11 | 7 | 3 | | 4 | 9 | | | | | | | | | | | | 7 |
| 1 | | 3 | | | | 7 | 8 | 9 | | 11 | | | | 6 | 10 | 2 | 4 | 5 | | | | | | | | | 8 |
| 1 | 2 | 3 | | 5 | 6 | 7 | 8 | 9 | 10 | 11 | | | | | | | 4 | | | | | | | | | | 9 |
| 1 | 2 | 3 | 4 | 5 | 6 | 7 | 8 | 9 | | 11 | | | | | | | | | 10 | | | | | | | | 10 |
| 1 | 2 | 3 | 4 | | 6 | 7 | 8 | 9 | | 11 | | | | | | | | 5 | 10 | | | | | | | | 11 |
| 1 | 2 | 3 | | 5 | 6 | | 8 | 9 | | 11 | 7 | | | 4 | | | | | 10 | | | | | | | | 12 |
| 1 | 2 | 3 | 4 | 5 | 6 | 7 | 8 | 9 | | 11 | | | | | | | | | 10 | | | | | | | | 13 |
| 1 | 2 | 3 | 4 | 5 | 6 | 7 | 8 | 9 | | 11 | | | | | | | | | 10 | | | | | | | | 14 |
| 1 | 2 | 3 | 4 | 5 | 6 | 7 | | 9 | 8 | 11 | | | | | | | | | 10 | | | | | | | | 15 |
| 1 | | 3 | 4 | | 6 | 7 | | 9 | 8 | 11 | | | | | | | | 5 | 10 | 2 | | | | | | | 16 |
| 1 | 2 | 3 | 4 | | 6 | 7 | | 9 | 8 | 11 | | | | | | | | 5 | 10 | | | | | | | | 17 |
| 1 | 2 | 3 | 4 | | | 7 | | 9 | 8 | 11 | | | | 6 | | | | 5 | 10 | | | | | | | | 18 |
| 1 | 2 | 3 | 4 | | | 7 | | 9 | 8 | 11 | | | | 6 | | | | 5 | 10 | | | | | | | | 19 |
| 1 | 2 | 3 | 4 | | | 7 | 8 | 9 | 10 | 11 | | | | | | | 6 | 5 | | | | | | | | | 20 |
| 1 | 2 | 3 | 4 | | | 7 | 8 | 9 | 10 | 11 | | | | | | | 6 | 5 | | | | | | | | | 21 |
| 1 | | 3 | 4 | | | 7 | 8 | 9 | 10 | 11 | | | | | | | 6 | 5 | | 2 | | | | | | | 22 |
| 1 | 2 | 3 | 4 | 5 | | 7 | 8 | 9 | 10 | 11 | | | | | | | | 6 | | | | | | | | | 23 |
| 1 | 2 | 3 | 4 | | 6 | 7 | 8 | 9 | 10 | 11 | | | | | | | | 5 | | | | | | | | | 24 |
| 1 | 2 | 3 | 4 | | 6 | 7 | 8 | 9 | 10 | 11 | | | | | | | | 5 | | | | | | | | | 25 |
| 1 | | 3 | | 5 | | 7 | | 8 | 10 | 11 | | | | | | 2 | | 6 | | | 4 | 9 | | | | | 26 |
| 1 | | 3 | 4 | 5 | | 7 | | 9 | 10 | | | | | | | 2 | | 6 | | | | | 8 | 11 | | | 27 |
| 1 | | 3 | 4 | 5 | 6 | 7 | | 8 | | 11 | | | | | | 2 | | | 10 | | | 9 | | | | | 28 |
| 1 | | 3 | 4 | 5 | 6 | 7 | | 8 | 10 | 11 | | | | | | 2 | | | | | | 9 | | | | | 29 |
| 1 | | 3 | 4 | 5 | 6 | 7 | 8 | 9 | 10 | 11 | | | | | | 2 | | | | | | | | | | | 30 |
| 1 | | 3 | 4 | 5 | 6 | 7 | 8 | 9 | 10 | 11 | | | | | | 2 | | | | | | | | | | | 31 |
| 1 | | | 4 | 5 | 6 | 7 | 8 | 9 | 10 | 11 | | 3 | | | | 2 | | | | | | | | | | | 32 |
| 1 | | | 4 | 5 | 6 | 7 | 8 | 9 | 10 | 11 | | 3 | | | | 2 | | | | | | | | | | | 33 |
| 1 | | | 4 | 5 | 6 | 7 | 8 | 9 | 10 | 11 | | 3 | | | | 2 | | | | | | | | | | | 34 |
| 1 | | 3 | | 5 | 6 | 7 | 8 | 9 | 10 | 11 | | | | | | 2 | | | | | 4 | | | | | | 35 |
| 1 | | 3 | 4 | 5 | 6 | | 8 | 9 | 10 | 11 | | | 7 | | | 2 | | | | | | | | | | | 36 |
| 1 | | 3 | 4 | 5 | 6 | 7 | 8 | 9 | 10 | 11 | | | | | | 2 | | | | | | | | | | | 37 |
| | | 3 | 4 | 5 | 6 | 7 | 8 | 9 | 10 | 11 | | | | | | 2 | | | | | | | | | 1 | | 38 |
| | | 3 | 4 | 5 | 6 | 7 | 8 | 9 | | | | | | | 10 | 2 | | | | | | | | 11 | 1 | | 39 |
| | 2 | 3 | 4 | | 6 | 7 | 8 | 9 | | | | | | 5 | 10 | | | | | | | | | 11 | 1 | | 40 |
| | | 3 | 4 | 5 | 6 | 7 | 8 | 9 | | | | | | | 10 | 2 | | | | | | | | 11 | | 1 | 41 |
| | | 3 | 4 | 5 | 6 | 7 | | 9 | 8 | 11 | | | | | | 2 | | | | | | | | 10 | | 1 | 42 |
| 37 | 22 | 35 | 36 | 30 | 33 | 34 | 32 | 42 | 31 | 38 | 6 | 8 | 2 | 6 | 5 | 17 | 5 | 14 | 11 | 2 | 2 | 3 | 1 | 5 | 3 | 2 | |
| | | | | 4 | | 10 | 14 | 30 | 14 | 3 | 1 | | | | 1 | | | | 4 | | | 3 | 1 | 5 | | | |

| Wilkes H | Carr W | Collin G | McIntyre J | Davison T | Malloch G | Crooks S | Barclay R | Bedford H | Stephenson G | Mee G | Fereday D | Robson W | Alderman A | Scott A | Ruddy T | Cooper T | Robinson T | Barker J | Ramage P | Webb J | Nicholas J | Bowers J | Hope J | Robson JC | Hampton J | Kirby J | |
|---|---|---|---|---|---|---|---|---|---|---|---|---|---|---|---|---|---|---|---|---|---|---|---|---|---|---|---|
| 1 | 2 | 3 | 4 | | 6 | 7 | 8 | 9 | 10 | 11 | | | | | | | | 5 | | | | | | | | | 3 |
| 1 | 2 | 3 | 4 | | 6 | 7 | 8 | 9 | 10 | 11 | | | | | | | | 5 | | | | | | | | | 4 |
| 1 | | 3 | 4 | | 6 | 7 | 8 | 9 | | 11 | | | | | | 2 | | 5 | 10 | | | | | | | | R |
| 3 | 2 | 3 | 3 | | 3 | 3 | 3 | 3 | 2 | 3 | | | | | | 1 | | 3 | 1 | | | | | | | | |
| | | | | | | | 3 | 1 | 2 | | | | | | | | | | 1 | | | | | | | | |

# 1930-31

| | P | W | D | L | F | A | Pts |
|---|---|---|---|---|---|---|---|
| Arsenal | 42 | 28 | 10 | 4 | 127 | 59 | 66 |
| Aston Villa | 42 | 25 | 9 | 8 | 128 | 78 | 59 |
| Sheffield W | 42 | 22 | 8 | 12 | 102 | 75 | 52 |
| Portsmouth | 42 | 18 | 13 | 11 | 84 | 67 | 49 |
| Huddersfield T | 42 | 18 | 12 | 12 | 81 | 65 | 48 |
| Derby Co | 42 | 18 | 10 | 14 | 94 | 79 | 46 |
| Middlesbrough | 42 | 19 | 8 | 15 | 98 | 90 | 46 |
| Manchester C | 42 | 18 | 10 | 14 | 75 | 70 | 46 |
| Liverpool | 42 | 15 | 12 | 15 | 86 | 85 | 42 |
| Blackburn R | 42 | 17 | 8 | 17 | 83 | 84 | 42 |
| Sunderland | 42 | 16 | 9 | 17 | 89 | 85 | 41 |
| Chelsea | 42 | 15 | 10 | 17 | 64 | 67 | 40 |
| Grimsby T | 42 | 17 | 5 | 20 | 82 | 87 | 39 |
| Bolton W | 42 | 15 | 9 | 18 | 68 | 81 | 39 |
| Sheffield U | 42 | 14 | 10 | 18 | 78 | 84 | 38 |
| Leicester C | 42 | 16 | 6 | 20 | 80 | 95 | 38 |
| Newcastle U | 42 | 15 | 6 | 21 | 78 | 87 | 36 |
| West Ham U | 42 | 14 | 8 | 20 | 79 | 94 | 36 |
| Birmingham | 42 | 13 | 10 | 19 | 55 | 70 | 36 |
| Blackpool | 42 | 11 | 10 | 21 | 71 | 125 | 32 |
| Leeds U | 42 | 12 | 7 | 23 | 68 | 81 | 31 |
| Manchester U | 42 | 7 | 8 | 27 | 53 | 115 | 22 |

Manager: George Jobey.
Leading scorer: Jack Bowers, League 37, all matches 39.
League ever-present: Tommy Cooper.

- Jack Bowers smashed Derby's scoring records with 37 League goals, including four in a game three times, and 39 in all matches. One of George Jobey's most brilliant signings, Bowers was playing Midland League football for Scunthorpe and Lindsey United when he joined the Rams in May 1928.
- In January and February, he equalled the club record by scoring in six consecutive League games. Bowers hit 15 goals in those six games and, remarkably, Derby contrived to lose three of them.
- On 11 October, the Rams beat Arsenal 4–2, their 23rd consecutive home game without defeat. The run spanned just over a year and is the club record, equalled in 1995 and 1996.

## Division One

| Match No. | Date | | Venue | Opponents | Result | | Scorers | Atten |
|---|---|---|---|---|---|---|---|---|
| 1 | Aug | 30 | (a) | Leicester C | D | 1-1 | Stephenson | 20, |
| 2 | Sep | 3 | (h) | Leeds U | W | 4-1 | Barclay 2, Crooks, Stephenson | 13, |
| 3 | | 6 | (h) | Birmingham | D | 0-0 | | 15, |
| 4 | | 10 | (a) | Sunderland | W | 3-1 | Barclay, Bedford, Ramage | 23, |
| 5 | | 13 | (a) | Sheffield U | D | 3-3 | Crooks, Barclay, Ramage | 22, |
| 6 | | 17 | (h) | Sunderland | W | 4-1 | Bedford 3, Crooks | 8, |
| 7 | | 20 | (h) | Grimsby T | W | 1-0 | Bedford | 13, |
| 8 | | 27 | (h) | Manchester C | D | 1-1 | Bedford | 14, |
| 9 | Oct | 4 | (a) | Portsmouth | L | 0-2 | | 20, |
| 10 | | 11 | (h) | Arsenal | W | 4-2 | Stephenson 2, Bedford, Bowers | 29, |
| 11 | | 18 | (a) | Newcastle U | W | 5-2 | Crooks 2, Bedford, Bowers, Stephenson | 26, |
| 12 | | 25 | (h) | Sheffield W | L | 2-3 | Bowers, Stephenson | 23, |
| 13 | Nov | 1 | (a) | Bolton W | W | 2-1 | Bowers, Crooks | 15, |
| 14 | | 8 | (h) | Liverpool | D | 2-2 | Bedford, Stephenson | 14, |
| 15 | | 15 | (a) | Aston Villa | W | 6-4 | Crooks 2, McIntyre, Bowers, Randall, Stephenson | 37, |
| 16 | | 22 | (h) | West Ham U | D | 1-1 | Randall | 12, |
| 17 | | 29 | (a) | Middlesbrough | L | 1-4 | Barclay | 13, |
| 18 | Dec | 6 | (h) | Chelsea | W | 6-2 | Bowers 4, Stephenson 2 | 12, |
| 19 | | 13 | (a) | Manchester U | L | 1-2 | Bowers | 9, |
| 20 | | 20 | (h) | Huddersfield T | W | 4-1 | Bowers 2, Stephenson, Crooks | 13, |
| 21 | | 25 | (a) | Blackburn R | L | 0-1 | | 29, |
| 22 | | 26 | (h) | Blackburn R | D | 1-1 | Mee | 17, |
| 23 | | 27 | (h) | Leicester C | W | 1-0 | Ramage | 19, |
| 24 | Jan | 3 | (a) | Birmingham | W | 2-1 | Bowers 2 | 14, |
| 25 | | 17 | (h) | Sheffield U | W | 4-3 | Bowers 3, Ramage | 10, |
| 26 | | 31 | (a) | Manchester C | L | 3-4 | Bowers 2, Mee | 14, |
| 27 | Feb | 3 | (a) | Grimsby T | L | 3-5 | Bowers 3 | 8, |
| 28 | | 7 | (h) | Portsmouth | W | 5-1 | Bowers 4, Crooks (pen) | 12, |
| 29 | | 14 | (a) | Arsenal | L | 3-6 | Crooks, Barclay, Bowers | 34, |
| 30 | | 21 | (h) | Newcastle U | L | 1-5 | Barker | 17, |
| 31 | Mar | 7 | (h) | Bolton W | W | 4-1 | Bowers 2 (1 pen), Crooks, N.Robson | 8, |
| 32 | | 14 | (a) | Liverpool | D | 0-0 | | 29, |
| 33 | | 21 | (h) | Aston Villa | D | 1-1 | Ruddy | 24, |
| 34 | | 28 | (a) | West Ham U | W | 1-0 | Randall | 16, |
| 35 | Apr | 3 | (a) | Blackpool | L | 0-1 | | 22, |
| 36 | | 4 | (h) | Middlesbrough | L | 1-2 | Bowers | 13, |
| 37 | | 6 | (h) | Blackpool | W | 3-2 | Bowers 2, Crooks | 12, |
| 38 | | 11 | (a) | Chelsea | D | 1-1 | Barclay | 28, |
| 39 | | 18 | (h) | Manchester U | W | 6-1 | Bowers 4, N.Robson, Crooks | 6, |
| 40 | | 20 | (a) | Sheffield W | L | 2-3 | Crooks, Beeson (og) | 5, |
| 41 | | 25 | (a) | Huddersfield T | L | 0-3 | | 5, |
| 42 | May | 2 | (a) | Leeds U | L | 1-3 | Bowers | 11, |

FINAL LEAGUE POSITION: 6th in Division One

Appearan
Go

## FA Cup

| | | | | | | | | |
|---|---|---|---|---|---|---|---|---|
| 3 | Jan | 10 | (a) | Exeter C | L | 2-3 | Bowers 2 | 16, |

Appearan
Go

| Match | …kes H | Cooper T | Collin G | McIntyre J | Barker J | Malloch G | Crooks S | Barclay R | Bedford H | Stephenson G | Randall J | Jessop F | Ramage P | Webb J | Mee G | White A | Robson JC | Bowers J | Carr W | Scott A | Keen E | Robson N | Nicholas J | Kirby J | Davison T | Robson W | Ruddy T |
|---|---|---|---|---|---|---|---|---|---|---|---|---|---|---|---|---|---|---|---|---|---|---|---|---|---|---|---|
| 1 | | 2 | 3 | 4 | 5 | 6 | 7 | 8 | 9 | 10 | 11 | | | | | | | | | | | | | | | | |
| 2 | | 2 | 3 | 4 | 5 | 6 | 7 | 8 | 9 | 10 | 11 | | | | | | | | | | | | | | | | |
| 3 | | 2 | 3 | 4 | 5 | 6 | 7 | 8 | 9 | 10 | 11 | | | | | | | | | | | | | | | | |
| 4 | | 2 | 3 | 4 | 5 | | 7 | 8 | 9 | | 11 | 6 | 10 | | | | | | | | | | | | | | |
| 5 | | 2 | | 4 | 5 | | 7 | 8 | 9 | | 11 | 6 | 10 | 3 | | | | | | | | | | | | | |
| 6 | | 2 | 3 | 4 | 5 | | 7 | 8 | 9 | | | 6 | 10 | | 11 | | | | | | | | | | | | |
| 7 | | 2 | 3 | 4 | 5 | 6 | 7 | | 9 | | | | 10 | | | 8 | 11 | | | | | | | | | | |
| 8 | | 2 | 3 | 4 | 5 | 6 | 7 | 8 | 9 | | | | 10 | | | | 11 | | | | | | | | | | |
| 9 | | 2 | 3 | 4 | 5 | 6 | 7 | 8 | 9 | 10 | | | | | 11 | | | | | | | | | | | | |
| 10 | | 2 | 3 | 4 | 5 | 6 | 7 | | 8 | 10 | | | | | 11 | | | 9 | | | | | | | | | |
| 11 | | 2 | 3 | 4 | 5 | 6 | 7 | | 8 | 10 | | | | | 11 | | | 9 | | | | | | | | | |
| 12 | | 2 | 3 | 4 | 5 | 6 | 7 | | 8 | 10 | | | | | 11 | | | 9 | | | | | | | | | |
| 13 | | 2 | 3 | 4 | 5 | 6 | 7 | | 8 | 10 | 11 | | | | | | | 9 | | | | | | | | | |
| 14 | | 2 | 3 | 4 | | 6 | 7 | | 8 | 10 | 11 | | | | | | | 9 | 5 | | | | | | | | |
| 15 | | 2 | 3 | 4 | | 6 | 7 | | 8 | 10 | 11 | | | | | | | 9 | | 5 | | | | | | | |
| 16 | | 2 | 3 | 4 | | 6 | | | 8 | 10 | 7 | | | | | | 11 | 9 | | 5 | | | | | | | |
| 17 | | 2 | 3 | 4 | | 6 | | 8 | 5 | 10 | 7 | | | | | | 11 | 9 | | | | | | | | | |
| 18 | | 2 | 3 | 4 | | 6 | | | 8 | 10 | 7 | | | | 11 | | | 9 | | 5 | | | | | | | |
| 19 | | 2 | 3 | 4 | | 6 | | 8 | | 10 | 7 | | | | 11 | | | 9 | | 5 | | | | | | | |
| 20 | | 2 | 3 | 4 | | 6 | 7 | 8 | | 10 | 11 | 5 | | | | | | 9 | | | | | | | | | |
| 21 | | 2 | 3 | 4 | | 6 | 7 | 8 | | 10 | | 5 | | | 11 | | | 9 | | | | | | | | | |
| 22 | | 2 | 3 | | | 6 | 7 | | | 10 | | 5 | | | 11 | | | 9 | | | 4 | 8 | | | | | |
| 23 | | 2 | 3 | | | 6 | 7 | | | 8 | | 5 | 10 | | 11 | | | 9 | | | | | 4 | | | | |
| 24 | | 2 | 3 | | | 6 | 7 | | | | | 5 | 10 | | 11 | | | 9 | | | | 8 | 4 | 1 | | | |
| 25 | | 2 | 3 | 4 | | 6 | 7 | 8 | | | | | 10 | | 11 | | | 9 | | | | | | | 5 | | |
| 26 | | 2 | 3 | 4 | | 6 | 7 | 8 | | 10 | | | | | 11 | | | 9 | | | | | | | 5 | | |
| 27 | | 2 | | | | 6 | 7 | 8 | | 10 | | | | | 11 | | | 9 | | | 4 | | | | 5 | 3 | |
| 28 | | 2 | 3 | | | 6 | 7 | 8 | | | | 5 | 10 | | 11 | | | 9 | | | 4 | | | | | | |
| 29 | | 2 | 3 | 4 | | 6 | 7 | 8 | | | | 5 | 10 | | 11 | | | 9 | | | | | | | | | |
| 30 | | 2 | 3 | | 5 | 6 | 7 | 8 | | | | | 10 | | 11 | | | 9 | | | 4 | | | 1 | | | |
| 31 | | 2 | 3 | 4 | 5 | 6 | 7 | | | | | | 10 | | 11 | | | 9 | | | | 8 | | | | | |
| 32 | | 2 | 3 | 4 | 5 | | 7 | | | | | 6 | | | 11 | | | 9 | | | | 8 | | | | | 10 |
| 33 | | 2 | 3 | 4 | | 6 | 7 | | | | | 5 | | | 11 | | | 9 | | | | 8 | | | | | 10 |
| 34 | | 2 | 3 | 4 | 5 | 6 | | | | | 7 | | | | 11 | | | 9 | | | | 8 | | | | | 10 |
| 35 | | 2 | 3 | 4 | 5 | 6 | 7 | | | | | | | | 11 | | | 9 | | | | 8 | | | | | 10 |
| 36 | | 2 | 3 | 4 | 5 | 6 | 7 | | | | | | 10 | | 11 | 8 | | 9 | | | | | | | | | |
| 37 | | 2 | 3 | 4 | | | 7 | | | | | 6 | 10 | | 11 | | | 9 | | | | 8 | 5 | | | | |
| 38 | | 2 | 3 | | 5 | 6 | 7 | 8 | | | | | | | 11 | | | 9 | | | | 10 | 4 | | | | |
| 39 | | 2 | 3 | 4 | 5 | 6 | 7 | 8 | | | | | | | 11 | | | 9 | | | | 10 | | | | | |
| 40 | | 2 | 3 | | 5 | 6 | 7 | | | | 8 | | | | 11 | | | 9 | | | | 10 | 4 | | | | |
| 41 | | 2 | 3 | | 5 | 6 | 7 | | | | 8 | | | | 11 | | | 9 | | | | 10 | 4 | | | | |
| 42 | | 2 | 3 | 4 | 5 | 6 | 7 | 8 | | | | | | | 11 | | | 9 | | | | 10 | | | | | |
| | 0 | 42 | 40 | 33 | 24 | 37 | 37 | 21 | 18 | 20 | 16 | 13 | 14 | 1 | 29 | 2 | 4 | 33 | 1 | 4 | 4 | 13 | 6 | 2 | 3 | 1 | 4 |
| | | | | 1 | 1 | | 15 | 7 | 9 | 11 | 3 | | 4 | | 2 | | | 37 | | | | 2 | | | | | 1 |

1 own-goal

| Round | …kes H | Cooper T | Collin G | McIntyre J | Barker J | Malloch G | Crooks S | Barclay R | Bedford H | Stephenson G | Randall J | Jessop F | Ramage P | Webb J | Mee G | White A | Robson JC | Bowers J | Carr W | Scott A | Keen E | Robson N | Nicholas J | Kirby J | Davison T | Robson W | Ruddy T |
|---|---|---|---|---|---|---|---|---|---|---|---|---|---|---|---|---|---|---|---|---|---|---|---|---|---|---|---|
| 3 | | 2 | 3 | | | 6 | 7 | | | 8 | | 5 | 10 | | 11 | | | 9 | | | | | 4 | 1 | | | |
| | | 1 | 1 | | | 1 | 1 | | | 1 | | 1 | 1 | | 1 | | | 1 | | | | | 1 | 1 | | | |
| | | | | | | | | | | | | | | | | | | 2 | | | | | | | | | |

# 1931-32

| | P | W | D | L | F | A | Pts |
|---|---|---|---|---|---|---|---|
| Everton | 42 | 26 | 4 | 12 | 116 | 64 | 56 |
| Arsenal | 42 | 22 | 10 | 10 | 90 | 48 | 54 |
| Sheffield W | 42 | 22 | 6 | 14 | 96 | 82 | 50 |
| Huddersfield T | 42 | 19 | 10 | 13 | 80 | 63 | 48 |
| Aston Villa | 42 | 19 | 8 | 15 | 104 | 72 | 46 |
| WBA | 42 | 20 | 6 | 16 | 77 | 55 | 46 |
| Sheffield U | 42 | 20 | 6 | 16 | 80 | 75 | 46 |
| Portsmouth | 42 | 19 | 7 | 16 | 62 | 62 | 45 |
| Birmingham | 42 | 18 | 8 | 16 | 78 | 67 | 44 |
| Liverpool | 42 | 19 | 6 | 17 | 81 | 93 | 44 |
| Newcastle U | 42 | 18 | 6 | 18 | 80 | 87 | 42 |
| Chelsea | 42 | 16 | 8 | 18 | 69 | 73 | 40 |
| Sunderland | 42 | 15 | 10 | 17 | 67 | 73 | 40 |
| Manchester C | 42 | 13 | 12 | 17 | 83 | 73 | 38 |
| Derby Co | 42 | 14 | 10 | 18 | 71 | 75 | 38 |
| Blackburn R | 42 | 16 | 6 | 20 | 89 | 95 | 38 |
| Bolton W | 42 | 17 | 4 | 21 | 72 | 80 | 38 |
| Middlesbrough | 42 | 15 | 8 | 19 | 64 | 89 | 38 |
| Leicester C | 42 | 15 | 7 | 20 | 74 | 94 | 37 |
| Blackpool | 42 | 12 | 9 | 21 | 65 | 102 | 33 |
| Grimsby T | 42 | 13 | 6 | 23 | 67 | 98 | 32 |
| West Ham U | 42 | 12 | 7 | 23 | 62 | 107 | 31 |

Manager: George Jobey.
Leading scorer: Jack Bowers, League 25, all matches 26.

- Jack Nicholas, who made his debut in 1928, embarked on a formidable sequence. From September 1931, until the end of 1938–39, he played in 328 out of 331 League matches. He was ever-present four times.
- After raising the FA Cup as Derby's captain in 1946, the 36-year-old Nicholas played in the first three League games after World War Two.
- Tommy Cooper succeeded Johnny McIntyre as Derby captain in November. The following month, McIntyre joined Chesterfield after 369 appearances for the Rams.

## Division One

| Match No. | Date | | Venue | Opponents | Result | | Scorers | Atten |
|---|---|---|---|---|---|---|---|---|
| 1 | Aug | 29 | (a) | Blackpool | L | 1-2 | Bowers (pen) | 22 |
| 2 | Sep | 2 | (h) | Manchester C | W | 2-1 | Crooks, Bowers | 10 |
| 3 | | 5 | (h) | Sheffield U | L | 1-3 | Ruddy | 12 |
| 4 | | 9 | (a) | Manchester C | L | 0-3 | | 15 |
| 5 | | 12 | (a) | Blackburn R | L | 2-3 | Crooks, Ruddy | 10 |
| 6 | | 16 | (h) | Everton | W | 3-0 | Bowers 3 (1 pen) | 12, |
| 7 | | 19 | (h) | Portsmouth | W | 2-1 | Bowers, Lewis | 13 |
| 8 | | 23 | (a) | Everton | L | 1-2 | Bowers | 19, |
| 9 | | 26 | (a) | Middlesbrough | L | 2-5 | Bowers, Ramage | 13 |
| 10 | Oct | 3 | (a) | West Brom A | L | 0-4 | | 33 |
| 11 | | 10 | (h) | Birmingham | W | 2-1 | Bowers, Ramage | 12, |
| 12 | | 17 | (h) | Leicester C | D | 1-1 | Lewis | 14 |
| 13 | | 24 | (a) | Sheffield W | L | 1-3 | Lewis | 12 |
| 14 | | 31 | (h) | West Ham U | W | 5-1 | Crooks 2, Bowers, Ramage, Alderman | 10, |
| 15 | Nov | 7 | (a) | Chelsea | L | 1-2 | Bowers | 31, |
| 16 | | 14 | (h) | Newcastle U | D | 1-1 | Alderman | 12 |
| 17 | | 21 | (a) | Huddersfield T | L | 0-6 | | 11 |
| 18 | | 28 | (h) | Bolton W | W | 5-1 | N.Robson 2, Crooks, Bowers, Ramage | 9, |
| 19 | Dec | 5 | (a) | Aston Villa | L | 0-2 | | 32, |
| 20 | | 12 | (h) | Grimsby T | D | 3-3 | Crooks, Jessop, Alderman | 10, |
| 21 | | 19 | (a) | Liverpool | D | 1-1 | Ramage | 17, |
| 22 | | 26 | (h) | Sunderland | W | 3-1 | Bowers 2, Ramage | 23, |
| 23 | Jan | 1 | (a) | Sunderland | D | 0-0 | | 23, |
| 24 | | 2 | (h) | Blackpool | W | 5-0 | Crooks 2, Bowers, Ramage, Neal | 8, |
| 25 | | 16 | (a) | Sheffield U | L | 1-3 | Ramage | 21, |
| 26 | | 27 | (h) | Blackburn R | D | 1-1 | Bowers | 7, |
| 27 | | 30 | (a) | Portsmouth | L | 0-2 | | 17, |
| 28 | Feb | 6 | (h) | Middlesbrough | W | 5-2 | Bowers 2, Crooks, Cooper, Nicholas | 11, |
| 29 | | 17 | (h) | West Brom A | W | 3-1 | Bowers 2, Ramage | 8, |
| 30 | | 20 | (a) | Birmingham | D | 1-1 | Crooks | 17, |
| 31 | | 27 | (a) | Leicester C | D | 1-1 | J.C.Robson | 17, |
| 32 | Mar | 5 | (h) | Sheffield W | L | 0-1 | | 15, |
| 33 | | 12 | (a) | West Ham U | L | 1-2 | Barrett (og) | 19, |
| 34 | | 19 | (h) | Chelsea | W | 1-0 | Nicholas | 14, |
| 35 | | 25 | (a) | Arsenal | L | 1-2 | Bowers | 56, |
| 36 | | 26 | (a) | Newcastle U | D | 3-3 | Duncan 2, Bowers | 27, |
| 37 | | 28 | (h) | Arsenal | D | 1-1 | Alderman | 25, |
| 38 | Apr | 2 | (h) | Huddersfield T | W | 3-2 | Bowers 2, Ramage | 13, |
| 39 | | 9 | (a) | Bolton W | W | 2-1 | Duncan, Ramage | 7, |
| 40 | | 16 | (h) | Aston Villa | W | 3-1 | Crooks, Ramage, N.Robson | 14, |
| 41 | | 23 | (a) | Grimsby T | L | 1-2 | Bowers | 7, |
| 42 | | 30 | (h) | Liverpool | L | 1-2 | Hutchison | 11, |

FINAL LEAGUE POSITION: 15th in Division One

Appearan
Go

## FA Cup

| | | | | | | | | |
|---|---|---|---|---|---|---|---|---|
| 3 | Jan | 9 | (a) | Burnley | W | 4-0 | Neal 2, Alderman, Crooks | 16, |
| 4 | | 23 | (h) | Blackburn R | W | 3-2 | Ramage 2, Bowers | 30, |
| 5 | Feb | 13 | (a) | Manchester C | L | 0-3 | | 62, |

Appearan
Go

| Wilkes H | Cooper T | Collin G | McIntyre J | Barker J | Malloch G | Crooks S | Green R | Bowers J | Ramage P | Randall J | Carr W | Ruddy T | Mee G | Kirby J | Lewis W | Scott A | Jessop F | Neal R | Robson W | White A | Nicholas J | Keen E | Alderman A | Robson JC | Robson N | Reid S | Fabian H | Duncan D | Hutchison D | |
|---|---|---|---|---|---|---|---|---|---|---|---|---|---|---|---|---|---|---|---|---|---|---|---|---|---|---|---|---|---|---|
| | 2 | 3 | 4 | 5 | 6 | 7 | 8 | 9 | 10 | 11 | | | | | | | | | | | | | | | | | | | | 1 |
| | | 3 | 4 | 5 | 6 | 7 | | 9 | 10 | | 2 | 8 | 11 | | | | | | | | | | | | | | | | | 2 |
| | 2 | 3 | 4 | 5 | 6 | 7 | | 9 | | | | 10 | 11 | 1 | 8 | | | | | | | | | | | | | | | 3 |
| | 2 | 3 | 4 | | | 8 | | 9 | | 11 | | 10 | | | | 5 | 6 | 7 | | | | | | | | | | | | 4 |
| | 2 | | 4 | 5 | 6 | 7 | | 9 | | | | 10 | 11 | | | | | | 3 | 8 | | | | | | | | | | 5 |
| | 2 | 3 | | 5 | | 7 | | 9 | | | | 10 | 11 | | 8 | | 6 | | | | 4 | | | | | | | | | 6 |
| | 2 | 3 | | 5 | | 7 | | 9 | | | | 10 | 11 | | 8 | | 6 | | | | 4 | | | | | | | | | 7 |
| | 2 | 3 | | 5 | | 7 | | 9 | 10 | | | 8 | 11 | | | | 6 | | | | 4 | | | | | | | | | 8 |
| | 2 | 3 | | 5 | | | | 9 | 10 | | | 8 | 11 | | | | 6 | 7 | | | 4 | | | | | | | | | 9 |
| | 2 | 3 | | 5 | | 7 | | 9 | 10 | 11 | | | | | 8 | | | | | | 4 | 6 | | | | | | | | 10 |
| | 2 | 3 | | 5 | | 7 | | 9 | 10 | | | | 11 | | 8 | | | | | | 4 | 6 | | | | | | | | 11 |
| | 2 | 3 | | 5 | | | | 9 | 10 | | | | 11 | | 8 | | | 7 | | | 4 | 6 | | | | | | | | 12 |
| | 2 | 3 | | 5 | | 7 | | 9 | 10 | | | | 11 | | 8 | | | | | | 4 | 6 | | | | | | | | 13 |
| | 2 | 3 | | 5 | | 7 | | 9 | 10 | | | | 11 | | | | | | | | 4 | 6 | 8 | | | | | | | 14 |
| | 2 | 3 | | 5 | | | | 9 | 10 | 7 | | | | | | | | | | | 4 | 6 | 8 | 11 | | | | | | 15 |
| | 2 | 3 | | 5 | | 7 | | 9 | 10 | | | | | | | | | | | | 4 | 6 | 8 | 11 | | | | | | 16 |
| | 2 | 3 | | 5 | | 7 | | 9 | 10 | | | | | | | | | 11 | | | 4 | 6 | | | 8 | | | | | 17 |
| | 2 | 3 | | 5 | | 7 | | 9 | 10 | 11 | | | | | | | 6 | | | | 4 | | | | 8 | | | | | 18 |
| | 2 | 3 | | 5 | | 7 | | 9 | 10 | 11 | | | | | 8 | | 6 | | | | 4 | | | | | | | | | 19 |
| | 2 | | | | 6 | 7 | | 9 | 10 | | | | 11 | | | | 5 | | | | 4 | | 8 | | | 3 | | | | 20 |
| | 2 | 3 | | 5 | | 7 | | 9 | 10 | | | | | 1 | | | 6 | | | | 4 | | 8 | 11 | | | | | | 21 |
| | 2 | 3 | | 5 | | 7 | | 9 | 10 | | | | | | | | 6 | 11 | | | 4 | | 8 | | | | | | | 22 |
| | 2 | 3 | | 5 | | 7 | | 9 | 10 | | | | | | | | 6 | 11 | | | 4 | | 8 | | | | | | | 23 |
| | 2 | 3 | | 5 | | 7 | | 9 | 10 | | | | | | | | 6 | 11 | | | 4 | | 8 | | | | | | | 24 |
| | 2 | 3 | | 5 | | 7 | | 9 | 10 | | | | | | | | 6 | 11 | | | 4 | | 8 | | | | | | | 25 |
| | 2 | 3 | | 5 | | 7 | | 9 | 10 | | | | | | | | 6 | 11 | | | 4 | | 8 | | | | | | | 26 |
| | 2 | 3 | | 5 | | 7 | | 9 | 10 | | | | | | | | 6 | 11 | | | 4 | | 8 | | | | | | | 27 |
| | 2 | 3 | | 5 | | 7 | | 9 | 10 | | | | | | | | 6 | | | | 4 | | 8 | 11 | | | | | | 28 |
| | | 3 | | 5 | | 7 | | 9 | 10 | | 2 | | | | | | | | | | 4 | 6 | | 11 | 8 | | | | | 29 |
| | | 3 | | 5 | | 7 | | 9 | | | 2 | | | | | | | | | | 4 | 6 | | 11 | 10 | | 8 | | | 30 |
| | | 3 | | 5 | | 7 | | | 10 | | 2 | | | | | | | | | | 4 | 6 | | 11 | 9 | | 8 | | | 31 |
| | | 3 | | 5 | | 7 | | 9 | | | 2 | | | | | | | | | | 4 | 6 | | 11 | 10 | | 8 | | | 32 |
| | | 3 | | 5 | | 7 | | 9 | 10 | | 2 | | | | | | | | | | 4 | 6 | | | 8 | | | 11 | | 33 |
| | 2 | 3 | | 5 | | 7 | | 9 | 10 | | | | | | | | | | | | 4 | 6 | | | 8 | | | 11 | | 34 |
| | 2 | 3 | | 5 | | 7 | | 9 | 10 | | | | | | | | | | | | 4 | 6 | | | 8 | | | 11 | | 35 |
| | | 3 | | 5 | | 7 | | 9 | 10 | | 2 | | | | | | | | | | 4 | 6 | | | 8 | | | 11 | | 36 |
| | | 3 | | 5 | | | | 9 | 10 | | 2 | | | | | | | | | | 4 | 6 | 7 | | 8 | | | 11 | | 37 |
| | | 3 | | 5 | | 7 | | 9 | 10 | | 2 | | | | | | | | | | 4 | 6 | | | 8 | | | 11 | | 38 |
| | 2 | 3 | | 5 | | | | 9 | 10 | 7 | | | | | | | | | | | 4 | 6 | | | 8 | | | 11 | | 39 |
| | 2 | 3 | | 5 | | 7 | | 9 | 10 | | | | | | | | | | | | 4 | 6 | | | 8 | | | 11 | | 40 |
| | 2 | 3 | | 5 | | 7 | | 9 | 10 | | | | | | | | | | | | 4 | 6 | | | | | | 11 | 8 | 41 |
| | 2 | 3 | | 5 | | 7 | | 9 | 10 | | | | | | | | | | | | 4 | 6 | | | | | | 11 | 8 | 42 |
| 0 | 33 | 40 | 5 | 40 | 5 | 37 | 1 | 41 | 35 | 7 | 9 | 8 | 12 | 2 | 8 | 1 | 16 | 10 | 1 | 1 | 37 | 22 | 13 | 8 | 14 | 1 | 3 | 10 | 2 | |
| | 1 | | | | | 11 | | 25 | 12 | | | 2 | | | 3 | | 1 | 1 | | | 2 | | 4 | 1 | 3 | | | 3 | 1 | |

1 own-goal

| | | | | | | | | | | | | | | | | | | | | | | | | | | | | | | |
|---|---|---|---|---|---|---|---|---|---|---|---|---|---|---|---|---|---|---|---|---|---|---|---|---|---|---|---|---|---|---|
| 1 | 2 | 3 | | 5 | | 7 | | 9 | 10 | | | | | | | | 6 | 11 | | | 4 | | 8 | | | | | | | 3 |
| 1 | 2 | 3 | | 5 | | 7 | | 9 | 10 | | | | | | | | 6 | 11 | | | 4 | | 8 | | | | | | | 4 |
| | 2 | 3 | | 5 | | 7 | | 9 | 10 | | | | | | | | 6 | | | | 4 | | 8 | 11 | | | | | | 5 |
| 3 | 3 | 3 | | 3 | | 3 | | 3 | 3 | | | | | | | | 3 | 2 | | | 3 | | 3 | 1 | | | | | | |
| | | | | | | 1 | | 1 | 2 | | | | | | | | | 2 | | | | | 1 | | | | | | | |

# 1932-33

| | P | W | D | L | F | A | Pts |
|---|---|---|---|---|---|---|---|
| Arsenal | 42 | 25 | 8 | 9 | 118 | 61 | 58 |
| Aston Villa | 42 | 23 | 8 | 11 | 92 | 67 | 54 |
| Sheffield W | 42 | 21 | 9 | 12 | 80 | 68 | 51 |
| WBA | 42 | 20 | 9 | 13 | 83 | 70 | 49 |
| Newcastle U | 42 | 22 | 5 | 15 | 71 | 63 | 49 |
| Huddersfield T | 42 | 18 | 11 | 13 | 66 | 53 | 47 |
| Derby Co | 42 | 15 | 14 | 13 | 76 | 69 | 44 |
| Leeds U | 42 | 15 | 14 | 13 | 59 | 62 | 44 |
| Portsmouth | 42 | 18 | 7 | 17 | 74 | 76 | 43 |
| Sheffield U | 42 | 17 | 9 | 16 | 74 | 80 | 43 |
| Everton | 42 | 16 | 9 | 17 | 81 | 74 | 41 |
| Sunderland | 42 | 15 | 10 | 17 | 63 | 80 | 40 |
| Birmingham | 42 | 14 | 11 | 17 | 57 | 57 | 39 |
| Liverpool | 42 | 14 | 11 | 17 | 79 | 84 | 39 |
| Blackburn R | 42 | 14 | 10 | 18 | 76 | 102 | 38 |
| Manchester C | 42 | 16 | 5 | 21 | 68 | 71 | 37 |
| Middlesbrough | 42 | 14 | 9 | 19 | 63 | 73 | 37 |
| Chelsea | 42 | 14 | 7 | 21 | 63 | 73 | 35 |
| Leicester C | 42 | 11 | 13 | 18 | 75 | 89 | 35 |
| Wolves | 42 | 13 | 9 | 20 | 80 | 96 | 35 |
| Bolton W | 42 | 12 | 9 | 21 | 78 | 92 | 33 |
| Blackpool | 42 | 14 | 5 | 23 | 69 | 85 | 33 |

Manager: George Jobey.
Leading scorer: Jack Bowers, League 35, all matches 43.
League ever-present: George Collin.

- Jack Bowers, leading scorer in the First Division, added eight FA Cup goals to beat his Rams record with 43 in the season. It remains unchallenged.
- The FA Cup sixth-round tie against Sunderland attracted a record 34,218 to the Baseball Ground. The gate for the replay at Roker Park, 75,118, remains the highest to see a Sunderland home game.
- Dally Duncan became the first to be capped by Scotland while a Derby player when he appeared against Wales in October. He earned 14 caps.

## Division One

| Match No. | Date | | Venue | Opponents | Result | | Scorers | Atten |
|---|---|---|---|---|---|---|---|---|
| 1 | Aug | 27 | (a) | Leeds U | W | 2-0 | Bowers, Duncan | 16, |
| 2 | | 31 | (h) | Blackburn R | W | 2-1 | Bowers 2 | 17, |
| 3 | Sep | 3 | (h) | Sheffield W | W | 2-0 | Ramage, Duncan | 18, |
| 4 | | 10 | (a) | West Brom A | L | 0-2 | | 30, |
| 5 | | 17 | (h) | Birmingham | D | 2-2 | Ramage, Duncan | 16, |
| 6 | | 19 | (a) | Blackburn R | D | 3-3 | Crooks, Robson, Duncan | 16, |
| 7 | | 24 | (a) | Sunderland | W | 2-0 | Bowers, Duncan | 19, |
| 8 | Oct | 1 | (h) | Manchester C | W | 4-0 | Bowers 2, Crooks, Duncan (pen) | 13, |
| 9 | | 8 | (a) | Arsenal | D | 3-3 | Crooks, Roberts 2 (ogs) | 32, |
| 10 | | 15 | (h) | Everton | W | 2-0 | Bowers 2 | 23, |
| 11 | | 22 | (a) | Chelsea | W | 3-1 | Bowers 2, Duncan | 37, |
| 12 | | 29 | (h) | Huddersfield T | L | 2-3 | Bowers, Duncan | 19, |
| 13 | Nov | 5 | (a) | Middlesbrough | W | 3-0 | Bowers, Barker, Ramage | 11, |
| 14 | | 12 | (h) | Bolton W | W | 4-1 | Duncan 2, Bowers, Jessop | 14, |
| 15 | | 19 | (a) | Liverpool | L | 1-6 | Ramage | 22, |
| 16 | | 26 | (h) | Leicester C | W | 3-2 | Bowers 3 | 16, |
| 17 | Dec | 3 | (a) | Sheffield U | L | 3-4 | Bowers 2, Duncan | 19, |
| 18 | | 10 | (h) | Wolves | D | 4-4 | Crooks, Ramage, Duncan, Lumberg (og) | 13, |
| 19 | | 17 | (a) | Newcastle U | D | 0-0 | | 22, |
| 20 | | 24 | (h) | Aston Villa | D | 0-0 | | 26, |
| 21 | | 26 | (h) | Blackpool | D | 1-1 | Duncan | 21, |
| 22 | | 27 | (a) | Blackpool | L | 1-4 | Bowers | 19, |
| 23 | | 31 | (h) | Leeds U | W | 5-1 | Bowers 2, Crooks, Duncan, Jessop | 13, |
| 24 | Jan | 7 | (a) | Sheffield W | D | 0-0 | | 20, |
| 25 | | 21 | (h) | West Brom A | D | 2-2 | Bowers, Ramage | 15, |
| 26 | Feb | 1 | (a) | Birmingham | L | 1-3 | Fabian | 9, |
| 27 | | 4 | (h) | Sunderland | W | 3-0 | Bowers 3 | 15, |
| 28 | | 11 | (a) | Manchester C | L | 1-2 | Bowers | 33, |
| 29 | | 22 | (h) | Arsenal | D | 2-2 | Bowers 2 | 23, |
| 30 | | 25 | (a) | Everton | L | 2-4 | Bowers 2 | 14, |
| 31 | Mar | 11 | (a) | Huddersfield T | D | 0-0 | | 14, |
| 32 | | 25 | (a) | Bolton W | D | 1-1 | Bowers | 9, |
| 33 | | 29 | (h) | Chelsea | L | 0-1 | | 7, |
| 34 | Apr | 1 | (h) | Liverpool | D | 1-1 | Bowers | 7, |
| 35 | | 5 | (h) | Middlesbrough | D | 2-2 | Bowden, Griffiths (og) | 6, |
| 36 | | 8 | (a) | Leicester C | L | 0-4 | | 18, |
| 37 | | 14 | (a) | Portsmouth | L | 0-2 | | 22, |
| 38 | | 15 | (h) | Sheffield U | W | 3-0 | Bowers, Ramage, Hutchison (pen) | 9, |
| 39 | | 17 | (h) | Portsmouth | W | 2-0 | Bowers 2 | 11, |
| 40 | | 22 | (a) | Wolves | L | 1-3 | Duncan | 21, |
| 41 | | 29 | (h) | Newcastle U | W | 3-2 | Duncan 2, Randall | 6, |
| 42 | May | 6 | (a) | Aston Villa | L | 0-2 | | 32, |

FINAL LEAGUE POSITION: 7th in Division One

Appearan
Gc

## FA Cup

| | | | | | | | | |
|---|---|---|---|---|---|---|---|---|
| 3 | Jan | 14 | (a) | Wolves | W | 6-3 | Bowers 3, Duncan 2, Crooks | 31, |
| 4 | | 28 | (a) | Southend U | W | 3-2 | Bowers 2, Fabian | 15, |
| 5 | Feb | 18 | (h) | Aldershot | W | 2-0 | Bowers 2 | 30, |
| 6 | Mar | 4 | (h) | Sunderland | D | 4-4 | Duncan 2, Ramage, Bowers | 34, |
| R | | 8 | (a) | Sunderland | W | 1-0** | Ramage | 75, |
| SF | | 18 | (n*) | Manchester C | L | 2-3 | Fabian, Crooks | 51, |

*Played at Leeds Road, Huddersfield.
**after extra-time

Appearan
Gc

| Match | Wilkes H | Cooper T | Collin G | Nicholas J | Barker J | Keen E | Crooks S | Robson N | Bowers J | Ramage P | Duncan D | Hutchison D | Carr W | Jessop F | Webb J | Alderman A | Fabian H | Kirby J | Bowden O | Reid S | Hann R | Randall J |
|---|---|---|---|---|---|---|---|---|---|---|---|---|---|---|---|---|---|---|---|---|---|---|
| 1 | 1 | 2 | 3 | 4 | 5 | 6 | 7 | 8 | 9 | 10 | 11 | | | | | | | | | | | |
| 2 | 1 | 2 | 3 | 4 | 5 | 6 | 7 | 8 | 9 | 10 | 11 | | | | | | | | | | | |
| 3 | 1 | 2 | 3 | 4 | 5 | 6 | 7 | 8 | | 10 | 11 | 9 | | | | | | | | | | |
| 4 | 1 | 2 | 3 | 4 | 5 | 6 | 7 | | 9 | 10 | 11 | 8 | | | | | | | | | | |
| 5 | 1 | 2 | 3 | 4 | 5 | 6 | 7 | | 9 | 10 | 11 | 8 | | | | | | | | | | |
| 6 | 1 | 2 | 3 | 4 | 5 | 6 | 7 | 8 | 9 | 10 | 11 | | | | | | | | | | | |
| 7 | 1 | 2 | 3 | 4 | 5 | 6 | 7 | 8 | 9 | 10 | 11 | | | | | | | | | | | |
| 8 | 1 | | 3 | 4 | 5 | 6 | 7 | | 9 | 10 | 11 | 8 | 2 | | | | | | | | | |
| 9 | 1 | 2 | 3 | 4 | | 6 | 7 | | 9 | 10 | 11 | 8 | | 5 | | | | | | | | |
| 10 | 1 | 2 | 3 | 4 | | 6 | 7 | | 9 | 10 | 11 | 8 | | 5 | | | | | | | | |
| 11 | 1 | 2 | 3 | 4 | 5 | 6 | 7 | | 9 | 10 | 11 | 8 | | | | | | | | | | |
| 12 | 1 | 2 | 3 | 4 | 5 | 6 | 7 | | 9 | 10 | 11 | 8 | | | | | | | | | | |
| 13 | 1 | 2 | 3 | 4 | 5 | 6 | 7 | | 9 | 10 | 11 | | | 8 | | | | | | | | |
| 14 | 1 | | 3 | 4 | 5 | 6 | 7 | | 9 | 10 | 11 | | | 8 | 2 | | | | | | | |
| 15 | 1 | | 3 | 4 | 5 | 6 | 7 | | 9 | 10 | 11 | | | 8 | 2 | | | | | | | |
| 16 | 1 | 2 | 3 | 4 | 5 | 6 | 7 | 8 | 9 | 10 | 11 | | | | | | | | | | | |
| 17 | 1 | 2 | 3 | 4 | 5 | 6 | 7 | 8 | 9 | 10 | 11 | | | | | | | | | | | |
| 18 | 1 | 2 | 3 | 4 | 5 | 6 | 7 | 8 | 9 | 10 | 11 | | | | | | | | | | | |
| 19 | 1 | 2 | 3 | 4 | | 6 | 7 | | 9 | 10 | 11 | | | 5 | | 8 | | | | | | |
| 20 | 1 | 2 | 3 | 4 | 5 | 6 | | | 9 | 10 | 11 | | | | | 8 | 7 | | | | | |
| 21 | 1 | 2 | 3 | 4 | 5 | 6 | | | 9 | | 11 | 8 | | 10 | | | 7 | | | | | |
| 22 | 1 | 2 | 3 | | 5 | | | | 9 | | 11 | 10 | 4 | 6 | | 8 | 7 | | | | | |
| 23 | | | 3 | 4 | 5 | 6 | 7 | | 9 | | 11 | | | 10 | 2 | | 8 | 1 | | | | |
| 24 | | 2 | 3 | 4 | 5 | 6 | 7 | | 9 | 10 | 11 | | | 8 | | | | 1 | | | | |
| 25 | | 2 | 3 | 4 | 5 | 6 | 7 | | 9 | 10 | 11 | | | 8 | | | | 1 | | | | |
| 26 | | 2 | 3 | 4 | 5 | 6 | 7 | | 9 | 10 | 11 | | | | | | 8 | 1 | | | | |
| 27 | | 2 | 3 | 4 | 5 | 6 | 7 | | 9 | 10 | 11 | | | 8 | | | | 1 | | | | |
| 28 | | 2 | 3 | 4 | 5 | 6 | 7 | | 9 | 10 | 11 | | | | | | 8 | 1 | | | | |
| 29 | | 2 | 3 | 4 | 5 | 6 | 7 | | 9 | 10 | 11 | | | | | | 8 | 1 | | | | |
| 30 | | 2 | 3 | 4 | 5 | 6 | 7 | | 9 | 10 | 11 | | | 8 | | | | 1 | | | | |
| 31 | | 2 | 3 | 4 | 5 | 6 | 7 | | 9 | 10 | 11 | | | | | | 8 | 1 | | | | |
| 32 | | 2 | 3 | 4 | 5 | 6 | | | 9 | 10 | 11 | 7 | | | | | | 1 | 8 | | | |
| 33 | | | 3 | 4 | 5 | 6 | | | 9 | 10 | | 7 | | | | | | 1 | | 2 | 6 | 11 |
| 34 | | | 3 | 4 | 5 | 6 | | | 9 | 10 | | 7 | | | | | | 1 | 8 | 2 | | 11 |
| 35 | | 2 | 3 | 4 | 5 | 6 | | | 9 | 10 | 11 | 7 | | | | | | 1 | 8 | | | |
| 36 | | 2 | 3 | 4 | 5 | 6 | | | 9 | 10 | 11 | 7 | | | | | | 1 | 8 | | | |
| 37 | | 2 | 3 | 4 | 5 | 6 | | | 9 | 10 | 11 | 8 | | | | | | 1 | | | | 7 |
| 38 | | 2 | 3 | 4 | 5 | 6 | | | 9 | 10 | 11 | 8 | | | | | | 1 | | | | 7 |
| 39 | | 2 | 3 | 4 | 5 | 6 | | | 9 | 10 | 11 | 8 | | | | | | 1 | | | | 7 |
| 40 | | 2 | 3 | 4 | 5 | 6 | | | 9 | 10 | 11 | 8 | | | | | 7 | 1 | | | | |
| 41 | | 2 | 3 | 4 | 5 | 6 | | | 9 | 10 | 11 | 8 | | | | | | 1 | | | | 7 |
| 42 | | 2 | 3 | 4 | 5 | 6 | | | 9 | 10 | 11 | 8 | | | | | | 1 | | | | 7 |
| | 22 | 36 | 42 | 41 | 39 | 41 | 28 | 8 | 41 | 39 | 40 | 21 | 2 | 13 | 3 | 3 | 9 | 20 | 4 | 2 | 1 | 7 |
| | | | | | 1 | | 5 | 1 | 35 | 7 | 17 | 1 | | 2 | | | 1 | | 1 | | | 1 |

4 own-goals

| Round | Wilkes H | Cooper T | Collin G | Nicholas J | Barker J | Keen E | Crooks S | Robson N | Bowers J | Ramage P | Duncan D | Hutchison D | Carr W | Jessop F | Webb J | Alderman A | Fabian H | Kirby J | Bowden O | Reid S | Hann R | Randall J |
|---|---|---|---|---|---|---|---|---|---|---|---|---|---|---|---|---|---|---|---|---|---|---|
| 3 | | 2 | 3 | | 5 | 6 | 7 | | 9 | 10 | 11 | | | 4 | | | 8 | 1 | | | | |
| 4 | | 2 | 3 | 4 | 5 | 6 | 7 | | 9 | 10 | 11 | | | | | | 8 | 1 | | | | |
| 5 | | 2 | 3 | 4 | 5 | 6 | 7 | | 9 | 10 | 11 | | | 8 | | | | 1 | | | | |
| 6 | | 2 | 3 | 4 | 5 | 6 | 7 | | 9 | 10 | 11 | | | 8 | | | | 1 | | | | |
| R | | 2 | 3 | 4 | 5 | 6 | 7 | | 9 | 10 | 11 | | | | | | 8 | 1 | | | | |
| SF | | 2 | 3 | 4 | 5 | 6 | 7 | | 9 | 10 | 11 | | | | | | 8 | 1 | | | | |
| | | 6 | 6 | 5 | 6 | 6 | 6 | | 6 | 6 | 6 | | | 3 | | | 4 | 6 | | | | |
| | | | | | | | 2 | | 8 | 2 | 4 | | | | | | 2 | | | | | |

# 1933-34

| | P | W | D | L | F | A | Pts |
|---|---|---|---|---|---|---|---|
| Arsenal | 42 | 25 | 9 | 8 | 75 | 47 | 59 |
| Huddersfield T | 42 | 23 | 10 | 9 | 90 | 61 | 56 |
| Tottenham H | 42 | 21 | 7 | 14 | 79 | 56 | 49 |
| Derby Co | 42 | 17 | 11 | 14 | 68 | 54 | 45 |
| Manchester C | 42 | 17 | 11 | 14 | 65 | 72 | 45 |
| Sunderland | 42 | 16 | 12 | 14 | 81 | 56 | 44 |
| WBA | 42 | 17 | 10 | 15 | 78 | 70 | 44 |
| Blackburn R | 42 | 18 | 7 | 17 | 74 | 81 | 43 |
| Leeds U | 42 | 17 | 8 | 17 | 75 | 66 | 42 |
| Portsmouth | 42 | 15 | 12 | 15 | 52 | 55 | 42 |
| Sheffield W | 42 | 16 | 9 | 17 | 62 | 67 | 41 |
| Stoke C | 42 | 15 | 11 | 16 | 58 | 71 | 41 |
| Aston Villa | 42 | 14 | 12 | 16 | 78 | 75 | 40 |
| Everton | 42 | 12 | 16 | 14 | 62 | 63 | 40 |
| Wolves | 42 | 14 | 12 | 16 | 74 | 86 | 40 |
| Middlesbrough | 42 | 16 | 7 | 19 | 68 | 80 | 39 |
| Leicester C | 42 | 14 | 11 | 17 | 59 | 74 | 39 |
| Liverpool | 42 | 14 | 10 | 18 | 79 | 87 | 38 |
| Chelsea | 42 | 14 | 8 | 20 | 67 | 69 | 36 |
| Birmingham | 42 | 12 | 12 | 18 | 54 | 56 | 36 |
| Newcastle U | 42 | 10 | 14 | 18 | 68 | 77 | 34 |
| Sheffield U | 42 | 12 | 7 | 23 | 58 | 101 | 31 |

Manager: George Jobey.
Leading scorer: Jack Bowers, League 34, all matches 37.
League ever-present: Jack Nicholas.

- Tommy Cooper captained England three times during the season and the summer tour, against Scotland, Hungary and Czechoslovakia. John Goodall and Steve Bloomer had previously led England while Derby players.
- For the second time, Jack Bowers scored in six consecutive League games, this time the first six. He is the only Derby player to do this twice.
- The double-decker stand at the Osmaston End was opened for this season, further increasing the capacity, and the Baseball Ground record was again lifted in an FA Cup tie, 37,727 for the fourth round against Wolves.

## Division One

| Match No. | Date | Venue | Opponents | Result | | Scorers | Attendance |
|---|---|---|---|---|---|---|---|
| 1 | Aug 26 | (a) | Middlesbrough | L | 1-3 | Bowers | 14,57 |
| 2 | 30 | (h) | Everton | D | 1-1 | Bowers | 23,07 |
| 3 | Sep 2 | (h) | Blackburn R | D | 1-1 | Bowers (pen) | 15,51 |
| 4 | 9 | (a) | Newcastle U | D | 1-1 | Bowers | 23,94 |
| 5 | 16 | (h) | Leeds U | W | 3-1 | Bowers 3 | 16,58 |
| 6 | 23 | (a) | Stoke C | W | 4-0 | Bowers 3, Crooks | 32,24 |
| 7 | 30 | (a) | West Brom A | L | 1-5 | Groves | 24,59 |
| 8 | Oct 7 | (h) | Birmingham | W | 4-0 | Bowers 3, Ramage | 17,40 |
| 9 | 14 | (a) | Sheffield W | D | 1-1 | Ramage | 14,65 |
| 10 | 21 | (h) | Huddersfield T | D | 1-1 | Bowers | 20,86 |
| 11 | 28 | (a) | Portsmouth | L | 0-1 | | 17,54 |
| 12 | Nov 4 | (h) | Leicester C | W | 2-1 | Bowers, Crooks | 22,10 |
| 13 | 11 | (a) | Chelsea | W | 2-0 | Bowers, Duncan | 24,42 |
| 14 | 18 | (h) | Liverpool | W | 3-1 | Bowers, Nicholas, Duncan | 15,58 |
| 15 | 25 | (a) | Tottenham H | W | 2-1 | Bowers, Duncan | 41,46 |
| 16 | Dec 2 | (h) | Wolves | W | 3-1 | Bowers 2, Groves | 16,56 |
| 17 | 9 | (a) | Aston Villa | W | 2-0 | Crooks, Groves | 30,47 |
| 18 | 16 | (h) | Sheffield U | W | 5-1 | Crooks 2, Bowers 2, Duncan | 14,90 |
| 19 | 23 | (a) | Sunderland | D | 0-0 | | 24,7 |
| 20 | 25 | (h) | Manchester C | W | 4-1 | Bowers 2, Ramage 2 | 32,3 |
| 21 | 26 | (a) | Manchester C | L | 0-2 | | 57,2 |
| 22 | 30 | (h) | Middlesbrough | W | 2-0 | Hutchison 2 | 17,38 |
| 23 | Jan 1 | (a) | Everton | W | 3-0 | Bowers, Duncan, Alderman | 24,5 |
| 24 | 6 | (a) | Blackburn R | L | 1-2 | Crooks | 16,9 |
| 25 | 20 | (h) | Newcastle U | D | 1-1 | Wileman | 18,7 |
| 26 | 31 | (a) | Leeds U | W | 2-0 | Bowers, Duncan | 11,7 |
| 27 | Feb 3 | (h) | Stoke C | W | 5-1 | Ramage 2, Duncan, Bowers, Crooks | 20,4 |
| 28 | 10 | (h) | West Brom A | D | 1-1 | Keen | 20,1 |
| 29 | 21 | (a) | Birmingham | L | 1-2 | Bowers | 12,3 |
| 30 | 24 | (h) | Sheffield W | D | 1-1 | Bowers | 18,9 |
| 31 | Mar 3 | (a) | Huddersfield T | L | 0-2 | | 21,9 |
| 32 | 10 | (h) | Portsmouth | L | 0-1 | | 13,4 |
| 33 | 17 | (h) | Sunderland | D | 0-0 | | 13,7 |
| 34 | 24 | (h) | Chelsea | W | 1-0 | Duncan | 13,6 |
| 35 | 30 | (a) | Arsenal | L | 0-1 | | 69,0 |
| 36 | 31 | (a) | Liverpool | L | 2-4 | Groves, Ramage | 31,3 |
| 37 | Apr 2 | (h) | Arsenal | L | 2-4 | Groves, Dobbs | 32,1 |
| 38 | 7 | (h) | Tottenham H | W | 4-3 | Bowers 4 | 14,2 |
| 39 | 14 | (a) | Wolves | L | 0-3 | | 17,9 |
| 40 | 19 | (a) | Leicester C | L | 0-2 | | 8,8 |
| 41 | 21 | (h) | Aston Villa | D | 1-1 | Bowers | 14,1 |
| 42 | 28 | (a) | Sheffield U | L | 0-2 | | 4,9 |

FINAL LEAGUE POSITION: 4th in Division One

Appearances
Goals

## FA Cup

| | | | | | | | |
|---|---|---|---|---|---|---|---|
| 3 | Jan 13 | (a) | Bristol C | D | 1-1 | Nicholas | 34,2 |
| R | 17 | (h) | Bristol C | W | 1-0* | Bowers | 24,2 |
| 4 | 27 | (h) | Wolves | W | 3-0 | Bowers 2, Crooks | 37,7 |
| 5 | Feb 17 | (a) | Arsenal | L | 0-1 | | 66,9 |

*after extra-time

Appearances
Goals

| | Kirby J | Cooper T | Collin G | Nicholas J | Barker J | Keen E | Crooks S | Hutchison D | Bowers J | Groves A | Duncan D | Ramage P | Reid S | Randall J | Webb J | Jessop F | Scott A | Alderman A | Wileman S | Dobbs A | Bowden O | Hann R | Blore V |
|---|---|---|---|---|---|---|---|---|---|---|---|---|---|---|---|---|---|---|---|---|---|---|---|
| 1 | 1 | 2 | 3 | 4 | 5 | 6 | 7 | 8 | 9 | 10 | 11 | | | | | | | | | | | | |
| 2 | 1 | 2 | 3 | 4 | 5 | 6 | 7 | 8 | 9 | 10 | 11 | | | | | | | | | | | | |
| 3 | 1 | 2 | 3 | 4 | 5 | 6 | 7 | | 9 | 8 | 11 | 10 | | | | | | | | | | | |
| 4 | 1 | 2 | | 4 | 5 | 6 | 7 | | 9 | 8 | 11 | 10 | 3 | | | | | | | | | | |
| 5 | 1 | 2 | | 4 | 5 | 6 | 7 | | 9 | 8 | 11 | 10 | 3 | | | | | | | | | | |
| 6 | 1 | 2 | 3 | 4 | 5 | 6 | 7 | | 9 | 8 | 11 | 10 | | | | | | | | | | | |
| 7 | 1 | 2 | 3 | 4 | 5 | 6 | 7 | | 9 | 8 | 11 | 10 | | | | | | | | | | | |
| 8 | 1 | 2 | 3 | 4 | 5 | 6 | 7 | | 9 | 8 | 11 | 10 | | | | | | | | | | | |
| 9 | 1 | 2 | 3 | 4 | 5 | 6 | | 9 | | 8 | 11 | 10 | | 7 | | | | | | | | | |
| 10 | 1 | 2 | 3 | 4 | 5 | 6 | 7 | | 9 | 8 | 11 | 10 | | | | | | | | | | | |
| 11 | 1 | 2 | 3 | 4 | 5 | 6 | | | 9 | 8 | 11 | 10 | | 7 | | | | | | | | | |
| 12 | 1 | 2 | 3 | 4 | 5 | 6 | 7 | | 9 | 8 | 11 | 10 | | | | | | | | | | | |
| 13 | 1 | 2 | 3 | 4 | 5 | 6 | 7 | | 9 | 8 | 11 | 10 | | | | | | | | | | | |
| 14 | 1 | 2 | 3 | 4 | 5 | 6 | 7 | | 9 | 8 | 11 | 10 | | | | | | | | | | | |
| 15 | 1 | 2 | 3 | 4 | 5 | 6 | 7 | | 9 | 8 | 11 | 10 | | | | | | | | | | | |
| 16 | 1 | | 3 | 4 | 5 | 6 | 7 | | 9 | 8 | 11 | 10 | | | 2 | | | | | | | | |
| 17 | 1 | | 3 | 4 | 5 | 6 | 7 | | 9 | 8 | 11 | 10 | | | 2 | | | | | | | | |
| 18 | 1 | | 3 | 4 | 5 | 6 | 7 | | 9 | 8 | 11 | 10 | | | 2 | | | | | | | | |
| 19 | 1 | 2 | 3 | 4 | 5 | 6 | 7 | 8 | 9 | | 11 | 10 | | | | | | | | | | | |
| 20 | 1 | 2 | 3 | 4 | | 6 | 7 | | 9 | 8 | 11 | 10 | | | | 5 | | | | | | | |
| 21 | 1 | | 3 | 4 | | 6 | 7 | 8 | 9 | | 11 | 10 | | | 2 | 5 | | | | | | | |
| 22 | 1 | | 3 | 4 | | 6 | 7 | 8 | 9 | | 11 | 10 | | | 2 | | 5 | | | | | | |
| 23 | 1 | | 3 | 4 | | 6 | 7 | | 9 | | 11 | | | | 2 | | 5 | 8 | 10 | | | | |
| 24 | 1 | | 3 | 4 | | 6 | 7 | | 9 | | 11 | | | | 2 | | 5 | 8 | 10 | | | | |
| 25 | 1 | 2 | 3 | 4 | | 6 | 7 | | 9 | | 11 | 10 | | | | | 5 | | 8 | | | | |
| 26 | 1 | 2 | 3 | 4 | 5 | 6 | | | 9 | 8 | 11 | | | 7 | | | | | 10 | | | | |
| 27 | 1 | 2 | 3 | 4 | 5 | 6 | 7 | | 9 | 8 | 11 | 10 | | | | | | | | | | | |
| 28 | 1 | 2 | | 4 | 5 | 6 | 7 | | | | | 10 | 3 | 11 | | | | | 8 | 9 | | | |
| 29 | 1 | 2 | 3 | 4 | 5 | 6 | 7 | | 9 | | | 10 | | 11 | | | | | | | 8 | | |
| 30 | 1 | 2 | 3 | 4 | 5 | 6 | 7 | | 9 | 8 | | 10 | | 11 | | | | | | | | | |
| 31 | 1 | 2 | 3 | 4 | 5 | 6 | 7 | | 9 | | | 10 | | 11 | | | | | | | 8 | | |
| 32 | 1 | 2 | 3 | 4 | 5 | 6 | | | 9 | 8 | | 10 | | 11 | | | | | | | 7 | | |
| 33 | 1 | 2 | 3 | 4 | 5 | 6 | 7 | | 9 | 8 | | 10 | | 11 | | | | | | | | | |
| 34 | 1 | 2 | 3 | 4 | 5 | 6 | 7 | | 9 | 8 | 11 | 10 | | | | | | | | | | | |
| 35 | 1 | 2 | 3 | 4 | 5 | 6 | 7 | | 9 | | 11 | 10 | | | | | | | | | 8 | | |
| 36 | 1 | 2 | 3 | 4 | 5 | 6 | 7 | | | 8 | | 10 | | 11 | | | | | | 9 | | | |
| 37 | 1 | 2 | 3 | 4 | 5 | 6 | 7 | | | 8 | | 10 | | 11 | | | | | | 9 | | | |
| 38 | 1 | | | 4 | | 6 | 7 | | 9 | 8 | | 10 | 3 | 11 | 2 | | | | | | | 5 | |
| 39 | 1 | | | 4 | 5 | | | | | 8 | | 10 | 3 | 11 | 2 | | | | 7 | | 9 | 6 | |
| 40 | | 2 | | 4 | 5 | 6 | 7 | | 9 | | | 10 | 3 | 11 | | | | | | | | 8 | 1 |
| 41 | | 2 | | 4 | 5 | 6 | 7 | | 9 | | | 10 | 3 | 11 | | | | | | | | 8 | 1 |
| 42 | 1 | 2 | | 4 | | 6 | 7 | | 9 | | | 10 | 3 | 11 | | | | | | | 8 | 5 | |
| | 40 | 33 | 34 | 42 | 34 | 41 | 37 | 6 | 37 | 29 | 29 | 37 | 8 | 16 | 9 | 2 | 4 | 2 | 6 | 3 | 6 | 5 | 2 |
| | | | | 1 | | 1 | 7 | 2 | 34 | 5 | 8 | 7 | | | | | | 1 | 1 | 1 | | | |

| | Kirby J | Cooper T | Collin G | Nicholas J | Barker J | Keen E | Crooks S | Hutchison D | Bowers J | Groves A | Duncan D | Ramage P | Reid S | Randall J | Webb J | Jessop F | Scott A | Alderman A | Wileman S | Dobbs A | Bowden O | Hann R | Blore V |
|---|---|---|---|---|---|---|---|---|---|---|---|---|---|---|---|---|---|---|---|---|---|---|---|
| 3 | 1 | 2 | 3 | 4 | 5 | 6 | 7 | | 9 | 8 | 11 | 10 | | | | | | | | | | | |
| R | 1 | 2 | 3 | 4 | | 6 | 7 | 8 | 9 | | 11 | 10 | | | | | 5 | | | | | | |
| 4 | 1 | 2 | 3 | 4 | 5 | 6 | 7 | | 9 | 8 | 11 | | | | | | | | 10 | | | | |
| 5 | 1 | 2 | 3 | 4 | 5 | 6 | 7 | | 9 | | 11 | 10 | | | | | | | 8 | | | | |
| | 4 | 4 | 4 | 4 | 3 | 4 | 4 | 1 | 4 | 2 | 4 | 3 | | | | | 1 | | 2 | | | | |
| | | | | 1 | | | 1 | | 3 | | | | | | | | | | | | | | |

# 1934-35

| | P | W | D | L | F | A | Pts |
|---|---|---|---|---|---|---|---|
| Arsenal | 42 | 23 | 12 | 7 | 115 | 46 | 58 |
| Sunderland | 42 | 19 | 16 | 7 | 90 | 51 | 54 |
| Sheffield W | 42 | 18 | 13 | 11 | 70 | 64 | 49 |
| Manchester C | 42 | 20 | 8 | 14 | 82 | 67 | 48 |
| Grimsby T | 42 | 17 | 11 | 14 | 78 | 60 | 45 |
| Derby Co | 42 | 18 | 9 | 15 | 81 | 66 | 45 |
| Liverpool | 42 | 19 | 7 | 16 | 85 | 88 | 45 |
| Everton | 42 | 16 | 12 | 14 | 89 | 88 | 44 |
| WBA | 42 | 17 | 10 | 15 | 83 | 83 | 44 |
| Stoke C | 42 | 18 | 6 | 18 | 71 | 70 | 42 |
| Preston NE | 42 | 15 | 12 | 15 | 62 | 67 | 42 |
| Chelsea | 42 | 16 | 9 | 17 | 73 | 82 | 41 |
| Aston Villa | 42 | 14 | 13 | 15 | 74 | 88 | 41 |
| Portsmouth | 42 | 15 | 10 | 17 | 71 | 72 | 40 |
| Blackburn R | 42 | 14 | 11 | 17 | 66 | 78 | 39 |
| Huddersfield T | 42 | 14 | 10 | 18 | 76 | 71 | 38 |
| Wolves | 42 | 15 | 8 | 19 | 88 | 94 | 38 |
| Leeds U | 42 | 13 | 12 | 17 | 75 | 92 | 38 |
| Birmingham | 42 | 13 | 10 | 19 | 63 | 81 | 36 |
| Middlesbrough | 42 | 10 | 14 | 18 | 70 | 90 | 34 |
| Leicester C | 42 | 12 | 9 | 21 | 61 | 86 | 33 |
| Tottenham H | 42 | 10 | 10 | 22 | 54 | 93 | 30 |

Manager: George Jobey.
Leading scorer: Hughie Gallacher, League 23, all matches 24.
League ever-present: Peter Ramage.

- Derby equalled the highest League score in their history when they beat West Bromwich Albion 9–3 on 8 December.
- They had previously scored nine without reply on two occasions, against Wolves in 1891 and Sheffield Wednesday in 1899.
- A knee operation kept out Jack Bowers for six months and, in November, George Jobey signed Hughie Gallacher from Chelsea for £2,750. Gallacher was one of the great centre-forwards and, in December, scored all five goals against Blackburn Rovers at Ewood Park.

## Division One

| Match No. | Date | | Venue | Opponents | Result | | Scorers | Atten |
|---|---|---|---|---|---|---|---|---|
| 1 | Aug | 25 | (h) | Chelsea | W | 3-0 | Crooks, Bowers, Ramage | 20 |
| 2 | | 27 | (a) | Huddersfield T | L | 0-1 | | 8 |
| 3 | Sep | 1 | (a) | Aston Villa | L | 2-3 | Ramage, Morton (og) | 44 |
| 4 | | 5 | (h) | Huddersfield T | W | 4-1 | Bowers 2 (1 pen), Duncan, Ramage | 19 |
| 5 | | 8 | (h) | Stoke C | L | 0-2 | | 22 |
| 6 | | 15 | (h) | Leicester C | D | 1-1 | Bowers | 25 |
| 7 | | 22 | (a) | Sunderland | W | 4-1 | Bowers 3, Duncan | 25 |
| 8 | | 29 | (h) | Tottenham H | W | 2-1 | Stockill 2 | 15 |
| 9 | Oct | 6 | (a) | Preston NE | W | 1-0 | Crooks | 24 |
| 10 | | 13 | (h) | Grimsby T | L | 1-4 | Duncan | 21, |
| 11 | | 20 | (a) | Manchester C | W | 1-0 | Crooks | 44, |
| 12 | | 27 | (h) | Middlesbrough | W | 2-0 | Ramage, Duncan | 15 |
| 13 | Nov | 3 | (a) | Sheffield W | L | 0-1 | | 19 |
| 14 | | 10 | (h) | Birmingham | D | 1-1 | Gallacher | 20 |
| 15 | | 17 | (a) | Portsmouth | L | 1-5 | Gallacher | 19 |
| 16 | | 24 | (h) | Liverpool | L | 1-2 | Ramage | 17 |
| 17 | Dec | 1 | (a) | Leeds U | L | 2-4 | Ramage, Stockill | 16 |
| 18 | | 8 | (h) | West Brom A | W | 9-3 | Crooks 3, Stockill 3, Gallacher 2, Nicholas | 14, |
| 19 | | 15 | (a) | Blackburn R | W | 5-2 | Gallacher 5 | 12, |
| 20 | | 22 | (h) | Arsenal | W | 3-1 | Stockill 2, Gallacher (pen) | 26, |
| 21 | | 25 | (a) | Wolves | L | 1-5 | Ramage | 36, |
| 22 | | 26 | (h) | Wolves | W | 2-0 | Crooks, Gallacher | 35, |
| 23 | | 29 | (a) | Chelsea | D | 1-1 | Miller (og) | 50, |
| 24 | Jan | 1 | (a) | Everton | D | 2-2 | Groves, Crooks | 31, |
| 25 | | 5 | (h) | Aston Villa | D | 1-1 | Groves | 24, |
| 26 | | 19 | (a) | Stoke C | D | 1-1 | Groves | 25, |
| 27 | | 31 | (a) | Leicester C | W | 1-0 | Gallacher | 14, |
| 28 | Feb | 2 | (h) | Sunderland | W | 3-1 | Gallacher, Groves, Hall (og) | 24, |
| 29 | | 9 | (a) | Tottenham H | D | 2-2 | Gallacher, Duncan | 42, |
| 30 | | 23 | (a) | Grimsby T | W | 3-1 | Gallacher 3 | 12, |
| 31 | Mar | 2 | (h) | Manchester C | L | 1-2 | Gallacher | 27, |
| 32 | | 9 | (a) | Middlesbrough | D | 1-1 | Groves | 13, |
| 33 | | 20 | (h) | Sheffield W | W | 4-0 | Groves, Ramage, Duncan, Gallacher | 15, |
| 34 | | 23 | (a) | Birmingham | L | 2-3 | Duncan, Gallacher | 11, |
| 35 | | 30 | (h) | Portsmouth | L | 0-1 | | 14, |
| 36 | Apr | 6 | (a) | Liverpool | W | 3-1 | Crooks, Bowers, Bird | 20, |
| 37 | | 10 | (h) | Preston NE | L | 0-3 | | 8, |
| 38 | | 13 | (h) | Leeds U | L | 1-2 | Crooks | 11, |
| 39 | | 20 | (a) | West Brom A | L | 3-4 | Gallacher 2 (1 pen), Groves | 16, |
| 40 | | 22 | (h) | Everton | W | 4-1 | Ramage, Duncan, Gallacher, Hughes | 17, |
| 41 | | 27 | (h) | Blackburn R | D | 1-1 | Groves | 8, |
| 42 | May | 4 | (a) | Arsenal | W | 1-0 | Ramage | 36, |

FINAL LEAGUE POSITION: 6th in Division One

Appearar

Gc

## FA Cup

| | | | | | | | | |
|---|---|---|---|---|---|---|---|---|
| 3 | Jan | 12 | (a) | York C | W | 1-0 | Crooks | 13, |
| 4 | | 26 | (h) | Swansea T | W | 3-0 | Duncan, Groves, Gallacher | 28, |
| 5 | Feb | 16 | (a) | Everton | L | 1-3 | Crooks | 62, |

Appearar

Gc

| rby J | Cooper T | Collin G | Nicholas J | Barker J | Keen E | Crooks S | Groves A | Bowers J | Ramage P | Randall J | Bird D | Jessop F | Duncan D | Bell D | Stockill R | Udall E | Hann R | Wileman S | Gallacher H | Blore V | Hughes A | Reid S | Philbin J | Webb J | |
|---|---|---|---|---|---|---|---|---|---|---|---|---|---|---|---|---|---|---|---|---|---|---|---|---|---|
| | 2 | 3 | 4 | 5 | 6 | 7 | 8 | 9 | 10 | 11 | | | | | | | | | | | | | | | 1 |
| | 2 | 3 | 4 | 5 | 6 | | 8 | 9 | 10 | 7 | 11 | | | | | | | | | | | | | | 2 |
| | 2 | 3 | 4 | | 6 | | 8 | 9 | 10 | 7 | | 5 | 11 | | | | | | | | | | | | 3 |
| | 2 | 3 | 5 | | 6 | | 8 | 9 | 10 | 7 | | | 11 | 4 | | | | | | | | | | | 4 |
| | 2 | 3 | 5 | | 6 | | 8 | 9 | 10 | 7 | | | 11 | 4 | | | | | | | | | | | 5 |
| | 2 | 3 | 5 | | 6 | 7 | | 9 | 10 | | | | 11 | 4 | 8 | | | | | | | | | | 6 |
| | 2 | 3 | 4 | 5 | 6 | 7 | | 9 | 10 | | | | 11 | | 8 | | | | | | | | | | 7 |
| | | 3 | 4 | | 6 | 7 | | 9 | 10 | | | | 11 | | 8 | 2 | 5 | | | | | | | | 8 |
| | 2 | 3 | 4 | 5 | 6 | 7 | | | 10 | | | | 11 | | 8 | | | 9 | | | | | | | 9 |
| | 2 | 3 | 4 | 5 | 6 | 7 | | | 10 | | | | 11 | | 8 | | | 9 | | | | | | | 10 |
| | 2 | 3 | 4 | 5 | | 7 | 8 | | 10 | | | | 11 | | 9 | | 6 | | | | | | | | 11 |
| | 2 | 3 | 4 | 5 | | 7 | 8 | | 10 | | | | 11 | | 9 | | 6 | | | | | | | | 12 |
| | 2 | 3 | 4 | 5 | | 7 | 8 | | 10 | | | | 11 | | 9 | | 6 | | | | | | | | 13 |
| | 2 | 3 | 4 | 5 | | 7 | | | 10 | | | | 11 | | 8 | | 6 | | 9 | | | | | | 14 |
| | 2 | 3 | 4 | 5 | | 7 | | | 10 | | 11 | | | | 8 | | 6 | | 9 | | | | | | 15 |
| | 2 | 3 | 4 | 5 | | 7 | | | 10 | | | | 11 | | 8 | | 6 | | 9 | | | | | | 16 |
| | 2 | 3 | 4 | 5 | 6 | 7 | | | 10 | | | | 11 | | 8 | | | | 9 | 1 | | | | | 17 |
| | | 3 | 4 | 5 | | 7 | | | 10 | | | | 11 | | 8 | 2 | 6 | | 9 | 1 | | | | | 18 |
| | | 3 | 4 | 5 | | 7 | | | 10 | | | | 11 | | 8 | 2 | 6 | | 9 | 1 | | | | | 19 |
| | | 3 | 4 | 5 | | 7 | | | 10 | | | | 11 | | 8 | 2 | 6 | | 9 | | | | | | 20 |
| | | 3 | 4 | 5 | 6 | 7 | | | 10 | | 11 | | | | 8 | 2 | | | 9 | | | | | | 21 |
| | | 3 | 4 | 5 | | 7 | | | 10 | | | | 11 | | 8 | 2 | 6 | | 9 | | | | | | 22 |
| | | 3 | 4 | 5 | | | 8 | | 10 | | | | 11 | | | 2 | 6 | | 9 | | 7 | | | | 23 |
| | | 3 | 4 | 5 | | 7 | 8 | | 10 | | | | 11 | | | 2 | 6 | | 9 | | | | | | 24 |
| | | 3 | 4 | 5 | | 7 | 8 | | 10 | | | | 11 | | | 2 | 6 | | 9 | | | | | | 25 |
| | | 3 | 4 | 5 | | 7 | 8 | | 10 | 11 | | | | | | 2 | 6 | | 9 | | | | | | 26 |
| | | 3 | 4 | 5 | | 7 | 8 | | 10 | | | | 11 | | | 2 | 6 | | 9 | | | | | | 27 |
| | | 3 | 4 | 5 | | 7 | 8 | | 10 | | | | 11 | | | 2 | 6 | | 9 | | | | | | 28 |
| | | 3 | 4 | 5 | | 7 | 8 | | 10 | | | | 11 | | | 2 | 6 | | 9 | | | | | | 29 |
| | | 3 | 4 | 5 | | 7 | 8 | | 10 | | | | 11 | | | 2 | 6 | | 9 | 1 | | | | | 30 |
| | | 3 | 4 | 5 | | 7 | 8 | | 10 | | | | 11 | | | 2 | 6 | | 9 | 1 | | | | | 31 |
| | | 3 | 4 | 5 | | 7 | 8 | | 10 | | | | 11 | | | 2 | 6 | | 9 | 1 | | | | | 32 |
| | | 3 | 4 | 5 | | 7 | 8 | | 10 | | | | 11 | | | 2 | 6 | | 9 | 1 | | | | | 33 |
| | | | 4 | 5 | | 7 | 8 | | 10 | | | | 11 | | | 2 | 6 | | 9 | 1 | | 3 | | | 34 |
| | | 3 | 4 | 5 | | 7 | 8 | | 10 | | | | 11 | | | 2 | 6 | | 9 | 1 | | | | | 35 |
| | | 3 | 4 | | 6 | 7 | 8 | 9 | 10 | | 11 | 5 | | | | 2 | | | | 1 | | | | | 36 |
| | | 3 | 4 | | 6 | 7 | 8 | 9 | 10 | | | 5 | 11 | | | 2 | | | | 1 | | | | | 37 |
| | | | | 5 | 6 | 7 | | | 10 | | | | 11 | 4 | | 2 | | | 9 | 1 | | 3 | 8 | | 38 |
| | | | 4 | 5 | 6 | 7 | 8 | | 10 | | | | 11 | | | 2 | | | 9 | 1 | | 3 | | | 39 |
| | | | 4 | 5 | 6 | | 8 | | 10 | | | | 11 | | | 2 | | | 9 | | 7 | | | 3 | 40 |
| | | | 4 | 5 | 6 | 7 | 8 | | 10 | | | | 11 | | | | | | 9 | | | 3 | | 2 | 41 |
| | | | 4 | 5 | 6 | 7 | 8 | | 10 | | | 3 | 11 | | | 2 | | | 9 | | | | | | 42 |
| 9 | 16 | 36 | 41 | 35 | 19 | 36 | 27 | 10 | 42 | 6 | 4 | 4 | 36 | 4 | 17 | 25 | 24 | 2 | 27 | 13 | 2 | 4 | 1 | 2 | |
| | | | 1 | | | 10 | 8 | 8 | 10 | | 1 | | 8 | | 8 | | | | 23 | | 1 | | | | |

3 own-goals

| rby J | Cooper T | Collin G | Nicholas J | Barker J | Keen E | Crooks S | Groves A | Bowers J | Ramage P | Randall J | Bird D | Jessop F | Duncan D | Bell D | Stockill R | Udall E | Hann R | Wileman S | Gallacher H | Blore V | Hughes A | Reid S | Philbin J | Webb J | |
|---|---|---|---|---|---|---|---|---|---|---|---|---|---|---|---|---|---|---|---|---|---|---|---|---|---|
| | | 3 | 4 | 5 | | 7 | 8 | | 10 | | | | 11 | | | 2 | 6 | | 9 | | | | | | 3 |
| | | 3 | 4 | 5 | | 7 | 8 | | 10 | | | | 11 | | | 2 | 6 | | 9 | | | | | | 4 |
| | | 3 | 4 | 5 | | 7 | 8 | | 10 | | | | 11 | | | 2 | 6 | | 9 | | | | | | 5 |
| | | 3 | 3 | 3 | | 3 | 3 | | 3 | | | | 3 | | | 3 | 3 | | 3 | | | | | | |
| | | | | | | 2 | 1 | | | | | | 1 | | | | | | 1 | | | | | | |

# 1935-36

| | P | W | D | L | F | A | Pts |
|---|---|---|---|---|---|---|---|
| Sunderland | 42 | 25 | 6 | 11 | 109 | 74 | 56 |
| Derby Co | 42 | 18 | 12 | 12 | 61 | 52 | 48 |
| Huddersfield T | 42 | 18 | 12 | 12 | 59 | 56 | 48 |
| Stoke C | 42 | 20 | 7 | 15 | 57 | 57 | 47 |
| Brentford | 42 | 17 | 12 | 13 | 81 | 60 | 46 |
| Arsenal | 42 | 15 | 15 | 12 | 78 | 48 | 45 |
| Preston NE | 42 | 18 | 8 | 16 | 67 | 64 | 44 |
| Chelsea | 42 | 15 | 13 | 14 | 65 | 72 | 43 |
| Manchester C | 42 | 17 | 8 | 17 | 68 | 60 | 42 |
| Portsmouth | 42 | 17 | 8 | 17 | 54 | 67 | 42 |
| Leeds U | 42 | 15 | 11 | 16 | 66 | 64 | 41 |
| Birmingham | 42 | 15 | 11 | 16 | 61 | 63 | 41 |
| Bolton W | 42 | 14 | 13 | 15 | 67 | 76 | 41 |
| Middlesbrough | 42 | 15 | 10 | 17 | 84 | 70 | 40 |
| Wolves | 42 | 15 | 10 | 17 | 77 | 76 | 40 |
| Everton | 42 | 13 | 13 | 16 | 89 | 89 | 39 |
| Grimsby T | 42 | 17 | 5 | 20 | 65 | 73 | 39 |
| WBA | 42 | 16 | 6 | 20 | 89 | 88 | 38 |
| Liverpool | 42 | 13 | 12 | 17 | 60 | 64 | 38 |
| Sheffield W | 42 | 13 | 12 | 17 | 63 | 77 | 38 |
| Aston Villa | 42 | 13 | 9 | 20 | 81 | 110 | 35 |
| Blackburn R | 42 | 12 | 9 | 21 | 55 | 96 | 33 |

Manager: George Jobey.
Leading scorer: Hughie Gallacher, League 15, all matches 16.
League ever-present: Jack Kirby, Jack Nicholas.

- Derby were First Division runners-up for the third time in their history, eight points behind Arsenal. They did not improve on this until their first Championship in 1971–72.
- The Normanton End stand opened for this season so, in a decade, the Rams had three new stands that lasted until the stadium was demolished following the move to Pride Park.
- The last rise in the Baseball Ground attendance record before World War Two, 37,830 for the fourth-round FA Cup tie against Nottingham Forest.
- Derby County Reserves won the Central League for the first time.

## Division One

| Match No. | Date | | Venue | Opponents | Result | | Scorers | Atten |
|---|---|---|---|---|---|---|---|---|
| 1 | Aug | 31 | (a) | Everton | L | 0-4 | | 43 |
| 2 | Sep | 2 | (a) | Preston NE | L | 0-1 | | 28 |
| 3 | | 7 | (h) | Bolton W | W | 4-0 | Gallacher (pen), Ramage, Duncan, Groves | 25 |
| 4 | | 11 | (h) | Preston NE | W | 2-0 | Groves, Gallacher | 21 |
| 5 | | 14 | (a) | Huddersfield T | D | 1-1 | Groves | 21 |
| 6 | | 18 | (h) | Brentford | W | 2-1 | Groves, Gallacher | 21 |
| 7 | | 21 | (h) | Middlesbrough | W | 3-2 | Napier 2, Gallacher | 27 |
| 8 | | 28 | (a) | Aston Villa | W | 2-0 | Boyd, Gallacher | 49 |
| 9 | Oct | 5 | (h) | Wolves | W | 3-1 | Nicholas, Ramage, Bird | 20 |
| 10 | | 12 | (a) | Sheffield W | L | 0-1 | | 34 |
| 11 | | 19 | (h) | Blackburn R | W | 1-0 | Duncan | 18 |
| 12 | | 26 | (a) | Stoke C | D | 0-0 | | 27 |
| 13 | Nov | 2 | (h) | Manchester C | W | 3-0 | Napier 2, Gallacher | 28 |
| 14 | | 9 | (a) | Arsenal | D | 1-1 | Ramage | 54 |
| 15 | | 16 | (h) | Birmingham | D | 2-2 | Napier, Bowers | 23 |
| 16 | | 23 | (a) | Liverpool | D | 0-0 | | 31 |
| 17 | | 30 | (h) | West Brom A | W | 2-0 | Napier, Jessop (pen) | 21 |
| 18 | Dec | 7 | (a) | Leeds U | L | 0-1 | | 21 |
| 19 | | 14 | (h) | Grimsby T | W | 2-0 | Crooks, Bowers | 17 |
| 20 | | 21 | (a) | Sunderland | L | 1-3 | Bowers | 33 |
| 21 | | 25 | (a) | Portsmouth | L | 0-3 | | 21 |
| 22 | | 26 | (h) | Portsmouth | D | 1-1 | Gallacher | 21 |
| 23 | | 28 | (h) | Everton | D | 3-3 | Keen, Ramage, Jessop (pen) | 20 |
| 24 | Jan | 4 | (a) | Bolton W | W | 2-0 | Gallacher, Crooks | 31 |
| 25 | | 18 | (h) | Huddersfield T | W | 2-0 | Ramage, Halford | 18 |
| 26 | | 29 | (a) | Middlesbrough | W | 3-0 | Bowers 2, Halford | 7 |
| 27 | Feb | 1 | (h) | Aston Villa | L | 1-3 | Bowers | 30 |
| 28 | | 8 | (a) | Wolves | D | 0-0 | | 23 |
| 29 | | 19 | (h) | Sheffield W | W | 3-1 | Bowers 2, Crooks | 14 |
| 30 | | 22 | (a) | Blackburn R | D | 0-0 | | 14 |
| 31 | Mar | 4 | (h) | Arsenal | L | 0-4 | | 17 |
| 32 | | 7 | (a) | West Brom A | W | 3-0 | Gallacher 2, Nicholas | 18 |
| 33 | | 14 | (h) | Stoke C | L | 0-1 | | 20 |
| 34 | | 21 | (a) | Birmingham | W | 3-2 | Gallacher 2, Duncan | 25 |
| 35 | | 28 | (h) | Liverpool | D | 2-2 | Crooks, Stockill | 16 |
| 36 | Apr | 4 | (a) | Manchester C | L | 0-1 | | 25 |
| 37 | | 10 | (a) | Chelsea | D | 1-1 | Gallacher | 54 |
| 38 | | 11 | (h) | Leeds U | W | 2-1 | Hagan 2 | 15 |
| 39 | | 13 | (h) | Chelsea | D | 1-1 | Gallacher | 21 |
| 40 | | 18 | (a) | Grimsby T | L | 1-4 | Hagan | 11 |
| 41 | | 25 | (h) | Sunderland | W | 4-0 | Stockill 2, Halford, Gallacher | 15 |
| 42 | May | 2 | (a) | Brentford | L | 0-6 | | 20 |

FINAL LEAGUE POSITION: 2nd in Division One

Appearan

Gc

## FA Cup

| | | | | | | | | |
|---|---|---|---|---|---|---|---|---|
| 3 | Jan | 11 | (h) | Dartford | W | 3-2 | Gallacher, Crooks, Napier | 27 |
| 4 | | 25 | (h) | Nottingham F | W | 2-0 | Halford, Bowers | 37 |
| 5 | Feb | 15 | (a) | Bradford C | W | 1-0 | Bowers | 33 |
| 6 | | 29 | (a) | Fulham | L | 0-3 | | 37 |

Appearan

Gc

| by J | Udall E | Reid S | Nicholas J | Barker J | Keen E | Crooks S | Napier C | Gallacher H | Ramage P | Duncan D | Collin G | Groves A | Bowers J | Jessop F | Boyd J | Bird D | Hann R | Summers J | Hagan J | Halford D | Webb J | Stockill R | Roberts E | Howe J | |
|---|---|---|---|---|---|---|---|---|---|---|---|---|---|---|---|---|---|---|---|---|---|---|---|---|---|
| | 2 | 3 | 4 | 5 | 6 | 7 | 8 | 9 | 10 | 11 | | | | | | | | | | | | | | | 1 |
| | 2 | | 4 | 5 | 6 | 7 | | | 10 | 11 | 3 | 8 | 9 | | | | | | | | | | | | 2 |
| | 2 | | 4 | 5 | 6 | 7 | | 9 | 10 | 11 | 3 | 8 | | | | | | | | | | | | | 3 |
| | 2 | | 4 | 5 | 6 | 7 | | 9 | 10 | 11 | 3 | 8 | | | | | | | | | | | | | 4 |
| | 2 | | 4 | 5 | 6 | 7 | | 9 | 10 | 11 | 3 | 8 | | | | | | | | | | | | | 5 |
| | 2 | | 4 | 5 | 6 | 7 | | 9 | 10 | 11 | 3 | 8 | | | | | | | | | | | | | 6 |
| | 2 | | 4 | 5 | 6 | 7 | 8 | 9 | 10 | 11 | | | | 3 | | | | | | | | | | | 7 |
| | 2 | | 4 | 5 | 6 | | 8 | 9 | 10 | 11 | | | | 3 | 7 | | | | | | | | | | 8 |
| | 2 | | 4 | 5 | 6 | | | 9 | 10 | | | 8 | | 3 | 7 | 11 | | | | | | | | | 9 |
| | 2 | | 4 | 5 | 6 | | 8 | | 10 | 11 | | | 9 | 3 | 7 | | | | | | | | | | 10 |
| | 2 | | 4 | | 6 | 7 | 8 | 9 | 10 | 11 | | | | 3 | | | 5 | | | | | | | | 11 |
| | 2 | | 4 | 5 | 6 | 7 | 8 | 9 | 10 | 11 | | | | 3 | | | | | | | | | | | 12 |
| | 2 | | 4 | 5 | 6 | 7 | 8 | 9 | 10 | 11 | | | | 3 | | | | | | | | | | | 13 |
| | 2 | | 4 | 5 | 6 | 7 | 9 | | 10 | 11 | | 8 | | 3 | | | | | | | | | | | 14 |
| | 2 | | 4 | 5 | 6 | 7 | 8 | | 10 | 11 | | | 9 | 3 | | | | | | | | | | | 15 |
| | 2 | | 4 | 5 | 6 | | 8 | | 10 | 11 | | | 9 | 3 | 7 | | | | | | | | | | 16 |
| | 2 | | 4 | 5 | 6 | | 8 | | 10 | 11 | | | 9 | 3 | 7 | | | | | | | | | | 17 |
| | 2 | | 4 | 5 | 6 | | 8 | | 10 | 11 | | | 9 | 3 | 7 | | | | | | | | | | 18 |
| | 2 | | 4 | 5 | 6 | 7 | 8 | | 10 | 11 | | | 9 | 3 | | | | | | | | | | | 19 |
| | 2 | | 4 | 5 | 6 | | 8 | | 10 | 11 | | | 9 | 3 | | | | 7 | | | | | | | 20 |
| | 2 | | 4 | 5 | 6 | | 7 | | 10 | 11 | | 8 | 9 | 3 | | | | | | | | | | | 21 |
| | 2 | | 4 | 5 | 6 | | 8 | 9 | 10 | 11 | | | | 3 | | | | 7 | | | | | | | 22 |
| | 2 | | 4 | 5 | 6 | | 8 | 9 | 10 | 11 | | | | 3 | | | | | 7 | | | | | | 23 |
| | 2 | | 4 | 5 | 6 | 7 | 8 | 9 | 10 | | | | | 3 | | | | | | 11 | | | | | 24 |
| | 2 | | 4 | 5 | 6 | 7 | 8 | | 10 | | | | 9 | 3 | | | | | | 11 | | | | | 25 |
| | 2 | | 4 | 5 | 6 | 7 | 8 | | 10 | | | | 9 | 3 | | | | | | 11 | | | | | 26 |
| | 2 | | 4 | 5 | 6 | 7 | 8 | | 10 | | | | 9 | 3 | | | | | | 11 | | | | | 27 |
| | 2 | | 4 | 5 | 6 | 7 | 8 | | 10 | | 3 | | 9 | | | | | | | 11 | | | | | 28 |
| | 2 | | 4 | 5 | 6 | 7 | | | 10 | 11 | 3 | | 9 | | | | | | 8 | | | | | | 29 |
| | 2 | | 4 | 5 | 6 | 7 | 8 | | 10 | 11 | 3 | | 9 | | | | | | | | | | | | 30 |
| | | | 4 | 5 | 6 | 7 | | | 10 | 11 | 3 | | 9 | | | | | | 8 | | 2 | | | | 31 |
| | | | 4 | 5 | | 7 | | 9 | | 11 | 3 | | | | | | 6 | | | | 2 | 8 | 10 | | 32 |
| | | | 4 | 5 | | 7 | | 9 | | 11 | 3 | | | | | | 6 | | | | 2 | 8 | 10 | | 33 |
| | | | 4 | 5 | | 7 | | 9 | | 11 | 3 | | | | | | 6 | | | | 2 | 8 | 10 | | 34 |
| | 2 | | 4 | 5 | | 7 | | 9 | | 11 | | | | | | | 6 | | | | 3 | 8 | 10 | | 35 |
| | 2 | | 4 | | 6 | | 11 | 9 | 10 | | | | | | 7 | | 5 | | | | 3 | 8 | | | 36 |
| | 2 | | 4 | 5 | | 7 | | 9 | 10 | 11 | | | | | | | 6 | | | | 3 | 8 | | | 37 |
| | 2 | | 4 | 5 | 6 | 7 | | | | 11 | 3 | | 9 | | | | | | 8 | | | 10 | | | 38 |
| | 2 | | 4 | 5 | 6 | 7 | | 9 | | 11 | 3 | | | | | | | | 8 | | | 10 | | | 39 |
| | 2 | | 4 | 5 | 6 | 7 | 10 | 9 | | 11 | 3 | | | | | | | | 8 | | | | | | 40 |
| | 2 | | 4 | 5 | 6 | | | 9 | | | | | | | 7 | | | | 8 | 11 | | 10 | | 3 | 41 |
| | 2 | | 4 | 5 | 6 | | 10 | 9 | | 11 | | | | | | | | | 7 | | | 8 | | 3 | 42 |
| 2 | 38 | 1 | 42 | 40 | 37 | 29 | 26 | 24 | 33 | 34 | 15 | 8 | 17 | 21 | 8 | 1 | 7 | 2 | 8 | 6 | 7 | 10 | 4 | 2 | |
| | | | 2 | | 1 | 4 | 6 | 15 | 5 | 3 | | 4 | 8 | 2 | 1 | 1 | | | 3 | 3 | | 3 | | | |

| by J | Udall E | Reid S | Nicholas J | Barker J | Keen E | Crooks S | Napier C | Gallacher H | Ramage P | Duncan D | Collin G | Groves A | Bowers J | Jessop F | Boyd J | Bird D | Hann R | Summers J | Hagan J | Halford D | Webb J | Stockill R | Roberts E | Howe J | |
|---|---|---|---|---|---|---|---|---|---|---|---|---|---|---|---|---|---|---|---|---|---|---|---|---|---|
| | 2 | | 4 | 5 | 6 | 7 | 8 | 9 | 10 | | | | | 3 | | | | | | 11 | | | | | 3 |
| | 2 | | 4 | 5 | 6 | 7 | 8 | | 10 | | | | 9 | 3 | | | | | | 11 | | | | | 4 |
| | 2 | | 4 | 5 | 6 | 7 | 8 | | 10 | | 3 | | 9 | | | | | | | 11 | | | | | 5 |
| | 2 | | 4 | 5 | 6 | 7 | 8 | | 10 | 11 | 3 | | 9 | | | | | | | | | | | | 6 |
| | 4 | | 4 | 4 | 4 | 4 | 4 | 1 | 4 | 1 | 2 | | 3 | 2 | | | | | | 3 | | | | | |
| | | | | | | 1 | 1 | 1 | | | | | 2 | | | | | | | 1 | | | | | |

# 1936-37

| | P | W | D | L | F | A | Pts |
|---|---|---|---|---|---|---|---|
| Manchester C | 42 | 22 | 13 | 7 | 107 | 61 | 57 |
| Charlton A | 42 | 21 | 12 | 9 | 58 | 49 | 54 |
| Arsenal | 42 | 18 | 16 | 8 | 80 | 49 | 52 |
| Derby Co | 42 | 21 | 7 | 14 | 96 | 90 | 49 |
| Wolves | 42 | 21 | 5 | 16 | 84 | 67 | 47 |
| Brentford | 42 | 18 | 10 | 14 | 82 | 78 | 46 |
| Middlesbrough | 42 | 19 | 8 | 15 | 74 | 71 | 46 |
| Sunderland | 42 | 19 | 6 | 17 | 89 | 87 | 44 |
| Portsmouth | 42 | 17 | 10 | 15 | 62 | 66 | 44 |
| Stoke C | 42 | 15 | 12 | 15 | 72 | 57 | 42 |
| Birmingham | 42 | 13 | 15 | 14 | 64 | 60 | 41 |
| Grimsby T | 42 | 17 | 7 | 18 | 86 | 81 | 41 |
| Chelsea | 42 | 14 | 13 | 15 | 52 | 55 | 41 |
| Preston NE | 42 | 14 | 13 | 15 | 56 | 67 | 41 |
| Huddersfield T | 42 | 12 | 15 | 15 | 62 | 64 | 39 |
| WBA | 42 | 16 | 6 | 20 | 77 | 98 | 38 |
| Everton | 42 | 14 | 9 | 19 | 81 | 78 | 37 |
| Liverpool | 42 | 12 | 11 | 19 | 62 | 84 | 35 |
| Leeds U | 42 | 15 | 4 | 23 | 60 | 80 | 34 |
| Bolton W | 42 | 10 | 14 | 18 | 43 | 66 | 34 |
| Manchester U | 42 | 10 | 12 | 20 | 55 | 78 | 32 |
| Sheffield W | 42 | 9 | 12 | 21 | 53 | 69 | 30 |

Manager: George Jobey.
Leading scorer: Dai Astley, League 25, all matches 29.

- Jack Barker was captain of England in the last of his 11 internationals, a 2–1 defeat by Wales at Ninian Park. Errington Keen and Sammy Crooks also played.
- Welsh international Dai Astley, signed from Aston Villa, made a marvellous start with 29 goals in 30 League and Cup games, including three hat-tricks.
- George Jobey raided Aston Villa again in February, increasing his forward power with the signing of Ronnie Dix.
- Ken Scattergood, son of former Derby and England goalkeeper Ernald, had a disastrous debut in goal when Everton put seven past him on Christmas Day. To his credit, he kept West Bromwich Albion out on Boxing Day.

## Division One

| Match No. | Date | | Venue | Opponents | Result | | Scorers | Atter |
|---|---|---|---|---|---|---|---|---|
| 1 | Aug | 29 | (a) | West Brom A | W | 3-1 | Stockill, Bowers, Napier | 30 |
| 2 | Sep | 2 | (a) | Sunderland | L | 2-3 | Napier 2 | 42 |
| 3 | | 5 | (h) | Manchester U | W | 5-4 | Bowers 4, Crooks | 21 |
| 4 | | 9 | (h) | Sunderland | W | 3-0 | Keen, Napier, Hagan | 29 |
| 5 | | 12 | (a) | Sheffield W | W | 3-2 | Bowers, Napier, Duncan | 25 |
| 6 | | 19 | (h) | Preston NE | L | 1-2 | Duncan | 22 |
| 7 | | 23 | (h) | Wolves | W | 5-1 | Duncan 2, Bowers 2, Crooks | 18 |
| 8 | | 26 | (a) | Arsenal | D | 2-2 | Stockill, Bowers | 61 |
| 9 | Oct | 3 | (h) | Brentford | L | 2-3 | Bowers, Crooks | 24 |
| 10 | | 10 | (a) | Bolton W | W | 3-1 | Napier 2, Bowers | 27 |
| 11 | | 17 | (a) | Manchester C | L | 2-3 | Bowers, Jessop (pen) | 21 |
| 12 | | 24 | (h) | Portsmouth | L | 1-3 | Stockill | 23 |
| 13 | | 31 | (a) | Chelsea | D | 1-1 | Nicholas | 15 |
| 14 | Nov | 7 | (h) | Stoke C | D | 2-2 | Duncan, Hagan | 23 |
| 15 | | 14 | (a) | Charlton A | L | 0-2 | | 34 |
| 16 | | 21 | (h) | Grimsby T | W | 3-1 | Astley 2, Stockill | 17, |
| 17 | | 28 | (a) | Liverpool | D | 3-3 | Duncan, Stockill, Crooks (pen) | 27 |
| 18 | Dec | 5 | (h) | Leeds U | W | 5-3 | Astley 2, Ramage, Duncan, Keen | 15, |
| 19 | | 12 | (a) | Birmingham | W | 1-0 | Ramage | 8 |
| 20 | | 19 | (h) | Middlesbrough | L | 0-2 | | 16 |
| 21 | | 25 | (a) | Everton | L | 0-7 | | 32 |
| 22 | | 26 | (h) | West Brom A | W | 1-0 | Stockill | 29 |
| 23 | | 28 | (h) | Everton | W | 3-1 | Astley 3 | 22 |
| 24 | Jan | 2 | (a) | Manchester U | D | 2-2 | Astley, Ramage | 31, |
| 25 | | 9 | (h) | Sheffield W | W | 3-2 | Napier, Ramage, Astley | 16, |
| 26 | | 23 | (a) | Preston NE | L | 2-5 | Stockill 2 | 15, |
| 27 | Feb | 3 | (h) | Arsenal | W | 5-4 | Astley 3, Stockill 2 | 22, |
| 28 | | 6 | (a) | Brentford | L | 2-6 | Astley 2 | 31, |
| 29 | | 13 | (h) | Bolton W | W | 3-0 | Astley 2, Napier | 23, |
| 30 | | 24 | (h) | Manchester C | L | 0-5 | | 12, |
| 31 | | 27 | (a) | Portsmouth | W | 2-1 | Astley, Dix | 16, |
| 32 | Mar | 6 | (h) | Chelsea | D | 1-1 | Stockill | 15, |
| 33 | | 13 | (a) | Stoke C | W | 2-1 | Crooks, Napier | 20, |
| 34 | | 20 | (h) | Charlton A | W | 5-0 | Crooks, Napier, Duncan, Astley, Dix | 21, |
| 35 | | 27 | (a) | Grimsby T | W | 4-3 | Crooks 2, Astley, Dix | 13, |
| 36 | | 29 | (h) | Huddersfield T | D | 3-3 | Napier, Astley, Dix | 30, |
| 37 | | 30 | (a) | Huddersfield T | L | 0-2 | | 20, |
| 38 | Apr | 3 | (h) | Liverpool | W | 4-1 | Nicholas, Napier, Astley, Dix | 13, |
| 39 | | 10 | (a) | Leeds U | L | 0-2 | | 20, |
| 40 | | 17 | (h) | Birmingham | W | 3-1 | Crooks, Stockill, Astley | 10, |
| 41 | | 24 | (a) | Middlesbrough | W | 3-1 | Astley 2, Duncan | 18, |
| 42 | May | 1 | (a) | Wolves | L | 1-3 | Astley | 12, |

FINAL LEAGUE POSITION: 4th in Division One

Appearar
G

## FA Cup

| | | | | | | | | |
|---|---|---|---|---|---|---|---|---|
| 3 | Jan | 16 | (a) | Bradford PA | W | 4-0 | Napier, Astley, Duncan, Stockill | 21, |
| 4 | | 30 | (h) | Brentford | W | 3-0 | Astley 3 | 27, |
| 5 | Feb | 20 | (a) | Millwall | L | 1-2 | Keen | 48, |

Appearar
G

| Kirby J | Udall E | Howe J | Nicholas J | Barker J | Keen E | Crooks S | Stockill R | Bowers J | Napier C | Duncan D | Jessop F | Hann R | Hagan J | Wileman S | Boyd J | Ramage P | Wilson A | Bell D | Astley D | Scattergood K | Webb J | Jeffries A | Dix R | Parkin R | Travis H | |
|---|---|---|---|---|---|---|---|---|---|---|---|---|---|---|---|---|---|---|---|---|---|---|---|---|---|---|
| 1 | 2 | 3 | 4 | 5 | 6 | 7 | 8 | 9 | 10 | 11 | | | | | | | | | | | | | | | | 1 |
| 1 | 2 | | 4 | 5 | 6 | 7 | 8 | 9 | 10 | 11 | 3 | | | | | | | | | | | | | | | 2 |
| 1 | 2 | 3 | 4 | | 6 | 7 | 8 | 9 | 10 | 11 | | 5 | | | | | | | | | | | | | | 3 |
| 1 | 2 | | 4 | 5 | 6 | 7 | | 9 | 10 | 11 | 3 | | 8 | | | | | | | | | | | | | 4 |
| 1 | 2 | | 4 | 5 | 6 | 7 | | 9 | 10 | 11 | 3 | | 8 | | | | | | | | | | | | | 5 |
| 1 | 2 | | 4 | 5 | 6 | 7 | | 9 | 10 | 11 | 3 | | 8 | | | | | | | | | | | | | 6 |
| 1 | 2 | | 4 | | 6 | 7 | 8 | 9 | 10 | 11 | 3 | 5 | | | | | | | | | | | | | | 7 |
| 1 | 2 | | 4 | 5 | 6 | 7 | 8 | 9 | 10 | 11 | 3 | | | | | | | | | | | | | | | 8 |
| 1 | 2 | | 4 | 5 | 6 | 7 | 8 | 9 | 10 | 11 | 3 | | | | | | | | | | | | | | | 9 |
| 1 | 2 | | 4 | 5 | 6 | 7 | 8 | 9 | 10 | 11 | 3 | | | | | | | | | | | | | | | 10 |
| 1 | 2 | | 4 | | | | 8 | 9 | 10 | 11 | 3 | 5 | | 6 | 7 | | | | | | | | | | | 11 |
| 1 | 2 | | 4 | 5 | 6 | 7 | 8 | 9 | 10 | 11 | 3 | | | | | | | | | | | | | | | 12 |
| 1 | 2 | | 4 | 5 | 6 | 7 | 8 | 9 | | | 3 | | | | | 10 | 11 | | | | | | | | | 13 |
| 1 | 2 | 3 | 4 | 5 | 6 | 7 | | 9 | 10 | 11 | | | 8 | | | | | | | | | | | | | 14 |
| 1 | | 3 | 4 | 5 | 6 | 7 | | 9 | 10 | 11 | | | | | | | | 2 | 8 | | | | | | | 15 |
| 1 | | 3 | 2 | 5 | 6 | 7 | 8 | | 10 | 11 | | 4 | | | | | | | 9 | | | | | | | 16 |
| 1 | | 3 | 2 | 5 | 6 | 7 | 8 | | 10 | 11 | | 4 | | | | | | | 9 | | | | | | | 17 |
| 1 | | 3 | 2 | 5 | 6 | 7 | 8 | | | 11 | | 4 | | | | 10 | | | 9 | | | | | | | 18 |
| 1 | | 3 | 2 | 5 | 6 | 7 | | | | 11 | | 4 | 8 | | | 10 | | | 9 | | | | | | | 19 |
| 1 | | 3 | 2 | 5 | 6 | 7 | 8 | | | 11 | | 4 | | | | 10 | | | 9 | | | | | | | 20 |
| | | 3 | 2 | 5 | 6 | 7 | | | 10 | 11 | | 4 | 8 | | | | | | 9 | 1 | | | | | | 21 |
| | 2 | 3 | 4 | 5 | 6 | | 9 | | 8 | 11 | | | 7 | | | 10 | | | | 1 | | | | | | 22 |
| | 2 | 3 | 4 | 5 | 6 | | | | 8 | 11 | | | 7 | | | 10 | | | 9 | 1 | | | | | | 23 |
| | 2 | 3 | 4 | 5 | 6 | | | | 8 | 11 | | | 7 | | | 10 | | | 9 | 1 | | | | | | 24 |
| | | 3 | | 5 | 6 | | | | 8 | 11 | | 4 | 7 | | | 10 | | | 9 | 1 | 2 | | | | | 25 |
| | | 3 | 2 | 5 | 6 | | 7 | | 8 | 11 | | 4 | | | | 10 | | | 9 | 1 | | | | | | 26 |
| | | 3 | 4 | 5 | 6 | | 8 | | | 11 | | | | | | 10 | | 2 | 9 | 1 | | 7 | | | | 27 |
| | | 3 | 4 | 5 | 6 | | 8 | | | 11 | | | | | | 10 | | 2 | 9 | 1 | | 7 | | | | 28 |
| | | 3 | 4 | 5 | 6 | 7 | | | 10 | 11 | | | | | | | | 2 | 9 | 1 | | | 8 | | | 29 |
| | 2 | 3 | 4 | 5 | 6 | 7 | | | 11 | | | | | | | 10 | | | 9 | 1 | | | 8 | | | 30 |
| 1 | | 3 | 4 | 5 | | 7 | 10 | | 11 | | | 6 | | | | | | 2 | 9 | | | | 8 | | | 31 |
| 1 | | 3 | 4 | 5 | | 7 | 10 | | 11 | | | 6 | | | | | | 2 | 9 | | | | 8 | | | 32 |
| 1 | | 3 | 4 | | 6 | 7 | | | 10 | 11 | | 5 | | | | | | 2 | 9 | | | | 8 | | | 33 |
| 1 | | 3 | 4 | 5 | | 7 | | | 10 | 11 | | 6 | | | | | | 2 | 9 | | | | 8 | | | 34 |
| 1 | | 3 | 4 | 5 | | 7 | | | 10 | 11 | | 6 | | | | | | 2 | 9 | | | | 8 | | | 35 |
| | | 3 | 4 | 5 | | 7 | | | 10 | 11 | | 6 | | | | | | 2 | 9 | | | | 8 | 1 | | 36 |
| | | 3 | 4 | 5 | 6 | 7 | | | | 11 | | | | | | | | 2 | 8 | 1 | | | 10 | | 9 | 37 |
| | | 3 | 4 | 5 | | 7 | | | 10 | 11 | | 6 | | | | | | 2 | 9 | 1 | | | 8 | | | 38 |
| | | 3 | 4 | | 6 | 7 | | | 10 | 11 | | 5 | | | | | | 2 | 9 | 1 | | | 8 | | | 39 |
| | | | 4 | 5 | | 7 | 11 | | | | 3 | 6 | | | | 10 | | 2 | 9 | 1 | | | 8 | | | 40 |
| | | 3 | 4 | 5 | | 7 | | | | 11 | | 6 | | | | 10 | | 2 | 9 | 1 | | | 8 | | | 41 |
| 1 | | 3 | 4 | 5 | | 7 | | | | 11 | | 6 | | | | 10 | | 2 | 9 | | | | 8 | | | 42 |
| 26 | 18 | 30 | 41 | 37 | 32 | 34 | 21 | 15 | 32 | 37 | 12 | 22 | 10 | 1 | 1 | 15 | 1 | 16 | 27 | 15 | 1 | 2 | 14 | 1 | 1 | |
| | | | 2 | | 2 | 9 | 12 | 12 | 13 | 9 | 1 | | 2 | | | 4 | | | 25 | | | | 5 | | | |

| Kirby J | Udall E | Howe J | Nicholas J | Barker J | Keen E | Crooks S | Stockill R | Bowers J | Napier C | Duncan D | Jessop F | Hann R | Hagan J | Wileman S | Boyd J | Ramage P | Wilson A | Bell D | Astley D | Scattergood K | Webb J | Jeffries A | Dix R | Parkin R | Travis H | |
|---|---|---|---|---|---|---|---|---|---|---|---|---|---|---|---|---|---|---|---|---|---|---|---|---|---|---|
| | | 3 | 2 | 5 | 6 | | 7 | | 8 | 11 | | 4 | | | | 10 | | | 9 | 1 | | | | | | 3 |
| | | 3 | 4 | 5 | 6 | | 8 | | 10 | 11 | | | 7 | | | | | 2 | 9 | 1 | | | | | | 4 |
| | | 3 | 4 | 5 | 6 | 7 | 8 | | 10 | 11 | | | | | | | | 2 | 9 | 1 | | | | | | 5 |
| | | 3 | 3 | 3 | 3 | 1 | 3 | | 3 | 3 | | 1 | 1 | | | 1 | | 2 | 3 | 3 | | | | | | |
| | | | | | 1 | | 1 | | 1 | 1 | | | | | | | | | 4 | | | | | | | |

# 1937-38

| | P | W | D | L | F | A | Pts |
|---|---|---|---|---|---|---|---|
| Arsenal | 42 | 21 | 10 | 11 | 77 | 44 | 52 |
| Wolves | 42 | 20 | 11 | 11 | 72 | 49 | 51 |
| Preston NE | 42 | 16 | 17 | 9 | 64 | 44 | 49 |
| Charlton A | 42 | 16 | 14 | 12 | 65 | 51 | 46 |
| Middlesbrough | 42 | 19 | 8 | 15 | 72 | 65 | 46 |
| Brentford | 42 | 18 | 9 | 15 | 69 | 59 | 45 |
| Bolton W | 42 | 15 | 15 | 12 | 64 | 60 | 45 |
| Sunderland | 42 | 14 | 16 | 12 | 55 | 57 | 44 |
| Leeds U | 42 | 14 | 15 | 13 | 64 | 69 | 43 |
| Chelsea | 42 | 14 | 13 | 15 | 65 | 65 | 41 |
| Liverpool | 42 | 15 | 11 | 16 | 65 | 71 | 41 |
| Blackpool | 42 | 16 | 8 | 18 | 61 | 66 | 40 |
| Derby Co | 42 | 15 | 10 | 17 | 66 | 87 | 40 |
| Everton | 42 | 16 | 7 | 19 | 79 | 75 | 39 |
| Huddersfield T | 42 | 17 | 5 | 20 | 55 | 68 | 39 |
| Leicester C | 42 | 14 | 11 | 17 | 54 | 75 | 39 |
| Stoke C | 42 | 13 | 12 | 17 | 58 | 59 | 38 |
| Birmingham | 42 | 10 | 18 | 14 | 58 | 62 | 38 |
| Portsmouth | 42 | 13 | 12 | 17 | 62 | 68 | 38 |
| Grimsby T | 42 | 13 | 12 | 17 | 51 | 68 | 38 |
| Manchester C | 42 | 14 | 8 | 20 | 80 | 77 | 36 |
| WBA | 42 | 14 | 8 | 20 | 74 | 91 | 36 |

Manager: George Jobey.

Leading scorer: Dai Astley, League/all matches 17.

League ever-present: Dai Astley, Jack Nicholas.

- On 29 January, Manchester City won 7–1 at the Baseball Ground, the heaviest home defeat in Derby's history.
- They lost by the same score to Middlesbrough in 1959 and Liverpool in 1991.
- Tim Ward, a £100 signing from Cheltenham Town, took over from England international Errington Keen in January and played in the last 20 games. At the end of the season, Keen moved into the Southern League with Chelmsford City.

## Division One

| Match No. | Date | | Venue | Opponents | Result | | Scorers | Atter |
|---|---|---|---|---|---|---|---|---|
| 1 | Aug | 28 | (a) | Leicester C | D | 0-0 | | 37 |
| 2 | Sep | 1 | (h) | Wolves | L | 1-2 | Astley | 23 |
| 3 | | 4 | (h) | Sunderland | D | 2-2 | Astley, Crooks | 21 |
| 4 | | 6 | (a) | Wolves | D | 2-2 | Napier 2 | 28 |
| 5 | | 11 | (a) | Stoke C | L | 1-8 | Astley | 32 |
| 6 | | 15 | (h) | Everton | W | 2-1 | Dix, Jeffries | 14 |
| 7 | | 18 | (a) | Manchester C | L | 1-6 | Dix | 32 |
| 8 | | 25 | (h) | Arsenal | W | 2-0 | Napier, Duncan | 33 |
| 9 | Oct | 2 | (a) | Blackpool | D | 1-1 | Jessop (pen) | 29 |
| 10 | | 9 | (h) | Brentford | L | 1-3 | Duncan | 19 |
| 11 | | 16 | (h) | Middlesbrough | D | 1-1 | Stockill | 15 |
| 12 | | 23 | (a) | Birmingham | L | 0-1 | | 23 |
| 13 | | 30 | (h) | West Brom A | W | 5-3 | Crooks 2, Dix 2, Robbins (og) | 13 |
| 14 | Nov | 6 | (a) | Charlton A | W | 2-1 | Travis, Crooks | 27 |
| 15 | | 13 | (h) | Leeds U | D | 2-2 | Astley, Travis | 15 |
| 16 | | 20 | (a) | Portsmouth | L | 0-4 | | 19 |
| 17 | | 27 | (h) | Preston NE | D | 1-1 | Napier | 14, |
| 18 | Dec | 4 | (a) | Liverpool | W | 4-3 | Dix, Astley, Napier, Nicholas (pen) | 19 |
| 19 | | 11 | (h) | Chelsea | W | 4-0 | Dix 2, Astley, Griffith (og) | 12 |
| 20 | | 18 | (a) | Grimsby T | D | 0-0 | | 8 |
| 21 | | 27 | (h) | Bolton W | W | 4-2 | Astley 2, Duncan 2 | 31, |
| 22 | Jan | 1 | (h) | Leicester C | L | 0-1 | | 24, |
| 23 | | 15 | (a) | Sunderland | L | 0-2 | | 16, |
| 24 | | 22 | (a) | Bolton W | W | 2-0 | Astley 2 | 26, |
| 25 | | 29 | (h) | Manchester C | L | 1-7 | Astley | 13, |
| 26 | Feb | 2 | (h) | Stoke C | W | 4-1 | Duncan 2, Astley, Crooks | 9, |
| 27 | | 5 | (a) | Arsenal | L | 0-3 | | 47, |
| 28 | | 12 | (h) | Blackpool | W | 3-1 | Astley 2, Dix | 12, |
| 29 | | 19 | (a) | Brentford | W | 3-2 | Nicholas (pen), Dix, Brinton | 20, |
| 30 | | 26 | (a) | Middlesbrough | L | 2-4 | Brinton, Astley | 21, |
| 31 | Mar | 5 | (h) | Birmingham | D | 0-0 | | 14, |
| 32 | | 12 | (a) | West Brom A | L | 2-4 | Nicholas (pen), Dix | 25, |
| 33 | | 19 | (h) | Charlton A | W | 3-2 | Dix, Astley, Hagan | 15, |
| 34 | | 26 | (a) | Leeds U | W | 2-0 | Dix, Crooks | 19, |
| 35 | Apr | 2 | (h) | Portsmouth | W | 1-0 | Dix | 13, |
| 36 | | 9 | (a) | Preston NE | L | 1-4 | Hagan | 13, |
| 37 | | 16 | (h) | Liverpool | W | 4-1 | Nicholas, Crooks, Dix, Astley | 16, |
| 38 | | 18 | (h) | Huddersfield T | L | 0-4 | | 19, |
| 39 | | 19 | (a) | Huddersfield T | L | 0-2 | | 25, |
| 40 | | 23 | (a) | Chelsea | L | 0-3 | | 25, |
| 41 | | 30 | (h) | Grimsby T | L | 1-2 | Duncan | 8, |
| 42 | May | 7 | (a) | Everton | D | 1-1 | Duncan | 18, |

FINAL LEAGUE POSITION: 13th in Division One

Appearan
Go

## FA Cup

| | | | | | | | | |
|---|---|---|---|---|---|---|---|---|
| 3 | Jan | 8 | (h) | Stoke C | L | 1-2 | Nicholas (pen) | 28, |

Appearan
Go

| Scattergood K | Bell D | Howe J | Nicholas J | Barker J | Keen E | Crooks S | Dix R | Astley D | Napier C | Duncan D | Stockill R | Hagan J | Jessop F | Hann R | Jeffries A | Travis H | Wright H | Bailey L | Kirby J | Ward T | Jones V | Alton T | Brinton J | Wilcox G | King F | |
|---|---|---|---|---|---|---|---|---|---|---|---|---|---|---|---|---|---|---|---|---|---|---|---|---|---|---|
| | 2 | 3 | 4 | 5 | 6 | 7 | 8 | 9 | 10 | 11 | | | | | | | | | | | | | | | | 1 |
| | 2 | 3 | 4 | 5 | 6 | 7 | 8 | 9 | 10 | 11 | | | | | | | | | | | | | | | | 2 |
| | 2 | 3 | 4 | 5 | 6 | 7 | 8 | 9 | 10 | 11 | | | | | | | | | | | | | | | | 3 |
| | 2 | 3 | 4 | 5 | 6 | 7 | 8 | 9 | 11 | | 10 | | | | | | | | | | | | | | | 4 |
| | 2 | 3 | 4 | 5 | 6 | 7 | 10 | 9 | | 11 | | 8 | | | | | | | | | | | | | | 5 |
| | 2 | | 4 | 5 | | | 10 | 8 | | 11 | | | 3 | 6 | 7 | 9 | | | | | | | | | | 6 |
| | 2 | | 4 | 5 | 6 | | 8 | 9 | 10 | 11 | | | 3 | | 7 | | | | | | | | | | | 7 |
| | 2 | 3 | 4 | 5 | 6 | 7 | 8 | 9 | 10 | 11 | | | | | | | 1 | | | | | | | | | 8 |
| | 2 | | 4 | | 6 | 7 | 8 | 9 | | 11 | 10 | | 3 | | | | 1 | 5 | | | | | | | | 9 |
| | 2 | 3 | 4 | | 6 | 7 | 8 | 9 | | 11 | 10 | | | | | | 1 | 5 | | | | | | | | 10 |
| | 2 | 3 | 4 | | 6 | 7 | | 9 | 10 | 11 | 8 | | | 5 | | | | | 1 | | | | | | | 11 |
| | 2 | 3 | 4 | | 6 | | | 9 | 10 | 11 | 8 | | | 5 | 7 | | | | 1 | | | | | | | 12 |
| | 2 | 3 | 4 | | 6 | 7 | 10 | 8 | 11 | | | | | 5 | | 9 | | | 1 | | | | | | | 13 |
| | 2 | 3 | 4 | | 6 | 7 | 10 | 8 | 11 | | | | | 5 | | 9 | 1 | | | | | | | | | 14 |
| | 2 | 3 | 4 | | 6 | | 10 | 8 | | 11 | | | | 5 | 7 | 9 | 1 | | | | | | | | | 15 |
| | 2 | 3 | 4 | | 6 | | | 8 | | 11 | 10 | | | 5 | 7 | 9 | 1 | | | | | | | | | 16 |
| | 2 | 3 | 4 | | 6 | 7 | 8 | 9 | 10 | 11 | | | | 5 | | | 1 | | | | | | | | | 17 |
| | 2 | 3 | 4 | | 6 | 7 | 8 | 9 | 10 | 11 | | | | 5 | | | 1 | | | | | | | | | 18 |
| | 2 | 3 | 4 | | 6 | 7 | 8 | 9 | 10 | 11 | | | | 5 | | | 1 | | | | | | | | | 19 |
| | 2 | 3 | 4 | | 6 | 7 | 8 | 9 | 10 | 11 | | | | 5 | | | 1 | | | | | | | | | 20 |
| | 2 | 3 | 4 | | 6 | 7 | 8 | 9 | 10 | 11 | | | | 5 | | | 1 | | | | | | | | | 21 |
| | 2 | 3 | 4 | | 6 | 7 | 8 | 9 | 10 | 11 | | | | 5 | | | 1 | | | | | | | | | 22 |
| | 2 | 3 | 4 | | | 7 | | 9 | | 11 | 10 | 8 | | | | | 1 | 5 | | 6 | | | | | | 23 |
| | 2 | 3 | 5 | | 4 | 7 | 8 | 9 | 10 | 11 | | | | | | | 1 | | | 6 | | | | | | 24 |
| | 2 | 3 | 5 | | 4 | 7 | 8 | 9 | 10 | 11 | | | | | | | 1 | | | 6 | | | | | | 25 |
| | 2 | 3 | 4 | 5 | | 7 | 10 | 9 | | 11 | | | | | | | | | 1 | 6 | 8 | | | | | 26 |
| | 2 | 3 | 4 | 5 | | 7 | 10 | 9 | | 11 | | | | | | | | | 1 | 6 | 8 | | | | | 27 |
| | 2 | 3 | 4 | 5 | | 7 | 8 | 9 | 10 | 11 | | | | | | | | | 1 | 6 | | | | | | 28 |
| | | 3 | 4 | 5 | | 7 | 8 | 9 | | | 10 | | | | | | | | 1 | 6 | | 2 | 11 | | | 29 |
| | | 3 | 4 | | | 7 | 8 | 9 | 10 | | | | | 5 | | | | | 1 | 6 | | 2 | 11 | | | 30 |
| | | 3 | 4 | 5 | | 7 | 8 | 9 | 10 | | | | | | | | | | 1 | 6 | | 2 | 11 | | | 31 |
| | 2 | 3 | 4 | 5 | | 7 | 8 | 9 | 10 | | | | | | | | | | 1 | 6 | | | 11 | | | 32 |
| | | 3 | 4 | 5 | | 7 | 10 | 9 | | | | 8 | | | | | 1 | | | 6 | | | 11 | 2 | | 33 |
| | | 3 | 4 | 5 | | 7 | 10 | 9 | | | | 8 | | | | | 1 | | | 6 | | | 11 | 2 | | 34 |
| | | 3 | 4 | 5 | | 7 | 10 | 9 | | 11 | | 8 | | | | | 1 | | | 6 | | | | 2 | | 35 |
| | | 3 | 4 | 5 | | 7 | 10 | 9 | | 11 | | 8 | | | | | 1 | | | 6 | | | | 2 | | 36 |
| | | 3 | 4 | 5 | | 7 | 10 | 9 | | 11 | | 8 | | | | | 1 | | | 6 | | | | 2 | | 37 |
| | | 3 | 4 | 5 | | 7 | 10 | 9 | | 11 | | 8 | | | | | 1 | | | 6 | | | | 2 | | 38 |
| | | 3 | 4 | | | 7 | 10 | 9 | | | | 8 | | | | | 1 | 5 | | 6 | | | 11 | 2 | | 39 |
| | | 3 | 4 | | | 7 | 10 | 9 | | | | 8 | | | | | | 5 | | 6 | | | 11 | 2 | 1 | 40 |
| | 2 | 3 | 4 | 5 | | 7 | 10 | 9 | | 11 | | 8 | | | | | | | | 6 | | | | | 1 | 41 |
| | 2 | 3 | 4 | | | 7 | 10 | 8 | | 11 | | | | | | 9 | | 5 | | 6 | | | | | 1 | 42 |
| | 31 | 39 | 42 | 21 | 23 | 37 | 38 | 42 | 22 | 31 | 8 | 11 | 3 | 14 | 5 | 6 | 22 | 6 | 10 | 20 | 2 | 3 | 8 | 8 | 3 | |
| | | | 4 | | | 7 | 14 | 17 | 5 | 8 | 1 | 2 | 1 | | 1 | 2 | | | | | | | 2 | | | |

2 own-goals

| | | | | | | | | | | | | | | | | | | | | | | | | | | |
|---|---|---|---|---|---|---|---|---|---|---|---|---|---|---|---|---|---|---|---|---|---|---|---|---|---|---|
| | 2 | 3 | 4 | | 6 | 7 | 8 | 9 | 10 | 11 | | | | | | | 1 | 5 | | | | | | | | 3 |
| | 1 | 1 | 1 | | 1 | 1 | 1 | 1 | 1 | 1 | | | | | | | 1 | 1 | | | | | | | | |
| | | | 1 | | | | | | | | | | | | | | | | | | | | | | | |

# 1938-39

| | P | W | D | L | F | A | Pts |
|---|---|---|---|---|---|---|---|
| Everton | 42 | 27 | 5 | 10 | 88 | 52 | 59 |
| Wolves | 42 | 22 | 11 | 9 | 88 | 39 | 55 |
| Charlton A | 42 | 22 | 6 | 14 | 75 | 59 | 50 |
| Middlesbrough | 42 | 20 | 9 | 13 | 93 | 74 | 49 |
| Arsenal | 42 | 19 | 9 | 14 | 55 | 41 | 47 |
| Derby Co | 42 | 19 | 8 | 15 | 66 | 55 | 46 |
| Stoke C | 42 | 17 | 12 | 13 | 71 | 68 | 46 |
| Bolton W | 42 | 15 | 15 | 12 | 67 | 58 | 45 |
| Preston NE | 42 | 16 | 12 | 14 | 63 | 59 | 44 |
| Grimsby T | 42 | 16 | 11 | 15 | 61 | 69 | 43 |
| Liverpool | 42 | 14 | 14 | 14 | 62 | 63 | 42 |
| Aston Villa | 42 | 16 | 9 | 17 | 71 | 60 | 41 |
| Leeds U | 42 | 16 | 9 | 17 | 59 | 67 | 41 |
| Manchester U | 42 | 11 | 16 | 15 | 57 | 65 | 38 |
| Blackpool | 42 | 12 | 14 | 16 | 56 | 68 | 38 |
| Sunderland | 42 | 13 | 12 | 17 | 54 | 67 | 38 |
| Portsmouth | 42 | 12 | 13 | 17 | 47 | 70 | 37 |
| Brentford | 42 | 14 | 8 | 20 | 53 | 74 | 36 |
| Huddersfield T | 42 | 12 | 11 | 19 | 58 | 64 | 35 |
| Chelsea | 42 | 12 | 9 | 21 | 64 | 80 | 33 |
| Birmingham | 42 | 12 | 8 | 22 | 62 | 84 | 32 |

Manager: George Jobey.
Leading scorers: Ronnie Dix, Dave McCulloch, League/all matches 16.
League ever-present: Ronnie Dix, Dally Duncan, Ralph Hann, Jack Nicholas.

- Four players appeared in every League game, equalling the numbers in 1893–94 and 1895–96. This has never been repeated for the Rams.
- Scottish international Dave McCulloch was George Jobey's record signing when he arrived from Brentford for £9,500. He added two caps while with the Rams but lost his peak years to World War Two.
- After Ronnie Dix played for England against Norway in November, Derby fielded an international forward line: Sammy Crooks (England), Dai Astley (Wales), Dave McCulloch (Scotland), Ronnie Dix (England), Dally Duncan (Scotland).
- This lasted until Astley moved to Blackpool in January.

## Division One

| Match No. | Date | | Venue | Opponents | Result | | Scorers | Attendan |
|---|---|---|---|---|---|---|---|---|
| 1 | Aug | 27 | (h) | Wolves | D | 2-2 | Travis, Cullis (og) | 19,97 |
| 2 | | 31 | (h) | Huddersfield T | W | 1-0 | Dix | 13,37 |
| 3 | Sep | 3 | (a) | Aston Villa | W | 1-0 | Travis | 49,60 |
| 4 | | 7 | (a) | Huddersfield T | L | 0-3 | | 11,29 |
| 5 | | 10 | (h) | Sunderland | W | 1-0 | Dix | 19,37 |
| 6 | | 14 | (a) | Arsenal | W | 2-1 | Duncan, Stockill | 25,75 |
| 7 | | 17 | (a) | Grimsby T | D | 1-1 | Stockill | 12,45 |
| 8 | | 24 | (h) | Stoke C | W | 5-0 | Dix 2, Stockill 2, Duncan | 20,91 |
| 9 | Oct | 1 | (h) | Blackpool | W | 2-1 | Crooks, Duncan | 21,58 |
| 10 | | 8 | (a) | Brentford | W | 3-1 | Stockill, Dix, Crooks | 23,53 |
| 11 | | 15 | (a) | Birmingham | L | 0-3 | | 27,85 |
| 12 | | 22 | (h) | Manchester U | W | 5-1 | McCulloch 2, Dix, Crooks, Vose (og) | 26,61 |
| 13 | | 29 | (a) | Chelsea | W | 2-0 | Dix, Astley | 37,91 |
| 14 | Nov | 5 | (h) | Preston NE | W | 2-0 | Crooks, McCulloch | 33,29 |
| 15 | | 12 | (a) | Charlton A | L | 0-1 | | 41,81 |
| 16 | | 19 | (h) | Bolton W | W | 3-0 | Dix, Astley, Hubbick (og) | 26,0 |
| 17 | | 26 | (a) | Leeds U | W | 4-1 | McCulloch 2, Dix, Crooks | 34,15 |
| 18 | Dec | 3 | (h) | Liverpool | D | 2-2 | Crooks, McCulloch | 24,75 |
| 19 | | 10 | (a) | Leicester C | W | 3-2 | McCulloch 2, Dix | 29,7 |
| 20 | | 17 | (h) | Middlesbrough | L | 1-4 | McCulloch | 17,1 |
| 21 | | 24 | (a) | Wolves | D | 0-0 | | 25,3 |
| 22 | | 26 | (a) | Everton | D | 2-2 | Dix, McCulloch | 55,4 |
| 23 | | 27 | (h) | Everton | W | 2-1 | Duncan, McCulloch | 35,6 |
| 24 | | 31 | (h) | Aston Villa | W | 2-1 | Dix, Astley | 25,75 |
| 25 | Jan | 14 | (a) | Sunderland | L | 0-1 | | 25,8 |
| 26 | | 28 | (a) | Stoke C | L | 0-3 | | 33,2 |
| 27 | Feb | 1 | (h) | Grimsby T | W | 4-1 | Dix 2, Crooks, Duncan | 11,1 |
| 28 | | 4 | (a) | Blackpool | D | 2-2 | Duncan, Hinchcliffe | 15,9 |
| 29 | | 11 | (h) | Brentford | L | 1-2 | Nicholas (pen) | 19,7 |
| 30 | | 18 | (h) | Birmingham | L | 0-1 | | 15,4 |
| 31 | | 25 | (a) | Manchester U | D | 1-1 | McCulloch | 37,1 |
| 32 | Mar | 8 | (h) | Chelsea | L | 0-1 | | 6,6 |
| 33 | | 11 | (a) | Preston NE | L | 1-4 | McCulloch | 14,6 |
| 34 | | 18 | (h) | Charlton A | W | 3-1 | Stamps 2, Nicholas (pen) | 13,1 |
| 35 | | 25 | (a) | Bolton W | L | 1-2 | Atkinson (og) | 20,5 |
| 36 | Apr | 1 | (h) | Leeds U | W | 1-0 | McCulloch | 11,2 |
| 37 | | 7 | (a) | Portsmouth | W | 3-1 | Dix 2, Duncan | 36,8 |
| 38 | | 8 | (a) | Liverpool | L | 1-2 | McCulloch | 25,9 |
| 39 | | 10 | (h) | Portsmouth | L | 0-1 | | 17,0 |
| 40 | | 15 | (h) | Leicester C | D | 1-1 | Stamps | 11,9 |
| 41 | | 22 | (a) | Middlesbrough | L | 0-2 | | 13,6 |
| 42 | | 29 | (h) | Arsenal | L | 1-2 | McCulloch | 10,1 |

FINAL LEAGUE POSITION: 6th in Division One

Appearanc
Go

## FA Cup

| | | | | | | | |
|---|---|---|---|---|---|---|---|
| 3 | Jan | 7 | (h) | Everton | L | 0-1 | 22,2 |

Appearan
Go

| oulton F | Nicholas J | Howe J | Hann R | Barker J | Ward T | Crooks S | Astley D | Travis H | Dix R | Duncan D | Bell D | Jeffries A | Hagan J | Stockill R | McCulloch D | Bailey L | Hinchcliffe T | Wright H | Steel W | McLachlan S | Stamps J | Wilcox G | |
|---|---|---|---|---|---|---|---|---|---|---|---|---|---|---|---|---|---|---|---|---|---|---|---|
| | 2 | 3 | 4 | 5 | 6 | 7 | 8 | 9 | 10 | 11 | | | | | | | | | | | | | 1 |
| | 2 | 3 | 4 | 5 | 6 | 7 | 8 | 9 | 10 | 11 | | | | | | | | | | | | | 2 |
| | 2 | 3 | 4 | 5 | 6 | 7 | 8 | 9 | 10 | 11 | | | | | | | | | | | | | 3 |
| | 2 | 3 | 6 | 5 | | | 8 | 9 | 10 | 11 | 4 | 7 | | | | | | | | | | | 4 |
| | 2 | 3 | 4 | 5 | 6 | | 8 | 9 | 10 | 11 | | | 7 | | | | | | | | | | 5 |
| | 2 | 3 | 4 | 5 | 6 | 7 | 8 | | 10 | 11 | | | | 9 | | | | | | | | | 6 |
| | 2 | 3 | 4 | 5 | 6 | 7 | 8 | | 10 | 11 | | | | 9 | | | | | | | | | 7 |
| | 2 | 3 | 4 | 5 | 6 | 7 | 8 | | 10 | 11 | | | | 9 | | | | | | | | | 8 |
| | 2 | 3 | 4 | 5 | 6 | 7 | 8 | | 10 | 11 | | | | 9 | | | | | | | | | 9 |
| | 2 | 3 | 4 | 5 | 6 | 7 | 8 | | 10 | 11 | | | | 9 | | | | | | | | | 10 |
| | 2 | 3 | 4 | 5 | 6 | 7 | 8 | | 10 | 11 | | | | 9 | | | | | | | | | 11 |
| | 2 | 3 | 4 | 5 | 6 | 7 | | | 10 | 11 | | | | 8 | 9 | | | | | | | | 12 |
| | 2 | 3 | 4 | | 6 | 7 | 8 | | 10 | 11 | | | | | 9 | 5 | | | | | | | 13 |
| | 2 | 3 | 4 | 5 | 6 | 7 | 8 | | 10 | 11 | | | | | 9 | | | | | | | | 14 |
| | 2 | 3 | 4 | 5 | 6 | 7 | 8 | | 10 | 11 | | | | | 9 | | | | | | | | 15 |
| | 2 | 3 | 4 | 5 | 6 | 7 | 8 | | 10 | 11 | | | | | 9 | | | | | | | | 16 |
| | 2 | 3 | 4 | 5 | 6 | 7 | 8 | | 10 | 11 | | | | | 9 | | | | | | | | 17 |
| | 2 | 3 | 4 | 5 | 6 | 7 | 8 | | 10 | 11 | | | | | 9 | | | | | | | | 18 |
| | 2 | 3 | 4 | 5 | 6 | 7 | 8 | | 10 | 11 | | | | | 9 | | | | | | | | 19 |
| | 2 | 3 | 4 | 5 | 6 | 7 | 8 | | 10 | 11 | | | | | 9 | | | | | | | | 20 |
| | 2 | 3 | 4 | | 6 | 7 | 8 | | 10 | 11 | | | | | 9 | 5 | | | | | | | 21 |
| | 2 | 3 | 4 | | 6 | 7 | 8 | | 10 | 11 | | | | | 9 | 5 | | | | | | | 22 |
| | 2 | 3 | 4 | | 6 | 7 | 8 | | 10 | 11 | | | | | 9 | 5 | | | | | | | 23 |
| | 2 | 3 | 4 | | 6 | 7 | 8 | | 10 | 11 | | | | | 9 | 5 | | | | | | | 24 |
| | 2 | 3 | 4 | | 6 | 7 | 8 | | 10 | 11 | | | | | 9 | 5 | | | | | | | 25 |
| | 2 | 3 | 4 | | 6 | 7 | | | 10 | 11 | | | | | 9 | 5 | 8 | | | | | | 26 |
| | 2 | 3 | 4 | | 6 | 7 | | | 10 | 11 | | | | | 9 | 5 | 8 | | | | | | 27 |
| | 2 | 3 | 4 | | 6 | | | | 10 | 11 | | 7 | | | 9 | 5 | 8 | 1 | | | | | 28 |
| | 2 | 3 | 4 | | 6 | | | | 10 | 11 | | 7 | | | 9 | 5 | 8 | 1 | | | | | 29 |
| | 2 | 3 | 4 | | 6 | 7 | | | 10 | 11 | | | | | 9 | 5 | 8 | | | | | | 30 |
| | 2 | | 4 | | 6 | 7 | | | 10 | 11 | | | | 8 | 9 | 5 | | | 3 | | | | 31 |
| | 2 | | 4 | | 6 | 7 | | | 10 | 11 | | | | 8 | 9 | 5 | | | 3 | | | | 32 |
| | 2 | | 6 | 5 | | 7 | | | 10 | 11 | | | | 8 | 9 | | | 1 | 3 | 4 | | | 33 |
| | 2 | | 4 | 5 | 6 | 7 | | | 8 | 11 | | | | | 9 | | | | 3 | | 10 | | 34 |
| | 2 | | 4 | | 6 | 7 | | | 8 | 11 | | | | | 9 | 5 | | | 3 | | 10 | | 35 |
| | 2 | | 4 | | 6 | | | | 8 | 11 | | 7 | | | 9 | 5 | | | 3 | | 10 | | 36 |
| | 2 | | 4 | | 6 | | | | 8 | 11 | | 7 | | | 9 | 5 | | | 3 | | 10 | | 37 |
| | 2 | | 4 | | 6 | 7 | | | 8 | 11 | | | | | 9 | 5 | 10 | | 3 | | | | 38 |
| | 2 | | 4 | 5 | 6 | | | | 8 | 11 | | 7 | | | 9 | | | | 3 | | 10 | | 39 |
| | 2 | | 4 | | 6 | | | | 8 | 11 | | 7 | | | 9 | 5 | | | | | 10 | 3 | 40 |
| | 2 | | 4 | | 6 | | | | 8 | 11 | | 7 | | | 9 | 5 | | | 3 | | 10 | | 41 |
| | 2 | | 4 | | 6 | 7 | | | 8 | 11 | | | | | 9 | 5 | | | 3 | | 10 | | 42 |
| 9 | 42 | 30 | 42 | 22 | 40 | 33 | 24 | 5 | 42 | 42 | 1 | 8 | 1 | 10 | 31 | 20 | 6 | 3 | 11 | 1 | 8 | 1 | |
| | 2 | | | | | 7 | 3 | 2 | 16 | 7 | | | | 5 | 16 | | 1 | | | | 3 | | |

4 own-goals

| | | | | | | | | | | | | | | | | | | | | | | | |
|---|---|---|---|---|---|---|---|---|---|---|---|---|---|---|---|---|---|---|---|---|---|---|---|
| | 2 | 3 | 4 | | 6 | 7 | 8 | | 10 | 11 | | | | | 9 | 5 | | | | | | | 3 |
| | 1 | 1 | 1 | | 1 | 1 | 1 | | 1 | 1 | | | | | 1 | 1 | | | | | | | |
| | | | | | | | | | | | | | | | | | | | | | | | |

# 1945-46

## FA Cup

| Round | Date | | Venue | Opponents | Result | | Scorers | Atten |
|---|---|---|---|---|---|---|---|---|
| 3 | Jan | 5 | (a) | Luton T | W | 6-0 | Stamps 4, Crooks, Carter | 16 |
| | | 9 | (h) | Luton T | W | 3-0 | Carter 2, Morrison | 16 |
| 4 | | 26 | (h) | West Brom A | W | 1-0 | Doherty | 31 |
| | | 30 | (a) | West Brom A | W | 3-1 | Carter, Stamps (pen), Harrison | 37 |
| 5 | Feb | 9 | (a) | Brighton & HA | W | 4-1 | Doherty 2 (1 pen), Carter 2 | 22 |
| | | 13 | (h) | Brighton & HA | W | 6-0 | Carter 3, Doherty 2, Crooks | 32 |
| 6 | Mar | 2 | (a) | Aston Villa | W | 4-3 | Doherty 2, Carter, Crooks | 76 |
| | | 9 | (h) | Aston Villa | D | 1-1 | Carter | 32 |
| SF | | 23 | (n*) | Birmingham City | D | 1-1 | Carter | 65 |
| R | | 27 | (n‡) | Birmingham City | W | 4-0† | Doherty 2, Stamps 2 | §80 |
| F | Apr | 27 | (n#) | Charlton A | W | 4-1† | Stamps 2, Doherty, H.Turner (og) | 98 |

*Played at Hillsborough, Sheffield. ‡Played at Maine Road, Manchester. †after extra-time

Appeara

§Record attendance for a midweek game between two Football League clubs outside an FA Cup final.

G

#Played at Wembley Stadium.

| ulton F | Nicholas J | Parr J | Bullions J | Leuty L | Ward T | Crooks S | Carter H | Stamps J | Doherty P | Morrison A | Eggleston T | Musson W | Harrison R | Duncan D | Townsend W | Woodley V | Howe J | |
|---|---|---|---|---|---|---|---|---|---|---|---|---|---|---|---|---|---|---|
| | 2 | 3 | 4 | 5 | 6 | 7 | 8 | 9 | 10 | 11 | | | | | | | | 3 |
| | 2 | 3 | 4 | 5 | | 7 | 8 | 9 | 10 | 11 | 6 | | | | | | | |
| | 2 | 3 | 4 | 5 | | | 8 | | 10 | 9 | | 6 | 7 | 11 | | | | 4 |
| | 2 | 3 | 4 | 5 | | | 8 | 10 | | 9 | | 6 | 7 | 11 | | | | |
| | 2 | 3 | 4 | 5 | | | 8 | | 10 | 9 | | 6 | 7 | 11 | | | | 5 |
| | 2 | 3 | 4 | 5 | | 7 | 8 | | 10 | 9 | | 6 | | 11 | | | | |
| | 2 | 3 | 4 | 5 | | 7 | 8 | 9 | 10 | | | 6 | | 11 | 1 | | | 6 |
| | 2 | 3 | 4 | 5 | | 7 | 8 | 9 | 10 | | | 6 | | 11 | 1 | | | |
| | 2 | 3 | 4 | 5 | | | 8 | 9 | 10 | | | 6 | 7 | 11 | | 1 | | SF |
| | 2 | 3 | 4 | | | | 8 | 9 | 10 | | | 6 | 7 | 11 | | 1 | 5 | R |
| | 2 | | 4 | 5 | | | 8 | 9 | 10 | | | 6 | 7 | 11 | | 1 | 3 | F |
| | 11 | 10 | 11 | 10 | 1 | 5 | 11 | 8 | 10 | 6 | 1 | 9 | 6 | 9 | 2 | 3 | 2 | |
| | | | | | | 3 | 12 | 9 | 10 | 1 | | | 1 | | | | | |

1 own-goal

# 1946-47

| | P | W | D | L | F | A | Pts |
|---|---|---|---|---|---|---|---|
| Liverpool | 42 | 25 | 7 | 10 | 84 | 52 | 57 |
| Manchester U | 42 | 22 | 12 | 8 | 95 | 54 | 56 |
| Wolves | 42 | 25 | 6 | 11 | 98 | 56 | 56 |
| Stoke C | 42 | 24 | 7 | 11 | 90 | 53 | 55 |
| Blackpool | 42 | 22 | 6 | 14 | 71 | 70 | 50 |
| Sheffield U | 42 | 21 | 7 | 14 | 89 | 75 | 49 |
| Preston NE | 42 | 18 | 11 | 13 | 76 | 74 | 47 |
| Aston Villa | 42 | 18 | 9 | 15 | 67 | 53 | 45 |
| Sunderland | 42 | 18 | 8 | 16 | 65 | 66 | 44 |
| Everton | 42 | 17 | 9 | 16 | 62 | 67 | 43 |
| Middlesbrough | 42 | 17 | 8 | 17 | 73 | 68 | 42 |
| Portsmouth | 42 | 16 | 9 | 17 | 66 | 60 | 41 |
| Arsenal | 42 | 16 | 9 | 17 | 72 | 70 | 41 |
| Derby Co | 42 | 18 | 5 | 19 | 73 | 79 | 41 |
| Chelsea | 42 | 16 | 7 | 19 | 69 | 84 | 39 |
| Grimsby T | 42 | 13 | 12 | 17 | 61 | 82 | 38 |
| Blackburn R | 42 | 14 | 8 | 20 | 45 | 53 | 36 |
| Bolton W | 42 | 13 | 8 | 21 | 57 | 69 | 34 |
| Charlton A | 42 | 11 | 12 | 19 | 57 | 71 | 34 |
| Huddersfield T | 42 | 13 | 7 | 22 | 53 | 79 | 33 |
| Brentford | 42 | 9 | 7 | 26 | 45 | 88 | 25 |
| Leeds U | 42 | 6 | 6 | 30 | 45 | 90 | 18 |

Manager: Stuart McMillan.
Leading scorer: Raich Carter League 19, all matches 21.

- The players who won the FA Cup in April 1946 never appeared together in the first League season after World War Two. Four had left before the following summer.
- Dally Duncan became Luton Town's player-coach in October and Peter Doherty, having been refused permission by the Derby directors to take over the Arboretum Hotel, joined Huddersfield Town in December.
- Vic Woodley returned to Bath City in May 1947, and Cup-winning captain Jack Nicholas retired at the age of 36 after 383 appearances.
- Chick Musson missed only one match. He was never an ever-present but played 41 League games in each of the first five post-war seasons.

## Division One

| Match No. | Date | | Venue | Opponents | Result | | Scorers | Atten |
|---|---|---|---|---|---|---|---|---|
| 1 | Aug | 31 | (a) | Sunderland | L | 2-3 | Stamps, Doherty (pen) | 48 |
| 2 | Sep | 4 | (h) | Portsmouth | W | 2-0 | Carter, Stamps | 21 |
| 3 | | 7 | (h) | Aston Villa | L | 1-2 | Carter | 28 |
| 4 | | 11 | (a) | Huddersfield T | L | 2-5 | Stamps, Broome | 18 |
| 5 | | 14 | (a) | Stoke C | L | 2-3 | Carter, Doherty (pen) | 35 |
| 6 | | 21 | (a) | Arsenal | W | 1-0 | Broome | 60 |
| 7 | | 28 | (h) | Blackpool | L | 1-2 | Broome | 25 |
| 8 | Oct | 5 | (a) | Brentford | W | 3-0 | Carter, Stamps, Doherty | 34 |
| 9 | | 12 | (h) | Blackburn R | W | 2-1 | Stamps 2 | 25 |
| 10 | | 19 | (h) | Middlesbrough | D | 1-1 | Carter | 28 |
| 11 | | 26 | (a) | Sheffield U | L | 2-3 | Carter, Broome | 43 |
| 12 | Nov | 2 | (h) | Preston NE | D | 2-2 | Doherty 2 | 28 |
| 13 | | 9 | (a) | Manchester U | L | 1-4 | Carter | 57 |
| 14 | | 16 | (h) | Liverpool | L | 1-4 | Carter | 28 |
| 15 | | 23 | (a) | Bolton W | L | 1-5 | Broome | 28 |
| 16 | | 30 | (h) | Chelsea | W | 3-1 | Morrison 2, Broome | 27 |
| 17 | Dec | 7 | (a) | Charlton A | W | 4-2 | Morrison 2, Stamps, Broome | 24, |
| 18 | | 14 | (h) | Grimsby T | W | 4-1 | Morrison 2, Broome 2 | 18, |
| 19 | | 21 | (a) | Leeds U | W | 2-1 | Carter, Stamps | 21 |
| 20 | | 25 | (a) | Everton | L | 1-4 | Carter | 32, |
| 21 | | 26 | (h) | Everton | W | 5-1 | Doherty 2, Harrison 2, Ward | 29 |
| 22 | | 28 | (h) | Sunderland | W | 5-1 | Carter 2, Stamps 2, Morrison | 30 |
| 23 | Jan | 4 | (a) | Aston Villa | L | 0-2 | | 50 |
| 24 | | 18 | (h) | Stoke C | W | 3-0 | Carter, Stamps, Harrison | 31 |
| 25 | Feb | 1 | (a) | Blackpool | L | 1-2 | Carter | 16, |
| 26 | | 15 | (a) | Blackburn R | D | 1-1 | Broome | 31 |
| 27 | | 22 | (a) | Middlesbrough | L | 0-1 | | 32, |
| 28 | Mar | 1 | (h) | Brentford | W | 2-1 | Broome 2 | 18, |
| 29 | | 15 | (h) | Manchester U | W | 4-3 | Broome 2, Carter, Antonio | 19, |
| 30 | | 22 | (a) | Liverpool | D | 1-1 | Stamps | 50, |
| 31 | | 29 | (h) | Bolton W | L | 1-3 | Stamps | 18, |
| 32 | Apr | 5 | (a) | Chelsea | L | 0-3 | | 52, |
| 33 | | 7 | (h) | Wolves | W | 2-1 | Stamps 2 (1 pen) | 31, |
| 34 | | 8 | (a) | Wolves | L | 2-7 | Carter 2 | 41, |
| 35 | | 12 | (h) | Charlton A | W | 1-0 | Broome | 19, |
| 36 | | 19 | (a) | Grimsby T | L | 0-2 | | 16, |
| 37 | | 26 | (h) | Leeds U | W | 2-1 | Carter, Stamps (pen) | 10, |
| 38 | May | 3 | (h) | Huddersfield T | W | 1-0 | Broome | 16, |
| 39 | | 10 | (h) | Arsenal | L | 0-1 | | 19, |
| 40 | | 17 | (h) | Sheffield U | L | 1-2 | Morrison | 17, |
| 41 | | 26 | (a) | Preston NE | D | 1-1 | Stamps (pen) | 17, |
| 42 | | 31 | (a) | Portsmouth | W | 2-1 | Carter, Broome | 20, |

FINAL LEAGUE POSITION: 14th in Division One

Appearar

G

## FA Cup

| | | | | | | | | |
|---|---|---|---|---|---|---|---|---|
| 3 | Jan | 11 | (a) | Bournemouth | W | 2-0 | Ward, Carter | 18, |
| 4 | | 25 | (a) | Chelsea | D | 2-2 | Stamps, Carter | 49, |
| R | | 29 | (h) | Chelsea | W | 1-0* | Stamps | 19, |
| 5 | Feb | 8 | (a) | Liverpool | L | 0-1 | | 44, |

*after extra-time

Appearar

G

| oodley V | Nicholas J | Howe J | Bullions J | Leuty L | Musson W | Walsh W | Carter H | Stamps J | Doherty P | Morrison A | Crooks S | Parr J | Ward T | Broome F | Duncan D | Powell K | Mozley B | Harrison R | Grant A | McLachlan S | Peart R | Poppitt J | Antonio G | Townsend W | Wilcox G | McGill J | McCormick H | |
|---|---|---|---|---|---|---|---|---|---|---|---|---|---|---|---|---|---|---|---|---|---|---|---|---|---|---|---|---|
| | 2 | 3 | 4 | 5 | 6 | 7 | 8 | 9 | 10 | 11 | | | | | | | | | | | | | | | | | | 1 |
| | 2 | 3 | 4 | 5 | 6 | | 8 | 9 | 10 | 11 | 7 | | | | | | | | | | | | | | | | | 2 |
| | 2 | 3 | 4 | 5 | 6 | | 8 | 9 | 10 | 11 | 7 | | | | | | | | | | | | | | | | | 3 |
| | | 3 | | 5 | 6 | | 8 | 9 | 10 | 11 | | 2 | 4 | 7 | | | | | | | | | | | | | | 4 |
| | | 3 | | 5 | 6 | | 8 | 9 | 10 | 11 | | 2 | 4 | 7 | | | | | | | | | | | | | | 5 |
| | | 3 | | 5 | 6 | | 8 | 9 | 10 | | | 2 | 4 | 7 | 11 | | | | | | | | | | | | | 6 |
| | | 3 | | 5 | 6 | | | 10 | | 9 | 7 | 2 | 4 | 8 | 11 | | | | | | | | | | | | | 7 |
| | | 3 | | 5 | 6 | | 8 | 9 | 10 | | | 2 | 4 | 7 | | 11 | | | | | | | | | | | | 8 |
| | | 3 | | 5 | 6 | | 8 | 9 | 10 | | | 2 | 4 | 7 | | 11 | | | | | | | | | | | | 9 |
| | | 3 | | 5 | 6 | | 8 | 9 | 10 | | | 2 | 4 | 7 | | 11 | | | | | | | | | | | | 10 |
| | | 3 | | 5 | 6 | | 8 | 9 | 10 | | | 2 | 4 | 7 | | 11 | | | | | | | | | | | | 11 |
| | | 5 | | | 6 | | | 8 | 10 | | | 3 | 4 | 9 | | 11 | 2 | 7 | | | | | | | | | | 12 |
| | | 6 | | 5 | | | 8 | 11 | 10 | | | 3 | 4 | 9 | | | 2 | 7 | | | | | | | | | | 13 |
| | | 2 | 4 | 5 | 6 | | 8 | 9 | 10 | | | 3 | | 7 | | 11 | | | 1 | | | | | | | | | 14 |
| | | 2 | 4 | 5 | 6 | | 8 | 9 | 10 | | | 3 | | 7 | | 11 | | | 1 | | | | | | | | | 15 |
| | | 3 | 4 | 5 | 6 | | 8 | 10 | | 9 | | | | 7 | | 11 | 2 | | 1 | | | | | | | | | 16 |
| | | 3 | 4 | | 6 | | 8 | 10 | | 9 | | | | 7 | | 11 | 2 | | 1 | 5 | | | | | | | | 17 |
| | | 3 | 4 | 5 | 6 | | 8 | 10 | | 9 | | | | 7 | | 11 | 2 | | 1 | | | | | | | | | 18 |
| | | | 4 | 5 | 6 | | 8 | 10 | | 9 | | 3 | | | | 11 | 2 | 7 | 1 | | | | | | | | | 19 |
| | | 3 | 4 | 5 | 6 | | 8 | 10 | | 9 | | | | 7 | | 11 | 2 | | 1 | | | | | | | | | 20 |
| | | 3 | 4 | 5 | 6 | | 8 | | 10 | 9 | | | 11 | | | | 2 | 7 | 1 | | | | | | | | | 21 |
| | | 3 | 4 | 5 | 6 | | 8 | 10 | | 9 | | | 11 | | | | 2 | 7 | 1 | | | | | | | | | 22 |
| | | 3 | 4 | 5 | 6 | | | 10 | | 9 | | | 8 | | | 11 | 2 | 7 | 1 | | | | | | | | | 23 |
| | | 3 | | 5 | 6 | | 8 | 10 | | 9 | | | 4 | 11 | | | 2 | 7 | 1 | | | | | | | | | 24 |
| | | 3 | | 5 | 6 | | 8 | 10 | | | | | 4 | 11 | | | 2 | 7 | | | 9 | | | | | | | 25 |
| | 2 | 3 | | 5 | 6 | | 8 | 10 | | | | | 4 | 11 | | | | 7 | | | | 9 | | | | | | 26 |
| | 2 | 3 | | 5 | 6 | | 8 | 10 | | | | | 4 | 11 | | | | 7 | | | | 9 | | | | | | 27 |
| | 2 | 3 | | 5 | 6 | | 8 | 10 | | 9 | | | 4 | 11 | | | | 7 | | | | | | | | | | 28 |
| | 2 | 3 | | 5 | 6 | | 8 | 9 | | | | | 4 | 11 | | | | 7 | | | | | 10 | | | | | 29 |
| | 2 | 3 | | 5 | 6 | | | 10 | | 9 | | | 4 | 11 | | | | 7 | | | | | 8 | | | | | 30 |
| | | | | 5 | 6 | | 8 | 9 | | | | | 4 | 11 | | | 2 | 7 | | | | 3 | 10 | | | | | 31 |
| | 2 | | | 5 | 6 | | 8 | 9 | | | | | 4 | 11 | | | 3 | 7 | | | | | 10 | | | | | 32 |
| | | | | 5 | 6 | | 8 | 9 | | | | 3 | 4 | 11 | | | 2 | 7 | | | | | 10 | | | | | 33 |
| | | | | 5 | 6 | | 8 | 9 | | | | 3 | 4 | 11 | | | 2 | 7 | | | | | 10 | | | | | 34 |
| | | 3 | | 5 | 6 | | | 10 | | 9 | | | 4 | 11 | | | 2 | 7 | | | | | 8 | | | | | 35 |
| | | 5 | | | 6 | | 8 | 9 | | | | 3 | 4 | 11 | | | 2 | 7 | | | | | 10 | | | | | 36 |
| | | | | 5 | 6 | | 8 | 9 | | | | 3 | 4 | 11 | | | 2 | 7 | | | | | 10 | 1 | | | | 37 |
| | | | | | 6 | | | | | | | 3 | 4 | 9 | | | | 7 | | 5 | | | 10 | | 2 | 8 | 11 | 38 |
| | | 3 | | | 6 | | | 10 | | | | | 4 | 9 | | | | 7 | | 5 | | | | | 2 | 8 | 11 | 39 |
| | | 3 | | | 6 | | | 10 | | 9 | | | 4 | 7 | | | | | | 5 | | | | | 2 | 8 | 11 | 40 |
| | | 3 | | | 6 | | | 9 | | | | | 4 | 7 | | | 2 | 8 | | 5 | | | 10 | | | | 11 | 41 |
| | | 3 | | | 6 | | 8 | 9 | | | | | 4 | 7 | | | 2 | | | 5 | | | | | | 10 | 11 | 42 |
| 0 | 9 | 35 | 13 | 34 | 41 | 1 | 33 | 40 | 15 | 19 | 3 | 18 | 32 | 35 | 2 | 13 | 21 | 23 | 11 | 6 | 1 | 3 | 11 | 1 | 3 | 4 | 5 | |
| | | | | | | | 19 | 17 | 7 | 8 | | | 1 | 17 | | | | 3 | | | | | 1 | | | | | |

| oodley V | Nicholas J | Howe J | Bullions J | Leuty L | Musson W | Walsh W | Carter H | Stamps J | Doherty P | Morrison A | Crooks S | Parr J | Ward T | Broome F | Duncan D | Powell K | Mozley B | Harrison R | Grant A | McLachlan S | Peart R | Poppitt J | Antonio G | Townsend W | Wilcox G | McGill J | McCormick H | |
|---|---|---|---|---|---|---|---|---|---|---|---|---|---|---|---|---|---|---|---|---|---|---|---|---|---|---|---|---|
| | | 3 | 4 | 5 | 6 | | 8 | 10 | | 9 | | | 11 | | | | 2 | 7 | 1 | | | | | | | | | 3 |
| | | 3 | | 5 | 6 | | 8 | 10 | | 9 | | | 4 | 11 | | | 2 | 7 | 1 | | | | | | | | | 4 |
| | | 3 | | 5 | 6 | | 8 | 10 | | 9 | | | 4 | 11 | | | 2 | 7 | 1 | | | | | | | | | R |
| | | 3 | | 5 | 6 | | 8 | 10 | | 9 | | | 4 | 11 | | | 2 | 7 | | | | | | | | | | 5 |
| | | 4 | 1 | 4 | 4 | | 4 | 4 | | 4 | | | 4 | 3 | | | 4 | 4 | 3 | | | | | | | | | |
| | | | | | | | 2 | 2 | | | | | 1 | | | | | | | | | | | | | | | |

# 1947-48

| | P | W | D | L | F | A | Pts |
|---|---|---|---|---|---|---|---|
| Arsenal | 42 | 23 | 13 | 6 | 81 | 32 | 59 |
| Manchester U | 42 | 19 | 14 | 9 | 81 | 48 | 52 |
| Burnley | 42 | 20 | 12 | 10 | 56 | 43 | 52 |
| Derby Co | 42 | 19 | 12 | 11 | 77 | 57 | 50 |
| Wolves | 42 | 19 | 9 | 14 | 83 | 70 | 47 |
| Aston Villa | 42 | 19 | 9 | 14 | 65 | 57 | 47 |
| Preston NE | 42 | 20 | 7 | 15 | 67 | 68 | 47 |
| Portsmouth | 42 | 19 | 7 | 16 | 68 | 50 | 45 |
| Blackpool | 42 | 17 | 10 | 15 | 57 | 41 | 44 |
| Manchester C | 42 | 15 | 12 | 15 | 52 | 47 | 42 |
| Liverpool | 42 | 16 | 10 | 16 | 65 | 61 | 42 |
| Sheffield U | 42 | 16 | 10 | 16 | 65 | 70 | 42 |
| Charlton A | 42 | 17 | 6 | 19 | 57 | 66 | 40 |
| Everton | 42 | 17 | 6 | 19 | 52 | 66 | 40 |
| Stoke C | 42 | 14 | 10 | 18 | 41 | 55 | 38 |
| Middlesbrough | 42 | 14 | 9 | 19 | 71 | 73 | 37 |
| Bolton W | 42 | 16 | 5 | 21 | 46 | 58 | 37 |
| Chelsea | 42 | 14 | 9 | 19 | 53 | 71 | 37 |
| Huddersfield T | 42 | 12 | 12 | 18 | 51 | 60 | 36 |
| Sunderland | 42 | 13 | 10 | 19 | 56 | 67 | 36 |
| Blackburn R | 42 | 11 | 10 | 21 | 54 | 72 | 32 |
| Grimsby T | 42 | 8 | 6 | 28 | 45 | 111 | 22 |

Manager: Stuart McMillan.
Leading scorers: Raich Carter, Reg Harrison, League 15. Reg Harrison, all matches 18.

- In May 1947, Billy Steel played and scored for Great Britain in their 6–1 defeat of the Rest of Europe at Hampden Park. The match, watched by 134,000, was to mark the United Kingdom countries rejoining FIFA.
- The following month, Steel joined Derby from Greenock Morton for a British record fee of £15,500, helping the Rams to the FA Cup semi-final.
- Arsenal opened the season with an unbeaten run of 17 games but Reg Harrison's goal ended it in November, in front of the biggest Baseball Ground attendance since 1936.
- Raich Carter marked his final appearance for Derby with the winner against Blackpool before joining Hull City as player and assistant manager. It was his 50th peacetime goal for the Rams, to go with another 55 in wartime competitions.

## Division One

| Match No. | Date | | Venue | Opponents | Result | | Scorers | Atten. |
|---|---|---|---|---|---|---|---|---|
| 1 | Aug | 23 | (h) | Huddersfield T | D | 0-0 | | 30 |
| 2 | | 26 | (a) | Burnley | W | 2-0 | Carter, Stamps | 43 |
| 3 | | 30 | (a) | Chelsea | L | 0-1 | | 59 |
| 4 | Sep | 3 | (h) | Burnley | D | 1-1 | Broome | 32 |
| 5 | | 6 | (h) | Everton | W | 1-0 | Harrison | 29 |
| 6 | | 10 | (h) | Manchester C | D | 0-0 | | 31 |
| 7 | | 13 | (a) | Wolves | L | 0-1 | | 53 |
| 8 | | 17 | (a) | Manchester C | L | 2-3 | Broome, Carter | 38 |
| 9 | | 20 | (h) | Aston Villa | L | 1-3 | Harrison | 32 |
| 10 | | 27 | (a) | Sunderland | D | 1-1 | Harrison | 54 |
| 11 | Oct | 4 | (h) | Grimsby T | W | 4-1 | Morrison 2, Broome, Antonio | 24 |
| 12 | | 11 | (a) | Portsmouth | D | 0-0 | | 43 |
| 13 | | 18 | (h) | Bolton W | W | 2-1 | Broome, Morrison | 24 |
| 14 | | 25 | (a) | Liverpool | D | 2-2 | Steel 2 | 49 |
| 15 | Nov | 1 | (h) | Middlesbrough | W | 4-2 | Morrison 2, Broome, Carter | 32 |
| 16 | | 8 | (a) | Sheffield U | W | 2-1 | Broome, Carter | 51 |
| 17 | | 15 | (h) | Manchester U | D | 1-1 | Harrison | 32 |
| 18 | | 22 | (a) | Charlton A | W | 5-1 | Harrison 3, Carter, Oliver | 39 |
| 19 | | 29 | (h) | Arsenal | W | 1-0 | Harrison | 35 |
| 20 | Dec | 6 | (a) | Preston NE | L | 4-7 | Morrison 3, Howe (pen) | 28 |
| 21 | | 13 | (h) | Stoke C | D | 1-1 | Steel | 24 |
| 22 | | 20 | (a) | Huddersfield T | L | 1-2 | Morrison | 27 |
| 23 | | 25 | (a) | Blackburn R | W | 4-3 | Carter 2, Steel, Morrison | 30 |
| 24 | | 27 | (h) | Blackburn R | W | 5-0 | Carter 2, Harrison 2, Morrison | 25 |
| 25 | Jan | 3 | (h) | Chelsea | W | 5-1 | Stamps 2, Steel 2, Carter | 27 |
| 26 | | 17 | (a) | Everton | W | 3-1 | Stamps 2, Steel | 51, |
| 27 | Feb | 14 | (h) | Sunderland | W | 5-1 | Carter 4, Morrison | 35 |
| 28 | | 21 | (a) | Grimsby T | W | 3-2 | Stamps 2, Morrison | 11, |
| 29 | Mar | 20 | (a) | Middlesbrough | D | 1-1 | Stamps (pen) | 24 |
| 30 | | 26 | (a) | Blackpool | D | 2-2 | Stamps, Harrison | 30 |
| 31 | | 27 | (h) | Sheffield U | D | 1-1 | Harrison | 26 |
| 32 | | 29 | (h) | Blackpool | W | 1-0 | Carter | 34 |
| 33 | | 31 | (h) | Liverpool | L | 0-4 | | 16 |
| 34 | Apr | 3 | (a) | Manchester U | L | 0-1 | | 50 |
| 35 | | 7 | (a) | Aston Villa | D | 2-2 | Stamps (pen), Harrison | 30, |
| 36 | | 10 | (h) | Charlton A | L | 0-3 | | 18, |
| 37 | | 14 | (h) | Wolves | L | 1-2 | Stamps | 17, |
| 38 | | 17 | (a) | Arsenal | W | 2-1 | Stamps, Steel | 49, |
| 39 | | 21 | (a) | Bolton W | W | 3-0 | Broome, Harrison, Aspinall (og) | 25, |
| 40 | | 24 | (h) | Preston NE | W | 2-1 | Broome, Harrison | 19, |
| 41 | | 28 | (h) | Portsmouth | W | 2-1 | Broome, Stamps | 15, |
| 42 | May | 1 | (a) | Stoke C | L | 0-1 | | 19, |

FINAL LEAGUE POSITION: 4th in Division One

Appearar
G

## FA Cup

| | | | | | | | | |
|---|---|---|---|---|---|---|---|---|
| 3 | Jan | 10 | (h) | Chesterfield | W | 2-0 | Stamps, Harrison | 34, |
| 4 | | 24 | (a) | Crewe A | W | 3-0 | Steel 2, Harrison | 14, |
| 5 | Feb | 7 | (a) | Middlesbrough | W | 2-1 | Harrison, Stamps | 43, |
| 6 | | 28 | (a) | Queen's Park R | D | 1-1* | Steel | 28, |
| R | Mar | 6 | (h) | Queen's Park R | W | 5-0 | Stamps 2, Carter 2, Steel | 31, |
| SF | | 13 | (n‡) | Manchester U | L | 1-3 | Steel | 60, |

‡Played at Hillsborough, Sheffield
*after extra-time

Appearar
G

| Mozley B | Howe J | Ward T | Leuty L | Musson W | Broome F | Carter H | Stamps J | Steel W | McGill J | Townsend W | Harrison R | Morrison A | Smith F | Bullions J | McCormick H | Antonio G | Oliver A | Miller D | Parr J | Wallace J | Poppitt J | Payne F | |
|---|---|---|---|---|---|---|---|---|---|---|---|---|---|---|---|---|---|---|---|---|---|---|---|
| 2 | 3 | 4 | 5 | 6 | 7 | 8 | 9 | 10 | 11 | | | | | | | | | | | | | | 1 |
| 2 | 3 | 4 | 5 | 6 | 11 | 8 | 9 | 10 | | 1 | 7 | | | | | | | | | | | | 2 |
| 2 | 3 | 4 | 5 | 6 | 11 | 8 | | 10 | | 1 | 7 | 9 | | | | | | | | | | | 3 |
| 2 | 3 | 4 | 5 | 6 | 11 | 8 | | 10 | | 1 | 7 | | 9 | | | | | | | | | | 4 |
| 2 | 3 | 4 | 5 | 6 | | 8 | | 10 | | 1 | 7 | | | 9 | 11 | | | | | | | | 5 |
| 2 | 3 | 4 | 5 | 6 | | 8 | | | 10 | 1 | 7 | | | 9 | 11 | | | | | | | | 6 |
| 2 | 3 | 4 | 5 | 6 | | 8 | | 10 | | 1 | 7 | | | | | 9 | 11 | | | | | | 7 |
| 2 | 3 | 4 | 5 | 6 | 9 | 8 | | 10 | | 1 | 7 | | | | | | 11 | | | | | | 8 |
| 2 | 3 | | 5 | 6 | 9 | 8 | | 10 | | 1 | 7 | | | 4 | | | 11 | | | | | | 9 |
| 2 | 3 | 4 | 5 | 6 | 11 | 8 | | 10 | | 1 | 7 | | | | | | | 9 | | | | | 10 |
| 2 | 3 | 4 | 5 | 6 | 11 | 8 | | | | 1 | 7 | 9 | | | | 10 | | | | | | | 11 |
| 2 | 3 | 4 | 5 | 6 | 11 | 8 | | | | 1 | 7 | 9 | | | | 10 | | | | | | | 12 |
| 2 | 3 | | 5 | 6 | 11 | | | 10 | | 1 | 7 | 9 | | 4 | | 8 | | | | | | | 13 |
| 2 | 3 | 4 | 5 | 6 | 11 | | | 10 | | 1 | 7 | 9 | | | | 8 | | | | | | | 14 |
| 2 | 3 | 4 | 5 | 6 | 7 | 8 | | 10 | | 1 | | 9 | | | | | 11 | | | | | | 15 |
| 2 | 3 | 4 | 5 | 6 | 7 | 8 | | 10 | | 1 | | 9 | | | | | 11 | | | | | | 16 |
| 2 | 3 | 4 | 5 | 6 | | 8 | | 10 | | 1 | 7 | 9 | | | | | 11 | | | | | | 17 |
| 2 | 3 | 4 | 5 | 6 | | 8 | | 10 | | 1 | 7 | 9 | | | | | 11 | | | | | | 18 |
| 2 | 3 | 4 | 5 | 6 | | 8 | | 10 | | 1 | 7 | 9 | | | | | 11 | | | | | | 19 |
| 2 | 3 | 4 | 5 | 6 | | 8 | | 10 | | 1 | 7 | 9 | | | | | 11 | | | | | | 20 |
| 2 | 3 | 4 | 5 | 6 | | 8 | | 10 | | 1 | 7 | 9 | | | | | 11 | | | | | | 21 |
| 2 | 3 | 4 | 5 | 6 | 11 | 8 | | 10 | | 1 | 7 | 9 | | | | | | | | | | | 22 |
| 2 | | 4 | 5 | 6 | | 8 | 9 | 10 | | 1 | 7 | 11 | | | | | | | 3 | | | | 23 |
| 2 | | 4 | 5 | 6 | | 8 | 9 | 10 | | 1 | 7 | 11 | | | | | | | 3 | | | | 24 |
| 2 | | 4 | 5 | 6 | | 8 | 9 | 10 | | 1 | 7 | 11 | | | | | | | 3 | | | | 25 |
| 2 | 3 | | 5 | 6 | | 8 | 9 | 10 | | 1 | 7 | 11 | | | | 4 | | | | | | | 26 |
| 2 | 3 | 4 | 5 | 6 | | 8 | 9 | 10 | | | 7 | 11 | | | | | | | | 1 | | | 27 |
| 2 | 3 | 4 | 5 | 6 | | 8 | 9 | 10 | | | 7 | 11 | | | | | | | | 1 | | | 28 |
| | 3 | 4 | 5 | 6 | | 8 | 9 | 10 | | | 7 | 11 | | | | | | | | 1 | 2 | | 29 |
| | 3 | 4 | 5 | 6 | | 8 | 9 | 10 | | | 7 | 11 | | | | | | | | 1 | 2 | | 30 |
| | 3 | 4 | 5 | 6 | | 8 | 9 | 10 | | | 7 | 11 | | | | | | | | 1 | 2 | | 31 |
| 2 | 3 | 4 | 5 | 6 | | 8 | 9 | 10 | | | 7 | 11 | | | | | | | | 1 | | | 32 |
| 2 | 5 | 4 | | 6 | 8 | | 9 | 10 | | | 7 | 11 | | | | | | | | 1 | 3 | | 33 |
| 2 | 3 | 4 | 5 | 6 | 11 | | 10 | 8 | | | 7 | 9 | | | | | | | | 1 | | | 34 |
| 2 | 3 | 4 | 5 | 6 | 11 | | 10 | | 8 | | 7 | 9 | | | | | | | | 1 | | | 35 |
| 2 | 3 | 4 | 5 | 6 | 11 | | 10 | | 8 | | 7 | 9 | | | | | | | | 1 | | | 36 |
| 2 | 3 | 4 | 5 | | 11 | | 10 | 8 | | | 7 | 9 | | | | 6 | | | | 1 | | | 37 |
| 2 | 3 | 4 | 5 | 6 | 11 | | 10 | 8 | | | 7 | 9 | | | | | | | | 1 | | | 38 |
| 2 | 3 | 4 | 5 | 6 | 11 | | 10 | 8 | | | 7 | 9 | | | | | | | | 1 | | | 39 |
| 2 | 3 | 4 | 5 | 6 | 11 | | 10 | 8 | | | 7 | 9 | | | | | | | | 1 | | | 40 |
| 2 | 3 | 4 | 5 | 6 | 11 | | 10 | 8 | | | 7 | 9 | | | | | | | | 1 | | | 41 |
| 2 | 3 | 4 | 5 | 6 | 11 | | 10 | 8 | | | 7 | 9 | | | | | | | | 1 | | | 42 |
| 39 | 39 | 39 | 41 | 41 | 24 | 30 | 22 | 37 | 4 | 25 | 39 | 33 | 1 | 4 | 2 | 7 | 10 | 1 | 3 | 16 | 4 | | |
| | 1 | | | | 9 | 15 | 13 | 8 | | | 15 | 13 | | | | 1 | 1 | | | | | | |

1 own-goal

| Mozley B | Howe J | Ward T | Leuty L | Musson W | Broome F | Carter H | Stamps J | Steel W | McGill J | Townsend W | Harrison R | Morrison A | Smith F | Bullions J | McCormick H | Antonio G | Oliver A | Miller D | Parr J | Wallace J | Poppitt J | Payne F | |
|---|---|---|---|---|---|---|---|---|---|---|---|---|---|---|---|---|---|---|---|---|---|---|---|
| 2 | 3 | 4 | 5 | 6 | 7 | | 9 | 10 | | 1 | 8 | 11 | | | | | | | | | | | 3 |
| 2 | 3 | 4 | 5 | 6 | | 8 | 9 | 10 | | 1 | 7 | 11 | | | | | | | | | | | 4 |
| 2 | 3 | 4 | 5 | 6 | | 8 | 9 | 10 | | | 7 | 11 | | | | | | | | | | 1 | 5 |
| 2 | 3 | 4 | 5 | 6 | | 8 | 9 | 10 | | | 7 | 11 | | | | | | | | 1 | | | 6 |
| 2 | 3 | 4 | 5 | 6 | | 8 | 9 | 10 | | | 7 | 11 | | | | | | | | 1 | | | R |
| 2 | 3 | 4 | 5 | 6 | | 8 | 9 | 10 | | | 7 | 11 | | | | | | | | 1 | | | SF |
| 6 | 6 | 6 | 6 | 6 | 1 | 5 | 6 | 6 | | 2 | 6 | 6 | | | | | | | | 3 | | 1 | |
| | | | | | | 2 | 4 | 5 | | | 3 | | | | | | | | | | | | |

# 1948-49

| | P | W | D | L | F | A | Pts |
|---|---|---|---|---|---|---|---|
| Portsmouth | 42 | 25 | 8 | 9 | 84 | 42 | 58 |
| Manchester U | 42 | 21 | 11 | 10 | 77 | 44 | 53 |
| Derby Co | 42 | 22 | 9 | 11 | 74 | 55 | 53 |
| Newcastle U | 42 | 20 | 12 | 10 | 70 | 56 | 52 |
| Arsenal | 42 | 18 | 13 | 11 | 74 | 44 | 49 |
| Wolves | 42 | 17 | 12 | 13 | 79 | 66 | 46 |
| Manchester C | 42 | 15 | 15 | 12 | 47 | 51 | 45 |
| Sunderland | 42 | 13 | 17 | 12 | 49 | 58 | 43 |
| Charlton A | 42 | 15 | 12 | 15 | 63 | 67 | 42 |
| Aston Villa | 42 | 16 | 10 | 16 | 60 | 76 | 42 |
| Stoke C | 42 | 16 | 9 | 17 | 66 | 68 | 41 |
| Liverpool | 42 | 13 | 14 | 15 | 53 | 43 | 40 |
| Chelsea | 42 | 12 | 14 | 16 | 69 | 68 | 38 |
| Bolton W | 42 | 14 | 10 | 18 | 59 | 68 | 38 |
| Burnley | 42 | 12 | 14 | 16 | 43 | 50 | 38 |
| Blackpool | 42 | 11 | 16 | 15 | 54 | 67 | 38 |
| Birmingham C | 42 | 11 | 15 | 16 | 36 | 38 | 37 |
| Everton | 42 | 13 | 11 | 18 | 41 | 63 | 37 |
| Middlesbrough | 42 | 11 | 12 | 19 | 46 | 57 | 34 |
| Huddersfield T | 42 | 12 | 10 | 20 | 40 | 69 | 34 |
| Preston N.E. | 42 | 11 | 11 | 20 | 62 | 75 | 33 |
| Sheffield U | 42 | 11 | 11 | 20 | 57 | 78 | 33 |

Manager: Stuart McMillan.
Leading scorers: Frank Broome, Billy Steel, League 14. Billy Steel, all matches 15.
League ever-present: Frank Broome.

- In March, Derby again broke the British record by paying Manchester United £24,500 for Johnny Morris, an FA Cup winner in the previous season's victory over Blackpool.
- Morris scored 13 goals in his first 13 games and earned selection for England in the post-season tour to Norway and France.
- The Rams finished third, a position they did not equal or improve on for 23 years, until the first Championship.
- Derby's FA Cup sixth-round tie at Portsmouth set an attendance record for Fratton Park, 51,385. It has never been beaten.

## Division One

| Match No. | Date | | Venue | Opponents | Result | | Scorers | Atte |
|---|---|---|---|---|---|---|---|---|
| 1 | Aug | 21 | (a) | Manchester U | W | 2-1 | Harrison, Broome | 52 |
| 2 | | 25 | (h) | Huddersfield T | W | 4-1 | Powell 2, Steel, Thompson | 31 |
| 3 | | 28 | (h) | Sheffield U | W | 2-1 | Broome, Howe (pen) | 32 |
| 4 | Sep | 1 | (a) | Huddersfield T | D | 1-1 | Thompson | 24 |
| 5 | | 4 | (a) | Aston Villa | D | 1-1 | Harrison | 50 |
| 6 | | 6 | (a) | Blackpool | D | 1-1 | Steel | 30 |
| 7 | | 11 | (h) | Sunderland | D | 2-2 | Thompson, Broome | 29 |
| 8 | | 15 | (h) | Blackpool | W | 3-1 | Broome 2, Stamps | 32 |
| 9 | | 18 | (a) | Wolves | D | 2-2 | Harrison, Steel | 51 |
| 10 | | 25 | (h) | Bolton W | W | 1-0 | Broome | 33 |
| 11 | Oct | 2 | (a) | Liverpool | D | 0-0 | | 53 |
| 12 | | 9 | (h) | Preston NE | W | 1-0 | Harrison | 31 |
| 13 | | 16 | (a) | Everton | W | 1-0 | Stamps | 53 |
| 14 | | 23 | (h) | Chelsea | W | 2-1 | Stamps, Broome | 29 |
| 15 | | 30 | (a) | Birmingham C | W | 1-0 | Steel | 52 |
| 16 | Nov | 6 | (h) | Middlesbrough | W | 2-0 | Stamps, Steel | 34 |
| 17 | | 13 | (a) | Newcastle U | L | 0-3 | | 64 |
| 18 | | 20 | (h) | Portsmouth | W | 1-0 | Steel | 34 |
| 19 | | 27 | (a) | Manchester C | L | 1-2 | Harrison | 45 |
| 20 | Dec | 4 | (h) | Charlton A | W | 5-1 | Stamps 2, Steel 2, Broome | 28 |
| 21 | | 11 | (a) | Stoke C | L | 2-4 | Powell, Taft | 39 |
| 22 | | 18 | (h) | Manchester U | L | 1-3 | Mozley | 31 |
| 23 | | 25 | (a) | Arsenal | D | 3-3 | Harrison, Broome, Powell | 40 |
| 24 | | 27 | (h) | Arsenal | W | 2-1 | Steel, Broome | 33 |
| 25 | Jan | 1 | (a) | Sheffield U | L | 1-3 | Leuty | 41 |
| 26 | | 22 | (a) | Sunderland | L | 1-2 | Powell | 52 |
| 27 | Feb | 5 | (h) | Wolves | W | 3-2 | Broome 2, Powell | 31 |
| 28 | | 19 | (a) | Bolton W | L | 0-4 | | 37 |
| 29 | Mar | 5 | (a) | Preston NE | D | 0-0 | | 22 |
| 30 | | 12 | (h) | Everton | W | 3-2 | Stamps, Steel, Broome | 33 |
| 31 | | 19 | (a) | Portsmouth | L | 0-1 | | 43 |
| 32 | | 26 | (h) | Manchester C | W | 2-0 | Morris, Walsh (og) | 29 |
| 33 | Apr | 2 | (a) | Middlesbrough | L | 0-1 | | 38 |
| 34 | | 9 | (h) | Newcastle U | L | 2-4 | Morris, Stamps(pen) | 24 |
| 35 | | 15 | (a) | Burnley | L | 1-3 | Morris | 30 |
| 36 | | 16 | (a) | Chelsea | W | 3-0 | Steel, Broome, Morris | 60 |
| 37 | | 18 | (h) | Burnley | W | 2-0 | Stamps, Steel | 26 |
| 38 | | 23 | (h) | Birmingham C | W | 1-0 | Stamps | 25 |
| 39 | | 27 | (h) | Aston Villa | D | 2-2 | Morris, Parry | 23 |
| 40 | | 30 | (a) | Charlton A | W | 5-1 | Morris 3, Stamps, Steel | 23 |
| 41 | May | 4 | (h) | Liverpool | W | 3-0 | Morris 2, Steel | 22 |
| 42 | | 7 | (h) | Stoke C | W | 4-1 | Morris 3, Harrison | 28 |

FINAL LEAGUE POSITION: 3rd in Division One

Appeara
G

## FA Cup

| | | | | | | | | |
|---|---|---|---|---|---|---|---|---|
| 3 | Jan | 8 | (h) | Southport | W | 4-1 | Harrison 2, Powell 2 | 28 |
| 4 | | 29 | (h) | Arsenal | W | 1-0 | Steel | 31 |
| 5 | Feb | 12 | (h) | Cardiff C | W | 2-1 | Taft, Harrison | 35 |
| 6 | | 26 | (a) | Portsmouth | L | 1-2 | Stamps | 51 |

Appearar
G

| wnsend W | Mozley B | Howe J | Ward T | Leuty L | Musson W | Harrison R | Stamps J | Thompson C | Steel W | Broome F | Powell T | Poppitt J | Parr J | Walker C | Taft D | Clamp E | McLachlan S | Webster T | Morris J | Oliver A | Parry J | Cushlow R | |
|---|---|---|---|---|---|---|---|---|---|---|---|---|---|---|---|---|---|---|---|---|---|---|---|
| | 2 | 3 | 4 | 5 | 6 | 7 | 8 | 9 | 10 | 11 | | | | | | | | | | | | | 1 |
| | 2 | 3 | 4 | 5 | 6 | 7 | | 9 | 10 | 11 | 8 | | | | | | | | | | | | 2 |
| | 2 | 3 | 4 | 5 | 6 | 7 | | 9 | 10 | 11 | 8 | | | | | | | | | | | | 3 |
| | 2 | 3 | 4 | 5 | 6 | 7 | | 9 | 10 | 11 | 8 | | | | | | | | | | | | 4 |
| | 2 | 3 | 4 | 5 | 6 | 7 | | 9 | 10 | 11 | 8 | | | | | | | | | | | | 5 |
| | 2 | 3 | 4 | 5 | 6 | 7 | 8 | 9 | 10 | 11 | | | | | | | | | | | | | 6 |
| | 2 | 3 | 4 | 5 | 6 | 7 | 8 | 9 | 10 | 11 | | | | | | | | | | | | | 7 |
| | 2 | 3 | 4 | 5 | 6 | 7 | 8 | 9 | 10 | 11 | | | | | | | | | | | | | 8 |
| | 2 | 3 | 4 | 5 | 6 | 7 | 8 | 9 | 10 | 11 | | | | | | | | | | | | | 9 |
| | 2 | 3 | 4 | 5 | 6 | 7 | 8 | 9 | 10 | 11 | | | | | | | | | | | | | 10 |
| | | 3 | 4 | 5 | 6 | 7 | 8 | 9 | 10 | 11 | | 2 | | | | | | | | | | | 11 |
| | | | 4 | 5 | 6 | 7 | | 9 | 10 | 11 | 8 | 2 | 3 | | | | | | | | | | 12 |
| | 2 | | 4 | 5 | 6 | 7 | 9 | | 10 | 11 | 8 | | 3 | | | | | | | | | | 13 |
| | | | 4 | 5 | 6 | 7 | 10 | 9 | | 11 | 8 | 2 | 3 | | | | | | | | | | 14 |
| | | 3 | 4 | 5 | 6 | 7 | 9 | | 10 | 11 | 8 | 2 | | | | | | | | | | | 15 |
| | 2 | 3 | 4 | 5 | 6 | 7 | 9 | | 10 | 11 | 8 | | | | | | | | | | | | 16 |
| | 2 | 3 | 4 | 5 | 6 | 7 | 9 | | 10 | 11 | 8 | | | | | | | | | | | | 17 |
| | 2 | 3 | 4 | 5 | 6 | 7 | 9 | | 10 | 11 | 8 | | | | | | | | | | | | 18 |
| | | 3 | 4 | 5 | | 7 | 9 | | 10 | 11 | 8 | | 2 | 6 | | | | | | | | | 19 |
| | 2 | 3 | 4 | 5 | 6 | 7 | 9 | | 10 | 11 | 8 | | | | | | | | | | | | 20 |
| | 2 | 3 | 4 | 5 | 6 | 7 | | | 10 | 11 | 8 | | | | 9 | | | | | | | | 21 |
| | 2 | | 4 | 5 | 6 | 7 | 9 | | 10 | 11 | 8 | | 3 | | | | | | | | | | 22 |
| | | 3 | 4 | 5 | 6 | 7 | | | 10 | 11 | 8 | | 2 | | 9 | | | | | | | | 23 |
| | | 3 | 4 | 5 | 6 | 7 | | | 10 | 11 | 8 | | 2 | | 9 | | | | | | | | 24 |
| | | 3 | 4 | 5 | 6 | 7 | | | 10 | 11 | 8 | | 2 | | 9 | 1 | | | | | | | 25 |
| | | 3 | 4 | 5 | 6 | 7 | | | 10 | 11 | 8 | | 2 | | 9 | | | | | | | | 26 |
| | | 3 | | 5 | 6 | 7 | | | 10 | 11 | 8 | | 2 | | 9 | | 4 | | | | | | 27 |
| | | 3 | | 5 | 6 | 7 | 9 | | 10 | 11 | 8 | | 2 | | | | 4 | | | | | | 28 |
| | 4 | 3 | | 5 | 6 | 7 | 9 | | 10 | 11 | 8 | | 2 | | | | | 1 | | | | | 29 |
| | 4 | 3 | | 5 | 6 | 7 | 9 | | 10 | 11 | | | 2 | | | | | 1 | 8 | | | | 30 |
| | 4 | 3 | | 5 | 6 | 7 | 10 | 9 | | 11 | | | 2 | | | | | 1 | 8 | | | | 31 |
| | 4 | 3 | | 5 | 6 | 7 | 9 | | 10 | 11 | | | 2 | | | | | 1 | 8 | | | | 32 |
| | 4 | 3 | | 5 | 6 | 7 | 9 | | 10 | 11 | | | 2 | | | | | 1 | 8 | | | | 33 |
| | 3 | | 4 | | 6 | 7 | 9 | | | 11 | | | 2 | | | | 5 | 1 | 8 | 10 | | | 34 |
| | 2 | 3 | 4 | 5 | 6 | 7 | 9 | | 10 | 11 | | | | | | | | 1 | 8 | | | | 35 |
| | 2 | 3 | 4 | 5 | 6 | 7 | 9 | | 10 | 11 | | | | | | | | 1 | 8 | | | | 36 |
| | 2 | 3 | 4 | 5 | 6 | 7 | 9 | | 10 | 11 | | | | | | | | 1 | 8 | | | | 37 |
| | 2 | 3 | 4 | 5 | 6 | 7 | 9 | | 10 | 11 | | | | | | | | 1 | 8 | | | | 38 |
| | 2 | 3 | 4 | 5 | 6 | 7 | 9 | | | 11 | | | | | | | | 1 | 8 | | 10 | | 39 |
| | 2 | 3 | 4 | 5 | 6 | | 8 | | 10 | 7 | | | | | | | | 1 | 8 | 11 | | | 40 |
| | 2 | 3 | 4 | | 6 | | 9 | | 10 | 7 | | | | | | | | 1 | 8 | 11 | | 5 | 41 |
| | 2 | 3 | 4 | 5 | 6 | 7 | 9 | | 10 | 11 | | | | | | | | 1 | 8 | | | | 42 |
| [illegible] | 31 | 37 | 35 | 40 | 41 | 40 | 31 | 14 | 38 | 42 | 22 | 4 | 17 | 1 | 6 | 1 | 3 | 14 | 13 | 3 | 1 | 1 | |
| | 1 | 1 | | 1 | | 7 | 11 | 3 | 14 | 14 | 6 | | | | 1 | | | | 13 | | 1 | | |

1 own-goal

| | | | | | | | | | | | | | | | | | | | | | | |
|---|---|---|---|---|---|---|---|---|---|---|---|---|---|---|---|---|---|---|---|---|---|---|
| | 3 | 4 | 5 | 6 | 7 | | | 10 | | 8 | | 2 | | 9 | | | | | 11 | | | 3 |
| | 3 | 4 | 5 | 6 | 7 | | | 10 | 11 | 8 | | 2 | | 9 | | | | | | | | 4 |
| | 3 | | 5 | 6 | 7 | | | 10 | 11 | 8 | | 2 | | 9 | | 4 | | | | | | 5 |
| 4 | 3 | | 5 | 6 | 7 | 9 | | 10 | 11 | 8 | | 2 | | | | | | | | | | 6 |
| 1 | 4 | 2 | 4 | 4 | 4 | 1 | | 4 | 3 | 4 | | 4 | | 3 | | 1 | | | 1 | | | |
| | | | | | 3 | 1 | | 1 | | 2 | | | | 1 | | | | | | | | |

# 1949-50

| | P | W | D | L | F | A | Pts |
|---|---|---|---|---|---|---|---|
| Portsmouth | 42 | 22 | 9 | 11 | 74 | 38 | 53 |
| Wolves | 42 | 20 | 13 | 9 | 76 | 49 | 53 |
| Sunderland | 42 | 21 | 10 | 11 | 83 | 62 | 52 |
| Manchester U | 42 | 18 | 14 | 10 | 69 | 44 | 50 |
| Newcastle U | 42 | 19 | 12 | 11 | 77 | 55 | 50 |
| Arsenal | 42 | 19 | 11 | 12 | 79 | 55 | 49 |
| Blackpool | 42 | 17 | 15 | 10 | 46 | 35 | 49 |
| Liverpool | 42 | 17 | 14 | 11 | 64 | 54 | 48 |
| Middlesbrough | 42 | 20 | 7 | 15 | 59 | 48 | 47 |
| Burnley | 42 | 16 | 13 | 13 | 40 | 40 | 45 |
| Derby Co | 42 | 17 | 10 | 15 | 69 | 61 | 44 |
| Aston Villa | 42 | 15 | 12 | 15 | 61 | 61 | 42 |
| Chelsea | 42 | 12 | 16 | 14 | 58 | 65 | 40 |
| W.B.A. | 42 | 14 | 12 | 16 | 47 | 53 | 40 |
| Huddersfield T | 42 | 14 | 9 | 19 | 52 | 73 | 37 |
| Bolton W | 42 | 10 | 14 | 18 | 45 | 59 | 34 |
| Fulham | 42 | 10 | 14 | 18 | 41 | 54 | 34 |
| Everton | 42 | 10 | 14 | 18 | 42 | 66 | 34 |
| Stoke C | 42 | 11 | 12 | 19 | 45 | 75 | 34 |
| Charlton A | 42 | 13 | 6 | 23 | 53 | 65 | 32 |
| Manchester C | 42 | 8 | 13 | 21 | 36 | 68 | 29 |
| Birmingham C | 42 | 7 | 14 | 21 | 31 | 67 | 28 |

Manager: Stuart McMillan.
Leading scorer: Jack Stamps, League 22, all matches 29.

- Bert Mozley became one of a rare breed, a Derby-born Rams player who appeared for England. He made his debut against the Republic of Ireland at Goodison Park and won two more caps.
- The Baseball Ground attendance record was established when 38,063 watched the FA Cup fifth-round tie against Northampton Town in February. It survived until capacity was extended by the building of the Ley Stand in 1969.
- Another FA Cup winner left when Jack Howe joined Huddersfield Town in October. He was 34 and had been at the Baseball Ground for 13 years, spending World War Two with the Cameron Highlanders.

## Division One

| Match No. | Date | | Venue | Opponents | Result | | Scorers | Att |
|---|---|---|---|---|---|---|---|---|
| 1 | Aug | 20 | (h) | Manchester U | L | 0-1 | | 3 |
| 2 | | 23 | (a) | Aston Villa | D | 1-1 | Steel | 5 |
| 3 | | 27 | (a) | Chelsea | W | 2-1 | Stamps, Broome | 5 |
| 4 | | 31 | (h) | Aston Villa | W | 3-2 | Morris 2, Stamps | 3 |
| 5 | Sep | 3 | (h) | Stoke C | L | 2-3 | Broome, A.Oliver | 2 |
| 6 | | 5 | (a) | Bolton W | D | 0-0 | | 2 |
| 7 | | 10 | (a) | Burnley | W | 1-0 | Stamps | 3 |
| 8 | | 17 | (h) | Sunderland | W | 3-2 | Broome 2, Morris | 3 |
| 9 | | 24 | (a) | Liverpool | L | 1-3 | Morris | 5 |
| 10 | Oct | 1 | (h) | Arsenal | L | 1-2 | Broome | 3 |
| 11 | | 8 | (h) | Wolves | L | 1-2 | Stamps | 3 |
| 12 | | 15 | (a) | Portsmouth | L | 1-3 | Stamps (pen) | 3 |
| 13 | | 22 | (h) | Huddersfield T | W | 4-2 | McLaren 2, Harrison, Steel | 2 |
| 14 | | 29 | (a) | Everton | W | 2-1 | Harrison, McLaren | 3 |
| 15 | Nov | 5 | (h) | Middlesbrough | W | 1-0 | Harrison | 2 |
| 16 | | 12 | (a) | Blackpool | L | 0-1 | | 1 |
| 17 | | 26 | (a) | Fulham | D | 0-0 | | 3 |
| 18 | Dec | 3 | (h) | Manchester C | W | 7-0 | Morris 2, Stamps 2, McLaren 2, Steel | 2 |
| 19 | | 10 | (a) | Charlton A | W | 3-1 | Ward, Stamps, Steel | 3 |
| 20 | | 17 | (a) | Manchester U | W | 1-0 | Stamps | 3 |
| 21 | | 24 | (h) | Chelsea | D | 2-2 | McLaren 2 | 2 |
| 22 | | 26 | (a) | Birmingham C | D | 2-2 | Stamps, McLaren | 4 |
| 23 | | 27 | (h) | Birmingham C | W | 4-1 | Stamps 3, Mozley | 3 |
| 24 | | 31 | (a) | Stoke C | W | 3-1 | Harrison, Morris, Stamps (pen) | 3 |
| 25 | Jan | 14 | (h) | Burnley | D | 1-1 | Attwell (og) | 3 |
| 26 | | 21 | (a) | Sunderland | L | 1-6 | Powell | 6 |
| 27 | Feb | 4 | (h) | Liverpool | D | 2-2 | Steel, McLaren | 3 |
| 28 | | 18 | (a) | Arsenal | L | 0-1 | | 6 |
| 29 | | 25 | (a) | Wolves | L | 1-4 | Wilkins | 4 |
| 30 | Mar | 8 | (h) | Portsmouth | W | 2-1 | Stamps 2 | 1 |
| 31 | | 11 | (a) | Newcastle U | L | 1-2 | Stamps | 4 |
| 32 | | 18 | (h) | Fulham | W | 2-1 | Ward, Stamps | 1 |
| 33 | | 25 | (a) | Middlesbrough | L | 1-3 | Morris | 3 |
| 34 | | 29 | (h) | Newcastle U | D | 1-1 | Morris | 1 |
| 35 | Apr | 1 | (h) | Blackpool | D | 0-0 | | 2 |
| 36 | | 7 | (h) | West Brom A | W | 3-1 | McLaren 2, Stamps | 2 |
| 37 | | 8 | (a*) | Huddersfield T | L | 0-2 | | 3 |
| 38 | | 10 | (a) | West Brom A | L | 0-1 | | 31 |
| 39 | | 15 | (h) | Everton | W | 2-0 | McLaren, Moore (og) | 15 |
| 40 | | 22 | (a) | Manchester C | D | 2-2 | Mynard, Morris | 53 |
| 41 | | 29 | (h) | Charlton A | L | 1-2 | Mynard | 11 |
| 42 | May | 5 | (h) | Bolton W | W | 4-0 | Stamps 3, Barrass (og) | 1 |

FINAL LEAGUE POSITION: 11th in Division One

*Played at Elland Road, Leeds.

Appeara

G

## FA Cup

| | | | | | | | | |
|---|---|---|---|---|---|---|---|---|
| 3 | Jan | 7 | (a) | Manchester C | W | 5-3 | Stamps 3 (1 pen), Steel, Powell | 53 |
| 4 | | 28 | (a) | Bury | D | 2-2 | Powell, Stamps | 33 |
| R | Feb | 1 | (h) | Bury | W | 5-2 | Stamps 3, Morris, Powell | 28 |
| 5 | | 11 | (h) | Northampton T | W | 4-2 | McLaren 2, Morris, Steel | 38 |
| 6 | Mar | 4 | (h) | Everton | L | 1-2 | Powell | 32 |

Appeara

G

| ebster T | Mozley B | Howe J | Ward T | Leuty L | Musson W | Harrison R | Morris J | Stamps J | Steel W | Broome F | Oliver A | Parkin G | Powell T | Parr J | Mynard L | Poppitt J | Cushlow R | McLaren H | Oliver K | Townsend W | Thompson C | Brown H | Wilkins R | Mays A | McLachlan S | |
|---|---|---|---|---|---|---|---|---|---|---|---|---|---|---|---|---|---|---|---|---|---|---|---|---|---|---|
| | 2 | 3 | 4 | 5 | 6 | 7 | 8 | 9 | 10 | 11 | | | | | | | | | | | | | | | | 1 |
| | 2 | 3 | 4 | 5 | 6 | 7 | 8 | 9 | 10 | 11 | | | | | | | | | | | | | | | | 2 |
| | 2 | 3 | 4 | 5 | 6 | 7 | 8 | 9 | 10 | 11 | | | | | | | | | | | | | | | | 3 |
| | 2 | 3 | 4 | 5 | 6 | 7 | 8 | 9 | 10 | 11 | | | | | | | | | | | | | | | | 4 |
| | 2 | 3 | 4 | 5 | 6 | | 8 | | 10 | 11 | 7 | 9 | | | | | | | | | | | | | | 5 |
| | 2 | 3 | 4 | 5 | 6 | | 8 | | 10 | 11 | 7 | | 9 | | | | | | | | | | | | | 6 |
| | 2 | 3 | 4 | 5 | 6 | 7 | 8 | 9 | 10 | 11 | | | | | | | | | | | | | | | | 7 |
| | 2 | 3 | 4 | 5 | 6 | 7 | 8 | 9 | 10 | 11 | | | | | | | | | | | | | | | | 8 |
| | 2 | | 4 | 5 | 6 | 7 | 8 | 9 | 10 | 11 | | | | 3 | | | | | | | | | | | | 9 |
| | 2 | 3 | 4 | 5 | 6 | 7 | 8 | 10 | | 9 | | | | | 11 | | | | | | | | | | | 10 |
| | 2 | 3 | 4 | 5 | 6 | 7 | | 9 | 10 | 11 | | | 8 | | | | | | | | | | | | | 11 |
| | | 3 | 4 | | 6 | 7 | | 9 | 10 | | | | 8 | | | 2 | 5 | 11 | | | | | | | | 12 |
| | 2 | | 4 | | 6 | 7 | | 9 | 10 | | | | 8 | 3 | | | | 11 | 5 | | | | | | | 13 |
| | 2 | | 4 | 5 | 6 | 7 | | 9 | | | 11 | | 8 | 3 | | | | 10 | | 1 | | | | | | 14 |
| | 2 | | | | 6 | 7 | | 9 | 10 | | | | 8 | 3 | | | | 11 | 5 | 1 | 4 | | | | | 15 |
| | 2 | | 4 | | 6 | 7 | | 9 | 10 | | | | 8 | 3 | | | | 11 | 5 | 1 | | | | | | 16 |
| | | | 4 | | 6 | | 8 | 9 | 10 | | | | 7 | 3 | | 2 | | 11 | 5 | 1 | | | | | | 17 |
| | | | 4 | | 6 | | 8 | 9 | 10 | | | | 7 | 3 | | 2 | | 11 | 5 | 1 | | | | | | 18 |
| | 2 | | 4 | | 6 | | 8 | 9 | 10 | | | | 7 | 3 | | | | 11 | 5 | 1 | | | | | | 19 |
| | 2 | | 4 | | 6 | | 8 | 9 | 10 | | | | 7 | 3 | | | | 11 | 5 | 1 | | | | | | 20 |
| | 2 | | 4 | | | | 8 | 9 | 10 | | | | 7 | 3 | | | | 11 | 5 | 1 | 6 | | | | | 21 |
| | 2 | | 4 | | 6 | | 8 | 9 | 10 | | | | 7 | 3 | | | | 11 | 5 | | | 1 | | | | 22 |
| | 2 | | 4 | | 6 | 7 | 8 | 9 | 10 | | | | 11 | 3 | | | | | 5 | 1 | | | | | | 23 |
| | 2 | | 4 | | 6 | 7 | 8 | 9 | 10 | | | | 11 | 3 | | | | | 5 | 1 | | | | | | 24 |
| | 2 | | 4 | | 6 | | 8 | 9 | 10 | | | | 7 | 3 | | | | 11 | 5 | 1 | | | | | | 25 |
| | 2 | | 4 | 5 | 6 | | 8 | 9 | 10 | | | | 7 | 3 | | | | 11 | | 1 | | | | | | 26 |
| | 2 | | 4 | 5 | 6 | | 8 | | 10 | | | | 7 | 3 | | | | 11 | | 1 | | | 9 | | | 27 |
| | 2 | | 4 | 5 | 6 | 7 | 8 | 9 | | | | | 10 | 3 | | | | 11 | | 1 | | | | | | 28 |
| | 2 | | 4 | 5 | 6 | | 8 | | 10 | | | | 7 | 3 | | | | 11 | | 1 | | | 9 | | | 29 |
| | 2 | | 4 | | 6 | | 8 | 9 | 10 | | | | 11 | 3 | 7 | | | | 5 | 1 | | | | | | 30 |
| | 2 | | 4 | | 6 | | 8 | 9 | | | | 10 | | 3 | 7 | | | 11 | 5 | 1 | | | | | | 31 |
| | 2 | | 8 | | 6 | | | 9 | | | | 10 | | 3 | | 7 | | 11 | 5 | 1 | | | | 4 | | 32 |
| | 2 | | 4 | | 6 | | 8 | 9 | | | | 10 | | 3 | | 7 | | 11 | 5 | 1 | | | | | | 33 |
| | 2 | | 4 | | 6 | | 8 | 9 | 10 | | | 7 | | 3 | | | | 11 | 5 | 1 | | | | | | 34 |
| | 2 | | 4 | | 6 | | 8 | 9 | 10 | | | | | 3 | 7 | | | 11 | 5 | 1 | | | | | | 35 |
| | 2 | | 4 | | 6 | | 8 | 9 | 10 | | | | | 3 | 7 | | | 11 | 5 | 1 | | | | | | 36 |
| | 2 | | 4 | | 6 | | 8 | 9 | 10 | | | | | 3 | 7 | | | 11 | 5 | 1 | | | | | | 37 |
| | 2 | | 4 | | 6 | | 8 | 9 | 10 | | | | | 3 | 7 | | | 11 | 5 | | | 1 | | | | 38 |
| | 2 | | 4 | | 6 | | 8 | 10 | | | | 9 | | 3 | 7 | | | 11 | 5 | | | 1 | | | | 39 |
| | 2 | | 4 | | 6 | | 8 | 10 | | | | 9 | | 3 | 7 | | | 11 | 5 | | | 1 | | | | 40 |
| | 2 | | 4 | | 6 | | 8 | | 10 | | | 9 | | | 7 | | | 11 | 5 | | | 1 | | | 3 | 41 |
| | 2 | | 4 | | 6 | | | 8 | 10 | | | 9 | | | 7 | | | 11 | 5 | | | 1 | | | 3 | 42 |
| 3 | 39 | 11 | 41 | 16 | 41 | 17 | 34 | 37 | 34 | 11 | 3 | 9 | 21 | 29 | 11 | 5 | 1 | 28 | 25 | 23 | 2 | 6 | 2 | 1 | 2 | Apps |
| | 1 | | 2 | | | 4 | 10 | 22 | 5 | 5 | 1 | | 1 | | 2 | | | 12 | | | | | 1 | | | Goals |

3 own-goals

| ebster T | Mozley B | Howe J | Ward T | Leuty L | Musson W | Harrison R | Morris J | Stamps J | Steel W | Broome F | Oliver A | Parkin G | Powell T | Parr J | Mynard L | Poppitt J | Cushlow R | McLaren H | Oliver K | Townsend W | Thompson C | Brown H | Wilkins R | Mays A | McLachlan S | |
|---|---|---|---|---|---|---|---|---|---|---|---|---|---|---|---|---|---|---|---|---|---|---|---|---|---|---|
| | 2 | | 4 | | 6 | | 8 | 9 | 10 | | | | 7 | 3 | | | | 11 | 5 | 1 | | | | | | 3 |
| | 2 | | 4 | 5 | 6 | | 8 | 9 | 10 | | | | 7 | 3 | | | | 11 | | 1 | | | | | | 4 |
| | 2 | | 4 | 5 | 6 | | 8 | 9 | 10 | | | | 7 | 3 | | | | 11 | | 1 | | | | | | R |
| | 2 | | 4 | 5 | 6 | | 8 | 9 | 10 | | | | 7 | 3 | | | | 11 | | 1 | | | | | | 5 |
| | 2 | | 4 | | 6 | 7 | 8 | 9 | 10 | | | | 11 | 3 | | | | | 5 | 1 | | | | | | 6 |
| | 5 | | 5 | 3 | 5 | 1 | 5 | 5 | 5 | | | | 5 | 5 | | | | 4 | 2 | 5 | | | | | | Cup Apps |
| | | | | | | | 2 | 7 | 2 | | | | 4 | | | | | 2 | | | | | | | | Cup Goals |

# 1950-51

| | P | W | D | L | F | A | Pts |
|---|---|---|---|---|---|---|---|
| Tottenham H | 42 | 25 | 10 | 7 | 82 | 44 | 60 |
| Manchester U | 42 | 24 | 8 | 10 | 74 | 40 | 56 |
| Blackpool | 42 | 20 | 10 | 12 | 79 | 53 | 50 |
| Newcastle U | 42 | 18 | 13 | 11 | 62 | 53 | 49 |
| Arsenal | 42 | 19 | 9 | 14 | 73 | 56 | 47 |
| Middlesbrough | 42 | 18 | 11 | 13 | 76 | 65 | 47 |
| Portsmouth | 42 | 16 | 15 | 11 | 71 | 68 | 47 |
| Bolton W | 42 | 19 | 7 | 16 | 64 | 61 | 45 |
| Liverpool | 42 | 16 | 11 | 15 | 53 | 59 | 43 |
| Burnley | 42 | 14 | 14 | 14 | 48 | 43 | 42 |
| Derby Co | 42 | 16 | 8 | 18 | 81 | 75 | 40 |
| Sunderland | 42 | 12 | 16 | 14 | 63 | 73 | 40 |
| Stoke C | 42 | 13 | 14 | 15 | 50 | 59 | 40 |
| Wolves | 42 | 15 | 8 | 19 | 74 | 61 | 38 |
| Aston Villa | 42 | 12 | 13 | 17 | 66 | 68 | 37 |
| W.B.A. | 42 | 13 | 11 | 18 | 53 | 61 | 37 |
| Charlton A | 42 | 14 | 9 | 19 | 63 | 80 | 37 |
| Fulham | 42 | 13 | 11 | 18 | 52 | 68 | 37 |
| Huddersfield T | 42 | 15 | 6 | 21 | 64 | 92 | 36 |
| Chelsea | 42 | 12 | 8 | 22 | 53 | 65 | 32 |
| Sheffield W | 42 | 12 | 8 | 22 | 64 | 83 | 32 |
| Everton | 42 | 12 | 8 | 22 | 48 | 86 | 32 |

Manager: Stuart McMillan.
Leading scorer: Jack Lee, League 28, all matches 29.

- Jack Lee was 29 when he joined Derby from Leicester City in June 1950. Stuart McMillan said he would play for England and, in November, he scored in a 4–1 victory over Northern Ireland at Windsor Park.
- It was Lee's only cap and it was more than 20 years before Roy McFarland became the next Derby player to win full England honours. Lee scored four goals in the memorable 6–5 victory over Sunderland in December.
- Jack Stamps, who scored four against Blackpool in September, became the sixth player to reach 100 goals for the club with one in the victory over Huddersfield Town on 4 November.
- Billy Steel set another transfer record in September when he joined Dundee for £23,000, then the most paid by a Scottish club.

## Division One

| Match No. | Date | | Venue | Opponents | Result | | Scorers | Atter |
|---|---|---|---|---|---|---|---|---|
| 1 | Aug | 19 | (a) | Sunderland | L | 0-1 | | 52 |
| 2 | | 23 | (h) | Wolves | L | 1-2 | Stamps | 31 |
| 3 | | 26 | (h) | Aston Villa | W | 4-2 | Lee 2, Harrison, Powell | 26 |
| 4 | | 28 | (a) | Wolves | W | 3-2 | Lee 2, Morris | 46 |
| 5 | Sep | 2 | (a) | Stoke C | L | 1-4 | Morris | 27 |
| 6 | | 6 | (h) | Charlton A | W | 5-0 | Lee 3, Stamps, Powell | 21 |
| 7 | | 9 | (a) | Liverpool | L | 0-1 | | 50 |
| 8 | | 16 | (h) | Fulham | W | 3-2 | Lee 2, Stamps | 25 |
| 9 | | 23 | (a) | Bolton W | L | 0-3 | | 36 |
| 10 | | 30 | (h) | Blackpool | W | 4-1 | Stamps 4 | 32 |
| 11 | Oct | 7 | (h) | West Brom A | D | 1-1 | Stamps | 27 |
| 12 | | 14 | (a) | Newcastle U | L | 1-3 | Lee | 54 |
| 13 | | 21 | (h) | Sheffield W | W | 4-1 | Stamps 2 (1 pen), Morris, McLaren | 31 |
| 14 | | 28 | (a) | Arsenal | L | 1-3 | Lee | 62 |
| 15 | Nov | 4 | (h) | Huddersfield T | W | 3-0 | Harrison, Stamps, McLaren | 21 |
| 16 | | 11 | (a) | Middlesbrough | D | 1-1 | Lee | 36 |
| 17 | | 18 | (h) | Burnley | D | 1-1 | Morris | 21 |
| 18 | | 25 | (a) | Chelsea | W | 2-1 | Lee, Morris | 26 |
| 19 | Dec | 2 | (h) | Portsmouth | L | 2-3 | Ward, Harrison | 23 |
| 20 | | 9 | (a) | Everton | W | 2-1 | Harrison, Morris | 37 |
| 21 | | 16 | (h) | Sunderland | W | 6-5 | Lee 4, McLaren 2 | 15 |
| 22 | | 23 | (a) | Aston Villa | D | 1-1 | Stamps | 28 |
| 23 | | 25 | (h) | Tottenham H | D | 1-1 | Stamps | 32 |
| 24 | | 26 | (a) | Tottenham H | L | 1-2 | McLaren | 59 |
| 25 | | 30 | (h) | Stoke C | D | 1-1 | Lee | 19 |
| 26 | Jan | 13 | (h) | Liverpool | L | 1-2 | Lee | 21 |
| 27 | | 20 | (a) | Fulham | W | 5-3 | Lee 3, Stamps 2 | 28 |
| 28 | Feb | 3 | (h) | Bolton W | D | 2-2 | Stamps, Morris | 19 |
| 29 | | 17 | (a) | Blackpool | L | 1-3 | McLaren | 21 |
| 30 | | 24 | (a) | West Brom A | W | 2-1 | Harrison, Stamps | 33 |
| 31 | Mar | 3 | (h) | Newcastle U | L | 1-2 | Lee | 25 |
| 32 | | 17 | (h) | Arsenal | W | 4-2 | Lee 2, McLaren 2 | 22 |
| 33 | | 23 | (a) | Manchester U | L | 0-2 | | 43 |
| 34 | | 24 | (a) | Huddersfield T | L | 0-2 | | 25 |
| 35 | | 26 | (h) | Manchester U | L | 2-4 | Harrison, Stamps | 25 |
| 36 | | 31 | (h) | Middlesbrough | W | 6-0 | Morris 2, Harrison, Lee, McLaren, Mays | 16 |
| 37 | Apr | 7 | (a) | Burnley | L | 0-1 | | 21 |
| 38 | | 14 | (h) | Chelsea | W | 1-0 | Harrison | 16 |
| 39 | | 18 | (a) | Sheffield W | L | 3-4 | Lee 2, Stamps | 40 |
| 40 | | 21 | (a) | Portsmouth | D | 2-2 | Stamps, Revell | 29 |
| 41 | | 28 | (h) | Everton | L | 0-1 | | 9 |
| 42 | May | 5 | (a) | Charlton A | W | 2-1 | Morris, Parry | 17 |

FINAL LEAGUE POSITION: 11th in Division One

Appearar

G

## FA Cup

| | | | | | | | | |
|---|---|---|---|---|---|---|---|---|
| 3 | Jan | 6 | (h) | West Brom A | D | 2-2 | Stamps 2 | 24 |
| R | | 10 | (a) | West Brom A | W | 1-0 | Stamps | 33 |
| 4 | | 27 | (h) | Birmingham C | L | 1-3 | Lee | 37 |

Appearar

G

| wn H | Mozley B | Parr J | Ward T | Oliver K | Musson W | Harrison R | Stamps J | Lee J | Morris J | Powell T | McLachlan S | Scott K | Parry J | McLaren H | Savin K | Webster T | Mynard L | Mays A | Revell C | Bell C | Sharman D | |
|---|---|---|---|---|---|---|---|---|---|---|---|---|---|---|---|---|---|---|---|---|---|---|
| | 2 | 3 | 4 | 5 | 6 | 7 | 8 | 9 | 10 | 11 | | | | | | | | | | | | 1 |
| | 2 | | 4 | 5 | 6 | 7 | 8 | 9 | 10 | 11 | 3 | | | | | | | | | | | 2 |
| | 2 | 3 | 5 | | 6 | 7 | 8 | 9 | 10 | 11 | 4 | | | | | | | | | | | 3 |
| | 2 | 3 | 5 | | 6 | 7 | 8 | 9 | 10 | 11 | 4 | | | | | | | | | | | 4 |
| | 2 | 3 | 5 | | 6 | 7 | 8 | 9 | 10 | 11 | 4 | | | | | | | | | | | 5 |
| | 2 | 3 | 5 | | 6 | 7 | 8 | 9 | 10 | 11 | 4 | | | | | | | | | | | 6 |
| | 2 | 3 | 5 | | 6 | 7 | 8 | 9 | 10 | 11 | 4 | | | | | | | | | | | 7 |
| | 2 | 3 | 5 | | 6 | 7 | 8 | 9 | 10 | 11 | 4 | | | | | | | | | | | 8 |
| | 2 | 3 | 5 | | 6 | 7 | 8 | 9 | 10 | 11 | 4 | | | | | | | | | | | 9 |
| | 2 | 3 | 4 | 5 | 6 | | 8 | 9 | 10 | 11 | | 7 | | | | | | | | | | 10 |
| | 2 | 3 | 4 | 5 | 6 | | 8 | | 10 | 11 | | 7 | 9 | | | | | | | | | 11 |
| | 2 | 3 | 4 | 5 | 6 | | 8 | 9 | 10 | 7 | | | | 11 | | | | | | | | 12 |
| | 2 | 3 | 4 | 5 | 6 | | 8 | 9 | 10 | 7 | | | | 11 | | | | | | | | 13 |
| | 2 | 3 | 4 | 5 | 6 | | 8 | 9 | 10 | 7 | | | | 11 | | | | | | | | 14 |
| | 2 | 3 | 4 | 5 | 6 | 7 | 8 | 9 | | 10 | | | | 11 | | | | | | | | 15 |
| | 2 | 3 | 4 | 5 | 6 | 7 | 8 | 9 | 10 | 11 | | | | | | | | | | | | 16 |
| | 2 | 3 | 4 | 5 | 6 | 7 | 8 | 9 | 10 | | | | | 11 | | | | | | | | 17 |
| | 2 | 3 | 4 | 5 | 6 | 7 | | 9 | 10 | 8 | | | | 11 | | | | | | | | 18 |
| | 2 | 3 | 4 | 5 | 6 | 7 | | 9 | 10 | 8 | | | | 11 | | | | | | | | 19 |
| | 2 | 3 | 4 | 5 | 6 | 7 | 8 | 9 | 10 | | | | | 11 | | | | | | | | 20 |
| | 2 | 3 | 4 | 5 | 6 | 7 | 8 | 9 | 10 | | | | | 11 | | | | | | | | 21 |
| | 2 | 3 | 4 | 5 | 6 | 7 | 8 | 9 | 10 | | | | | 11 | | | | | | | | 22 |
| | 2 | 3 | 4 | 5 | 6 | 7 | 8 | 9 | 10 | | | | | 11 | | | | | | | | 23 |
| | 2 | 3 | 4 | 5 | 6 | 7 | 8 | 9 | 10 | | | | | 11 | | | | | | | | 24 |
| | 2 | 3 | 4 | 5 | 6 | 7 | | 9 | 10 | 8 | | | | 11 | | | | | | | | 25 |
| | 2 | 3 | 4 | 5 | 6 | 7 | 8 | 9 | | 10 | | | | 11 | | | | | | | | 26 |
| | 2 | | 4 | 5 | 6 | | 8 | 9 | 7 | 10 | | | | 11 | 3 | | | | | | | 27 |
| | 2 | 3 | 4 | 5 | 6 | 7 | 9 | | 10 | 8 | | | | 11 | | | | | | | | 28 |
| | 2 | 3 | 4 | 5 | 6 | | 8 | 9 | 10 | | | | | 11 | | 1 | 7 | | | | | 29 |
| | 3 | 2 | 4 | 5 | 6 | 7 | 8 | 9 | 10 | | | | | 11 | | 1 | | | | | | 30 |
| | 3 | 2 | 4 | 5 | | 7 | 8 | 9 | 10 | | | | | 11 | | 1 | | 6 | | | | 31 |
| | 2 | | | 5 | 6 | 7 | 8 | 9 | 10 | | | | | 11 | | 1 | | 4 | 3 | | | 32 |
| | 2 | | | 5 | 6 | 7 | 8 | 9 | 10 | | | | | 11 | | 1 | | 4 | 3 | | | 33 |
| | | | | 5 | 6 | 7 | 8 | 9 | 10 | | | | | 11 | | 1 | | 4 | 3 | 2 | | 34 |
| | | | | 5 | 6 | 7 | 8 | 9 | 10 | | | | | 11 | | 1 | | 4 | 3 | 2 | | 35 |
| | | | | 5 | 6 | 7 | 8 | 9 | 10 | | | | | 11 | | 1 | | 4 | 3 | 2 | | 36 |
| | | | | 5 | 6 | 7 | 8 | 9 | 10 | | | | | 11 | | 1 | | 4 | 3 | 2 | | 37 |
| | 2 | | | 5 | 6 | 7 | | 9 | 10 | 8 | | | | 11 | | | | 4 | 3 | | 1 | 38 |
| | 2 | | | 5 | 6 | 7 | 8 | 9 | | | | | 10 | | | | 11 | 4 | 3 | | 1 | 39 |
| | 2 | 3 | | 5 | 6 | 7 | 8 | 9 | | | | | 10 | | | | | 4 | 11 | | | 40 |
| | 2 | | | 5 | 6 | 7 | 8 | 9 | | | | | 10 | 11 | | | | 4 | 3 | | | 41 |
| | 2 | | | 5 | 6 | 7 | 9 | | 8 | | | | 10 | | | | 11 | 4 | 3 | | | 42 |
| | 38 | 30 | 31 | 35 | 41 | 35 | 38 | 39 | 37 | 23 | 8 | 2 | 5 | 27 | 1 | 9 | 3 | 12 | 11 | 4 | 2 | |
| | | | 1 | | | 8 | 20 | 28 | 10 | 2 | | | 1 | 9 | | | | 1 | 1 | | | |

| wn H | Mozley B | Parr J | Ward T | Oliver K | Musson W | Harrison R | Stamps J | Lee J | Morris J | Powell T | McLachlan S | Scott K | Parry J | McLaren H | Savin K | Webster T | Mynard L | Mays A | Revell C | Bell C | Sharman D | |
|---|---|---|---|---|---|---|---|---|---|---|---|---|---|---|---|---|---|---|---|---|---|---|
| | 2 | 3 | 4 | 5 | 6 | 7 | 8 | 9 | 10 | | | | | 11 | | | | | | | | 3 |
| | 2 | 3 | 4 | 5 | 6 | 7 | 8 | 9 | 10 | | | | | 11 | | | | | | | | R |
| | 2 | 3 | 4 | 5 | 6 | | 8 | 9 | 7 | 10 | | | | 11 | | | | | | | | 4 |
| | 3 | 3 | 3 | 3 | 3 | 2 | 3 | 3 | 3 | 1 | | | | 3 | | | | | | | | |
| | | | | | | | 3 | 1 | | | | | | | | | | | | | | |

# 1951-52

| | P | W | D | L | F | A | Pts |
|---|---|---|---|---|---|---|---|
| Manchester U | 42 | 23 | 11 | 8 | 95 | 52 | 57 |
| Tottenham H | 42 | 22 | 9 | 11 | 76 | 51 | 53 |
| Arsenal | 42 | 21 | 11 | 10 | 80 | 61 | 53 |
| Portsmouth | 42 | 20 | 8 | 14 | 68 | 58 | 48 |
| Bolton W | 42 | 19 | 10 | 13 | 65 | 61 | 48 |
| Aston Villa | 42 | 19 | 9 | 14 | 79 | 70 | 47 |
| Preston N.E. | 42 | 17 | 12 | 13 | 74 | 54 | 46 |
| Newcastle U | 42 | 18 | 9 | 15 | 98 | 73 | 45 |
| Blackpool | 42 | 18 | 9 | 15 | 64 | 64 | 45 |
| Charlton A | 42 | 17 | 10 | 15 | 68 | 63 | 44 |
| Liverpool | 42 | 12 | 19 | 11 | 57 | 61 | 43 |
| Sunderland | 42 | 15 | 12 | 15 | 70 | 61 | 42 |
| W.B.A. | 42 | 14 | 13 | 15 | 74 | 77 | 41 |
| Burnley | 42 | 15 | 10 | 17 | 56 | 63 | 40 |
| Manchester C | 42 | 13 | 13 | 16 | 58 | 61 | 39 |
| Wolves | 42 | 12 | 14 | 16 | 73 | 73 | 38 |
| Derby Co | 42 | 15 | 7 | 20 | 63 | 80 | 37 |
| Middlesbrough | 42 | 15 | 6 | 21 | 64 | 88 | 36 |
| Chelsea | 42 | 14 | 8 | 20 | 52 | 72 | 36 |
| Stoke C | 42 | 12 | 7 | 23 | 49 | 88 | 31 |
| Huddersfield T | 42 | 10 | 8 | 24 | 49 | 82 | 28 |
| Fulham | 42 | 8 | 11 | 23 | 58 | 77 | 27 |

Manager: Stuart McMillan.
Leading scorers: Jack Parry, League 11. Jack Parry, Johnny Morris, all matches 11.
League ever-present: Reg Harrison, Ray Middleton.

- Goalkeeper Ray Middleton, signed from Chesterfield in June, was a Justice of the Peace, the only active professional footballer to act as a magistrate.
- Middleton spent three seasons with Derby before he was appointed as Boston United's player-manager.
- Derby were clearly declining and 17th was their lowest position in the First Division since they were promoted in 1925–26. There was worse to come.

## Division One

| Match No. | Date | | Venue | Opponents | Result | | Scorers | Atte |
|---|---|---|---|---|---|---|---|---|
| 1 | Aug | 18 | (h) | Sunderland | L | 3-4 | Morris 2, McLaren | 24 |
| 2 | | 22 | (a) | Wolves | W | 2-1 | Harrison, Powell | 37 |
| 3 | | 25 | (a) | Aston Villa | L | 1-4 | Powell | 37 |
| 4 | | 29 | (h) | Wolves | L | 1-3 | Parry | 26 |
| 5 | Sep | 1 | (h) | Stoke C | W | 4-2 | Stamps 2, Powell, Mountford (og) | 20 |
| 6 | | 5 | (a) | Chelsea | W | 1-0 | Parry | 25 |
| 7 | | 8 | (h) | Manchester C | L | 1-3 | Parry | 22 |
| 8 | | 15 | (a) | Arsenal | L | 1-3 | Harrison | 47 |
| 9 | | 22 | (h) | Blackpool | D | 1-1 | Revell | 26 |
| 10 | | 29 | (a) | Liverpool | L | 0-2 | | 40 |
| 11 | Oct | 6 | (a) | Manchester U | L | 1-2 | Stamps | 41 |
| 12 | | 13 | (h) | Tottenham H | W | 4-2 | Parry 2, McLaren, Willis (og) | 27 |
| 13 | | 20 | (a) | Preston NE | W | 1-0 | McLaren | 26 |
| 14 | | 27 | (h) | Burnley | W | 1-0 | Wilkins | 21 |
| 15 | Nov | 3 | (a) | Charlton A | D | 3-3 | McLaren, Parry, Wilkins | 26 |
| 16 | | 10 | (h) | Fulham | W | 5-0 | Harrison, McLaren, Parry, Wilkins, McLachlan | 20 |
| 17 | | 17 | (a) | Middlesbrough | D | 0-0 | | 25 |
| 18 | | 24 | (h) | West Brom A | W | 2-1 | Oliver, McLaren | 21 |
| 19 | Dec | 1 | (a) | Newcastle U | L | 1-2 | McLaren | 49 |
| 20 | | 8 | (h) | Bolton W | W | 5-2 | Morris 2, Harrison, McLaren, Wilkins | 23 |
| 21 | | 15 | (a) | Sunderland | L | 0-3 | | 36 |
| 22 | | 22 | (h) | Aston Villa | D | 1-1 | McLaren | 21 |
| 23 | | 25 | (a) | Huddersfield T | D | 1-1 | Morris (pen) | 28 |
| 24 | | 26 | (h) | Huddersfield T | W | 2-1 | Harrison, McLaren | 24 |
| 25 | | 29 | (a) | Stoke C | L | 1-3 | Barrowcliffe | 27 |
| 26 | Jan | 5 | (a) | Manchester C | L | 2-4 | Morris (pen), Lee | 37 |
| 27 | | 19 | (h) | Arsenal | L | 1-2 | Powell | 28 |
| 28 | | 26 | (a) | Blackpool | L | 1-2 | Wilkins | 18 |
| 29 | Feb | 2 | (a) | Bolton W | W | 2-1 | Morris, Wilkins | 26 |
| 30 | | 9 | (h) | Liverpool | D | 1-1 | Morris | 22 |
| 31 | | 16 | (h) | Manchester U | L | 0-3 | | 27 |
| 32 | Mar | 1 | (a) | Tottenham H | L | 0-5 | | 44 |
| 33 | | 8 | (h) | Preston NE | W | 4-3 | Harrison, Morris (pen), Nielson, Lee | 22 |
| 34 | | 15 | (a) | Burnley | W | 1-0 | Lee | 25 |
| 35 | | 22 | (h) | Charlton A | L | 1-3 | Lee | 18 |
| 36 | Apr | 5 | (h) | Middlesbrough | W | 3-1 | Powell, Stamps, Parry | 10 |
| 37 | | 11 | (a) | Portsmouth | L | 1-3 | Parry | 36 |
| 38 | | 12 | (a) | West Brom A | L | 0-1 | | 27 |
| 39 | | 14 | (h) | Portsmouth | W | 1-0 | Parry | 21 |
| 40 | | 19 | (h) | Newcastle U | L | 1-3 | Parry | 18 |
| 41 | May | 1 | (a) | Fulham | L | 0-3 | | 10 |
| 42 | | 3 | (h) | Chelsea | D | 1-1 | Morris | 8 |

FINAL LEAGUE POSITION: 17th in Division One

Appeara
G

## FA Cup

| | | | | | | | | |
|---|---|---|---|---|---|---|---|---|
| 3 | Jan | 12 | (a) | Middlesbrough | D | 2-2 | Morris, Nielson | 35 |
| R | | 16 | (h) | Middlesbrough | L | 0-2 | | 30 |

Appeara
G

| ddleton R | Mozley B | Revell C | Mays A | Oliver K | Walker C | Harrison R | Powell T | Stamps J | Morris J | McLaren H | Parry J | Barrowcliffe G | Nielson N | Wilkins R | McLachlan S | Bell C | Musson W | Lee J | Parr J | Rowe N | Wheatley S | Straw R | |
|---|---|---|---|---|---|---|---|---|---|---|---|---|---|---|---|---|---|---|---|---|---|---|---|
| | 2 | 3 | 4 | 5 | 6 | 7 | 8 | 9 | 10 | 11 | | | | | | | | | | | | | 1 |
| | 2 | 3 | 4 | 5 | 6 | 7 | 8 | 9 | 10 | 11 | | | | | | | | | | | | | 2 |
| | 2 | 3 | 4 | 5 | 6 | 7 | 8 | 9 | 10 | 11 | | | | | | | | | | | | | 3 |
| | 2 | 3 | 4 | 5 | 6 | 7 | 8 | 9 | 10 | | 11 | | | | | | | | | | | | 4 |
| | 2 | 6 | 4 | 5 | | 7 | 8 | 9 | 10 | | 11 | 3 | | | | | | | | | | | 5 |
| | 2 | 6 | 4 | 5 | | 7 | 8 | 9 | 10 | | 11 | 3 | | | | | | | | | | | 6 |
| | 2 | 6 | 4 | 5 | | 7 | 8 | 9 | 10 | | 11 | 3 | | | | | | | | | | | 7 |
| | 9 | | 6 | 5 | | 7 | 10 | 8 | 4 | | 11 | 3 | 2 | | | | | | | | | | 8 |
| | 2 | 11 | 6 | 5 | | 7 | 10 | 8 | 4 | | 9 | 3 | | | | | | | | | | | 9 |
| | 2 | 11 | 6 | 5 | | 7 | | 8 | 4 | | 10 | 3 | | 9 | | | | | | | | | 10 |
| | 2 | | | 5 | | 7 | | 9 | 8 | 11 | 10 | 3 | | | 4 | 6 | | | | | | | 11 |
| | 2 | | | 5 | | 7 | 10 | | 8 | 11 | 9 | 3 | | | 4 | 6 | | | | | | | 12 |
| | 2 | | | 5 | | 7 | 10 | | 8 | 11 | 9 | 3 | | | 4 | 6 | | | | | | | 13 |
| | 2 | | | 5 | | 7 | 10 | | 8 | 11 | | 3 | | 9 | 4 | 6 | | | | | | | 14 |
| | 2 | | | 5 | | 7 | | | 8 | 11 | 10 | 3 | | 9 | 4 | 6 | | | | | | | 15 |
| | 2 | | | 5 | | 7 | | | 8 | 11 | 10 | 3 | | 9 | 4 | 6 | | | | | | | 16 |
| | 2 | | | 5 | | 7 | | | 8 | 11 | 10 | 3 | | 9 | 4 | 6 | | | | | | | 17 |
| | 2 | | | 5 | | 7 | | | 8 | 11 | 10 | 3 | | 9 | 4 | 6 | | | | | | | 18 |
| | 2 | | | | | 7 | | | 8 | 11 | 10 | 3 | 5 | 9 | 4 | 6 | | | | | | | 19 |
| | 2 | | | 5 | | 7 | | | 8 | 11 | 10 | 3 | | 9 | 4 | 6 | | | | | | | 20 |
| | 2 | | | 5 | | 7 | | | 8 | 11 | 10 | 3 | 6 | 9 | 4 | | | | | | | | 21 |
| | 2 | | 6 | 5 | | 7 | | | 8 | 11 | 10 | 3 | | 9 | 4 | | | | | | | | 22 |
| | 2 | | | 5 | | 7 | | | 8 | 11 | 10 | 3 | | 9 | 4 | | 6 | | | | | | 23 |
| | 2 | | | 5 | | 7 | | | 8 | 11 | 10 | 3 | | 9 | 4 | | 6 | | | | | | 24 |
| | 2 | | | 5 | | 7 | | | 8 | 11 | 10 | 3 | | 9 | 4 | | 6 | | | | | | 25 |
| | 2 | | | 5 | | 7 | | 10 | 8 | 11 | | 3 | | | 4 | 6 | | 9 | | | | | 26 |
| | 2 | 3 | | 5 | | 7 | 10 | | 8 | 11 | | | | | 4 | 6 | | 9 | | | | | 27 |
| | 2 | 6 | | 5 | | 7 | 10 | | 8 | 11 | | | | 9 | 4 | | | | 3 | | | | 28 |
| | 2 | | | 5 | | 7 | 11 | 10 | 8 | | | | | 9 | 4 | 6 | | | 3 | | | | 29 |
| | 2 | | | 5 | | 7 | 11 | 10 | 8 | | | | | 9 | 4 | 6 | | | 3 | | | | 30 |
| | 2 | | | 5 | | 7 | 11 | 10 | 8 | | | | | 9 | 4 | 6 | | | 3 | | | | 31 |
| | 2 | | 4 | 5 | | 7 | 11 | 10 | 8 | | | | | | | 6 | | 9 | 3 | | | | 32 |
| | 2 | | 4 | | | 7 | 11 | 10 | 8 | | | | 5 | | | | 6 | 9 | 3 | | | | 33 |
| | 2 | | 4 | | | 7 | 11 | 10 | 8 | | | | 5 | | | | 6 | 9 | 3 | | | | 34 |
| | 2 | | 4 | | | 7 | 11 | 10 | 8 | | | | 5 | | | | 6 | 9 | 3 | | | | 35 |
| | | | 4 | | | 7 | 11 | 8 | | | 10 | | 5 | | 2 | | 6 | 9 | 3 | | | | 36 |
| | | | 4 | | | 7 | 11 | 8 | 9 | | 10 | | 5 | | 2 | | 6 | | 3 | | | | 37 |
| | | | 4 | | | 7 | 11 | 9 | 8 | | 10 | | 5 | | 2 | | 6 | | 3 | | | | 38 |
| | | | 4 | | | 7 | | 9 | 8 | 11 | 10 | | 5 | | 2 | | 6 | | 3 | | | | 39 |
| | | | | | | 7 | 11 | 9 | 8 | | 10 | | 5 | | 2 | 4 | 6 | | 3 | | | | 40 |
| | 3 | | | 6 | | 7 | 11 | 8 | 4 | | 9 | | 5 | | | | | 10 | | 2 | | | 41 |
| | 3 | | 4 | | | 11 | | | 8 | | 10 | | 5 | | | 6 | | | | 2 | 7 | 9 | 42 |
| 2 | 37 | 11 | 20 | 32 | 4 | 42 | 26 | 25 | 41 | 22 | 28 | 22 | 13 | 17 | 26 | 18 | 11 | 8 | 13 | 2 | 1 | 1 | |
| | | 1 | | 1 | | 6 | 5 | 4 | 10 | 10 | 11 | 1 | 1 | 6 | 1 | | | 4 | | | | | |

2 own-goals

| | | | | | | | | | | | | | | | | | | | | | | | |
|---|---|---|---|---|---|---|---|---|---|---|---|---|---|---|---|---|---|---|---|---|---|---|---|
| | 2 | | | 5 | | 7 | 10 | | 8 | 11 | | 3 | 9 | | 4 | 6 | | | | | | | 3 |
| | 2 | | | 5 | | 7 | 10 | | 8 | 11 | | 3 | 9 | | 4 | 6 | | | | | | | R |
| | 2 | | | 2 | | 2 | 2 | | 2 | 2 | | 2 | 2 | | 2 | 2 | | | | | | | |
| | | | | | | | | | 1 | | | | 1 | | | | | | | | | | |

# 1952-53

| | P | W | D | L | F | A | Pts |
|---|---|---|---|---|---|---|---|
| Arsenal | 42 | 21 | 12 | 9 | 97 | 64 | 54 |
| Preston N.E. | 42 | 21 | 12 | 9 | 85 | 60 | 54 |
| Wolves | 42 | 19 | 13 | 10 | 86 | 63 | 51 |
| W.B.A. | 42 | 21 | 8 | 13 | 66 | 60 | 50 |
| Charlton A | 42 | 19 | 11 | 12 | 77 | 63 | 49 |
| Burnley | 42 | 18 | 12 | 12 | 67 | 52 | 48 |
| Blackpool | 42 | 19 | 9 | 14 | 71 | 70 | 47 |
| Manchester U | 42 | 18 | 10 | 14 | 69 | 72 | 46 |
| Sunderland | 42 | 15 | 13 | 14 | 68 | 82 | 43 |
| Tottenham H | 42 | 15 | 11 | 16 | 78 | 69 | 41 |
| Aston Villa | 42 | 14 | 13 | 15 | 63 | 61 | 41 |
| Cardiff C | 42 | 14 | 12 | 16 | 54 | 46 | 40 |
| Middlesbrough | 42 | 14 | 11 | 17 | 70 | 77 | 39 |
| Bolton W | 42 | 15 | 9 | 18 | 61 | 69 | 39 |
| Portsmouth | 42 | 14 | 10 | 18 | 74 | 83 | 38 |
| Newcastle U | 42 | 14 | 9 | 19 | 59 | 70 | 37 |
| Liverpool | 42 | 14 | 8 | 20 | 61 | 82 | 36 |
| Sheffield W | 42 | 12 | 11 | 19 | 62 | 72 | 35 |
| Chelsea | 42 | 12 | 11 | 19 | 56 | 66 | 35 |
| Manchester C | 42 | 14 | 7 | 21 | 72 | 87 | 35 |
| Stoke C | 42 | 12 | 10 | 20 | 53 | 66 | 34 |
| Derby Co | 42 | 11 | 10 | 21 | 59 | 74 | 32 |

Manager: Stuart McMillan.
Leading scorer: Jack Lee, League 16, all matches 17.

- Jack Stamps scored his final goal for Derby in a victory over Stoke City at the Victoria Ground. It was his 100th League goal for the Rams and he is one of only seven players to achieve this for the club.
- Jimmy Dunn, an FA Cup winner with Wolverhampton Wanderers in 1949, was signed to add goals in the battle to stay up but was ruled out by a cartilage operation after only six appearances.
- Derby were soon in trouble, losing six of their first eight games, and were relegated after 20 seasons in the First Division, spanning World War Two. It remains their longest run in the top flight.

## Division One

| Match No. | Date | Venue | Opponents | Result | | Scorers | Atte. |
|---|---|---|---|---|---|---|---|
| 1 | Aug 23 | (a) | Bolton W | L | 0-2 | | 35 |
| 2 | 27 | (a) | Chelsea | D | 1-1 | Morris | 34 |
| 3 | 30 | (h) | Aston Villa | L | 0-1 | | 22 |
| 4 | Sep 3 | (h) | Chelsea | W | 3-2 | Lee, Straw, Parry | 15 |
| 5 | 6 | (a) | Sunderland | L | 1-2 | Hazledine | 40 |
| 6 | 10 | (h) | Manchester U | L | 2-3 | Harrison, Hazledine | 20 |
| 7 | 13 | (h) | Wolves | L | 2-3 | Hazledine 2 | 21 |
| 8 | 20 | (a) | Charlton A | L | 1-3 | Harrison | 26 |
| 9 | 27 | (h) | Arsenal | W | 2-0 | Straw, Stamps | 24 |
| 10 | Oct 4 | (a) | Burnley | W | 2-1 | Straw, Stamps | 26 |
| 11 | 11 | (h) | Tottenham H | D | 0-0 | | 27 |
| 12 | 18 | (a) | Sheffield W | L | 0-2 | | 51 |
| 13 | 25 | (h) | Cardiff C | D | 1-1 | Straw (pen) | 23 |
| 14 | Nov 1 | (a) | Newcastle U | L | 0-1 | | 44 |
| 15 | 8 | (h) | West Brom A | D | 1-1 | Powell | 26 |
| 16 | 15 | (a) | Middlesbrough | L | 0-1 | | 14 |
| 17 | 22 | (h) | Liverpool | W | 3-2 | McLaren 2, Dunn | 20 |
| 18 | 29 | (a) | Manchester C | L | 0-1 | | 23 |
| 19 | Dec 6 | (h) | Stoke C | W | 4-0 | Lee, Stamps, Dunn, Doyle (og) | 17 |
| 20 | 13 | (a) | Preston NE | L | 0-3 | | 19 |
| 21 | 20 | (h) | Bolton W | W | 4-3 | Lee 2, McLaren 2 | 12 |
| 22 | 26 | (h) | Portsmouth | W | 3-0 | Lee, Dunn, McLaren | 30 |
| 23 | 27 | (a) | Portsmouth | D | 2-2 | Lee 2 | 30 |
| 24 | Jan 1 | (a) | Manchester U | L | 0-1 | | 36 |
| 25 | 3 | (a) | Aston Villa | L | 0-3 | | 27 |
| 26 | 17 | (h) | Sunderland | W | 3-1 | Lee 2, Stamps | 21 |
| 27 | 24 | (a) | Wolves | L | 1-3 | Stamps (pen) | 29 |
| 28 | Feb 7 | (h) | Charlton A | D | 1-1 | Stamps | 18 |
| 29 | 18 | (a) | Arsenal | L | 2-6 | Harrison, McLaren | 32 |
| 30 | 21 | (h) | Burnley | L | 1-3 | Lee | 19 |
| 31 | Mar 7 | (h) | Sheffield W | W | 2-1 | Lee, Parry | 23 |
| 32 | 12 | (a) | Tottenham H | L | 2-5 | Hazledine, McLaren | 13 |
| 33 | 14 | (a) | Cardiff C | L | 0-2 | | 33 |
| 34 | 21 | (h) | Newcastle U | L | 0-2 | | 19 |
| 35 | 28 | (a) | West Brom A | D | 2-2 | Parry, Stamps | 17 |
| 36 | Apr 3 | (a) | Blackpool | L | 1-2 | McLaren | 27 |
| 37 | 4 | (h) | Middlesbrough | D | 3-3 | Hazledine, McLaren, Stamps | 17 |
| 38 | 6 | (h) | Blackpool | D | 1-1 | Lee | 24 |
| 39 | 11 | (a) | Liverpool | D | 1-1 | Lee | 34 |
| 40 | 18 | (h) | Manchester C | W | 5-0 | Lee 2, McLaren 2, Stamps | 15 |
| 41 | 25 | (a) | Stoke C | W | 2-1 | Lee, Stamps | 30 |
| 42 | 29 | (h) | Preston NE | L | 0-1 | | 31 |

FINAL LEAGUE POSITION: 22nd in Division One - Relegated

Appeara
G

## FA Cup

| | | | | | | | |
|---|---|---|---|---|---|---|---|
| 3 | Jan 10 | (h) | Chelsea | D | 4-4 | Lee, Parry, McLachlan, McLaren | 24 |
| R | 14 | (a) | Chelsea | L | 0-1* | | 38 |

*after extra-time

Appeara
G

| Middleton R | Mozley B | Barrowcliffe G | McLachlan S | Nielson N | Bell C | Harrison R | Morris J | Lee J | Hazledine D | McLaren H | Mays A | Straw R | Parry J | Patrick R | Parr J | Williams P | Powell T | Stamps J | Oliver K | Wilkins R | Dunn J | Musson W | Townsend W | Savin K | Wheatley S | Walker C | McQuillan D | Law C | |
|---|---|---|---|---|---|---|---|---|---|---|---|---|---|---|---|---|---|---|---|---|---|---|---|---|---|---|---|---|---|
| | 2 | 3 | 4 | 5 | 6 | 7 | 8 | 9 | 10 | 11 | | | | | | | | | | | | | | | | | | | 1 |
| | 2 | 3 | 4 | 5 | | 7 | 8 | 9 | 10 | 11 | 6 | | | | | | | | | | | | | | | | | | 2 |
| | 2 | 3 | 4 | 5 | | 7 | 8 | 9 | | 11 | 6 | 10 | | | | | | | | | | | | | | | | | 3 |
| | 2 | | | 5 | 3 | 7 | 4 | 10 | | 8 | 6 | 9 | 11 | | | | | | | | | | | | | | | | 4 |
| | | | 4 | 5 | 3 | 7 | | 10 | 8 | | 6 | 9 | 11 | 2 | | | | | | | | | | | | | | | 5 |
| | | | | 5 | 3 | 7 | 4 | 10 | 8 | | 6 | 9 | | | 2 | 11 | | | | | | | | | | | | | 6 |
| | 2 | 3 | | 5 | 4 | 7 | | 10 | 8 | | 6 | 9 | | | | 11 | | | | | | | | | | | | | 7 |
| | 2 | 3 | | 5 | 4 | 7 | | | 8 | | 6 | 9 | 11 | | | | 10 | | | | | | | | | | | | 8 |
| | 2 | 3 | | 5 | 4 | 7 | | | 8 | | 6 | 9 | | | | | 11 | 10 | | | | | | | | | | | 9 |
| | 2 | 3 | | 5 | 4 | 7 | | | 8 | | 6 | 9 | | | | | 11 | 10 | | | | | | | | | | | 10 |
| | 2 | 3 | | 5 | 4 | 7 | | | 8 | | 6 | 9 | | | | | 11 | 10 | | | | | | | | | | | 11 |
| | 2 | 3 | | 5 | 4 | 7 | | | 8 | | 6 | 9 | | | | | 11 | 10 | | | | | | | | | | | 12 |
| | 2 | 3 | | 5 | 4 | 7 | | | 8 | | 6 | 9 | | | | | 11 | 10 | | | | | | | | | | | 13 |
| | 2 | 3 | | 5 | 4 | 7 | | | | | 6 | 9 | 8 | | | | 11 | 10 | | | | | | | | | | | 14 |
| | 2 | 3 | | 9 | 4 | 7 | | | | | 6 | 8 | | | | | 11 | 10 | 5 | | | | | | | | | | 15 |
| | | 3 | | | 4 | 7 | | | | | 6 | | 8 | | 2 | | 11 | 10 | 5 | 9 | | | | | | | | | 16 |
| | | 3 | | 2 | 4 | 7 | | | | 11 | 6 | | 9 | | | | | 10 | 5 | | 8 | | | | | | | | 17 |
| | | 3 | 2 | | 4 | 7 | | | | 11 | 6 | | 9 | | | | | 10 | 5 | | 8 | | | | | | | | 18 |
| | 2 | 3 | | | 4 | 7 | | 9 | | 11 | 6 | | | | | | | 10 | 5 | | 8 | | | | | | | | 19 |
| | 2 | 3 | | | 4 | 7 | | 9 | | 11 | 6 | | | | | | | 10 | 5 | | 8 | | | | | | | | 20 |
| | 2 | 3 | | | 4 | | | 9 | | 11 | | | | | | | 7 | 10 | 5 | | 8 | 6 | | | | | | | 21 |
| | 2 | 3 | | | 4 | | | 9 | | 11 | | | | | | | 7 | 10 | 5 | | 8 | 6 | | | | | | | 22 |
| | 2 | 3 | | | 4 | | | 9 | | 11 | | | 8 | | | | 7 | 10 | 5 | | | 6 | | | | | | | 23 |
| | 2 | 3 | | | 4 | | | 9 | 8 | 11 | | | | | | | 7 | 10 | 5 | | | 6 | | | | | | | 24 |
| | 2 | 3 | 4 | | | | | 9 | 8 | 11 | | | | | | | 7 | 10 | 5 | | | 6 | | | | | | | 25 |
| | 2 | | 4 | | | | | 9 | 8 | 11 | | | | | | | | 10 | 5 | | | 6 | 1 | 3 | 7 | | | | 26 |
| | 2 | | 4 | | | | | | 8 | 11 | | | 9 | | | | | 10 | 5 | | | 6 | 1 | 3 | 7 | | | | 27 |
| | 2 | | 4 | | | | | 9 | 8 | 11 | | | | | | | | 10 | 5 | | | 6 | 1 | 3 | 7 | | | | 28 |
| | 2 | | | | | 7 | | 9 | | 11 | 4 | | | | | | 8 | 10 | 5 | | | 6 | | 3 | | | | | 29 |
| | 2 | | 4 | | | 7 | | 9 | | | | | 8 | | | | 11 | 10 | 5 | | | 6 | | 3 | | | | | 30 |
| | 2 | | 4 | 5 | | | | 9 | | 11 | 6 | | 8 | | | | 7 | 10 | | | | | | 3 | | | | | 31 |
| | 2 | | 4 | 5 | | | | 9 | 8 | 11 | 6 | 7 | | | | | | | 10 | | | | | 3 | | | | | 32 |
| | 2 | | | 5 | | | | 9 | 8 | 11 | 4 | 7 | 10 | | | | | | | | | | | 3 | | 6 | | | 33 |
| | 2 | | | 5 | | 7 | | 9 | 8 | 11 | 4 | | 10 | | | | | | | | | | | 3 | | 6 | | | 34 |
| | 2 | | | | | | | | 8 | 11 | 4 | | 7 | | | | | 10 | 5 | 9 | | | | 3 | | 6 | | | 35 |
| | 2 | | | | | | | | 8 | 11 | 4 | | 9 | | | | 7 | 10 | 5 | | | | | 3 | | 6 | | | 36 |
| | 2 | | | | | | | | 8 | 11 | 4 | | 9 | | | | 7 | 10 | 5 | | | | | 3 | | 6 | | | 37 |
| | 2 | | | | | | | 9 | 8 | 11 | 4 | | 10 | | | | | | 5 | | | | | 3 | | 6 | 7 | | 38 |
| | 2 | | | | | 7 | | 9 | | 11 | 4 | | | | | | 8 | 10 | 5 | | | 6 | | 3 | | | | | 39 |
| | 2 | | | | | | | 9 | | 7 | 4 | | | | | | 8 | 10 | 5 | | | 6 | | 3 | | | | 11 | 40 |
| | 2 | | | | | | | 9 | | 7 | 4 | | | | | | 8 | 10 | 5 | | | 6 | | 3 | | | | 11 | 41 |
| | 2 | | | | | | | 9 | | 7 | 4 | | | | | | 8 | 10 | 5 | | | 6 | | 3 | | | | 11 | 42 |
| 9 | 37 | 22 | 12 | 20 | 22 | 24 | 5 | 27 | 23 | 29 | 32 | 15 | 17 | 1 | 2 | 2 | 23 | 30 | 25 | 2 | 6 | 14 | 3 | 17 | 3 | 6 | 1 | 3 | |
| | | | | | | 3 | 1 | 16 | 6 | 11 | | 4 | 3 | | | | 1 | 10 | | | 3 | | | | | | | | |

1 own-goal

| Middleton R | Mozley B | Barrowcliffe G | McLachlan S | Nielson N | Bell C | Harrison R | Morris J | Lee J | Hazledine D | McLaren H | Mays A | Straw R | Parry J | Patrick R | Parr J | Williams P | Powell T | Stamps J | Oliver K | Wilkins R | Dunn J | Musson W | Townsend W | Savin K | Wheatley S | Walker C | McQuillan D | Law C | |
|---|---|---|---|---|---|---|---|---|---|---|---|---|---|---|---|---|---|---|---|---|---|---|---|---|---|---|---|---|---|
| | 2 | 3 | 4 | | | | | 9 | | 11 | | | 8 | | | | 7 | 10 | 5 | | | 6 | | | | | | | 3 |
| | 2 | 3 | 4 | | | 7 | | 9 | 8 | 11 | | | | | | | | 10 | 5 | | | 6 | 1 | | | | | | R |
| | 2 | 2 | 2 | | | 1 | | 2 | 1 | 2 | | | 1 | | | | 1 | 2 | 2 | | | 2 | 1 | | | | | | |
| | | | 1 | | | | | 1 | | 1 | | | 1 | | | | | | | | | | | | | | | | |

# 1953-54

| | P | W | D | L | F | A | Pts |
|---|---|---|---|---|---|---|---|
| Leicester C | 42 | 23 | 10 | 9 | 97 | 60 | 56 |
| Everton | 42 | 20 | 16 | 6 | 92 | 58 | 56 |
| Blackburn R | 42 | 23 | 9 | 10 | 86 | 50 | 55 |
| Nottingham F | 42 | 20 | 12 | 10 | 86 | 59 | 52 |
| Rotherham U | 42 | 21 | 7 | 14 | 80 | 67 | 49 |
| Luton T | 42 | 18 | 12 | 12 | 64 | 59 | 48 |
| Birmingham C | 42 | 18 | 11 | 13 | 78 | 58 | 47 |
| Fulham | 42 | 17 | 10 | 15 | 98 | 85 | 44 |
| Bristol R | 42 | 14 | 16 | 12 | 64 | 58 | 44 |
| Leeds U | 42 | 15 | 13 | 14 | 89 | 81 | 43 |
| Stoke C | 42 | 12 | 17 | 13 | 71 | 60 | 41 |
| Doncaster R | 42 | 16 | 9 | 17 | 59 | 63 | 41 |
| West Ham U | 42 | 15 | 9 | 18 | 67 | 69 | 39 |
| Notts Co | 42 | 13 | 13 | 16 | 54 | 74 | 39 |
| Hull C | 42 | 16 | 6 | 20 | 64 | 66 | 38 |
| Lincoln C | 42 | 14 | 9 | 19 | 65 | 83 | 37 |
| Bury | 42 | 11 | 14 | 17 | 54 | 72 | 36 |
| Derby Co | 42 | 12 | 11 | 19 | 64 | 82 | 35 |
| Plymouth A | 42 | 9 | 16 | 17 | 65 | 82 | 34 |
| Swansea T | 42 | 13 | 8 | 21 | 58 | 82 | 34 |
| Brentford | 42 | 10 | 11 | 21 | 40 | 78 | 31 |
| Oldham A | 42 | 8 | 9 | 25 | 40 | 89 | 25 |

Manager: Stuart McMillan until November, then Jack Barker.
Leading scorer: Hugh McLaren, League/all matches 11.

- As Derby continued to struggle, FA Cup-winning manager Stuart McMillan was dismissed in November after almost eight years in the job.
- Jack Barker, one of Derby's finest players of the 1930s, took over but could only delay the slide towards Division Three North.
- Brothers Don and Geoff Hazledine appeared during the season, although not in the same match. They were the first brothers to represent the Rams since before World War One.

## Division Two

| Match No. | Date | | Venue | Opponents | Result | | Scorers | Atte |
|---|---|---|---|---|---|---|---|---|
| 1 | Aug | 19 | (a) | Leicester C | D | 2-2 | Dunn, Lee | 35 |
| 2 | | 22 | (h) | Brentford | W | 4-1 | Lee 3, Powell | 18 |
| 3 | | 24 | (a) | Stoke C | D | 2-2 | Mays, Dunn | 23 |
| 4 | | 29 | (a) | Bristol R | L | 0-3 | | 20 |
| 5 | Sep | 2 | (h) | Stoke C | D | 1-1 | Dunn | 18 |
| 6 | | 5 | (h) | Lincoln C | W | 2-0 | Lee, Harrison | 21 |
| 7 | | 9 | (h) | Blackburn R | D | 2-2 | Nielson 2 | 15 |
| 8 | | 12 | (a) | Notts C | W | 1-0 | Nielson | 23 |
| 9 | | 19 | (h) | Hull C | W | 2-0 | Harrison, McLaren | 19 |
| 10 | | 26 | (a) | Everton | L | 2-3 | Nielson, McLaren | 54 |
| 11 | Oct | 3 | (h) | Oldham A | W | 3-1 | McLaren 2, Nielson | 18 |
| 12 | | 10 | (a) | Fulham | L | 2-5 | McLaren 2 | 25 |
| 13 | | 17 | (h) | West Ham U | W | 2-1 | McLaren, Powell | 17 |
| 14 | | 24 | (a) | Leeds U | L | 1-3 | Nielson | 26 |
| 15 | | 31 | (h) | Birmingham C | L | 2-4 | McLaren, Smith (og) | 18 |
| 16 | Nov | 7 | (a) | Nottingham F | L | 2-4 | McLaren, Wilkins | 31 |
| 17 | | 14 | (h) | Luton T | L | 1-2 | Wilkins | 15 |
| 18 | | 21 | (a) | Plymouth A | L | 2-3 | Dunn, Nielson (pen) | 19 |
| 19 | | 28 | (h) | Swansea T | W | 4-2 | Dunn 2, Harrison, Wilkins | 17 |
| 20 | Dec | 5 | (a) | Rotherham U | L | 2-5 | McLaren 2 | 14 |
| 21 | | 12 | (h) | Leicester C | W | 2-1 | Parry 2 | 28 |
| 22 | | 19 | (a) | Brentford | D | 0-0 | | 10 |
| 23 | | 25 | (a) | Bury | L | 0-4 | | 14 |
| 24 | | 26 | (h) | Bury | W | 3-1 | Powell, Lee, Parry | 17 |
| 25 | Jan | 1 | (a) | Blackburn R | W | 3-0 | Parry 2, Harrison | 33 |
| 26 | | 2 | (h) | Bristol R | L | 0-1 | | 16 |
| 27 | | 16 | (a) | Lincoln C | D | 2-2 | Powell, Law | 13 |
| 28 | | 23 | (h) | Notts C | D | 0-0 | | 18 |
| 29 | Feb | 6 | (a) | Hull C | L | 0-3 | | 23 |
| 30 | | 13 | (h) | Everton | L | 2-6 | Dunn 2 | 16 |
| 31 | | 20 | (a) | Oldham A | D | 0-0 | | 18 |
| 32 | | 27 | (h) | Fulham | D | 3-3 | Dunn 2, Straw | 13 |
| 33 | Mar | 6 | (a) | West Ham U | D | 0-0 | | 18 |
| 34 | | 13 | (h) | Leeds U | L | 0-2 | | 12 |
| 35 | | 20 | (a) | Birmingham C | L | 0-3 | | 18 |
| 36 | | 27 | (h) | Plymouth A | L | 1-4 | Straw | 9 |
| 37 | Apr | 3 | (a) | Swansea T | L | 1-2 | Parry | 11 |
| 38 | | 10 | (h) | Nottingham F | L | 1-2 | Powell | 21 |
| 39 | | 16 | (a) | Doncaster R | W | 3-1 | Law, Harrison, Wilkins | 11 |
| 40 | | 17 | (a) | Luton T | L | 1-2 | Bell | 12 |
| 41 | | 19 | (h) | Doncaster R | W | 2-0 | Barrowcliffe 2 | 14 |
| 42 | | 24 | (h) | Rotherham U | D | 1-1 | Lowell | 12 |

FINAL LEAGUE POSITION: 18th in Division Two

Appeara
G

## FA Cup

| | | | | | | | | |
|---|---|---|---|---|---|---|---|---|
| 3 | Jan | 9 | (h) | Preston NE | L | 0-2 | | 25 |

Appearar
G

| …dleton R | Mozley B | Bell C | Mays A | Oliver K | Musson W | Dunn J | Powell T | Lee J | Stamps J | Law C | Parry J | Barrowcliffe G | Walker C | Harrison R | Nielson N | McLaren H | Osman R | Hazledine D | Wilkins R | Savin K | Paul D | Patrick R | Davies G | Straw R | Hawden K | Hazledine G | McQuillan D | Webster T | Young R | Lowell E | |
|---|---|---|---|---|---|---|---|---|---|---|---|---|---|---|---|---|---|---|---|---|---|---|---|---|---|---|---|---|---|---|---|
| | 2 | 3 | 4 | 5 | 6 | 7 | 8 | 9 | 10 | 11 | | | | | | | | | | | | | | | | | | | | | 1 |
| | 2 | 3 | 4 | 5 | 6 | 7 | 8 | 9 | | 11 | 10 | | | | | | | | | | | | | | | | | | | | 2 |
| | 2 | 3 | 4 | 5 | 6 | 7 | 8 | 9 | | 11 | 10 | | | | | | | | | | | | | | | | | | | | 3 |
| | 2 | 3 | 4 | 5 | 6 | 7 | 8 | 9 | | 11 | 10 | | | | | | | | | | | | | | | | | | | | 4 |
| | 2 | 6 | 4 | 5 | | 8 | 7 | 9 | | 11 | 10 | 3 | | | | | | | | | | | | | | | | | | | 5 |
| | 2 | | 4 | 5 | | 8 | | 10 | | 11 | | 3 | 6 | 7 | 9 | | | | | | | | | | | | | | | | 6 |
| | 2 | | 4 | 5 | | 8 | | 10 | | 11 | | 3 | 6 | 7 | 9 | | | | | | | | | | | | | | | | 7 |
| | 2 | | 4 | 5 | | 8 | | 10 | | 11 | | 3 | 6 | 7 | 9 | | | | | | | | | | | | | | | | 8 |
| | 2 | | 4 | 5 | | | | 10 | | 11 | | 3 | 6 | 7 | 9 | 8 | | | | | | | | | | | | | | | 9 |
| | 2 | | 4 | 5 | | | | 10 | | 11 | | 3 | | 7 | 9 | 8 | 6 | | | | | | | | | | | | | | 10 |
| | 2 | | 4 | 5 | | | | 10 | | 11 | 7 | 3 | | | 9 | 8 | | 6 | | | | | | | | | | | | | 11 |
| | 2 | | 4 | 5 | | | | 10 | | 11 | 7 | 3 | | | | 8 | | 6 | 9 | | | | | | | | | | | | 12 |
| | 2 | 6 | 4 | 5 | | | 10 | 9 | | | 11 | | | 7 | | 8 | | | | 3 | | | | | | | | | | | 13 |
| | 2 | 6 | 4 | 5 | | | 10 | | | 11 | 7 | | | | 9 | 8 | | | | 3 | | | | | | | | | | | 14 |
| | 2 | | 4 | 5 | | 6 | 10 | | | 11 | 7 | | | | 9 | 8 | | | | 3 | | | | | | | | | | | 15 |
| | 2 | | 6 | 5 | | 10 | | | | 11 | 7 | | 4 | | | 8 | | | 9 | 3 | | | | | | | | | | | 16 |
| | | | 6 | 5 | | 10 | | | | 11 | 7 | | 4 | | | 8 | | | 9 | 3 | 1 | 2 | | | | | | | | | 17 |
| | 3 | 6 | 4 | | | 10 | 11 | | | | 7 | | | | 5 | 8 | | | 9 | | | 2 | | | | | | | | | 18 |
| | | 6 | 4 | | | 8 | 10 | | | | | 2 | | 7 | 5 | 11 | | | 9 | 3 | | | | | | | | | | | 19 |
| | | | 4 | | | 8 | 10 | | | | 9 | 2 | | 7 | 5 | 11 | | | | 3 | | | 6 | | | | | | | | 20 |
| | 2 | | 4 | | | 8 | 11 | | 10 | | 9 | 3 | | 7 | 5 | | | | | | | | 6 | | | | | | | | 21 |
| | 2 | | 4 | | | | 10 | | | 11 | 9 | 3 | | 7 | 5 | | | 8 | | | | | 6 | | | | | | | | 22 |
| | 2 | | 4 | | | | 8 | | | 11 | 9 | 3 | | 7 | 5 | 10 | | | | | | | 6 | | | | | | | | 23 |
| | 2 | | 4 | | | | 11 | 10 | | | 8 | 3 | 6 | 7 | 5 | | | | 9 | | | | | | | | | | | | 24 |
| | 2 | | 4 | | | | 11 | 10 | | | 8 | 3 | 6 | 7 | 5 | | | | | | | | | 9 | | | | | | | 25 |
| | 2 | | 4 | 6 | | | 11 | 10 | | | 8 | 3 | | 7 | 5 | | | | | | | | | 9 | | | | | | | 26 |
| | 2 | | 4 | | 6 | | 10 | | | 11 | 8 | 3 | | 7 | 5 | | | | 9 | | | | | | | | | | | | 27 |
| | 2 | | 4 | | 6 | 8 | 10 | | | 11 | 9 | 3 | | 7 | 5 | | | | | | | | | | | | | | | | 28 |
| | 2 | | 4 | | 6 | 8 | 10 | | | 11 | 9 | 3 | | 7 | 5 | | | | | | | | | | | | | | | | 29 |
| | 2 | | 4 | | 6 | 8 | 11 | 9 | | | 10 | 3 | | 7 | 5 | | | | | | | | | | | | | | | | 30 |
| | 2 | | 4 | | 6 | 8 | | 10 | | | 7 | 3 | | | 5 | | | | | | | | | | 9 | 11 | | | | | 31 |
| | 2 | | 4 | | 6 | 8 | 10 | | | 11 | | 3 | | | 5 | | | | | | | | | 9 | | | 7 | | | | 32 |
| | 2 | 5 | 4 | | | 8 | 10 | | | 11 | | 3 | 6 | | | | | | | | | | | 9 | | | 7 | | | | 33 |
| | 2 | 5 | 4 | | | 8 | 10 | | | 11 | | 3 | 6 | | | | | | | | | | | | 9 | | 7 | | | | 34 |
| | 2 | | 8 | 5 | 6 | 10 | 11 | | | | | 3 | 4 | | 9 | | | | | | | | | | | | 7 | | | | 35 |
| | 2 | | 4 | 5 | | 8 | 11 | 10 | | | 7 | 3 | 6 | | | | | | | | | | | 9 | | | | | | | 36 |
| | 2 | | 4 | 5 | 6 | 10 | 8 | | | 11 | 9 | 3 | | 7 | | | | | | | | | | | | | | 1 | | | 37 |
| | | 4 | | 5 | 6 | 10 | 8 | | | 11 | 9 | 2 | | 7 | | | | | | 3 | | | | | | | | 1 | | | 38 |
| | 2 | | 4 | | 6 | | 8 | | | 11 | 10 | 3 | | 7 | | | | | 9 | | | | | | | | | 1 | 5 | | 39 |
| | 2 | 6 | 4 | | | 10 | | | | 11 | 8 | 3 | | 7 | | | | | 9 | | | | | | | | | 1 | 5 | | 40 |
| | 2 | 8 | 4 | | 6 | | | | | 11 | 10 | 9 | | 7 | | | | | | 3 | | | | | | | | 1 | 5 | | 41 |
| | 2 | 8 | 4 | | 6 | | | | | 11 | | 9 | | 7 | | | | | | 3 | | | | | | | | 1 | 5 | 10 | 42 |
| 5 | 38 | 15 | 41 | 22 | 16 | 27 | 29 | 19 | 2 | 30 | 30 | 32 | 12 | 24 | 24 | 13 | 1 | 3 | 9 | 10 | 1 | 2 | 4 | 5 | 2 | 1 | 4 | 6 | 4 | 1 | |
| | | 1 | 1 | | | 10 | 5 | 6 | | 2 | 6 | 2 | | 5 | 7 | 11 | | | 4 | | | | | 2 | | | | | | 1 | |

1 own-goal

| …dleton R | Mozley B | Bell C | Mays A | Oliver K | Musson W | Dunn J | Powell T | Lee J | Stamps J | Law C | Parry J | Barrowcliffe G | Walker C | Harrison R | Nielson N | McLaren H | Osman R | Hazledine D | Wilkins R | Savin K | Paul D | Patrick R | Davies G | Straw R | Hawden K | Hazledine G | McQuillan D | Webster T | Young R | Lowell E | |
|---|---|---|---|---|---|---|---|---|---|---|---|---|---|---|---|---|---|---|---|---|---|---|---|---|---|---|---|---|---|---|---|
| | 2 | | 4 | | 6 | | | 9 | | | 8 | 3 | | 7 | 5 | 11 | | 10 | | | | | | | | | | | | | 3 |
| | 1 | | 1 | | 1 | | | 1 | | | 1 | 1 | | 1 | 1 | 1 | | 1 | | | | | | | | | | | | | |
| | | | | | | | | | | | | | | | | | | | | | | | | | | | | | | | |

# 1954-55

| | P | W | D | L | F | A | Pts |
|---|---|---|---|---|---|---|---|
| Birmingham C | 42 | 22 | 10 | 10 | 92 | 47 | 54 |
| Luton T | 42 | 23 | 8 | 11 | 88 | 53 | 54 |
| Rotherham U | 42 | 25 | 4 | 13 | 94 | 64 | 54 |
| Leeds U | 42 | 23 | 7 | 12 | 70 | 53 | 53 |
| Stoke C | 42 | 21 | 10 | 11 | 69 | 46 | 52 |
| Blackburn R | 42 | 22 | 6 | 14 | 114 | 79 | 50 |
| Notts Co | 42 | 21 | 6 | 15 | 74 | 71 | 48 |
| West Ham U | 42 | 18 | 10 | 14 | 74 | 70 | 46 |
| Bristol R | 42 | 19 | 7 | 16 | 75 | 70 | 45 |
| Swansea T | 42 | 17 | 9 | 16 | 86 | 83 | 43 |
| Liverpool | 42 | 16 | 10 | 16 | 92 | 96 | 42 |
| Middlesbrough | 42 | 18 | 6 | 18 | 73 | 82 | 42 |
| Bury | 42 | 15 | 11 | 16 | 77 | 72 | 41 |
| Fulham | 42 | 14 | 11 | 17 | 76 | 79 | 39 |
| Nottingham F | 42 | 16 | 7 | 19 | 58 | 62 | 39 |
| Lincoln C | 42 | 13 | 10 | 19 | 68 | 79 | 36 |
| Port Vale | 42 | 12 | 11 | 19 | 48 | 71 | 35 |
| Doncaster R | 42 | 14 | 7 | 21 | 58 | 95 | 35 |
| Hull C | 42 | 12 | 10 | 20 | 44 | 69 | 34 |
| Plymouth A | 42 | 12 | 7 | 23 | 57 | 82 | 31 |
| Ipswich T | 42 | 11 | 6 | 25 | 57 | 92 | 28 |
| Derby Co | 42 | 7 | 9 | 26 | 53 | 82 | 23 |

Manager: Jack Barker.
Leading scorers: Jimmy Dunn, Tommy Powell, League 8. Jimmy Dunn, Tommy Powell, Jesse Pye, all matches 8.

- Nine years after they won the FA Cup, Derby lost their status as full member of the Football League for the first time when they dropped into Division Three North.
- Reg Harrison was the last of the FA Cup winners to leave Derby, joining Boston United in July 1955. He returned to the Baseball Ground the following season in Boston's historic Cup victory.
- A 6–1 victory over Port Vale in February offered a spasm of hope with 15 games left but the Rams did not win again until their final match, when it was too late to matter. They lost 11 times in the next 14 outings.

## Division Two

| Match No. | Date | | Venue | Opponents | Result | | Scorers | Atter |
|---|---|---|---|---|---|---|---|---|
| 1 | Aug | 21 | (a) | Notts C | W | 3-2 | Barrowcliffe, Parry (pen), Dunn | 29 |
| 2 | | 25 | (h) | Fulham | L | 3-4 | Powell, Parry (pen), Dunn | 18 |
| 3 | | 28 | (h) | Liverpool | W | 3-2 | Barrowcliffe, Powell, Dunn | 18 |
| 4 | Sep | 1 | (a) | Fulham | L | 0-2 | | 26 |
| 5 | | 4 | (a) | Bristol R | L | 1-4 | Parry (pen) | 23 |
| 6 | | 8 | (h) | Blackburn R | L | 0-3 | | 15 |
| 7 | | 11 | (h) | Plymouth A | D | 2-2 | Parry, Powell | 12 |
| 8 | | 13 | (a) | Blackburn R | L | 2-5 | Powell, Dunn | 24 |
| 9 | | 18 | (a) | Port Vale | L | 0-3 | | 22 |
| 10 | | 25 | (h) | Doncaster R | W | 5-0 | Dunn 2, Parry (pen), Powell, Bell | 14 |
| 11 | Oct | 2 | (a) | Luton T | L | 0-2 | | 17 |
| 12 | | 9 | (h) | Leeds U | L | 2-4 | Upton, R.Harrison | 20 |
| 13 | | 16 | (a) | Bury | D | 2-2 | Dunn, Imlach | 13 |
| 14 | | 23 | (h) | Middlesbrough | L | 1-2 | Pye | 15 |
| 15 | | 30 | (a) | Birmingham C | D | 1-1 | McQuillan | 20 |
| 16 | Nov | 6 | (h) | Ipswich T | W | 2-0 | Upton, Powell | 11 |
| 17 | | 13 | (a) | Nottingham F | L | 0-3 | | 16 |
| 18 | | 20 | (h) | Rotherham U | L | 2-3 | Barrowcliffe 2 | 15 |
| 19 | | 27 | (a) | Stoke C | L | 1-3 | Pye | 18 |
| 20 | Dec | 4 | (h) | Lincoln C | W | 3-0 | Pye 3 | 10 |
| 21 | | 11 | (a) | Hull C | D | 1-1 | Pye | 16 |
| 22 | | 18 | (h) | Notts C | D | 1-1 | Powell | 15 |
| 23 | | 25 | (a) | West Ham U | L | 0-1 | | 23 |
| 24 | | 27 | (h) | West Ham U | D | 0-0 | | 20 |
| 25 | Jan | 1 | (a) | Liverpool | L | 0-2 | | 34 |
| 26 | | 22 | (a) | Plymouth | L | 0-1 | | 13 |
| 27 | Feb | 5 | (h) | Port Vale | W | 6-1 | Buchanan 2, Parry, Dunn, Imlach, Hayward (og) | 19 |
| 28 | | 12 | (a) | Doncaster R | L | 0-2 | | 9 |
| 29 | | 19 | (h) | Bristol R | D | 1-1 | Powell | 11 |
| 30 | | 26 | (a) | Leeds U | L | 0-1 | | 16 |
| 31 | Mar | 2 | (h) | Luton T | D | 0-0 | | 5 |
| 32 | | 5 | (h) | Bury | L | 2-3 | Parry (pen), Pye | 14 |
| 33 | | 12 | (a) | Middlesbrough | L | 1-3 | Buchanan | 20 |
| 34 | | 19 | (h) | Birmingham C | D | 0-0 | | 19 |
| 35 | | 26 | (a) | Ipswich T | L | 1-2 | K.Harrison | 13 |
| 36 | Apr | 2 | (h) | Nottingham F | L | 1-2 | Young | 18 |
| 37 | | 8 | (h) | Swansea T | L | 1-4 | Barrowcliffe | 14 |
| 38 | | 9 | (a) | Rotherham U | L | 1-2 | Barrowcliffe | 14 |
| 39 | | 11 | (a) | Swansea T | L | 0-3 | | 18 |
| 40 | | 16 | (h) | Stoke C | L | 1-2 | K.Harrison | 12 |
| 41 | | 23 | (a) | Lincoln C | L | 0-3 | | 9 |
| 42 | | 30 | (h) | Hull C | W | 3-0 | Ackerman 2, K.Harrison | 7 |

FINAL LEAGUE POSITION: 22nd in Division Two - Relegated

Appearar

G

## FA Cup

| | | | | | | | | |
|---|---|---|---|---|---|---|---|---|
| 3 | Jan | 8 | (h) | Manchester C | L | 1-3 | Pye | 23 |

Appearar

G

| | unter G | Patrick R | Barrowcliffe G | Mays A | Young R | Upton F | Cresswell P | Powell T | Parry J | Dunn J | Imlach S | Bell C | Harrison R | McQuillan D | Walker C | Oliver K | Straw R | Mozley B | Savin K | Davies G | Pye J | Webster T | Moran J | Clark B | Buchanan J | Harrison K | Ackerman A | Osman R |
|---|---|---|---|---|---|---|---|---|---|---|---|---|---|---|---|---|---|---|---|---|---|---|---|---|---|---|---|---|
| 1 | | 2 | 3 | 4 | 5 | 6 | 7 | 8 | 9 | 10 | 11 | | | | | | | | | | | | | | | | | |
| 2 | | 2 | 9 | | 5 | 6 | | 8 | 4 | 10 | 11 | 3 | 7 | | | | | | | | | | | | | | | |
| 3 | | 2 | 9 | | 5 | 6 | | 8 | 4 | 10 | 11 | 3 | 7 | | | | | | | | | | | | | | | |
| 4 | | 2 | 9 | | 5 | 6 | | 8 | 4 | | 11 | 3 | | 7 | 10 | | | | | | | | | | | | | |
| 5 | | 2 | | | | 6 | | 8 | 4 | | 11 | 3 | 7 | | 10 | 5 | 9 | | | | | | | | | | | |
| 6 | | | 9 | | | 6 | | 10 | 4 | | 11 | 8 | 7 | | | 5 | | 2 | 3 | | | | | | | | | |
| 7 | | | 9 | | | 6 | | 8 | 7 | 10 | | 5 | | 11 | | | | 2 | 3 | 4 | | | | | | | | |
| 8 | | | 9 | | | 6 | | 8 | 7 | 10 | | 5 | | 11 | | | | 2 | 3 | 4 | | | | | | | | |
| 9 | | | 9 | | 5 | 6 | | 8 | 4 | 10 | 11 | | | 7 | | | | 2 | 3 | | | | | | | | | |
| 10 | | | 3 | | 5 | 6 | | 8 | 4 | 10 | 11 | 9 | 7 | | | | | 2 | | | | | | | | | | |
| 11 | | | 3 | 4 | 5 | 6 | | 8 | | 10 | 11 | 9 | 7 | | | | | 2 | | | | | | | | | | |
| 12 | | | 3 | | 5 | 6 | | 8 | 4 | 10 | 11 | | 7 | | | | | 2 | | | 9 | | | | | | | |
| 13 | | | 3 | | 5 | 6 | | 8 | 4 | 10 | 11 | 7 | | | | | | 2 | | | 9 | | | | | | | |
| 14 | | | 3 | | 5 | 6 | | 8 | 4 | 10 | 11 | 7 | | | | | | 2 | | | 9 | | | | | | | |
| 15 | | | | | 5 | 6 | | 10 | 8 | | 11 | 4 | | 7 | | | | 2 | 3 | | 9 | 1 | | | | | | |
| 16 | | | | | 5 | 6 | | 10 | 8 | | 11 | 4 | | 7 | | | | 2 | 3 | | 9 | 1 | | | | | | |
| 17 | | | | | 5 | 6 | | 10 | | 8 | 11 | 4 | | 7 | | | | 2 | 3 | | 9 | 1 | | | | | | |
| 18 | | | 8 | 4 | 5 | 6 | | | | | 11 | | | 7 | | | | 2 | 3 | | 9 | 1 | 10 | | | | | |
| 19 | | 3 | 8 | 4 | 5 | 6 | | | | | 11 | | 7 | | | | | 2 | | | 9 | 1 | 10 | | | | | |
| 20 | | 3 | | 4 | 5 | 6 | | 10 | | 7 | 11 | 8 | | | | | | 2 | | | 9 | 1 | | | | | | |
| 21 | | 3 | | 4 | 5 | 6 | | 10 | 11 | 7 | | 8 | | | | | | 2 | | | 9 | 1 | | | | | | |
| 22 | | 3 | | 4 | 5 | 6 | | 10 | | 7 | 11 | 8 | | | | | | 2 | | | 9 | 1 | | | | | | |
| 23 | | 2 | | 4 | 5 | 6 | | 10 | 8 | 7 | 11 | | | | | | | | 3 | | 9 | 1 | | | | | | |
| 24 | | 2 | | 4 | 5 | 6 | | 10 | | 7 | 11 | 8 | | | | | | | 3 | | 9 | 1 | | | | | | |
| 25 | | 2 | | | 5 | 6 | | 10 | 8 | 7 | 11 | | | | | | | | 3 | | 9 | 1 | | 4 | | | | |
| 26 | | 2 | | | 5 | 6 | | 10 | | 8 | 11 | | | 7 | | | | | 3 | | 9 | 1 | | 4 | | | | |
| 27 | | 2 | | | | 6 | | | 10 | 8 | 11 | | | | | 5 | | | 3 | | 9 | 1 | | 4 | 7 | | | |
| 28 | | 2 | | | 5 | 6 | | | 10 | 8 | 11 | | | | | | | | 3 | | 9 | 1 | | 4 | 7 | | | |
| 29 | | 2 | | | 5 | 6 | | 10 | | | 11 | | | 8 | | | | | 3 | | 9 | 1 | | 4 | 7 | | | |
| 30 | | 2 | 9 | | | 6 | | 10 | | | 11 | | | 8 | | 5 | | | 3 | | | 1 | | 4 | 7 | | | |
| 31 | | 2 | 3 | | | 6 | | 10 | 8 | | 11 | | | | | 5 | | | | | 9 | 1 | | 4 | 7 | | | |
| 32 | | 2 | 3 | | | 6 | | 10 | 8 | | 11 | | | | | 5 | | | | | 9 | 1 | | 4 | 7 | | | |
| 33 | | 2 | 3 | | | 6 | | 10 | 8 | | 11 | | | | | 5 | | | | | 9 | 1 | | 4 | 7 | | | |
| 34 | | 2 | 3 | | 5 | 6 | | 4 | | | 11 | | | | | | | | | | 9 | 1 | | | 8 | 7 | 10 | |
| 35 | | 2 | 3 | | 5 | 6 | | 4 | | | 11 | | | | | | | | | | 9 | 1 | | | 8 | 7 | 10 | |
| 36 | | 2 | 3 | | 5 | 6 | | 4 | 8 | | 11 | | | | | | | | | | | 1 | | | 9 | 7 | 10 | |
| 37 | | 2 | 9 | | 5 | 3 | | 6 | 4 | | 11 | | | | | | | | | | | 1 | | | 8 | 7 | 10 | |
| 38 | | 2 | 9 | | 6 | 3 | | 10 | 8 | 11 | | | | | | 5 | | | | 4 | | | | | | 7 | | |
| 39 | | 2 | 9 | | 6 | 3 | | | 8 | 10 | | | 7 | | | 5 | | | | 4 | | | | | | 11 | | |
| 40 | | 2 | 9 | | 5 | 3 | | | 4 | | | | 7 | | | | | | | 6 | 8 | | | | | 11 | 10 | |
| 41 | | 2 | 3 | | 5 | 6 | | | 8 | 10 | 11 | | | | | | | | | 4 | | | | | | 7 | 9 | |
| 42 | | 2 | 3 | | 5 | | | | 8 | | 11 | | | | | | | | | 6 | 9 | | | | | 7 | 10 | 4 |
| | 9 | 29 | 28 | 9 | 33 | 41 | 1 | 34 | 30 | 24 | 36 | 18 | 10 | 11 | 2 | 9 | 1 | 17 | 16 | 7 | 25 | 23 | 2 | 9 | 11 | 9 | 7 | 1 |
| | | | 6 | | 1 | 2 | | 8 | 7 | 8 | 2 | 1 | 1 | 1 | | | | | | | 7 | | | | 3 | 3 | 2 | |

1 own-goal

| | unter G | Patrick R | Barrowcliffe G | Mays A | Young R | Upton F | Cresswell P | Powell T | Parry J | Dunn J | Imlach S | Bell C | Harrison R | McQuillan D | Walker C | Oliver K | Straw R | Mozley B | Savin K | Davies G | Pye J | Webster T | Moran J | Clark B | Buchanan J | Harrison K | Ackerman A | Osman R |
|---|---|---|---|---|---|---|---|---|---|---|---|---|---|---|---|---|---|---|---|---|---|---|---|---|---|---|---|---|
| 3 | | 2 | | | 5 | 6 | | 10 | 8 | 7 | 11 | | | | | | | | 3 | | 9 | 1 | | 4 | | | | |
| | | 1 | | | 1 | 1 | | 1 | 1 | 1 | 1 | | | | | | | | 1 | | 1 | 1 | | 1 | | | | |
| | | | | | | | | | | | | | | | | | | | | | 1 | | | | | | | |

# 1955-56

| | P | W | D | L | F | A | Pts |
|---|---|---|---|---|---|---|---|
| Grimsby T | 46 | 31 | 6 | 9 | 76 | 29 | 68 |
| Derby Co | 46 | 28 | 7 | 11 | 110 | 55 | 63 |
| Accrington S | 46 | 25 | 9 | 12 | 92 | 57 | 59 |
| Hartlepools U | 46 | 26 | 5 | 15 | 81 | 60 | 57 |
| Southport | 46 | 23 | 11 | 12 | 66 | 53 | 57 |
| Chesterfield | 46 | 25 | 4 | 17 | 94 | 66 | 54 |
| Stockport Co | 46 | 21 | 9 | 16 | 90 | 61 | 51 |
| Bradford C | 46 | 18 | 13 | 15 | 78 | 64 | 49 |
| Scunthorpe U | 46 | 20 | 8 | 18 | 75 | 63 | 48 |
| Workington | 46 | 19 | 9 | 18 | 75 | 63 | 47 |
| York C | 46 | 19 | 9 | 18 | 85 | 72 | 47 |
| Rochdale | 46 | 17 | 13 | 16 | 66 | 84 | 47 |
| Gateshead | 46 | 17 | 11 | 18 | 77 | 84 | 45 |
| Wrexham | 46 | 16 | 10 | 20 | 66 | 73 | 42 |
| Darlington | 46 | 16 | 9 | 21 | 60 | 73 | 41 |
| Tranmere R | 46 | 16 | 9 | 21 | 59 | 84 | 41 |
| Chester | 46 | 13 | 14 | 19 | 52 | 82 | 40 |
| Mansfield T | 46 | 14 | 11 | 21 | 84 | 81 | 39 |
| Halifax T | 46 | 14 | 11 | 21 | 66 | 76 | 39 |
| Oldham A | 46 | 10 | 18 | 18 | 76 | 86 | 38 |
| Carlisle U | 46 | 15 | 8 | 23 | 71 | 95 | 38 |
| Barrow | 46 | 12 | 9 | 25 | 61 | 83 | 33 |
| Bradford P.A. | 46 | 13 | 7 | 26 | 61 | 122 | 33 |
| Crewe A | 46 | 9 | 10 | 27 | 50 | 105 | 28 |

Manager: Harry Storer.
Leading scorer: Jack Parry, League 24, all matches 27.

- Harry Storer was the third successive former Derby player to become manager. He scored 63 goals in 274 Rams appearances, won two England caps and was one of Derbyshire's finest opening batsmen.
- Storer's first act was to sign Paddy Ryan, an FA Cup winner with West Bromwich Albion in 1954, for £3,000. Ryan supplied the leadership Storer wanted, on and off the field.
- For the first time, Derby scored a century of League goals, their 110 easily beating the top-flight club record of 96, twice achieved under George Jobey.
- But there was a major FA Cup shock for them when Boston United, from the Midland League, won 6–1 at the Baseball Ground. Boston included six former Derby players, including Reg Harrison, a Cup winner in 1946, and Geoff Hazledine, who scored a hat-trick.

## Division Three North

| Match No. | Date | | Venue | Opponents | Result | | Scorers | Atter |
|---|---|---|---|---|---|---|---|---|
| 1 | Aug | 20 | (h) | Mansfield T | W | 4-0 | Ackerman 2, Mays, Pye | 24 |
| 2 | | 23 | (a) | Southport | W | 5-2 | Ackerman 2, Parry, Pye, Powell | 8 |
| 3 | | 27 | (a) | Wrexham | L | 1-3 | Parry (pen) | 16 |
| 4 | | 31 | (h) | Southport | W | 2-0 | Ackerman, Parkinson (og) | 17 |
| 5 | Sep | 3 | (h) | Halifax T | W | 4-1 | Parry 2, Buchanan 2 | 18 |
| 6 | | 5 | (a) | Crewe A | L | 1-2 | Cooke (og) | 8 |
| 7 | | 10 | (a) | Bradford C | L | 1-2 | Straw | 19 |
| 8 | | 14 | (h) | Crewe A | D | 3-3 | Ackerman 2, Parry | 14 |
| 9 | | 17 | (h) | Scunthorpe U | D | 2-2 | Parry, Pye | 18 |
| 10 | | 19 | (a) | Hartlepools U | L | 0-2 | | 9 |
| 11 | | 24 | (a) | Oldham A | D | 1-1 | Tate | 9 |
| 12 | | 28 | (h) | York C | W | 3-2 | Ackerman 2, Pye | 13 |
| 13 | Oct | 1 | (h) | Workington | D | 2-2 | Parry, Powell | 17 |
| 14 | | 8 | (h) | Chesterfield | W | 3-0 | Pye, Powell, Cresswell | 22 |
| 15 | | 15 | (a) | Gateshead | W | 4-2 | Parry, Pye, Powell, Buchanan | 6 |
| 16 | | 22 | (h) | Bradford PA | W | 4-0 | Parry 2, Mays, Buchanan | 17 |
| 17 | | 29 | (a) | Grimsby T | L | 1-2 | Powell | 19 |
| 18 | Nov | 5 | (h) | Carlisle U | W | 3-0 | Pye 2, Powell | 17 |
| 19 | | 12 | (a) | Chester | W | 5-2 | Mays 2, Parry, Pye, Todd | 10 |
| 20 | | 26 | (a) | Accrington S | L | 0-2 | | 10 |
| 21 | Dec | 3 | (h) | Darlington | W | 6-2 | Parry 3, Todd 2, Powell | 15 |
| 22 | | 17 | (a) | Mansfield T | D | 1-1 | Cresswell | 9, |
| 23 | | 24 | (h) | Wrexham | W | 2-0 | Parry 2 | 14 |
| 24 | | 26 | (a) | Stockport C | L | 1-2 | Straw | 11, |
| 25 | | 27 | (h) | Stockport C | W | 2-0 | Pye, Straw | 20 |
| 26 | | 31 | (a) | Halifax T | D | 2-2 | Ryan, Parry | 9, |
| 27 | Jan | 14 | (h) | Bradford C | W | 4-1 | Parry 2, Pye 2 | 15 |
| 28 | | 21 | (a) | Scunthorpe U | W | 2-0 | Parry, Upton | 10 |
| 29 | | 28 | (a) | Rochdale | W | 5-0 | Woodhead 2, Parry, Powell, Straw | 7 |
| 30 | Feb | 11 | (a) | Workington | W | 3-0 | Powell, Straw, Woodhead | 8 |
| 31 | | 18 | (a) | Chesterfield | L | 0-2 | | 22 |
| 32 | | 25 | (h) | Gateshead | W | 4-1 | Pye 2, Mays, Parry | 19, |
| 33 | Mar | 3 | (a) | Bradford PA | W | 4-2 | Ryan, Parry, Straw, Woodhead | 11 |
| 34 | | 7 | (h) | Barrow | W | 2-1 | Parry, Woodhead | 23 |
| 35 | | 10 | (h) | Grimsby T | L | 1-3 | Powell | 33 |
| 36 | | 17 | (a) | Barrow | W | 2-1 | Ryan, Woodhead | 6 |
| 37 | | 19 | (h) | Oldham A | W | 2-0 | Straw 2 | 19 |
| 38 | | 24 | (h) | Chester | W | 3-1 | Pye 2, Straw | 16, |
| 39 | | 30 | (a) | Tranmere R | W | 1-0 | Barrowcliffe (pen) | 13, |
| 40 | | 31 | (a) | Carlisle U | W | 3-0 | Ryan, Powell, Straw | 7, |
| 41 | Apr | 2 | (h) | Tranmere R | D | 0-0 | | 24, |
| 42 | | 7 | (h) | Accrington S | W | 6-2 | Ackerman 4, Straw 2 | 22, |
| 43 | | 14 | (a) | Darlington | L | 0-1 | | 4, |
| 44 | | 21 | (h) | Rochdale | W | 2-0 | Ackerman, Straw | 13, |
| 45 | | 23 | (a) | York C | L | 0-1 | | 14, |
| 46 | | 28 | (h) | Hartlepools U | W | 3-2 | Ackerman, Powell, Straw | 10, |

FINAL LEAGUE POSITION: 2nd in Division Three North

Appearar

G

## FA Cup

| | | | | | | | | |
|---|---|---|---|---|---|---|---|---|
| 1 | Nov | 19 | (a) | Crook Town | D | 2-2 | Straw, Parry | 9, |
| R | | 23 | (h) | Crook Town | W | 5-1 | Straw 2, Parry 2, Pye | 14, |
| 2 | Dec | 10 | (h) | Boston U | L | 1-6 | Pye (pen) | 23, |

Appearar

G

| | ...ster T | Barrowcliffe G | Savin K | Mays A | McDonnell M | Ryan R | Harrison K | Parry J | Ackerman A | Pye J | Powell T | Upton F | White W | Buchanan J | Place C | Paul D | Straw R | Millin A | Patrick R | McQuillan D | Davies G | Tate G | Young R | Cresswell P | Oliver K | Todd T | Woodhead D | Martin R | Clark B |
|---|---|---|---|---|---|---|---|---|---|---|---|---|---|---|---|---|---|---|---|---|---|---|---|---|---|---|---|---|---|
| 1 | | 2 | 3 | 4 | 5 | 6 | 7 | 8 | 9 | 10 | 11 | | | | | | | | | | | | | | | | | | |
| 2 | | 2 | 3 | 4 | 5 | 6 | 7 | 8 | 9 | 10 | 11 | | | | | | | | | | | | | | | | | | |
| 3 | | 2 | 3 | 4 | 5 | 10 | 7 | 8 | 9 | | 11 | 6 | | | | | | | | | | | | | | | | | |
| 4 | | 2 | 3 | 4 | 5 | 6 | | 8 | 9 | 10 | 11 | | 1 | 7 | | | | | | | | | | | | | | | |
| 5 | | 2 | 3 | 4 | 5 | 6 | | 8 | 9 | 10 | | | 1 | 7 | 11 | | | | | | | | | | | | | | |
| 6 | | 2 | 3 | 4 | 5 | 6 | | 8 | 9 | 10 | | | 1 | 7 | 11 | | | | | | | | | | | | | | |
| 7 | | 2 | 3 | 4 | 5 | 6 | | 8 | | 10 | | | | 7 | | 1 | 9 | 11 | | | | | | | | | | | |
| 8 | | 3 | | 4 | 5 | 6 | 11 | 8 | 9 | 10 | | | | 7 | | | | | 2 | | | | | | | | | | |
| 9 | | | | 4 | 5 | 6 | | 8 | 9 | 10 | | 3 | | 7 | | | | | 2 | 11 | | | | | | | | | |
| 10 | | | | 4 | 5 | 3 | | 8 | 10 | 9 | 11 | | | 7 | | | | | 2 | | 6 | | | | | | | | |
| 11 | | 2 | | 4 | 5 | 6 | | 8 | | 9 | 11 | 3 | | 10 | | | | | | | | 7 | | | | | | | |
| 12 | | 2 | | 4 | 5 | 6 | | 8 | 9 | 10 | 11 | | | 7 | | | | | | | 3 | | | | | | | | |
| 13 | | 2 | | 4 | | 6 | | 8 | 9 | | 10 | 3 | | 7 | | | | | | 11 | | | 5 | | | | | | |
| 14 | | 2 | | 4 | 5 | 6 | | 8 | 9 | 10 | 11 | 3 | | | | | | | | | | | | 7 | | | | | |
| 15 | | 2 | | 4 | | 6 | | 8 | | 9 | 11 | 3 | | 10 | | | | | | | | | | 7 | 5 | | | | |
| 16 | | 2 | | 4 | 5 | 6 | | 8 | | 10 | 11 | 3 | | 9 | | | | | | | | | | 7 | | | | | |
| 17 | | 2 | | 4 | 5 | 6 | | 8 | | 9 | 11 | 3 | | 10 | | | | | | | | | | 7 | | | | | |
| 18 | | 2 | | 4 | 5 | 6 | 7 | 8 | 9 | 10 | 11 | 3 | | | | | | | | | | | | | | | | | |
| 19 | | 2 | | 4 | 5 | 6 | 7 | 8 | | 10 | 11 | 3 | | | | | | | | | | | | | | 9 | | | |
| 20 | | 2 | | 4 | 5 | | | 8 | | 10 | 11 | 3 | | | | | | | | | 6 | | | 7 | | 9 | | | |
| 21 | | 2 | | 4 | 5 | 6 | | 8 | | 10 | 11 | 3 | | | | | | | | | | | | 7 | | 9 | | | |
| 22 | | | 3 | 4 | | 6 | | 8 | | 10 | 11 | | | | | | | | 2 | | | | 5 | 7 | | 9 | | | |
| 23 | | | 3 | 4 | | 6 | | 8 | | 10 | 11 | | | | | | 9 | | 2 | | | | 5 | 7 | | | | | |
| 24 | | | 3 | 4 | | 10 | | 8 | | 11 | | 6 | | | | | 9 | | 2 | | | | 5 | 7 | | | | | |
| 25 | | 11 | 3 | 4 | | 8 | | | | 10 | | 6 | | | | | 9 | | 2 | | | | | 7 | 5 | | | | |
| 26 | | | 3 | 4 | | 8 | | 7 | | 10 | 11 | 6 | | | | | 9 | | 2 | | | | 5 | | | | | | |
| 27 | | | 3 | 4 | | 6 | | 8 | | 10 | 7 | | | | | | 9 | | 2 | | | | | | 5 | | 11 | | |
| 28 | | | 3 | 4 | | 10 | | 8 | | | 7 | 6 | | | | | 9 | | 2 | | | | | | 5 | | 11 | | |
| 29 | | | 3 | 4 | | 10 | | 8 | | | 7 | 6 | | | | | 9 | | 2 | | | | | | 5 | | 11 | | |
| 30 | | | 3 | 4 | | 10 | | 8 | | | 7 | 6 | | | | | 9 | | 2 | | | | | | 5 | | 11 | | |
| 31 | | | 3 | 4 | | 10 | | 8 | | | 7 | 6 | | | | | 9 | | 2 | | | | | | 5 | | 11 | | |
| 32 | | | 3 | 4 | | 6 | | 8 | 9 | 10 | 7 | | | | | | | | 2 | | | | | | 5 | | 11 | | |
| 33 | | | 3 | 4 | | 10 | | 8 | | | 7 | 6 | | | | | 9 | | 2 | | | | | | 5 | | 11 | | |
| 34 | | | 3 | 4 | | 10 | | 8 | | | 7 | 6 | | | | | 9 | | 2 | | | | | | 5 | | 11 | | |
| 35 | | | 3 | 4 | | 10 | | 8 | | 9 | 7 | 6 | | | | | | | 2 | | | | | | 5 | | 11 | | |
| 36 | | 2 | | 4 | | 8 | | | | | 10 | 6 | | 7 | | | 9 | | | | | | | | 5 | | 11 | 3 | |
| 37 | | 2 | | 4 | | 10 | | | | 8 | 7 | 6 | | | | | 9 | | | | | | | | 5 | | 11 | 3 | |
| 38 | | 2 | | | | 10 | | | | 8 | 7 | 6 | | | | | 9 | | | | | | | | 5 | | 11 | 3 | 4 |
| 39 | | 2 | | 4 | | 8 | | | | | 10 | 6 | | 7 | | | 9 | | | | | | | | 5 | | 11 | 3 | |
| 40 | | 3 | | 4 | 2 | 10 | | | | 8 | 7 | 6 | | | | | 9 | | | | | | | | 5 | | 11 | | |
| 41 | | 3 | | 4 | 2 | 10 | | | | 8 | 7 | 6 | | | | | 9 | | | | | | | | 5 | | 11 | | |
| 42 | | 3 | | 4 | 2 | 8 | | | 10 | | 7 | 6 | | | | | 9 | | | | | | | | 5 | | 11 | | |
| 43 | | 2 | | 4 | | 8 | | | 10 | | 7 | 6 | | | | | 9 | | | | | | | | 5 | | 11 | 3 | |
| 44 | | 2 | | 4 | | 8 | | | 10 | | 7 | 6 | | | | | 9 | | | | | | | | 5 | | 11 | 3 | |
| 45 | | 2 | | 4 | | 10 | | | 8 | | 7 | 6 | | | | | 9 | | | | | | | | 5 | | 11 | 3 | |
| 46 | | 2 | | 4 | | 10 | | | 8 | | 7 | 6 | | | | | 9 | | | | | | | | 5 | | 11 | 3 | |
| | 2 | 31 | 21 | 45 | 22 | 45 | 6 | 34 | 19 | 31 | 39 | 33 | 3 | 15 | 2 | 1 | 23 | 1 | 17 | 2 | 3 | 1 | 5 | 10 | 22 | 4 | 20 | 8 | 1 |
| | | 1 | | 5 | | 4 | | 24 | 15 | 16 | 12 | 1 | | 4 | | | 14 | | | | | 1 | | 2 | | 3 | 6 | | |

2 own-goals

| | ...ster T | Barrowcliffe G | Savin K | Mays A | McDonnell M | Ryan R | Harrison K | Parry J | Ackerman A | Pye J | Powell T | Upton F | White W | Buchanan J | Place C | Paul D | Straw R | Millin A | Patrick R | McQuillan D | Davies G | Tate G | Young R | Cresswell P | Oliver K | Todd T | Woodhead D | Martin R | Clark B |
|---|---|---|---|---|---|---|---|---|---|---|---|---|---|---|---|---|---|---|---|---|---|---|---|---|---|---|---|---|---|
| 1 | | 2 | | 4 | 5 | 6 | 7 | 8 | | 10 | 11 | 3 | | | | | 9 | | | | | | | | | | | | |
| R | | 2 | | 4 | 5 | 6 | | 8 | | 10 | 11 | 3 | | | | | 9 | | | | | | | 7 | | | | | |
| 2 | | 2 | | 4 | 5 | 6 | | 8 | | 10 | 11 | 3 | | | | | | | | | | | | 7 | | 9 | | | |
| | | 3 | | 3 | 3 | 3 | 1 | 3 | | 3 | 3 | 3 | | | | | 2 | | | | | | | 2 | | 1 | | | |
| | | | | | | | | 3 | | 2 | | | | | | | 3 | | | | | | | | | | | | |

# 1956-57

| | P | W | D | L | F | A | Pts |
|---|---|---|---|---|---|---|---|
| Derby Co | 46 | 26 | 11 | 9 | 111 | 53 | 63 |
| Hartlepools U | 46 | 25 | 9 | 12 | 90 | 63 | 59 |
| Accrington S | 46 | 25 | 8 | 13 | 95 | 64 | 58 |
| Workington | 46 | 24 | 10 | 12 | 93 | 63 | 58 |
| Stockport Co | 46 | 23 | 8 | 15 | 91 | 75 | 54 |
| Chesterfield | 46 | 22 | 9 | 15 | 96 | 79 | 53 |
| York C | 46 | 21 | 10 | 15 | 75 | 61 | 52 |
| Hull C | 46 | 21 | 10 | 15 | 84 | 69 | 52 |
| Bradford C | 46 | 22 | 8 | 16 | 78 | 68 | 52 |
| Barrow | 46 | 21 | 9 | 16 | 76 | 62 | 51 |
| Halifax T | 46 | 21 | 7 | 18 | 65 | 70 | 49 |
| Wrexham | 46 | 19 | 10 | 17 | 97 | 74 | 48 |
| Rochdale | 46 | 18 | 12 | 16 | 65 | 65 | 48 |
| Scunthorpe U | 46 | 15 | 15 | 16 | 71 | 69 | 45 |
| Carlisle U | 46 | 16 | 13 | 17 | 76 | 85 | 45 |
| Mansfield T | 46 | 17 | 10 | 19 | 91 | 90 | 44 |
| Gateshead | 46 | 17 | 10 | 19 | 72 | 90 | 44 |
| Darlington | 46 | 17 | 8 | 21 | 82 | 95 | 42 |
| Oldham A | 46 | 12 | 15 | 19 | 66 | 74 | 39 |
| Bradford P.A. | 46 | 16 | 3 | 27 | 66 | 93 | 35 |
| Chester | 46 | 10 | 13 | 23 | 55 | 84 | 33 |
| Southport | 46 | 10 | 12 | 24 | 52 | 94 | 32 |
| Tranmere R | 46 | 7 | 13 | 26 | 51 | 91 | 27 |
| Crewe A | 46 | 6 | 9 | 31 | 43 | 110 | 21 |

Manager: Harry Storer.
Leading scorer: Ray Straw, League/all matches 37.

- Ray Straw, whose heading ability was finely served by Tommy Powell and Dennis Woodhead, equalled Jack Bowers' 26-year-old club record with 37 League goals as Derby surged out of the Third Division North.
- Straw, signed from Ilkeston Town in 1951, equalled another club record with goals in six consecutive games in September. Derby beat the previous season's record with 111 goals.
- Derby's average home attendance in two Third Division North seasons was more than 19,000. As away teams collected a share of the gate receipts, other clubs were sorry to see them promoted.
- The vital Easter games against Chesterfield attracted 56,398 spectators to Saltergate and the Baseball Ground.

## Division Three North

| Match No. | Date | | Venue | Opponents | Result | | Scorers | Attenda |
|---|---|---|---|---|---|---|---|---|
| 1 | Aug | 18 | (h) | Gateshead | W | 5-3 | Parry 2, Woodhead 2, Ackerman | 19,05 |
| 2 | | 22 | (a) | Chester | D | 2-2 | Ackerman, Woodhead | 12,1 |
| 3 | | 25 | (a) | Bradford PA | L | 2-3 | Parry, Suddards (og) | 13,7 |
| 4 | | 29 | (h) | Chester | W | 3-0 | Barrowcliffe (pen), Straw. Parry | 20,0 |
| 5 | Sep | 1 | (h) | Darlington | D | 1-1 | Ackerman | 19,3 |
| 6 | | 5 | (a) | Wrexham | W | 2-0 | Straw, Anderson (og) | 10,5 |
| 7 | | 8 | (a) | Barrow | D | 2-2 | Straw, Ackerman | 8,65 |
| 8 | | 12 | (h) | Wrexham | W | 1-0 | Straw | 19,0 |
| 9 | | 15 | (h) | Hull C | W | 1-0 | Straw | 20,1 |
| 10 | | 19 | (h) | Rochdale | W | 3-0 | Straw 2, Barrowcliffe | 19,4 |
| 11 | | 22 | (a) | Workington | L | 1-2 | Straw | 13,9 |
| 12 | | 26 | (a) | Rochdale | L | 1-3 | Ryan | 4,8 |
| 13 | | 29 | (h) | Halifax T | W | 6-0 | Straw 3, Mays, Crowshaw, Pye | 16,3 |
| 14 | Oct | 6 | (a) | Hartlepools U | L | 1-2 | Parry | 12,0 |
| 15 | | 13 | (h) | Bradford C | L | 0-2 | | 19,3 |
| 16 | | 20 | (a) | Mansfield T | W | 2-1 | Ryan, Bradley (og) | 16,3 |
| 17 | | 27 | (h) | Carlisle U | W | 3-0 | Mays, Ryan, Parry | 15,2 |
| 18 | Nov | 3 | (a) | Accrington S | D | 0-0 | | 9,9 |
| 19 | | 10 | (h) | Tranmere R | W | 4-0 | Straw 3, Parry | 13,9 |
| 20 | | 24 | (h) | Oldham A | W | 3-2 | Straw 2, Ryan | 15,3 |
| 21 | Dec | 1 | (a) | Stockport C | L | 2-3 | Straw, Ryan | 11,4 |
| 22 | | 15 | (a) | Gateshead | D | 1-1 | Barrowcliffe (pen) | 3,9 |
| 23 | | 22 | (h) | Bradford PA | W | 6-1 | Crowshaw 2, Buchanan 2, Wyer, Woodhead | 7,6 |
| 24 | | 25 | (h) | Scunthorpe U | W | 4-0 | Woodhead 2, Ryan, Barrowcliffe (pen) | 11,2 |
| 25 | | 26 | (a) | Scunthorpe U | W | 4-1 | Straw 2, Ryan, Hubbard (og) | 4,1 |
| 26 | | 29 | (a) | Darlington | D | 1-1 | Straw | 7,1 |
| 27 | Jan | 5 | (a) | Crewe A | W | 5-2 | Crowshaw 2, Buchanan 2, Straw | 5,4 |
| 28 | | 12 | (h) | Barrow | D | 3-3 | Crowshaw, Buchanan, Straw | 17,5 |
| 29 | | 19 | (a) | Hull C | D | 3-3 | Ryan, Straw, Brown | 14,5 |
| 30 | | 26 | (h) | Crewe A | W | 4-0 | Brown 2, Woodhead, Mays | 19,7 |
| 31 | Feb | 2 | (h) | Workington | L | 2-3 | Straw, Woodhead | 25,3 |
| 32 | | 9 | (a) | Halifax T | L | 0-1 | | 8,5 |
| 33 | | 16 | (h) | Hartlepools U | W | 2-0 | Ryan, Brown | 24,6 |
| 34 | Mar | 2 | (h) | Mansfield T | W | 4-0 | Straw 2, Brown 2 | 22,9 |
| 35 | | 9 | (a) | Carlisle U | W | 3-1 | Brown 2, Woodhead | 11,4 |
| 36 | | 16 | (h) | Accrington S | D | 2-2 | Mays, Ryan | 24,2 |
| 37 | | 23 | (a) | Tranmere R | W | 1-0 | Woodhead (pen) | 8,0 |
| 38 | | 30 | (h) | York C | W | 1-0 | Straw | 21,6 |
| 39 | Apr | 3 | (a) | Bradford C | W | 2-0 | Straw 2 | 18,3 |
| 40 | | 6 | (a) | Oldham A | W | 2-1 | Ryan, Brown | 10,2 |
| 41 | | 13 | (h) | Stockport C | W | 2-0 | Woodhead (pen), Straw | 22,9 |
| 42 | | 19 | (a) | Chesterfield | D | 2-2 | Straw, Davies | 26,5 |
| 43 | | 20 | (a) | Southport | L | 2-3 | Straw, Woodhead (pen) | 8,0 |
| 44 | | 22 | (h) | Chesterfield | W | 7-1 | Straw 3, Powell, Ryan, Woodhead, Hutchinson (og) | 29,8 |
| 45 | | 27 | (h) | Southport | W | 2-0 | Straw 2 | 25,9 |
| 46 | | 29 | (a) | York C | D | 1-1 | Woodhead | 9,4 |

FINAL LEAGUE POSITION: 1st in Division Three North – Promoted

Appearan
Go

## FA Cup

| | | | | | | | | |
|---|---|---|---|---|---|---|---|---|
| 1 | Nov | 17 | (h) | Bradford C | W | 2-1 | Woodhead, Powell | 22,5 |
| 2 | Dec | 8 | (h) | New Brighton | L | 1-3 | Ryan | 23, |

Appearan
Go

| ster T | Barrowcliffe G | Martin R | Mays A | Oliver K | Ryan R | Powell T | Parry J | Straw R | Ackerman A | Woodhead D | Crowshaw A | McDonnell M | Upton F | Pye J | Davies G | Cresswell P | Buchanan J | Wyer P | Brown G | Adlington T | Young R | Clark B | |
|---|---|---|---|---|---|---|---|---|---|---|---|---|---|---|---|---|---|---|---|---|---|---|---|
| | 2 | 3 | 4 | 5 | 6 | 7 | 8 | 9 | 10 | 11 | | | | | | | | | | | | | 1 |
| | 2 | 3 | 4 | 5 | 6 | 7 | 8 | 9 | 10 | 11 | | | | | | | | | | | | | 2 |
| | 2 | 3 | 4 | 5 | 6 | 7 | 8 | 9 | 10 | 11 | | | | | | | | | | | | | 3 |
| | 2 | 3 | 4 | 5 | 6 | | 8 | 9 | 10 | 11 | 7 | | | | | | | | | | | | 4 |
| | 2 | 3 | 4 | 5 | 6 | 7 | 8 | 9 | 10 | 11 | | | | | | | | | | | | | 5 |
| | 2 | 3 | 4 | | 10 | 7 | 8 | 9 | | 11 | | 5 | 6 | | | | | | | | | | 6 |
| | 2 | 3 | 4 | | 8 | 7 | | 9 | 10 | 11 | | 5 | 6 | | | | | | | | | | 7 |
| | 2 | 3 | 4 | | | 7 | | 9 | 10 | 11 | | 5 | 6 | 8 | | | | | | | | | 8 |
| | 2 | 3 | 4 | | 8 | 7 | | 9 | 10 | 11 | | 5 | 6 | | | | | | | | | | 9 |
| | 2 | 3 | 4 | | 10 | 7 | | 9 | 8 | 11 | | 5 | 6 | | | | | | | | | | 10 |
| | 2 | 3 | 4 | | 10 | 7 | | 9 | | | 11 | 5 | 6 | 8 | | | | | | | | | 11 |
| | 2 | 3 | 4 | | 10 | 7 | 8 | 9 | | | 11 | 5 | | | 6 | | | | | | | | 12 |
| | 2 | 3 | 4 | | 6 | 7 | 8 | 9 | | | 11 | 5 | | 10 | | | | | | | | | 13 |
| | 2 | 3 | 4 | | 6 | 7 | 8 | 9 | | | 11 | 5 | | 10 | | | | | | | | | 14 |
| | 2 | 3 | 4 | | 6 | 7 | 8 | 9 | | 11 | | 5 | | 10 | | | | | | | | | 15 |
| | 2 | 3 | 4 | | 8 | 11 | 7 | 9 | 10 | | | 5 | | | 6 | | | | | | | | 16 |
| | 2 | 3 | 4 | | 10 | 11 | 8 | 9 | | | | 5 | | | 6 | 7 | | | | | | | 17 |
| | 2 | 3 | 4 | | 10 | 11 | 8 | 9 | | | 7 | 5 | | | 6 | | | | | | | | 18 |
| | 2 | 3 | 4 | | 10 | 11 | 8 | 9 | | 7 | | 5 | | | 6 | | | | | | | | 19 |
| | 2 | 3 | 4 | | 10 | 11 | 8 | 9 | | 7 | | 5 | | | 6 | | | | | | | | 20 |
| | 2 | 3 | 4 | | 10 | 11 | 8 | 9 | | 7 | | 5 | | | 6 | | | | | | | | 21 |
| | 2 | 3 | 4 | | 10 | | 8 | 9 | | | 11 | 5 | | | 6 | | 7 | | | | | | 22 |
| | 2 | 3 | 4 | | 10 | | | | | 7 | 11 | 5 | | | 6 | | 9 | 8 | | | | | 23 |
| | 2 | 3 | 4 | | 10 | | | | | 7 | 11 | 5 | | | 6 | | 9 | 8 | | | | | 24 |
| | 2 | 3 | 4 | | 10 | 8 | | 9 | | 7 | 11 | 5 | | | 6 | | | | | | | | 25 |
| | 2 | 3 | 4 | | 10 | 8 | | 9 | | 7 | 11 | 5 | | | 6 | | | | | | | | 26 |
| | 2 | 3 | 4 | | 10 | 8 | | 9 | | | 11 | 5 | | | 6 | | 7 | | | | | | 27 |
| | 2 | 3 | 4 | | 10 | 8 | | 9 | | | 11 | 5 | | | 6 | | 7 | | | | | | 28 |
| | 2 | 3 | 4 | | 10 | | | 9 | | | 11 | 5 | 6 | | | | 7 | | 8 | | | | 29 |
| | 2 | 3 | 4 | | 10 | | | 9 | | 7 | 11 | 5 | 6 | | | | | | 8 | 1 | | | 30 |
| | 2 | 3 | 4 | | 10 | | | 9 | | 7 | 11 | 5 | 6 | | | | | | 8 | | | | 31 |
| | 2 | 3 | 4 | | 10 | | | 9 | | 7 | 11 | | | | 6 | | | | 8 | | 5 | | 32 |
| | | 3 | 4 | | 10 | 7 | | 9 | | 11 | | 2 | | | 6 | | | | 8 | | 5 | | 33 |
| | 2 | 3 | | | 10 | 7 | | 9 | | 11 | | | | | 6 | | | | 8 | | 5 | 4 | 34 |
| | 3 | | 4 | | 10 | 7 | | 9 | | 11 | | 2 | | | 6 | | | | 8 | | 5 | | 35 |
| | 3 | | 4 | | 10 | 7 | | 9 | | 11 | | 2 | | | 6 | | | | 8 | | 5 | | 36 |
| | 3 | | 4 | 5 | 10 | 7 | | 9 | | 11 | | 2 | | | 6 | | | | 8 | | | | 37 |
| | 3 | | 4 | 5 | 10 | 7 | | 9 | | 11 | | 2 | | | 6 | | | | 8 | | | | 38 |
| | 3 | | 4 | 5 | 10 | 7 | | 9 | | 11 | | 2 | | | 6 | | | | 8 | | | | 39 |
| | 3 | | 4 | 5 | 10 | 7 | | 9 | | 11 | | 2 | | | 6 | | | | 8 | | | | 40 |
| | 3 | | 4 | 5 | 10 | 7 | | 9 | | 11 | | 2 | | | 6 | | | | 8 | | | | 41 |
| | 3 | | 4 | 5 | 10 | 7 | | 9 | | 11 | | 2 | | | 6 | | | | 8 | | | | 42 |
| | 3 | | 4 | 5 | 10 | 7 | | 9 | | 11 | | 2 | | | 6 | | | | 8 | | | | 43 |
| | 3 | | 4 | | 10 | 7 | 8 | 9 | | 11 | | 2 | | | 6 | | | | | | 5 | | 44 |
| | 3 | | 4 | | 10 | 7 | | 9 | | 11 | | 2 | | | 6 | | | | 8 | | 5 | | 45 |
| | 3 | | 4 | | 10 | 7 | | 9 | | 11 | | 2 | | | 6 | | | | 8 | | 5 | | 46 |
| 5 | 45 | 34 | 45 | 12 | 45 | 38 | 18 | 44 | 10 | 35 | 17 | 39 | 9 | 5 | 29 | 1 | 6 | 2 | 17 | 1 | 8 | 1 | |
| | 4 | | 4 | | 12 | 1 | 7 | 37 | 4 | 14 | 6 | | | 1 | 1 | | 5 | 1 | 9 | | | | |

5 own-goals

| | | | | | | | | | | | | | | | | | | | | | | |
|---|---|---|---|---|---|---|---|---|---|---|---|---|---|---|---|---|---|---|---|---|---|---|
| 2 | 3 | 4 | | 10 | 11 | 8 | 9 | | 7 | | 5 | | | 6 | | | | | | | | 1 |
| 2 | 3 | 4 | | 10 | 11 | 8 | 9 | | 7 | | 5 | | | 6 | | | | | | | | 2 |
| 2 | 2 | 2 | | 2 | 2 | 2 | 2 | | 2 | | 2 | | | 2 | | | | | | | | |
| | | | | 1 | 1 | | | | 1 | | | | | | | | | | | | | |

# 1957-58

| | P | W | D | L | F | A | Pts |
|---|---|---|---|---|---|---|---|
| West Ham U | 42 | 23 | 11 | 8 | 101 | 54 | 57 |
| Blackburn R | 42 | 22 | 12 | 8 | 93 | 57 | 56 |
| Charlton A | 42 | 24 | 7 | 11 | 107 | 69 | 55 |
| Liverpool | 42 | 22 | 10 | 10 | 79 | 54 | 54 |
| Fulham | 42 | 20 | 12 | 10 | 97 | 59 | 52 |
| Sheffield U | 42 | 21 | 10 | 11 | 75 | 50 | 52 |
| Middlesbrough | 42 | 19 | 7 | 16 | 83 | 74 | 45 |
| Ipswich T | 42 | 16 | 12 | 14 | 68 | 69 | 44 |
| Huddersfield T | 42 | 14 | 16 | 12 | 63 | 66 | 44 |
| Bristol R | 42 | 17 | 8 | 17 | 85 | 80 | 42 |
| Stoke C | 42 | 18 | 6 | 18 | 75 | 73 | 42 |
| Leyton O | 42 | 18 | 5 | 19 | 77 | 79 | 41 |
| Grimsby T | 42 | 17 | 6 | 19 | 86 | 83 | 40 |
| Barnsley | 42 | 14 | 12 | 16 | 70 | 74 | 40 |
| Cardiff C | 42 | 14 | 9 | 19 | 63 | 77 | 37 |
| Derby Co | 42 | 14 | 8 | 20 | 60 | 81 | 36 |
| Bristol C | 42 | 13 | 9 | 20 | 63 | 88 | 35 |
| Rotherham U | 42 | 14 | 5 | 23 | 65 | 101 | 33 |
| Swansea T | 42 | 11 | 9 | 22 | 72 | 99 | 31 |
| Lincoln C | 42 | 11 | 9 | 22 | 55 | 82 | 31 |
| Notts Co | 42 | 12 | 6 | 24 | 44 | 80 | 30 |
| Doncaster R | 42 | 8 | 11 | 23 | 56 | 88 | 27 |

Manager: Harry Storer.
Leading scorer: Reg Ryan, League/all matches 14.

- Ray Straw joined Coventry City in November after scoring 60 goals in 98 appearances for the Rams. He made his debut in the First Division, played in the Second and broke records in the Third North.
- Coventry were in the Third South until, at the end of the season, the regional split turned into Divisions Three and Four.
- Straw helped Coventry to promotion from the Fourth and became the first man to play in six divisions of the Football League. He also helped Mansfield Town to promotion.
- In a moderate season, Derby never won more than two games in succession – and managed that only twice.

## Division Two

| Match No. | Date | | Venue | Opponents | Result | | Scorers | Atte |
|---|---|---|---|---|---|---|---|---|
| 1 | Aug | 24 | (a) | Fulham | L | 0-2 | | 27 |
| 2 | | 26 | (a) | Bristol R | L | 2-5 | Ryan, Parry | 25 |
| 3 | | 31 | (h) | Barnsley | L | 1-4 | Powell | 22 |
| 4 | Sep | 4 | (h) | Bristol R | W | 2-1 | Parry, Darwin | 20 |
| 5 | | 7 | (a) | West Ham U | L | 1-2 | Brown | 18 |
| 6 | | 11 | (a) | Lincoln C | D | 1-1 | Mays | 12 |
| 7 | | 14 | (h) | Sheffield U | W | 2-0 | Mays, G.Shaw (og) | 22 |
| 8 | | 18 | (h) | Lincoln C | W | 3-2 | Mays, Ryan, Parry | 18 |
| 9 | | 21 | (a) | Blackburn R | L | 1-3 | Ryan | 18 |
| 10 | | 28 | (h) | Ipswich T | D | 2-2 | Brown, Ryan | 18 |
| 11 | Oct | 5 | (a) | Notts C | L | 0-1 | | 23 |
| 12 | | 12 | (a) | Cardiff C | L | 2-3 | Parry, Darwin | 15 |
| 13 | | 19 | (h) | Liverpool | W | 2-1 | Woodhead, Darwin | 22 |
| 14 | | 26 | (a) | Middlesbrough | L | 2-3 | Parry, Upton | 30 |
| 15 | Nov | 2 | (h) | Leyton O | W | 2-0 | Parry, Darwin | 20 |
| 16 | | 9 | (a) | Charlton A | D | 2-2 | Mays (pen), Ryan | 18 |
| 17 | | 16 | (h) | Doncaster R | W | 1-0 | Parry | 20 |
| 18 | | 23 | (a) | Rotherham U | W | 2-0 | Mays (pen), Powell | 12 |
| 19 | | 30 | (h) | Huddersfield T | L | 2-4 | Ryan 2 | 20 |
| 20 | Dec | 7 | (a) | Grimsby T | L | 2-3 | Powell, Ryan | 12 |
| 21 | | 14 | (h) | Stoke C | D | 0-0 | | 24 |
| 22 | | 21 | (h) | Fulham | D | 3-3 | Ryan, Parry, Darwin | 21, |
| 23 | | 25 | (a) | Bristol C | L | 1-2 | Ryan | 17 |
| 24 | | 26 | (h) | Bristol C | W | 5-2 | Parry 2, Ryan, Woodhead, Darwin | 25, |
| 25 | | 28 | (a) | Barnsley | L | 0-3 | | 21 |
| 26 | Jan | 11 | (h) | West Ham U | L | 2-3 | Mays, Ryan | 21 |
| 27 | | 18 | (a) | Sheffield U | W | 1-0 | Darwin | 20, |
| 28 | Feb | 1 | (h) | Blackburn R | L | 0-3 | | 20, |
| 29 | | 8 | (a) | Ipswich T | D | 2-2 | Brown 2 | 15, |
| 30 | | 15 | (h) | Notts C | W | 2-1 | Ryan, Woodhead | 21 |
| 31 | | 22 | (h) | Rotherham U | L | 3-4 | Darwin 2, Parry | 17 |
| 32 | Mar | 5 | (a) | Liverpool | L | 0-2 | | 30 |
| 33 | | 8 | (h) | Middlesbrough | W | 2-1 | Brown 2 | 17 |
| 34 | | 15 | (a) | Leyton O | D | 1-1 | Brown | 13, |
| 35 | | 22 | (h) | Charlton A | L | 1-3 | Brown | 17 |
| 36 | | 29 | (a) | Doncaster R | W | 2-1 | Woodhead, Parry | 8, |
| 37 | Apr | 5 | (h) | Cardiff C | L | 0-2 | | 15, |
| 38 | | 7 | (h) | Swansea T | W | 1-0 | Darwin | 14, |
| 39 | | 8 | (a) | Swansea T | L | 0-7 | | 15, |
| 40 | | 12 | (a) | Huddersfield T | D | 0-0 | | 12, |
| 41 | | 19 | (h) | Grimsby T | W | 1-0 | Ryan | 13, |
| 42 | | 26 | (a) | Stoke C | L | 1-2 | Barrowcliffe (pen) | 10, |

FINAL LEAGUE POSITION: 16th in Division Two

Appearar
G

## FA Cup

| | | | | | | | |
|---|---|---|---|---|---|---|---|
| 3 | Jan | 4 | (a) | Middlesbrough | L | 0-5 | 29, |

Appearar
G

| oster T | McDonnell M | Barrowcliffe G | Mays A | Young R | Davies G | Powell T | Brown G | Straw R | Ryan R | Woodhead D | Parry J | Smith M | Darwin G | Upton F | Oliver K | Moore L | Oxford K | Clark B | Martin R | Womack R | Crowshaw A | Richmond J | |
|---|---|---|---|---|---|---|---|---|---|---|---|---|---|---|---|---|---|---|---|---|---|---|---|
| | 2 | 3 | 4 | 5 | 6 | 7 | 8 | 9 | 10 | 11 | | | | | | | | | | | | | 1 |
| | 2 | 3 | 4 | 5 | 6 | 7 | | 9 | 10 | 11 | 8 | | | | | | | | | | | | 2 |
| | 2 | 3 | 4 | 5 | 6 | 7 | | 9 | 10 | 11 | 8 | | | | | | | | | | | | 3 |
| | 5 | 2 | 4 | | 6 | 7 | 11 | | 10 | | 8 | 3 | 9 | | | | | | | | | | 4 |
| | 5 | | 4 | | 2 | 7 | 11 | | 10 | | 8 | 3 | 9 | 6 | | | | | | | | | 5 |
| | 5 | 2 | 4 | | 6 | 7 | 10 | 9 | 8 | 11 | | 3 | | | | | | | | | | | 6 |
| | 5 | 2 | 4 | | 6 | 7 | 10 | | 8 | 11 | 9 | 3 | | | | | | | | | | | 7 |
| | 5 | 2 | 4 | | 6 | 7 | 10 | | 8 | 11 | 9 | 3 | | | | | | | | | | | 8 |
| | 5 | 2 | 4 | | 6 | 7 | | | 8 | 11 | 9 | 3 | 10 | | | | | | | | | | 9 |
| | | 2 | 4 | 5 | 6 | | 7 | | 8 | 11 | 9 | 3 | 10 | | | | | | | | | | 10 |
| | | 2 | 4 | | 3 | 7 | | 9 | 10 | 11 | 8 | | | 6 | 5 | | | | | | | | 11 |
| | | 2 | 4 | | 3 | 7 | | | 10 | 11 | 8 | | 9 | 6 | 5 | | | | | | | | 12 |
| | 5 | 2 | 4 | | 3 | 7 | | | 10 | 11 | 8 | | 9 | 6 | | | | | | | | | 13 |
| | 5 | 2 | 4 | | 3 | 7 | | | 10 | 11 | 8 | | 9 | 6 | | | | | | | | | 14 |
| | 5 | 2 | 4 | | 3 | 7 | | | 10 | 11 | 8 | | 9 | 6 | | | | | | | | | 15 |
| | 5 | 2 | 4 | | 3 | 7 | | | 10 | 11 | 8 | | 9 | 6 | | | | | | | | | 16 |
| | 5 | 2 | 4 | | 3 | 7 | | | 10 | 11 | 8 | | 9 | 6 | | | | | | | | | 17 |
| | | 2 | 4 | | 3 | 7 | | | 10 | 11 | 8 | | 9 | 6 | | 5 | | | | | | | 18 |
| | | 2 | 4 | | 3 | 7 | | | 10 | 11 | 8 | | 9 | 6 | | 5 | | | | | | | 19 |
| | 5 | 2 | 4 | | 3 | 7 | | | 10 | 11 | 8 | | 9 | 6 | | | | | | | | | 20 |
| | 5 | 2 | 4 | | 3 | 7 | | | 10 | 11 | 8 | | 9 | 6 | | | 1 | | | | | | 21 |
| | 5 | 2 | | | 3 | 7 | | | 10 | 11 | 8 | | 9 | 6 | | | 1 | 4 | | | | | 22 |
| | 5 | 2 | | | 3 | 7 | | | 10 | 11 | 8 | | 9 | 6 | | | 1 | 4 | | | | | 23 |
| | 5 | 2 | | | 3 | 7 | | | 10 | 11 | 8 | | 9 | 6 | | | 1 | 4 | | | | | 24 |
| | 5 | 2 | | | 3 | | 7 | | 10 | 11 | 8 | | 9 | 6 | | | 1 | 4 | | | | | 25 |
| | 2 | | 4 | | 3 | 7 | | | 10 | 11 | 8 | | 9 | 6 | | 5 | 1 | | | | | | 26 |
| | 2 | 3 | 4 | | 6 | 7 | | | 10 | 11 | 8 | | 9 | | | 5 | 1 | | | | | | 27 |
| | 2 | 3 | 4 | | 6 | 7 | | | 10 | 11 | 8 | | 9 | | | 5 | 1 | | | | | | 28 |
| | 2 | | 4 | | 3 | 7 | 9 | | 10 | 11 | 8 | | | 6 | | 5 | 1 | | | | | | 29 |
| | 2 | | | | 4 | 7 | 9 | | 10 | 11 | 8 | | | 6 | | 5 | 1 | | 3 | | | | 30 |
| | 2 | | 4 | | 3 | 7 | 9 | | | 11 | 8 | | 10 | 6 | | 5 | 1 | | | | | | 31 |
| | 5 | 2 | | | 3 | 7 | 9 | | 4 | 11 | 8 | | 10 | 6 | | | 1 | | | | | | 32 |
| | 5 | 2 | | | 3 | 7 | 9 | | 4 | 11 | 8 | | 10 | 6 | | | 1 | | | | | | 33 |
| | 5 | 2 | | | 3 | 7 | 9 | | 4 | 11 | 8 | | 10 | 6 | | | 1 | | | | | | 34 |
| | 5 | 2 | | | 3 | 7 | 9 | | 4 | 11 | 8 | | 10 | 6 | | | 1 | | | | | | 35 |
| | 5 | | 4 | | 2 | 7 | 9 | | 10 | 11 | 8 | | | 6 | | | 1 | | 3 | | | | 36 |
| | 5 | | 4 | | 2 | 7 | 9 | | 10 | 11 | 8 | | | 6 | | | 1 | | 3 | | | | 37 |
| | | 2 | | 5 | | 7 | 10 | | 4 | | 8 | | 9 | 6 | | | 1 | | 3 | 11 | | | 38 |
| | | 2 | 8 | 5 | | | | | 4 | | 10 | | 9 | 6 | | | 1 | | 3 | 11 | 7 | | 39 |
| | | 2 | | | | | 9 | | 10 | 11 | 7 | | 8 | 4 | | 5 | 1 | | 3 | | | 6 | 40 |
| | | 2 | | | | 7 | 9 | | 10 | 11 | 8 | | | 4 | | 5 | 1 | | 3 | | | 6 | 41 |
| | | 2 | | | | 7 | 9 | | 10 | 11 | 8 | | | 6 | | 5 | 1 | 4 | 3 | | | | 42 |
| | 32 | 35 | 29 | 6 | 37 | 38 | 21 | 5 | 41 | 38 | 40 | 7 | 29 | 31 | 2 | 11 | 22 | 5 | 8 | 2 | 1 | 2 | |
| | | 1 | 6 | | | 3 | 8 | | 14 | 4 | 12 | | 10 | 1 | | | | | | | | | |

1 own-goal

| | | | | | | | | | | | | | | | | | | | | | | | |
|---|---|---|---|---|---|---|---|---|---|---|---|---|---|---|---|---|---|---|---|---|---|---|---|
| | 5 | 2 | 4 | | 3 | 7 | | | 10 | 11 | 8 | | 9 | 6 | | | 1 | | | | | | 3 |
| | 1 | 1 | 1 | | 1 | 1 | | | 1 | 1 | 1 | | 1 | 1 | | | 1 | | | | | | |
| | | | | | | | | | | | | | | | | | | | | | | | |

# 1958-59

| | P | W | D | L | F | A | Pts |
|---|---|---|---|---|---|---|---|
| Sheffield W | 42 | 28 | 6 | 8 | 106 | 48 | 62 |
| Fulham | 42 | 27 | 6 | 9 | 96 | 61 | 60 |
| Sheffield U | 42 | 23 | 7 | 12 | 82 | 48 | 53 |
| Liverpool | 42 | 24 | 5 | 13 | 87 | 62 | 53 |
| Stoke C | 42 | 21 | 7 | 14 | 72 | 58 | 49 |
| Bristol R | 42 | 18 | 12 | 12 | 80 | 64 | 48 |
| Derby Co | 42 | 20 | 8 | 14 | 74 | 71 | 48 |
| Charlton A | 42 | 18 | 7 | 17 | 92 | 90 | 43 |
| Cardiff C | 42 | 18 | 7 | 17 | 65 | 65 | 43 |
| Bristol C | 42 | 17 | 7 | 18 | 74 | 70 | 41 |
| Swansea T | 42 | 16 | 9 | 17 | 79 | 81 | 41 |
| Brighton & H.A. | 42 | 15 | 11 | 16 | 74 | 90 | 41 |
| Middlesbrough | 42 | 15 | 10 | 17 | 87 | 71 | 40 |
| Huddersfield T | 42 | 16 | 8 | 18 | 62 | 55 | 40 |
| Sunderland | 42 | 16 | 8 | 18 | 64 | 75 | 40 |
| Ipswich T | 42 | 17 | 6 | 19 | 62 | 77 | 40 |
| Leyton O | 42 | 14 | 8 | 20 | 71 | 78 | 36 |
| Scunthorpe U | 42 | 12 | 9 | 21 | 55 | 84 | 33 |
| Lincoln C | 42 | 11 | 7 | 24 | 63 | 93 | 29 |
| Rotherham U | 42 | 10 | 9 | 23 | 42 | 82 | 29 |
| Grimsby T | 42 | 9 | 10 | 23 | 62 | 90 | 28 |
| Barnsley | 42 | 10 | 7 | 25 | 55 | 91 | 27 |

Manager: Harry Storer.
Leading scorer: Jack Parry, League 15, all matches 16.
League ever-present: Geoff Barrowcliffe.

- Derbyshire were grateful when Harry Storer signed Ray Swallow from Arsenal in September.
- Swallow had played first-class cricket for MCC against Scotland and represented Derbyshire from 1959 to 1963.
- Paddy Ryan, whose influence was so important in the Third Division North title, moved to Coventry City in September.
- Ralph Hunt, a centre-forward who spent the season with the Rams, died following a car crash in December 1964, when he was a Chesterfield player.

## Division Two

| Match No. | Date | Venue | Opponents | Result | | Scorers | Atter |
|---|---|---|---|---|---|---|---|
| 1 | Aug 23 | (a) | Huddersfield T | D | 1-1 | Hunt | 16 |
| 2 | 30 | (h) | Leyton O | L | 1-2 | Hunt | 22 |
| 3 | Sep 3 | (h) | Bristol R | W | 3-2 | Hannigan, Hunt, Brown | 20 |
| 4 | 6 | (a) | Scunthorpe U | D | 2-2 | Hunt 2 | 13 |
| 5 | 10 | (a) | Ipswich T | D | 1-1 | Brown | 15 |
| 6 | 13 | (h) | Sheffield W | L | 1-4 | Cargill | 24 |
| 7 | 17 | (h) | Ipswich T | W | 3-2 | Mays 2, Swallow | 19 |
| 8 | 20 | (a) | Fulham | L | 2-4 | Cargill, Mays | 31 |
| 9 | 22 | (a) | Bristol R | L | 1-2 | Hunt | 14 |
| 10 | 27 | (h) | Lincoln C | W | 1-0 | Hunt | 18 |
| 11 | Oct 4 | (a) | Sunderland | L | 0-3 | | 23 |
| 12 | 11 | (a) | Barnsley | D | 0-0 | | 11 |
| 13 | 18 | (h) | Rotherham U | D | 1-1 | Swallow | 16 |
| 14 | 22 | (a) | Stoke C | L | 1-2 | Swallow | 20 |
| 15 | 25 | (a) | Sheffield U | W | 2-1 | Barrowcliffe, Swallow | 20 |
| 16 | Nov 1 | (h) | Cardiff C | L | 1-3 | Barrowcliffe | 17 |
| 17 | 8 | (a) | Grimsby T | L | 0-3 | | 11 |
| 18 | 15 | (h) | Liverpool | W | 3-2 | Hannigan, Hunt, Darwin | 16 |
| 19 | 22 | (a) | Middlesbrough | L | 0-5 | | 16 |
| 20 | 29 | (h) | Charlton A | W | 3-2 | Parry 2, Cargill | 11, |
| 21 | Dec 6 | (a) | Bristol C | W | 3-1 | Parry, Hunt, Darwin | 20 |
| 22 | 13 | (h) | Brighton & HA | L | 1-3 | Upton | 14, |
| 23 | 20 | (h) | Huddersfield T | W | 3-1 | Powell, Cargill (pen), Darwin | 13 |
| 24 | 26 | (h) | Swansea T | W | 3-1 | Davies, Parry, Darwin | 23, |
| 25 | 27 | (a) | Swansea T | D | 4-4 | Hannigan, Powell, Cargill, Darwin | 19 |
| 26 | Jan 3 | (a) | Leyton O | W | 3-1 | Parry 2, Powell | 11, |
| 27 | 17 | (h) | Scunthorpe U | W | 3-1 | Darwin 2, Hannigan | 13 |
| 28 | 31 | (a) | Sheffield W | D | 1-1 | Darwin | 30 |
| 29 | Feb 7 | (h) | Fulham | W | 2-0 | Hannigan, Darwin | 21 |
| 30 | 14 | (a) | Lincoln C | W | 4-1 | Upton, Hannigan, Powell, Darwin | 11, |
| 31 | 21 | (h) | Sunderland | W | 2-0 | Upton, Parry | 24 |
| 32 | 28 | (h) | Grimsby T | W | 3-0 | Parry 3 | 22, |
| 33 | Mar 7 | (a) | Rotherham U | L | 0-3 | | 10, |
| 34 | 14 | (h) | Sheffield U | W | 2-1 | Parry 2 | 22 |
| 35 | 21 | (a) | Cardiff C | D | 0-0 | | 14, |
| 36 | 28 | (h) | Barnsley | W | 3-0 | Parry, Cargill, Darwin | 18 |
| 37 | 30 | (h) | Stoke C | W | 3-0 | Thompson 2, Parry | 24, |
| 38 | Apr 4 | (a) | Liverpool | L | 0-3 | | 38, |
| 39 | 11 | (h) | Middlesbrough | L | 0-3 | | 19, |
| 40 | 18 | (a) | Charlton A | W | 2-1 | Parry, Hunt | 10, |
| 41 | 22 | (a) | Brighton & HA | L | 1-3 | Swallow (pen) | 21, |
| 42 | 25 | (h) | Bristol C | W | 4-1 | Swallow 2, Hannigan, Powell | 12, |

FINAL LEAGUE POSITION: 7th in Division Two

Appearar
G

## FA Cup

| | | | | | | | |
|---|---|---|---|---|---|---|---|
| 3 | Jan 10 | (h) | Preston NE | D | 2-2 | Parry, Darwin | 29, |
| R | 19 | (a) | Preston NE | L | 2-4* | Cargill 2 (1 pen) | 29, |

*after extra-time

Appearar
G

| rd K | Barrowcliffe G | Davies G | Ryan R | Moore L | Upton F | Hannigan J | Parry J | Hunt R | Powell T | Cargill D | Mays A | Darwin G | Brown G | Adlington T | Swallow R | Smith M | Newbery P | Young R | Woodhead D | Thompson P | Martin R | Mitchell J | Scarborough B | |
|---|---|---|---|---|---|---|---|---|---|---|---|---|---|---|---|---|---|---|---|---|---|---|---|---|
| | 2 | 3 | 4 | 5 | 6 | 7 | 8 | 9 | 10 | 11 | | | | | | | | | | | | | | 1 |
| | 2 | 3 | 4 | 5 | 6 | 7 | 8 | 9 | 10 | 11 | | | | | | | | | | | | | | 2 |
| | 2 | 3 | | 5 | 6 | 7 | | 9 | | 11 | 4 | 8 | 10 | | | | | | | | | | | 3 |
| | 2 | 3 | | 5 | 6 | 7 | | 9 | | 11 | 4 | 8 | 10 | | | | | | | | | | | 4 |
| | 2 | 3 | | 5 | 6 | 7 | 4 | 9 | | 11 | | 8 | 10 | | | | | | | | | | | 5 |
| | 2 | 3 | | 5 | 6 | 7 | 4 | 9 | | 11 | | 8 | 10 | | | | | | | | | | | 6 |
| | 2 | 3 | | 5 | | | 6 | 9 | 7 | 11 | 4 | 8 | | 1 | 10 | | | | | | | | | 7 |
| | 2 | 3 | | 5 | | | 4 | 9 | 7 | 11 | 6 | 8 | | 1 | 10 | | | | | | | | | 8 |
| | 2 | 3 | | 5 | 6 | | 8 | 9 | 7 | 11 | 4 | | | | 10 | | | | | | | | | 9 |
| | 2 | | | 5 | 6 | | 8 | 9 | 7 | 11 | 4 | | | | 10 | 3 | | | | | | | | 10 |
| | 2 | 3 | | 5 | 6 | | 4 | 10 | 7 | 11 | | | | | 8 | | 9 | | | | | | | 11 |
| | 2 | 3 | | 5 | 6 | | 4 | 10 | 7 | 11 | | 9 | | | 8 | | | | | | | | | 12 |
| | 2 | 3 | | | 6 | | 4 | 10 | 7 | 11 | | 9 | | | 8 | | | 5 | | | | | | 13 |
| | 2 | 3 | | | 6 | | 4 | 9 | 7 | 11 | | | | | 8 | | | 5 | 10 | | | | | 14 |
| | 9 | 3 | | | 6 | 7 | 4 | 10 | 11 | | | | | | 8 | 2 | | 5 | | | | | | 15 |
| | 9 | 3 | | | 6 | 7 | 4 | 10 | 11 | | | | | | 8 | 2 | | 5 | | | | | | 16 |
| | 2 | 3 | | 5 | 6 | 7 | 4 | 10 | 11 | | | | | | 8 | | | | | 9 | | | | 17 |
| | 2 | 6 | | 5 | | 7 | 8 | 9 | | 11 | 4 | 10 | | | | | | | | | 3 | | | 18 |
| | 2 | 6 | | 5 | | 7 | 8 | 9 | | 11 | 4 | 10 | | | | | | | | | 3 | | | 19 |
| | 2 | 6 | | | 4 | 7 | 8 | 9 | | 11 | | 10 | | | | | | 5 | | | 3 | | | 20 |
| | 2 | 6 | | | 4 | 7 | 8 | 9 | | 11 | | 10 | | | | | | 5 | | | 3 | | | 21 |
| | 2 | 6 | | | 4 | 7 | 8 | 9 | | 11 | | 10 | | | | | | 5 | | | 3 | | | 22 |
| | 2 | 6 | | | 4 | | 8 | | 7 | 11 | | 10 | | | | | | 5 | | 9 | 3 | | | 23 |
| | 2 | 6 | | 5 | | | 8 | | 7 | 11 | 4 | 10 | | | | | | | | 9 | 3 | | | 24 |
| | 2 | 6 | | 5 | | 9 | 8 | | 7 | 11 | 4 | 10 | | | | | | | | | 3 | | | 25 |
| | 2 | 6 | | 5 | | 9 | 8 | | 7 | 11 | 4 | 10 | | | | | | | | | 3 | | | 26 |
| | 2 | 6 | | 5 | | 9 | 8 | | 7 | 11 | 4 | 10 | | | | | | | | | 3 | | | 27 |
| | 2 | 3 | | 5 | 6 | 9 | 8 | | 7 | 11 | 4 | 10 | | | | | | | | | | | | 28 |
| | 2 | 3 | | 5 | 6 | 9 | 8 | | 7 | 11 | 4 | 10 | | | | | | | | | | | | 29 |
| | 2 | 3 | | 5 | 6 | 9 | 8 | | 7 | 11 | 4 | 10 | | | | | | | | | | | | 30 |
| | 2 | 3 | | 5 | 6 | 9 | 8 | | 7 | 11 | 4 | 10 | | | | | | | | | | | | 31 |
| | 2 | | | 5 | 6 | 9 | 8 | | 7 | 11 | 4 | 10 | | | | | | | | | 3 | | | 32 |
| | 2 | | | 5 | 6 | 9 | 8 | | 7 | 11 | 4 | 10 | | | | | | | | | 3 | | | 33 |
| | 2 | 3 | | 5 | 6 | 9 | 8 | | 7 | 11 | 4 | 10 | | | | | | | | | | | | 34 |
| | 2 | 3 | | 5 | 6 | 9 | 8 | | 7 | 11 | 4 | 10 | | | | | | | | | | | | 35 |
| | 2 | 3 | | 5 | 4 | | 8 | | 7 | 11 | | 10 | 6 | | | | | | | 9 | | | | 36 |
| | 2 | 6 | | 5 | 4 | | 8 | | 7 | 11 | | 10 | | | | | 3 | | | 9 | | | | 37 |
| | 2 | 6 | | 5 | 4 | | 8 | | 7 | 11 | | 10 | | | | | 3 | | | 9 | | | | 38 |
| | 2 | 3 | | 5 | 6 | | 8 | | | 11 | 4 | 10 | | | 7 | | | | | 9 | | | | 39 |
| | 2 | 6 | | 5 | 4 | | 8 | 9 | | 11 | | 10 | | | 7 | | | | | | 3 | | | 40 |
| | 2 | 6 | | 5 | 4 | | 8 | 9 | 7 | 11 | | | | | 10 | | | | | | 3 | 1 | | 41 |
| | 2 | 6 | | 5 | 4 | 9 | | | 7 | | | | 10 | | 8 | | | | | | 3 | 1 | 11 | 42 |
| | 42 | 39 | 2 | 34 | 34 | 26 | 39 | 24 | 31 | 38 | 21 | 31 | 6 | 2 | 15 | 5 | 1 | 8 | 1 | 7 | 15 | 2 | 1 | |
| | 2 | 1 | | | 3 | 7 | 15 | 10 | 5 | 6 | 3 | 11 | 2 | | 7 | | | | | 2 | | | | |

| | | | | | | | | | | | | | | | | | | | | | | | |
|---|---|---|---|---|---|---|---|---|---|---|---|---|---|---|---|---|---|---|---|---|---|---|---|
| 2 | 6 | | 5 | | 9 | 8 | | 7 | 11 | 4 | 10 | | | | | | | | | 3 | | | 3 |
| 2 | 6 | | 5 | | 9 | 8 | | 7 | 11 | 4 | 10 | | | | | | | | | 3 | | | R |
| 2 | 2 | | 2 | | 2 | 2 | | 2 | 2 | 2 | 2 | | | | | | | | | 2 | | | |
| | | | | | | 1 | | | 2 | | 1 | | | | | | | | | | | | |

# 1959-60

| | P | W | D | L | F | A | Pts |
|---|---|---|---|---|---|---|---|
| Aston Villa | 42 | 25 | 9 | 8 | 89 | 43 | 59 |
| Cardiff C | 42 | 23 | 12 | 7 | 90 | 62 | 58 |
| Liverpool | 42 | 20 | 10 | 12 | 90 | 66 | 50 |
| Sheffield U | 42 | 19 | 12 | 11 | 68 | 51 | 50 |
| Middlesbrough | 42 | 19 | 10 | 13 | 90 | 64 | 48 |
| Huddersfield T | 42 | 19 | 9 | 14 | 73 | 52 | 47 |
| Charlton A | 42 | 17 | 13 | 12 | 90 | 87 | 47 |
| Rotherham U | 42 | 17 | 13 | 12 | 61 | 60 | 47 |
| Bristol R | 42 | 18 | 11 | 13 | 72 | 78 | 47 |
| Leyton O | 42 | 15 | 14 | 13 | 76 | 61 | 44 |
| Ipswich T | 42 | 19 | 6 | 17 | 78 | 68 | 44 |
| Swansea T | 42 | 15 | 10 | 17 | 82 | 84 | 40 |
| Lincoln C | 42 | 16 | 7 | 19 | 75 | 78 | 39 |
| Brighton & H.A. | 42 | 13 | 12 | 17 | 67 | 76 | 38 |
| Scunthorpe U | 42 | 13 | 10 | 19 | 57 | 71 | 36 |
| Sunderland | 42 | 12 | 12 | 18 | 52 | 65 | 36 |
| Stoke C | 42 | 14 | 7 | 21 | 66 | 83 | 35 |
| Derby Co | 42 | 14 | 7 | 21 | 61 | 77 | 35 |
| Plymouth A | 42 | 13 | 9 | 20 | 61 | 89 | 35 |
| Portsmouth | 42 | 10 | 12 | 20 | 59 | 77 | 32 |
| Hull C | 42 | 10 | 10 | 22 | 48 | 76 | 30 |
| Bristol C | 42 | 11 | 5 | 26 | 60 | 97 | 27 |

Manager: Harry Storer.
Leading scorer: Peter Thompson, League 11, all matches 12.

- Derby's heaviest home defeat was equalled on 29 August, when Middlesbrough won 7–1 at the Baseball Ground. Brian Clough was in the Middlesbrough side but did not score, something that did not amuse him. Alan Peacock grabbed the headlines with four of Middlesbrough's goals.
- Three Derbyshire cricketers appeared for the Rams, Ian Hall and Ian Buxton joining Ray Swallow. They were the last of the footballer-cricketers at Derby.
- Republic of Ireland winger Paddy Fagan signed from Manchester City in March. He played in the FA Cup final for City in 1955 and his father also won an Irish cap.

## Division Two

| Match No. | Date | | Venue | Opponents | Result | | Scorers | Atte |
|---|---|---|---|---|---|---|---|---|
| 1 | Aug | 22 | (a) | Sheffield U | L | 1-2 | Cargill (pen) | 25 |
| 2 | | 26 | (h) | Rotherham U | D | 1-1 | Parry | 20 |
| 3 | | 29 | (h) | Middlesbrough | L | 1-7 | Parry | 19 |
| 4 | | 31 | (a) | Rotherham U | W | 2-1 | Barrowcliffe, Cargill (pen) | 13 |
| 5 | Sep | 5 | (a) | Stoke C | L | 1-2 | Darwin | 21 |
| 6 | | 9 | (h) | Cardiff C | L | 1-2 | Swallow | 17 |
| 7 | | 12 | (a) | Plymouth A | W | 5-0 | Thompson 2, Hannigan, Parry, Daykin | 22 |
| 8 | | 16 | (a) | Cardiff C | L | 0-2 | | 21 |
| 9 | | 19 | (h) | Liverpool | L | 1-2 | Thompson | 18 |
| 10 | | 26 | (a) | Charlton A | L | 1-6 | Thompson | 18 |
| 11 | Oct | 3 | (h) | Bristol C | W | 3-0 | Upton, Hannigan, Thompson | 16 |
| 12 | | 10 | (h) | Portsmouth | W | 1-0 | Swallow | 17 |
| 13 | | 17 | (a) | Sunderland | L | 1-3 | Darwin | 27 |
| 14 | | 24 | (h) | Aston Villa | D | 2-2 | Parry, Hannigan | 26 |
| 15 | | 31 | (a) | Lincoln C | L | 2-6 | Davies, Darwin | 12 |
| 16 | Nov | 7 | (h) | Leyton O | D | 1-1 | Darwin | 13 |
| 17 | | 14 | (a) | Huddersfield T | D | 2-2 | Upton, Brown | 9 |
| 18 | | 21 | (h) | Ipswich T | W | 3-0 | Buxton 2, Swallow | 14 |
| 19 | | 28 | (a) | Bristol R | L | 1-2 | Mays (pen) | 15 |
| 20 | Dec | 5 | (h) | Swansea T | L | 1-2 | Hannigan | 13 |
| 21 | | 12 | (a) | Brighton & HA | L | 0-2 | | 11 |
| 22 | | 19 | (h) | Sheffield U | D | 1-1 | Buxton | 11 |
| 23 | | 26 | (a) | Scunthorpe U | L | 2-3 | Barrowcliffe, Buxton | 13 |
| 24 | | 28 | (h) | Scunthorpe U | W | 3-0 | Upton, Parry, Hannigan | 17 |
| 25 | Jan | 2 | (a) | Middlesbrough | L | 0-3 | | 32 |
| 26 | | 16 | (h) | Stoke C | W | 2-0 | Powell, Darwin | 13 |
| 27 | | 23 | (h) | Plymouth A | W | 1-0 | Upton | 15 |
| 28 | Feb | 20 | (a) | Bristol C | W | 1-0 | Swallow | 14 |
| 29 | | 24 | (h) | Charlton A | L | 1-2 | Hannigan | 15 |
| 30 | | 27 | (a) | Portsmouth | W | 3-2 | Hannigan 2, Swallow | 13 |
| 31 | Mar | 5 | (h) | Sunderland | L | 0-1 | | 16 |
| 32 | | 15 | (a) | Aston Villa | L | 2-3 | Darwin, Swallow | 37 |
| 33 | | 19 | (h) | Bristol R | W | 1-0 | Hannigan | 13 |
| 34 | | 26 | (a) | Leyton O | L | 0-3 | | 10 |
| 35 | Apr | 2 | (h) | Huddersfield T | W | 3-2 | Thompson 2, Hannigan | 13 |
| 36 | | 6 | (a) | Liverpool | L | 1-4 | Thompson | 19 |
| 37 | | 9 | (a) | Ipswich T | D | 1-1 | Hall | 11 |
| 38 | | 15 | (a) | Hull C | D | 1-1 | Fagan | 13 |
| 39 | | 16 | (h) | Brighton & HA | L | 0-1 | | 14 |
| 40 | | 18 | (h) | Hull C | L | 1-3 | Darwin | 11 |
| 41 | | 23 | (a) | Swansea T | W | 3-1 | Davies, Darwin, Thompson | 9 |
| 42 | | 30 | (h) | Lincoln C | W | 3-1 | Thompson 2, Darwin | 10 |

FINAL LEAGUE POSITION: 18th in Division Two

Appeara
G

## FA Cup

| | | | | | | | | |
|---|---|---|---|---|---|---|---|---|
| 3 | Jan | 9 | (h) | Manchester U | L | 2-4 | Thompson, Barrowcliffe (pen) | 33 |

Appeara
G

| ord K | Conwell A | Barrowcliffe G | Upton F | Moore L | Davies G | Powell T | Parry J | Hannigan J | Darwin G | Cargill D | Swallow R | Thompson P | Mays A | Young R | Mitchell J | Daykin B | Martin R | Hall I | Brown G | Bowers J | Buxton I | Adlington T | Smith M | Richmond J | Fagan F | Newbery P | |
|---|---|---|---|---|---|---|---|---|---|---|---|---|---|---|---|---|---|---|---|---|---|---|---|---|---|---|---|
| | 2 | 3 | 4 | 5 | 6 | 7 | 8 | 9 | 10 | 11 | | | | | | | | | | | | | | | | | 1 |
| | 2 | 3 | 4 | 5 | 6 | 7 | 8 | 9 | 10 | 11 | | | | | | | | | | | | | | | | | 2 |
| | 2 | 3 | 4 | 5 | 6 | | 8 | | 10 | 11 | 7 | 9 | | | | | | | | | | | | | | | 3 |
| | | 2 | 6 | | 3 | | 8 | | 10 | 11 | 7 | 9 | 4 | 5 | | | | | | | | | | | | | 4 |
| | 2 | | 6 | | 3 | 11 | 8 | | 10 | | 7 | 9 | 4 | 5 | | | | | | | | | | | | | 5 |
| | 2 | | 6 | 5 | 3 | 11 | 8 | | 10 | | 7 | 9 | 4 | | 1 | | | | | | | | | | | | 6 |
| | | 2 | 6 | 5 | 3 | | 10 | 9 | | 11 | 7 | 8 | | | 1 | 4 | | | | | | | | | | | 7 |
| | | 2 | 6 | 5 | 3 | | 10 | 9 | | 11 | 7 | 8 | | | 1 | 4 | | | | | | | | | | | 8 |
| | | 2 | 6 | | 3 | 11 | 10 | 9 | | | 7 | 8 | | 5 | 1 | 4 | | | | | | | | | | | 9 |
| | 3 | 2 | 4 | | 6 | 11 | 10 | 9 | | | 7 | 8 | | 5 | | | | | | | | | | | | | 10 |
| | | 2 | 4 | 5 | 6 | | | 11 | 10 | | 7 | 9 | | | | | 3 | 8 | | | | | | | | | 11 |
| | | 2 | 4 | 5 | 6 | | | 9 | 10 | 11 | 7 | 8 | | | | | 3 | | | | | | | | | | 12 |
| | | 2 | 4 | 5 | 6 | | 8 | | 10 | 11 | 7 | 9 | | | | | 3 | | | | | | | | | | 13 |
| | | 2 | 4 | 5 | 6 | 7 | 8 | 11 | 10 | | | 9 | | | | | 3 | | | | | | | | | | 14 |
| | | 2 | 4 | 5 | 6 | 7 | 8 | 11 | 10 | | | 9 | | | | | 3 | | | | | | | | | | 15 |
| | | 2 | 6 | | 3 | 7 | 8 | 11 | 10 | | | | 4 | 5 | | | | | 9 | | | | | | | | 16 |
| | 3 | 2 | 6 | | | 7 | | 9 | | | 8 | | 4 | 5 | | | | | 10 | 11 | | | | | | | 17 |
| | 3 | 2 | 6 | 5 | | 7 | | 11 | | | 8 | | 4 | | | | | | 10 | | 9 | | | | | | 18 |
| | 3 | 2 | 6 | 5 | | 7 | | 11 | | | 8 | | 4 | | | | | | 10 | | 9 | | | | | | 19 |
| | 3 | 2 | | 5 | 6 | 11 | | 9 | 10 | | 7 | | 4 | | | | | 8 | | | | 1 | | | | | 20 |
| | | | 6 | | 3 | | 8 | 11 | 10 | | 7 | | 4 | 5 | | | | | 9 | | | 1 | 2 | | | | 21 |
| | | | 4 | | | | | 11 | | | 7 | | | 5 | | | 3 | 8 | 10 | | 9 | 1 | 2 | 6 | | | 22 |
| | | 2 | 4 | | | | 7 | 11 | | | | | | 5 | | | 3 | 8 | 10 | | 9 | | | 6 | | | 23 |
| | 3 | 2 | 4 | | 6 | 7 | 8 | 11 | | | | 9 | | 5 | | | | | 10 | | | | | | | | 24 |
| | 3 | 2 | 4 | | 6 | 7 | 8 | 11 | | | | 9 | | 5 | | | | | 10 | | | | | | | | 25 |
| | 2 | | 6 | | | 11 | | 7 | 10 | | | 8 | 4 | 5 | | | 3 | | | | 9 | | | | | | 26 |
| | 2 | 9 | 6 | | | 8 | | 11 | 10 | | 7 | | 4 | 5 | | | 3 | | | | | | | | | | 27 |
| | 2 | | 6 | | | 8 | | 9 | 10 | 11 | 7 | | 4 | 5 | | | 3 | | | | | | | | | | 28 |
| | 2 | | | | 6 | 8 | | 9 | 10 | 11 | 7 | | 4 | 5 | | | 3 | | | | | | | | | | 29 |
| | 2 | | 4 | | 6 | | 8 | 9 | 10 | 11 | 7 | | | 5 | | | 3 | | | | | 1 | | | | | 30 |
| | 2 | | | | 6 | 8 | 4 | 9 | 10 | 11 | 7 | | | 5 | | | 3 | | | | | 1 | | | | | 31 |
| | 2 | | | | 6 | | 8 | 9 | 10 | 11 | 7 | | 4 | 5 | | | 3 | | | | | 1 | | | | | 32 |
| | 2 | | | | 6 | | 8 | 9 | 10 | | 7 | | 4 | 5 | | | 3 | | | | | 1 | | | 11 | | 33 |
| | 2 | | | | 6 | | 8 | 9 | 10 | | 7 | | 4 | 5 | | | 3 | | | | | 1 | | | 11 | | 34 |
| | 3 | 2 | 6 | | | 10 | 4 | 11 | | | | 9 | | 5 | | | | 8 | | | | | | | 7 | | 35 |
| | 3 | 2 | 6 | | | 10 | 4 | 11 | | | | 9 | | 5 | | | | 8 | | | | | | | 7 | | 36 |
| | 2 | | 6 | | 3 | 10 | 4 | 11 | | | | 9 | | 5 | | | | 8 | | | | | | | 7 | | 37 |
| | 2 | | 6 | | 3 | | 4 | 11 | | | 10 | 9 | | 5 | | | | 8 | | | | | | | 7 | | 38 |
| | 3 | 2 | 6 | | | | 4 | 11 | | | 10 | | | 5 | | | | 8 | | | | | | | 7 | 9 | 39 |
| | 3 | 2 | | | | | 6 | 9 | 10 | 11 | | | 4 | | | | | 8 | | | | | 5 | | 7 | | 40 |
| | 3 | 2 | 4 | | 6 | | 8 | | 10 | | 7 | 9 | | | | | | | | | | | 5 | | 11 | | 41 |
| | 3 | 2 | 4 | | 6 | | 8 | | 10 | | 7 | 9 | | | | | | | | | | | 5 | | 11 | | 42 |
| | 29 | 28 | 35 | 14 | 30 | 23 | 31 | 35 | 26 | 14 | 29 | 22 | 17 | 25 | 4 | 3 | 16 | 10 | 9 | 1 | 5 | 8 | 5 | 2 | 10 | 1 | |
| | | 2 | 4 | | 2 | 1 | 5 | 10 | 9 | 2 | 6 | 11 | 1 | | | 1 | | 1 | 1 | | 4 | | | | 1 | | |

| | | | | | | | | | | | | | | | | | | | | | | | | | | |
|---|---|---|---|---|---|---|---|---|---|---|---|---|---|---|---|---|---|---|---|---|---|---|---|---|---|---|
| 3 | 2 | 4 | | 6 | 7 | 8 | 11 | | | | 9 | | 5 | | | | | 10 | | | | | | | | 3 |
| 1 | 1 | 1 | | 1 | 1 | 1 | 1 | | | | 1 | | 1 | | | | | 1 | | | | | | | | |
| | 1 | | | | | | | | | | 1 | | | | | | | | | | | | | | | |

# 1960-61

| | P | W | D | L | F | A | Pts |
|---|---|---|---|---|---|---|---|
| Ipswich T | 42 | 26 | 7 | 9 | 100 | 55 | 59 |
| Sheffield U | 42 | 26 | 6 | 10 | 81 | 51 | 58 |
| Liverpool | 42 | 21 | 10 | 11 | 87 | 58 | 52 |
| Norwich C | 42 | 20 | 9 | 13 | 70 | 53 | 49 |
| Middlesbrough | 42 | 18 | 12 | 12 | 83 | 74 | 48 |
| Sunderland | 42 | 17 | 13 | 12 | 75 | 60 | 47 |
| Swansea T | 42 | 18 | 11 | 13 | 77 | 73 | 47 |
| Southampton | 42 | 18 | 8 | 16 | 84 | 81 | 44 |
| Scunthorpe U | 42 | 14 | 15 | 13 | 69 | 64 | 43 |
| Charlton A | 42 | 16 | 11 | 15 | 97 | 91 | 43 |
| Plymouth A | 42 | 17 | 8 | 17 | 81 | 82 | 42 |
| Derby Co | 42 | 15 | 10 | 17 | 80 | 80 | 40 |
| Luton T | 42 | 15 | 9 | 18 | 71 | 79 | 39 |
| Leeds U | 42 | 14 | 10 | 18 | 75 | 83 | 38 |
| Rotherham U | 42 | 12 | 13 | 17 | 65 | 64 | 37 |
| Brighton & H.A. | 42 | 14 | 9 | 19 | 61 | 75 | 37 |
| Bristol R | 42 | 15 | 7 | 20 | 73 | 92 | 37 |
| Stoke C | 42 | 12 | 12 | 18 | 51 | 59 | 36 |
| Leyton O | 42 | 14 | 8 | 20 | 55 | 78 | 36 |
| Huddersfield T | 42 | 13 | 9 | 20 | 62 | 71 | 35 |
| Portsmouth | 42 | 11 | 11 | 20 | 64 | 91 | 33 |
| Lincoln C | 42 | 8 | 8 | 26 | 48 | 95 | 24 |

Manager: Harry Storer.
Leading scorer: Bill Curry, League 19, all matches 20.
League ever-present: Tony Conwell.

- Bill Curry, who won an England Under-23 cap when he was with Newcastle United, joined Derby from Brighton and Hove Albion in September for £12,000.
- Curry was leading scorer, either on his own or jointly, for three seasons and gave the Rams team an extra flourish, appreciated by supporters. He worked particularly well with Barry Hutchinson, signed in July after spending most of his Chesterfield career at wing-half.
- Jack Parry scored his 100th goal for Derby County in a 3–2 home defeat by Swansea Town on 25 February. After starring in attack in Division Three North, until injured in a clash with Grimsby Town defender Ray de Gruchy, Parry spent much of his career in midfield.

## Division Two

| Match No. | Date | | Venue | Opponents | Result | | Scorers | Atte |
|---|---|---|---|---|---|---|---|---|
| 1 | Aug | 20 | (h) | Brighton & HA | W | 4-1 | Swallow, Thompson, Darwin, Fagan | 14 |
| 2 | | 24 | (a) | Middlesbrough | W | 2-1 | Thompson, Darwin | 18 |
| 3 | | 27 | (a) | Ipswich T | L | 1-4 | Parry | 12 |
| 4 | | 31 | (h) | Middlesbrough | W | 1-0 | Swallow | 19 |
| 5 | Sep | 3 | (h) | Scunthorpe U | L | 2-5 | Swallow, Fagan | 16 |
| 6 | | 7 | (a) | Southampton | L | 1-5 | Fagan | 21 |
| 7 | | 10 | (a) | Leyton O | L | 1-2 | Newbery | 10 |
| 8 | | 14 | (h) | Southampton | D | 2-2 | Fagan, Newbery | 12 |
| 9 | | 17 | (h) | Stoke C | D | 1-1 | Conwell | 14 |
| 10 | | 24 | (h) | Bristol R | D | 1-1 | Fagan | 12 |
| 11 | Oct | 1 | (a) | Liverpool | L | 0-1 | | 24 |
| 12 | | 8 | (a) | Swansea T | L | 1-2 | Hall | 8 |
| 13 | | 15 | (h) | Luton T | W | 4-1 | Curry 2, Hutchinson, Barrowcliffe (pen) | 13 |
| 14 | | 22 | (a) | Lincoln C | W | 4-3 | Curry 3, Hall | 9 |
| 15 | | 29 | (h) | Portsmouth | W | 6-2 | Curry 2, Powell 2, Hall, Hutchinson | 17 |
| 16 | Nov | 5 | (a) | Huddersfield T | W | 3-1 | Curry, Hall, Hutchinson | 11 |
| 17 | | 12 | (h) | Sunderland | D | 1-1 | Hutchinson | 21 |
| 18 | | 19 | (a) | Plymouth A | L | 2-4 | Thompson, Hutchinson | 18 |
| 19 | | 26 | (h) | Norwich C | D | 0-0 | | 16 |
| 20 | Dec | 3 | (a) | Charlton A | L | 1-3 | Young | 6 |
| 21 | | 10 | (h) | Sheffield U | W | 2-0 | Hall, Hannigan | 16 |
| 22 | | 17 | (a) | Brighton & HA | L | 2-3 | Curry, Hall | 12 |
| 23 | | 24 | (h) | Leeds U | L | 2-3 | Hall 2 | 15 |
| 24 | | 27 | (a) | Leeds U | D | 3-3 | Powell 2, Curry | 18 |
| 25 | Jan | 14 | (a) | Scunthorpe U | W | 2-1 | Powell, Hall | 10 |
| 26 | | 21 | (h) | Leyton O | W | 3-1 | Barrowcliffe 2 (2 pens), Hall | 11 |
| 27 | Feb | 11 | (a) | Bristol R | D | 1-1 | Parry | 11 |
| 28 | | 18 | (h) | Liverpool | L | 1-4 | Barrowcliffe (pen) | 16 |
| 29 | | 25 | (h) | Swansea T | L | 2-3 | Curry, Parry | 8 |
| 30 | Mar | 4 | (a) | Luton T | D | 1-1 | Curry | 13 |
| 31 | | 11 | (h) | Lincoln C | W | 3-1 | Hutchinson 2, Curry | 10 |
| 32 | | 20 | (a) | Stoke C | L | 1-2 | Curry | 6 |
| 33 | | 25 | (h) | Huddersfield T | D | 1-1 | Hutchinson | 9 |
| 34 | Apr | 1 | (a) | Norwich C | W | 2-0 | Curry, Hutchinson | 22 |
| 35 | | 3 | (h) | Rotherham U | W | 3-0 | Thompson, Parry, Hannigan | 12 |
| 36 | | 4 | (a) | Rotherham U | D | 1-1 | Hutchinson | 6 |
| 37 | | 8 | (h) | Plymouth A | W | 4-1 | Curry 2, Powell, Hutchinson | 12 |
| 38 | | 15 | (a) | Sunderland | W | 2-1 | Curry, Hutchinson | 21 |
| 39 | | 19 | (a) | Sheffield U | L | 1-3 | Hutchinson | 21 |
| 40 | | 22 | (h) | Charlton A | L | 2-3 | Curry, Upton | 10 |
| 41 | | 24 | (h) | Ipswich T | L | 1-4 | Hutchinson | 13 |
| 42 | | 29 | (a) | Portsmouth | L | 2-3 | Hutchinson 2 | 9 |

FINAL LEAGUE POSITION: 12th in Division Two

Appeara
G

## FA Cup

| | | | | | | | | |
|---|---|---|---|---|---|---|---|---|
| 3 | Jan | 7 | (a) | Brighton & HA | L | 1-3 | Thompson | 18 |

Appeara
G

## League Cup

| | | | | | | | | |
|---|---|---|---|---|---|---|---|---|
| 1 | Oct | 11 | (a) | Watford | W | 5-2 | Buxton, Hall, Hutchinson, Cargill, Porter (og) | 10 |
| 2 | | 19 | (h) | Barnsley | W | 3-0 | Hutchinson, Curry, Barrowcliffe (pen) | 11 |
| 3 | Nov | 14 | (h) | Norwich C | L | 1-4 | Hutchinson | 21 |

Appeara
G

| …ord K | Barrowcliffe G | Conwell A | Upton F | Young R | Davies G | Swallow R | Powell T | Thompson P | Darwin G | Fagan F | Parry J | Adlington T | Cargill D | Moore L | Smith M | Newbery P | Hannigan J | Buxton I | Curry W | Hall I | Hutchinson B | Bowers J | Scarborough B | Hopkinson M | |
|---|---|---|---|---|---|---|---|---|---|---|---|---|---|---|---|---|---|---|---|---|---|---|---|---|---|
| | 2 | 3 | 4 | 5 | 6 | 7 | 8 | 9 | 10 | 11 | | | | | | | | | | | | | | | 1 |
| | 2 | 3 | 4 | 5 | 6 | 7 | 8 | 9 | 10 | 11 | | | | | | | | | | | | | | | 2 |
| | 2 | 3 | 4 | 5 | 6 | 7 | | 9 | 10 | 11 | 8 | | | | | | | | | | | | | | 3 |
| | 2 | 3 | 4 | 5 | 6 | 7 | 8 | 9 | | 11 | 10 | 1 | | | | | | | | | | | | | 4 |
| | 2 | 3 | 4 | 5 | 6 | 10 | | 9 | | 7 | 8 | 1 | 11 | | | | | | | | | | | | 5 |
| | 2 | 3 | 4 | 5 | 6 | 7 | 8 | 9 | 10 | 11 | | 1 | | | | | | | | | | | | | 6 |
| | | 3 | 4 | | 6 | 7 | 8 | | 10 | | | 1 | 11 | 2 | 5 | 9 | | | | | | | | | 7 |
| | 2 | 3 | 4 | | 6 | 7 | 8 | | 10 | 11 | | 1 | | | 5 | 9 | | | | | | | | | 8 |
| | 2 | 3 | 6 | 5 | | 7 | 8 | | 10 | 11 | 4 | 1 | | | | 9 | | | | | | | | | 9 |
| | 2 | 3 | 6 | 5 | | 7 | 8 | | | 11 | 4 | 1 | | | | | 9 | 10 | | | | | | | 10 |
| | 2 | 3 | 6 | 5 | | 7 | 8 | | 10 | | 4 | 1 | 11 | | | | | | 9 | | | | | | 11 |
| | 2 | 3 | 6 | 5 | | 7 | | | | | 4 | 1 | 11 | | | | | | 9 | 8 | 10 | | | | 12 |
| | 2 | 3 | 6 | 5 | | 7 | 11 | | | | 4 | 1 | | | | | | | 9 | 8 | 10 | | | | 13 |
| | 2 | 3 | 6 | 5 | | 7 | 11 | | | | 4 | 1 | | | | | | | 9 | 8 | 10 | | | | 14 |
| | 2 | 3 | 6 | 5 | | 7 | 11 | | | | 4 | 1 | | | | | | | 9 | 8 | 10 | | | | 15 |
| | 2 | 3 | 6 | | | 7 | 11 | | | | 4 | 1 | | | 5 | | | | 9 | 8 | 10 | | | | 16 |
| | 2 | 3 | 6 | | | 7 | 11 | | | | 4 | 1 | | | 5 | | | | 9 | 8 | 10 | | | | 17 |
| | 2 | 3 | 6 | | | 7 | | 9 | | 11 | 4 | 1 | | 5 | | | | | | 8 | 10 | | | | 18 |
| | | 2 | 6 | 5 | 3 | 7 | | 9 | | 11 | 4 | 1 | | | | | | | | 8 | 10 | | | | 19 |
| | | 2 | 6 | 5 | 3 | 7 | | | | | 4 | 1 | | | | | | | 9 | 8 | 10 | 11 | | | 20 |
| | | 2 | 6 | 5 | 3 | | | | | | 4 | 1 | | | | | 7 | | 9 | 8 | 10 | 11 | | | 21 |
| | | 2 | 6 | 5 | 3 | | 11 | | | | 4 | 1 | | | | | 7 | | 9 | 8 | 10 | | | | 22 |
| | | 2 | 6 | 5 | 3 | | 11 | | | | 4 | 1 | | | | | 7 | | 9 | 8 | 10 | | | | 23 |
| | 2 | 3 | 6 | | | 7 | 11 | 10 | | | 4 | 1 | | 5 | | | | | 9 | 8 | | | | | 24 |
| | 2 | 3 | 6 | | | 7 | 11 | | | | 4 | | | 5 | | | | | 9 | 8 | 10 | | | | 25 |
| | 2 | 3 | 6 | | | 7 | 11 | | | | 4 | | | 5 | | | | | 9 | 8 | 10 | | | | 26 |
| | 2 | 3 | 6 | | | 7 | 11 | | | | 4 | | | 5 | | | | | 9 | 8 | 10 | | | | 27 |
| | 2 | 3 | 6 | | | 7 | | | | 11 | 4 | | | 5 | | | | | 9 | 8 | 10 | | | | 28 |
| | 2 | 3 | 6 | 5 | | 7 | 11 | 9 | | | 4 | | | | | | | | 10 | 8 | | | | | 29 |
| | 2 | 3 | 4 | 5 | 6 | 7 | | 9 | | | 8 | 1 | | | | | | | 10 | | | 11 | | | 30 |
| | 2 | 3 | 6 | 5 | | | 7 | | | | 4 | 1 | | | | | | | 9 | 8 | 10 | | 11 | | 31 |
| | 2 | 3 | 6 | 5 | | | 7 | | | | 4 | 1 | | | | | | | 9 | 8 | 10 | | 11 | | 32 |
| | 2 | 3 | 6 | 5 | | | 7 | | | | 4 | 1 | | | | | | | 9 | 8 | 10 | | 11 | | 33 |
| | 2 | 3 | 6 | 5 | | | 7 | 8 | | | 4 | | | | | | 11 | | 9 | | 10 | | | | 34 |
| | 2 | 3 | 6 | 5 | | | 7 | 8 | | | 4 | | | | | | 11 | | 9 | | 10 | | | | 35 |
| | 2 | 3 | 6 | 5 | | 7 | | 8 | | | 4 | | | | | | 11 | | 9 | | 10 | | | | 36 |
| | 2 | 3 | | 5 | | | 7 | 8 | | | 4 | | | | | | 11 | | 9 | | 10 | | | 6 | 37 |
| | 2 | 3 | 6 | 5 | | 8 | 7 | | | | 4 | | | | | | 11 | | 9 | | 10 | | | | 38 |
| | 2 | 3 | 6 | | | | 7 | | | | 4 | | | 5 | | | 11 | | 9 | 8 | 10 | | | | 39 |
| | 2 | 3 | 5 | | | 7 | 11 | | | | 4 | | | | | | | | 9 | | 10 | 8 | | 6 | 40 |
| | 2 | 3 | 6 | 5 | | 7 | | 8 | | 11 | 4 | | | | | | | | 9 | | 10 | | | | 41 |
| | 2 | 3 | 6 | | | | | 8 | | 11 | 4 | | | | 5 | | 7 | | 9 | | 10 | | | | 42 |
| | 36 | 42 | 41 | 29 | 14 | 31 | 30 | 17 | 8 | 14 | 37 | 25 | 4 | 8 | 5 | 3 | 11 | 1 | 30 | 22 | 28 | 4 | 3 | 2 | |
| | 4 | 1 | 1 | 1 | | 3 | 6 | 4 | 2 | 5 | 4 | | | | | 2 | 2 | | 19 | 10 | 16 | | | | |

| …ord K | Barrowcliffe G | Conwell A | Upton F | Young R | Davies G | Swallow R | Powell T | Thompson P | Darwin G | Fagan F | Parry J | Adlington T | Cargill D | Moore L | Smith M | Newbery P | Hannigan J | Buxton I | Curry W | Hall I | Hutchinson B | Bowers J | Scarborough B | Hopkinson M | |
|---|---|---|---|---|---|---|---|---|---|---|---|---|---|---|---|---|---|---|---|---|---|---|---|---|---|
| | 2 | 3 | 6 | | | 7 | 11 | 10 | | | 4 | 1 | | 5 | | | | | 9 | 8 | | | | | 3 |
| | 1 | 1 | 1 | | | 1 | 1 | 1 | | | 1 | 1 | | 1 | | | | | 1 | 1 | | | | | |
| | | | | | | | | 1 | | | | | | | | | | | | | | | | | |

| …ord K | Barrowcliffe G | Conwell A | Upton F | Young R | Davies G | Swallow R | Powell T | Thompson P | Darwin G | Fagan F | Parry J | Adlington T | Cargill D | Moore L | Smith M | Newbery P | Hannigan J | Buxton I | Curry W | Hall I | Hutchinson B | Bowers J | Scarborough B | Hopkinson M | |
|---|---|---|---|---|---|---|---|---|---|---|---|---|---|---|---|---|---|---|---|---|---|---|---|---|---|
| | 2 | 3 | 6 | 5 | | 7 | | | | | 4 | 1 | 11 | | | | | 9 | | 8 | 10 | | | | 1 |
| | 2 | 3 | 6 | 5 | | 7 | | | | | 4 | 1 | | | | | | | 9 | 8 | 10 | 11 | | | 2 |
| | 2 | 3 | 6 | | | 7 | | | | 11 | 4 | 1 | | | 5 | | | | 9 | 8 | 10 | | | | 3 |
| | 3 | 3 | 3 | 2 | | 3 | | | | 1 | 3 | 3 | 1 | | 1 | | | 1 | 2 | 3 | 3 | 1 | | | |
| | 1 | | | | | | | | | | | | 1 | | | | | 1 | 1 | 1 | 3 | | | | |

1 own-goal

# 1961-62

| | P | W | D | L | F | A | Pts |
|---|---|---|---|---|---|---|---|
| Liverpool | 42 | 27 | 8 | 7 | 99 | 43 | 62 |
| Leyton O | 42 | 22 | 10 | 10 | 69 | 40 | 54 |
| Sunderland | 42 | 22 | 9 | 11 | 85 | 50 | 53 |
| Scunthorpe U | 42 | 21 | 7 | 14 | 86 | 71 | 49 |
| Plymouth A | 42 | 19 | 8 | 15 | 75 | 75 | 46 |
| Southampton | 42 | 18 | 9 | 15 | 77 | 62 | 45 |
| Huddersfield T | 42 | 16 | 12 | 14 | 67 | 59 | 44 |
| Stoke C | 42 | 17 | 8 | 17 | 55 | 57 | 42 |
| Rotherham U | 42 | 16 | 9 | 17 | 70 | 76 | 41 |
| Preston N.E. | 42 | 15 | 10 | 17 | 55 | 57 | 40 |
| Newcastle U | 42 | 15 | 9 | 18 | 64 | 58 | 39 |
| Middlesbrough | 42 | 16 | 7 | 19 | 76 | 72 | 39 |
| Luton T | 42 | 17 | 5 | 20 | 69 | 71 | 39 |
| Walsall | 42 | 14 | 11 | 17 | 70 | 75 | 39 |
| Charlton A | 42 | 15 | 9 | 18 | 69 | 75 | 39 |
| Derby Co | 42 | 14 | 11 | 17 | 68 | 75 | 39 |
| Norwich C | 42 | 14 | 11 | 17 | 61 | 70 | 39 |
| Bury | 42 | 17 | 5 | 20 | 52 | 76 | 39 |
| Leeds U | 42 | 12 | 12 | 18 | 50 | 61 | 36 |
| Swansea T | 42 | 12 | 12 | 18 | 61 | 83 | 36 |
| Bristol R | 42 | 13 | 7 | 22 | 53 | 81 | 33 |
| Brighton & H.A. | 42 | 10 | 11 | 21 | 42 | 86 | 31 |

Manager: Harry Storer.
Leading scorer: Bill Curry, League 18, all matches 25.

- After seven seasons at the Baseball Ground, Harry Storer's management career came to a close. He was 64.
- Storer revived the Rams after relegation to the Third North and did much to reduce the overdraft but was unable to make significant progress in the Second Division. He won promotions with Coventry City and Birmingham City as well as the Rams.
- Des Palmer, a Welsh international who made his name with Swansea Town but suffered a severe knee injury when he joined Liverpool, spent the season with Derby. He had played in South Africa with Johannesburg Ramblers to regain fitness.
- Reg Matthews, who kept goal for England when a Third Division player with Coventry, joined Derby from Chelsea in October.

## Division Two

| Match No. | Date | | Venue | Opponents | Result | | Scorers | Atte |
|---|---|---|---|---|---|---|---|---|
| 1 | Aug | 19 | (a) | Middlesbrough | W | 4-3 | Curry 2, Palmer 2 | 15 |
| 2 | | 23 | (h) | Luton T | W | 2-0 | Curry, Hutchinson | 18 |
| 3 | | 26 | (h) | Walsall | L | 1-3 | Hutchinson | 26 |
| 4 | | 30 | (a) | Luton T | L | 2-4 | Hall 2 | 15 |
| 5 | Sep | 2 | (a) | Stoke C | D | 1-1 | Parry | 13 |
| 6 | | 6 | (h) | Swansea T | W | 6-3 | Swallow 2 (1 pen), Curry 2, Hutchinson, Griffiths (og) | 14 |
| 7 | | 9 | (a) | Leyton O | L | 0-2 | | 12 |
| 8 | | 16 | (h) | Preston NE | W | 3-2 | Davies, Hutchinson, Powell | 13 |
| 9 | | 19 | (a) | Swansea T | L | 1-3 | Thompson | 13 |
| 10 | | 23 | (a) | Plymouth A | W | 3-2 | Swallow 2, Fincham (og) | 13 |
| 11 | | 30 | (h) | Huddersfield T | W | 1-0 | Hutchinson | 13 |
| 12 | Oct | 7 | (h) | Sunderland | D | 1-1 | Curry | 16 |
| 13 | | 14 | (a) | Rotherham U | D | 2-2 | Curry 2 | 12 |
| 14 | | 21 | (h) | Liverpool | W | 2-0 | Curry, Hopkinson | 27 |
| 15 | | 28 | (a) | Charlton A | L | 0-4 | | 12 |
| 16 | Nov | 4 | (h) | Bury | W | 3-0 | Palmer (pen), Curry, Havenhand | 15 |
| 17 | | 11 | (a) | Bristol R | W | 4-1 | Havenhand 3, Thompson | 10 |
| 18 | | 18 | (h) | Scunthorpe U | D | 2-2 | Roby, Havenhand | 21 |
| 19 | | 25 | (a) | Norwich C | L | 2-3 | Roby, Palmer | 16 |
| 20 | Dec | 2 | (h) | Leeds U | D | 3-3 | Palmer (pen), Hutchinson, Bell (og) | 16 |
| 21 | | 9 | (a) | Brighton & HA | W | 2-1 | Curry, Hutchinson | 10 |
| 22 | | 16 | (h) | Middlesbrough | W | 3-2 | Curry 3 | 15 |
| 23 | | 23 | (a) | Walsall | L | 0-2 | | 9 |
| 24 | | 26 | (h) | Southampton | D | 1-1 | Havenhand | 20 |
| 25 | | 30 | (a) | Southampton | L | 1-2 | Roby | 12 |
| 26 | Jan | 13 | (h) | Stoke C | W | 2-0 | Palmer, Havenhand | 18 |
| 27 | | 20 | (h) | Leyton O | L | 1-2 | Curry | 22 |
| 28 | Feb | 3 | (a) | Preston NE | L | 0-1 | | 12 |
| 29 | | 10 | (h) | Plymouth A | D | 2-2 | Curry, Havenhand | 15 |
| 30 | | 24 | (a) | Sunderland | L | 1-2 | Curry | 22 |
| 31 | Mar | 3 | (h) | Rotherham U | D | 1-1 | Havenhand | 12 |
| 32 | | 10 | (a) | Liverpool | L | 1-4 | Havenhand | 38 |
| 33 | | 17 | (h) | Charlton A | L | 0-1 | | 12 |
| 34 | | 24 | (a) | Bury | D | 2-2 | Curry, Havenhand | 7 |
| 35 | | 31 | (h) | Bristol R | W | 4-1 | Havenhand 3, Stephenson | 8 |
| 36 | Apr | 6 | (a) | Scunthorpe U | L | 0-2 | | 7 |
| 37 | | 9 | (a) | Huddersfield T | L | 0-4 | | 8 |
| 38 | | 14 | (h) | Norwich C | D | 1-1 | Moore | 8 |
| 39 | | 20 | (a) | Newcastle U | L | 0-3 | | 33 |
| 40 | | 21 | (a) | Leeds U | D | 0-0 | | 11 |
| 41 | | 23 | (h) | Newcastle U | L | 1-2 | Bowers | 10 |
| 42 | | 28 | (h) | Brighton & HA | W | 2-0 | Hutchinson, Bowers | 6 |

FINAL LEAGUE POSITION: 16th in Division Two

Appeara
G

## FA Cup

| | | | | | | | | |
|---|---|---|---|---|---|---|---|---|
| 3 | Jan | 6 | (a) | Leeds U | D | 2-2 | Curry, Swallow | 27 |
| R | | 10 | (h) | Leeds U | W | 3-1 | Curry 2, Bell (og) | 28 |
| 4 | | 27 | (a) | Charlton A | L | 1-2 | Curry | 34 |

Appeara
G

## League Cup

| | | | | | | | | |
|---|---|---|---|---|---|---|---|---|
| 1 | Sep | 14 | (a) | Notts C | D | 2-2 | Hall, Hutchinson | 14 |
| R | | 27 | (h) | Notts C | W | 3-2 | Roby, Curry, Hall | 12 |
| 2 | Oct | 4 | (a) | Portsmouth | D | 1-1 | Thompson | 11 |
| R | Nov | 1 | (h) | Portsmouth | L | 2-4 | Curry 2 | 13 |

Appeara
G

| ord K | Barrowcliffe G | Conwell A | Parry J | Young R | Davies G | Roby D | Palmer D | Curry W | Hutchinson B | Swallow R | Hall I | Hopkinson M | Powell T | Thompson P | Moore L | Bowers J | Havenhand K | Matthews R | Daykin B | Waller P | Stephenson R | Buxton I | Webster R | Richmond J | Williamson M | Adlington T | |
|---|---|---|---|---|---|---|---|---|---|---|---|---|---|---|---|---|---|---|---|---|---|---|---|---|---|---|---|
| | 2 | 3 | 4 | 5 | 6 | 7 | 8 | 9 | 10 | 11 | | | | | | | | | | | | | | | | | 1 |
| | 2 | 3 | 4 | 5 | 6 | 7 | | 9 | 10 | 11 | 8 | | | | | | | | | | | | | | | | 2 |
| | 2 | 3 | 4 | 5 | 6 | 7 | 8 | 9 | 10 | 11 | | | | | | | | | | | | | | | | | 3 |
| | 2 | 3 | 4 | 5 | 6 | 7 | 10 | 9 | | 11 | 8 | | | | | | | | | | | | | | | | 4 |
| | | 2 | 4 | 5 | 3 | 7 | | 9 | 10 | 11 | 8 | 6 | | | | | | | | | | | | | | | 5 |
| | | 2 | 4 | 5 | 3 | 7 | | 9 | 10 | 11 | 8 | 6 | | | | | | | | | | | | | | | 6 |
| | | 2 | 4 | 5 | 3 | 7 | | | 10 | 11 | | 6 | 8 | 9 | | | | | | | | | | | | | 7 |
| | | 2 | 4 | | 3 | 7 | | 9 | 10 | 11 | | 6 | 8 | | 5 | | | | | | | | | | | | 8 |
| | 2 | 3 | 4 | | 5 | 7 | | 9 | | 11 | 10 | 6 | | 8 | | | | | | | | | | | | | 9 |
| | 2 | 3 | 8 | | 4 | 7 | | 9 | | 11 | 10 | 6 | | | 5 | | | | | | | | | | | | 10 |
| | | 2 | 4 | | 3 | 7 | | 9 | 10 | | 8 | 6 | 11 | | 5 | | | | | | | | | | | | 11 |
| | 2 | | 4 | | 3 | 7 | | 9 | 10 | | | 6 | | 8 | 5 | 11 | | | | | | | | | | | 12 |
| | 2 | | 4 | 5 | 3 | 7 | 11 | 9 | 10 | | | 6 | | | | | 8 | | | | | | | | | | 13 |
| | | 2 | 4 | 5 | 3 | 7 | 11 | 9 | 10 | | | 6 | | | | | 8 | | | | | | | | | | 14 |
| | | 2 | 4 | 5 | 3 | 7 | 11 | 9 | 10 | | | 6 | | | | | 8 | | | | | | | | | | 15 |
| | | 2 | 4 | | 3 | 7 | 10 | 9 | | | | 6 | | | 5 | 11 | 8 | 1 | | | | | | | | | 16 |
| | | 2 | 4 | | 3 | 7 | 11 | 9 | | | | 6 | | 10 | 5 | | 8 | 1 | | | | | | | | | 17 |
| | | 2 | 4 | | 3 | 7 | 11 | 9 | | | | 6 | | 10 | 5 | | 8 | 1 | | | | | | | | | 18 |
| | | 2 | 4 | | 3 | 7 | 11 | 9 | | | | 6 | | 10 | 5 | | 8 | 1 | | | | | | | | | 19 |
| | | 2 | 4 | 5 | 3 | 7 | 11 | 9 | 10 | | | 6 | | | | | 8 | 1 | | | | | | | | | 20 |
| | 2 | | 4 | | 3 | 7 | | 9 | 10 | 11 | | 6 | | | 5 | | 8 | 1 | | | | | | | | | 21 |
| | 2 | | 4 | | 3 | 7 | | 9 | 10 | 11 | | 6 | | | 5 | | 8 | 1 | | | | | | | | | 22 |
| | 2 | 3 | 4 | | 5 | 7 | | 9 | 10 | 11 | | 6 | | | | | 8 | 1 | | | | | | | | | 23 |
| | 2 | 3 | 4 | | 6 | 7 | 11 | 9 | 10 | | | | | | 5 | | 8 | 1 | | | | | | | | | 24 |
| | 2 | 3 | 4 | | | 7 | 11 | 9 | 10 | | | 6 | | | 5 | | 8 | 1 | | | | | | | | | 25 |
| | 2 | | 4 | | | 7 | 11 | 9 | | 10 | | 6 | | | 5 | | 8 | | 3 | | | | | | | | 26 |
| | 2 | | 4 | | 3 | 7 | 11 | 9 | | 10 | | 6 | | | 5 | | 8 | 1 | | | | | | | | | 27 |
| | 2 | | 4 | | 3 | 7 | | 9 | | 11 | | 6 | | | 5 | | 8 | 1 | | 10 | | | | | | | 28 |
| | 2 | | 4 | | 3 | 7 | | 9 | | 11 | 10 | 6 | | | 5 | | 8 | 1 | | | | | | | | | 29 |
| | 2 | | 4 | | 3 | 7 | | 9 | | 11 | 10 | 6 | | | 5 | | 8 | 1 | | | | | | | | | 30 |
| | 2 | | 4 | | 3 | 11 | | 9 | | 10 | | 6 | | | 5 | | 8 | 1 | | | 7 | | | | | | 31 |
| | 2 | 3 | 4 | | 6 | 11 | | 9 | | 7 | | | | | 5 | | 8 | 1 | | | | 10 | | | | | 32 |
| | 2 | 3 | 4 | | 6 | 11 | | 9 | | 7 | | | | | 5 | | 8 | | | | | 10 | | | | | 33 |
| | 2 | | 10 | | 3 | 7 | | 9 | | | | 6 | | | 5 | 11 | 8 | 1 | | | | | 4 | | | | 34 |
| | 2 | | 10 | | 3 | 11 | | 9 | | | | 6 | | | 5 | | 8 | 1 | | | 7 | | 4 | | | | 35 |
| | 2 | | 10 | | 3 | 11 | | 9 | | | | 6 | | | 5 | | 8 | 1 | | | 7 | | 4 | | | | 36 |
| | 2 | | 10 | | 3 | 11 | | 9 | | | 7 | 6 | | | 5 | | 8 | 1 | | | | | 4 | | | | 37 |
| | 2 | 3 | 6 | | | 7 | | 9 | | 11 | 10 | | | | 5 | | 8 | 1 | | | | | 4 | | | | 38 |
| | 2 | 3 | | | | 7 | 11 | 9 | 10 | 8 | | 6 | | | 5 | | | 1 | | | | | 4 | | | | 39 |
| | 2 | 3 | | 4 | 6 | | 11 | 9 | 10 | 8 | 7 | | | | 5 | | | 1 | | | | | | | | | 40 |
| | 2 | 3 | | 4 | 6 | 7 | 11 | 9 | 10 | | | | | | 5 | 8 | | 1 | | | | | | | | | 41 |
| | 2 | | | | | 7 | | 9 | 10 | | | 6 | | | 5 | 8 | | 1 | | | | | 4 | 3 | 11 | | 42 |
| 7 | 30 | 27 | 38 | 13 | 37 | 41 | 18 | 41 | 22 | 24 | 12 | 32 | 3 | 6 | 29 | 5 | 26 | 25 | 1 | 1 | 3 | 2 | 7 | 1 | 1 | | |
| | | | 1 | | 1 | 3 | 6 | 18 | 8 | 4 | 2 | 1 | 1 | 2 | 1 | 2 | 14 | | | | 1 | | | | | | |

3 own-goals

| ord K | Barrowcliffe G | Conwell A | Parry J | Young R | Davies G | Roby D | Palmer D | Curry W | Hutchinson B | Swallow R | Hall I | Hopkinson M | Powell T | Thompson P | Moore L | Bowers J | Havenhand K | Matthews R | Daykin B | Waller P | Stephenson R | Buxton I | Webster R | Richmond J | Williamson M | Adlington T | |
|---|---|---|---|---|---|---|---|---|---|---|---|---|---|---|---|---|---|---|---|---|---|---|---|---|---|---|---|
| | 2 | | 4 | | 3 | 7 | 11 | 9 | | 10 | | 6 | | | 5 | | 8 | 1 | | | | | | | | | 3 |
| | 2 | | 4 | | 3 | 7 | 11 | 9 | | 10 | | 6 | | | 5 | | 8 | 1 | | | | | | | | | R |
| | 2 | | 4 | | 3 | 7 | | 9 | 10 | 11 | | 6 | | | 5 | | 8 | 1 | | | | | | | | | 4 |
| | 3 | | 3 | | 3 | 3 | 2 | 3 | 1 | 3 | | 3 | | | 3 | | 3 | 3 | | | | | | | | | |
| | | | | | | | | 4 | | 1 | | | | | | | | | | | | | | | | | |

1 own-goal

| ord K | Barrowcliffe G | Conwell A | Parry J | Young R | Davies G | Roby D | Palmer D | Curry W | Hutchinson B | Swallow R | Hall I | Hopkinson M | Powell T | Thompson P | Moore L | Bowers J | Havenhand K | Matthews R | Daykin B | Waller P | Stephenson R | Buxton I | Webster R | Richmond J | Williamson M | Adlington T | |
|---|---|---|---|---|---|---|---|---|---|---|---|---|---|---|---|---|---|---|---|---|---|---|---|---|---|---|---|
| | | 2 | 4 | | 3 | 7 | | 9 | 10 | 11 | 8 | 6 | | | 5 | | | | | | | | | | | | 1 |
| | | 2 | 4 | | 3 | 7 | 10 | 9 | | | 8 | 6 | 11 | | 5 | | | | | | | | | | | | R |
| | | 2 | 4 | | 3 | 7 | | 9 | 10 | 11 | | 6 | | 8 | 5 | | | | | | | | | | | | 2 |
| | | 2 | 4 | 5 | 3 | 7 | | 9 | 10 | | 8 | 6 | 11 | | | | | | | | | | | | | 1 | R |
| | | 4 | 4 | 1 | 4 | 4 | 1 | 4 | 3 | 2 | 3 | 4 | 2 | 1 | 3 | | | | | | | | | | | 1 | |
| | | | | | | 1 | | 3 | 1 | | 2 | | | 1 | | | | | | | | | | | | | |

# 1962-63

| | P | W | D | L | F | A | Pts |
|---|---|---|---|---|---|---|---|
| Stoke C | 42 | 20 | 13 | 9 | 73 | 50 | 53 |
| Chelsea | 42 | 24 | 4 | 14 | 81 | 42 | 52 |
| Sunderland | 42 | 20 | 12 | 10 | 84 | 55 | 52 |
| Middlesbrough | 42 | 20 | 9 | 13 | 86 | 85 | 49 |
| Leeds U | 42 | 19 | 10 | 13 | 79 | 53 | 48 |
| Huddersfield T | 42 | 17 | 14 | 11 | 63 | 50 | 48 |
| Newcastle U | 42 | 18 | 11 | 13 | 79 | 59 | 47 |
| Bury | 42 | 18 | 11 | 13 | 51 | 47 | 47 |
| Scunthorpe U | 42 | 16 | 12 | 14 | 57 | 59 | 44 |
| Cardiff C | 42 | 18 | 7 | 17 | 83 | 73 | 43 |
| Southampton | 42 | 17 | 8 | 17 | 72 | 67 | 42 |
| Plymouth A | 42 | 15 | 12 | 15 | 76 | 73 | 42 |
| Norwich C | 42 | 17 | 8 | 17 | 80 | 79 | 42 |
| Rotherham U | 42 | 17 | 6 | 19 | 67 | 74 | 40 |
| Swansea T | 42 | 15 | 9 | 18 | 51 | 72 | 39 |
| Portsmouth | 42 | 13 | 11 | 18 | 63 | 79 | 37 |
| Preston N.E. | 42 | 13 | 11 | 18 | 59 | 74 | 37 |
| Derby Co | 42 | 12 | 12 | 18 | 61 | 72 | 36 |
| Grimsby T | 42 | 11 | 13 | 18 | 55 | 66 | 35 |
| Charlton A | 42 | 13 | 5 | 24 | 62 | 94 | 31 |
| Walsall | 42 | 11 | 9 | 22 | 53 | 89 | 31 |
| Luton T | 42 | 11 | 7 | 24 | 61 | 84 | 29 |

Manager: Tim Ward.
Leading scorers: Bill Curry, League 21. Bill Curry, Barry Hutchinson, all matches 22.
League ever-present: Jack Parry.

- Tim Ward, another former Derby player, replaced Harry Storer, having previously managed Barnsley and Grimsby Town. He also had eight days in charge of Exeter City before Barnsley called him back. They had not released his playing registration.
- Like Storer before him, Ward was frustrated by lack of funds and a cautious boardroom but made some signings who were to play a part in Derby's greatest days.
- One of the future champions, Ron Webster, was already there. Webster went on to play under six managers and worked for three more when he returned as Youth team coach.

## Division Two

| Match No. | Date | | Venue | Opponents | Result | | Scorers | Atte |
|---|---|---|---|---|---|---|---|---|
| 1 | Aug | 18 | (a) | Huddersfield T | D | 3-3 | Barrowcliffe (pen), Curry, Hutchinson | 10 |
| 2 | | 22 | (h) | Stoke C | D | 1-1 | Stuart (og) | 24 |
| 3 | | 25 | (h) | Cardiff C | L | 1-2 | Bowers | 14 |
| 4 | | 29 | (a) | Stoke C | D | 3-3 | Curry 2, Hutchinson | 19 |
| 5 | Sep | 1 | (a) | Portsmouth | L | 0-1 | | 21 |
| 6 | | 8 | (h) | Preston NE | W | 1-0 | Buxton | 11 |
| 7 | | 12 | (a) | Newcastle U | D | 0-0 | | 34 |
| 8 | | 15 | (a) | Plymouth A | L | 1-2 | Buxton | 16 |
| 9 | | 19 | (h) | Newcastle U | L | 0-1 | | 14 |
| 10 | | 22 | (h) | Grimsby T | L | 2-4 | Roby, Curry | 12 |
| 11 | | 29 | (a) | Norwich C | L | 0-2 | | 22 |
| 12 | Oct | 6 | (a) | Sunderland | L | 0-3 | | 35 |
| 13 | | 13 | (h) | Leeds U | D | 0-0 | | 13 |
| 14 | | 19 | (a) | Swansea T | L | 0-2 | | 8 |
| 15 | | 26 | (h) | Chelsea | L | 1-3 | Parry | 12 |
| 16 | Nov | 3 | (a) | Luton T | W | 2-1 | Curry, Hutchinson | 7 |
| 17 | | 10 | (h) | Southampton | W | 3-1 | Hutchinson 2, Knapp (og) | 9 |
| 18 | | 16 | (a) | Scunthorpe U | L | 1-2 | Hutchinson | 6 |
| 19 | | 24 | (h) | Bury | D | 0-0 | | 12 |
| 20 | | 30 | (a) | Rotherham U | D | 2-2 | Hutchinson 2 | 9 |
| 21 | Dec | 8 | (h) | Charlton A | L | 2-3 | Roby 2 | 9 |
| 22 | | 15 | (h) | Huddersfield T | W | 2-1 | Curry, Hutchinson | 9 |
| 23 | | 22 | (a) | Cardiff C | L | 0-1 | | 12 |
| 24 | Feb | 23 | (h) | Sunderland | D | 2-2 | Curry, Hutchinson | 15 |
| 25 | Mar | 2 | (a) | Leeds U | L | 1-3 | Barrowcliffe | 22 |
| 26 | | 9 | (h) | Swansea T | L | 0-2 | | 8 |
| 27 | | 16 | (a) | Walsall | W | 3-1 | Barrowcliffe, Parry, Hutchinson | 7 |
| 28 | | 20 | (h) | Plymouth A | W | 3-2 | Curry 2, Hutchinson | 10 |
| 29 | | 23 | (h) | Luton T | W | 1-0 | Hutchinson | 10 |
| 30 | | 27 | (a) | Chelsea | L | 1-3 | Curry | 19 |
| 31 | Apr | 6 | (h) | Scunthorpe U | W | 6-2 | Curry 2, Barrowcliffe (pen), Young, Hutchinson, Brownsword (og) | 8 |
| 32 | | 12 | (a) | Middlesbrough | L | 1-5 | Curry | 11 |
| 33 | | 13 | (a) | Bury | D | 3-3 | Curry 2, Hutchinson | 5 |
| 34 | | 15 | (h) | Middlesbrough | D | 3-3 | Hutchinson, Barrowcliffe, Swallow | 13 |
| 35 | | 20 | (h) | Rotherham U | W | 3-2 | Curry 2, Hutchinson | 10 |
| 36 | | 24 | (h) | Walsall | W | 2-0 | Barrowcliffe (pen), Webster | 11 |
| 37 | | 27 | (a) | Charlton A | D | 0-0 | | 10 |
| 38 | May | 1 | (a) | Southampton | L | 0-5 | | 10 |
| 39 | | 4 | (a) | Grimsby T | D | 0-0 | | 12 |
| 40 | | 6 | (h) | Norwich C | W | 3-0 | Hutchinson 2, Curry | 9 |
| 41 | | 10 | (h) | Portsmouth | W | 4-0 | Curry 3, Hutchinson | 10 |
| 42 | | 18 | (a) | Preston NE | L | 0-1 | | 8 |

FINAL LEAGUE POSITION: 18th in Division Two

Appeara
G

## FA Cup

| | | | | | | | | |
|---|---|---|---|---|---|---|---|---|
| 3 | Feb | 4 | (h) | Peterborough U | W | 2-0 | Hutchinson 2 | 14 |
| 4 | Mar | 4 | (a) | Leyton O | L | 0-3 | | 12, |

Appeara
G

## League Cup

| | | | | | | | | |
|---|---|---|---|---|---|---|---|---|
| 2 | Sep | 26 | (h) | Blackburn R | D | 1-1 | Curry | 9 |
| R | Oct | 2 | (a) | Blackburn R | L | 1-3 | Bowers | 6 |

Appeara
G

| Oxford K | Barrowcliffe G | Young R | Webster R | Moore L | Hopkinson M | Roby D | Parry J | Curry W | Hutchinson B | Swallow R | Bowers J | Stephenson R | Waller P | Buxton I | McCann J | Ferguson R | Cullen M | Richmond J | Matthews R | Richardson J | Williamson M | |
|---|---|---|---|---|---|---|---|---|---|---|---|---|---|---|---|---|---|---|---|---|---|---|
| 1 | 2 | 3 | 4 | 5 | 6 | 7 | 8 | 9 | 10 | 11 | | | | | | | | | | | | 1 |
| 1 | 2 | 3 | 4 | 5 | 6 | 7 | 8 | 9 | 10 | 11 | | | | | | | | | | | | 2 |
| 1 | 2 | 3 | | 5 | 6 | 7 | 4 | 9 | 10 | 11 | 8 | | | | | | | | | | | 3 |
| 1 | 2 | 3 | | 5 | 6 | 7 | 4 | 9 | 10 | 11 | 8 | | | | | | | | | | | 4 |
| 1 | 2 | 3 | | 5 | 6 | 7 | 4 | 9 | 10 | | 11 | 8 | | | | | | | | | | 5 |
| 1 | 2 | 3 | | 5 | 6 | 7 | 8 | | | | 11 | 10 | 4 | 9 | | | | | | | | 6 |
| 1 | 2 | 3 | | 5 | 6 | 7 | 8 | | | 11 | 10 | | 4 | 9 | | | | | | | | 7 |
| 1 | 2 | 3 | | 5 | 6 | 7 | 9 | 10 | | 11 | | | 4 | 8 | | | | | | | | 8 |
| 1 | 2 | 3 | | 5 | 6 | 7 | 8 | 9 | | 11 | 10 | | 4 | | | | | | | | | 9 |
| 1 | 2 | 3 | | 5 | 6 | 7 | 8 | 9 | | | 10 | | 4 | | 11 | | | | | | | 10 |
| 1 | 2 | 3 | | 5 | | 7 | 4 | 9 | | | | 8 | 6 | 10 | 11 | | | | | | | 11 |
| 1 | 2 | 3 | | 5 | | | 4 | 9 | 10 | | 7 | 8 | 6 | | 11 | | | | | | | 12 |
| 1 | 2 | 3 | | 5 | | 7 | 4 | 9 | | | | 8 | 6 | 10 | 11 | | | | | | | 13 |
| 1 | 2 | | | 5 | | 7 | 4 | 9 | | | | 8 | 6 | 10 | 11 | 3 | | | | | | 14 |
| 1 | 2 | | | 5 | | 7 | 4 | 9 | | | | 8 | 6 | 10 | 11 | 3 | | | | | | 15 |
| 1 | 2 | 4 | | 5 | | 7 | 8 | 9 | 10 | | | | 6 | | 11 | 3 | | | | | | 16 |
| 1 | 2 | 4 | | 5 | | 7 | 8 | 9 | 10 | | | | 6 | | 11 | 3 | | | | | | 17 |
| 1 | 2 | 4 | | 5 | | 7 | 8 | 9 | 10 | | | | 6 | | 11 | 3 | | | | | | 18 |
| 1 | 2 | 4 | | 5 | | 7 | 8 | 9 | 10 | | | | 6 | | 11 | 3 | | | | | | 19 |
| 1 | 2 | 4 | | | | 7 | 6 | | 10 | | | | 5 | 9 | 11 | 3 | 8 | | | | | 20 |
| 1 | 2 | | | | | 7 | 6 | | 10 | | | | 5 | 9 | 11 | 3 | 8 | 4 | | | | 21 |
| 1 | 2 | | | | 6 | 7 | 4 | 9 | 10 | | | | 5 | | 11 | 3 | 8 | | | | | 22 |
| 1 | 2 | | | 5 | 6 | 7 | 4 | 9 | 10 | | | | | | 11 | 3 | 8 | | | | | 23 |
| 1 | 2 | 5 | | | 6 | 7 | 4 | 9 | 10 | | | | | | 11 | 3 | 8 | | | | | 24 |
| 1 | 2 | 6 | | 5 | | 7 | 4 | 9 | 10 | | | | | | 11 | 3 | 8 | | | | | 25 |
| | 2 | | | 5 | 6 | | 8 | 9 | 10 | | | 7 | 4 | | 11 | 3 | | | 1 | | | 26 |
| | 2 | 4 | | 5 | 8 | 7 | 6 | 9 | 10 | | | | | | 11 | 3 | | | 1 | | | 27 |
| | 2 | 4 | | 5 | 8 | 7 | 6 | 9 | 10 | | | | | | 11 | 3 | | | 1 | | | 28 |
| | 2 | 4 | | 5 | 8 | 7 | 6 | 9 | 10 | | | | | | 11 | 3 | | | 1 | | | 29 |
| | 2 | 4 | | 5 | | 7 | 6 | 9 | 10 | | | | 8 | | 11 | 3 | | | 1 | | | 30 |
| | 2 | 4 | | 5 | | | 6 | 9 | 10 | 7 | | | 8 | | 11 | 3 | | | 1 | | | 31 |
| | 2 | 4 | | 5 | | 7 | 6 | 9 | 10 | | | | 8 | | 11 | 3 | | | 1 | | | 32 |
| | 2 | 4 | 8 | 5 | | | 6 | 9 | 10 | 7 | | | | | 11 | 3 | | | | | | 33 |
| | 2 | 4 | 8 | 5 | | | 6 | 9 | 10 | 7 | | | | | 11 | 3 | | | | | | 34 |
| | 2 | 4 | | 5 | | | 6 | 9 | 10 | 7 | | | 8 | | 11 | 3 | | | 1 | | | 35 |
| | 2 | 4 | 8 | 5 | | | 6 | 9 | 10 | 7 | | | | | 11 | 3 | | | 1 | | | 36 |
| | 2 | 4 | 8 | 5 | | | 6 | 9 | 10 | 7 | | | | | 11 | 3 | | | 1 | | | 37 |
| | | 4 | 7 | 5 | | | 6 | 9 | 10 | | | | | | 11 | 3 | 8 | | 1 | 2 | | 38 |
| | | 2 | 4 | 5 | | | 6 | 9 | 10 | 7 | | | | | 11 | 3 | 8 | | 1 | | | 39 |
| | 2 | 4 | 8 | 5 | | | 6 | 9 | 10 | 7 | | | | | | 3 | | | 1 | | 11 | 40 |
| | 2 | 4 | 8 | 5 | | | 6 | 9 | 10 | | 7 | | | | | 3 | | | 1 | | 11 | 41 |
| | 2 | | 4 | 5 | | | 6 | 9 | 10 | | 7 | | | | 8 | 3 | | | 1 | | 11 | 42 |
| 7 | 40 | 35 | 11 | 38 | 17 | 29 | 42 | 38 | 33 | 15 | 10 | 8 | 22 | 9 | 31 | 29 | 8 | 1 | 15 | 1 | 3 | |
| | 6 | 1 | 1 | | | 3 | 2 | 21 | 20 | 1 | 1 | | | 2 | | | | | | | | |

3 own-goals

| | | | | | | | | | | | | | | | | | | | | | | |
|---|---|---|---|---|---|---|---|---|---|---|---|---|---|---|---|---|---|---|---|---|---|---|
| | 2 | 5 | | | 6 | 7 | 4 | 9 | 10 | | | | | | 11 | 3 | 8 | | | | | 3 |
| | 2 | 4 | | 5 | | | 8 | 9 | 10 | | | 7 | 6 | | 11 | 3 | | | | | | 4 |
| | 2 | 2 | | 1 | 1 | 1 | 2 | 2 | 2 | | | 1 | 1 | | 2 | 2 | 1 | | | | | |
| | | | | | | | | | 2 | | | | | | | | | | | | | |

| | | | | | | | | | | | | | | | | | | | | | | |
|---|---|---|---|---|---|---|---|---|---|---|---|---|---|---|---|---|---|---|---|---|---|---|
| | 2 | 3 | | 5 | | 7 | 4 | 9 | | | 11 | 8 | 6 | 10 | | | | | | | | 2 |
| | 2 | 3 | | 5 | | 7 | 4 | 9 | | | 11 | 8 | 6 | 10 | | | | | | | | R |
| | 2 | 2 | | 2 | | 2 | 2 | 2 | | | 2 | 2 | 2 | 2 | | | | | | | | |
| | | | | | | | | 1 | | | 1 | | | | | | | | | | | |

# 1963-64

| | P | W | D | L | F | A | Pts |
|---|---|---|---|---|---|---|---|
| Leeds U | 42 | 24 | 15 | 3 | 71 | 34 | 63 |
| Sunderland | 42 | 25 | 11 | 6 | 81 | 37 | 61 |
| Preston N.E. | 42 | 23 | 10 | 9 | 79 | 54 | 56 |
| Charlton A | 42 | 19 | 10 | 13 | 76 | 70 | 48 |
| Southampton | 42 | 19 | 9 | 14 | 100 | 73 | 47 |
| Manchester C | 42 | 18 | 10 | 14 | 84 | 66 | 46 |
| Rotherham U | 42 | 19 | 7 | 16 | 90 | 78 | 45 |
| Newcastle U | 42 | 20 | 5 | 17 | 74 | 69 | 45 |
| Portsmouth | 42 | 16 | 11 | 15 | 79 | 70 | 43 |
| Middlesbrough | 42 | 15 | 11 | 16 | 67 | 52 | 41 |
| Northampton T | 42 | 16 | 9 | 17 | 58 | 60 | 41 |
| Huddersfield T | 42 | 15 | 10 | 17 | 57 | 64 | 40 |
| Derby Co | 42 | 14 | 11 | 17 | 56 | 67 | 39 |
| Swindon T | 42 | 14 | 10 | 18 | 57 | 69 | 38 |
| Cardiff C | 42 | 14 | 10 | 18 | 56 | 81 | 38 |
| Leyton O | 42 | 13 | 10 | 19 | 54 | 72 | 36 |
| Norwich C | 42 | 11 | 13 | 18 | 64 | 80 | 35 |
| Bury | 42 | 13 | 9 | 20 | 57 | 73 | 35 |
| Swansea T | 42 | 12 | 9 | 21 | 63 | 74 | 33 |
| Plymouth A | 42 | 8 | 16 | 18 | 45 | 67 | 32 |
| Grimsby T | 42 | 9 | 14 | 19 | 47 | 75 | 32 |
| Scunthorpe U | 42 | 10 | 10 | 22 | 52 | 82 | 30 |

Manager: Tim Ward.
Leading scorer: Alan Durban, League 9, all matches 11.
League ever-present: Geoff Barrowcliffe, Reg Matthews.

- Jack Parry's 100th League goal, like his 100th in all competitions, was scored against Swansea Town, on 28 August. He is one of only seven Derby players to achieve this.
- Alan Durban cost £10,000 when he was signed from Cardiff City in July 1963. It was the start of 10 increasingly successful seasons with the Rams.
- Derby made their usual immediate exit from the FA Cup. In Tim Ward's five seasons as manager, the Rams survived the third round only once, in 1962–63.

## Division Two

| Match No. | Date | Venue | Opponents | Result | | Scorers | Attendar |
|---|---|---|---|---|---|---|---|
| 1 | Aug 24 | (a) | Newcastle U | L | 1-3 | McCann | 35,2 |
| 2 | 28 | (h) | Swansea T | W | 3-0 | Hutchinson 2, Parry | 15,8 |
| 3 | 31 | (h) | Huddersfield T | W | 2-0 | Barrowcliffe (pen), Hughes | 14,7 |
| 4 | Sep 3 | (a) | Swansea T | L | 1-2 | Hutchinson | 9,9 |
| 5 | 7 | (a) | Northampton T | W | 1-0 | Hutchinson | 14,6 |
| 6 | 11 | (h) | Leyton O | W | 1-0 | Hughes | 17,6 |
| 7 | 14 | (a) | Plymouth A | D | 0-0 | | 12,4 |
| 8 | 18 | (a) | Leyton O | L | 0-3 | | 11,4 |
| 9 | 21 | (h) | Charlton A | D | 1-1 | Barrowcliffe (pen) | 13,0 |
| 10 | 28 | (a) | Grimsby T | W | 3-1 | Durban 2, Cullen | 9,0 |
| 11 | Oct 5 | (h) | Preston NE | L | 1-2 | Hopkinson | 14,1 |
| 12 | 8 | (a) | Bury | W | 2-1 | Durban, Hutchinson | 8,1 |
| 13 | 16 | (h) | Sunderland | L | 0-3 | | 20,3 |
| 14 | 19 | (a) | Leeds U | D | 2-2 | Hutchinson, McCann | 28,8 |
| 15 | 26 | (h) | Manchester C | L | 1-3 | Buxton | 15,6 |
| 16 | Nov 2 | (a) | Portsmouth | D | 1-1 | Hutchinson | 15,6 |
| 17 | 16 | (a) | Norwich C | L | 0-3 | | 16,0 |
| 18 | 23 | (h) | Cardiff C | W | 2-1 | Hopkinson, Waller | 11,8 |
| 19 | 30 | (a) | Swindon T | D | 0-0 | | 16,0 |
| 20 | Dec 7 | (h) | Rotherham U | L | 1-4 | Durban | 10,5 |
| 21 | 14 | (h) | Newcastle U | L | 1-2 | Waller | 9,3 |
| 22 | 21 | (a) | Huddersfield T | D | 0-0 | | 6,0 |
| 23 | 26 | (a) | Middlesbrough | L | 0-3 | | 18,4 |
| 24 | 28 | (h) | Middlesbrough | D | 2-2 | Curry, Nurse (og) | 11,5 |
| 25 | Jan 11 | (h) | Northampton T | D | 0-0 | | 10,1 |
| 26 | 18 | (h) | Plymouth A | W | 3-1 | Curry 2, Hughes | 6, |
| 27 | 25 | (h) | Scunthorpe U | D | 2-2 | Curry, Moore | 9,1 |
| 28 | Feb 1 | (a) | Charlton A | L | 0-2 | | 16,5 |
| 29 | 8 | (h) | Grimsby T | D | 0-0 | | 10, |
| 30 | 17 | (a) | Preston NE | W | 2-0 | Durban, Webster | 17, |
| 31 | 22 | (a) | Sunderland | L | 0-3 | | 43, |
| 32 | 29 | (h) | Norwich C | W | 2-1 | Moore, Hughes | 8, |
| 33 | Mar 7 | (a) | Manchester C | L | 2-3 | Durban, Buxton | 11, |
| 34 | 14 | (h) | Bury | W | 2-1 | Durban, Bowers | 5, |
| 35 | 20 | (a) | Scunthorpe U | L | 2-3 | Hughes, Buxton | 7, |
| 36 | 28 | (h) | Leeds U | D | 1-1 | Cullen | 16, |
| 37 | 30 | (h) | Southampton | W | 3-2 | Parry, Durban, Buxton | 11, |
| 38 | Apr 1 | (a) | Southampton | L | 4-6 | Barrowcliffe 2, Bowers 2 | 11, |
| 39 | 4 | (a) | Cardiff C | L | 1-2 | Hughes | 8, |
| 40 | 11 | (h) | Swindon T | W | 3-0 | Barrowcliffe (pen), Curry, Cullen | 9, |
| 41 | 18 | (a) | Rotherham U | L | 0-2 | | 9, |
| 42 | 25 | (h) | Portsmouth | W | 3-1 | Cullen 2, Durban | 7, |

FINAL LEAGUE POSITION: 13th in Division Two

Appearan

Gc

## FA Cup

| | | | | | | | |
|---|---|---|---|---|---|---|---|
| 3 | Jan 4 | (a) | Liverpool | L | 0-5 | | 46, |

Appearan

Gc

## League Cup

| | | | | | | | |
|---|---|---|---|---|---|---|---|
| 2 | Sep 25 | (a) | Portsmouth | L | 2-3 | Durban 2 | 12, |

Appearan

Gc

| Match | Barrowcliffe G | Ferguson R | Young R | Moore L | Parry J | Hughes G | Durban A | Curry W | Hutchinson B | McCann J | Hopkinson M | Buxton I | Williamson M | Cullen M | Swallow R | Waller P | Webster R | Bowers J | McAndrew R |
|---|---|---|---|---|---|---|---|---|---|---|---|---|---|---|---|---|---|---|---|
| 1 | 2 | 3 | 4 | 5 | 6 | 7 | 8 | 9 | 10 | 11 | | | | | | | | | |
| 2 | 2 | 3 | 5 | | 4 | 7 | 8 | 9 | 10 | 11 | 6 | | | | | | | | |
| 3 | 2 | 3 | 5 | | 4 | 7 | 8 | 9 | 10 | 11 | 6 | | | | | | | | |
| 4 | 2 | 3 | 5 | | 4 | 7 | 8 | 9 | 10 | 11 | 6 | | | | | | | | |
| 5 | 2 | 3 | 5 | | 4 | 7 | 8 | 9 | 10 | 11 | 6 | | | | | | | | |
| 6 | 2 | 3 | 5 | | 4 | 7 | 8 | 9 | 10 | 11 | 6 | | | | | | | | |
| 7 | 2 | 3 | 5 | | 4 | 7 | 8 | 9 | 10 | 11 | 6 | | | | | | | | |
| 8 | 2 | 3 | 5 | | 4 | 7 | 8 | | 10 | 11 | 6 | 9 | | | | | | | |
| 9 | 2 | 3 | 5 | | 4 | 7 | 8 | | 10 | | 6 | 9 | 11 | | | | | | |
| 10 | 2 | 3 | 5 | | 4 | 7 | 8 | | | | 6 | 9 | | 10 | 11 | | | | |
| 11 | 2 | 3 | 5 | | 4 | 7 | 8 | 9 | | | 6 | 10 | | | 11 | | | | |
| 12 | 2 | 3 | 5 | | | 7 | 8 | 9 | 10 | 11 | 6 | | | | | 4 | | | |
| 13 | 2 | 3 | 5 | | | 7 | 8 | 9 | 10 | 11 | 6 | | | | | 4 | | | |
| 14 | 2 | 3 | 5 | | 10 | 7 | 8 | | 9 | 11 | 6 | | | | | 4 | | | |
| 15 | 2 | 3 | 5 | | 6 | 7 | 8 | | 10 | 11 | | 9 | | | | 4 | | | |
| 16 | 2 | 3 | 5 | | 10 | 7 | 8 | | 9 | 11 | 6 | | | | | 4 | | | |
| 17 | 2 | 3 | 5 | | 10 | | 8 | | 9 | 11 | 6 | | 7 | | | 4 | | | |
| 18 | 2 | 3 | 5 | | 10 | 7 | 8 | | 9 | 11 | 6 | | | | | 4 | | | |
| 19 | 2 | 3 | 5 | | 10 | | 8 | | 9 | 11 | 6 | | | | 7 | 4 | | | |
| 20 | 2 | 3 | 5 | | 10 | | 8 | | 9 | 11 | 6 | | | | 7 | 4 | | | |
| 21 | 2 | 3 | 5 | | 10 | 7 | 8 | | 9 | | 6 | | 11 | | | 4 | | | |
| 22 | 2 | 3 | 5 | | 6 | 7 | | 9 | 10 | 11 | | | | | | 4 | 8 | | |
| 23 | 2 | 3 | 5 | | 6 | 7 | | 9 | 10 | 11 | | | | | | 4 | 8 | | |
| 24 | 2 | 3 | 5 | | 6 | | | 9 | | 11 | | | 10 | | | 4 | 8 | 7 | |
| 25 | 2 | 3 | 4 | 5 | 6 | 7 | | 9 | | 11 | | | 10 | | | 8 | | | |
| 26 | 2 | 3 | 4 | 5 | 8 | 7 | | 9 | 10 | | | | 11 | | | 6 | | | |
| 27 | 2 | 3 | 4 | 5 | 8 | 7 | | 9 | 10 | 11 | | | | | | 6 | | | |
| 28 | 2 | 3 | 4 | 5 | 6 | 7 | 8 | 9 | 10 | 11 | | | | | | | | | |
| 29 | 2 | 3 | 4 | 5 | 6 | 7 | | 9 | | | | 10 | 11 | 8 | | | | | |
| 30 | 2 | 3 | 5 | | 6 | 7 | 10 | | | | | 9 | 11 | 8 | | | 4 | | |
| 31 | 2 | 3 | | 5 | 6 | 7 | 10 | | | 11 | | 9 | | | | 4 | | 8 | |
| 32 | 2 | 3 | | 5 | 6 | 7 | 10 | | | | | 9 | | 8 | | 4 | | 11 | |
| 33 | 2 | 3 | | 5 | 6 | 7 | 10 | | | | | 9 | | 8 | | 4 | | 11 | |
| 34 | 2 | 3 | 5 | | 6 | 7 | 10 | | | | | 9 | | 8 | | 4 | | 11 | |
| 35 | 2 | 3 | 5 | | 6 | 7 | 10 | | | | | 9 | | 8 | | 4 | | 11 | |
| 36 | 2 | 3 | 5 | | 6 | 7 | 10 | | | | | 9 | | 8 | | | 4 | 11 | |
| 37 | 2 | 3 | 5 | | 6 | 7 | 10 | | | | | 9 | | 8 | | | 4 | 11 | |
| 38 | 2 | 3 | 5 | | 6 | 7 | | 9 | | | | | | 8 | | 10 | 4 | 11 | |
| 39 | 2 | 3 | 5 | | 6 | 7 | 10 | 9 | | | | | | 8 | | | 4 | 11 | |
| 40 | 2 | | 5 | | 6 | 7 | 10 | 9 | | | | | | 8 | | | 4 | 11 | 3 |
| 41 | 2 | 3 | | 5 | 6 | 7 | 10 | | | | | 9 | | 8 | | | 4 | 11 | |
| 42 | 2 | 3 | 5 | | 6 | 7 | 10 | | | | | 9 | | 8 | | | 4 | 11 | |
| | 42 | 41 | 38 | 10 | 40 | 38 | 34 | 21 | 24 | 24 | 19 | 16 | 8 | 14 | 4 | 22 | 11 | 13 | 1 |
| | 5 | | | 2 | 2 | 6 | 9 | 5 | 7 | 2 | 2 | 4 | | 5 | | 2 | 1 | 3 | |

1 own-goal

| Round | Barrowcliffe G | Ferguson R | Young R | Moore L | Parry J | Hughes G | Durban A | Curry W | Hutchinson B | McCann J | Hopkinson M | Buxton I | Williamson M | Cullen M | Swallow R | Waller P | Webster R | Bowers J | McAndrew R |
|---|---|---|---|---|---|---|---|---|---|---|---|---|---|---|---|---|---|---|---|
| 3 | 2 | 3 | 5 | | 6 | 7 | | 9 | | 11 | | | 10 | | | 4 | 8 | | |
| | 1 | 1 | 1 | | 1 | 1 | | 1 | | 1 | | | 1 | | | 1 | 1 | | |
| | | | | | | | | | | | | | | | | | | | |

| Round | Barrowcliffe G | Ferguson R | Young R | Moore L | Parry J | Hughes G | Durban A | Curry W | Hutchinson B | McCann J | Hopkinson M | Buxton I | Williamson M | Cullen M | Swallow R | Waller P | Webster R | Bowers J | McAndrew R |
|---|---|---|---|---|---|---|---|---|---|---|---|---|---|---|---|---|---|---|---|
| 2 | 2 | 3 | 5 | | 4 | | 8 | | | | 6 | 9 | 11 | 10 | 7 | | | | |
| | 1 | 1 | 1 | | 1 | | 1 | | | | 1 | 1 | 1 | 1 | 1 | | | | |
| | | | | | | | 2 | | | | | | | | | | | | |

# 1964-65

| | P | W | D | L | F | A | Pts |
|---|---|---|---|---|---|---|---|
| Newcastle U | 42 | 24 | 9 | 9 | 81 | 45 | 57 |
| Northampton T | 42 | 20 | 16 | 6 | 66 | 50 | 56 |
| Bolton W | 42 | 20 | 10 | 12 | 80 | 58 | 50 |
| Southampton | 42 | 17 | 14 | 11 | 83 | 63 | 48 |
| Ipswich T | 42 | 15 | 17 | 10 | 74 | 67 | 47 |
| Norwich C | 42 | 20 | 7 | 15 | 61 | 57 | 47 |
| Crystal Palace | 42 | 16 | 13 | 13 | 55 | 51 | 45 |
| Huddersfield T | 42 | 17 | 10 | 15 | 53 | 51 | 44 |
| Derby Co | 42 | 16 | 11 | 15 | 84 | 79 | 43 |
| Coventry C | 42 | 17 | 9 | 16 | 72 | 70 | 43 |
| Manchester C | 42 | 16 | 9 | 17 | 63 | 62 | 41 |
| Preston N.E. | 42 | 14 | 13 | 15 | 76 | 81 | 41 |
| Cardiff C | 42 | 13 | 14 | 15 | 64 | 57 | 40 |
| Rotherham U | 42 | 14 | 12 | 16 | 70 | 69 | 40 |
| Plymouth A | 42 | 16 | 8 | 18 | 63 | 79 | 40 |
| Bury | 42 | 14 | 10 | 18 | 60 | 66 | 38 |
| Middlesbrough | 42 | 13 | 9 | 20 | 70 | 76 | 35 |
| Charlton A | 42 | 13 | 9 | 20 | 64 | 75 | 35 |
| Leyton O | 42 | 12 | 11 | 19 | 50 | 72 | 35 |
| Portsmouth | 42 | 12 | 10 | 20 | 56 | 77 | 34 |
| Swindon T | 42 | 14 | 5 | 23 | 63 | 81 | 33 |
| Swansea T | 42 | 11 | 10 | 21 | 62 | 84 | 32 |

Manager: Tim Ward
Leading scorers: Alan Durban, Eddie Thomas, League 22, all matches 24.
League ever-present: Alan Durban, Jack Parry, Ron Webster.

- On 17 April, Jack Parry became only the third player to complete 500 appearances for Derby, following Jimmy Methven and Steve Bloomer. Parry was born in Derby and, apart from a final season with Boston United, spent his whole career at the Baseball Ground.
- In August and September, Eddie Thomas became the eighth Derby player to score in six consecutive League matches. Uniquely, he did it in his first six appearances after signing from Swansea Town.
- When he left Derby, Ward admitted that signing Thomas from Swansea Town for £3,500 worked against him because the directors expected him to find equally gifted players for under £5,000.

## Division Two

| Match No. | Date | | Venue | Opponents | Result | | Scorers | Attendar |
|---|---|---|---|---|---|---|---|---|
| 1 | Aug | 22 | (a) | Crystal Palace | W | 3-2 | Bowers, Durban, Hughes | 22,9 |
| 2 | | 26 | (h) | Norwich C | L | 0-1 | | 13,7 |
| 3 | | 29 | (h) | Bury | W | 3-1 | Durban, Thomas, Atherton (og) | 8,8 |
| 4 | Sep | 2 | (a) | Norwich C | L | 2-5 | Thomas 2 | 18,4 |
| 5 | | 5 | (a) | Leyton Orient | W | 4-1 | Bowers 2, Buxton, Thomas | 9,1 |
| 6 | | 9 | (h) | Coventry C | W | 2-1 | Bowers, Thomas | 32,8 |
| 7 | | 12 | (h) | Charlton A | D | 4-4 | Durban, Thomas, Cleevely, Bailey (og) | 13,5 |
| 8 | | 15 | (a) | Coventry C | W | 2-0 | Durban, Thomas | 38,2 |
| 9 | | 19 | (a) | Manchester C | L | 0-2 | | 16,2 |
| 10 | | 26 | (h) | Portsmouth | W | 4-0 | Barrowcliffe (pen), Durban, Curry, Harris (og) | 13,1 |
| 11 | Oct | 3 | (a) | Swindon T | L | 2-4 | Barrowcliffe (pen), Thomas | 15,2 |
| 12 | | 7 | (h) | Huddersfield T | W | 2-0 | Durban, Thomas | 13,6 |
| 13 | | 10 | (a) | Cardiff C | L | 1-2 | Thomas | 8,3 |
| 14 | | 17 | (h) | Preston NE | W | 3-1 | Young (pen), Buxton, Thomas | 12,6 |
| 15 | | 24 | (a) | Ipswich T | L | 1-2 | Buxton | 12,7 |
| 16 | | 31 | (h) | Plymouth A | W | 3-2 | Thomas 2, Curry | 11,6 |
| 17 | Nov | 7 | (a) | Bolton W | L | 1-3 | Durban | 12,9 |
| 18 | | 14 | (h) | Middlesbrough | D | 3-3 | Durban, Thomas, Curry | 11,9 |
| 19 | | 21 | (a) | Newcastle U | D | 2-2 | Durban, Thomas | 31,0 |
| 20 | | 28 | (h) | Northampton T | D | 2-2 | Durban, Buxton | 17,3 |
| 21 | Dec | 5 | (a) | Southampton | D | 3-3 | Durban 2, Hughes | 14,4 |
| 22 | | 12 | (h) | Crystal Palace | D | 3-3 | Thomas 2, Young | 11,8 |
| 23 | | 19 | (a) | Bury | L | 1-2 | Curry | 4,8 |
| 24 | | 28 | (a) | Rotherham U | D | 1-1 | Durban | 8,6 |
| 25 | Jan | 2 | (h) | Leyton Orient | W | 1-0 | Webb (og) | 12,9 |
| 26 | | 16 | (a) | Charlton A | W | 3-1 | Durban 2, Buxton | 8,9 |
| 27 | | 30 | (h) | Manchester C | W | 2-0 | Durban, Hughes | 14,7 |
| 28 | Feb | 6 | (a) | Portsmouth | L | 1-3 | Thomas | 12,4 |
| 29 | | 13 | (h) | Swindon T | W | 4-1 | Parry 2, Buxton, Bowers | 10,2 |
| 30 | | 20 | (h) | Cardiff C | W | 1-0 | Webster | 10,8 |
| 31 | | 27 | (a) | Preston NE | D | 2-2 | Hughes, Thomas | 12,9 |
| 32 | Mar | 6 | (h) | Southampton | W | 2-1 | Buxton, Durban | 13,5 |
| 33 | | 13 | (a) | Plymouth A | D | 1-1 | Bowers | 9,7 |
| 34 | | 20 | (h) | Bolton W | L | 2-3 | Durban, Hatton (og) | 16,1 |
| 35 | | 24 | (h) | Rotherham U | D | 2-2 | Barrowcliffe (pen), Bowers | 11,7 |
| 36 | | 27 | (a) | Middlesbrough | W | 2-1 | Durban, Thomas | 12,7 |
| 37 | Apr | 3 | (h) | Newcastle U | L | 0-3 | | 19,6 |
| 38 | | 10 | (a) | Northampton T | D | 2-2 | Durban 2 | 17,9 |
| 39 | | 17 | (h) | Ipswich T | L | 2-3 | Bowers, Durban | 11, |
| 40 | | 19 | (h) | Swansea T | L | 3-4 | Parry, Buxton, Bowers | 7,4 |
| 41 | | 20 | (a) | Swansea T | L | 1-2 | Thomas | 11, |
| 42 | | 27 | (a) | Huddersfield T | L | 1-3 | Thomas | 10, |

FINAL LEAGUE POSITION: 9th in Division Two

Appearan
Gc

## FA Cup

| | | | | | | | | |
|---|---|---|---|---|---|---|---|---|
| 3 | Jan | 9 | (a) | Plymouth A | L | 2-4 | Durban, Hopkinson | 15, |

Appearan
G

## League Cup

| | | | | | | | | |
|---|---|---|---|---|---|---|---|---|
| 2 | Sep | 23 | (a) | Chester | L | 4-5 | Thomas 2, Durban, Butler (og) | 9, |

Appearar
G

rews R

| Barrowcliffe G | Ferguson R | Webster R | Young R | Parry J | Hughes G | Cullen M | Buxton I | Durban A | Bowers J | Thomas E | Saxton R | Cleevely N | Richardson J | Curry W | Hopkinson M | Boulton C | Rhodes A | Roby D | |
|---|---|---|---|---|---|---|---|---|---|---|---|---|---|---|---|---|---|---|---|
| 2 | 3 | 4 | 5 | 6 | 7 | 8 | 9 | 10 | 11 | | | | | | | | | | 1 |
| 2 | 3 | 4 | 5 | 6 | 7 | 8 | 9 | 10 | 11 | | | | | | | | | | 2 |
| 2 | 3 | 4 | 5 | 6 | 7 | | 9 | 10 | 11 | 8 | | | | | | | | | 3 |
| 2 | 3 | 4 | | 6 | 7 | | 9 | 10 | 11 | 8 | 5 | | | | | | | | 4 |
| 2 | 3 | 4 | 5 | 6 | 7 | | 9 | 10 | 11 | 8 | | | | | | | | | 5 |
| 2 | 3 | 4 | 5 | 6 | 7 | | 9 | 10 | 11 | 8 | | | | | | | | | 6 |
| 2 | 3 | 4 | 5 | 6 | 7 | | 9 | 10 | | 8 | | 11 | | | | | | | 7 |
| | 3 | 4 | 5 | 6 | 7 | | 9 | 10 | | 8 | | 11 | 2 | | | | | | 8 |
| 2 | 3 | 4 | 5 | 6 | 7 | | 9 | 10 | | 8 | | 11 | | | | | | | 9 |
| 2 | 3 | 4 | 5 | 6 | 7 | | 9 | 10 | | 8 | | | | 11 | | | | | 10 |
| 2 | 3 | 4 | 5 | 6 | 7 | | 9 | 10 | | 8 | | | | 11 | | | | | 11 |
| | 3 | 4 | 5 | 6 | 7 | | 9 | 10 | | 8 | | | 2 | 11 | | | | | 12 |
| | 3 | 4 | 5 | 6 | 7 | | 9 | 10 | | 8 | | | 2 | 11 | | | | | 13 |
| | 3 | 4 | 5 | 6 | 7 | | 9 | 10 | | 8 | | | 2 | 11 | | | | | 14 |
| | 3 | 4 | 5 | 6 | 7 | | 9 | 10 | | 8 | | | 2 | 11 | | | | | 15 |
| | 3 | 4 | 5 | 6 | 7 | | 9 | 10 | | 8 | | | 2 | 11 | | | | | 16 |
| | 3 | 4 | 5 | 6 | 7 | | 9 | 10 | | 8 | | | 2 | 11 | | | | | 17 |
| 2 | 3 | 4 | 5 | 6 | 7 | | 9 | 10 | | 8 | | | | 11 | | | | | 18 |
| 2 | 3 | 4 | 5 | 6 | 7 | | 9 | 10 | | 8 | | | | 11 | | | | | 19 |
| 2 | 3 | 4 | 5 | 6 | 7 | | 9 | 10 | 8 | | | | | 11 | | | | | 20 |
| 2 | 3 | 4 | 5 | 6 | 7 | | 9 | 10 | | | | | | 11 | 8 | | | | 21 |
| 2 | 3 | 4 | 5 | 6 | 7 | | 9 | 10 | | 8 | | | | 11 | | | | | 22 |
| 2 | | 4 | 5 | 6 | 7 | | 9 | 10 | | 8 | | | 3 | 11 | | | | | 23 |
| 2 | 3 | 4 | 5 | 6 | | | 9 | 10 | | 8 | | | | 11 | 7 | | | | 24 |
| 2 | 3 | 4 | 5 | 6 | 7 | | 9 | 10 | | 8 | | | | 11 | | | | | 25 |
| 2 | 3 | 4 | 5 | 6 | 7 | | 9 | 10 | | 8 | | | | 11 | | | | | 26 |
| 2 | 3 | 4 | 5 | 6 | 7 | | 9 | 10 | | 8 | | | | 11 | | | | | 27 |
| 2 | 3 | 4 | 5 | 6 | 7 | | 9 | 10 | 11 | 8 | | | | | | | | | 28 |
| 2 | 3 | 4 | 5 | 6 | 7 | | 9 | 10 | 11 | 8 | | | | | | | | | 29 |
| 2 | 3 | 4 | 5 | 6 | 7 | | 9 | 10 | 11 | 8 | | | | | | | | | 30 |
| 2 | 3 | 4 | 5 | 6 | 7 | | 9 | 10 | 11 | 8 | | | | | | | | | 31 |
| 2 | 3 | 4 | 5 | 6 | 7 | | 9 | 10 | 11 | 8 | | | | | | | | | 32 |
| 2 | 3 | 4 | 5 | 6 | 7 | | 9 | 10 | 11 | 8 | | | | | | | | | 33 |
| 2 | 3 | 4 | 5 | 6 | 7 | | 9 | 10 | 11 | 8 | | | | | | | | | 34 |
| 2 | 3 | 4 | 5 | 6 | 7 | | 9 | 10 | 11 | 8 | | | | | | | | | 35 |
| 2 | 3 | 4 | 5 | 6 | 7 | | 9 | 10 | 11 | 8 | | | | | | | | | 36 |
| 2 | 3 | 4 | 5 | 6 | 7 | | 9 | 10 | 11 | 8 | | | | | | 1 | | | 37 |
| 2 | 3 | 4 | 5 | 6 | 7 | | 9 | 10 | 11 | 8 | | | | | | 1 | | | 38 |
| 2 | 3 | 4 | 5 | 6 | 7 | | 9 | 10 | 11 | 8 | | | | | | 1 | | | 39 |
| 2 | 3 | 4 | 5 | 6 | 7 | | 9 | 10 | 11 | 8 | | | | | | 1 | | | 40 |
| 2 | 3 | 4 | | 6 | 7 | | | 10 | 11 | 9 | | | | | 8 | 1 | 5 | | 41 |
| 5 | 3 | 4 | | 6 | 7 | | | 10 | 11 | 9 | | | 2 | | 8 | 1 | | | 42 |
| 35 | 41 | 42 | 39 | 42 | 41 | 2 | 40 | 42 | 22 | 38 | 1 | 3 | 9 | 18 | 4 | 6 | 1 | | |
| 3 | | 1 | 2 | 3 | 4 | | 8 | 22 | 9 | 22 | | 1 | | 4 | | | | | |

5 own-goals

| | | | | | | | | | | | | | | | | | | | |
|---|---|---|---|---|---|---|---|---|---|---|---|---|---|---|---|---|---|---|---|
| 2 | 3 | 4 | 5 | 6 | | | | 10 | | 8 | | | | 11 | 9 | | | 7 | 3 |
| 1 | 1 | 1 | 1 | 1 | | | | 1 | | 1 | | | | 1 | 1 | | | 1 | |
| | | | | | | | | 1 | | | | | | | 1 | | | | |

| | | | | | | | | | | | | | | | | | | | |
|---|---|---|---|---|---|---|---|---|---|---|---|---|---|---|---|---|---|---|---|
| | 3 | 4 | 5 | 6 | 7 | | 9 | 10 | | 8 | | 11 | 2 | | | | | | 2 |
| | 1 | 1 | 1 | 1 | 1 | | 1 | 1 | | 1 | | 1 | 1 | | | | | | |
| | | | | | | | | 1 | | 2 | | | | | | | | | |

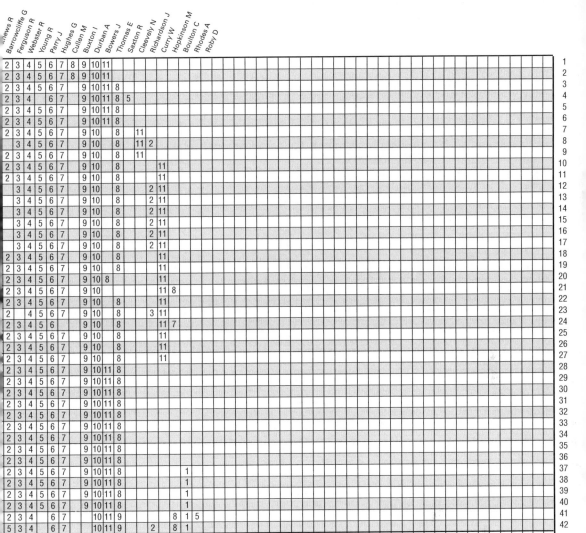

1 own-goal

# 1965-66

| | P | W | D | L | F | A | Pts |
|---|---|---|---|---|---|---|---|
| Manchester C | 42 | 22 | 15 | 5 | 76 | 44 | 59 |
| Southampton | 42 | 22 | 10 | 10 | 85 | 56 | 54 |
| Coventry C | 42 | 20 | 13 | 9 | 73 | 53 | 53 |
| Huddersfield T | 42 | 19 | 13 | 10 | 62 | 36 | 51 |
| Bristol C | 42 | 17 | 17 | 8 | 63 | 48 | 51 |
| Wolves | 42 | 20 | 10 | 12 | 87 | 61 | 50 |
| Rotherham U | 42 | 16 | 14 | 12 | 75 | 74 | 46 |
| Derby Co | 42 | 16 | 11 | 15 | 71 | 68 | 43 |
| Bolton W | 42 | 16 | 9 | 17 | 62 | 59 | 41 |
| Birmingham C | 42 | 16 | 9 | 17 | 70 | 75 | 41 |
| Crystal Palace | 42 | 14 | 13 | 15 | 47 | 52 | 41 |
| Portsmouth | 42 | 16 | 8 | 18 | 74 | 78 | 40 |
| Norwich C | 42 | 12 | 15 | 15 | 52 | 52 | 39 |
| Carlisle U | 42 | 17 | 5 | 20 | 60 | 63 | 39 |
| Ipswich T | 42 | 15 | 9 | 18 | 58 | 66 | 39 |
| Charlton A | 42 | 12 | 14 | 16 | 61 | 70 | 38 |
| Preston N.E. | 42 | 11 | 15 | 16 | 62 | 70 | 37 |
| Plymouth A | 42 | 12 | 13 | 17 | 54 | 63 | 37 |
| Bury | 42 | 14 | 7 | 21 | 62 | 76 | 35 |
| Cardiff C | 42 | 12 | 10 | 20 | 71 | 91 | 34 |
| Middlesbrough | 42 | 10 | 13 | 19 | 58 | 86 | 33 |
| Leyton O | 42 | 5 | 13 | 24 | 38 | 80 | 23 |

Manager: Tim Ward.
Leading scorers: Alan Durban, League 17. Alan Durban, Eddie Thomas, all matches 17.
League ever-present: Gordon Hughes, Reg Matthews.

- Substitutes were allowed in League matches for the first time, although a player had to be injured before being replaced. Bobby Saxton was Derby's first sub, taking over from Geoff Barrowcliffe after 14 minutes of an opening-day home defeat by Southampton.
- Saxton was close to claiming the record. The distinction of being the first League substitute belongs to Keith Peacock, on for Charlton Athletic after 13 minutes.
- On 7 September, Geoff Barrowcliffe followed Jack Parry to 500 senior appearances for the Rams. Both were one-club men with the ability to climb higher in the game had they played in a more successful side.
- Derby equalled their worst start in the League by losing the first four games. It previously happened in 1899.

## Division Two

| Match No. | Date | | Venue | Opponents | Result | | Scorers | Atte |
|---|---|---|---|---|---|---|---|---|
| 1 | Aug | 21 | (h) | Southampton | L | 0-3 | | 13 |
| 2 | | 25 | (a) | Cardiff C | L | 1-2 | Hughes | 15 |
| 3 | | 28 | (a) | Bury | L | 1-4 | Buxton | 6 |
| 4 | Sep | 1 | (h) | Cardiff C | L | 1-5 | Hughes | 10 |
| 5 | | 4 | (h) | Norwich C | W | 3-1 | Cleevely 2, Bowers | 8 |
| 6 | | 7 | (a) | Carlisle U | L | 1-2 | Bowers | 16 |
| 7 | | 11 | (a) | Wolves | L | 0-4 | | 17 |
| 8 | | 14 | (h) | Carlisle U | W | 3-1 | Hodgson 2, Buxton | 11 |
| 9 | | 18 | (h) | Rotherham U | L | 1-3 | Parry | 11 |
| 10 | | 25 | (a) | Manchester C | L | 0-1 | | 20 |
| 11 | Oct | 2 | (h) | Bristol C | W | 2-1 | Hughes, Thomas | 11 |
| 12 | | 9 | (a) | Portsmouth | D | 1-1 | Buxton | 15 |
| 13 | | 16 | (h) | Bolton W | W | 2-0 | Durban 2 | 11 |
| 14 | | 23 | (a) | Ipswich T | D | 2-2 | Buxton 2 | 12 |
| 15 | | 30 | (h) | Birmingham C | W | 5-3 | Thomas 2, Upton 2, Durban | 12 |
| 16 | Nov | 6 | (a) | Leyton Orient | D | 0-0 | | 5 |
| 17 | | 13 | (h) | Middlesbrough | W | 5-0 | Hodgson 3, Durban 2 | 12 |
| 18 | | 20 | (a) | Huddersfield T | W | 3-1 | Durban, Hodgson, Richardson (pen) | 14 |
| 19 | | 27 | (h) | Crystal Palace | W | 4-0 | Thomas, Durban, Hodgson, Upton (pen) | 13 |
| 20 | Dec | 4 | (a) | Preston NE | L | 0-2 | | 10 |
| 21 | | 11 | (h) | Charlton A | W | 2-0 | Hughes, Buxton | 12 |
| 22 | | 18 | (a) | Bolton W | W | 1-0 | Bowers | 8 |
| 23 | | 27 | (a) | Plymouth A | D | 0-0 | | 11 |
| 24 | Jan | 1 | (h) | Portsmouth | W | 3-1 | Buxton, Thomas, Hughes | 21 |
| 25 | | 8 | (a) | Middlesbrough | D | 0-0 | | 11 |
| 26 | | 15 | (h) | Ipswich T | D | 2-2 | Buxton, Durban | 14 |
| 27 | | 29 | (a) | Southampton | L | 1-3 | Bowers | 16 |
| 28 | Feb | 5 | (h) | Bury | W | 4-1 | Webster, Buxton, Durban, Upton | 12 |
| 29 | | 19 | (a) | Norwich C | W | 1-0 | Buxton | 19 |
| 30 | | 26 | (h) | Wolves | D | 2-2 | Thomas 2 | 27 |
| 31 | Mar | 5 | (h) | Plymouth A | L | 1-2 | Durban | 15 |
| 32 | | 12 | (a) | Rotherham U | L | 0-3 | | 10 |
| 33 | | 19 | (h) | Manchester C | L | 1-2 | Thomas | 22 |
| 34 | | 25 | (a) | Bristol C | D | 1-1 | Thomas | 13 |
| 35 | Apr | 2 | (h) | Leyton Orient | L | 1-3 | Thomas | 6 |
| 36 | | 9 | (a) | Birmingham C | D | 5-5 | Durban 3, Buxton, Thomas (og) | 13 |
| 37 | | 11 | (h) | Coventry C | W | 1-0 | Durban | 21 |
| 38 | | 12 | (a) | Coventry C | L | 2-3 | Thomas, Kearns (og) | 25 |
| 39 | | 16 | (h) | Huddersfield T | W | 4-1 | Thomas 2, Buxton, Durban | 15 |
| 40 | | 23 | (a) | Crystal Palace | D | 1-1 | Hughes | 11 |
| 41 | | 30 | (h) | Preston NE | W | 1-0 | Durban | 11 |
| 42 | May | 7 | (a) | Charlton A | D | 2-2 | Durban, Hodgson | 10 |

FINAL LEAGUE POSITION: 8th in Division Two

Appeara
Substi
G

## FA Cup

| | | | | | | | | |
|---|---|---|---|---|---|---|---|---|
| 3 | Jan | 22 | (h) | Manchester U | L | 2-5 | Richardson (pen), Upton | 33 |

Appeara
G

## League Cup

| | | | | | | | | |
|---|---|---|---|---|---|---|---|---|
| 2 | Sep | 22 | (a) | Hull C | D | 2-2 | Thomas 2 | 15 |
| R | | 29 | (h) | Hull C | W | 4-3 | Thomas 2, Buxton, Hodgson | 9 |
| 3 | Oct | 13 | (h) | Reading | D | 1-1 | Hughes | 10 |
| R | | 20 | (a) | Reading | L | 0-2 | | 8 |

Appeara
G

Substitutes:
First substitute (No.12) is distinguished by **bold**;
Second substitute (No.13) is distinguished by <u>underline</u>; Third substitute (No.14) is distinguished by *italic*.

| Matthews R | Barrowcliffe G | Ferguson R | Webster R | Young R | Parry J | Hughes G | Thomas E | Buxton I | Durban A | Hodgson W | Saxton R | Waller P | Bowers J | Hopkinson M | Cleevely N | Upton F | Richardson J | Daniel P | |
|---|---|---|---|---|---|---|---|---|---|---|---|---|---|---|---|---|---|---|---|
| | **2** | 3 | 4 | 5 | 6 | 7 | 8 | 9 | 10 | 11 | 12 | | | | | | | | 1 |
| | | 3 | 2 | 5 | 6 | 7 | 8 | 9 | 10 | 11 | 4 | | | | | | | | 2 |
| | | 3 | 2 | 5 | 6 | 7 | 8 | 9 | 10 | 11 | 4 | | | | | | | | 3 |
| | 2 | 3 | 4 | 5 | 6 | 7 | | | 10 | 11 | | 8 | 9 | | | | | | 4 |
| | 2 | 3 | 4 | 5 | 6 | 7 | | | 12 | 10 | | | 9 | **8** | 11 | | | | 5 |
| | 2 | 3 | 4 | 5 | 6 | 7 | | | 8 | 10 | | | 9 | | 11 | | | | 6 |
| | 2 | 3 | **4** | 5 | 6 | 7 | | | 8 | 10 | | | 9 | 12 | 11 | | | | 7 |
| | | 3 | 2 | 5 | 6 | 7 | | 9 | 8 | 10 | | | | | 11 | 4 | | | 8 |
| | 2 | 3 | 8 | 5 | 6 | 7 | | 9 | | 10 | | | | | 11 | 4 | | | 9 |
| | | 3 | 4 | 5 | | 7 | 8 | 9 | 10 | 11 | | | | | | 6 | 2 | | 10 |
| | | | 4 | | | 7 | 8 | 9 | 10 | 11 | 5 | | | | | 6 | 2 | 3 | 11 |
| | | | **4** | 12 | | 7 | 8 | 9 | 10 | 11 | 5 | | | | | 6 | 2 | 3 | 12 |
| | | | | | 4 | 7 | 8 | 9 | 10 | 11 | 5 | | | | | 6 | 2 | 3 | 13 |
| | 2 | | **4** | | 12 | 7 | 8 | 9 | 10 | 11 | 5 | | | | | 6 | | 3 | 14 |
| | | | 4 | | | 7 | 8 | 9 | 10 | 11 | 5 | | | | | 6 | 2 | 3 | 15 |
| | | | 4 | | | 7 | 8 | 9 | 10 | 11 | 5 | | | | | 6 | 2 | 3 | 16 |
| | | | | | | 7 | 8 | 9 | 10 | 11 | 5 | 4 | | | | 6 | 2 | 3 | 17 |
| | | | 4 | | | 7 | 8 | | 10 | 11 | 5 | 12 | 9 | | | 6 | **2** | 3 | 18 |
| | | | 2 | | | 7 | 8 | 9 | 10 | 11 | 5 | 4 | | | | 6 | | 3 | 19 |
| | | | 4 | | | 7 | 8 | 9 | 10 | 11 | 5 | | | | | 6 | 2 | 3 | 20 |
| | | | 4 | | | 7 | 8 | 9 | 10 | | 5 | | 11 | | | 6 | 2 | 3 | 21 |
| | | | 4 | | | 7 | 8 | 9 | 10 | | 5 | | 11 | | | 6 | 2 | 3 | 22 |
| | | | 2 | | | 7 | 8 | 9 | 10 | 11 | 5 | 4 | | | | 6 | | 3 | 23 |
| | | | 4 | | | 7 | 8 | 9 | 10 | 11 | 5 | | | | | 6 | 2 | 3 | 24 |
| | | | 4 | | | 7 | 8 | 9 | 10 | 11 | 5 | | | | | 6 | 2 | 3 | 25 |
| | | | 4 | | | 7 | 8 | 9 | 10 | 11 | 5 | | | | | 6 | 2 | 3 | 26 |
| | | | 4 | | | 7 | | 9 | 10 | 11 | 5 | | 8 | | | 6 | 2 | 3 | 27 |
| | | | 4 | | | 7 | 8 | 9 | 10 | 11 | 5 | | | | | 6 | 2 | 3 | 28 |
| | | | 4 | | | 7 | 8 | 9 | 10 | 11 | 5 | | | | | 6 | 2 | 3 | 29 |
| | | | 4 | | | 7 | 8 | 9 | 10 | 11 | 5 | | | | | 6 | 2 | 3 | 30 |
| | | | 4 | | | 7 | 8 | 9 | 10 | | 5 | | | | 11 | 6 | 2 | 3 | 31 |
| | | | 4 | | | 7 | 8 | 9 | 10 | 11 | 5 | | | | | 6 | 2 | 3 | 32 |
| | | | 4 | | | 7 | 8 | 9 | 10 | 11 | 5 | | | | | 6 | 2 | 3 | 33 |
| | | | 4 | | | 7 | 8 | 9 | 10 | | 5 | | 11 | | | 6 | 2 | 3 | 34 |
| | | | 4 | | | 7 | 8 | 9 | 10 | | 5 | | 11 | | | 6 | 2 | 3 | 35 |
| | | | 4 | | | 7 | 8 | 9 | 10 | | 5 | | | 11 | | 6 | 2 | 3 | 36 |
| | | | 4 | | | 7 | 8 | 9 | 10 | 11 | 5 | 6 | | | | | 2 | 3 | 37 |
| | | | 4 | | | 7 | 8 | 9 | 10 | 11 | 5 | 6 | | | | | 2 | 3 | 38 |
| | | | 4 | | | 7 | 8 | 9 | 10 | 11 | 5 | 6 | | | | | 2 | 3 | 39 |
| | | | 4 | | | 7 | 8 | 9 | 10 | 11 | 5 | 6 | | | | | 2 | 3 | 40 |
| | | | 4 | | | 7 | 8 | 9 | 10 | 11 | 5 | 6 | | | | | 2 | 3 | 41 |
| | | | 4 | | | 7 | 8 | | 10 | 11 | 5 | 6 | | | | 9 | 2 | 3 | 42 |
| 2 | 7 | 10 | 40 | 10 | 10 | 42 | 35 | 36 | 40 | 36 | 34 | 10 | 10 | 2 | 6 | 30 | 30 | 32 | |
| | | | | 1 | 1 | | | | 1 | | 1 | 1 | | 1 | | | | | |
| | | | 1 | | 1 | 6 | 13 | 12 | 17 | 8 | | | 4 | | 2 | 4 | 1 | | |

2 own-goals

| Matthews R | Barrowcliffe G | Ferguson R | Webster R | Young R | Parry J | Hughes G | Thomas E | Buxton I | Durban A | Hodgson W | Saxton R | Waller P | Bowers J | Hopkinson M | Cleevely N | Upton F | Richardson J | Daniel P | |
|---|---|---|---|---|---|---|---|---|---|---|---|---|---|---|---|---|---|---|---|
| | | | 4 | | | 7 | 8 | 9 | 10 | 11 | 5 | | | | | 6 | 2 | 3 | 3 |
| | | | 1 | | | 1 | 1 | 1 | 1 | 1 | 1 | | | | | 1 | 1 | 1 | |
| | | | | | | | | | | | | | | | | 1 | 1 | | |

| Matthews R | Barrowcliffe G | Ferguson R | Webster R | Young R | Parry J | Hughes G | Thomas E | Buxton I | Durban A | Hodgson W | Saxton R | Waller P | Bowers J | Hopkinson M | Cleevely N | Upton F | Richardson J | Daniel P | |
|---|---|---|---|---|---|---|---|---|---|---|---|---|---|---|---|---|---|---|---|
| | | 3 | 4 | 5 | 6 | 7 | 8 | 9 | 10 | 11 | | | | | | | 2 | | 2 |
| | | 3 | 4 | 5 | | 7 | 8 | 9 | 10 | 11 | | | | 6 | | | 2 | | R |
| | | | | | 4 | 7 | 8 | 9 | 10 | 11 | 5 | | | | | 6 | 2 | 3 | 3 |
| | | | | | 4 | 7 | 8 | 9 | 10 | 11 | 5 | | | | | 6 | 2 | 3 | R |
| | | 2 | 2 | 2 | 3 | 4 | 4 | 4 | 4 | 4 | 2 | | | 1 | | 2 | 4 | 2 | |
| | | | | | | 1 | 4 | 1 | | 1 | | | | | | | | | |

# 1966-67

| | P | W | D | L | F | A | Pts |
|---|---|---|---|---|---|---|---|
| Coventry C | 42 | 23 | 13 | 6 | 74 | 43 | 59 |
| Wolves | 42 | 25 | 8 | 9 | 88 | 48 | 58 |
| Carlisle U | 42 | 23 | 6 | 13 | 71 | 54 | 52 |
| Blackburn R | 42 | 19 | 13 | 10 | 56 | 46 | 51 |
| Ipswich T | 42 | 17 | 16 | 9 | 70 | 54 | 50 |
| Huddersfield T | 42 | 20 | 9 | 13 | 58 | 46 | 49 |
| Crystal Palace | 42 | 19 | 10 | 13 | 61 | 55 | 48 |
| Millwall | 42 | 18 | 9 | 15 | 49 | 58 | 45 |
| Bolton W | 42 | 14 | 14 | 14 | 64 | 58 | 42 |
| Birmingham C | 42 | 16 | 8 | 18 | 70 | 66 | 40 |
| Norwich C | 42 | 13 | 14 | 15 | 49 | 55 | 40 |
| Hull C | 42 | 16 | 7 | 19 | 77 | 72 | 39 |
| Preston N.E. | 42 | 16 | 7 | 19 | 65 | 67 | 39 |
| Portsmouth | 42 | 13 | 13 | 16 | 59 | 70 | 39 |
| Bristol C | 42 | 12 | 14 | 16 | 56 | 62 | 38 |
| Plymouth A | 42 | 14 | 9 | 19 | 59 | 58 | 37 |
| Derby Co | 42 | 12 | 12 | 18 | 68 | 72 | 36 |
| Rotherham U | 42 | 13 | 10 | 19 | 61 | 70 | 36 |
| Charlton A | 42 | 13 | 9 | 20 | 49 | 53 | 35 |
| Cardiff C | 42 | 12 | 9 | 21 | 61 | 87 | 33 |
| Northampton T | 42 | 12 | 6 | 24 | 47 | 84 | 30 |
| Bury | 42 | 11 | 6 | 25 | 49 | 83 | 28 |

Manager: Tim Ward.
Leading scorer: Kevin Hector, League/all matches 16.

- In September, Derby astonished their supporters by paying almost £40,000 for Bradford forward Kevin Hector. It was Derby's record fee and signs of such ambition had been alien to the Baseball Ground for years.
- Hector was 21 when he moved but already had 113 League goals in 176 games for the Park Avenue club. His home debut, against Huddersfield Town, thrilled fans, although Alan Durban scored three of the four goals.
- Despite Hector's success, Tim Ward's contract was not renewed at the end of the season. The directors picked the team for the final game, giving Ronnie Metcalfe his solitary League appearance.

## Division Two

| Match No. | Date | Venue | Opponents | Result | | Scorers | Atten |
|---|---|---|---|---|---|---|---|
| 1 | Aug 20 | (h) | Blackburn R | L | 2-3 | Upton, Durban | 14 |
| 2 | 23 | (a) | Carlisle U | D | 0-0 | | 13 |
| 3 | 27 | (a) | Bolton W | L | 1-3 | Thomas | 11 |
| 4 | 31 | (h) | Carlisle U | L | 0-1 | | 12 |
| 5 | Sep 3 | (h) | Charlton A | L | 0-2 | | 10 |
| 6 | 6 | (a) | Ipswich T | L | 3-4 | Thomas 2, Durban | 15 |
| 7 | 10 | (a) | Northampton T | W | 2-0 | Waller, Buxton | 10 |
| 8 | 17 | (a) | Crystal Palace | L | 1-2 | Hodgson | 17 |
| 9 | 24 | (h) | Huddersfield T | W | 4-3 | Durban 3, Hector | 15 |
| 10 | 28 | (h) | Ipswich T | D | 2-2 | Richardson (pen), Hector | 18 |
| 11 | Oct 1 | (a) | Cardiff C | D | 1-1 | Durban | 6 |
| 12 | 8 | (h) | Millwall | W | 5-1 | Webster, Buxton, Hodgson, Hector, Jones (og) | 16 |
| 13 | 15 | (a) | Rotherham U | D | 0-0 | | 11 |
| 14 | 22 | (h) | Preston NE | W | 5-1 | Buxton 2, Hughes, Thomas, Hector | 18 |
| 15 | 29 | (a) | Bury | D | 2-2 | Hughes, Hector | 6 |
| 16 | Nov 5 | (h) | Coventry C | L | 1-2 | Hodgson | 22 |
| 17 | 12 | (a) | Norwich C | L | 1-4 | Buxton | 13 |
| 18 | 19 | (h) | Birmingham C | L | 1-2 | Hector (pen) | 17 |
| 19 | 26 | (a) | Portsmouth | W | 3-0 | Hector, Buxton, Durban | 13 |
| 20 | Dec 3 | (h) | Hull C | L | 2-3 | Thomas, Hodgson | 18 |
| 21 | 10 | (a) | Plymouth A | W | 2-1 | Buxton, Hodgson | 11 |
| 22 | 17 | (a) | Blackburn R | D | 0-0 | | 10 |
| 23 | 24 | (a) | Wolves | L | 3-5 | Durban 2, Richardson (pen) | 24 |
| 24 | 26 | (h) | Wolves | L | 0-3 | | 28 |
| 25 | 31 | (h) | Bolton W | D | 2-2 | Buxton, Waller | 14 |
| 26 | Jan 7 | (a) | Charlton A | L | 1-3 | Buxton | 9 |
| 27 | 14 | (h) | Northampton T | W | 4-3 | Hector, Hodgson, Durban, Waller | 14 |
| 28 | 21 | (h) | Crystal Palace | W | 2-0 | Hodgson 2 | 15 |
| 29 | Feb 4 | (a) | Huddersfield T | L | 0-1 | | 17 |
| 30 | 11 | (h) | Cardiff C | D | 1-1 | Hector (pen) | 14 |
| 31 | 25 | (a) | Millwall | L | 2-3 | Hector 2 | 12 |
| 32 | Mar 4 | (h) | Bury | W | 3-1 | Hector 2 (1 pen), Hopkinson | 14 |
| 33 | 18 | (a) | Preston NE | L | 0-2 | | 14 |
| 34 | 25 | (h) | Rotherham U | W | 2-0 | Hector, Hodgson | 14 |
| 35 | 27 | (h) | Bristol C | W | 2-0 | Thomas, Low (og) | 15 |
| 36 | 28 | (a) | Bristol C | L | 1-4 | Buxton | 20 |
| 37 | Apr 1 | (a) | Coventry C | D | 2-2 | Hector, Thomas | 32 |
| 38 | 8 | (h) | Norwich C | D | 1-1 | Hector | 12 |
| 39 | 15 | (a) | Birmingham C | L | 0-2 | | 15 |
| 40 | 22 | (h) | Portsmouth | D | 0-0 | | 11 |
| 41 | 27 | (a) | Hull C | W | 3-1 | Hughes 2, Thomas | 19 |
| 42 | May 6 | (h) | Plymouth A | D | 1-1 | Draper | 11 |

FINAL LEAGUE POSITION: 17th in Division Two

Appeara
Substit
G

## FA Cup

| | | | | | | | |
|---|---|---|---|---|---|---|---|
| 3 | Jan 28 | (a) | Norwich C | L | 0-3 | | 21 |

Appeara
G

## League Cup

| | | | | | | | |
|---|---|---|---|---|---|---|---|
| 2 | Sep 14 | (a) | Coventry C | L | 1-2 | Hodgson | 14 |

Appeara
G

ws R

| Richardson J | Webster R | Upton F | Saxton R | Waller P | Hughes G | Thomas E | Buxton I | Durban A | Hodgson W | Daniel P | Draper D | Hopkinson M | Hector K | Cholerton W | Boulton C | Cleevely N | Metcalfe R | |
|---|---|---|---|---|---|---|---|---|---|---|---|---|---|---|---|---|---|---|
| 2 | 3 | 4 | 5 | 6 | 7 | 8 | 9 | 10 | 11 | | | | | | | | | 1 |
| 2 | 4 | 6 | 5 | 7 | | 8 | 9 | 10 | 11 | 3 | | | | | | | | 2 |
| 2 | 4 | 6 | 5 | 7 | | 8 | 9 | 10 | 11 | 3 | | | | | | | | 3 |
| 2 | 4 | 6 | 5 | 7 | | 8 | 9 | 10 | 11 | 3 | | | | | | | | 4 |
| | 2 | 6 | 5 | 4 | 7 | 9 | | 10 | | 3 | 8 | 11 | | | | | | 5 |
| 2 | 4 | | 5 | 6 | 7 | 9 | | 10 | | 3 | 8 | 11 | | | | | | 6 |
| 2 | 4 | | 5 | 6 | 7 | 8 | 9 | | 11 | 3 | 10 | | | | | | | 7 |
| 2 | 4 | | 5 | 6 | 7 | 9 | | | 11 | 3 | 10 | | 8 | | | | | 8 |
| 2 | 4 | | 5 | 6 | 7 | | 9 | 10 | 11 | 3 | | | 8 | | | | | 9 |
| 2 | 4 | | 5 | 6 | 7 | | 9 | 10 | 11 | 3 | | | 8 | | | | | 10 |
| 2 | 4 | | 5 | 6 | | | 9 | 10 | 11 | | | 7 | 8 | 3 | | | | 11 |
| 2 | 4 | | 5 | 6 | 7 | | 9 | 10 | 11 | 3 | | | 8 | | | | | 12 |
| 2 | 4 | | 5 | 6 | 7 | 8 | 9 | 10 | 11 | 3 | | | | | | | | 13 |
| 2 | 4 | | 5 | 6 | 7 | 10 | 9 | | 11 | 3 | | | 8 | | | | | 14 |
| 2 | 4 | | 5 | 6 | 7 | | 9 | 10 | 11 | 3 | | | 8 | | | | | 15 |
| 2 | 4 | | 5 | **6** | 7 | 12 | 9 | 10 | 11 | 3 | | | 8 | | | | | 16 |
| 2 | 4 | | 5 | | 7 | 6 | 9 | 10 | 11 | 12 | | **3** | 8 | | | | | 17 |
| 2 | 4 | | **5** | 6 | 7 | 12 | 9 | 10 | 11 | 3 | | | 8 | | | | | 18 |
| 2 | 4 | | | 5 | 7 | 6 | 9 | 10 | 11 | 3 | | | 8 | | | | | 19 |
| 2 | 4 | | | 5 | 7 | 6 | 9 | 10 | 11 | 3 | | | 8 | | | | | 20 |
| 2 | 4 | | 5 | 6 | | 7 | 9 | 10 | 11 | 3 | | | 8 | | | | | 21 |
| 2 | 4 | | 5 | 6 | | 7 | 9 | 10 | 11 | 3 | | | 8 | | | | | 22 |
| 2 | 4 | | 5 | 6 | 7 | | 9 | 10 | 11 | | | 3 | 8 | | | | | 23 |
| 2 | 4 | | | 5 | 7 | 6 | 9 | 10 | 11 | | | 3 | 8 | | | | | 24 |
| 2 | 4 | | 5 | 6 | 7 | | 9 | 10 | 11 | | | 3 | 8 | | | | | 25 |
| | 2 | | 5 | 6 | 7 | 4 | 9 | 10 | 11 | | | 3 | 8 | | | | | 26 |
| 2 | 4 | | 5 | 6 | 7 | | 9 | 10 | 11 | | | 3 | 8 | | | | | 27 |
| 2 | 4 | | 5 | 6 | 7 | | 9 | 10 | 11 | | | 3 | 8 | | | | | 28 |
| 2 | 4 | | 5 | 6 | 7 | | 9 | 10 | **11** | | | 3 | 8 | | 1 | 12 | | 29 |
| 2 | 4 | | 5 | 6 | 7 | | 9 | 10 | | | | 3 | 8 | | 1 | 11 | | 30 |
| 2 | 4 | | 5 | 6 | 7 | 10 | 9 | | | | | 3 | 8 | | 1 | 11 | | 31 |
| 2 | 4 | | 5 | 6 | 7 | 9 | | | 10 | | | 3 | 8 | | 1 | 11 | | 32 |
| | 4 | | 5 | 6 | 7 | 9 | | | 10 | 2 | | 3 | 8 | | 1 | 11 | | 33 |
| 3 | 4 | | 5 | 6 | 7 | 9 | | 10 | 11 | 2 | | | 8 | | 1 | | | 34 |
| 3 | **4** | | 5 | 6 | 7 | 9 | 12 | 10 | 11 | 2 | | | 8 | | 1 | | | 35 |
| 3 | | | 5 | 6 | 7 | 4 | 9 | 10 | 11 | 2 | | | 8 | | 1 | | | 36 |
| 3 | | | 5 | 6 | 7 | 4 | 9 | 10 | | 2 | | 12 | **8** | | 1 | 11 | | 37 |
| | 3 | | 5 | 6 | 7 | 4 | 9 | 10 | | 2 | | | 8 | | 1 | 11 | | 38 |
| | 3 | | 5 | 6 | 7 | 4 | 9 | 10 | 11 | 2 | 8 | | | | 1 | | | 39 |
| | 3 | | 5 | 6 | 7 | 4 | 9 | 10 | 11 | 2 | 8 | | | | 1 | | | 40 |
| 3 | 4 | | 5 | 6 | 7 | 8 | 9 | 10 | | 2 | 11 | | | | 1 | | | 41 |
| 3 | 4 | | 5 | 6 | 7 | 9 | | 10 | | 2 | 8 | | | | 1 | | 11 | 42 |
| 36 | 40 | 5 | 39 | 41 | 36 | 29 | 34 | 36 | 34 | 29 | 8 | 15 | 30 | 1 | 14 | 6 | 1 | |
| | | | | | | 2 | 1 | | | 1 | | 1 | | | | 1 | | |
| 2 | 1 | 1 | | 3 | 4 | 8 | 10 | 10 | 9 | | 1 | 1 | 16 | | | | | |

2 own-goals

| | | | | | | | | | | | | | | | | | |
|---|---|---|---|---|---|---|---|---|---|---|---|---|---|---|---|---|---|
| | 4 | | 5 | 6 | 7 | | 9 | 10 | 11 | | | 3 | 8 | | 1 | 2 | 3 |
| | 1 | | 1 | 1 | 1 | | 1 | 1 | 1 | | | 1 | 1 | | 1 | 1 | |
| | | | | | | | | | | | | | | | | | |

| | | | | | | | | | | | | |
|---|---|---|---|---|---|---|---|---|---|---|---|---|
| 2 | 4 | | 5 | 6 | 7 | 8 | 9 | | 11 | 3 | 10 | 3 |
| 1 | 1 | | 1 | 1 | 1 | 1 | 1 | | 1 | 1 | 1 | |
| | | | | | | | | | 1 | | | |

# 1967-68

| | P | W | D | L | F | A | Pts |
|---|---|---|---|---|---|---|---|
| Ipswich T | 42 | 22 | 15 | 5 | 79 | 44 | 59 |
| Q.P.R. | 42 | 25 | 8 | 9 | 67 | 36 | 58 |
| Blackpool | 42 | 24 | 10 | 8 | 71 | 43 | 58 |
| Birmingham C | 42 | 19 | 14 | 9 | 83 | 51 | 52 |
| Portsmouth | 42 | 18 | 13 | 11 | 68 | 55 | 49 |
| Middlesbrough | 42 | 17 | 12 | 13 | 60 | 54 | 46 |
| Millwall | 42 | 14 | 17 | 11 | 62 | 50 | 45 |
| Blackburn R | 42 | 16 | 11 | 15 | 56 | 49 | 43 |
| Norwich C | 42 | 16 | 11 | 15 | 60 | 65 | 43 |
| Carlisle U | 42 | 14 | 13 | 15 | 58 | 52 | 41 |
| Crystal Palace | 42 | 14 | 11 | 17 | 56 | 56 | 39 |
| Bolton W | 42 | 13 | 13 | 16 | 60 | 63 | 39 |
| Cardiff C | 42 | 13 | 12 | 17 | 60 | 66 | 38 |
| Huddersfield T | 42 | 13 | 12 | 17 | 46 | 61 | 38 |
| Charlton A | 42 | 12 | 13 | 17 | 63 | 68 | 37 |
| Aston Villa | 42 | 15 | 7 | 20 | 54 | 64 | 37 |
| Hull C | 42 | 12 | 13 | 17 | 58 | 73 | 37 |
| Derby Co | 42 | 13 | 10 | 19 | 71 | 78 | 36 |
| Bristol C | 42 | 13 | 10 | 19 | 48 | 62 | 36 |
| Preston N.E. | 42 | 12 | 11 | 19 | 43 | 65 | 35 |
| Rotherham U | 42 | 10 | 11 | 21 | 42 | 76 | 31 |
| Plymouth A | 42 | 9 | 9 | 24 | 38 | 72 | 27 |

Manager: Brian Clough.
Leading scorer: Kevin Hector, League 21, all matches 24.
League ever-present: John O'Hare.

- On the recommendation of former Sunderland and England inside-forward Len Shackleton, Derby engaged Brian Clough from Hartlepools United as manager. Clough insisted on bringing Peter Taylor, once Burton Albion's manager, as his assistant.
- Clough's first three signings were John O'Hare, Roy McFarland and Alan Hinton for a total outlay of £75,000. Between them, they made 1,154 (1,125 + 29) appearances and scored 212 goals. Value for money.
- Derby reached the semi-finals of the League Cup for the first and, so far, only time. On the way, they helped to set the attendance record at Sincil Bank for their replay victory over Lincoln City.
- Reg Matthews passed Harry Maskrey's 222 appearances and ended with 246, a record for a Rams goalkeeper.
- Despite the quality of the signings, the Rams finished one place lower than in Tim Ward's final season.

## Division Two

| Match No. | Date | | Venue | Opponents | Result | | Scorers |
|---|---|---|---|---|---|---|---|
| 1 | Aug | 19 | (h) | Charlton A | W | 3-2 | O'Hare, Hector, King (og) |
| 2 | | 26 | (a) | Crystal Palace | L | 0-1 | |
| 3 | | 28 | (a) | Rotherham U | W | 3-1 | Hector (pen), O'Hare, Buxton |
| 4 | Sep | 2 | (h) | Aston Villa | W | 3-1 | Durban 2, Hector (pen) |
| 5 | | 6 | (a) | Norwich C | L | 2-3 | Hughes, Durban |
| 6 | | 9 | (a) | QPR | W | 1-0 | Hector |
| 7 | | 16 | (h) | Plymouth A | W | 1-0 | Everitt (og) |
| 8 | | 23 | (a) | Cardiff C | W | 5-1 | Hector 3, O'Hare 2 |
| 9 | | 27 | (h) | Rotherham U | W | 4-1 | Hector 2, O'Hare, Hughes |
| 10 | | 30 | (h) | Portsmouth | L | 0-1 | |
| 11 | Oct | 7 | (h) | Millwall | D | 3-3 | Hector, Saxton, Gilchrist (og) |
| 12 | | 14 | (a) | Ipswich T | L | 0-4 | |
| 13 | | 21 | (h) | Huddersfield T | W | 1-0 | Barker |
| 14 | | 28 | (a) | Bolton W | L | 3-5 | Hector, O'Hare, Durban |
| 15 | Nov | 4 | (h) | Birmingham C | D | 2-2 | Durban, Barker |
| 16 | | 10 | (a) | Bristol C | L | 0-1 | |
| 17 | | 18 | (h) | Carlisle U | L | 0-1 | |
| 18 | | 25 | (a) | Hull C | L | 0-3 | |
| 19 | Dec | 2 | (h) | Middlesbrough | L | 2-4 | Hector, O'Hare |
| 20 | | 9 | (a) | Blackpool | D | 1-1 | O'Hare |
| 21 | | 16 | (a) | Charlton A | W | 2-1 | Barker, Curtis(og) |
| 22 | | 23 | (h) | Crystal Palace | D | 1-1 | Durban |
| 23 | | 26 | (a) | Blackburn R | L | 0-3 | |
| 24 | | 30 | (h) | Blackburn R | D | 2-2 | Hector, Barker |
| 25 | Jan | 6 | (a) | Aston Villa | L | 1-2 | Hector |
| 26 | | 20 | (a) | Plymouth A | W | 4-3 | Hinton 2, O'Hare, Barker |
| 27 | Feb | 3 | (h) | Cardiff C | L | 3-4 | Durban, Hector, Hinton |
| 28 | | 10 | (a) | Portsmouth | L | 2-3 | Hector, Barker |
| 29 | | 17 | (h) | QPR | W | 4-0 | Hector, McFarland, Hinton, Stewart |
| 30 | | 24 | (a) | Millwall | D | 1-1 | Durban |
| 31 | Mar | 2 | (h) | Ipswich T | L | 2-3 | Hector, Barker |
| 32 | | 9 | (h) | Norwich C | D | 1-1 | Barker |
| 33 | | 16 | (a) | Huddersfield T | L | 1-3 | McFarland |
| 34 | | 23 | (h) | Bolton W | W | 2-1 | O'Hare, Hinton |
| 35 | Apr | 2 | (a) | Birmingham C | L | 1-3 | O'Hare |
| 36 | | 6 | (h) | Bristol C | W | 3-1 | Barker 2, Hector (pen) |
| 37 | | 13 | (a) | Carlisle U | D | 1-1 | Durban |
| 38 | | 15 | (h) | Preston NE | L | 1-2 | Hinton (pen) |
| 39 | | 16 | (a) | Preston NE | D | 1-1 | O'Hare |
| 40 | | 20 | (h) | Hull C | L | 1-2 | Richardson |
| 41 | | 27 | (a) | Middlesbrough | D | 2-2 | Hector 2 |
| 42 | May | 4 | (h) | Blackpool | L | 1-3 | Robson |

FINAL LEAGUE POSITION: 18th in Division Two

Appear.
Subst

## FA Cup

| | | | | | | | |
|---|---|---|---|---|---|---|---|
| 3 | Jan | 27 | (a) | Leeds U | L | 0-2 | |

Appear.
Subst

## League Cup

| | | | | | | | |
|---|---|---|---|---|---|---|---|
| 2 | Sep | 13 | (h) | Hartlepools U | W | 4-0 | O'Hare 3, Hodgson |
| 3 | Oct | 11 | (h) | Birmingham C | W | 3-1 | Hector, Hopkinson, O'Hare |
| 4 | Nov | 1 | (h) | Lincoln C | D | 1-1 | Barker |
| R | | 15 | (a) | Lincoln C | W | 3-0 | O'Hare 2, Hector |
| 5 | | 29 | (h) | Darlington | W | 5-4 | Durban 2, Hughes, Barker, O'Neill (og) |
| SF | Jan | 17 | (h) | Leeds U | L | 0-1 | |
| SF | Feb | 7 | (a) | Leeds U | L | 2-3 | Hector, Stewart |

Appear.
Subst.

…hews R

| Daniel P | Hopkinson M | Webster R | Saxton R | Waller P | Hughes G | Durban A | O'Hare J | Hector K | Hodgson W | Thomas E | Richardson J | McFarland R | Buxton I | Hinton A | Wright P | Barker R | Butlin B | Boulton C | Stewart A | Robson J | Walker J | |
|---|---|---|---|---|---|---|---|---|---|---|---|---|---|---|---|---|---|---|---|---|---|---|
| 2 | 3 | 4 | 5 | 6 | 7 | 8 | 9 | 10 | 11 | | | | | | | | | | | | | 1 |
| 2 | 3 | 4 | 5 | **6** | 7 | 8 | 9 | 10 | 11 | 12 | | | | | | | | | | | | 2 |
| 2 | | 4 | 6 | | 7 | | 9 | 10 | 11 | | 3 | 5 | 8 | | | | | | | | | 3 |
| 2 | | 4 | 6 | | 7 | 8 | 9 | 10 | 11 | | 3 | 5 | | | | | | | | | | 4 |
| 2 | | 4 | 6 | | 7 | 8 | 9 | 10 | 11 | | 3 | 5 | | | | | | | | | | 5 |
| 2 | | 4 | 6 | | 7 | 8 | 9 | 10 | 11 | | 3 | 5 | | | | | | | | | | 6 |
| 2 | | 4 | 6 | | 7 | 8 | 9 | 10 | 11 | | 3 | 5 | | | | | | | | | | 7 |
| 2 | | 4 | | 6 | 7 | 8 | 9 | 10 | 11 | | 3 | 5 | | | | | | | | | | 8 |
| 2 | | 4 | | 6 | 7 | 8 | 9 | 10 | | | 3 | 5 | | 11 | | | | | | | | 9 |
| 2 | | 4 | 6 | | 7 | 8 | 9 | 10 | | | 3 | 5 | | 11 | | | | | | | | 10 |
| | | 4 | 6 | | 7 | 8 | 9 | 10 | | | 3 | 5 | | 11 | 2 | | | | | | | 11 |
| | 12 | **4** | 6 | | 7 | 8 | 9 | 10 | | | 3 | 5 | | 11 | 2 | | | | | | | 12 |
| | 6 | 4 | 12 | | 7 | | 9 | 10 | | | **3** | 5 | | 11 | 2 | 8 | | | | | | 13 |
| 3 | | 4 | 6 | | 7 | 8 | 9 | 10 | | | | 5 | | 11 | 2 | | | | | | | 14 |
| | 3 | 4 | 6 | | 7 | 8 | 9 | 10 | | | | 5 | | | 2 | 11 | | | | | | 15 |
| | 3 | **4** | 6 | 11 | 7 | 8 | 9 | 10 | | | | 5 | | | 2 | 12 | | | | | | 16 |
| | 3 | 4 | | 6 | 7 | 11 | 9 | 10 | | | | 5 | | 12 | 2 | | **8** | | | | | 17 |
| | 3 | 4 | 6 | | **7** | 8 | 9 | 10 | | | | 5 | | 11 | 2 | 12 | | | | | | 18 |
| | | 4 | | | 7 | 8 | 9 | 10 | | | 3 | 5 | | 11 | 2 | | | 1 | 6 | | | 19 |
| | | 2 | 4 | | 7 | 11 | 9 | 10 | | | 3 | 5 | | | | 8 | | | 6 | | | 20 |
| | | 2 | 4 | | 7 | 11 | 9 | 10 | | | 3 | 5 | | | | 8 | | | 6 | | | 21 |
| | | 2 | 4 | | 7 | 11 | 9 | 10 | | | | 5 | | | 3 | 8 | | | 6 | | | 22 |
| | | 2 | 4 | | 7 | 11 | 9 | 10 | | | | 5 | | | 3 | 8 | | | 6 | | | 23 |
| 3 | | 2 | 4 | | 7 | 8 | 9 | 10 | | | | 5 | | | | 8 | | | 6 | | | 24 |
| | | 2 | 4 | | 7 | 11 | 9 | 10 | | | 3 | 5 | | | | 8 | | | 6 | | | 25 |
| 2 | | 4 | | | 7 | **8** | 9 | 10 | | | 3 | 5 | | 11 | | 12 | | | 6 | | | 26 |
| 2 | | 4 | | | 7 | 8 | **9** | 10 | | | 3 | 5 | | 11 | | 12 | | | 6 | | | 27 |
| 2 | | 4 | | | | 7 | 9 | 10 | | | 3 | 5 | | 11 | | 8 | | | 6 | | | 28 |
| | 3 | 4 | | 12 | | 7 | 9 | 10 | | | **2** | 5 | | 11 | | 8 | | | 6 | | | 29 |
| | 3 | **4** | | | | 7 | 9 | 10 | | | 2 | 5 | | 11 | 12 | 8 | | | 6 | | | 30 |
| | 3 | | | | | 7 | 9 | 10 | | | 2 | 5 | | 11 | | 8 | | | 6 | 4 | | 31 |
| | 3 | | | | | 7 | 9 | 10 | | | 2 | 5 | | 11 | | 8 | | | 6 | 4 | | 32 |
| | 3 | 4 | | | | 7 | 9 | 10 | | | 2 | 5 | | 11 | | 8 | | | 6 | | | 33 |
| | 6 | 2 | | | | 8 | 10 | 11 | | | 3 | 5 | | 7 | | 9 | | 1 | 4 | | | 34 |
| | 6 | 2 | | | | 8 | 7 | 9 | | | 3 | 5 | | 11 | | 10 | | 1 | 4 | | | 35 |
| | 6 | 2 | | | | 7 | 9 | 10 | | | 3 | 5 | | 11 | | 8 | | 1 | 4 | | | 36 |
| | 6 | 2 | | | | 7 | 9 | 10 | | | 3 | 5 | | 11 | | 8 | | 1 | 4 | | | 37 |
| | 6 | 2 | | | | 7 | 9 | 10 | | | 3 | 5 | | 11 | | 8 | | | 4 | | | 38 |
| | 2 | 4 | | | | 7 | 9 | 10 | | | 3 | 5 | | 11 | | 8 | | | 6 | | | 39 |
| | 3 | 4 | | | | 10 | 7 | | | | 2 | 5 | | 11 | | 8 | 9 | | 6 | | | 40 |
| | 3 | 2 | | | | 7 | 9 | 10 | | | | 5 | | 11 | | 8 | | | 6 | 4 | | 41 |
| | 3 | | | | | | 9 | 10 | | | | 5 | | 7 | 2 | 8 | | | 6 | 4 | 11 | 42 |
| 15 | 21 | 39 | 20 | 6 | 27 | 39 | 42 | 41 | 8 | | 30 | 40 | 1 | 25 | 12 | 23 | 2 | 5 | 24 | 4 | 1 | |
| | 1 | | 1 | 1 | | | | | | 1 | | | | 1 | 1 | 4 | | | | | | |
| | | | 1 | | 2 | 9 | 12 | 21 | | | 1 | 2 | 1 | 6 | | 10 | | | 1 | 1 | | |

4 own-goals

| | | | | | | | | | | | | | | | | | | | | | | |
|---|---|---|---|---|---|---|---|---|---|---|---|---|---|---|---|---|---|---|---|---|---|---|
| 2 | | 4 | 5 | | 7 | | 9 | 10 | | | 3 | 6 | | 11 | | | | | 8 | | | 3 |
| 1 | | 1 | 1 | | 1 | | 1 | 1 | | | 1 | 1 | | 1 | | | | | 1 | | | |
| | | | | | | | | | | | | | | | | | | | | | | |
| | | | | | | | | | | | | | | | | | | | | | | |

| | | | | | | | | | | | | | | | | | | | | | | | |
|---|---|---|---|---|---|---|---|---|---|---|---|---|---|---|---|---|---|---|---|---|---|---|---|
| | 3 | 4 | 5 | | 7 | 8 | 9 | 10 | 11 | | 2 | | 6 | | | | | | | | | | 2 |
| 2 | 11 | 4 | 5 | 6 | 7 | 8 | 9 | 10 | | | 3 | | | | | | | | | | | | 3 |
| 2 | 3 | 4 | 5 | 6 | 7 | 8 | 9 | 10 | | | | | | | | 11 | | | | | | | 4 |
| 2 | 3 | 4 | 5 | 6 | 7 | 11 | 9 | **10** | | | | | | | | | 8 | | | | | 12 | R |
| 2 | | 4 | 5 | 6 | 7 | 11 | 9 | 10 | | | 3 | | | | | 8 | | | | | | | 5 |
| 2 | | 4 | 5 | | 7 | 11 | 9 | 10 | | | 3 | | | | | 8 | | | 6 | | | | SF |
| 2 | | 4 | | 6 | 7 | 11 | 9 | 10 | | | 3 | | | | | 8 | | | 6 | | | | SF |
| 6 | 4 | 7 | 6 | 5 | 7 | 7 | 7 | 7 | 1 | | 5 | | 1 | | | 4 | 1 | | 2 | | | | |
| | | | | | | | | | | | | | | | | | | | | | | 1 | |
| | 1 | | | | 1 | 2 | 6 | 3 | 1 | | | | | | | 2 | | | 1 | | | | |

1 own-goal

# 1968-69

| | P | W | D | L | F | A | Pts |
|---|---|---|---|---|---|---|---|
| Derby Co | 42 | 26 | 11 | 5 | 65 | 32 | 63 |
| Crystal Palace | 42 | 22 | 12 | 8 | 70 | 47 | 56 |
| Charlton A | 42 | 18 | 14 | 10 | 61 | 52 | 50 |
| Middlesbrough | 42 | 19 | 11 | 12 | 58 | 49 | 49 |
| Cardiff C | 42 | 20 | 7 | 15 | 67 | 54 | 47 |
| Huddersfield T | 42 | 17 | 12 | 13 | 53 | 46 | 46 |
| Birmingham C | 42 | 18 | 8 | 16 | 73 | 59 | 44 |
| Blackpool | 42 | 14 | 15 | 13 | 51 | 41 | 43 |
| Sheffield U | 42 | 16 | 11 | 15 | 61 | 50 | 43 |
| Millwall | 42 | 17 | 9 | 16 | 57 | 49 | 43 |
| Hull C | 42 | 13 | 16 | 13 | 59 | 52 | 42 |
| Carlisle U | 42 | 16 | 10 | 16 | 46 | 49 | 42 |
| Norwich C | 42 | 15 | 10 | 17 | 53 | 56 | 40 |
| Preston N.E. | 42 | 12 | 15 | 15 | 38 | 44 | 39 |
| Portsmouth | 42 | 12 | 14 | 16 | 58 | 58 | 38 |
| Bristol C | 42 | 11 | 16 | 15 | 46 | 53 | 38 |
| Bolton W | 42 | 12 | 14 | 16 | 55 | 67 | 38 |
| Aston Villa | 42 | 12 | 14 | 16 | 37 | 48 | 38 |
| Blackburn R | 42 | 13 | 11 | 18 | 52 | 63 | 37 |
| Oxford U | 42 | 12 | 9 | 21 | 34 | 55 | 33 |
| Bury | 42 | 11 | 8 | 23 | 51 | 80 | 30 |
| Fulham | 42 | 7 | 11 | 24 | 40 | 81 | 25 |

Manager: Brian Clough.
Leading scorer: Kevin Hector, League 16, all matches 20.
League ever-present: Les Green, Roy McFarland, John Robson.
Player of the season: Roy McFarland.

- Dave Mackay, who looked likely to rejoin Heart of Midlothian, was persuaded to sign for Derby from Tottenham Hotspur. Mackay, a massive influence in Tottenham's League and FA Cup double team, was Brian Clough's most imaginative signing and became joint Footballer of the Year with Tony Book of Manchester City.
- An extra ingredient was required and Willie Carlin's £60,000 signing from Sheffield United in August provided it. With Carlin and Alan Durban in midfield, the promotion campaign took off.
- From 15 March, when they beat Huddersfield Town, Derby won nine consecutive matches to set a club record. Their 10 away wins equalled the record set in 1955–56 and they did not lose anywhere after a home defeat by Crystal Palace on 5 March.
- Derby were back in the First Division after an absence of 16 years and set about building the Ley Stand to increase capacity.

## Division Two

| Match No. | Date | Venue | Opponents | Result | | Scorers | Att |
|---|---|---|---|---|---|---|---|
| 1 | Aug 10 | (a) | Blackburn R | D | 1-1 | McFarland | 1 |
| 2 | 17 | (h) | Blackpool | D | 1-1 | O'Hare | 2 |
| 3 | 20 | (a) | Sheffield U | L | 0-2 | | 2 |
| 4 | 24 | (a) | Huddersfield T | L | 0-2 | | 1 |
| 5 | 28 | (h) | Hull C | D | 2-2 | Barker, Hector | 2 |
| 6 | 31 | (h) | Oxford U | W | 2-0 | McFarland, O'Hare | 2 |
| 7 | Sep 7 | (h) | Aston Villa | W | 3-1 | Hector 2, Hinton | 2 |
| 8 | 14 | (a) | Bristol C | D | 0-0 | | 1 |
| 9 | 18 | (h) | Fulham | W | 1-0 | Hinton | 2 |
| 10 | 21 | (h) | Millwall | W | 1-0 | Durban | 2 |
| 11 | 28 | (a) | Bolton W | W | 2-1 | Walker, Barker | 1 |
| 12 | Oct 5 | (a) | Middlesbrough | D | 0-0 | | 2 |
| 13 | 9 | (a) | Hull C | L | 0-1 | | 2 |
| 14 | 12 | (h) | Preston NE | W | 1-0 | Hinton | 2 |
| 15 | 19 | (a) | Portsmouth | W | 1-0 | Hector | 2 |
| 16 | 26 | (h) | Birmingham C | W | 1-0 | Carlin | 3 |
| 17 | Nov 9 | (h) | Charlton A | W | 2-1 | O'Hare, Hector | 25 |
| 18 | 16 | (a) | Cardiff C | D | 1-1 | Durban | 1 |
| 19 | 23 | (h) | Carlisle U | D | 3-3 | Mackay, O'Hare, Carlin | 2 |
| 20 | 30 | (a) | Crystal Palace | W | 2-1 | McFarland, Carlin | 20 |
| 21 | Dec 7 | (h) | Norwich C | D | 1-1 | McFarland | 24 |
| 22 | 14 | (a) | Preston NE | D | 0-0 | | 12 |
| 23 | 21 | (h) | Portsmouth | W | 2-1 | Hector 2 | 22 |
| 24 | 26 | (h) | Middlesbrough | W | 3-2 | Hinton 2 (1 pen), McFarland | 34 |
| 25 | Jan 11 | (h) | Bury | W | 2-0 | McFarland, O'Hare | 24 |
| 26 | 14 | (a) | Birmingham C | D | 1-1 | Hector | 3 |
| 27 | 18 | (a) | Charlton A | L | 0-2 | | 30 |
| 28 | 25 | (a) | Bury | W | 1-0 | O'Hare | 15 |
| 29 | Feb 1 | (h) | Cardiff C | W | 2-0 | Hector 2 | 34 |
| 30 | Mar 1 | (h) | Blackburn R | W | 4-2 | Hector, O'Hare, Carlin, Wignall | 26 |
| 31 | 5 | (h) | Crystal Palace | L | 0-1 | | 31 |
| 32 | 8 | (a) | Blackpool | W | 3-2 | McFarland, O'Hare, Hinton (pen) | 18 |
| 33 | 11 | (a) | Carlisle U | D | 1-1 | Hector | 12 |
| 34 | 15 | (h) | Huddersfield T | W | 1-0 | McFarland | 28 |
| 35 | 22 | (a) | Oxford U | W | 2-0 | Hector 2 | 18 |
| 36 | 29 | (a) | Aston Villa | W | 1-0 | Simmons (og) | 49 |
| 37 | Apr 2 | (a) | Fulham | W | 1-0 | Wignall | 18 |
| 38 | 5 | (h) | Bolton W | W | 5-1 | McFarland, O'Hare, Hector, Carlin, Wignall | 30 |
| 39 | 7 | (h) | Sheffield U | W | 1-0 | Durban | 34 |
| 40 | 12 | (a) | Millwall | W | 1-0 | Carlin | 13 |
| 41 | 16 | (a) | Norwich C | W | 4-1 | Carlin 2, O'Hare, Wignall | 13 |
| 42 | 19 | (h) | Bristol C | W | 5-0 | Durban 3, Hinton, Hector | 31 |

FINAL LEAGUE POSITION: 1st in Division Two – Promoted

Appeara
Substi
G

## FA Cup

| | | | | | | | |
|---|---|---|---|---|---|---|---|
| 3 | Jan 4 | (a) | Burnley | L | 1-3 | Durban | 22 |

Appeara
Substi
G

## League Cup

| | | | | | | | |
|---|---|---|---|---|---|---|---|
| 1 | Aug 14 | (h) | Chesterfield | W | 3-0 | Hector, Hinton, Humphreys (og) | 21 |
| 2 | Sep 4 | (h) | Stockport C | W | 5-1 | Hinton 4, Hector | 21 |
| 3 | 25 | (a) | Chelsea | D | 0-0 | | 26 |
| R | Oct 2 | (h) | Chelsea | W | 3-1 | Mackay, Durban, Hector | 34 |
| 4 | 16 | (a) | Everton | D | 0-0 | | 44 |
| R | 23 | (h) | Everton | W | 1-0 | Hector | 34 |
| 5 | 30 | (h) | Swindon T | D | 0-0 | | 35 |
| R | Nov 5 | (a) | Swindon T | L | 0-1 | | 26 |

Appeara
Substi
G

| en L | Richardson J | Robson J | Stewart A | McFarland R | Mackay D | Walker J | Barker R | O'Hare J | Hector K | Hinton A | Webster R | Carlin W | Durban A | McGovern J | Daniel P | Wignall F | Butlin B | |
|---|---|---|---|---|---|---|---|---|---|---|---|---|---|---|---|---|---|---|
| | 2 | 3 | 4 | 5 | 6 | 7 | 8 | 9 | 10 | 11 | | | | | | | | 1 |
| | 2 | 3 | 4 | 5 | 6 | 7 | 8 | 9 | 10 | 11 | | | | | | | | 2 |
| | | 3 | 4 | 5 | 6 | 7 | 8 | 9 | 10 | 11 | 2 | | | | | | | 3 |
| | | 3 | 4 | 5 | 6 | 7 | 10 | 9 | 10 | 11 | 2 | | | | | | | 4 |
| | | 3 | | 5 | 6 | 7 | 8 | 9 | 10 | 11 | 2 | 4 | | | | | | 5 |
| | | 3 | | 5 | 6 | 11 | | 9 | 10 | 7 | 2 | 8 | 4 | | | | | 6 |
| | | 3 | | 5 | 6 | **7** | 12 | 9 | 10 | 11 | 2 | 8 | 4 | | | | | 7 |
| | | 3 | | 5 | 6 | 7 | | 9 | 10 | 11 | 2 | 8 | 4 | | | | | 8 |
| | | 3 | | 5 | 6 | 7 | | 9 | 10 | 11 | 2 | 8 | 4 | | | | | 9 |
| | | 3 | | 5 | 6 | **7** | 12 | 9 | 10 | 11 | 2 | 8 | 4 | | | | | 10 |
| | | 3 | | 5 | 6 | 7 | 9 | | 10 | 11 | 2 | 8 | 4 | | | | | 11 |
| | | 3 | | 5 | 6 | 7 | | 9 | 10 | 11 | 2 | 8 | 4 | | | | | 12 |
| | | 3 | | 5 | 6 | 7 | | 9 | 10 | 11 | 2 | 8 | 4 | | | | | 13 |
| | | 3 | | 5 | 6 | 7 | | 9 | 10 | 11 | 22 | 8 | 4 | | | | | 14 |
| | | 3 | | 5 | 6 | | 9 | 7 | 10 | 11 | 2 | 8 | 4 | | | | | 15 |
| | | 3 | | 5 | 6 | 7 | 12 | 9 | 10 | **11** | 2 | 8 | 4 | | | | | 16 |
| | | 3 | | 5 | 6 | 11 | | 9 | 10 | | 2 | 8 | 4 | 7 | | | | 17 |
| | | 3 | | 5 | 6 | 7 | | 9 | 10 | 11 | | 8 | 4 | | 2 | | | 18 |
| | | 3 | | 5 | 6 | | | 9 | 10 | 11 | | 8 | 4 | 7 | 2 | | | 19 |
| | | 3 | | 5 | 6 | 7 | | 9 | 10 | 11 | 2 | 8 | 4 | | | | | 20 |
| | | 3 | | 5 | 6 | **7** | 12 | 9 | 10 | 11 | 2 | 8 | 4 | | | | | 21 |
| | | 3 | | 5 | 6 | 7 | | 9 | 10 | 11 | 2 | 8 | 4 | | | | | 22 |
| | 3 | 6 | | 5 | | 7 | | 9 | 10 | 11 | 2 | 8 | 4 | | | | | 23 |
| | | 3 | | 5 | 6 | 7 | | 9 | 10 | 11 | 2 | 8 | 4 | | | | | 24 |
| | 3 | 4 | | 5 | **6** | 12 | | 9 | | 11 | 2 | 8 | 10 | 7 | | | | 25 |
| | | 3 | | 5 | 6 | 8 | | 9 | 10 | 11 | 2 | | 4 | 7 | | | | 26 |
| | | 3 | | 5 | 6 | | | 9 | 10 | 11 | 2 | 8 | 4 | 7 | | | | 27 |
| | | 3 | | 5 | **6** | 12 | | 9 | 10 | 11 | 2 | 8 | 4 | 7 | | | | 28 |
| | | 3 | | 5 | 6 | | | 9 | 10 | 11 | 2 | 8 | 4 | 7 | | | | 29 |
| | | 3 | | 5 | 6 | | | 9 | 10 | 11 | 2 | **8** | 4 | 7 | | 12 | | 30 |
| | | 3 | | 5 | 6 | 12 | | 9 | 8 | 11 | 2 | | 4 | **7** | | 10 | | 31 |
| | | 3 | | 5 | 6 | | | 9 | 10 | 11 | 2 | 8 | 4 | 7 | | | | 32 |
| | | 3 | | 5 | 6 | | | 9 | 10 | 11 | 2 | 8 | 4 | 7 | | | | 33 |
| | | 3 | | 5 | 6 | | | 9 | 10 | 11 | 2 | 8 | 4 | 7 | | | | 34 |
| | | 3 | | 5 | 6 | | | 9 | 10 | 11 | 2 | 8 | 4 | 7 | | | | 35 |
| | | 3 | | 5 | 6 | | | 9 | 10 | 11 | 2 | 8 | 4 | 7 | | | | 36 |
| | | 3 | | 5 | 6 | | | 9 | 10 | 11 | 2 | 8 | 4 | **7** | | 12 | | 37 |
| | | 3 | | 5 | 6 | | | 9 | 10 | 11 | 2 | 8 | 4 | | | 7 | | 38 |
| | | 3 | | 5 | 6 | | | 9 | 10 | 11 | 2 | 8 | 4 | | | 7 | | 39 |
| | | 3 | | 5 | 6 | | | 9 | 10 | 11 | 2 | 8 | 4 | 7 | | | | 40 |
| | | 3 | | 5 | 6 | | | 9 | 10 | 11 | 2 | 8 | | 4 | | 7 | | 41 |
| | | 3 | | 5 | 6 | | | 9 | 10 | 11 | 2 | 8 | 4 | 7 | | | | 42 |
| | 4 | 42 | 4 | 42 | 41 | 23 | 7 | 41 | 41 | 41 | 38 | 36 | 36 | 18 | 2 | 4 | | |
| | | | | | | 3 | 4 | | | | | | | | | 2 | | |
| | | | | 9 | 1 | 1 | 2 | 10 | 16 | 7 | | 8 | 6 | | | 4 | | |

1 own-goal

| | | | | | | | | | | | | | | | | | |
|---|---|---|---|---|---|---|---|---|---|---|---|---|---|---|---|---|---|
| 3 | 6 | | 5 | | | | 9 | 10 | 11 | 2 | 8 | 4 | 7 | | | | 3 |
| 1 | 1 | | 1 | | | | 1 | 1 | 1 | 1 | 1 | 1 | 1 | | | | |
| | | | | | | | | | | | | | | | | | |
| | | | | | | | | | | | | 1 | | | | | |

| | | | | | | | | | | | | | | | | | |
|---|---|---|---|---|---|---|---|---|---|---|---|---|---|---|---|---|---|
| 2 | 3 | 4 | 5 | 6 | 7 | 8 | 9 | 10 | 11 | | | | | | | | 1 |
| | 3 | 4 | 5 | 6 | 7 | | 9 | 10 | 11 | 2 | | 8 | | | | | 2 |
| | 3 | | 5 | 6 | 7 | | 9 | 10 | 11 | 2 | 8 | 4 | | | | | 3 |
| | 3 | | 5 | 6 | 7 | | 9 | 10 | 11 | 2 | 8 | 4 | | | | | R |
| | 3 | | 5 | 6 | 7 | | 9 | 10 | 11 | 2 | 8 | 4 | | | | | 4 |
| | 3 | | 5 | 6 | 7 | | 9 | 10 | 11 | 2 | 8 | 4 | | | | | R |
| | 3 | | 5 | 6 | 11 | 7 | 9 | 10 | | 2 | 8 | 4 | | | | | 5 |
| | 3 | | 5 | 6 | 11 | 7 | | 10 | | 2 | 8 | 4 | | | | 9 | R |
| 1 | 8 | 2 | 8 | 8 | 8 | 3 | 7 | 8 | 6 | 7 | 6 | 7 | | | | 1 | |
| | | | | | | | | | | | | | | | | | |
| | | | | 1 | | | | 4 | 5 | | | 1 | | | | | |

1 own-goal

# 1969-70

| | P | W | D | L | F | A | Pts |
|---|---|---|---|---|---|---|---|
| Everton | 42 | 29 | 8 | 5 | 72 | 34 | 66 |
| Leeds U | 42 | 21 | 15 | 6 | 84 | 49 | 57 |
| Chelsea | 42 | 21 | 13 | 8 | 70 | 50 | 55 |
| Derby Co | 42 | 22 | 9 | 11 | 64 | 37 | 53 |
| Liverpool | 42 | 20 | 11 | 11 | 65 | 42 | 51 |
| Coventry C | 42 | 19 | 11 | 12 | 58 | 48 | 49 |
| Newcastle U | 42 | 17 | 13 | 12 | 57 | 35 | 47 |
| Manchester U | 42 | 14 | 17 | 11 | 66 | 61 | 45 |
| Stoke C | 42 | 15 | 15 | 12 | 56 | 52 | 45 |
| Manchester C | 42 | 16 | 11 | 15 | 55 | 48 | 43 |
| Tottenham H | 42 | 17 | 9 | 16 | 54 | 55 | 43 |
| Arsenal | 42 | 12 | 18 | 12 | 51 | 49 | 42 |
| Wolves | 42 | 12 | 16 | 14 | 55 | 57 | 40 |
| Burnley | 42 | 12 | 15 | 15 | 56 | 61 | 39 |
| Nottingham F | 42 | 10 | 18 | 14 | 50 | 71 | 38 |
| W.B.A. | 42 | 14 | 9 | 19 | 58 | 66 | 37 |
| West Ham U | 42 | 12 | 12 | 18 | 51 | 60 | 36 |
| Ipswich T | 42 | 10 | 11 | 21 | 40 | 63 | 31 |
| Southampton | 42 | 6 | 17 | 19 | 46 | 67 | 29 |
| Crystal Palace | 42 | 6 | 15 | 21 | 34 | 68 | 27 |
| Sunderland | 42 | 6 | 14 | 22 | 30 | 68 | 26 |
| Sheffield W | 42 | 8 | 9 | 25 | 40 | 71 | 25 |

Manager: Brian Clough.
Leading scorers: John O'Hare, League 13. Kevin Hector, John O'Hare, all matches 16.
League ever-present: Les Green, Alan Hinton.
Player of the season: John O'Hare.

- The attendance record at the Baseball Ground was set on 20 September, when 41,826 saw Dave Mackay lead the Rams to a 5–0 victory over his former club, Tottenham Hotspur.
- It was Derby's 22nd consecutive League match without defeat, the club record. It began in March and ended on 27 September when Sheffield Wednesday beat them at Hillsborough.
- Terry Hennessey became Derby's first £100,000 player when he was signed from Nottingham Forest in February. He and Alan Durban played for Wales in the Home International Tournament while John O'Hare was winning his first Scotland caps.
- The Rams finished fourth, their best in Division One since they were third in 1948–49, and qualified for the UEFA Cup. They were not allowed to take their place after a League disciplinary commission found them guilty of administrative irregularities.

## Division One

| Match No. | Date | | Venue | Opponents | Result | | Scorers | Att |
|---|---|---|---|---|---|---|---|---|
| 1 | Aug | 9 | (h) | Burnley | D | 0-0 | | 2 |
| 2 | | 12 | (a) | Ipswich T | W | 1-0 | McFarland | 2 |
| 3 | | 16 | (a) | Coventry C | D | 1-1 | McFarland | 4 |
| 4 | | 20 | (h) | Ipswich T | W | 3-1 | Hinton 2 (1 pen), Carlin | 3 |
| 5 | | 23 | (h) | Stoke C | D | 0-0 | | 3 |
| 6 | | 27 | (a) | Wolves | D | 1-1 | Hinton | 4 |
| 7 | | 30 | (a) | West Brom A | W | 2-0 | Hector, Mackay | 3 |
| 8 | Sep | 6 | (h) | Everton | W | 2-1 | O'Hare, Hector | 3 |
| 9 | | 10 | (h) | Southampton | W | 3-0 | Durban, Carlin, Hector | 3 |
| 10 | | 13 | (a) | Newcastle U | W | 1-0 | McFarland | 3 |
| 11 | | 20 | (h) | Tottenham H | W | 5-0 | Durban 2, Carlin, O'Hare, Hector | 4 |
| 12 | | 27 | (a) | Sheffield W | L | 0-1 | | 4 |
| 13 | Oct | 4 | (h) | Manchester U | W | 2-0 | Hector, Fitzpatrick (og) | 4 |
| 14 | | 8 | (h) | Coventry C | L | 1-3 | Durban | 3 |
| 15 | | 11 | (a) | Chelsea | D | 2-2 | O'Hare, Hector | 5 |
| 16 | | 18 | (h) | Manchester C | L | 0-1 | | 4 |
| 17 | | 25 | (a) | Leeds U | L | 0-2 | | 4 |
| 18 | Nov | 1 | (h) | Liverpool | W | 4-0 | Hector 2, McGovern, O'Hare | 4 |
| 19 | | 8 | (a) | Arsenal | L | 0-4 | | 4 |
| 20 | | 15 | (h) | Sunderland | W | 3-0 | Durban 2, Ashurst (og) | 3 |
| 21 | | 22 | (a) | West Ham U | L | 0-3 | | 3 |
| 22 | | 29 | (h) | Nottingham F | L | 0-2 | | 3 |
| 23 | Dec | 6 | (a) | Crystal P | W | 1-0 | Hector | 2 |
| 24 | | 13 | (h) | Newcastle U | W | 2-0 | McGovern, Hinton | 3 |
| 25 | | 20 | (a) | Everton | L | 0-1 | | 4 |
| 26 | | 26 | (a) | Stoke C | L | 0-1 | | 3 |
| 27 | | 27 | (h) | West Brom A | W | 2-0 | O'Hare 2 | 35 |
| 28 | Jan | 10 | (a) | Tottenham H | L | 1-2 | Carlin | 3 |
| 29 | | 17 | (h) | Sheffield W | W | 1-0 | O'Hare | 32 |
| 30 | | 31 | (a) | Manchester U | L | 0-1 | | 5 |
| 31 | Feb | 11 | (h) | Chelsea | D | 2-2 | Durban, Hector | 35 |
| 32 | | 14 | (a) | Burnley | D | 1-1 | O'Hare | 1 |
| 33 | | 21 | (h) | Arsenal | W | 3-2 | O'Hare, Hector, Mackay | 35 |
| 34 | | 28 | (a) | Liverpool | W | 2-0 | O'Hare, Hennessey | 4 |
| 35 | Mar | 7 | (h) | West Ham U | W | 3-0 | Durban, O'Hare, Hinton (pen) | 35 |
| 36 | | 14 | (a) | Nottingham F | W | 3-1 | Durban, O'Hare, O'Kane (og) | 4 |
| 37 | | 21 | (h) | Crystal P | W | 3-1 | Carlin, Hector, Hinton (pen) | 30 |
| 38 | | 27 | (a) | Manchester C | W | 1-0 | McFarland | 42 |
| 39 | | 28 | (a) | Sunderland | D | 1-1 | McGovern | 18 |
| 40 | | 30 | (h) | Leeds U | W | 4-1 | McFarland, Carlin, O'Hare, Wignall | 41 |
| 41 | Apr | 4 | (h) | Wolves | W | 2-0 | Wignall, Hennessey | 33 |
| 42 | | 15 | (a) | Southampton | D | 1-1 | McGovern | 21 |

FINAL LEAGUE POSITION: 4th in Division One

Appeara
Substi
G

## FA Cup

| | | | | | | | | |
|---|---|---|---|---|---|---|---|---|
| 3 | Jan | 3 | (a) | Preston NE | D | 1-1 | Durban | 21 |
| R | | 7 | (h) | Preston NE | W | 4-1 | Hector 2, Durban 2 | 25 |
| 4 | | 24 | (h) | Sheffield U | W | 3-0 | O'Hare 2, Durban | 41 |
| 5 | Feb | 7 | (a) | Queen's Park R | L | 0-1 | | 27 |

Appeara
Substi
G

## League Cup

| | | | | | | | | |
|---|---|---|---|---|---|---|---|---|
| 2 | Sep | 3 | (a) | Hartlepool | W | 3-1 | McFarland, Carlin, Hinton (pen) | 7 |
| 3 | | 24 | (h) | Hull C | W | 3-1 | O'Hare, Hector, Hinton | 31 |
| 4 | Oct | 14 | (a) | Crystal P | D | 1-1 | Carlin | 30 |
| R | | 29 | (h) | Crystal P | W | 3-0 | Hinton 2, Hector | 33 |
| 5 | Nov | 12 | (h) | Manchester U | D | 0-0 | | 38 |
| R | | 19 | (a) | Manchester U | L | 0-1 | | 57 |

Appeara
Substit
G

| en L | Webster R | Robson J | Durban A | McFarland R | Mackay D | McGovern J | Carlin W | O'Hare J | Hector K | Hinton A | Wignall F | Rhodes A | Daniel P | Stewart A | Walker J | Hennessey T | |
|---|---|---|---|---|---|---|---|---|---|---|---|---|---|---|---|---|---|
| | 2 | 3 | 4 | 5 | 6 | 7 | 8 | 9 | 10 | 11 | | | | | | | 1 |
| | 2 | 3 | 4 | 5 | 6 | 7 | 8 | 9 | 10 | 11 | | | | | | | 2 |
| | 2 | 3 | 4 | 5 | 6 | 7 | 8 | 9 | 10 | 11 | | | | | | | 3 |
| | 2 | 3 | 4 | **5** | 6 | 7 | 8 | 9 | 10 | 11 | 12 | | | | | | 4 |
| | 2 | 3 | 4 | | 6 | 7 | 8 | 9 | **10** | 11 | 12 | 5 | | | | | 5 |
| | 2 | 3 | 4 | 5 | 6 | 7 | 8 | 9 | 10 | 11 | | | | | | | 6 |
| | 2 | 3 | 4 | 5 | 6 | 7 | 8 | 9 | 10 | 11 | | | | | | | 7 |
| | 2 | 3 | 4 | 5 | 6 | 7 | 8 | 9 | 10 | 11 | | | | | | | 8 |
| | 2 | 3 | 4 | 5 | 6 | 7 | 8 | 9 | 10 | 11 | | | | | | | 9 |
| | 2 | 3 | 4 | 5 | 6 | 7 | 8 | 9 | 10 | 11 | | | | | | | 10 |
| | 2 | 3 | **4** | 5 | 6 | 7 | 8 | 9 | 10 | 11 | 12 | | | | | | 11 |
| | 2 | 3 | 4 | 5 | 6 | 7 | 8 | 9 | 10 | 11 | | | | | | | 12 |
| | | 3 | 4 | 5 | 6 | 7 | 8 | 9 | 10 | 11 | | | 2 | | | | 13 |
| | | 3 | 4 | 5 | 6 | 7 | 8 | 9 | 10 | 11 | | | 2 | | | | 14 |
| | | 3 | 4 | 5 | 6 | 7 | 8 | 9 | 10 | 11 | | | 2 | | | | 15 |
| | 2 | 3 | 4 | | 6 | 7 | 8 | 9 | 10 | 11 | | | 5 | | | | 16 |
| | 2 | | 4 | 5 | 6 | 7 | 8 | 9 | 10 | 11 | | | 3 | | | | 17 |
| | 2 | | 4 | 5 | 6 | 7 | 8 | 9 | 10 | 11 | | | 3 | | | | 18 |
| | 2 | 3 | 4 | 5 | 6 | 7 | 8 | 9 | 10 | 11 | | | | | | | 19 |
| | 2 | 3 | 4 | 5 | 6 | 7 | 8 | 9 | 10 | 11 | | | | | | | 20 |
| | 2 | **3** | 4 | 5 | 6 | 7 | 8 | 9 | 10 | 11 | | | | 12 | | | 21 |
| | 2 | 3 | 4 | 5 | 6 | 7 | 8 | 9 | 10 | 11 | | | | | | | 22 |
| | 2 | 3 | 4 | 5 | 6 | 7 | 8 | 9 | 10 | 11 | | | | | | | 23 |
| | 2 | 3 | 4 | 5 | 6 | 7 | 8 | 9 | 10 | 11 | | | | | | | 24 |
| | 2 | 3 | 4 | 5 | 6 | | 8 | 9 | 10 | 11 | | | | | 7 | | 25 |
| | 2 | 3 | 4 | 5 | 6 | **7** | | 9 | 10 | 11 | 12 | | | | 8 | | 26 |
| | 2 | 3 | 4 | 5 | 6 | 7 | | 9 | 10 | 11 | 8 | | | | | | 27 |
| | 2 | | 4 | 5 | 6 | 7 | 8 | | 10 | 11 | 9 | | 3 | | | | 28 |
| | | 3 | 4 | 5 | 6 | 7 | 8 | 9 | 10 | 11 | | | 2 | | | | 29 |
| | 2 | 3 | | 5 | 6 | 7 | 8 | 9 | 10 | 11 | 12 | | | **4** | | | 30 |
| | 2 | 3 | 7 | 5 | 6 | | 8 | 9 | 10 | 11 | | | | | | 4 | 31 |
| | 2 | 3 | 7 | 5 | 6 | | 8 | 9 | 10 | 11 | | | | | | 4 | 32 |
| | 2 | 3 | 7 | 5 | 6 | | 8 | 9 | 10 | 11 | | | | | | 4 | 33 |
| | 2 | 3 | 7 | 5 | 6 | 12 | **8** | 9 | 10 | 11 | | | | | | 4 | 34 |
| | 2 | 3 | 7 | 5 | 6 | | 8 | 9 | 10 | 11 | | | | | | 4 | 35 |
| | 2 | 3 | 7 | 5 | 6 | | 8 | 9 | | 11 | 10 | | | | | 4 | 36 |
| | 2 | 3 | 7 | 5 | 6 | | 8 | 9 | 10 | 11 | | | | | | 4 | 37 |
| | 2 | 3 | 4 | 5 | | 7 | 8 | 9 | 10 | 11 | | | | | | 6 | 38 |
| | 2 | 3 | 4 | 5 | | **7** | 8 | 9 | 10 | 11 | 12 | | | | | 6 | 39 |
| | 2 | 3 | 4 | 5 | | | 8 | 9 | 10 | 11 | 7 | | | | | 6 | 40 |
| | 2 | 3 | 4 | | 6 | | 8 | 9 | 10 | 11 | 7 | | | | | 5 | 41 |
| | 2 | 3 | 4 | | 6 | 7 | 8 | 9 | 10 | 11 | | | | | | 5 | 42 |
| | 38 | 39 | 41 | 38 | 39 | 32 | 40 | 41 | 41 | 42 | 5 | 1 | 8 | 1 | 2 | 12 | |
| | | | | | | 1 | | | | | 6 | | | 1 | | | |
| | | | 9 | 5 | 2 | 4 | 6 | 13 | 12 | 6 | 2 | | | | | 2 | |

3 own-goals

| | | | | | | | | | | | | | | | | |
|---|---|---|---|---|---|---|---|---|---|---|---|---|---|---|---|---|
| | 3 | 4 | 5 | 6 | 7 | 8 | | 10 | 11 | 9 | | 2 | | | | 3 |
| 2 | 3 | 4 | 5 | 6 | 7 | 8 | | 10 | 11 | 9 | | | | | | R |
| 2 | 3 | 4 | 5 | 6 | 7 | 8 | 9 | 10 | 11 | | | | | | | 4 |
| 2 | 3 | 4 | 5 | 6 | 7 | 8 | 9 | 10 | 11 | | | | | | | 5 |
| 3 | 4 | 4 | 4 | 4 | 4 | 4 | 2 | 4 | 4 | 2 | | 1 | | | | |
| | | | | | | | | | | | | | | | | |
| | | 4 | | | | | 2 | 2 | | | | | | | | |

| | | | | | | | | | | | | | | | | |
|---|---|---|---|---|---|---|---|---|---|---|---|---|---|---|---|---|
| 2 | 3 | 4 | 5 | 6 | 7 | 8 | 9 | 10 | 11 | | | | | | | 2 |
| 2 | 3 | 4 | **5** | 6 | 7 | 8 | 9 | 10 | 11 | 12 | | | | | | 3 |
| 2 | 3 | 4 | 5 | 6 | 7 | 8 | 9 | 10 | **11** | 12 | | | | | | 4 |
| 2 | | 4 | 5 | 6 | 7 | 8 | 9 | 10 | 11 | | | 3 | | | | R |
| 2 | 3 | 4 | 5 | 6 | 7 | 8 | 9 | 10 | 11 | | | | | | | 5 |
| 2 | 3 | 4 | 5 | 6 | 7 | 8 | 9 | 10 | 11 | | | | | | | R |
| 6 | 5 | 6 | 6 | 6 | 6 | 6 | 6 | 6 | 6 | | | 1 | | | | |
| | | | | | | | | | | 2 | | | | | | |
| | | | 1 | | | 2 | 1 | 2 | 4 | | | | | | | |

# 1970-71

| | P | W | D | L | F | A | Pts |
|---|---|---|---|---|---|---|---|
| Arsenal | 42 | 29 | 7 | 6 | 71 | 29 | 65 |
| Leeds U | 42 | 27 | 10 | 5 | 72 | 30 | 64 |
| Tottenham H | 42 | 19 | 14 | 9 | 54 | 33 | 52 |
| Wolves | 42 | 22 | 8 | 12 | 64 | 54 | 52 |
| Liverpool | 42 | 17 | 17 | 8 | 42 | 24 | 51 |
| Chelsea | 42 | 18 | 15 | 9 | 52 | 42 | 51 |
| Southampton | 42 | 17 | 12 | 13 | 56 | 44 | 46 |
| Manchester U | 42 | 16 | 11 | 15 | 65 | 66 | 43 |
| Derby Co | 42 | 16 | 10 | 16 | 56 | 54 | 42 |
| Coventry C | 42 | 16 | 10 | 16 | 37 | 38 | 42 |
| Manchester C | 42 | 12 | 17 | 13 | 47 | 42 | 41 |
| Newcastle U | 42 | 14 | 13 | 15 | 44 | 46 | 41 |
| Stoke C | 42 | 12 | 13 | 17 | 44 | 48 | 37 |
| Everton | 42 | 12 | 13 | 17 | 54 | 60 | 37 |
| Huddersfield T | 42 | 11 | 14 | 17 | 40 | 49 | 36 |
| Nottingham F | 42 | 14 | 8 | 20 | 42 | 61 | 36 |
| W.B.A. | 42 | 10 | 15 | 17 | 58 | 75 | 35 |
| Crystal Palace | 42 | 12 | 11 | 19 | 39 | 57 | 35 |
| Ipswich T | 42 | 12 | 10 | 20 | 42 | 48 | 34 |
| West Ham U | 42 | 10 | 14 | 18 | 47 | 60 | 34 |
| Burnley | 42 | 7 | 13 | 22 | 29 | 63 | 27 |
| Blackpool | 42 | 4 | 15 | 23 | 34 | 66 | 23 |

Manager: Brian Clough.
Leading scorer: John O'Hare, League 13, all matches 15.
League ever-present: Kevin Hector, Dave Mackay, John O'Hare.
Player of the season: Dave Mackay.

- Derby, denied a place in Europe, won the Watney Cup, beating Fulham, Sheffield United and Manchester United. It was an out-of-season invitation tournament and appearances are not included in players' records.
- Archie Gemmill was signed from Preston North End for £66,000 in September as Brian Clough and Peter Taylor continued to develop the team. They considered Willie Carlin's job was complete and he moved to Leicester City in October.
- Roy McFarland was Derby's first England player since 1950 when he appeared against Malta in February. On the same day, Archie Gemmill won his first Scotland cap, against Belgium.
- Derby raised their transfer record again in February when they paid Sunderland £170,000 for Colin Todd. Dave Mackay ended three great years, signing off with the first ever-present season of his career and joining Swindon Town.

## Division One

| Match No. | Date | | Venue | Opponents | Result | | Scorers | Att |
|---|---|---|---|---|---|---|---|---|
| 1 | Aug | 15 | (a) | Chelsea | L | 1-2 | O'Hare | 4 |
| 2 | | 19 | (a) | Wolves | W | 4-2 | McGovern 2, Durban, O'Hare | 2 |
| 3 | | 22 | (h) | Stoke C | W | 2-0 | Hinton (pen), Wignall | 3 |
| 4 | | 26 | (h) | Ipswich T | W | 2-0 | Hector, Harper (og) | 3 |
| 5 | | 29 | (a) | Huddersfield T | D | 0-0 | | 2 |
| 6 | Sep | 2 | (h) | Coventry C | L | 3-4 | McGovern, Hector, Hinton | 3 |
| 7 | | 5 | (h) | Newcastle U | L | 1-2 | O'Hare | 3 |
| 8 | | 12 | (a) | Southampton | L | 0-4 | | 1 |
| 9 | | 19 | (h) | Burnley | W | 1-0 | Hinton | 2 |
| 10 | | 26 | (a) | West Brom A | L | 1-2 | O'Hare | 3 |
| 11 | Oct | 3 | (h) | Tottenham H | D | 1-1 | Hinton (pen) | 3 |
| 12 | | 10 | (a) | Everton | D | 1-1 | McGovern | 4 |
| 13 | | 17 | (h) | Chelsea | L | 1-2 | O'Hare | 3 |
| 14 | | 24 | (h) | Leeds U | L | 0-2 | | 3 |
| 15 | | 31 | (a) | Arsenal | L | 0-2 | | 4 |
| 16 | Nov | 7 | (h) | Liverpool | D | 0-0 | | 3 |
| 17 | | 14 | (a) | Manchester C | D | 1-1 | O'Hare | 3 |
| 18 | | 21 | (h) | Blackpool | W | 2-0 | McFarland, Hector | 2 |
| 19 | | 28 | (a) | Nottingham F | W | 4-2 | McGovern, O'Hare, Wignall, Gemmill | 3 |
| 20 | Dec | 5 | (h) | West Ham U | L | 2-4 | Durban, Wignall | 3 |
| 21 | | 12 | (a) | Crystal P | D | 0-0 | | 2 |
| 22 | | 19 | (a) | Stoke C | L | 0-1 | | 2 |
| 23 | | 26 | (h) | Manchester U | D | 4-4 | Mackay, Hector, Wignall, Gemmill | 3 |
| 24 | Jan | 9 | (h) | Wolves | L | 1-2 | Gemmill (pen) | 3 |
| 25 | | 16 | (a) | Ipswich T | W | 1-0 | O'Hare | 2 |
| 26 | Feb | 6 | (a) | West Ham U | W | 4-1 | Hector 2, Hinton 2 | 2 |
| 27 | | 17 | (h) | Crystal P | W | 1-0 | Mackay | 2 |
| 28 | | 20 | (a) | Blackpool | W | 1-0 | O'Hare | 1 |
| 29 | | 27 | (h) | Arsenal | W | 2-0 | McFarland, Hector | 3 |
| 30 | Mar | 6 | (a) | Leeds U | L | 0-1 | | 3 |
| 31 | | 13 | (h) | Manchester C | D | 0-0 | | 3 |
| 32 | | 20 | (a) | Liverpool | L | 0-2 | | 4 |
| 33 | | 27 | (a) | Newcastle U | L | 1-3 | Hector | 2 |
| 34 | | 31 | (h) | Nottingham F | L | 1-2 | Hector | 3 |
| 35 | Apr | 3 | (h) | Huddersfield T | W | 3-2 | Hinton 2 (1 pen), Hector | 2 |
| 36 | | 7 | (a) | Tottenham H | L | 1-2 | Hinton | 2 |
| 37 | | 10 | (a) | Manchester U | W | 2-1 | O'Hare 2 | 44 |
| 38 | | 12 | (h) | Southampton | D | 0-0 | | 2 |
| 39 | | 17 | (h) | Everton | W | 3-1 | O'Hare 2, Hector | 2 |
| 40 | | 24 | (a) | Burnley | W | 2-1 | McGovern, Durban | 1 |
| 41 | | 27 | (a) | Coventry C | D | 0-0 | | 2 |
| 42 | May | 1 | (h) | West Brom A | W | 2-0 | Hinton, Durban | 3 |

FINAL LEAGUE POSITION: 9th in Division One

Appeara
Substi
G

## FA Cup

| | | | | | | | | |
|---|---|---|---|---|---|---|---|---|
| 3 | Jan | 2 | (a) | Chester | W | 2-1 | Wignall, Gemmill | 1 |
| 4 | | 23 | (h) | Wolves | W | 2-1 | Hinton (pen), O'Hare | 40 |
| 5 | Feb | 13 | (a) | Everton | L | 0-1 | | 5 |

Appeara
Substi
G

## League Cup

| | | | | | | | | |
|---|---|---|---|---|---|---|---|---|
| 2 | Sep | 8 | (h) | Halifax T | W | 3-1 | Durban 2, Hector | 2 |
| 3 | Oct | 7 | (h) | Millwall | W | 4-2 | Hinton (pen), McGovern, Mackay, O'Hare | 2 |
| 4 | | 27 | (a) | Coventry C | L | 0-1 | | 2 |

Appeara
Substi
G

**Derby County played in the Watney Cup (see Rams in Other Competitions)**

| Webster R | Robson J | Durban A | McFarland R | Mackay D | McGovern J | Carlin W | O'Hare J | Hector K | Hinton A | Wignall F | Hennessey T | Rhodes A | Richardson J | Walker J | Gemmill A | Daniel P | Butlin B | Boulton C | Todd C | Bourne J | |
|---|---|---|---|---|---|---|---|---|---|---|---|---|---|---|---|---|---|---|---|---|---|
| 2 | 3 | 4 | 5 | 6 | 7 | 8 | 9 | 10 | **11** | 12 | | | | | | | | | | | 1 |
| 2 | 3 | **4** | 5 | 6 | 7 | 8 | 9 | 10 | 11 | 12 | | | | | | | | | | | 2 |
| 2 | 3 | | 5 | 6 | 7 | 8 | 9 | 10 | 11 | 12 | **4** | | | | | | | | | | 3 |
| 2 | 3 | **4** | 5 | 6 | 7 | 8 | 9 | 10 | 11 | 12 | | | | | | | | | | | 4 |
| 2 | 3 | | 5 | 6 | 4 | 8 | 9 | 10 | 11 | 7 | | | | | | | | | | | 5 |
| 2 | 3 | | 5 | 6 | 7 | 8 | 9 | 10 | 11 | 4 | | | | | | | | | | | 6 |
| 2 | 3 | 4 | 5 | 6 | 7 | 8 | 9 | **10** | 11 | 12 | | | | | | | | | | | 7 |
| 2 | 3 | **4** | | 6 | 7 | 8 | 9 | 10 | 11 | 12 | | | | | | | | | | | 8 |
| | 3 | **4** | | 6 | | 8 | 9 | 10 | 11 | 12 | | 5 | | 7 | | | | | | | 9 |
| | 3 | 4 | | 6 | | 8 | 9 | 10 | 11 | | | 5 | 2 | | 7 | | | | | | 10 |
| 2 | 3 | **4** | | 6 | 12 | 8 | 9 | 10 | 11 | | | 5 | 2 | | 7 | 5 | | | | | 11 |
| 2 | 3 | | 5 | 6 | 4 | 8 | 9 | 10 | 11 | | | | | | 7 | | | | | | 12 |
| 2 | 3 | | | 6 | 4 | 8 | 9 | 10 | 11 | | | | | | 7 | 5 | | | | | 13 |
| 2 | 3 | | 5 | 6 | 8 | | 9 | 10 | 11 | | 4 | | | | 7 | | | | | | 14 |
| 2 | 3 | 8 | 5 | 6 | | | 9 | 10 | 11 | | 4 | | | | 7 | | | | | | 15 |
| 2 | 3 | 4 | 5 | 6 | 8 | | 9 | 10 | 11 | | | | | | 7 | | | | | | 16 |
| 2 | 3 | | 5 | 6 | 7 | | 9 | 10 | 11 | | 4 | | | | 8 | | | | | | 17 |
| 2 | 3 | 8 | 5 | 6 | | | 9 | 10 | 11 | | 4 | | | | 7 | | | | | | 18 |
| 2 | 3 | 4 | | 6 | 7 | | 9 | 10 | | 8 | 5 | | | | 11 | | | | | | 19 |
| 2 | 3 | 4 | | 6 | 7 | | 9 | 10 | | 8 | 5 | | | | 11 | | | | | | 20 |
| 2 | 3 | 7 | 5 | 6 | | | 9 | 10 | | 8 | **4** | | | | 11 | 12 | | | | | 21 |
| 2 | 3 | 7 | 5 | 6 | 12 | | 9 | 10 | | | 4 | | | | 11 | | **8** | | | | 22 |
| 2 | | 7 | 5 | 6 | | | 9 | 10 | | 8 | 4 | | | | 11 | 3 | | | | | 23 |
| 2 | | 12 | 5 | **6** | 7 | | 9 | 10 | | 8 | 4 | | | | 11 | 3 | | 1 | | | 24 |
| 2 | 3 | 8 | 5 | 6 | 7 | | 9 | 10 | | | 4 | | | | 11 | | | 1 | | | 25 |
| 2 | 3 | 4 | 5 | 6 | 7 | | 9 | 10 | 11 | | | | | | 8 | | | 1 | | | 26 |
| 2 | 3 | 4 | 5 | 6 | 7 | | 9 | 10 | 11 | | | | | | 8 | | | 1 | | | 27 |
| 2 | 3 | 4 | 5 | 6 | 7 | | 9 | 10 | 11 | | | | | | 8 | | | 1 | | | 28 |
| 2 | | | 5 | 6 | 7 | | 9 | 10 | 11 | | | | 3 | | 8 | | | 1 | 4 | | 29 |
| 2 | 3 | | 5 | 6 | 7 | | 9 | 10 | 11 | | | | | | 8 | | | 1 | 4 | | 30 |
| 2 | | | 5 | 6 | 7 | | 9 | 10 | 11 | | | | 3 | | 8 | | | 1 | 4 | | 31 |
| 2 | 12 | | 5 | 6 | 7 | | **9** | 10 | 11 | | | | 3 | | 8 | | | 1 | 4 | | 32 |
| 2 | 3 | 12 | 5 | 6 | **7** | | 9 | 10 | | 8 | | | | | 11 | | | 1 | 4 | | 33 |
| 2 | | | 5 | 6 | | | 9 | 10 | 11 | 8 | | | 3 | | 7 | | | 1 | 4 | | 34 |
| 2 | | | 5 | 6 | | | 9 | 10 | 11 | 8 | | | 3 | | 7 | | | 1 | 4 | | 35 |
| 2 | | | 5 | 6 | 7 | | 9 | 10 | 11 | | | | 3 | | 8 | | | 1 | 4 | | 36 |
| | 3 | 4 | 5 | 6 | 7 | | 9 | 10 | 11 | | | | | | 8 | | | 1 | 2 | | 37 |
| | 3 | 4 | 5 | 6 | 7 | | 9 | 10 | 11 | | | | | | 8 | | | 1 | 2 | | 38 |
| | 3 | 4 | 5 | 6 | 7 | | 9 | 10 | 11 | | | | | | 8 | | | 1 | 2 | | 39 |
| | 3 | 4 | 5 | 6 | 7 | | 9 | 10 | 11 | | | | | | | | | 1 | 2 | 8 | 40 |
| 12 | 3 | 4 | 5 | 6 | 7 | | 9 | 10 | 11 | | | | | | | | | 1 | 2 | **8** | 41 |
| | 3 | 4 | 5 | 6 | 7 | | 9 | 10 | 11 | | | | | | 8 | | | 1 | 2 | | 42 |
| 34 | 34 | 26 | 35 | 42 | 32 | 13 | 42 | 42 | 34 | 10 | 12 | 3 | 8 | 1 | 31 | 4 | 1 | 19 | 14 | 2 | |
| 1 | 1 | 2 | | | 2 | | | | | 7 | | | | | | 1 | | | | | |
| | | 4 | 2 | 2 | 6 | | 13 | 11 | 10 | 4 | | | | | 3 | | | | | | |

1 own-goal

| Webster R | Robson J | Durban A | McFarland R | Mackay D | McGovern J | Carlin W | O'Hare J | Hector K | Hinton A | Wignall F | Hennessey T | Rhodes A | Richardson J | Walker J | Gemmill A | Daniel P | Butlin B | Boulton C | Todd C | Bourne J | |
|---|---|---|---|---|---|---|---|---|---|---|---|---|---|---|---|---|---|---|---|---|---|
| 2 | | | 5 | 6 | 7 | | 9 | 10 | | 8 | 4 | | | | 11 | 3 | | 1 | | | 3 |
| 2 | 3 | 4 | 5 | 6 | 7 | | 9 | 10 | 11 | | | | | | 8 | | | 1 | | | 4 |
| 2 | 3 | 4 | 5 | 6 | 7 | | 9 | 10 | 11 | | | | | | 8 | | | 1 | | | 5 |
| 3 | 2 | 2 | 3 | 3 | 3 | | 3 | 3 | 2 | 1 | 1 | | | | 3 | 1 | | 3 | | | |
| | | | | | | | | | | | | | | | | | | | | | |
| | | | | | | | 1 | | 1 | 1 | | | | | 1 | | | | | | |

| Webster R | Robson J | Durban A | McFarland R | Mackay D | McGovern J | Carlin W | O'Hare J | Hector K | Hinton A | Wignall F | Hennessey T | Rhodes A | Richardson J | Walker J | Gemmill A | Daniel P | Butlin B | Boulton C | Todd C | Bourne J | |
|---|---|---|---|---|---|---|---|---|---|---|---|---|---|---|---|---|---|---|---|---|---|
| 2 | 3 | 4 | **5** | | | 8 | 9 | 10 | 11 | 7 | | 6 | | | | 12 | | | | | 2 |
| 2 | 3 | | 5 | 6 | 4 | 8 | 9 | 10 | 11 | 7 | | | | | | | | | | | 3 |
| 2 | 3 | 8 | 5 | 6 | 7 | | 9 | 10 | 11 | | 4 | | | | | | | | | | 4 |
| 3 | 3 | 2 | 3 | 2 | 2 | 2 | 3 | 3 | 3 | 2 | 1 | 1 | | | | | | | | | |
| | | | | | | | | | | | | | | | | 1 | | | | | |
| | | 2 | | 1 | 1 | | 1 | 1 | 1 | | | | | | | | | | | | |

# 1971-72

| | P | W | D | L | F | A | Pts |
|---|---|---|---|---|---|---|---|
| Derby Co | 42 | 24 | 10 | 8 | 69 | 33 | 58 |
| Leeds U | 42 | 24 | 9 | 9 | 73 | 31 | 57 |
| Liverpool | 42 | 24 | 9 | 9 | 64 | 30 | 57 |
| Manchester C | 42 | 23 | 11 | 8 | 77 | 45 | 57 |
| Arsenal | 42 | 22 | 8 | 12 | 58 | 40 | 52 |
| Tottenham H | 42 | 19 | 13 | 10 | 63 | 42 | 51 |
| Chelsea | 42 | 18 | 12 | 12 | 58 | 49 | 48 |
| Manchester U | 42 | 19 | 10 | 13 | 69 | 61 | 48 |
| Wolves | 42 | 18 | 11 | 13 | 65 | 57 | 47 |
| Sheffield U | 42 | 17 | 12 | 13 | 61 | 60 | 46 |
| Newcastle U | 42 | 15 | 11 | 16 | 49 | 52 | 41 |
| Leicester C | 42 | 13 | 13 | 16 | 41 | 46 | 39 |
| Ipswich T | 42 | 11 | 16 | 15 | 39 | 53 | 38 |
| West Ham U | 42 | 12 | 12 | 18 | 47 | 51 | 36 |
| Everton | 42 | 9 | 18 | 15 | 37 | 48 | 36 |
| W.B.A. | 42 | 12 | 11 | 19 | 42 | 54 | 35 |
| Stoke C | 42 | 10 | 15 | 17 | 39 | 56 | 35 |
| Coventry C | 42 | 9 | 15 | 18 | 44 | 67 | 33 |
| Southampton | 42 | 12 | 7 | 23 | 52 | 80 | 31 |
| Crystal Palace | 42 | 8 | 13 | 21 | 39 | 65 | 29 |
| Nottingham F | 42 | 8 | 9 | 25 | 47 | 81 | 25 |
| Huddersfield T | 42 | 6 | 13 | 23 | 27 | 59 | 25 |

Manager: Brian Clough.
Leading scorer: Alan Hinton, League 15, all matches 20.
League ever-present: Colin Boulton, Kevin Hector.
Player of the season: Colin Todd.

- Derby County's greatest season. They were League Champions for the first time, won the Texaco Cup and the Reserves lifted the Central League title.
- Only 16 players were used in the League season. Three of them, Tony Bailey, Steve Powell and Jim Walker, made only 10 (6 + 4) appearances between them and another, Frank Wignall, joined Mansfield Town in November. They would have signed Ian Storey-Moore had Nottingham Forest not declined to complete the forms.
- Steve Powell made his Rams debut in the Texaco Cup match against Stoke City on 20 October, aged 16 years and 30 days. At the time, he was the youngest player to appear for Derby, taking the record from Roy Patrick (16/277 in 1952).
- Kevin Hector scored his 100th goal for the Rams in the FA Cup victory over Notts County.
- Alan Durban made his 27th and final appearance for Wales against Northern Ireland at the Racecourse, Wrexham, on 27 May. He became Derby's most capped player, passing Sammy Crooks' 26 for England.

## Division One

| Match No. | Date | | Venue | Opponents | Result | | Scorers | Atte |
|---|---|---|---|---|---|---|---|---|
| 1 | Aug | 14 | (h) | Manchester U | D | 2-2 | Wignall, Hector | 35 |
| 2 | | 18 | (h) | West Ham U | W | 2-0 | Wignall, O'Hare | 36 |
| 3 | | 21 | (a) | Leicester C | W | 2-0 | Hector, Hinton (pen) | 35 |
| 4 | | 24 | (a) | Coventry C | D | 2-2 | Wignall, O'Hare | 27 |
| 5 | | 28 | (h) | Southampton | D | 2-2 | McGovern, Hector | 2 |
| 6 | | 31 | (a) | Ipswich T | D | 0-0 | | 18 |
| 7 | Sep | 4 | (a) | Everton | W | 2-0 | Wignall, Hector | 41 |
| 8 | | 11 | (h) | Stoke C | W | 4-0 | Todd, Gemmill, O'Hare, Hinton | 32 |
| 9 | | 18 | (a) | Chelsea | D | 1-1 | McFarland | 42 |
| 10 | | 25 | (h) | West Brom A | D | 0-0 | | 30 |
| 11 | Oct | 2 | (a) | Newcastle U | W | 1-0 | Hinton | 32 |
| 12 | | 9 | (h) | Tottenham H | D | 2-2 | Todd, McFarland | 35 |
| 13 | | 16 | (a) | Manchester U | L | 0-1 | | 53 |
| 14 | | 23 | (h) | Arsenal | W | 2-1 | O'Hare, Hinton (pen) | 36 |
| 15 | | 30 | (a) | Nottingham F | W | 2-0 | Robson, Hinton (pen) | 37 |
| 16 | Nov | 6 | (h) | Crystal P | W | 3-0 | Wignall, Hector, Bell (og) | 30 |
| 17 | | 13 | (a) | Wolves | L | 1-2 | O'Hare | 32 |
| 18 | | 20 | (h) | Sheffield U | W | 3-0 | Hinton 2 (2 pens), Hector | 35 |
| 19 | | 27 | (a) | Huddersfield T | L | 1-2 | McGovern | 15 |
| 20 | Dec | 4 | (h) | Manchester C | W | 3-1 | Webster, Durban, Hinton (pen) | 35 |
| 21 | | 11 | (a) | Liverpool | L | 2-3 | O'Hare 2 | 44 |
| 22 | | 18 | (h) | Everton | W | 2-0 | Hinton 2 | 27 |
| 23 | | 27 | (a) | Leeds U | L | 0-3 | | 44 |
| 24 | Jan | 1 | (h) | Chelsea | W | 1-0 | Gemmill | 33 |
| 25 | | 8 | (a) | Southampton | W | 2-1 | O'Hare, Durban | 19 |
| 26 | | 22 | (a) | West Ham U | D | 3-3 | Hector, Hinton, Durban | 31 |
| 27 | | 29 | (h) | Coventry C | W | 1-0 | Robson | 29 |
| 28 | Feb | 12 | (a) | Arsenal | L | 0-2 | | 52 |
| 29 | | 19 | (h) | Nottingham F | W | 4-0 | Hinton 2, Hector, O'Hare | 31 |
| 30 | Mar | 4 | (h) | Wolves | W | 2-1 | Hinton (pen), McFarland | 33 |
| 31 | | 11 | (a) | Tottenham H | W | 1-0 | Hinton (pen) | 36 |
| 32 | | 18 | (h) | Leicester C | W | 3-0 | O'Hare, Hector, Durban | 34 |
| 33 | | 22 | (h) | Ipswich T | W | 1-0 | Hector | 26 |
| 34 | | 25 | (a) | Stoke C | D | 1-1 | Durban | 33 |
| 35 | | 28 | (a) | Crystal P | W | 1-0 | Walker | 21 |
| 36 | Apr | 1 | (h) | Leeds U | W | 2-0 | O'Hare, Hunter (og) | 38 |
| 37 | | 3 | (h) | Newcastle U | L | 0-1 | | 38 |
| 38 | | 5 | (a) | West Brom A | D | 0-0 | | 32 |
| 39 | | 8 | (a) | Sheffield U | W | 4-0 | Gemmill, O'Hare, Hector, Durban | 38 |
| 40 | | 15 | (h) | Huddersfield T | W | 3-0 | McFarland, O'Hare, Hector | 31 |
| 41 | | 22 | (a) | Manchester C | L | 0-2 | | 55 |
| 42 | May | 1 | (h) | Liverpool | W | 1-0 | McGovern | 39 |

FINAL LEAGUE POSITION: 1st in Division One – Champions

Appeara
Substi
G

## FA Cup

| | | | | | | | | |
|---|---|---|---|---|---|---|---|---|
| 3 | Jan | 15 | (h) | Shrewsbury T | W | 2-0 | Hector 2 | 33 |
| 4 | Feb | 5 | (h) | Notts C | W | 6-0 | Durban 3, Robson, Hector, Hinton (pen) | 39 |
| 5 | | 26 | (h) | Arsenal | D | 2-2 | Durban, Hinton (pen) | 39 |
| R | | 29 | (a) | Arsenal | D | 0-0* | | 63 |
| 2R | Mar | 13 | (n‡) | Arsenal | L | 0-1 | | 40 |

*after extra-time. ‡Played at Filbert Street, Leicester

Appeara
Substi
G

## League Cup

| | | | | | | | | |
|---|---|---|---|---|---|---|---|---|
| 2 | Sep | 8 | (h) | Leeds U | D | 0-0 | | 36 |
| R | | 27 | (a) | Leeds U | L | 0-2 | | 29 |

Appeara
Substit
G

**Derby County played in the Texaco Cup (see Rams in Other Competitions)**

…ton C

| Webster R | Robson J | McGovern J | Hennessey T | Todd C | Gemmill A | Wignall F | O'Hare J | Hector K | Hinton A | McFarland R | Durban A | Powell S | Walker J | Bailey A | |
|---|---|---|---|---|---|---|---|---|---|---|---|---|---|---|---|
| 2 | 3 | 4 | 5 | 6 | 7 | 8 | 9 | 10 | 11 | | | | | | 1 |
| 2 | 3 | 4 | 5 | 6 | 7 | 8 | 9 | 10 | 11 | | | | | | 2 |
| 2 | 3 | 4 | 5 | 6 | 7 | 8 | 9 | 10 | 11 | | | | | | 3 |
| 2 | 3 | 4 | | 6 | 7 | 8 | 9 | 10 | 11 | 5 | | | | | 4 |
| | 3 | 6 | 4 | 2 | 7 | | 9 | 10 | 11 | 5 | 8 | | | | 5 |
| | 3 | 6 | 4 | 2 | 7 | 9 | | 10 | 11 | 5 | 8 | | | | 6 |
| 2 | 3 | 6 | | 4 | 7 | 9 | | 10 | 11 | 5 | 8 | | | | 7 |
| 2 | 3 | | | 4 | 6 | 8 | 9 | 10 | 11 | 5 | 7 | | | | 8 |
| 2 | 3 | 6 | | 4 | 7 | 8 | 9 | 10 | 11 | 5 | | | | | 9 |
| 2 | 3 | 12 | | 4 | 6 | 8 | 9 | 10 | 11 | 5 | **7** | | | | 10 |
| 2 | 3 | 7 | 4 | 6 | | | 9 | 10 | 11 | 5 | 8 | | | | 11 |
| **2** | 3 | 6 | | 4 | 7 | 12 | 9 | 10 | 11 | 5 | 8 | | | | 12 |
| | 3 | 6 | 4 | 2 | 7 | | 9 | 10 | 11 | 5 | 8 | | | | 13 |
| **2** | 3 | 6 | | 4 | 7 | | 9 | 10 | 11 | 5 | 8 | 12 | | | 14 |
| 2 | 3 | 7 | | 6 | 8 | | 9 | 10 | 11 | 5 | | 4 | | | 15 |
| 2 | 3 | 6 | 5 | 4 | | 8 | 9 | 10 | 11 | | 7 | | | | 16 |
| 2 | 3 | 7 | 6 | 4 | 8 | | 9 | 10 | 11 | 5 | | | | | 17 |
| 2 | 3 | 7 | 6 | 4 | 8 | | 9 | 10 | 11 | 5 | | | | | 18 |
| 2 | 3 | 7 | 6 | 4 | 8 | | 9 | 10 | 11 | 5 | | | | | 19 |
| 2 | 3 | 6 | | 4 | 8 | | 9 | 10 | 11 | 5 | 7 | | | | 20 |
| 3 | | 6 | 4 | **2** | 8 | | 9 | 10 | 11 | 5 | 7 | | 12 | | 21 |
| 2 | 3 | 6 | 4 | | 8 | | 9 | 10 | 11 | 5 | 7 | | | | 22 |
| 2 | 3 | 7 | 6 | | 8 | | 9 | 10 | 11 | 5 | | | | 4 | 23 |
| 2 | 3 | 6 | | 4 | 8 | | 9 | 10 | 11 | 5 | 7 | | | | 24 |
| 2 | 3 | 7 | | 6 | 8 | | 9 | 10 | 11 | 5 | 4 | | | | 25 |
| 2 | 3 | 7 | | 6 | 8 | | 9 | 10 | 11 | 5 | 4 | | | | 26 |
| 2 | 3 | 7 | | 6 | 8 | | 9 | 10 | 11 | 5 | 4 | | | | 27 |
| 2 | 3 | 7 | | 6 | 8 | | 9 | 10 | 11 | 5 | 4 | | | | 28 |
| 2 | 3 | 7 | | 6 | 8 | | 9 | 10 | 11 | 5 | 4 | | | | 29 |
| 2 | 3 | 7 | | 6 | 8 | | 9 | 10 | 11 | 5 | 4 | | | | 30 |
| 2 | 3 | 7 | 4 | 6 | 8 | | 9 | 10 | 11 | 5 | | | | | 31 |
| 2 | 3 | 7 | **8** | 6 | 11 | | 9 | 10 | | 5 | 4 | | 12 | | 32 |
| 2 | 3 | 7 | | 6 | 8 | | 9 | 10 | **11** | 5 | 4 | | 12 | | 33 |
| 2 | 3 | 7 | | 6 | 8 | | 9 | 10 | | 5 | 4 | | 11 | | 34 |
| 2 | 3 | | 7 | 6 | 8 | | 9 | 10 | | 5 | 4 | | 11 | | 35 |
| 2 | 3 | 7 | | 6 | 8 | | 9 | 10 | | 5 | 4 | | 11 | | 36 |
| 2 | 3 | 7 | | 6 | 8 | | 9 | 10 | 11 | 5 | 4 | | | | 37 |
| 2 | 3 | 7 | | 6 | 8 | | 9 | 10 | 11 | 5 | 4 | | | | 38 |
| 2 | 3 | 7 | | 6 | 8 | | 9 | 10 | 11 | 5 | 4 | | | | 39 |
| 2 | 3 | 7 | | 6 | 8 | | 9 | 10 | 11 | 5 | 4 | | | | 40 |
| **2** | 3 | 7 | 12 | 6 | 8 | | 9 | 10 | 11 | 5 | 4 | | | | 41 |
| | 3 | 7 | | 6 | 8 | | 9 | 10 | 11 | 5 | 4 | 2 | | | 42 |
| 38 | 41 | 39 | 17 | 40 | 40 | 10 | 40 | 42 | 38 | 38 | 31 | 2 | 3 | 1 | |
| | | 1 | 1 | | | 1 | | | | | | 1 | 3 | | |
| 1 | 2 | 3 | | 2 | 3 | 5 | 13 | 12 | 15 | 4 | 6 | | 1 | | |

2 own-goals

| Webster R | Robson J | McGovern J | Hennessey T | Todd C | Gemmill A | Wignall F | O'Hare J | Hector K | Hinton A | McFarland R | Durban A | Powell S | |
|---|---|---|---|---|---|---|---|---|---|---|---|---|---|
| 2 | 3 | 7 | | 6 | 8 | | 9 | 10 | 11 | 5 | 4 | | 3 |
| 2 | 3 | 7 | | 6 | 8 | | **9** | 10 | 11 | 5 | 4 | 12 | 4 |
| 2 | 3 | 7 | | 6 | 8 | | 9 | 10 | 11 | 5 | 4 | | 5 |
| 2 | 3 | 7 | | 6 | 8 | | 9 | 10 | 11 | 5 | 4 | | R |
| 2 | 3 | **7** | 12 | 6 | 8 | | 9 | 10 | 11 | 5 | 4 | | 2R |
| 5 | 5 | 5 | | 5 | 5 | | 5 | 5 | 5 | 5 | 5 | | |
| | | | 1 | | | | | | | | | 1 | |
| | 1 | | | | | | | 3 | 2 | | 4 | | |

| Webster R | Robson J | McGovern J | Hennessey T | Todd C | Gemmill A | Wignall F | O'Hare J | Hector K | Hinton A | McFarland R | Durban A | |
|---|---|---|---|---|---|---|---|---|---|---|---|---|
| 2 | 3 | | | 4 | 6 | 8 | 9 | 10 | 11 | 5 | 7 | 2 |
| 2 | 3 | 7 | | 4 | 6 | 8 | 9 | 10 | 11 | 5 | | R |
| 2 | 2 | 1 | | 2 | 2 | 2 | 2 | 2 | 2 | 2 | 1 | |

# 1972-73

| | P | W | D | L | F | A | Pts |
|---|---|---|---|---|---|---|---|
| Liverpool | 42 | 25 | 10 | 7 | 72 | 42 | 60 |
| Arsenal | 42 | 23 | 11 | 8 | 57 | 43 | 57 |
| Leeds U | 42 | 21 | 11 | 10 | 71 | 45 | 53 |
| Ipswich T | 42 | 17 | 14 | 11 | 55 | 45 | 48 |
| Wolves | 42 | 18 | 11 | 13 | 66 | 54 | 47 |
| West Ham U | 42 | 17 | 12 | 13 | 67 | 53 | 46 |
| Derby Co | 42 | 19 | 8 | 15 | 56 | 54 | 46 |
| Tottenham H | 42 | 16 | 13 | 13 | 58 | 48 | 45 |
| Newcastle U | 42 | 16 | 13 | 13 | 60 | 51 | 45 |
| Birmingham C | 42 | 15 | 12 | 15 | 53 | 54 | 42 |
| Manchester C | 42 | 15 | 11 | 16 | 57 | 60 | 41 |
| Chelsea | 42 | 13 | 14 | 15 | 49 | 51 | 40 |
| Southampton | 42 | 11 | 18 | 13 | 47 | 52 | 40 |
| Sheffield U | 42 | 15 | 10 | 17 | 51 | 59 | 40 |
| Stoke C | 42 | 14 | 10 | 18 | 61 | 56 | 38 |
| Leicester C | 42 | 10 | 17 | 15 | 40 | 46 | 37 |
| Everton | 42 | 13 | 11 | 18 | 41 | 49 | 37 |
| Manchester U | 42 | 12 | 13 | 17 | 44 | 60 | 37 |
| Coventry C | 42 | 13 | 9 | 20 | 40 | 55 | 35 |
| Norwich C | 42 | 11 | 10 | 21 | 36 | 63 | 32 |
| Crystal Palace | 42 | 9 | 12 | 21 | 41 | 58 | 30 |
| W.B.A. | 42 | 9 | 10 | 23 | 38 | 62 | 28 |

Manager: Brian Clough.
Leading scorer: Kevin Hector, League 14, all matches 23.
Player of the season: Kevin Hector.

- When the European Cup was inaugurated in 1955, Derby County were in the Third Division North. Now they were England's representatives, reaching the semi-finals before losing to Juventus.
- Derby broke the British transfer record for the first time since Johnny Morris arrived in 1949 to sign David Nish from Leicester City for £225,000 in August.
- Roger Davies, a record signing from non-League when the Rams paid Worcester City £12,000 for him in September 1971, began to make his mark, particularly with a hat-trick in the memorable FA Cup replay victory over Tottenham Hotspur at White Hart Lane.
- Kevin Hector became the seventh player to complete 100 League goals for Derby when he scored at Coventry on 14 April.
- Colin Boulton missed two games through suspension in April, ending a run of 131 consecutive competitive matches going back to January 1971, when he replaced Les Green in goal.

## Division One

| Match No. | Date | | Venue | Opponents | Result | | Scorers | Att |
|---|---|---|---|---|---|---|---|---|
| 1 | Aug | 12 | (a) | Southampton | D | 1-1 | Hinton | 2 |
| 2 | | 15 | (a) | Crystal P | D | 0-0 | | 2 |
| 3 | | 19 | (h) | Chelsea | L | 1-2 | Hector | 3 |
| 4 | | 23 | (h) | Manchester C | W | 1-0 | Walker | 3 |
| 5 | | 26 | (a) | Norwich C | L | 0-1 | | 2 |
| 6 | | 29 | (a) | Everton | L | 0-1 | | 3 |
| 7 | Sep | 2 | (h) | Liverpool | W | 2-1 | O'Hare, Hinton | 3 |
| 8 | | 9 | (a) | West Brom A | L | 1-2 | McFarland | 1 |
| 9 | | 16 | (h) | Birmingham C | W | 1-0 | Hector | 3 |
| 10 | | 23 | (a) | Manchester U | L | 0-3 | | 4 |
| 11 | | 30 | (h) | Tottenham H | W | 2-1 | Hector, Hinton (pen) | 3 |
| 12 | Oct | 7 | (a) | Leeds U | L | 0-5 | | 3 |
| 13 | | 14 | (h) | Leicester C | W | 2-1 | Hinton (pen), Hennessey | 3 |
| 14 | | 21 | (a) | Ipswich T | L | 1-3 | Hinton (pen) | 1 |
| 15 | | 28 | (h) | Sheffield U | W | 2-1 | Todd, O'Hare | 3 |
| 16 | Nov | 4 | (a) | Manchester C | L | 0-4 | | 3 |
| 17 | | 11 | (h) | Crystal P | D | 2-2 | Hinton, Powell | 2 |
| 18 | | 18 | (a) | West Ham U | W | 2-1 | Hector 2 | 2 |
| 19 | | 25 | (h) | Arsenal | W | 5-0 | McFarland, McGovern, Hector, Hinton, Davies | 31 |
| 20 | Dec | 2 | (a) | Wolves | W | 2-1 | Hector, Hennesey | 2 |
| 21 | | 9 | (h) | Coventry C | W | 2-0 | Gemmill, Hinton (pen) | 31 |
| 22 | | 16 | (h) | Newcastle U | D | 1-1 | Hector | 2 |
| 23 | | 23 | (a) | Stoke C | L | 0-4 | | 2 |
| 24 | | 26 | (h) | Manchester U | W | 3-1 | McFarland 2, Hinton | 3 |
| 25 | | 30 | (a) | Chelsea | D | 1-1 | O'Hare | 2 |
| 26 | Jan | 6 | (h) | Norwich C | W | 1-0 | Hinton (pen) | 2 |
| 27 | | 20 | (a) | Liverpool | D | 1-1 | Davies | 45 |
| 28 | | 27 | (h) | West Brom A | W | 2-0 | Hinton (pen), Davies | 2 |
| 29 | Feb | 10 | (a) | Birmingham C | L | 0-2 | | 38 |
| 30 | | 14 | (h) | Stoke C | L | 0-3 | | 22 |
| 31 | | 17 | (h) | Southampton | W | 4-0 | Hector 2, Hinton, McCarthy (og) | 26 |
| 32 | | 28 | (a) | Newcastle U | L | 0-2 | | 34 |
| 33 | Mar | 3 | (h) | Leeds U | L | 2-3 | Durban, Hector | 38 |
| 34 | | 10 | (a) | Leicester C | D | 0-0 | | 29 |
| 35 | | 24 | (a) | Sheffield U | L | 1-3 | Davies | 24 |
| 36 | | 31 | (a) | Arsenal | W | 1-0 | Powell | 45 |
| 37 | Apr | 14 | (a) | Coventry C | W | 2-0 | O'Hare, Hector | 22 |
| 38 | | 18 | (a) | Tottenham H | L | 0-1 | | 22 |
| 39 | | 21 | (h) | West Ham U | D | 1-1 | Gemmill (pen) | 28 |
| 40 | | 28 | (h) | Everton | W | 3-1 | Gemmill (pen), Hinton, Nish | 24 |
| 41 | | 30 | (h) | Ipswich T | W | 3-0 | Hector 2, Davies | 20 |
| 42 | May | 4 | (h) | Wolves | W | 3-0 | Davies 2, McFarland | 31 |

FINAL LEAGUE POSITION: 7th in Division One

Appeara
Substi
G

## FA Cup

| | | | | | | | | |
|---|---|---|---|---|---|---|---|---|
| 3 | Jan | 13 | (a) | Peterborough U | W | 1-0 | Davies | 20 |
| 4 | Feb | 3 | (h) | Tottenham H | D | 1-1 | Davies | 37 |
| R | | 7 | (a) | Tottenham H | W | 5-3* | Davies 3, Hector 2 | 52 |
| 5 | | 24 | (h) | Queen's Park R | W | 4-2 | Hector 3, Davies | 38 |
| 6 | Mar | 17 | (h) | Leeds U | L | 0-1 | | 38 |

*after extra-time

Appeara
Substi
G

## League Cup

| | | | | | | | | |
|---|---|---|---|---|---|---|---|---|
| 2 | Sep | 5 | (a) | Swindon T | W | 1-0 | Hennessey | 15 |
| 3 | Oct | 4 | (h) | Chelsea | D | 0-0 | | 28 |
| R | | 9 | (a) | Chelsea | L | 2-3 | Hinton, McGovern | 26 |

Appeara
Substi
G

**Derby County played in the European Cup (see Rams in Europe)**

| on C | Webster R | Robson J | Durban A | McFarland R | Todd C | McGovern J | Gemmill A | O'Hare J | Hector K | Hinton A | Hennessey T | Walker J | Powell S | Lewis A | Nish D | Daniel P | Davies R | Butlin B | Sims J | Parry A | Moseley G | |
|---|---|---|---|---|---|---|---|---|---|---|---|---|---|---|---|---|---|---|---|---|---|---|
| | 2 | 3 | 4 | 5 | 6 | 7 | 8 | 9 | 10 | 11 | | | | | | | | | | | | 1 |
| | 2 | 3 | 4 | | 6 | 7 | 8 | 9 | 10 | 11 | 5 | | | | | | | | | | | 2 |
| | 2 | 3 | 4 | 5 | 6 | 7 | 8 | 9 | 10 | | | 11 | | | | | | | | | | 3 |
| | | | | 5 | 6 | 7 | 8 | 9 | 10 | | 4 | 11 | 2 | 3 | | | | | | | | 4 |
| | | | 12 | 5 | 6 | 7 | 8 | 9 | 10 | | **4** | 11 | 2 | | 3 | | | | | | | 5 |
| | | | | 5 | 6 | 7 | 8 | 9 | 10 | | 4 | 11 | 2 | | 3 | | | | | | | 6 |
| | | | | 5 | 6 | 7 | 8 | 9 | 10 | 11 | 4 | | 2 | | 3 | | | | | | | 7 |
| | | | | 5 | 6 | 7 | 8 | 9 | 10 | 11 | 4 | | 2 | | 3 | | | | | | | 8 |
| | | | | 5 | 6 | 7 | 8 | 9 | 10 | 11 | 4 | | 2 | | 3 | | | | | | | 9 |
| | | | | 5 | 6 | 7 | 8 | 9 | 10 | 11 | 4 | | 2 | | 3 | | | | | | | 10 |
| | | 2 | 12 | 5 | 6 | 7 | 8 | 9 | 10 | 11 | **4** | | | | 3 | | | | | | | 11 |
| | | 2 | 4 | 5 | 6 | | 8 | 9 | 10 | 11 | | | | | 3 | 7 | | | | | | 12 |
| | | 2 | | 5 | 6 | 7 | | 9 | 10 | 11 | 4 | | 8 | | 3 | | | | | | | 13 |
| | | 2 | 11 | 5 | 6 | 7 | | | 10 | 9 | 4 | | 8 | | 3 | | | | | | | 14 |
| | | 3 | | 5 | 6 | 7 | | 9 | 10 | 11 | 4 | | 2 | | 8 | | | | | | | 15 |
| | | 3 | 12 | 5 | 6 | 7 | | | | **11** | 4 | | 2 | | 8 | | 9 | 10 | | | | 16 |
| | 2 | 3 | | 5 | 6 | 7 | | 9 | 10 | 11 | | | 4 | | 8 | | | | | | | 17 |
| | 2 | | | 5 | 6 | 7 | 8 | 9 | 10 | 11 | 4 | | | | 3 | | | | | | | 18 |
| | 2 | | | 5 | 6 | 7 | 8 | | 10 | 11 | 4 | | | | 3 | | 9 | | | | | 19 |
| | 2 | | | | 6 | 7 | 8 | 9 | 10 | 11 | 4 | | | | 3 | 5 | | | | | | 20 |
| | 2 | | | | 6 | 7 | 8 | 4 | 10 | 11 | | | | | 3 | 5 | 9 | | | | | 21 |
| | 2 | | | 5 | 6 | 7 | 8 | 4 | 10 | 11 | | | | | **3** | | 9 | | 12 | | | 22 |
| | 2 | | | 5 | 6 | 7 | 8 | 9 | 10 | 11 | 4 | | | 3 | | | | | | | | 23 |
| | 2 | | | 5 | 6 | 7 | 8 | | 10 | 11 | 4 | | | | | 3 | 9 | | | | | 24 |
| | 2 | | | 5 | 6 | 7 | | 8 | 10 | 11 | 4 | | | | | 3 | 9 | | | | | 25 |
| | | | | 5 | 6 | 7 | 8 | 4 | 10 | 11 | | | | | 2 | 3 | 9 | | | | | 26 |
| | 2 | | | 5 | 6 | 7 | | 8 | 10 | | 4 | | 11 | | 3 | | 9 | | | | | 27 |
| | 2 | | | 5 | 6 | 7 | 8 | | 10 | 11 | 4 | | | | 3 | | 9 | | | | | 28 |
| | 2 | | 4 | 5 | | 7 | 11 | | 10 | | | | | | 3 | | 9 | | 8 | 6 | | 29 |
| | 2 | | 4 | | 6 | | 8 | | 10 | | | **11** | | | 3 | 5 | 9 | | 7 | 12 | | 30 |
| | 2 | | | 5 | 6 | 7 | 8 | 4 | 10 | 11 | | | | | 3 | | 9 | | | | | 31 |
| | **2** | | 12 | 5 | 6 | 7 | 8 | 4 | 10 | | | | 11 | | 3 | | 9 | | | | | 32 |
| | | | 11 | 5 | 6 | 7 | 8 | 4 | 10 | | | | 2 | | 3 | | 9 | | | | | 33 |
| | **2** | | 12 | 5 | 6 | 7 | 8 | 4 | 10 | | | | 11 | | | 3 | 9 | | | | | 34 |
| | 2 | | 11 | 5 | 6 | **7** | 8 | 9 | 10 | | | | 4 | | 3 | | 12 | | | | | 35 |
| | 2 | | | 5 | 6 | 7 | | 8 | 10 | | | | 11 | | 3 | | 9 | | | 4 | | 36 |
| | 2 | | **4** | 5 | 6 | 7 | 8 | 9 | 10 | | | | 11 | | 3 | | | | | 12 | | 37 |
| | 2 | | 12 | 5 | 6 | **7** | 8 | 9 | 10 | | | | 11 | | 3 | | | | | 4 | 1 | 38 |
| | | | 12 | 5 | 6 | 7 | 8 | 9 | 10 | | | | 11 | | 2 | 3 | | | | **4** | 1 | 39 |
| | 2 | | 7 | 5 | 6 | | 8 | | 10 | 11 | | | 4 | | 3 | | 9 | | | | | 40 |
| | 2 | | | 5 | 6 | 7 | 8 | 4 | 10 | 11 | | | | | 3 | | 9 | | | | | 41 |
| | 2 | | | 5 | 6 | 7 | 8 | 4 | 10 | 11 | | | | | 3 | | 9 | | | | | 42 |
| | 26 | 10 | 11 | 38 | 41 | 39 | 34 | 34 | 41 | 27 | 21 | 5 | 22 | 2 | 34 | 9 | 19 | 1 | 2 | 4 | 2 | |
| | | | 7 | | | | | | | | | | | | | | 1 | | 1 | 2 | | |
| | | | 1 | 5 | 1 | 1 | 3 | 4 | 14 | 13 | 2 | 1 | 2 | | 1 | | 7 | | | | | |

1 own-goal

| Webster R | Robson J | Durban A | McFarland R | Todd C | McGovern J | Gemmill A | O'Hare J | Hector K | Hinton A | Hennessey T | Walker J | Powell S | Lewis A | Nish D | Daniel P | Davies R | |
|---|---|---|---|---|---|---|---|---|---|---|---|---|---|---|---|---|---|
| | | 4 | 5 | 6 | 7 | 8 | 11 | 10 | | 12 | | | | 2 | 3 | **9** | 3 |
| 2 | | | 5 | 6 | 7 | 8 | 11 | 10 | | 4 | | | | 3 | | 9 | 4 |
| 2 | | 12 | 5 | 6 | 7 | 8 | 11 | 10 | | **4** | | | | 3 | | 9 | R |
| 2 | | 12 | 5 | 6 | 7 | 8 | 4 | 10 | **11** | | | | | 3 | | 9 | 5 |
| 2 | | 12 | 5 | 6 | 7 | 8 | 4 | 10 | | | | **11** | | 3 | | 9 | 6 |
| 4 | | 1 | 5 | 5 | 5 | 5 | 5 | 5 | 1 | 2 | | 1 | | 5 | 1 | 5 | |
| | | 3 | | | | | | | | 1 | | | | | | | |
| | | | | | | | | 5 | | | | | | | | 6 | |

| Webster R | Robson J | Durban A | McFarland R | Todd C | McGovern J | Gemmill A | O'Hare J | Hector K | Hinton A | Hennessey T | Walker J | Powell S | Lewis A | Nish D | |
|---|---|---|---|---|---|---|---|---|---|---|---|---|---|---|---|
| | | 12 | 5 | 6 | 7 | **8** | 9 | 10 | 11 | 4 | | 2 | | 3 | 2 |
| | | 4 | 5 | 6 | 7 | 8 | 9 | 10 | 11 | | | 2 | | 3 | 3 |
| | 2 | | 5 | 6 | 7 | 8 | 9 | 10 | 11 | | | 4 | | 3 | R |
| | 1 | 1 | 3 | 3 | 3 | 3 | 3 | 3 | 3 | 1 | | 3 | | 3 | |
| | | 1 | | | | | | | | | | | | | |
| | | | | | 1 | | | | 1 | 1 | | | | | |

# 1973-74

| | P | W | D | L | F | A | Pts |
|---|---|---|---|---|---|---|---|
| Leeds U | 42 | 24 | 14 | 4 | 66 | 31 | 62 |
| Liverpool | 42 | 22 | 13 | 7 | 52 | 31 | 57 |
| Derby Co | 42 | 17 | 14 | 11 | 52 | 42 | 48 |
| Ipswich T | 42 | 18 | 11 | 13 | 67 | 58 | 47 |
| Stoke C | 42 | 15 | 16 | 11 | 54 | 42 | 46 |
| Burnley | 42 | 16 | 14 | 12 | 56 | 53 | 46 |
| Everton | 42 | 16 | 12 | 14 | 50 | 48 | 44 |
| Q.P.R. | 42 | 13 | 17 | 12 | 56 | 52 | 43 |
| Leicester C | 42 | 13 | 16 | 13 | 51 | 41 | 42 |
| Arsenal | 42 | 14 | 14 | 14 | 49 | 51 | 42 |
| Tottenham H | 42 | 14 | 14 | 14 | 45 | 50 | 42 |
| Wolves | 42 | 13 | 15 | 14 | 49 | 49 | 41 |
| Sheffield U | 42 | 14 | 12 | 16 | 44 | 49 | 40 |
| Manchester C | 42 | 14 | 12 | 16 | 39 | 46 | 40 |
| Newcastle U | 42 | 13 | 12 | 17 | 49 | 48 | 38 |
| Coventry C | 42 | 14 | 10 | 18 | 43 | 54 | 38 |
| Chelsea | 42 | 12 | 13 | 17 | 56 | 60 | 37 |
| West Ham U | 42 | 11 | 15 | 16 | 55 | 60 | 37 |
| Birmingham C | 42 | 12 | 13 | 17 | 52 | 64 | 37 |
| Southampton | 42 | 11 | 14 | 17 | 47 | 68 | 36 |
| Manchester U | 42 | 10 | 12 | 20 | 38 | 48 | 32 |
| Norwich C | 42 | 7 | 15 | 20 | 37 | 62 | 29 |

Manager: Brian Clough until October, then Dave Mackay.
Leading scorer: Kevin Hector, League/all matches 19.
League ever-present: Colin Boulton, Kevin Hector.
Player of the season: Ron Webster.

- Brian Clough and Peter Taylor resigned in October following a lengthy dispute with chairman Sam Longson and other directors. It was only 18 months after Derby's first League title and a Protest Movement was formed to put pressure on the board.
- Jimmy Gordon, the trainer-coach, had one match in charge, a 2–1 home victory over Leicester City, before Dave Mackay left Nottingham Forest to become manager.
- It was difficult for Mackay and his assistant Des Anderson as they went through six League and two League Cup games without victory before winning at Newcastle.
- Mackay spent £80,000 on Rod Thomas from Swindon Town in November and £200,000 on Bruce Rioch from Aston Villa in February. The manager had the Rams back on track and third place earned them a UEFA Cup spot.

## Division One

| Match No. | Date | | Venue | Opponents | Result | | Scorers | Att |
|---|---|---|---|---|---|---|---|---|
| 1 | Aug | 25 | (h) | Chelsea | W | 1-0 | McGovern | 3 |
| 2 | | 29 | (h) | Manchester C | W | 1-0 | Hinton | 3 |
| 3 | Sep | 1 | (a) | Birmingham C | D | 0-0 | | 3 |
| 4 | | 4 | (a) | Liverpool | L | 0-2 | | 4 |
| 5 | | 8 | (h) | Everton | W | 2-1 | Davies, Hector | 2 |
| 6 | | 12 | (h) | Liverpool | W | 3-1 | McFarland, Davies, Hector | 3 |
| 7 | | 15 | (a) | Burnley | D | 1-1 | Davies | 2 |
| 8 | | 18 | (a) | Coventry C | L | 0-1 | | 2 |
| 9 | | 22 | (h) | Southampton | W | 6-2 | Hector 3, Davies 2, Hinton (pen) | 2 |
| 10 | | 29 | (a) | Tottenham H | L | 0-1 | | 3 |
| 11 | Oct | 6 | (h) | Norwich C | D | 1-1 | Davies | 2 |
| 12 | | 13 | (a) | Manchester U | W | 1-0 | Hector | 4 |
| 13 | | 20 | (h) | Leicester C | W | 2-1 | McGovern, Hector | 3 |
| 14 | | 27 | (a) | West Ham U | D | 0-0 | | 3 |
| 15 | Nov | 3 | (h) | Queen's Park R | L | 1-2 | Gemmill (pen) | 2 |
| 16 | | 10 | (a) | Ipswich T | L | 0-3 | | 2 |
| 17 | | 17 | (a) | Sheffield U | L | 0-3 | | 2 |
| 18 | | 24 | (h) | Leeds U | D | 0-0 | | 3 |
| 19 | Dec | 8 | (h) | Arsenal | D | 1-1 | McFarland | 2 |
| 20 | | 15 | (a) | Newcastle U | W | 2-0 | Davies, Hinton | 1 |
| 21 | | 22 | (h) | Tottenham H | W | 2-0 | Hinton 2 | 2 |
| 22 | | 26 | (a) | Stoke C | D | 0-0 | | 2 |
| 23 | | 29 | (a) | Everton | L | 1-2 | Hector | 37 |
| 24 | Jan | 1 | (h) | Birmingham C | D | 1-1 | Bourne | 31 |
| 25 | | 12 | (h) | Burnley | W | 5-1 | Hector 3, Bourne 2 | 2 |
| 26 | | 19 | (a) | Chelsea | D | 1-1 | Bourne | 27 |
| 27 | Feb | 2 | (h) | Newcastle U | W | 1-0 | McFarland | 2 |
| 28 | | 6 | (a) | Manchester C | L | 0-1 | | 22 |
| 29 | | 16 | (h) | Manchester U | D | 2-2 | Nish, Hector | 2 |
| 30 | | 23 | (a) | Norwich C | W | 4-2 | Bourne 2, Davies, Hector | 2 |
| 31 | Mar | 2 | (h) | Stoke C | D | 1-1 | Bourne | 28 |
| 32 | | 5 | (a) | Southampton | D | 1-1 | Newton | 17 |
| 33 | | 9 | (h) | West Ham U | D | 1-1 | Rioch (pen) | 24 |
| 34 | | 16 | (a) | Leicester C | W | 1-0 | McFarland | 30 |
| 35 | | 23 | (h) | Ipswich T | W | 2-0 | Hector, Rioch (pen) | 23 |
| 36 | | 30 | (a) | Queen's Park R | D | 0-0 | | 1 |
| 37 | Apr | 6 | (a) | Leeds U | L | 0-2 | | 37 |
| 38 | | 9 | (a) | Wolves | L | 0-4 | | 23 |
| 39 | | 13 | (h) | Sheffield U | W | 4-1 | Hector 3, Davies | 25 |
| 40 | | 15 | (h) | Coventry C | W | 1-0 | Hector | 23 |
| 41 | | 20 | (a) | Arsenal | L | 0-2 | | 26 |
| 42 | | 27 | (h) | Wolves | W | 2-0 | Powell, Hector | 26 |

FINAL LEAGUE POSITION: 3rd in Division One

Appeara
Substi
G

## FA Cup

| | | | | | | | | |
|---|---|---|---|---|---|---|---|---|
| 3 | Jan | 5 | (h) | Boston U | D | 0-0 | | 25 |
| R | | 9 | (a) | Boston U | W | 6-1 | Gemmill 3 (1 pen), Bourne 2, Nish | 9 |
| 4 | | 27 | (a) | Coventry C | D | 0-0 | | 40 |
| R | | 30 | (h) | Coventry C | L | 0-1* | | 31 |

*after extra-time

Appeara
Substi
G

## League Cup

| | | | | | | | | |
|---|---|---|---|---|---|---|---|---|
| 2 | Oct | 8 | (h) | Sunderland | D | 2-2 | Nish, Davies | 29 |
| R | | 29 | (a) | Sunderland | D | 1-1* | Gemmill | 38 |
| 2R | | 31 | (a) | Sunderland | L | 0-3 | | 38 |

*after extra-time

Appeara
Substi
G

| Webster R | Nish D | Powell S | McFarland R | Todd C | McGovern J | Gemmill A | Davies R | Hector K | Hinton A | O'Hare J | Newton H | Daniel P | Walker J | Thomas R | Bourne J | Rioch B | |
|---|---|---|---|---|---|---|---|---|---|---|---|---|---|---|---|---|---|
| 2 | 3 | 4 | 5 | 6 | 7 | 8 | 9 | 10 | 11 | | | | | | | | 1 |
| 2 | 3 | 4 | 5 | 6 | 7 | 8 | 9 | 10 | 11 | | | | | | | | 2 |
| 2 | 3 | 4 | 5 | 6 | 7 | 8 | | 10 | 11 | 9 | | | | | | | 3 |
| 2 | 3 | 4 | 5 | 6 | 7 | 8 | | 10 | 11 | 9 | | | | | | | 4 |
| 2 | 3 | 4 | 5 | 6 | 7 | 8 | 9 | 10 | 11 | | | | | | | | 5 |
| 2 | 3 | 4 | 5 | 6 | 7 | 8 | 9 | 10 | 11 | | | | | | | | 6 |
| 2 | 3 | 4 | 5 | 6 | 7 | 8 | 9 | 10 | 11 | | | | | | | | 7 |
| 2 | 3 | **4** | 5 | 6 | 7 | 8 | 9 | 10 | 11 | 12 | | | | | | | 8 |
| 2 | 3 | 4 | 5 | 6 | 7 | 8 | 9 | 10 | 11 | | | | | | | | 9 |
| 2 | 3 | 4 | 5 | 6 | 7 | 11 | | 10 | | 9 | 8 | | | | | | 10 |
| 2 | 3 | 4 | | 6 | | 8 | 9 | 10 | 11 | | 7 | 5 | | | | | 11 |
| 2 | 3 | | 5 | 6 | 7 | 8 | 9 | 10 | 11 | | 4 | | | | | | 12 |
| 2 | 3 | | 5 | 6 | 7 | 8 | 9 | 10 | 11 | | 4 | | | | | | 13 |
| 2 | 3 | | 5 | 6 | 7 | 8 | 9 | 10 | 11 | | 4 | | | | | | 14 |
| | 3 | | 5 | 6 | 7 | 8 | 9 | 10 | 11 | | 4 | 2 | | | | | 15 |
| 2 | 3 | | 5 | 6 | 7 | 8 | | 10 | 11 | 9 | 4 | | | | | | 16 |
| | 3 | | 5 | 6 | 7 | 8 | | 10 | 11 | 9 | 4 | 2 | | | | | 17 |
| 2 | 3 | | 5 | 6 | 7 | 8 | 12 | 10 | 11 | **9** | 4 | | | | | | 18 |
| 2 | 3 | | 5 | 6 | 7 | 8 | 9 | 10 | 11 | | 4 | | | | | | 19 |
| 2 | 3 | | 5 | 6 | 7 | 8 | 9 | 10 | 11 | | 4 | | | | | | 20 |
| 2 | 3 | | 5 | 6 | 7 | 8 | 9 | 10 | 11 | | 4 | | | | | | 21 |
| 2 | 3 | | 5 | 6 | 7 | 8 | **9** | 10 | 11 | | 4 | | 12 | | | | 22 |
| 2 | | 12 | 5 | 6 | 7 | 8 | | 10 | 11 | **9** | 4 | | | 3 | | | 23 |
| 2 | | | 5 | 6 | 7 | 8 | | 10 | 11 | | 4 | | | 3 | 9 | | 24 |
| 2 | 3 | 4 | 5 | 6 | 7 | 8 | | 10 | 11 | | | | | | 9 | | 25 |
| 2 | 3 | 7 | 5 | 6 | | 8 | | 10 | 11 | | 4 | | | | 9 | | 26 |
| 2 | 3 | 7 | 5 | 6 | 11 | | 9 | 10 | | | 4 | | | | 8 | | 27 |
| 2 | 3 | 7 | 5 | | 11 | | 9 | 10 | 12 | | 4 | 6 | | | **8** | | 28 |
| 2 | 3 | 7 | 5 | | | 8 | 9 | 10 | | | 4 | 6 | | | 11 | | 29 |
| 2 | 3 | 7 | 5 | 6 | | 8 | 9 | 10 | | | | | | | 11 | 4 | 30 |
| 2 | 3 | 7 | 5 | 6 | | 8 | 9 | 10 | | | | | | | 11 | 4 | 31 |
| 2 | 3 | 7 | 5 | 6 | | | **9** | 10 | 12 | | 8 | | | | 11 | 4 | 32 |
| 2 | 3 | 7 | 5 | 6 | | | **9** | 10 | 12 | | 8 | | | | 11 | 4 | 33 |
| 2 | 3 | 7 | 5 | 6 | | 8 | 9 | 10 | | | | | | | 11 | 4 | 34 |
| | 3 | 7 | 5 | 6 | | 8 | 9 | 10 | | | | | | 2 | 11 | 4 | 35 |
| 2 | 3 | 7 | | 6 | | 8 | 9 | 10 | | | | 5 | | | 11 | 4 | 36 |
| 2 | 3 | 7 | | 6 | | 8 | 9 | 10 | 12 | | | 5 | | | 11 | **4** | 37 |
| 2 | 3 | 7 | | 6 | | 8 | 9 | 10 | | | | 5 | | | 11 | 4 | 38 |
| 2 | 3 | 7 | 5 | 6 | | 8 | 9 | 10 | | | | | | | 11 | 4 | 39 |
| 2 | 3 | 7 | 5 | 6 | | 8 | 9 | 10 | | | | | | | 11 | 4 | 40 |
| 2 | 3 | 7 | 5 | 6 | | 8 | 9 | 10 | | | | | | | 11 | 4 | 41 |
| | 3 | 7 | 5 | 6 | | 8 | 9 | 10 | | | | | | 2 | 11 | 4 | 42 |
| 38 | 40 | 29 | 38 | 40 | 26 | 38 | 32 | 42 | 25 | 7 | 21 | 8 | | 4 | 19 | 13 | |
| | | 1 | | | | | 1 | | 4 | 1 | | | 1 | | | | |
| | 1 | 1 | 4 | | 2 | 1 | 9 | 19 | 5 | | 1 | | | | 7 | 2 | |

| | | | | | | | | | | | | | | | | | |
|---|---|---|---|---|---|---|---|---|---|---|---|---|---|---|---|---|---|
| 2 | | 7 | **5** | 6 | | 8 | | 10 | 11 | | 4 | 12 | | 3 | 9 | | 3 |
| 2 | 3 | **7** | | 6 | | 8 | | 10 | 11 | | 4 | 5 | 12 | | 9 | | R |
| 2 | 3 | 7 | 5 | 6 | | 8 | | 10 | 11 | | 4 | | | | 9 | | 4 |
| 2 | 3 | **7** | 5 | 6 | | 8 | 12 | 10 | 11 | | 4 | | | | 9 | | R |
| 4 | 3 | 4 | 3 | 4 | | 4 | | 4 | 4 | | 4 | 1 | | 1 | 4 | | |
| | | | | | | | 1 | | | | | 1 | 1 | | | | |
| | 1 | | | | | 3 | | | | | | | | | 2 | | |

| | | | | | | | | | | | | | | | | | |
|---|---|---|---|---|---|---|---|---|---|---|---|---|---|---|---|---|---|
| 2 | 3 | | 5 | 6 | 7 | 8 | 9 | 10 | 11 | | 4 | | | | | | 2 |
| 2 | 3 | | 5 | 6 | **7** | 8 | 9 | 10 | 11 | 12 | 4 | | | | | | R |
| **2** | 3 | | 5 | 6 | 7 | 8 | 9 | 10 | 11 | 12 | 4 | | | | | | 2R |
| 3 | 3 | | 3 | 3 | 3 | 3 | 3 | 3 | 3 | | 3 | | | | | | |
| | | | | | | | | | | 2 | | | | | | | |
| | 1 | | | | | 1 | 1 | | | | | | | | | | |

# 1974-75

| | P | W | D | L | F | A | Pts |
|---|---|---|---|---|---|---|---|
| Derby Co | 42 | 21 | 11 | 10 | 67 | 49 | 53 |
| Liverpool | 42 | 20 | 11 | 11 | 60 | 39 | 51 |
| Ipswich T | 42 | 23 | 5 | 14 | 66 | 44 | 51 |
| Everton | 42 | 16 | 18 | 8 | 56 | 42 | 50 |
| Stoke C | 42 | 17 | 15 | 10 | 64 | 48 | 49 |
| Sheffield U | 42 | 18 | 13 | 11 | 58 | 51 | 49 |
| Middlesbrough | 42 | 18 | 12 | 12 | 54 | 40 | 48 |
| Manchester C | 42 | 18 | 10 | 14 | 54 | 54 | 46 |
| Leeds U | 42 | 16 | 13 | 13 | 57 | 49 | 45 |
| Burnley | 42 | 17 | 11 | 14 | 68 | 67 | 45 |
| Q.P.R. | 42 | 16 | 10 | 16 | 54 | 54 | 42 |
| Wolves | 42 | 14 | 11 | 17 | 57 | 54 | 39 |
| West Ham U | 42 | 13 | 13 | 16 | 58 | 59 | 39 |
| Coventry C | 42 | 12 | 15 | 15 | 51 | 62 | 39 |
| Newcastle U | 42 | 15 | 9 | 18 | 59 | 72 | 39 |
| Arsenal | 42 | 13 | 11 | 18 | 47 | 49 | 37 |
| Birmingham C | 42 | 14 | 9 | 19 | 53 | 61 | 37 |
| Leicester C | 42 | 12 | 12 | 18 | 46 | 60 | 36 |
| Tottenham H | 42 | 13 | 8 | 21 | 52 | 63 | 34 |
| Luton T | 42 | 11 | 11 | 20 | 47 | 65 | 33 |
| Chelsea | 42 | 9 | 15 | 18 | 42 | 72 | 33 |
| Carlisle U | 42 | 12 | 5 | 25 | 43 | 59 | 29 |

Manager: Dave Mackay.
Leading scorers: Bruce Rioch, League 15. Kevin Hector, all matches 21.
League ever-present: Colin Boulton, Bruce Rioch.
Player of the season: Peter Daniel.

- Roy McFarland suffered an Achilles tendon injury while playing for England against Northern Ireland in May 1974, and was unable to appear until the last four matches. Archie Gemmill took over as captain and Peter Daniel, a Derby professional since 1964, had a great season in defence.
- Francis Lee was an inspired signing in August, £100,000 from Manchester City at the age of 30.
- On 21 December, at Luton, Ron Webster became the fifth player to complete 500 appearances for the Rams.
- Although eight players appeared in both Championship sides, only Colin Boulton played in all 84 games of the two successful seasons. During the second year, he overtook Reg Matthews's 246 appearances and went on to reach 344, still the record for a Derby goalkeeper.
- Roger Davies was the first Derby player to score five goals in a game since Hughie Gallacher in 1934. Davies bagged them in the 5–0 victory over Luton Town on 29 March.

## Division One

| Match No. | Date | | Venue | Opponents | Result | | Scorers |
|---|---|---|---|---|---|---|---|
| 1 | Aug | 17 | (a) | Everton | D | 0-0 | |
| 2 | | 21 | (h) | Coventry C | D | 1-1 | Lee |
| 3 | | 24 | (h) | Sheffield U | W | 2-0 | Davies, Hector |
| 4 | | 27 | (a) | Coventry C | D | 1-1 | Davies |
| 5 | | 31 | (a) | Tottenham H | L | 0-2 | |
| 6 | Sep | 7 | (h) | Newcastle U | D | 2-2 | Davies, Lee |
| 7 | | 14 | (a) | Birmingham C | L | 2-3 | Rioch, Davies |
| 8 | | 21 | (h) | Burnley | W | 3-2 | Rioch (pen), Hector, Lee |
| 9 | | 25 | (h) | Chelsea | W | 4-1 | Webster, Rioch, Hector, Daniel |
| 10 | | 28 | (a) | Stoke C | D | 1-1 | Lee |
| 11 | Oct | 5 | (a) | West Ham U | D | 2-2 | Hector, Lee |
| 12 | | 12 | (h) | Leicester C | W | 1-0 | Rioch |
| 13 | | 15 | (a) | Sheffield U | W | 2-1 | Lee 2 |
| 14 | | 19 | (a) | Carlisle U | L | 0-3 | |
| 15 | | 26 | (h) | Middlesbrough | L | 2-3 | Hector, Hinton |
| 16 | Nov | 2 | (a) | Leeds U | W | 1-0 | Lee |
| 17 | | 9 | (h) | QPR | W | 5-2 | Hector 3, Lee, Rioch |
| 18 | | 16 | (a) | Arsenal | L | 1-3 | Rioch (pen) |
| 19 | | 23 | (h) | Ipswich T | W | 2-0 | Rioch, Hector |
| 20 | Dec | 7 | (a) | Liverpool | D | 2-2 | Davies, Bourne |
| 21 | | 14 | (h) | Everton | L | 0-1 | |
| 22 | | 21 | (a) | Luton T | L | 0-1 | |
| 23 | | 26 | (h) | Birmingham C | W | 2-1 | Rioch, Bourne |
| 24 | | 28 | (a) | Manchester C | W | 2-1 | Lee, Newton |
| 25 | Jan | 11 | (h) | Liverpool | W | 2-0 | Lee, Newton |
| 26 | | 18 | (a) | Wolves | W | 1-0 | Newton |
| 27 | Feb | 1 | (a) | QPR | L | 1-4 | Rioch |
| 28 | | 8 | (h) | Leeds U | D | 0-0 | |
| 29 | | 22 | (h) | Arsenal | W | 2-1 | Powell 2 |
| 30 | | 25 | (a) | Ipswich T | L | 0-3 | |
| 31 | Mar | 1 | (h) | Tottenham H | W | 3-1 | Rioch, Daniel, Davies |
| 32 | | 8 | (a) | Chelsea | W | 2-1 | Daniel, Hinton |
| 33 | | 15 | (h) | Stoke C | L | 1-2 | Hector |
| 34 | | 22 | (a) | Newcastle U | W | 2-0 | Nish, Rioch |
| 35 | | 29 | (h) | Luton T | W | 5-0 | Davies 5 |
| 36 | | 31 | (a) | Burnley | W | 5-2 | Hector 2, Davies, Nish, Rioch |
| 37 | Apr | 1 | (h) | Manchester C | W | 2-1 | Rioch 2 |
| 38 | | 5 | (a) | Middlesbrough | D | 1-1 | Hector |
| 39 | | 9 | (h) | Wolves | W | 1-0 | Lee |
| 40 | | 12 | (h) | West Ham U | W | 1-0 | Rioch |
| 41 | | 19 | (a) | Leicester C | D | 0-0 | |
| 42 | | 26 | (h) | Carlisle U | D | 0-0 | |

FINAL LEAGUE POSITION: 1st in Division One – Champions

Appear.
Subst

## FA Cup

| | | | | | | | |
|---|---|---|---|---|---|---|---|
| 3 | Jan | 3 | (a) | Orient | D | 2-2 | Todd 2 |
| R | | 8 | (h) | Orient | W | 2-1 | Lee, Rioch |
| 4 | | 27 | (h) | Bristol R | W | 2-0 | Hector, Rioch (pen) |
| 5 | Feb | 18 | (h) | Leeds U | L | 0-1 | |

Appeara
Subst

## League Cup

| | | | | | | | |
|---|---|---|---|---|---|---|---|
| 2 | Sep | 11 | (a) | Portsmouth | W | 5-1 | Hector 2, Lee, Rioch, Roberts (og) |
| 3 | Oct | 8 | (a) | Southampton | L | 0-5 | |

Appeara
Subst.

**Derby County played in the UEFA Cup (see Rams in Europe)**

| ton C | Webster R | Nish D | Rioch B | Daniel P | Todd C | Powell S | Gemmill A | Davies R | Hector K | Lee F | Bourne J | Newton H | Thomas R | Hinton A | McFarland R | |
|---|---|---|---|---|---|---|---|---|---|---|---|---|---|---|---|---|
| | 2 | 3 | 4 | 5 | 6 | 7 | 8 | 9 | **10** | 11 | 12 | | | | | 1 |
| | 2 | 3 | 4 | 5 | 6 | 7 | 8 | 9 | **10** | 11 | 12 | | | | | 2 |
| | 2 | 3 | **4** | | 6 | 7 | 8 | 9 | 10 | 11 | 12 | 5 | | | | 3 |
| | 2 | 3 | 4 | | 6 | 7 | 8 | 9 | 10 | 11 | | | 5 | | | 4 |
| | 2 | 3 | 4 | 5 | 6 | | 8 | 9 | 10 | **11** | 12 | 7 | | | | 5 |
| | 2 | 3 | **4** | 5 | 6 | | 8 | 9 | 10 | 11 | 12 | 7 | | | | 6 |
| | 2 | 3 | 4 | 5 | 6 | **7** | 8 | 9 | 10 | 11 | | 12 | | | | 7 |
| | 2 | 3 | 4 | 5 | 6 | | 8 | 9 | 10 | 11 | | 7 | | | | 8 |
| | 2 | 3 | 4 | 5 | 6 | | 8 | 9 | 10 | 11 | | 7 | | | | 9 |
| | 2 | 3 | **4** | 5 | 6 | 12 | 8 | 9 | 10 | 11 | | 7 | | | | 10 |
| | 2 | 3 | 4 | 5 | 6 | | 8 | 9 | 10 | 11 | | 7 | | | | 11 |
| | 2 | 3 | 4 | 5 | 6 | | 8 | 9 | 10 | 11 | | 7 | | | | 12 |
| | 2 | 3 | 4 | 5 | 6 | | 8 | 9 | 10 | 11 | | 7 | | | | 13 |
| | 2 | 3 | 4 | 5 | 6 | | 8 | 9 | 10 | 11 | | 7 | | | | 14 |
| | 2 | 3 | **4** | 5 | | 6 | 8 | 9 | 10 | 11 | | 7 | | 12 | | 15 |
| | 2 | 3 | 4 | 5 | | 6 | 8 | 9 | 10 | 11 | | 7 | | | | 16 |
| | 2 | 3 | 4 | 5 | | 6 | **8** | 9 | 10 | 11 | 12 | 7 | | | | 17 |
| | 2 | 3 | 4 | 5 | 6 | | 8 | 9 | 10 | 11 | | 7 | | | | 18 |
| | 2 | 3 | 4 | 5 | 6 | | 8 | 9 | 10 | 11 | | 7 | | | | 19 |
| | 2 | | 4 | 5 | 6 | | 8 | 12 | **10** | 11 | 9 | 7 | 3 | | | 20 |
| | 2 | | 4 | 5 | 6 | | 8 | 9 | | 11 | **10** | 7 | 3 | 12 | | 21 |
| | 2 | | 4 | 5 | 6 | | 8 | **9** | | 11 | 10 | 7 | 3 | 12 | | 22 |
| | 2 | 3 | 4 | 5 | 6 | | 8 | 9 | | 11 | 10 | 7 | | | | 23 |
| | 2 | 3 | 4 | 5 | 6 | | 8 | 9 | | 11 | 10 | 7 | | | | 24 |
| | | 3 | 4 | 5 | 6 | | 8 | 9 | 10 | 11 | | 7 | 2 | | | 25 |
| | | 3 | 4 | 5 | 6 | | 8 | 9 | 10 | 11 | | 7 | 2 | | | 26 |
| | | 3 | 4 | 5 | 6 | | 8 | 9 | 10 | **11** | 12 | 7 | 2 | | | 27 |
| | | 3 | 4 | 5 | 6 | | 8 | **9** | 10 | 11 | 12 | 7 | 2 | | | 28 |
| | | 3 | 4 | 5 | 6 | 8 | | | 10 | 11 | 9 | 7 | 2 | | | 29 |
| | | 3 | 4 | 5 | 6 | 12 | 8 | | 10 | **11** | 9 | 7 | 2 | | | 30 |
| | | 3 | 4 | 5 | **6** | 12 | 8 | 9 | 10 | | | 7 | 2 | 11 | | 31 |
| | | 3 | 4 | 5 | 6 | | 8 | 9 | 10 | | | 7 | 2 | 11 | | 32 |
| | | 3 | 4 | 5 | 6 | | 8 | 9 | 10 | | | 7 | 2 | 11 | | 33 |
| | | 3 | 4 | 5 | 6 | | 8 | 9 | 10 | | 12 | **7** | 2 | 11 | | 34 |
| | | 3 | 4 | 5 | 6 | 7 | 8 | 9 | 10 | | | | 2 | 11 | | 35 |
| | | 3 | 4 | 5 | 6 | 7 | 8 | 9 | 10 | | | | 2 | 11 | | 36 |
| | | 3 | 4 | 5 | 6 | 7 | 8 | 9 | 10 | | | | 2 | 11 | | 37 |
| | | **3** | 4 | 5 | 6 | | 8 | 9 | 10 | | 12 | 7 | 2 | 11 | | 38 |
| | | | 4 | 5 | 6 | | 8 | 9 | 10 | 11 | | 7 | 2 | | 3 | 39 |
| | | 3 | 4 | | 6 | | 8 | **9** | 10 | 11 | | 7 | 2 | 12 | 5 | 40 |
| | | 3 | 4 | | 6 | | 8 | 9 | 10 | 11 | | 7 | 2 | | 5 | 41 |
| | | 3 | 4 | | 6 | | 8 | 9 | 10 | **11** | | 7 | 2 | 12 | 5 | 42 |
| | 24 | 38 | 42 | 37 | 39 | 12 | 41 | 39 | 38 | 34 | 7 | 35 | 22 | 8 | 4 | |
| | | | | | | 3 | | 1 | | | 10 | 1 | | 5 | | |
| | 1 | 2 | 15 | 3 | | 2 | | 12 | 13 | 12 | 2 | 3 | | 2 | | |

| | | | | | | | | | | | | | | | |
|---|---|---|---|---|---|---|---|---|---|---|---|---|---|---|---|
| 2 | 3 | 4 | 5 | 6 | | 8 | 9 | | 11 | **10** | 7 | | 12 | | 3 |
| **2** | 3 | 4 | 5 | 6 | | 8 | 9 | | 11 | 10 | 7 | | 12 | | R |
| | 3 | 4 | 5 | 6 | | 8 | 9 | 10 | **11** | 12 | 7 | 2 | | | 4 |
| | 3 | 4 | 5 | 6 | 8 | | 12 | 10 | 11 | **9** | 7 | 2 | | | 5 |
| 2 | 4 | 4 | 4 | 4 | 1 | 3 | 3 | 2 | 4 | 3 | 4 | 2 | | | |
| | | | | | | | 1 | | | 1 | | | 2 | | |
| | | 2 | | 2 | | | | 1 | 1 | | | | | | |

| | | | | | | | | | | | | | | | |
|---|---|---|---|---|---|---|---|---|---|---|---|---|---|---|---|
| **2** | 3 | 4 | 5 | 6 | 7 | 8 | 9 | 10 | 11 | | 12 | | | | 2 |
| 2 | 3 | 4 | 5 | 6 | | 8 | 9 | 10 | 11 | 12 | **7** | | | | 3 |
| 2 | 2 | 2 | 2 | 2 | 1 | 2 | 2 | 2 | 2 | | 1 | | | | |
| | | | | | | | | | | 1 | 1 | | | | |
| | | 1 | | | | | | 2 | 1 | | | | | | |

1 own-goal

# 1975-76

| | P | W | D | L | F | A | Pts |
|---|---|---|---|---|---|---|---|
| Liverpool | 42 | 23 | 14 | 5 | 66 | 31 | 60 |
| Q.P.R. | 42 | 24 | 11 | 7 | 67 | 33 | 59 |
| Manchester U | 42 | 23 | 10 | 9 | 68 | 42 | 56 |
| Derby Co | 42 | 21 | 11 | 10 | 75 | 58 | 53 |
| Leeds U | 42 | 21 | 9 | 12 | 65 | 46 | 51 |
| Ipswich T | 42 | 16 | 14 | 12 | 54 | 48 | 46 |
| Leicester C | 42 | 13 | 19 | 10 | 48 | 51 | 45 |
| Manchester C | 42 | 16 | 11 | 15 | 64 | 46 | 43 |
| Tottenham H | 42 | 14 | 15 | 13 | 63 | 63 | 43 |
| Norwich C | 42 | 16 | 10 | 16 | 58 | 58 | 42 |
| Everton | 42 | 15 | 12 | 15 | 60 | 66 | 42 |
| Stoke C | 42 | 15 | 11 | 16 | 48 | 50 | 41 |
| Middlesbrough | 42 | 15 | 10 | 17 | 46 | 45 | 40 |
| Coventry C | 42 | 13 | 14 | 15 | 47 | 57 | 40 |
| Newcastle U | 42 | 15 | 9 | 18 | 71 | 62 | 39 |
| Aston Villa | 42 | 11 | 17 | 14 | 51 | 59 | 39 |
| Arsenal | 42 | 13 | 10 | 19 | 47 | 53 | 36 |
| West Ham U | 42 | 13 | 10 | 19 | 48 | 71 | 36 |
| Birmingham C | 42 | 13 | 7 | 22 | 57 | 75 | 33 |
| Wolves | 42 | 10 | 10 | 22 | 51 | 68 | 30 |
| Burnley | 42 | 9 | 10 | 23 | 43 | 66 | 28 |
| Sheffield U | 42 | 6 | 10 | 26 | 33 | 82 | 22 |

Manager: Dave Mackay.
Leading scorer: Charlie George, League 16, all matches 24.
League ever-present: Archie Gemmill, Colin Todd.
Player of the season: Charlie George.

- Charlie George made his competitive debut for Derby at Wembley in the Charity Shield victory over West Ham United. He was signed from Arsenal for a bargain £100,000 in July.
- George had a brilliant season, including four goals in the two-leg European Cup defeat by Real Madrid, and was named Midlands Player of the Season.
- Until George dislocated a shoulder against Stoke City at the Baseball Ground in March, the Rams had a chance of a League and Cup Double. They lost to Manchester United in the FA Cup semi-final and were fourth in the League, ending with a flourish at Ipswich in the final game of Francis Lee's career.
- Archie Gemmill became the first Derby player to lead Scotland when he was appointed captain against Wales in May.

## Division One

| Match No. | Date | | Venue | Opponents | Result | | Scorers | Att |
|---|---|---|---|---|---|---|---|---|
| 1 | Aug | 16 | (a) | Sheffield U | D | 1-1 | George | 3 |
| 2 | | 19 | (a) | Coventry C | D | 1-1 | McFarland | 2 |
| 3 | | 23 | (h) | QPR | L | 1-5 | McFarland | 2 |
| 4 | | 27 | (h) | Newcastle U | W | 3-2 | Lee, Hector, Craig (og) | 2 |
| 5 | | 30 | (a) | Everton | L | 0-2 | | 3 |
| 6 | Sep | 6 | (h) | Burnley | W | 3-0 | Gemmill, Lee, Hector | 2 |
| 7 | | 13 | (a) | Tottenham H | W | 3-2 | Lee, Hector, George | 2 |
| 8 | | 20 | (h) | Manchester C | W | 1-0 | Lee | 2 |
| 9 | | 24 | (h) | Manchester U | W | 2-1 | George 2 | 3 |
| 10 | | 27 | (a) | Stoke C | L | 0-1 | | 2 |
| 11 | Oct | 4 | (h) | Ipswich T | W | 1-0 | Lee | 2 |
| 12 | | 11 | (a) | Norwich C | D | 0-0 | | 2 |
| 13 | | 18 | (h) | Wolves | W | 3-2 | Hector 2, Lee | 2 |
| 14 | | 25 | (a) | Liverpool | D | 1-1 | Lee | 4 |
| 15 | Nov | 1 | (h) | Leeds U | W | 3-2 | George (pen), Gemmill, Davies | 3 |
| 16 | | 8 | (a) | Arsenal | W | 1-0 | Hector | 3 |
| 17 | | 15 | (h) | West Ham U | W | 2-1 | Rioch, George | 3 |
| 18 | | 22 | (a) | Wolves | D | 0-0 | | 2 |
| 19 | | 29 | (h) | Middlesbrough | W | 3-2 | Newton, Gemmill, Lee | 2 |
| 20 | Dec | 6 | (a) | Birmingham C | L | 1-2 | George | 3 |
| 21 | | 13 | (a) | QPR | D | 1-1 | Rioch | 2 |
| 22 | | 20 | (h) | Sheffield U | W | 3-2 | Nish, George, Garner (og) | 2 |
| 23 | | 26 | (a) | Leicester C | L | 1-2 | James | 2 |
| 24 | | 27 | (h) | Aston Villa | W | 2-0 | George (pen), Powell | 3 |
| 25 | Jan | 10 | (h) | Tottenham H | L | 2-3 | Powell, Davies | 2 |
| 26 | | 17 | (a) | Burnley | W | 2-1 | George, James | 2 |
| 27 | | 31 | (h) | Coventry C | W | 2-0 | George 2 (1 pen) | 2 |
| 28 | Feb | 7 | (a) | Newcastle U | L | 3-4 | Rioch, George, Powell | 4 |
| 29 | | 18 | (h) | Arsenal | W | 2-0 | James 2 | 2 |
| 30 | | 21 | (a) | West Ham U | W | 2-1 | Rioch, George | 2 |
| 31 | | 25 | (a) | Manchester U | D | 1-1 | Rioch | 5 |
| 32 | | 28 | (h) | Liverpool | D | 1-1 | George (pen) | 3 |
| 33 | Mar | 2 | (a) | Leeds U | D | 1-1 | Gemmill | 4 |
| 34 | | 13 | (h) | Norwich C | W | 3-1 | Rioch, Gemmill, James | 2 |
| 35 | | 20 | (a) | Middlesbrough | W | 2-0 | Hector, George | 2 |
| 36 | | 24 | (h) | Stoke C | D | 1-1 | Rioch (pen) | 3 |
| 37 | | 27 | (h) | Birmingham C | W | 4-2 | Nish, Rioch, Davies, James | 2 |
| 38 | Apr | 10 | (a) | Manchester C | L | 3-4 | Rioch 2, Todd | 4 |
| 39 | | 17 | (h) | Leicester C | D | 2-2 | Lee 2 | 3 |
| 40 | | 19 | (a) | Aston Villa | L | 0-1 | | 3 |
| 41 | | 20 | (h) | Everton | L | 1-3 | Rioch | 2 |
| 42 | | 24 | (a) | Ipswich T | W | 6-2 | Lee 2, Hector 2, Rioch 2 (1 pen) | 2 |

FINAL LEAGUE POSITION: 4th in Division One

Appeara
Substi
(

## FA Charity Shield

| | | | | | | | | |
|---|---|---|---|---|---|---|---|---|
| | Aug | 9 | (n*) | West Ham U | W | 2-0 | Hector, McFarland | 5 |

*Played at Wembley

Appeara
Subst

## FA Cup

| | | | | | | | | |
|---|---|---|---|---|---|---|---|---|
| 3 | Jan | 3 | (h) | Everton | W | 2-1 | George 2 | 3 |
| 4 | | 24 | (h) | Liverpool | W | 1-0 | Davies | 3 |
| 5 | Feb | 14 | (h) | Southend U | W | 1-0 | Rioch | 3 |
| 6 | Mar | 6 | (h) | Newcastle U | W | 4-2 | Rioch 2, Newton, George | 3 |
| SF | Apr | 3 | (n*) | Manchester U | L | 0-2 | | 5 |

*Played at Hillsborough

Appeara
Substi
G

## League Cup

| | | | | | | | | |
|---|---|---|---|---|---|---|---|---|
| 2 | Sep | 10 | (h) | Huddersfield T | W | 2-1 | Rioch, George | 2 |
| 3 | Oct | 7 | (a) | Middlesbrough | L | 0-1 | | 2 |

Appeara
Substi
G

**Derby County played in the European Cup (see Rams in Europe)**

ton C

| Thomas R | Nish D | Rioch B | McFarland R | Todd C | Newton H | Gemmill A | Lee F | Bourne J | George C | Hinton A | Hector K | Webster R | Moseley G | Davies R | Powell S | James L | Daniel P | Macken A | King J | |
|---|---|---|---|---|---|---|---|---|---|---|---|---|---|---|---|---|---|---|---|---|
| 2 | 3 | 4 | 5 | 6 | 7 | 8 | 9 | **10** | 11 | 12 | | | | | | | | | | 1 |
| 2 | 3 | 4 | 5 | 6 | 7 | 8 | 9 | 10 | 11 | | | | | | | | | | | 2 |
| 2 | 3 | 4 | 5 | 6 | 7 | 8 | **9** | | 11 | 12 | 10 | | | | | | | | | 3 |
| 2 | 3 | 4 | 5 | 6 | 7 | 8 | 9 | | 11 | | 10 | | | | | | | | | 4 |
| 5 | 3 | 4 | | 6 | 7 | 8 | **9** | | **11** | 12 | 10 | 2 | | | | | | | | 5 |
| 5 | 3 | 4 | | 6 | 7 | 8 | 9 | | 11 | | 10 | 2 | | | | | | | | 6 |
| 2 | 3 | 4 | 5 | 6 | 7 | 8 | 9 | | 11 | | 10 | | 1 | | | | | | | 7 |
| 2 | 3 | 4 | 5 | 6 | 7 | 8 | 9 | | 11 | | 10 | | | | | | | | | 8 |
| 2 | 3 | 4 | 5 | 6 | 7 | 8 | **9** | | 11 | | 10 | | | 12 | | | | | | 9 |
| 2 | 3 | 4 | 5 | 6 | 7 | 8 | | 9 | 11 | | 10 | | | | | | | | | 10 |
| 2 | 3 | 4 | 5 | 6 | | 8 | 9 | | 11 | | 10 | | | | 7 | | | | | 11 |
| 2 | 3 | 4 | 5 | 6 | | 8 | **9** | | 11 | | 10 | | | 12 | 7 | | | | | 12 |
| 2 | 3 | 4 | 5 | 6 | 7 | 8 | 9 | | **11** | | 10 | | | 12 | | | | | | 13 |
| 2 | 3 | 4 | 5 | 6 | **7** | 8 | 9 | | 11 | | 10 | | | 12 | | | | | | 14 |
| 5 | 3 | **4** | | 6 | 7 | 8 | 9 | | 11 | | 10 | 2 | | 12 | | | | | | 15 |
| 2 | 3 | 4 | 5 | 6 | 7 | 8 | 9 | | 11 | | 10 | | | | | | | | | 16 |
| 2 | 3 | 4 | 5 | 6 | 7 | 8 | 9 | | 11 | | 10 | | | | | | | | | 17 |
| 5 | 3 | 4 | | 6 | 7 | 8 | 9 | | 11 | | 10 | 2 | | | | | | | | 18 |
| 2 | 3 | 4 | 5 | 6 | 7 | 8 | 9 | | 11 | | 10 | | | | | | | | | 19 |
| 2 | 3 | 4 | 5 | 6 | **7** | 8 | 9 | | 11 | | 10 | | | | | 12 | | | | 20 |
| 2 | 3 | 4 | 5 | 6 | 7 | 8 | 9 | | 10 | | | | | | | 11 | | | | 21 |
| 2 | 3 | 4 | 5 | 6 | 7 | 8 | | | **10** | | 12 | | | 9 | | 11 | | | | 22 |
| 2 | | **4** | 5 | 6 | 7 | 8 | | | 10 | | 12 | | | 9 | | 11 | 3 | | | 23 |
| 2 | | | | 6 | 3 | 8 | | | 10 | | | | | 9 | 7 | 11 | 5 | 4 | | 24 |
| 2 | | 4 | 5 | 6 | 3 | 8 | | | 10 | | 12 | | | 9 | **7** | 11 | | | | 25 |
| 2 | 3 | 4 | 5 | 6 | | 8 | 9 | | 10 | | | | 1 | | 7 | 11 | | | | 26 |
| 2 | | 4 | 5 | 6 | 3 | 8 | **9** | | 10 | | | | 1 | 12 | 7 | 11 | | | | 27 |
| 2 | 3 | 4 | 5 | 6 | | 8 | **9** | | 10 | | | | 1 | 12 | 7 | 11 | | | | 28 |
| 2 | 3 | 4 | 5 | 6 | | 8 | | | 10 | | 9 | | 1 | | 7 | 11 | | | | 29 |
| 2 | 3 | 4 | 5 | 6 | | 8 | | | 10 | | 9 | | 1 | | 7 | 11 | | | | 30 |
| 2 | 3 | 4 | 5 | 6 | | 8 | | | 10 | | 9 | | 1 | | 7 | 11 | | | | 31 |
| 2 | 3 | | 5 | 6 | 4 | 8 | | | 10 | | 9 | | 1 | 12 | **7** | 11 | | | | 32 |
| 2 | 3 | | 5 | 6 | 4 | 8 | | 7 | 10 | | 9 | | 1 | 12 | | **11** | | | | 33 |
| | 3 | 4 | 5 | 6 | | 8 | | | | | 9 | 2 | 1 | 10 | 7 | 11 | | | | 34 |
| 2 | 3 | | 5 | 6 | 4 | 8 | | | 10 | | 9 | | 1 | | 7 | 11 | | | | 35 |
| 2 | 3 | 4 | 5 | 6 | | 8 | | | **10** | | 9 | | 1 | 12 | 7 | 11 | | | | 36 |
| 2 | 3 | 4 | **5** | 6 | 12 | 8 | | | | | 9 | | 1 | 10 | 7 | 11 | | | | 37 |
| **2** | 3 | 4 | 5 | 6 | 12 | 8 | 9 | | | | | | 1 | 10 | 7 | 11 | | | | 38 |
| 2 | 3 | **4** | 5 | 6 | 12 | 8 | 9 | | | | | | 1 | 10 | 7 | 11 | | | | 39 |
| 2 | | 4 | 5 | 6 | 3 | 8 | 9 | | | | | | 1 | 12 | 7 | 11 | | **10** | | 40 |
| **2** | | 4 | 5 | 6 | 3 | 8 | 9 | | | | 10 | | 1 | 12 | 7 | 11 | | | | 41 |
| | | 4 | **5** | 6 | 3 | 8 | 9 | | | | 10 | 2 | 1 | 12 | 7 | | | | 11 | 42 |
| 40 | 35 | 38 | 37 | 42 | 30 | 42 | 28 | 4 | 35 | | 29 | 6 | 18 | 8 | 20 | 21 | 2 | 2 | 1 | |
| | | | | | 3 | | | | | 3 | 3 | | | 13 | | 1 | | | | |
| | 2 | 13 | 2 | 1 | 1 | 5 | 12 | | 16 | | 9 | | | 3 | 3 | 6 | | | | |

2 own-goals

| | | | | | | | | | | | | | | | | | | | |
|---|---|---|---|---|---|---|---|---|---|---|---|---|---|---|---|---|---|---|---|
| 2 | 3 | 4 | 5 | 6 | 7 | 8 | 9 | | 11 | | 10 | | | | | | | | |
| 1 | 1 | 1 | 1 | 1 | 1 | 1 | 1 | | 1 | | 1 | | | | | | | | |
| | | | | | | | | | | | | | | | | | | | |
| | | | 1 | | | | | | | | 1 | | | | | | | | |

| | | | | | | | | | | | | | | | | | | | | |
|---|---|---|---|---|---|---|---|---|---|---|---|---|---|---|---|---|---|---|---|---|
| 2 | | 4 | | 6 | 3 | 8 | | | 10 | | | | | 9 | 7 | 11 | 5 | | | 3 |
| 2 | 3 | 4 | 5 | 6 | | 8 | 9 | | 10 | | | | 1 | 12 | 7 | **11** | | | | 4 |
| 2 | 3 | 4 | 5 | 6 | | 8 | 12 | | 10 | | | | 1 | **9** | 7 | 11 | | | | 5 |
| 2 | 3 | 4 | 5 | 6 | **7** | 8 | | | 10 | | 9 | | 1 | 12 | | 11 | | | | 6 |
| 2 | 3 | 4 | 5 | 6 | | 8 | 12 | | | | **9** | | 1 | 10 | 7 | 11 | | | | SF |
| 5 | 4 | 5 | 4 | 5 | 2 | 5 | 1 | | 4 | | 2 | | 4 | 3 | 4 | 5 | 1 | | | |
| | | | | | | | 2 | | | 1 | | | | 2 | | | | | | |
| | | 3 | | | 1 | | | | 3 | | | | | 1 | | | | | | |

| | | | | | | | | | | | | | | | | | | | | |
|---|---|---|---|---|---|---|---|---|---|---|---|---|---|---|---|---|---|---|---|---|
| **2** | 3 | 4 | 5 | 6 | 7 | 8 | **9** | | 11 | 12 | 10 | | | | | | | | | 2 |
| 2 | 3 | 4 | 5 | 6 | | 8 | 9 | | 11 | | 10 | | | | 7 | | | | | 3 |
| 2 | 2 | 2 | 2 | 2 | 1 | 2 | 2 | | 2 | | 2 | | | | 1 | | | | | |
| | | | | | | | | | | 1 | | | | | | | | | | |
| | | 1 | | | | | | | 1 | | | | | | | | | | | |

# 1976-77

| | P | W | D | L | F | A | Pts |
|---|---|---|---|---|---|---|---|
| Liverpool | 42 | 23 | 11 | 8 | 62 | 33 | 57 |
| Manchester C | 42 | 21 | 14 | 7 | 60 | 34 | 56 |
| Ipswich T | 42 | 22 | 8 | 12 | 66 | 39 | 52 |
| Aston Villa | 42 | 22 | 7 | 13 | 76 | 50 | 51 |
| Newcastle U | 42 | 18 | 13 | 11 | 64 | 49 | 49 |
| Manchester U | 42 | 18 | 11 | 13 | 71 | 62 | 47 |
| W.B.A. | 42 | 16 | 13 | 13 | 62 | 56 | 45 |
| Arsenal | 42 | 16 | 11 | 15 | 64 | 59 | 43 |
| Everton | 42 | 14 | 14 | 14 | 62 | 64 | 42 |
| Leeds U | 42 | 15 | 12 | 15 | 48 | 51 | 42 |
| Leicester C | 42 | 12 | 18 | 12 | 47 | 60 | 42 |
| Middlesbrough | 42 | 14 | 13 | 15 | 40 | 45 | 41 |
| Birmingham C | 42 | 13 | 12 | 17 | 63 | 61 | 38 |
| Q.P.R. | 42 | 13 | 12 | 17 | 47 | 52 | 38 |
| Derby Co | 42 | 9 | 19 | 14 | 50 | 55 | 37 |
| Norwich C | 42 | 14 | 9 | 19 | 47 | 64 | 37 |
| West Ham U | 42 | 11 | 14 | 17 | 46 | 65 | 36 |
| Bristol C | 42 | 11 | 13 | 18 | 38 | 48 | 35 |
| Coventry C | 42 | 10 | 15 | 17 | 48 | 59 | 35 |
| Sunderland | 42 | 11 | 12 | 19 | 46 | 54 | 34 |
| Stoke C | 42 | 10 | 14 | 18 | 28 | 51 | 34 |
| Tottenham H | 42 | 12 | 9 | 21 | 48 | 72 | 33 |

Manager: Dave Mackay until November, then Colin Murphy.
Leading scorers: Leighton James, League 9. Charlie George, all matches 17.
Player of the season: Leighton James.

- Kevin Hector scored five goals in the biggest win in Derby's history, 12–0 over Republic of Ireland club Finn Harps in the UEFA Cup on 15 September. He was the sixth player to record 500 appearances for the Rams, reaching the mark at Villa Park on 2 March.
- Bruce Rioch, an emergency centre-forward, scored four in the 8–2 rout of Tottenham Hotspur at the Baseball Ground on 16 October.
- Dave Mackay and Des Anderson were dismissed in November. Like Brian Clough and Peter Taylor, they lasted only 18 months after winning the title. Colin Murphy, brought in by Mackay as Reserve-team coach, was initially temporary manager and asked to continue after Derby's unsuccessful attempt to bring back Clough and Taylor in February.
- Roy McFarland's 28th and last England appearance, against Italy in Rome, made him Derby's most capped player, one ahead of Alan Durban.
- Ron Webster beat Steve Bloomer's 62-year-old club record of 525 appearances when he played at Roker Park, Sunderland, on 23 April.

## Division One

| Match No. | Date | | Venue | Opponents | Result | | Scorers | Att |
|---|---|---|---|---|---|---|---|---|
| 1 | Aug | 21 | (a) | Newcastle U | D | 2-2 | George, Nish | 3 |
| 2 | | 25 | (h) | Middlesbrough | D | 0-0 | | 2 |
| 3 | | 28 | (h) | Manchester U | D | 0-0 | | 3 |
| 4 | Sep | 4 | (a) | Leeds U | L | 0-2 | | 3 |
| 5 | | 11 | (h) | Liverpool | L | 2-3 | George, Neal (og) | 2 |
| 6 | | 18 | (a) | Norwich C | D | 0-0 | | 2 |
| 7 | | 25 | (h) | West Brom A | D | 2-2 | McFarland 2 | 2 |
| 8 | Oct | 2 | (a) | Birmingham C | L | 1-5 | James | 2 |
| 9 | | 16 | (h) | Tottenham H | W | 8-2 | Rioch 4, George 3 (1 pen), Todd, Thomas | 2 |
| 10 | | 23 | (a) | Stoke C | L | 0-1 | | 2 |
| 11 | | 30 | (h) | Bristol C | W | 2-0 | George, Hector | 2 |
| 12 | Nov | 6 | (a) | QPR | D | 1-1 | Thomas | 2 |
| 13 | | 20 | (a) | Everton | L | 0-2 | | 2 |
| 14 | | 27 | (h) | Sunderland | W | 1-0 | James | 2 |
| 15 | Dec | 4 | (a) | Manchester C | L | 2-3 | James 2 | 3 |
| 16 | | 15 | (h) | Arsenal | D | 0-0 | | 2 |
| 17 | | 18 | (a) | Ipswich T | D | 0-0 | | 2 |
| 18 | | 27 | (h) | Leicester C | W | 1-0 | James | 3 |
| 19 | Jan | 15 | (a) | Middlesbrough | L | 0-2 | | 1 |
| 20 | | 22 | (h) | Newcastle U | W | 4-2 | Hales 2, McFarland, Powell | 2 |
| 21 | Feb | 5 | (a) | Manchester U | L | 1-3 | Macken | 5 |
| 22 | | 12 | (h) | Leeds U | L | 0-1 | | 2 |
| 23 | | 19 | (a) | Liverpool | L | 1-3 | Hector | 4 |
| 24 | Mar | 2 | (a) | Aston Villa | L | 0-4 | | 3 |
| 25 | | 5 | (a) | West Brom A | L | 0-1 | | 1 |
| 26 | | 9 | (h) | Coventry C | D | 1-1 | Daniel | 2 |
| 27 | | 12 | (h) | Birmingham C | D | 0-0 | | 25 |
| 28 | | 15 | (a) | Bristol C | D | 2-2 | Hales, Daly | 1 |
| 29 | | 23 | (a) | Tottenham H | D | 0-0 | | 2 |
| 30 | Apr | 2 | (h) | Stoke C | W | 2-0 | James, Daly (pen) | 2 |
| 31 | | 6 | (h) | Norwich C | D | 2-2 | James, Powell | 21 |
| 32 | | 9 | (h) | Aston Villa | W | 2-1 | Hales, James | 2 |
| 33 | | 12 | (a) | Leicester C | D | 1-1 | Powell | 2 |
| 34 | | 16 | (h) | Everton | L | 2-3 | Daly 2 (1 pen) | 2 |
| 35 | | 20 | (h) | West Ham U | D | 1-1 | Daly (pen) | 21 |
| 36 | | 23 | (a) | Sunderland | D | 1-1 | Powell | 3 |
| (a) | | 25 | (a) | Coventry C | L | 0-2 | | 1 |
| 38 | | 30 | (h) | Manchester C | W | 4-0 | Daly (pen), Gemmill, Hector, Daniel | 2 |
| 39 | May | 3 | (a) | Arsenal | D | 0-0 | | 26 |
| 40 | | 7 | (a) | West Ham U | D | 2-2 | James, McGiven (og) | 32 |
| 41 | | 11 | (h) | QPR | W | 2-0 | McFarland, Daly | 21 |
| 42 | | 14 | (h) | Ipswich T | D | 0-0 | | 24 |

FINAL LEAGUE POSITION: 15th in Division One

Appeara
Substi
G

## FA Cup

| Round | Date | | Venue | Opponents | Result | | Scorers | Att |
|---|---|---|---|---|---|---|---|---|
| 3 | Jan | 8 | (a) | Blackpool | D | 0-0 | | 19 |
| R | | 19 | (h) | Blackpool | W | 3-2 | Hales, James, George | 21 |
| 4 | | 29 | (a) | Colchester U | D | 1-1 | Hales | 14 |
| R | Feb | 2 | (h) | Colchester U | W | 1-0 | James | 22 |
| 5 | | 26 | (h) | Blackburn R | W | 3-1 | George 2 (1 pen), Hector | 30 |
| 6 | Mar | 19 | (a) | Everton | L | 0-2 | | 42 |

Appeara
Substi
G

## League Cup

| Round | Date | | Venue | Opponents | Result | | Scorers | Att |
|---|---|---|---|---|---|---|---|---|
| 2 | Aug | 31 | (a) | Doncaster R | W | 2-1 | George, Rioch | 14 |
| 3 | Sep | 22 | (h) | Notts C | D | 1-1 | George (pen) | 24 |
| R | Oct | 4 | (a) | Notts C | W | 2-1 | Rioch 2 | 16 |
| 4 | | 26 | (a) | Brighton & HA | D | 1-1 | James | 33 |
| R | Nov | 8 | (h) | Brighton & HA | W | 2-1 | Todd, Hector | 25 |
| 5 | Dec | 1 | (h) | Bolton W | L | 1-2 | George (pen) | 26 |

Appeara
Substi
G

**Derby County played in the UEFA Cup (see Rams in Europe)**

| Thomas R | Nish D | Rioch B | McFarland R | Todd C | Newton H | Gemmill A | George C | Hector K | James L | Daniel P | King J | Bourne J | Carruthers E | Macken A | Webster R | Powell S | Boulton C | Hales D | Langan D | Daly G | O'Riordan D | |
|---|---|---|---|---|---|---|---|---|---|---|---|---|---|---|---|---|---|---|---|---|---|---|
| 2 | 3 | 4 | 5 | 6 | 7 | 8 | 9 | 10 | 11 | | | | | | | | | | | | | 1 |
| 2 | 3 | 10 | 5 | 6 | 7 | 8 | | | 11 | 4 | 9 | | | | | | | | | | | 2 |
| 2 | 3 | 4 | 5 | 6 | 7 | 8 | 9 | | 11 | | | **10** | 12 | | | | | | | | | 3 |
| 2 | 3 | 9 | 5 | 6 | **7** | 8 | 10 | | 11 | | 12 | | | 4 | | | | | | | | 4 |
| 2 | 3 | 4 | 5 | 6 | 7 | 8 | 10 | 9 | 11 | | | | | | | | | | | | | 5 |
| 2 | 3 | 4 | 5 | 6 | 7 | 8 | 10 | 9 | 11 | | | | | | | | | | | | | 6 |
| | 3 | 4 | 5 | 6 | **7** | 8 | 10 | 9 | 11 | | | | | 12 | 2 | | | | | | | 7 |
| 2 | 3 | 4 | | **6** | 7 | 8 | 9 | | 11 | 5 | 12 | | | 10 | | | | | | | | 8 |
| 2 | 3 | 9 | 5 | 6 | | 8 | 10 | | 11 | | | | | 4 | | 7 | | | | | | 9 |
| 2 | 3 | 9 | 5 | 6 | | | 10 | | 11 | 12 | 8 | | | **4** | | 7 | | | | | | 10 |
| 2 | | 9 | 5 | 6 | 3 | | **10** | 12 | 11 | | 8 | | | 4 | | 7 | | | | | | 11 |
| 2 | | 9 | 5 | 6 | 3 | 8 | | 10 | 11 | | | | | 4 | | 7 | 1 | | | | | 12 |
| 2 | | 9 | | 6 | 3 | 8 | | **10** | 11 | 5 | | 12 | | 4 | | 7 | 1 | | | | | 13 |
| 2 | | | 5 | 6 | 3 | 8 | | 10 | 11 | | | 9 | | 4 | | 7 | 1 | | | | | 14 |
| 2 | | | | 6 | 3 | 8 | 10 | | 11 | 5 | | 9 | | 4 | | 7 | 1 | | | | | 15 |
| 2 | | | 5 | 6 | 3 | 8 | 10 | | 11 | | | | | 4 | | 7 | 1 | 9 | | | | 16 |
| 2 | | | 5 | 6 | 3 | 8 | 10 | | 11 | | | | | 4 | | 7 | 1 | 9 | | | | 17 |
| 2 | | | 5 | 6 | 8 | | 10 | | 11 | 3 | | | | 4 | | 7 | 1 | 9 | | | | 18 |
| 2 | | | 5 | 6 | 3 | 8 | 10 | | 11 | | | 12 | | 4 | | **7** | 1 | 9 | | | | 19 |
| | | | 5 | 6 | | 8 | | 10 | **11** | 3 | | 12 | | 4 | 2 | 7 | 1 | 9 | | | | 20 |
| 2 | | | 5 | 6 | | | | 10 | 11 | 3 | 8 | | | 4 | | 7 | 1 | 9 | | | | 21 |
| | | | | 6 | 3 | | 10 | 8 | 11 | 5 | 4 | 12 | | | | **7** | 1 | 9 | 2 | | | 22 |
| | | | | 6 | 7 | | 10 | 8 | **11** | 5 | 4 | | | 12 | 3 | | 1 | 9 | 2 | | | 23 |
| | | | | 6 | 7 | | 10 | 9 | 11 | 5 | 4 | | | 8 | 3 | | 1 | | 2 | | | 24 |
| 3 | | | | 6 | 7 | | 10 | 9 | 11 | 5 | 4 | | | 8 | | | 1 | | 2 | | | 25 |
| 3 | | | **5** | 6 | | | 10 | 7 | 11 | 12 | | | | 8 | | | 1 | 9 | 2 | 4 | | 26 |
| | | | | 6 | | | 10 | 8 | 11 | 5 | | | | | 3 | 7 | 1 | 9 | 2 | 4 | | 27 |
| | | | | 6 | | | 10 | 8 | 11 | 5 | | | | | 3 | 7 | 1 | 9 | 2 | 4 | | 28 |
| | | | | 6 | 7 | | **10** | 9 | 11 | 5 | 8 | | | | 3 | | 1 | | 2 | 4 | 12 | 29 |
| | | | 5 | | 7 | 8 | | 10 | 11 | | | | | | 3 | 6 | 1 | 9 | 2 | 4 | | 30 |
| | | | 5 | 6 | | 8 | 10 | **9** | 11 | | | | | | 3 | 7 | 1 | 12 | 2 | 4 | | 31 |
| | | | 5 | 6 | | 8 | 10 | | 11 | | | | | | 3 | 7 | 1 | 9 | 2 | 4 | | 32 |
| | | | 5 | 6 | | 8 | 10 | | 11 | | | | | | 3 | 7 | 1 | 9 | 2 | 4 | | 33 |
| | | | | 6 | 12 | 8 | | 10 | 11 | 5 | | | | | **3** | 7 | 1 | 9 | 2 | 4 | | 34 |
| | | | 5 | 6 | | 8 | | 10 | 11 | | | | | | 3 | 7 | 1 | 9 | 2 | 4 | | 35 |
| | | | 5 | 6 | 12 | 8 | | 10 | 11 | | | | | | 3 | 7 | 1 | 9 | 2 | **4** | | 36 |
| | | | 5 | 6 | | 10 | | 9 | 11 | 7 | | | | | 3 | 8 | | | 2 | 4 | | 37 |
| | | | 5 | 6 | 11 | 8 | | 10 | | 9 | | | | | 3 | 7 | 1 | | 2 | 4 | | 38 |
| | | | 5 | 6 | 11 | 8 | | 10 | | 3 | | | | | 2 | 7 | 1 | | 9 | 4 | | 39 |
| | | | 5 | 6 | | 8 | 10 | 9 | 11 | | | | | | 3 | 7 | 1 | | 2 | 4 | | 40 |
| | | | 5 | 6 | | 8 | 10 | 9 | 11 | | | | | | 3 | 7 | 1 | | 2 | 4 | | 41 |
| | | | 5 | 6 | | 8 | 10 | 9 | | 3 | 11 | | | | | 7 | 1 | | 2 | 4 | | 42 |
| 21 | 10 | 13 | 31 | 41 | 25 | 30 | 29 | 28 | 39 | 19 | 10 | 3 | | 18 | 19 | 29 | 30 | 17 | 21 | 17 | | |
| | | | | | 2 | | | 1 | | 2 | 2 | 4 | 1 | 2 | | | | 1 | | | 1 | |
| 2 | 1 | 4 | 4 | 1 | | 1 | 5 | 3 | 9 | 2 | | | | 1 | | 4 | | 4 | | 7 | | |

2 own-goals

| Thomas R | Nish D | Rioch B | McFarland R | Todd C | Newton H | Gemmill A | George C | Hector K | James L | Daniel P | King J | Bourne J | Carruthers E | Macken A | Webster R | Powell S | Boulton C | Hales D | Langan D | Daly G | O'Riordan D | |
|---|---|---|---|---|---|---|---|---|---|---|---|---|---|---|---|---|---|---|---|---|---|---|
| | | | 5 | 6 | 3 | 8 | 10 | | 11 | 2 | | | | 4 | | 7 | 1 | 9 | | | | 3 |
| 2 | | | 5 | 6 | 3 | 8 | **10** | | 11 | | | 12 | | 4 | | 7 | 1 | 9 | | | | R |
| | | | 5 | 6 | | 8 | | 10 | 11 | 3 | | | | 4 | 2 | 7 | 1 | 9 | | | | 4 |
| 2 | | | 5 | 6 | 8 | | | 10 | 11 | 3 | | 12 | | 4 | | 7 | 1 | **9** | | | | R |
| | | | 5 | 6 | 7 | | 10 | 8 | 11 | | 4 | | | 12 | 3 | | 1 | **9** | 2 | | | 5 |
| | | | | 6 | 4 | | 10 | 8 | 11 | 5 | 12 | | | | 3 | 7 | 1 | **9** | 2 | | | 6 |
| 2 | | | 5 | 6 | 5 | 3 | 4 | 4 | 6 | 4 | 1 | | | 4 | 3 | 5 | 6 | 6 | 2 | | | |
| | | | | | | | | | | | 1 | 2 | | 1 | | | | | | | | |
| | | | | | | | 3 | 1 | 2 | | | | | | | | | 2 | | | | |

| Thomas R | Nish D | Rioch B | McFarland R | Todd C | Newton H | Gemmill A | George C | Hector K | James L | Daniel P | King J | Bourne J | Carruthers E | Macken A | Webster R | Powell S | Boulton C | Hales D | Langan D | Daly G | O'Riordan D | |
|---|---|---|---|---|---|---|---|---|---|---|---|---|---|---|---|---|---|---|---|---|---|---|
| 2 | 3 | 9 | 5 | 6 | 7 | 8 | 10 | | 11 | | **4** | | | 12 | | | | | | | | 2 |
| 2 | 3 | 4 | 5 | 6 | 7 | 8 | 10 | 9 | 11 | | | | | | | | | | | | | 3 |
| 2 | 3 | 9 | | 6 | | 8 | 10 | | 11 | 5 | 12 | | | **4** | | 7 | | | | | | R |
| 2 | | 9 | 5 | 6 | 3 | 8 | 10 | | 11 | | | | | 4 | | 7 | | | | | | 4 |
| 2 | | 9 | 5 | 6 | 3 | 8 | | 10 | 11 | | 12 | | | **4** | | 7 | 1 | | | | | R |
| 2 | | 4 | **5** | 6 | 3 | 8 | 10 | | 11 | | | 9 | | 12 | | 7 | 1 | | | | | 5 |
| 6 | 3 | 6 | 5 | 6 | 5 | 6 | 5 | 2 | 6 | 1 | 1 | 1 | | 3 | | 4 | 2 | | | | | |
| | | | | | | | | | | | 2 | | | 2 | | | | | | | | |
| | | 3 | | 1 | | | 3 | 1 | 1 | | | | | | | | | | | | | |

# 1977-78

| | P | W | D | L | F | A | Pts |
|---|---|---|---|---|---|---|---|
| Nottingham F | 42 | 25 | 14 | 3 | 69 | 24 | 64 |
| Liverpool | 42 | 24 | 9 | 9 | 65 | 34 | 57 |
| Everton | 42 | 22 | 11 | 9 | 76 | 45 | 55 |
| Arsenal | 42 | 21 | 10 | 11 | 60 | 37 | 52 |
| Manchester C | 42 | 20 | 12 | 10 | 74 | 51 | 52 |
| W.B.A. | 42 | 18 | 14 | 10 | 62 | 53 | 50 |
| Coventry C | 42 | 18 | 12 | 12 | 75 | 62 | 48 |
| Aston Villa | 42 | 18 | 10 | 14 | 57 | 42 | 46 |
| Leeds U | 42 | 18 | 10 | 14 | 63 | 53 | 46 |
| Manchester U | 42 | 16 | 10 | 16 | 67 | 63 | 42 |
| Birmingham C | 42 | 16 | 9 | 17 | 55 | 60 | 41 |
| Derby Co | 42 | 14 | 13 | 15 | 54 | 59 | 41 |
| Norwich C | 42 | 11 | 18 | 13 | 52 | 66 | 40 |
| Middlesbrough | 42 | 12 | 15 | 15 | 42 | 54 | 39 |
| Wolves | 42 | 12 | 12 | 18 | 51 | 64 | 36 |
| Chelsea | 42 | 11 | 14 | 17 | 46 | 69 | 36 |
| Bristol C | 42 | 11 | 13 | 18 | 49 | 53 | 35 |
| Ipswich T | 42 | 11 | 13 | 18 | 47 | 61 | 35 |
| Q.P.R. | 42 | 9 | 15 | 18 | 47 | 64 | 33 |
| West Ham U | 42 | 12 | 8 | 22 | 52 | 69 | 32 |
| Newcastle U | 42 | 6 | 10 | 26 | 42 | 78 | 22 |
| Leicester C | 42 | 5 | 12 | 25 | 26 | 70 | 22 |

Manager: Colin Murphy until September, then Tommy Docherty.
Leading scorers: Charlie George, League 11. Gerry Daly, all matches 12.
League ever-present: David Langan.
Player of the season: David Langan.

- Colin Murphy watched the home match against Leeds United as manager, knowing that Tommy Docherty was on his way to the Baseball Ground to replace him.
- Docherty was constantly active in the transfer market but the one major success was Steve Buckley, who cost £163,000 when he arrived from Luton Town in January.
- Buckley, first choice at left-back for the next eight years, played on Derby's doorstep in his early days, for Ilkeston Town and Burton Albion.
- Don Masson, signed in exchange for Leighton James, and Bruce Rioch were in the Scotland team for an unsuccessful venture to the World Cup finals in Argentina. Rioch was Scotland's captain.

## Division One

| Match No. | Date | | Venue | Opponents | Result | | Scorers |
|---|---|---|---|---|---|---|---|
| 1 | Aug | 20 | (a) | Coventry C | L | 1-3 | Nish |
| 2 | | 24 | (h) | Ipswich T | D | 0-0 | |
| 3 | | 27 | (a) | Nottingham F | L | 0-3 | |
| 4 | Sep | 3 | (h) | Manchester U | L | 0-1 | |
| 5 | | 10 | (a) | Chelsea | D | 1-1 | Daly (pen) |
| 6 | | 17 | (h) | Leeds U | D | 2-2 | Hughes, Gemmill |
| 7 | | 24 | (a) | Liverpool | L | 0-1 | |
| 8 | Oct | 1 | (h) | Middlesbrough | W | 4-1 | Daly (pen), Hector, Hughes, Powell |
| 9 | | 4 | (a) | Wolves | W | 2-1 | Hughes 2 |
| 10 | | 8 | (a) | Newcastle U | W | 2-1 | McFarland, Hughes |
| 11 | | 15 | (h) | West Brom A | D | 1-1 | George |
| 12 | | 22 | (a) | Birmingham C | L | 1-3 | O'Riordan |
| 13 | | 29 | (h) | Norwich C | D | 2-2 | Daly, Hughes |
| 14 | Nov | 5 | (h) | Everton | L | 0-1 | |
| 15 | | 12 | (a) | Bristol C | L | 1-3 | Rioch |
| 16 | | 19 | (h) | West Ham U | W | 2-1 | Rioch, Nish |
| 17 | | 26 | (a) | Arsenal | W | 3-1 | Powell, Ryan, Rioch |
| 18 | Dec | 3 | (h) | Manchester C | W | 2-1 | Hughes, Ryan |
| 19 | | 10 | (a) | Leicester C | D | 1-1 | Hughes |
| 20 | | 17 | (h) | Bristol C | W | 1-0 | Todd |
| 21 | | 26 | (a) | QPR | D | 0-0 | |
| 22 | | 27 | (h) | Aston Villa | L | 0-3 | |
| 23 | | 31 | (a) | Ipswich T | W | 2-1 | George, Ryan |
| 24 | Jan | 2 | (h) | Coventry C | W | 4-2 | George 3 (1 pen), Daly |
| 25 | | 14 | (h) | Nottingham F | D | 0-0 | |
| 26 | | 21 | (a) | Manchester U | L | 0-4 | |
| 27 | Feb | 25 | (a) | Middlesbrough | L | 1-3 | Daly |
| 28 | Mar | 4 | (h) | Newcastle U | D | 1-1 | George (pen) |
| 29 | | 8 | (h) | Liverpool | W | 4-2 | Daly 2. George, Crawford |
| 30 | | 11 | (h) | Chelsea | D | 1-1 | Daniel |
| 31 | | 18 | (h) | Birmingham C | L | 1-3 | Curran |
| 32 | | 25 | (a) | Aston Villa | D | 0-0 | |
| 33 | | 27 | (h) | QPR | W | 2-0 | Daly, George |
| 34 | | 29 | (a) | Norwich C | D | 0-0 | |
| 35 | Apr | 1 | (a) | Everton | L | 1-2 | George |
| 36 | | 8 | (h) | Wolves | W | 3-1 | Daly, Ryan, Masson |
| 37 | | 12 | (a) | Leeds U | L | 0-2 | |
| 38 | | 15 | (a) | West Ham U | L | 0-3 | |
| 39 | | 18 | (a) | West Brom A | L | 0-1 | |
| 40 | | 22 | (h) | Leicester C | W | 4-1 | George 2, Rioch, Buckley |
| 41 | | 29 | (a) | Manchester C | D | 1-1 | Daly |
| 42 | May | 9 | (h) | Arsenal | W | 3-0 | Curran, Chesters, Hill |

FINAL LEAGUE POSITION: 12th in Division One

Appear
Subst

## FA Cup

| | | | | | | | |
|---|---|---|---|---|---|---|---|
| 3 | Jan | 7 | (h) | Southend U | W | 3-2 | Masson, Ryan, Young (og) |
| 4 | Feb | 1 | (h) | Birmingham C | W | 2-1 | Daly, Masson |
| 5 | | 22 | (h) | West Brom U | L | 2-3 | Rioch 2 |

Appeara
Subst

## League Cup

| | | | | | | | |
|---|---|---|---|---|---|---|---|
| 2 | Aug | 31 | (h) | Orient | W | 3-1 | Hector, Daly (pen), Hales |
| 3 | Oct | 26 | (a) | Liverpool | L | 0-2 | |

Appeara
Subst

on C

| Langan D | Nish D | Daly G | McFarland R | Todd C | O'Riordan D | King J | Hales D | Hector K | Hughes W | Gemmill A | Webster R | Powell S | Thomas R | George C | James L | Hunt D | Macken A | Daniel P | Middleton J | Ryan G | Masson D | Rioch B | Curran E | Chesters C | Bartlett P | Buckley S | Crawford A | Corish R | Hill G | Blockley J | |
|---|---|---|---|---|---|---|---|---|---|---|---|---|---|---|---|---|---|---|---|---|---|---|---|---|---|---|---|---|---|---|---|
| 2 | 3 | 4 | 5 | 6 | 7 | 8 | 9 | 10 | 11 | | | | | | | | | | | | | | | | | | | | | | 1 |
| 2 | **3** | 4 | 5 | 6 | 7 | | 9 | 10 | 11 | 8 | 12 | | | | | | | | | | | | | | | | | | | | 2 |
| 2 | 3 | 4 | **5** | 6 | | | 9 | 10 | 11 | 8 | 12 | 7 | | | | | | | | | | | | | | | | | | | 3 |
| 2 | **3** | 4 | | 6 | | | 9 | | 12 | 8 | | 7 | 5 | 10 | 11 | | | | | | | | | | | | | | | | 4 |
| 2 | | 4 | | 6 | | | 9 | | 7 | 8 | 12 | 3 | 5 | 10 | **11** | | | | | | | | | | | | | | | | 5 |
| 2 | 3 | 4 | **5** | 6 | | | | | 9 | 8 | | 7 | | 10 | | 11 | 12 | | | | | | | | | | | | | | 6 |
| 2 | 3 | 4 | | 6 | | | | 8 | 9 | | | 7 | | 10 | 11 | | | 5 | | | | | | | | | | | | | 7 |
| 2 | 3 | 4 | 5 | 6 | | | | 8 | 9 | | | 10 | | | 11 | | | | 1 | 7 | | | | | | | | | | | 8 |
| 2 | 3 | 4 | 5 | | 12 | | | 8 | 9 | | | 7 | | 10 | **11** | | | 6 | 1 | | | | | | | | | | | | 9 |
| 2 | **3** | 4 | 5 | | 12 | | | 8 | 9 | | | 7 | | 10 | | | | 6 | 1 | 11 | | | | | | | | | | | 10 |
| 2 | 3 | 4 | 5 | 6 | | | | | 9 | | | 7 | | 10 | 11 | | | | 1 | 8 | | | | | | | | | | | 11 |
| 2 | 3 | 4 | **5** | 6 | 12 | | | 8 | 9 | | | 7 | | 10 | 11 | | | | 1 | | | | | | | | | | | | 12 |
| 2 | 3 | 4 | | 6 | | | | 8 | 9 | | | 7 | | | | | | 5 | 1 | 11 | 10 | | | | | | | | | | 13 |
| 2 | 3 | 4 | | | | | | 8 | 9 | | | 7 | | | | | | 5 | | 11 | 10 | 6 | | | | | | | | | 14 |
| 2 | 3 | | 5 | 6 | | | | 8 | 9 | | | 7 | | | | | | | 1 | 11 | 10 | 4 | | | | | | | | | 15 |
| 2 | 3 | | 5 | 6 | | | | | 8 | | | | | 10 | | | | | 1 | 11 | 9 | 4 | 7 | | | | | | | | 16 |
| 2 | 3 | | 5 | 6 | | | | | | | | 8 | | 10 | | | | | 1 | 11 | 9 | 4 | 7 | | | | | | | | 17 |
| 2 | 3 | | 5 | 6 | | | | | 8 | | | | | 10 | | | | | 1 | 11 | 9 | 4 | 7 | | | | | | | | 18 |
| **2** | 3 | 8 | | 6 | | | | | 12 | | | 5 | | 10 | | | | | 1 | 11 | 9 | 4 | 7 | | | | | | | | 19 |
| 2 | **3** | 4 | 5 | 6 | | | | | 8 | | | 12 | | 10 | | | | | 1 | 11 | 9 | | 7 | | | | | | | | 20 |
| 2 | | 4 | | 6 | | | | | | | | 5 | | 10 | | | | 3 | 1 | 11 | 9 | 8 | 7 | | | | | | | | 21 |
| 2 | | 4 | | 6 | | | | | | | | 8 | | | | 5 | | 3 | 1 | 11 | 9 | | 7 | 10 | | | | | | | 22 |
| 2 | | 4 | | 6 | | | | | | | | 8 | | 10 | | 5 | | 3 | 1 | **11** | 9 | | 7 | 12 | | | | | | | 23 |
| 2 | | 4 | | 6 | | | | | | | | 8 | | **10** | | 5 | | 3 | 1 | | 9 | | 7 | 12 | 11 | | | | | | 24 |
| 2 | | 8 | | 6 | | | | | | | | 12 | | 10 | | | | 5 | 1 | **11** | 9 | 4 | 7 | | | 3 | | | | | 25 |
| 2 | | 8 | | | | | | | | | | 6 | | 10 | | | | 5 | 1 | **11** | 9 | 4 | 7 | | 12 | 3 | | | | | 26 |
| 2 | | 8 | | | | | | | | | | 6 | | 10 | | 5 | | | 1 | | 9 | 4 | 7 | 11 | | 3 | | | | | 27 |
| 2 | | 8 | 5 | | | | | | | | | 12 | | 10 | | | | 6 | 1 | | 9 | **4** | 7 | | 11 | 3 | | | | | 28 |
| 2 | | 8 | 5 | | | | | | | | | 4 | | 10 | | | | 6 | 1 | | 9 | | 7 | | | 3 | 11 | | | | 29 |
| 2 | | 8 | **5** | | | | | | | | | 4 | | 10 | | | | 6 | 1 | | 9 | | 7 | | 12 | 3 | 11 | | | | 30 |
| 2 | | 8 | | | | | | | | | | 6 | | 10 | | | | 5 | 1 | | **9** | 4 | 7 | | | 3 | 11 | 12 | | | 31 |
| 2 | | 8 | | 6 | | | | | | | | 4 | | 10 | | | | 5 | 1 | | 9 | | 7 | | 11 | 3 | | | | | 32 |
| 2 | | 8 | 5 | 6 | | | | | | | | 9 | | 10 | | | | | 1 | 11 | | 4 | 7 | | | 3 | | | | | 33 |
| 2 | | 8 | 5 | 6 | | | | | | | | **9** | | 10 | | | | 12 | 1 | 11 | | 4 | 7 | | | 3 | | | | | 34 |
| 2 | | 8 | 5 | 6 | | | | | | | | | | 10 | | | | 9 | 1 | 11 | | **4** | 7 | | 12 | 3 | | | | | 35 |
| 2 | | 8 | 5 | 6 | | | | | | | | 4 | | 10 | | | | | 1 | 11 | 9 | | 7 | | | 3 | | | | | 36 |
| 2 | | 8 | 5 | 6 | | | | | | | | 4 | | 10 | | | | | 1 | 11 | 9 | | **7** | | 12 | 3 | | | | | 37 |
| 2 | 11 | 8 | 5 | 6 | | | | | | | | **7** | | 10 | | | | | 1 | | 9 | 4 | | | 12 | 3 | | | | | 38 |
| 2 | | 8 | 5 | **6** | | | | | | | | | | 10 | | | | 12 | 1 | 11 | | 4 | 7 | 9 | | 3 | | | | | 39 |
| 2 | 6 | 8 | | | | | | | | | | 5 | | 10 | | | | | 1 | **11** | | 4 | 7 | 9 | 12 | 3 | | | | | 40 |
| 2 | | 8 | 5 | 6 | | | | | | | | | | 10 | | | | | 1 | 11 | | 4 | 7 | 9 | | 3 | | | | | 41 |
| 2 | | | 5 | 6 | | | | | | | | 8 | | 10 | | | | | 1 | | | 4 | 7 | 9 | | 3 | | | 11 | | 42 |
| 42 | 21 | 37 | 26 | 32 | 2 | 1 | 5 | 11 | 17 | 5 | | 32 | 2 | 34 | 7 | 5 | | 17 | 34 | 24 | 23 | 20 | 26 | 6 | 3 | 18 | 3 | | 1 | | |
| | | | | | 3 | | | | 2 | | 3 | 3 | | | | | 1 | 2 | | | | | | 2 | 6 | | | 1 | | | |
| | 2 | 10 | 1 | 1 | 1 | | | 1 | 8 | 1 | | 2 | | 11 | | | | 1 | | 4 | 1 | 4 | 2 | 1 | | 1 | 1 | | 1 | | |

| Langan D | Nish D | Daly G | McFarland R | Todd C | O'Riordan D | King J | Hales D | Hector K | Hughes W | Gemmill A | Webster R | Powell S | Thomas R | George C | James L | Hunt D | Macken A | Daniel P | Middleton J | Ryan G | Masson D | Rioch B | Curran E | Chesters C | Bartlett P | Buckley S | Crawford A | Corish R | Hill G | Blockley J | |
|---|---|---|---|---|---|---|---|---|---|---|---|---|---|---|---|---|---|---|---|---|---|---|---|---|---|---|---|---|---|---|---|
| 2 | | 8 | | 6 | | | | | | | | 5 | | 10 | | | | 3 | 1 | 11 | 9 | 4 | 7 | | | | | | | | 3 |
| 2 | | 8 | | | | | | | | | | 6 | | 10 | | | | 5 | 1 | 11 | 9 | 4 | **7** | | | 3 | 12 | | | | 4 |
| 2 | | 8 | | | | | | | | | | **6** | | 10 | | | | 11 | 1 | | 9 | 4 | 7 | | | 3 | 12 | | | 5 | 5 |
| 3 | | 3 | | 1 | | | | | | | | 3 | | 3 | | | | 3 | 3 | 2 | 3 | 3 | 3 | | | 2 | | | | 1 | |
| | | | | | | | | | | | | | | | | | | | | | | | | | | | 2 | | | | |
| | | 1 | | | | | | | | | | | | | | | | | | 1 | 2 | 2 | | | | | | | | | |

1 own-goal

| Langan D | Nish D | Daly G | McFarland R | Todd C | O'Riordan D | King J | Hales D | Hector K | Hughes W | Gemmill A | Webster R | Powell S | Thomas R | George C | James L | Hunt D | Macken A | Daniel P | Middleton J | Ryan G | Masson D | Rioch B | Curran E | Chesters C | Bartlett P | Buckley S | Crawford A | Corish R | Hill G | Blockley J | |
|---|---|---|---|---|---|---|---|---|---|---|---|---|---|---|---|---|---|---|---|---|---|---|---|---|---|---|---|---|---|---|---|
| 2 | 3 | 4 | | 6 | | | 9 | 10 | | 8 | | 7 | 5 | | 11 | | | | | | | | | | | | | | | | 2 |
| 2 | 3 | **4** | | 6 | 12 | | | 8 | 9 | | | 7 | | 10 | | | | 5 | | 11 | | | | | | | | | | | 3 |
| 2 | 2 | 2 | | 2 | | | 1 | 2 | 1 | 1 | | 2 | 1 | 1 | 1 | | | 1 | | 1 | | | | | | | | | | | |
| | | | | | 1 | | | | | | | | | | | | | | | | | | | | | | | | | | |
| | | 1 | | | | | 1 | 1 | | | | | | | | | | | | | | | | | | | | | | | |

# 1978-79

| | P | W | D | L | F | A | Pts |
|---|---|---|---|---|---|---|---|
| Liverpool | 42 | 30 | 8 | 4 | 85 | 16 | 68 |
| Nottingham F | 42 | 21 | 18 | 3 | 61 | 26 | 60 |
| W.B.A. | 42 | 24 | 11 | 7 | 72 | 35 | 59 |
| Everton | 42 | 17 | 17 | 8 | 52 | 40 | 51 |
| Leeds U | 42 | 18 | 14 | 10 | 70 | 52 | 50 |
| Ipswich T | 42 | 20 | 9 | 13 | 63 | 49 | 49 |
| Arsenal | 42 | 17 | 14 | 11 | 61 | 48 | 48 |
| Aston Villa | 42 | 15 | 16 | 11 | 59 | 49 | 46 |
| Manchester U | 42 | 15 | 15 | 12 | 60 | 63 | 45 |
| Coventry C | 42 | 14 | 16 | 12 | 58 | 68 | 44 |
| Tottenham H | 42 | 13 | 15 | 14 | 48 | 61 | 41 |
| Middlesbrough | 42 | 15 | 10 | 17 | 57 | 50 | 40 |
| Bristol C | 42 | 15 | 10 | 17 | 47 | 51 | 40 |
| Southampton | 42 | 12 | 16 | 14 | 47 | 53 | 40 |
| Manchester C | 42 | 13 | 13 | 16 | 58 | 56 | 39 |
| Norwich C | 42 | 7 | 23 | 12 | 51 | 57 | 37 |
| Bolton W | 42 | 12 | 11 | 19 | 54 | 75 | 35 |
| Wolves | 42 | 13 | 8 | 21 | 44 | 68 | 34 |
| Derby Co | 42 | 10 | 11 | 21 | 44 | 71 | 31 |
| Q.P.R. | 42 | 6 | 13 | 23 | 45 | 73 | 25 |
| Birmingham C | 42 | 6 | 10 | 26 | 37 | 64 | 22 |
| Chelsea | 42 | 5 | 10 | 27 | 44 | 92 | 20 |

Manager: Tommy Docherty.
Leading scorer: Gerry Daly, League/all matches 13.
League ever-present: Steve Buckley.
Player of the season: Steve Powell.

- Although Tommy Docherty kept Derby in the First Division, he was unpopular with supporters. There was a sense of relief when, in May, he resigned to start a second spell as manager of Queen's Park Rangers.
- Docherty's signings from Glentoran, Billy Caskey and Vic Moreland, were capped by Northern Ireland, the first Derby players since Arthur Stewart 10 years earlier.
- Charlie George joined Southampton in December, another crowd favourite sold by Docherty.

## Division One

| Match No. | Date | Venue | Opponents | Result | | Scorers | Att |
|---|---|---|---|---|---|---|---|
| 1 | Aug 19 | (h) | Manchester C | D | 1-1 | George | 2 |
| 2 | 22 | (a) | Everton | L | 1-2 | Nish | 4 |
| 3 | 26 | (a) | Birmingham C | D | 1-1 | Daly | 2 |
| 4 | Sep 2 | (h) | Coventry C | L | 0-2 | | 2 |
| 5 | 9 | (a) | Bolton W | L | 1-2 | Daly | 2 |
| 6 | 16 | (h) | West Brom A | W | 3-2 | Daly, Powell, Duncan | 2 |
| 7 | 23 | (h) | Southampton | W | 2-1 | George, Carter | 2 |
| 8 | 30 | (a) | Norwich C | L | 0-3 | | 1 |
| 9 | Oct 7 | (h) | Chelsea | W | 1-0 | Harris (og) | 2 |
| 10 | 14 | (a) | Liverpool | L | 0-5 | | 4 |
| 11 | 21 | (h) | Tottenham H | D | 2-2 | Buckley, Duncan | 2 |
| 12 | 28 | (a) | Leeds U | L | 0-4 | | 2 |
| 13 | Nov 4 | (h) | Wolves | W | 4-1 | Daly, Hill, Duncan, Caskey | 2 |
| 14 | 11 | (a) | Manchester C | W | 2-1 | Daly (pen), Duncan | 3 |
| 15 | 18 | (h) | Birmingham C | W | 2-1 | Buckley, Daly | 2 |
| 16 | 21 | (a) | Coventry C | L | 2-4 | Daly (pen), Caskey | 2 |
| 17 | 25 | (h) | QPR | W | 2-1 | Daniel, Caskey | 1 |
| 18 | Dec 2 | (a) | Bristol C | L | 0-1 | | 1 |
| 19 | 9 | (h) | Manchester U | L | 1-3 | Daly | 2 |
| 20 | 16 | (a) | Arsenal | L | 0-2 | | 2 |
| 21 | 23 | (h) | Aston Villa | D | 0-0 | | 2 |
| 22 | 26 | (a) | Nottingham F | D | 1-1 | Daly (pen) | 3 |
| 23 | Feb 3 | (a) | Southampton | W | 2-1 | Powell, Duncan | 2 |
| 24 | 10 | (h) | Norwich C | D | 1-1 | Buckley | 1 |
| 25 | 24 | (h) | Liverpool | L | 0-2 | | 2 |
| 26 | 28 | (h) | Ipswich T | L | 0-1 | | 1 |
| 27 | Mar 3 | (a) | Tottenham H | L | 0-2 | | 2 |
| 28 | 10 | (h) | Leeds U | L | 0-1 | | 2 |
| 29 | 13 | (a) | Middlesbrough | L | 1-3 | Daly (pen) | 1 |
| 30 | 21 | (h) | Bolton W | W | 3-0 | McFarland 2, Daly | 1 |
| 31 | 24 | (h) | Everton | D | 0-0 | | 2 |
| 32 | 26 | (a) | West Brom A | L | 1-2 | Crawford | 1 |
| 33 | 31 | (a) | QPR | D | 2-2 | Daly, Crawford | 1 |
| 34 | Apr 4 | (a) | Chelsea | D | 1-1 | McFarland | 1 |
| 35 | 7 | (h) | Bristol C | L | 0-1 | | 1 |
| 36 | 11 | (a) | Aston Villa | D | 3-3 | Greenwood, Powell, Gibson (og) | 2 |
| (a) | 14 | (h) | Nottingham F | L | 1-2 | Webb | 3 |
| 38 | 16 | (a) | Ipswich T | L | 1-2 | Crawford | 1 |
| 39 | 21 | (h) | Arsenal | W | 2-0 | Buckley, Daly | 1 |
| 40 | 24 | (a) | Wolves | L | 0-4 | | 1 |
| 41 | 28 | (a) | Manchester U | D | 0-0 | | 4 |
| 42 | May 5 | (h) | Middlesbrough | L | 0-3 | | 1 |

FINAL LEAGUE POSITION: 19th in Division One

Appeara
Subst
(

## FA Cup

| | | | | | | | |
|---|---|---|---|---|---|---|---|
| 3 | Jan 16 | (a) | Preston NE | L | 0-3 | | 1 |

Appeara
Subst
(

## League Cup

| | | | | | | | |
|---|---|---|---|---|---|---|---|
| 2 | Aug 30 | (a) | Leicester C | W | 1-0 | Hill | 1 |
| 3 | Oct 3 | (a) | Southampton | L | 0-1 | | 1 |

Appeara
Substi
(

| | Langan D | Buckley S | Daly G | McFarland R | Todd C | Powell S | Nish D | Ryan G | George C | Hill G | Daniel P | Chesters C | Carter S | McCaffery A | Duncan J | Rioch B | Caskey W | Moreland V | Clark J | Bartlett P | Clayton J | McKellar D | Webb D | Wicks S | Greenwood R | Spooner S | Crawford A | Emson P |
|---|---|---|---|---|---|---|---|---|---|---|---|---|---|---|---|---|---|---|---|---|---|---|---|---|---|---|---|---|
| 1 | 2 | 3 | 4 | 5 | 6 | 7 | 8 | 9 | 10 | 11 | | | | | | | | | | | | | | | | | | |
| 2 | 2 | 3 | 4 | 5 | 6 | 7 | 8 | 9 | 10 | 11 | | | | | | | | | | | | | | | | | | |
| 3 | 2 | 3 | 4 | 5 | | **7** | 8 | 9 | 10 | 11 | 6 | 12 | | | | | | | | | | | | | | | | |
| 4 | 2 | 3 | 4 | 5 | 6 | 9 | **8** | 11 | 10 | | 12 | | 7 | | | | | | | | | | | | | | | |
| 5 | 2 | 3 | 4 | 5 | 6 | 9 | 8 | 11 | 10 | | | | 7 | | | | | | | | | | | | | | | |
| 6 | 2 | 3 | 4 | 5 | | 8 | 12 | **11** | | | | | 7 | 6 | 9 | 10 | | | | | | | | | | | | |
| 7 | 2 | 3 | 4 | | | 6 | | | 10 | | | | 7 | 5 | **9** | 8 | 11 | 12 | | | | | | | | | | |
| 8 | 2 | 3 | 4 | 5 | | 7 | 11 | | | | | | | 6 | | 8 | 9 | | 10 | | | | | | | | | |
| 9 | 2 | 3 | 4 | | | 8 | | | 10 | | | | 7 | 5 | | 12 | 9 | **6** | 11 | | | | | | | | | |
| 10 | 2 | 3 | 4 | | | 8 | 12 | | **10** | | | | 7 | 5 | | | 9 | 6 | 11 | | | | | | | | | |
| 11 | 2 | 3 | 4 | | | 8 | 12 | | | | | | 7 | 5 | 9 | | | 6 | | **10** | 11 | | | | | | | |
| 12 | 2 | 3 | 4 | | | 8 | | | | 11 | 5 | | 7 | | 9 | | | 6 | | 10 | | | | | | | | |
| 13 | 2 | 3 | 4 | 5 | | 8 | | | | 11 | | | 7 | | 9 | | 10 | 6 | | | | | | | | | | |
| 14 | 2 | 3 | 4 | 5 | | 8 | | | | 11 | | | 7 | | 9 | | 10 | 6 | | | | | | | | | | |
| 15 | 2 | 3 | 4 | | | 8 | | | | 11 | 5 | | 7 | | | | 10 | 6 | 9 | | | | | | | | | |
| 16 | 2 | 3 | 4 | | | 8 | 12 | | | 11 | 5 | | 7 | | | | **9** | 6 | 10 | | | | | | | | | |
| 17 | 2 | 3 | 4 | | | 8 | | | | | 5 | | 7 | | 9 | | 10 | 6 | 11 | | | | | | | | | |
| 18 | 2 | 3 | 4 | **5** | | 8 | | | | 12 | | | 7 | | 9 | | 10 | 6 | 11 | | | | | | | | | |
| 19 | 2 | 3 | 4 | | | 5 | | | | 11 | | | 7 | | 9 | | 10 | 6 | 8 | | | | | | | | | |
| 20 | | 3 | 4 | | | 8 | | | | 11 | 5 | | 7 | | 10 | | 9 | 6 | 2 | | | 1 | | | | | | |
| 21 | 2 | 3 | 4 | 5 | | 8 | | | | 11 | | | 7 | | | | 9 | 12 | 10 | | | 1 | **6** | | | | | |
| 22 | 2 | 3 | 4 | 5 | | 8 | | | | 11 | | | **7** | | | | 9 | 12 | 10 | | | 1 | 6 | | | | | |
| 23 | 2 | 3 | | 5 | | 8 | | | | | | | | | **10** | 4 | 9 | 12 | 7 | | | 1 | | 6 | 11 | | | |
| 24 | 2 | 3 | | 5 | | 8 | | | | | | | 7 | | 9 | 4 | | | 10 | | | 1 | | 6 | 11 | | | |
| 25 | 2 | 3 | 4 | 5 | | 8 | | | | | | | 7 | | | 10 | 9 | 6 | | | | 1 | | | 11 | | | |
| 26 | 2 | 3 | 4 | 5 | | 8 | | | | | | | 7 | | 12 | 10 | **9** | | | | | 1 | | 6 | 11 | | | |
| 27 | 2 | 3 | 4 | 5 | | 8 | | | | | | | | | 10 | | 9 | | | | | 1 | | 6 | 11 | 7 | | |
| 28 | 2 | 3 | 4 | | | 8 | | | | | | | | | **10** | | 9 | | 7 | | | 1 | 5 | 6 | 11 | | 12 | |
| 29 | 2 | 3 | 4 | | | 8 | | | | | | | | | | | 9 | 7 | | | | 1 | 6 | 5 | 11 | | 10 | |
| 30 | 2 | 3 | 4 | 5 | | 8 | | | | | | | 7 | | | | | 10 | | | | | | 6 | 9 | | 11 | |
| 31 | 2 | 3 | 4 | 5 | | 8 | | | | | | | 7 | | | | | 10 | | | | | | 6 | 9 | | 11 | |
| 32 | 2 | 3 | **4** | 5 | | 8 | | | | | | | 7 | | | | | 10 | | | | | 12 | 6 | 9 | | 11 | |
| 33 | 2 | 3 | 4 | 5 | | 8 | | | | 12 | | | **7** | | | | | 10 | | | | | | 6 | 9 | | 11 | |
| 34 | 2 | 3 | 4 | 5 | | 8 | | | | | | | **7** | | | | 12 | 10 | | | | | | 6 | 9 | | 11 | |
| 35 | 2 | 3 | **4** | | | 8 | | | | | | | 7 | | | | 12 | 10 | | | | | 5 | 6 | 9 | | 11 | |
| 36 | 2 | 3 | | 5 | | 8 | | | | | | | | | | | 4 | 10 | | | | | | 6 | 9 | | 11 | 7 |
| 37 | 2 | 3 | | | | 8 | | | | | | | 7 | | | | | 4 | | | | 1 | 5 | 6 | 9 | | 11 | 10 |
| 38 | 2 | 3 | | | | 8 | | | | | | | 7 | | | | | 4 | | | | 1 | 5 | 6 | 9 | | 11 | 10 |
| 39 | 2 | 3 | 4 | | | 8 | | | | | | | | | | | | 10 | | | | 1 | 5 | 6 | 9 | | 11 | 7 |
| 40 | | 3 | 4 | | | 8 | | | | | | | | | | | | 10 | 2 | | | 1 | 5 | 6 | 9 | | 11 | 7 |
| 41 | 2 | 3 | 4 | 5 | | 8 | | | | | | | | | 9 | | | 10 | 7 | | | 1 | | 6 | 11 | | | |
| 42 | 2 | 3 | 4 | | | | | | | | | | | | 9 | | **8** | 6 | 7 | 10 | | 1 | | 5 | 12 | | | 11 |
| | 40 | 42 | 37 | 24 | 4 | 41 | 6 | 6 | 8 | 12 | 6 | | 29 | 6 | 16 | 7 | 22 | 27 | 17 | 3 | 1 | 16 | 9 | 19 | 19 | 1 | 12 | 6 |
| | | | | | | | 4 | | | 2 | 1 | 1 | | | 1 | 1 | 2 | 4 | | | | | 1 | | 1 | | 1 | |
| | | 4 | 13 | 3 | | 3 | 1 | | 2 | 1 | 1 | | 1 | | 5 | | 3 | | | | | | 1 | | 1 | | 3 | |

2 own-goals

| | Langan D | Buckley S | Daly G | McFarland R | Todd C | Powell S | Nish D | Ryan G | George C | Hill G | Daniel P | Chesters C | Carter S | McCaffery A | Duncan J | Rioch B | Caskey W | Moreland V | Clark J | Bartlett P | Clayton J | McKellar D | Webb D | Wicks S | Greenwood R | Spooner S | Crawford A | Emson P |
|---|---|---|---|---|---|---|---|---|---|---|---|---|---|---|---|---|---|---|---|---|---|---|---|---|---|---|---|---|
| 3 | 2 | 3 | 4 | 5 | | 8 | | | | **11** | | | 7 | | 12 | | 9 | | 10 | | | 1 | 6 | | | | | |
| | 1 | 1 | 1 | 1 | | 1 | | | | 1 | | | 1 | | | | 1 | | 1 | | | 1 | 1 | | | | | |
| | | | | | | | | | | | | | | | 1 | | | | | | | | | | | | | |
| | | | | | | | | | | | | | | | | | | | | | | | | | | | | |

| | Langan D | Buckley S | Daly G | McFarland R | Todd C | Powell S | Nish D | Ryan G | George C | Hill G | Daniel P | Chesters C | Carter S | McCaffery A | Duncan J | Rioch B | Caskey W | Moreland V | Clark J | Bartlett P | Clayton J | McKellar D | Webb D | Wicks S | Greenwood R | Spooner S | Crawford A | Emson P |
|---|---|---|---|---|---|---|---|---|---|---|---|---|---|---|---|---|---|---|---|---|---|---|---|---|---|---|---|---|
| 2 | 2 | 3 | 4 | 5 | | | 8 | 9 | 10 | **11** | 7 | 12 | | 6 | | | | | | | | | | | | | | |
| 3 | 2 | 3 | 4 | **5** | | 7 | | | 10 | | 11 | | | 6 | | | 9 | 12 | 8 | | | | | | | | | |
| | 2 | 2 | 2 | 2 | | 1 | 1 | 1 | 2 | 1 | 2 | | | 2 | 1 | | 1 | | 1 | | | | | | | | | |
| | | | | | | | | | | | | 1 | | | | | | 1 | | | | | | | | | | |
| | | | | | | | | | | 1 | | | | | | | | | | | | | | | | | | |

# 1979-80

| | P | W | D | L | F | A | Pts |
|---|---|---|---|---|---|---|---|
| Liverpool | 42 | 25 | 10 | 7 | 81 | 30 | 60 |
| Manchester U | 42 | 24 | 10 | 8 | 65 | 35 | 58 |
| Ipswich T | 42 | 22 | 9 | 11 | 68 | 39 | 53 |
| Arsenal | 42 | 18 | 16 | 8 | 52 | 36 | 52 |
| Nottingham F | 42 | 20 | 8 | 14 | 63 | 43 | 48 |
| Wolves | 42 | 19 | 9 | 14 | 58 | 47 | 47 |
| Aston Villa | 42 | 16 | 14 | 12 | 51 | 50 | 46 |
| Southampton | 42 | 18 | 9 | 15 | 65 | 53 | 45 |
| Middlesbrough | 42 | 16 | 12 | 14 | 50 | 44 | 44 |
| W.B.A. | 42 | 11 | 19 | 12 | 54 | 50 | 41 |
| Leeds U | 42 | 13 | 14 | 15 | 46 | 50 | 40 |
| Norwich C | 42 | 13 | 14 | 15 | 58 | 66 | 40 |
| Crystal Palace | 42 | 12 | 16 | 14 | 41 | 50 | 40 |
| Tottenham H | 42 | 15 | 10 | 17 | 52 | 62 | 40 |
| Coventry C | 42 | 16 | 7 | 19 | 56 | 66 | 39 |
| Brighton & H.A. | 42 | 11 | 15 | 16 | 47 | 57 | 37 |
| Manchester C | 42 | 12 | 13 | 17 | 43 | 66 | 37 |
| Stoke C | 42 | 13 | 10 | 19 | 44 | 58 | 36 |
| Everton | 42 | 9 | 17 | 16 | 43 | 51 | 35 |
| Bristol C | 42 | 9 | 13 | 20 | 37 | 66 | 31 |
| Derby Co | 42 | 11 | 8 | 23 | 47 | 67 | 30 |
| Bolton W | 42 | 5 | 15 | 22 | 38 | 73 | 25 |

Manager: Colin Addison.
Leading scorer: Alan Biley, League/all matches 9.
League ever-present: Steve Buckley.
Player of the season: Steve Buckley.

- Colin Addison brought in Grimsby Town manager John Newman as his assistant.
- Steve Wicks and Gordon Hill rejoined Tommy Docherty by moving to Queen's Park Rangers.
- Addison spent heavily in an attempt to preserve Derby's First Division status. Barry Powell, Alan Biley and David Swindlehurst cost more that £1million between them. Swindlehurst, initially on loan from Crystal Palace, was Derby's first £400,000 player.
- After 11 seasons and two Championships, the Rams slipped back into the Second Division. Another decline was setting in.

## Division One

| Match No. | Date | | Venue | Opponents | Result | | Scorers | Atte |
|---|---|---|---|---|---|---|---|---|
| 1 | Aug | 18 | (a) | West Brom A | D | 0-0 | | 2 |
| 2 | | 22 | (h) | Wolves | L | 0-1 | | 2 |
| 3 | | 25 | (h) | Everton | L | 0-1 | | 1 |
| 4 | Sep | 1 | (a) | Crystal P | L | 0-4 | | 2 |
| 5 | | 8 | (h) | Arsenal | W | 3-2 | McCaffery, Langan, Duncan | 1 |
| 6 | | 15 | (a) | Manchester U | L | 0-1 | | 5 |
| 7 | | 22 | (h) | Middlesbrough | W | 1-0 | Duncan | 1 |
| 8 | | 29 | (a) | Southampton | L | 0-4 | | 2 |
| 9 | Oct | 6 | (h) | Bolton W | W | 4-0 | Duncan 2, Emson 2 | 1 |
| 10 | | 9 | (a) | Wolves | D | 0-0 | | 3 |
| 11 | | 13 | (a) | Tottenham H | L | 0-1 | | 3 |
| 12 | | 20 | (h) | Aston Villa | L | 1-3 | Emson | 2 |
| 13 | | 27 | (a) | Stoke C | L | 2-3 | Hill 2 | 1 |
| 14 | Nov | 3 | (h) | West Brom A | W | 2-1 | Hill, Emery | 2 |
| 15 | | 10 | (a) | Bristol C | W | 2-0 | Moreland, Duncan | 1 |
| 16 | | 17 | (h) | Ipswich T | L | 0-1 | | 1 |
| 17 | | 24 | (h) | Nottingham F | W | 4-1 | Duncan 2, Daly, Emery | 27 |
| 18 | Dec | 1 | (a) | Brighton & HA | L | 0-2 | | 2 |
| 19 | | 8 | (h) | Norwich C | D | 0-0 | | 1 |
| 20 | | 15 | (a) | Manchester C | L | 0-3 | | 27 |
| 21 | | 22 | (h) | Liverpool | L | 1-3 | Davies (pen) | 24 |
| 22 | | 26 | (h) | Coventry C | L | 1-2 | Clark | 1 |
| 23 | | 29 | (a) | Everton | D | 1-1 | Davies | 22 |
| 24 | Jan | 1 | (a) | Leeds U | L | 0-1 | | 24 |
| 25 | | 12 | (h) | Crystal P | L | 1-2 | Osgood | 16 |
| 26 | | 19 | (a) | Arsenal | L | 0-2 | | 22 |
| 27 | Feb | 2 | (h) | Manchester U | L | 1-3 | B.Powell | 27 |
| 28 | | 9 | (a) | Middlesbrough | L | 0-3 | | 15 |
| 29 | | 16 | (h) | Southampton | D | 2-2 | Davies, B.Powell | 16 |
| 30 | | 23 | (h) | Tottenham H | W | 2-1 | McCaffery, Biley | 21 |
| 31 | Mar | 1 | (a) | Aston Villa | L | 0-1 | | 28 |
| 32 | | 8 | (h) | Stoke C | D | 2-2 | Biley, Osgood | 22 |
| 33 | | 15 | (a) | Bolton W | W | 2-1 | Swindlehurst, Biley | 13 |
| 34 | | 22 | (h) | Bristol C | D | 3-3 | Biley 3 (1 pen) | 17 |
| 35 | | 29 | (a) | Ipswich T | D | 1-1 | Swindlehurst | 19 |
| 36 | Apr | 5 | (h) | Leeds U | W | 2-0 | B.Powell, Emson | 22 |
| 37 | | 7 | (a) | Coventry C | L | 1-2 | McCaffery | 19 |
| 38 | | 8 | (a) | Liverpool | L | 0-3 | | 4 |
| 39 | | 12 | (h) | Brighton & HA | W | 3-0 | Biley 2 (1 pen), Osgood | 17 |
| 40 | | 19 | (a) | Nottingham F | L | 0-1 | | 32 |
| 41 | | 26 | (h) | Manchester C | W | 3-1 | Swindlehurst, Biley (pen), Reid (og) | 22 |
| 42 | May | 3 | (a) | Norwich C | L | 2-4 | McCaffery, Swindlehurst | 15 |

FINAL LEAGUE POSITION: 21st in Division One – Relegated

Appeara
Substi
G

## FA Cup

| | | | | | | | | |
|---|---|---|---|---|---|---|---|---|
| 3 | Jan | 5 | (a) | Bristol C | L | 2-6 | Davies, Daly | 13 |

Appeara
Substi
G

## League Cup

| | | | | | | | | |
|---|---|---|---|---|---|---|---|---|
| 2 | Aug | 29 | (h) | Middlesbrough | L | 0-1 | | 15 |
| 2 | Sep | 4 | (a) | Middlesbrough | D | 1-1 | Crawford | 19 |

Appeara
Substi
G

| ton J | Langan D | Buckley S | Rioch B | McFarland R | Wicks S | McCaffery A | Moreland V | Caskey W | Greenwood R | Hill G | Daly G | Crawford A | Webb D | Duncan J | Powell S | Carter S | Davies R | Emery S | Osgood K | Emson P | Spooner S | Powell B | McKellar D | Clark J | Bartlett P | Whymark T | Biley A | Cherry S | Swindlehurst D | Wilson K | Richards W | |
|---|---|---|---|---|---|---|---|---|---|---|---|---|---|---|---|---|---|---|---|---|---|---|---|---|---|---|---|---|---|---|---|---|
| | 2 | 3 | 4 | 5 | 6 | 7 | 8 | **9** | 10 | 11 | 12 | | | | | | | | | | | | | | | | | | | | | 1 |
| | 2 | 3 | | 5 | 6 | 7 | 8 | **9** | 10 | 11 | 4 | 12 | | | | | | | | | | | | | | | | | | | | 2 |
| | 2 | 3 | 7 | 5 | 6 | 8 | | **9** | 10 | 11 | 4 | 12 | | | | | | | | | | | | | | | | | | | | 3 |
| | 2 | 3 | 7 | 5 | | 8 | | | 10 | 11 | **4** | 12 | 6 | 9 | | | | | | | | | | | | | | | | | | 4 |
| | 2 | 3 | | | 5 | 8 | 7 | | | 11 | | **10** | 6 | 9 | 4 | 12 | | | | | | | | | | | | | | | | 5 |
| | 2 | 3 | | | 5 | 8 | 7 | | | 11 | | 12 | 6 | **9** | 4 | 10 | | | | | | | | | | | | | | | | 6 |
| | 2 | 3 | | 5 | | 6 | | | 12 | | **4** | | | 9 | 8 | 7 | 10 | 11 | | | | | | | | | | | | | | 7 |
| | 2 | 3 | | **5** | | 6 | 11 | | 12 | | | | | 9 | 8 | 7 | 10 | 4 | | | | | | | | | | | | | | 8 |
| | 2 | 3 | 4 | | | 5 | 8 | | | | | | | 9 | | | 10 | 7 | 6 | 11 | | | | | | | | | | | | 9 |
| | 2 | 3 | 4 | | | 5 | 8 | | 12 | | | | | **9** | | | 10 | 7 | 6 | 11 | | | | | | | | | | | | 10 |
| | 2 | 3 | 4 | | | 5 | 8 | 9 | 10 | | | | | | | | | 7 | 6 | **11** | 12 | | | | | | | | | | | 11 |
| | 2 | 3 | 4 | | | 5 | 8 | | 9 | | | | | | | | 10 | 7 | 6 | 11 | | | | | | | | | | | | 12 |
| | **2** | 3 | 4 | | | 5 | | | 12 | 11 | | | | 9 | | | 10 | 7 | 6 | | | 8 | | | | | | | | | | 13 |
| | 2 | 3 | 4 | | | 5 | | | | 11 | | | | 9 | | | 10 | 7 | 6 | | | 8 | 1 | | | | | | | | | 14 |
| | 2 | 3 | | | | 5 | 11 | | | | | | | 9 | | | 10 | 7 | 6 | | | 8 | 1 | 4 | | | | | | | | 15 |
| | 2 | 3 | **4** | | | 5 | | | | 11 | | | | 9 | | | 10 | 7 | 6 | | | 8 | 1 | 12 | | | | | | | | 16 |
| | 2 | 3 | | | | | | | | | **4** | | 5 | 9 | | | 10 | 7 | 6 | 12 | | 8 | 1 | 11 | | | | | | | | 17 |
| | 2 | 3 | | | | 12 | | | | | 4 | | 5 | 9 | | | | 7 | 6 | | | 8 | 1 | 11 | **10** | | | | | | | 18 |
| | 2 | 3 | 11 | | | | | | | | 4 | | 5 | 9 | | | 10 | 7 | 6 | | | 8 | 1 | | | | | | | | | 19 |
| | 2 | 3 | 11 | | | | | | | | 4 | | 5 | 9 | | | **10** | 7 | 6 | 12 | | 8 | 1 | | | | | | | | | 20 |
| | 2 | 3 | 11 | | | | | | | | 4 | | 5 | | | | 10 | 7 | 6 | | | 8 | 1 | | | 9 | | | | | | 21 |
| | 2 | 3 | | | | | | | | | 4 | | 5 | | | | 10 | 12 | 6 | 11 | | 8 | 1 | 7 | | **9** | | | | | | 22 |
| | 2 | 3 | | | | | | | | | 4 | | 5 | 9 | | | 10 | | 6 | 11 | | 8 | 1 | 7 | | | | | | | | 23 |
| | 2 | 3 | | | | | | | 9 | | 4 | | **5** | | 12 | | 10 | | 6 | 11 | | 8 | 1 | 7 | | | | | | | | 24 |
| | | 3 | | | | | 11 | | | | 4 | | | | 5 | | 10 | 2 | 6 | 12 | | 8 | 1 | **7** | | | 9 | | | | | 25 |
| | | 3 | | | | | | | | | 4 | | 5 | | 7 | | 10 | 2 | 6 | 11 | | 8 | 1 | | | | 9 | | | | | 26 |
| | 2 | 3 | | | | 12 | | | | | 4 | | 5 | | 7 | | 10 | | 6 | 11 | | 8 | 1 | | | | **9** | | | | | 27 |
| | 2 | 3 | | 5 | | 7 | | | | | 8 | | 6 | | | | 10 | | 4 | 12 | | **11** | 1 | | | | 9 | | | | | 28 |
| | 2 | 3 | | | | 5 | | | | | | | 6 | | **4** | | 10 | 7 | | 11 | | 8 | | 12 | | | 9 | 1 | | | | 29 |
| | 2 | 3 | | 5 | | 4 | | | | | | | **6** | | | | 10 | 7 | 12 | 11 | | 8 | | | | | 9 | 1 | | | | 30 |
| | 2 | 3 | | 5 | | | | | | | | | | | 4 | | | 7 | 6 | 11 | | 8 | 1 | | | | 9 | | 10 | | | 31 |
| | 2 | 3 | | 5 | | 12 | | | | | | | | | 4 | | | **7** | 6 | 11 | | 8 | 1 | | | | 9 | | 10 | | | 32 |
| | 2 | 3 | | 5 | | | | | | | | | | | 4 | | | 7 | 6 | 11 | | | 1 | 8 | | | 9 | | 10 | | | 33 |
| | 2 | 3 | | 5 | | 12 | | | | | | | | | 4 | | | **7** | 6 | 11 | | 8 | 1 | | | | 9 | | 10 | | | 34 |
| | 2 | 3 | | 5 | | 12 | | | | | 7 | | | | 4 | | | | 6 | **11** | | 8 | 1 | | | | 9 | | 10 | | | 35 |
| | 2 | 3 | | 5 | | 12 | | | | | **7** | | | | 4 | | | | 6 | 11 | | 8 | 1 | | | | 9 | | 10 | | | 36 |
| | 2 | 3 | | 5 | | 4 | | | | | | | | | | | | 7 | 6 | 11 | | **8** | 1 | 12 | | | 9 | | 10 | | | 37 |
| | 2 | 3 | | 5 | | 4 | | | | | | | | | | | | 7 | 6 | **11** | | | 1 | 8 | | | 9 | | 10 | 12 | | 38 |
| | 2 | 3 | | 5 | | 4 | | | | | | | | | | | | 7 | 6 | 12 | | | 1 | 8 | | | 9 | | **10** | 11 | | 39 |
| | 2 | 3 | | 5 | | 4 | | | | | | | | | 7 | | | | 6 | 12 | | | 1 | 8 | | | 9 | | 10 | **11** | | 40 |
| | 2 | 3 | | 5 | | 4 | | | | | 6 | | | | 7 | | | | | 11 | | 8 | | | | | 9 | 1 | 10 | | | 41 |
| | 2 | 3 | | **5** | | 4 | | | | | 6 | | | | 7 | | | | 8 | | | | | | | | 9 | 1 | 10 | 11 | 12 | 42 |
| | 40 | 42 | 13 | 20 | 5 | 25 | 11 | 4 | 7 | 9 | 20 | 1 | 16 | 16 | 17 | 3 | 22 | 26 | 31 | 20 | | 25 | 25 | 11 | 1 | 2 | 18 | 4 | 12 | 3 | | |
| | | | | | | 6 | | | 4 | | 1 | 4 | | | 1 | 1 | | 1 | 1 | 6 | 1 | | | 3 | | | | | | 1 | 1 | |
| | 1 | | | | | 4 | 1 | | | 3 | 1 | | | 7 | | | 3 | 2 | 3 | 4 | | 3 | | 1 | | | 9 | | 4 | | | |

1 own-goal

| ton J | Langan D | Buckley S | Rioch B | McFarland R | Wicks S | McCaffery A | Moreland V | Caskey W | Greenwood R | Hill G | Daly G | Crawford A | Webb D | Duncan J | Powell S | Carter S | Davies R | Emery S | Osgood K | Emson P | Spooner S | Powell B | McKellar D | Clark J | Bartlett P | Whymark T | Biley A | Cherry S | Swindlehurst D | Wilson K | Richards W | |
|---|---|---|---|---|---|---|---|---|---|---|---|---|---|---|---|---|---|---|---|---|---|---|---|---|---|---|---|---|---|---|---|---|
| | | 3 | | | | | 11 | | 9 | | 4 | | | | 5 | | 10 | 2 | 6 | 12 | | 8 | 1 | **7** | | | | | | | | 3 |
| | | 1 | | | | | 1 | | 1 | | 1 | | | | 1 | | 1 | 1 | 1 | | | 1 | 1 | 1 | | | | | | | | |
| | | | | | | | | | | | | | | | | | | | | 1 | | | | | | | | | | | | |
| | | | | | | | | | | | 1 | | | | | | 1 | | | | | | | | | | | | | | | |

| ton J | Langan D | Buckley S | Rioch B | McFarland R | Wicks S | McCaffery A | Moreland V | Caskey W | Greenwood R | Hill G | Daly G | Crawford A | Webb D | Duncan J | Powell S | Carter S | Davies R | Emery S | Osgood K | Emson P | Spooner S | Powell B | McKellar D | Clark J | Bartlett P | Whymark T | Biley A | Cherry S | Swindlehurst D | Wilson K | Richards W | |
|---|---|---|---|---|---|---|---|---|---|---|---|---|---|---|---|---|---|---|---|---|---|---|---|---|---|---|---|---|---|---|---|---|
| | 2 | 3 | 7 | 5 | | 8 | | | **10** | 11 | 4 | 12 | 6 | 9 | | | | | | | | | | | | | | | | | | 2 |
| | 2 | 3 | | **5** | | 8 | 4 | | | | | 11 | 6 | 9 | | 7 | | | | 12 | | | | 10 | | | | | | | | 2 |
| | 2 | 2 | 1 | 2 | | 2 | 1 | | 1 | 1 | 1 | 1 | 2 | 2 | | 1 | | | | | | | | 1 | | | | | | | | |
| | | | | | | | | | | | | 1 | | | | | | | | 1 | | | | | | | | | | | | |
| | | | | | | | | | | | | 1 | | | | | | | | | | | | | | | | | | | | |

# 1980-81

| | P | W | D | L | F | A | Pts |
|---|---|---|---|---|---|---|---|
| West Ham U | 42 | 28 | 10 | 4 | 79 | 29 | 66 |
| Notts Co | 42 | 18 | 17 | 7 | 49 | 38 | 53 |
| Swansea C | 42 | 18 | 14 | 10 | 64 | 44 | 50 |
| Blackburn R | 42 | 16 | 18 | 8 | 42 | 29 | 50 |
| Luton T | 42 | 18 | 12 | 12 | 61 | 46 | 48 |
| Derby Co | 42 | 15 | 15 | 12 | 57 | 52 | 45 |
| Grimsby T | 42 | 15 | 15 | 12 | 44 | 42 | 45 |
| Q.P.R. | 42 | 15 | 13 | 14 | 56 | 46 | 43 |
| Watford | 42 | 16 | 11 | 15 | 50 | 45 | 43 |
| Sheffield W | 42 | 17 | 8 | 17 | 53 | 51 | 42 |
| Newcastle U | 42 | 14 | 14 | 14 | 30 | 45 | 42 |
| Chelsea | 42 | 14 | 12 | 16 | 46 | 41 | 40 |
| Cambridge U | 42 | 17 | 6 | 19 | 53 | 65 | 40 |
| Shrewsbury T | 42 | 11 | 17 | 14 | 46 | 47 | 39 |
| Oldham A | 42 | 12 | 15 | 15 | 39 | 48 | 39 |
| Wrexham | 42 | 12 | 14 | 16 | 43 | 45 | 38 |
| Orient | 42 | 13 | 12 | 17 | 52 | 56 | 38 |
| Bolton W | 42 | 14 | 10 | 18 | 61 | 66 | 38 |
| Cardiff C | 42 | 12 | 12 | 18 | 44 | 60 | 36 |
| Preston N.E. | 42 | 11 | 14 | 17 | 41 | 62 | 36 |
| Bristol C | 42 | 7 | 16 | 19 | 29 | 51 | 30 |
| Bristol R | 42 | 5 | 13 | 24 | 34 | 65 | 23 |

Manager: Colin Addison.
Leading scorer: David Swindlehurst, League/all matches 11.
League ever-present: Roger Jones.
Player of the season: Roger Jones.

- Roy McFarland became the seventh and, so far, last to complete 500 appearances for the Rams when he played against Sheffield Wednesday on 4 October. McFarland was released at the end of the season and became player-manager of Bradford City.
- Kevin Hector returned to Derby in October and went on to beat Ron Webster's appearances record. When he left in 1982, Hector had played in 589 (581 + 8) games for the Rams.
- Steve Buckley ended a run of 117 consecutive League matches and 127 in all competitions on 8 November.
- Barry Powell spent summer 1981 in the North American Soccer League with Portland Timbers.
- Other players with Derby connections involved in the NASL before it folded in 1984: Terry Adlington, Colin Boulton, Jeff Bourne, Billy Caskey, Mick Coop, Bob Corish, Gerry Daly, Peter Daniel, Roger Davies, Archie Gemmill, Charlie George, Trevor Hebberd, Kevin Hector, Gordon Hill, Alan Hinton, Tony Macken, Don Masson, Gary Mills, Vic Moreland, David Nish, John O'Hare, Donald O'Riordan, Steve Powell, Bruce Rioch, Colin Todd, Dave Watson, Ron Webster, Trevor Whymark.

## Division Two

| Match No. | Date | | Venue | Opponents | Result | | Scorers | Att |
|---|---|---|---|---|---|---|---|---|
| 1 | Aug | 16 | (a) | Cambridge U | L | 0-3 | | |
| 2 | | 20 | (h) | Chelsea | W | 3-2 | B.Powell (pen), Biley, Chivers (og) | 2 |
| 3 | | 23 | (a) | Luton T | W | 2-1 | Swindlehurst, Osgood | 1 |
| 4 | | 30 | (h) | Bolton W | W | 1-0 | Swindlehurst | 1 |
| 5 | Sep | 6 | (h) | Blackburn R | D | 2-2 | Biley 2 | 1 |
| 6 | | 13 | (a) | Grimsby T | W | 1-0 | Swindlehurst | 1 |
| 7 | | 20 | (h) | Wrexham | L | 0-1 | | 1 |
| 8 | | 27 | (a) | Orient | L | 0-1 | | |
| 9 | Oct | 4 | (h) | Sheffield W | W | 3-1 | Biley, Emson, Grant (og) | 1 |
| 10 | | 7 | (a) | Watford | D | 1-1 | Osgood | 1 |
| 11 | | 11 | (a) | Swansea C | L | 1-3 | Osgood (pen) | 1 |
| 12 | | 18 | (h) | Queen's Park R | D | 3-3 | Sheridan 2, Emson | 1 |
| 13 | | 25 | (a) | Bristol C | D | 2-2 | Emson, Wilson | 1 |
| 14 | Nov | 1 | (h) | Shrewsbury T | D | 1-1 | Biley | 1 |
| 15 | | 8 | (a) | Notts C | D | 0-0 | | 1 |
| 16 | | 12 | (a) | Chelsea | W | 3-1 | Clark, Wilson, Reid | 1 |
| 17 | | 15 | (h) | Cambridge U | L | 0-3 | | 1 |
| 18 | | 22 | (a) | Bristol R | D | 1-1 | Emson | |
| 19 | | 26 | (h) | West Ham U | W | 2-0 | Clark, Biley | 1 |
| 20 | | 29 | (h) | Cardiff C | D | 1-1 | Wilson | 1 |
| 21 | Dec | 6 | (a) | Preston NE | W | 3-0 | Biley, Swindlehurst, Hector | |
| 22 | | 13 | (h) | Watford | D | 1-1 | Hector | 1 |
| 23 | | 20 | (a) | West Ham U | L | 1-3 | Swindlehurst (pen) | 2 |
| 24 | | 26 | (h) | Oldham A | W | 4-1 | Biley 2, Swindlehurst 2 | 1 |
| 25 | | 27 | (a) | Newcastle U | W | 2-0 | McFarland, Boam (og) | 2 |
| 26 | Jan | 10 | (h) | Bristol R | W | 2-1 | Biley, Gillies (og) | 1 |
| 27 | | 24 | (a) | Bolton W | L | 1-3 | Wilson | |
| 28 | | 31 | (h) | Luton T | D | 2-2 | Wilson, Hector | 1 |
| 29 | Feb | 7 | (h) | Grimsby T | W | 2-1 | Emery, Swindlehurst | 1 |
| 30 | | 14 | (a) | Blackburn R | L | 0-1 | | 1 |
| 31 | | 21 | (h) | Orient | D | 1-1 | McFarland | 1 |
| 32 | | 28 | (a) | Wrexham | D | 2-2 | Swindlehurst (pen), Sheridan | |
| 33 | Mar | 7 | (a) | Sheffield W | D | 0-0 | | 2 |
| 34 | | 21 | (a) | Queen's Park R | L | 1-3 | B.Powell | |
| 35 | | 28 | (h) | Bristol C | W | 1-0 | Swindlehurst | 1 |
| 36 | | 31 | (h) | Swansea C | L | 0-1 | | 1 |
| 37 | Apr | 4 | (a) | Shrewsbury T | L | 0-1 | | |
| 38 | | 11 | (h) | Notts C | D | 2-2 | Osgood (pen), Wilson | 1 |
| 39 | | 18 | (h) | Newcastle U | W | 2-0 | McFarland, Wilson | 1 |
| 40 | | 20 | (a) | Oldham A | W | 2-0 | Buckley, Clayton | |
| 41 | May | 2 | (a) | Cardiff C | D | 0-0 | | |
| 42 | | 6 | (h) | Preston NE | L | 1-2 | Swindlehurst | 1 |

FINAL LEAGUE POSITION: 6th in Division Two

Appeara
Subst

## FA Cup

| | | | | | | | |
|---|---|---|---|---|---|---|---|
| 3 | Jan | 3 | (h) | Bristol C | D | 0-0 | 1 |
| R | | 7 | (a) | Bristol C | L | 0-2 | 1 |

Appeara
Substi
G

## League Cup

| | | | | | | | |
|---|---|---|---|---|---|---|---|
| 2 | Aug | 26 | (a) | Queen's Park R | D | 0-0 | 1 |
| R | Sep | 3 | (h) | Queen's Park R | D | 0-0 | 1 |

Derby lost 5-3 on penalties after extra-time

Appeara
Substi
G

| Emery S | Buckley S | Powell S | McFarland R | Ramage A | Clark J | Powell B | Biley A | Swindlehurst D | Emson P | Osgood K | Richards W | Wilson K | Skivington G | Hector K | Sheridan F | Reid A | Clayton J | Duncan J | Gibson A | Spooner S | |
|---|---|---|---|---|---|---|---|---|---|---|---|---|---|---|---|---|---|---|---|---|---|
| 2 | 3 | 4 | 5 | 6 | 7 | 8 | 9 | 10 | 11 | | | | | | | | | | | | 1 |
| 2 | 3 | 4 | | 6 | 7 | 8 | 9 | 10 | 11 | 5 | | | | | | | | | | | 2 |
| 2 | 3 | 4 | | 6 | 7 | 8 | 9 | 10 | **11** | 5 | 12 | | | | | | | | | | 3 |
| 2 | 3 | 4 | | 6 | 7 | 8 | 9 | **10** | 11 | 5 | | 12 | | | | | | | | | 4 |
| 2 | 3 | 4 | | 6 | 7 | 8 | 9 | | 11 | 5 | | 10 | | | | | | | | | 5 |
| 2 | 3 | 4 | | 6 | | 8 | 9 | 10 | 11 | 5 | | | 7 | | | | | | | | 6 |
| 2 | 3 | 4 | | 6 | | 8 | 9 | 10 | 11 | 5 | | | 7 | | | | | | | | 7 |
| 2 | 3 | 4 | 5 | 12 | | 8 | 9 | 10 | 11 | 6 | | | **7** | | | | | | | | 8 |
| 2 | 3 | 4 | 5 | | 7 | 8 | 9 | 10 | 11 | 6 | | | | | | | | | | | 9 |
| 2 | 3 | 4 | 5 | **7** | 12 | 8 | 9 | 10 | 11 | 6 | | | | | | | | | | | 10 |
| 2 | 3 | 4 | **5** | | 7 | 8 | | 9 | 11 | 6 | | | 12 | 10 | | | | | | | 11 |
| 2 | 3 | 5 | | | | 8 | | | 11 | 6 | | 9 | 7 | 10 | 4 | | | | | | 12 |
| 2 | 3 | 5 | | | 8 | | 9 | | 11 | 6 | | 12 | **7** | 10 | 4 | | | | | | 13 |
| 2 | 3 | 5 | | | 7 | | 9 | 10 | 11 | 6 | | | | 8 | 4 | | | | | | 14 |
| 2 | 3 | 5 | | | 7 | | 9 | 8 | 11 | 6 | | 10 | 4 | | | | | | | | 15 |
| 2 | | 5 | | 6 | 7 | | 9 | 8 | **11** | 3 | | 10 | 4 | | | 12 | | | | | 16 |
| | | 5 | | 6 | 4 | **7** | 9 | 8 | | 3 | | 10 | 2 | | | 12 | 11 | | | | 17 |
| | | 5 | | 6 | 4 | 7 | 9 | 8 | 11 | 3 | | 10 | 2 | | | | | | | | 18 |
| | | 2 | 5 | 6 | 4 | 7 | 9 | 8 | 11 | | 3 | 10 | | | | | | | | | 19 |
| | | 2 | 5 | 6 | 4 | **7** | 9 | 8 | 11 | 12 | 3 | 10 | | | | | | | | | 20 |
| | | 2 | 5 | 6 | 4 | | 9 | 10 | 11 | | 3 | | | 8 | | 7 | | | | | 21 |
| | | 2 | **5** | 6 | 4 | | 9 | 10 | 11 | | 3 | 12 | | 8 | | 7 | | | | | 22 |
| 2 | | 7 | | 6 | 4 | | 9 | 10 | 11 | 5 | 3 | | | 8 | | | | | | | 23 |
| 2 | | 7 | 5 | 6 | 4 | | 9 | 10 | 11 | | 3 | | | **8** | | 12 | | | | | 24 |
| 2 | | 7 | 5 | 6 | 4 | | 9 | 10 | 11 | | 3 | | | 8 | | | | | | | 25 |
| 2 | 3 | 4 | 5 | 6 | | 8 | 9 | 10 | 11 | | | | | | | 7 | | | | | 26 |
| 2 | 3 | 4 | 5 | | | 7 | 9 | | 11 | 6 | | 10 | | 8 | | | | | | | 27 |
| 2 | 3 | 4 | 5 | | | 7 | 9 | | 11 | 6 | | 10 | | 8 | | | | | | | 28 |
| 2 | 3 | 4 | 5 | | | 7 | 9 | **6** | 11 | 12 | | 10 | | 8 | | | | | | | 29 |
| 2 | 3 | | 5 | 6 | | 7 | 9 | 4 | 11 | 12 | | **10** | | 8 | | | | | | | 30 |
| 2 | 3 | | **5** | 6 | | 7 | 9 | 10 | | 12 | | 11 | | 8 | | 4 | | | | | 31 |
| 2 | 3 | | | 6 | 12 | | | 10 | | 5 | | 9 | | 8 | 4 | 7 | **11** | | | | 32 |
| **2** | 3 | | 5 | 6 | | | | 10 | 12 | | | 9 | | 8 | 4 | 7 | 11 | | | | 33 |
| 2 | 3 | 6 | 5 | | | 7 | | 10 | 12 | | | 9 | | 8 | 4 | | **11** | | | | 34 |
| 2 | 3 | 4 | 5 | | | 6 | | 10 | 11 | | | 7 | | 8 | | | | 9 | | | 35 |
| 2 | 3 | 4 | **5** | | | 6 | | 10 | 11 | | | 7 | | 8 | 12 | | | 9 | | | 36 |
| 2 | 3 | 4 | | | | 6 | | 10 | | | | **9** | | 8 | 5 | 7 | 11 | | 12 | | 37 |
| 2 | 3 | 4 | | | | 6 | | | 11 | 5 | | 10 | | 8 | | 7 | | 9 | | | 38 |
| | 3 | 4 | 5 | | | 6 | | | 11 | 2 | | 10 | | 8 | | 7 | 9 | | | | 39 |
| | 3 | 4 | | | | 6 | | | 11 | 2 | | 10 | | 8 | 5 | 7 | 9 | | | | 40 |
| | 4 | | | | | | | 10 | 11 | 2 | 3 | **9** | | 8 | 5 | 7 | 12 | | | 6 | 41 |
| | 3 | | 5 | | | | | 10 | 11 | 2 | | **9** | | 8 | 4 | 7 | 12 | | | 6 | 42 |
| 32 | 32 | 36 | 23 | 23 | 20 | 29 | 29 | 34 | 36 | 26 | 8 | 24 | 9 | 25 | 10 | 12 | 7 | 3 | | 2 | |
| | | | | 1 | 2 | | | | 2 | 4 | 1 | 3 | 1 | | 1 | 3 | 2 | | 1 | | |
| 1 | 1 | | 3 | | 2 | 2 | 10 | 11 | 4 | 4 | | 7 | | 3 | 3 | 1 | 1 | | | | |

4 own-goals

| | | | | | | | | | | | | | | | | | | | | | |
|---|---|---|---|---|---|---|---|---|---|---|---|---|---|---|---|---|---|---|---|---|---|
| 2 | | 7 | 5 | 6 | **4** | | 9 | 10 | 11 | | 3 | | | 8 | | 12 | | | | | 3 |
| 2 | | 7 | | 6 | 4 | | 9 | 10 | 12 | 5 | 3 | | | 8 | | **11** | | | | | R |
| 2 | | 2 | 1 | 2 | 2 | | 2 | 2 | 1 | 1 | 2 | | | 2 | | 1 | | | | | |
| | | | | | | | | | 1 | | | | | | | 1 | | | | | |
| | | | | | | | | | | | | | | | | | | | | | |

| | | | | | | | | | | | | | | | | | | | | | |
|---|---|---|---|---|---|---|---|---|---|---|---|---|---|---|---|---|---|---|---|---|---|
| **2** | 3 | 4 | | 6 | 7 | 8 | 9 | 10 | 11 | 5 | 12 | | | | | | | | | | 2 |
| 2 | 3 | 4 | | 6 | 7 | 8 | 9 | **10** | 11 | 5 | | 12 | | | | | | | | | R |
| 2 | 2 | 2 | | 2 | 2 | 2 | 2 | 2 | 2 | 2 | | | | | | | | | | | |
| | | | | | | | | | | | 1 | 1 | | | | | | | | | |
| | | | | | | | | | | | | | | | | | | | | | |

# 1981-82

| | P | W | D | L | F | A | Pts |
|---|---|---|---|---|---|---|---|
| Luton T | 42 | 25 | 13 | 4 | 86 | 46 | 88 |
| Watford | 42 | 23 | 11 | 8 | 76 | 42 | 80 |
| Norwich C | 42 | 22 | 5 | 15 | 64 | 50 | 71 |
| Sheffield W | 42 | 20 | 10 | 12 | 55 | 51 | 70 |
| Q.P.R. | 42 | 21 | 6 | 15 | 65 | 43 | 69 |
| Barnsley | 42 | 19 | 10 | 13 | 59 | 41 | 67 |
| Rotherham U | 42 | 20 | 7 | 15 | 66 | 54 | 67 |
| Leicester C | 42 | 18 | 12 | 12 | 56 | 48 | 66 |
| Newcastle U | 42 | 18 | 8 | 16 | 52 | 50 | 62 |
| Blackburn R | 42 | 16 | 11 | 15 | 47 | 43 | 59 |
| Oldham A | 42 | 15 | 14 | 13 | 50 | 51 | 59 |
| Chelsea | 42 | 15 | 12 | 15 | 60 | 60 | 57 |
| Charlton A | 42 | 13 | 12 | 17 | 50 | 65 | 51 |
| Cambridge U | 42 | 13 | 9 | 20 | 48 | 53 | 48 |
| Crystal Palace | 42 | 13 | 9 | 20 | 34 | 45 | 48 |
| Derby Co | 42 | 12 | 12 | 18 | 53 | 68 | 48 |
| Grimsby T | 42 | 11 | 13 | 18 | 53 | 65 | 46 |
| Shrewsbury T | 42 | 11 | 13 | 18 | 37 | 57 | 46 |
| Bolton W | 42 | 13 | 7 | 22 | 39 | 61 | 46 |
| Cardiff C | 42 | 12 | 8 | 22 | 45 | 61 | 44 |
| Wrexham | 42 | 11 | 11 | 20 | 40 | 56 | 44 |
| Orient | 42 | 10 | 9 | 23 | 36 | 61 | 39 |

Manager: Colin Addison until January, then John Newman.
Leading scorer: Kevin Wilson, League/all matches 9.
Player of the season: Steve Buckley.

- Kevin Hector scored his 200th Derby goal in a League Cup tie against West Ham United on 2 October. Only Steve Bloomer (332) has more.
- Colin Addison was dismissed in January and John Newman, who expected to leave at the same time, was persuaded to stay as manager.
- Charlie George, on non-contract terms with AFC Bournemouth, returned to Derby in March and helped to keep Derby clear of relegation.
- Other late signings John McAlle and John Barton were valuable but the club was struggling from the chairman down.

## Division Two

| Match No. | Date | | Venue | Opponents | Result | | Scorers | Att |
|---|---|---|---|---|---|---|---|---|
| 1 | Aug | 29 | (h) | Orient | L | 1-2 | Hector | 1 |
| 2 | Sep | 1 | (a) | Cambridge U | W | 2-1 | Swindlehurst, Emery | |
| 3 | | 5 | (a) | Shrewsbury T | L | 1-4 | Swindlehurst | |
| 4 | | 12 | (h) | Leicester C | W | 3-1 | Ramage, Hector, Buckley | 1 |
| 5 | | 19 | (a) | Sheffield W | D | 1-1 | S.Powell | 2 |
| 6 | | 23 | (h) | Bolton W | L | 0-2 | | 1 |
| 7 | | 26 | (h) | Queen's Park R | W | 3-1 | Hector 2, Ramage | 1 |
| 8 | Oct | 3 | (a) | Charlton A | L | 1-2 | Emson | |
| 9 | | 10 | (a) | Newcastle U | L | 0-3 | | 1 |
| 10 | | 17 | (h) | Blackburn R | D | 1-1 | B.Powell | 1 |
| 11 | | 24 | (a) | Crystal P | W | 1-0 | Swindlehurst | 1 |
| 12 | | 31 | (h) | Grimsby T | D | 1-1 | Clayton | 1 |
| 13 | Nov | 7 | (a) | Luton T | L | 2-3 | Osgood, Clayton | 1 |
| 14 | | 14 | (h) | Wrexham | W | 2-1 | Buckley, Edwards (og) | 1 |
| 15 | | 21 | (a) | Norwich C | L | 1-4 | Osgood | 1 |
| 16 | | 25 | (h) | Cambridge U | W | 2-1 | Swindlehurst, Clayton | |
| 17 | | 28 | (h) | Chelsea | D | 1-1 | Osgood | 1 |
| 18 | Dec | 4 | (a) | Cardiff C | L | 0-1 | | |
| 19 | Jan | 16 | (a) | Orient | L | 2-3 | Hill, Fisher (og) | |
| 20 | | 23 | (h) | Oldham A | W | 1-0 | Swindlehurst | 1 |
| 21 | | 26 | (a) | Watford | L | 1-6 | Emson | 1 |
| 22 | | 30 | (h) | Sheffield W | W | 3-1 | Wilson 2, Sheridan | 1 |
| 23 | Feb | 2 | (a) | Rotherham U | L | 1-2 | Hill | |
| 24 | | 6 | (a) | Leicester C | L | 1-2 | Emson | 14 |
| 25 | | 13 | (h) | Charlton A | D | 1-1 | Sheridan | 1 |
| 26 | | 20 | (a) | Queen's Park R | L | 0-3 | | |
| 27 | | 27 | (h) | Newcastle U | D | 2-2 | Wilson, Emson | 1 |
| 28 | Mar | 6 | (a) | Blackburn R | L | 1-4 | Swindlehurst | |
| 29 | | 10 | (h) | Shrewsbury T | D | 1-1 | Wilson | |
| 30 | | 13 | (h) | Crystal P | W | 4-1 | Wilson 2, Buckley, Skivington | 1 |
| 31 | | 20 | (a) | Grimsby T | L | 0-1 | | 7 |
| 32 | | 27 | (h) | Luton T | D | 0-0 | | 1 |
| 33 | Apr | 3 | (a) | Wrexham | D | 1-1 | Emson | 4 |
| 34 | | 10 | (a) | Barnsley | D | 0-0 | | 1 |
| 35 | | 12 | (h) | Rotherham U | W | 3-1 | Wilson, Buckley, Skivington | 14 |
| 36 | | 17 | (h) | Norwich C | L | 0-2 | | 1 |
| 37 | | 24 | (a) | Chelsea | W | 2-0 | B.Powell, George | 1 |
| 38 | | 28 | (h) | Barnsley | L | 0-1 | | 1 |
| 39 | May | 1 | (h) | Cardiff C | D | 0-0 | | 1 |
| 40 | | 4 | (a) | Bolton W | L | 2-3 | Attley, George | |
| 41 | | 8 | (a) | Oldham A | D | 1-1 | Wilson | 4 |
| 42 | | 15 | (h) | Watford | W | 3-2 | Hector, Wilson, Buckley | 14 |

FINAL LEAGUE POSITION: 16th in Division Two

## FA Cup

| | | | | | | | | |
|---|---|---|---|---|---|---|---|---|
| 3 | Jan | 2 | (a) | Bolton W | L | 1-3 | B.Powell | 9 |

## League Cup

| | | | | | | | | |
|---|---|---|---|---|---|---|---|---|
| 2 | Oct | 7 | (h) | West Ham U | L | 2-3 | Hector, Stewart (og) | 1 |
| 2 | | 27 | (a) | West Ham U | L | 0-2 | | 21 |

| Coop M | Richards W | Powell S | Ramage A | Hector K | Spooner S | Reid A | Wilson K | Swindlehurst D | Emson P | Emery S | Buckley S | Powell B | Cherry S | Osgood K | Gamble F | Sheridan F | Skivington G | Clayton J | Gibson A | Money R | Dalziel I | Hill A | Banovic V | Attley B | Lovatt J | McAlle J | George C | Barton J | |
|---|---|---|---|---|---|---|---|---|---|---|---|---|---|---|---|---|---|---|---|---|---|---|---|---|---|---|---|---|---|
| 2 | 3 | 4 | 5 | 6 | 7 | 8 | **9** | 10 | 11 | 12 | | | | | | | | | | | | | | | | | | | 1 |
| 2 | 3 | 4 | 5 | 9 | 6 | 8 | | 10 | | 7 | 11 | | | | | | | | | | | | | | | | | | 2 |
| 2 | 3 | 4 | 5 | 9 | **6** | 8 | | 10 | 12 | 7 | 11 | | | | | | | | | | | | | | | | | | 3 |
| 2 | | 4 | 5 | 9 | | 8 | | 10 | 11 | 7 | 3 | 6 | | | | | | | | | | | | | | | | | 4 |
| 2 | | 4 | 5 | **9** | | 8 | 12 | 10 | 11 | 7 | 3 | 6 | | | | | | | | | | | | | | | | | 5 |
| 2 | | 4 | 5 | 9 | | 8 | 12 | 10 | **11** | 7 | 3 | 6 | 1 | | | | | | | | | | | | | | | | 6 |
| 2 | | 4 | 5 | 9 | | 8 | | 10 | 11 | | | 6 | 1 | 3 | **7** | 12 | | | | | | | | | | | | | 7 |
| 2 | | 4 | 5 | | 7 | 8 | 9 | **10** | 11 | | 3 | 6 | 1 | | 12 | | | | | | | | | | | | | | 8 |
| 2 | | 4 | **5** | 9 | | | | 10 | 11 | | 3 | 8 | 1 | | | 6 | 7 | 12 | | | | | | | | | | | 9 |
| 2 | | 4 | | | | 8 | | 10 | 11 | 7 | 3 | 6 | | | | 5 | | 9 | | | | | | | | | | | 10 |
| 2 | | 4 | | | | 8 | | 10 | 11 | 7 | 3 | 6 | | | | 5 | | 9 | | | | | | | | | | | 11 |
| 2 | | 4 | | 7 | | 8 | | 10 | **11** | | 3 | 6 | | | | 5 | | 9 | 12 | | | | | | | | | | 12 |
| 2 | | 4 | | 7 | | **8** | 10 | | 11 | | 3 | 6 | | 12 | | 5 | | 9 | | | | | | | | | | | 13 |
| 2 | | 4 | | 8 | | | | 10 | 11 | 7 | 3 | 6 | | 12 | | 5 | | **9** | | | | | | | | | | | 14 |
| 2 | | **4** | | 8 | | | | 10 | 11 | 7 | 3 | 6 | | 12 | | 5 | | 9 | | | | | | | | | | | 15 |
| 12 | 3 | | | 8 | | | | 10 | 11 | **7** | 4 | 6 | | 2 | | 5 | | 9 | | | | | | | | | | | 16 |
| 7 | **3** | | | 8 | | | | 10 | 11 | | 4 | 6 | | 2 | | 5 | 12 | 9 | | | | | | | | | | | 17 |
| 7 | 3 | | | **8** | | | 9 | 10 | 11 | | 4 | 6 | | 2 | | 5 | 12 | | | | | | | | | | | | 18 |
| | 3 | | | 7 | | | | 10 | 11 | 2 | 4 | 8 | | | | | | | | 5 | 6 | 9 | | | | | | | 19 |
| | | | | 7 | | | | 10 | 11 | 2 | 3 | 8 | | | | 5 | | | | 6 | 4 | 9 | | | | | | | 20 |
| | **11** | | | 7 | | | | 10 | 12 | 2 | 3 | 8 | | | | 5 | | | | 6 | 4 | 9 | | | | | | | 21 |
| | | | | 7 | | | 10 | | 11 | 2 | 3 | 8 | | | | 5 | 12 | | | 6 | **4** | 9 | 1 | | | | | | 22 |
| | 12 | | | 7 | | | 10 | | 11 | **2** | 3 | 8 | | | | 5 | 4 | | | 6 | | 9 | 1 | | | | | | 23 |
| | | **4** | | 7 | | | 8 | 10 | 11 | | 3 | | | | | 5 | 6 | 9 | | | | | 1 | 2 | 12 | | | | 24 |
| | | | | 7 | | | 10 | | 11 | | 3 | 8 | | | | 5 | 4 | 9 | | | | | 1 | 2 | | 6 | | | 25 |
| | | | | 7 | | | 10 | | 11 | | 3 | 8 | | | | 5 | 4 | 9 | | | | | 1 | 2 | | 6 | | | 26 |
| | | | | | | | 10 | | 11 | | 3 | 8 | | | | 5 | 4 | 9 | | | | | 1 | 7 | 2 | 6 | | | 27 |
| | | | | 4 | | | | 10 | 11 | | 3 | 8 | | | | | 5 | 9 | | | | | 1 | 7 | 2 | 6 | | | 28 |
| | | | | 7 | | | 9 | 10 | 11 | | 3 | 8 | | | | 5 | 4 | | | | | | 1 | **2** | 12 | 6 | | | 29 |
| | | | | 7 | | | 9 | 10 | 11 | | 3 | 8 | | | | 5 | 4 | | | | | | 1 | 2 | | 6 | | | 30 |
| | | | | 12 | | | 9 | 10 | 11 | | 3 | 8 | | | | 5 | 4 | | | | | | 1 | **2** | | 6 | 7 | | 31 |
| | | | | | | | 9 | 10 | 11 | | 3 | | | | | 5 | 4 | | | | | | 1 | 8 | | 6 | 7 | 2 | 32 |
| | | | | | | | 9 | 10 | 11 | | 3 | | | | | 5 | 4 | | | | | | 1 | 8 | | 6 | 7 | 2 | 33 |
| | | | | 12 | | | **9** | 10 | 11 | | 3 | | | | | 5 | 4 | | | | | | 1 | 8 | | 6 | 7 | 2 | 34 |
| | | | | | | | 9 | 10 | 11 | | 3 | | | | | 5 | 4 | | | | | | 1 | 8 | | 6 | 7 | 2 | 35 |
| | | | | 12 | | | **9** | 10 | 11 | | 3 | | | | | 5 | 4 | | | | | | 1 | 8 | | 6 | 7 | 2 | 36 |
| | | | | | | | | 10 | 11 | | 3 | 7 | | | | 5 | 4 | | | | | | 1 | 8 | | 6 | 9 | 2 | 37 |
| | | | | | | | 12 | 10 | 11 | | 3 | 7 | | | | 5 | **4** | | | | | | 1 | 8 | | 6 | 9 | 2 | 38 |
| | | | | | | | | 10 | 11 | | 3 | 7 | | | | 5 | 4 | | | | | | 1 | 8 | | 6 | 9 | 2 | 39 |
| | | | | | | | 12 | 10 | 11 | | 3 | 7 | | | | 5 | 4 | | | | | | 1 | 8 | | 6 | 9 | **2** | 40 |
| | | | | 12 | | | 9 | 10 | 11 | | 3 | 8 | | | | 5 | 4 | | | | | | 1 | 2 | | 6 | **7** | | 41 |
| | | | | 7 | | | 8 | 10 | 11 | | 3 | | | | | | 5 | | | | | 9 | 1 | 4 | | 6 | | 2 | 42 |
| 17 | 8 | 16 | 9 | 27 | 4 | 12 | 20 | 36 | 39 | 15 | 40 | 32 | 4 | 4 | 1 | 31 | 21 | 13 | | 5 | 4 | 6 | 21 | 19 | 2 | 18 | 11 | 10 | |
| 1 | 1 | | | 4 | | | 4 | | 2 | 1 | | | | 3 | 1 | 1 | 3 | 1 | 1 | | | | | | 2 | | | | |
| | | 1 | 2 | 5 | | | 9 | 6 | 5 | 1 | 5 | 2 | | 3 | | 2 | 2 | 3 | | | | 2 | | 1 | | | 2 | | |

2 own-goals

| Coop M | Richards W | Powell S | Ramage A | Hector K | Spooner S | Reid A | Wilson K | Swindlehurst D | Emson P | Emery S | Buckley S | Powell B | Cherry S | Osgood K | Gamble F | Sheridan F | Skivington G | Clayton J | Gibson A | Money R | Dalziel I | Hill A | Banovic V | Attley B | Lovatt J | McAlle J | George C | Barton J | |
|---|---|---|---|---|---|---|---|---|---|---|---|---|---|---|---|---|---|---|---|---|---|---|---|---|---|---|---|---|---|
| 2 | 3 | 4 | | | | | | 10 | 12 | | 6 | 8 | | | **11** | | | 9 | | 5 | 7 | | | | | | | | 3 |
| 1 | 1 | 1 | | | | | | 1 | | | 1 | 1 | | | 1 | | | 1 | | 1 | 1 | | | | | | | | |
| | | | | | | | | | 1 | | | | | | | | | | | | | | | | | | | | |
| | | | | | | | | | | | | 1 | | | | | | | | | | | | | | | | | |

| Coop M | Richards W | Powell S | Ramage A | Hector K | Spooner S | Reid A | Wilson K | Swindlehurst D | Emson P | Emery S | Buckley S | Powell B | Cherry S | Osgood K | Gamble F | Sheridan F | Skivington G | Clayton J | Gibson A | Money R | Dalziel I | Hill A | Banovic V | Attley B | Lovatt J | McAlle J | George C | Barton J | |
|---|---|---|---|---|---|---|---|---|---|---|---|---|---|---|---|---|---|---|---|---|---|---|---|---|---|---|---|---|---|
| 2 | | 4 | 5 | 9 | | | | 10 | 11 | | 3 | 8 | 1 | **6** | | | 7 | 12 | | | | | | | | | | | 2 |
| 2 | | 4 | | **7** | | 8 | | 10 | 11 | | 3 | 6 | | | | 5 | | 9 | 12 | | | | | | | | | | 2 |
| 2 | | 2 | 1 | 2 | | 1 | | 2 | 2 | | 2 | 2 | 1 | 1 | | 1 | 1 | 1 | | | | | | | | | | | |
| | | | | | | | | | | | | | | | | | | 1 | 1 | | | | | | | | | | |
| | | | | 1 | | | | | | | | | | | | | | | | | | | | | | | | | |

1 own-goal

# 1982-83

| | P | W | D | L | F | A | Pts |
|---|---|---|---|---|---|---|---|
| Q.P.R. | 42 | 26 | 7 | 9 | 77 | 36 | 85 |
| Wolves | 42 | 20 | 15 | 7 | 68 | 44 | 75 |
| Leicester C | 42 | 20 | 10 | 12 | 72 | 44 | 70 |
| Fulham | 42 | 20 | 9 | 13 | 64 | 47 | 69 |
| Newcastle U | 42 | 18 | 13 | 11 | 75 | 53 | 67 |
| Sheffield W | 42 | 16 | 15 | 11 | 60 | 47 | 63 |
| Oldham A | 42 | 14 | 19 | 9 | 64 | 47 | 61 |
| Leeds U | 42 | 13 | 21 | 8 | 51 | 46 | 60 |
| Shrewsbury T | 42 | 15 | 14 | 13 | 48 | 48 | 59 |
| Barnsley | 42 | 14 | 15 | 13 | 57 | 55 | 57 |
| Blackburn R | 42 | 15 | 12 | 15 | 58 | 58 | 57 |
| Cambridge U | 42 | 13 | 12 | 17 | 42 | 60 | 51 |
| Derby Co | 42 | 10 | 19 | 13 | 49 | 58 | 49 |
| Carlisle U | 42 | 12 | 12 | 18 | 68 | 70 | 48 |
| Crystal Palace | 42 | 12 | 12 | 18 | 43 | 52 | 48 |
| Middlesbrough | 42 | 11 | 15 | 16 | 46 | 67 | 48 |
| Charlton A | 42 | 13 | 9 | 20 | 63 | 86 | 48 |
| Chelsea | 42 | 11 | 14 | 17 | 51 | 61 | 47 |
| Grimsby T | 42 | 12 | 11 | 19 | 45 | 70 | 47 |
| Rotherham U | 42 | 10 | 15 | 17 | 45 | 68 | 45 |
| Burnley | 42 | 12 | 8 | 22 | 56 | 66 | 44 |
| Bolton W | 42 | 11 | 11 | 20 | 42 | 61 | 44 |

Manager: John Newman until November, then Peter Taylor.
Leading scorers: Bobby Davison, David Swindlehurst, League 8. David Swindlehurst, all matches 11.
League ever-present: Mick Brolly (41+1).
Player of the season: Steve Cherry.

- The arrival of Mike Watterson as chairman led to a change of management, Peter Taylor coming out of retirement to replace John Newman.
- Derby were in trouble with the League when Taylor appointed Roy McFarland as his assistant. Bradford City complained of an illegal approach and the Rams were fined.
- After losing 11 of their first 24 League matches, Derby laid foundations for survival under Taylor with an unbeaten run of 15 League games, from 22 January to 30 April.
- Taylor brought Archie Gemmill back to Derby to provide leadership but his most important signing was Bobby Davison, £80,000 from Halifax Town.

## Division Two

| Match No. | Date | | Venue | Opponents | Result | | Scorers |
|---|---|---|---|---|---|---|---|
| 1 | Aug | 28 | (h) | Carlisle U | L | 0-3 | |
| 2 | Sep | 4 | (a) | Queen's Park R | L | 1-4 | Gamble |
| 3 | | 8 | (h) | Chelsea | W | 1-0 | Buckley (pen) |
| 4 | | 11 | (h) | Middlesbrough | D | 1-1 | Dalziel (pen) |
| 5 | | 18 | (a) | Leeds U | L | 1-2 | Brolly |
| 6 | | 25 | (h) | Blackburn R | L | 1-2 | Dalziel |
| 7 | Oct | 2 | (a) | Charlton A | D | 1-1 | Gamble |
| 8 | | 9 | (h) | Cambridge U | D | 1-1 | Brolly |
| 9 | | 16 | (a) | Grimsby T | D | 1-1 | Swindlehurst |
| 10 | | 19 | (a) | Barnsley | D | 1-1 | Brolly |
| 11 | | 23 | (h) | Leicester C | L | 0-4 | |
| 12 | | 30 | (a) | Wolves | L | 1-2 | Wilson |
| 13 | Nov | 6 | (a) | Sheffield W | L | 0-2 | |
| 14 | | 13 | (h) | Bolton W | D | 0-0 | |
| 15 | | 20 | (h) | Oldham A | D | 2-2 | Swindlehurst, Dalziel |
| 16 | | 27 | (a) | Burnley | D | 1-1 | Richards |
| 17 | Dec | 4 | (h) | Rotherham U | W | 3-0 | Swindlehurst 2, Dalziel |
| 18 | | 11 | (a) | Fulham | L | 1-2 | Buckley |
| 19 | | 18 | (h) | Crystal P | D | 1-1 | Richards |
| 20 | | 27 | (a) | Newcastle U | L | 0-1 | |
| 21 | | 29 | (h) | Shrewsbury T | l | 2-3 | Davison 2 |
| 22 | Jan | 1 | (a) | Oldham A | D | 2-2 | Swindlehurst, Gemmill (pen) |
| 23 | | 3 | (h) | Queen's Park R | W | 2-0 | Swindlehurst, Mills |
| 24 | | 15 | (a) | Carlisle U | L | 0-3 | |
| 25 | | 22 | (h) | Leeds U | D | 3-3 | Swindlehurst, Davison, Gemmill (pen) |
| 26 | Feb | 5 | (a) | Chelsea | W | 3-1 | Mills, Gemmill (pen), Bumstead (og) |
| 27 | | 26 | (h) | Grimsby T | W | 2-0 | Davison, K.Moore (og) |
| 28 | Mar | 5 | (a) | Leicester C | D | 1-1 | Barton |
| 29 | | 12 | (h) | Wolves | D | 1-1 | Swindlehurst |
| 30 | | 15 | (a) | Cambridge U | D | 0-0 | |
| 31 | | 19 | (h) | Sheffield W | D | 0-0 | |
| 32 | | 26 | (a) | Bolton W | W | 2-0 | Brolly, Wilson |
| 33 | Apr | 2 | (a) | Shrewsbury T | D | 1-1 | Hooks |
| 34 | | 4 | (h) | Newcastle U | W | 2-1 | Hooks, Wilson |
| 35 | | 9 | (a) | Middlesbrough | W | 3-2 | Davison 2, Gemmill (pen) |
| 36 | | 13 | (h) | Charlton A | D | 1-1 | Gemmill |
| 37 | | 16 | (h) | Barnsley | D | 1-1 | Burns |
| 38 | | 23 | (a) | Rotherham U | D | 1-1 | Gemmill (pen) |
| 39 | | 30 | (h) | Burnley | W | 2-0 | Wilson, Davison |
| 40 | May | 2 | (a) | Blackburn R | L | 0-2 | |
| 41 | | 7 | (a) | Crystal P | L | 1-4 | Gilbert (og) |
| 42 | | 14 | (h) | Fulham | W | 1-0 | Davison |

FINAL LEAGUE POSITION: 13th in Division Two

Appeara
Subst

## FA Cup

| | | | | | | | |
|---|---|---|---|---|---|---|---|
| 3 | Jan | 8 | (h) | Nottingham F | W | 2-0 | Gemmill, Hill |
| 4 | | 29 | (h) | Chelsea | W | 2-1 | Wilson 2 |
| 5 | Feb | 19 | (h) | Manchester U | L | 0-1 | |

Appeara
Subst

## League Cup

| | | | | | | | |
|---|---|---|---|---|---|---|---|
| 1 | Aug | 31 | (a) | Halifax T | L | 1-2 | Swindlehurst |
| 1 | Sep | 15 | (h) | Halifax T | W | 5-2* | Buckley 2 (1 pen), Skivington, Hill, Wilson |
| 2 | Oct | 6 | (h) | Hartlepool U | W | 2-0 | Swindlehurst, Watson (og) |
| 2 | | 25 | (a) | Hartlepool U | L | 2-4‡ | Wilson, Brolly |
| 3 | Nov | 9 | (a) | Birmingham C | L | 1-3 | Swindlehurst |

*after extra-time ‡Derby County won on away goals rule.

Appeara
Substi

| Barton J | Attley B | Powell S | Foster G | McAlle J | Brolly M | Skivington G | Wilson K | Swindlehurst D | Reid A | Emson P | Gamble F | Hill A | Buckley S | Dalziel I | Blades P | Mills G | Cherry S | Gemmill A | Richards J | Davison R | Futcher P | Thomas A | Hooks P | Burns K | |
|---|---|---|---|---|---|---|---|---|---|---|---|---|---|---|---|---|---|---|---|---|---|---|---|---|---|
| 2 | 3 | 4 | 5 | 6 | 7 | **8** | 9 | 10 | 11 | 12 | | | | | | | | | | | | | | | 1 |
| 2 | 3 | **4** | 5 | 6 | 7 | 8 | | 10 | 11 | | 9 | 12 | | | | | | | | | | | | | 2 |
| **2** | 8 | | 5 | 6 | 7 | 4 | | 10 | | 12 | | 9 | 3 | 11 | | | | | | | | | | | 3 |
| | 2 | | 5 | 6 | 7 | 4 | | 10 | 8 | 11 | | 9 | | 3 | | | | | | | | | | | 4 |
| 2 | 8 | | **5** | | 7 | 4 | 10 | | | 12 | | 9 | 3 | 11 | 6 | | | | | | | | | | 5 |
| | 2 | 4 | 5 | 6 | 7 | 8 | | **10** | | | 9 | 12 | 3 | 11 | | | | | | | | | | | 6 |
| 2 | 4 | 6 | 5 | | 7 | | | 10 | | 12 | **8** | 9 | 3 | 11 | | | | | | | | | | | 7 |
| 2 | 4 | 6 | 5 | | 7 | | | 10 | | 12 | **8** | 9 | 3 | 11 | | | | | | | | | | | 8 |
| 2 | | 4 | 5 | 6 | 7 | | 9 | 10 | | 11 | | | | 3 | | 8 | | | | | | | | | 9 |
| 2 | | 4 | 5 | 6 | 7 | | 9 | 10 | | 11 | | | 3 | | | 8 | | | | | | | | | 10 |
| 2 | 4 | | 5 | 6 | 7 | | 9 | 10 | | 11 | | | 3 | | | 8 | | | | | | | | | 11 |
| 2 | | 4 | 5 | 6 | 7 | 8 | 9 | | | | | 10 | 3 | 11 | | | 1 | | | | | | | | 12 |
| 2 | | 4 | 5 | | 7 | 6 | 9 | | | | | 10 | 3 | 11 | | 8 | 1 | | | | | | | | 13 |
| 2 | | **4** | 5 | 6 | 7 | 12 | 8 | 10 | | | | 9 | 3 | 11 | | | 1 | | | | | | | | 14 |
| 2 | 4 | | 5 | 6 | 7 | | | 10 | | | | | 3 | 11 | | | 1 | 8 | 9 | | | | | | 15 |
| 2 | 4 | | 5 | | 7 | | | 10 | | | | | 3 | 11 | 6 | | 1 | 8 | 9 | | | | | | 16 |
| 2 | 4 | | 5 | | 7 | | | 10 | | | | | 3 | 11 | 6 | | 1 | 8 | **9** | 12 | | | | | 17 |
| 2 | 4 | | 5 | | 7 | | | 10 | | | | | 3 | 11 | 6 | | 1 | 8 | **9** | 12 | | | | | 18 |
| 2 | **4** | | 5 | | 7 | | | 10 | | | | | 3 | 11 | 6 | | 1 | 8 | 9 | 12 | | | | | 19 |
| **2** | 3 | | 5 | 4 | 12 | | | 10 | | | | | | 11 | | 6 | 1 | 8 | 9 | 7 | | | | | 20 |
| 12 | 3 | | 5 | 6 | 7 | | | 10 | | | | | | **11** | | 2 | 1 | 4 | 9 | 8 | | | | | 21 |
| 2 | 3 | | 5 | 6 | 7 | | | 10 | | | | | | | | 11 | 1 | 4 | 9 | 8 | | | | | 22 |
| 2 | 3 | | 5 | 6 | 7 | | | 10 | | | | | | | | 11 | 1 | 4 | 9 | 8 | | | | | 23 |
| 2 | 3 | | 5 | 4 | 7 | 12 | | 10 | | | | | | | **6** | 11 | 1 | | 9 | 8 | | | | | 24 |
| 2 | | | 5 | 6 | 7 | 12 | 9 | 10 | | | | | 3 | | | 11 | 1 | **4** | | 8 | | | | | 25 |
| 2 | 3 | 5 | | | 7 | | 9 | 10 | | | | | | | | 11 | 1 | 4 | | 8 | 6 | | | | 26 |
| 2 | | 5 | | | 7 | | 9 | 10 | | | | | 3 | | | 11 | 1 | 4 | | 8 | 6 | | | | 27 |
| 2 | | 5 | | | 7 | | | 10 | | | | 9 | 3 | | | 11 | 1 | 4 | | 8 | 6 | | | | 28 |
| 2 | | 5 | | | 7 | | | 10 | | | | 9 | 3 | | | 11 | 1 | 4 | | 8 | 6 | | | | 29 |
| 2 | | | 5 | | 7 | | | 10 | | | | 9 | 3 | | | 11 | 1 | 4 | | 8 | 6 | | | | 30 |
| 2 | | 4 | 5 | | 7 | | | 10 | | 11 | | | 3 | | | | 1 | 8 | | **9** | 6 | 12 | | | 31 |
| 2 | | 5 | | | 7 | | 9 | | | | | | 3 | | | 11 | 1 | 4 | | 8 | 6 | | 10 | | 32 |
| 2 | | 5 | | | 7 | | 9 | | | | | | 3 | | | 11 | 1 | 4 | | 8 | 6 | | 10 | | 33 |
| 2 | | **5** | | | 7 | | 9 | | | | | | 3 | | | 11 | 1 | 4 | | 8 | 6 | | 10 | 12 | 34 |
| 2 | | 5 | | 12 | 7 | | 9 | | | | | | 3 | | | | 1 | 4 | | 8 | 6 | | **10** | 11 | 35 |
| 2 | | 5 | | 12 | 7 | | 9 | | | 11 | | | **3** | | | | 1 | 4 | | 8 | 6 | | | 10 | 36 |
| 2 | | 5 | | | 7 | | 9 | | | 11 | | | | | | | 1 | 4 | | 8 | 6 | | 10 | 3 | 37 |
| 2 | | 5 | | 12 | 7 | | 9 | | | | | | | **11** | | | 1 | 4 | | 8 | 6 | | 10 | 3 | 38 |
| 2 | | **5** | | 12 | 7 | | 9 | | | 11 | | | | | | | 1 | 4 | | 8 | 6 | | 10 | 3 | 39 |
| 2 | 3 | | 5 | 4 | 7 | | 9 | | | 11 | | 10 | | | | | 1 | | | 8 | 6 | | | | 40 |
| 2 | 3 | | 5 | 4 | 7 | 10 | 9 | | | **11** | | 12 | | | | | 1 | | | 8 | 6 | | | | 41 |
| 2 | | | 5 | 12 | 7 | | 9 | | | 11 | | | | | | | 1 | **4** | | 8 | 6 | | 10 | 3 | 42 |
| 39 | 22 | 23 | 30 | 19 | 41 | 9 | 22 | 28 | 3 | 11 | 4 | 12 | 26 | 18 | 6 | 18 | 31 | 25 | 10 | 23 | 17 | | 8 | 6 | |
| 1 | | | | 5 | 1 | 3 | | | | 5 | | 3 | | | | | | | | 3 | | 1 | | 1 | |
| 1 | | | | | 4 | | 4 | 8 | | | 2 | | 2 | 4 | | 2 | | 6 | 2 | 8 | | | 2 | 1 | |

3 own-goals

| Barton J | Attley B | Powell S | Foster G | McAlle J | Brolly M | Skivington G | Wilson K | Swindlehurst D | Reid A | Emson P | Gamble F | Hill A | Buckley S | Dalziel I | Blades P | Mills G | Cherry S | Gemmill A | |
|---|---|---|---|---|---|---|---|---|---|---|---|---|---|---|---|---|---|---|---|
| 2 | 3 | | 5 | 6 | 7 | | 8 | 10 | | | | 9 | | 12 | | 11 | 1 | **4** | 3 |
| 2 | 3 | 4 | 5 | 6 | 7 | | 8 | 10 | | | | 9 | | | | 11 | 1 | | 4 |
| 2 | | 6 | 5 | 12 | 7 | | **8** | 10 | | | | 9 | 3 | | | 11 | 1 | 4 | 5 |
| 3 | 2 | 2 | 3 | 2 | 3 | | 3 | 3 | | | | 3 | 1 | | | 3 | 3 | 2 | |
| | | | | 1 | | | | | | | | | | 1 | | | | | |
| | | | | | | | 2 | | | | | 1 | | | | | | 1 | |

| Barton J | Attley B | Powell S | Foster G | McAlle J | Brolly M | Skivington G | Wilson K | Swindlehurst D | Reid A | Emson P | Gamble F | Hill A | Buckley S | Dalziel I | Blades P | Mills G | Cherry S | |
|---|---|---|---|---|---|---|---|---|---|---|---|---|---|---|---|---|---|---|
| 2 | 3 | 4 | 5 | 6 | 7 | 8 | **9** | 10 | 11 | 12 | | | | | | | | 1 |
| 2 | 8 | | 5 | 6 | 7 | 4 | 12 | 10 | | | | 9 | 3 | **11** | | | | 1 |
| 2 | 4 | 6 | 5 | | 7 | | | 10 | | 12 | 8 | **9** | 3 | 11 | | | | 2 |
| 2 | | | 5 | 6 | 7 | 11 | 9 | 10 | | | | | 3 | 12 | 4 | **8** | 1 | 2 |
| 2 | | 4 | 5 | 6 | 7 | | 12 | 10 | | | | 9 | 3 | 11 | | **8** | 1 | 3 |
| 5 | 3 | 3 | 5 | 4 | 5 | 3 | 2 | 5 | 1 | | 1 | 3 | 4 | 3 | 1 | 2 | 2 | |
| | | | | | | | 2 | | | 2 | | | | 1 | | | | |
| | | | | | 1 | 1 | 2 | 3 | | | | 1 | 2 | | | | | |

1 own-goal

# 1983-84

| | P | W | D | L | F | A | Pts |
|---|---|---|---|---|---|---|---|
| Chelsea | 42 | 25 | 13 | 4 | 90 | 40 | 88 |
| Sheffield W | 42 | 26 | 10 | 6 | 72 | 34 | 88 |
| Newcastle U | 42 | 24 | 8 | 10 | 85 | 53 | 80 |
| Manchester C | 42 | 20 | 10 | 12 | 66 | 48 | 70 |
| Grimsby T | 42 | 19 | 13 | 10 | 60 | 47 | 70 |
| Blackburn R | 42 | 17 | 16 | 9 | 57 | 46 | 67 |
| Carlisle U | 42 | 16 | 16 | 10 | 48 | 41 | 64 |
| Shrewsbury T | 42 | 17 | 10 | 15 | 49 | 53 | 61 |
| Brighton & H.A. | 42 | 17 | 9 | 16 | 69 | 60 | 60 |
| Leeds U | 42 | 16 | 12 | 14 | 55 | 56 | 60 |
| Huddersfield T | 42 | 14 | 15 | 13 | 56 | 49 | 57 |
| Fulham | 42 | 15 | 12 | 15 | 60 | 53 | 57 |
| Charlton A | 42 | 16 | 9 | 17 | 53 | 64 | 57 |
| Barnsley | 42 | 15 | 7 | 20 | 57 | 53 | 52 |
| Cardiff C | 42 | 15 | 6 | 21 | 53 | 66 | 51 |
| Portsmouth | 42 | 14 | 7 | 21 | 73 | 64 | 49 |
| Middlesbrough | 42 | 12 | 13 | 17 | 41 | 47 | 49 |
| Crystal Palace | 42 | 12 | 11 | 19 | 42 | 52 | 47 |
| Oldham A | 42 | 13 | 8 | 21 | 47 | 73 | 47 |
| Derby Co | 42 | 11 | 9 | 22 | 36 | 72 | 42 |
| Swansea C | 42 | 7 | 8 | 27 | 36 | 85 | 29 |
| Cambridge U | 42 | 4 | 12 | 26 | 28 | 77 | 24 |

Manager: Peter Taylor until April, then Roy McFarland.
Leading scorer: Bobby Davison, League 14, all matches 18.
Player of the season: Archie Gemmill.

- Derby were in financial trouble for much of the season. Inland Revenue and Customs and Excise instigated winding-up petitions in the High Court. Stuart Webb took over the running of the club and, with help from Robert Maxwell, the petitions were lifted in April.
- Although Derby reached the FA Cup sixth round, the season was a disaster and Peter Taylor left as soon as the Rams were clear of the High Court. Roy McFarland took over for the last nine matches.
- Nine years after winning the Cup, Derby were in Division Three North. The cycle was repeated as they again headed for Division Three nine years after the second Championship.

## Division Two

| Match No. | Date | Venue | Opponents | Result | | Scorers | Att |
|---|---|---|---|---|---|---|---|
| 1 | Aug 27 | (a) | Chelsea | L | 0-5 | | 1 |
| 2 | 29 | (h) | Sheffield W | D | 1-1 | Davison | 1 |
| 3 | Sep 3 | (h) | Swansea C | W | 2-1 | Davison, Campbell | |
| 4 | 6 | (a) | Brighton & HA | L | 0-1 | | 1 |
| 5 | 10 | (a) | Blackburn R | L | 1-5 | Campbell | |
| 6 | 17 | (h) | Oldham A | D | 2-2 | Campbell 2 | 1 |
| 7 | 24 | (a) | Charlton A | L | 0-1 | | |
| 8 | Oct 1 | (h) | Carlisle U | L | 1-4 | Davison | 1 |
| 9 | 8 | (h) | Barnsley | L | 0-2 | | 1 |
| 10 | 15 | (a) | Crystal P | W | 1-0 | Robertson | |
| 11 | 22 | (a) | Huddersfield T | L | 0-3 | | 1 |
| 12 | 29 | (h) | Grimsby T | L | 1-2 | Davison | 1 |
| 13 | Nov 5 | (a) | Cambridge U | W | 1-0 | Davison | |
| 14 | 12 | (h) | Middlesbrough | W | 1-0 | Davison | 1 |
| 15 | 19 | (h) | Leeds U | D | 1-1 | Davison | 1 |
| 16 | 26 | (a) | Manchester C | D | 1-1 | Plummer | 2 |
| 17 | Dec 3 | (h) | Newcastle U | W | 3-2 | Davison 2, Gemmill (pen) | 1 |
| 18 | 10 | (a) | Portsmouth | L | 0-3 | | 1 |
| 19 | 17 | (h) | Shrewsbury T | W | 1-0 | Plummer | 1 |
| 20 | 26 | (a) | Fulham | D | 2-2 | Wilson 2 | |
| 21 | 27 | (h) | Cardiff C | L | 2-3 | McAlle, Hooks | 1 |
| 22 | 31 | (a) | Swansea C | L | 0-2 | | |
| 23 | Jan 2 | (h) | Charlton A | L | 0-1 | | 1 |
| 24 | 14 | (h) | Chelsea | L | 1-2 | Plummer | 1 |
| 25 | 21 | (a) | Oldham A | L | 0-3 | | |
| 26 | Feb 4 | (a) | Carlisle U | L | 1-2 | Powell | |
| 27 | 11 | (h) | Blackburn R | D | 1-1 | Gemmill (pen) | 1 |
| 28 | 21 | (a) | Grimsby T | L | 1-2 | Garner | 8 |
| 29 | 25 | (h) | Huddersfield T | D | 1-1 | Robertson (pen) | 1 |
| 30 | Mar 3 | (h) | Cambridge U | W | 1-0 | Davison | 12 |
| 31 | 17 | (h) | Brighton & HA | L | 0-3 | | 1 |
| 32 | 20 | (a) | Middlesbrough | D | 0-0 | | 5 |
| 33 | 31 | (a) | Barnsley | L | 1-5 | Davison | |
| 34 | Apr 7 | (h) | Crystal P | W | 3-0 | Garner 3 | 10 |
| 35 | 10 | (a) | Sheffield W | L | 1-3 | Davison | 22 |
| 36 | 14 | (a) | Leeds U | D | 0-0 | | 12 |
| 37 | 21 | (h) | Fulham | W | 1-0 | Garner | 1 |
| 38 | 23 | (a) | Cardiff C | L | 0-1 | | 5 |
| 39 | 28 | (h) | Manchester C | W | 1-0 | Watson | 14 |
| 40 | May 5 | (a) | Newcastle U | L | 0-4 | | 35 |
| 41 | 9 | (h) | Portsmouth | W | 2-0 | Davison 2 | 1 |
| 42 | 12 | (a) | Shrewsbury T | L | 0-3 | | 5 |

FINAL LEAGUE POSITION: 20th in Division Two – Relegated

Appeara
Substi

## FA Cup

| | | | | | | | |
|---|---|---|---|---|---|---|---|
| 3 | Jan 7 | (a) | Cambridge U | W | 3-0 | Wilson, Plummer, McAlle | |
| 4 | Feb 1 | (h) | Telford U | W | 3-2 | Davison 3 | 2 |
| 5 | 18 | (h) | Norwich C | W | 2-1 | Gemmill (pen), Davison | 25 |
| 6 | Mar 10 | (a) | Plymouth A | D | 0-0 | | 34 |
| R | 14 | (h) | Plymouth A | L | 0-1 | | 26 |

Appeara
Subst

## League Cup

| | | | | | | | |
|---|---|---|---|---|---|---|---|
| 2 | Oct 5 | (h) | Birmingham C | L | 0-3 | | 1 |
| 2 | 25 | (a) | Birmingham C | L | 0-4 | | 7 |

Appeara
Substi

| | Barton J | Buckley S | Gemmill A | Powell S | Futcher P | Plummer C | Davison R | Campbell R | Hooks P | Robertson J | Attley B | McAlle J | O'Brien R | McFarland R | Hill A | Pratley R | Harbey G | Watson D | Wilson K | Blades P | Deacy E | Lane S | Findlay J | Garner A | Burns K | Banovic V | Devine S | |
|---|---|---|---|---|---|---|---|---|---|---|---|---|---|---|---|---|---|---|---|---|---|---|---|---|---|---|---|---|
| | 2 | **3** | 4 | 5 | 6 | 7 | 8 | 9 | 10 | 11 | 12 | | | | | | | | | | | | | | | | | 1 |
| | 2 | | 4 | **5** | 6 | 7 | 8 | 9 | 10 | 11 | 3 | 12 | | | | | | | | | | | | | | | | 2 |
| | 2 | | 4 | | 6 | 7 | 8 | 9 | 10 | 11 | | | 3 | 5 | | | | | | | | | | | | | | 3 |
| | 2 | | 4 | | 6 | 7 | | 9 | 10 | 11 | | 12 | 3 | **5** | 8 | | | | | | | | | | | | | 4 |
| | 2 | | 4 | | 6 | 8 | | 9 | 10 | 11 | 2 | 5 | 3 | | | | | | | | | | | | | | | 5 |
| | 2 | | 4 | | 6 | 7 | 8 | 9 | 10 | 11 | | | 3 | | | 5 | | | | | | | | | | | | 6 |
| | 2 | | 4 | 7 | 6 | | **8** | 9 | 10 | 11 | | | | 12 | | | 3 | 5 | | | | | | | | | | 7 |
| | **2** | | 4 | 7 | 6 | 12 | 8 | 9 | 10 | 11 | | | | | | | 3 | 5 | | | | | | | | | | 8 |
| | | | 4 | 10 | | 7 | 8 | | | 11 | | | | 6 | | | 3 | 5 | 9 | 2 | | | | | | | | 9 |
| | | | 4 | 2 | 6 | 7 | 8 | 9 | | 11 | | | | | | | 3 | 5 | 10 | | | | | | | | | 10 |
| | | | 4 | 2 | 6 | 7 | 8 | 9 | | 11 | | | | | | | 3 | 5 | 10 | | | | | | | | | 11 |
| | | | | 4 | 6 | 7 | 8 | 9 | 10 | 11 | | | | | | | 3 | 5 | 12 | | **2** | | | | | | | 12 |
| | | 3 | 4 | 6 | | | 8 | | 10 | 11 | 7 | | | | | | | 5 | 9 | | 2 | | | | | | | 13 |
| | | 3 | 4 | 6 | | 10 | 8 | | | **11** | 7 | | | 12 | | | | 5 | 9 | | 2 | | | | | | | 14 |
| | | 3 | 4 | | 6 | 10 | 8 | | | | 7 | | | 12 | | | | 5 | 9 | | 2 | **11** | | | | | | 15 |
| | | 3 | 4 | 6 | | 10 | 8 | | | | | 7 | | 12 | | | **11** | 5 | 9 | | 2 | | | | | | | 16 |
| | | 3 | 4 | 6 | | 10 | 8 | | | | 2 | 7 | | | | | 11 | 5 | 9 | | | | | | | | | 17 |
| | | 3 | 4 | 6 | | 10 | 8 | | | | 2 | 7 | | 12 | | | **11** | 5 | 9 | | | | | | | | | 18 |
| | | 3 | 4 | 6 | | 10 | 8 | | 11 | | 2 | 7 | | | | | | 5 | 9 | | | | | | | | | 19 |
| | | 3 | 4 | 6 | | 10 | 8 | | 11 | | 2 | 7 | | | | | | 5 | 9 | | | | | | | | | 20 |
| | | 3 | 4 | 6 | | 10 | 8 | | 11 | | 2 | 7 | | | | | | 5 | 9 | | | | | | | | | 21 |
| | | 3 | 4 | 6 | | 10 | 8 | | 11 | | 2 | 7 | | | | | | 5 | 9 | | | | | | | | | 22 |
| | 2 | 3 | 4 | 6 | | 10 | 8 | | 11 | | | 7 | | | | | | 5 | 9 | | | | 1 | | | | | 23 |
| | 2 | 3 | 4 | 6 | | 10 | 8 | | 11 | | | 7 | | | | | | 5 | 9 | | | | | | | | | 24 |
| | 2 | 3 | 4 | 6 | 7 | 10 | 8 | | | 11 | | | | | | | | 5 | 9 | | | | | | | | | 25 |
| | 2 | 3 | 4 | 6 | 7 | 12 | 8 | | | 11 | | | | | | | **10** | 5 | 9 | | | | | | | | | 26 |
| | 2 | 3 | 4 | 6 | 7 | | 8 | | 10 | 11 | | | | | | | | 5 | 9 | | | | | | | | | 27 |
| | 2 | 3 | 4 | **6** | 7 | 12 | 8 | | | 11 | | | | | | | | 5 | 9 | | | | | 10 | | | | 28 |
| | 2 | 3 | 4 | | 7 | | 8 | | | 11 | | 6 | | | | | | | 9 | | | | | 10 | 5 | | | 29 |
| | 2 | 3 | 4 | 6 | 7 | 12 | 8 | | | 11 | | | | | | | | | 9 | | | | | **10** | 5 | | | 30 |
| | 2 | 3 | | 4 | | 7 | 8 | | | | | 11 | | | | | | 5 | 9 | | | | | 10 | 6 | 1 | | 31 |
| | 2 | 3 | | 4 | | | 8 | | | 11 | 7 | 10 | | | | | | 5 | 9 | | | | | | 6 | 1 | | 32 |
| | 2 | 3 | | 4 | | | 8 | | | 11 | 7 | **10** | | | | | | 5 | 9 | | | | | | 6 | 1 | 12 | 33 |
| | | 3 | 4 | 6 | | | 8 | | | 11 | | | | | | | **10** | 5 | 12 | | | | | 9 | 2 | | 7 | 34 |
| | | 3 | 4 | 6 | | | 8 | | | 11 | | | | | | | 10 | 5 | | | | | | 9 | 2 | | 7 | 35 |
| | | 3 | 4 | 6 | | | 8 | | | **11** | | | | | | | 10 | 5 | 12 | 2 | | | | 9 | | | 7 | 36 |
| | | 3 | 4 | 6 | | | 8 | | | 11 | | | | | | | 10 | 5 | 12 | 2 | | | | **9** | | | 7 | 37 |
| | | 3 | 4 | 6 | | | 8 | | | 11 | | | | | | 12 | 10 | 5 | | **2** | | | | 9 | | | 7 | 38 |
| | | 3 | 4 | 6 | | | 8 | | | 11 | | | | | | | 10 | 5 | 12 | | | | | **9** | 2 | | 7 | 39 |
| | | 3 | 4 | 6 | | | 8 | | | 11 | | | | | | | 10 | 5 | 12 | | | | | **9** | 2 | | 7 | 40 |
| | | 3 | 4 | 6 | | | 8 | | | 11 | | | | | | | 10 | 5 | 12 | | | | | 9 | 2 | | **7** | 41 |
| | | 3 | 4 | 6 | | | 8 | | | 11 | | | | | | | 10 | 5 | 12 | | | | | **9** | 2 | | 7 | 42 |
| | 19 | 31 | 38 | 36 | 18 | 23 | 40 | 11 | 17 | 31 | 13 | 14 | 4 | 3 | 1 | 1 | 19 | 34 | 24 | 4 | 5 | 1 | 1 | 13 | 11 | 3 | 9 | |
| | | | | | | 4 | | | | | 1 | 2 | | 5 | | 1 | | | 8 | | | | | | | | 1 | |
| | | | 2 | 1 | | 3 | 14 | 4 | 1 | 2 | | 1 | | | | | | 1 | 2 | | | | | 5 | | | | |

| | Barton J | Buckley S | Gemmill A | Powell S | Futcher P | Plummer C | Davison R | Campbell R | Hooks P | Robertson J | Attley B | McAlle J | O'Brien R | McFarland R | Hill A | Pratley R | Harbey G | Watson D | Wilson K | Blades P | Deacy E | Lane S | Findlay J | Garner A | Burns K | Banovic V | Devine S | |
|---|---|---|---|---|---|---|---|---|---|---|---|---|---|---|---|---|---|---|---|---|---|---|---|---|---|---|---|
| 2 | 3 | 4 | 6 | | 10 | 8 | | 11 | | | 7 | | | | | | 5 | 9 | | | | | | | | | 3 |
| 2 | 3 | 4 | 6 | 7 | 10 | 8 | | | 11 | | | | | | | | 5 | 9 | | | | | | | | | 4 |
| 2 | 3 | 4 | 6 | 7 | 12 | 8 | | | 11 | | | | | | | | 5 | 9 | | | | | **10** | | | | 5 |
| 2 | 3 | 4 | 6 | 7 | | 8 | | **10** | 11 | | | | | | | | 12 | 9 | | | | | | 5 | | | 6 |
| 2 | 3 | 4 | 6 | 7 | 10 | **8** | | | 11 | | | | | | | | 12 | 9 | | | | | | 5 | | | R |
| 5 | 5 | 5 | 5 | 4 | 3 | 5 | | 2 | 4 | | 1 | | | | | | 3 | 5 | | | | | 1 | 2 | | | |
| | | | | | 1 | | | | | | | | | | | | 2 | | | | | | | | | | |
| | | 1 | | | 1 | 4 | | | | | 1 | | | | | | | 1 | | | | | | | | | |

| Barton J | Buckley S | Gemmill A | Powell S | Futcher P | Plummer C | Davison R | Campbell R | Hooks P | Robertson J | Attley B | McAlle J | O'Brien R | McFarland R | Hill A | Pratley R | Harbey G | Watson D | Wilson K | Blades P | Deacy E | Lane S | Findlay J | Garner A | Burns K | Banovic V | Devine S | |
|---|---|---|---|---|---|---|---|---|---|---|---|---|---|---|---|---|---|---|---|---|---|---|---|---|---|---|---|
| | | 4 | 6 | | 7 | 8 | | 10 | 11 | 2 | | | | | | 3 | 5 | 9 | | | | | | | | | 2 |
| | | | | 6 | 7 | 8 | 9 | 2 | 11 | | | | 4 | | | 3 | 5 | 10 | | | | | | | | | 2 |
| | | 1 | 1 | 1 | 2 | 2 | 1 | 2 | 2 | 1 | | | 1 | | | 2 | 2 | 2 | | | | | | | | | |

# 1984-85

| | P | W | D | L | F | A | Pts |
|---|---|---|---|---|---|---|---|
| Bradford C* | 46 | 28 | 10 | 8 | 77 | 45 | 94 |
| Millwall | 46 | 26 | 12 | 8 | 73 | 42 | 90 |
| Hull C | 46 | 25 | 12 | 9 | 78 | 49 | 87 |
| Gillingham | 46 | 25 | 8 | 13 | 80 | 62 | 83 |
| Bristol C | 46 | 24 | 9 | 13 | 74 | 47 | 81 |
| Bristol R | 46 | 21 | 12 | 13 | 66 | 48 | 75 |
| Derby Co | 46 | 19 | 13 | 14 | 65 | 54 | 70 |
| York C | 46 | 20 | 9 | 17 | 70 | 57 | 69 |
| Reading | 46 | 19 | 12 | 15 | 68 | 62 | 69 |
| Bournemouth | 46 | 19 | 11 | 16 | 57 | 46 | 68 |
| Walsall | 46 | 18 | 13 | 15 | 58 | 52 | 67 |
| Rotherham U | 46 | 18 | 11 | 17 | 55 | 55 | 65 |
| Brentford | 46 | 16 | 14 | 16 | 62 | 64 | 62 |
| Doncaster R | 46 | 17 | 8 | 21 | 72 | 74 | 59 |
| Plymouth A | 46 | 15 | 14 | 17 | 62 | 65 | 59 |
| Wigan A | 46 | 15 | 14 | 17 | 60 | 64 | 59 |
| Bolton W | 46 | 16 | 6 | 24 | 69 | 75 | 54 |
| Newport Co | 46 | 13 | 13 | 20 | 55 | 67 | 52 |
| Lincoln C* | 46 | 11 | 18 | 17 | 50 | 51 | 51 |
| Swansea C | 46 | 12 | 11 | 23 | 53 | 80 | 47 |
| Burnley | 46 | 11 | 13 | 22 | 60 | 73 | 46 |
| Orient | 46 | 11 | 13 | 22 | 51 | 76 | 46 |
| Preston N.E. | 46 | 13 | 7 | 26 | 51 | 100 | 46 |
| Cambridge U | 46 | 4 | 9 | 33 | 37 | 95 | 21 |

*Includes one match abandoned at 0-0 after 40 minutes. Result stands.

Manager: Arthur Cox.
Leading scorer: Bobby Davison, League 24, all matches 26.
League ever-present: Steve Buckley, Bobby Davison.
Player of the season: Bobby Davison.

- Arthur Cox steered Newcastle United back to the First Division but left over a contractual dispute to take over at Derby, their ninth manager in under 11 years. Roy McFarland stayed as his assistant.
- Derby's Centenary Year. Robert Maxwell now owned the club but, as he also owned Oxford United, one of his sons, Ian, was installed as chairman.
- Kevin Wilson, who scored only twice in 1983–84, hit four goals against Hartlepool United in the League Cup. He also scored seven in the first 10 League games before suffering a broken arm.
- When he recovered, he moved to Ipswich Town for £150,000 in January and went on to win 42 caps for Northern Ireland. The money raised from Wilson's transfer helped to fund three important signings, Trevor Christie, Gary Micklewhite and Geraint Williams.
- Bobby Davison was the first Derby forward to pass 20 League goals in a season since Kevin Hector in 1967–68.

## Division Three

| Match No. | Date | Venue | Opponents | Result | | Scorers | Att |
|---|---|---|---|---|---|---|---|
| 1 | Aug 25 | (a) | Bournemouth | L | 0-1 | | |
| 2 | Sep 1 | (h) | Bolton W | W | 3-2 | Wilson 3 | 1 |
| 3 | 8 | (a) | Preston NE | L | 1-2 | Wilson | |
| 4 | 15 | (h) | Burnley | D | 2-2 | Taylor, Davison | 1 |
| 5 | 19 | (h) | Bristol C | W | 1-0 | Wilson | 1 |
| 6 | 22 | (a) | Reading | D | 0-0 | | |
| 7 | 29 | (h) | Lincoln C | W | 2-0 | Wilson, Burns | 1, |
| 8 | Oct 2 | (a) | Millwall | L | 1-2 | Wilson | |
| 9 | 6 | (a) | Bristol R | L | 1-2 | Davison | |
| 10 | 13 | (h) | Plymouth A | W | 3-1 | Davison 2, Buckley (pen) | 1 |
| 11 | 20 | (h) | Hull C | W | 3-1 | Davison, Biggins, Taylor | 1 |
| 12 | 23 | (a) | Walsall | D | 0-0 | | |
| 13 | 27 | (a) | Rotherham U | L | 0-2 | | |
| 14 | Nov 7 | (h) | Brentford | W | 1-0 | Davison | 1 |
| 15 | 10 | (a) | Bradford C | L | 1-3 | Palmer | |
| 16 | 24 | (h) | Wigan A | D | 2-2 | Davison 2 | 1 |
| 17 | 28 | (h) | Doncaster R | W | 3-1 | Davison 3 | 1 |
| 18 | Dec 1 | (a) | Cambridge U | W | 2-0 | Powell, Davison | |
| 19 | 15 | (h) | Orient | W | 1-0 | Garner | 1 |
| 20 | 22 | (h) | Newport C | D | 3-3 | Garner, Davison, Robertson | 1 |
| 21 | 26 | (a) | Gillingham | L | 2-3 | Buckley, Davison | |
| 22 | 29 | (a) | Swansea C | W | 5-1 | Davison, Wilson, Buckley, Garner, Palmer | 5 |
| 23 | Jan 1 | (h) | York C | W | 1-0 | Davison | 16 |
| 24 | 12 | (a) | Bolton W | L | 0-3 | | 6 |
| 25 | 30 | (h) | Bournemouth | L | 2-3 | Pratley, Buckley (pen) | 9 |
| 26 | Feb 2 | (a) | Lincoln C | D | 0-0 | | 5 |
| 27 | 22 | (a) | Doncaster R | L | 1-2 | Davison | 5 |
| 28 | 26 | (a) | Bristol C | L | 0-3 | | 8 |
| 29 | Mar 2 | (h) | Rotherham U | D | 1-1 | Christie | 1 |
| 30 | 6 | (h) | Walsall | W | 2-0 | Christie, Hooks | 9 |
| 31 | 9 | (a) | Hull C | L | 2-3 | Buckley (pen), Christie | 9 |
| 32 | 13 | (h) | Preston NE | W | 2-0 | Hindmarch, Buckley (pen) | 8 |
| 33 | 16 | (a) | Plymouth A | W | 1-0 | Davison | 6 |
| 34 | 23 | (h) | Bristol R | D | 0-0 | | 1 |
| 35 | 30 | (a) | Brentford | D | 1-1 | Micklewhite | 4 |
| 36 | Apr 3 | (h) | Millwall | L | 1-2 | Micklewhite | 1 |
| 37 | 6 | (h) | Gillingham | W | 1-0 | Davison | 1 |
| 38 | 8 | (a) | York C | D | 1-1 | Davison | 6 |
| 39 | 13 | (h) | Bradford C | D | 0-0 | | 14 |
| 40 | 17 | (h) | Reading | W | 4-1 | Micklewhite, Buckley, Davison, Christie | 7 |
| 41 | 20 | (a) | Wigan A | L | 0-2 | | 4 |
| 42 | 23 | (a) | Burnley | W | 1-0 | Christie | 3 |
| 43 | 27 | (h) | Cambridge U | W | 1-0 | Davison | 8 |
| 44 | May 4 | (a) | Orient | D | 2-2 | Micklewhite, Davison | 3 |
| 45 | 6 | (h) | Swansea C | D | 1-1 | Christie | 1 |
| 46 | 11 | (a) | Newport C | W | 3-1 | Christie (pen), Davison, Harbey | 4 |

FINAL LEAGUE POSITION: 7th in Division Three

Appeara
Subst
(

## FA Cup

| | | | | | | | |
|---|---|---|---|---|---|---|---|
| 1 | Nov 17 | (a) | Hartlepool U | L | 1-2 | Buckley (pen) | 7 |

Appeara
Substi
(

## League Cup

| | | | | | | | |
|---|---|---|---|---|---|---|---|
| 1 | Aug 29 | (h) | Hartlepool U | W | 5-1 | Wilson 4, Powell | 9 |
| 1 | Sep 5 | (a) | Hartlepool U | W | 1-0 | Robertson (pen) | 1 |
| 2 | 25 | (a) | Ipswich T | L | 2-4 | Wilson 2 | 10 |
| 2 | Oct 10 | (h) | Ipswich T | D | 1-1 | Buckley (pen) | 14 |

Appeara
Substi
G

**Derby County played in the Freight/Rover Trophy (see Rams in Other Competitions)**

| Palmer C | Buckley S | Richardson P | Powell S | Burns K | Taylor K | Wilson K | Davison R | Hooks P | Robertson J | Hindmarch R | Burridge J | Streete F | Biggins S | Pratley R | Lewis M | Garner A | Blades P | Ablett G | Christie T | Micklewhite G | Sutton S | Devine S | Williams G | Harbey G | |
|---|---|---|---|---|---|---|---|---|---|---|---|---|---|---|---|---|---|---|---|---|---|---|---|---|---|
| 2 | 3 | 4 | 5 | 6 | 7 | 8 | 9 | 10 | 11 | | | | | | | | | | | | | | | | 1 |
| 2 | 3 | 12 | 4 | 6 | 7 | 8 | 9 | **10** | 11 | 5 | | | | | | | | | | | | | | | 2 |
| 2 | 3 | 12 | 4 | **6** | 7 | 8 | 9 | 10 | 11 | 5 | | | | | | | | | | | | | | | 3 |
| 2 | 3 | 12 | 4 | 6 | 7 | 8 | 9 | 10 | **11** | 5 | | | | | | | | | | | | | | | 4 |
| 2 | 3 | | 4 | 6 | 7 | 8 | 9 | 10 | 11 | 5 | | | | | | | | | | | | | | | 5 |
| 2 | 3 | | 4 | 6 | 7 | 8 | 9 | 10 | 11 | | 1 | 5 | | | | | | | | | | | | | 6 |
| 2 | 3 | 12 | **4** | 6 | 7 | 8 | 9 | 10 | 11 | | 1 | 5 | | | | | | | | | | | | | 7 |
| 2 | 3 | 4 | | 6 | 7 | 8 | 9 | 10 | 11 | | 1 | 5 | | | | | | | | | | | | | 8 |
| 2 | 3 | 12 | 4 | 6 | 7 | 8 | 9 | **10** | 11 | | 1 | 5 | | | | | | | | | | | | | 9 |
| 2 | 3 | | 4 | 6 | 7 | 8 | 9 | 10 | 11 | | 1 | 5 | | | | | | | | | | | | | 10 |
| 2 | 3 | | 4 | 6 | 7 | | 9 | 10 | 11 | | 1 | 5 | 8 | | | | | | | | | | | | 11 |
| 2 | 3 | | 4 | 6 | 7 | | 9 | 10 | 11 | | | 5 | 8 | | | | | | | | | | | | 12 |
| 2 | 3 | 12 | 4 | 6 | 7 | | 9 | **10** | 11 | | | 5 | 8 | | | | | | | | | | | | 13 |
| 2 | 3 | | 4 | 6 | 7 | | 9 | 10 | 11 | | | | 8 | 5 | | | | | | | | | | | 14 |
| 2 | 3 | 7 | 4 | 6 | | | 9 | 10 | 11 | | | | 8 | 5 | | | | | | | | | | | 15 |
| 2 | 3 | | 4 | | 7 | | 9 | **10** | 11 | | | 5 | 8 | 12 | 6 | | | | | | | | | | 16 |
| 2 | 3 | | 4 | | 7 | | 9 | | 11 | | | 5 | | 6 | 10 | 8 | | | | | | | | | 17 |
| 2 | 3 | | 4 | | 7 | | 9 | | 11 | | | 5 | | 6 | 10 | 8 | | | | | | | | | 18 |
| 2 | 3 | | 4 | 6 | 7 | | 9 | | 11 | | | 5 | | | 10 | 8 | | | | | | | | | 19 |
| 2 | 3 | 12 | **4** | 6 | 7 | | 9 | | 11 | | | 5 | | | 10 | 8 | | | | | | | | | 20 |
| 2 | 3 | 7 | | 6 | | 11 | 9 | | | | | 5 | | 4 | 10 | 8 | | | | | | | | | 21 |
| 2 | 3 | 4 | | | 7 | 8 | **9** | | | | | 5 | 12 | 6 | 10 | 11 | | | | | | | | | 22 |
| 2 | 3 | 4 | | | 7 | 8 | 9 | | | | | 5 | | 6 | 10 | 11 | | | | | | | | | 23 |
| | 3 | 4 | | 12 | **7** | | 9 | | | | | 5 | 8 | 6 | 10 | 11 | 2 | | | | | | | | 24 |
| | 3 | | 4 | 2 | | | 9 | | **11** | | | 5 | 12 | 6 | 10 | 8 | | 7 | | | | | | | 25 |
| 2 | 3 | | 4 | | | | 9 | | 11 | | | 6 | | 6 | 10 | **8** | 12 | 7 | | | | | | | 26 |
| | 3 | | | | | | 9 | 12 | 11 | | | 6 | 7 | 5 | 4 | | 2 | **8** | 10 | | | | | | 27 |
| | 3 | | **4** | | | | 9 | 12 | 11 | | | 6 | | 5 | 10 | | 2 | | 8 | 7 | | | | | 28 |
| | 3 | | | | | | 9 | 10 | 11 | 5 | | 6 | | | 4 | | 2 | | 8 | 7 | 1 | | | | 29 |
| 2 | 3 | | | | | | 9 | 10 | 11 | 5 | | | | | 4 | | 6 | | 8 | 7 | 1 | | | | 30 |
| 2 | 3 | | | | | | 9 | 10 | **11** | 5 | | | | | 4 | | 6 | 12 | 8 | 7 | 1 | | | | 31 |
| 2 | 3 | | | | | | 9 | **10** | 11 | 5 | | | | | 4 | | 6 | 12 | 8 | 7 | 1 | | | | 32 |
| 2 | 3 | | 12 | | | | 9 | | **11** | 5 | | | | | 4 | | 6 | | 8 | 7 | 1 | 10 | | | 33 |
| | 3 | | 4 | | | | 9 | **10** | 11 | 5 | | 2 | | | | | 6 | 12 | 8 | 7 | 1 | | | | 34 |
| | 3 | | | | | | 9 | | 11 | 5 | | 2 | | | 4 | | 6 | | 8 | 7 | 1 | | 10 | | 35 |
| | 3 | | | | | | 9 | | 11 | 5 | | 2 | | | **4** | | 6 | | 8 | 7 | 1 | | 10 | 12 | 36 |
| | 3 | | 4 | | | | 9 | | 11 | 5 | | 2 | | | | 12 | 6 | | **8** | 7 | 1 | | 10 | | 37 |
| | 3 | | 4 | | | | 9 | | | 5 | | 2 | | | | | 6 | | 8 | 7 | 1 | | 10 | 11 | 38 |
| | 3 | | 4 | | | | 9 | | 11 | 5 | | 2 | | | | | 6 | | 8 | 7 | 1 | | 10 | | 39 |
| | 3 | | **4** | | | | 9 | | 11 | 5 | | 2 | | | | 12 | 6 | | 8 | 7 | 1 | | 10 | | 40 |
| | 3 | | | | | | 9 | | 11 | 5 | | 2 | | | | 4 | 6 | | 8 | 7 | 1 | | 10 | | 41 |
| 2 | 3 | | | | | | 9 | | 11 | 5 | | | | | | **4** | 6 | | 8 | 7 | 1 | | 10 | 12 | 42 |
| 2 | 3 | | | | | | 9 | | 11 | 5 | | | | | | 4 | 6 | | 8 | 7 | | | 10 | | 43 |
| 2 | 3 | | | | | | 9 | | 11 | 5 | | | | | 4 | | 6 | | 8 | 7 | | | 10 | | 44 |
| 2 | 3 | | | | | | 9 | | **11** | 5 | | | | | 4 | 12 | 6 | | 8 | 7 | | | 10 | | 45 |
| 2 | 3 | | | | | | 9 | | 11 | 5 | | | | | | | 6 | | 8 | 7 | | | 10 | 4 | 46 |
| 33 | 46 | 7 | 27 | 19 | 22 | 13 | 46 | 21 | 41 | 22 | 6 | 30 | 8 | 12 | 22 | 13 | 21 | 3 | 20 | 19 | 14 | 1 | 12 | 2 | |
| | | 7 | 1 | 1 | | | | 2 | | | | | 2 | 1 | | 3 | 1 | 3 | | | | | | 2 | |
| 2 | 7 | | 1 | 1 | 2 | 8 | 24 | 1 | 1 | 1 | | | 1 | 1 | | 3 | | | 7 | 4 | | | | 1 | |

| | | | | | | | | | | | | | | | |
|---|---|---|---|---|---|---|---|---|---|---|---|---|---|---|---|
| 2 | 3 | 7 | 4 | **6** | | | 9 | 10 | 11 | | | 5 | 8 | 12 | 1 |
| 1 | 1 | 1 | 1 | 1 | | | 1 | 1 | 1 | | | 1 | 1 | | |
| | | | | | | | | | | | | | | 1 | |
| | 1 | | | | | | | | | | | | | | |

| | | | | | | | | | | | | | |
|---|---|---|---|---|---|---|---|---|---|---|---|---|---|
| 2 | 3 | 12 | 4 | 6 | 7 | 8 | 9 | **10** | 11 | 5 | | | 1 |
| 2 | 3 | 12 | 4 | 6 | 7 | 8 | **9** | 10 | 11 | 5 | | | 1 |
| 2 | 3 | | 4 | 6 | 7 | 8 | 9 | 10 | 11 | | 1 | 5 | 2 |
| 2 | 3 | | 4 | 6 | 7 | 8 | 9 | 10 | 11 | | 1 | 5 | 2 |
| 4 | 4 | | 4 | 4 | 4 | 4 | 4 | 4 | 4 | 2 | 2 | 2 | |
| | | 2 | | | | | | | | | | | |
| | 1 | | 1 | | | 6 | | | 1 | | | | |

# 1985-86

| | P | W | D | L | F | A | Pts |
|---|---|---|---|---|---|---|---|
| Reading | 46 | 29 | 7 | 10 | 67 | 51 | 94 |
| Plymouth A | 46 | 26 | 9 | 11 | 88 | 53 | 87 |
| Derby Co | 46 | 23 | 15 | 8 | 80 | 41 | 84 |
| Wigan A | 46 | 23 | 14 | 9 | 82 | 48 | 83 |
| Gillingham | 46 | 22 | 13 | 11 | 81 | 54 | 79 |
| Walsall | 46 | 22 | 9 | 15 | 90 | 64 | 75 |
| York C | 46 | 20 | 11 | 15 | 77 | 58 | 71 |
| Notts Co | 46 | 19 | 14 | 13 | 71 | 60 | 71 |
| Bristol C | 46 | 18 | 14 | 14 | 69 | 60 | 68 |
| Brentford | 46 | 18 | 12 | 16 | 58 | 61 | 66 |
| Doncaster R | 46 | 16 | 16 | 14 | 45 | 52 | 64 |
| Blackpool | 46 | 17 | 12 | 17 | 66 | 55 | 63 |
| Darlington | 46 | 15 | 13 | 18 | 61 | 78 | 58 |
| Rotherham U | 46 | 15 | 12 | 19 | 61 | 59 | 57 |
| Bournemouth | 46 | 15 | 9 | 22 | 65 | 72 | 54 |
| Bristol R | 46 | 14 | 12 | 20 | 51 | 75 | 54 |
| Chesterfield | 46 | 13 | 14 | 19 | 61 | 64 | 53 |
| Bolton W | 46 | 15 | 8 | 23 | 54 | 68 | 53 |
| Newport Co | 46 | 11 | 18 | 17 | 52 | 65 | 51 |
| Bury | 46 | 12 | 13 | 21 | 63 | 67 | 49 |
| Lincoln C | 46 | 10 | 16 | 20 | 55 | 77 | 46 |
| Cardiff C | 46 | 12 | 9 | 25 | 53 | 83 | 45 |
| Wolves | 46 | 11 | 10 | 25 | 57 | 98 | 43 |
| Swansea C | 46 | 11 | 10 | 25 | 43 | 87 | 43 |

Manager: Arthur Cox.
Leading scorer: Bobby Davison, League 17, all matches 23.
League ever-present: Steve Buckley, Ross MacLaren, Gary Micklewhite.
Player of the season: Ross MacLaren.

- Having started with free transfers a year earlier, Arthur Cox was able to raise the quality of his squad. Jeff Chandler, Ross MacLaren and Steve McClaren were all signed after transfer tribunal adjudications.
- John Gregory was signed from Queen's Park Rangers for £100,000 in November, 18 months after he played for England.
- Derby played 60 competitive matches in the season, their highest total, and clinched promotion on Cup final eve by beating Rotherham United at the Baseball Ground. They were third but Play-offs had yet to be introduced.
- Steve Buckley ended his Rams career with his 122nd consecutive League appearance, the only Derby player to achieve two League centuries.
- The Rams won the Central League, the first Third Division club to achieve it.

## Division Three

| Match No. | Date | Venue | Opponents | Result | | Scorers |
|---|---|---|---|---|---|---|
| 1 | Aug 17 | (h) | Bournemouth | W | 3-0 | Chandler 2, Christie |
| 2 | 24 | (a) | Wigan A | L | 1-2 | Chandler |
| 3 | 26 | (h) | Wolves | W | 4-2 | Christie 2, Lewis, Davison |
| 4 | 31 | (a) | Bristol R | D | 0-0 | |
| 5 | Sep 7 | (h) | Blackpool | L | 1-2 | Davison |
| 6 | 14 | (a) | Bury | D | 1-1 | Hindmarch |
| 7 | 17 | (a) | Bristol C | D | 1-1 | Davison |
| 8 | 21 | (h) | Chesterfield | D | 0-0 | |
| 9 | 28 | (a) | Cardiff C | W | 2-0 | MacLaren (pen), Christie |
| 10 | Oct 2 | (h) | Swansea C | W | 5-1 | Davison 2, Christie, Micklewhite, Chandler |
| 11 | 5 | (h) | Notts C | W | 2-0 | Chandler (pen), Davison |
| 12 | 19 | (h) | York C | W | 2-1 | Garner 2 |
| 13 | 22 | (a) | Gillingham | W | 2-1 | Garner, Chandler |
| 14 | 26 | (h) | Plymouth A | L | 1-2 | Davison |
| 15 | Nov 2 | (a) | Rotherham U | D | 1-1 | Williams |
| 16 | 6 | (a) | Brentford | D | 3-3 | Hindmarch 2, Davison |
| 17 | 9 | (h) | Lincoln C | W | 7-0 | Hindmarch 2, Micklewhite 2, Chandler, Davison, Garner |
| 18 | 23 | (a) | Bolton W | W | 1-0 | Micklewhite |
| 19 | 30 | (h) | Reading | D | 1-1 | Davison |
| 20 | Dec 15 | (a) | Doncaster R | W | 3-0 | Davison 2, Micklewhite |
| 21 | 22 | (h) | Wigan A | W | 1-0 | Christie |
| 22 | 28 | (a) | Wolves | W | 4-0 | Williams, Christie, Davison, Gregory |
| 23 | Jan 18 | (a) | Bournemouth | D | 1-1 | Micklewhite |
| 24 | Feb 1 | (a) | Blackpool | W | 1-0 | Garner |
| 25 | 8 | (a) | York C | W | 3-1 | Micklewhite 2, Christie |
| 26 | 22 | (a) | Chesterfield | L | 0-1 | |
| 27 | Mar 1 | (h) | Cardiff C | W | 2-1 | Gregory, MacLaren |
| 28 | 8 | (a) | Notts C | W | 3-0 | Davison 2, Micklewhite |
| 29 | 12 | (h) | Walsall | W | 3-1 | Chandler, Williams, Hart (og) |
| 30 | 15 | (h) | Darlington | D | 1-1 | Christie |
| 31 | 19 | (h) | Bristol C | W | 2-0 | Gregory, Christie |
| 32 | 22 | (a) | Plymouth A | L | 1-4 | Christie |
| 33 | 29 | (h) | Newport C | D | 1-1 | Gregory |
| 34 | 31 | (a) | Walsall | D | 1-1 | MacLaren |
| 35 | Apr 5 | (h) | Brentford | D | 1-1 | Micklewhite |
| 36 | 7 | (h) | Gillingham | W | 2-0 | Davison, Micklewhite |
| 37 | 9 | (h) | Bristol R | L | 0-2 | |
| 38 | 12 | (a) | Lincoln C | W | 1-0 | Davison |
| 39 | 19 | (h) | Bolton W | W | 2-1 | Buckley, Williams |
| 40 | 22 | (a) | Newport C | D | 1-1 | Christie |
| 41 | 26 | (a) | Reading | L | 0-1 | |
| 42 | 30 | (h) | Bury | D | 1-1 | MacLaren (pen) |
| 43 | May 3 | (h) | Doncaster R | D | 1-1 | Hindmarch |
| 44 | 6 | (a) | Swansea C | W | 3-0 | Christie 2 (1 pen), Chandler |
| 45 | 9 | (h) | Rotherham U | W | 2-1 | Gee, Christie (pen) |
| 46 | 12 | (a) | Darlington | L | 1-2 | Gee |

FINAL LEAGUE POSITION: 3rd in Division Three – Promoted

Appear
Subs

## FA Cup

| | | | | | | |
|---|---|---|---|---|---|---|
| 1 | Nov 16 | (h) | Crewe A | W | 5-1 | Davison 2, Christie 2, Chandler (pen) |
| 2 | Dec 9 | (h) | Telford U | W | 6-1 | Chandler 3, Micklewhite 2, Gregory |
| 3 | Jan 4 | (a) | Gillingham | D | 1-1 | Garner |
| R | 13 | (h) | Gillingham | W | 3-1* | Micklewhite, Garner, Christie |
| 4 | 25 | (a) | Sheffield U | W | 1-0 | Hindmarch |
| 5 | Feb 26 | (h) | Sheffield W | D | 1-1 | Davison |
| R | Mar 5 | (a) | Sheffield W | L | 0-2 | |

*after extra-time

Appear
Subs

## League Cup

| | | | | | | |
|---|---|---|---|---|---|---|
| 1 | Aug 21 | (h) | Hartlepool U | W | 3-0 | Davison 2, McClaren |
| 1 | Sep 4 | (a) | Hartlepool U | L | 0-0 | |
| 2 | 25 | (h) | Leicester C | W | 2-0 | MacLaren (pen), Chandler |
| 2 | Oct 9 | (a) | Leicester C | D | 1-1 | Davison |
| 3 | 30 | (h) | Nottingham F | L | 1-2 | Chandler (pen) |

Appear
Subs

**Derby County played in the Freight/Rover Trophy (see Rams in Other Competitions)**

| Streete F | Buckley S | Lewis M | Hindmarch R | MacLaren R | Micklewhite G | Christie T | Davison R | McClaren S | Chandler J | Blades P | Palmer C | Williams G | Garner A | Harbey G | Gregory J | Pratley R | Gee P | Steele E | Thomas M | |
|---|---|---|---|---|---|---|---|---|---|---|---|---|---|---|---|---|---|---|---|---|
| 2 | 3 | 4 | 5 | 6 | 7 | 8 | 9 | 10 | 11 | | | | | | | | | | | 1 |
| 2 | 3 | **4** | 5 | 6 | 7 | 8 | 9 | 10 | 11 | 12 | | | | | | | | | | 2 |
| 2 | 3 | 4 | 5 | 6 | 7 | 8 | 9 | **10** | 11 | 12 | | | | | | | | | | 3 |
| 2 | 3 | 4 | 5 | 6 | 7 | 8 | 9 | 10 | **11** | 12 | | | | | | | | | | 4 |
| 2 | 3 | 4 | 5 | 6 | 7 | 8 | 9 | 10 | 11 | | | | | | | | | | | 5 |
| | 3 | | 5 | 6 | 7 | 8 | 9 | **10** | 11 | 12 | 2 | 4 | | | | | | | | 6 |
| | 3 | | 5 | 6 | 7 | 8 | 9 | 10 | 11 | | 2 | 4 | | | | | | | | 7 |
| | 3 | | 5 | 6 | 7 | 8 | 9 | 10 | 11 | | 2 | 4 | | | | | | | | 8 |
| | 3 | | 5 | 6 | 7 | 8 | 9 | **10** | 11 | 12 | 2 | 4 | | | | | | | | 9 |
| | 3 | | 5 | 6 | 7 | 8 | 9 | 10 | 11 | | 2 | 4 | | | | | | | | 10 |
| | 3 | | 5 | 6 | 7 | 8 | 9 | **10** | 11 | | 2 | 4 | 12 | | | | | | | 11 |
| | 3 | | 5 | 6 | 7 | **8** | 9 | 10 | 11 | | 2 | 4 | 12 | | | | | | | 12 |
| | 3 | | 5 | 6 | 7 | | 9 | 10 | 11 | | 2 | 4 | 8 | | | | | | | 13 |
| | 3 | | 5 | 6 | 7 | 8 | 9 | **10** | 11 | | 2 | 4 | 12 | | | | | | | 14 |
| | 3 | | 5 | 6 | 7 | 8 | 9 | 10 | 11 | 12 | **2** | 4 | | | | | | | | 15 |
| | 3 | | 5 | 6 | 7 | 8 | 9 | | 11 | 2 | | 4 | 10 | | | | | | | 16 |
| | 3 | | 5 | 6 | 7 | 8 | **9** | | 11 | 2 | | 4 | 10 | 12 | | | | | | 17 |
| | 3 | | 5 | 6 | 7 | 8 | 9 | | **11** | 2 | | 4 | 12 | | 10 | | | | | 18 |
| | 3 | | 5 | 6 | 7 | 8 | **9** | | 11 | 2 | | 4 | 12 | | 10 | | | | | 19 |
| | 3 | | 5 | 6 | 7 | 8 | 9 | | 11 | 2 | | 4 | 10 | | | | | | | 20 |
| | 3 | | 5 | 6 | 7 | 8 | 9 | | **11** | 2 | | 4 | 12 | | 10 | | | | | 21 |
| | 3 | | 5 | 6 | 7 | 8 | 9 | | 11 | 2 | | 4 | | | 10 | | | | | 22 |
| | 3 | | 5 | 6 | 7 | 8 | | | 11 | 2 | | 4 | 9 | | 10 | | | | | 23 |
| | 3 | | | 6 | 7 | 8 | | | 11 | 2 | | 4 | 9 | | 10 | 5 | | | | 24 |
| | 3 | | | 6 | 7 | 8 | | | **11** | 2 | | 4 | 9 | 12 | 10 | 5 | | | | 25 |
| | 3 | | 5 | 6 | 7 | 8 | | | 11 | 2 | | 4 | 9 | | 10 | | | | | 26 |
| | 3 | | 5 | 6 | 7 | 8 | 9 | | 11 | 2 | | 4 | | | 10 | | | | | 27 |
| | 3 | | 5 | 6 | 7 | 8 | 9 | | 11 | 2 | | 4 | | | 10 | | | | | 28 |
| | 3 | | 5 | 6 | 7 | 8 | | | 11 | 2 | | 4 | | | 10 | | 9 | | | 29 |
| | 3 | | 5 | 6 | 7 | 8 | 9 | | 11 | 2 | | 4 | | | 10 | | | 1 | | 30 |
| | 3 | | | 6 | 7 | 8 | 9 | | 11 | 2 | | 4 | | | 10 | 5 | | 1 | | 31 |
| | 3 | | | 6 | 7 | 8 | 9 | | 11 | 2 | | 4 | | | 10 | 5 | | 1 | | 32 |
| | 3 | | **5** | 6 | 7 | 8 | 9 | | | 2 | | 4 | 12 | | 10 | | | 1 | 11 | 33 |
| | 3 | | | 6 | 7 | 8 | 9 | 12 | | 2 | | 4 | | | **10** | 5 | | 1 | 11 | 34 |
| | 3 | | 5 | 6 | 7 | 8 | 9 | 10 | | 2 | | 4 | | | | | | 1 | 11 | 35 |
| | 3 | | | 6 | 7 | 8 | 9 | 10 | | 2 | | 4 | | | | 5 | | 1 | 11 | 36 |
| | 3 | | | 6 | 7 | 8 | 9 | 10 | | 2 | | 4 | 12 | | | 5 | | 1 | **11** | 37 |
| | 3 | | 5 | 6 | 7 | 8 | 9 | 10 | | **2** | | 4 | | 12 | | | | 1 | 11 | 38 |
| | 3 | | 5 | 6 | 7 | 8 | 9 | 10 | | | 2 | 4 | | | | | | 1 | 11 | 39 |
| | 3 | | 5 | 6 | 7 | 8 | 9 | 10 | | | 2 | 4 | | | | | | 1 | 11 | 40 |
| | 3 | | 5 | 6 | 7 | 8 | 9 | 4 | | | 2 | 12 | | | 10 | | | 1 | **11** | 41 |
| | 3 | | 5 | 6 | 7 | 8 | 9 | | 11 | | 2 | 4 | | | 10 | | | 1 | | 42 |
| | 3 | | 5 | 6 | 7 | 8 | **9** | | 11 | | 2 | 4 | | | 10 | | 12 | | | 43 |
| | 3 | | 5 | 6 | 7 | 8 | 9 | | 11 | | 2 | 4 | | | 10 | | | | | 44 |
| | 3 | | 5 | 6 | 7 | 8 | 9 | | 11 | | 2 | **4** | | | 10 | | 12 | | | 45 |
| | **3** | | 5 | 6 | 7 | 8 | 9 | | 12 | 4 | 2 | | | | 10 | | 11 | | | 46 |
| 5 | 46 | 5 | 39 | 46 | 46 | 45 | 41 | 22 | 36 | 24 | 18 | 39 | 8 | | 22 | 7 | 2 | 13 | 9 | |
| | | | | | | | | 1 | 1 | 6 | | 1 | 8 | 3 | | | 2 | | | |
| | 1 | 1 | 6 | 4 | 11 | 15 | 17 | | 9 | | | 4 | 5 | | 4 | | 2 | | | |

1 own-goal

| Streete F | Buckley S | Lewis M | Hindmarch R | MacLaren R | Micklewhite G | Christie T | Davison R | McClaren S | Chandler J | Blades P | Palmer C | Williams G | Garner A | Harbey G | Gregory J | Pratley R | Gee P | Steele E | Thomas M | |
|---|---|---|---|---|---|---|---|---|---|---|---|---|---|---|---|---|---|---|---|---|
| | 3 | | 5 | 6 | 7 | 8 | 9 | | 11 | 2 | | 4 | | | 10 | | | | | 1 |
| | 3 | | 5 | 6 | 7 | 8 | 9 | | 11 | 2 | | 4 | 12 | | **10** | | | | | 2 |
| | 3 | | 5 | 6 | 7 | 8 | | | **11** | 2 | | 4 | 9 | 12 | 10 | | | | | 3 |
| | 3 | | 5 | 6 | 7 | 8 | | | **11** | 2 | | 4 | 9 | 12 | 10 | | | | | R |
| | 3 | | 5 | 6 | 7 | 8 | | | 11 | 2 | | 4 | 9 | | 10 | | | | | 4 |
| | 3 | | 5 | 6 | 7 | 8 | 9 | | 11 | 2 | | 4 | | | 10 | | | | | 5 |
| | 3 | | 5 | 6 | 7 | 8 | **9** | | 11 | 2 | | 4 | 12 | | 10 | | | | | R |
| | 7 | | 7 | 7 | 7 | 7 | 4 | | 7 | 7 | | 7 | 3 | | 7 | | | | | |
| | | | | | | | | | | | | | 2 | 2 | | | | | | |
| | | | 1 | | 3 | 3 | 3 | | 4 | | | | 2 | | 1 | | | | | |

| Streete F | Buckley S | Lewis M | Hindmarch R | MacLaren R | Micklewhite G | Christie T | Davison R | McClaren S | Chandler J | Blades P | Palmer C | Williams G | Garner A | Harbey G | Gregory J | Pratley R | Gee P | Steele E | Thomas M | |
|---|---|---|---|---|---|---|---|---|---|---|---|---|---|---|---|---|---|---|---|---|
| 2 | 3 | 4 | 5 | 6 | 7 | 8 | 9 | 10 | 11 | | | | | | | | | | | 1 |
| 2 | 3 | 4 | 5 | 6 | 7 | 8 | 9 | 10 | **11** | 12 | | | | | | | | | | 1 |
| | **3** | | 5 | 6 | 7 | 8 | 9 | 10 | 11 | | 2 | 4 | 12 | | | | | | | 2 |
| | 3 | | 5 | 6 | 7 | 8 | 9 | 10 | **11** | 12 | 2 | 4 | | | | | | | | 2 |
| | 3 | | 5 | 6 | 7 | 8 | 9 | 10 | 11 | | 2 | **4** | 12 | | | | | | | 3 |
| 2 | 5 | 2 | 5 | 5 | 5 | 5 | 5 | 5 | 5 | | 3 | 3 | | | | | | | | |
| | | | | | | | | | | 2 | | | 2 | | | | | | | |
| | | | | 1 | | | 3 | 1 | 2 | | | | | | | | | | | |

# 1986-87

| | P | W | D | L | F | A | Pts |
|---|---|---|---|---|---|---|---|
| Derby Co | 42 | 25 | 9 | 8 | 64 | 38 | 84 |
| Portsmouth | 42 | 23 | 9 | 10 | 53 | 28 | 78 |
| Oldham A | 42 | 22 | 9 | 11 | 65 | 44 | 75 |
| Leeds U | 42 | 19 | 11 | 12 | 58 | 44 | 68 |
| Ipswich T | 42 | 17 | 13 | 12 | 59 | 43 | 64 |
| Crystal Palace | 42 | 19 | 5 | 18 | 51 | 53 | 62 |
| Plymouth A | 42 | 16 | 13 | 13 | 62 | 57 | 61 |
| Stoke C | 42 | 16 | 10 | 16 | 63 | 53 | 58 |
| Sheffield U | 42 | 15 | 13 | 14 | 50 | 49 | 58 |
| Bradford C | 42 | 15 | 10 | 17 | 62 | 62 | 55 |
| Barnsley | 42 | 14 | 13 | 15 | 49 | 52 | 55 |
| Blackburn R | 42 | 15 | 10 | 17 | 45 | 55 | 55 |
| Reading | 42 | 14 | 11 | 17 | 52 | 59 | 53 |
| Hull C | 42 | 13 | 14 | 15 | 41 | 55 | 53 |
| W.B.A. | 42 | 13 | 12 | 17 | 51 | 49 | 51 |
| Millwall | 42 | 14 | 9 | 19 | 39 | 45 | 51 |
| Huddersfield T | 42 | 13 | 12 | 17 | 54 | 61 | 51 |
| Shrewsbury T | 42 | 15 | 6 | 21 | 41 | 53 | 51 |
| Birmingham C | 42 | 11 | 17 | 14 | 47 | 59 | 50 |
| Sunderland | 42 | 12 | 12 | 18 | 49 | 59 | 48 |
| Grimsby T | 42 | 10 | 14 | 18 | 39 | 59 | 44 |
| Brighton & H.A. | 42 | 9 | 12 | 21 | 37 | 54 | 39 |

Manager: Arthur Cox.
Leading scorer: Bobby Davison, League 19, all matches 22.
League ever-present: John Gregory, Ross MacLaren, Gary Micklewhite.
Player of the season: Geraint Williams.

- Derby lost their opening home game to Oldham Athletic but were undefeated at the Baseball Ground for the remainder of the season. Between January and April, they were unbeaten in 13 League games anywhere.
- Their 11 away victories set a new club record as they won the title with six points to spare.
- Phil Gee, signed from Gresley Rovers in August 1985, was an ideal partner for Bobby Davison and, after an early injury, Mark Lillis was unable to regain his place.
- Promotions in successive seasons established Arthur Cox as one of Derby's most effective managers.

## Division Two

| Match No. | Date | | Venue | Opponents | Result | | Scorers |
|---|---|---|---|---|---|---|---|
| 1 | Aug | 23 | (h) | Oldham A | L | 0-1 | |
| 2 | | 30 | (a) | Birmingham C | D | 1-1 | Gregory |
| 3 | Sep | 6 | (h) | Crystal P | W | 1-0 | Gregory (pen) |
| 4 | | 13 | (a) | Grimsby T | W | 1-0 | Davison |
| 5 | | 20 | (h) | Millwall | D | 1-1 | Davison |
| 6 | | 27 | (a) | West Brom A | L | 0-2 | |
| 7 | Oct | 1 | (h) | Sunderland | W | 3-2 | Forsyth, Davison, Sage |
| 8 | | 4 | (a) | Huddersfield T | L | 0-2 | |
| 9 | | 11 | (h) | Hull C | D | 1-1 | Gee |
| 10 | | 18 | (a) | Shrewsbury T | W | 1-0 | Gee |
| 11 | | 21 | (a) | Portsmouth | L | 1-3 | Gregory |
| 12 | | 25 | (h) | Brighton & HA | W | 4-1 | Gee 2, Gregory, Sage |
| 13 | Nov | 1 | (a) | Stoke C | W | 2-0 | Williams, Gee |
| 14 | | 8 | (h) | Ipswich T | W | 2-1 | Micklewhite, Davison |
| 15 | | 15 | (a) | Barnsley | W | 1-0 | Gee |
| 16 | | 22 | (h) | Sheffield U | W | 2-0 | Micklewhite, Gregory |
| 17 | | 29 | (a) | Leeds U | L | 0-2 | |
| 18 | Dec | 6 | (h) | Reading | W | 3-0 | Davison 3 |
| 19 | | 13 | (a) | Plymouth A | D | 1-1 | Micklewhite |
| 20 | | 21 | (h) | Grimsby T | W | 4-0 | Davison 2, Micklewhite, Gee |
| 21 | | 26 | (a) | Bradford C | W | 1-0 | Gregory (pen) |
| 22 | | 27 | (h) | Barnsley | W | 3-2 | Gee, Gregory, Davison |
| 23 | Jan | 3 | (a) | Crystal P | L | 0-1 | |
| 24 | | 24 | (a) | Oldham A | W | 4-1 | Davison, Gregory (pen), Gee, Micklewhite |
| 25 | Feb | 7 | (h) | Birmingham C | D | 2-2 | Gee 2 |
| 26 | | 14 | (a) | Sunderland | W | 2-1 | Gregory, Davison |
| 27 | | 21 | (h) | West Brom A | D | 1-1 | Gregory |
| 28 | | 28 | (a) | Millwall | W | 1-0 | Callaghan |
| 29 | Mar | 4 | (h) | Portsmouth | D | 0-0 | |
| 30 | | 7 | (a) | Brighton & HA | W | 1-0 | Gee |
| 31 | | 14 | (h) | Shrewsbury T | W | 3-1 | Davison 2, Callaghan |
| 32 | | 18 | (h) | Blackburn R | W | 3-2 | Davison 2, Keeley (og) |
| 33 | | 21 | (a) | Hull C | D | 1-1 | Hindmarch |
| 34 | Apr | 4 | (a) | Ipswich T | W | 2-0 | Callaghan, Davison |
| 35 | | 8 | (h) | Huddersfield T | W | 2-0 | Gregory, Gee |
| 36 | | 11 | (h) | Stoke C | D | 0-0 | |
| 37 | | 17 | (a) | Blackburn R | L | 1-3 | Hindmarch |
| 38 | | 20 | (h) | Bradford C | W | 1-0 | Lillis |
| 39 | | 25 | (a) | Sheffield U | W | 1-0 | Gee |
| 40 | May | 2 | (h) | Leeds U | W | 2-1 | Gee, Davison |
| 41 | | 4 | (a) | Reading | L | 0-2 | |
| 42 | | 9 | (h) | Plymouth A | W | 4-2 | Davison, Callaghan, Micklewhite, Gregory |

FINAL LEAGUE POSITION: 1st in Division Two – Promoted

Appear
Subst

## FA Cup

| | | | | | | | |
|---|---|---|---|---|---|---|---|
| 3 | Jan | 26 | (a) | Sheffield W | L | 0-1 | |

Appear
Subst

## League Cup

| | | | | | | | |
|---|---|---|---|---|---|---|---|
| 1 | Aug | 27 | (h) | Chester C | L | 0-1 | |
| 1 | Sep | 3 | (a) | Chester C | W | 2-1* | Gee, Davison |
| 2 | | 24 | (h) | West Brom A | W | 4-1 | Davison 2, Chandler, Micklewhite |
| 2 | Oct | 7 | (a) | West Brom A | W | 1-0 | Gee |
| 3 | | 29 | (h) | Aston Villa | D | 1-1 | Harbey |
| R | Nov | 4 | (a) | Aston Villa | L | 1-2 | Williams |

*Derby County won on away goals rule after extra-time.

Appear
Subst

**Derby County played in the Full Members' Cup (see Rams in Other Competitions)**

| igton M | Sage M | Forsyth M | Gregory J | Pratley R | MacLaren R | Micklewhite G | Lillis M | Davison R | Cross S | Chandler J | Gee P | Williams G | Garner A | Penney D | Hindmarch R | Harbey G | Callaghan N | Blades P | Steele E | |
|---|---|---|---|---|---|---|---|---|---|---|---|---|---|---|---|---|---|---|---|---|
| | 2 | 3 | 4 | 5 | 6 | 7 | 8 | 9 | 10 | **11** | 12 | | | | | | | | | 1 |
| | 2 | 3 | 10 | 5 | 6 | 7 | 8 | 9 | | 11 | | 4 | | | | | | | | 2 |
| | 2 | 3 | 10 | 5 | 6 | 7 | **8** | 9 | | 11 | 12 | 4 | | | | | | | | 3 |
| | 2 | 3 | 10 | 5 | 6 | 7 | | 9 | | 11 | 8 | 4 | | | | | | | | 4 |
| | 2 | 3 | 10 | 5 | 6 | 7 | | 9 | | 11 | 8 | 4 | | | | | | | | 5 |
| | 2 | 3 | 10 | 5 | 6 | 7 | | 9 | 12 | 11 | **8** | 4 | | | | | | | | 6 |
| | 2 | 3 | 10 | 5 | 6 | 7 | | 9 | | 11 | 8 | 4 | | | | | | | | 7 |
| | 2 | 3 | 10 | 5 | 6 | 7 | | 9 | | 11 | **8** | 4 | 12 | | | | | | | 8 |
| | 2 | 3 | 10 | 5 | 6 | 7 | | 9 | | 11 | **8** | 4 | | 12 | | | | | | 9 |
| | 2 | 3 | 10 | | 6 | 7 | | 9 | 12 | | **8** | 4 | | | 5 | 11 | | | | 10 |
| | 2 | 3 | 10 | | 6 | 7 | | 9 | | | 8 | 4 | | | 5 | 11 | | | | 11 |
| | 2 | 3 | 10 | | 6 | 7 | | **9** | | | 8 | 4 | 12 | | 5 | 11 | | | | 12 |
| | 2 | 3 | 10 | | 6 | 7 | | 9 | | | 8 | 4 | | | 5 | 11 | | | | 13 |
| | 2 | 3 | 10 | | 6 | 7 | | 9 | | | 8 | 4 | | | 5 | 11 | | | | 14 |
| | 2 | 3 | 10 | | 6 | 7 | | 9 | 11 | | 8 | 4 | | | 5 | | | | | 15 |
| | 2 | 3 | 10 | | 6 | 7 | | 9 | | | 8 | 4 | | | 5 | 11 | | | | 16 |
| | 2 | 3 | 10 | | 6 | 7 | | 9 | 12 | | 8 | 4 | | | 5 | **11** | | | | 17 |
| | 2 | 3 | 10 | | 6 | 7 | 12 | 9 | | | **8** | 4 | | | 5 | 11 | | | | 18 |
| | 2 | 3 | 10 | | 6 | 7 | 12 | 9 | | | **8** | 4 | | | 5 | 11 | | | | 19 |
| | 2 | 3 | **10** | | 6 | 7 | 12 | 9 | | | 8 | 4 | | | 5 | 11 | | | | 20 |
| | 2 | 3 | 10 | | 6 | 7 | | 9 | | | 8 | 4 | | | 5 | 11 | | | | 21 |
| | 2 | 3 | 10 | | 6 | 7 | | 9 | | | 8 | 4 | | | 5 | 11 | | | | 22 |
| | 2 | 3 | 10 | | 6 | 7 | 12 | 9 | | | 8 | 4 | | | 5 | **11** | | | | 23 |
| | 2 | | 10 | | 6 | 7 | | 9 | 11 | | 8 | 4 | | | 5 | 3 | | | | 24 |
| | 2 | 3 | 10 | | 6 | 7 | 4 | 9 | | | 8 | | | | 5 | | 11 | | | 25 |
| | **2** | 3 | 10 | | 6 | 7 | 12 | 9 | | | 8 | 4 | | | 5 | | 11 | | | 26 |
| | | 3 | 10 | | 6 | 7 | | 9 | | | 8 | 4 | | | 5 | | 11 | 2 | | 27 |
| | | 3 | 10 | | 6 | 7 | | 9 | | | 8 | 4 | | | 5 | | 11 | 2 | | 28 |
| | | 3 | 10 | | 6 | 7 | | 9 | | | 8 | 4 | | | 5 | | 11 | 2 | | 29 |
| | | 3 | 10 | | 6 | 7 | | 9 | | | 8 | 4 | | | 5 | | 11 | 2 | | 30 |
| | | 3 | 10 | | 6 | 7 | | 9 | | | 8 | 4 | | | 5 | | 11 | 2 | | 31 |
| | | 3 | 10 | | 6 | 7 | | 9 | | | 8 | 4 | | | 5 | | 11 | 2 | | 32 |
| | | 3 | 10 | | 6 | 7 | | 9 | | | 8 | 4 | | | 5 | | 11 | 2 | | 33 |
| | | 3 | 10 | | 6 | 7 | | 9 | | | 8 | 4 | | | 5 | | 11 | 2 | | 34 |
| | | 3 | 10 | | 6 | 7 | | 9 | | | 8 | 4 | | | 5 | | 11 | 2 | 1 | 35 |
| | | 3 | 10 | | 6 | 7 | | 9 | | | 8 | 4 | | | 5 | | 11 | 2 | 1 | 36 |
| | | 3 | 10 | | 6 | 7 | 12 | **9** | | | 8 | 4 | | | 5 | | 11 | 2 | 1 | 37 |
| | | 3 | 10 | | 6 | 7 | 9 | | | | 8 | 4 | | | 5 | | 11 | 2 | 1 | 38 |
| | | 3 | 10 | | 6 | 7 | 9 | | | | 8 | 4 | | | 5 | | 11 | 2 | 1 | 39 |
| | | 3 | 10 | | 6 | 7 | | 9 | | | 8 | 4 | | | 5 | | 11 | 2 | 1 | 40 |
| | | **3** | 10 | | 6 | 7 | 12 | 9 | | | 8 | 4 | | | 5 | | 11 | 2 | 1 | 41 |
| | | 3 | 10 | | 6 | 7 | 12 | 9 | | | **8** | 4 | | | 5 | | 11 | 2 | 1 | 42 |
| | 26 | 41 | 42 | 9 | 42 | 42 | 6 | 40 | 3 | 9 | 39 | 40 | | | 33 | 14 | 18 | 16 | 8 | |
| | | | | | | | 8 | | 3 | | 2 | | 2 | 1 | | | | | | |
| | 2 | 1 | 12 | | | 6 | 1 | 19 | | | 15 | 1 | | | 2 | | 4 | | | |

1 own-goal

| Sage M | Forsyth M | Gregory J | Pratley R | MacLaren R | Micklewhite G | Lillis M | Davison R | Cross S | Chandler J | Gee P | Williams G | Garner A | Penney D | Hindmarch R | Harbey G | Callaghan N | Blades P | Steele E | |
|---|---|---|---|---|---|---|---|---|---|---|---|---|---|---|---|---|---|---|---|
| 2 | | 10 | | 6 | 7 | 12 | 9 | **11** | | 8 | 4 | | | 5 | 3 | | | | 3 |
| 1 | | 1 | | 1 | 1 | | 1 | 1 | | 1 | 1 | | | 1 | 1 | | | | |
| | | | | | | 1 | | | | | | | | | | | | | |
| | | | | | | | | | | | | | | | | | | | |

| Sage M | Forsyth M | Gregory J | Pratley R | MacLaren R | Micklewhite G | Lillis M | Davison R | Cross S | Chandler J | Gee P | Williams G | Garner A | Penney D | Hindmarch R | Harbey G | Callaghan N | Blades P | Steele E | |
|---|---|---|---|---|---|---|---|---|---|---|---|---|---|---|---|---|---|---|---|
| 2 | 3 | 4 | 5 | 6 | 7 | 8 | 9 | **10** | | 11 | 12 | 13 | | | | | | | 1 |
| 2 | 3 | 10 | 5 | 6 | 7 | **8** | 9 | 13 | 11 | 12 | 4 | | | | | | | | 1 |
| 2 | 3 | 10 | 5 | 6 | 7 | | 9 | | 11 | 8 | 4 | | | | | | | | 2 |
| 2 | 3 | 10 | 5 | 6 | 7 | | 9 | 13 | | 8 | 4 | | 12 | | **11** | | | | 2 |
| 2 | 3 | 10 | | 6 | 7 | | 9 | | | 8 | 4 | | | 5 | 11 | | | | 3 |
| 2 | 3 | 10 | | 6 | 7 | 13 | 9 | | | 8 | 4 | | 12 | 5 | **11** | | | | R |
| 6 | 6 | 6 | 4 | 6 | 6 | 2 | 6 | 1 | 2 | 5 | 5 | 1 | | 2 | 3 | | | | |
| | | | | | | 1 | | 2 | | 1 | 1 | | 2 | | | | | | |
| | | | | | 1 | | 3 | | 1 | 2 | 1 | | | | 1 | | | | |

# 1987-88

| | P | W | D | L | F | A | Pts |
|---|---|---|---|---|---|---|---|
| Liverpool | 40 | 26 | 12 | 2 | 87 | 24 | 90 |
| Manchester U | 40 | 23 | 12 | 5 | 71 | 38 | 81 |
| Nottingham F | 40 | 20 | 13 | 7 | 67 | 39 | 73 |
| Everton | 40 | 19 | 13 | 8 | 53 | 27 | 70 |
| Q.P.R. | 40 | 19 | 10 | 11 | 48 | 38 | 67 |
| Arsenal | 40 | 18 | 12 | 10 | 58 | 39 | 66 |
| Wimbledon | 40 | 14 | 15 | 11 | 58 | 47 | 57 |
| Newcastle U | 40 | 14 | 14 | 12 | 55 | 53 | 56 |
| Luton T | 40 | 14 | 11 | 15 | 57 | 58 | 53 |
| Coventry C | 40 | 13 | 14 | 13 | 46 | 53 | 53 |
| Sheffield W | 40 | 15 | 8 | 17 | 52 | 66 | 53 |
| Southampton | 40 | 12 | 14 | 14 | 49 | 53 | 50 |
| Tottenham H | 40 | 12 | 11 | 17 | 38 | 48 | 47 |
| Norwich C | 40 | 12 | 9 | 19 | 40 | 52 | 45 |
| Derby Co | 40 | 10 | 13 | 17 | 35 | 45 | 43 |
| West Ham U | 40 | 9 | 15 | 16 | 40 | 52 | 42 |
| Charlton A | 40 | 9 | 15 | 16 | 38 | 52 | 42 |
| Chelsea | 40 | 9 | 15 | 16 | 50 | 68 | 42 |
| Portsmouth | 40 | 7 | 14 | 19 | 36 | 66 | 35 |
| Watford | 40 | 7 | 11 | 22 | 27 | 51 | 32 |
| Oxford U | 40 | 6 | 13 | 21 | 44 | 80 | 31 |

Manager: Arthur Cox.
Leading scorers: Phil Gee, John Gregory, League/all matches 6.
League ever-present: Nigel Callaghan, Peter Shilton, Geraint Williams.
Player of the season: Michael Forsyth.

- Once Derby were in the First Division, Robert Maxwell took over as chairman. His son Ian became vice-chairman and another son, Kevin, assumed control of Oxford United.
- Derby signed two England internationals from Southampton, goalkeeper Peter Shilton and centre-half Mark Wright. The £760,000 fee for Wright beat the Derby record of £410,000, set seven years earlier for David Swindlehurst.
- Gary Micklewhite, an ever-present since he made his debut in February 1985, was out injured for the match against Sheffield Wednesday on 19 September, ending a run of 112 consecutive League appearances.
- From 12 December to 10 February, Derby suffered eight successive defeats, equalling their worst runs in 1888 and 1965. It was hard work but the Rams finished eight points clear of relegation.

## Division One

| Match No. | Date | | Venue | Opponents | Result | | Scorers | Att |
|---|---|---|---|---|---|---|---|---|
| 1 | Aug | 15 | (h) | Luton T | W | 1-0 | Gregory | 1 |
| 2 | | 19 | (a) | Queen's Park R | D | 1-1 | Gee | 1 |
| 3 | | 29 | (h) | Wimbledon | L | 0-1 | | 1 |
| 4 | Sep | 5 | (h) | Portsmouth | D | 0-0 | | 1 |
| 5 | | 12 | (a) | Norwich C | W | 2-1 | Davison, Gregory (pen) | 1 |
| 6 | | 19 | (h) | Sheffield W | D | 2-2 | Gregory, Forsyth | 1 |
| 7 | | 26 | (h) | Oxford U | L | 0-1 | | 1 |
| 8 | | 29 | (a) | Liverpool | L | 0-4 | | 4 |
| 9 | Oct | 3 | (a) | West Ham U | D | 1-1 | Gee | 1 |
| 10 | | 10 | (h) | Nottingham F | L | 0-1 | | 2 |
| 11 | | 17 | (a) | Charlton A | W | 1-0 | Cross | |
| 12 | | 24 | (a) | Arsenal | L | 1-2 | Garner | 3 |
| 13 | | 31 | (h) | Coventry C | W | 2-0 | Garner 2 | 1 |
| 14 | Nov | 14 | (a) | Newcastle U | D | 0-0 | | 2 |
| 15 | | 22 | (h) | Chelsea | W | 2-0 | Cross, Gregory | 1 |
| 16 | | 28 | (a) | Southampton | W | 2-1 | Gee, Garner | 1 |
| 17 | Dec | 5 | (h) | Watford | D | 1-1 | Wright | 1 |
| 18 | | 12 | (a) | Everton | L | 0-3 | | 2 |
| 19 | | 20 | (h) | Tottenham H | L | 1-2 | Gregory | 1 |
| 20 | | 26 | (h) | Norwich C | L | 1-2 | Wright | 1 |
| 21 | | 28 | (a) | Sheffield W | L | 1-2 | Gee | 2 |
| 22 | Jan | 1 | (a) | Wimbledon | L | 1-2 | Callaghan | |
| 23 | | 16 | (a) | Luton T | L | 0-1 | | |
| 24 | Feb | 6 | (a) | Portsmouth | L | 1-2 | Wright | 1 |
| 25 | | 10 | (h) | Manchester U | L | 1-2 | McMinn | 2 |
| 26 | | 20 | (a) | Oxford U | D | 0-0 | | |
| 27 | | 27 | (h) | West Ham U | W | 1-0 | Callaghan | 1 |
| 28 | Mar | 1 | (a) | Tottenham H | D | 0-0 | | 1 |
| 29 | | 5 | (h) | Charlton A | D | 1-1 | Callaghan (pen) | 1 |
| 30 | | 16 | (h) | Liverpool | D | 1-1 | Forsyth | 2 |
| 31 | | 19 | (a) | Coventry C | W | 3-0 | Forsyth, Gee, Williams | 1 |
| 32 | | 26 | (h) | Arsenal | D | 0-0 | | 1 |
| 33 | | 30 | (a) | Nottingham F | L | 1-2 | Foster (og) | 2 |
| 34 | Apr | 2 | (a) | Manchester U | L | 1-4 | Cross | 4 |
| 35 | | 4 | (h) | Newcastle U | W | 2-1 | Gee, Micklewhite | 1 |
| 36 | | 9 | (a) | Chelsea | L | 0-1 | | 1 |
| 37 | | 13 | (h) | Queen's Park R | L | 0-2 | | 1 |
| 38 | | 23 | (h) | Southampton | W | 2-0 | Gregory, Stapleton | 1 |
| 39 | | 30 | (a) | Watford | D | 1-1 | Callaghan | 1 |
| 40 | May | 2 | (h) | Everton | D | 0-0 | | 1 |

FINAL LEAGUE POSITION: 15th in Division One

Appeara
Subst

## FA Cup

| | | | | | | | | |
|---|---|---|---|---|---|---|---|---|
| 3 | Jan | 9 | (h) | Chelsea | L | 1-3 | Penney | 1 |

Appeara
Subst

## League Cup

| | | | | | | | | |
|---|---|---|---|---|---|---|---|---|
| 2 | Sep | 22 | (a) | Southend U | L | 0-1 | | |
| 2 | Oct | 7 | (h) | Southend U | D | 0-0 | | 1 |

Appeara
Subst

**Derby County played in the Full Members' Cup (see Rams in Other Competitions)**

| Sage M | Forsyth M | Williams G | Hindmarch R | MacLaren R | Micklewhite G | Gee P | Davison R | Gregory J | Callaghan N | Wright M | Blades P | Lillis M | Garner A | Cross S | Lewis M | Penney D | McClaren S | McCord B | McMinn K | Stapleton F | |
|---|---|---|---|---|---|---|---|---|---|---|---|---|---|---|---|---|---|---|---|---|---|
| 2 | 3 | 4 | 5 | 6 | 7 | 8 | 9 | 10 | 11 | | | | | | | | | | | | 1 |
| 2 | 3 | 4 | 5 | 6 | 7 | 8 | 9 | 10 | 11 | | | | | | | | | | | | 2 |
| 2 | 3 | 4 | **5** | | 7 | 8 | 9 | 10 | 11 | 6 | 12 | 13 | | | | | | | | | 3 |
| 2 | 3 | 4 | | 6 | 7 | **8** | 9 | 10 | 11 | 5 | | | 12 | | | | | | | | 4 |
| 2 | 3 | 4 | | 6 | 7 | **8** | 9 | 10 | 11 | 5 | | | 12 | | | | | | | | 5 |
| 7 | 3 | 4 | | 6 | | **8** | 9 | 10 | 11 | 5 | 2 | | 12 | | | | | | | | 6 |
| 7 | 3 | 4 | | 6 | | 8 | **9** | 10 | 11 | 5 | 2 | | 12 | 13 | | | | | | | 7 |
| 7 | 3 | 4 | | 6 | | **8** | 9 | 10 | 11 | 5 | 2 | | 12 | | | | | | | | 8 |
| 7 | 3 | 4 | | 6 | | 8 | 9 | 10 | 7 | 5 | | | | 11 | | | | | | | 9 |
| **2** | 3 | 4 | | 12 | | 8 | | 10 | 7 | 5 | 6 | | 9 | 11 | | | | | | | 10 |
| | 3 | 4 | | 2 | | | 9 | 10 | 7 | 5 | 6 | | 8 | 11 | | | | | | | 11 |
| | 3 | 4 | | 2 | | 12 | 9 | 10 | 7 | 5 | 6 | | **8** | 11 | 13 | | | | | | 12 |
| | 3 | 4 | | 2 | | | 9 | 10 | 7 | 5 | 6 | | 8 | 11 | | | | | | | 13 |
| | 3 | 4 | | 2 | | 12 | 9 | 10 | 7 | 5 | 6 | | **8** | 11 | | | | | | | 14 |
| | 3 | 4 | | 2 | | 9 | | 10 | 7 | 5 | 6 | | 8 | 11 | | | | | | | 15 |
| | 3 | 4 | | 2 | | 9 | | **10** | 7 | 5 | 6 | | 8 | 11 | 12 | 13 | | | | | 16 |
| | 3 | 4 | | 2 | | 9 | | **10** | 7 | 5 | 6 | | 8 | 11 | 12 | 13 | | | | | 17 |
| | 3 | 4 | | 2 | | 8 | | | **7** | 5 | 6 | | 9 | 11 | 10 | 12 | 13 | | | | 18 |
| | 3 | 4 | | 2 | | 9 | | 10 | 7 | 5 | 6 | | 8 | **11** | 13 | 12 | | | | | 19 |
| | 3 | 4 | | 2 | | 9 | | 10 | 7 | 5 | 6 | | 8 | | | 11 | | | | | 20 |
| 13 | 3 | 4 | | 2 | | 9 | | 10 | 7 | 5 | 6 | | 8 | | 12 | **11** | | | | | 21 |
| | 3 | 4 | | 2 | | 9 | | 10 | 7 | 5 | 6 | | | | | 8 | | 11 | | | 22 |
| | 3 | 4 | | 2 | | 8 | | 10 | 7 | 5 | 6 | | 9 | | | | 11 | | | | 23 |
| | 3 | 4 | | 2 | | 8 | | **10** | 11 | 5 | 6 | | 9 | | 12 | 13 | | | 7 | | 24 |
| | 3 | 4 | 6 | 2 | | 9 | | 10 | **11** | 5 | | | 12 | | 8 | 13 | | | 7 | | 25 |
| | 3 | 4 | 6 | | | 9 | | 10 | 11 | 5 | 2 | | | | 8 | | | | 7 | | 26 |
| | 3 | 4 | 6 | 12 | | 9 | | 10 | 11 | 5 | **2** | | 13 | | 8 | | | | 7 | | 27 |
| | 3 | 4 | 6 | 13 | | 9 | | 10 | 11 | 5 | 2 | | 12 | | 8 | | | | **7** | | 28 |
| | 3 | 4 | 6 | | | 9 | | 10 | 11 | 5 | 2 | | 12 | | **8** | | | | 7 | | 29 |
| | 3 | 4 | 6 | | 12 | 9 | | 10 | 11 | 5 | 2 | | 13 | | 8 | | | | **7** | | 30 |
| | 3 | 4 | 6 | 13 | 12 | 9 | | 10 | 11 | 5 | 2 | | | | 8 | | | | | **7** | 31 |
| | 3 | 4 | 6 | | 12 | **9** | | 10 | 11 | 5 | 2 | | | | 8 | | | | | 7 | 32 |
| | 3 | 4 | 6 | 13 | 12 | 9 | | 10 | 11 | 5 | 2 | | | | **8** | | | | | 7 | 33 |
| | 3 | 4 | 6 | | 7 | **9** | | 10 | 11 | 5 | 2 | | | 12 | | | | | | 8 | 34 |
| | 3 | 4 | 6 | 12 | 7 | 9 | | 10 | 11 | 5 | **2** | | | | | | | | | 8 | 35 |
| | 3 | 4 | 6 | 12 | 7 | 9 | | 10 | 11 | 5 | **2** | | | 13 | | | | | | 8 | 36 |
| | 3 | 4 | 6 | 13 | **7** | 9 | | 10 | 11 | 5 | 2 | | | 12 | | | | | | 8 | 37 |
| 3 | | 4 | 6 | 2 | 7 | 9 | | 10 | 11 | 5 | | | | | | | | | | 8 | 38 |
| **2** | 3 | 4 | 6 | 12 | 7 | 9 | | 10 | 11 | 5 | | | | | | | | | | 8 | 39 |
| | 3 | 4 | 6 | 2 | 7 | 9 | | 10 | 11 | 5 | | | | | | | | | | 8 | 40 |
| 12 | 39 | 40 | 19 | 25 | 12 | 36 | 13 | 39 | 40 | 38 | 30 | | 14 | 11 | 10 | 3 | 1 | 1 | 7 | 10 | |
| 1 | | | | 9 | 4 | 2 | | | | | 1 | 1 | 10 | 4 | 6 | 6 | 1 | | | | |
| | 3 | 1 | | | 1 | 6 | 1 | 6 | 4 | 3 | | | 4 | 3 | | | | | 1 | 1 | |

1 own-goal

| | | | | | | | | | | | | | | | | | | | | | |
|---|---|---|---|---|---|---|---|---|---|---|---|---|---|---|---|---|---|---|---|---|---|
| | 3 | 4 | | 2 | | 9 | | 10 | 7 | 5 | 6 | | 13 | | 12 | 8 | | **11** | | | 3 |
| | 1 | 1 | | 1 | | 1 | | 1 | 1 | 1 | 1 | | | | | 1 | | 1 | | | |
| | | | | | | | | | | | | | 1 | | 1 | | | | | | |
| | | | | | | | | | | | | | | | | 1 | | | | | |

| | | | | | | | | | | | | | | | | | | | | | |
|---|---|---|---|---|---|---|---|---|---|---|---|---|---|---|---|---|---|---|---|---|---|
| 7 | 3 | 4 | | 6 | | **8** | 9 | 10 | 11 | 5 | 2 | | 12 | | | | | | | | 2 |
| 2 | 3 | 4 | | 6 | | 8 | | 10 | 7 | 5 | 13 | | 9 | **11** | | 12 | | | | | 2 |
| 2 | 2 | 2 | | 2 | | 2 | 1 | 2 | 2 | 2 | 1 | | 1 | 1 | | | | | | | |
| | | | | | | | | | | | 1 | | 1 | | | 1 | | | | | |
| | | | | | | | | | | | | | | | | | | | | | |

# 1988-89

| | P | W | D | L | F | A | Pts |
|---|---|---|---|---|---|---|---|
| Arsenal | 38 | 22 | 10 | 6 | 73 | 36 | 76 |
| Liverpool | 38 | 22 | 10 | 6 | 65 | 28 | 76 |
| Nottingham F | 38 | 17 | 13 | 8 | 64 | 43 | 64 |
| Norwich C | 38 | 17 | 11 | 10 | 48 | 45 | 62 |
| Derby Co | 38 | 17 | 7 | 14 | 40 | 38 | 58 |
| Tottenham H | 38 | 15 | 12 | 11 | 60 | 46 | 57 |
| Coventry C | 38 | 14 | 13 | 11 | 47 | 42 | 55 |
| Everton | 38 | 14 | 12 | 12 | 50 | 45 | 54 |
| Q.P.R. | 38 | 14 | 11 | 13 | 43 | 37 | 53 |
| Millwall | 38 | 14 | 11 | 13 | 47 | 52 | 53 |
| Manchester U | 38 | 13 | 12 | 13 | 45 | 35 | 51 |
| Wimbledon | 38 | 14 | 9 | 15 | 50 | 46 | 51 |
| Southampton | 38 | 10 | 15 | 13 | 52 | 66 | 45 |
| Charlton A | 38 | 10 | 12 | 16 | 44 | 58 | 42 |
| Sheffield W | 38 | 10 | 12 | 16 | 34 | 51 | 42 |
| Luton T | 38 | 10 | 11 | 17 | 42 | 52 | 41 |
| Aston Villa | 38 | 9 | 13 | 16 | 45 | 56 | 40 |
| Middlesbrough | 38 | 9 | 12 | 17 | 44 | 61 | 39 |
| West Ham U | 38 | 10 | 8 | 20 | 37 | 62 | 38 |
| Newcastle U | 38 | 7 | 10 | 21 | 32 | 63 | 31 |

Manager: Arthur Cox.
Leading scorer: Dean Saunders, League 14, all matches 15.
League ever-present: Paul Blades, Michael Forsyth, Peter Shilton.
Player of the season: Mark Wright.

- The Rams added significantly to their quality in summer by signing Paul Goddard from Newcastle United and Trevor Hebberd from Oxford United.
- Dean Saunders became Derby's first £1 million player when he was signed from Oxford United in October. Robert Maxwell owned both clubs.
- Only three years after climbing out of the Third Division, Derby were fifth in the First. They would have been back in Europe but for the ban on English clubs in the wake of the Heysel disaster of 1985.
- As Peter Shilton said: 'It was a battling fifth.' Derby needed to strengthen further if they were to consolidate but the club's relationship with Robert Maxwell became increasingly troubled.

## Division One

| Match No. | Date | | Venue | Opponents | Result | | Scorers | At |
|---|---|---|---|---|---|---|---|---|
| 1 | Aug | 27 | (h) | Middlesbrough | W | 1-0 | Goddard | 1 |
| 2 | Sep | 3 | (a) | Millwall | L | 0-1 | | |
| 3 | | 10 | (h) | Newcastle U | W | 2-0 | Hebberd, Goddard | 1 |
| 4 | | 17 | (a) | Nottingham F | D | 1-1 | Hebberd | 2 |
| 5 | | 24 | (h) | QPR | L | 0-1 | | 1 |
| 6 | Oct | 1 | (a) | Southampton | D | 0-0 | | 1 |
| 7 | | 8 | (h) | Norwich C | L | 0-1 | | 1 |
| 8 | | 22 | (h) | Charlton A | D | 0-0 | | 1 |
| 9 | | 29 | (h) | Wimbledon | W | 4-1 | Saunders 2, Sage, Micklewhite | 1 |
| 10 | Nov | 5 | (a) | Tottenham H | W | 3-1 | McMinn 2, Saunders | 2 |
| 11 | | 12 | (h) | Manchester U | D | 2-2 | Saunders, Hebberd | 2 |
| 12 | | 19 | (a) | Aston Villa | W | 2-1 | Saunders, Goddard | 2 |
| 13 | | 26 | (h) | Arsenal | W | 2-1 | Callaghan, Gee | 2 |
| 14 | Dec | 3 | (a) | Sheffield W | D | 1-1 | Callaghan (pen) | 2 |
| 15 | | 10 | (h) | Luton T | L | 0-1 | | 1 |
| 16 | | 17 | (a) | Coventry C | W | 2-0 | Saunders, McMinn | 1 |
| 17 | | 26 | (h) | Liverpool | L | 0-1 | | 2 |
| 18 | | 31 | (h) | Millwall | L | 0-1 | | 1 |
| 19 | Jan | 2 | (a) | Newcastle U | W | 1-0 | Wright | 3 |
| 20 | | 14 | (h) | West Ham U | L | 1-2 | Saunders | 1 |
| 21 | | 21 | (a) | QPR | W | 1-0 | Williams | |
| 22 | Feb | 4 | (h) | Southampton | W | 3-1 | Hebberd, Goddard, Saunders (pen) | 1 |
| 23 | | 11 | (a) | Norwich C | L | 0-1 | | 1 |
| 24 | | 25 | (h) | Everton | W | 3-2 | Goddard 2, Saunders | 1 |
| 25 | Mar | 1 | (a) | Wimbledon | L | 0-4 | | |
| 26 | | 11 | (h) | Tottenham H | D | 1-1 | Saunders | 1 |
| 27 | | 18 | (a) | Middlesbrough | W | 1-0 | McMinn | 1 |
| 28 | | 25 | (h) | Nottingham F | L | 0-2 | | 2 |
| 29 | | 29 | (a) | Liverpool | L | 0-1 | | 4 |
| 30 | Apr | 1 | (h) | Coventry C | W | 1-0 | Blades | 1 |
| 31 | | 8 | (a) | West Ham U | D | 1-1 | Micklewhite | 1 |
| 32 | | 15 | (a) | Manchester U | W | 2-0 | Micklewhite, Goddard | 3 |
| 33 | | 22 | (h) | Sheffield W | W | 1-0 | Saunders | 1 |
| 34 | | 29 | (a) | Luton T | L | 0-3 | | |
| 35 | May | 6 | (h) | Aston Villa | W | 2-1 | Saunders, Hebberd | 1 |
| 36 | | 10 | (a) | Charlton A | L | 0-3 | | |
| 37 | | 13 | (a) | Arsenal | W | 2-1 | Saunders 2 (1 pen) | 4 |
| 38 | | 15 | (a) | Everton | L | 0-1 | | 1 |

FINAL LEAGUE POSITION: 5th in Division One

Appeara
Subst

## FA Cup

| | | | | | | | | |
|---|---|---|---|---|---|---|---|---|
| 3 | Jan | 7 | (h) | Southampton | D | 1-1 | Hebberd | 17 |
| R | | 10 | (a) | Southampton | W | 2-1 | McMinn, Callaghan | 16 |
| 4 | | 28 | (a) | Watford | L | 1-2 | Micklewhite | 20 |

Appeara
Subst.
(

## League Cup

| | | | | | | | | |
|---|---|---|---|---|---|---|---|---|
| 2 | Sep | 28 | (h) | Southend U | W | 1-0 | Hebberd | 9 |
| 2 | Oct | 11 | (a) | Southend U | W | 2-1 | Penney, Hebberd | 4 |
| 3 | Nov | 1 | (a) | West Ham U | L | 0-5 | | 14 |

Appeara
Substi
G

**Derby County played in the Full Members' Cup (see Rams in Other Competitions)**

n P

| Sage M | Forsyth M | Williams G | Wright M | Blades P | Micklewhite G | Chiedozie J | Goddard P | Hebberd T | Callaghan N | Gee P | Pickering N | McMinn K | Cross S | Penney D | Hindmarch R | Saunders D | Patterson M | |
|---|---|---|---|---|---|---|---|---|---|---|---|---|---|---|---|---|---|---|
| 2 | 3 | 4 | 5 | 6 | 7 | 8 | 9 | 10 | 11 | | | | | | | | | 1 |
| 2 | 3 | 4 | 5 | 6 | 7 | **8** | 9 | 10 | 11 | 12 | 13 | | | | | | | 2 |
| 2 | 3 | 4 | 5 | 6 | | | 9 | 10 | 11 | 8 | 12 | **7** | 13 | | | | | 3 |
| 2 | 3 | 4 | 5 | 6 | | | 9 | 10 | 11 | **8** | | 7 | 12 | | | | | 4 |
| 2 | 3 | 4 | 5 | 6 | 12 | | 9 | 10 | 11 | | 13 | **7** | 8 | | | | | 5 |
| 2 | 3 | 4 | 5 | 6 | | | 9 | 10 | | | 11 | 7 | | 8 | | | | 6 |
| 2 | 3 | 4 | 5 | 6 | | | 9 | 10 | | | 11 | 7 | | 8 | | | | 7 |
| 2 | 3 | 4 | | 6 | | | 9 | 10 | | | 11 | 7 | | 8 | 5 | | | 8 |
| 2 | 3 | 4 | | 6 | 12 | | 9 | 10 | **11** | | | 7 | | | 5 | 8 | | 9 |
| 2 | 3 | | 5 | 6 | | | 9 | 10 | 11 | | | 7 | 4 | | | 8 | | 10 |
| 2 | 3 | 4 | 5 | 6 | 12 | | 9 | 10 | **11** | | | 7 | | | | 8 | | 11 |
| 2 | 3 | 4 | 5 | 6 | 12 | | 9 | 10 | **11** | | | 7 | | | | 8 | | 12 |
| 2 | 3 | 4 | 5 | 6 | | | | 10 | 11 | 9 | | 7 | | | | 8 | | 13 |
| 2 | 3 | 4 | 5 | 6 | 12 | | | 10 | 11 | **9** | | 7 | | | | 8 | | 14 |
| | 3 | 4 | 5 | 6 | | | **9** | 10 | 11 | 12 | | 7 | | | | 8 | 2 | 15 |
| | 3 | 4 | 5 | 2 | | | 9 | 10 | 11 | | | 7 | | | 6 | 8 | | 16 |
| | 3 | 4 | 5 | 2 | 13 | | **9** | 10 | 11 | | | 7 | 12 | | 6 | 8 | | 17 |
| | 3 | 4 | 5 | 2 | 13 | | 9 | **10** | 11 | | | 7 | 12 | | 6 | 8 | | 18 |
| | 3 | 4 | 5 | 2 | | | 9 | 10 | 11 | | | 7 | | | 6 | 8 | | 19 |
| | 3 | 4 | 5 | 2 | | | | 10 | 11 | 9 | | **7** | 13 | 12 | 6 | 8 | | 20 |
| | 3 | 4 | 5 | 2 | | | | 10 | **11** | 9 | | 7 | 12 | | 6 | 8 | | 21 |
| | 3 | 4 | | 6 | 11 | | 9 | 10 | | | | 7 | 2 | | 5 | 8 | | 22 |
| | 3 | 4 | 5 | 2 | 11 | | 9 | **10** | | | | 7 | 12 | 13 | 6 | 8 | | 23 |
| | 3 | 4 | 5 | 2 | 7 | | 9 | 10 | | | 11 | | | | 6 | 8 | | 24 |
| | 3 | 4 | 5 | 2 | **7** | | 9 | 10 | | | 11 | | 13 | 12 | 6 | 8 | | 25 |
| | 3 | 4 | 5 | 2 | 11 | | **9** | 10 | | | | 7 | 12 | | 6 | 8 | | 26 |
| | 3 | 4 | 5 | 2 | 11 | | | | | 9 | | 7 | 10 | | 6 | 8 | | 27 |
| | 3 | 4 | 5 | 2 | 11 | | | 10 | | **9** | | 7 | 12 | | 6 | 8 | | 28 |
| | 3 | 4 | 5 | 2 | 11 | | | **10** | | | | 7 | 9 | 12 | 6 | 8 | | 29 |
| | 3 | 4 | 5 | 2 | 11 | | 9 | 10 | | | | 7 | | | 6 | 8 | | 30 |
| | 3 | 4 | 5 | 2 | 11 | | **9** | 10 | | | | 7 | 12 | | 6 | 8 | | 31 |
| | 3 | 4 | 5 | 2 | 11 | | 9 | 10 | | | | 7 | | | 6 | 8 | | 32 |
| | 3 | 4 | 5 | 2 | 11 | | 9 | 10 | | | | 7 | | | 6 | 8 | | 33 |
| | 3 | 4 | 5 | 2 | 11 | | **9** | 10 | | 12 | | 7 | 13 | | 6 | 8 | | 34 |
| | 3 | 4 | 5 | 2 | 11 | | 9 | 10 | | | | 7 | | | 6 | 8 | | 35 |
| | 3 | 4 | 5 | 2 | 11 | | 9 | 10 | | | | **7** | | 12 | 6 | 8 | | 36 |
| 2 | 3 | 4 | | 5 | 11 | | 9 | 10 | | | | | 7 | | 6 | 8 | | 37 |
| 2 | 3 | 4 | | 5 | 11 | | **9** | 10 | | 13 | | | 7 | 12 | 6 | 8 | | 38 |
| 16 | 38 | 37 | 33 | 38 | 19 | 2 | 31 | 37 | 18 | 8 | 5 | 32 | 7 | 3 | 25 | 30 | 1 | |
| | | | | | 7 | | | | | 4 | 3 | | 12 | 6 | | | | |
| 1 | | 1 | 1 | 1 | 3 | | 7 | 5 | 2 | 1 | | 4 | | | | 14 | | |

| | | | | | | | | | | | | | | | | | | |
|---|---|---|---|---|---|---|---|---|---|---|---|---|---|---|---|---|---|---|
| | 3 | 4 | 5 | 2 | 13 | | **9** | 10 | 11 | | | 7 | 12 | | 6 | 8 | | 3 |
| | 3 | 4 | 5 | 2 | | | | 10 | 11 | 9 | | 7 | | | 6 | 8 | | R |
| | 3 | 4 | | 2 | 13 | | 12 | 10 | 11 | **9** | | 7 | 5 | | 6 | 8 | | 4 |
| | 3 | 3 | 2 | 3 | | | 1 | 3 | 3 | 2 | | 3 | 1 | | 3 | 3 | | |
| | | | | | 2 | | 1 | | | | | | 1 | | | | | |
| | | | | | 1 | | | 1 | 1 | | | 1 | | | | | | |

| | | | | | | | | | | | | | | | | | | |
|---|---|---|---|---|---|---|---|---|---|---|---|---|---|---|---|---|---|---|
| 2 | 3 | 4 | 5 | 6 | 12 | | 9 | 10 | | | 11 | 7 | | **8** | | | | 2 |
| 2 | 3 | 4 | 5 | 6 | | | 9 | 10 | | | 11 | 7 | | 8 | | | | 2 |
| 2 | 3 | 4 | | 6 | 12 | | 9 | 10 | 11 | **8** | | 7 | 13 | | 5 | | | 3 |
| 3 | 3 | 3 | 2 | 3 | | | 3 | 3 | 1 | 1 | 2 | 3 | | 2 | 1 | | | |
| | | | | | 2 | | | | | | | | 1 | | | | | |
| | | | | | | | | 2 | | | | | | 1 | | | | |

# 1989-90

| | P | W | D | L | F | A | Pts |
|---|---|---|---|---|---|---|---|
| Liverpool | 38 | 23 | 10 | 5 | 78 | 37 | 79 |
| Aston Villa | 38 | 21 | 7 | 10 | 57 | 38 | 70 |
| Tottenham H | 38 | 19 | 6 | 13 | 59 | 47 | 63 |
| Arsenal | 38 | 18 | 8 | 12 | 54 | 38 | 62 |
| Chelsea | 38 | 16 | 12 | 10 | 58 | 50 | 60 |
| Everton | 38 | 17 | 8 | 13 | 57 | 46 | 59 |
| Southampton | 38 | 15 | 10 | 13 | 71 | 63 | 55 |
| Wimbledon | 38 | 13 | 16 | 9 | 47 | 40 | 55 |
| Nottingham F | 38 | 15 | 9 | 14 | 55 | 47 | 54 |
| Norwich C | 38 | 13 | 14 | 11 | 44 | 42 | 53 |
| Q.P.R. | 38 | 13 | 11 | 14 | 45 | 44 | 50 |
| Coventry C | 38 | 14 | 7 | 17 | 39 | 59 | 49 |
| Manchester U | 38 | 13 | 9 | 16 | 46 | 47 | 48 |
| Manchester C | 38 | 12 | 12 | 14 | 43 | 52 | 48 |
| Crystal Palace | 38 | 13 | 9 | 16 | 42 | 66 | 48 |
| Derby Co | 38 | 13 | 7 | 18 | 43 | 40 | 46 |
| Luton T | 38 | 10 | 13 | 15 | 43 | 57 | 43 |
| Sheffield W | 38 | 11 | 10 | 17 | 35 | 51 | 43 |
| Charlton A | 38 | 7 | 9 | 22 | 31 | 57 | 30 |
| Millwall | 38 | 5 | 11 | 22 | 39 | 65 | 26 |

Manager: Arthur Cox.
Leading scorer: Dean Saunders, League 11, all matches 21.
League ever-present: Michael Forsyth, Dean Saunders, Geraint Williams.
Player of the season: Mark Wright.

- Peter Shilton replaced Roy McFarland as Derby's most capped player when he kept goal against Holland in Cagliari during the 1990 World Cup finals. It was Shilton's 29th appearance as a Rams player and he extended this to 34 out of his record 125 caps, earned with five clubs.
- Shilton was captain against Egypt and Italy in the World Cup finals and Mark Wright was also in the England side.
- Shilton's first absence for the Rams, on 31 March, ended a run of 124 consecutive games, 108 in the League.
- Paul Goddard, the ideal partner for Dean Saunders, joined Millwall for £800,000 in December. Although it was then the highest fee received by Derby, it was a shock move and an indication that Robert Maxwell was curbing the finances.

## Division One

| Match No. | Date | | Venue | Opponents | Result | | Scorers | At |
|---|---|---|---|---|---|---|---|---|
| 1 | Aug | 19 | (a) | Charlton A | D | 0-0 | | |
| 2 | | 23 | (h) | Wimbledon | D | 1-1 | Hebberd | 1 |
| 3 | | 26 | (h) | Manchester U | W | 2-0 | Goddard, Saunders (pen) | 2 |
| 4 | | 30 | (a) | Nottingham F | L | 1-2 | Hodge (og) | 2 |
| 5 | Sep | 9 | (h) | Liverpool | L | 0-3 | | 2 |
| 6 | | 16 | (a) | QPR | W | 1-0 | Saunders | 1 |
| 7 | | 23 | (h) | Southampton | L | 0-1 | | 1 |
| 8 | | 30 | (a) | Aston Villa | L | 0-1 | | 1 |
| 9 | Oct | 14 | (h) | Crystal P | W | 3-1 | Goddard 2, Saunders (pen) | |
| 10 | | 21 | (h) | Chelsea | L | 0-1 | | 1 |
| 11 | | 28 | (a) | Arsenal | D | 1-1 | Goddard | 3 |
| 12 | Nov | 4 | (a) | Luton T | L | 0-1 | | |
| 13 | | 11 | (h) | Manchester C | W | 6-0 | Saunders 2 (2 pens), Wright, Hebberd, Goddard, Micklewhite | 1 |
| 14 | | 18 | (h) | Sheffield W | W | 2-0 | Goddard, Saunders | 1 |
| 15 | | 25 | (a) | Tottenham H | W | 2-1 | Saunders, Goddard | 2 |
| 16 | Dec | 2 | (h) | Charlton A | W | 2-0 | Saunders, Micklewhite | 1 |
| 17 | | 9 | (a) | Wimbledon | D | 1-1 | Goddard | |
| 18 | | 16 | (a) | Norwich C | L | 0-1 | | 1 |
| 19 | | 26 | (h) | Everton | L | 0-1 | | 2 |
| 20 | | 30 | (h) | Coventry C | W | 4-1 | Hebberd 2, Pickering, Ramage | 1 |
| 21 | Jan | 1 | (a) | Millwall | D | 1-1 | Pickering | 1 |
| 22 | | 13 | (a) | Manchester U | W | 2-1 | Wright, Pickering | 3 |
| 23 | | 20 | (h) | Nottingham F | L | 0-2 | | 2 |
| 24 | Feb | 10 | (h) | QPR | W | 2-0 | Gee, Saunders | 1 |
| 25 | | 24 | (h) | Tottenham H | W | 2-1 | Saunders, Harford | 1 |
| 26 | Mar | 3 | (a) | Sheffield W | L | 0-1 | | 2 |
| 27 | | 10 | (a) | Southampton | L | 1-2 | Saunders | 1 |
| 28 | | 17 | (h) | Aston Villa | L | 0-1 | | 2 |
| 29 | | 20 | (a) | Crystal P | D | 1-1 | Wright | 1 |
| 30 | | 24 | (h) | Arsenal | L | 1-3 | Briscoe | 1 |
| 31 | | 31 | (a) | Chelsea | D | 1-1 | Harford | 1 |
| 32 | Apr | 7 | (a) | Coventry C | L | 0-1 | | 1 |
| 33 | | 14 | (h) | Millwall | W | 2-0 | Harford 2 | 1 |
| 34 | | 16 | (a) | Everton | L | 1-2 | Wright | 2 |
| 35 | | 21 | (h) | Norwich C | L | 0-2 | | 1 |
| 36 | | 28 | (a) | Manchester C | W | 1-0 | Wright | 2 |
| 37 | May | 1 | (a) | Liverpool | L | 0-1 | | 3 |
| 38 | | 5 | (h) | Luton T | L | 2-3 | Wright, P.Williams | 1 |

FINAL LEAGUE POSITION: 16th in Division One

Appear
Subst

## FA Cup

| | | | | | | | | |
|---|---|---|---|---|---|---|---|---|
| 3 | Jan | 7 | (a) | Port Vale | D | 1-1 | Hebberd | 1 |
| R | | 10 | (h) | Port Vale | L | 2-3 | Ramage, Francis | 2 |

Appear
Subst

## League Cup

| | | | | | | | | |
|---|---|---|---|---|---|---|---|---|
| 2 | Sep | 19 | (a) | Cambridge U | L | 1-2 | Goddard | 5 |
| 2 | Oct | 4 | (h) | Cambridge U | W | 5-0 | Saunders 3, Goddard, McMinn | 1 |
| 3 | | 25 | (h) | Sheffield W | W | 2-1 | Saunders 2 (1 pen) | 1 |
| 4 | Nov | 22 | (h) | West Brom A | W | 2-0 | McMinn 2 | 2 |
| 5 | Jan | 17 | (a) | West Ham U | D | 1-1 | Saunders | 2 |
| R | | 24 | (h) | West Ham U | D | 0-0 | | 2 |
| 2R | | 31 | (a) | West Ham U | L | 1-2 | Saunders | 2 |

Appear
Subst

**Derby County played in the Full Members' Cup (see Rams in Other Competitions)**

| Sage M | Forsyth M | Williams G | Wright M | Hindmarch R | McMinn K | Saunders D | Goddard P | Pickering N | Micklewhite G | Cross S | Gee P | Hebberd T | Blades P | Ramage C | McCord B | Harford M | Patterson M | Francis K | Davidson J | Briscoe R | Williams P | Hayward S | Taylor M | |
|---|---|---|---|---|---|---|---|---|---|---|---|---|---|---|---|---|---|---|---|---|---|---|---|---|
| 2 | 3 | 4 | 5 | 6 | **7** | 8 | 9 | 10 | 11 | 12 | | | | | | | | | | | | | | 1 |
| 2 | 3 | 4 | 5 | 6 | 7 | 8 | **9** | 10 | 11 | | 12 | 13 | | | | | | | | | | | | 2 |
| | 3 | 4 | 5 | 6 | **7** | 8 | 9 | | 11 | 12 | | 10 | 2 | | | | | | | | | | | 3 |
| | 3 | 4 | 5 | 6 | 7 | 8 | **9** | | 11 | 13 | 12 | 10 | 2 | | | | | | | | | | | 4 |
| | 3 | 4 | 5 | 6 | **7** | 8 | 9 | 12 | 11 | | | 10 | 2 | | | | | | | | | | | 5 |
| | 3 | 4 | 5 | 6 | 7 | 8 | 9 | | 11 | | | 10 | 2 | | | | | | | | | | | 6 |
| 12 | 3 | 4 | 5 | 6 | 7 | 8 | 9 | 10 | 11 | | 13 | | **2** | | | | | | | | | | | 7 |
| 2 | 3 | 4 | 5 | | 7 | 8 | **9** | | 11 | | 12 | 10 | 6 | | | | | | | | | | | 8 |
| 2 | 3 | 4 | 5 | | 7 | 8 | 9 | 12 | 11 | | | 10 | **6** | | | | | | | | | | | 9 |
| 2 | 3 | 4 | 5 | | 7 | 8 | 9 | 12 | 11 | | | **10** | 6 | | | | | | | | | | | 10 |
| 2 | 3 | 4 | 5 | | 7 | 8 | 9 | 12 | 11 | | | 10 | **6** | | | | | | | | | | | 11 |
| 2 | 3 | 4 | 5 | | 7 | 8 | 9 | | 11 | | | 10 | 6 | | | | | | | | | | | 12 |
| 2 | 3 | 4 | 5 | | 7 | 8 | 9 | | 11 | | | 10 | 6 | | | | | | | | | | | 13 |
| 2 | 3 | 4 | 5 | | 7 | 8 | 9 | | 11 | | | 10 | 6 | | | | | | | | | | | 14 |
| 2 | 3 | 4 | 5 | 6 | **7** | 8 | 9 | 12 | 11 | | | 10 | | | | | | | | | | | | 15 |
| 2 | 3 | 4 | 5 | 6 | | 8 | | 7 | 11 | | | 10 | | 9 | | | | | | | | | | 16 |
| 2 | 3 | 4 | 5 | 6 | | 8 | 9 | 7 | 11 | | | 10 | | | | | | | | | | | | 17 |
| 2 | 3 | 4 | 5 | **6** | | 8 | 9 | 7 | 11 | 13 | | 10 | 12 | | | | | | | | | | | 18 |
| 2 | 3 | 4 | 5 | | | 8 | 9 | 7 | | **11** | | 10 | 6 | 13 | 12 | | | | | | | | | 19 |
| 2 | 3 | 4 | **5** | | | 8 | | 7 | | 12 | | 10 | 6 | 9 | 11 | | | | | | | | | 20 |
| 2 | 3 | 4 | | 5 | | 8 | | 7 | | 12 | | 10 | 6 | 9 | **11** | | | | | | | | | 21 |
| 2 | 3 | 4 | 5 | 6 | | 8 | | 7 | | 11 | | 10 | | 9 | | | | | | | | | | 22 |
| 2 | 3 | 4 | 5 | 6 | | 8 | | **7** | | | | 10 | | | 12 | 9 | 11 | 13 | | | | | | 23 |
| 2 | 3 | 4 | 5 | | | 8 | | | | | 7 | 10 | | | | 9 | | | 6 | 11 | | | | 24 |
| 2 | 3 | 4 | 5 | 6 | | 8 | | 11 | | | **7** | | | 12 | | 9 | 10 | | | | | | | 25 |
| 2 | 3 | 4 | 5 | 6 | | 8 | | 11 | | | 7 | | | 12 | | **9** | 10 | | | 13 | | | | 26 |
| 2 | 3 | 4 | | 5 | | 8 | | 11 | | | **7** | | 6 | 13 | | 9 | 10 | 12 | | | | | | 27 |
| 2 | 3 | 4 | 5 | | | 8 | | 11 | | | | | 6 | **10** | | 9 | 7 | 13 | | 12 | | | | 28 |
| 2 | 3 | 4 | 5 | | | 8 | | 11 | | | | | 6 | | | 9 | **7** | | | 10 | 12 | | | 29 |
| 2 | 3 | 4 | 5 | 6 | | 8 | | **10** | | | | | | | | 9 | | | | 11 | 7 | 12 | | 30 |
| 2 | 3 | 4 | 5 | 6 | | 8 | | **10** | | | | | | | | 9 | | 13 | | 11 | 7 | 12 | 1 | 31 |
| 2 | 3 | 4 | 5 | 6 | | 8 | | | | | | | | | | 9 | | 13 | 12 | 11 | **7** | 10 | 1 | 32 |
| 2 | 3 | 4 | 5 | 6 | | 8 | | | | | | | | | | 9 | 7 | | | 11 | 10 | | | 33 |
| 2 | 3 | 4 | 5 | 6 | | 8 | | | | | | | | | | 9 | **7** | 12 | | 11 | 10 | | 1 | 34 |
| 2 | 3 | 4 | **5** | 6 | | 8 | | | | | | | | | | 9 | 7 | 13 | 12 | 11 | 10 | | | 35 |
| 2 | 3 | 4 | 5 | 6 | | 8 | | | | | | | | 11 | | 9 | | | 7 | | 10 | | | 36 |
| 2 | 3 | 4 | 5 | 6 | | 8 | | | | | | | | **11** | | 9 | | 12 | 7 | | 10 | | | 37 |
| 2 | 3 | 4 | 5 | 6 | | 8 | | | | | | 12 | | **11** | | 9 | | | 7 | | 10 | | | 38 |
| 33 | 38 | 38 | 36 | 26 | 15 | 38 | 18 | 18 | 18 | 2 | 4 | 21 | 18 | 8 | 2 | 16 | 9 | | 4 | 8 | 9 | 1 | 3 | |
| 1 | | | | | | | | 5 | | 6 | 4 | 2 | 1 | 4 | 2 | | | 8 | 2 | 2 | 1 | 2 | | |
| | | | 6 | | | 11 | 8 | 3 | 2 | | 1 | 4 | | 1 | | 4 | | | | 1 | 1 | | | |

1 own-goal

| | | | | | | | | | | | | | | | | | | | |
|---|---|---|---|---|---|---|---|---|---|---|---|---|---|---|---|---|---|---|---|
| 2 | 3 | 4 | | 5 | | 8 | | 7 | | 12 | | 10 | **6** | 9 | 11 | | | 13 | 3 |
| 2 | 3 | 4 | 5 | 6 | | 8 | | 7 | | | | 10 | | **9** | 11 | | | 12 | R |
| 2 | 2 | 2 | 1 | 2 | | 2 | | 2 | | | | 2 | 1 | 2 | 2 | | | | |
| | | | | | | | | | | 1 | | | | | | | | 2 | |
| | | | | | | | | | | | | 1 | | 1 | | | | 1 | |

| | | | | | | | | | | | | | | | | | | | | | | | | |
|---|---|---|---|---|---|---|---|---|---|---|---|---|---|---|---|---|---|---|---|---|---|---|---|---|
| | 3 | 4 | 5 | 6 | 7 | 8 | 9 | 12 | 11 | | | **10** | 2 | | | | | | | | | | | 2 |
| 2 | 3 | 4 | 5 | | 7 | 8 | 9 | | 11 | | | 10 | 6 | | | | | | | | | | | 2 |
| 2 | 3 | 4 | 5 | | 7 | 8 | 9 | | 11 | | | 10 | 6 | | | | | | | | | | | 3 |
| 2 | 3 | 4 | 5 | | 7 | 8 | 9 | | 11 | 12 | | 10 | **6** | | | | | | | | | | | 4 |
| 2 | 3 | 4 | 5 | 6 | | 8 | | 7 | | **11** | | 10 | | 9 | | | 12 | 13 | | | | | | 5 |
| 2 | 3 | 4 | 5 | 6 | | 8 | | | | | | 10 | | | **11** | 9 | 7 | 13 | | 12 | | | 1 | R |
| 2 | 3 | 4 | | | | 8 | | | | | | 10 | | 12 | | 9 | 5 | **7** | 6 | 11 | | | 1 | 2R |
| 6 | 7 | 7 | 6 | 3 | 4 | 7 | 4 | 1 | 4 | 1 | | 7 | 4 | 1 | 1 | 2 | 2 | 1 | 1 | 1 | | | 2 | |
| | | | | | | | | 1 | | 1 | | | | 1 | | | 1 | 2 | | 1 | | | | |
| | | | | | 3 | 7 | 2 | | | | | | | | | | | | | | | | | |

# 1990-91

| | P | W | D | L | F | A | Pts |
|---|---|---|---|---|---|---|---|
| Arsenal* | 38 | 24 | 13 | 1 | 74 | 18 | 83 |
| Liverpool | 38 | 23 | 7 | 8 | 77 | 40 | 76 |
| Crystal Palace | 38 | 20 | 9 | 9 | 50 | 41 | 69 |
| Leeds U | 38 | 19 | 7 | 12 | 65 | 47 | 64 |
| Manchester C | 38 | 17 | 11 | 10 | 64 | 53 | 62 |
| Manchester U** | 38 | 16 | 12 | 10 | 58 | 45 | 59 |
| Wimbledon | 38 | 14 | 14 | 10 | 53 | 46 | 56 |
| Nottingham F | 38 | 14 | 12 | 12 | 65 | 50 | 54 |
| Everton | 38 | 13 | 12 | 13 | 50 | 46 | 51 |
| Tottenham H | 38 | 11 | 16 | 11 | 51 | 50 | 49 |
| Chelsea | 38 | 13 | 10 | 15 | 58 | 69 | 49 |
| Q.P.R. | 38 | 12 | 10 | 16 | 44 | 53 | 46 |
| Sheffield U | 38 | 13 | 7 | 18 | 36 | 55 | 46 |
| Southampton | 38 | 12 | 9 | 17 | 58 | 69 | 45 |
| Norwich C | 38 | 13 | 6 | 19 | 41 | 64 | 45 |
| Coventry C | 38 | 11 | 11 | 16 | 42 | 49 | 44 |
| Aston Villa | 38 | 9 | 14 | 15 | 46 | 58 | 41 |
| Luton T | 38 | 10 | 7 | 21 | 42 | 61 | 37 |
| Sunderland | 38 | 8 | 10 | 20 | 38 | 60 | 34 |
| Derby Co | 38 | 5 | 9 | 24 | 37 | 75 | 24 |

*Arsenal had two points deducted for disciplinary reasons.

**Manchester United had one point deducted for disciplinary reasons.

Manager: Arthur Cox.
Leading scorer: Dean Saunders, League 17, all matches 21.
League ever-present: Dean Saunders.
Player of the season: Dean Saunders.

- Dean Saunders missed only one match in his time at Derby, a League Cup tie for which he was ineligible. He left with runs of 130 consecutive appearances and 106 in the League.
- At the end of the season, Saunders (£2.9 million) and Mark Wright (£2.3 million) joined Liverpool. Much of the cash from record incoming fees was used to pay off Robert Maxwell, who became a liability to the Rams.
- Mark Wright captained England against the USSR at Wembley in May.
- Injury ruled out Geraint Williams after he completed 100 consecutive games in November and Michael Forsyth appeared in 124 consecutive matches to January.
- Unable to buy or even sign players on loan, Derby had a disastrous season. Between December and April, they endured a club record 20 League games, including nine at home, without a victory and equalled their worst home defeat in March when Liverpool beat them 7–1.

## Division One

| Match No. | Date | | Venue | Opponents | Result | | Scorers | Att |
|---|---|---|---|---|---|---|---|---|
| 1 | Aug | 25 | (a) | Chelsea | L | 1-2 | Saunders | 2 |
| 2 | | 29 | (h) | Sheffield U | D | 1-1 | Saunders | 1 |
| 3 | Sep | 1 | (h) | Wimbledon | D | 1-1 | Saunders (pen) | 12 |
| 4 | | 8 | (a) | Tottenham H | L | 0-3 | | 2 |
| 5 | | 15 | (h) | Aston Villa | L | 0-2 | | 1 |
| 6 | | 22 | (a) | Norwich C | L | 1-2 | Patterson | 1 |
| 7 | | 29 | (h) | Crystal P | L | 0-2 | | 1 |
| 8 | Oct | 6 | (a) | Liverpool | L | 0-2 | | 3 |
| 9 | | 20 | (h) | Manchester C | D | 1-1 | Saunders | 1 |
| 10 | | 27 | (a) | Southampton | W | 1-0 | Harford | 1 |
| 11 | Nov | 3 | (h) | Luton T | W | 2-1 | Saunders (pen), Callaghan | 1 |
| 12 | | 10 | (h) | Manchester U | D | 0-0 | | 2 |
| 13 | | 17 | (a) | Leeds U | L | 0-3 | | 2 |
| 14 | | 24 | (h) | Nottingham F | W | 2-1 | Ramage, Saunders | 2 |
| 15 | Dec | 1 | (a) | Sunderland | W | 2-1 | Saunders, Harford | 2 |
| 16 | | 15 | (h) | Chelsea | L | 4-6 | Saunders 2, Hebberd, Micklewhite | 1 |
| 17 | | 23 | (h) | QPR | D | 1-1 | Saunders | 1 |
| 18 | | 26 | (a) | Arsenal | L | 0-3 | | 2 |
| 19 | | 29 | (a) | Everton | L | 0-2 | | 2 |
| 20 | Jan | 1 | (h) | Coventry C | D | 1-1 | Harford | 1 |
| 21 | | 12 | (a) | Wimbledon | L | 1-3 | Harford | 4 |
| 22 | | 20 | (h) | Tottenham H | L | 0-1 | | 17 |
| 23 | | 26 | (a) | Sheffield U | L | 0-1 | | 18 |
| 24 | Feb | 2 | (a) | Aston Villa | L | 2-3 | Harford, Sage | 21 |
| 25 | | 23 | (h) | Norwich C | D | 0-0 | | 14 |
| 26 | Mar | 2 | (h) | Sunderland | D | 3-3 | Saunders 3 (1 pen) | 16 |
| 27 | | 16 | (a) | Crystal P | L | 1-2 | Micklewhite | 14 |
| 28 | | 23 | (h) | Liverpool | L | 1-7 | Saunders (pen) | 20 |
| 29 | | 30 | (h) | Arsenal | L | 0-2 | | 18 |
| 30 | Apr | 1 | (a) | QPR | D | 1-1 | Harford | 12 |
| 31 | | 10 | (a) | Nottingham F | L | 0-1 | | 25 |
| 32 | | 13 | (a) | Coventry C | L | 0-3 | | 11 |
| 33 | | 16 | (a) | Manchester U | L | 1-3 | P.Williams | 32 |
| 34 | | 20 | (a) | Manchester C | L | 1-2 | Harford | 24 |
| 35 | | 23 | (h) | Leeds U | L | 0-1 | | 12 |
| 36 | May | 4 | (h) | Southampton | W | 6-2 | P.Williams 3 (1 pen), Saunders 2, Phillips | 11 |
| 37 | | 8 | (h) | Everton | L | 2-3 | Harford (pen), Saunders | 12 |
| 38 | | 11 | (a) | Luton T | L | 0-2 | | 12 |

FINAL LEAGUE POSITION: 20th in Division One – Relegated

Appeara
Substi
G

## FA Cup

| | | | | | | | | |
|---|---|---|---|---|---|---|---|---|
| 3 | Jan | 5 | (a) | Newcastle U | L | 0-2 | | 19 |

Appeara
Substi

## League Cup

| | | | | | | | | |
|---|---|---|---|---|---|---|---|---|
| 2 | Sep | 25 | (a) | Carlisle U | D | 1-1 | Saunders | 7 |
| 2 | Oct | 10 | (h) | Carlisle U | W | 1-0 | Saunders | 12 |
| 3 | | 31 | (h) | Sunderland | W | 6-0 | Harford 3, Ramage 2, Bennett (og) | 16 |
| 4 | Nov | 28 | (a) | Sheffield W | D | 1-1 | Saunders | 25 |
| R | Dec | 12 | (h) | Sheffield W | L | 1-2 | Micklewhite | 17 |

Appeara
Substi
G

**Derby County played in the Full Members' Cup (see Rams in Other Competitions)**

| Shilton P | Sage M | Forsyth M | Williams G | Wright M | Davidson J | Micklewhite G | Saunders D | Harford M | Ramage C | Williams P | Patterson M | Hebberd T | Watson A | Francis K | Callaghan N | Cross S | Gee P | Pickering N | Briscoe R | Kavanagh J | Taylor M | McMinn K | Wilson I | Phillips J | Hayward S | |
|---|---|---|---|---|---|---|---|---|---|---|---|---|---|---|---|---|---|---|---|---|---|---|---|---|---|---|
| 1 | 2 | 3 | 4 | 5 | 6 | 7 | 8 | 9 | 10 | **11** | 12 | | | | | | | | | | | | | | | 1 |
| 1 | 2 | 3 | 4 | 5 | | 7 | 8 | 9 | 6 | 11 | | 10 | | | | | | | | | | | | | | 2 |
| 1 | 2 | 3 | 4 | 5 | | **7** | 8 | 9 | 10 | 11 | | 13 | 6 | 12 | | | | | | | | | | | | 3 |
| 1 | 2 | 3 | 4 | 5 | | **7** | 8 | 9 | 10 | 11 | 13 | 12 | 6 | | | | | | | | | | | | | 4 |
| 1 | | 3 | 4 | 5 | | 7 | 8 | 9 | | 11 | 2 | 10 | 6 | | | | | | | | | | | | | 5 |
| 1 | 12 | 3 | 4 | 5 | 11 | 7 | 8 | 9 | | | **2** | 10 | 6 | 13 | | | | | | | | | | | | 6 |
| 1 | 2 | 3 | 4 | 5 | | **7** | 8 | 9 | | 10 | | 12 | 6 | | 11 | | | | | | | | | | | 7 |
| 1 | 2 | 6 | 4 | 5 | | 7 | 8 | 9 | 10 | 3 | | | | | 11 | | | | | | | | | | | 8 |
| 1 | 2 | 6 | 4 | 5 | | 7 | 8 | 9 | **10** | | | 12 | | | 11 | 3 | | | | | | | | | | 9 |
| 1 | 2 | 6 | 4 | 5 | | 7 | 8 | 9 | 10 | | | | | | 11 | 3 | | | | | | | | | | 10 |
| 1 | 2 | 6 | 4 | 5 | | 7 | 8 | | 10 | | | | | | 11 | 3 | 9 | | | | | | | | | 11 |
| 1 | **2** | 6 | 4 | 5 | | 7 | 8 | 9 | 10 | | | | | | 11 | 3 | | 12 | | | | | | | | 12 |
| 1 | | 6 | 4 | 5 | | 7 | 8 | 9 | 10 | | 12 | 13 | | | 11 | **3** | | 2 | | | | | | | | 13 |
| 1 | | 6 | **4** | 5 | | 7 | 8 | 9 | 12 | | 3 | 10 | | | 11 | | | 2 | | | | | | | | 14 |
| 1 | | 6 | | 5 | | | 8 | 9 | 4 | | 2 | 10 | | | 11 | | | 3 | 7 | | | | | | | 15 |
| | 2 | 6 | | 5 | | 7 | 8 | 9 | **4** | 12 | | 10 | | | 11 | | | 3 | | | | | | | | 16 |
| | 2 | 6 | | 5 | | 7 | 8 | 9 | 12 | 4 | | **10** | | | 11 | | | 3 | | 13 | | | | | | 17 |
| | 2 | 6 | | 5 | 13 | 7 | 8 | 9 | 10 | **4** | | | | | 11 | | | 3 | | 12 | 1 | | | | | 18 |
| | 2 | 6 | | 5 | | **7** | 8 | 9 | 10 | 4 | | | | | | 11 | 13 | 3 | | 12 | 1 | | | | | 19 |
| | 2 | 6 | | 5 | 12 | | 8 | 9 | 10 | **4** | | | | | | 11 | | 3 | | 7 | 1 | | | | | 20 |
| | 2 | | | 5 | 12 | | 8 | 9 | | | 4 | 10 | | | | 7 | | **3** | 11 | 6 | | | | | | 21 |
| | 2 | | 4 | 5 | | **7** | 8 | 9 | | | 12 | 10 | | | | 3 | | 11 | | 6 | | | | | | 22 |
| | 2 | 6 | 4 | 5 | | 7 | 8 | 9 | | | | 10 | | | | 3 | | | | | | 11 | | | | 23 |
| | 2 | 6 | 4 | 5 | | 7 | 8 | 9 | | | | 10 | | | | 3 | | | | | | 11 | | | | 24 |
| | 2 | 6 | 4 | 5 | | 7 | 8 | 9 | | | | 12 | | | | 3 | | | | | | **11** | 10 | | | 25 |
| | 2 | 6 | 4 | 5 | | 7 | 8 | 9 | | | | | | | | 3 | | | | | | 11 | 10 | | | 26 |
| | 2 | 6 | 4 | 5 | | 7 | 8 | | | | | 11 | | | | 3 | | | | | | 9 | 10 | | | 27 |
| | 2 | 6 | 4 | 5 | | 7 | 8 | 9 | | | | 12 | | | | 3 | | | | | | 11 | **10** | | | 28 |
| | 2 | 6 | 4 | 5 | | 7 | 8 | 9 | | | | | | | | 3 | | | | | | 11 | 10 | | | 29 |
| | 2 | 6 | 4 | 5 | | 7 | 8 | 9 | | | | | | | | 3 | | 11 | | | | | 10 | | | 30 |
| | 2 | 6 | 4 | **5** | | 7 | 8 | 9 | | 13 | | | | | | 3 | | | | 12 | | 11 | 10 | | | 31 |
| | 2 | 6 | 4 | 5 | | 7 | 8 | 9 | | | | | | | | 3 | | | | | | 11 | 10 | | | 32 |
| | 2 | 6 | 4 | 5 | | 7 | 8 | 9 | | 11 | | | | | | | | | | 3 | 1 | | 10 | | | 33 |
| | 2 | | 4 | 5 | | 7 | 8 | 9 | | 11 | 12 | | | | | 13 | | 3 | | 6 | 1 | | **10** | | | 34 |
| | 2 | **3** | 4 | 5 | | 7 | 8 | 9 | | 10 | | 12 | | | | | | | 13 | | 1 | 11 | | 6 | | 35 |
| | 2 | 3 | 4 | **5** | | 7 | 8 | 9 | | 10 | | | | | | | | | | 12 | | 11 | | 6 | | 36 |
| | 2 | 5 | 4 | | | 7 | 8 | 9 | | 10 | | | | | | | | | | 12 | 1 | 11 | **3** | 6 | 13 | 37 |
| | 2 | 3 | 4 | 5 | | 7 | 8 | 9 | | 10 | 6 | 13 | | | | 12 | | | | | | **11** | | | | 38 |
| | 33 | 35 | 31 | 37 | 2 | 35 | 38 | 36 | 15 | 17 | 6 | 12 | 5 | | 12 | 19 | 1 | 12 | 2 | 5 | 7 | 13 | 11 | 3 | | |
| | 1 | | | | 3 | | | | 2 | 2 | 5 | 9 | | 2 | | 2 | 1 | 1 | 1 | 6 | | | | | 1 | |
| | 1 | | | | | 2 | 17 | 8 | 1 | 4 | 1 | 1 | | | 1 | | | | | | | | | 1 | | |

| Shilton P | Sage M | Forsyth M | Williams G | Wright M | Davidson J | Micklewhite G | Saunders D | Harford M | Ramage C | Williams P | Patterson M | Hebberd T | Watson A | Francis K | Callaghan N | Cross S | Gee P | Pickering N | Briscoe R | Kavanagh J | Taylor M | McMinn K | Wilson I | Phillips J | Hayward S | |
|---|---|---|---|---|---|---|---|---|---|---|---|---|---|---|---|---|---|---|---|---|---|---|---|---|---|---|
| | 2 | 6 | | 5 | 12 | | 8 | 9 | 7 | | | | | **10** | | 11 | 13 | 3 | | 4 | | | | | | 3 |
| | 1 | 1 | | 1 | | | 1 | 1 | 1 | | | | | 1 | | 1 | | 1 | | 1 | | | | | | |
| | | | | | 1 | | | | | | | | | | | | 1 | | | | | | | | | |
| | | | | | | | | | | | | | | | | | | | | | | | | | | |

| Shilton P | Sage M | Forsyth M | Williams G | Wright M | Davidson J | Micklewhite G | Saunders D | Harford M | Ramage C | Williams P | Patterson M | Hebberd T | Watson A | Francis K | Callaghan N | Cross S | Gee P | Pickering N | Briscoe R | Kavanagh J | Taylor M | McMinn K | Wilson I | Phillips J | Hayward S | |
|---|---|---|---|---|---|---|---|---|---|---|---|---|---|---|---|---|---|---|---|---|---|---|---|---|---|---|
| | 2 | 6 | 4 | 5 | | 7 | 8 | 9 | 11 | 3 | | 10 | | | | | | | | | | | | | | 2 |
| | 2 | 6 | 4 | 5 | | 7 | 8 | 9 | 10 | | | | | | | | | 3 | 11 | | | | | | | 2 |
| | 2 | 6 | 4 | 5 | | 7 | 8 | 9 | 10 | | | | | | | 3 | | 11 | | | | | | | | 3 |
| | | 6 | | 5 | | 7 | 8 | 9 | 4 | | 2 | 10 | | | | | | 3 | 11 | | | | | | | 4 |
| | 12 | 6 | | 5 | | 7 | 8 | 9 | **4** | | 2 | 10 | | | | | 13 | 3 | 11 | | | | | | | R |
| | 3 | 5 | 3 | 5 | | 5 | 5 | 5 | 5 | 1 | 2 | 3 | | | | 1 | | 4 | 3 | | | | | | | |
| | 1 | | | | | | | | | | | | | | | | 1 | | | | | | | | | |
| | | | | | | 1 | 3 | 3 | 2 | | | | | | | | | | | | | | | | | |

1 own-goal

# 1991-92

| Team | P | W | D | L | F | A | Pts |
|---|---|---|---|---|---|---|---|
| Ipswich T | 46 | 24 | 12 | 10 | 70 | 50 | 84 |
| Middlesbrough | 46 | 23 | 11 | 12 | 58 | 41 | 80 |
| Derby Co | 46 | 23 | 9 | 14 | 69 | 51 | 78 |
| Leicester C | 46 | 23 | 8 | 15 | 62 | 55 | 77 |
| Cambridge U | 46 | 19 | 17 | 10 | 65 | 47 | 74 |
| Blackburn R | 46 | 21 | 11 | 14 | 70 | 53 | 74 |
| Charlton A | 46 | 20 | 11 | 15 | 54 | 48 | 71 |
| Swindon T | 46 | 18 | 15 | 13 | 69 | 55 | 69 |
| Portsmouth | 46 | 19 | 12 | 15 | 65 | 51 | 69 |
| Watford | 46 | 18 | 11 | 17 | 51 | 48 | 65 |
| Wolves | 46 | 18 | 10 | 18 | 61 | 54 | 64 |
| Southend U | 46 | 17 | 11 | 18 | 63 | 63 | 62 |
| Bristol R | 46 | 16 | 14 | 16 | 60 | 63 | 62 |
| Tranmere R | 46 | 14 | 19 | 13 | 56 | 56 | 61 |
| Millwall | 46 | 17 | 10 | 19 | 64 | 71 | 61 |
| Barnsley | 46 | 16 | 11 | 19 | 46 | 57 | 59 |
| Bristol C | 46 | 13 | 15 | 18 | 55 | 71 | 54 |
| Sunderland | 46 | 14 | 11 | 21 | 61 | 65 | 53 |
| Grimsby | 46 | 14 | 11 | 21 | 47 | 62 | 53 |
| Newcastle U | 46 | 13 | 13 | 20 | 66 | 84 | 52 |
| Oxford U | 46 | 13 | 11 | 22 | 66 | 73 | 50 |
| Plymouth A | 46 | 13 | 9 | 24 | 42 | 64 | 48 |
| Brighton & H.A. | 46 | 12 | 11 | 23 | 56 | 77 | 47 |
| Port Vale | 46 | 10 | 15 | 21 | 42 | 59 | 45 |

Manager: Arthur Cox.
Leading scorer: Paul Williams, League 13, all matches 16.
League ever-present: Andy Comyn.
Player of the season: Ted McMinn.

- Bobby Davison returned on loan from Leeds United and became the 10th player to score 100 goals for the Rams. He reached his century in a 2–2 draw with Newcastle United at St James' Park on 28 September.
- Derby set a club record by winning 12 away games in the League but had to settle for a place in the Play-offs.
- After buying out Robert Maxwell, Derby were short of money until Lionel Pickering, an Ashbourne man who founded and directed the Derby Trader, bought the majority shareholding in November.
- Derby twice raised their transfer record in March. Paul Kitson cost £1.3 million from Leicester City, Phil Gee and Ian Ormondroyd going to Filbert Street as part of the deal. Ten days later, Tommy Johnson was signed from Notts County for £1.375 million.

## Division Two

| Match No. | Date | | Venue | Opponents | Result | | Scorers | Attenda |
|---|---|---|---|---|---|---|---|---|
| 1 | Aug | 17 | (a) | Sunderland | D | 1-1 | Harford | 20,6 |
| 2 | | 21 | (h) | Middlesbrough | W | 2-0 | Comyn, Harford | 12,8 |
| 3 | | 24 | (h) | Southend U | L | 1-2 | P.Williams | 12,2 |
| 4 | Sep | 1 | (a) | Charlton A | W | 2-0 | P.Williams, Harford | 6,6 |
| 5 | | 4 | (h) | Blackburn R | L | 0-2 | | 12,0 |
| 6 | | 7 | (h) | Barnsley | D | 1-1 | P.Williams | 10,5 |
| 7 | | 13 | (a) | Cambridge U | D | 0-0 | | 7,9 |
| 8 | | 18 | (a) | Oxford U | L | 0-2 | | 4,4 |
| 9 | | 21 | (h) | Brighton & Hove A | W | 3-1 | Davison, Patterson, P.Williams (pen) | 12,0 |
| 10 | | 28 | (a) | Newcastle U | D | 2-2 | Davison, Ormondroyd | 17,8 |
| 11 | Oct | 5 | (h) | Bristol C | W | 4-1 | Davison 2, Micklewhite, Aizlewood (og) | 11,8 |
| 12 | | 12 | (a) | Swindon T | W | 2-1 | P.Williams, Gee | 12,0 |
| 13 | | 19 | (h) | Portsmouth | W | 2-0 | McMinn, P.Williams | 13,1 |
| 14 | | 26 | (a) | Millwall | W | 2-1 | Davison, Ormondroyd | 7,6 |
| 15 | Nov | 2 | (h) | Tranmere R | L | 0-1 | | 11,5 |
| 16 | | 6 | (a) | Port Vale | L | 0-1 | | 8,5 |
| 17 | | 9 | (a) | Wolves | W | 3-2 | Davison, Ormondroyd, Bennett (og) | 15,6 |
| 18 | | 16 | (h) | Ipswich T | W | 1-0 | Davison | 12,4 |
| 19 | | 23 | (a) | Bristol R | W | 3-2 | Patterson, P.Williams (pen), Davison | 6,5 |
| 20 | | 30 | (h) | Leicester C | L | 1-2 | Ormondroyd | 19,3 |
| 21 | Dec | 7 | (a) | Watford | W | 2-1 | Ormondroyd 2 | 8,3 |
| 22 | | 26 | (h) | Grimsby T | D | 0-0 | | 16,3 |
| 23 | | 28 | (h) | Charlton A | L | 1-2 | Ormondroyd | 14,3 |
| 24 | Jan | 1 | (a) | Middlesbrough | D | 1-1 | Chalk | 16,2 |
| 25 | | 11 | (a) | Southend U | L | 0-1 | | 8,2 |
| 26 | | 18 | (h) | Sunderland | L | 1-2 | G.Williams | 15,3 |
| 27 | Feb | 1 | (a) | Portsmouth | W | 1-0 | Gabbiadini | 12, |
| 28 | | 8 | (h) | Millwall | L | 0-2 | | 12,7 |
| 29 | | 11 | (a) | Blackburn R | L | 0-2 | | 14,8 |
| 30 | | 15 | (h) | Bristol R | W | 1-0 | Coleman | 11,1 |
| 31 | | 22 | (a) | Leicester C | W | 2-1 | Ormondroyd, Simpson | 18,1 |
| 32 | | 29 | (h) | Watford | W | 3-1 | P.Williams 3 (1 pen) | 14, |
| 33 | Mar | 7 | (a) | Plymouth A | D | 1-1 | Simpson | 8, |
| 34 | | 11 | (h) | Port Vale | W | 3-1 | G.Williams, Simpson, Gabbiadini | 15, |
| 35 | | 14 | (a) | Tranmere R | L | 3-4 | Kitson, Coleman, Simpson | 10, |
| 36 | | 21 | (h) | Wolves | L | 1-2 | Kitson | 21, |
| 37 | | 25 | (h) | Plymouth A | W | 2-0 | Johnson, McMinn | 13, |
| 38 | | 28 | (a) | Ipswich T | L | 1-2 | Simpson | 15, |
| 39 | Apr | 1 | (h) | Cambridge U | D | 0-0 | | 15, |
| 40 | | 4 | (a) | Barnsley | W | 3-0 | Simpson, Forsyth, P.Williams (pen) | 10, |
| 41 | | 7 | (a) | Grimsby T | W | 1-0 | Gabbiadini | 7, |
| 42 | | 11 | (h) | Oxford U | D | 2-2 | Simpson, P.Williams (pen) | 15, |
| 43 | | 15 | (a) | Brighton & Hove A | W | 2-1 | Gabbiadini 2 | 8, |
| 44 | | 20 | (h) | Newcastle U | W | 4-1 | Ramage 2, P.Williams (pen), Kitson | 21, |
| 45 | | 25 | (a) | Bristol C | W | 2-1 | Gabbiadini, Micklewhite | 16, |
| 46 | May | 2 | (h) | Swindon T | W | 2-1 | Kitson, Johnson | 22, |

FINAL LEAGUE POSITION: 3rd in Division Two

Appearar
Substit
G

## Play-offs

| | | | | | | | | |
|---|---|---|---|---|---|---|---|---|
| 1 | May | 10 | (a) | Blackburn R | L | 2-4 | Gabbiadini, Johnson | 19, |
| 2 | | 13 | (h) | Blackburn R | W | 2-1 | Comyn, McMinn | 22 |

Appeara
Substit
G

## FA Cup

| | | | | | | | | |
|---|---|---|---|---|---|---|---|---|
| 3 | Jan | 4 | (a) | Burnley | D | 2-2 | Chalk, Comyn | 18 |
| R | | 25 | (h) | Burnley | W | 2-0 | P.Williams, Ormondroyd | 18 |
| 4 | Feb | 5 | (h) | Aston Villa | L | 3-4 | Gee 2, P.Williams | 22 |

Appeara
Substi
G

## League Cup

| | | | | | | | | |
|---|---|---|---|---|---|---|---|---|
| 2 | Sep | 25 | (h) | Ipswich T | D | 0-0 | | 10 |
| 2 | Oct | 8 | (a) | Ipswich T | W | 2-0 | Gee, P.Williams (pen) | 8 |
| 3 | | 29 | (a) | Oldham A | L | 1-2 | Forsyth | 11 |

Appeara
Substi
G

**Derby County played in the Full Members' Cup (see Rams in Other Competitions)**

| Shilton P | Sage M | Forsyth M | Williams G | Coleman S | Comyn A | Micklewhite G | Gee P | Harford M | Williams P | McMinn K | Cross S | Pickering N | Taylor M | Hayward S | Ramage C | Stallard M | Patterson M | Ormondroyd I | Davison R | Kavanagh J | Chalk M | Davidson J | Sturridge D | Gabbiadini M | Simpson P | Round S | Kitson P | Johnson T | Sutton S | |
|---|---|---|---|---|---|---|---|---|---|---|---|---|---|---|---|---|---|---|---|---|---|---|---|---|---|---|---|---|---|---|
| 1 | 2 | 3 | 4 | 5 | 6 | 7 | **8** | 9 | 10 | 11 | 12 | | | | | | | | | | | | | | | | | | | 1 |
| 1 | 2 | 3 | 4 | 5 | 6 | 7 | 8 | 9 | 10 | 11 | | | | | | | | | | | | | | | | | | | | 2 |
| 1 | 2 | 3 | 4 | 5 | 6 | 7 | **8** | 9 | 10 | 11 | | 12 | | | | | | | | | | | | | | | | | | 3 |
| | 2 | 3 | 4 | 5 | 6 | 7 | 8 | 9 | 10 | **11** | 12 | | 1 | | | | | | | | | | | | | | | | | 4 |
| 1 | 2 | 3 | 4 | 5 | 6 | 7 | **8** | 9 | 10 | 11 | 12 | | | 13 | | | | | | | | | | | | | | | | 5 |
| 1 | 2 | 3 | 4 | 5 | 6 | 7 | 8 | 9 | 10 | **11** | 12 | | | | | | | | | | | | | | | | | | | 6 |
| 1 | 2 | 3 | 4 | 5 | 6 | 7 | 8 | | 10 | 11 | | | | 12 | **9** | | | | | | | | | | | | | | | 7 |
| 1 | 2 | 3 | 4 | 5 | 6 | 7 | **8** | | 10 | 11 | | | | 9 | | 12 | 13 | | | | | | | | | | | | | 8 |
| 1 | 2 | 3 | 4 | 5 | 6 | **7** | | | 10 | 11 | | | | | | | 12 | 8 | 9 | | | | | | | | | | | 9 |
| 1 | **2** | 3 | 4 | 5 | 6 | 7 | | | 10 | 11 | | | | | | | 12 | 8 | 9 | | | | | | | | | | | 10 |
| 1 | 2 | 3 | 4 | 5 | 6 | 7 | | | 10 | 11 | | | | | | | | 8 | 9 | | | | | | | | | | | 11 |
| 1 | | 3 | 4 | 5 | 6 | 7 | 9 | | 10 | 11 | | | | | | | 2 | 8 | | | | | | | | | | | | 12 |
| 1 | 2 | 3 | 4 | 5 | 6 | 7 | 9 | | 10 | 11 | | | | | | | | 8 | | | | | | | | | | | | 13 |
| 1 | 2 | 3 | 4 | 5 | 6 | 7 | | | 10 | 11 | | | | | | | | 8 | 9 | | | | | | | | | | | 14 |
| 1 | 2 | 3 | 4 | 5 | 6 | 7 | **11** | | 10 | | | | | | | | 12 | 8 | 9 | | | | | | | | | | | 15 |
| 1 | 2 | 3 | 4 | 5 | 6 | 7 | 11 | | 10 | | | | | | | | | 8 | 9 | | | | | | | | | | | 16 |
| 1 | 2 | 3 | 4 | 5 | 6 | 7 | 11 | | 10 | | | | | | | | | 8 | 9 | | | | | | | | | | | 17 |
| 1 | **2** | 3 | 4 | 5 | 6 | 7 | | | 10 | 11 | | | | 12 | | | | 8 | 9 | | | | | | | | | | | 18 |
| 1 | | 3 | 4 | | 6 | 7 | 13 | | 10 | 11 | | | | **5** | | | 2 | 8 | 9 | 12 | | | | | | | | | | 19 |
| 1 | | | 4 | 5 | 6 | 7 | | | 10 | 11 | | | | | | | 2 | 8 | 9 | 3 | | | | | | | | | | 20 |
| 1 | | 3 | 4 | 5 | 6 | 7 | 9 | | 10 | 11 | | | | | | | 2 | 8 | | | | | | | | | | | | 21 |
| 1 | | 3 | 4 | 5 | 6 | 7 | **9** | | 10 | 11 | | | | | | | 2 | 8 | | | 12 | | | | | | | | | 22 |
| 1 | | 3 | 4 | 5 | 6 | **7** | 9 | | 10 | 11 | | | | | | | 2 | 8 | | 12 | 13 | | | | | | | | | 23 |
| 1 | | 3 | 4 | 5 | 6 | | | | 10 | 11 | | | | | | 9 | 2 | 8 | | | 7 | | | | | | | | | 24 |
| 1 | | **3** | 4 | 5 | 6 | | | | | | | | | 13 | | 9 | 2 | 8 | | 12 | 7 | 10 | 11 | | | | | | | 25 |
| | | 3 | 4 | 5 | 6 | **7** | 9 | | | 11 | | | | 10 | | | | 8 | | 2 | 12 | | | | | | | | | 26 |
| | | 3 | 4 | 5 | 6 | | | | 10 | 11 | | | | | | | | 8 | | 2 | 7 | | | 9 | | | | | | 27 |
| | | 3 | 4 | 5 | 6 | 12 | | | 10 | 11 | | | | | | | | 8 | | 2 | **7** | | | 9 | | | | | | 28 |
| | | 3 | 4 | 5 | 6 | 7 | | | 10 | 11 | | | | | | | | 8 | | 2 | | | | 9 | | | | | | 29 |
| | | 3 | 4 | 5 | 6 | 7 | 12 | | 10 | 11 | | | | | | | | 8 | | 2 | | | | **9** | | | | | | 30 |
| | | 3 | 4 | 5 | 6 | | | | 10 | 7 | | | | | | | | 8 | | 2 | | | | 9 | 11 | | | | | 31 |
| | | 3 | 4 | 5 | 6 | | | | 10 | 7 | | | | | | | | 8 | | 2 | | | | 9 | 11 | | | | | 32 |
| | | | 4 | 5 | 6 | 12 | | | 10 | **7** | | | 1 | | | | | 8 | | 2 | | | | 9 | 11 | 3 | | | | 33 |
| | | | 4 | 5 | 6 | 7 | | | 10 | | | | 1 | | | | | | | 2 | | | | 9 | 11 | 3 | 8 | | | 34 |
| | | 3 | 4 | 5 | 6 | | | | 10 | | | | 1 | | | | | | | 2 | | | | 9 | 11 | | 8 | 7 | | 35 |
| | | 3 | 4 | 5 | 6 | | | | 10 | 12 | | | 1 | | | | | | | 2 | | | | 9 | **11** | | 8 | 7 | | 36 |
| | | 3 | 4 | 5 | 6 | | | | **10** | 12 | | | | | | | | | | 2 | | | | 9 | 11 | | 8 | 7 | 1 | 37 |
| | | 3 | 4 | 5 | 6 | | | | | 10 | | | | | | | | | | 2 | | | | 9 | 11 | | 8 | 7 | 1 | 38 |
| | | 3 | 4 | 5 | 6 | | | | | 10 | | | | | | | | | | 2 | | | | 9 | 11 | | 8 | 7 | 1 | 39 |
| | | 3 | | 5 | 6 | | | | 4 | **10** | | | | | | | | | | 2 | | | | 9 | 11 | 12 | 8 | 7 | 1 | 40 |
| | | 3 | | 5 | 6 | | | | 4 | | | | | | 10 | | | | | 2 | | | | 9 | 11 | | 8 | 7 | 1 | 41 |
| | | 3 | | 5 | 6 | | | | 4 | | | | | | 10 | | | | | 2 | | | | 9 | 11 | | 8 | 7 | 1 | 42 |
| | | 3 | | 5 | 6 | 8 | | | 4 | | | | | | 10 | | | | | 2 | | | | 9 | 11 | | | 7 | 1 | 43 |
| | | 3 | | | 6 | | | | 4 | 5 | | | | | 10 | | | | | 2 | | | | 9 | 11 | | 8 | 7 | 1 | 44 |
| | | 3 | | | 6 | 12 | | | 4 | 5 | | | | | 10 | | | | | 2 | | | | 9 | 11 | | **8** | 7 | 1 | 45 |
| | | 3 | | 5 | 6 | 12 | | | | 4 | | | | | 10 | | | | | 2 | | | | **9** | 11 | | 8 | 7 | 1 | 46 |
| | 17 | 43 | 39 | 43 | 46 | 28 | 17 | 6 | 41 | 35 | | | 5 | 3 | 7 | 2 | 8 | 25 | 10 | 22 | 4 | 1 | 1 | 20 | 16 | 2 | 12 | 12 | 10 | |
| | | | | | | 4 | 2 | | | 2 | 4 | 1 | | 4 | | 1 | 4 | | | 3 | 3 | | | | | 1 | | | | |
| | | 1 | 2 | 2 | 1 | 2 | 1 | 3 | 13 | 2 | | | | | 2 | | 2 | 8 | 8 | | 1 | | | 6 | 7 | | 4 | 2 | | |

2 own-goals

| | | | | | | | | | | | | | | | | | | | | | | | | | | | | | | |
|---|---|---|---|---|---|---|---|---|---|---|---|---|---|---|---|---|---|---|---|---|---|---|---|---|---|---|---|---|---|---|
| | | 3 | | 5 | 6 | 13 | | | 10 | **4** | | | | | 12 | | | | | 2 | | | | 9 | 11 | | 8 | 7 | 1 | 1 |
| | | 3 | | 5 | 6 | | | | 10 | 4 | | | | | | | | | | 2 | | | | 9 | 11 | | 8 | 7 | 1 | 2 |
| | | 2 | | 2 | 2 | | | | 2 | 2 | | | | | | | | | | 2 | | | | 2 | 2 | | 2 | 2 | 2 | |
| | | | | | | 1 | | | | | | | | | 1 | | | | | | | | | | | | | | | |
| | | | | | 1 | | | | | 1 | | | | | | | | | | | | | | 1 | | | | 1 | | |

| | | | | | | | | | | | | | | | | | | | | | | | | | | | | | | |
|---|---|---|---|---|---|---|---|---|---|---|---|---|---|---|---|---|---|---|---|---|---|---|---|---|---|---|---|---|---|---|
| | | 3 | 4 | 5 | 6 | | | | 10 | 11 | | | | | | 9 | 2 | 8 | | | 7 | | | | | | | | | 3 |
| | | 3 | 4 | 5 | 6 | | 9 | | 10 | 11 | | | | | | | | 8 | | 2 | 7 | | | | | | | | | R |
| | | 3 | 4 | 5 | 6 | | 9 | | 10 | 11 | | | | | | 13 | | 8 | | **2** | 7 | 12 | | | | | | | | 4 |
| | | 3 | 3 | 3 | 3 | | 2 | | 3 | 3 | | | | | | 1 | 1 | 3 | | 2 | 3 | | | | | | | | | |
| | | | | | | | | | | | | | | | | 1 | | | | | | 1 | | | | | | | | |
| | | | | | 1 | | 2 | | 2 | | | | | | | | | 1 | | | 1 | | | | | | | | | |

| | | | | | | | | | | | | | | | | | | | | | | | | | | | | | | |
|---|---|---|---|---|---|---|---|---|---|---|---|---|---|---|---|---|---|---|---|---|---|---|---|---|---|---|---|---|---|---|
| | 2 | 3 | 4 | 5 | 6 | **7** | 9 | | 10 | 11 | | | | 13 | | | 12 | 8 | | | | | | | | | | | | 2 |
| | | 3 | 4 | 5 | 6 | 7 | 9 | | 10 | 11 | | | | | | | 2 | 8 | | | | | | | | | | | | 2 |
| | 2 | 3 | 4 | 5 | 6 | 7 | **9** | | 10 | 11 | | | | 12 | | | | 8 | | | | | | | | | | | | 3 |
| | 2 | 3 | 3 | 3 | 3 | 3 | 3 | | 3 | 3 | | | | | | | 1 | 3 | | | | | | | | | | | | |
| | | | | | | | | | | | | | | 2 | | | 1 | | | | | | | | | | | | | |
| | | 1 | | | | | 1 | | 1 | | | | | | | | | | | | | | | | | | | | | |

# 1992-93

| | P | W | D | L | F | A | Pts |
|---|---|---|---|---|---|---|---|
| Newcastle U | 46 | 29 | 9 | 8 | 92 | 38 | 96 |
| West Ham U | 46 | 26 | 10 | 10 | 81 | 41 | 88 |
| Portsmouth | 46 | 26 | 10 | 10 | 80 | 46 | 88 |
| Tranmere R | 46 | 23 | 10 | 13 | 72 | 56 | 79 |
| Swindon T | 46 | 21 | 13 | 12 | 74 | 59 | 76 |
| Leicester C | 46 | 22 | 10 | 14 | 71 | 64 | 76 |
| Millwall | 46 | 18 | 16 | 12 | 65 | 53 | 70 |
| Derby Co | 46 | 19 | 9 | 18 | 68 | 57 | 66 |
| Grimsby | 46 | 19 | 7 | 20 | 58 | 57 | 64 |
| Peterborough U | 46 | 16 | 14 | 16 | 55 | 63 | 62 |
| Wolves | 46 | 16 | 13 | 17 | 57 | 56 | 61 |
| Charlton A | 46 | 16 | 13 | 17 | 49 | 46 | 61 |
| Barnsley | 46 | 17 | 9 | 20 | 56 | 60 | 60 |
| Oxford U | 46 | 14 | 14 | 18 | 53 | 56 | 56 |
| Bristol C | 46 | 14 | 14 | 18 | 49 | 67 | 56 |
| Watford | 46 | 14 | 13 | 19 | 57 | 71 | 55 |
| Notts Co | 46 | 12 | 16 | 18 | 55 | 70 | 52 |
| Southend U | 46 | 13 | 13 | 20 | 54 | 64 | 52 |
| Birmingham C | 46 | 13 | 12 | 21 | 50 | 72 | 51 |
| Luton T | 46 | 10 | 21 | 15 | 48 | 62 | 51 |
| Sunderland | 46 | 13 | 11 | 22 | 50 | 64 | 50 |
| Brentford | 46 | 13 | 10 | 23 | 52 | 71 | 49 |
| Cambridge U | 46 | 11 | 16 | 19 | 48 | 69 | 49 |
| Bristol R | 46 | 10 | 11 | 25 | 55 | 87 | 41 |

Manager: Arthur Cox.
Leading scorer: Paul Kitson, League 17, all matches 24.
Player of the season: Marco Gabbiadini.

- The formation of the FA Premiership brought misleading name changes. The Second Division, in which Derby were playing, became the First Division.
- Craig Short was Derby's record signing in September when they paid Notts County £2.65 million for the central-defender.
- Between 3 October and 20 December, the Rams set a club record with seven consecutive away wins.
- Derby reached the final of the Anglo-Italian Cup, losing to Cremonese at Wembley. They played 64 competitive matches, beating the 60 in 1985–86.

## Division One

| Match No. | Date | | Venue | Opponents | Result | | Scorers | Attendar |
|---|---|---|---|---|---|---|---|---|
| 1 | Aug | 15 | (a) | Peterborough U | L | 0-1 | | 9,95 |
| 2 | | 22 | (h) | Newcastle U | L | 1-2 | Pembridge | 17,52 |
| 3 | | 26 | (a) | Leicester C | L | 2-3 | Simpson 2 | 17,73 |
| 4 | | 29 | (a) | Watford | D | 0-0 | | 9,8 |
| 5 | Sep | 6 | (h) | Bristol C | L | 3-4 | Simpson 3 | 12,73 |
| 6 | | 12 | (a) | Barnsley | D | 1-1 | Kitson | 8,4 |
| 7 | | 20 | (a) | West Ham U | D | 1-1 | Miklosko (og) | 11,4 |
| 8 | | 26 | (h) | Southend U | W | 2-0 | Gabbiadini, Simpson (pen) | 15,1 |
| 9 | Oct | 3 | (a) | Cambridge U | W | 3-1 | Simpson 2 (1 pen), Gabbiadini | 6,1 |
| 10 | | 11 | (h) | Oxford U | L | 0-1 | | 14,2 |
| 11 | | 17 | (a) | Luton T | W | 3-1 | Kitson 2, Johnson | 8,8 |
| 12 | | 24 | (h) | Charlton A | W | 4-3 | Gabbiadini, Minto (og), Pembridge, Simpson | 15,4 |
| 13 | | 31 | (a) | Wolves | W | 2-0 | Kitson, Short | 17,2 |
| 14 | Nov | 3 | (a) | Notts C | W | 2-0 | Pembridge, Kitson | 14,2 |
| 15 | | 7 | (h) | Millwall | L | 1-2 | Pembridge | 16,9 |
| 16 | | 14 | (a) | Bristol R | W | 2-1 | Kitson, Johnson | 6,6 |
| 17 | | 21 | (h) | Sunderland | L | 0-1 | | 17,5 |
| 18 | | 28 | (h) | Tranmere R | L | 1-2 | Kitson | 15,6 |
| 19 | Dec | 6 | (a) | Swindon T | W | 4-2 | Johnson, Pembridge, Kuhl, McMinn | 9,4 |
| 20 | | 12 | (h) | Birmingham C | W | 3-1 | Johnson, Kitson, Williams | 16,6 |
| 21 | | 20 | (a) | Grimsby T | W | 2-0 | Johnson, Kitson | 6,4 |
| 22 | | 26 | (a) | Brentford | L | 1-2 | Kitson | 10,2 |
| 23 | | 28 | (h) | Portsmouth | L | 2-4 | Johnson, Kitson | 21,4 |
| 24 | Jan | 10 | (h) | West Ham U | L | 0-2 | | 13,7 |
| 25 | | 16 | (a) | Southend U | D | 0-0 | | 4,2 |
| 26 | | 31 | (a) | Newcastle U | D | 1-1 | Johnson | 27,3 |
| 27 | Feb | 6 | (h) | Peterborough U | L | 2-3 | Kitson 2 | 16,0 |
| 28 | | 10 | (h) | Barnsley | W | 3-0 | Gabbiadini, Kitson, Williams | 13,0 |
| 29 | | 20 | (h) | Watford | L | 1-2 | Pembridge (pen) | 15,1 |
| 30 | | 24 | (h) | Leicester C | W | 2-0 | Forsyth, Gabbiadini | 17,5 |
| 31 | | 27 | (a) | Oxford U | W | 1-0 | Williams | 7,4 |
| 32 | Mar | 3 | (h) | Cambridge U | D | 0-0 | | 13,9 |
| 33 | | 10 | (h) | Bristol R | W | 3-1 | Short, Williams, Gabbiadini | 13,2 |
| 34 | | 13 | (a) | Millwall | L | 0-1 | | 9,3 |
| 35 | | 21 | (h) | Swindon T | W | 2-1 | Kitson, Pembridge (pen) | 12, |
| 36 | | 24 | (a) | Sunderland | L | 0-1 | | 17,2 |
| 37 | Apr | 2 | (a) | Tranmere R | L | 1-2 | Simpson | 7, |
| 38 | | 6 | (a) | Birmingham C | D | 1-1 | Johnson | 15, |
| 39 | | 10 | (h) | Brentford | W | 3-2 | Kitson, Gabbiadini, Simpson | 12, |
| 40 | | 12 | (a) | Portsmouth | L | 0-3 | | 23, |
| 41 | | 17 | (h) | Grimsby T | W | 2-1 | Simpson, Kitson | 12, |
| 42 | | 20 | (a) | Bristol C | D | 0-0 | | 8, |
| 43 | | 24 | (h) | Luton T | D | 1-1 | Short | 13, |
| 44 | May | 1 | (a) | Charlton A | L | 1-2 | Gabbiadini | 7, |
| 45 | | 5 | (h) | Notts C | W | 2-0 | McMinn, Pembridge (pen) | 13, |
| 46 | | 8 | (h) | Wolves | W | 2-0 | Gabbiadini, Hayward | 15, |

FINAL LEAGUE POSITION: 8th in Division One

Appearar
Substit
G

## FA Cup

| | | | | | | | | |
|---|---|---|---|---|---|---|---|---|
| 3 | Jan | 2 | (h) | Stockport C | W | 2-1 | Short, Miller (og) | 17, |
| 4 | | 23 | (a) | Luton T | W | 5-1 | Pembridge 3, Short, Gabbiadini | 9, |
| 5 | Feb | 13 | (h) | Bolton W | W | 3-1 | Short 2, Williams | 20, |
| 6 | Mar | 8 | (h) | Sheffield W | D | 3-3 | Nicholson, Gabbiadini, Kitson | 22, |
| R | | 17 | (a) | Sheffield W | L | 0-1 | | 32, |

Appearar
Substit
G

## League Cup

| | | | | | | | | |
|---|---|---|---|---|---|---|---|---|
| 2 | Sep | 23 | (a) | Southend U | L | 0-1 | | 2 |
| 2 | Oct | 7 | (h) | Southend U | W | 7-0 | Kitson 2, Gabbiadini 2, Martin (og), Simpson, Johnson | 13 |
| 3 | | 28 | (h) | Arsenal | D | 1-1 | Simpson (pen) | 22 |
| R | Dec | 1 | (a) | Arsenal | L | 1-2 | Pembridge (pen) | 24 |

Appeara
Substi
G

**Derby County played in the Anglo-Italian Cup (see Rams in Other Competitions)**

| ll S | Kavanagh J | Forsyth M | Pembridge M | Coleman S | Wassall D | Johnson T | Kitson P | Gabbiadini M | Williams P | Simpson P | McMinn K | Comyn A | Micklewhite G | Patterson M | Taylor M | Short C | Sturridge D | Kuhl M | Goulooze R | Hayward S | Nicholson S | Round S | Stallard M | Ramage C | |
|---|---|---|---|---|---|---|---|---|---|---|---|---|---|---|---|---|---|---|---|---|---|---|---|---|---|
| | 2 | 3 | 4 | 5 | 6 | 7 | **8** | 9 | 10 | 11 | 12 | | | | | | | | | | | | | | 1 |
| | 2 | 3 | 4 | 5 | 6 | 7 | 8 | **9** | 10 | 11 | 12 | | | | | | | | | | | | | | 2 |
| | 2 | 3 | 4 | 5 | 6 | 9 | 8 | | 10 | 11 | 7 | | | | | | | | | | | | | | 3 |
| | 2 | 3 | 4 | 5 | 6 | **9** | 8 | 13 | 10 | 11 | 7 | 12 | | | | | | | | | | | | | 4 |
| | 2 | 3 | 4 | 5 | 6 | 9 | 8 | **7** | 10 | 11 | | 13 | 12 | | | | | | | | | | | | 5 |
| | | 3 | **4** | 5 | 6 | 7 | 8 | 9 | 10 | 11 | | 12 | | 2 | | | | | | | | | | | 6 |
| | | 3 | 6 | 12 | 5 | 7 | 8 | 9 | **10** | 11 | | 2 | | | 1 | 4 | 13 | | | | | | | | 7 |
| | | 3 | 6 | 12 | 5 | 7 | 9 | 10 | | 11 | | 2 | | | | 4 | | **8** | | | | | | | 8 |
| | | 3 | 6 | 13 | 5 | **7** | 9 | 10 | | 11 | | 2 | | | | 4 | | 8 | 12 | | | | | | 9 |
| | | 3 | 6 | | 5 | **7** | 9 | 10 | | 11 | | 2 | | | | 4 | | 8 | 12 | | | | | | 10 |
| | | 3 | 6 | | 5 | 7 | 9 | 10 | | **11** | 12 | 2 | | | | 4 | | 8 | | | | | | | 11 |
| | | 3 | 6 | | 5 | **7** | 9 | 10 | | 11 | 12 | 2 | | | | 4 | | 8 | 13 | | | | | | 12 |
| | | 3 | 6 | | 5 | 7 | 9 | 10 | | 11 | | 2 | | | | 4 | | 8 | | | | | | | 13 |
| | | 3 | 6 | | 5 | 7 | **9** | 10 | | 11 | 12 | 2 | | | | 4 | | 8 | | | | | | | 14 |
| | | 3 | 6 | 13 | 5 | 7 | **9** | 10 | | 11 | 12 | 2 | | | | 4 | | 8 | | | | | | | 15 |
| | | 3 | 6 | | 5 | 7 | 9 | 10 | | 11 | | 2 | | | | 4 | | 8 | | | | | | | 16 |
| | | 3 | 6 | | 5 | 7 | 9 | 10 | | **11** | 12 | 2 | | | | 4 | | 8 | 13 | | | | | | 17 |
| | | 3 | 6 | 5 | | 7 | 9 | 10 | | 11 | | 2 | | | | 4 | | 8 | | | | | | | 18 |
| | | 3 | 6 | 5 | | **7** | 9 | 10 | 11 | | 12 | | | | | 4 | | 8 | 2 | | | | | | 19 |
| | 2 | 3 | 6 | 5 | | 7 | 9 | 10 | 11 | | | | | | | 4 | | 8 | | | | | | | 20 |
| | | 3 | 6 | | 5 | 7 | 9 | 10 | 11 | | | | | | 1 | 4 | | 8 | 2 | | | | | | 21 |
| | | 3 | 6 | | 5 | **7** | 9 | 10 | 11 | | 12 | | | | | 4 | | 8 | 2 | | | | | | 22 |
| | | 3 | 6 | 12 | 5 | 7 | 9 | 10 | 11 | | 13 | | | | | 4 | | 8 | **2** | | | | | | 23 |
| | 2 | 3 | 6 | | 5 | **10** | 9 | 12 | | 11 | 7 | | | | | 4 | | 8 | | | | | | | 24 |
| | 2 | 3 | 6 | | 5 | 7 | 9 | 10 | | | | | | | | 4 | | 8 | | 11 | | | | | 25 |
| | 2 | 3 | 6 | | **5** | 7 | 9 | 10 | | | 12 | | | 11 | | 4 | | 8 | | | | | | | 26 |
| | 2 | 3 | 6 | 5 | | **7** | 9 | 10 | | 12 | 11 | | | | | 4 | | 8 | | | | | | | 27 |
| | | 3 | 6 | 4 | | | 9 | 10 | 7 | 11 | | | | 2 | 1 | 5 | | 8 | | | | | | | 28 |
| | | 3 | 6 | 4 | | | 9 | 10 | 7 | 11 | 12 | | | 2 | 1 | 5 | | **8** | | | | | | | 29 |
| | | 3 | 6 | | | 11 | 9 | 10 | 7 | | **8** | | | 2 | 1 | 5 | | | 12 | | 4 | | | | 30 |
| | | 3 | | | | 11 | 9 | 10 | 7 | | | | | 2 | 1 | 5 | | | 6 | 8 | 4 | | | | 31 |
| | | 3 | | | | **11** | 9 | 10 | 7 | 12 | | | | 2 | 1 | 5 | | | 6 | 8 | 4 | | | | 32 |
| | | 3 | 6 | | | 11 | 9 | 10 | 7 | | | | | 2 | 1 | 5 | | 8 | | | 4 | | | | 33 |
| | | 3 | 6 | | | | 9 | 10 | 7 | 11 | | | | 2 | 1 | 5 | | | 8 | | 4 | | | | 34 |
| | | 3 | 6 | 12 | | 11 | 9 | 10 | | | | | 7 | | 1 | **5** | | 8 | | | 4 | 2 | 13 | | 35 |
| | | 3 | 6 | 5 | | 11 | 9 | **10** | | 12 | | | 7 | | 1 | | | 8 | | | 4 | 2 | | | 36 |
| | | | | 6 | | 13 | 9 | 10 | | 11 | | 12 | **7** | 2 | 1 | 5 | | 8 | | | 3 | 4 | | | 37 |
| | | | | 6 | | 10 | | | | 11 | | | **7** | 4 | 1 | 5 | 12 | 8 | | 13 | 3 | 2 | 9 | | 38 |
| | | | 6 | 4 | | | 9 | 10 | | 11 | | | | | 1 | 5 | 7 | 8 | | | 3 | 2 | | | 39 |
| | | | **6** | 4 | | | 9 | 10 | | 11 | | | | 12 | 1 | 5 | 7 | 8 | | | 3 | 2 | 13 | | 40 |
| | | 5 | 6 | 12 | | | 9 | **10** | | 11 | | 4 | | 2 | 1 | | 7 | 8 | | | 3 | | 13 | | 41 |
| | | 4 | 6 | | | | 9 | 10 | | 11 | | | | 2 | 1 | 5 | 7 | 8 | | | 3 | | | | 42 |
| | | 4 | 6 | 12 | | | 9 | 10 | | 11 | | | | 2 | 1 | 5 | 7 | **8** | | | 3 | | 13 | | 43 |
| | | 4 | 6 | | | | 9 | 10 | | 11 | | | 12 | 2 | 1 | 5 | **7** | | | 8 | 3 | | | | 44 |
| | | 4 | 6 | | | | **9** | 10 | | 11 | 12 | | | 2 | 1 | 5 | 7 | | | 8 | 3 | | | | 45 |
| | | | 6 | | 4 | | | 10 | | 11 | 7 | | | 2 | 1 | 5 | **9** | | | 8 | 3 | | | 12 | 46 |
| | 10 | 41 | 42 | 17 | 24 | 34 | 44 | 42 | 19 | 32 | 6 | 13 | 4 | 17 | 21 | 38 | 8 | 32 | 7 | 6 | 17 | 6 | 1 | | |
| | | | | 8 | | 1 | | 2 | | 3 | 13 | 4 | 2 | 1 | | | 2 | | 5 | 1 | | | 4 | 1 | |
| | | 1 | 8 | | | 8 | 17 | 9 | 4 | 12 | 2 | | | | | 3 | | 1 | | 1 | | | | | |

2 own-goals

| | | | | | | | | | | | | | | | | | | | | | | | |
|---|---|---|---|---|---|---|---|---|---|---|---|---|---|---|---|---|---|---|---|---|---|---|---|
| 2 | 3 | 6 | | 5 | 7 | **9** | 10 | 11 | 13 | 12 | | | | | 4 | | 8 | | | | | | 3 |
| 2 | 3 | 6 | | 5 | 7 | 9 | 10 | | | | | 12 | | | 4 | | 8 | **11** | | | | | 4 |
| | 3 | 6 | 4 | | | 9 | 10 | 7 | 11 | | | | 2 | 1 | 5 | | 8 | | | | | | 5 |
| | 3 | 6 | | | 11 | 9 | 10 | 7 | | | | | 2 | 1 | 5 | | 8 | | | 4 | | | 6 |
| | | 6 | 3 | | 11 | 9 | 10 | | | | 12 | | **2** | 1 | 5 | | 8 | | 7 | 4 | | 13 | R |
| 2 | 4 | 5 | 2 | 2 | 4 | 5 | 5 | 3 | 1 | | | | 3 | 3 | 5 | | 5 | 1 | 1 | 2 | | | |
| | | | | | | | | | 1 | 1 | 1 | 1 | | | | | | | | | | 1 | |
| | | 3 | | | | 1 | 2 | 1 | | | | | | | 4 | | | | | 1 | | | |

1 own-goal

| | | | | | | | | | | | | | | | | | | | |
|---|---|---|---|---|---|---|---|---|---|---|---|---|---|---|---|---|---|---|---|
| | 3 | 6 | 8 | 5 | 7 | 9 | 10 | | 11 | | 2 | | | | 4 | | | | 2 |
| | 3 | 6 | 13 | 5 | 7 | 9 | 10 | | 11 | | 2 | | | | 4 | | **8** | 12 | 2 |
| | 3 | 6 | | 5 | 7 | 9 | 10 | | 11 | | 2 | | | | 4 | | 8 | | 3 |
| | 3 | 6 | 5 | | 7 | 9 | 10 | 13 | | **11** | 2 | 12 | | | 4 | | 8 | | R |
| | 4 | 4 | 2 | 3 | 4 | 4 | 4 | | 3 | 1 | 4 | | | | 4 | | 3 | | |
| | | | 1 | | | | | 1 | | | | 1 | | | | | | 1 | |
| | | 1 | | | 1 | 2 | 2 | | 2 | | | | | | | | | | |

1 own-goal

# 1993-94

| | P | W | D | L | F | A | Pts |
|---|---|---|---|---|---|---|---|
| Crystal Palace | 46 | 27 | 9 | 10 | 73 | 46 | 90 |
| Nottingham F | 46 | 23 | 14 | 9 | 74 | 49 | 83 |
| Millwall | 46 | 19 | 17 | 10 | 58 | 49 | 74 |
| Leicester C | 46 | 19 | 16 | 11 | 72 | 59 | 73 |
| Tranmere R | 46 | 21 | 9 | 16 | 69 | 53 | 72 |
| Derby Co | 46 | 20 | 11 | 15 | 73 | 68 | 71 |
| Notts Co | 46 | 20 | 8 | 18 | 65 | 69 | 68 |
| Wolverh'pton W | 46 | 17 | 17 | 12 | 60 | 47 | 68 |
| Middlesbrough | 46 | 18 | 13 | 15 | 66 | 54 | 67 |
| Stoke C | 46 | 18 | 13 | 15 | 57 | 59 | 67 |
| Charlton A | 46 | 19 | 8 | 19 | 61 | 58 | 65 |
| Sunderland | 46 | 19 | 8 | 19 | 54 | 57 | 65 |
| Bristol C | 46 | 16 | 16 | 14 | 47 | 50 | 64 |
| Bolton W | 46 | 15 | 14 | 17 | 63 | 64 | 59 |
| Southend U | 46 | 17 | 8 | 21 | 63 | 67 | 59 |
| Grimsby | 46 | 13 | 20 | 13 | 52 | 47 | 59 |
| Portsmouth | 46 | 15 | 13 | 18 | 52 | 58 | 58 |
| Barnsley | 46 | 16 | 7 | 23 | 55 | 67 | 55 |
| Watford | 46 | 15 | 9 | 22 | 66 | 80 | 54 |
| Luton T | 46 | 14 | 11 | 21 | 56 | 60 | 53 |
| W.B.A. | 46 | 13 | 12 | 21 | 60 | 69 | 51 |
| Birmingham C | 46 | 13 | 12 | 21 | 52 | 69 | 51 |
| Oxford U | 46 | 13 | 10 | 23 | 54 | 75 | 49 |
| Peterborough U | 46 | 8 | 13 | 25 | 48 | 76 | 37 |

Manager: Arthur Cox until October, then Roy McFarland.
Leading scorers: Marco Gabbiadini, Tommy Johnson, Paul Kitson, League 13. Tommy Johnson, all matches 19.
League ever-present: Martin Taylor.
Player of the season: Martin Taylor.

- After more than nine years at the Baseball Ground, a severe back problem forced Arthur Cox's resignation. Roy McFarland took over and steered Derby to the Play-offs for the second time.
- They survived pitch invasions at the New Den when beating Millwall but lost to Leicester City at Wembley.
- When John Harkes played for the United States against Switzerland in Detroit in the 1994 World Cup finals, he was the first Derby representative in international football outside the five nations of the British Isles.
- Since then, contracted or loan players at Derby have appeared for a further 17 countries.

## Division One

| Match No. | Date | | Venue | Opponents | Result | | Scorers | Att |
|---|---|---|---|---|---|---|---|---|
| 1 | Aug | 14 | (h) | Sunderland | W | 5-0 | Pembridge 2 (1 pen), Gabbiadini, Kitson, Short | 1 |
| 2 | | 18 | (a) | Nottingham F | D | 1-1 | Forsyth | 2 |
| 3 | | 21 | (a) | Middlesbrough | L | 0-3 | | 1 |
| 4 | | 28 | (h) | Bristol C | W | 1-0 | Gabbiadini | 1 |
| 5 | Sep | 4 | (a) | Birmingham C | L | 0-3 | | 1 |
| 6 | | 11 | (h) | Peterborough U | W | 2-0 | Gabbiadini, Johnson | 1 |
| 7 | | 18 | (a) | Millwall | D | 0-0 | | |
| 8 | | 25 | (a) | Notts C | L | 1-4 | Gabbiadini | 1 |
| 9 | Oct | 3 | (h) | West Brom A | W | 5-3 | Simpson 2, Kitson, Pembridge (pen), Short | 1 |
| 10 | | 9 | (h) | Luton T | W | 2-1 | Kitson, Johnson | 1 |
| 11 | | 16 | (a) | Portsmouth | L | 2-3 | Johnson, Kitson | 1 |
| 12 | | 23 | (h) | Crystal P | W | 3-1 | Harkes, Kitson, Pembridge | 1 |
| 13 | | 30 | (a) | Bolton W | W | 2-0 | Pembridge, Simpson | 1 |
| 14 | Nov | 2 | (a) | Charlton A | W | 2-1 | Simpson, Pembridge | |
| 15 | | 7 | (h) | Wolves | L | 0-4 | | 1 |
| 16 | | 13 | (a) | Oxford U | L | 0-2 | | |
| 17 | | 20 | (h) | Grimsby T | W | 2-1 | Short, Pembridge (pen) | 1 |
| 18 | | 27 | (h) | Southend U | L | 1-3 | Simpson | 1 |
| 19 | Dec | 5 | (a) | Wolves | D | 2-2 | Gabbiadini 2 | 1 |
| 20 | | 18 | (a) | Sunderland | L | 0-1 | | 1 |
| 21 | | 27 | (a) | Barnsley | W | 1-0 | Kitson | 1 |
| 22 | | 28 | (h) | Leicester C | W | 3-2 | Pembridge, Gabbiadini, Johnson | 1 |
| 23 | Jan | 1 | (a) | Stoke C | L | 1-2 | Gabbiadini | 1 |
| 24 | | 3 | (h) | Tranmere R | W | 4-0 | Gabbiadini 3, Williams | 1 |
| 25 | | 15 | (h) | Portsmouth | W | 1-0 | Johnson | 1 |
| 26 | | 22 | (a) | Luton T | L | 1-2 | Forsyth | |
| 27 | | 29 | (h) | Watford | L | 1-2 | Kitson | 1 |
| 28 | Feb | 5 | (a) | Crystal P | D | 1-1 | Charles | 1 |
| 29 | | 12 | (h) | Bolton W | W | 2-0 | Pembridge, Gabbiadini | 1 |
| 30 | | 19 | (a) | Watford | W | 4-3 | Kitson, Johnson, Gabbiadini, Watson (og) | |
| 31 | | 22 | (h) | Middlesbrough | L | 0-1 | | 1 |
| 32 | | 26 | (h) | Birmingham C | D | 1-1 | Johnson | 1 |
| 33 | Mar | 5 | (a) | Bristol C | D | 0-0 | | |
| 34 | | 12 | (h) | Millwall | D | 0-0 | | 1 |
| 35 | | 16 | (a) | Peterborough U | D | 2-2 | Johnson, Nicholson | 7 |
| 36 | | 26 | (a) | West Brom A | W | 2-1 | Johnson, Simpson | 17 |
| 37 | | 29 | (a) | Tranmere R | L | 0-4 | | 7 |
| 38 | Apr | 2 | (h) | Barnsley | W | 2-0 | Johnson, Harkes | 14 |
| 39 | | 5 | (a) | Leicester C | D | 3-3 | Kitson 2, Willis (og) | 2 |
| 40 | | 9 | (h) | Stoke C | W | 4-2 | Simpson, Pembridge, Kitson, Butler (og) | 16 |
| 41 | | 16 | (h) | Charlton A | W | 2-0 | Johnson, Kitson | 15 |
| 42 | | 20 | (h) | Notts C | D | 1-1 | Dijkstra (og) | 18 |
| 43 | | 23 | (a) | Grimsby T | D | 1-1 | Kitson | 7 |
| 44 | | 27 | (h) | Nottingham F | L | 0-2 | | 19 |
| 45 | | 30 | (h) | Oxford U | W | 2-1 | Pembridge (pen), Johnson | 16 |
| 46 | May | 8 | (a) | Southend U | L | 3-4 | Simpson 2, Johnson | 8 |

FINAL LEAGUE POSITION: 6th in Division One

Appeara
Substi
G

## Play-offs

| | | | | | | | | |
|---|---|---|---|---|---|---|---|---|
| SF1 | May | 15 | (h) | Millwall | W | 2-0 | Cowans, Johnson | 17 |
| SF2 | | 18 | (a) | Millwall | W | 3-1 | Gabbiadini, Johnson, Van den Hauwe (og) | 16 |
| F | | 30 | (n*) | Leicester C | L | 1-2 | Johnson | 73 |

*Final at Wembley Stadium

Appeara
Substi
G

## FA Cup

| | | | | | | | | |
|---|---|---|---|---|---|---|---|---|
| 3 | Jan | 8 | (a) | Oldham A | L | 1-2 | Johnson | 12 |

Appeara
Substi
G

## League Cup

| | | | | | | | | |
|---|---|---|---|---|---|---|---|---|
| 2 | Sep | 22 | (a) | Exeter C | W | 3-1 | Kitson, Simpson, Gabbiadini | 5 |
| 2 | Oct | 6 | (h) | Exeter C | W | 2-0 | Gabbiadini, Johnson | 10 |
| 3 | | 27 | (h) | Tottenham H | L | 0-1 | | 19 |

Appeara
Substi
G

**Derby County played in the Anglo-Italian Cup (see Rams in Other Competitions)**

| Charles G | Forsyth M | Kuhl M | Short C | Wassall D | Simpson P | Williams P | Kitson P | Gabbiadini M | Pembridge M | Harkes J | Ramage C | Johnson T | Kavanagh J | Coleman S | Hayward S | Nicholson S | Ratcliffe K | Cowans G | |
|---|---|---|---|---|---|---|---|---|---|---|---|---|---|---|---|---|---|---|---|
| 2 | 3 | 4 | 5 | 6 | 7 | 8 | 9 | 10 | 11 | | | | | | | | | | 1 |
| 2 | 3 | 4 | 5 | 6 | | 8 | 9 | 10 | 11 | 7 | | | | | | | | | 2 |
| 2 | 3 | 4 | 5 | 6 | | | 9 | 10 | 11 | 7 | **8** | 12 | 13 | | | | | | 3 |
| 2 | 3 | 4 | 5 | 6 | | 8 | 9 | 10 | 11 | 7 | | | | | | | | | 4 |
| 2 | 3 | 4 | 5 | | 11 | 8 | 9 | 10 | | 7 | | | | 6 | | | | | 5 |
| 2 | 3 | 4 | 5 | 6 | 11 | 8 | 9 | 10 | | | | 7 | | | | | | | 6 |
| 2 | 3 | 4 | 5 | 6 | 7 | 8 | 9 | 10 | 11 | | | | | | | | | | 7 |
| 2 | 3 | 4 | 5 | 6 | 7 | 8 | 9 | **10** | 11 | | | 12 | | | | | | | 8 |
| 2 | 3 | 4 | 5 | 6 | 7 | 8 | 9 | **10** | 11 | 13 | | 12 | | | | | | | 9 |
| | 3 | | 5 | 6 | 11 | | 9 | 10 | 4 | 7 | | 8 | 2 | | | | | | 10 |
| 2 | 3 | | 5 | 6 | 11 | | 9 | **10** | 4 | 7 | | 8 | 13 | | 12 | | | | 11 |
| | 3 | 4 | 5 | 6 | 11 | | 9 | | 10 | 7 | | 8 | 2 | | | | | | 12 |
| 8 | 3 | 4 | 5 | **6** | 11 | 12 | 9 | | 10 | 7 | | | 2 | | | | | | 13 |
| 8 | 3 | 4 | 5 | 6 | 11 | | 9 | | 10 | 7 | | | 2 | | | | | | 14 |
| 2 | 3 | **4** | 5 | | 11 | 12 | 9 | | 10 | 7 | | 8 | 6 | | | | | | 15 |
| 2 | 3 | | 5 | | 11 | 10 | 9 | | | 7 | | 8 | 13 | **6** | 12 | 4 | | | 16 |
| 2 | 3 | | 5 | 6 | 11 | 12 | 9 | 10 | 4 | 7 | | **8** | | | | | | | 17 |
| 2 | 3 | | 5 | 6 | 11 | | 9 | 10 | 4 | 7 | | 8 | | | | | | | 18 |
| 2 | 3 | 4 | 5 | 6 | 11 | | 9 | 10 | 8 | 7 | | | | | | | | | 19 |
| 2 | 3 | 4 | 5 | 6 | **11** | 13 | 9 | 10 | 8 | 7 | | 12 | | | | | | | 20 |
| 2 | 3 | 4 | 5 | 6 | | 11 | **9** | 10 | 8 | 7 | 13 | 12 | | | | | | | 21 |
| 2 | 3 | 4 | 5 | 6 | | 11 | | **10** | 8 | 7 | 12 | 9 | | | | | | | 22 |
| 2 | 3 | **4** | 5 | 6 | 12 | 11 | | 10 | | 7 | 8 | 9 | 13 | | | | | | 23 |
| 2 | 3 | 4 | 5 | 6 | 12 | 11 | | 10 | 8 | **7** | | 9 | | | | | | | 24 |
| 2 | 3 | 4 | 5 | 6 | | 11 | 9 | 10 | 8 | | | 7 | | | | | | | 25 |
| 2 | 3 | 4 | | 6 | 13 | | 9 | 10 | 8 | | | 7 | 12 | | | 5 | **11** | | 26 |
| 2 | **3** | 4 | | 6 | 13 | | 9 | 10 | 8 | | 11 | 7 | 12 | | | 5 | | | 27 |
| 2 | | 4 | | | | 3 | | 10 | 8 | | | 9 | 6 | | | 5 | 11 | 7 | 28 |
| 2 | | 4 | 5 | | 12 | 6 | 9 | 10 | **8** | | | 11 | 13 | | | 3 | | 7 | 29 |
| 2 | | | 5 | | 12 | 6 | 9 | 10 | 8 | | | 11 | | | **4** | 3 | | 7 | 30 |
| 2 | | **4** | 5 | | 12 | 6 | 9 | 10 | 8 | | | 11 | | | | 3 | | 7 | 31 |
| 2 | | 4 | 5 | | | 6 | 9 | 10 | 8 | | | 11 | | | | 3 | | 7 | 32 |
| 2 | | **4** | 5 | | | 6 | 9 | 10 | 8 | | | 12 | | | | 3 | 11 | 7 | 33 |
| **2** | | | 5 | | | | 9 | 10 | 8 | 12 | | 11 | 4 | | | 3 | 6 | 7 | 34 |
| 2 | | | 5 | | | | 9 | 10 | | 8 | | 11 | 4 | | | 3 | 6 | 7 | 35 |
| 2 | | | 5 | | 11 | 6 | 9 | **10** | 12 | 4 | | 8 | | | | 3 | | 7 | 36 |
| 2 | | | 5 | | 11 | 6 | 9 | 10 | 12 | **4** | | 8 | | | | 3 | | 7 | 37 |
| 2 | | | 5 | | 11 | 6 | 9 | | 10 | 4 | | 8 | | | | 3 | | 7 | 38 |
| 2 | | | 5 | | | 6 | 9 | 12 | 10 | 4 | | **8** | | | | 3 | 11 | 7 | 39 |
| 2 | | | 5 | | 11 | 6 | 9 | | 10 | 4 | | 8 | | | | 3 | | 7 | 40 |
| 2 | | | 5 | | 11 | 6 | 9 | 12 | 10 | 4 | | **8** | | | | 3 | | 7 | 41 |
| 2 | | | 5 | | 11 | 6 | 9 | 12 | 10 | 4 | | 8 | | | | 3 | | **7** | 42 |
| 2 | | | 5 | | 11 | 6 | 9 | 12 | 10 | 4 | | **8** | 13 | | | 3 | | 7 | 43 |
| **2** | | | 5 | | 11 | 6 | 9 | 8 | 10 | 4 | | | 12 | | 13 | 3 | | 7 | 44 |
| 2 | | | 5 | | 11 | 6 | **9** | 12 | 10 | 4 | | 8 | 13 | | | 3 | | 7 | 45 |
| | 12 | | 5 | 6 | 11 | | | 13 | 10 | 4 | | 8 | 2 | | 9 | **3** | | 7 | 46 |
| 43 | 27 | 27 | 43 | 25 | 27 | 30 | 41 | 33 | 39 | 31 | 3 | 31 | 9 | 2 | 2 | 22 | 6 | 19 | |
| | 1 | | | | 7 | 4 | | 6 | 2 | 2 | 2 | 6 | 10 | | 3 | | | | |
| 1 | 2 | | 3 | | 9 | 1 | 13 | 13 | 11 | 2 | | 13 | | | | 1 | | | |

4 own-goals

| Charles G | Forsyth M | Kuhl M | Short C | Wassall D | Simpson P | Williams P | Kitson P | Gabbiadini M | Pembridge M | Harkes J | Ramage C | Johnson T | Kavanagh J | Coleman S | Hayward S | Nicholson S | Ratcliffe K | Cowans G | |
|---|---|---|---|---|---|---|---|---|---|---|---|---|---|---|---|---|---|---|---|
| 2 | 3 | | 5 | | 11 | 6 | | 9 | 10 | 4 | | 8 | | | | | | 7 | SF1 |
| **2** | 3 | | 5 | | 11 | 6 | | 9 | 10 | 4 | | 8 | 12 | | 13 | | | 7 | SF2 |
| 2 | **3** | | 5 | | 11 | 6 | 12 | 9 | 10 | 4 | | 8 | | | | | | 7 | F |
| 3 | 3 | | 3 | | 3 | 3 | | 3 | 3 | 3 | | 3 | | | | | | 3 | |
| | | | | | | | 1 | | | | | | 1 | | 1 | | | | |
| | | | | | | | | 1 | | | | 3 | | | | | | 1 | |

1 own-goal

| Charles G | Forsyth M | Kuhl M | Short C | Wassall D | Simpson P | Williams P | Kitson P | Gabbiadini M | Pembridge M | Harkes J | Ramage C | Johnson T | Kavanagh J | Coleman S | Hayward S | Nicholson S | Ratcliffe K | Cowans G | |
|---|---|---|---|---|---|---|---|---|---|---|---|---|---|---|---|---|---|---|---|
| 2 | **3** | 4 | 5 | 6 | 7 | 11 | | 10 | 8 | | 12 | 9 | | | | | | | 3 |
| 1 | 1 | 1 | 1 | 1 | 1 | 1 | | 1 | 1 | | | 1 | | | | | | | |
| | | | | | | | | | | | 1 | | | | | | | | |
| | | | | | | | | | | | | 1 | | | | | | | |

| Charles G | Forsyth M | Kuhl M | Short C | Wassall D | Simpson P | Williams P | Kitson P | Gabbiadini M | Pembridge M | Harkes J | Ramage C | Johnson T | Kavanagh J | Coleman S | Hayward S | Nicholson S | Ratcliffe K | Cowans G | |
|---|---|---|---|---|---|---|---|---|---|---|---|---|---|---|---|---|---|---|---|
| 2 | 3 | 4 | 5 | 6 | 11 | 8 | 9 | 10 | 7 | | | | | | | | | | 2 |
| 2 | 3 | | 5 | 6 | 11 | **8** | 9 | 10 | 4 | 7 | | 12 | 13 | | | | | | 2 |
| 12 | 3 | 4 | 5 | 6 | 11 | 13 | 9 | | 10 | 7 | | 8 | **2** | | | | | | 3 |
| 2 | 3 | 2 | 3 | 3 | 3 | 2 | 3 | 2 | 3 | 2 | | 1 | 1 | | | | | | |
| 1 | | | | | | 1 | | | | | | 1 | 1 | | | | | | |
| | | | | | 1 | | 1 | 2 | | | | 1 | | | | | | | |

# 1994-95

| | P | W | D | L | F | A | Pts |
|---|---|---|---|---|---|---|---|
| Middlesbrough | 46 | 23 | 13 | 10 | 67 | 40 | 82 |
| Reading | 46 | 23 | 10 | 13 | 58 | 44 | 79 |
| Bolton W | 46 | 21 | 14 | 11 | 67 | 45 | 77 |
| Wolves | 46 | 21 | 13 | 12 | 77 | 61 | 76 |
| Tranmere R | 46 | 22 | 10 | 14 | 67 | 58 | 76 |
| Barnsley | 46 | 20 | 12 | 14 | 63 | 52 | 72 |
| Watford | 46 | 19 | 13 | 14 | 52 | 46 | 70 |
| Sheffield U | 46 | 17 | 17 | 12 | 74 | 55 | 68 |
| Derby Co | 46 | 18 | 12 | 16 | 66 | 51 | 66 |
| Grimsby | 46 | 17 | 14 | 15 | 62 | 56 | 65 |
| Stoke C | 46 | 16 | 15 | 15 | 50 | 53 | 63 |
| Millwall | 46 | 16 | 14 | 16 | 60 | 60 | 62 |
| Southend U | 46 | 18 | 8 | 20 | 54 | 73 | 62 |
| Oldham A | 46 | 16 | 13 | 17 | 60 | 60 | 61 |
| Charlton A | 46 | 16 | 11 | 19 | 58 | 66 | 59 |
| Luton T | 46 | 15 | 13 | 18 | 61 | 64 | 58 |
| Port Vale | 46 | 15 | 13 | 18 | 58 | 64 | 58 |
| Portsmouth | 46 | 15 | 13 | 18 | 53 | 63 | 58 |
| W.B.A. | 46 | 16 | 10 | 20 | 51 | 57 | 58 |
| Sunderland | 46 | 12 | 18 | 16 | 41 | 45 | 54 |
| Swindon T | 46 | 12 | 12 | 22 | 54 | 73 | 48 |
| Burnley | 46 | 11 | 13 | 22 | 49 | 74 | 46 |
| Bristol C | 46 | 11 | 12 | 23 | 42 | 63 | 45 |
| Notts Co | 46 | 9 | 13 | 24 | 45 | 66 | 40 |

Manager: Roy McFarland.
Leading scorer: Marco Gabbiadini, League 11, all matches 13.
Player of the season: Craig Short.

- Martin Taylor, the last Derby player to achieve an ever-present League season, suffered a double fracture of the left leg in a clash with Dave Regis as the Rams lost to Southend United at Roots Hall in October.
- Taylor did not play for the Rams for 29 months but went on to revive his career with Wycombe Wanderers.
- Important players left during the season. Paul Kitson joined Newcastle United for £2.25 million in September before a joint £2.9 million deal took Gary Charles and Tommy Johnson to Aston Villa.
- Roy McFarland, knowing his contract would not be renewed, said his farewells in the final home match against Southend. Billy McEwan stood in for the last game, at Watford.

## Division One

| Match No. | Date | | Venue | Opponents | Result | | Scorers | Atte |
|---|---|---|---|---|---|---|---|---|
| 1 | Aug | 13 | (a) | Barnsley | L | 1-2 | Pembridge | |
| 2 | | 20 | (h) | Luton T | D | 0-0 | | 1 |
| 3 | | 27 | (a) | Millwall | L | 1-4 | Sturridge | |
| 4 | | 31 | (h) | Middlesbrough | L | 0-1 | | 1 |
| 5 | Sep | 3 | (h) | Grimsby T | W | 2-1 | Charles, Pembridge | 1 |
| 6 | | 11 | (a) | Swindon T | D | 1-1 | Kitson | |
| 7 | | 13 | (a) | Bristol C | W | 2-0 | Kitson, Carsley | |
| 8 | | 17 | (h) | Oldham A | W | 2-1 | Carsley, Short | 1 |
| 9 | | 25 | (h) | Stoke C | W | 3-0 | Hodge, Gabbiadini, Charles | 1 |
| 10 | Oct | 1 | (a) | Bolton W | L | 0-1 | | 1 |
| 11 | | 8 | (h) | Watford | D | 1-1 | Hodge | 1 |
| 12 | | 16 | (a) | Southend U | L | 0-1 | | |
| 13 | | 23 | (a) | Notts C | D | 0-0 | | |
| 14 | | 29 | (h) | Charlton A | D | 2-2 | Short, Johnson | 1 |
| 15 | Nov | 2 | (h) | Reading | L | 1-2 | Gabbiadini | 1 |
| 16 | | 6 | (a) | Portsmouth | W | 1-0 | Gabbiadini | |
| 17 | | 12 | (a) | Sheffield U | L | 1-2 | Simpson (pen) | 1 |
| 18 | | 19 | (h) | Port Vale | W | 2-0 | Johnson 2 | 1 |
| 19 | | 27 | (a) | Wolves | W | 2-0 | Johnson, Stallard | 22 |
| 20 | Dec | 3 | (h) | Notts C | D | 0-0 | | 14 |
| 21 | | 11 | (a) | Luton T | D | 0-0 | | |
| 22 | | 17 | (h) | Barnsley | W | 1-0 | Johnson | 1 |
| 23 | | 26 | (a) | Tranmere R | L | 1-3 | Johnson | 1 |
| 24 | | 31 | (a) | Sunderland | D | 1-1 | Johnson | 1 |
| 25 | Jan | 2 | (h) | West Brom A | D | 1-1 | Trollope | 16 |
| 26 | | 14 | (a) | Charlton A | W | 4-3 | Gabbiadini 2, Short, Stallard | |
| 27 | | 22 | (h) | Portsmouth | W | 3-0 | Simpson 3 | 1 |
| 28 | Feb | 4 | (h) | Sheffield U | L | 2-3 | Williams, Kavanagh | 15 |
| 29 | | 11 | (a) | Reading | L | 0-1 | | |
| 30 | | 21 | (a) | Port Vale | L | 0-1 | | |
| 31 | | 26 | (h) | Bolton W | W | 2-1 | Yates, Mills | 1 |
| 32 | Mar | 4 | (a) | Stoke C | D | 0-0 | | 13 |
| 33 | | 7 | (a) | Grimsby T | W | 1-0 | Pembridge | 5 |
| 34 | | 11 | (h) | Millwall | W | 3-2 | Pembridge, Trollope, Gabbiadini | 12 |
| 35 | | 15 | (h) | Burnley | W | 4-0 | Mills, Trollope, Simpson (pen), Gabbiadini | 13 |
| 36 | | 18 | (a) | Middlesbrough | W | 4-2 | Mills 2, Pembridge, Gabbiadini | 18 |
| 37 | | 22 | (h) | Swindon T | W | 3-1 | Simpson (pen), Pembridge, Mills | 16 |
| 38 | | 25 | (a) | Oldham A | L | 0-1 | | 7 |
| 39 | Apr | 1 | (h) | Bristol C | W | 3-1 | Gabbiadini, Williams, Wrack | 14 |
| 40 | | 8 | (h) | Sunderland | L | 0-1 | | 15 |
| 41 | | 12 | (h) | Wolves | D | 3-3 | Simpson 2 (1 pen), Gabbiadini | 16 |
| 42 | | 15 | (a) | Burnley | L | 1-3 | Trollope | 11 |
| 43 | | 17 | (h) | Tranmere R | W | 5-0 | Pembridge 2, Mills, Williams, Gabbiadini | 13 |
| 44 | | 22 | (a) | West Brom A | D | 0-0 | | 15 |
| 45 | | 29 | (h) | Southend U | L | 1-2 | Mills | 12 |
| 46 | May | 7 | (a) | Watford | L | 1-2 | Pembridge | 8 |

FINAL LEAGUE POSITION: 9th in Division One

Appeara
Substi
G

## FA Cup

| | | | | | | | | |
|---|---|---|---|---|---|---|---|---|
| 3 | Jan | 7 | (a) | Everton | L | 0-1 | | 29 |

Appeara
Substi

## League Cup

| | | | | | | | | |
|---|---|---|---|---|---|---|---|---|
| 2 | Sep | 20 | (a) | Reading | L | 1-3 | Gabbiadini | 6 |
| 2 | | 28 | (h) | Reading | W | 2-0* | Gabbiadini, Williams | 9 |
| 3 | Oct | 26 | (a) | Portsmouth | W | 1-0 | Simpson | 8 |
| 4 | Nov | 30 | (a) | Swindon T | L | 1-2 | Stallard | 8 |

* won on the away goals rule

Appeara
Substi
G

**Derby County played in the Anglo-Italian Cup (see Rams in Other Competitions)**

| Charles G | Forsyth M | Hayward S | Short C | Williams P | Cowans G | Gabbiadini M | Kitson P | Pembridge M | Simpson P | Harkes J | Wassall D | Johnson T | Nicholson S | Kuhl M | Sturridge D | Kavanagh J | Hodge S | Stallard M | Carsley L | Davies W | Sutton S | Trollope P | Wrack D | Sutton W | Yates D | Hoult R | Mills L | Boden C | Ashbee I | Cooper K | Quy A | |
|---|---|---|---|---|---|---|---|---|---|---|---|---|---|---|---|---|---|---|---|---|---|---|---|---|---|---|---|---|---|---|---|---|
| 2 | **3** | 4 | 5 | 6 | 7 | 8 | 9 | 10 | 11 | 12 | 13 | | | | | | | | | | | | | | | | | | | | | 1 |
| 2 | 3 | 4 | 5 | | 7 | 12 | 9 | 10 | 11 | | 6 | **8** | | | | | | | | | | | | | | | | | | | | 2 |
| 2 | 5 | 8 | | | 7 | | **9** | 10 | 11 | | 6 | | 3 | 4 | 12 | 13 | | | | | | | | | | | | | | | | 3 |
| 2 | 3 | | 5 | | 7 | | 9 | 10 | 11 | | 6 | | | | 8 | 12 | **4** | 13 | | | | | | | | | | | | | | 4 |
| 2 | 3 | | 5 | | 7 | | 9 | 10 | 12 | **11** | 6 | | | | 8 | | 4 | | | | | | | | | | | | | | | 5 |
| 2 | 3 | | 5 | 6 | 7 | 8 | 9 | 10 | | | | | | | | | 4 | | 11 | | | | | | | | | | | | | 6 |
| 2 | 3 | | 5 | 6 | 7 | 8 | **9** | 10 | 12 | | | | | | | | 4 | | 11 | | | | | | | | | | | | | 7 |
| 2 | 3 | | 5 | 6 | 7 | 8 | 9 | 10 | 13 | 12 | | | | | | | 4 | | **11** | | | | | | | | | | | | | 8 |
| 2 | 3 | | 5 | 6 | 7 | 8 | | 10 | 13 | 12 | | 9 | | | | | 4 | | **11** | | | | | | | | | | | | | 9 |
| 2 | 3 | | 5 | 6 | **7** | | | 10 | 9 | 11 | 12 | | | | 8 | | 4 | | 13 | | | | | | | | | | | | | 10 |
| 2 | 3 | | | 6 | 7 | | | 10 | | 11 | 5 | | | | 8 | | 4 | | | 9 | | | | | | | | | | | | 11 |
| 2 | 3 | | 5 | 6 | 7 | | | **10** | *12* | 11 | 14 | | | | 8 | | 4 | | 9 | | 13 | | | | | | | | | | | 12 |
| 2 | 3 | | 5 | 6 | 7 | | | | | **11** | | 10 | | | 9 | | 4 | 12 | 8 | | 1 | | | | | | | | | | | 13 |
| 2 | 3 | | 5 | 6 | 7 | 10 | | | 11 | | 4 | 9 | | | | | | | 8 | | 1 | | | | | | | | | | | 14 |
| 2 | 3 | | 5 | 6 | 7 | 10 | | | 11 | | 4 | 9 | | | | | | | 8 | | 1 | | | | | | | | | | | 15 |
| 2 | 3 | | **5** | 6 | 7 | 10 | | | 11 | | | 9 | | 4 | | 12 | | | 8 | | 1 | | | | | | | | | | | 16 |
| 2 | **3** | | | 6 | 7 | 10 | | | 11 | | 5 | 9 | | 4 | | 12 | | 13 | 8 | | 1 | | | | | | | | | | | 17 |
| | | | 5 | 6 | | | | | 11 | 7 | | 9 | 3 | 4 | | 2 | | 10 | 8 | | 1 | | | | | | | | | | | 18 |
| | | | 5 | 6 | | | | | 11 | 7 | | 9 | 3 | 4 | | 2 | | 10 | 8 | | 1 | | | | | | | | | | | 19 |
| | | | 5 | 6 | | | | | 11 | 7 | | 9 | 3 | 4 | | 2 | | 10 | 8 | | 1 | | | | | | | | | | | 20 |
| | | | 5 | 6 | | | | | 11 | 7 | | 9 | | 4 | 3 | 2 | | 10 | 8 | | 1 | | | | | | | | | | | 21 |
| | 3 | | | 6 | | | | | **11** | 7 | 5 | 9 | | 4 | | 2 | | 10 | 8 | | 1 | 12 | | | | | | | | | | 22 |
| 2 | | | | 6 | | 12 | | | **11** | 7 | 5 | 9 | | 4 | | 3 | | 10 | 8 | | 1 | | | | | | | | | | | 23 |
| | **3** | | 5 | 6 | | | | | | 7 | 13 | 9 | 4 | | | 2 | | 10 | 8 | | 1 | 11 | 12 | | | | | | | | | 24 |
| | | | 5 | 6 | | | | | 11 | **7** | | | 3 | | | 2 | | 10 | 8 | 12 | 1 | 4 | 9 | | | | | | | | | 25 |
| | 6 | | 5 | | | 10 | | | 11 | | 7 | | 3 | | | 2 | | 9 | 8 | | 1 | 4 | | | | | | | | | | 26 |
| | 6 | | **5** | | | 10 | | | 11 | | 7 | | 3 | | | 2 | | 9 | | | 1 | 4 | 12 | 8 | | | | | | | | 27 |
| | 12 | | 5 | 6 | | 10 | | | 11 | | 7 | | **3** | | | 2 | | 9 | | | 1 | 4 | 13 | 8 | | | | | | | | 28 |
| | | | 5 | 6 | | 10 | | | 11 | | 12 | | 3 | | | **7** | | 9 | 8 | | 1 | 4 | 13 | | 2 | | | | | | | 29 |
| | | | 5 | 6 | | 10 | | | 11 | 13 | 2 | | 3 | | | | | **9** | 8 | | 1 | 7 | 12 | | 4 | | | | | | | 30 |
| | | | 5 | | | 10 | | | 11 | 7 | | | 3 | | | 2 | | | **8** | | | 4 | 12 | | 6 | 1 | 9 | | | | | 31 |
| | | | 5 | | | 10 | | 8 | 11 | 7 | 12 | | 3 | | | **2** | | | | | | 4 | | | 6 | 1 | 9 | | | | | 32 |
| | | | 5 | | | 10 | | 8 | 11 | 7 | 2 | | 3 | | | | | | | | | 4 | | | 6 | 1 | 9 | | | | | 33 |
| | | | 5 | 6 | | 10 | | 8 | 11 | 7 | 12 | | **3** | | | | | | | | | 4 | 13 | | 2 | 1 | 9 | | | | | 34 |
| | | | **5** | 6 | | 10 | | 8 | 11 | 7 | 3 | | | | | | | | | | | 4 | 12 | 13 | 2 | 1 | 9 | | | | | 35 |
| | | | 5 | 6 | | 10 | | 8 | 11 | 7 | 3 | | | | | | | | | | | 4 | 12 | | 2 | 1 | **9** | | | | | 36 |
| | | | 5 | 6 | | 10 | | 8 | 11 | 7 | 3 | | | | | | | | | | | 4 | 12 | | 2 | 1 | **9** | | | | | 37 |
| | | | 5 | 6 | | 10 | | 8 | 11 | 7 | 3 | | | | | 13 | | | | | | 4 | 12 | | 2 | 1 | **9** | | | | | 38 |
| | | | | 6 | | 10 | | 8 | 11 | 7 | 3 | | | | 13 | 5 | | | | | | 4 | 12 | | **2** | 1 | 9 | | | | | 39 |
| | | | | 6 | | 10 | | 8 | **11** | 7 | 3 | | | | 13 | 5 | | | | | | 4 | 2 | | | 1 | 9 | 12 | | | | 40 |
| | | | 5 | 6 | | 10 | | 8 | 11 | 7 | 3 | | | | | 2 | | | | | | 4 | | | | 1 | 9 | | | | | 41 |
| | | | 5 | 6 | | 10 | | 8 | 11 | 7 | 3 | | | | | **2** | | | | | | 4 | 13 | | | 1 | 9 | 12 | | | | 42 |
| | | | **5** | 6 | | 10 | | 8 | 11 | 7 | 3 | | | | | | | | | | | 4 | | 12 | | 1 | 9 | 2 | | | | 43 |
| | | | 5 | 6 | | 10 | | 8 | 11 | 7 | 3 | | | | | | | | | | | 4 | 12 | | | 1 | 9 | **2** | | | | 44 |
| | | | | 6 | | 10 | | **8** | 11 | 7 | | | | | 12 | 5 | | | | | | 4 | | 13 | | 1 | 9 | 2 | 3 | | | 45 |
| | | | | 6 | | **10** | | 8 | 7 | 2 | | | | | 12 | 5 | | | | | 1 | 4 | | 3 | | | 9 | 11 | | 13 | | 46 |
| 18 | 21 | 3 | 37 | 37 | 17 | 30 | 8 | 27 | 37 | 29 | 25 | 14 | 15 | 9 | 7 | 20 | 10 | 13 | 22 | 1 | 19 | 23 | 2 | 3 | 11 | 15 | 16 | 4 | 1 | | | |
| | 1 | | | | | 2 | | | 5 | 4 | 7 | | | | 5 | 5 | | 3 | 1 | 1 | 1 | 1 | 14 | 3 | | | | 2 | | 1 | | |
| 2 | | | 3 | 3 | | 11 | 2 | 9 | 8 | | | 7 | | | 1 | 1 | 2 | 2 | 2 | | | 4 | 1 | | 1 | | 7 | | | | | |

| Charles G | Forsyth M | Hayward S | Short C | Williams P | Cowans G | Gabbiadini M | Kitson P | Pembridge M | Simpson P | Harkes J | Wassall D | Johnson T | Nicholson S | Kuhl M | Sturridge D | Kavanagh J | Hodge S | Stallard M | Carsley L | Davies W | Sutton S | Trollope P | Wrack D | Sutton W | Yates D | Hoult R | Mills L | Boden C | Ashbee I | Cooper K | Quy A | |
|---|---|---|---|---|---|---|---|---|---|---|---|---|---|---|---|---|---|---|---|---|---|---|---|---|---|---|---|---|---|---|---|---|
| | 12 | | 5 | 6 | | 10 | | | 11 | | 7 | | 3 | | | 2 | | 9 | 8 | | 1 | | 13 | **4** | | | | | | | | 3 |
| | | | 1 | 1 | | 1 | | | 1 | | 1 | | 1 | | | 1 | | 1 | 1 | | 1 | | | 1 | | | | | | | | |
| | 1 | | | | | | | | | | | | | | | | | | | | | | 1 | | | | | | | | | |
| | | | | | | | | | | | | | | | | | | | | | | | | | | | | | | | | |

| Charles G | Forsyth M | Hayward S | Short C | Williams P | Cowans G | Gabbiadini M | Kitson P | Pembridge M | Simpson P | Harkes J | Wassall D | Johnson T | Nicholson S | Kuhl M | Sturridge D | Kavanagh J | Hodge S | Stallard M | Carsley L | Davies W | Sutton S | Trollope P | Wrack D | Sutton W | Yates D | Hoult R | Mills L | Boden C | Ashbee I | Cooper K | Quy A | |
|---|---|---|---|---|---|---|---|---|---|---|---|---|---|---|---|---|---|---|---|---|---|---|---|---|---|---|---|---|---|---|---|---|
| 2 | 3 | | 5 | 6 | 7 | 8 | | 10 | | 4 | | 9 | | | | | | | 11 | | | | | | | | | | | | | 2 |
| 2 | 3 | | 5 | 6 | 7 | 8 | | 10 | 12 | 4 | 11 | **9** | | | | | | | 13 | | | | | | | | | | | | | 2 |
| 2 | 3 | | 5 | 6 | 7 | 10 | | | 11 | | 4 | *9* | | | | 13 | | 14 | 8 | | **1** | | | | | | | | | | 12 | 3 |
| | | | 5 | 6 | | | | | 11 | **7** | | 9 | 3 | 4 | 12 | 2 | | 10 | 8 | | 1 | | | | | | | | | | | 4 |
| 3 | 3 | | 4 | 4 | 3 | 3 | | 2 | 2 | 3 | 2 | 4 | 1 | 1 | | 1 | | 1 | 3 | | 2 | | | | | | | | | | | |
| | | | | | | | | | 1 | | | | | | 1 | 1 | | 1 | 1 | | | | | | | | | | | | 1 | |
| | | | | 1 | | 2 | | | 1 | | | | | | | | | 1 | | | | | | | | | | | | | | |

# 1995-96

| | P | W | D | L | F | A | Pts |
|---|---|---|---|---|---|---|---|
| Sunderland | 46 | 22 | 17 | 7 | 59 | 33 | 83 |
| Derby Co | 46 | 21 | 16 | 9 | 71 | 51 | 79 |
| Crystal Palace | 46 | 20 | 15 | 11 | 67 | 48 | 75 |
| Stoke C | 46 | 20 | 13 | 13 | 60 | 49 | 73 |
| Leicester C | 46 | 19 | 14 | 13 | 66 | 60 | 71 |
| Charlton A | 46 | 17 | 20 | 9 | 57 | 45 | 71 |
| Ipswich T | 46 | 19 | 12 | 15 | 79 | 69 | 69 |
| Huddersfield T | 46 | 17 | 12 | 17 | 61 | 58 | 63 |
| Sheffield U | 46 | 16 | 14 | 16 | 57 | 54 | 62 |
| Barnsley | 46 | 14 | 18 | 14 | 60 | 66 | 60 |
| W.B.A. | 46 | 16 | 12 | 18 | 60 | 68 | 60 |
| Port Vale | 46 | 15 | 15 | 16 | 59 | 66 | 60 |
| Tranmere R | 46 | 14 | 17 | 15 | 64 | 60 | 59 |
| Southend U | 46 | 15 | 14 | 17 | 52 | 61 | 59 |
| Birmingham C | 46 | 15 | 13 | 18 | 61 | 64 | 58 |
| Norwich C | 46 | 14 | 15 | 17 | 59 | 55 | 57 |
| Grimsby | 46 | 14 | 14 | 18 | 55 | 69 | 56 |
| Oldham A | 46 | 14 | 14 | 18 | 54 | 50 | 56 |
| Reading | 46 | 13 | 17 | 16 | 54 | 63 | 56 |
| Wolves | 46 | 13 | 16 | 17 | 56 | 62 | 55 |
| Portsmouth | 46 | 13 | 13 | 20 | 61 | 69 | 52 |
| Millwall | 46 | 13 | 13 | 20 | 43 | 63 | 52 |
| Watford | 46 | 10 | 18 | 18 | 62 | 70 | 48 |
| Luton T | 46 | 11 | 12 | 23 | 40 | 64 | 45 |

Manager: Jim Smith.
Leading scorer: Dean Sturridge, League/all matches 20.
Player of the season: Dean Yates.

- Jim Smith appointed former Rams player Steve McClaren as his assistant. The partnership worked perfectly until McClaren left for Manchester United in February 1999.
- Because many of Arthur Cox's captures held their value, Smith was able to make profitable exchange deals and was not in the red until Ashley Ward arrived from Norwich City in March.
- Smith pulled off an inspired signing when Croatian international Igor Stimac joined Derby from Hajduk Split for £1.57 million in October. Stimac made his debut in a 5–1 defeat at Tranmere: then the season took off.
- From 11 November to 5 March, Derby were unbeaten in 20 League games. Although behind the 22 achieved in 1969, it is the best run inside one season. This included a 4–1 win over Birmingham City, Derby's first victory at St Andrew's since October 1948.

## Division One

| Match No. | Date | | Venue | Opponents | Result | | Scorers |
|---|---|---|---|---|---|---|---|
| 1 | Aug | 13 | (h) | Port Vale | D | 0-0 | |
| 2 | | 19 | (a) | Reading | L | 2-3 | Sturridge, Preece |
| 3 | | 26 | (h) | Grimsby T | D | 1-1 | Sturridge |
| 4 | | 30 | (a) | Wolves | L | 0-3 | |
| 5 | Sep | 2 | (a) | Luton T | W | 2-1 | Sturridge 2 |
| 6 | | 10 | (h) | Leicester C | L | 0-1 | |
| 7 | | 13 | (h) | Southend U | W | 1-0 | Sturridge |
| 8 | | 16 | (a) | Portsmouth | D | 2-2 | Van der Laan, Flynn |
| 9 | | 23 | (a) | Barnsley | L | 0-2 | |
| 10 | Oct | 1 | (h) | Millwall | D | 2-2 | Willems, Van der Laan |
| 11 | | 7 | (a) | Sheffield U | W | 2-0 | Gabbiadini, Willems |
| 12 | | 14 | (h) | Ipswich T | D | 1-1 | Gabbiadini |
| 13 | | 22 | (a) | Stoke C | D | 1-1 | Van der Laan |
| 14 | | 28 | (h) | Oldham A | W | 2-1 | Van der Laan, Simpson |
| 15 | Nov | 4 | (a) | Tranmere R | L | 1-5 | Stimac |
| 16 | | 11 | (h) | West Brom A | W | 3-0 | Gabbiadini 2, Sturridge (pen) |
| 17 | | 18 | (h) | Charlton A | W | 2-0 | Willems, Gabbiadini |
| 18 | | 21 | (a) | Birmingham C | W | 4-1 | Sturridge, Willems, Gabbiadini, D.Powell |
| 19 | | 25 | (a) | Crystal P | D | 0-0 | |
| 20 | Dec | 2 | (h) | Sheffield U | W | 4-2 | Willems 2 (1 pen), Sturridge, Gabbiadini |
| 21 | | 9 | (h) | Barnsley | W | 4-1 | Carsley, Gabbiadini, Sturridge, Willems (pen) |
| 22 | | 16 | (a) | Millwall | W | 1-0 | Sturridge |
| 23 | | 23 | (h) | Sunderland | W | 3-1 | Gabbiadini, Willems (pen), Sturridge |
| 24 | | 26 | (a) | Huddersfield T | W | 1-0 | Willems |
| 25 | Jan | 1 | (h) | Norwich C | W | 2-1 | Willems, Gabbiadini |
| 26 | | 13 | (h) | Reading | W | 3-0 | Sturridge 2, Flynn |
| 27 | | 20 | (a) | Port Vale | D | 1-1 | Sturridge |
| 28 | Feb | 3 | (a) | Grimsby T | D | 1-1 | D.Powell |
| 29 | | 10 | (h) | Wolves | D | 0-0 | |
| 30 | | 17 | (a) | Southend U | W | 2-1 | Simpson, Willems |
| 31 | | 21 | (h) | Luton T | D | 1-1 | D.Powell |
| 32 | | 24 | (h) | Portsmouth | W | 3-2 | Yates, Sturridge, Gabbiadini |
| 33 | | 28 | (a) | Leicester C | D | 0-0 | |
| 34 | Mar | 2 | (h) | Huddersfield T | W | 3-2 | Simpson 2, Van der Laan |
| 35 | | 5 | (a) | Watford | D | 0-0 | |
| 36 | | 9 | (a) | Sunderland | L | 0-3 | |
| 37 | | 16 | (h) | Watford | D | 1-1 | Simpson (pen) |
| 38 | | 23 | (a) | Norwich C | L | 0-1 | |
| 39 | | 30 | (h) | Stoke C | W | 3-1 | Sturridge 2, D.Powell |
| 40 | Apr | 2 | (a) | Ipswich T | L | 0-1 | |
| 41 | | 6 | (a) | Oldham A | W | 1-0 | Simpson (pen) |
| 42 | | 8 | (h) | Tranmere R | W | 6-2 | Simpson 3, D.Powell, Yates, Sturridge |
| 43 | | 14 | (a) | Charlton A | D | 0-0 | |
| 44 | | 20 | (h) | Birmingham C | D | 1-1 | Simpson |
| 45 | | 28 | (h) | Crystal P | W | 2-1 | Sturridge, Van der Laan |
| 46 | May | 5 | (a) | West Brom A | L | 2-3 | Sturridge, Ward |

FINAL LEAGUE POSITION: 2nd in Division One – Promoted

Appear...
Subst...

## FA Cup

| | | | | | | | |
|---|---|---|---|---|---|---|---|
| 3 | Jan | 7 | (h) | Leeds U | L | 2-4 | Gabbiadini, Simpson |

Appeara...
Subst...

## League Cup

| | | | | | | | |
|---|---|---|---|---|---|---|---|
| 2 | Sep | 19 | (a) | Shrewsbury T | W | 3-1 | Simpson, Stallard, Gabbiadini |
| 2 | Oct | 4 | (h) | Shrewsbury T | D | 1-1 | Willems |
| 3 | | 25 | (h) | Leeds U | L | 0-1 | |

Appeara...
Subst...

| Flynn S | Wassall D | Rowett G | Powell D | Harkes J | Van der Laan R | Trollope P | Stallard M | Gabbiadini M | Simpson P | Preece D | Sturridge D | Willems R | Kavanagh J | Nicholson S | Webster S | Carsley L | Hoult R | Yates D | Wrack D | Stimac I | Boden C | Powell C | Hodges G | Carbon M | Ward A | Sutton W | Cooper K | |
|---|---|---|---|---|---|---|---|---|---|---|---|---|---|---|---|---|---|---|---|---|---|---|---|---|---|---|---|---|
| 2 | 3 | 4 | 5 | 6 | 7 | 8 | 9 | 10 | 11 | 12 | 13 | | | | | | | | | | | | | | | | | 1 |
| 2 | 3 | 4 | 5 | 6 | 7 | 8 | 9 | | 11 | 13 | 12 | 10 | 14 | | | | | | | | | | | | | | | 2 |
| 4 | 5 | | 6 | 13 | 7 | 3 | | | 11 | 10 | 8 | 9 | 2 | 12 | | | | | | | | | | | | | | 3 |
| 4 | | | 6 | 11 | 7 | 12 | | | | 10 | 8 | | 2 | 3 | 5 | 9 | | | | | | | | | | | | 4 |
| 9 | 12 | | 6 | 11 | 7 | | | | 13 | 10 | 8 | | 2 | 3 | 5 | 4 | 1 | | | | | | | | | | | 5 |
| 3 | 6 | | 10 | 11 | 7 | | | 9 | 12 | 14 | 8 | | 2 | 3 | 5 | 4 | 1 | | | | | | | | | | | 6 |
| 9 | 6 | | | 11 | 7 | | | 10 | | 4 | 8 | | 2 | 3 | | | 1 | 5 | 12 | | | | | | | | | 7 |
| 9 | 6 | | | 11 | 7 | 13 | | 10 | 12 | 4 | 8 | | 2 | 3 | | | 1 | 5 | 14 | | | | | | | | | 8 |
| 9 | 6 | | | | 7 | | 8 | 10 | 11 | 4 | | | 2 | 3 | | 12 | 1 | 5 | | | | | | | | | | 9 |
| 9 | 6 | 3 | 10 | | 7 | 13 | | | 11 | 4 | | 8 | 2 | | | | | 5 | 12 | | | | | | | | | 10 |
| 9 | | 6 | 11 | | 7 | | | 10 | 14 | 4 | | 8 | | 3 | | 2 | 12 | 5 | 13 | | | | | | | | | 11 |
| | | 6 | 11 | | 7 | | | 10 | 13 | 4 | 12 | 9 | | 3 | | 2 | 1 | 5 | 8 | | | | | | | | | 12 |
| 3 | | 6 | | | 7 | 11 | | 10 | 12 | 4 | | 9 | | 3 | | 2 | 1 | 5 | 8 | | | | | | | | | 13 |
| 8 | | 6 | 4 | | 7 | | | 10 | 11 | | | 9 | | 3 | | 2 | 1 | 5 | 12 | | | | | | | | | 14 |
| 8 | | 2 | 4 | | 7 | | | 10 | 11 | | 12 | 9 | | 3 | | | 1 | 5 | | 6 | | | | | | | | 15 |
| 12 | | 2 | 4 | | 7 | | | 10 | | | 8 | 9 | | | | 11 | 1 | 5 | | 6 | 3 | | | | | | | 16 |
| 12 | | 2 | 4 | | 7 | | | 10 | | | 8 | 9 | | | | 11 | 1 | 5 | | 6 | 3 | | | | | | | 17 |
| 12 | | 2 | 4 | | 7 | | | 10 | 13 | | 8 | 9 | | | | 11 | 1 | 5 | | 6 | 3 | | | | | | | 18 |
| | | 2 | 4 | | 7 | | | 10 | 12 | | 8 | 9 | | | | 11 | 1 | 5 | | 6 | 3 | | | | | | | 19 |
| 13 | | 2 | 4 | | 7 | 12 | | 10 | | | 8 | 9 | | 3 | | 11 | 1 | 5 | | 6 | | | | | | | | 20 |
| 7 | | 2 | 4 | | | 12 | | 10 | 13 | | 8 | 9 | | 3 | | 11 | 1 | 5 | 14 | 6 | | | | | | | | 21 |
| 7 | | 2 | 4 | | | | | 10 | 12 | | 8 | 9 | | 3 | | 11 | 1 | 5 | | 6 | | | | | | | | 22 |
| 7 | | 2 | 4 | | | | | 10 | 12 | | 8 | 9 | | 3 | | 11 | 1 | 5 | | 6 | | | | | | | | 23 |
| 14 | | 2 | 4 | | 7 | 12 | | 10 | 13 | | 8 | 9 | | 3 | | 11 | 1 | 5 | | 6 | | | | | | | | 24 |
| 8 | | 2 | 4 | | 7 | 13 | | 10 | 12 | | | 9 | | 3 | | 11 | 1 | 5 | 14 | 6 | | | | | | | | 25 |
| 4 | 6 | 2 | | | 7 | | | | 10 | | 8 | 9 | | 3 | | 11 | 1 | 5 | | | | | | | | | | 26 |
| 11 | | 2 | 4 | | 7 | | | 10 | 12 | | 8 | 9 | | 3 | | | 1 | 5 | | 6 | | | | | | | | 27 |
| 11 | 2 | | 4 | | 7 | | | 10 | 12 | | 8 | 9 | | | | | 1 | 5 | | 6 | | 3 | | | | | | 28 |
| | | 2 | 4 | | 7 | | | 10 | | | 8 | 9 | | | | 11 | 1 | 5 | | 6 | | 3 | | | | | | 29 |
| 13 | | 2 | 4 | | 7 | | | 12 | 10 | | 8 | 9 | | | | 11 | 1 | 5 | | 6 | | 3 | | | | | | 30 |
| 13 | | 2 | 4 | | 7 | | | 12 | 10 | | 8 | 9 | | | | 11 | 1 | 5 | | 6 | | 3 | 14 | | | | | 31 |
| 11 | 6 | 2 | 4 | | 7 | | | 12 | 10 | | 8 | 9 | | | | | 1 | 5 | | | | 3 | 13 | | | | | 32 |
| 11 | | 2 | 4 | | 7 | | | 12 | 10 | | 8 | 9 | | | | 13 | 1 | 5 | | 6 | | 3 | | | | | | 33 |
| 11 | | 2 | 4 | | 7 | | | 12 | 10 | | 8 | 9 | | | | 13 | 1 | 5 | | 6 | | 3 | 14 | | | | | 34 |
| 11 | | 2 | 4 | | 7 | | | 10 | | | 8 | 9 | | | | 13 | 1 | 5 | | 6 | | 3 | 12 | | | | | 35 |
| 12 | | 2 | 4 | | 7 | | | 10 | 9 | | 8 | | | | | 11 | 1 | 5 | | 6 | | 3 | 13 | 14 | | | | 36 |
| 7 | 6 | 2 | 4 | | | | | 10 | 9 | | 8 | | | | | 11 | 1 | 5 | | | | 3 | 12 | 13 | | | | 37 |
| 7 | 2 | 14 | | | | | | 10 | 13 | | 12 | 9 | | | | 11 | 1 | 5 | | 6 | | 3 | 4 | | 8 | | | 38 |
| 7 | 2 | | 4 | | | | | 10 | 13 | | 12 | 9 | | | | 11 | 1 | 5 | | 6 | | 3 | | | 8 | | | 39 |
| 6 | 2 | | 4 | | 7 | | | 10 | 13 | | 8 | 12 | | | | 11 | 1 | 5 | | | | 3 | 14 | | 9 | | | 40 |
| 12 | | 2 | 4 | | 7 | 13 | | 10 | 9 | | 8 | | | | | 11 | 1 | 5 | | 6 | | 3 | | | | | | 41 |
| 14 | | 2 | 4 | | 7 | 13 | | 10 | 9 | | 8 | | | | | 11 | 1 | 5 | | 6 | | 3 | | 12 | | | | 42 |
| 12 | | 2 | 4 | | 7 | 13 | | 10 | 9 | | 8 | | | | | 11 | 1 | 5 | | 6 | | 3 | | | 14 | | | 43 |
| | | 2 | | | 7 | 4 | | 12 | 9 | | | 10 | | | | 11 | 1 | 5 | | 6 | | 3 | 14 | 13 | 8 | | | 44 |
| 11 | | 2 | | | 7 | 4 | | 10 | 9 | | 8 | 12 | | | | | 1 | | | 6 | | 3 | | 5 | 13 | | | 45 |
| 7 | 2 | | | | | 4 | | | 9 | | 8 | | | | | 11 | 1 | | 13 | | | 3 | | 5 | 10 | 6 | 12 | 46 |
| 29 | 16 | 34 | 37 | 7 | 39 | 7 | 3 | 33 | 21 | 10 | 33 | 31 | 8 | 19 | 3 | 31 | 40 | 38 | 2 | 27 | 4 | 19 | 1 | 2 | 5 | 1 | | |
| 13 | 1 | 1 | | 1 | | 10 | | 6 | 18 | 3 | 6 | 2 | 1 | 1 | | 4 | 1 | | 8 | | | | 8 | 4 | 2 | | 1 | |
| 2 | | | 5 | | 6 | | | 11 | 10 | 1 | 20 | 11 | | | | 1 | | 2 | | 1 | | | | | 1 | | | |

| | | | | | | | | | | | | | | | | | | | | | |
|---|---|---|---|---|---|---|---|---|---|---|---|---|---|---|---|---|---|---|---|---|---|
| 8 | | 2 | | | 7 | 12 | | 10 | 11 | | | 9 | 4 | 3 | | | 1 | 5 | 13 | 6 | 3 |
| 1 | | 1 | | | 1 | | | 1 | 1 | | | 1 | 1 | 1 | | | 1 | 1 | | 1 | |
| | | | | | | 1 | | | | | | | | | | | | | 1 | | |
| | | | | | | | | 1 | 1 | | | | | | | | | | | | |

| | | | | | | | | | | | | | | | | | | | | |
|---|---|---|---|---|---|---|---|---|---|---|---|---|---|---|---|---|---|---|---|---|
| 9 | 6 | | | | 7 | 12 | 8 | 10 | 11 | 4 | | | 2 | 3 | | | 1 | 5 | 13 | 2 |
| 8 | | 6 | 11 | | 7 | | | 10 | | 4 | | 9 | | 3 | | 2 | | 5 | 12 | 2 |
| 8 | | 6 | 13 | | 7 | 4 | | 10 | 11 | | | 9 | | 3 | | 2 | 1 | 5 | 12 | 3 |
| 3 | 1 | 2 | 1 | | 3 | 1 | 1 | 3 | 2 | 2 | | 2 | 1 | 3 | | 2 | 2 | 3 | | |
| | | | 1 | | | 1 | | | | | | | | | | | | | 3 | |
| | | | | | | | 1 | 1 | 1 | | | 1 | | | | | | | | |

# 1996-97

| | P | W | D | L | F | A | Pts |
|---|---|---|---|---|---|---|---|
| Manchester U | 38 | 21 | 12 | 5 | 76 | 44 | 75 |
| Newcastle U | 38 | 19 | 11 | 8 | 73 | 40 | 68 |
| Arsenal | 38 | 19 | 11 | 8 | 62 | 32 | 68 |
| Liverpool | 38 | 19 | 11 | 8 | 62 | 37 | 68 |
| Aston Villa | 38 | 17 | 10 | 11 | 47 | 34 | 61 |
| Chelsea | 38 | 16 | 11 | 11 | 58 | 55 | 59 |
| Sheffield W | 38 | 14 | 15 | 9 | 50 | 51 | 57 |
| Wimbledon | 38 | 15 | 11 | 12 | 49 | 46 | 56 |
| Leicester C | 38 | 12 | 11 | 15 | 46 | 54 | 47 |
| Tottenham H | 38 | 13 | 7 | 18 | 44 | 51 | 46 |
| Leeds U | 38 | 11 | 13 | 14 | 28 | 38 | 46 |
| Derby Co | 38 | 11 | 13 | 14 | 45 | 58 | 46 |
| Blackburn R | 38 | 9 | 15 | 14 | 42 | 43 | 42 |
| West Ham U | 38 | 10 | 12 | 16 | 39 | 48 | 42 |
| Everton | 38 | 10 | 12 | 16 | 44 | 57 | 42 |
| Southampton | 38 | 10 | 11 | 17 | 50 | 56 | 41 |
| Coventry C | 38 | 9 | 14 | 15 | 38 | 54 | 41 |
| Sunderland | 38 | 10 | 10 | 18 | 35 | 53 | 40 |
| Middlesbrough* | 38 | 10 | 12 | 16 | 51 | 60 | 39 |
| Nottingham F | 38 | 6 | 16 | 16 | 31 | 59 | 34 |

*Middlesbrough deducted 3 points

Manager: Jim Smith.
Leading scorer: Dean Sturridge, League 11, all matches 14.
Player of the season: Chris Powell.

- Jim Smith signed two players from the European Championship finals for Derby's first tilt at the Premiership, Danish defender Jacob Laursen and Croatian midfield player Aljosa Asanovic.
- Wimbledon's victory at the Baseball Ground on 28 September ended a sequence of 23 home matches without defeat. That equalled the club record set in 1929 and 1930.
- Paul McGrath arrived from Aston Villa in October and, despite his ailing knees, proved a magnificent short-term signing, adding class and presence to the defence.
- Paulo Wanchope scored one of Derby's greatest goals on his debut against Manchester United at Old Trafford. Costa Ricans Wanchope and Mauricio Solis were signed in transfer deadline week, along with Estonian goalkeeper Mart Poom.
- The final match, against Arsenal, ended 102 years at the Baseball Ground, although Reserve fixtures continued there. Ashley Ward scored Derby's last League goal at their old home, in a 3–1 defeat by Arsenal.

## Premiership

| Match No. | Date | | Venue | Opponents | Result | | Scorers |
|---|---|---|---|---|---|---|---|
| 1 | Aug | 17 | (h) | Leeds U | D | 3-3 | Sturridge 2, Simpson |
| 2 | | 21 | (a) | Tottenham H | D | 1-1 | Dailly |
| 3 | | 24 | (a) | Aston Villa | L | 0-2 | |
| 4 | Sep | 4 | (h) | Manchester U | D | 1-1 | Laursen |
| 5 | | 9 | (a) | Blackburn R | W | 2-1 | Willems, Flynn |
| 6 | | 14 | (h) | Sunderland | W | 1-0 | Asanovic (pen) |
| 7 | | 21 | (a) | Sheffield W | D | 0-0 | |
| 8 | | 28 | (h) | Wimbledon | L | 0-2 | |
| 9 | Oct | 12 | (h) | Newcastle U | L | 0-1 | |
| 10 | | 19 | (a) | Nottingham F | D | 1-1 | Dailly |
| 11 | | 27 | (a) | Liverpool | L | 1-2 | Ward |
| 12 | Nov | 2 | (h) | Leicester C | W | 2-0 | Ward, Whitlow (og) |
| 13 | | 17 | (h) | Middlesbrough | W | 2-1 | Asanovic, Ward |
| 14 | | 23 | (a) | West Ham U | D | 1-1 | Sturridge |
| 15 | | 30 | (h) | Coventry C | W | 2-1 | Asanovic (pen), Ward |
| 16 | Dec | 7 | (a) | Arsenal | D | 2-2 | Sturridge, D.Powell |
| 17 | | 16 | (h) | Everton | L | 0-1 | |
| 18 | | 21 | (a) | Southampton | L | 1-3 | Dailly |
| 19 | | 26 | (a) | Sunderland | L | 0-2 | |
| 20 | | 28 | (h) | Blackburn R | D | 0-0 | |
| 21 | Jan | 11 | (a) | Wimbledon | D | 1-1 | Willems |
| 22 | | 18 | (a) | Chelsea | L | 1-3 | Asanovic |
| 23 | | 29 | (a) | Leeds U | D | 0-0 | |
| 24 | Feb | 1 | (h) | Liverpool | L | 0-1 | |
| 25 | | 15 | (h) | West Ham U | W | 1-0 | Asanovic (pen) |
| 26 | | 19 | (h) | Sheffield W | D | 2-2 | Sturridge, Stimac |
| 27 | | 22 | (a) | Leicester C | L | 2-4 | Sturridge 2 |
| 28 | Mar | 1 | (h) | Chelsea | W | 3-2 | Minto (og), Asanovic (pen), Ward |
| 29 | | 5 | (a) | Middlesbrough | L | 1-6 | Simpson |
| 30 | | 15 | (a) | Everton | L | 0-1 | |
| 31 | | 22 | (h) | Tottenham H | W | 4-2 | Van der Laan, Trollop, Sturridge, Ward |
| 32 | Apr | 5 | (a) | Manchester U | W | 3-2 | Ward, Wanchope, Sturridge |
| 33 | | 9 | (h) | Southampton | D | 1-1 | Ward |
| 34 | | 12 | (h) | Aston Villa | W | 2-1 | Rowett, Van der Laan |
| 35 | | 19 | (a) | Newcastle U | L | 1-3 | Sturridge |
| 36 | | 23 | (h) | Nottingham F | D | 0-0 | |
| 37 | May | 3 | (a) | Coventry C | W | 2-1 | Rowett, Sturridge |
| 38 | | 11 | (h) | Arsenal | L | 1-3 | Ward |

FINAL LEAGUE POSITION: 12th in Premiership

Appear

Subst

## FA Cup

| | | | | | | | |
|---|---|---|---|---|---|---|---|
| 3 | Jan | 21 | (a) | Gillingham | W | 2-0 | Van der Laan, Willems |
| 4 | | 25 | (h) | Aston Villa | W | 3-1 | Sturridge, Van der Laan, Willems |
| 5 | Feb | 26 | (h) | Coventry C | W | 3-2 | Sturridge, Van der Laan, Ward |
| 6 | Mar | 8 | (h) | Middlesbrough | L | 0-2 | |

Appear

Subst

## League Cup

| | | | | | | | |
|---|---|---|---|---|---|---|---|
| 2 | Sep | 17 | (a) | Luton T | L | 0-1 | |
| 2 | | 25 | (h) | Luton T | D | 2-2 | Simpson, Sturridge |

Appear

Subst

| Parker P | Powell C | Laursen J | Yates D | Rowett G | Asanovic A | Dailly C | Sturridge D | Gabbiadini M | Powell D | Flynn S | Willems R | Simpson P | Stimac I | Van der Laan R | Carbon M | Ward A | Carsley L | McGrath P | Trollope P | Rahmberg M | Taylor M | Poom M | Wanchope P | Solis M | Cooper K | |
|---|---|---|---|---|---|---|---|---|---|---|---|---|---|---|---|---|---|---|---|---|---|---|---|---|---|---|
| 2 | 3 | **4** | 5 | 6 | 7 | 8 | 9 | 10 | *11* | 12 | 13 | 14 | | | | | | | | | | | | | | 1 |
| 2 | 3 | 4 | | 6 | 7 | 8 | 9 | **10** | 11 | 14 | 12 | 13 | 5 | | | | | | | | | | | | | 2 |
| 2 | 3 | 4 | | **6** | 7 | 10 | | 13 | 11 | 8 | *9* | 14 | 5 | 12 | | | | | | | | | | | | 3 |
| | 3 | 2 | | 4 | 7 | 8 | *9* | 14 | 11 | 13 | **10** | 12 | 5 | | 6 | | | | | | | | | | | 4 |
| | 3 | 2 | | 4 | 7 | 8 | 9 | 12 | 11 | 13 | **10** | | 5 | | 6 | | | | | | | | | | | 5 |
| | 3 | 2 | | 4 | 7 | 10 | | 9 | 11 | | | 13 | 5 | 8 | **6** | 12 | | | | | | | | | | 6 |
| 6 | 3 | 2 | | 4 | | 7 | 9 | **10** | 11 | | | 13 | 5 | | | 12 | 8 | | | | | | | | | 7 |
| | 3 | 2 | | **4** | *7* | 8 | 9 | 14 | 11 | | | 13 | 5 | | 6 | 10 | 12 | | | | | | | | | 8 |
| | *3* | 2 | | 4 | 7 | 8 | **9** | 12 | 11 | 13 | | 14 | 6 | | | 10 | | 5 | | | | | | | | 9 |
| | 3 | **2** | | 4 | 7 | 8 | | | 11 | | *10* | 14 | 6 | | 13 | 9 | 12 | 5 | | | | | | | | 10 |
| | 3 | 2 | | 4 | 7 | *8* | | | 11 | 12 | **10** | 14 | 6 | | | 9 | 13 | 5 | | | | | | | | 11 |
| | 3 | 2 | 6 | 4 | 7 | **8** | 12 | | 11 | 10 | | 13 | | | | 9 | | 5 | | | | | | | | 12 |
| | 3 | 2 | 6 | 4 | *7* | **8** | 9 | | | 11 | 13 | 14 | | | | 10 | 12 | 5 | | | | | | | | 13 |
| | 3 | **2** | 6 | 4 | 7 | | 9 | | 11 | 8 | | | | | | 10 | 12 | 5 | | | | | | | | 14 |
| | | 3 | 4 | 2 | 7 | 12 | 9 | | 11 | 8 | | | 6 | | | 10 | 13 | **5** | | | | | | | | 15 |
| | 3 | 2 | | 4 | **7** | 12 | 9 | | 11 | 8 | | | 6 | | 13 | 10 | | 5 | | | | | | | | 16 |
| | 3 | 2 | | 4 | **7** | 13 | 9 | 12 | 11 | 8 | | | 6 | | | 10 | | 5 | | | | | | | | 17 |
| | 3 | 2 | **4** | 6 | *7* | 10 | | 13 | 11 | 8 | 14 | | 5 | | | 9 | 12 | | | | | | | | | 18 |
| | 3 | 2 | 12 | 4 | | 7 | 9 | 13 | 11 | *8* | | | **6** | | | 10 | 14 | 5 | | | | | | | | 19 |
| | 3 | 2 | 5 | 4 | 7 | **8** | 9 | 13 | 12 | | | | 6 | | | 10 | 11 | | | | | | | | | 20 |
| | 3 | 2 | **4** | 6 | 7 | 13 | 9 | | 12 | 8 | 14 | | | | | *10* | 11 | 5 | | | | | | | | 21 |
| | 3 | 2 | | 4 | 7 | 13 | 9 | | 11 | | 12 | | | | 6 | **10** | 8 | 5 | | | | | | | | 22 |
| | 3 | 4 | | | 7 | 6 | | 9 | 12 | | **10** | 13 | | 8 | | | 2 | 5 | 11 | | | | | | | 23 |
| | 3 | **4** | | 6 | 7 | | 9 | | 10 | 13 | | 14 | | 8 | *12* | | 2 | 5 | 11 | | | | | | | 24 |
| | 3 | | | 4 | 7 | 10 | 9 | | | | | | 6 | 8 | | | 2 | 5 | 11 | | | | | | | 25 |
| | 3 | | | 4 | 7 | 10 | 9 | | | | | | 6 | **8** | | 12 | 2 | 5 | 11 | | | | | | | 26 |
| | **3** | 12 | | 4 | 7 | *2* | 9 | | | | | 13 | 6 | | | 10 | 8 | 5 | 11 | 14 | | | | | | 27 |
| | | 4 | | 3 | 7 | 6 | 9 | | 11 | | | | 5 | 8 | | 10 | 2 | | | | | | | | | 28 |
| | | **3** | | 4 | 7 | 6 | 9 | | 11 | | 13 | 14 | 5 | 8 | | 10 | *2* | 12 | | | | | | | | 29 |
| | 3 | 4 | | 6 | 7 | 8 | | | 10 | | | 12 | | | 13 | 9 | **2** | 5 | 11 | | 1 | | | | | 30 |
| | 3 | 4 | | | 7 | 6 | 9 | | 13 | | | | | 8 | **10** | 12 | 2 | 5 | 11 | | 1 | | | | | 31 |
| | 3 | 2 | | | | 6 | 9 | | 7 | | | 12 | | 8 | | 10 | | 5 | 4 | | | 1 | **11** | | | 32 |
| | 3 | 5 | | 4 | 7 | 6 | 9 | | 11 | | 14 | | | *8* | | 10 | | | 2 | | | **1** | 13 | | | 33 |
| | 3 | 4 | | 2 | **7** | 6 | 9 | | 13 | | | | | 8 | | *10* | | 5 | 11 | | | | 14 | 12 | | 34 |
| | **3** | 4 | | 2 | 7 | 6 | 9 | | 12 | | | | | *8* | | 10 | | 5 | 11 | | | | 13 | 14 | | 35 |
| | 3 | 5 | | 4 | 7 | 6 | 9 | | | | | | | 8 | | 12 | 2 | | 11 | | 1 | | **10** | | | 36 |
| | 3 | 4 | 12 | 5 | | 6 | 9 | | 7 | | 13 | | | 8 | | 10 | **2** | | 11 | | | 1 | | | | 37 |
| | 3 | 2 | | 4 | 7 | 6 | | | **11** | | *10* | 14 | | 8 | | 9 | 13 | 5 | 12 | | | 1 | | | | 38 |
| 4 | 35 | 35 | 8 | 35 | 34 | 31 | 29 | 5 | 27 | 10 | 7 | | 21 | 15 | 6 | 25 | 15 | 23 | 13 | | 3 | 4 | 2 | | | |
| | | 1 | 2 | | | 5 | 1 | 9 | 6 | 7 | 9 | 19 | | 1 | 4 | 5 | 9 | 1 | 1 | 1 | | | 3 | 2 | | |
| | | 1 | | 2 | 6 | 3 | 11 | | 1 | 1 | 2 | 2 | 1 | 2 | | 9 | | | 1 | | | | 1 | | | |

2 own-goals

| | | | | | | | | | | | | | | | | | | | | | | | | | | |
|---|---|---|---|---|---|---|---|---|---|---|---|---|---|---|---|---|---|---|---|---|---|---|---|---|---|---|
| | 3 | 4 | | 6 | | 8 | 9 | | **11** | 7 | *10* | 13 | | 12 | 14 | | 2 | 5 | | | | | | | | 3 |
| | 3 | | | **6** | 7 | 4 | 9 | | | | 10 | 12 | | 8 | | | 2 | 5 | 11 | | | | | | | 4 |
| | | 4 | | 5 | 7 | 6 | 9 | | 11 | | | | | 8 | | 10 | 2 | | 3 | | | | | | | 5 |
| | 3 | | | 12 | 7 | 6 | | 14 | 11 | **4** | *10* | 13 | 5 | | | 9 | 2 | | 8 | | 1 | | | | | 6 |
| | 3 | 2 | | 3 | 3 | 4 | 3 | | 3 | 2 | 3 | | 1 | 2 | | 2 | 4 | 2 | 3 | | 1 | | | | | |
| | | | | 1 | | | | 1 | | | | 3 | | 1 | 1 | | | | | | | | | | | |
| | | | | | | | 3 | | | | 1 | | | 3 | | 1 | | | | | | | | | | |

| | | | | | | | | | | | | | | | | | | | | | | | | | | |
|---|---|---|---|---|---|---|---|---|---|---|---|---|---|---|---|---|---|---|---|---|---|---|---|---|---|---|
| 6 | 3 | 2 | | 4 | 7 | 11 | | | | | | 10 | 5 | **8** | | 9 | 12 | | | | | | | | 13 | 2 |
| *4* | | **2** | | 5 | | 11 | 9 | 10 | 8 | | | 7 | | 12 | 6 | 13 | 3 | | | | | | | | 14 | 2 |
| 2 | 1 | 2 | | 2 | 1 | 2 | 1 | 1 | 1 | | | 2 | 1 | 1 | 1 | 1 | 1 | | | | | | | | | |
| | | | | | | | | | | | | | | 1 | | 1 | 1 | | | | | | | | 2 | |
| | | | | | | | 1 | | | | | 1 | | | | | | | | | | | | | | |

# 1997-98

| | P | W | D | L | F | A | Pts |
|---|---|---|---|---|---|---|---|
| Arsenal | 38 | 23 | 9 | 6 | 68 | 33 | 78 |
| Manchester U | 38 | 23 | 8 | 7 | 73 | 26 | 77 |
| Liverpool | 38 | 18 | 11 | 9 | 68 | 42 | 65 |
| Chelsea | 38 | 20 | 3 | 15 | 71 | 43 | 63 |
| Leeds U | 38 | 17 | 8 | 13 | 57 | 46 | 59 |
| Blackburn R | 38 | 16 | 10 | 12 | 57 | 52 | 58 |
| Aston Villa | 38 | 17 | 6 | 15 | 49 | 48 | 57 |
| West Ham U | 38 | 16 | 8 | 14 | 56 | 57 | 56 |
| Derby Co | 38 | 16 | 7 | 15 | 52 | 49 | 55 |
| Leicester C | 38 | 13 | 14 | 11 | 51 | 41 | 53 |
| Coventry C | 38 | 12 | 16 | 10 | 46 | 44 | 52 |
| Southampton | 38 | 14 | 6 | 18 | 50 | 55 | 48 |
| Newcastle U | 38 | 11 | 11 | 16 | 35 | 44 | 44 |
| Tottenham H | 38 | 11 | 11 | 16 | 44 | 56 | 44 |
| Wimbledon | 38 | 10 | 14 | 14 | 34 | 46 | 44 |
| Sheffield W | 38 | 12 | 8 | 18 | 52 | 67 | 44 |
| Everton | 38 | 9 | 13 | 16 | 41 | 56 | 40 |
| Bolton W | 38 | 9 | 13 | 16 | 41 | 61 | 40 |
| Barnsley | 38 | 10 | 5 | 23 | 37 | 82 | 35 |
| Crystal Palace | 38 | 8 | 9 | 21 | 37 | 71 | 33 |

Manager: Jim Smith.
Leading scorer: Paulo Wanchope, League 13, all matches 17.
Player of the season: Francesco Baiano.

- Ashley Ward, Derby's last League scorer at the Baseball Ground, was their first at Pride Park but it counted for nothing because the opening game against Wimbledon was abandoned when the floodlights failed.
- In September and October, Francesco Baiano, signed from Fiorentina, equalled the club record by scoring in six consecutive League games. He scored twice in a 5–2 victory over Sheffield Wednesday, the first time Derby had won at Hillsborough, including FA Cup semi-finals, since September 1936.
- The first 30,000 attendance at Pride Park, for the visit of Manchester United on 18 October.
- Five Derby players were involved in the 1998 World Cup finals in France, their biggest representation in the tournament. Two, Deon Burton and Darryl Powell, were with Jamaica. The others were Christian Dailly (Scotland), Jacob Laursen (Denmark) and Igor Stimac (Croatia).

## Premiership

| Match No. | Date | | Venue | Opponents | Result | | Scorers |
|---|---|---|---|---|---|---|---|
| 1 | Aug | 9 | (a) | Blackburn Rovers | L | 0-1 | |
| 2 | | 23 | (a) | Tottenham H | L | 0-1 | |
| 3 | | 30 | (h) | Barnsley | W | 1-0 | Eranio (pen) |
| 4 | Sep | 13 | (h) | Everton | W | 3-1 | Hunt, C.Powell, Sturridge |
| 5 | | 20 | (a) | Aston Villa | L | 1-2 | Baiano |
| 6 | | 24 | (a) | Sheffield W | W | 5-2 | Baiano 2, Laursen, Wanchope, Burton |
| 7 | | 27 | (h) | Southampton | W | 4-0 | Eranio (pen), Wanchope, Baiano, Carsley |
| 8 | Oct | 6 | (a) | Leicester C | W | 2-1 | Baiano 2 |
| 9 | | 18 | (h) | Manchester U | D | 2-2 | Baiano, Wanchope |
| 10 | | 22 | (h) | Wimbledon | D | 1-1 | Baiano |
| 11 | | 25 | (a) | Liverpool | L | 0-4 | |
| 12 | Nov | 1 | (h) | Arsenal | W | 3-0 | Wanchope 2, Sturridge |
| 13 | | 8 | (a) | Leeds U | L | 3-4 | Sturridge 2, Asanovic (pen) |
| 14 | | 22 | (h) | Coventry C | W | 3-1 | Baiano, Eranio (pen), Wanchope |
| 15 | | 29 | (a) | Chelsea | L | 0-4 | |
| 16 | Dec | 6 | (h) | West Ham U | W | 2-0 | Miklosko (og), Sturridge |
| 17 | | 14 | (a) | Bolton W | D | 3-3 | Baiano 2, Eranio |
| 18 | | 17 | (a) | Newcastle U | D | 0-0 | |
| 19 | | 20 | (h) | Crystal P | D | 0-0 | |
| 20 | | 26 | (h) | Newcastle U | W | 1-0 | Eranio (pen) |
| 21 | | 28 | (a) | Barnsley | L | 0-1 | |
| 22 | Jan | 11 | (h) | Blackburn R | W | 3-1 | Sturridge 2, Wanchope |
| 23 | | 17 | (a) | Wimbledon | D | 0-0 | |
| 24 | | 31 | (h) | Tottenham H | W | 2-1 | Sturridge, Wanchope |
| 25 | Feb | 7 | (h) | Aston Villa | L | 0-1 | |
| 26 | | 14 | (a) | Everton | W | 2-1 | Stimac, Wanchope |
| 27 | | 21 | (a) | Manchester U | L | 0-2 | |
| 28 | | 28 | (h) | Sheffield W | W | 3-0 | Wanchope 2, Rowett |
| 29 | Mar | 15 | (h) | Leeds U | L | 0-5 | |
| 30 | | 28 | (a) | Coventry C | L | 0-1 | |
| 31 | Apr | 5 | (h) | Chelsea | L | 0-1 | |
| 32 | | 11 | (a) | West Ham U | D | 0-0 | |
| 33 | | 13 | (h) | Bolton W | W | 4-0 | Burton 2, Wanchope, Baiano |
| 34 | | 18 | (a) | Crystal P | L | 1-3 | Bohinen |
| 35 | | 26 | (h) | Leicester C | L | 0-4 | |
| 36 | | 29 | (a) | Arsenal | L | 0-1 | |
| 37 | May | 2 | (a) | Southampton | W | 2-0 | Dailly, Sturridge |
| 38 | | 10 | (h) | Liverpool | W | 1-0 | Wanchope |

FINAL LEAGUE POSITION: 9th in Premiership

Appear
Subs

## FA Cup

| | | | | | | | |
|---|---|---|---|---|---|---|---|
| 3 | Jan | 3 | (h) | Southampton | W | 2-0 | C.Powell, Baiano (pen) |
| 4 | | 24 | (a) | Coventry C | L | 0-2 | |

Appear
Subs

## League Cup

| | | | | | | | |
|---|---|---|---|---|---|---|---|
| 2 | Sep | 16 | (a) | Southend U | W | 1-0 | Wanchope |
| 2 | Oct | 1 | (h) | Southend U | W | 5-0 | Rowett 2, Sturridge, Trollope, Wanchope |
| 3 | | 15 | (a) | Tottenham H | W | 2-1 | Wanchope 2 |
| 4 | Nov | 18 | (h) | Newcastle U | L | 0-1 | |

Appear
Subs

| Poom M | Eranio S | Powell C | Laursen J | Stimac I | Dailly C | Carsley L | Van der Laan R | Carbon M | Simpson P | Hunt J | Ward A | Burton D | Powell D | Sturridge D | Solis M | Baiano F | Rowett G | Trollope P | Asanovic A | Wanchope P | Kozluk R | Yates D | Elliott S | Willems R | Delap R | Hoult R | Bohinen L | |
|---|---|---|---|---|---|---|---|---|---|---|---|---|---|---|---|---|---|---|---|---|---|---|---|---|---|---|---|---|
| 1 | 2 | 3 | 4 | 5 | 6 | 7 | *8* | **9** | 10 | 11 | 12 | 13 | 14 | | | | | | | | | | | | | | | 1 |
| 1 | 2 | 3 | 4 | 5 | 6 | 7 | 8 | | | *11* | 9 | **10** | 13 | 12 | 14 | | | | | | | | | | | | | 2 |
| 1 | **2** | 3 | 4 | 5 | 6 | 7 | 8 | | | 11 | 9 | | | 14 | | *10* | 12 | 13 | | | | | | | | | | 3 |
| 1 | | 3 | **4** | 5 | 6 | 8 | 12 | | | *11* | | | 14 | 9 | | 10 | 2 | 13 | *7* | | | | | | | | | 4 |
| 1 | 2 | 3 | 4 | | 6 | 8 | | | | **11** | | 13 | | 9 | | *10* | 5 | 7 | 12 | 14 | | | | | | | | 5 |
| 1 | 7 | 3 | 4 | 5 | 6 | 8 | | | | 12 | | 11 | | | | **10** | 2 | | | 9 | | | | | | | | 6 |
| 1 | 7 | 3 | 4 | 5 | 6 | 8 | | | | | | 11 | | | | 10 | **2** | 12 | | 9 | | | | | | | | 7 |
| 1 | **7** | 3 | 4 | 5 | 6 | 8 | 14 | | | | | 10 | | 13 | | *11* | 2 | 12 | | 9 | | | | | | | | 8 |
| 1 | | 3 | 4 | | 5 | 8 | *7* | | | 13 | | 12 | | 10 | | **11** | 2 | 6 | | 9 | | | | | | | | 9 |
| 1 | | 3 | 4 | | 5 | 8 | | | | | | 13 | 12 | 10 | | 11 | 2 | 6 | **7** | 9 | | | | | | | | 10 |
| 1 | | 3 | 4 | | 5 | | | | | 12 | | 11 | 8 | 13 | **7** | 10 | | 6 | | 9 | 2 | | | | | | | 11 |
| 1 | | 3 | 4 | | | 8 | | 5 | | | | 14 | 6 | 10 | **7** | *11* | 2 | 13 | | 9 | 12 | | | | | | | 12 |
| 1 | | 3 | 4 | | 5 | 8 | | **6** | | 13 | | | *7* | 9 | | 10 | 2 | 14 | *11* | | 12 | | | | | | | 13 |
| 1 | 7 | 3 | **4** | | 5 | 8 | | | | 13 | | | 12 | 10 | | 11 | 6 | | | 9 | 2 | | | | | | | 14 |
| 1 | 7 | 3 | | | 6 | 8 | | | | 14 | | 12 | 13 | 10 | | *11* | 4 | | | **9** | 2 | 5 | | | | | | 15 |
| 1 | **7** | 3 | | 5 | 6 | 8 | | | | 12 | | | 13 | 10 | | 11 | 4 | | | 9 | 2 | | | | | | | 16 |
| 1 | 7 | 3 | | 5 | 6 | 8 | | | | | | 13 | 12 | 10 | | 11 | 4 | | | 9 | **2** | | | | | | | 17 |
| 1 | 2 | 3 | | | | 8 | | | | 14 | | *11* | 7 | **9** | | 10 | 4 | | | 12 | | 5 | 6 | 13 | | | | 18 |
| 1 | 2 | 3 | | 5 | | 8 | | | | | | 11 | 7 | | | 10 | 4 | | | 9 | | 12 | **6** | 13 | | | | 19 |
| 1 | **2** | 3 | 12 | 5 | | 8 | | | | | | 14 | 7 | *10* | | 11 | 4 | | | 9 | | 6 | | 13 | | | | 20 |
| 1 | 2 | 3 | **6** | | | 8 | | 12 | | | | 14 | 7 | 10 | | 13 | 4 | | | *9* | | 5 | | 11 | | | | 21 |
| 1 | | 3 | 2 | 5 | | | | | | 7 | | 13 | | 10 | | 11 | 8 | | | 9 | | 4 | **6** | 12 | | | | 22 |
| 1 | | 3 | 4 | 5 | | | | | | 7 | | 10 | | | | 11 | 2 | | | 9 | | 6 | | 8 | | | | 23 |
| 1 | 2 | 3 | 4 | 5 | | 8 | | | | | | | **7** | 10 | | 11 | 12 | | | 9 | | 6 | | 13 | | | | 24 |
| 1 | 7 | 3 | 4 | 5 | 10 | 8 | | | | | | | 13 | 9 | | 11 | 2 | | | | | **6** | | 12 | | | | 25 |
| 1 | 7 | 3 | | 5 | 6 | 8 | | | | | | | 12 | 10 | | | 4 | | | 9 | | | | **11** | 2 | | | 26 |
| 1 | 7 | 3 | | 5 | 6 | 8 | | | | | | | | 10 | | 11 | 4 | | | 9 | | | | 12 | **2** | | | 27 |
| 1 | **7** | | 4 | 5 | 6 | 8 | | | | 12 | | 10 | 3 | | | 11 | 2 | | | 9 | | | | | 13 | | | 28 |
| 1 | **7** | 13 | *4* | 5 | 6 | 8 | | | | 12 | | 10 | 3 | | | 11 | 2 | | | 9 | | | | | 14 | | | 29 |
| 1 | | 3 | 4 | 5 | 6 | 8 | | | | | | 12 | **7** | | 14 | *10* | 13 | | | 9 | | | | | 2 | 1 | 11 | 30 |
| 1 | | 3 | **4** | | 6 | 8 | | | | 12 | | 13 | | 10 | 14 | 11 | 5 | | | 9 | | | | | 2 | 1 | *7* | 31 |
| 1 | 7 | 3 | | 5 | 6 | 8 | | | | | | 12 | | **10** | | 13 | 4 | | | 9 | | | | | 2 | | 11 | 32 |
| 1 | **7** | 3 | | | 6 | | 4 | | | | | *10* | | 14 | 12 | 11 | 5 | | | 9 | 13 | | | | 2 | | 8 | 33 |
| 1 | | 3 | | 5 | 6 | 8 | **7** | | | 13 | | *10* | | 14 | | 12 | 4 | | | 9 | | | | | 2 | | 11 | 34 |
| 1 | | *3* | 4 | | 6 | 2 | **7** | | | | | 14 | | 10 | 13 | 11 | 5 | | | 9 | | | | | 12 | | 8 | 35 |
| 1 | | 3 | 4 | | 6 | 8 | | | | | | 12 | **7** | 10 | 13 | | 5 | | | 9 | | | | | 2 | | 11 | 36 |
| 1 | | 12 | 4 | | 6 | 8 | 13 | | | | | 14 | | 10 | *7* | | 5 | | | *9* | **2** | | | | 3 | | 11 | 37 |
| 1 | | 3 | 4 | | 6 | 8 | | | | | | 13 | 12 | 10 | | 11 | 5 | | | 9 | | | | | 2 | | **7** | 38 |
| 6 | 23 | 35 | 27 | 22 | 30 | 34 | 7 | 3 | 1 | 7 | 2 | 12 | 12 | 24 | 3 | 30 | 32 | 4 | 3 | 30 | 6 | 8 | 3 | 3 | 10 | 2 | 9 | |
| | | 2 | 1 | | | | 3 | 1 | | 12 | 1 | 17 | 11 | 6 | 6 | 3 | 3 | 6 | 1 | 2 | 3 | 1 | | 7 | 3 | | | |
| | 5 | 1 | 1 | 1 | 1 | 1 | | | | 1 | | 3 | | 9 | | 12 | 1 | | 1 | 13 | | | | | | | 1 | |

1 own-goal

| | | | | | | | | | | | | | | | | | | | | | | | | | |
|---|---|---|---|---|---|---|---|---|---|---|---|---|---|---|---|---|---|---|---|---|---|---|---|---|---|
| | 3 | | 5 | | 8 | | | | | | 11 | 7 | | | 10 | **6** | | | 9 | 2 | 4 | 12 | 13 | | 3 |
| 2 | 3 | 4 | 5 | 14 | 8 | | | | | | *11* | 7 | | | **10** | 13 | | | 9 | | 6 | | 12 | | 4 |
| 1 | 2 | 1 | 2 | | 2 | | | | | | 2 | 2 | | | 2 | 1 | | | 2 | 1 | 2 | | | | |
| | | | | 1 | | | | | | | | | | | | 1 | | | | | | 1 | 2 | | |
| | 1 | | | | | | | | | | | | | | 1 | | | | | | | | | | |

| | | | | | | | | | | | | | | | | | | | | | | | | | | |
|---|---|---|---|---|---|---|---|---|---|---|---|---|---|---|---|---|---|---|---|---|---|---|---|---|---|---|
| | 3 | | | 4 | | 8 | | 12 | **11** | | | *7* | 10 | | | 5 | 13 | | 9 | 2 | | 6 | | | | 2 |
| | 3 | 5 | | 4 | | 13 | | 14 | 12 | | | | 10 | 7 | | **2** | 8 | 11 | *9* | | | 6 | | | 1 | 2 |
| | 3 | | | 4 | 8 | 6 | | | 12 | | 11 | | 10 | 13 | | 5 | 7 | | **9** | 2 | | | | | | 3 |
| 2 | 3 | 4 | | 6 | 8 | | | | **7** | | | | 10 | 12 | 11 | 5 | | | 9 | | | | | | | 4 |
| 1 | 4 | 2 | | 4 | 2 | 2 | | | 2 | | 1 | 1 | 4 | 1 | 1 | 4 | 2 | 1 | 4 | 2 | | 2 | | | 1 | |
| | | | | | | 1 | | 2 | 2 | | | | | 2 | | | 1 | | | | | | | | | |
| | | | | | | | | | | | | | 1 | | | 2 | 1 | | 4 | | | | | | | |

# 1998-99

| | P | W | D | L | F | A | Pts |
|---|---|---|---|---|---|---|---|
| Manchester U | 38 | 22 | 13 | 3 | 80 | 37 | 79 |
| Arsenal | 38 | 22 | 12 | 4 | 59 | 17 | 78 |
| Chelsea | 38 | 20 | 15 | 3 | 57 | 30 | 75 |
| Leeds U | 38 | 18 | 13 | 7 | 62 | 34 | 67 |
| West Ham U | 38 | 16 | 9 | 13 | 46 | 53 | 57 |
| Aston Villa | 38 | 15 | 10 | 13 | 51 | 46 | 55 |
| Liverpool | 38 | 15 | 9 | 14 | 68 | 49 | 54 |
| Derby Co | 38 | 13 | 13 | 12 | 40 | 45 | 52 |
| Middlesbrough | 38 | 12 | 15 | 11 | 48 | 54 | 51 |
| Leicester C | 38 | 12 | 13 | 13 | 40 | 46 | 49 |
| Tottenham H | 38 | 11 | 14 | 13 | 47 | 50 | 47 |
| Sheffield W | 38 | 13 | 7 | 18 | 41 | 42 | 46 |
| Newcastle U | 38 | 11 | 13 | 14 | 48 | 54 | 46 |
| Everton | 38 | 11 | 10 | 17 | 42 | 47 | 43 |
| Coventry C | 38 | 11 | 9 | 18 | 39 | 51 | 42 |
| Wimbledon | 38 | 10 | 12 | 16 | 40 | 63 | 42 |
| Southampton | 38 | 11 | 8 | 19 | 37 | 64 | 41 |
| Charlton A | 38 | 8 | 12 | 18 | 41 | 56 | 36 |
| Blackburn R | 38 | 7 | 14 | 17 | 38 | 52 | 35 |
| Nottingham F | 38 | 7 | 9 | 22 | 35 | 69 | 30 |

Manager: Jim Smith.
Leading scorers: Deon Burton, Paulo Wanchope, League 9. Deon Burton, all matches 12.
Player of the season: Jacob Laursen.

- Derby reached their peak under Jim Smith, finishing eighth in the Premiership. They appeared to have consolidated but, from then on, it was a constant battle to stay afloat.
- After playing in the opening match, Scottish international Christian Daily joined Blackburn Rovers. The £5.35 million fee, then comfortably the highest Derby had ever received, was too tempting to reject.
- The first representative match at Pride Park was an England Under-21 international against France on 9 February. The attendance, 32,865, was the highest at the stadium to that date and set a record for an England Under-21 match anywhere.
- For the third time in seven years, Derby reached the sixth round of the FA Cup. They lost to Nwankwo Kanu's late goal at Highbury and have not been further than the fourth round since then.

## Premiership

| Match No. | Date | | Venue | Opponents | Result | | Scorers | A |
|---|---|---|---|---|---|---|---|---|
| 1 | Aug | 15 | (a) | Blackburn R | D | 0-0 | | |
| 2 | | 22 | (h) | Wimbledon | D | 0-0 | | |
| 3 | | 29 | (a) | Middlesbrough | D | 1-1 | Wanchope | |
| 4 | Sep | 9 | (h) | Sheffield W | W | 1-0 | Sturridge | |
| 5 | | 12 | (a) | Charlton A | W | 2-1 | Wanchope, Baiano | |
| 6 | | 19 | (h) | Leicester C | W | 2-0 | Schnoor, Wanchope | |
| 7 | | 26 | (a) | Aston Villa | L | 0-1 | | |
| 8 | Oct | 3 | (h) | Tottenham H | L | 0-1 | | |
| 9 | | 17 | (a) | Newcastle U | L | 1-2 | Burton | |
| 10 | | 24 | (h) | Manchester U | D | 1-1 | Burton | |
| 11 | | 31 | (h) | Leeds U | D | 2-2 | Schnoor (pen), Sturridge | |
| 12 | Nov | 7 | (a) | Liverpool | W | 2-1 | Harper, Wanchope | |
| 13 | | 16 | (a) | Nottingham F | D | 2-2 | Dorigo (pen), Carbonari | |
| 14 | | 22 | (h) | West Ham U | L | 0-2 | | |
| 15 | | 28 | (a) | Southampton | W | 1-0 | Carbonari | |
| 16 | Dec | 5 | (h) | Arsenal | D | 0-0 | | |
| 17 | | 12 | (h) | Chelsea | D | 2-2 | Carbonari, Sturridge | |
| 18 | | 19 | (a) | Coventry C | D | 1-1 | Carsley | |
| 19 | | 26 | (a) | Everton | D | 0-0 | | |
| 20 | | 28 | (h) | Middlesbrough | W | 2-1 | Sturridge, Hunt | |
| 21 | Jan | 9 | (a) | Wimbledon | L | 1-2 | Wanchope | |
| 22 | | 16 | (h) | Blackburn R | W | 1-0 | Burton | |
| 23 | | 30 | (a) | Sheffield W | W | 1-0 | Prior | |
| 24 | Feb | 3 | (a) | Manchester U | L | 0-1 | | |
| 25 | | 7 | (h) | Everton | W | 2-1 | Burton 2 | |
| 26 | | 20 | (h) | Charlton A | L | 0-2 | | |
| 27 | | 27 | (a) | Tottenham H | D | 1-1 | Burton | |
| 28 | Mar | 10 | (h) | Aston Villa | W | 2-1 | Baiano, Burton | |
| 29 | | 13 | (h) | Liverpool | W | 3-2 | Wanchope 2, Burton | |
| 30 | | 20 | (a) | Leeds U | L | 1-4 | Baiano (pen) | |
| 31 | Apr | 3 | (h) | Newcastle U | L | 3-4 | Burton, Baiano (pen), Wanchope | |
| 32 | | 10 | (h) | Nottingham F | W | 1-0 | Carbonari | |
| 33 | | 17 | (a) | West Ham U | L | 1-5 | Wanchope | |
| 34 | | 24 | (h) | Southampton | D | 0-0 | | |
| 35 | May | 2 | (a) | Arsenal | L | 0-1 | | |
| 36 | | 5 | (a) | Leicester C | W | 2-1 | Sturridge, Beck | |
| 37 | | 8 | (h) | Coventry C | D | 0-0 | | |
| 38 | | 16 | (a) | Chelsea | L | 1-2 | Carbonari | |

FINAL LEAGUE POSITION: 8th in Premiership

Appea
Subs

## FA Cup

| | | | | | | | | |
|---|---|---|---|---|---|---|---|---|
| 3 | Jan | 2 | (a) | Plymouth A | W | 3-0 | Burton 2, Eranio (pen) | 1 |
| 4 | | 23 | (a) | Swansea C | W | 1-0 | Harper | 1 |
| 5 | Feb | 13 | (a) | Huddersfield T | D | 2-2 | Burton, Dorigo (pen) | 2 |
| 5 | | 24 | (h) | Huddersfield T | W | 3-1 | Baiano 2, Dorigo | 2 |
| 6 | Mar | 6 | (a) | Arsenal | L | 0-1 | | |

Appear
Subs

## League Cup

| | | | | | | | | |
|---|---|---|---|---|---|---|---|---|
| 2 | Sep | 16 | (h) | Manchester C | D | 1-1 | Delap | 2 |
| 2 | | 23 | (a) | Manchester C | W | 1-0 | Wanchope | 1 |
| 3 | Oct | 28 | (h) | Arsenal | L | 1-2 | Sturridge | 2 |

Appear
Subs

| Delap R | Schnoor S | Dailly C | Carbonari H | Laursen J | Powell D | Carsley L | Wanchope P | Sturridge D | Baiano F | Elliott S | Bohinen L | Burton D | Prior S | Stimac I | Eranio S | Kozluk R | Harper K | Dorigo A | Bridge-Wilkinson M | Poom M | Hunt J | Christie M | Borbokis V | Launders B | Beck M | Murray A | Robinson M | Boertien P | |
|---|---|---|---|---|---|---|---|---|---|---|---|---|---|---|---|---|---|---|---|---|---|---|---|---|---|---|---|---|---|
| 2 | 3 | 4 | 5 | **6** | 7 | 8 | *9* | 10 | 11 | 12 | 13 | 14 | | | | | | | | | | | | | | | | | 1 |
| 2 | 3 | | | 6 | 7 | 8 | 9 | 10 | 12 | | **11** | | 4 | 5 | 13 | | | | | | | | | | | | | | 2 |
| 12 | **3** | | | 4 | 7 | 8 | 9 | 10 | 13 | 6 | 11 | | | 5 | 2 | | | | | | | | | | | | | | 3 |
| *2* | 3 | | | 6 | 13 | 8 | 9 | 10 | 11 | | **7** | | 4 | 5 | 12 | 14 | | | | | | | | | | | | | 4 |
| 2 | **3** | | | 6 | 12 | 8 | 9 | 10 | 11 | | 7 | | 4 | 5 | 13 | | | | | | | | | | | | | | 5 |
| 2 | 3 | | | 6 | 7 | 8 | 9 | 10 | | 12 | 11 | | 4 | **5** | | | 13 | | | | | | | | | | | | 6 |
| 3 | | | 5 | 6 | 7 | 8 | 9 | 10 | 12 | | 11 | | 4 | | 13 | **3** | | | | | | | | | | | | | 7 |
| 2 | 3 | | *5* | 6 | 7 | 8 | 9 | 12 | 10 | | **11** | 14 | 4 | | 13 | | | | | | | | | | | | | | 8 |
| 2 | 12 | | 5 | 6 | 3 | 8 | 9 | 10 | 11 | | | 13 | 4 | | **7** | | | | | | | | | | | | | | 9 |
| 2 | 3 | | | **6** | 7 | 8 | 9 | 10 | | | | 11 | 4 | 5 | | | | 12 | | | | | | | | | | | 10 |
| | 8 | | | 4 | 7 | | 9 | **10** | 13 | *6* | 11 | 12 | | 5 | | 2 | 14 | 3 | | | | | | | | | | | 11 |
| **2** | | | 5 | 4 | 7 | | 9 | | | 6 | 11 | 10 | | | | 12 | 8 | 3 | 13 | | | | | | | | | | 12 |
| | | | 5 | 2 | 8 | | 9 | 12 | | 6 | 11 | 10 | 4 | | | | **7** | 3 | | 13 | | | | | | | | | 13 |
| 2 | | | 5 | 6 | *7* | 12 | 9 | 10 | **11** | | 8 | | 4 | | 14 | | 13 | 3 | | 1 | | | | | | | | | 14 |
| 2 | | | 5 | 6 | 7 | 8 | 9 | 10 | | | **11** | 13 | 4 | | | | 12 | 3 | | 1 | | | | | | | | | 15 |
| 2 | | | 5 | 6 | 7 | | 9 | 10 | | | 11 | | 4 | | **8** | | 12 | 3 | | 1 | | | | | | | | | 16 |
| 2 | 14 | | **5** | 6 | 7 | | 9 | 12 | 10 | | *11* | | 4 | | 8 | | 13 | 3 | | 1 | | | | | | | | | 17 |
| 2 | | | 5 | 6 | 7 | 13 | 9 | 10 | | 12 | 11 | | 4 | | | | **8** | *3* | | 1 | 14 | | | | | | | | 18 |
| 10 | | | 5 | **3** | 7 | 8 | 9 | | | 6 | | | 4 | | 11 | 2 | 12 | | | 1 | 13 | | | | | | | | 19 |
| | | | 5 | 2 | 3 | 8 | 9 | *10* | | 6 | 11 | | 4 | | **7** | 12 | 14 | | | 1 | 13 | | | | | | | | 20 |
| | | | 5 | 2 | *7* | 8 | 9 | 10 | | 6 | 12 | 14 | 4 | | **11** | | 13 | 3 | | 1 | | | | | | | | | 21 |
| | 6 | | 5 | | | 8 | | 10 | 11 | | **7** | 9 | 4 | | 2 | 13 | 12 | 3 | | 1 | | | | | | | | | 22 |
| | 14 | | 5 | 2 | | 8 | | **9** | 11 | | *7* | | 4 | 6 | 13 | | 10 | 3 | | | | 12 | | | | | | | 23 |
| | | | 5 | 2 | 7 | 8 | 9 | | | | 11 | 12 | 4 | 6 | | | **10** | 3 | | | 13 | | | | | | | | 24 |
| | | | 5 | **2** | 12 | 8 | *9* | | 11 | | | 10 | 4 | 6 | 7 | | 13 | 3 | | | 14 | | | | | | | | 25 |
| **2** | | | | *6* | 7 | 8 | 12 | 9 | | | 13 | 10 | 4 | 5 | 11 | | 14 | 3 | | | | | | | | | | | 26 |
| | 6 | | 5 | 4 | | 8 | 9 | | *11* | | 7 | 10 | 12 | | **2** | | 13 | 3 | | | 14 | | | | | | | | 27 |
| | 3 | | | 6 | 7 | | **9** | | 11 | | 8 | 10 | 4 | 5 | 2 | | 12 | | | | | | | | | | | | 28 |
| | **3** | | 12 | 6 | 7 | | 9 | | 11 | | 8 | 10 | 4 | 5 | *2* | | 14 | | | | | | 13 | | | | | | 29 |
| | | | 5 | 2 | 7 | | | | 11 | 12 | *8* | 9 | 4 | **6** | | | 10 | | | 1 | | 13 | 3 | 14 | | | | | 30 |
| | 7 | | **5** | 6 | | | 12 | 13 | 11 | | 8 | 10 | 4 | | | | | 3 | | | | | 2 | | 9 | | | | 31 |
| | 3 | | 5 | 6 | 7 | | 9 | 12 | 11 | | 8 | *10* | 4 | | | | 13 | | | 14 | | | **2** | | | | | | 32 |
| | 6 | | 5 | 2 | 7 | | 9 | 10 | | | 8 | | 4 | | | | 12 | **3** | | | | | | | 11 | 13 | | | 33 |
| 12 | 3 | | 5 | 6 | 7 | | 9 | 13 | | | 8 | *10* | 4 | | 2 | | 14 | | | 1 | | | | | **11** | | | | 34 |
| 2 | | | 5 | 6 | 3 | | 9 | | | | 8 | **10** | 4 | | 7 | | *12* | | | 1 | | | | | 11 | 13 | 14 | | 35 |
| 2 | 3 | | 5 | 6 | | | 9 | 10 | | | **8** | | 4 | | 7 | | | | | 1 | | | | | 11 | 12 | | | 36 |
| *2* | 3 | | 5 | 6 | 8 | | 9 | 10 | 13 | | | | 4 | | **7** | | 14 | | | 1 | | | | | 11 | 12 | | | 37 |
| 2 | **3** | | 5 | 6 | 8 | | 9 | *10* | 11 | | | | 4 | | 7 | | 12 | | | 1 | | | | | 13 | | | 14 | 38 |
| 21 | 20 | 1 | 28 | 37 | 30 | 20 | 33 | 23 | 17 | 7 | 29 | 14 | 33 | 14 | 18 | 3 | 6 | 17 | | 15 | | | 3 | | 6 | | | | |
| 2 | 3 | | 1 | | 3 | 2 | 2 | 6 | 5 | 4 | 3 | 7 | 1 | | 7 | 4 | 21 | 1 | 1 | 2 | 6 | 2 | 1 | 1 | 1 | 4 | 1 | 1 | |
| | 2 | | 5 | | | 1 | 9 | 5 | 4 | | | 9 | 1 | | | | 1 | 1 | | | | | | | 1 | | | | |

| | | | | | | | | | | | | | | | | | | | | | | | | | | | | | |
|---|---|---|---|---|---|---|---|---|---|---|---|---|---|---|---|---|---|---|---|---|---|---|---|---|---|---|---|---|---|
| | | | 5 | 3 | | 8 | | 9 | | 6 | **11** | 10 | 4 | | 7 | 2 | 13 | | | 1 | 12 | | | | | | | | 3 |
| | 6 | | 5 | 2 | | 8 | | 9 | 11 | 13 | *7* | **10** | 4 | | | 14 | 12 | 3 | | 1 | | | | | | | | | 4 |
| | | | **5** | 2 | 12 | 8 | | 9 | *11* | | | 10 | 4 | 6 | 7 | | 13 | 3 | | | 14 | | | | | | | | 5 |
| 12 | 6 | | 5 | | | 8 | 9 | | 11 | | 7 | 10 | | **4** | 2 | | | 3 | | | | | | | | | | | 5 |
| | **3** | | | 4 | 7 | 8 | 9 | 10 | | | | 11 | 5 | 6 | 2 | | | | | | 12 | | | | | | | | 6 |
| | 3 | | 4 | 4 | 1 | 5 | 2 | 4 | 3 | 1 | 3 | 5 | 4 | 3 | 4 | 1 | | 3 | | 2 | | | | | | | | | |
| 1 | | | | | 1 | | | | | 1 | | | | | | 1 | 3 | | | | 3 | | | | | | | | |
| | | | | | | | | | 2 | | | 3 | | | 1 | | 1 | 2 | | | | | | | | | | | |

| | | | | | | | | | | | | | | | | | | | | | | | | | | | | | |
|---|---|---|---|---|---|---|---|---|---|---|---|---|---|---|---|---|---|---|---|---|---|---|---|---|---|---|---|---|---|
| 2 | | | | 4 | 3 | 8 | 9 | 10 | 11 | **6** | | | | 5 | 7 | | 12 | | | 1 | | | | | | | | | 2 |
| 6 | 3 | | | 4 | 7 | 12 | 9 | 10 | 11 | | | | 5 | | **8** | 2 | 13 | | | 1 | | | | | | | | | 2 |
| 2 | 5 | | | 6 | 7 | 8 | 14 | 9 | *11* | 12 | | 10 | **4** | | | | 13 | 3 | | 1 | | | | | | | | | 3 |
| 3 | 2 | | | 3 | 3 | 2 | 2 | 3 | 3 | 1 | | 1 | 2 | 1 | 2 | 1 | | 1 | | 3 | | | | | | | | | |
| | | | | | | 1 | 1 | | | 1 | | | | | | | 3 | | | | | | | | | | | | |
| 1 | | | | | | | 1 | 1 | | | | | | | | | | | | | | | | | | | | | |

# 1999-2000

| | P | W | D | L | F | A | Pts |
|---|---|---|---|---|---|---|---|
| Manchester U | 38 | 28 | 7 | 3 | 97 | 45 | 91 |
| Arsenal | 38 | 22 | 7 | 9 | 73 | 43 | 73 |
| Leeds U | 38 | 21 | 6 | 11 | 58 | 43 | 69 |
| Liverpool | 38 | 19 | 10 | 9 | 51 | 30 | 67 |
| Chelsea | 38 | 18 | 11 | 9 | 53 | 34 | 65 |
| Aston Villa | 38 | 15 | 13 | 10 | 46 | 35 | 58 |
| Sunderland | 38 | 16 | 10 | 12 | 57 | 56 | 58 |
| Leicester C | 38 | 16 | 7 | 15 | 55 | 55 | 55 |
| West Ham U | 38 | 15 | 10 | 13 | 52 | 53 | 55 |
| Tottenham H | 38 | 15 | 8 | 15 | 57 | 49 | 53 |
| Newcastle U | 38 | 14 | 10 | 14 | 63 | 54 | 52 |
| Middlesbrough | 38 | 14 | 10 | 14 | 46 | 52 | 52 |
| Everton | 38 | 12 | 14 | 12 | 59 | 49 | 50 |
| Coventry C | 38 | 12 | 8 | 18 | 47 | 54 | 44 |
| Southampton | 38 | 12 | 8 | 18 | 45 | 62 | 44 |
| Derby Co | 38 | 9 | 11 | 18 | 44 | 57 | 38 |
| Bradford C | 38 | 9 | 9 | 20 | 38 | 68 | 36 |
| Wimbledon | 38 | 7 | 12 | 19 | 46 | 74 | 33 |
| Sheffield W | 38 | 8 | 7 | 23 | 38 | 70 | 31 |
| Watford | 38 | 6 | 6 | 26 | 35 | 77 | 24 |

Manager: Jim Smith.
Leading scorer: Rory Delap, League/all matches 8.
Player of the season: Mart Poom.

- Derby spent heavily to stay in the Premiership. Seth Johnson, Craig Burley and Branko Strupar each cost £3 million. Lee Morris arrived for £2 million, rising with appearances.
- Signing Argentine Esteban Fuertes from Colon de Santa Fe proved a total disaster. He claimed Italian ancestry to qualify for an EU passport but, after a club training break in Portugal, was refused re-entry at Heathrow Airport in November.
- The passport was forged and Fuertes returned to Colon on loan before the Rams recouped their £2.3 million by selling him to RC Lens the following summer.
- Liverpool's visit on 18 March raised the Pride Park attendance record to 33,378.

## Premiership

| Match No. | Date | | Venue | Opponents | Result | | Scorers | Atte |
|---|---|---|---|---|---|---|---|---|
| 1 | Aug | 7 | (a) | Leeds U | D | 0-0 | | 4 |
| 2 | | 10 | (h) | Arsenal | L | 1-2 | Delap | 2 |
| 3 | | 14 | (h) | Middlesbrough | L | 1-3 | Burton | 2 |
| 4 | | 21 | (a) | Coventry C | L | 0-2 | | 1 |
| 5 | | 25 | (a) | Sheffield W | W | 2-0 | Delap, Sturridge | 2 |
| 6 | | 28 | (h) | Everton | W | 1-0 | Fuertes | 2 |
| 7 | Sep | 11 | (a) | Wimbledon | D | 2-2 | Carbonari, Johnson | 1 |
| 8 | | 18 | (h) | Sunderland | L | 0-5 | | 2 |
| 9 | | 25 | (h) | Bradford C | L | 0-1 | | 3 |
| 10 | Oct | 4 | (a) | Southampton | D | 3-3 | Delap, Laursen, Beck | 1 |
| 11 | | 16 | (h) | Tottenham H | L | 0-1 | | 2 |
| 12 | | 25 | (a) | Newcastle U | L | 0-2 | | 3 |
| 13 | | 30 | (h) | Chelsea | W | 3-1 | Delap 2, Burton | 2 |
| 14 | Nov | 6 | (a) | Liverpool | L | 0-2 | | 4 |
| 15 | | 20 | (h) | Manchester U | L | 1-2 | Delap | 3 |
| 16 | | 28 | (a) | Arsenal | L | 1-2 | Sturridge | 3 |
| 17 | Dec | 5 | (h) | Leeds U | L | 0-1 | | 2 |
| 18 | | 18 | (a) | Leicester C | W | 1-0 | Powell | 1 |
| 19 | | 26 | (h) | Aston Villa | L | 0-2 | | 3 |
| 20 | | 28 | (a) | West Ham U | D | 1-1 | Sturridge | 2 |
| 21 | Jan | 3 | (h) | Watford | W | 2-0 | Strupar 2 | 2 |
| 22 | | 15 | (a) | Middlesbrough | W | 4-1 | Christie 2, Burton, Burley | 3 |
| 23 | | 22 | (h) | Coventry C | D | 0-0 | | 2 |
| 24 | Feb | 5 | (h) | Sheffield W | D | 3-3 | Strupar, Burley, Srnicek (og) | 3 |
| 25 | | 12 | (a) | Everton | L | 1-2 | Nimni | 3 |
| 26 | | 26 | (a) | Sunderland | D | 1-1 | Christie | 41 |
| 27 | Mar | 4 | (h) | Wimbledon | W | 4-0 | Kinkladze, Christie, Burton, Sturridge | 2 |
| 28 | | 11 | (a) | Manchester U | L | 1-3 | Strupar | 61 |
| 29 | | 18 | (h) | Liverpool | L | 0-2 | | 3 |
| 30 | | 25 | (a) | Aston Villa | L | 0-2 | | 2 |
| 31 | Apr | 2 | (h) | Leicester C | W | 3-0 | Burley, Delap, Sturridge | 25 |
| 32 | | 8 | (a) | Watford | D | 0-0 | | 16 |
| 33 | | 15 | (h) | West Ham U | L | 1-2 | Sturridge | 31 |
| 34 | | 21 | (a) | Bradford C | D | 4-4 | Burley 2 (2 pens), Delap, Strupar | 1 |
| 35 | | 24 | (h) | Southampton | W | 2-0 | Powell, Christie | 2 |
| 36 | | 29 | (a) | Tottenham H | D | 1-1 | Carbonari | 33 |
| 37 | May | 6 | (h) | Newcastle U | D | 0-0 | | 32 |
| 38 | | 14 | (a) | Chelsea | L | 0-4 | | 35 |

FINAL LEAGUE POSITION: 16th in Premiership

Appeara
Substi
G

## FA Cup

| | | | | | | | | |
|---|---|---|---|---|---|---|---|---|
| 3 | Dec | 11 | (h) | Burnley | L | 0-1 | | 23 |

Appeara
Substi
G

## League Cup

| | | | | | | | | |
|---|---|---|---|---|---|---|---|---|
| 2 | Sep | 14 | (a) | Swansea C | D | 0-0 | | 6 |
| 2 | | 22 | (h) | Swansea C | W | 3-1 | Fuertes, Sturridge, Borbokis | 19 |
| 3 | Oct | 13 | (h) | Bolton Wanderers | L | 1-2 | Beck | 20 |

Appeara
Substi
G

| Delap R | Dorigo A | Prior S | Carbonari H | Laursen J | Powell D | Eranio S | Sturridge D | Baiano F | Johnson S | Burton D | Beck M | Borbokis V | Schnoor S | Harper K | Bohinen L | Hoult R | Fuertes E | Elliott S | Christie M | Murray A | Morris L | Robinson M | Nimni A | Kinkladze G | Burley C | Strupar B | Boertien P | Jackson R | Riggott C | |
|---|---|---|---|---|---|---|---|---|---|---|---|---|---|---|---|---|---|---|---|---|---|---|---|---|---|---|---|---|---|---|
|2|3|4|5|6|7|8|9|10|11|12|13|14||||||||||||||||||1|
|2||4|5|6|7|8||10|11|14|9|12|3|13||||||||||||||||2|
|2||4|5|6|7|8||11|3|10|9|12|13||14|||||||||||||||3|
|3||4|5|6|7|8|9||11|10|12|2||14|13|||||||||||||||4|
|10||4|5|6|7|13|14||11||12|2|3||8|1|9|||||||||||||5|
|10||4|5|6|7|12|14|13|11|||2|3||8|1|9|||||||||||||6|
|2||4|5|6|7|8||14|11|10|13||3||12|1|9|||||||||||||7|
|2||4|5|6|7|8||13|11||10||3|12|14|1|9|||||||||||||8|
|7|3|4|5||||10|11|8|||2||12||1|9|6|13|14||||||||||9|
|8|3|4|5|2|7||10||11||12|14|6|13||1|9|||||||||||||10|
|6|3|||4||2|13|12|8|10|9|7|5|||1||||14|11|||||||||11|
|6|3|14||4|7|2||10|8|13|9||5|||1|||12||11|||||||||12|
|2|3|12|5|4|7|8|||11|10||13|6|||1|9||||14|||||||||13|
|2|3|14|5|4|7|8|13||11|10||12|6|||1|9|||||||||||||14|
|2|3||5|4|8||9||11|||7|6||||||13|12||10||||||||15|
|2|3|6|5|4|8||9||11|10||||||||12||||14|7|13||||||16|
|2|13|12|5|4|7||9||3|10||||||||6|14|||||11|8|||||17|
|2|3|4||5|7||||11|10|||13|||||6||||9|||8|12||||18|
||3|4||5|7||||11|10|||12||8|||6|13|||14|||2|9||||19|
|||4|5|2|7||9||3||12||||11|||6||||10|||8|||||20|
|2|3|14|5|4|7||10||||||13|||||6||||12|11||8|9||||21|
|2|||5||7||||3|10|||4||11|||6|9||||12|13|8|||||22|
|2|||5|4|||||11|10|||3||7|||6|13|||||12|8|9||||23|
|2|3|||4||7|13||11||||5|||||6|10|||||12|8|9||||24|
||3|5||4||2|10||11|||||||||6|12|||13|14|7|8|9||||25|
|2|||5|4|11|7|14||3||||13|||||6|12|||||10|8|9||||26|
|2|||5|4|7|8|14||3|13|||12||11|||6|9|||||10||||||27|
|2|3||5|4||7|13||11||||8|||||6|9|||||10||12||||28|
|2|||5|4|7|8|13||3||||12|||||6|10|||||11||9||||29|
|2|||5|4|7|8|13||11||||3|||||6|12|||||10||9||||30|
|2|12||5|4|7||10||3||||6|||||14||13||||11|8|9||||31|
|2|12||5|4|7||10||3||||6||||||13|||||11|8|9||||32|
|2|3|||4|7||10||11||||5|||||6|12|||13|||8|9||||33|
|2|3||5|4|7||||11|||||||||6|10|||||12|8|9||||34|
|2|3|||4|7||||6||||5||||||10|13||||11|8|9|12|||35|
|2|||5|4|7||||6|10|||3||||||9|13||||11|8||12|||36|
||3||5|2|6||12|||10|||4||13||||9|7||||11|8|||14||37|
|2|3|||4|||7||11|10|||||6|||5|9|14|||||8|||13|12|38|
|34|20|15|29|36|31|17|14|5|36|15|5|6|22||8|10|8|18|10|1|2|3|2|12|18|13|||||
||3|5||||2|11|4||4|6|6|7|5|5|||2|11|7|1|5|2|5||2|2|2|1||
|8|||2|1|2||6||1|4|1||||||1||5||||1|1|5|5|||||

1 own-goal

| | | | | | | | | | | | | | | | | | | | | | | | | | | | | | | |
|---|---|---|---|---|---|---|---|---|---|---|---|---|---|---|---|---|---|---|---|---|---|---|---|---|---|---|---|---|---|---|
|10|3||5||4||9||13|14|12|2||||||6|||||7|11|8|||||3|
|1|1||1||1||1|||||1||||||1|||||1|1|1||||||
||||||||||1|1|1|||||||||||||||||||||
|||||||||||||||||||||||||||||||||

| | | | | | | | | | | | | | | | | | | | | | | | | | | | | | | |
|---|---|---|---|---|---|---|---|---|---|---|---|---|---|---|---|---|---|---|---|---|---|---|---|---|---|---|---|---|---|---|
||3|4|5|||||11|7||10|2||12|8|1|9|6|13||||||||14|||2|
|10|3|4||5|7||12|11|13|||2||14|8|1|9|6||||||||||||2|
|8|3|4||5||7|9|||13|10|2|12|11||1||6||||||||||||3|
|2|3|3|1|2|1|1|1|2|1||2|3||1|2|3|2|3||||||||||||
||||||||1||1|1|||1|2|||||1||||||||1||||
||||||||1||||1|1|||||1|||||||||||||

# 2000-01

| | P | W | D | L | F | A | Pts |
|---|---|---|---|---|---|---|---|
| Manchester U | 38 | 24 | 8 | 6 | 79 | 31 | 80 |
| Arsenal | 38 | 20 | 10 | 8 | 63 | 38 | 70 |
| Liverpool | 38 | 20 | 9 | 9 | 71 | 39 | 69 |
| Leeds U | 38 | 20 | 8 | 10 | 64 | 43 | 68 |
| Ipswich T | 38 | 20 | 6 | 12 | 57 | 42 | 66 |
| Chelsea | 38 | 17 | 10 | 11 | 68 | 45 | 61 |
| Sunderland | 38 | 15 | 12 | 11 | 46 | 41 | 57 |
| Aston Villa | 38 | 13 | 15 | 10 | 46 | 43 | 54 |
| Charlton A | 38 | 14 | 10 | 14 | 50 | 57 | 52 |
| Southampton | 38 | 14 | 10 | 14 | 40 | 48 | 52 |
| Newcastle U | 38 | 14 | 9 | 15 | 44 | 50 | 51 |
| Tottenham H | 38 | 13 | 10 | 15 | 47 | 54 | 49 |
| Leicester C | 38 | 14 | 6 | 18 | 39 | 51 | 48 |
| Middlesbrough | 38 | 9 | 15 | 14 | 44 | 44 | 42 |
| West Ham U | 38 | 10 | 12 | 16 | 45 | 50 | 42 |
| Everton | 38 | 11 | 9 | 18 | 45 | 59 | 42 |
| Derby Co | 38 | 10 | 12 | 16 | 37 | 59 | 42 |
| Manchester C | 38 | 8 | 10 | 20 | 41 | 65 | 34 |
| Coventry C | 38 | 8 | 10 | 20 | 36 | 63 | 34 |
| Bradford C | 38 | 5 | 11 | 22 | 30 | 70 | 26 |

Manager: Jim Smith.
Leading scorer: Malcolm Christie, League 8, all matches 12.
Player of the season: Chris Riggott.

- Another £3 million signing. After playing on loan from Ajax Amsterdam the previous season, Giorgi Kinkladze completed a £3 million move in April.
- Deon Burton's 35th appearance for Jamaica, against Honduras in April, took him past Peter Shilton as Derby's most capped player. He is the current holder of the record with 42 (36 + 6) appearances for Jamaica as a Rams player.
- England beat Mexico 4–1 at Pride Park in May, the first full international staged in Derby since a 2–1 victory over Ireland at the Baseball Ground in 1911.

## Premiership

| Match No. | Date | | Venue | Opponents | Result | | Scorers | Att |
|---|---|---|---|---|---|---|---|---|
| 1 | Aug | 19 | (h) | Southampton | D | 2-2 | Strupar, Burton | 2 |
| 2 | | 23 | (a) | Newcastle U | L | 2-3 | Strupar, Johnson | 5 |
| 3 | | 26 | (a) | Everton | D | 2-2 | Sturridge, Strupar | 3 |
| 4 | Sep | 6 | (h) | Middlesbrough | D | 3-3 | Christie 2, Strupar | 2 |
| 5 | | 10 | (h) | Charlton A | D | 2-2 | Christie, Valakari | 2 |
| 6 | | 16 | (a) | Sunderland | L | 1-2 | Christie | 4 |
| 7 | | 23 | (h) | Leeds U | D | 1-1 | Kinkladze | 2 |
| 8 | | 30 | (a) | Aston Villa | L | 1-4 | Riggott | 2 |
| 9 | Oct | 15 | (h) | Liverpool | L | 0-4 | | 3 |
| 10 | | 21 | (a) | Tottenham H | L | 1-3 | Riggott | 3 |
| 11 | | 28 | (a) | Leicester C | L | 1-2 | Delap | 2 |
| 12 | Nov | 6 | (h) | West Ham U | D | 0-0 | | 2 |
| 13 | | 11 | (a) | Arsenal | D | 0-0 | | 3 |
| 14 | | 18 | (h) | Bradford C | W | 2-0 | Christie, Delap | 3 |
| 15 | | 25 | (h) | Manchester U | L | 0-3 | | 3 |
| 16 | Dec | 2 | (a) | Ipswich T | W | 1-0 | Delap | 2 |
| 17 | | 9 | (a) | Chelsea | L | 1-4 | Riggott | 3 |
| 18 | | 16 | (h) | Coventry C | W | 1-0 | Christie | 2 |
| 19 | | 23 | (h) | Newcastle U | W | 2-0 | Carbonari, Burton | 2 |
| 20 | | 26 | (a) | Manchester C | D | 0-0 | | 3 |
| 21 | | 30 | (a) | Southampton | L | 0-1 | | 1 |
| 22 | Jan | 1 | (h) | Everton | W | 1-0 | Burton | 2 |
| 23 | | 13 | (a) | Middlesbrough | L | 0-4 | | 2 |
| 24 | | 20 | (h) | Manchester C | D | 1-1 | Powell | 3 |
| 25 | | 30 | (a) | Charlton A | L | 1-2 | Burley | 2 |
| 26 | Feb | 3 | (h) | Sunderland | W | 1-0 | Burley | 2 |
| 27 | | 10 | (a) | Leeds U | D | 0-0 | | 3 |
| 28 | | 24 | (h) | Aston Villa | W | 1-0 | Burton (pen) | 2 |
| 29 | Mar | 3 | (h) | Tottenham H | W | 2-1 | Strupar 2 (1 pen) | 2 |
| 30 | | 18 | (a) | Liverpool | D | 1-1 | Burton | 4 |
| 31 | | 31 | (a) | Coventry C | L | 0-2 | | 1 |
| 32 | Apr | 7 | (h) | Chelsea | L | 0-4 | | 2 |
| 33 | | 14 | (a) | West Ham U | L | 1-3 | Gudjonsson | 2 |
| 34 | | 16 | (h) | Leicester C | W | 2-0 | Boertien, Eranio | 2 |
| 35 | | 21 | (a) | Bradford C | L | 0-2 | | 1 |
| 36 | | 28 | (h) | Arsenal | L | 1-2 | Eranio | 2 |
| 37 | May | 5 | (a) | Manchester U | W | 1-0 | Christie | 6 |
| 38 | | 19 | (h) | Ipswich T | D | 1-1 | Christie | 3 |

FINAL LEAGUE POSITION: 17th in Premiership

Appeara
Substi
G

## FA Cup

| | | | | | | | | |
|---|---|---|---|---|---|---|---|---|
| 3 | Jan | 6 | (h) | West Brom A | W | 3-2 | Christie 2, Eranio | 1 |
| 4 | | 27 | (a) | Blackburn R | D | 0-0 | | 1 |
| R | Feb | 7 | (h) | Blackburn R | L | 2-5 | Riggott, Eranio | 1 |

Appeara
Substi
G

## League Cup

| | | | | | | | | |
|---|---|---|---|---|---|---|---|---|
| 2 | Sep | 19 | (h) | West Brom A | L | 1-2 | Burton | 1 |
| 2 | | 26 | (a) | West Brom A | W | 4-2 | Bragstad 2, Riggott, Burley | 1 |
| 3 | Nov | 1 | (h) | Norwich C | W | 3-0 | Delap, Burley (pen), Christie | 1 |
| 4 | | 29 | (a) | Fulham | L | 2-3 | Christie, Powell | 1 |

Appeara
Substi
G

| Eranio S | Higginbotham D | Blatsis C | Bragstad B | Valakari S | Delap R | Powell D | Strupar B | Morris L | Johnson S | Burton D | Elliott S | Sturridge D | Jackson R | Murray A | Schnoor S | Riggott C | Kinkladze G | Christie M | Carbonari H | Burley C | Bohinen L | Martin L | West T | O'Neil B | Mawene Y | Oakes A | Boertien P | Gudjonsson T | Bolder A | Evatt I | |
|---|---|---|---|---|---|---|---|---|---|---|---|---|---|---|---|---|---|---|---|---|---|---|---|---|---|---|---|---|---|---|---|
|2|3|4|5|6|7|8|*9*|**10**|11|12|13|14||||||||||||||||||||1|
|**7**|3|2|5|4||8|9|13|11|10|6|12||||||||||||||||||||2|
|7|3||5|4|||9||11|10|6|12|**2**|8|13|14|||||||||||||||||3|
|8|||5|**4**|2||*9*||11|10|6|7||14|3||12|13|||||||||||||||4|
|2|3||5|4|8||||11|10||**7**||13|6||12|9|||||||||||||||5|
|2|3||4|8||||14|11|10|*6*|12||13|||**7**|9|5||||||||||||||6|
|**2**|3||4|7|||||11|10||14|||6|12|13|*9*|5|8|||||||||||||7|
|2|3||5||12|7|||11|*10*||14|||**6**|4|13|9||8|||||||||||||8|
|2|||5|11|6|7|12||3|||13||||**4**|10|9||8|||||||||||||9|
||**3**||5||2|7||13|*6*|10||11|||12|4||9||8|14||||||||||||10|
|**11**||||2|9|7|||3|10|6||||5|4|13|12||8|||||||||||||11|
|||||12|10|**7**||14|3|13||||||6|4|11|9|5|8||*2*||||||||||12|
||6|||13|10|7||12|3|||14||||4|*11*|**9**|5|8||2||||||||||13|
|**7**|||||10|8||12|3|||13||||4|11|9|5|||2|6|||||||||14|
|13|||||10|7||12|3|||14||||4|11|9|*5*|||2|6|**8**||||||||15|
|**11**|14||||10|7||12|3|13||||||4||9|5|8||*2*|6|||||||||16|
||3||||10|7||13||12||||14||4||9|**5**|8|*11*|2|6|||||||||17|
|1|||||10|7||14|3|12||||13||4||*9*|5|8||**2**|6|||||||||18|
|**11**|||||2|7||13|3|10||||||4|12|9|5|8|||6|||||||||19|
||12||||2|**7**|||3|10||||||4|11|9|5|8||13|6|||||||||20|
|**7**|3||||2||||11|10||13||||4|12|9||8|||5||6|||||||21|
|7|3||||2||||11|10||||12||4|13|9|5|**8**|||6|||||||||22|
|7|*3*||||2|11|12|14||10||||||4|13|**9**|5|8|||||6|||||||23|
||3||||2|7||13||10||||**11**||||9|5|8||12|6||4|||||||24|
|13|3||12||2|7||||10||||||4||9|5|8||||11|**6**|||||||25|
|7|||||*2*|**11**||13||10||||12||4||9|5|8|||6|14||1|3|||||26|
|2|12||13|||7|11|14||10||||||4||*9*|5|8|||6|**3**||1||||||27|
||6||||2|7|**9**|11|3|10||||13||4|||||8|||5|||1|12|||||28|
||3||||2|7|**9**||11|12||||||4||10|5|8|||6|||1||13||||29|
|13|3||||2|7|||11|10||||||4||**9**|5|8|||6|||1||12||||30|
||6||||2|7|||3|10||||14|||13|9|5|*8*|||||4|**1**||11||||31|
||||||2|7|||11|10||||**8**||4|12|9|5||||6||||3|13||||32|
|**8**|3||||2|7||13|11|9||||||4|*10*|12|5||||6|||||14||||33|
|8|||||2|**7**|||11|9||||||4|10|13|5||||6||14||3|*12*||||34|
|8|||||2|||**11**|6|9||||7||4|10|12|5||||||||3|13||||35|
|7|6||||2||||11|13||||12||4|*10*|9|5|**8**||||||||3|14||||36|
|7|6||||8|||10|||||||||4|**11**|9|5||||||2||3|12|13|||37|
|7|6||||8||||||||12|||**4**|11|9|5||||||2||3|10|14|13|38|
|25|23|2|10|9|32|27|7|4|30|25|5|3|1|4|6|29|13|29|27|24|1|7|18|3|7|6|7|2||||
|3|3||2|2|1||2|16||7|1|11|1|10|2|2|11|5|||1|2||1|1||1|8|2|1||
|2||||1|3|1|6||1|5||1||||3|1|8|1|2|||||||1|1||||

| Eranio S | Higginbotham D | Blatsis C | Bragstad B | Valakari S | Delap R | Powell D | Strupar B | Morris L | Johnson S | Burton D | Elliott S | Sturridge D | Jackson R | Murray A | Schnoor S | Riggott C | Kinkladze G | Christie M | Carbonari H | Burley C | Bohinen L | Martin L | West T | O'Neil B | Mawene Y | Oakes A | Boertien P | Gudjonsson T | Bolder A | Evatt I | |
|---|---|---|---|---|---|---|---|---|---|---|---|---|---|---|---|---|---|---|---|---|---|---|---|---|---|---|---|---|---|---|---|
|**7**|3||||||||||10||||8||4|11|9|5|||2|||6||12||||3|
|**7**|3||4||10|||||||||11||||9|5|||2||8|6||12||||4|
|*7*|14|||||||13||10||||11||4||9|5|**8**||12|6|2||1|3||||R|
|3|2||1||1|||||2||||3||2|1|3|3|1||2|1|2|2|1|1|||||
||1|||||||1||||||||||||||1|||||2|||||
|2|||||||||||||||||1||2||||||||||||||

| Eranio S | Higginbotham D | Blatsis C | Bragstad B | Valakari S | Delap R | Powell D | Strupar B | Morris L | Johnson S | Burton D | Elliott S | Sturridge D | Jackson R | Murray A | Schnoor S | Riggott C | Kinkladze G | Christie M | Carbonari H | Burley C | Bohinen L | Martin L | West T | O'Neil B | Mawene Y | Oakes A | Boertien P | Gudjonsson T | Bolder A | Evatt I | |
|---|---|---|---|---|---|---|---|---|---|---|---|---|---|---|---|---|---|---|---|---|---|---|---|---|---|---|---|---|---|---|---|
|7|3||4|6|||||**11**|10||13|2|12|14||*8*|9|5||||||||||||2|
||3||5|2||7||13|11|**10**||12|||6|4||9||*8*|||||||||||2|
||12|||2|10|7||13|3||6||||**5**|4|11|9||8|||||||||||3|
||3||5||2|7|**9**||11|12|||||||4||10||8|||6||||||||4|
|1|3||3|3|2|3|1||4|2|1||1||2|3|2|4|1|3|||1||||||||
||1|||||||2||1||2||1|1||||||||||||||||||
||||2||1|1||||1||||||1||2||2|||||||||||||

# 2001-02

| | P | W | D | L | F | A | Pts |
|---|---|---|---|---|---|---|---|
| Arsenal | 38 | 26 | 9 | 3 | 79 | 36 | 87 |
| Liverpool | 38 | 24 | 8 | 6 | 67 | 30 | 80 |
| Manchester U | 38 | 24 | 5 | 9 | 87 | 45 | 77 |
| Newcastle U | 38 | 21 | 8 | 9 | 74 | 52 | 71 |
| Leeds U | 38 | 18 | 12 | 8 | 53 | 37 | 66 |
| Chelsea | 38 | 17 | 13 | 8 | 66 | 38 | 64 |
| West Ham U | 38 | 15 | 8 | 15 | 48 | 57 | 53 |
| Aston Villa | 38 | 12 | 14 | 12 | 46 | 47 | 50 |
| Tottenham H | 38 | 14 | 8 | 16 | 49 | 53 | 50 |
| Blackburn R | 38 | 12 | 10 | 16 | 55 | 51 | 46 |
| Southampton | 38 | 12 | 9 | 17 | 46 | 54 | 45 |
| Middlesbrough | 38 | 12 | 9 | 17 | 35 | 47 | 45 |
| Fulham | 38 | 10 | 14 | 14 | 36 | 44 | 44 |
| Charlton A | 38 | 10 | 14 | 14 | 38 | 49 | 44 |
| Everton | 38 | 11 | 10 | 17 | 45 | 57 | 43 |
| Bolton W | 38 | 9 | 13 | 16 | 44 | 62 | 40 |
| Sunderland | 38 | 10 | 10 | 18 | 29 | 51 | 40 |
| Ipswich T | 38 | 9 | 9 | 20 | 41 | 64 | 36 |
| Derby Co | 38 | 8 | 6 | 24 | 33 | 63 | 30 |
| Leicester C | 38 | 5 | 13 | 20 | 30 | 64 | 28 |

Manager: Jim Smith until October, Colin Todd until January, then John Gregory.
Leading scorers: Malcolm Christie, Fabrizio Ravanelli, League 9. Fabrizio Ravanelli, all matches 11.
Player of the season: Danny Higginbotham.

- For the first time, Derby had three managers in a season. Billy McEwan also stood in between Colin Todd and John Gregory. It was hardly surprising that the Rams struggled towards relegation.
- The Rams received the biggest transfer fee in their history when Seth Johnson moved to Leeds United for £7 million. He had a bad time with injuries and returned to Derby in 2005.
- Derby had used 32 players in a season six times. In this relegation season, they raised the total to 34.

## Premiership

| Match No. | Date | | Venue | Opponents | Result | | Scorers |
|---|---|---|---|---|---|---|---|
| 1 | Aug | 18 | (h) | Blackburn R | W | 2-1 | Ravanelli, Christie |
| 2 | | 21 | (a) | Ipswich T | L | 1-3 | Ravanelli |
| 3 | | 25 | (a) | Fulham | D | 0-0 | |
| 4 | Sep | 8 | (h) | West Ham U | D | 0-0 | |
| 5 | | 15 | (h) | Leicester C | L | 2-3 | Burton, Ravanelli (pen) |
| 6 | | 23 | (a) | Leeds U | L | 0-3 | |
| 7 | | 29 | (h) | Arsenal | L | 0-2 | |
| 8 | Oct | 15 | (a) | Tottenham H | L | 1-3 | Ravanelli |
| 9 | | 20 | (h) | Charlton A | D | 1-1 | Ravanelli |
| 10 | | 28 | (h) | Chelsea | D | 1-1 | Ravanelli |
| 11 | Nov | 3 | (a) | Middlesbrough | L | 1-5 | Ravanelli |
| 12 | | 17 | (h) | Southampton | W | 1-0 | Mawene |
| 13 | | 24 | (a) | Newcastle U | L | 0-1 | |
| 14 | Dec | 1 | (h) | Liverpool | L | 0-1 | |
| 15 | | 8 | (h) | Bolton W | W | 1-0 | Christie |
| 16 | | 12 | (a) | Manchester U | L | 0-5 | |
| 17 | | 15 | (a) | Everton | L | 0-1 | |
| 18 | | 22 | (h) | Aston Villa | W | 3-1 | Ravanelli, Carbone, Christie |
| 19 | | 26 | (a) | West Ham U | L | 0-4 | |
| 20 | | 29 | (a) | Blackburn R | W | 1-0 | Christie |
| 21 | Jan | 2 | (h) | Fulham | L | 0-1 | |
| 22 | | 12 | (a) | Aston Villa | L | 1-2 | Powell |
| 23 | | 19 | (h) | Ipswich T | L | 1-3 | Christie |
| 24 | | 29 | (a) | Charlton A | L | 0-1 | |
| 25 | Feb | 2 | (h) | Tottenham H | W | 1-0 | Morris |
| 26 | | 9 | (h) | Sunderland | L | 0-1 | |
| 27 | | 23 | (a) | Leicester C | W | 3-0 | Kinkladze, Strupar, Morris |
| 28 | Mar | 3 | (h) | Manchester U | D | 2-2 | Christie 2 |
| 29 | | 5 | (a) | Arsenal | L | 0-1 | |
| 30 | | 16 | (a) | Bolton W | W | 3-1 | Christie, Ravanelli, Higginbotham (pen) |
| 31 | | 23 | (h) | Everton | L | 3-4 | Strupar 2, Morris |
| 32 | | 30 | (a) | Chelsea | L | 1-2 | Strupar |
| 33 | Apr | 1 | (h) | Middlesbrough | L | 0-1 | |
| 34 | | 6 | (a) | Southampton | L | 0-2 | |
| 35 | | 13 | (h) | Newcastle U | L | 2-3 | Christie, Morris |
| 36 | | 20 | (a) | Liverpool | L | 0-2 | |
| 37 | | 27 | (h) | Leeds U | L | 0-1 | |
| 38 | May | 11 | (a) | Sunderland | D | 1-1 | Robinson |

FINAL LEAGUE POSITION: 19th in Premiership – Relegated

Appear
Subs

## FA Cup

| | | | | | | | |
|---|---|---|---|---|---|---|---|
| 3 | Jan | 6 | (h) | Bristol R | L | 1-3 | Ravanelli |

Appear
Subst

## League Cup

| | | | | | | | |
|---|---|---|---|---|---|---|---|
| 2 | Sep | 12 | (h) | Hull C | W | 3-0 | Burton 2, Kinkladze |
| 3 | Oct | 10 | (a) | Fulham | L | 2-5 | Burley, Ravanelli |

Appear
Subst

| Daino D | Boertien P | O'Neil B | Riggott C | Higginbotham D | Powell D | Burley C | Christie M | Ravanelli F | Morris L | Kinkladze G | Johnson S | Burton D | Murray A | Oakes A | Mawene Y | Jackson R | Feuer I | Valakari S | Zavagno L | Ducrocq P | Carbone B | Grenet F | Bolder A | Elliott S | Carbonari H | Barton W | Lee R | Strupar B | Foletti P | Evatt IR | Robinson M | Twigg G | |
|---|---|---|---|---|---|---|---|---|---|---|---|---|---|---|---|---|---|---|---|---|---|---|---|---|---|---|---|---|---|---|---|---|---|
|2|3|4|5|6|7|8|9|10|**11**|12||||||||||||||||||||||1|
|2|3|4|5|6|**7**|8|9|10|||11|12|13||||||||||||||||||||2|
||3|4|5|6|7|8|**9**|||12|11|10|13|1|2||||||||||||||||||3|
||3||5|6|7|8||10|12|11|4|**9**||1|2||||||||||||||||||4|
||3|4|5|6||8|12|10||11|7|9||1|**2**||||||||||||||||||5|
||3|4|5|6|7||9|10||12|11|13|**8**|1|2||||||||||||||||||6|
||3|4|5|6|7||9|10||12|11|13|**8**|1||2|||||||||||||||||7|
||||5|6|7|8|13|10||12|3|9|**11**||4||1|2|||||||||||||||8|
||||5|6|7|8|**9**|10||||12|||2||1|13|3|4|11||||||||||||9|
||||5|6|7|8|12|10||||**9**|||2||||3|4|11||||||||||||10|
||||5|6|7|8|12|10||||9|||2||||3|**4**|11||||||||||||11|
||13||5|6|7|8|12|10|||||||4||||3|11|9|**2**|||||||||||12|
||13||5|6|**7**|8|12|10|||||||4||||3|11|9|2|||||||||||13|
||||5|6|7||9|10|||||||4||||3|8|11|2|||||||||||14|
||||5|6|7||9|10||||13|||4||||3|8|**11**|2|12||||||||||15|
||13||5|6|||9|10||||12|14|1|**4**||||3|*8*|11|2|7||||||||||16|
||14||5||**7**||9|||13||10||1|4||||3|8|11|*2*|12|6|||||||||17|
||7||5|6|||13|10||*11*||14|||4||||3|8|9|**2**|12||||||||||18|
||11||5|6|7|||10||12|||||4||||3|**8**|9|2|13||||||||||19|
||12||4|6|7||9|10|||||||||||3|8|11|**2**|13||5||||||||20|
||14||4|6|7||9|10||||13|||||||3|**8**|11|2|12||*5*||||||||21|
||11||4|6|7||9|10||12|||||||||3|8||2|13|**5**|||||||||22|
||13||4|6|7||9|10||12||11||1||2||8|**3**||||||5||||||||23|
||3||5|6|7||9|10||12||||1|4|2||8||**11**|||||||||||||24|
||12|13|5|6|7||9|10|**11**|||||1||||4|3|8||||||2|||||||25|
||12||5|6|**4**||9|10|11|||13||1|||||3|7||||||2|8||||||26|
||11|||6|||10||14|*7*||||**1**||||13|3|8||2||||5|4|9|12||||27|
||11||5|6|||9|10|12|*7*||||1|||||3|**8**||||14||2|4|13|||||28|
||8|13|5|6|||10||11|**7**||||1||||14|3|||12||||2|4|*9*|||||29|
||11|8|5|6|||**9**|*10*|12|7||||1|||||3|||13||||2|4|14|||||30|
||11|8|5|6|||**9**|10|12|7|||||||||3|||||||2|4|13|1||||31|
||11||5|6||||10|12|7||||1||||8|3|||||13||2|4|**9**|||||32|
||8||5|6|||13|10|11|12||||1||||7|*3*|||||14||2|4|**9**|||||33|
||8||5|6|||9|10|11|*7*||||1|||||**3**|||14|12|||2|4|13|||||34|
||8||5|6|||**10**|12|*11*|7||||1||3||||||||14||2|4|9||13|||35|
||8||5|6|||10||11|7||||1||3||||||||||2|4|9|||||36|
||8||5|6|||10||**11**|7||||||3|||||||13|||2|4|*9*||12|14||37|
||11||5|6|||10|||||||||14|||*3*||||7|||2|4|**9**||8|12|13|38|
|2|23|8|37|37|23|11|27|30|9|13|7|8|3|20|17|6|2|6|26|19|13|12|2|2|3|14|13|8|1|1||||
||9|2|||||8|1|6|11||9|3|||1||3||||3|9|4||||4|1|2|2|1||
|||||1|1||9|9|4|1||1|||1||||||1|||||||4|||1|||

| Daino D | Boertien P | O'Neil B | Riggott C | Higginbotham D | Powell D | Burley C | Christie M | Ravanelli F | Morris L | Kinkladze G | Johnson S | Burton D | Murray A | Oakes A | Mawene Y | Jackson R | Feuer I | Valakari S | Zavagno L | Ducrocq P | Carbone B | Grenet F | Bolder A | Elliott S | Carbonari H | Barton W | Lee R | Strupar B | Foletti P | Evatt IR | Robinson M | Twigg G | |
|---|---|---|---|---|---|---|---|---|---|---|---|---|---|---|---|---|---|---|---|---|---|---|---|---|---|---|---|---|---|---|---|---|---|
||8|||6|||9|10|12||||||**4**||||3||11|2|7||5||||||||3|
||1|||1|||1|1|||||||1||||1||1|1|1||1|||||||||
||||||||||1|||||||||||||||||||||||||
|||||||||1||||||||||||||||||||||||||

| Daino D | Boertien P | O'Neil B | Riggott C | Higginbotham D | Powell D | Burley C | Christie M | Ravanelli F | Morris L | Kinkladze G | Johnson S | Burton D | Murray A | Oakes A | Mawene Y | Jackson R | Feuer I | Valakari S | Zavagno L | Ducrocq P | Carbone B | Grenet F | Bolder A | Elliott S | Carbonari H | Barton W | Lee R | Strupar B | Foletti P | Evatt IR | Robinson M | Twigg G | |
|---|---|---|---|---|---|---|---|---|---|---|---|---|---|---|---|---|---|---|---|---|---|---|---|---|---|---|---|---|---|---|---|---|---|
|13|3|12|5|6||8||10||7||9|11|1|2|||**4**|||||||||||||||2|
|2|||5|6|7|8|12|10|||3|9|**11**|1|4||||||||||||||||||3|
|1|1||2|2|1|2||2||1|1|2|2|2|2|||1|||||||||||||||
|1||1|||||1||||||||||||||||||||||||||
|||||||1||1||1||2|||||||||||||||||||||

# 2002-03

| | P | W | D | L | F | A | Pts |
|---|---|---|---|---|---|---|---|
| Portsmouth | 46 | 29 | 11 | 6 | 97 | 45 | 98 |
| Leicester C | 46 | 26 | 14 | 6 | 73 | 40 | 92 |
| Sheffield U | 46 | 23 | 11 | 12 | 72 | 52 | 80 |
| Reading | 46 | 25 | 4 | 17 | 61 | 46 | 79 |
| Wolves | 46 | 20 | 16 | 10 | 81 | 44 | 76 |
| Nottingham F | 46 | 20 | 14 | 12 | 82 | 50 | 74 |
| Ipswich T | 46 | 19 | 13 | 14 | 80 | 64 | 70 |
| Norwich C | 46 | 19 | 12 | 15 | 60 | 49 | 69 |
| Millwall | 46 | 19 | 9 | 18 | 59 | 69 | 66 |
| Wimbledon | 46 | 18 | 11 | 17 | 76 | 73 | 65 |
| Gillingham | 46 | 16 | 14 | 16 | 56 | 65 | 62 |
| Preston NE | 46 | 16 | 13 | 17 | 68 | 70 | 61 |
| Watford | 46 | 17 | 9 | 20 | 54 | 70 | 60 |
| Crystal Palace | 46 | 14 | 17 | 15 | 59 | 52 | 59 |
| Rotherham U | 46 | 15 | 14 | 17 | 62 | 62 | 59 |
| Burnley | 46 | 15 | 10 | 21 | 65 | 89 | 55 |
| Walsall | 46 | 15 | 9 | 22 | 57 | 69 | 54 |
| Derby Co | 46 | 15 | 7 | 24 | 55 | 74 | 52 |
| Bradford C | 46 | 14 | 10 | 22 | 51 | 73 | 52 |
| Coventry C | 46 | 12 | 14 | 20 | 46 | 62 | 50 |
| Stoke City | 46 | 12 | 14 | 20 | 45 | 69 | 50 |
| Sheffield W | 46 | 10 | 16 | 20 | 56 | 73 | 46 |
| Brighton & HA | 46 | 11 | 12 | 23 | 49 | 67 | 45 |
| Grimsby T | 46 | 9 | 12 | 25 | 48 | 85 | 39 |

Manager: John Gregory until March, then George Burley.
Leading scorers: Malcolm Christie, Lee Morris, League 8, all matches 9.
Player of the season: Giorgi Kinkladze.

- John Gregory was suspended in March, the club alleging serious misconduct. They never offered anything specific and the next board had to pay compensation to Gregory.
- George Burley was appointed as interim manager, taking over on a permanent basis in summer.
- Lee Holmes became the youngest player in Derby's history when he went on as substitute against Grimsby Town on Boxing Day, aged 15 years and 268 days. Nine days later, again as substitute at Brentford, he was the youngest to appear for any club in a full round of the FA Cup.
- The Rams beat their year-old record for most players used in a season, fielding 36.

## Division One

| Match No. | Date | | Venue | Opponents | Result | | Scorers | Att |
|---|---|---|---|---|---|---|---|---|
| 1 | Aug | 10 | (h) | Reading | W | 3-0 | Lee, Ravanelli, Christie | 3 |
| 2 | | 13 | (a) | Gillingham | L | 0-1 | | |
| 3 | | 17 | (a) | Grimsby T | W | 2-1 | Bolder 2 | |
| 4 | | 24 | (h) | Wolves | L | 1-4 | Christie | 2 |
| 5 | | 26 | (a) | Rotherham U | L | 1-2 | Strupar | |
| 6 | | 31 | (h) | Stoke C | W | 2-0 | Christie 2 | 2 |
| 7 | Sep | 7 | (h) | Burnley | L | 1-2 | Bolder | 2 |
| 8 | | 14 | (a) | Leicester C | L | 1-3 | Riggott | 3 |
| 9 | | 17 | (a) | Crystal P | W | 1-0 | Kinkladze | 1 |
| 10 | | 21 | (h) | Preston NE | L | 0-2 | | 2 |
| 11 | | 28 | (a) | Ipswich T | W | 1-0 | Carbonari | 2 |
| 12 | Oct | 5 | (h) | Walsall | D | 2-2 | Christie 2 | 2 |
| 13 | | 12 | (a) | Bradford C | D | 0-0 | | 1 |
| 14 | | 20 | (h) | Nottingham F | D | 0-0 | | 3 |
| 15 | | 26 | (a) | Millwall | L | 0-3 | | |
| 16 | | 30 | (h) | Sheffield U | W | 2-1 | McLeod, Burton | 2 |
| 17 | Nov | 2 | (a) | Sheffield W | W | 3-1 | Morris 2, McLeod | 1 |
| 18 | | 9 | (h) | Portsmouth | L | 1-2 | Higginbotham (pen) | 2 |
| 19 | | 16 | (a) | Brighton & HA | L | 0-1 | | |
| 20 | | 25 | (h) | Wimbledon | W | 3-2 | Elliott, Burton, Morris | 2 |
| 21 | | 30 | (a) | Norwich C | L | 0-1 | | 2 |
| 22 | Dec | 7 | (h) | Watford | W | 3-0 | Morris, Riggott, Burton | 2 |
| 23 | | 14 | (h) | Brighton & HA | W | 1-0 | Higginbotham (pen) | 2 |
| 24 | | 21 | (a) | Coventry C | L | 0-3 | | 1 |
| 25 | | 26 | (h) | Grimsby T | L | 1-3 | Morris | 2 |
| 26 | | 28 | (a) | Reading | L | 1-2 | Burley (pen) | 1 |
| 27 | Jan | 1 | (a) | Wolves | D | 1-1 | Christie | 2 |
| 28 | | 11 | (h) | Gillingham | D | 1-1 | Zavagno (pen) | 2 |
| 29 | | 18 | (a) | Stoke C | W | 3-1 | Christie, Zavagno, Morris | 1 |
| 30 | Feb | 1 | (h) | Rotherham U | W | 3-0 | Kinkladze, Bolder, McLeod | 2 |
| 31 | | 8 | (a) | Portsmouth | L | 2-6 | Morris, Kinkladze (pen) | 1 |
| 32 | | 15 | (h) | Sheffield W | D | 2-2 | Bolder 2 | 2 |
| 33 | | 22 | (a) | Burnley | L | 0-2 | | 1 |
| 34 | Mar | 1 | (h) | Leicester C | D | 1-1 | Burley | 2 |
| 35 | | 5 | (h) | Crystal P | L | 0-1 | | 2 |
| 36 | | 8 | (a) | Preston NE | L | 2-4 | Ravanelli 2 | 1 |
| 37 | | 15 | (h) | Bradford C | L | 1-2 | Morris | 2 |
| 38 | | 19 | (a) | Nottingham F | L | 0-3 | | 2 |
| 39 | | 22 | (a) | Sheffield U | L | 0-2 | | 1 |
| 40 | Apr | 5 | (h) | Norwich C | W | 2-1 | Burley, Kenton (og) | 2 |
| 41 | | 12 | (a) | Wimbledon | W | 2-0 | Valakari, Boertien | |
| 42 | | 16 | (h) | Millwall | L | 1-2 | Kinkladze | 2 |
| 43 | | 19 | (h) | Coventry C | W | 1-0 | Ravanelli | 2 |
| 44 | | 21 | (a) | Watford | L | 0-2 | | 1 |
| 45 | | 26 | (a) | Walsall | L | 2-3 | Valakari, Ravanelli | |
| 46 | May | 4 | (h) | Ipswich T | L | 1-4 | Lee | 2 |

FINAL LEAGUE POSITION: 18th in Division One

Appeara
Subst

## FA Cup

| | | | | | | | |
|---|---|---|---|---|---|---|---|
| 3 | Jan | 4 | A | Brentford | L | 0-1 | |

Appeara
Subst

## League Cup

| | | | | | | | | |
|---|---|---|---|---|---|---|---|---|
| 1 | Sep | 10 | A | Mansfield T | W | 3-1 | Morris, Christie, Evatt | |
| 2 | Oct | 2 | H | Oldham A | L | 1-2e | Higginbotham (pen) | |

Appeara
Subst

| Barton W | Boertien P | Lee R | Riggott C | Higginbotham D | Murray A | Bolder A | Christie M | Ravanelli F | Morris L | Jackson R | Twigg G | Evatt I | Strupar B | Tudgay M | Grenet F | Oakes A | Kinkladze G | Grant L | O'Neil B | Hunt L | Carbonari H | McLeod I | Burton D | Elliott S | Burley C | Mills P | Holmes L | Zavagno L | Chadwick N | Mooney T | Robinson M | Ritchie P | Valakari S | Camp L | |
|---|---|---|---|---|---|---|---|---|---|---|---|---|---|---|---|---|---|---|---|---|---|---|---|---|---|---|---|---|---|---|---|---|---|---|---|
| 2 | **3** | 4 | 5 | 6 | 7 | 8 | *9* | 10 | 11 | 12 | 13 | 14 | | | | | | | | | | | | | | | | | | | | | | | 1 |
| 2 | 3 | 4 | | 6 | *7* | 8 | 9 | 10 | 11 | **2** | | 12 | 13 | 14 | | | | | | | | | | | | | | | | | | | | | 2 |
| 2 | **3** | 4 | | 6 | 7 | 8 | 9 | 10 | 11 | | 13 | 5 | | | 12 | | | | | | | | | | | | | | | | | | | | 3 |
| 2 | | 4 | | 6 | 7 | 8 | 9 | | 12 | | **11** | 5 | 10 | 13 | 3 | 1 | | | | | | | | | | | | | | | | | | | 4 |
| 2 | 7 | **4** | | 6 | 12 | 8 | 9 | | 11 | | 13 | 5 | 10 | | 3 | 1 | | | | | | | | | | | | | | | | | | | 5 |
| 2 | 11 | 4 | 5 | 6 | **7** | 8 | 9 | | | 3 | | 13 | 10 | | | | 12 | | | | | | | | | | | | | | | | | | 6 |
| 2 | 11 | 4 | 5 | 6 | **7** | 8 | 9 | | 12 | 3 | | | 10 | | | 1 | | 13 | | | | | | | | | | | | | | | | | 7 |
| 2 | 3 | **4** | 5 | 6 | | 7 | 9 | | 11 | | 13 | 12 | | | | | 10 | | 8 | | | | | | | | | | | | | | | | 8 |
| 2 | 3 | | 5 | 6 | 7 | 8 | 9 | | 11 | | | 13 | | | | | 10 | | **4** | 12 | | | | | | | | | | | | | | | 9 |
| 2 | 3 | 4 | 5 | 6 | 13 | **7** | 9 | | 11 | | | | | | | | 10 | | 8 | 12 | | | | | | | | | | | | | | | 10 |
| 2 | 3 | 8 | 4 | 6 | 11 | 7 | **9** | | | | | 12 | | | | | | | | | 5 | 10 | | | | | | | | | | | | | 11 |
| | 3 | 8 | 4 | 6 | 11 | 7 | 9 | | | | 14 | 12 | | | | | 13 | | | 2 | **5** | *10* | | | | | | | | | | | | | 12 |
| | 3 | 8 | 5 | 6 | 11 | 7 | **9** | | 12 | | | 4 | | | | | | | | 2 | | 10 | | | | | | | | | | | | | 13 |
| | 3 | 8 | 5 | 6 | **11** | 7 | 9 | | | | | 4 | | | | | 12 | 1 | | 2 | | 10 | | | | | | | | | | | | | 14 |
| 2 | | | **5** | 6 | 7 | 8 | | | 9 | 3 | 13 | 4 | | | | | 11 | 14 | | 12 | | *10* | | | | | | | | | | | | | 15 |
| 5 | 3 | 8 | | 6 | | 7 | | | **9** | | | 4 | | | | | 11 | | | 2 | | 10 | 12 | 13 | | | | | | | | | | | 16 |
| 5 | 3 | 8 | | 6 | | 7 | | | **9** | | 13 | 4 | | | | | 11 | | | 2 | | *10* | 12 | 14 | | | | | | | | | | | 17 |
| 5 | 3 | 8 | 12 | 6 | | 7 | | 13 | 9 | | | 4 | | | | | 11 | 1 | | **2** | | *10* | 14 | | | | | | | | | | | | 18 |
| **2** | 3 | 8 | 5 | | | 7 | 9 | | | 12 | | 4 | | | | | 11 | 1 | | | | | 10 | 6 | | | | | | | | | | | 19 |
| 2 | 3 | 8 | 5 | 12 | | 13 | *9* | | 14 | | | **4** | | | | | | 1 | | | | 11 | 10 | 6 | 7 | | | | | | | | | | 20 |
| 2 | 3 | 8 | 4 | 6 | | 12 | | | 11 | | | 13 | | | | | | 1 | | | | 9 | **10** | 5 | 7 | | | | | | | | | | 21 |
| **2** | 3 | *8* | 4 | 6 | | 12 | 9 | | 11 | | | 14 | | | | | | 1 | | | | 13 | 10 | 5 | 7 | | | | | | | | | | 22 |
| 2 | 3 | 8 | *4* | **6** | 13 | | 9 | | 11 | | | 14 | | | | | | 1 | | | | 10 | | 5 | 7 | 12 | | | | | | | | | 23 |
| 2 | **3** | | 5 | | | 8 | 9 | | 11 | | | 4 | | | | | | 1 | | | | 10 | | 6 | 7 | 12 | | | | | | | | | 24 |
| 2 | *3* | 8 | 5 | | | 11 | 9 | | 10 | | | **4** | | | | | 13 | 1 | | | | 12 | | 6 | 7 | | 14 | | | | | | | | 25 |
| 3 | | | 5 | | 8 | 4 | 9 | | 11 | | | 13 | | 12 | | | | 1 | | | | **10** | | 6 | 7 | 2 | | | | | | | | | 26 |
| 2 | | | 5 | | 7 | 8 | 9 | | **11** | | | 4 | | | | | | 1 | | | | 10 | | 6 | | 3 | 12 | | | | | | | | 27 |
| 2 | 11 | | 5 | | | 7 | **9** | | 10 | 13 | | 4 | | 12 | | | 8 | 1 | | | | | | 6 | | | | 3 | | | | | | | 28 |
| | 11 | | | 6 | 12 | 4 | 9 | | *10* | 2 | | 5 | | 13 | | | **8** | 1 | | | | 14 | | | 7 | | | 3 | | | | | | | 29 |
| **2** | 11 | 4 | | | | 7 | | 13 | *9* | 12 | | 5 | | 14 | | | 8 | 1 | | | | 10 | | 6 | | | | 3 | | | | | | | 30 |
| 2 | 11 | 4 | | | | 7 | | | 9 | | | 5 | | | | | 8 | 1 | | | | 10 | | 6 | | | | 3 | | | | | | | 31 |
| 5 | 11 | 4 | | | | 7 | | 13 | *9* | 2 | | | | 14 | | | 8 | 1 | | | | 10 | | 6 | | 12 | | **3** | | | | | | | 32 |
| 5 | 11 | **4** | | | 12 | 7 | | 10 | 9 | 2 | | | | | | | 8 | 1 | | | | | | 6 | | | | 3 | | | | | | | 33 |
| | 3 | 4 | | | | 11 | | 10 | 9 | 2 | | | | | | | **8** | 1 | | | | | | 6 | 7 | 5 | | | 12 | | | | | | 34 |
| | *3* | 4 | | | **11** | 8 | | 10 | | 2 | | | | 13 | | | | 1 | | | | 14 | | 6 | 7 | 5 | | 12 | 9 | | | | | | 35 |
| 2 | 3 | 4 | | | | 7 | | 10 | | | | | | | | | 8 | 1 | | | | 12 | | 6 | 11 | 5 | | | **9** | | | | | | 36 |
| 2 | 3 | 4 | | | | **8** | | 10 | 11 | | | | | | | | 12 | 1 | | | | 13 | | 6 | 7 | *5* | | 14 | 9 | | | | | | 37 |
| 2 | **3** | 4 | | | | 8 | | 10 | | | | | | | | | | 1 | | | | 11 | | 6 | 7 | 5 | | 12 | 13 | 9 | | | | | 38 |
| *5* | 3 | 8 | | | 11 | 7 | | | | 12 | | | | | | | 14 | 1 | | 2 | | 10 | | 6 | | **4** | | | 9 | | 13 | | | | 39 |
| 4 | 3 | | | | | 13 | | 10 | | 2 | | | | | | 1 | 8 | | | | | 12 | | 6 | 7 | | | | | **9** | | 5 | 11 | | 40 |
| 4 | 3 | | | | 12 | **8** | | 9 | | 2 | | | | | | 1 | 10 | | | | | 13 | | | 7 | | | | | 6 | | 5 | 11 | | 41 |
| 4 | 3 | | | | | 8 | | 9 | | 2 | | | | | | **1** | 10 | 12 | | | | | | | 7 | 13 | | | | 6 | | 5 | 11 | | 42 |
| 4 | 3 | 8 | | | | 12 | | 9 | | 2 | | | | | | | 11 | 1 | | | | | | | 7 | 5 | | | | **10** | | 6 | 13 | | 43 |
| **4** | 3 | 14 | | | 13 | 8 | | 9 | | 2 | | | | | | | 10 | 1 | | | | | | | 7 | 5 | | | | 12 | | 6 | *11* | | 44 |
| | 3 | | | | 8 | 13 | | 9 | | 2 | | | | | | | | **1** | | | | 10 | | | 7 | 4 | | | | 6 | | 5 | 11 | 12 | 45 |
| **4** | 3 | 8 | | | | 13 | | *9* | | 2 | | 12 | | | | 1 | 11 | | | | | 14 | | | 7 | 6 | | | | 10 | | 5 | | | 46 |
| 39 | 42 | 34 | 21 | 22 | 17 | 38 | 24 | 16 | 26 | 16 | 1 | 18 | 4 | | 2 | 7 | 22 | 26 | 3 | 7 | 2 | 20 | 4 | 21 | 20 | 12 | | 6 | 4 | 7 | | 7 | 5 | | |
| | | 1 | 1 | 1 | 7 | 7 | | 3 | 4 | 5 | 7 | 12 | 1 | 8 | 1 | | 6 | 3 | | 3 | | 9 | 3 | 2 | | 4 | 2 | 3 | 2 | 1 | 1 | | 1 | 1 | |
| | 1 | 2 | 2 | 2 | | 6 | 8 | 5 | 8 | | | | 1 | | | | 4 | | | | 1 | 3 | 3 | 1 | 3 | | | 2 | | | | | 2 | | |

1 own-goal

| Barton W | Boertien P | Lee R | Riggott C | Higginbotham D | Murray A | Bolder A | Christie M | Ravanelli F | Morris L | Jackson R | Twigg G | Evatt I | Strupar B | Tudgay M | Grenet F | Oakes A | Kinkladze G | Grant L | O'Neil B | Hunt L | Carbonari H | McLeod I | Burton D | Elliott S | Burley C | Mills P | Holmes L | Zavagno L | Chadwick N | Mooney T | Robinson M | Ritchie P | Valakari S | Camp L | |
|---|---|---|---|---|---|---|---|---|---|---|---|---|---|---|---|---|---|---|---|---|---|---|---|---|---|---|---|---|---|---|---|---|---|---|---|
| 3 | 4 | | | | 7 | **8** | 9 | | 11 | | | 5 | | 10 | | | 12 | 1 | | | | | | 6 | | 2 | 14 | 13 | | | | | | | 3 |
| 1 | 1 | | | | 1 | 1 | 1 | | 1 | | | 1 | | 1 | | | | 1 | | | | | | 1 | | 1 | | | | | | | | | |
| | | | | | | | | | | | | | | | | | 1 | | | | | | | | | | 1 | 1 | | | | | | | |
| | | | | | | | | | | | | | | | | | | | | | | | | | | | | | | | | | | | |

| Barton W | Boertien P | Lee R | Riggott C | Higginbotham D | Murray A | Bolder A | Christie M | Ravanelli F | Morris L | Jackson R | Twigg G | Evatt I | Strupar B | Tudgay M | Grenet F | Oakes A | Kinkladze G | Grant L | O'Neil B | Hunt L | Carbonari H | McLeod I | Burton D | Elliott S | Burley C | Mills P | Holmes L | Zavagno L | Chadwick N | Mooney T | Robinson M | Ritchie P | Valakari S | Camp L | |
|---|---|---|---|---|---|---|---|---|---|---|---|---|---|---|---|---|---|---|---|---|---|---|---|---|---|---|---|---|---|---|---|---|---|---|---|
| *2* | 3 | 4 | 5 | 6 | | 7 | 9 | | 11 | | | 12 | **10** | | | | 13 | | 8 | 14 | | | | | | | | | | | | | | | 1 |
| **2** | 3 | *8* | 4 | 6 | 11 | 7 | 9 | | 13 | | | 14 | | | | | | | | 12 | 5 | 10 | | | | | | | | | | | | | 2 |
| 2 | 2 | 2 | 2 | 2 | 1 | 2 | 2 | | 1 | | | | 1 | | | | | | 1 | | 1 | 1 | | | | | | | | | | | | | |
| | | | | | | | | | 1 | | | 2 | | | | | 1 | | | 2 | | | | | | | | | | | | | | | |
| | | | | 1 | | | 1 | | 1 | | | 1 | | | | | | | | | | | | | | | | | | | | | | | |

# 2003-04

| | P | W | D | L | F | A | Pts |
|---|---|---|---|---|---|---|---|
| Norwich C | 46 | 28 | 10 | 8 | 79 | 39 | 94 |
| W.B.A. | 46 | 25 | 11 | 10 | 64 | 32 | 86 |
| Sunderland | 46 | 22 | 13 | 11 | 62 | 45 | 79 |
| West Ham U | 46 | 19 | 17 | 10 | 67 | 45 | 74 |
| Ipswich T | 46 | 21 | 10 | 15 | 84 | 72 | 73 |
| Crystal P | 46 | 21 | 10 | 15 | 72 | 61 | 73 |
| Wigan A | 46 | 18 | 17 | 11 | 60 | 45 | 71 |
| Sheffield U | 46 | 20 | 11 | 15 | 65 | 56 | 71 |
| Reading | 46 | 20 | 10 | 16 | 55 | 57 | 70 |
| Millwall | 46 | 18 | 15 | 13 | 55 | 48 | 69 |
| Stoke C | 46 | 18 | 12 | 16 | 58 | 55 | 66 |
| Coventry C | 46 | 17 | 14 | 15 | 67 | 54 | 65 |
| Cardiff C | 46 | 17 | 14 | 15 | 68 | 58 | 65 |
| Nottingham F | 46 | 15 | 14 | 16 | 61 | 58 | 60 |
| Preston NE | 46 | 15 | 14 | 17 | 69 | 71 | 59 |
| Watford | 46 | 15 | 12 | 19 | 54 | 68 | 57 |
| Rotherham U | 46 | 13 | 15 | 18 | 53 | 61 | 54 |
| Crewe Alex | 46 | 14 | 11 | 21 | 57 | 66 | 53 |
| Burnley | 46 | 13 | 14 | 19 | 60 | 77 | 53 |
| Derby Co | 46 | 13 | 13 | 20 | 53 | 67 | 52 |
| Gillingham | 46 | 14 | 9 | 23 | 48 | 67 | 51 |
| Walsall | 46 | 13 | 12 | 21 | 45 | 65 | 51 |
| Bradford C | 46 | 10 | 6 | 30 | 57 | 69 | 36 |
| Wimbledon | 46 | 8 | 5 | 33 | 41 | 89 | 29 |

Manager: George Burley.
Leading scorer: Ian Taylor, League 11, all matches 12.
Player of the season: Youl Mawene.

- For a second consecutive season 36 players appeared. Of these, Candido Costa was on loan for the season, Manel and Noel Whelan signed on short contracts and seven were temporary loans.
- Of the loan players, Mathias Svensson did well early in the season but the only one to make a major impact was Everton midfield player Leon Osman. Without him, Derby could well have been relegated and were not safe until the 45th match.
- After being voted Player of the season, Youl Mawene was not allowed the specified time to respond to a contract offer and joined Preston North End.

## Division One

| Match No. | Date | | Venue | Opponents | Result | | Scorers | Att |
|---|---|---|---|---|---|---|---|---|
| 1 | Aug | 9 | (h) | Stoke C | L | 0-3 | | 2 |
| 2 | | 16 | (a) | Gillingham | D | 0-0 | | |
| 3 | | 23 | (h) | Reading | L | 2-3 | Taylor (pen), Svensson | 1 |
| 4 | | 25 | (a) | Cardiff C | L | 1-4 | Svensson | 1 |
| 5 | | 30 | (h) | West Brom A | L | 0-1 | | 2 |
| 6 | Sep | 13 | (a) | Walsall | W | 1-0 | Junior | |
| 7 | | 17 | (h) | Watford | W | 3-2 | Taylor, Svensson, Junior | 1 |
| 8 | | 20 | (h) | Sunderland | D | 1-1 | Taylor | 2 |
| 9 | | 27 | (a) | Nottingham F | D | 1-1 | Junior | 2 |
| 10 | | 30 | (a) | Bradford C | W | 2-1 | Morris 2 | 1 |
| 11 | Oct | 4 | (h) | West Ham U | L | 0-1 | | 2 |
| 12 | | 11 | (h) | Wigan A | D | 2-2 | Taylor (pen), Morris | 1 |
| 13 | | 14 | (a) | Crystal P | D | 1-1 | Zavagno | 1 |
| 14 | | 18 | (a) | Crewe A | L | 0-3 | | |
| 15 | | 21 | (a) | Norwich C | L | 1-2 | Taylor (pen) | 1 |
| 16 | | 25 | (h) | Coventry C | L | 1-3 | Holmes | 2 |
| 17 | Nov | 1 | (a) | Preston NE | L | 0-3 | | 1 |
| 18 | | 8 | (h) | Ipswich T | D | 2-2 | Kennedy, Dichio | 1 |
| 19 | | 15 | (h) | Burnley | W | 2-0 | Morris, Taylor (pen) | 2 |
| 20 | | 22 | (a) | Millwall | D | 0-0 | | 1 |
| 21 | | 29 | (h) | Wimbledon | W | 3-1 | Herzig (og), Tudgay, Holmes | 2 |
| 22 | Dec | 6 | (a) | Ipswich T | L | 1-2 | Tudgay | 2 |
| 23 | | 13 | (a) | Rotherham U | D | 0-0 | | |
| 24 | | 26 | (a) | West Brom A | D | 1-1 | Costa | 2 |
| 25 | | 28 | (h) | Norwich C | L | 0-4 | | 2 |
| 26 | Jan | 10 | (a) | Stoke C | L | 1-2 | Morris | 1 |
| 27 | | 17 | (h) | Gillingham | W | 2-1 | Vincent, Edwards | 2 |
| 28 | | 28 | (h) | Sheffield U | W | 2-0 | Tudgay, McLeod | 2 |
| 29 | | 31 | (a) | Reading | L | 1-3 | Johnson | 1 |
| 30 | Feb | 7 | (h) | Cardiff C | D | 2-2 | Taylor, Osman | 2 |
| 31 | | 14 | (a) | Wigan A | L | 0-2 | | |
| 32 | | 21 | (h) | Crystal P | W | 2-1 | Manel, Osman | 2 |
| 33 | | 28 | (a) | Coventry C | L | 0-2 | | 1 |
| 34 | Mar | 3 | (h) | Crewe A | D | 0-0 | | 1 |
| 35 | | 13 | (h) | Rotherham U | W | 1-0 | Peschisolido | 2 |
| 36 | | 16 | (a) | Watford | L | 1-2 | Peschisolido | 1 |
| 37 | | 20 | (h) | Nottingham F | W | 4-2 | Taylor, Peschisolido 2, Tudgay | 3 |
| 38 | | 23 | (a) | Sheffield U | D | 1-1 | Taylor (pen) | 2 |
| 39 | | 27 | (a) | Sunderland | L | 1-2 | Taylor (pen) | 3 |
| 40 | Apr | 3 | (h) | Walsall | L | 0-1 | | 2 |
| 41 | | 10 | (a) | West Ham U | D | 0-0 | | 2 |
| 42 | | 12 | (h) | Bradford C | W | 3-2 | Osman, Taylor, Combe (og) | 2 |
| 43 | | 17 | (h) | Preston NE | W | 5-1 | Manel 2, Tudgay 2, Junior (pen) | 2 |
| 44 | | 24 | (a) | Burnley | L | 0-1 | | 1 |
| 45 | May | 1 | (h) | Millwall | W | 2-0 | Bolder, Reich | 2 |
| 46 | | 9 | (a) | Wimbledon | L | 0-1 | | |

FINAL LEAGUE POSITION: 20th in Division One

Appeara
Subst

## FA Cup

| | | | | | | | | |
|---|---|---|---|---|---|---|---|---|
| 3 | Jan | 3 | (a) | Ipswich T | L | 0-3 | | 1 |

Appeara
Subst

## League Cup

| | | | | | | | | |
|---|---|---|---|---|---|---|---|---|
| 1 | Aug | 12 | (a) | Huddersfield T | L | 1-2 | Taylor | 6 |

Appeara
Subst

| Hunt L | Jackson R | Caldwell G | Mills P | Elliott S | Costa C | Huddlestone T | McLeod I | Taylor I | Morris L | Labarthe Tome A | Boertien P | Bolder A | Grant L | Zavagno L | Johnson M | Bradbury L | Svensson M | Valakari S | Junior | Holmes L | Tudgay M | Dichio D | Walton D | Kennedy P | Mawene Y | Doyle N | Edwards R | Manel | Vincent J | Reich M | Osman L | Whelan ND | Kenna J | Peschisolido P | |
|---|---|---|---|---|---|---|---|---|---|---|---|---|---|---|---|---|---|---|---|---|---|---|---|---|---|---|---|---|---|---|---|---|---|---|---|
|**2**|3|4|5|6|7|8|9|10|*11*|12|13|14||||||||||||||||||||||1|
||2|5|||7|8|**9**|4|12||11|13|1|3|6|10||||||||||||||||||2|
||2|**5**|12||7|8||4|10||3||1||6||9|11|13|||||||||||||||3|
||2||5||7|8||4|**11**||3|13|1||6||9|12|10|||||||||||||||4|
||2||5||7|8||4|10||3||||**6**||9|11|12|||||||||||||||5|
||2|13|5|||8||4|11||12|||**3**|6||9|7|10|||||||||||||||6|
||2|12|5|||8||4|11||13|||3|**6**||9|*7*|10|14||||||||||||||7|
||2|6|5|||8||4|**7**||3||||||9|12|10|11||||||||||||||8|
||2|14|5||12|8||4|13|||||3|6||9|*7*|10|**11**||||||||||||||9|
||2|5|||**7**|8||4|10|||||3|6||9|12||11||||||||||||||10|
|||2|5||7|8||4|10|||||3|6||**9**|12||11|13|||||||||||||11|
||2||5|||8||10|9|||||3|6|||4||11|7|||||||||||||12|
||2||5|13|7|8||4|**9**|||||3|6|||10||11|12|||||||||||||13|
||2||5|14|12|8||4|**9**||||1|*3*|6|||*7*||11|13|10||||||||||||14|
||2||||13|8||4|9||||1|3|6|||**7**||11|12|10|5|||||||||||15|
||2||12||*7*|8|||9|||13|1|3|6||14|*4*||11||10|**5**|||||||||||16|
||||2|6|12||||*9*||13|7|1|||||4||**11**|14|10||3|5|8||||||||17|
||||2||12|8||4|9||||1||6|||**7**||11||10||3|5|||||||||18|
||2||12||*7*|8||4|9||13||1||6|||14||11||10||3|**5**|||||||||19|
||2|||||8||4|9||12|13|1||6|*10*||*7*||**11**|14|||3|5|||||||||20|
||2||13||7|**8**||4||||12|1|14|6|10||||*11*|9|||3|5|||||||||21|
||2||12||7||14|4||||11|1|3|**6**|9||8||13|*10*||||5|||||||||22|
||2||||7|||**4**||||8|1|3||10||12||11|9||5||6|||||||||23|
||2||||12|8||4|10|||11|1|3|6|9|||||**7**||||5|||||||||24|
||2||||12|**8**|13|4|9|||10|1|3|6|||||11|7||||5|||||||||25|
||||||13|8||4|11|||**7**|1|3|6|10|||||12||||5||2|9|||||||26|
||||||7|8||4||12||13|1||6||||||10||||5||2|**9**|3|11|||||27|
||||||7|8|12|||||13|1||6||||||10||||5||2|9|3|**11**|4||||28|
||13||||7|8|||||||1||6||||||10||||5||2|**9**|3|11|4|12|||29|
||14||||**7**|8|12|4|||||1||6||||||13||||5||*2*||3|11|10|9|||30|
||2|||||7|10|8|||||1||6||||||||||5||4|13|3|12|11|**9**|||31|
||3||||**7**|8|*9*|4||||13|1||6||||||||||5||2|14||11|10|12|||32|
||3|||||12|14|4||||7|1||6||||||13||||5||**2**|10||11|8|*9*|||33|
||2||||12|8|14|4|||3||1||6||||||*10*||||5|||9||**11**|7|13|||34|
||3||||7|8||4|||12||1||**6**|||||13|10||||5||||||11|14|2|*9*|35|
||*2*||||**7**|8||4||13|3||1|||||||14|10||12||5||||||11||6|9|36|
||**3**||||7|8||4|||12||1||6|||||13|10||||5||||||11||2|9|37|
||||||13|8||4|||3|7|1||**6**||||||*10*||12||5||2|9|||11|14|||38|
|||||||8||4|||11|12|1||6||||||||||5||**2**|10|||7||3|9|39|
||||||7|8||4|||**3**||1||6||||14||||||5||12|10||13|11||2|*9*|40|
||2|||||8||4||||12|1|||||||**11**|10||||5|||13|3||7||6|9|41|
||2||12||7|8||4||||13|1||||||||10||||5|||14|**3**||11||*6*|9|42|
||3|||||2||**4**||||7|1||6||||13||*8*||||5|14||10||12|11|||9|43|
||3|||||2||4||||**7**|1||6||||13||8||||5|||10||12|11|||9|44|
||3|||||8||4||||12|1||**6**||||14|13|7||||5|||*10*||11|||2|9|45|
||||||12|2||4||||8|1||6||||**10**||7||||5|||||11|||3|9|46|
|1|34|6|13|2|23|42|4|42|21||10|11|36|16|39|7|9|14|6|17|20|6|3|5|30|1|10|12|7|9|17|3|9|11||
||2|3|6|2|11|1|6||2|3|8|13||1|||1|6|6|6|9||2|||1|1|4||4||5||||
||||||1||1|11|5|||1||1|1||3||4|2|6|1||1|||1|3|1|1|3|||4||

2 own-goals

| | | | | | | | | | | | | | | | | | | | | | | | | | | | | | | | | | | | |
|---|---|---|---|---|---|---|---|---|---|---|---|---|---|---|---|---|---|---|---|---|---|---|---|---|---|---|---|---|---|---|---|---|---|---|---|
||||2|||8||4|11|||10|1|3|**6**|||||12|7||||5|||9|||||||3|
||||1|||1||1|1|||1|1|1|1||||||1||||1|||1|||||||
|||||||||||||||||||||1|||||||||||||||
|||||||||||||||||||||||||||||||||||||

| | | | | | | | | | | | | | | | | | | | | | | | | | | | | | | | | | | | |
|---|---|---|---|---|---|---|---|---|---|---|---|---|---|---|---|---|---|---|---|---|---|---|---|---|---|---|---|---|---|---|---|---|---|---|---|
||2|4|**5**|6|7|8|12|9|13|10|3||1|||||11|||||||||||||||||1|
||1|1|1|1|1|1||1||1|1||1|||||1|||||||||||||||||
||||||||1||1|||||||||||||||||||||||||||
|||||||||1|||||||||||||||||||||||||||

# 2004-05

| | P | W | D | L | F | A | Pts |
|---|---|---|---|---|---|---|---|
| Sunderland | 46 | 29 | 7 | 15 | 76 | 41 | 94 |
| Wigan | 46 | 25 | 12 | 9 | 79 | 35 | 87 |
| Ipswich T | 46 | 24 | 13 | 9 | 85 | 56 | 85 |
| Derby Co | 46 | 22 | 10 | 14 | 71 | 60 | 76 |
| Preston NE | 46 | 21 | 12 | 13 | 67 | 58 | 75 |
| West Ham U | 46 | 21 | 10 | 15 | 66 | 56 | 73 |
| Reading | 46 | 19 | 13 | 14 | 51 | 44 | 70 |
| Sheffield U | 46 | 18 | 13 | 15 | 57 | 56 | 67 |
| Wolves | 46 | 14 | 21 | 10 | 72 | 59 | 66 |
| Millwall | 46 | 18 | 12 | 16 | 51 | 45 | 66 |
| Q.P.R. | 46 | 17 | 11 | 18 | 54 | 58 | 62 |
| Stoke C | 46 | 17 | 10 | 19 | 36 | 38 | 61 |
| Burnley | 46 | 15 | 15 | 16 | 38 | 39 | 60 |
| Leeds U | 46 | 14 | 18 | 14 | 49 | 52 | 60 |
| Leicester C | 46 | 12 | 21 | 13 | 49 | 46 | 57 |
| Cardiff C | 46 | 13 | 15 | 18 | 48 | 51 | 54 |
| Plymouth Argyle | 46 | 14 | 11 | 21 | 52 | 64 | 53 |
| Watford | 46 | 12 | 16 | 18 | 52 | 59 | 52 |
| Coventry C | 46 | 13 | 13 | 20 | 61 | 73 | 52 |
| Brighton & H.A. | 46 | 13 | 12 | 21 | 40 | 65 | 51 |
| Crewe Alex | 46 | 12 | 14 | 20 | 66 | 86 | 50 |
| Gillingham | 46 | 12 | 14 | 20 | 45 | 66 | 50 |
| Nottingham F | 46 | 9 | 17 | 20 | 42 | 66 | 44 |
| Rotherham | 46 | 5 | 14 | 27 | 35 | 69 | 29 |

Manager: George Burley.
Leading scorer: Grzegorz Rasiak, League 16, all matches 17.
Player of the season: Inigo Idiakez.

- Another name change. The First Division, below the Premiership in status, became the Championship, so what is in reality the Third Division is now known as League One.
- The Rams equalled their 1991–92 record with 12 away wins in the League. As in the earlier season, they ended in the Play-offs.
- Before he played League football, Lewin Nyatanga set a record by going on as a substitute for Wales Under-21 against Germany at the age of 16 years and 174 days, their youngest at this level.
- Polish international striker Grzegorz Rasiak was the key to a vastly improved season. Derby moved sharply to sign him when a move from Dyskobolia Grodzisk Wielkopolski to Italian club AC Siena was never registered.
- George Burley left in summer, citing interference by director of football Murdo Mackay.

## Championship

| Match No. | Date | Venue | Opponents | Result | | Scorers | Att |
|---|---|---|---|---|---|---|---|
| 1 | Aug 7 | (a) | Leeds U | L | 0-1 | | 3 |
| 2 | 11 | (h) | Leicester C | L | 1-2 | Tudgay | 2 |
| 3 | 14 | (h) | Ipswich T | W | 3-2 | Reich 2, Idiakez | 2 |
| 4 | 21 | (a) | QPR | W | 2-0 | Smith, Tudgay | 1 |
| 5 | 28 | (h) | Crewe A | L | 2-4 | Tudgay, Idiakez | 2 |
| 6 | 30 | (a) | Stoke C | L | 0-1 | | 1 |
| 7 | Sep 11 | (h) | Reading | W | 2-1 | Smith, Tudgay | 2 |
| 8 | 18 | (a) | Cardiff C | W | 2-0 | Reich, Taylor | 1 |
| 9 | 22 | (a) | Millwall | L | 1-3 | Reich | |
| 10 | 25 | (h) | Wigan A | D | 1-1 | Smith | 2 |
| 11 | 29 | (h) | West Ham U | D | 1-1 | Johnson | 2 |
| 12 | Oct 2 | (a) | Sunderland | D | 0-0 | | 2 |
| 13 | 16 | (h) | Watford | D | 2-2 | Smith, Rasiak | 2 |
| 14 | 19 | (a) | Wolves | L | 0-2 | | 2 |
| 15 | 22 | (a) | Burnley | W | 2-0 | Tudgay, Reich | 1 |
| 16 | 30 | (h) | Rotherham U | W | 3-2 | Rasiak, Peschisolido, Vincent | 2 |
| 17 | Nov 3 | (h) | Brighton & HA | W | 3-0 | Rasiak 2, Smith | 2 |
| 18 | 6 | (a) | Watford | D | 2-2 | Taylor, Peschisolido | 1 |
| 19 | 13 | (a) | Gillingham | W | 2-0 | Rasiak, Taylor | |
| 20 | 20 | (h) | Sheffield U | L | 0-1 | | 2 |
| 21 | 27 | (a) | Preston NE | L | 0-3 | | 1 |
| 22 | Dec 4 | (h) | Coventry C | D | 2-2 | Rasiak, Peschisolido | 2 |
| 23 | 11 | (h) | Nottingham F | W | 3-0 | Rasiak 2, Smith | 3 |
| 24 | 18 | (a) | Plymouth A | W | 2-0 | Coughlan (og), Peschisolido | 1 |
| 25 | 26 | (a) | Wigan A | W | 2-1 | Rasiak, Smith | 1 |
| 26 | 28 | (h) | Millwall | L | 0-3 | | 2 |
| 27 | Jan 1 | (h) | Cardiff C | L | 0-1 | | 2 |
| 28 | 3 | (a) | Reading | W | 1-0 | Smith | 1 |
| 29 | 16 | (h) | Sunderland | L | 0-2 | | 2 |
| 30 | 23 | (a) | West Ham U | W | 2-1 | Rasiak 2 | 3 |
| 31 | 26 | (h) | Leeds U | W | 2-0 | Smith, Bolder | 2 |
| 32 | Feb 5 | (a) | Brighton & HA | W | 3-2 | Tudgay 2, Bisgaard | |
| 33 | 19 | (a) | Rotherham U | W | 3-1 | Rasiak, Tudgay, Idiakez (pen) | |
| 34 | 23 | (h) | Burnley | D | 1-1 | Peschisolido | 2 |
| 35 | 26 | (a) | Nottingham F | D | 2-2 | Rasiak 2 | 2 |
| 36 | Mar 2 | (h) | Wolves | D | 3-3 | Idiakez 2 (1 pen), Reich | 2 |
| 37 | 5 | (h) | Plymouth A | W | 1-0 | Idiakez | 2 |
| 38 | 16 | (h) | QPR | D | 0-0 | | 2 |
| 39 | Apr 2 | (a) | Ipswich T | L | 2-3 | Tudgay, Idiakez | 2 |
| 40 | 5 | (a) | Crewe A | W | 2-1 | Rasiak, Smith | |
| 41 | 9 | (h) | Stoke C | W | 3-1 | Rasiak, Bisgaard, Idiakez | 2 |
| 42 | 15 | (a) | Sheffield U | W | 1-0 | Bisgaard | 2 |
| 43 | 23 | (h) | Gillingham | W | 2-0 | Bisgaard, Peschisolido | 2 |
| 44 | 26 | (a) | Leicester C | L | 0-1 | | 2 |
| 45 | 30 | (a) | Coventry C | L | 2-6 | Bolder, Peschisolido | 2 |
| 46 | May 8 | (h) | Preston NE | W | 3-1 | Idiakez, Smith, Peschisolido | 3 |

FINAL LEAGUE POSITION: 4th in Championship

Appeara
Subst

## Play-offs

| | | | | | | | |
|---|---|---|---|---|---|---|---|
| SF1 | May 15 | (a) | Preston NE | L | 0-2 | | 2 |
| SF2 | 19 | (h) | Preston NE | D | 0-0 | | 3 |

Appeara
Subst
G

## FA Cup

| | | | | | | | |
|---|---|---|---|---|---|---|---|
| 3 | Jan 8 | (h) | Wigan A | W | 2-1 | Idiakez, Junior | 1 |
| 4 | 29 | (h) | Fulham | D | 1-1 | Tudgay | 2 |
| R | Feb 12 | (a) | Fulham | L | 2-4 | Rasiak, Peschisolido | 1 |

Appeara
Substi
G

## League Cup

| | | | | | | | |
|---|---|---|---|---|---|---|---|
| 1 | Aug 24 | (a) | Lincoln C | L | 1-3 | Idiakez | 4 |

Appeara
Substi
G

| | Kenna J | Jackson R | Taylor I | Mills P | Johnson M | Huddlestone T | Idiakez I | Tudgay M | Smith T | Bisgaard M | Bolder A | Junior | Reich M | Peschisolido P | Doyle N | Vincent J | Konjic M | Holmes L | Talbot J | Rasiak G | Grant L | Kaku B | Makin C | Boertien P |
|---|---|---|---|---|---|---|---|---|---|---|---|---|---|---|---|---|---|---|---|---|---|---|---|---|
| 1 | 2 | 3 | 4 | 5 | 6 | **7** | 8 | 9 | 10 | 11 | 12 | 13 | 14 | | | | | | | | | | | |
| 2 | 2 | 3 | 4 | | 6 | 5 | 8 | 12 | 10 | 7 | | 9 | **11** | 13 | | | | | | | | | | |
| 3 | | 3 | 4 | | 6 | 5 | 8 | 12 | *10* | 7 | 13 | **9** | 11 | 14 | 2 | | | | | | | | | |
| 4 | | 3 | *4* | | 6 | 5 | 8 | 9 | **10** | 7 | 14 | 13 | 11 | 12 | 2 | | | | | | | | | |
| 5 | | | 4 | | 6 | 5 | 8 | 9 | 10 | 7 | | 12 | **11** | | 2 | 3 | | | | | | | | |
| 6 | 2 | | 4 | | 6 | 5 | 8 | 9 | 11 | **7** | 10 | 13 | | 12 | | 3 | | | | | | | | |
| 7 | 2 | | **4** | | 6 | 12 | 8 | 7 | 10 | | | 9 | 11 | 13 | | 3 | 5 | | | | | | | |
| 8 | 2 | | 4 | | 6 | 10 | 8 | **9** | 7 | | 12 | 13 | 11 | | | 3 | 5 | | | | | | | |
| 9 | 2 | | 4 | | **6** | 10 | 8 | | 7 | | 12 | 9 | 11 | | | 3 | 5 | 13 | | | | | | |
| 10 | 2 | | 4 | 12 | | 6 | 8 | | 10 | | 7 | | 11 | 13 | | | 5 | | **3** | 9 | | | | |
| 11 | 2 | | 13 | | 6 | 4 | 8 | | 10 | | 7 | | **11** | 12 | | | 5 | | 3 | 9 | | | | |
| 12 | 2 | | 4 | 5 | 6 | 12 | **8** | | 10 | | 7 | | 11 | | | 3 | | | | 9 | | | | |
| 13 | 2 | 14 | 4 | 5 | 6 | **8** | | 10 | 7 | | 12 | 13 | 11 | | | 3 | | | | 9 | | | | |
| 14 | | 2 | 4 | 5 | 6 | 13 | | 7 | *10* | | 8 | | **11** | | | 3 | | 14 | | 9 | 12 | | | |
| 15 | | 2 | 4 | 5 | | 6 | 8 | 7 | | 12 | 10 | | **11** | | | 3 | | | | 9 | 1 | | | |
| 16 | 2 | | 13 | | 6 | 5 | 8 | 10 | | **7** | 4 | | 11 | 12 | | 3 | | | | 9 | | | | |
| 17 | 2 | | 12 | 13 | 6 | 5 | 8 | 14 | *7* | | **4** | | 11 | 10 | | 3 | | | | 9 | | | | |
| 18 | 2 | | 4 | 12 | **6** | 5 | 8 | | *7* | 14 | 10 | | 11 | 13 | | 3 | | | | 9 | | | | |
| 19 | | **2** | 4 | 12 | 6 | 5 | 8 | | 11 | 14 | 7 | | 13 | *10* | | 3 | | | | 9 | | | | |
| 20 | 2 | | 12 | | 6 | 5 | 8 | 13 | 7 | 14 | **4** | | 11 | 10 | | *3* | | | | 9 | | | | |
| 21 | 2 | | 4 | | 6 | 5 | 8 | 13 | 7 | 12 | | | *11* | 14 | | 3 | | | | 9 | | **10** | | |
| 22 | 3 | 2 | 12 | 5 | **6** | 4 | 8 | 14 | *10* | 7 | | | 11 | 13 | | | | | | 9 | | | | |
| 23 | 2 | 3 | 4 | 13 | 6 | 5 | *8* | | 11 | 7 | 14 | | 12 | **10** | | | | | | 9 | | | | |
| 24 | 2 | 3 | 4 | | 6 | 5 | | 13 | **11** | 7 | | | 12 | 10 | | | | | | 9 | | 8 | | |
| 25 | 2 | 3 | 4 | | 6 | 5 | 8 | | 12 | 7 | | | 11 | **10** | | | | | | 9 | | 13 | | |
| 26 | 2 | 3 | 12 | | 6 | 5 | 8 | 14 | *10* | 7 | | | 11 | 13 | | | | | | 9 | | **4** | | |
| 27 | **2** | 3 | 4 | | 6 | 5 | 8 | 13 | 11 | 7 | | | 12 | 10 | | | | | | 9 | | | | |
| 28 | 2 | 3 | | 5 | 6 | 4 | 8 | 13 | 10 | **7** | 12 | | 11 | | | | | | | 9 | | | | |
| 29 | 2 | 3 | 14 | 5 | 6 | 4 | 8 | | 10 | *7* | | 13 | **11** | 12 | | | | | | 9 | | | | |
| 30 | 2 | 3 | 4 | 5 | | 6 | 8 | 12 | 11 | **7** | 10 | 14 | 13 | | | | | | | *9* | | | | |
| 31 | 2 | **3** | 4 | 5 | 12 | 6 | 8 | 13 | 7 | *10* | 14 | | 11 | | | | | | | 9 | | | | |
| 32 | 2 | | 4 | 5 | 3 | 6 | 8 | 11 | 7 | 10 | 13 | 12 | | | | | | | | **9** | | | | |
| 33 | 2 | | | 5 | | 6 | 8 | 7 | **11** | 10 | 4 | | 12 | | | | 13 | | | 9 | | | 3 | |
| 34 | 2 | | | **5** | | 6 | 8 | 7 | | 10 | 4 | | 11 | 13 | | | 12 | | | 9 | | | 3 | |
| 35 | 2 | | 13 | | | 6 | 8 | 11 | | 7 | 4 | 12 | | **10** | | | 5 | | | 9 | | | 3 | |
| 36 | 2 | | 13 | 5 | | 6 | 8 | 11 | *10* | | 4 | **7** | 14 | 12 | | | | | | 9 | | | 3 | |
| 37 | 2 | | 13 | | | 6 | 8 | **7** | 11 | 10 | 4 | | | 12 | | | 5 | | | 9 | | | 3 | |
| 38 | 2 | | | | | 6 | 8 | 11 | **7** | 10 | 4 | | 12 | 13 | | | 5 | | | 9 | | | 3 | |
| 39 | 2 | | | 5 | | 6 | 8 | **11** | 7 | 10 | 4 | | | 12 | | | | | | 9 | | | 3 | |
| 40 | 2 | | | 12 | **6** | 5 | 8 | 7 | 11 | 10 | 4 | 13 | | | | | | | | 9 | | | 3 | |
| 41 | 2 | | | | 6 | 4 | 8 | 11 | 7 | 10 | 13 | | | 12 | | | 5 | | | **9** | | | 3 | |
| 42 | 2 | | 14 | | *6* | 4 | **8** | 7 | 11 | 10 | 12 | | | 13 | | | 5 | | | 9 | | | 3 | |
| 43 | 2 | | 13 | 12 | **6** | 4 | | | *7* | 11 | 8 | | 14 | 10 | | | 5 | | | 9 | | | 3 | |
| 44 | 2 | | 13 | | 6 | 4 | | | 7 | 10 | 8 | 14 | 11 | 12 | | | *5* | | | **9** | | | 3 | |
| 45 | 2 | | **4** | | 6 | | 8 | 9 | 11 | 7 | 10 | 13 | | 12 | | | 5 | | | | | | 3 | |
| 46 | 2 | 3 | 12 | | 6 | 5 | **8** | | 11 | 7 | 4 | | *10* | 9 | | | 14 | 13 | | | | | | |
| | 40 | 18 | 25 | 15 | 35 | 42 | 41 | 22 | 41 | 31 | 24 | 5 | 27 | 10 | 3 | 15 | 13 | | 2 | 35 | 1 | 3 | 13 | |
| | | 1 | 14 | 7 | 1 | 3 | | 12 | 1 | 5 | 12 | 13 | 10 | 22 | | | 3 | 3 | | | 1 | 1 | | |
| | | | 3 | | 1 | | 9 | 9 | 11 | 4 | 2 | | 6 | 8 | | 1 | | | | 16 | | | | |

1 own-goal

| | Kenna J | Jackson R | Taylor I | Mills P | Johnson M | Huddlestone T | Idiakez I | Tudgay M | Smith T | Bisgaard M | Bolder A | Junior | Reich M | Peschisolido P | Doyle N | Vincent J | Konjic M | Holmes L | Talbot J | Rasiak G | Grant L | Kaku B | Makin C | Boertien P |
|---|---|---|---|---|---|---|---|---|---|---|---|---|---|---|---|---|---|---|---|---|---|---|---|---|
| SF1 | 2 | 3 | 4 | 12 | **6** | 8 | | | 11 | 10 | 13 | | 7 | 9 | | | 5 | | | | | | | |
| SF2 | 2 | 3 | 13 | | | 6 | 8 | | **11** | 7 | 4 | | 12 | 10 | | | 5 | | | 9 | | | | |
| | 2 | 2 | 1 | | 1 | 2 | 1 | | 2 | 2 | 1 | | 1 | 2 | | | 2 | | | 1 | | | | |
| | | | 1 | 1 | | | | | | | 1 | | 1 | | | | | | | | | | | |
| | | | | | | | | | | | | | | | | | | | | | | | | |

| | Kenna J | Jackson R | Taylor I | Mills P | Johnson M | Huddlestone T | Idiakez I | Tudgay M | Smith T | Bisgaard M | Bolder A | Junior | Reich M | Peschisolido P | Doyle N | Vincent J | Konjic M | Holmes L | Talbot J | Rasiak G | Grant L | Kaku B | Makin C | Boertien P |
|---|---|---|---|---|---|---|---|---|---|---|---|---|---|---|---|---|---|---|---|---|---|---|---|---|
| 3 | | 2 | 4 | 5 | | 6 | 8 | **9** | 10 | 7 | 13 | 12 | 11 | | | | | | | | | | | 3 |
| 4 | 2 | | 4 | 5 | 3 | 6 | 8 | 12 | 7 | 10 | | | **11** | | | | | | | 9 | | | | |
| R | 2 | | | 5 | 6 | | 8 | 7 | **11** | 10 | 4 | *12* | | 13 | 14 | | | | | 9 | | | | 3 |
| | 2 | 1 | 2 | 3 | 2 | 2 | 3 | 2 | 3 | 3 | 1 | | 2 | | | | | | | 2 | | | | 2 |
| | | | | | | | | 1 | | | 1 | 2 | | 1 | 1 | | | | | | | | | |
| | | | | | | | 1 | 1 | | | | 1 | | 1 | | | | | | 1 | | | | |

| | Kenna J | Jackson R | Taylor I | Mills P | Johnson M | Huddlestone T | Idiakez I | Tudgay M | Smith T | Bisgaard M | Bolder A | Junior | Reich M | Peschisolido P | Doyle N | Vincent J | Konjic M | Holmes L | Talbot J | Rasiak G | Grant L | Kaku B | Makin C | Boertien P |
|---|---|---|---|---|---|---|---|---|---|---|---|---|---|---|---|---|---|---|---|---|---|---|---|---|
| 1 | 12 | **2** | 13 | | 6 | 5 | 8 | 9 | | | *4* | 14 | 11 | 10 | | 3 | | 7 | | | | | | |
| | | 1 | | | 1 | 1 | 1 | 1 | | | 1 | | 1 | 1 | | 1 | | 1 | | | | | | |
| | 1 | | 1 | | | | | | | | | 1 | | | | | | | | | | | | |
| | | | | | | | 1 | | | | | | | | | | | | | | | | | |

# 2005-06

| | P | W | D | L | F | A | Pts |
|---|---|---|---|---|---|---|---|
| Reading | 46 | 31 | 13 | 2 | 99 | 32 | 106 |
| Sheffield U | 46 | 26 | 12 | 8 | 76 | 46 | 90 |
| Watford | 46 | 22 | 15 | 9 | 77 | 53 | 81 |
| Preston | 46 | 20 | 20 | 6 | 59 | 30 | 80 |
| Leeds U | 46 | 21 | 15 | 10 | 57 | 38 | 78 |
| Crystal P | 46 | 21 | 12 | 13 | 67 | 48 | 75 |
| Wolves | 46 | 16 | 19 | 11 | 50 | 42 | 67 |
| Coventry C | 46 | 16 | 15 | 15 | 62 | 65 | 63 |
| Norwich C | 46 | 18 | 8 | 20 | 56 | 65 | 62 |
| Luton T | 46 | 17 | 10 | 19 | 66 | 67 | 61 |
| Cardiff C | 46 | 16 | 12 | 18 | 58 | 59 | 60 |
| Southampton | 46 | 13 | 19 | 14 | 49 | 50 | 58 |
| Stoke C | 46 | 17 | 7 | 22 | 54 | 63 | 58 |
| Plymouth Argyle | 46 | 13 | 17 | 16 | 39 | 46 | 56 |
| Ipswich T | 46 | 14 | 14 | 18 | 53 | 66 | 56 |
| Leicester C | 46 | 13 | 15 | 18 | 51 | 59 | 54 |
| Burnley | 46 | 14 | 12 | 20 | 46 | 54 | 54 |
| Hull C | 46 | 12 | 16 | 18 | 49 | 55 | 52 |
| Sheffield W | 46 | 13 | 13 | 20 | 39 | 52 | 52 |
| Derby C | 46 | 10 | 20 | 16 | 53 | 67 | 50 |
| QPR | 46 | 12 | 14 | 20 | 50 | 65 | 50 |
| Crewe | 46 | 9 | 15 | 22 | 57 | 86 | 42 |
| Millwall | 46 | 8 | 16 | 22 | 35 | 62 | 40 |
| Brighton & HA | 46 | 7 | 17 | 22 | 39 | 71 | 38 |

Manager: Phil Brown to January, then Terry Westley.
Leading scorer: Inigo Idiakez, League/all matches 11.
Player of the season: Tommy Smith.

- Derby used 39 players, more than ever before. Two, Lee Grant and Mo Konjic, appeared only in the Carling Cup. A remarkable total of 22 players made debuts for the Rams and 12 of them were on loan.

- The Rams drew 20 of their Championship games, the most in their League history.

- John Sleightholme resigned as chairman and Murdo Mackay ceased to be director of football before, at the end of April, a local consortium took control of the club. It was led by Peter Gadsby, who had been vice-chairman under Lionel Pickering.

- Ted McMinn, a former player signed by Arthur Cox, had his right leg amputated below the knee and was granted a testimonial. His match on 1 May, between a Derby legends team and the Rangers side that won nine successive Scottish Championships, attracted 33,475, a record for Pride Park.

## Championship

| Match No. | Date | | Venue | Opponents | Result | | Scorers |
|---|---|---|---|---|---|---|---|
| 1 | Aug | 6 | H | Brighton & HA | D | 1-1 | Peschisolido |
| 2 | | 8 | A | Preston NE | D | 1-1 | Idiakez (pen) |
| 3 | | 13 | A | Plymouth A | W | 2-0 | Rasiak, Bisgaard |
| 4 | | 20 | H | Cardiff C | W | 2-1 | Bisgaard, Idiakez (pen) |
| 5 | | 27 | A | Burnley | D | 2-2 | Idiakez, Rasiak |
| 6 | | 29 | H | Watford | L | 1-2 | Bolder |
| 7 | Sep | 11 | A | Crewe A | D | 1-1 | Bisgaard |
| 8 | | 14 | H | Coventry C | D | 1-1 | Bisgaard |
| 9 | | 18 | H | Southampton | D | 2-2 | Idiakez (pen), Davies |
| 10 | | 24 | A | Sheffield U | L | 1-2 | Peschisolido |
| 11 | | 28 | A | Leeds U | L | 1-3 | Gregan (og) |
| 12 | Oct | 1 | H | Leicester C | D | 1-1 | El Hamdaoui |
| 13 | | 15 | H | Stoke C | W | 2-1 | Idiakez, Peschisolido |
| 14 | | 18 | A | Wolves | D | 1-1 | El Hamdaoui |
| 15 | | 22 | A | Hull C | L | 1-2 | Idiakez (pen) |
| 16 | | 29 | H | QPR | L | 1-2 | Blackstock |
| 17 | Nov | 2 | H | Ipswich T | D | 3-3 | Blackstock 2, Tudgay |
| 18 | | 5 | A | Sheffield W | L | 1-2 | Tudgay |
| 19 | | 18 | H | Wolverhampton W | L | 0-3 | |
| 20 | | 22 | A | Stoke C | W | 2-1 | Smith, Nyatanga |
| 21 | | 26 | A | Brighton & HA | D | 0-0 | |
| 22 | Dec | 3 | H | Norwich C | W | 2-0 | Davies 2 |
| 23 | | 10 | H | Preston NE | D | 1-1 | Smith (pen) |
| 24 | | 17 | A | Cardiff C | D | 0-0 | |
| 25 | | 26 | H | Luton T | D | 1-1 | Idiakez |
| 26 | | 28 | A | Crystal Palace | L | 0-2 | |
| 27 | | 31 | H | Reading | D | 2-2 | S Johnson 2 |
| 28 | Jan | 2 | A | Millwall | L | 1-2 | S Johnson |
| 29 | | 14 | H | Crewe A | W | 5-1 | Peschisolido, M Johnson, Smith 2, Idiakez |
| 30 | | 21 | A | Coventry C | L | 1-6 | Peschisolido |
| 31 | Feb | 1 | H | Sheffield U | L | 0-1 | |
| 32 | | 4 | A | Southampton | D | 0-0 | |
| 33 | | 11 | H | Leeds U | D | 0-0 | |
| 34 | | 14 | A | Leicester C | D | 2-2 | El Hamdaoui, Stearman (og) |
| 35 | | 18 | A | Norwich C | L | 0-2 | |
| 36 | | 25 | H | Plymouth A | W | 1-0 | Bolder |
| 37 | Mar | 4 | A | Watford | D | 2-2 | Lisbie, Barnes |
| 38 | | 11 | H | Burnley | W | 3-0 | Smith, Idiakez, Moore |
| 39 | | 18 | A | Luton T | L | 0-1 | |
| 40 | | 25 | H | Crystal P | W | 2-1 | Idiakez 2 |
| 41 | Apr | 1 | A | Reading | L | 0-5 | |
| 42 | | 8 | H | Millwall | W | 1-0 | Smith |
| 43 | | 15 | A | QPR | D | 1-1 | Smith |
| 44 | | 17 | H | Hull C | D | 1-1 | Smith (pen) |
| 45 | | 22 | A | Ipswich T | L | 0-2 | |
| 46 | | 30 | H | Sheffield W | L | 0-2 | |

FINAL LEAGUE POSITION: 20th in Championship

Appeara
Subs

## FA Cup

| | | | | | | | |
|---|---|---|---|---|---|---|---|
| 3 | Jan | 7 | H | Burnley | W | 2-1 | Peschisolido 2 |
| 4 | | 28 | A | Colchester U | L | 1-3 | Smith (pen) |

Appeara
Subs

## League Cup

| | | | | | | | |
|---|---|---|---|---|---|---|---|
| 1 | Aug | 24 | H | Grimsby T | L | 0-1 | |

Appeara
Subst

| Edworthy M | Jackson R | Thirlwell P | Davies A | Johnson M | Bisgaard M | Idiakez I | Rasiak G | Peschisolido P | Smith T | Tudgay M | Holmes L | Bolder A | Mills P | Johnson S | Kenna J | Barnes G | Fadiga K | Holdsworth D | Whittingham P | John S | El Hamdaoui M | Poole K | Jackson J | Nyatanga L | Thorne E | Blackstock D | Doyle N | Graham D | Hajto T | Moore D | Wright A | Lisbie K | Ainsworth L | McIndoe M | Addison M | Grant L | Konjic M | |
|---|---|---|---|---|---|---|---|---|---|---|---|---|---|---|---|---|---|---|---|---|---|---|---|---|---|---|---|---|---|---|---|---|---|---|---|---|---|---|
| 2 | 3 | 4 | 5 | 6 | 7 | 8 | 9 | **10** | 11 | 12 | 13 | | | | | | | | | | | | | | | | | | | | | | | | | | | 1 |
| 2 | 3 | | 5 | 6 | 7 | 8 | 9 | **10** | 11 | 13 | | 4 | 12 | | | | | | | | | | | | | | | | | | | | | | | | | 2 |
| 2 | 3 | 10 | 5 | 6 | 7 | 8 | 9 | | **11** | 12 | | 4 | | | | | | | | | | | | | | | | | | | | | | | | | | 3 |
| 2 | 3 | 10 | 5 | 6 | **7** | 8 | 9 | | 11 | 12 | | 4 | | 13 | | | | | | | | | | | | | | | | | | | | | | | | 4 |
| 2 | 3 | 10 | 5 | *6* | 7 | 8 | 9 | 12 | 11 | 14 | | **4** | | 13 | | | | | | | | | | | | | | | | | | | | | | | | 5 |
| | 3 | 10 | 5 | 6 | 7 | 8 | 9 | 14 | **11** | 13 | | *4* | | 12 | 2 | | | | | | | | | | | | | | | | | | | | | | | 6 |
| | | 10 | 5 | 6 | 7 | 8 | | 13 | 11 | **9** | | 4 | | 3 | 2 | 12 | | | | | | | | | | | | | | | | | | | | | | 7 |
| 2 | | **10** | | 6 | 7 | 8 | | 14 | 11 | 9 | | 4 | | 3 | 5 | | 12 | 13 | | | | | | | | | | | | | | | | | | | | 8 |
| **2** | | | 5 | 6 | 7 | 8 | | 14 | 11 | | | | | 10 | 12 | | 4 | | 3 | *9* | 13 | | | | | | | | | | | | | | | | | 9 |
| | | | 5 | 6 | *7* | 8 | | 13 | 11 | | | **4** | | 10 | 2 | | 14 | | 3 | 9 | 12 | | | | | | | | | | | | | | | | | 10 |
| | | | 5 | 6 | 7 | | | 10 | 11 | | | 13 | | 8 | 2 | | **4** | 14 | 3 | *9* | 12 | | | | | | | | | | | | | | | | | 11 |
| | | | **5** | 6 | 7 | 8 | | 10 | 11 | | | 12 | | 4 | 2 | | | 14 | 3 | *9* | 13 | 1 | | | | | | | | | | | | | | | | 12 |
| | | | 5 | 6 | 7 | 8 | | *10* | 11 | 12 | | | | 4 | 2 | | | | 3 | | **9** | 1 | 13 | 14 | | | | | | | | | | | | | | 13 |
| | | | | 6 | *7* | 8 | | 10 | 11 | 14 | | | | 4 | 2 | | | | 3 | 12 | **9** | 1 | 13 | 5 | | | | | | | | | | | | | | 14 |
| 6 | | | 5 | | 7 | 8 | | 10 | **11** | 13 | | | | 4 | 2 | | | | 3 | 9 | | 1 | 12 | | | | | | | | | | | | | | | 15 |
| | | 12 | | 6 | 7 | 8 | | *10* | | 14 | | | | 4 | **2** | | | | 11 | 9 | | 1 | 3 | | 5 | 13 | | | | | | | | | | | | 16 |
| 2 | | | | 6 | 7 | 8 | | | | 9 | | | | 4 | | 12 | | | 3 | | | 1 | **11** | | 5 | 10 | | | | | | | | | | | | 17 |
| | | 13 | | 6 | **7** | 8 | | 12 | | 9 | | | | 4 | 2 | | | | 3 | | | | 11 | | 5 | 10 | | | | | | | | | | | | 18 |
| | 2 | | 5 | **6** | 7 | 8 | | 13 | 11 | 9 | | | | 4 | | | | | 3 | | | | | | 12 | 10 | | | | | | | | | | | | 19 |
| 2 | 3 | 7 | 5 | | | **8** | | | 11 | 9 | | 12 | | 4 | | | | | | | | | | 6 | | 10 | 13 | | | | | | | | | | | 20 |
| 2 | 3 | *7* | 5 | | 12 | 8 | | | 11 | **9** | | 14 | | 4 | | | | | | | | | | 6 | | 10 | | 13 | | | | | | | | | | 21 |
| 2 | 3 | 7 | 5 | | | 8 | | | 11 | 9 | | 4 | | | | | | | | | | | | 6 | | 10 | | | | | | | | | | | | 22 |
| 2 | 3 | 7 | 5 | | 12 | 8 | | | 11 | **9** | | 4 | | 13 | | | | | | | | | | 6 | | *10* | | 14 | | | | | | | | | | 23 |
| | 2 | 7 | 5 | 3 | 12 | 8 | | | 11 | **9** | | | | 4 | | | | | | | | | | 6 | | 10 | | 13 | | | | | | | | | | 24 |
| | 2 | 7 | 5 | 3 | 13 | 8 | | 14 | 11 | 10 | | 12 | | **4** | | | | | | | | | | 6 | | | | *9* | | | | | | | | | | 25 |
| | 2 | 10 | 5 | 3 | **7** | 8 | | 13 | 11 | | 12 | 14 | | 4 | | | | | | | | | | 6 | | | | *9* | | | | | | | | | | 26 |
| 2 | 3 | 13 | 5 | 12 | | 8 | | 14 | **10** | | 7 | 4 | | 11 | | | | | | | | | | 6 | | | | *9* | | | | | | | | | | 27 |
| 2 | 3 | | | 5 | | 8 | | 12 | 7 | | 11 | **4** | | 10 | | 13 | | | | | | | | 6 | | | | 9 | | | | | | | | | | 28 |
| 2 | 12 | 13 | | **3** | 14 | 8 | | 10 | 7 | | 11 | | | 4 | 5 | | | | | | | | | 6 | | | | *9* | | | | | | | | | | 29 |
| 2 | | | 12 | 3 | 13 | 8 | | 10 | 7 | | 11 | 14 | | *4* | **5** | | | | | | | | | 6 | | | | 9 | | | | | | | | | | 30 |
| 2 | 12 | | | 3 | | 8 | | 13 | 7 | | **11** | 4 | | | | *10* | | | | | | | | | | | 14 | 9 | 5 | 6 | | | | | | | | 31 |
| 2 | 12 | | | **3** | 13 | 8 | | | 7 | | 11 | 4 | | | | *10* | | | | | | | | | | | 14 | 9 | 5 | 6 | | | | | | | | 32 |
| 3 | **2** | | | | 7 | | | 14 | 11 | | 13 | 4 | | | | 8 | | | | | 10 | | | | | | 12 | *9* | 5 | 6 | | | | | | | | 33 |
| 2 | | 12 | | | 7 | | | 13 | 11 | | | 4 | | | 3 | 8 | | | | | **10** | | | | | | | 9 | 5 | 6 | | | | | | | | 34 |
| 2 | | | | | | 8 | | 12 | 7 | | **11** | 4 | | | 3 | 10 | | | | | | | | | | | | 9 | 5 | 6 | | | | | | | | 35 |
| 2 | | | | | | 4 | | **10** | 11 | | 12 | 7 | | | | 8 | | | | | | | | 6 | | | | | | 5 | 3 | 9 | 13 | | | | | 36 |
| 2 | | | | | | 8 | | 12 | 7 | | 11 | 4 | | | | 10 | | | | | | | | 6 | | | | | | 5 | 3 | **9** | | | | | | 37 |
| 2 | | 12 | | | | 8 | | 14 | 7 | | 13 | 4 | | | | **10** | | | | | | | | 6 | | | | | | 5 | 3 | *9* | | 11 | | | | 38 |
| 2 | | | | | | 8 | | 13 | 7 | | 12 | 4 | | | | 10 | | | | | | | | 6 | | | | | | 5 | 3 | 9 | | **11** | | | | 39 |
| | 2 | | | | | 8 | | | 7 | | | 4 | | | | 10 | | | | | | | | 6 | | | | | | 5 | 3 | 9 | | 11 | | | | 40 |
| | 2 | | | | 12 | 8 | | 9 | 7 | | | **4** | | | | 10 | | | | | | | | 6 | | | | | | 5 | 3 | | 13 | 11 | | | | 41 |
| 2 | 14 | | | | | 8 | | | 11 | | | 12 | | **4** | | 7 | | | | | 10 | | | 6 | | | | | | 5 | *3* | 9 | | 13 | | | | 42 |
| | 2 | | | 3 | | 12 | | 13 | 11 | | 14 | **4** | | 8 | | 7 | | | | | | | | 6 | | | | | | 5 | | 9 | | *10* | | | | 43 |
| 2 | 12 | 4 | | **3** | 10 | 8 | | 9 | 7 | | *11* | 14 | | | | 13 | | | | | | | | 6 | | | | | | | | | | | 5 | | | 44 |
| 2 | 14 | | | 3 | *9* | 8 | | | 7 | | 13 | 12 | | 4 | | 10 | | | | | | | | 6 | | | | | | | | | | **11** | 5 | | | 45 |
| 2 | | | | 3 | 7 | | | **9** | 11 | | 12 | 8 | | 4 | | 10 | | | | | | | | 6 | | | | | | 5 | | | | 13 | | | | 46 |
| 30 | 20 | 15 | 22 | 30 | 25 | 41 | 6 | 14 | 43 | 11 | 9 | 25 | | 26 | 15 | 15 | 2 | | 11 | 6 | 5 | 6 | 3 | 23 | 3 | 8 | | 11 | 5 | 14 | 7 | 7 | | 6 | 2 | | | |
| | 6 | 6 | 1 | 1 | 8 | 1 | | 20 | | 10 | 9 | 10 | 1 | 4 | 1 | 4 | 2 | 3 | | 1 | 4 | | 3 | 1 | 1 | 1 | 4 | 3 | | | | | 2 | 2 | | | | |
| | | | 3 | 1 | 4 | 11 | 2 | 5 | 8 | 2 | | 2 | | 3 | | 1 | | | | | 3 | | | 1 | | 3 | | | | 1 | | 1 | | | | | | |

2 own-goals

| Edworthy M | Jackson R | Thirlwell P | Davies A | Johnson M | Bisgaard M | Idiakez I | Rasiak G | Peschisolido P | Smith T | Tudgay M | Holmes L | Bolder A | Mills P | Johnson S | Kenna J | Barnes G | Fadiga K | Holdsworth D | Whittingham P | John S | El Hamdaoui M | Poole K | Jackson J | Nyatanga L | Thorne E | Blackstock D | Doyle N | Graham D | Hajto T | Moore D | Wright A | Lisbie K | Ainsworth L | McIndoe M | Addison M | Grant L | Konjic M | |
|---|---|---|---|---|---|---|---|---|---|---|---|---|---|---|---|---|---|---|---|---|---|---|---|---|---|---|---|---|---|---|---|---|---|---|---|---|---|---|
| 2 | | 4 | | 3 | | 10 | | **9** | 7 | | 11 | 12 | | 8 | 5 | | | | | | | 1 | | 6 | | | | | | | | | | | | | | R3 |
| | | 8 | 5 | 3 | 7 | 10 | | **9** | 11 | | 13 | 4 | | | | | | 12 | | | | | | 6 | | | | | 2 | | | | | | | | | R4 |
| 1 | | 2 | 1 | 2 | 1 | 2 | | 2 | 2 | | 1 | 1 | | 1 | 1 | | | | | | | 1 | | 2 | | | | | 1 | | | | | | | | | |
| | | | | | | | | | | | 1 | 1 | | | | | | 1 | | | | | | | | | | | | | | | | | | | | |
| | | | | | | | | 2 | 1 | | | | | | | | | | | | | | | | | | | | | | | | | | | | | |

| Edworthy M | Jackson R | Thirlwell P | Davies A | Johnson M | Bisgaard M | Idiakez I | Rasiak G | Peschisolido P | Smith T | Tudgay M | Holmes L | Bolder A | Mills P | Johnson S | Kenna J | Barnes G | Fadiga K | Holdsworth D | Whittingham P | John S | El Hamdaoui M | Poole K | Jackson J | Nyatanga L | Thorne E | Blackstock D | Doyle N | Graham D | Hajto T | Moore D | Wright A | Lisbie K | Ainsworth L | McIndoe M | Addison M | Grant L | Konjic M | |
|---|---|---|---|---|---|---|---|---|---|---|---|---|---|---|---|---|---|---|---|---|---|---|---|---|---|---|---|---|---|---|---|---|---|---|---|---|---|---|
| 13 | 2 | | | | | | 12 | *10* | 7 | 9 | **11** | 4 | | 8 | 6 | 14 | | | | | | | | 3 | | | | | | | | | | | | 1 | 5 | R1 |
| | 1 | | | | | | | 1 | 1 | 1 | 1 | 1 | | 1 | 1 | | | | | | | | | 1 | | | | | | | | | | | | 1 | 1 | |
| 1 | | | | | | | 1 | | | | | | | | | 1 | | | | | | | | | | | | | | | | | | | | | | |
| | | | | | | | | | | | | | | | | | | | | | | | | | | | | | | | | | | | | | | |

# Rams in Europe

## European Cup

### 1972-73

**Round 1: v FK Zeljeznicar Sarajevo (Yugoslavia).**
**Sep 13, 1st leg (h) 2-0.**
*McFarland, Gemmill.*
Boulton, Powell, Daniel, Hennessey, McFarland, Todd, McGovern, Gemmill, O'Hare, Hector, Hinton.
Att: 27,350.

**Sep 27, 2nd leg (a) 2-1 (aggregate 4-1).**
*Hinton, O,Hare.*
Boulton, Daniel, Robson, Hennessey, McFarland, Todd, McGovern, Gemmill, O'Hare, Hector, Hinton.
Att: 60,000.

**Round 2: v SL Benfica (Portugal).**
**Oct 25, 1st leg (h) 3-0.**
*McFarland, Hector, McGovern.*
Boulton, Robson, Daniel, Hennessey, McFarland, Todd, McGovern, Gemmill, O,Hare, Hector, Hinton.
Att: 38,100.

**Nov 8, 2nd leg (a) 0-0 (aggregate 3-0).**
Boulton, Webster, Robson, Hennessey, McFarland, Todd, McGovern, Gemmill, O,Hare, Hector, Hinton.
Att: 75,000.

**Round 3: v Spartak Trnava (Czechoslovakia).**
**Mar 7, 1st leg (a) 0-1.**
Boulton, Powell, Nish, O'Hare, McFarland, Todd, McGovern, Gemmill, Davies, Hector, Durban.
Att: 28,000.

**Mar 21, 2nd leg (h) 2-0 (aggregate 2-1).**
*Hector 2.*
Boulton, Webster, Nish, O'Hare, McFarland, Todd, McGovern, Gemmill, Davies, Hector, Hinton.
Att: 36,472.

**Semi-final: v Juventus (Italy).**
**Apr 11, 1st leg (a) 1-3.**
*Hector.*
Boulton, Webster, Nish, Durban, McFarland, Todd, McGovern, Hector, O'Hare, Gemmill, Powell.
Att: 72,000.

**Apr 25, 2nd leg (h) 0-0 (aggregate 1-3).**
Boulton, Webster, Nish, Powell (Durban), Daniel (Sims), Todd, McGovern, O'Hare, Davies, Hector, Hinton.
Att: 35,350.

Dino Zoff denies the Rams again in the European Cup semi-final tie in the second leg at the Baseball Ground.

### 1975-76

**Round 1: v Slovan Bratislava (Czechoslovakia).**
**Sep 17, 1st leg (a) 0-1.**
Boulton, Thomas, Nish, Rioch, McFarland, Todd, Newton, Gemmill, Lee (Bourne), Powell, George.
Att: 45,000.

**Oct 1, 2nd leg (h) 3-0 (aggregate 3-1).**
*Lee 2, Bourne.*
Boulton, Thomas, Nish, Rioch, McFarland, Todd, Newton (Bourne), Gemmill, Lee, Hector, George.
Att: 30,888.

**Round 2: v Real Madrid (Spain).**
**Oct 22, 1st leg (h) 4-1.**
*George 3 (2 pen), Nish.*
Boulton, Thomas, Nish, Rioch, McFarland, Todd, Newton, Gemmill, Lee, Hector (Bourne), George (Davies).
Att: 34,839.

**Nov 5, 2nd leg (a) 1-5 [after extra-time] (aggregate 5-6).**
*George.*
Boulton, Thomas, Nish, Powell, McFarland, Todd, Newton, Gemmill, Davies, Hector (Bourne [Hinton]), George.
Att: 120,000.

# UEFA Cup

### 1974-75

**Round 1: v Servette Geneva (Switzerland).**
**Sep 18, 1st leg (h) 4-1.**
*Hector 2, Daniel, Lee.*
Boulton, Webster, Nish, Rioch, Daniel, Todd, Newton (Hinton), Gemmill, Bourne, Hector, Lee.
Att: 17,716.

**Oct 2, 2nd leg (a) 2-1 (aggregate 6-2).**
*Lee, Hector.*
Boulton, Webster, Nish, Rioch, Daniel, Todd, Newton, Gemmill, Bourne, Hector, Lee.
Att: 9,600.

Charlie George beats Real Madrid's goalkeeper Miguel from the penalty spot to complete his hat-trick and the Rams' scoring in the great 4-1 European Cup triumph at the Baseball Ground in October 1975.

**Round 2: v Atletico Madrid (Spain).**
**Oct 23, 1st leg (h) 2-2.**
*Nish, Rioch (pen).*
Boulton, Webster, Nish, Rioch, Daniel, Todd, Newton, Gemmill, Bourne (Hinton), Hector, Lee.
Att: 29,347.

**Nov 6, 2nd leg (a) 2-2 (aggregate 4-4). Derby won 7-6 on penalties after extra-time.**
*Rioch, Hector.*
Boulton, Webster, Nish, Rioch, Daniel, Powell, Newton, Gemmill, Davies, Hector, Lee.
Att: 35,000.

**Round 3: v Velez Mostar (Yugoslavia).**
**Nov 27, 1st leg (h) 3-1.**
*Bourne 2, Hinton.*
Boulton, Webster, Nish, Rioch, Daniel, Todd, Newton, Gemmill, Davies (Bourne), Hector, Lee (Hinton).
Att: 26,131.

**Dec 11, 2nd leg (a) 1-4 (aggregate 4-5).**
*Hector.*
Boulton, Webster, Thomas, Rioch, Daniel, Todd, Newton, Gemmill, Bourne (Davies), Hector, Lee (Hinton).
Att: 15,000.

Plenty of goals at the Baseball Ground as Kevin Hector scores one of his five goals in the Rams' record 12-0 defeat of Finn Harps in the 1976-77 UEFA Cup.

## 1976-77

**Round 1: v Finn Harps (Republic of Ireland).**
**Sep 15, 1st leg (h), 12-0.**
*Hector 5, George 3, James 3, Rioch.*
Moseley, Thomas, Nish, Rioch, McFarland, Todd (King), Macken, Gemmill, Hector, George, James.
Att: 13,353.

**Sep 29, 2nd leg (a) 4-1 (aggregate 16-1).**
*Hector 2, George 2.*
Moseley, Thomas, Nish, Rioch, McFarland (Webster), Todd, Newton, Gemmill (Macken), Hector, George, James.
Att: 2,217.

**Round 2: v AEK Athens (Greece).**
**Oct 20, 1st leg (a) 0-2.**
Moseley, Thomas, Nish, Macken, McFarland, Todd, Powell, Gemmill (King), Rioch, George, James.
Att: 32,000.

**Nov 3, 2nd leg (h) 2-3 (aggregate 2-5).**
*George, Rioch.*
Moseley, Thomas (Macken), Newton, Rioch, McFarland, Todd, Powell, Gemmill, Hector, George (Bourne), James.
Att: 28,000.

# Rams in Other Competitions

## Watney Cup

### 1970-71

**Round 1:**
**Aug 1, v Fulham (a) 5-3, after extra-time.**
*Hector 2, Durban 2, O'Hare.*
Green, Webster, Robson, Durban, McFarland, Mackay (Daniel), Wignall, Carlin, O'Hare, Hector, Hinton (McGovern).
Att: 18,501.

**Semi-final:**
**Aug 5, v Sheffield United (h) 1-0.**
*McGovern.*
Green, Webster, Robson, Durban, McFarland, Mackay, McGovern, Carlin, O'Hare (Wignall), Hector, Hinton.
Att: 25,322.

**Final:**
**Aug 8, v Manchester United (h) 4-1.**
*McFarland, Hinton, Durban, Mackay.*
Green, Webster, Robson, Durban, McFarland, Mackay, McGovern, Carlin, O'Hare, Hector, Hinton.
Att: 32,049.

## Texaco Cup

### 1971-72

**Round 1: v Dundee United.**
**Sep 15, 1st leg (h) 6-2.**
*Durban, Hector, Walker, O'Hare, Hinton, Robson.*
Boulton, Webster, Robson, Todd, Hennessey, McGovern, Bourne, Durban (Walker), O'Hare, Hector, Hinton.
Att: 20,059.

**Sep 29, 2nd leg (a) 2-3 (aggregate 8-5).**
*Hinton, Butlin.*
Boulton, Daniel, Robson, Hennessey, Bailey, Gemmill, McGovern, Wignall, Butlin, Walker, Hinton.
Att: 6,000.

**Round 2: v Stoke City.**
**Oct 20, 1st leg (h) 3-2.**
*O'Hare 2, Hector.*
Boulton, Daniel, Lewis, Hennessey (Bailey), McFarland, Todd, Wignall, Powell, O'Hare, Hector, Hinton.
Att: 21,487.

**Nov 3, 2nd leg (a) 1-1 (aggregate 4-3).**
*Wignall.*
Boulton, Webster, Robson, Todd, Hennessey, McGovern, Durban, Wignall, O'Hare, Hector, Hinton.
Att: 23,461.

**Semi-final: v Newcastle United.**
**Nov 24, 1st leg (h) 1-0.**
*O'Hare.*
Boulton, Webster, Robson, Todd, McFarland, Hennessey, McGovern, Gemmill, O'Hare, Hector, Hinton.
Att: 20,201.

**Dec 8, 2nd leg (a) 3-2, after extra-time (aggregate 4-2).**
*McGovern, Todd, Walker.*
Boulton, Todd, Webster, Hennessey, Bailey, Daniel, Durban, McGovern, O'Hare, Hector, Hinton (Walker).
Att: 37,000.

**Final: v Airdrieonians.**
**Jan 26, 1st leg (a) 0-0.**
Boulton, Webster, Robson, Todd, Daniel, Hennessey, Parry, Gemmill, Butlin, Walker, Hinton.
Att: 16,000.

**Apr 26, 2nd leg (h) 2-1 (aggregate 2-1).**
*Hinton (pen), Davies.*
Boulton, Powell, Robson, Durban, Daniel, Hennessey, McGovern, Butlin, Davies, Hector, Hinton.
Att: 25,102.

# Associate Members' Cup (Freight Rover Trophy)

## 1984-85

**Round 1: v Walsall.**
**Feb 6, 1st leg (h) 1-0.**
*Davison.*
Steele, Palmer, Buckley, Powell (Blades), Pratley, Hooks, Ablett (Biggins), Garner, Davison, Lewis, Robertson.
Att: 3,950.

**Feb 19, 2nd leg (a) 3-5 (aggregate 4-5).**
*Christie, Davison, Taylor.*
Steele, Blades, Buckley, Lewis, Pratley, Streete, Ablett, Taylor (Hooks), Davison, Christie, Robertson.
Att: 3,663.

## 1985-86

**Southern Qualifying Group.**
**Jan 15, v Brentford (a) 0-0.**
Steele, Palmer, Harbey, Lewis, Pratley, Blades, Penney, Gee, Biggins, McClaren (Gregory), Garner (Chandler).
Att: 2,531.

**Jan 22, v Gillingham (h) 0-2.**
Wallington, Blades, Buckley, Williams (Harbey), Hindmarch, MacLaren, Micklewhite, Christie (Gee), Garner, Gregory, Chandler.
Att: 3,721.

# Full Members' Cup

## 1986-87

**Round 1:**
**Sep 16, v Oldham Athletic (a) 1-0.**
*Micklewhite.*
Wallington, Sage, Forsyth, G.Williams, Pratley, MacLaren, Micklewhite, Gee, Davison, Gregory, Chandler.
Att: 3,074.
**Round 2:**
**Nov 12, v Aston Villa (a) 1-4.**
*Micklewhite.*
Wallington, Sage, Forsyth, G.Williams, Hindmarch, MacLaren, Micklewhite, Gee, Davison, Gregory (Penney), Harbey (Cross).
Att: 5,124.

## 1987-88 (Simod Cup)

**Round 1:**
**Nov 25, v Birmingham City (h) 3-1 (after extra-time).**
*McCord, Garner, Trewick (og).*
Shilton, MacLaren, Forsyth, G.Williams, Wright, Blades, Callaghan, Garner, Gee (Penney), Gregory (McCord), Cross.
Att: 8,227.

**Round 2:**
**Dec 23, v Swindon Town (a) 1-2.**
*Penney.*
Shilton, Sage, Forsyth, G.Williams, Hindmarch, Blades, Callaghan, Garner (Penney), Gee, Lewis, McClaren.
Att: 8,133.

## 1988-89 (Simod Cup)

**Round 1:**
**Nov 9, v AFC Bournemouth (h) 1-0.**
*Saunders.*
Shilton, Patterson, Forsyth, G.Williams, Wright, Blades (Cross), McMinn, Saunders, Goddard, Hebberd, Callaghan.
Att: 7,897.

**Round 2:**
**Nov 23, v Aston Villa (h) 2-1.**
*Micklewhite 2.*
Shilton, Sage, Forsyth, G.Williams, Wright, Blades, McMinn, Saunders, Goddard (Cross), Hebberd, Micklewhite.
Att: 10,086.

**Round 3:**
**Dec 21, v Wimbledon (a) 0-0. Wimbledon won 4-3 on penalties after extra-time.**
Shilton, Blades, Forsyth, G.Williams, Wright, Hindmarch, McMinn, Saunders, Goddard (Cross), Hebberd, Callaghan.
Att: 1,386.

## 1989-90 (Zenith Data Systems Cup)

**Round 2:**
**Nov 29, v West Bromwich Albion (a) 5-0.**
*Saunders 3, Goddard, Micklewhite.*
Shilton, Sage, Forsyth, G.Williams, Wright (Cross), Hindmarch, Pickering, Saunders (Francis), Goddard, Hebberd, Micklewhite.
Att: 4,880.

**Round 3:**
**Dec 20, v Newcastle United (a) 2-3, after extra-time.**
*Cross 2.*
Shilton, Sage, Forsyth, G.Williams, Wright, Hindmarch (Blades), Gee (Ramage), Saunders, Goddard, Hebberd, Cross.
Att:6,800.

## 1990-91 (Zenith Data Systems Cup)

**Round 2:**
**Dec 19, v Coventry City (h) 1-0.**
*Callaghan.*
Taylor, Sage, Pickering, P.Williams, Kavanagh, Forsyth, Micklewhite, Saunders, Harford, Hebberd (Ramage), Callaghan.
Att: 7,270.

**Northern quarter-final:**
**Jan 22, v Leeds United (a) 1-2.**
*Saunders.*
Shilton, Sage, Forsyth, G.Williams, Wright, Kavanagh, Cross, Saunders, Harford, Hebberd (Patterson), Pickering.
Att: 6,334.

## 1991-92 (Zenith Data Systems Cup)

**Round 2:**
**Oct 22, v Middlesbrough (a) 2-4, after extra-time.**
*Micklewhite, Stallard.*
Taylor, Patterson, Forsyth, Hayward, Coleman, Comyn, Micklewhite, Stallard (Chalk), Gee, P.Williams (Davidson), McMinn.
Att: 6,385.

# Anglo-Italian Cup

## 1992-93

**Preliminary round:**
**Sep 2, v Notts County (h) 4-2.**
*Williams, Pembridge, Simpson, Gabbiadini.*
Sutton, Kavanagh, Forsyth, Pembridge, Coleman, Wassall, McMinn (Gabbiadini), Kitson, Johnson, Williams, Simpson.
Att: 6,767.

**Sep 29, v Barnsley (a) 2-1.**
*Pembridge, Goulooze.*
Sutton, Comyn, Forsyth, Coleman, Wassall, Pembridge, Johnson, Goulooze (Kavanagh), Kitson, Gabbiadini (Hayward), Simpson.
Att: 3,960.

**International Group B:**
**Nov 11, v Pisa (h) 3-0.**
*Johnson, Forsyth, Pembridge.*
Sutton, Comyn, Forsyth, Coleman, Wassall, Pembridge, Johnson, Williams, McMinn, Gabbiadini, Simpson.
Att: 8,059.

**Nov 24, v Cosenza (a) 3-0.**
*Comyn, Kitson, Gabbiadini.*
Sutton, Comyn, Forsyth, Coleman, Wassall (Kavanagh), Pembridge, Johnson, Williams, Kitson, Gabbiadini, McMinn.
Att: 4,263.

**Dec 8, v US Cremonese (h) 1-3.**
*Kitson.*
Sutton, Goulooze (Kavanagh), Forsyth, Coleman, Wassall, Pembridge, McMinn (Hayward), Williams, Kitson, Gabbiadini, Simpson.
Att: 7,050.

**Dec 16, v Reggiana (a) 3-0.**
*Kitson, Pembridge, Gabbiadini.*
Taylor, Kavanagh, Forsyth, Comyn, Coleman, Pembridge, Johnson (Simpson), Hayward, Kitson (Micklewhite), Gabbiadini, McMinn.
Att: 598.

**Semi-final: v Brentford.**
**Jan 27, 1st leg (a) 4-3.**
*Patterson 2, Gabbiadini, Kitson.*
Sutton, Kavanagh, Forsyth, Coleman, Wassall, Pembridge, Johnson, Comyn, Kitson, Gabbiadini, Patterson.
Att: 5,227.

**Feb 3, 2nd leg (h) 1-2 (aggregate 5-5. Derby won on away goals).**
*Gabbiadini.*
Sutton, Kavanagh, Forsyth, Coleman, Comyn, Pembridge, Johnson, McMinn (Williams), Kitson, Gabbiadini (Micklewhite), Patterson.
Att: 14,494.

**Final: v US Cremonese.**
**Mar 27, (Wembley) 1-3.**
*Gabbiadini.*
Taylor, Patterson, Forsyth, Nicholson, Coleman, Pembridge, Micklewhite, Goulooze (Hayward), Kitson, Gabbiadini, Johnson (Simpson).
Att: 37,024.

## 1993-94

**Preliminary round:**
**Aug 31, v Notts County (a) 2-3.**
*Harkes, Johnson.*
Taylor, Charles, Forsyth, Kuhl, Short, Wassall, Harkes, Pembridge, Kitson, Johnson, Simpson.
Att: 3,276.

**Sep 8, v Nottingham Forest (h) 3-2.**
*Simpson, Kitson, Kuhl.*
Taylor, Charles, Forsyth, Kuhl, Short, Wassall, Johnson, Williams, Kitson, Gabbiadini, Simpson.
Att: 6,654.

## 1994-95

**International Group B:**
**Aug 24, v Ancona (a) 1-2.**
*Pembridge.*
Taylor, Charles, Forsyth, Kuhl, Nicholson (Kavanagh), Wassall, Stallard, Hayward (Cowans), Gabbiadini, Pembridge, Simpson.
Att: 748.

**Sep 6, v Cesena (h) 6-1.**
*Kitson 4, Hodge 2.*
Taylor, Charles (Kavanagh), Nicholson, Hodge, Short, Wassall, Cowans, Carsley, Kitson, Gabbiadini (Sturridge), Simpson.
Att: 2,010.

**Oct 5, v Piacenza (a) 1-1.**
*Williams.*
Sutton, Charles, Nicholson (Kavanagh), Carsley (Davies), Wassall, Williams, Cowans, Sturridge, Harkes, Pembridge, Simpson.
Att: 1,710.

**Nov 15, v Udinese (h) 3-1.**
*Johnson 2, Stallard.*
Sutton, Charles (Kavanagh), Nicholson, Kuhl, Short, Williams, Harkes, Carsley, Johnson (Cooper), Stallard, Sturridge.
Att: 1,562 .

# Other appearances by competition

## Test Match (1894-95)

S. Bloomer 1, J. Cox 1, P. Francis 1, A. Goodall 1, J. Goodall 1, J. Leiper 1, J. McMillan 1, J. Methven 1, J. Paul 1, J. Robinson 1, J. Staley 1.
*Goalscorers: Bloomer 1, McMillan 1.*

## Texaco Cup (1971-72)

C. Boulton 8, T. Hennessey 8, A. Hinton 8, K. Hector 6, J. McGovern 6, J. Robson 6, C. Todd 6, P. Daniel 5, J. O'Hare 5, R. Webster 5, A. Durban 4, J. Walker 2/2, B. Butlin 3, A. Gemmill 3, F. Wignall 3, A. Bailey 2/1, R. McFarland 2, S. Powell 2, J. Bourne 1, R. Davies 1, A. Lewis 1, A. Parry 1.
*Goalscorers: O'Hare 4, Hinton 3, Hector 2, Walker 2, Butlin 1, Davies 1, Durban 1, McGovern 1, Robson 1, Todd 1, Wignall 1.*

## European Cup (1972-73 and 1975-76)

C. Boulton 12, C. Todd 12, A. Gemmill 11, K. Hector 11, R. McFarland 11, J. McGovern 8, D. Nish 8, J. O'Hare 8, A. Hinton 6/1, S. Powell 6, R. Davies 4/1, P. Daniel 4, C. George 4, T. Hennessey 4, H. Newton 4, R. Thomas 4, R. Webster 4, J. Bourne 0/4, F. Lee 3, B. Rioch 3, J. Robson 3, A. Durban 2/1, J. Sims 0/1.
*Goalscorers: George 4, Hector 4, Lee 2, McFarland 2, Bourne 1, Gemmill 1, Hinton 1, McGovern 1, Nish 1, O'Hare 1.*

## UEFA Cup (1974-75 and 1976-77)

A. Gemmill 10, B. Rioch 10, K. Hector 9, C. Todd 9, H. Newton 8, D. Nish 8, R. Webster 6/1, C. Boulton 6, P. Daniel 6, F. Lee 6, J. Bourne 4/2, R. Thomas 5, C. George 4, L. James 4, R. McFarland 4, G. Moseley 4, A. Macken 2/2, A. Hinton 0/4, S. Powell 3, R. Davies 2/1, J. King 0/2.
*Goalscorers: Hector 12, George 6, Rioch 4, James 3, Bourne 2, Lee 2, Daniel 1, Hinton 1, Nish 1.*

## FA Charity Shield (1975–76)

C. Boulton 1, A. Gemmill 1, C. George 1, K. Hector 1, F. Lee 1, R. McFarland 1, H. Newton 1, D. Nish 1, B. Rioch 1, R. Thomas 1, C. Todd 1.
*Goalscorers: Hector 1, McFarland 1.*

## Associate Members' (Freight/Rover) Trophy (1984-85 and 1985-86)

P. Blades 3/1, S. Buckley 3, A. Garner 3, M. Lewis 3, R. Pratley 3, E. Steele 3, G. Ablett 2, T. Christie 2, R. Davison 2, C. Palmer 2, J. Robertson 2, S. Biggins 1/1, J. Chandler 1/1, P. Gee 1/1, J. Gregory 1/1, G. Harbey 1/1, P. Hooks 1/1, R. Hindmarch 1, S. McClaren 1, R. MacLaren 1, G. Micklewhite 1, D. Penney 1, S. Powell 1, F. Streete 1, K. Taylor 1, M. Wallington 1, G. Williams 1.
*Goalscorers: Davison 2, Christie 1, Taylor 1.*

## Full Members' (Simod) Cup (1986-87 to 1991-92)

M. Forsyth 12, G. Williams 10, M. Sage 8, P. Shilton 8, S. Cross 3/5, T. Hebberd 7, D. Saunders 7, M. Wright 7, P. Gee 6, G. Micklewhite 6, P. Blades 5/1, N. Callaghan 5, P. Goddard 5, R. Hindmarch 5, K. McMinn 4, J. Gregory 3, R. MacLaren 3, N. Pickering 3, M. Patterson 2/1, D. Penney 0/3, R. Davison 2, A. Garner 2, M. Harford 2, J. Kavanagh 2, M. Taylor 2, M. Wallington 2, P. Williams 2, C. Ramage 0/2, J. Chandler 1, S. Coleman 1, A. Comyn 1, G. Harbey 1, S. Hayward 1, M. Lewis 1, S. McClaren 1, R. Pratley 1, M. Stallard 1, M. Chalk 0/1, J. Davidson 0/1, K. Francis 0/1, B. McCord 0/1.
*Goalscorers: Micklewhite 6, Saunders 5, Cross 2, Callaghan 1, Garner 1, Goddard 1, McCord 1, Penney 1, Stallard 1, Trewick (Birmingham City) og 1.*

### Division Two Play-offs (1991-92 and 1993–94)

M. Forsyth 5, M. Gabbiadini 5, T. Johnson 5, P. Simpson 5, P. Williams 5, G. Charles 3, G. Cowans 3, J. Harkes 3, M. Pembridge 3, C. Short 3, M. Taylor 3, J. Kavanagh 2/1, P. Kitson 2/1, S. Coleman 2, A. Comyn 2, K. McMinn 2, S. Sutton 2, S. Hayward 0/1, G. Micklewhite 0/1, C. Ramage 0/1.

*Goalscorers: Johnson 4, Gabbiadini 2, Comyn 1, Cowans 1, McMinn 1, Van Den Hauwe (Millwall) og 1.*

### Anglo-Italian Cup (1992–93, 1993–94 and 1994–95)

M. Forsyth 12, M. Pembridge 12, M. Gabbiadini 11/1, T. Johnson 11, P. Kitson 11, D. Wassall 11, P. Simpson 9/2, J. Kavanagh 4/7, S. Coleman 9, S. Sutton 9, P. Williams 7/1, G. Charles 6, A. Comyn 6, K. McMinn 6, M. Taylor 6, S. Nicholson 5, S. Hayward 2/3, M. Kuhl 4, C. Short 4, L. Carsley 3, R. Goulooze 3, J. Harkes 3, M. Patterson 3, G. Cowans 2/1, D. Sturridge 2/1, G. Micklewhite 1/2, M. Stallard 2, S. Hodge 1, K. Cooper 0/1, W. Davies 0/1.

*Goalscorers: Kitson 9, Gabbiadini 6, Pembridge 5, Johnson 4, Hodge 2, Patterson 2, Simpson 2, Williams 2, Comyn 1, Forsyth 1, Goulooze 1, Harkes 1, Kuhl 1, Stallard 1.*

# Records

## 100 Consecutive Appearances

### League

| | | |
|---|---|---|
| 151 | Archie Goodall | Oct 1892 to Sep 1897 |
| 122 | Steve Buckley | Nov 1983 to May 1986 |
| 117 | Steve Buckley | Jan 1978 to Nov 1980 |
| 112 | Gary Micklewhite | Feb 1985 to Sep 1987 |
| 108 | Peter Shilton | Aug 1987 to Mar 1990 |
| 107 | Les Green | Aug 1968 to Dec 1970 |
| 106 | Dean Saunders | Oct 1988 to May 1991 |
| 105 | Bobby Davison | Sep 1983 to Dec 1985 |
| 105 | Kevin Hector | Mar 1970 to Oct 1972 |
| 104 | Jack Nicholas | Jan 1937 to Sep 1946 |

### All Matches

| | | |
|---|---|---|
| 167 | Archie Goodall | Oct 1892 to Sep 1897 |
| 131 | Colin Boulton | Jan 1971 to April 1973 |
| 130 | Dean Saunders | Nov 1988 to May 1991 |
| 130 | Colin Todd | Nov 1974 to Mar 1977 |
| 129 | Les Green | Aug 1968 to Dec 1970 |
| 127 | Steve Buckley | Jan 1978 to Nov 1980 |
| 126 | Bobby Davison | Sep 1983 to Dec 1985 |
| 124 | Michael Forsyth | April 1988 to Jan 1991 |
| 124 | Peter Shilton | Aug 1987 to Mar 1990 |
| 120 | Jack Nicholas | Jan 1937 to Sep 1946 |
| 119 | Steve Buckley | Nov 1983 to Jan 1986 |
| 115 | Colin Boulton | Apr 1973 to Sep 1975 |
| 113 | Kevin Hector | Nov 1972 to Dec 1974 |
| 109 | Jack Nicholas | Jan 1933 to Apr 1935 |
| 100 | Geraint Williams | Nov 1988 to Nov 1990 |

## Individual Scoring Feats

### Six goals in a game

S. Bloomer v Sheffield Wednesday (h), Division One, 21 Jan 1899.

### Five goals in a game

A. Higgins v Aston Villa (h), Football League, 28 Dec 1889.

J. McMillan v Wolves (h), Football League, 10 Jan 1891.

J. Moore v Crystal Palace (h), Division Two, 25 Dec 1922.

H. Gallacher v Blackburn Rovers (a), Division One, 15 Dec 1934.

R. Davies v Luton Town (h), Division One, 29 Mar, 1975.

K. Hector v Finn Harps (h), UEFA Cup, 15 Sep 1976.

### Four goals in a game

A. Higgins v Aston Villa (h), Football League, 9 Mar 1889.

S. Bloomer v Wolves (h), Division One, 19 Sep 1896.

J. Stevenson v Blackburn Rovers (h), Division One, 21 Nov 1896.

A. Bentley v Barnsley (a), Division Two, 14 Sep 1907.

A. Bentley v Leeds City (h), Division Two, 19 Oct 1907.

A. Bentley v Leeds City (a), Division Two, 19 Sep 1908.

H. Leonard v Fulham (h), Division Two, 4 Nov 1911.

J. Lyons v Rotherham County (h), Division Two, 29 Apr 1922.

H. Storer v Bristol City (a), Division Two, 29 Sep 1923.

H. Storer v Nelson (h), Division Two, 26 Dec 1923.

A. Fairclough v Fulham (h), Division Two, 13 Sep 1924.

H. Bedford v Bradford City (a), FA Cup, 8 Jan 1927.

J. Whitehouse v Sheffield Wednesday (h), Division One, 19 Mar 1927.

H. Bedford v Cardiff City (h), Division One, 31 Mar 1928.

H. Bedford v West Ham United (h), Division One, 8 Dec 1928.

G. Stephenson v Grimsby Town (h), Division One, 14 Dec 1929.

J. Bowers v Chelsea (h), Division One, 6 Dec 1930.

J. Bowers v Portsmouth (h), Division One, 7 Feb 1931.

J. Bowers v Manchester United (h), Division One, 18 Apr 1931.

J. Bowers v Tottenham Hotspur (h), Division One, 7 Apr 1934.

J. Bowers v Manchester United (h), Division One, 5 Sep 1936.

J. Stamps v Luton Town (a), FA Cup, 5 Jan 1946.

H. Carter v Sunderland (h), Division One, 14 Feb 1948.

J. Stamps v Blackpool (h), Division One, 30 Sep 1950.

J. Lee v Sunderland (h), Division One, 16 Dec 1950.

A. Ackerman v Accrington Stanley (h), Division Three North, 7 Apr 1956.

A. Hinton v Stockport County (h), League Cup, 4 Sep 1968.

B. Rioch v Tottenham Hotspur (h), Division One, 16 Oct 1976.

K. Wilson v Hartlepool United (h), League Cup, 29 Aug 1984.

P. Kitson v Cesena (h), Anglo-Italian Cup, 6 Sep 1994.

## Three goals in a game

| | |
|---|---|
| 18 times | S. Bloomer |
| 11 | J. Bowers |
| 10 | H. Bedford |
| 6 | K. Hector |
| 5 | J. Bauchop, A. Bentley, J. Goodall |
| 4 | A. Durban, J. Stamps |
| 3 | D. Astley, W. Curry, R. Davison, C. George, J. Lee, D. Saunders, P. Simpson, R. Straw |
| 2 | K. Havenhand, J. McMillan, J. Morris, J. Parry, B. Spilsbury |
| 1 | T. Arkesden, R. Barclay, H. Barnes, A. Biley, J. Boag, H. Carter, J. Chandler, S. Crooks, R. Davies, A. Fairclough, N. Fordham, M. Gabbiadini, H. Gallacher, A. Garner, E. Garry, A. Gemmill, J. Gill, M. Harford, R. Harrison, W. Hodgkinson, W. Hodgson, L. James, H. Leonard, J. Miller, J. Moore, A. Morrison, J. O'Hare, W. Paterson, M. Pembridge, J. Pye, G. Stephenson, R. Stockill, H. Storer, B. Warren, P. Williams, K. Wilson |

Steve Bloomer scored 18 hat-tricks for Derby.

## Top 20 Scorers

| All Matches | | | League Matches | | |
|---|---|---|---|---|---|
| 1. | Steve Bloomer | 332 | 1. | Steve Bloomer | 293 |
| 2. | Kevin Hector | 201 | 2. | Jack Bowers | 167 |
| 3. | Jack Bowers | 183 | 3. | Kevin Hector | 155 |
| 4. | Harry Bedford | 152 | 4. | Harry Bedford | 142 |
| 5. | Jack Stamps | 126 | 5. | Jack Parry | 105 |
| =6. | Alf Bentley | 112 | 6. | Sammy Crooks | 101 |
| =6. | Alan Durban | 112 | 7. | Jack Stamps | 100 |
| 8. | Sammy Crooks | 111 | 8. | Alf Bentley | 99 |
| 9. | Jack Parry | 110 | 9. | Alan Durban | 93 |
| 10. | Bobby Davison | 106 | 10. | Bobby Davison | 91 |
| 11. | Jackie Whitehouse | 86 | 11. | Jackie Whitehouse | 82 |
| 12. | John Goodall | 85 | 12. | John Goodall | 76 |
| 13. | Alan Hinton | 83 | 13. | Jimmy Moore | 75 |
| 14. | Jimmy Moore | 82 | 14. | Horace Barnes | 74 |
| 15. | John O'Hare | 81 | 15. | Harry Leonard | 72 |
| 16. | Horace Barnes | 78 | 16. | Jimmy Bauchop | 68 |
| 17. | Bill Curry | 76 | 17. | Bill Curry | 67 |
| 18. | Harry Leonard | 73 | 18. | John O'Hare | 65 |
| 19. | Jimmy Bauchop | 72 | 19. | Alan Hinton | 64 |
| 20. | Douglas Duncan | 69 | 20. | Douglas Duncan | 63 |

Totals include League, FA Cup, League Cup, League Test Match, League Play-offs, FA Charity Shield, European Cup, UEFA Cup, Texaco Cup, Freight/Rover Trophy, Full Members' Cup and the Anglo-Italian Cup. The Watney Cup is not included as it was played out of season and, in some years, with experimental laws.

## Top 20 Appearances

| All Matches | | | League Matches | | |
|---|---|---|---|---|---|
| 1. | Kevin Hector | 581/8 | 1. | Kevin Hector | 478/8 |
| 2. | Ron Webster | 530/5 | 2. | Jack Parry | 482/1 |
| 3. | Roy McFarland | 525/5 | 3. | Geoff Barrowcliffe | 475 |
| 4. | Steve Bloomer | 525 | 4. | Steve Bloomer | 474 |
| 5. | Jack Parry | 516/1 | 5. | Jimmy Methven | 458 |
| 6. | Jimmy Methven | 511 | 6. | Ron Webster | 451/4 |
| 7. | Geoff Barrowcliffe | 503 | 7. | Roy McFarland | 437/5 |
| 8. | Sammy Crooks | 445 | 8. | Sammy Crooks | 408 |
| 9. | Archie Goodall | 423 | =9. | Archie Goodall | 380 |
| 10. | Steve Powell | 409/11 | =9. | Tommy Powell | 380 |
| 11. | Tommy Powell | 406 | 11. | Steve Powell | 342/10 |
| 12. | Michael Forsyth | 403/3 | 12. | Johnny McIntyre | 349 |
| 13. | Archie Gemmill | 404 | 13. | Jack Nicholas | 347 |
| 14. | Alan Durban | 388/15 | 14. | Alan Durban | 336/10 |
| 15. | Jack Nicholas | 383 | 15. | Jack Barker | 326 |
| 16. | Colin Todd | 371 | 16. | Michael Forsyth | 323/2 |
| 17. | Johnny McIntyre | 369 | 17. | Archie Gemmill | 324 |
| 18. | Steve Buckley | 366 | 18. | Steve Buckley | 323 |
| 19. | Jack Barker | 353 | 19. | George Collin | 309 |
| 20. | Colin Boulton | 344 | 20. | Jack Atkin | 308 |

Totals include League, FA Cup, League Cup, League Test Match, League Play-offs, FA Charity Shield, European Cup, UEFA Cup, Texaco Cup, Freight/Rover Trophy, Full Members' Cup and the Anglo-Italian Cup. The Watney Cup is not included as it was played out of season and, in some years, with experimental laws.

# Rams in Wartime

WHEN World War One was declared in August 1914, the football authorities decided to carry on, despite criticism that it was unpatriotic to do so. For Derby County, of course, it was as well they did, and in 1914–15 they won promotion to Division One. The Rams played one season in the wartime Midland Section, in 1915–16, before closing down for the duration with most of the players guesting for other clubs, particularly Notts County. When peace came in November 1918, it was too late to start a proper Football League competition, but in April 1919, the Rams played in the small Midland Victory League to prepare themselves for the resumption of League soccer proper that August.

Twenty years later, war with Germany again interrupted the soccer programme. This time the League closed down after two weekends, and the three matches of the 1939–40 season which Derby did manage to play are not included in the career records of the players in this book.

The Rams were offered a place in a substitute competition, but after playing a friendly match against Leeds United at the Baseball Ground towards the end of September 1939, to test public opinion, Derby County decided to suspend operations when fewer than 2,000 spectators turned up.

Rams players still in the surrounding district turned out for several local clubs, both League and non-League, and on Christmas Day 1941, a match against a Royal Air Force team heralded the return of soccer to the Baseball Ground.

The Rams played several more matches in the second half of that season, relying heavily on youngsters and guest players, and with Jack Nicholas manager in all but name.

Nicholas received valuable assistance from Jack Webb, the pre-war full-back, and in 1942–43 the Rams began to play in the Football League North. There was a strange look about the competitions at this time. The League programme was run two halves up to Christmas, at which point a champion club was declared, with another 'half' being contested in the New Year, although this was further confused by the Football League War Cup, and later, the Midland Cup.

Matches in these competitions also counted towards the second period of the Football League North. The Football League War Cup was run, in the first part, on a league qualifying basis, with successful teams then meeting in a home and away knockout competition.

The Rams played in the Football League North up to and including 1944–45, in which season they won the second period championship, beating Liverpool in a decider on Whit Monday. The Rams had finished runners-up to Huddersfield Town in the first period which ended at Christmas. This season Derby did the 'double', winning the Midland Cup after a two-leg final against Aston Villa. In 1945–46, with the FA Cup restarted on a two-leg basis – the Rams won it – Derby moved to the Football League South. This was a more familiar 42-match programme, in preparation for the resumption of the Football League in 1946–47. Derby County finished fourth in the Football League South which was won by Birmingham City.

Matches against teams representing the Police Athletic Association, the Army Commands, the Royal Air Force and other organisations were important because they included peacetime full-time professional players and often international stars.

Wartime soccer was often a lottery. When Bradford arrived at the Baseball Ground for a Midland Section match in April 1916, they had only seven men. The Rams lent them four reserves, namely Palethorpe, Haynes, Davis and Leigh, and went on to win 6–1.

**1915–16**

**MIDLAND SECTION**

**Sep 4 v Leeds City (h) 1–3**
*Leonard*
Lawrence; Atkin, Smith, Walker, Barbour, Bagshaw, Quantrill, Benfield, Leonard, Moore, Donald.
*Att: 2,000*

**Sep 11 v Hull City (a) 2–4**
*Leonard, Brooks*
Stone; Atkin, Smith, Walker, Barker, Povey, McMillan, Leigh, Leonard, Whittingham, Brooks.
*Att: 4,000*

**Sep 18 v Nottingham Forest (h) 3–4**
*Leonard 3*
Lawrence; Atkin, Smith, Walker, Barbour, Bagshaw, Benfield, Leigh, Leonard, Brooks, Donald.
*Att: 3,000*

**Sep 25 v Barnsley (a) 1–1**
*Leonard*
Stone; Atkin, Barbour, Walker, Povey, Brooks, Grimes, Leigh, Leonard, Benfield, Donald.
*Att: 3,000*

**Oct 2 v Leicester Fosse (h) 1–1**
*Leigh*
Stone; Atkin, Barbour, Walker, Povey, Benfield, Grimes, Leigh, Leonard, Moore, Donald.
*Att: 2,000*

**Oct 9 v Sheffield United (a) 0–2**
Stone; Atkin, F.Flanders, Walker, Povey, Barbour, Grimes, Leigh, Leonard, Moore, Donald.

**Oct 16 v Bradford City (h) 5–2**
*Leonard 3, Benfield, Leigh*
Stone; Atkin, F.Flanders, Walker, B.Hall, Barbour, Grimes, Leigh, Leonard, Benfield, Donald.
*Att: 2,000*

**Oct 23 v Huddersfield Town (a) 1–4**
*Leigh*
Stone; Atkin, F.Flanders, Walker, B.Hall, Smelt, Whittingham, Leigh, Leonard, Brooks, Donald.

**Oct 30 v Grimsby Town (h) 3–2**
*Leonard, Leigh, Pattinson (og)*
Stone; Atkin, F.Flanders, Walker, B.Hall, Brooks, Grimes, Leigh, Leonard, Meakin, Donald.
*Att: 3,000*

**Nov 6 v Notts County (a) 0–5**
Stone; Barbour, F.Flanders, Walker, B.Hall, E.Hall, Grimes, Leigh, Leonard, Brooks, Quantrill.

**Nov 13 v Lincoln City (h) 2–4**
*Crisp 2*
Stone; Atkin, F.Flanders, Barbour, E.Hall, Brooks, Grimes, Leigh, Leonard, Crisp, Donald.
*Att: 1,000*

**Nov 20 v Sheffield Wednesday (h) 1–5**
*Leigh*
Stone; Barbour, F.Flanders, Walker, E.Hall, Brooks, Grimes, Leigh, Leonard, Quantrill, Donald.

**Nov 27 v Bradford City (a) 3–2**
*Leonard 2, Leigh*
Barnett; Barbour, F.Flanders, Walker, Fletcher, Brooks, Grimes, Leigh, Leonard, Quantrill, Donald.

**Dec 4 v Leeds City (a) 1–4**
*Quantrill*
Stone; Barbour, F.Flanders, E.Hall, Fletcher, Brooks, Grimes, Leigh, Leonard, Quantrill, Donald.
*Att: 1,500*

**Dec 11 v Hull City (h) 3–1**
*Leonard 3*
Barnett; Atkin, F.Flanders, Barbour, Fletcher, Brooks, Jephcott, Leigh, Leonard, Donald, Kerle.
*Att: 1,000*

**Dec 18 v Nottingham Forest (a) 0–5**
Barnett; Atkin, F.Flanders, Barbour, Fletcher, B.Hall, Brooks, Leigh, Leonard, Moore, Donald.

**Dec 25 v Barnsley (h) 0–1**
Lawrence; Atkin, Skelton, Barbour, Crooks, Brooks, Walker, Leigh, Fletcher, Moore, Quantrill.
*Att: 2,000*

**Jan 1 v Leicester Fosse (a) 0–2**
Stone; Atkin, Barbour, Roe, Crooks, Fletcher, Walker, Brooks, Leonard, Quantrill, Donald.

**Jan 8 v Sheffield United (h) 2–1**
*Leonard, Donald*
Lawrence; Atkin, Skelton, Walker, Fletcher, Brooks, Jephcott, Leigh, Leonard, Quantrill, Donald.

**Jan 15 v Bradford City (a) 0–5**
Stone; Atkin, Brooks, Roe, Walker, Robinson, Moore, Leigh, Leonard, Quantrill, Donald.

**Jan 22 v Huddersfield Town (h) 1–4**
*Leonard*
Stone; Atkin, Heywood, Walker, Fletcher, Brooks, Grimes, Benfield, Leonard, Burton, Donald.

**Jan 29 v Grimsby Town (a) 1–2**
*Burton*

Alf Quantrill

Stone; Atkin, Haynes, Paxton, Fletcher, Walker, Quantrill, Greenlay, Leonard, Burton, Donald.

**Feb 5 v Notts County (h) 2–0**

*Leonard, Burton*

Lawrence; Atkin, Haynes, Walker, Fletcher, Brooks, Jephcott, Greenlay, Leonard, Burton, Donald.

**Feb 12 v Lincoln City (a) 0–1**

Stone; Atkin, Haynes, Walker, Fletcher, Brooks, Quantrill, Davis, Leonard, Burton, Donald.

**Feb 19 v Sheffield Wednesday (a) 0–5**

Palethorpe; Haynes, Skelton, Walker, Fletcher, Brooks, Davis, Congreve, Leonard, Burton, Donald.

**Apr 21 v Bradford (h) 6–1**

*Whitehouse 4, Donald, Taylor (og)*

Lawrence; Weston, Pennington, Walker, Benfield, Richards, Jephcott, Moore, Burton, Whitehouse, Timmins.

**Appearances:** Leonard 24, Donald 22, Walker 22, Atkin 20, Brooks 19, Leigh 18, Barbour 16, Stone 16, Fletcher (Glossop) 12, Grimes 12, F.Flanders (Newport County) 11, Quantrill 11, Benfield 7, Moore 7, Burton (Ilkeston United) 6, Lawrence 6, B.Hall (South Shields) 5, E.Hall (South Shields) 4, Haynes 4, Jephcott (West Brom) 4, Povey 4, Barnett (Leicester Fosse) 3, Skelton 3, Smith 3, Bagshaw 2, Crooks 2, Davis 2, Greenlay 2, Roe 2, Whittingham 2, Congreve 1, Crisp (West Brom) 1, Heywood (Ilkeston United) 1, Kerle 1, McMillan 1, Meakin 1, Palethorpe 1, Paxton 1, Pennington (Blackburn R) 1, Richards 1, Robinson 1, Smelt 1, Timmins 1, Weston 1, Whitehouse (Redditch) 1.

**Goalscorers:** Leonard 18, Leigh 6, Whitehouse 4, Burton 2, Crisp 2, Benfield 1, Brooks 1, Donald 1, Moore 1, Quantrill 1. Opponents own-goals: Pattinson (Grimsby T) 1, Taylor (Bradford) 1.

**Midland Section, Principal Tournament**

| | P | W | D | L | F | A | Pts |
|---|---|---|---|---|---|---|---|
| Nottingham Forest | 26 | 15 | 5 | 6 | 48 | 25 | 35 |
| Sheffield United | 26 | 12 | 7 | 7 | 51 | 36 | 31 |
| Huddersfield Town | 26 | 12 | 5 | 9 | 43 | 36 | 29 |
| Bradford City | 26 | 12 | 4 | 10 | 52 | 32 | 28 |
| Leicester Fosse | 26 | 11 | 6 | 9 | 42 | 34 | 28 |
| Barnsley | 26 | 12 | 4 | 10 | 46 | 55 | 28 |
| Sheffield Wednesday | 26 | 11 | 5 | 10 | 46 | 43 | 27 |
| Notts County | 26 | 10 | 6 | 10 | 39 | 36 | 26 |
| Lincoln City | 26 | 12 | 2 | 12 | 54 | 54 | 26 |
| Leeds City | 26 | 10 | 5 | 11 | 39 | 43 | 25 |
| Hull City | 26 | 10 | 3 | 13 | 42 | 58 | 23 |
| Bradford | 26 | 9 | 4 | 13 | 46 | 46 | 22 |
| Grimsby Town | 26 | 7 | 6 | 13 | 31 | 46 | 20 |
| DERBY COUNTY | 26 | 7 | 2 | 17 | 39 | 74 | 16 |

**1916**

**SUBSIDIARY TOURNAMENT**

**Mar 4 v Nottingham Forest (a) 0–3**

Palethorpe; Atkin, Haynes, Walker, Fletcher, Brooks, Greenlay, Davis, Leonard, Burton, Quantrill.

**Mar 11 v Leicester Fosse (h) 2–5**
*Burton, Leigh*
Palethorpe; Atkin, Haynes, Walker, Richards, Brooks, Fletcher, Leigh, Leonard, Burton, Quantrill.
**Mar 18 v Notts County (a) 1–3**
*Leonard*
Palethorpe; Atkin, Haynes, Walker, Richards, Brooks, Moore, Powell, Leonard, Burton, Timmins.
**Mar 25 v Chesterfield Town (h) 2–1**
*Burton, Leonard*
Pearson; Atkin, Weston, Walker, Hawley, Brooks, Jephcott, Davis, Leonard, Burton, Timmins.
**Apr 1 v Stoke (h) 4–2**
*Burton 3, Whitehouse*
Palethorpe; Atkin, Haynes, Walker, Hawley, Richards, Jephcott, Moore, Burton, Whitehouse, Timmins.
**Apr 8 v Nottingham Forest (h) 4–1**
*Burton 2, Davis, Timmins*
Pearson; Atkin, Weston, Walker, Hawley, Richards, Jephcott, Davis, Burton, Whitehouse, Timmins.
**Apr 15 v Leicester Fosse (a) 2–3**
*Whitehouse 2*
Palethorpe; Atkin, Weston, Walker, Hawley, Richards, Haynes, Davis, Burton, Whitehouse, Moore.
**Apr 22 v Notts County (h) 2–3**
*Burton 2*
Lawrence; Atkin, Haynes, Walker, Hawley, Richards, Reader, Moore, Burton, Whitehouse, Timmins.
**Apr 24 v Stoke (a) 1–6**
*Moore*
Haynes; Atkin, Brooks, Walker, Hawley, Richards, Reader, Leigh, Moore, Greaves, Timmins.
**Apr 29 v Chesterfield Town (a) 6–1**
*Moore 2, Whitehouse 2, Jephcott 2*
Pearson; Pennington, Weston, Walker, Hawley, Richards, Jephcott, Burton, Moore, Whitehouse, Timmins.
**Appearances:** Walker 10, Atkin 9, Burton (Ilkeston United) 9, Richards 8, Hawley (Sheffield U) 7, Haynes 7, Timmins 7, Moore 6, Brooks 5, Palethorpe 5, Whitehouse (Redditch) 5, Davis 4, Leonard 4, Jephcott (West Brom) 4, Weston (Aston Villa) 4, Pearson (West Brom) 3, Fletcher 2, Leigh 2, Quantrill 2, Reader 2, Greaves (Stoke) 1, Greenlay 1, Lawrence 1, Powell 1, Pennington (Blackburn R) 1.
**Goalscorers:** Burton 9, Whitehouse 5, Moore 3, Jephcott 2, Leonard 2, Davis 1, Leigh 1, Timmins 1.

**Subsidiary Tournament, Southern Division**

| | P | W | D | L | F | A | Pts |
|---|---|---|---|---|---|---|---|
| Nottingham Forest | 10 | 7 | 0 | 3 | 28 | 12 | 14 |
| Notts County | 10 | 5 | 3 | 2 | 16 | 13 | 13 |
| Leicester Fosse | 10 | 3 | 3 | 4 | 15 | 19 | 9 |
| Stoke | 10 | 4 | 0 | 6 | 21 | 18 | 8 |
| DERBY COUNTY | 10 | 4 | 0 | 6 | 24 | 28 | 8 |
| Chesterfield Town | 10 | 3 | 2 | 5 | 15 | 29 | 8 |

Six thousand people turned up to see Steve Bloomer captain The Pick of the Derby Wartime League against the Royal Engineers of Newark a few weeks before Christmas 1918.

**1919**
**MIDLAND VICTORY LEAGUE**
**Mar 15 v Wolverhampton Wanderers (a) 1–1**
*Leonard*
Lawrence; Atkin, Townley, Poole, Barbour, Walker, Thornewell, Leigh, Leonard, Robinson, Moore.
**Mar 22 v Aston Villa (a) 1–3**
*Leonard*
Lawrence; Atkin, Barbour, Bagshaw, Crookes, Walker, Thornewell, Ritchie, Leonard, Robinson, Moore.
**Mar 29 v Aston Villa (h) 3–2**
*Hawley, Leonard, Whitehouse*
Lawrence; Atkin, Barbour, Bagshaw, Hawley, Walker, Thornewell, Whitehouse, Leonard, Moore, Burton.
**Apr 5 v West Bromwich Albion (a) 1–3**
*Stone*
Lawrence; Atkin, Barbour, Walker, Bagshaw, Martin, Moore, Robinson, Leonard, Whitehouse, Stone.
**Apr 12 v West Bromwich Albion (h) 1–0**
*Leonard*
Lawrence; Atkin, Barbour, Walker, Bagshaw, Martin, Thompson, Howard, Leonard, Moore, Quantrill.
**Apr 19 v Wolverhampton Wanderers (h) 4–0**
*Burton 3, Leonard*

The Rams Midland Victory League team which lost 3-1 at West Brom in April 1919. Back row (left to right): G. Thornewell, J. Atkin, J. Bagshaw, G. Lawrence, H. Walker, Arthur Latham (trainer). Seated: J. Moore, J. Whitehouse, H. Leonard, A. Robinson, Stone. On ground: T. Barbour, B. Martin.

Lawrence; Atkin, Barbour, Boxley, Bagshaw, Martin, Thornewell, Moore, Leonard, Burton, Quantrill.

**Appearances:** Atkin 6, Barbour 6, Lawrence 6, Leonard 6, Moore 6, Bagshaw 5, Walker 5, Thornewell 4, Martin 3, Robinson 3, Burton 2, Quantrill 2, Whitehouse 2, Boxley 1, Crookes 1, Hawley 1, Howard 1, Leigh 1, Poole 1, Ritchie 1, Stone 1, Thompson 1, Townley 1.
**Goalscorers:** Leonard 5, Burton 3, Hawley 1, Stone 1, Whitehouse 1.

**Midland Victory League**

| | P | W | D | L | F | A | Pts |
|---|---|---|---|---|---|---|---|
| Nottingham Forest | 10 | 7 | 0 | 3 | 28 | 12 | 14 |
| West Bromwich A | 6 | 3 | 1 | 2 | 12 | 5 | 7 |
| **DERBY COUNTY** | **6** | **3** | **1** | **2** | **11** | **9** | **7** |
| Wolverhampton W | 6 | 2 | 3 | 1 | 9 | 9 | 7 |
| Aston Villa | 6 | 1 | 1 | 4 | 9 | 18 | 3 |

**1939–40**
**FIRST DIVISION**
**Aug 26 v Sunderland (a) 0–3**
Boulton; Nicholas, Howe, Hann, Barker, Ward, Walsh, Wilson, McCulloch, Stamps, Duncan.
*Att: 21,859*
**Aug 30 v Portsmouth (h) 2–0**
*Redfern, Duncan*
Boulton; Wilcox, Howe, Nicholas, Barker, Hann, Walsh, Redfern, McCulloch, Stamps, Duncan.
*Att: 10,211*
**Sep 2 v Aston Villa (h) 1–0**
*Nicholas (pen)*
Boulton; Wilcox, Howe, Nicholas, Barker, Ward, Walsh, Redfern, McCulloch, Stamps, Duncan.
*Att: 8,039*
**Friendly**
**Sep 30 v Leeds United (h) 1–3**
*Crooks*
Wood; Wilcox, Alton, Nicholas, Barker, Hann,

Crooks, Stamps, V.Jones, Hinchcliffe, Duncan.
*Att: 1,805*

**1941–42**
**MATCHES IN AID OF THE MAYOR OF DERBY'S WAR FUND**
**Dec 25 v RAF XI (h) 1–3**
*Bowers*
Allsop; Parr, Pallett, Hann, Nicholas, Musson, Crooks, Powell, Bowers, Ramage, Duncan.
*Att: 10,000*
**Jan 10 v Czechoslovakian Armed Forces (h) 11–4**
*McCormick 4 (1 pen), Ramage 3, Collins 2, Bowers, Quinn*
Allsop; Parr, Pallett, Musson, Nicholas, Mulranen, Collins, McCormick, Bowers, Ramage, Quinn.
*Att: 10,000*
**Feb 7 v Anti-Aircraft Command (h) 1–4**
*Ramage*
Allsop; Parr, Williams, Nicholas, A. Young, Riches, Crooks, McCormick, Bowers, Ramage, Duncan.
**Feb 21 v Belgian Army XI (h) 3–3**
*Elvin, Bowers, Gee*
Savage; Parr, Hewitt, L.Young, Nicholas, Roper, Watkin, Elvin, Bowers, Ramage, Gee.
**Mar 21 v Birmingham (h) 2–2**
*Ward, Dixon*
Boulton; Miller, Parr, Nicholas, Caddick, Ward, Smith, Dixon, Morrisroe, Ramage, Lewis.
**Apr 6 v RAF XI (h) 0–0**
Boulton; Parr, Howe, Musson, Nicholas, Townsend, Lawrence, Dewis, Bowers, Ramage, Hunt.

**MATCHES IN AID OF DERBY CIVIL DEFENCE BENEVOLENT FUND**
**May 2 v Army XI (h) 3–2**
*Duncan 2, Bowers*
Prince; Hampshire, Parr, Nicholas, Barker, Hann, Crooks, Harris, Bowers, Ramage, Duncan.
**May 30 v Pick of Derby & District Senior League (h) 5–4**
*Bowers 2, Staley 2, Prince*
Prince; Parr, Pallett, Hibbs, Hann, Townsend, Kinnerley, Powell, Bowers, Ramage, Staley.

**Appearances:** Parr 8, Ramage 8, Bowers 7, Nicholas 7, Allsop 3, Crooks 3, Duncan 3, Hann 3, Musson 3, Pallett 3, Boulton 2, McCormick (Spurs) 2, Powell 2, Prince 2, Townsend (Nottm F) 2, Barker 1, Caddick (Bolton W) 1, Collins (Wolves) 1, Dewis (Leicester C) 1, Dixon (Northampton T) 1, Elvin (Rotherham U) 1, Gee (Charlton A) 1, Hampshire 1, Harris 1, Hewitt (RAF) 1, Hibbs 1, Howe 1, Hunt (West Brom) 1, Kinnerley 1, Lawrence 1, Lewis (Swansea T) 1, Miller (Northampton T) 1, Morrisroe (Old Derbeians and RAF) 1, Mulranen (Corinthians) 1, Quinn (Everton) 1, Riches (Hull C) 1, Roper (Leeds U) 1, Savage (Leeds U) 1, Smith (Aberdeen) 1, Staley 1, Watkin (Aston Villa) 1, Ward 1, Williams 1, A. Young (Huddersfield T) 1, L. Young (Reading) 1.
**Goalscorers:** Bowers 6, McCormick 4, Ramage 4, Collins 2, Duncan 2, Staley 2, Dixon 1, Elvin 1, Gee 1, Prince 1, Quinn 1, Ward 1.

**1942–43**
**FOOTBALL LEAGUE NORTH (First Period)**
**Aug 29 v Notts County (a) 6–1**
*Beattie (pen), Challenger, Lyman, Ramage, Duncan, Sharman (og)*
Townsend; Parr, Beattie, Challenger, Nicholas, Hann, Crooks, Powell, Lyman, Ramage, Duncan.
*Att: 3,000*
**Sep 5 v Notts County (h) 2–0**
*Crooks, Duncan*
Townsend; Nicholas, Parr, Bailey, T. Smith, Hann, Crooks, Powell, Westland, Ramage, Duncan.
*Att: 8,000*
**Sep 12 v Birmingham (a) 5–0**
*Powell 4, Lyman*
Townsend; Nicholas, Parr, Challenger, T. Smith, Hann, Crooks, Powell, Lyman, Ramage, Duncan.
*Att: 6,500*
**Sep 19 v Birmingham (h) 3–1**
*Nicholas (pen), Lyman, Duncan*
Townsend; Nicholas, Parr, Challenger, Bailey, Hann, Crooks, Powell, Lyman, Ramage, Duncan.
*Att: 6,500*
**Sep 26 v Stoke City (a) 2–5**
*Challenger, Duncan*
Townsend; Nicholas, Parr, Challenger, Bailey, Hann, S.Smith, Powell, Lyman, Ramage, Duncan.
*Att: 5,000*
**Oct 3 v Stoke City (h) 0–1**
Townsend; Wilcox, Beattie, Hann, Nicholas, Ward, Crooks, Powell, Lyman, Ramage, Duncan.
*Att: 11,000*

**Oct 10 v Nottingham Forest (a) 1–5**
*Lyman*
Townsend; Nicholas, Parr, Hann, Challenger, Ramage, Crooks, Powell, Lyman, H.Jones, Duncan.
*Att: 5,000*
**Oct 17 v Nottingham Forest (h) 3–2**
*Powell 2, Crooks*
Townsend; Nicholas, Parr, Hann, Attwood, Weaver, Crooks, Powell, Lyman, Westland, Duncan.
*Att: 10,000*
**Oct 24 v West Bromwich Albion (h) 4–0**
*Nicholas, Crooks, Lyman, Smith (og)*
Townsend; Parr, Beattie, Nicholas, T. Smith, Weaver, Crooks, Powell, Lyman, Stamps, Duncan.
*Att: 9,000*
**Oct 31 v West Bromwich Albion (a) 3–3**
*Nicholas, Lyman, Weaver*
Townsend; Parr, Beattie, Nicholas, T. Smith, Attwood, D.Smith, Powell, Lyman, Weaver, Duncan.
*Att: 5,000*
**Nov 7 v Leicester City (a) 3–2**
*Weaver, Powell, Duncan*
Townsend; Parr, Beattie, Nicholas, T. Smith, Weaver, Crooks, Powell, Lyman, Westland, Duncan.
*Att: 8,500*
**Nov 14 v Leicester City (h) 5–3**
*Duncan 3, Lyman 2*
Townsend; Parr, McDonald, Nicholas, Griffiths, Weaver, Crooks, Powell, Lyman, Westland, Duncan.
*Att: 9,000*
**Nov 21 v Wolverhampton Wanderers (a) 1–8**
*Lyman*
Townsend; Parr, Pallett, Hibbs, Nicholas, Hann, Challenger, Powell, Lyman, Ramage, Duncan.
*Att: 3,000*
**Nov 28 v Wolverhampton Wanderers (h) 3–1**
*Powell 2, Lyman*
Townsend; Parr, Beattie, Nicholas, T. Smith, Weaver, Crooks, Powell, Lyman, Westland, Bivens.
*Att: 9,000*
**Dec 5 v Aston Villa (h) 4–2**
*Westland 2, Crooks, Lyman*
Townsend; Parr, Bacuzzi, Nicholas, T. Smith, Weaver, Crooks, Powell, Lyman, Westland, Duncan.
*Att: 7,000*
**Dec 12 v Aston Villa (a) 0–2**
Townsend; Bacuzzi, Parr, Hibbs, Nicholas, Weaver, Crooks, Powell, Lyman, Westland, Bivens.
*Att: 7,000*
**Dec 19 v Mansfield Town (a) 1–1**
*Duncan*
Townsend; Parr, Trim, Hibbs, G. Marriott, Weaver, Crooks, Shaw, Lyman, Westland, Duncan.
*Att: 2,500*
**Dec 25 v Mansfield Town (h) 5–0**
*Lyman 3, Powell, D.Smith*
Townsend; Parr, Trim, Ward, Nicholas, Weaver, D. Smith, Powell, Lyman, Westland, Duncan.
*Att: 8,000*

**FOOTBALL LEAGUE WAR CUP QUALIFYING COMPETITION**

**Dec 26 v Notts County (a) 3–2**
*Lyman, Crooks, Duncan*
Townsend; Nicholas, Parr, Ward, T. Smith, Weaver, D.Smith, Powell, Lyman, Crooks, Duncan.
*Att: 15,000*
**Jan 2 v Notts County (h) 1–2**
*Duncan*
Townsend; Parr, Trim, Nicholas, T. Smith, Weaver, Crooks, Westland, Lyman, Stamps, Duncan.
*Att: 7,000*
**Jan 9 v Mansfield Town (h) 10–0**
*McCulloch 5, Duncan 3, Lyman, Nicholas*
Townsend; Parr, Challinor, Nicholas, Leuty, Weaver, Crooks, Powell, McCulloch, Lyman, Duncan.
*Att: 7,000*
**Jan 16 v Mansfield Town (a) 1–1**
*Crooks*
Townsend; Parr, Trim, Hann, Leuty, Weaver, Crooks, Powell, Lyman, Ramage, Duncan.
*Att: 2,500*
**Jan 23 v Chesterfield (a) 2–0**
*Sinclair 2*
Townsend; Parr, Trim, Hann, T. Smith, Weaver, Crooks, Sinclair, Lyman, Rawcliffe, Duncan.
*Att: 9,017*
**Jan 30 v Chesterfield (h) 1–1**
*McCulloch*
Townsend; Parr, Trim, Nicholas, Vose, Beattie, Crooks, Gardiner, McCulloch, Lyman, Duncan.
*Att: 7,000*

**Feb 6 v Nottingham Forest (a) 1–4**
*Weaver*
Townsend; Parr, Beattie, Tunstall, T. Smith, Weaver, Crooks, Powell, W.G. Richardson, Lyman, Duncan.
*Att: 10,000*
**Feb 13 v Nottingham Forest (h) 3–1**
*Duncan 2, Ramage*
Townsend; Parr, Wilcox, Nicholas, T. Smith, Weaver, Crooks, W.G. Richardson, Lyman, Ramage, Duncan.
*Att: 7,000*
**Feb 20 v Stoke City (a) 0–4**
Townsend; Parr, Trim, Hibbs, Vose, Hann, Crooks, Powell, Lyman, Weaver, Duncan.
*Att: 6,000*
**Feb 27 v Stoke City (h) 0–1**
Townsend; Delaney, Beattie, Corkhill, T. Smith, Weaver, Richards, Crooks, McCulloch, Lyman, Duncan.
*Att: 10,000*

**FOOTBALL LEAGUE WAR CUP KNOCK-OUT COMPETITION**
**Round 1 (1st leg)**
**Mar 6 v Notts County (h) 1–3**
*Lyman*
Townsend; Delaney, Beattie, Eggleston, Webber, Weaver, McCormick, Powell, McCulloch, Lyman, Duncan.
*Att: 10,540*
**Round 1 (2nd leg)**
**Mar 13 v Notts County (a) 2–2 (aggregate 3–5)**
*Fisher, Crooks*
Townsend; Delaney, Trim, Parr, T. Smith, Weaver, Fisher, Lyman, McCulloch, Crooks, Duncan.
*Att: 15,100*

**FOOTBALL LEAGUE NORTH (Second Period)**
**Other matches**
**Mar 20 v Leicester City (h) 3–2**
*Attwood 2, Duncan*
Townsend; Delaney, Butler, Riddell, Weaver, Ward, Lyman, Powell, Attwood, Tunstall, Duncan.
*Att; 5,000*
**Mar 27 v Leicester City (a) 1–3**
*Attwood*
Townsend; Delaney, Parr, Riddell, T. Smith, Weaver, Crooks, Powell, Attwood, Tunstall, Duncan.
*Att: 4,000*
**Apr 3 v Coventry City (h) 1–1**
*Lyman*
Townsend; Parr, Trim, Baxter, T. Smith, Pithie, Crooks, Powell, Lyman, Stamps, Duncan.
*Att: 6,000*
**Apr 10 v Coventry City (a) 1–0**
*Attwood*
Townsend; Parr, Delaney, Pithie, Vose, Weaver, Alex Collins, Alan Collins, Attwood, Tunstall, Bivens.
*Att: 6,034*
**Apr 17 v Stoke City (h) 2–1**
*Lyman 2*
Townsend; Parr, Butler, Nicholas, Vose, Pithie, Crooks, Powell, Lyman, Tunstall, Bivens.
*Att: 5,000*
**Apr 24 v Crewe Alexandra (a) 4–0**
*Crooks 2, Lyman, Bivens*
Townsend; Parr, Butler, Pithie, Vose, Weaver, Crooks, Powell, Lyman, Grace, Bivens.
*Att: 5,000*
**Apr 26 v Crewe Alexandra (h) 1–3**
*Lyman*
Townsend; Parr, Trim, Nicholas, Leuty, Musson, Crooks, Powell, Lyman, Riddell, Bivens.
*Att: 4,000*
**May 1 v Wolverhampton Wanderers (h) 3–3**
*Crooks 3*
Boulton; Delaney, Trim, Hibbs, Nicholas, Pithie, Crooks, Powell, Lyman, Grace, Bivens.
*Att: 5,000*

**Appearances (League and Cup only):** Townsend 37, Lyman (Spurs) 35, Parr 33, Crooks 31, Duncan 31, Powell 30, Nicholas 25, Weaver (Chelsea) 25, T. Smith (Preston NE) 10, Ramage 10, Westland (Stoke C) 10, Bivens 7, Delaney (Arsenal) 7, Challenger (Wolves) 6, Attwood 5, Hibbs 5, McCulloch 5, Pithie (Hibernian) 5, Tunstall 5, Vose (Manchester U) 5, Ward 4, Bailey 3, Butler (Corinthians) 3, Leuty 3, Riddell 3, D.Smith 3, Stamps 3, Bacuzzi (Fulham) 2, Grace 2, Richardson (West Brom) 2, Wilcox 2, Baxter (Nottm F) 1, Boulton 1, Challinor (Stoke C) 1, Alex Collins (Dundee) 1, Allan Collins (Kilmarnock) 1, Corkhill (Cardiff C) 1, Eggleston 1, Fisher (Millwall) 1, Gardiner (Portsmouth) 1, Griffiths (Port Vale) 1, H. Jones 1, Marriott 1, McCormick (Spurs) 1, McDonald (Glasgow R) 1,

Musson 1, Pallett 1, Rawcliffe (Wolves) 1, Rickards (Notts County) 1, Shaw 1, Sinclair (Third Lanark) 1, S. Smith (Aberdeen) 1, Webber (Southampton) 1.

**Goalscorers (League and Cup only):** Lyman 22, Duncan 17, Crooks 12, Powell 10, McCulloch 6, Attwood 4, Nicholas 4 (1 pen), Weaver 3, Challenger 2, Ramage 2, Sinclair 2, Westland 2, Beattie 1 (pen), Bivens 1, Fisher 1, D.Smith 1. Opponents own-goals: Sharman (Notts County) 1, J.Smith (West Brom) 1.

**Friendly**

**May 15 v National Police XI (h) 2–0**
*Patterson, L.Jones*
Townsend; Trim, Howe, Baxter, Nicholas, Paterson, Crooks, L.Jones, Lyman, Stamps, Beaumont.
*Att: 3,500*

Nicholas (2) and Tuntsall scored in a 3–0 win over an RAF XI at Tutbury on 8 May 1943 but no teams were published.

**Football League North**

| | P | W | D | L | F | A | Pts | Pos |
|---|---|---|---|---|---|---|---|---|
| (First Period) | 18 | 11 | 2 | 5 | 51 | 37 | 24 | 9th |
| (Second Period) | 20 | 8 | 5 | 7 | 41 | 34 | 21 | 18th |

When the Rams met Mansfield Town in 1942–43, the Stags fielded George Hannah at right-half. Hannah had been on the Derby staff before the war without breaking into the first team. He was transferred to Port Vale in 1938. Hannah's return to the Baseball Ground was hardly a happy one – Derby won 10–0.

**1943–44**

**FOOTBALL LEAGUE NORTH (First Period)**

**Aug 28 v West Bromwich Albion (a) 2–3**
*Attwood, Duncan*
Townsend; Parr, Trim, Challenger, Leuty, Pithie, Crooks, Airlie, Attwood, Hinchcliffe, Duncan.
*Att: 4,000*

**Sep 4 v West Bromwich Albion (h) 1–5**
*Hinchcliffe*
Boulton; Nicholas, Parr, Challenger, Leuty, Hann, Crooks, Hinchcliffe, Attwood, Grace, Bivens.
*Att: 7,000*

**Sep 11 v Notts County (a) 1–3**
*Nicholas*
Townsend; Parr, Trim, Nicholas, Leuty, Hann, Slack, Powell, Hinchcliffe, Grace, Bivens.
*Att: 8,000*

**Sep 18 v Notts County (h) 4–2**
*Crooks (pen), Challenger, Hold, Hinchcliffe*
Townsend; Nicholas, Parr, Challenger, Leuty, Hann, Crooks, Powell, Hold, Hinchcliffe, Duncan.
*Att: 7,000*

**Sep 25 v Stoke City (a) 1–5**
*Crooks*
Townsend; Parr, Firth, Hibbs, Leuty, Musson, Crooks, Powell, Challenger, Hinchcliffe, Duncan.
*Att: 4,000*

**Oct 2 v Stoke City (h) 2–2**
*Nicholas, Duncan*
Boulton; Parr, Howe, Nicholas, Leuty, Hann, T. Jones, Powell, Thompson, Crooks, Duncan.
*Att: 8,000*

**Oct 9 v Birmingham (h) 5–3**
*Carter 3, Stamps 2*
Townsend; Trim, Firth, Nicholas, Leuty, Hann, Crooks, Powell, Stamps, Carter, Duncan.
*Att: 8,000*

**Oct 16 v Birmingham (a) 3–3**
*Stamps, T. Jones, Duncan*
Townsend; Nicholas, Parr, Challenger, Leuty, Musson, T. Jones, Powell, Stamps, Crooks, Duncan.
*Att: 4,500*

**Oct 23 v Nottingham Forest (a) 3–4**
*Duncan, Carter, Wilkinson (og)*
Townsend; Parr, Delaney, Nicholas, Leuty, Challenger, T. Jones, Carter, Heyden, Powell, Duncan.
*Att: 7,000*

**Oct 30 v Nottingham Forest (h) 3–1**
*Nicholas 2 (1 pen), Carter*
Boulton; Parr, Ancell, Challenger, Leuty, Ward, T. Jones, Carter, Nicholas, Crooks, Duncan.
*Att: 8,000*

**Nov 6 v Leicester City (a) 1–0**
*T. Jones*
Townsend; Brigham, Ancell, Leuty, Vose, Ward, T. Jones, Powell, Nicholas, Crooks, Duncan.
*Att: 9,000*

**Nov 13 v Leicester City (h) 3–2**
*Carter, Rodgers, Nicholas*
Townsend; Trim, Ancell, Nicholas, Vose, Ward, T.

Jones, Crooks, Rodgers, Carter, Duncan.
*Att: 7,000*
**Nov 20 v Wolverhampton Wanderers (a) 3–1**
*Nicholas 2 (1 pen), Bivens*
Townsend; Brigham, Parr, Challenger, Vose, Leuty, T. Jones, Crooks, Nicholas, Carter, Bivens.
*Att: 6,000*
**Nov 27 v Wolverhampton Wanderers (h) 2–2**
*Carter 2*
Townsend; Brigham, Trim, Ward, Leuty, Lambert, T. Jones, Powell, Rodgers, Carter, Bivens.
*Att: 7,000*
**Dec 4 v Aston Villa (a) 1–0**
*Powell*
Swindin; Brigham, Trim, Nicholas, Leuty, Ward, T. Jones, Crooks, Powell, Carter, Bivens.
*Att: 10,000*
**Dec 11 v Aston Villa (h) 3–3**
*Crooks, Powell, Carter*
Swindin; Parr, Trim, Nicholas, Leuty, Ward, T. Jones, Crooks, Powell, Carter, Duncan.
*Att: 10,000*
**Dec 18 v Mansfield Town (a) 1–3**
*Crooks*
Swindin; Parr, Smith, Leuty, Vose, Ward, T. Jones, Crooks, Powell, Fisher, Duncan.
*Att; 3,500*
**Dec 25 v Mansfield Town (h) 4–3**
*Conway 2, Grace, Duncan*
Townsend; Brigham, Delaney, Musson, Vose, Ward, Fisher, Jeffrey, Conway, Grace, Duncan.
*Att: 8,000*

**FOOTBALL LEAGUE WAR CUP QUALIFYING COMPETITION**
**Dec 27 v Nottingham Forest (h) 2–1**
*Powell, Duncan*
Swindin; Brigham, Delaney, Nicholas, Leuty, Trim, T. Jones, Crooks, Powell, Carter, Duncan.
*Att: 17,795*
**Jan 1 v Nottingham Forest (a) 1–1**
*Carter*
Townsend; Delaney, Trim, Leuty, Vose, Ward, T. Jones, Crooks, Conway, Carter, Duncan.
*Att: 9,000*
**Jan 8 v Leicester City (h) 0–1**
John; Delaney, Trim, Challenger, Vose, Leuty, T. Jones, Crooks, Nicholas, Carter, Duncan.
*Att: 10,000*
**Jan 15 v Leicester City (a) 0–1**
Swindin; Parr, Trim, Challenger, Vose, Leuty, T. Jones, Powell, Nicholas, Conway, Duncan.
*Att: 10,000*
**Jan 22 v Sheffield Wednesday (a) 1–3**
*Duncan*
Swindin; Parr, Delaney, Challenger, Vose, Leuty, T. Jones, Knott, Conway, Ward, Duncan.
*Att: 9,000*
**Jan 29 v Sheffield Wednesday (h) 4–1**
*Carter 2, Mountford, Bowyer*
Swindin; Brigham, Trim, Nicholas, Leuty, Ward, T. Jones, Bowyer, Mountford, Carter, Grace.
*Att: 10,000*
**Feb 5 v Notts County (a) 2–0**
*Bowyer, Knight*
Swindin; Brigham, Trim, Hann, Leuty, Musson, T. Jones, Bowyer, Knight, Powell, Duncan.
*Att: 7,000*
**Feb 12 v Notts County (h) 7–3**
*McCulloch 3, Nicholas 2, Bowyer, Woodward*
Boulton; Brigham, Trim, Nicholas, Leuty, Hann, Crooks, Bowyer, McCulloch, Woodward, Duncan.
*Att: 8,000*
**Feb 19 v Mansfield Town (h) 0–1**
Swindin; Brigham, Trim, Nicholas, Leuty, Hann, T. Jones, Powell, Knight, Crooks, Duncan.
*Att: 6,000*
**Feb 26 v Mansfield Town (a) 3–2**
*Woodward 2, Carter*
John; Brigham, Leuty, Hann, Vose, Ward, Crooks, Carter, Mountford, Woodward, Duncan.
*Att: 11,783*

**FOOTBALL LEAGUE WAR CUP KNOCK-OUT COMPETITION**
**Round 1 (1st leg)**
**Mar 4 v Coventry City (h) 2–1**
*McKay, Duncan*
Swindin; Nicholas, Trim, Hann, Leuty, Ward, T. Jones, Carter, McKay, Egan, Duncan.
*Att: 11,901*
**Round 1 (2nd leg)**
**Mar 11 v Coventry City (a) 0–3 (aggregate 2–4)**
Swindin; Nicholas, Trim, Hann, Leuty, Ward, Crooks, H. Jones, McKay, Egan, Duncan.
*Att: 12,172*

**MIDLAND CUP**

**Round 1 (1st leg)**

**Apr 1 v Stoke City (h) 1–3**

*Harrison*

Swindin; Griffiths, Trim, Nicholas, Leuty, Hann, Crooks, Harrison, McCulloch, Grace, Duncan.

*Att: 9,000*

**Round 1 (2nd leg)**

**Apr 8 v Stoke City (a) 1–1 (aggregate 2–4)**

*Grace*

Swindin; Parr, Trim, Lambert, Leuty, Musson, T. Jones, Crooks, Knight, Grace, Duncan.

*Att: 7,000*

**FOOTBALL LEAGUE NORTH (Second Period)**

**Other matches**

**Mar 18 v Leeds United (h) 2–2**

*Knight, Grace*

Swindin; Parr, Trim, Hann, Leuty, Ward, T. Jones, Crooks, Knight, Grace, Duncan.

*Att: 6,000*

**Mar 25 v Crewe Alexandra (h) 4–0**

*Musson (pen), Spacey, Crooks, Duncan*

Townsend; Nicholas, Parr, Hann, Leuty, Musson, T. Jones, Spacey, Grace, Crooks, Duncan.

*Att: 5,000*

**Apr 10 v Chesterfield (h) 1–1**

*Crooks*

Townsend; Parr, Trim, Lambert, Leuty, Musson, T. Jones, Tapping, Knight, Crooks, Duncan.

*Att: 8,000*

**Apr 15 v Rotherham United (a) 2–0**

*Slack, Powell*

Townsend; Nicholas, Parr, Riddell, Leuty, Musson, Slack, Powell, Lyman, Tapping, Duncan.

*Att: 8,000*

**Apr 22 v Rotherham United (h) 0–0**

Townsend; Parr, Trim, Nicholas, Leuty, Musson, Slack, Powell, Lyman, Crooks, Duncan.

*Att: 4,000*

**Apr 29 v Leicester City (h) 0–2**

Townsend; Parr, Trim, Nicholas, Leuty, Musson, Crooks, Tapping, Knight, Lyman, Duncan.

*Att: 3,000*

**May 6 v Leicester City (a) 0–1**

Townsend; Nicholas, Parr, Tapping, Leuty, Musson, Slack, Knight, Lyman, Powell, Duncan.

*Att: 3,000*

**Football League North**

| | P | W | D | L | F | A | Pts | Pos |
|---|---|---|---|---|---|---|---|---|
| (First Period) | 18 | 8 | 4 | 6 | 43 | 45 | 20 | 19th |
| (Second Period) | 21 | 8 | 5 | 8 | 33 | 28 | 21 | 23rd |

**Appearances (League and Cup only):** Leuty 37, Duncan 33, Crooks 28, Nicholas 27, T. Jones 24, Trim (Nottm F) 23, Parr 22, Powell 19, Townsend 19, Ward 15, Carter (Sunderland) 14, Hann 14, Swindin (Arsenal) 14, Brigham (Stoke C) 11, Challenger (Wolves) 11, Musson 11, Vose (Manchester U) 10, Grace 8, Knight 7, Delaney (Arsenal) 6, Bivens 5, Hinchcliffe 5, Boulton 4, Conway (Glasgow C) 4, Lyman (Spurs) 4, Slack 4, Tapping (Blackpool) 4, Ancell (Newcastle U) 3, Bowyer (Stoke C) 3, Lambert (Corinthians) 3, Attwood 2, Egan (Nottm F) 2, Firth (Bradford) 2, Fisher (Millwall) 2, John (Swansea T) 2, McCulloch 2, McKay (Glasgow R) 2, Mountford (Stoke C) 2, Rodgers (Huddersfield T) 2, Stamps 2, Woodward (Fulham) 2, Airlie (Glasgow C) 1, Griffiths (Manchester U) 1, Harrison 1, Heyden 1, Hibbs 1, Hold (Aldershot) 1, Howe 1, Jeffrey 1, H. Jones 1, Knott (Hull C) 1, Pithie (Hibernian) 1, Riddell 1, Spacey 1, Thompson (Bolton W) 1. (Trim was transferred to Derby County in December 1943.)

**Goalscorers (League and Cup only):** Carter 13, Duncan 9, Nicholas 9 (2 pen), Crooks 6 (1 pen), Powell 4, Bowyer 3, Grace 3, McCulloch 3, Stamps 3, Woodward 3, Conway 2, Hinchcliffe 2, T. Jones 2, Knight 2, Attwood 1, Bivens 1, Challenger 1, Harrison 1, Hold 1, McKay 1, Mountford 1, Musson 1 (pen), Rodgers 1, Slack 1, Spacey 1. Opponents own-goal: Wilkinson (Nottm F) 1.

**Match in aid of Police Benevolent Fund:**

**May 13 v Huddersfield Town (h) 3–4**

*Bowyer (pen), Carter, Duncan*

Townsend; McCall, Trim, Nicholas, Leuty, Baxter, Isaacs, Bowyer, Dodds, Carter, Duncan.

Stanley Matthews and Len Shackleton guested for Huddersfield.

When the Rams lost 2–0 at Barnsley in September 1944, it could hardly have been described as Derby's lucky day. The problem of wartime travel meant that goalkeeper Frank Boulton was stranded in Birmingham. Reserve 'keeper Vanham was sent for, but he arrived at Derby Bus Station a few minutes after the Rams team coach had departed, and it was left to Jack Nicholas to demonstrate his versatility by keeping goal. Although Derby lost, Nicholas performed valiantly and was in no way to blame.

**1944–45**

**FOOTBALL LEAGUE NORTH (First Period)**

**Aug 26 v Nottingham Forest (a) 0–0**
Bilton; Parr, Trim, Tapping, Leuty, Musson, Crooks, Carter, Knight, Doherty, Duncan.
*Att: 13,294*

**Sep 2 v Nottingham Forest (h) 5–0**
*Tapping 3, Powell, Baxter (og)*
Bilton; Marshall, Trim, Bullions, Leuty, Musson, Crooks, Powell, Tapping, Doherty, Duncan.
*Att: 9,936*

**Sep 9 v Barnsley (h) 1–2**
*Powell*
Bilton; Parr, Trim, Bullions, Leuty, Musson, Crooks, Powell, Tapping, Bert Brown, Duncan.
*Att: 12,897*

**Sep 16 v Barnsley (a) 0–2**
Nicholas; Parr, Trim, Bullions, Leuty, Musson, Crooks, Powell, Wainwright, Doherty, Kinnerley.
*Att: 6,268*

**Sep 23 v Doncaster Rovers (a) 4–1**
*Tapping 3, Duncan*
Boulton; Parr, Marshall, Bullions, Leuty, Musson, Crooks, Powell, Tapping, Carter, Duncan.
*Att:* 8,029

**Sep 30 v Doncaster Rovers (h) 4–1**
*Crooks 2, Tapping, Doherty*
Boulton; Parr, Trim, Baird, Leuty, Musson, Crooks, Powell, Tapping, Doherty, Duncan.
*Att: 9,524*

**Oct 7 v Grimsby Town (h) 3–2**
*Powell, Baird, Duncan*
Bilton; Parr, Trim, Bullions, Leuty, Musson, Crooks, Powell, Tapping, Baird, Duncan.
*Att: 11,659*

**Oct 14 v Grimsby Town (a) 1–3**
*Wainwright*
Vanham; Parr, Trim, Bullions, Leuty, Musson, T. Jones, Powell, Wainwright, Morrison, Duncan.
*Att: 5,365*

**Oct 21 v Sheffield United (h) 4–2**
*Doherty 2 (1 pen), Tapping 2*
Vanham; Parr, Trim, Bullions, Leuty, Musson, T. Jones, Powell, Tapping, Doherty, Morrison.
*Att: 9,650*

**Oct 28 v Sheffield United (a) 2–0**
*Tapping, Doherty*
Townsend; Nicholas, Parr, Bullions, Leuty, Musson, Morrison, Powell, Tapping, Doherty, Duncan.
*Att: 10,600*

**Nov 4 v Notts County (a) 4–1**
*Doherty 3, Duncan*
Savage; Nicholas, Parr, Bullions, Leuty, Musson, Tapping, Carter, Powell, Doherty, Duncan.
*Att: 10,300*

**Nov 11 v Notts County (h) 6–3**
*S. Smith 2, Carter 2, Doherty 2*
Savage; Parr, Trim, Bullions, Leuty, Musson, S. Smith, Carter, Powell, Doherty, Duncan.
*Att: 12,000*

**Nov 18 v Chesterfield (h) 3–1**
*Doherty 2, Bullions*
Savage; Parr, Trim, Bullions, Leuty, Musson, S. Smith, Powell, Harrison, Doherty, Duncan.
*Att: 12,000*

**Nov 25 v Chesterfield (a) 1–0**
*Harrison*
Savage; Parr, Trim, Bullions, Leuty, Musson, S. Smith, Harrison, Morrison, Powell, Duncan.
*Att: 4,700*

**Dec 2 v Mansfield Town (a) 4–0**
*Carter, Lyman, Doherty, Duncan*
Savage; Parr, Trim, Bullions, Leuty, Musson, S. Smith, Carter, Lyman, Doherty, Duncan.
*Att: 9,854*

**Dec 9 v Mansfield Town (h) 7–1**
*Doherty 3, Carter 2, Lyman, Duncan*
Savage; Parr, Trim, Bullions, Leuty, Musson, S. Smith, Carter, Lyman, Doherty, Duncan.
*Att: 13,796*

**Dec 16 v Rotherham United (h) 4–0**
*Doherty 2 (1 pen), Slack, Carter*
Savage; Parr, Trim, Bullions, Leuty, Musson, Slack, Carter, Lyman, Doherty, Duncan.
*Att: 10,897*

**Dec 23 v Rotherham United (a) 1–0**
*Lyman*
Savage; Nicholas, Parr, Bullions, Leuty, Musson, S. Smith, Powell, Lyman, Carter, Duncan.
*Att: 11,784*

**FOOTBALL LEAGUE WAR CUP QUALIFYING COMPETITION**

**Dec 25 v Chesterfield (h) 2–2**
*Lyman 2*
Savage; Nicholas, Parr, Bullions, Leuty, Musson, S. Smith, Powell, Lyman, Carter, Duncan.
*Att: 10,000*

**Dec 30 v Chesterfield (a) 1–0**
*Crooks*
Savage; Parr, Trim, Bullions, Leuty, Musson, Crooks, Carter, Lyman, Doherty, Duncan.
*Att: 10,987*

**Jan 6 v Nottingham Forest (a) 1–1**
*Lyman*
Savage; Parr, Trim, Bullions, Leuty, Musson, Crooks, Carter, Lyman, Doherty, Duncan.
*Att: 18,790*

**Jan 13 v Nottingham Forest (h) 3–0**
*Carter 2, Doherty*
Savage; Parr, Trim, Bullions, Leuty, Musson, Crooks, Carter, Lyman, Doherty, Duncan.
*Att: 12,715*

**Jan 20 v Notts County (h) 7–0**
*Carter 2, Lyman 2, Duncan, Crooks, Doherty*
Savage; Parr, Trim, Bullions, Leuty, Musson, Crooks, Carter, Lyman, Doherty, Duncan.
*Att: 6,218*

**Jan 27 v Notts County (a) 4–2**
*Carter 3, Crooks*
Savage; Nicholas, Parr, Bullions, Leuty, Musson, Crooks, Carter, Lyman, Doherty, Duncan.
*Att: 5,139*

**Feb 3 v Mansfield Town (a) 8–1**
*Carter 4, Lyman 3, Duncan*
Savage; Parr, Trim, Bullions, Leuty, Musson, Crooks, Carter, Lyman, Morrison, Duncan.
*Att: 7,280*

**Feb 10 v Mansfield Town (h) 7–1**
*Lyman 3, Crooks 2, Powell, Doherty*
Savage; Parr, Trim, Bullions, Leuty, Musson, Crooks, Powell, Lyman, Doherty, Duncan.
*Att: 12,570*

**Feb 17 v Leicester City (a) 2–2**
*Crooks, Duncan*
Savage; Parr, Trim, Bullions, Leuty, Musson, Crooks, Knight, Lyman, Doherty, Duncan.
*Att: 17,546*

**Feb 24 v Leicester City (h) 3–0**
*Doherty 2, Howe (og)*
Savage; Nicholas, Parr, Bullions, Leuty, Musson, Crooks, Carter, Lyman, Doherty, Duncan.
*Att: 18,621*

**FOOTBALL LEAGUE WAR CUP KNOCK-OUT COMPETITION**

**Round 1 (1st leg)**
**Mar 24 v Leicester City (a) 1–2**
*Lyman*
Bilton; Parr, Trim, Bullions, Leuty, Musson, Crooks, Harrison, Lyman, Carter, Johnston.
*Att: 19,074*

**Round 1 (2nd leg)**
**Mar 31 v Leicester City (h) 2–0 (aggregate 3–2)**
*Carter, Leuty*
Williams; Parr, Trim, Bullions, Leuty, Musson, Crooks, Carter, Lyman, Morrison, Duncan.
Att: 24,900

**Round 2 (1st leg)**
**Apr 7 v Doncaster Rovers (a) 2–1**
*Powell, Duncan*
Williams; Parr, Trim, Bullions, Leuty, Musson, Crooks, Powell, Lyman, Carter, Duncan.
*Att: 23,899*

**Round 2 (2nd leg)**
**Apr 14 v Doncaster Rovers (h) 1–4 (aggregate 3–5)**
*T. Jones*
Savage; Parr, Trim, Nicholas, Leuty, Ward, T. Jones, Powell, Lyman, Crooks, Duncan.
*Att: 19,062*

**FOOTBALL LEAGUE NORTH (Second Period) Other Matches**

**Dec 26 v Stoke City (a) 2–4**
*Carter 2*
Savage; Nicholas, Parr, Bullions, Leuty, Musson, S. Smith, Carter, Lyman, Morrison, Duncan.
*Att: 5,600*

**Mar 3 v Huddersfield Town (a) 4–0**
*Wainwright 2, Carter, Doherty*
Savage; Nicholas, Parr, Bullions, Leuty, Musson, T. Jones, Carter, Wainwright, Doherty, Duncan.
*Att: 13,798*

**Mar 10 v Huddersfield Town (h) 2–1**
*Carter 2*
Savage; Parr, Trim, Bullions, Leuty, Musson, Crooks, Powell, Lyman, Carter, Duncan.
*Att: 17,428*

**Mar 17 v Sheffield United (h) 3–2**
*Doherty (pen), Morrison, Lyman*
Savage; Nicholas, Trim, Bullions, Lambert, Musson, Crooks, Baird, Lyman, Doherty, Morrison.
*Att: 14,003*
**Apr 2 v Stoke City (h) 2–1**
*Lyman, Doherty*
Eccles; Nicholas, Parr, Bullions, Leuty, Musson, T. Jones, Carter, Lyman, Doherty, Duncan.
*Att: 21,791*
**May 21 v Liverpool (h) 1–0**
*Doherty*
Grant; Parr, Stephen, Bullions, Leuty, Baxter, Crooks, Carter, Jordan, Doherty, Duncan.
*Att: 16,723*

**MIDLAND CUP**
**Round 1 (1st leg)**
**Apr 21 v Northampton Town (a) 1–2**
*Carter*
Savage; Parr, Butler, Bullions, Leuty, Musson, T. Jones, Carter, Lyman, Doherty, Duncan.
*Att: 4,552*
**Round 1 (2nd leg)**
**Apr 28 v Northampton Town (h) 5–0 (aggregate 6–2)**
*Carter 2, Duncan 2, Doherty (pen)*
Savage; Nicholas, Parr, Bullions, Leuty, Musson, T. Jones, Carter, Lyman, Doherty, Duncan.
*Att: 7,357*
**Semi-final (1st leg)**
**May 5 v Leicester City (h) 3–1**
*Doherty 2, Lyman*
Savage; Nicholas, Parr, Bullions, Leuty, Baxter, T. Jones, Powell, Lyman, Doherty, Duncan.
*Att: 7,270*
**Semi-final (2nd leg)**
**May 12 v Leicester City (a) 2–1 (aggregate 5–2)**
*Crooks, Doherty*
Savage; Nicholas, Parr, Bullions, Leuty, Baxter, Crooks, Carter, T. Jones, Doherty, Duncan.
*Att: 9,000*
**Final (1st leg)**
**May 19 v Aston Villa (a) 3–0**
*Carter 3*
Grant; Nicholas, Parr, Bullions, Leuty, Baxter, Crooks, Powell, Jordan, Carter, Duncan.
*Att: 24,000*
**Final (2nd leg)**
**May 26 v Aston Villa (h) 6–0 (aggregate 9–0)**
*Doherty 5, Jordan*
Grant; Nicholas, Parr, Bullions, Leuty, Baxter, Crooks, Powell, Jordan, Doherty, Duncan.
*Att: 16,218*

Midland Cup winners Sammy Crooks, Jack Nicholas and Dally Duncan.

**Appearances (League and Cup only):** Leuty 43, Parr 42, Bullions 41, Duncan 40, Musson 38, Doherty (Manchester C) 29, Carter (Sunderland) 28, Savage (Queen of the South) 27, Trim 27, Crooks 26, Lyman (Spurs) 25, Powell 22, Nicholas 17, T. Jones 9, Tapping (Blackpool) 9, Morrison 8, Smith (Aberdeen) 8, Baxter (Nottm F) 5, Bilton 5, Baird (Huddersfield T) 3, Grant (Leicester C) 3, Harrison 3, Jordan (Doncaster R) 3, Wainwright 3, Boulton 2, Knight 2, Marshall (Burnley) 2, Vanham 2, Williams (Walsall) 2, Brown (Charlton A) 1, Butler 1, Eccles 1, Johnston (Nottm F) 1, Kinnerley 1, Lambert 1, Slack 1, Stephen (Bradford) 1, Townsend 1, Ward 1.
**Goalscorers (League and Cup only):** Doherty 35 (4 pen), Carter 29, Lyman 18, Duncan 11, Tapping 10, Crooks 9 Powell 5, Wainwright 3, Smith 2, Baird 1, Bullions 1, Harrison 1, Jones 1, Jordan 1, Leuty 1, Morris 1, Slack 1. Opponents own-goal: Baxter (Nottm F) 1, Howe (Leicester C) 1.

**Football League North**

| | P | W | D | L | F | A | Pts | Pos |
|---|---|---|---|---|---|---|---|---|
| (First Period) | 18 | 14 | 1 | 3 | 54 | 19 | 29 | 2nd |
| (Second Period) | 26 | 19 | 3 | 4 | 78 | 28 | 41 | 1st |

**VE DAY CELEBRATION MATCH**
**May 9 v Nottingham Forest (h) 2–2**
*Doherty 2*
Stretton; Parr, Moran, Bullions, Leuty, Attwood, T. Jones, Carter, Lyman, Doherty, Duncan.
*Att: 6,901*

In May 1945, a Horsley Woodhouse coal merchant was fined £1 10s (£1.50) plus costs, after being found guilty by Derby magistrates for 'misuse of petrol'. His crime? He had driven his son to the Baseball Ground to watch the Rams.

**1945–46**
**FOOTBALL LEAGUE SOUTH**
**Aug 25 v Fulham (h) 5–2**
*Lyman 2, Powell, Morrison, Duncan*
Boulton; Nicholas, Parr, Bullions, Leuty, Musson, Crooks, Powell, Lyman, Morrison, Duncan.
*Att: 15,000*
**Sep 1 v Fulham (a) 1–2**
*Doherty*
Boulton; Nicholas, Trim, Bullions, Leuty, Musson, Crooks, Powell, Harrison, Doherty, Duncan.
*Att: 21,217*
**Sep 8 v Plymouth Argyle (a) 4–0**
*Harrison 2, Morrison, Musson*
Boulton; Nicholas, Parr, Bullions, Leuty, Musson, Crooks, Powell, Harrison, Morrison, Duncan.
*Att: 16,953*
**Sep 12 v Brentford (a) 0–0**
Boulton; Nicholas, Parr, Bullions, Leuty, Musson, Crooks, Powell, Lyman, Morrison, Duncan.
*Att: 11,000*
**Sep 15 v Plymouth Argyle (h) 3–1**
*Musson, Morrison, Duncan*
Boulton; Parr, Trim, Bullions, Nicholas, Musson, Crooks, Powell, Lyman, Morrison, Duncan.
*Att: 15,220*
**Sep 19 v Chelsea (a) 0–3**
Savage; Nicholas, Parr, Bullions, Leuty, Musson, Crooks, Powell, Lyman, Morrison, Duncan.
*Att: 17,000*
**Sep 22 v Portsmouth (h) 3–1**
*Morrison 2, Doherty*
Savage; Nicholas, Parr, Bullions, Leuty, Musson, Crooks, Powell, Morrison, Doherty, Duncan.
*Att: 19,362*
**Sep 29 v Portsmouth (a) 0–3**
Savage; Nicholas, Parr, Bullions, Leuty, Musson, Beasley, Powell, Price, Morrison, Duncan.
*Att: 28,000*
**Oct 6 v Nottingham Forest (a) 1–1**
*Doherty*
Savage; Nicholas, Parr, Bullions, Leuty, Musson, Crooks, Powell, Morrison, Doherty, Duncan.
*Att: 30,130*
**Oct 13 v Nottingham Forest (h) 3–2**
*Price 3*
Savage; Nicholas, Parr, Bullions, Leuty, Musson, Crooks, Powell, Price, Doherty, Duncan.
*Att: 22,271*
**Oct 20 v Newport County (h) 4–1**
*Duncan 2, Doherty, Powell*
Boulton; Nicholas, Parr, Hann, Leuty, Musson, Crooks, Powell, Morrison, Doherty, Duncan.
*Att: 16,688*
**Oct 27 v Newport County (a) 4–1**
*Morrison 3, Doherty*
Boulton; Nicholas, Trim, Hann, Leuty, Musson, Crooks, Powell, Morrison, Doherty, Duncan.
*Att: 14,000*

**Nov 3 v Wolverhampton Wanderers (a) 0–1**
Boulton; Parr, Trim, Hann, Nicholas, Musson, Harrison, Powell, Morrison, Doherty, Duncan.
*Att: 23,000*

**Nov 10 v Wolverhampton Wanderers (h) 2–0**
*Morrison, Doherty*
Boulton; Nicholas, Parr, Hann, Leuty, Musson, Crooks, Harrison, Morrison, Doherty, Duncan.
*Att: 22,836*

**Nov 17 v West Ham United (h) 5–1**
*Harrison 2, Doherty 2, Walker (og)*
Boulton; Nicholas, Parr, Hann, Leuty, Musson, Crooks, Harrison, Morrison, Doherty, Duncan.
*Att: 21,935*

**Nov 24 v West Ham United (a) 3–2**
*Stamps, Doherty, Duncan*
Boulton; Nicholas, Parr, Eggleston, Leuty, Morrison, Crooks, Harrison, Stamps, Doherty, Duncan.
*Att: 28,500*

**Dec 1 v West Bromwich Albion (a) 3–2**
*Doherty 2, Stamps*
Boulton; Nicholas, Parr, Bullions, Leuty, Eggleston, Morrison, Harrison, Stamps, Doherty, Duncan.
*Att: 26,000*

**Dec 8 v West Bromwich Albion (h) 3–3**
*Harrison, Carter, McCulloch*
Boulton; Nicholas, Parr, Eggleston, Leuty, Morrison, Harrison, Carter, McCulloch, Doherty, Duncan.
*Att: 29,018*

**Dec 15 v Birmingham City (h) 0–2**
Boulton; Nicholas, Parr, Eggleston, Leuty, Hann, Harrison, Stamps, McCulloch, Doherty, Duncan.
*Att: 20,328*

**Dec 22 v Birmingham City (a) 0–1**
Boulton; Nicholas, Parr, Bullions, Leuty, Ward, Harrison, Carter, Morrison, Doherty, Duncan.
*Att: 30,000*

**Dec 25 v Tottenham Hotspur (a) 5–2**
*Doherty 2, Carter, Morrison, Duncan*
Boulton; Nicholas, Parr, Bullions, Leuty, Ward, Harrison, Carter, Morrison, Doherty, Duncan.
*Att: 33,000*

**Dec 26 v Tottenham Hotspur (h) 2–0**
*Carter, Morrison*
Boulton; Nicholas, Parr, Bullions, Leuty, Ward, Harrison, Carter, Morrison, Doherty, Duncan.
*Att: 30,823*

**Dec 29 v Brentford (h) 3–2**
*Carter 2, Doherty*
Boulton; Nicholas, Parr, Bullions, Leuty, Ward, Harrison, Carter, Morrison, Doherty, Duncan.
*Att: 22,751*

**Jan 12 v Millwall (h) 8–1**
*Morrison 3, Carter 2, Harrison, Doherty, Duncan*
Boulton; Nicholas, Parr, Bullions, Leuty, Eggleston, Harrison, Carter, Morrison, Doherty, Duncan.
*Att: 20,174*

**Jan 19 v Millwall (a) 2–1**
*Carter, Doherty*
Boulton; Nicholas, Parr, Bullions, Leuty, Eggleston, Harrison, Carter, Morrison, Doherty, Duncan.
*Att: 20,000*

**Feb 2 v Southampton (h) 8–1**
*Morrison 3, Stamps 3, Harrison, Duncan*
Boulton; Nicholas, Parr, Bullions, Leuty, Musson, Harrison, Carter, Morrison, Stamps, Duncan.
*Att: 19,608*

**Feb 16 v Swansea Town (h) 2–1**
*Morrison, Doherty (pen)*
Boulton; Nicholas, Parr, Bullions, Leuty, Musson, Crooks, Carter, Morrison, Doherty, Duncan.
*Att: 22,825*

**Feb 21 v Swansea Town (a) 3–2**
*Carter, Stamps, Doherty*
Bilton; Nicholas, Parr, Bullions, Leuty, Musson, Crooks, Carter, Stamps, Doherty, Brinton.
*Att: 25,000*

**Feb 23 v Leicester City (a) 1–1**
*Powell*
Bilton; Nicholas, Parr, Bullions, Leuty, Musson, Crooks, Powell, Harrison, Stamps, Duncan.
*Att: 21,640*

**Mar 14 v Coventry City (a) 1–3**
*Doherty (pen)*
Woodley; Nicholas, Parr, Bullions, Leuty, Musson, Harrison, Carter, Morrison, Doherty, Shearer.
*Att: 14,246*

**Mar 16 v Coventry City (h) 3–0**
*Stamps 2, Doherty*
Woodley; Nicholas, Parr, Bullions, Leuty, Musson, Harrison, Carter, Stamps, Doherty, Duncan.
*Att: 21,877*

**Mar 30 v Luton Town (a) 1–1**
*Carter*

The forward line for the League South game against West Brom at the Baseball Ground in December 1945. Reg Harrison, Raich Carter, Dave McCulloch, Peter Doherty, Dally Duncan.

Woodley; Nicholas, Parr, Bullions, Howe, Musson, Harrison, Carter, Stamps, Doherty, Morrison.
*Att: 18,507*

**Apr 3 v Luton Town (h) 4–3**
*Doherty 2, Simpson, Gager (og)*
Boulton; Nicholas, Parr, Bullions, Howe, Musson, Simpson, Carter, McCulloch, Doherty, Morrison.
*Att: 16,490*

**Apr 6 v Aston Villa (a) 1–4**
*Cummings (og)*
Griffiths; Nicholas, Trim, Eggleston, Howe, Musson, Harrison, Carter, McCulloch, Doherty, Morrison.
*Att: 50,000*

**Apr 10 v Leicester City (h) 4–1**
*Duncan 2, Doherty (pen), Carter*
Allsop; Nicholas, Howe, Bullions, Leuty, Eggleston, Slack, Carter, Stamps, Doherty, Duncan.
*Att: 15,541*

**Apr 13 v Aston Villa (h) 0–1**
Allsop; Nicholas, Howe, Bullions, Leuty, Musson, Harrison, Carter, Stamps, Doherty, Duncan.
*Att: 27,936*

**Apr 19 v Arsenal (h) 1–1**
*Male (og)*
Woodley; Nicholas, Howe, Bullions, Leuty, Musson, Harrison, Carter, Stamps, Doherty, Duncan.
*Att: 28,156*

**Apr 20 v Charlton Athletic (a) 1–2**
*Stamps*
Woodley; Nicholas, Howe, Bullions, Leuty, Musson, Crooks, Harrison, McCulloch, Stamps, Morrison.
*Att: 50,000*

**Apr 22 v Arsenal (a) 1–0**
*Stamps*
Woodley; Nicholas, Howe, Bullions, Leuty, Musson, Harrison, Carter, Stamps, Doherty, Duncan.
*Att: 27,540*

**Apr 29 v Southampton (a) 2–4**
*McCulloch, Stamps*

Woodley; Nicholas, Howe, Bullions, Leuty, Ward, Harrison, Stamps, McCulloch, Doherty, Morrison.
*Att: 22,000*
**May 1 v Charlton Athletic (h) 3–1**
*Carter, Stamps, Doherty*
Woodley; Nicholas, Howe, Bullions, Leuty, Musson, Harrison, Carter, Stamps, Doherty, Duncan.
*Att: 30,000*
**May 4 v Chelsea (h) 1–1**
*Carter*
Boulton; Nicholas, Howe, Bullions, Leuty, Musson, Harrison, Carter, McCulloch, Stamps, Duncan.
*Att: 27,000*

**Appearances (Football League South):** Nicholas 42, Leuty 37, Duncan 35, Bullions 33, Doherty (Manchester C) 32, Parr 31, Morrison 30, Musson 30, Harrison 28, Boulton 24, Carter (Sunderland) 21, Crooks 18, Stamps 16, Powell 14, Howe 11, Eggleston 8, Woodley 8, McCulloch 7, Hann 6, Savage (Queen of the South) 5, Trim 5, Ward 5, Lyman (Spurs) 4, Allsop 2, Bilton 2, Price (Huddersfield T) 2, Beasley (Spurs) 1, Brinton 1, Griffiths 1, Shearer 1, Simpson (Coventry C) 1, Slack 1.
(Carter and Doherty were transferred to Derby County in December 1945).
**Goalscorers (Football League South):** Doherty 24 (3 pens), Morrison 18, Carter 13, Stamps 12, Duncan 10, Harrison 7, Powell 3, Price 3, Lyman 2, McCulloch 2, Musson 2, Simpson 1. Opponents own-goals: Cummings (Aston Villa) 1, Gager (Luton T) 1, Male (Arsenal) 1, Walker (West Ham U) 1.

**VJ DAY CELEBRATION MATCH**
**Aug 16 v Nottingham Forest (a) 4–1**
*Attwood 2, Carter, Duncan*
Watson; Nicholas, Parr, Bullions, Leuty, Musson, Jones, Powell, Attwood, Carter, Duncan.

**Football League South**

| | P | W | D | L | F | A | Pts |
|---|---|---|---|---|---|---|---|
| Birmingham City | 42 | 28 | 5 | 9 | 96 | 45 | 61 |
| Aston Villa | 42 | 25 | 11 | 6 | 106 | 58 | 61 |
| Charlton Athletic | 42 | 25 | 10 | 7 | 92 | 45 | 60 |
| DERBY COUNTY | 42 | 24 | 7 | 11 | 101 | 62 | 55 |
| West Brom A | 42 | 22 | 8 | 12 | 104 | 69 | 52 |
| Wolverhampton W | 42 | 20 | 11 | 11 | 75 | 48 | 51 |
| West Ham United | 42 | 20 | 11 | 11 | 94 | 76 | 51 |
| Fulham | 42 | 20 | 10 | 12 | 93 | 73 | 50 |
| Tottenham H | 42 | 22 | 3 | 17 | 78 | 81 | 47 |
| Chelsea | 42 | 19 | 6 | 17 | 92 | 80 | 44 |
| Arsenal | 42 | 16 | 11 | 15 | 76 | 73 | 43 |
| Millwall | 42 | 17 | 8 | 17 | 79 | 105 | 42 |
| Coventry C | 42 | 15 | 10 | 17 | 70 | 69 | 40 |
| Brentford | 42 | 14 | 10 | 18 | 82 | 72 | 38 |
| Nottingham F | 42 | 12 | 13 | 17 | 72 | 73 | 37 |
| Southampton | 42 | 14 | 9 | 19 | 97 | 105 | 37 |
| Swansea Town | 42 | 15 | 7 | 20 | 90 | 112 | 37 |
| Luton Town | 42 | 13 | 7 | 22 | 60 | 92 | 33 |
| Portsmouth | 42 | 11 | 6 | 25 | 66 | 87 | 28 |
| Leicester City | 42 | 8 | 7 | 27 | 57 | 101 | 23 |
| Newport County | 42 | 9 | 2 | 31 | 52 | 125 | 20 |
| Plymouth Argyle | 42 | 3 | 8 | 31 | 39 | 120 | 14 |

# Rams Internationals

UNTIL 1993 and the signing of United States international John Harkes, the list of Derby County players winning representative honours was confined to the countries making up the British Isles. Since then, 19 more nations have been added. Some players appeared in internationals while on loan to Derby and are marked by an asterisk(*). Players belong to clubs holding their permanent registration. In the case of Giorgi Kinkladze, this applies only to his appearance against Israel: before his next cap, he joined Derby permanently. The Republic of Ireland first played as a separate nation in 1924 but Eire-born players appeared for Northern Ireland until after World War Two. [Correct to 30 June 2006]

## ENGLAND

**Bagshaw J.J.** 1919–20 v Ireland (1).

**Barker J.W.** 1934–35 v Wales, Italy, Northern Ireland, Scotland, Holland; 1935–36 v Northern Ireland, Germany, Wales, Scotland, Austria; 1936–37 v Wales (11).

**Bloomer S.** 1894–95 v Ireland, Scotland; 1895–96 v Ireland, Wales; 1896–97 v Ireland, Wales, Scotland; 1897–98 v Scotland; 1898–99 v Ireland, Wales, Scotland; 1899–1900 v Scotland; 1900–01 v Wales, Scotland; 1901–02 v Wales, Ireland, Scotland; 1903–04 v Scotland; 1904–05 v Ireland, Wales, Scotland (21).

**Bowers J.W.A.** 1933–34 v Northern Ireland, Wales, Scotland (3).

**Buckley F.C.** 1913–14 v Ireland (1).

**Carter H.S.** 1946–47 v Northern Ireland, Republic of Ireland, Wales, Holland, Scotland, France, Switzerland (7).

**Cooper T.** 1927–28 v Northern Ireland; 1928–29 v Northern Ireland, Wales, Scotland, France, Belgium, Spain; 1930–31 v France; 1931–32 v Wales, Spain; 1932–33 v Scotland; 1933–34 v Scotland, Hungary, Czechoslovakia; 1934–35 v Wales (15).

**Cox J.D.** 1891–92 v Ireland (1).

**Crooks S.D.** 1929–30 v Scotland, Germany, Austria; 1930–31 v Northern Ireland, Wales, Scotland, France, Belgium; 1931–32 v Northern Ireland, Wales, Spain, Scotland; 1932–33 v Northern Ireland, Wales, Austria; 1933–34 v Northern Ireland, Wales, France, Scotland, Hungary, Czechoslovakia; 1934–35 v Northern Ireland; 1935–36 v Wales, Scotland; 1936–37 v Wales, Hungary (26).

**Davis G.H.** 1903–04 v Wales, Ireland (2).

**Dix R.W.** 1938–39 v Norway (1).

**George C.F.** 1976–77 v Republic of Ireland (1).

**Goodall J.** 1890–91 v Wales, Scotland; 1891–92 v Scotland; 1892–93 v Wales; 1893–94 v Scotland; 1894–95 v Ireland, Scotland; 1895–96 v Wales, Scotland; 1897–98 v Wales (10).

**Hector K.J.** 1973–74 v Poland (sub), Italy (sub) (2).

**Howe J.R.** 1947–48 v Italy; 1948–49 v Northern Ireland, Scotland (3).

**Johnson S.A.M.** 2000–01 v Italy (sub) (1).

**Keen E.R.L.** 1932–33 v Austria; 1936–37 v Wales, Northern Ireland, Hungary (4).

**Kinsey G.** 1895–96 v Ireland, Wales (2).

**Lee J.** 1950–51 v Northern Ireland (1).

**McFarland R.L.** 1970–71 v Malta, Greece, Malta, Northern Ireland, Scotland; 1971–72 v Switzerland, Greece, West Germany, Wales, Scotland; 1972–73 v Wales, Wales, Northern Ireland, Wales, Scotland, Czechoslovakia, Poland, USSR, Italy; 1973–74 v Austria, Poland, Italy, Wales, Northern Ireland; 1975–76 v Czechoslovakia, Scotland; 1976–77 v Republic of Ireland, Italy (28).

**Maskrey H.M.** 1907–08 v Ireland (1).
**Moore J.** 1922–23 v Sweden (1).
**Morris J.** 1948–49 v Norway, France; 1949–50 v Republic of Ireland (3).
**Mozley B.** 1949–50 v Republic of Ireland, Wales, Northern Ireland (3).
**Nish D.J.** 1972–73 v Northern Ireland; 1973–74 v Portugal, Wales, Northern Ireland, Scotland (5).
**Quantrill A.E.** 1919–20 v Wales, Scotland; 1920–21 v Ireland, Wales (4).
**Richards G.H.** 1908–09 v Austria (1).
**Robinson J.W.** 1896–97 v Ireland, Scotland (2).
**Scattergood E.O.** 1912–13 v Wales (1).
**Shilton P.L.** 1987–88 v West Germany, Turkey, Yugoslavia, Holland, Scotland, Colombia, Switzerland, Republic of Ireland, Holland; 1988–89 v Denmark, Sweden, Greece, Albania, Albania, Chile, Scotland, Poland, Denmark; 1989–90 v Sweden, Poland, Italy, Yugoslavia, Brazil, Czechoslovakia, Denmark, Uruguay, Tunisia, Republic of Ireland, Holland, Egypt, Belgium, Cameroon, West Germany, Italy (34).
**Stephenson G.T.** 1927–28 v France, Belgium (2).
**Storer H.** 1923–24 v France; 1927–28 v Northern Ireland (2).
**Thornewell G.** 1922–23 v Sweden, Sweden; 1923–24 v France; 1924–25 v France (4).
**Todd C.** 1971–72 v Northern Ireland; 1973–74 v Portugal, Wales, Northern Ireland, Scotland, Argentina, East Germany, Bulgaria, Yugoslavia; 1974–75 v Portugal (sub), West Germany, Cyprus, Cyprus, Northern Ireland, Wales, Scotland; 1975–76 v Switzerland, Czechoslovakia, Portugal, Northern Ireland, Scotland, Brazil, Finland; 1976–77 v Republic of Ireland, Finland, Holland (sub), Northern Ireland (27).
**Turner J.A.** 1897–98 v Ireland (1).
**Ward T.V.** 1947–48 v Belgium; 1948–49 v Wales (2).
**Warren B.** 1905–06 v Ireland, Wales, Scotland; 1906–07 v Ireland, Wales, Scotland; 1907–08 v Ireland, Wales, Scotland, Austria, Austria, Hungary, Bohemia (13).
**Wright M.** 1987–88 v Israel, Holland (sub), Colombia, Switzerland, Republic of Ireland, Holland; 1989–90 v Czechoslovakia (sub), Tunisia (sub), Holland, Egypt, Belgium, Cameroon, West Germany, Italy; 1990–91 v Hungary, Poland, Republic of Ireland, Cameroon, Republic of Ireland, USSR, Argentina, Australia, New Zealand, Malaysia (24).
[**Spilsbury B.W.** 1884–85 v Ireland; 1885–86 v Ireland, Scotland (3). Spilsbury appeared for England as a Cambridge University player but also represented Derby County in Cup and League between 1885 and 1889.]

## SCOTLAND

**Burley C.W.** 1999–2000 v Holland, Republic of Ireland; 2000–01 v Croatia, Australia, Belgium, San Marino; 2001–02 v Croatia, Belgium, Latvia; 2002–03 v Austria (10).
**Dailly C.E.** 1996–97 v Wales, Malta, Belarus; 1997–98 v Belarus, Latvia, France, Denmark, Finland, Colombia, United States, Brazil, Norway, Morocco (13).
**Duncan D.** 1932–33 v Wales, England; 1933–34 v Wales, Austria; 1934–35 v Wales, England; 1935–36 v Wales, Northern Ireland, England; 1936–37 v Germany, Northern Ireland, Wales, England; 1937–38 v Wales (14).
**Gallacher H.K.** 1934–35 v England (1).
**Gemmill A.** 1970–71 v Belgium; 1971–72 v Portugal, Holland, Peru, Northern Ireland, Wales, England; 1975–76 v Denmark, Romania, Wales, Northern Ireland, England; 1976–77 v Finland, Czechoslovakia, Wales, Wales, Northern Ireland (sub), England (sub), Chile (sub), Argentina, Brazil; 1977–78 v East Germany (sub) (22).

**McCulloch D.** 1938–39 v Wales, Hungary (2).
**Masson D.S.** 1977–78 v Northern Ireland, England, Peru (3).
**Napier C.E.** 1936–37 v Northern Ireland, Austria (2).
**O'Hare J.** 1969–70 v Northern Ireland, Wales, England; 1970–71 v Denmark, Belgium, Wales, Northern Ireland; 1971–72 v Portugal, Belgium, Holland (sub), Peru, Northern Ireland, Wales (13).
**O'Neil B.** 2000–01 v Australia (1).
**Rioch B.D.** 1974–75 v Portugal, Wales, Northern Ireland, England, Romania; 1975–76 v Denmark, Denmark, Romania, Wales, Northern Ireland, England; 1976–77 v Finland, Czechoslovakia, Wales; 1977–78 v Northern Ireland, England, Peru, Holland (18).
**Robertson J.N.** 1983–84 v Uruguay, Belgium (2).
**Steel W.** 1947–48 v Northern Ireland, Wales, England, France; 1948–49 v Wales, Northern Ireland, England, France; 1949–50 v Northern Ireland, Wales, England, Switzerland, Portugal, France (14).

## WALES

**Astley D.J.** 1938–39 v England, Scotland (2).
**Durban W.A.** 1965–66 v Brazil (sub); 1966–67 v Northern Ireland; 1967–68 v England, Scotland, Northern Ireland, West Germany; 1968–69 v West Germany, East Germany, Scotland, England, Northern Ireland; 1969–70 v East Germany, Italy, England, Scotland, Northern Ireland; 1970–71 v Romania, Czechoslovakia, Scotland, England, Northern Ireland, Finland; 1971–72 v Finland, Czechoslovakia, England, Scotland, Northern Ireland (27).
***Edwards R.O.** 2003–04 v Scotland , Hungary (sub) (2).
**Hennessey W.T.** 1969–70 v England, Scotland, Northern Ireland; 1971–72 v Finland, Czechoslovakia, England, Scotland; 1972–73 v England (8).
**James L.** 1975–76 v Yugoslavia, Scotland, England, Northern Ireland, Yugoslavia; 1976–77 v West Germany, Scotland, Czechoslovakia, Scotland, England, Northern Ireland; 1977–78 v Kuwait, Kuwait (13).
**Morris C.R.** 1900–01 v Scotland, England, Ireland; 1901–02 v England; 1902–03 v England, Scotland, Ireland; 1903–04 v Ireland; 1904–05 v Scotland, England, Ireland; 1905–06 v Scotland; 1906–07 v Scotland; 1907–08 v Scotland, England; 1908–09 v Scotland, England, Ireland; 1909–10 v Scotland, England, Ireland (21).
**Nyatanga L.J.** 2005–06 v Paraguay, Trinidad and Tobago (sub) (2).
**Pembridge M.A.** 1991–92 v Holland, Japan (sub); 1992–93 v Belgium (sub), Republic of Ireland; 1993–94 v Norway (sub); 1994–95 v Albania (sub), Moldova, Georgia (sub) (8).
**Saunders D.N.** 1988–89 v Israel, Sweden, West Germany; 1989–90 v Finland, Holland, West Germany, Sweden, Costa Rica; 1990–91 v Denmark, Belgium, Luxembourg, Republic of Ireland, Belgium, Iceland, Poland, West Germany (16).
**Thomas R.J.** 1973–74 v England, Scotland, Northern Ireland; 1974–75 v Hungary, Luxembourg, Hungary, Luxembourg, Scotland, England, Northern Ireland; 1975–76 v Austria, Yugoslavia, England; 1976–77 v Czechoslovakia, Scotland, England, Northern Ireland; 1977–78 v Kuwait, Scotland (19).
**Trollope P.J.** 1996–97 v Scotland; 1997–98 v Brazil (sub) (2).
**Williams D.G.** 1987–88 v Czechoslovakia, Yugoslavia, Sweden, Malta, Italy; 1988–89 v Holland, Israel, Sweden, West Germany; 1989–90 v Finland, Holland (11).

## NORTHERN IRELAND (and Ireland before 1924)

**Caskey W.T.** 1978–79 v Bulgaria, England, Bulgaria, England, Scotland (sub), Denmark (sub); 1979–80 v England (sub) (7).

**Doherty P.D.** 1946–47 v England (1).
**Goodall A.L.** 1898–99 v Wales, Scotland; 1899–1900 v Wales, England; 1900–01 v England; 1901–02 v Scotland; 1902–03 v England, Wales (8).
**Halligan W.** 1910–11 v Wales (1).
**Mercer J.T.** 1903–04 v England, Wales; 1904–05 v Scotland (3).
**Moreland V.** 1978–79 v Bulgaria (sub), Bulgaria (sub), England, Scotland; 1979–80 v England, Republic of Ireland (6).
**O'Brien M.T.** 1926–27 v Wales (1).
**Reid S.E.** 1933–34 v England, Wales; 1935–36 v England (3).
**Stewart A.** 1967–68 v Wales; 1968–69 v Israel, Turkey (sub), Turkey (4).

### REPUBLIC OF IRELAND

**Carsley L.K.** 1997–98 v Romania, Belgium (sub), Belgium, Czech Republic, Argentina, Mexico; 1998–99 v Croatia (sub), Malta (sub), Paraguay (sub) (9).
**Daly G.A.** 1976–77 v France, Bulgaria; 1977–78 v Bulgaria, Turkey, Denmark; 1978–79 v Northern Ireland, England, Denmark, Bulgaria; 1979–80 v Northern Ireland, England, Cyprus, Switzerland, Argentina (14).
**Delap R.J.** 1997–98 v Czech Republic (sub), Argentina (sub), Mexico (sub); 1999–2000 v Turkey, Turkey, Greece (sub) (6).
**Fagan F.** 1959–60 v Chile, West Germany, Sweden; 1960–61 v Wales, Norway, Scotland (6).
**Langan D.F.** 1977–78 v Turkey, Norway; 1979–80 v Switzerland, Argentina (4).
**McGrath P.** 1996–97 v Wales (1).
**Macken A.** 1976–77 v Spain (1).
**O'Brien M.T.** 1926–27 v Italy (1).
**Ryan G.J.** 1977–78 v Turkey (1).
**Ryan R.A.** 1955–56 v Spain (1).
***Stapleton F.A.** 1987–88 v Romania, Yugoslavia, Norway, England, USSR, Holland (6).

## *Nations Outside the British Isles*

### AUSTRALIA

**Blatsis C.** 2000–01 v South Korea (sub), Colombia (2).

### BELGIUM

**Strupar B.** 1999–2000 v Portugal, Holland, Denmark, Sweden, Italy, Turkey (sub); 2000–01 v Croatia; 2001–02 v Slovakia, Algeria (sub), Japan (sub), Tunisia (11).

### CANADA

**Peschisolido P.P.** 2003–04 v Wales (sub), Belize, Belize (sub); 2004–05 v Guatemala, Honduras (5).

### COSTA RICA

**Solis M.** 1996–97 v El Salvador, Canada, Brazil, Colombia, Mexico; 1997–98 v El Salvador, Jamaica, Mexico (8).
**Wanchope P.** 1996–97 v El Salvador, Jamaica, Canada; 1997–98 v Mexico, Cuba, United States; 1998–99 v Ecuador, Belize, Honduras, El Salvador, Chile (11).

## CROATIA

**Asanovic A.** 1996–97 v Bosnia–Herzegovina, Greece, Morocco, Czech Republic, Denmark, Slovenia, Greece, Japan; 1997–98 v Bosnia–Herzegovina (sub), Denmark, Ukraine (sub), Ukraine (12).
**Stimac I.** 1995–96 v South Korea, Israel, England, Republic of Ireland, Turkey, Denmark, Germany; 1996–97 v Greece, Morocco, Czech Republic; 1997–98 v Bosnia–Herzegovina, Denmark, Poland, Slovakia, Iran, Australia, Jamaica, Japan, Argentina (sub), Romania, Germany, France, Holland; 1998–99 v Republic of Ireland, Macedonia, Denmark; 1999–2000 v Yugoslavia, Malta, Republic of Ireland (29).

## DENMARK

**Beck M.V.** 1999–2000 v Sweden (sub), France (sub), Czech Republic (3).
**Laursen J.** 1996–97 v Sweden, Slovenia, Greece, France, Croatia, Slovenia, Bosnia–Herzegovina; 1997–98 v Bosnia–Herzegovina, Scotland, Sweden (sub), France; 1999–2000 v Holland (sub), Israel (sub) (13).

## ESTONIA

**Poom M.** 1996–97 v Scotland, Austria, Latvia, Azerbaijan, Sweden, Andorra (sub); 1997–98 v Austria, Latvia, Sweden, Faroe Islands; 1998–99 v Bosnia–Herzegovina, Scotland, Czech Republic, Georgia, Cyprus, Lithuania, Czech Republic, Lithuania; 1999–2000 v Faroe Islands, Scotland, Luxembourg, Belarus, Georgia; 2000–01 v Portugal, Andorra, Republic of Ireland, Krygystan, Finland; 2001–02 v Greece, Kazakhstan, Poland, San Marino; 2002–03 v Azerbaijan, Moldova, Croatia, Belgium, Iceland (37).

## FINLAND

**Valakari S.J.** 2000–01 v Norway, Albania, Greece, England; 2001–02 v South Korea, Portugal (sub), Macedonia (sub), Latvia (sub); 2002–03 v Barbados, Trinidad and Tobago, Northern Ireland, Iceland, Norway, Serbia and Montenegro, Italy; 2003–04 v Denmark, Azerbaijan (sub) (17).

## GEORGIA

***Kinkladze G.** 1999–2000 v Israel, Azerbaijan, Estonia; 2000–01 v Lithuania, Italy, Romania, Israel, Hungary (sub); 2001–02 v Hungary, Lithuania, Romania, Ukraine; 2002–03 v Turkey, Switzerland, Republic of Ireland (15).

## ICELAND

***Gudjonsson T.** 2000–01 v Bulgaria, Malta (2).

## ISRAEL

***Nimni A.** 1999–2000 v Russia (1).

## JAMAICA

**Burton D.J.** 1997–98 v Trinidad and Tobago, Canada, Costa Rica, United States, El Salvador, Mexico, Brazil, Guatemala, El Salvador, Mexico, Brazil, Nigeria, Wales, Saudi Arabia, South Korea, South Korea, Croatia, Argentina, Japan (sub); 1998–99 v Costa Rica (sub); 1999–2000 v Cayman Islands (sub), Cayman Islands, Colombia (sub), Honduras; Summer 2000 v Romania, Cuba, St Vincent (sub), Honduras; 2000–01 v El Salvador, El Salvador, Bolivia, Bulgaria, Trinidad and Tobago, Mexico, Honduras, Costa Rica, Trinidad and Tobago; 2001–02 v Mexico, Honduras, United States (sub), Nigeria; 2002–03 v Nigeria (42).

**Johnson M.O.** 2003–04 v Australia (1).
**Powell D.A.** 1997–98 v Wales (sub), Macedonia, South Korea, Croatia (sub), Argentina; 1998–99 v Costa Rica, Norway, Sweden (sub); Summer 2000 v Cuba, Barbados, Trinidad and Tobago, St Vincent, Honduras; 2000–01 v Bolivia, Bulgaria, Trinidad and Tobago, Mexico, Trinidad and Tobago; 2001–02 v Mexico (19).

## NIGERIA
**West T.** 2000–01 v Zambia, Sudan, Ghana, Sierra Leone, Liberia (5).

## NORWAY
**Bohinen L.** 1998–99 v Greece (sub) (1).
**Bragstad B.O.** 2000–01 v Finland (1).

## POLAND
**Rasiak G.** 2004–05 v Austria, France (sub), Belarus (sub), Northern Ireland (sub); 2005–06 Serbia and Montenegro, Israel (sub) (6).

## SWEDEN
***Rahmberg M.** 1996–97 v Romania, Thailand, Japan (sub), Thailand (4).

## TRINIDAD AND TOBAGO
***John S.** 2005–06 v Panama, Mexico, Bahrein, Bahrein (4).

## UNITED STATES
**Harkes J.A.** 1993–94 v Switzerland, Colombia, Romania; Summer 1995 v Nigeria, Mexico, Colombia, Chile, Bolivia, Argentina, Mexico, Brazil (11).

## ENGLAND 'B'
**Forsyth M.E.** 1989–90 v Yugoslavia (1).
**Hill G.A.** 1977–78 v Malaysia, New Zealand (three times), Singapore (5).
**Leuty L.H.** 1948–49 v Finland, Holland; 1949–50 v Holland (3).
**Morris J.** 1948–49 v Finland (1).

## SCOTLAND 'B'
***McIndoe M.** 2005–06 v Turkey (1).

## WALES 'B'
**Pembridge M.A.** 1993–94 v Scotland (1).

## REPUBLIC OF IRELAND 'B'
**Delap R.J.** 1997–98 v Northern Ireland (1).

## *Wartime and Victory INTERNATIONALS*
## ENGLAND
**Bagshaw J.J.** 1919–20 v Wales (1).
**Carter H.S.** 1945–46 v Switzerland, France (2).

## SCOTLAND

**McCulloch D.** 1939–40 v England (1).

## WALES

**Redfern W.J.** 1939–40 v England (1).

## NORTHERN IRELAND

**Doherty P.D.** 1945–46 v Wales (1).

# *Under-23 INTERNATIONALS*

## ENGLAND

**Davies R.** 1973–74 v Scotland (sub) (1).
**McFarland R.L.** 1968–69 v Holland, Holland, Belgium, Portugal; 1969–70 v Scotland (5).
**Powell S.** 1974–75 v Scotland (1).
**Robson J.D.** 1970–71 v West Germany, Sweden, Scotland; 1971–72 v Wales, Scotland, East Germany (6).
**Todd C.** 1970–71 v Scotland; 1971–72 v Wales; 1974–75 v Wales (3).

## SCOTLAND

**McGovern J.P.** 1971–72 v Wales; 1972–73 v Wales (2).
**O'Hare J.** 1969–70 v France, England, Wales (3).

## WALES

**Durban W.A.** 1963–64 v England, Scotland, Northern Ireland (3).

# *Under-21 INTERNATIONALS*

## ENGLAND

**Camp L.M.J.** 2004–05 v Spain (sub), Holland (sub); 2005–06 v Denmark (sub), Norway (sub) (4).
**Carbon M.P.** 1995–96 v Croatia (sub); 1996–97 v Georgia, Italy, Switzerland (4).
**Christie M.N.** 2000–01 v Finland (sub), Spain, Finland, Albania, Mexico, Greece; 2001–02 v Holland (sub), Greece (sub), Holland, Slovenia, Portugal (11).
**Elliott S.W.** 1997–98 v France (sub), Argentina (2).
**Forsyth M.E.** 1987–88 v Switzerland (1).
**Grant L.A.** 2002–03 v Italy (sub); 2003–04 v Portugal, Turkey, Sweden (sub) (4).
**Huddlestone T.A.** 2004–05 v Holland, Germany, Azerbaijan (3).
**Johnson S.A.M.** 1998–99 v Sweden, Bulgaria; 1999–2000 v Denmark, Argentina (sub), Yugoslavia, Italy, Turkey; 2000–01 v Finland; 2001–02 v Holland (sub), Albania (sub) (10).
**Johnson T.** 1991–92 v Mexico, Czechoslovakia (sub) (2).
**Kitson P.** 1991–92 v Mexico, Czechoslovakia, France (3).
**Kozluk R.** 1997–98 v France, Argentina (sub) (2).
**Ramage C.D.** 1990–91 v Poland (sub), Wales; 1991–92 v France (sub) (3).
**Riggott C.M.** 2000–01 v Spain (sub), Finland (sub), Albania, Mexico (sub); 2001–02 v Holland (sub), Slovenia, Portugal, Switzerland, Italy (9).
***Whittingham P.M.** 2005–06 v Poland, France, France (sub) (3).

**Williams P.D.** 1990–91 v Senegal, Mexico, USSR; 1991–92 v Germany, Turkey, Poland (6).

## WALES

**Clark J.** 1978–79 v England (1).
**Nyatanga L.J.** 2004–05 v Germany (sub); 2005–06 v Malta, England, Poland, Germany, Azerbaijan, Cyprus, Estonia (8).

## REPUBLIC OF IRELAND

**Carsley L.K.** 1995–96 v Portugal (1).

## PORTUGAL

***Costa C.A.M.** 2003–04 v Belarus, Slovakia (sub), Sweden (sub), Italy (sub) (4).

## *Football League REPRESENTATIVES*

**Barker J.W.** 1934–35 v Scottish League; 1935–36 v Irish League; 1936–37 v Irish League (3).
**Bedford H.** 1925–26 v Scottish League (1).
**Bloomer S.** 1896–97 v Irish League, Scottish League; 1897–98 v Irish League; 1898–99 v Irish League, Scottish League; 1899–1900 v Irish League, Scottish League; 1900–01 v Irish League; 1901–02 v Irish League, Scottish League; 1902–03 v Irish League; 1903–04 v Irish League, Scottish League; 1904–05 v Scottish League; 1910–11 v Scottish League (15).
**Bowers J.W.A.** 1933–34 v Irish League, Scottish League (2).
**Carter H.S.** 1946–47 v Scottish League (1).
**Cooper T.** 1926–27 v Irish League; 1928–29 v Irish League; 1932–33 v Irish League; 1934–35 v Irish League, Scottish League (5).
**Crooks S.D.** 1930–31 v Irish League, Scottish League; 1931–32 v Scottish League; 1933–34 v Irish League; 1936–37 v Scottish League (5).
**Dix R.W.** 1938–39 v Scottish League (1).
**Goodall J.** 1890–91 v Football Alliance; 1891–92 v Scottish League; 1893–94 v Scottish League; 1895–96 v Scottish League (4).
**Hector K.J.** 1970–71 v Irish League; 1971–72 v League of Ireland; 1973–74 v Scottish League (sub) (3).
**Keen E.R.L.** 1936–37 v Scottish League (1).
**Leuty L.H.** 1947–48 v Scottish League; 1948–49 v League of Ireland (2).
**Maskrey H.M.** 1905–06 v Irish League (1).
**McFarland R.L.** 1969–70 v Scottish League; 1970–71 v Scottish League; 1971–72 v League of Ireland; 1972–73 v Scottish League; 1973–74 v Scottish League; 1975–76 v Scottish League (6).
**Morris J.** 1949–50 v Irish League; 1950–51 v Irish League, Scottish League (3).
**Mozley B.** 1947–48 v Scottish League (1).
**Musson W.U.** 1949–50 v Irish League (1).
**Nish D.J.** 1972–73 v Scottish League; 1973–74 v Scottish League (2).
**Robson J.D.** 1970–71 v Irish League (1).
**Saunders D.N.** 1990–91 v Italian League (sub) (1).
**Shilton P.L.** 1987–88 v Rest of the World (1).
**Todd C.** 1971–72 v Scottish League; 1973–74 v Scottish League (2).
**Warren B.** 1905–06 v Scottish League; 1906–07 v Irish League, Scottish League; 1907–08 v Scottish League (4).
**Wright M.** 1990–91 v Italian League (1).

## *Unofficial* INTERNATIONALS

Wartime and Victory internationals did not earn full caps and are regarded as unofficial. Derby County players appeared in several similar fixtures, such as Players' Union matches, aimed to create revenue for the organisation, tours against nations emerging in the football sense and fund-raising occasions, especially after crowd disasters.

Jack Cox played against Germany twice and a Germany/Austria combination on the FA tour in November 1899. He refereed another of the games against Germany.

Steve Bloomer scored twice as the English Professionals beat Germany 10–0 at Hyde Road, Manchester, in September 1901. Bloomer played for England against Scotland at Ibrox Park, Glasgow, in April 1902. This was a full international but part of a stand collapsed. The death toll was 26 and 587 were later compensated for their injuries. The game was completed but declared unofficial.

George Richards played in two of the three meetings with South Africa on an FA tour from May to July 1910.

Horace Barnes scored both goals as England beat Scotland 2–0 in a Players' Union international at Shawfield Park, Glasgow, in April 1914.

Mick O'Brien played for the Irish Free State against Italy B at Lansdowne Road, Dublin, in April 1927.

Dally Duncan played against the United States twice and Eastern Canada during the Scottish FA tour of May and June 1935. He scored a hat-trick in the first game, Scotland winning 5–1 at the Polo Grounds, New York. Hughie Gallacher played in the second game against the United States, scoring once in a 4–1 victory at the Newark High School Stadium, New Jersey.

Duncan was again on the winning side when Scotland beat England 4–2 at Hampden Park, a match for the King George V Jubilee Trust Fund.

Leon Leuty played for England in a 2–2 draw with Scotland at Maine Road, Manchester, in August 1946, a match in aid of the Bolton Disaster Fund.

Billy Steel scored in both games as Scotland beat the American Soccer League and the United States at the Triborough Stadium, New York, in May and June 1949.

Tim Ward played in a 1–0 victory over the United States at the Triborough Stadium in June 1950. It was the only representative game and Bert Mozley was also a member of the FA team that won 10 of the 11 fixtures on the tour to the US and Canada.

Norman Nielson played for the Anglo-South African XI against South Africa at Highbury in November 1953.

In September 1894, John and Archie Goodall played for the Rest of the Football League against Champions Aston Villa in a testimonial match for William McGregor, the founder of the League.

Jimmy Moore played for the Football League against a Nottingham XI at Meadow Lane in December 1913. It was a testimonial for Tom Harris, a member of the management committee and director of Notts County.

In May 1935, Jack Barker and Sammy Crooks represented the Football League against West Bromwich Albion at The Hawthorns in a match celebrating the jubilee of King George V. The League used the game to test a system of two referees.

Reg Ryan played for the Third Division North against the Third South at Peel Park, Accrington, in October 1955 and scored a penalty in a 3–3 draw.

Albert Mays played in the following season's fixture at Highfield Road, Coventry.

The Football League began a series of representative matches against the Italian Serie B in 1990–91 and Derby County players were involved in three of them. Simon Coleman and Paul Williams played in Caserta in March 1992. Lee Carsley was picked in Andria in February 1995 and

Mark Stallard went on as substitute to score the winner in a 3–2 victory. Gary Rowett and Dean Sturridge, as a substitute, played at the Alfred McAlpine Stadium, Huddersfield, in November 1995. Lee Camp kept goal for the League Under-21 against Italian Serie B at the Kingston Communications Stadium, Hull, in February 2006.

Lewin Nyatanga played for Wales against a Basque XI in May 2006.

When Derby County played at The Valley on 12 November 1938, they fielded an all-international forward line of Sammy Crooks (England), Dai Astley (Wales), Dave McCulloch (Scotland), Ronnie Dix (England) and Dally Duncan (Scotland), following Dix's scoring debut against Norway three days earlier. This was not, however, the first time the Rams had fielded a front line made up entirely of international players. Two years previously, almost to the day, and on the same Charlton ground, Crooks, Astley, Jack Bowers (England), Charlie Napier (Scotland) and Duncan had played. It was the only time this forward line appeared in Derby colours. The match was Astley's debut but the last game for Bowers, who was transferred to Leicester City shortly afterwards.

# Rams Career Records

Below are the career records (Football League, FA Premiership, FA Cup, and League Cup) of every Rams first-team player since the club's first FA Cup match in 1884. The years given are the first years of seasons. Thus, 1946 means 1946-47. FA Premiership and Football League appearances are classified together under League. In the 'Others' list are all the competitions not accounted for in the rest of the table. This list contains figures for the 1894-95 Test Match, 1975 FA Charity Shield, Texaco Cup, European Cup, UEFA Cup, Freight/Rover Trophy, Full Members' Cup, League Play-offs and the Anglo-Italian Cup. It should be noted that in 1889-90 the Rams fielded only ten men at Preston. Substitute appearances given to the right of full appearances (eg 26/2).

| | | LEAGUE | | FA CUP | | FL CUP | | OTHERS | | TOTAL | |
|---|---|---|---|---|---|---|---|---|---|---|---|
| Player | Played | App | Gls | App | Gls | App | Gls | App | Gls | App | Gls |
| ABBOTT S.W. | 1911 | 1 | 0 | 0 | 0 | 0 | 0 | 0 | 0 | 1 | 0 |
| ABBOTT W.L. | 1893 | 4 | 1 | 0 | 0 | 0 | 0 | 0 | 0 | 4 | 1 |
| ABDALLAH T. | 1920-21 | 15 | 1 | 0 | 0 | 0 | 0 | 0 | 0 | 15 | 1 |
| ABLETT G.I. | 1984 | 3/3 | 0 | 0 | 0 | 0 | 0 | 2 | 0 | 5/3 | 0 |
| ACKERMAN A.A.E. | 1954-56 | 36 | 21 | 0 | 0 | 0 | 0 | 0 | 0 | 36 | 21 |
| ADDISON M.V.E. | 2005 | 2 | 0 | 0 | 0 | 0 | 0 | 0 | 0 | 2 | 0 |
| ADLINGTON T. | 1956-61 | 36 | 0 | 1 | 0 | 4 | 0 | 0 | 0 | 41 | 0 |
| AINSWORTH C. | 1908 | 8 | 0 | 0 | 0 | 0 | 0 | 0 | 0 | 8 | 0 |
| AINSWORTH F. | 1919 | 1 | 0 | 0 | 0 | 0 | 0 | 0 | 0 | 1 | 0 |
| AINSWORTH L.G.R. | 2005 | 0/2 | 0 | 0 | 0 | 0 | 0 | 0 | 0 | 0/2 | 0 |
| ALDERMAN A.E. | 1928-33 | 21 | 5 | 3 | 1 | 0 | 0 | 0 | 0 | 24 | 6 |
| ALLAN J. | 1893-94 | 36 | 8 | 4 | 1 | 0 | 0 | 0 | 0 | 40 | 9 |
| ALLEN H. | 1898-99 | 15 | 3 | 5 | 2 | 0 | 0 | 0 | 0 | 20 | 5 |
| ALTON T.W. | 1937 | 3 | 0 | 0 | 0 | 0 | 0 | 0 | 0 | 3 | 0 |
| ANTONIO G.R. | 1946-47 | 18 | 2 | 0 | 0 | 0 | 0 | 0 | 0 | 18 | 2 |
| ARKESDEN T.A. | 1898-1900 | 50 | 14 | 1 | 0 | 0 | 0 | 0 | 0 | 51 | 14 |
| ARMSTRONG A.S. | 1906-07 | 4 | 1 | 0 | 0 | 0 | 0 | 0 | 0 | 4 | 1 |
| ASANOVIC A. | 1996-97 | 37/1 | 7 | 3 | 0 | 2 | 0 | 0 | 0 | 42/1 | 7 |
| ASHBEE I.M. | 1994 | 1 | 0 | 0 | 0 | 0 | 0 | 0 | 0 | 1 | 0 |
| ASTLEY D.J. | 1936-38 | 93 | 45 | 5 | 4 | 0 | 0 | 0 | 0 | 98 | 49 |
| ATKIN J.T. | 1907-21 | 308 | 3 | 17 | 0 | 0 | 0 | 0 | 0 | 325 | 3 |
| ATTLEY B.R. | 1981-83 | 54/1 | 1 | 2 | 0 | 4 | 0 | 0 | 0 | 60/1 | 1 |
| BACON A. | 1925-27 | 8 | 3 | 1 | 0 | 0 | 0 | 0 | 0 | 9 | 3 |
| BAGSHAW J.J. | 1906-19 | 226 | 6 | 14 | 0 | 0 | 0 | 0 | 0 | 240 | 6 |
| BAIANO F. | 1997-99 | 52/12 | 16 | 5 | 3 | 6 | 0 | 0 | 0 | 63/12 | 19 |
| BAILEY A.D. | 1971 | 1 | 0 | 0 | 0 | 0 | 0 | 2/1 | 0 | 3/1 | 0 |
| BAILEY H.P. | 1909 | 3 | 0 | 0 | 0 | 0 | 0 | 0 | 0 | 3 | 0 |
| BAILEY L.A. | 1937-38 | 26 | 0 | 2 | 0 | 0 | 0 | 0 | 0 | 28 | 0 |
| BAKER J. | 1890 | 8 | 0 | 2 | 0 | 0 | 0 | 0 | 0 | 10 | 0 |
| BAKER W.E. | 1914-20 | 44 | 7 | 0 | 0 | 0 | 0 | 0 | 0 | 44 | 7 |
| BAKEWELL G. | 1884-90 | 49 | 9 | 15 | 3 | 0 | 0 | 0 | 0 | 64 | 12 |
| BALKWILL A. | 1901 | 11 | 1 | 0 | 0 | 0 | 0 | 0 | 0 | 11 | 1 |
| BANOVIC V. | 1981-83 | 35 | 0 | 0 | 0 | 3 | 0 | 0 | 0 | 38 | 0 |
| BARBOUR T.P. | 1908-20 | 273 | 3 | 21 | 0 | 0 | 0 | 0 | 0 | 294 | 3 |
| BARCLAY R. | 1928-30 | 61 | 23 | 3 | 3 | 0 | 0 | 0 | 0 | 64 | 26 |
| BARKER F.C. | 1903-04 | 4 | 2 | 0 | 0 | 0 | 0 | 0 | 0 | 4 | 2 |
| BARKER J.W. | 1928-38 | 326 | 2 | 27 | 0 | 0 | 0 | 0 | 0 | 353 | 2 |
| BARKER R.J. | 1967-68 | 30/8 | 12 | 0 | 0 | 7 | 2 | 0 | 0 | 37/8 | 14 |
| BARNES G.G. | 2005 | 15/4 | 1 | 0 | 0 | 0/1 | 0 | 0 | 0 | 15/5 | 1 |
| BARNES H. | 1908-13 | 153 | 74 | 14 | 4 | 0 | 0 | 0 | 0 | 167 | 78 |
| BARNES J. | 1921 | 4 | 0 | 0 | 0 | 0 | 0 | 0 | 0 | 4 | 0 |
| BARROWCLIFFE G. | 1951-65 | 475 | 37 | 22 | 1 | 6 | 1 | 0 | 0 | 503 | 39 |

| Player | Played | LEAGUE App | LEAGUE Gls | FA CUP App | FA CUP Gls | FL CUP App | FL CUP Gls | OTHERS App | OTHERS Gls | TOTAL App | TOTAL Gls |
|---|---|---|---|---|---|---|---|---|---|---|---|
| BARTLETT P.J. | 1977-79 | 7/6 | 0 | 0 | 0 | 0 | 0 | 0 | 0 | 7/6 | 0 |
| BARTON J.S. | 1981-83 | 68/1 | 1 | 8 | 0 | 5 | 0 | 0 | 0 | 81/1 | 1 |
| BARTON W.D. | 2001-02 | 53 | 0 | 1 | 0 | 2 | 0 | 0 | 0 | 56 | 0 |
| BAUCHOP J.R. | 1909-12 | 126 | 68 | 9 | 4 | 0 | 0 | 0 | 0 | 135 | 72 |
| BAYLISS H.H.R. | 1920 | 1 | 0 | 0 | 0 | 0 | 0 | 0 | 0 | 1 | 0 |
| BECK M.V. | 1998-99 | 11/7 | 2 | 0/1 | 0 | 2 | 1 | 0 | 0 | 13/8 | 3 |
| BEDFORD H. | 1925-30 | 203 | 142 | 15 | 10 | 0 | 0 | 0 | 0 | 218 | 152 |
| BELL C. | 1950-54 | 77 | 2 | 2 | 0 | 0 | 0 | 0 | 0 | 79 | 2 |
| BELL D. | 1934-38 | 52 | 0 | 3 | 0 | 0 | 0 | 0 | 0 | 55 | 0 |
| BELLHOUSE E.W. | 1888 | 2 | 0 | 0 | 0 | 0 | 0 | 0 | 0 | 2 | 0 |
| BENFIELD T.C. | 1914 | 38 | 15 | 1 | 0 | 0 | 0 | 0 | 0 | 39 | 15 |
| BENTLEY A. | 1906-10 | 151 | 99 | 17 | 13 | 0 | 0 | 0 | 0 | 168 | 112 |
| BESTWICK T.H. | 1886-88 | 1 | 0 | 6 | 0 | 0 | 0 | 0 | 0 | 7 | 0 |
| BETTS A.C. | 1911-13 | 71 | 0 | 3 | 0 | 0 | 0 | 0 | 0 | 74 | 0 |
| BEVAN F.E.W. | 1907-09 | 51 | 17 | 1 | 1 | 0 | 0 | 0 | 0 | 52 | 18 |
| BIGGINS S.J. | 1984-85 | 8/2 | 1 | 1 | 0 | 0 | 0 | 1/1 | 0 | 10/3 | 1 |
| BILEY A.P. | 1979-80 | 47 | 19 | 2 | 0 | 2 | 0 | 0 | 0 | 51 | 19 |
| BIRD D.W.C. | 1934-35 | 5 | 2 | 0 | 0 | 0 | 0 | 0 | 0 | 5 | 2 |
| BIRDSALL G. | 1921 | 8 | 0 | 0 | 0 | 0 | 0 | 0 | 0 | 8 | 0 |
| BISGAARD M. | 2004-05 | 56/13 | 8 | 4 | 0 | 0 | 0 | 2 | 0 | 62/13 | 8 |
| BLACKETT J. | 1900 | 17 | 1 | 0 | 0 | 0 | 0 | 0 | 0 | 17 | 1 |
| BLACKSTOCK D.A. | 2005 | 8/1 | 3 | 0 | 0 | 0 | 0 | 0 | 0 | 8/1 | 3 |
| BLADES P.A. | 1982-89 | 157/9 | 1 | 12 | 0 | 9/3 | 0 | 8/2 | 0 | 186/14 | 1 |
| BLATSIS C. | 2000 | 2 | 0 | 0 | 0 | 0 | 0 | 0 | 0 | 2 | 0 |
| BLESSINGTON J. | 1899 | 2 | 0 | 0 | 0 | 0 | 0 | 0 | 0 | 2 | 0 |
| BLOCKLEY J.P. | 1977 | 0 | 0 | 1 | 0 | 0 | 0 | 0 | 0 | 1 | 0 |
| BLOOMER P. | 1895 | 1 | 0 | 0 | 0 | 0 | 0 | 0 | 0 | 1 | 0 |
| BLOOMER S. | 1892-1905 1910-13 | 474 | 293 | 50 | 38 | 0 | 0 | 1 | 1 | 525 | 332 |
| BLORE V. | 1933-34 | 15 | 0 | 0 | 0 | 0 | 0 | 0 | 0 | 15 | 0 |
| BOAG J. | 1896-1903 | 117 | 27 | 23 | 10 | 0 | 0 | 0 | 0 | 140 | 37 |
| BODEN C.D. | 1994-95 | 8/2 | 0 | 0 | 0 | 0 | 0 | 0 | 0 | 8/2 | 0 |
| BOERTIEN P. | 1998-2004 | 82/21 | 2 | 5/2 | 0 | 4/1 | 0 | 0 | 0 | 91/24 | 2 |
| BOHINEN L. | 1997-2000 | 47/9 | 1 | 3 | 0 | 2 | 0 | 0 | 0 | 52/9 | 1 |
| BOLDER A.P. | 2000-05 | 100/53 | 11 | 5/2 | 0 | 4 | 0 | 1/1 | 0 | 110/56 | 11 |
| BORBOKIS V. | 1998-99 | 9/7 | 0 | 1 | 0 | 3 | 1 | 0 | 0 | 13/7 | 1 |
| BOSWORTH S. | 1898 | 2 | 1 | 0 | 0 | 0 | 0 | 0 | 0 | 2 | 1 |
| BOULTON C.D. | 1964-77 | 272 | 0 | 29 | 0 | 16 | 0 | 27 | 0 | 344 | 0 |
| BOULTON F.P. | 1938-45 | 39 | 0 | 7 | 0 | 0 | 0 | 0 | 0 | 46 | 0 |
| BOURNE J.A. | 1970-76 | 35/14 | 9 | 7/3 | 2 | 1/1 | 0 | 5/6 | 3 | 48/24 | 14 |
| BOWDEN O. | 1932-33 | 10 | 1 | 0 | 0 | 0 | 0 | 0 | 0 | 10 | 1 |
| BOWER T.A. | 1886 | 0 | 0 | 1 | 0 | 0 | 0 | 0 | 0 | 1 | 0 |
| BOWERS J.A. | 1959-65 | 65 | 19 | 0 | 0 | 3 | 1 | 0 | 0 | 68 | 20 |
| BOWERS J.W.A. | 1928-36 | 203 | 167 | 17 | 16 | 0 | 0 | 0 | 0 | 220 | 183 |
| BOWLER G.H. | 1912 | 1 | 0 | 0 | 0 | 0 | 0 | 0 | 0 | 1 | 0 |
| BOXLEY H.H. | 1919 | 7 | 0 | 0 | 0 | 0 | 0 | 0 | 0 | 7 | 0 |
| BOYD J.M. | 1935-36 | 9 | 1 | 0 | 0 | 0 | 0 | 0 | 0 | 9 | 1 |
| BRADBURY J.J.L. | 1899 | 7 | 1 | 0 | 0 | 0 | 0 | 0 | 0 | 7 | 1 |
| BRADBURY L.M. | 2003 | 7 | 0 | 0 | 0 | 0 | 0 | 0 | 0 | 7 | 0 |
| BRAGSTAD B.O. | 2000 | 10/2 | 0 | 1 | 0 | 3 | 2 | 0 | 0 | 14/2 | 2 |
| BRAND R. | 1890 | 3 | 0 | 0 | 0 | 0 | 0 | 0 | 0 | 3 | 0 |
| BRIDGE-WILKINSON M. | 1998 | 0/1 | 0 | 0 | 0 | 0 | 0 | 0 | 0 | 0/1 | 0 |
| BRINTON J.V. | 1937 | 8 | 2 | 0 | 0 | 0 | 0 | 0 | 0 | 8 | 2 |
| BRISCOE R.D. | 1989-90 | 10/3 | 1 | 0 | 0 | 4/1 | 0 | 0 | 0 | 14/4 | 1 |
| BROLLY M.J. | 1982 | 41/1 | 4 | 3 | 0 | 5 | 1 | 0 | 0 | 49/1 | 5 |
| BROMAGE E. | 1888-89 | 17 | 0 | 1 | 0 | 0 | 0 | 0 | 0 | 18 | 0 |
| BROMAGE E. | 1923-26 | 4 | 2 | 2 | 1 | 0 | 0 | 0 | 0 | 6 | 3 |
| BROMAGE H. | 1899-1901 | 5 | 0 | 0 | 0 | 0 | 0 | 0 | 0 | 5 | 0 |
| BROOKS G. | 1914 | 33 | 0 | 1 | 0 | 0 | 0 | 0 | 0 | 34 | 0 |

| Player | Played | LEAGUE App | LEAGUE Gls | FA CUP App | FA CUP Gls | FL CUP App | FL CUP Gls | OTHERS App | OTHERS Gls | TOTAL App | TOTAL Gls |
|---|---|---|---|---|---|---|---|---|---|---|---|
| BROOKS J.T. | 1894 | 3 | 0 | 0 | 0 | 0 | 0 | 0 | 0 | 3 | 0 |
| BROOME F.H. | 1946-49 | 112 | 45 | 7 | 0 | 0 | 0 | 0 | 0 | 119 | 45 |
| BROWN G. | 1956-59 | 53 | 20 | 1 | 0 | 0 | 0 | 0 | 0 | 54 | 20 |
| BROWN H.T. | 1949-50 | 37 | 0 | 3 | 0 | 0 | 0 | 0 | 0 | 40 | 0 |
| BUCHANAN J. | 1954-56 | 32 | 12 | 0 | 0 | 0 | 0 | 0 | 0 | 32 | 12 |
| BUCKLEY F.C. | 1911-13 | 92 | 3 | 5 | 0 | 0 | 0 | 0 | 0 | 97 | 3 |
| BUCKLEY S. | 1977-85 | 323 | 21 | 19 | 1 | 21 | 3 | 3 | 0 | 366 | 25 |
| BULLIONS J.L. | 1945-47 | 17 | 0 | 12 | 0 | 0 | 0 | 0 | 0 | 29 | 0 |
| BUNYAN C. | 1889-91 | 9 | 0 | 2 | 0 | 0 | 0 | 0 | 0 | 11 | 0 |
| BURLEY C.W. | 1999-2002 | 73 | 10 | 2 | 0 | 5 | 3 | 0 | 0 | 80 | 13 |
| BURNS K. | 1982-84 | 36/2 | 2 | 3 | 0 | 4 | 0 | 0 | 0 | 43/2 | 2 |
| BURRIDGE J. | 1984 | 6 | 0 | 0 | 0 | 2 | 0 | 0 | 0 | 8 | 0 |
| BURTON D.J. | 1997-2002 | 78/47 | 25 | 9/1 | 3 | 6/2 | 3 | 0 | 0 | 93/50 | 31 |
| BURTON J.H. | 1897-98 | 10 | 3 | 0 | 0 | 0 | 0 | 0 | 0 | 10 | 3 |
| BURTON N. | 1919-20 | 56 | 16 | 5 | 2 | 0 | 0 | 0 | 0 | 61 | 18 |
| BUTLIN B.D. | 1967-72 | 4 | 0 | 0 | 0 | 2 | 0 | 3 | 1 | 9 | 1 |
| BUTTERWORTH C.E. | 1891 | 1 | 0 | 0 | 0 | 0 | 0 | 0 | 0 | 1 | 0 |
| BUXTON I.R. | 1959-67 | 144/1 | 41 | 2 | 0 | 11 | 2 | 0 | 0 | 157/1 | 43 |
| CALDWELL G. | 2003 | 6/3 | 0 | 0 | 0 | 1 | 0 | 0 | 0 | 7/3 | 0 |
| CALLAGHAN N.I. | 1986-88 1990 | 88 | 11 | 4 | 1 | 3 | 0 | 5 | 1 | 100 | 13 |
| CALLAN W.G. | 1921 | 1 | 0 | 0 | 0 | 0 | 0 | 0 | 0 | 1 | 0 |
| CALLENDER R.H. | 1913 | 5 | 0 | 0 | 0 | 0 | 0 | 0 | 0 | 5 | 0 |
| CAMP L.M.J. | 2002-05 | 85/1 | 0 | 4 | 0 | 1 | 0 | 2 | 0 | 92/1 | 0 |
| CAMPBELL R.M. | 1983 | 11 | 4 | 0 | 0 | 1 | 0 | 0 | 0 | 12 | 4 |
| CARBON M.P. | 1995-97 | 11/9 | 0 | 0/1 | 0 | 1 | 0 | 0 | 0 | 12/10 | 0 |
| CARBONARI H.A. | 1998-2002 | 89/1 | 9 | 9 | 0 | 3 | 0 | 0 | 0 | 101/1 | 9 |
| CARBONE B. | 2001 | 13 | 1 | 1 | 0 | 0 | 0 | 0 | 0 | 14 | 1 |
| CARGILL D.A. | 1958-60 | 56 | 8 | 2 | 2 | 1 | 1 | 0 | 0 | 59 | 11 |
| CARLIN W. | 1968-70 | 89 | 14 | 5 | 0 | 14 | 2 | 0 | 0 | 108 | 16 |
| CARR W.P. | 1925-32 | 102 | 0 | 7 | 0 | 0 | 0 | 0 | 0 | 109 | 0 |
| CARRUTHERS E. | 1976 | 0/1 | 0 | 0 | 0 | 0 | 0 | 0 | 0 | 0/1 | 0 |
| CARSLEY L.K. | 1994-98 | 122/16 | 5 | 12 | 0 | 10/3 | 0 | 3 | 0 | 147/19 | 5 |
| CARTER H.S. | 1945-47 | 63 | 34 | 20 | 16 | 0 | 0 | 0 | 0 | 83 | 50 |
| CARTER S.C. | 1978-79 | 32/1 | 1 | 1 | 0 | 1 | 0 | 0 | 0 | 34/1 | 1 |
| CASKEY W.T. | 1978-79 | 26/2 | 3 | 1 | 0 | 1 | 0 | 0 | 0 | 28/2 | 3 |
| CHADWICK N.G. | 2002 | 4/2 | 0 | 0 | 0 | 0 | 0 | 0 | 0 | 4/2 | 0 |
| CHALK M.P.G. | 1991 | 4/3 | 1 | 3 | 1 | 0 | 0 | 0/1 | 0 | 7/4 | 2 |
| CHALMERS B. | 1890 | 20 | 1 | 2 | 0 | 0 | 0 | 0 | 0 | 22 | 1 |
| CHANDLER A. | 1919-24 | 169 | 0 | 14 | 0 | 0 | 0 | 0 | 0 | 183 | 0 |
| CHANDLER J.G. | 1985-86 | 45/1 | 9 | 7 | 4 | 7 | 3 | 2/1 | 0 | 61/2 | 16 |
| CHARLES G.A. | 1993-94 | 61 | 3 | 1 | 0 | 5/1 | 0 | 9 | 0 | 76/1 | 3 |
| CHATTERTON W. | 1884-88 | 5 | 1 | 1 | 0 | 0 | 0 | 0 | 0 | 6 | 1 |
| CHERRY S.R. | 1979-83 | 77 | 0 | 8 | 0 | 5 | 0 | 0 | 0 | 90 | 0 |
| CHESTERS C.W. | 1977-78 | 6/3 | 1 | 0 | 0 | 0/1 | 0 | 0 | 0 | 6/4 | 1 |
| CHIEDOZIE J.O. | 1988 | 2 | 0 | 0 | 0 | 0 | 0 | 0 | 0 | 2 | 0 |
| CHOLERTON W. | 1966 | 1 | 0 | 0 | 0 | 0 | 0 | 0 | 0 | 1 | 0 |
| CHRISTIE M.N. | 1998-2002 | 90/26 | 30 | 5 | 2 | 6/2 | 3 | 0 | 0 | 101/28 | 35 |
| CHRISTIE T.J. | 1984-85 | 65 | 22 | 7 | 3 | 5 | 0 | 2 | 1 | 79 | 26 |
| CLAMP E. | 1948 | 1 | 0 | 0 | 0 | 0 | 0 | 0 | 0 | 1 | 0 |
| CLARK B. | 1954-57 | 16 | 0 | 1 | 0 | 0 | 0 | 0 | 0 | 17 | 0 |
| CLARK J. | 1978-80 | 48/5 | 3 | 4 | 0 | 4 | 0 | 0 | 0 | 56/5 | 3 |
| CLAYTON J. | 1978-81 | 21/3 | 4 | 1 | 0 | 1/1 | 0 | 0 | 0 | 23/4 | 4 |
| CLEAVER F.L. | 1905-06 | 11 | 3 | 1 | 0 | 0 | 0 | 0 | 0 | 12 | 3 |
| CLEEVELY N.R. | 1964-66 | 15/1 | 3 | 1 | 0 | 1 | 0 | 0 | 0 | 17/1 | 3 |
| CLIFTON G. | 1886-88 | 1 | 0 | 2 | 0 | 0 | 0 | 0 | 0 | 3 | 0 |
| COLEMAN S. | 1991-93 | 62/8 | 2 | 5 | 0 | 5/1 | 0 | 12 | 0 | 84/9 | 2 |
| COLLIN G. | 1927-35 | 309 | 0 | 25 | 0 | 0 | 0 | 0 | 0 | 334 | 0 |
| COMYN A.J. | 1991-92 | 59/4 | 1 | 3/1 | 1 | 7 | 0 | 9 | 2 | 78/5 | 4 |

| Player | Played | LEAGUE App | LEAGUE Gls | FA CUP App | FA CUP Gls | FL CUP App | FL CUP Gls | OTHERS App | OTHERS Gls | TOTAL App | TOTAL Gls |
|---|---|---|---|---|---|---|---|---|---|---|---|
| CONWELL A. | 1959-61 | 98 | 1 | 2 | 0 | 7 | 0 | 0 | 0 | 107 | 1 |
| COOKE J.A. | 1898-99 | 11 | 2 | 0 | 0 | 0 | 0 | 0 | 0 | 11 | 2 |
| COOP M.A. | 1981 | 17/1 | 0 | 1 | 0 | 2 | 0 | 0 | 0 | 20/1 | 0 |
| COOPER G.F. | 1885 | 0 | 0 | 3 | 0 | 0 | 0 | 0 | 0 | 3 | 0 |
| COOPER K.L. | 1994-96 | 0/2 | 0 | 0 | 0 | 0/2 | 0 | 0/1 | 0 | 0/5 | 0 |
| COOPER L. | 1885-91 | 50 | 23 | 8 | 4 | 0 | 0 | 0 | 0 | 58 | 27 |
| COOPER T. | 1925-34 | 248 | 1 | 18 | 0 | 0 | 0 | 0 | 0 | 266 | 1 |
| CORISH R. | 1977 | 0/1 | 0 | 0 | 0 | 0 | 0 | 0 | 0 | 0/1 | 0 |
| COSTA C.A.M. da | 2003 | 23/11 | 1 | 0 | 0 | 1 | 0 | 0 | 0 | 24/11 | 1 |
| COWANS G.S. | 1993-94 | 36 | 0 | 0 | 0 | 3 | 0 | 5/1 | 1 | 44/1 | 1 |
| COWELL W. | 1926 | 1 | 0 | 0 | 0 | 0 | 0 | 0 | 0 | 1 | 0 |
| COX J.D. | 1890-99 | 212 | 7 | 25 | 0 | 0 | 0 | 1 | 0 | 238 | 7 |
| CRAWFORD A. | 1977-79 | 16/5 | 4 | 0/2 | 0 | 1/1 | 1 | 0 | 0 | 17/8 | 5 |
| CRAWFORD J. | 1900-01 | 42 | 1 | 1 | 0 | 0 | 0 | 0 | 0 | 43 | 1 |
| CRESSWELL P.F. | 1954-56 | 12 | 2 | 2 | 0 | 0 | 0 | 0 | 0 | 14 | 2 |
| CRILLY T. | 1922-27 | 197 | 0 | 14 | 0 | 0 | 0 | 0 | 0 | 211 | 0 |
| CROOKS S.D. | 1927-46 | 408 | 101 | 37 | 10 | 0 | 0 | 0 | 0 | 445 | 111 |
| CROPPER W. | 1886 | 0 | 0 | 1 | 0 | 0 | 0 | 0 | 0 | 1 | 0 |
| CROSS S.C. | 1986-91 | 42/31 | 3 | 3/2 | 0 | 4/4 | 0 | 3/5 | 2 | 52/42 | 5 |
| CROWSHAW A.A. | 1956-57 | 18 | 6 | 0 | 0 | 0 | 0 | 0 | 0 | 18 | 6 |
| CRUMP F. | 1899 | 6 | 1 | 0 | 0 | 0 | 0 | 0 | 0 | 6 | 1 |
| CULLEN M.J. | 1962-64 | 24 | 5 | 1 | 0 | 1 | 0 | 0 | 0 | 26 | 5 |
| CURRAN E. | 1977 | 26 | 2 | 3 | 0 | 0 | 0 | 0 | 0 | 29 | 2 |
| CURRY W.M. | 1960-64 | 148 | 67 | 8 | 4 | 8 | 5 | 0 | 0 | 164 | 76 |
| CUSHLOW R. | 1948-49 | 2 | 0 | 0 | 0 | 0 | 0 | 0 | 0 | 2 | 0 |
| DAFT T. | 1890 | 3 | 0 | 0 | 0 | 0 | 0 | 0 | 0 | 3 | 0 |
| DAILLY C.E. | 1996-98 | 62/5 | 4 | 4/1 | 0 | 6 | 0 | 0 | 0 | 72/6 | 4 |
| DAINO D. | 2001 | 2 | 0 | 0 | 0 | 1/1 | 0 | 0 | 0 | 3/1 | 0 |
| DALY G.A. | 1976-79 | 111/1 | 31 | 5 | 2 | 5 | 1 | 0 | 0 | 121/1 | 34 |
| DALZIEL I. | 1981-82 | 22 | 4 | 1/1 | 0 | 3/1 | 0 | 0 | 0 | 26/2 | 4 |
| DANIEL P.A. | 1965-78 | 188/7 | 7 | 18/1 | 0 | 16/1 | 0 | 15 | 1 | 237/9 | 8 |
| DARWIN G.H. | 1957-60 | 94 | 32 | 3 | 1 | 0 | 0 | 0 | 0 | 97 | 33 |
| DAVIDSON J.S. | 1989-91 | 7/5 | 0 | 0/2 | 0 | 1 | 0 | 0/1 | 0 | 8/8 | 0 |
| DAVIES A.J. | 2005 | 22/1 | 3 | 1 | 0 | 0 | 0 | 0 | 0 | 23/1 | 3 |
| DAVIES F. | 1902 | 1 | 0 | 0 | 0 | 0 | 0 | 0 | 0 | 1 | 0 |
| DAVIES G. | 1953-61 | 200 | 5 | 9 | 0 | 4 | 0 | 0 | 0 | 213 | 5 |
| DAVIES R. | 1971-75<br>1979 | 120/16 | 34 | 12/4 | 8 | 5 | 1 | 7/2 | 1 | 144/22 | 44 |
| DAVIES W. | 1994 | 1/1 | 0 | 0 | 0 | 0 | 0 | 0/1 | 0 | 1/2 | 0 |
| DAVIS G.H. | 1900-07 | 134 | 27 | 21 | 2 | 0 | 0 | 0 | 0 | 155 | 29 |
| DAVIS J.W. | 1904-09 | 138 | 9 | 15 | 4 | 0 | 0 | 0 | 0 | 153 | 13 |
| DAVISON R. | 1982-87<br>1991 | 213/3 | 91 | 11 | 7 | 18 | 6 | 4 | 2 | 246/3 | 106 |
| DAVISON T.R. | 1925-30 | 83 | 5 | 2 | 0 | 0 | 0 | 0 | 0 | 85 | 5 |
| DAYKIN R.B. | 1959-61 | 4 | 1 | 0 | 0 | 0 | 0 | 0 | 0 | 4 | 1 |
| DEACY E.S. | 1983 | 5 | 0 | 0 | 0 | 0 | 0 | 0 | 0 | 5 | 0 |
| DELAP R.J. | 1997-2000 | 97/6 | 11 | 2/1 | 0 | 7 | 2 | 0 | 0 | 106/7 | 13 |
| DEVINE S.B. | 1983-84 | 10/1 | 0 | 0 | 0 | 0 | 0 | 0 | 0 | 10/1 | 0 |
| DEVONSHIRE W.J. | 1914 | 7 | 1 | 0 | 0 | 0 | 0 | 0 | 0 | 7 | 1 |
| DICHIO D.S.E. | 2003 | 6 | 1 | 0 | 0 | 0 | 0 | 0 | 0 | 6 | 1 |
| DILLY T. | 1907 | 10 | 2 | 0 | 0 | 0 | 0 | 0 | 0 | 10 | 2 |
| DIX R.W. | 1936-38 | 94 | 35 | 2 | 0 | 0 | 0 | 0 | 0 | 96 | 35 |
| DOBBS A. | 1933 | 3 | 1 | 0 | 0 | 0 | 0 | 0 | 0 | 3 | 1 |
| DOCHERTY J. | 1893-94 | 35 | 0 | 3 | 0 | 0 | 0 | 0 | 0 | 38 | 0 |
| DOCKERY G. | 1893 | 5 | 0 | 0 | 0 | 0 | 0 | 0 | 0 | 5 | 0 |
| DOHERTY P.D. | 1945-46 | 15 | 7 | 10 | 10 | 0 | 0 | 0 | 0 | 25 | 17 |
| DONAGHY E. | 1926 | 6 | 0 | 0 | 0 | 0 | 0 | 0 | 0 | 6 | 0 |
| DONALD D.M. | 1909-11 | 45 | 2 | 0 | 0 | 0 | 0 | 0 | 0 | 45 | 2 |
| DORIGO A.R. | 1998-99 | 37/4 | 1 | 4 | 2 | 4 | 0 | 0 | 0 | 45/4 | 3 |

| Player | Played | LEAGUE App | LEAGUE Gls | FA CUP App | FA CUP Gls | FL CUP App | FL CUP Gls | OTHERS App | OTHERS Gls | TOTAL App | TOTAL Gls |
|---|---|---|---|---|---|---|---|---|---|---|---|
| DOYLE N.L.R. | 2003-05 | 4/5 | 0 | 0/1 | 0 | 0 | 0 | 0 | 0 | 4/6 | 0 |
| DRAPER D. | 1966 | 8 | 1 | 0 | 0 | 1 | 0 | 0 | 0 | 9 | 1 |
| DUCROCQ P. | 2001 | 19 | 0 | 0 | 0 | 0 | 0 | 0 | 0 | 19 | 0 |
| DUNCAN D. | 1931-46 | 261 | 63 | 28 | 6 | 0 | 0 | 0 | 0 | 289 | 69 |
| DUNCAN J.P. | 1978-80 | 35/1 | 12 | 0/1 | 0 | 2 | 0 | 0 | 0 | 37/2 | 12 |
| DUNN G. | 1890 | 1 | 0 | 0 | 0 | 0 | 0 | 0 | 0 | 1 | 0 |
| DUNN J. | 1952-54 | 57 | 21 | 1 | 0 | 0 | 0 | 0 | 0 | 58 | 21 |
| DURBAN W.A. | 1963-72 | 336/10 | 93 | 16/3 | 10 | 30/1 | 8 | 6/1 | 1 | 388/15 | 112 |
| EADIE W.P. | 1914 | 31 | 0 | 0 | 0 | 0 | 0 | 0 | 0 | 31 | 0 |
| EDWARDS J.W. | 1908 | 2 | 1 | 0 | 0 | 0 | 0 | 0 | 0 | 2 | 1 |
| EDWARDS R.O. | 2003 | 10/1 | 1 | 0 | 0 | 0 | 0 | 0 | 0 | 10/1 | 1 |
| EDWORTHY M. | 2005 | 30 | 0 | 1 | 0 | 0/1 | 0 | 0 | 0 | 31/1 | 0 |
| EGGLESTON T. | 1945 | 0 | 0 | 1 | 0 | 0 | 0 | 0 | 0 | 1 | 0 |
| EKINS F.G. | 1891-92 | 18 | 3 | 0 | 0 | 0 | 0 | 0 | 0 | 18 | 3 |
| EL HAMDAOUI M. | 2005 | 5/4 | 3 | 0 | 0 | 0 | 0 | 0 | 0 | 5/4 | 3 |
| ELLIOTT S.W. | 1997-2003 | 58/15 | 1 | 3/2 | 0 | 8/1 | 0 | 0 | 0 | 69/18 | 1 |
| EMERY S.R. | 1979-81 | 73/2 | 4 | 3 | 0 | 2 | 0 | 0 | 0 | 78/2 | 4 |
| EMSON P.D. | 1978-82 | 112/15 | 13 | 1/3 | 0 | 4/3 | 0 | 0 | 0 | 117/21 | 13 |
| ERANIO S. | 1997-2000 | 83/12 | 7 | 8 | 3 | 5 | 0 | 0 | 0 | 96/12 | 10 |
| EVANS G. | 1884-86 | 0 | 0 | 5 | 6 | 0 | 0 | 0 | 0 | 5 | 6 |
| EVANS W. | 1907 | 1 | 0 | 0 | 0 | 0 | 0 | 0 | 0 | 1 | 0 |
| EVATT I.R. | 2000-02 | 19/15 | 0 | 1 | 0 | 0/2 | 1 | 0 | 0 | 20/17 | 1 |
| EXHAM P.G. | 1884 | 0 | 0 | 1 | 0 | 0 | 0 | 0 | 0 | 1 | 0 |
| FABIAN A.H. | 1931-32 | 12 | 1 | 4 | 2 | 0 | 0 | 0 | 0 | 16 | 3 |
| FADIGA K. | 2005 | 2/2 | 0 | 0 | 0 | 0 | 0 | 0 | 0 | 2/2 | 0 |
| FAGAN F. | 1959-60 | 24 | 6 | 0 | 0 | 1 | 0 | 0 | 0 | 25 | 6 |
| FAIRCLOUGH A. | 1924-26 | 37 | 26 | 0 | 0 | 0 | 0 | 0 | 0 | 37 | 26 |
| FAZACKERLEY S.N. | 1925 | 3 | 2 | 0 | 0 | 0 | 0 | 0 | 0 | 3 | 2 |
| FELLOWS P.J. | 1913 | 2 | 1 | 0 | 0 | 0 | 0 | 0 | 0 | 2 | 1 |
| FEREDAY D.T. | 1928-29 | 16 | 2 | 1 | 0 | 0 | 0 | 0 | 0 | 17 | 2 |
| FERGUSON A. | 1888-90 | 49 | 0 | 2 | 0 | 0 | 0 | 0 | 0 | 51 | 0 |
| FERGUSON R.B. | 1962-65 | 121 | 0 | 4 | 0 | 4 | 0 | 0 | 0 | 129 | 0 |
| FEUER A.I. | 2001 | 2 | 0 | 0 | 0 | 0 | 0 | 0 | 0 | 2 | 0 |
| FIFE | 1889 | 2 | 0 | 0 | 0 | 0 | 0 | 0 | 0 | 2 | 0 |
| FINDLAY J.W. | 1983 | 1 | 0 | 0 | 0 | 0 | 0 | 0 | 0 | 1 | 0 |
| FINDLAY T. | 1922-23 | 4 | 0 | 0 | 0 | 0 | 0 | 0 | 0 | 4 | 0 |
| FISHER W. | 1896 | 11 | 5 | 4 | 3 | 0 | 0 | 0 | 0 | 15 | 8 |
| FLANDERS F. | 1910 | 13 | 0 | 3 | 0 | 0 | 0 | 0 | 0 | 16 | 0 |
| FLETCHER F. | 1894 | 3 | 0 | 0 | 0 | 0 | 0 | 0 | 0 | 3 | 0 |
| FLETCHER T. | 1904-06 | 33 | 8 | 2 | 1 | 0 | 0 | 0 | 0 | 35 | 9 |
| FLOWERS J. | 1885 | 0 | 0 | 2 | 0 | 0 | 0 | 0 | 0 | 2 | 0 |
| FLYNN S.M. | 1995-96 | 39/20 | 3 | 3 | 0 | 3 | 0 | 0 | 0 | 45/20 | 3 |
| FOLETTI P. | 2001 | 1/1 | 0 | 0 | 0 | 0 | 0 | 0 | 0 | 1/1 | 0 |
| FORD D. | 1898 | 6 | 0 | 0 | 0 | 0 | 0 | 0 | 0 | 6 | 0 |
| FORDHAM N.M. | 1913-14 | 13 | 5 | 1 | 1 | 0 | 0 | 0 | 0 | 14 | 6 |
| FORMAN F. | 1894 | 8 | 0 | 0 | 0 | 0 | 0 | 0 | 0 | 8 | 0 |
| FORMAN F.R. | 1892 | 4 | 3 | 0 | 0 | 0 | 0 | 0 | 0 | 4 | 3 |
| FORSYTH M.E. | 1986-94 | 323/2 | 8 | 15/1 | 0 | 36 | 1 | 29 | 1 | 403/3 | 10 |
| FOSTER G.W. | 1982 | 30 | 0 | 3 | 0 | 5 | 0 | 0 | 0 | 38 | 0 |
| FOX W. | 1925 | 1 | 0 | 0 | 0 | 0 | 0 | 0 | 0 | 1 | 0 |
| FRAIL M.J. | 1897 | 10 | 0 | 0 | 0 | 0 | 0 | 0 | 0 | 10 | 0 |
| FRANCIS K.M.D. | 1989-90 | 0/10 | 0 | 1/2 | 1 | 1/2 | 0 | 0/1 | 0 | 2/15 | 1 |
| FRANCIS P.O. | 1893-95 | 16 | 6 | 3 | 1 | 0 | 0 | 1 | 0 | 20 | 7 |
| FRITH R.W. | 1910 | 1 | 0 | 0 | 0 | 0 | 0 | 0 | 0 | 1 | 0 |
| FRYER J.S. | 1897-1902 | 173 | 0 | 26 | 0 | 0 | 0 | 0 | 0 | 199 | 0 |
| FUERTES E.O. | 1999 | 8 | 1 | 0 | 0 | 2 | 1 | 0 | 0 | 10 | 2 |
| FULTON W. | 1901 | 13 | 1 | 0 | 0 | 0 | 0 | 0 | 0 | 13 | 1 |
| FUTCHER P. | 1982-83 | 35 | 0 | 4 | 0 | 1 | 0 | 0 | 0 | 40 | 0 |
| GABBIADINI M. | 1991-96 | 163/25 | 50 | 8/1 | 3 | 13 | 7 | 16/1 | 8 | 200/27 | 68 |

| Player | Played | LEAGUE App | LEAGUE Gls | FA CUP App | FA CUP Gls | FL CUP App | FL CUP Gls | OTHERS App | OTHERS Gls | TOTAL App | TOTAL Gls |
|---|---|---|---|---|---|---|---|---|---|---|---|
| GALLACHER H.K. | 1934-35 | 51 | 38 | 4 | 2 | 0 | 0 | 0 | 0 | 55 | 40 |
| GALLOWAY S.R. | 1922-24 | 66 | 25 | 10 | 5 | 0 | 0 | 0 | 0 | 76 | 30 |
| GAMBLE F. | 1981-82 | 5/1 | 2 | 1 | 0 | 1 | 0 | 0 | 0 | 7/1 | 2 |
| GARDEN H.W. | 1892 | 1 | 0 | 0 | 0 | 0 | 0 | 0 | 0 | 1 | 0 |
| GARDNER W. | 1920 | 5 | 1 | 0 | 0 | 0 | 0 | 0 | 0 | 5 | 1 |
| GARNER A. | 1983-87 | 48/23 | 17 | 4/3 | 2 | 1/4 | 0 | 5 | 1 | 58/30 | 20 |
| GARRY E. | 1907-12 | 120 | 18 | 9 | 1 | 0 | 0 | 0 | 0 | 129 | 19 |
| GEE P.J. | 1985-91 | 107/17 | 26 | 6/1 | 2 | 11/2 | 3 | 7/1 | 0 | 131/21 | 31 |
| GEMMILL A. | 1970-77 | | | | | | | | | | |
| | 1982-83 | 324 | 25 | 35 | 6 | 20 | 1 | 25 | 1 | 404 | 33 |
| GEORGE C.F. | 1975-78 | | | | | | | | | | |
| | 1981 | 117 | 36 | 11 | 6 | 10 | 4 | 9 | 10 | 147 | 56 |
| GIBSON A.M. | 1980-81 | 0/2 | 0 | 0 | 0 | 0/1 | 0 | 0 | 0 | 0/3 | 0 |
| GILCHRIST L. | 1904 | 11 | 0 | 0 | 0 | 0 | 0 | 0 | 0 | 11 | 0 |
| GILL J. | 1925-27 | 65 | 35 | 1 | 0 | 0 | 0 | 0 | 0 | 66 | 35 |
| GILLET L.F. | 1884 | 0 | 0 | 1 | 0 | 0 | 0 | 0 | 0 | 1 | 0 |
| GODDARD P. | 1988-89 | 49 | 15 | 1/1 | 0 | 7 | 2 | 5 | 1 | 62/1 | 18 |
| GOLBY J.A. | 1922 | 1 | 0 | 0 | 0 | 0 | 0 | 0 | 0 | 1 | 0 |
| GOODALL A.L. | 1889-1902 | 380 | 48 | 42 | 4 | 0 | 0 | 1 | 0 | 423 | 52 |
| GOODALL J. | 1889-98 | 211 | 76 | 26 | 9 | 0 | 0 | 1 | 0 | 238 | 85 |
| GOODCHILD G. | 1896 | 2 | 0 | 0 | 0 | 0 | 0 | 0 | 0 | 2 | 0 |
| GORHAM C. | 1884 | 0 | 0 | 1 | 0 | 0 | 0 | 0 | 0 | 1 | 0 |
| GOULOOZE R. | 1992 | 7/5 | 0 | 1 | 0 | 0/1 | 0 | 3 | 1 | 11/6 | 1 |
| GRAHAM D.A.W. | 2005 | 11/3 | 0 | 0 | 0 | 0 | 0 | 0 | 0 | 11/3 | 0 |
| GRANT A.F. | 1946-47 | 12 | 0 | 3 | 0 | 0 | 0 | 0 | 0 | 15 | 0 |
| GRANT L.A. | 2002-05 | 63/4 | 0 | 2 | 0 | 2 | 0 | 0 | 0 | 67/4 | 0 |
| GREEN J. | 1894 | 7 | 0 | 0 | 0 | 0 | 0 | 0 | 0 | 7 | 0 |
| GREEN L. | 1968-70 | 107 | 0 | 5 | 0 | 17 | 0 | 0 | 0 | 129 | 0 |
| GREEN R.E. | 1931 | 1 | 0 | 0 | 0 | 0 | 0 | 0 | 0 | 1 | 0 |
| GREENWOOD R.T. | 1978-79 | 26/5 | 1 | 1 | 0 | 1 | 0 | 0 | 0 | 28/5 | 1 |
| GREGORY J.C. | 1985-87 | 103 | 22 | 9 | 1 | 8 | 0 | 4/1 | 0 | 124/1 | 23 |
| GRENET F. | 2001-02 | 14/4 | 0 | 1 | 0 | 0 | 0 | 0 | 0 | 15/4 | 0 |
| GRIMES W.J. | 1909-14 | 161 | 11 | 8 | 0 | 0 | 0 | 0 | 0 | 169 | 11 |
| GROVES A. | 1933-35 | 64 | 17 | 5 | 1 | 0 | 0 | 0 | 0 | 69 | 18 |
| GUDJONSSON T. | 2001 | 2/8 | 1 | 0 | 0 | 0 | 0 | 0 | 0 | 2/8 | 1 |
| GWYNNE Revd L.H. | 1887 | 0 | 0 | 1 | 0 | 0 | 0 | 0 | 0 | 1 | 0 |
| HADDOW D. | 1890 | 16 | 0 | 0 | 0 | 0 | 0 | 0 | 0 | 16 | 0 |
| HAGAN J. | 1935-38 | 30 | 7 | 1 | 0 | 0 | 0 | 0 | 0 | 31 | 7 |
| HAIG J. | 1898 | 3 | 0 | 0 | 0 | 0 | 0 | 0 | 0 | 3 | 0 |
| HAJTO T. | 2005 | 5 | 0 | 1 | 0 | 0 | 0 | 0 | 0 | 6 | 0 |
| HALES D.D. | 1976-77 | 22/1 | 4 | 6 | 2 | 1 | 1 | 0 | 0 | 29/1 | 7 |
| HALEY W.T. | 1924-26 | 9 | 1 | 2 | 0 | 0 | 0 | 0 | 0 | 11 | 1 |
| HALFORD D. | 1935 | 6 | 3 | 3 | 1 | 0 | 0 | 0 | 0 | 9 | 4 |
| HALL B. | 1903-10 | 245 | 11 | 24 | 3 | 0 | 0 | 0 | 0 | 269 | 14 |
| HALL I.W. | 1959-61 | 44 | 13 | 1 | 0 | 6 | 3 | 0 | 0 | 51 | 16 |
| HALLIGAN W. | 1909-10 | 22 | 8 | 0 | 0 | 0 | 0 | 0 | 0 | 22 | 8 |
| HAMILTON J. | 1894 | 12 | 2 | 0 | 0 | 0 | 0 | 0 | 0 | 12 | 2 |
| HAMPTON J.W. | 1927-29 | 12 | 0 | 0 | 0 | 0 | 0 | 0 | 0 | 12 | 0 |
| HANDLEY G. | 1897-98 | 15 | 2 | 0 | 0 | 0 | 0 | 0 | 0 | 15 | 2 |
| HANN R. | 1932-38 | 115 | 0 | 5 | 0 | 0 | 0 | 0 | 0 | 120 | 0 |
| HANNAY J. | 1920 | 1 | 0 | 0 | 0 | 0 | 0 | 0 | 0 | 1 | 0 |
| HANNIGAN J.L. | 1958-60 | 72 | 19 | 3 | 0 | 0 | 0 | 0 | 0 | 75 | 19 |
| HARBEY G.K. | 1983-86 | 35/5 | 1 | 1/2 | 0 | 5 | 1 | 2/1 | 0 | 43/8 | 2 |
| HARBOUR H. | 1888 | 1 | 0 | 0 | 0 | 0 | 0 | 0 | 0 | 1 | 0 |
| HARDCASTLE D.S. | 1905 | 5 | 1 | 1 | 0 | 0 | 0 | 0 | 0 | 6 | 1 |
| HARDMAN J.A. | 1913-14 | 14 | 0 | 1 | 0 | 0 | 0 | 0 | 0 | 15 | 0 |
| HARDY A. | 1891-92 | 3 | 1 | 0 | 0 | 0 | 0 | 0 | 0 | 3 | 1 |
| HARDY J.J. | 1924 | 3 | 0 | 0 | 0 | 0 | 0 | 0 | 0 | 3 | 0 |
| HARFORD M.G. | 1989-91 | 58 | 15 | 1 | 0 | 7 | 3 | 2 | 0 | 68 | 18 |

| Player | Played | LEAGUE App | LEAGUE Gls | FA CUP App | FA CUP Gls | FL CUP App | FL CUP Gls | OTHERS App | OTHERS Gls | TOTAL App | TOTAL Gls |
|---|---|---|---|---|---|---|---|---|---|---|---|
| HARKES J.A. | 1993-95 | 67/7 | 2 | 0 | 0 | 5 | 0 | 6 | 1 | 78/7 | 3 |
| HARPER K.P. | 1998-99 | 6/26 | 1 | 0/3 | 1 | 1/5 | 0 | 0 | 0 | 7/34 | 2 |
| HARRISON K. | 1954-55 | 15 | 3 | 1 | 0 | 0 | 0 | 0 | 0 | 16 | 3 |
| HARRISON R.F. | 1945-54 | 254 | 52 | 27 | 7 | 0 | 0 | 0 | 0 | 281 | 59 |
| HARRISON T.W. | 1901 | 1 | 0 | 0 | 0 | 0 | 0 | 0 | 0 | 1 | 0 |
| HART J.L. | 1925-26 | 4 | 3 | 0 | 0 | 0 | 0 | 0 | 0 | 4 | 3 |
| HARVEY J.A.H. | 1894 | 5 | 0 | 0 | 0 | 0 | 0 | 0 | 0 | 5 | 0 |
| HASLAM H.B. | 1900-01 | 8 | 0 | 0 | 0 | 0 | 0 | 0 | 0 | 8 | 0 |
| HAVENHAND K. | 1961 | 26 | 14 | 3 | 0 | 0 | 0 | 0 | 0 | 29 | 14 |
| HAWDEN K. | 1953 | 2 | 0 | 0 | 0 | 0 | 0 | 0 | 0 | 2 | 0 |
| HAYWARD S.L. | 1989-94 | 15/11 | 1 | 1 | 0 | 0/2 | 0 | 3/4 | 0 | 19/17 | 1 |
| HAYWOOD F. | 1906 | 1 | 0 | 0 | 0 | 0 | 0 | 0 | 0 | 1 | 0 |
| HAZELDINE D. | 1952-53 | 26 | 6 | 2 | 0 | 0 | 0 | 0 | 0 | 28 | 6 |
| HAZELDINE G. | 1953 | 1 | 0 | 0 | 0 | 0 | 0 | 0 | 0 | 1 | 0 |
| HEBBERD T.N. | 1988-90 | 70/11 | 10 | 5 | 2 | 13 | 2 | 7 | 0 | 95/11 | 14 |
| HECTOR K.J. | 1966-77<br>1980-81 | 478/8 | 155 | 34 | 12 | 42 | 15 | 27 | 19 | 581/8 | 201 |
| HENNESSEY W.T. | 1969-72 | 62/1 | 4 | 3/2 | 0 | 2 | 1 | 12 | 0 | 79/3 | 5 |
| HICKINBOTTOM E.T. | 1888-93 | 50 | 0 | 3 | 0 | 0 | 0 | 0 | 0 | 53 | 0 |
| HICKLING W. | 1903 | 9 | 0 | 0 | 0 | 0 | 0 | 0 | 0 | 9 | 0 |
| HIGGINBOTHAM D.J. | 2000-02 | 82/4 | 3 | 3/1 | 0 | 7/1 | 1 | 0 | 0 | 92/6 | 4 |
| HIGGINS A.F. | 1888-89 | 42 | 25 | 3 | 1 | 0 | 0 | 0 | 0 | 45 | 26 |
| HILL A.R. | 1981-83 | 19/3 | 2 | 3 | 1 | 3 | 1 | 0 | 0 | 25/3 | 4 |
| HILL G.A. | 1977-79 | 22/2 | 5 | 1 | 0 | 2 | 1 | 0 | 0 | 25/2 | 6 |
| HINCHCLIFFE T. | 1938 | 6 | 1 | 0 | 0 | 0 | 0 | 0 | 0 | 6 | 1 |
| HIND F. | 1889 | 1 | 0 | 0 | 0 | 0 | 0 | 0 | 0 | 1 | 0 |
| HINDMARCH R. | 1984-89 | 164 | 9 | 13 | 1 | 13 | 0 | 6 | 0 | 196 | 10 |
| HINTON A.T. | 1967-75 | 240/13 | 64 | 18/2 | 3 | 23/1 | 11 | 14/5 | 5 | 295/21 | 83 |
| HODGE S.B. | 1994 | 10 | 2 | 0 | 0 | 0 | 0 | 1 | 2 | 11 | 4 |
| HODGES G.P. | 1995 | 1/8 | 0 | 0 | 0 | 0 | 0 | 0 | 0 | 1/8 | 0 |
| HODGKINSON W.H. | 1903 | 16 | 9 | 0 | 0 | 0 | 0 | 0 | 0 | 16 | 9 |
| HODGSON W. | 1965-67 | 78 | 17 | 2 | 0 | 6 | 3 | 0 | 0 | 86 | 20 |
| HOFFMAN E.H. | 1922 | 1 | 0 | 0 | 0 | 0 | 0 | 0 | 0 | 1 | 0 |
| HOLDSWORTH D.C. | 2005 | 0/3 | 0 | 0/1 | 0 | 0 | 0 | 0 | 0 | 0/4 | 0 |
| HOLMES L.D. | 2002-05 | 26/20 | 2 | 1/3 | 0 | 2 | 0 | 0 | 0 | 29/23 | 2 |
| HOLMES S. | 1889-90 | 21 | 8 | 1 | 0 | 0 | 0 | 0 | 0 | 22 | 8 |
| HOLYOAKE J.E. | 1901 | 1 | 0 | 0 | 0 | 0 | 0 | 0 | 0 | 1 | 0 |
| HOOKS P. | 1982-84 | 46/2 | 4 | 3 | 0 | 6 | 0 | 1/1 | 0 | 56/3 | 4 |
| HOPE J. | 1926-29 | 9 | 2 | 0 | 0 | 0 | 0 | 0 | 0 | 9 | 2 |
| HOPEWELL W. | 1888 | 5 | 0 | 0 | 0 | 0 | 0 | 0 | 0 | 5 | 0 |
| HOPKINS W. | 1890 | 8 | 0 | 0 | 0 | 0 | 0 | 0 | 0 | 8 | 0 |
| HOPKINSON M.E. | 1960-67 | 112/3 | 4 | 6 | 1 | 10 | 1 | 0 | 0 | 128/3 | 6 |
| HOULT R. | 1994<br>1995-99 | 121/2 | 0 | 7 | 0 | 8 | 0 | 0 | 0 | 136/2 | 0 |
| HOUNSFIELD R.E. | 1904-05 | 23 | 4 | 3 | 0 | 0 | 0 | 0 | 0 | 26 | 4 |
| HOWARD F. | 1899 | 1 | 0 | 0 | 0 | 0 | 0 | 0 | 0 | 1 | 0 |
| HOWARD F.J. | 1919 | 5 | 0 | 0 | 0 | 0 | 0 | 0 | 0 | 5 | 0 |
| HOWE J.R. | 1935-49 | 223 | 2 | 21 | 0 | 0 | 0 | 0 | 0 | 244 | 2 |
| HUDDLESTONE T.A. | 2003-04 | 84/4 | 0 | 3 | 0 | 2 | 0 | 2 | 0 | 91/4 | 0 |
| HUGHES A. | 1934 | 2 | 1 | 0 | 0 | 0 | 0 | 0 | 0 | 2 | 1 |
| HUGHES G. | 1963-67 | 184 | 22 | 4 | 0 | 13 | 2 | 0 | 0 | 201 | 24 |
| HUGHES W. | 1977 | 17/2 | 8 | 0 | 0 | 1 | 0 | 0 | 0 | 18/2 | 8 |
| HUNT A. | 1904-05 | 15 | 1 | 0 | 0 | 0 | 0 | 0 | 0 | 15 | 1 |
| HUNT D. | 1977 | 5 | 0 | 0 | 0 | 0 | 0 | 0 | 0 | 5 | 0 |
| HUNT J. | 1901-03<br>1905 | 5 | 0 | 0 | 0 | 0 | 0 | 0 | 0 | 5 | 0 |
| HUNT J.R. | 1997-98 | 7/18 | 2 | 0/3 | 0 | 2/2 | 0 | 0 | 0 | 9/23 | 2 |
| HUNT L.J. | 2002-03 | 8/3 | 0 | 0 | 0 | 0/2 | 0 | 0 | 0 | 8/5 | 0 |
| HUNT R.A.R. | 1958 | 24 | 10 | 0 | 0 | 0 | 0 | 0 | 0 | 24 | 10 |

| | | LEAGUE | | FA CUP | | FL CUP | | OTHERS | | TOTAL | |
|---|---|---|---|---|---|---|---|---|---|---|---|
| Player | Played | App | Gls | App | Gls | App | Gls | App | Gls | App | Gls |
| HUNTER G.I. | 1954 | 19 | 0 | 0 | 0 | 0 | 0 | 0 | 0 | 19 | 0 |
| HURST W. | 1922 | 3 | 0 | 0 | 0 | 0 | 0 | 0 | 0 | 3 | 0 |
| HUTCHINSON F. | 1886 | 0 | 0 | 1 | 0 | 0 | 0 | 0 | 0 | 1 | 0 |
| HUTCHINSON J.B. | 1960-63 | 107 | 51 | 3 | 2 | 6 | 4 | 0 | 0 | 116 | 57 |
| HUTCHISON D. | 1931-33 | 29 | 4 | 1 | 0 | 0 | 0 | 0 | 0 | 30 | 4 |
| IDIAKEZ I. | 2004-05 | 82/1 | 20 | 5 | 1 | 1 | 1 | 1 | 0 | 89/1 | 22 |
| IMLACH J.J.S. | 1954 | 36 | 2 | 1 | 0 | 0 | 0 | 0 | 0 | 37 | 2 |
| JACKSON J. | 2005 | 3/3 | 0 | 0 | 0 | 0 | 0 | 0 | 0 | 3/3 | 0 |
| JACKSON J.H. | 1921 | 13 | 4 | 1 | 0 | 0 | 0 | 0 | 0 | 14 | 4 |
| JACKSON R. | 1999-2005 | 95/18 | 0 | 1 | 0 | 4 | 0 | 2 | 0 | 102/18 | 0 |
| JAMES L. | 1975-77 | 67/1 | 15 | 11 | 2 | 7 | 1 | 4 | 3 | 89/1 | 21 |
| JARDINE R.J. | 1889 | 1 | 1 | 0 | 0 | 0 | 0 | 0 | 0 | 1 | 1 |
| EFFRIES A. | 1936-38 | 15 | 1 | 0 | 0 | 0 | 0 | 0 | 0 | 15 | 1 |
| JESSOP F.S. | 1930-37 | 84 | 7 | 9 | 0 | 0 | 0 | 0 | 0 | 93 | 7 |
| JOHN S. | 2005 | 6/1 | 0 | 0 | 0 | 0 | 0 | 0 | 0 | 6/1 | 0 |
| JOHNSON M.O. | 2003-05 | 104/2 | 3 | 5 | 0 | 1 | 0 | 1 | 0 | 111/2 | 3 |
| JOHNSON S.A.M. | 1999-2001 2005 | 99/4 | 5 | 1/1 | 0 | 7/1 | 0 | 0 | 0 | 107/6 | 5 |
| JOHNSON T. | 1991-94 | 91/7 | 30 | 5 | 1 | 9/1 | 2 | 16 | 8 | 121/8 | 41 |
| JOHNSTON J.M. | 1923 | 1 | 0 | 0 | 0 | 0 | 0 | 0 | 0 | 1 | 0 |
| JONES N.E. | 1922 | 3 | 0 | 0 | 0 | 0 | 0 | 0 | 0 | 3 | 0 |
| JONES R. | 1980-81 | 59 | 0 | 3 | 0 | 3 | 0 | 0 | 0 | 65 | 0 |
| JONES V.A. | 1937 | 2 | 0 | 0 | 0 | 0 | 0 | 0 | 0 | 2 | 0 |
| JUNIOR | 2003-04 | 11/19 | 4 | 0/2 | 1 | 0/1 | 0 | 0 | 0 | 11/22 | 5 |
| KAKU B. | 2004 | 3/1 | 0 | 0 | 0 | 0 | 0 | 0 | 0 | 3/1 | 0 |
| KAVANAGH J.C. | 1990-95 | 74/25 | 1 | 7 | 0 | 3/2 | 0 | 8/8 | 0 | 92/35 | 1 |
| KEAY W. | 1893-94 | 24 | 7 | 5 | 0 | 0 | 0 | 0 | 0 | 29 | 7 |
| KEEN E.R.L. | 1930-37 | 219 | 4 | 18 | 1 | 0 | 0 | 0 | 0 | 237 | 5 |
| KEETLEY F. | 1921-25 | 76 | 8 | 6 | 0 | 0 | 0 | 0 | 0 | 82 | 8 |
| KELHAM H. | 1908 | 1 | 0 | 0 | 0 | 0 | 0 | 0 | 0 | 1 | 0 |
| KELLY D. | 1926-27 | 5 | 0 | 0 | 0 | 0 | 0 | 0 | 0 | 5 | 0 |
| KENNA J.J. | 2003-05 | 64/1 | 0 | 3 | 0 | 1/1 | 0 | 2 | 0 | 70/2 | 0 |
| KENNEDY P.H.J. | 2003 | 5 | 1 | 0 | 0 | 0 | 0 | 0 | 0 | 5 | 1 |
| KIDD J. | 1919-21 | 20 | 0 | 1 | 0 | 0 | 0 | 0 | 0 | 21 | 0 |
| KIFFORD J. | 1898-99 | 6 | 0 | 0 | 0 | 0 | 0 | 0 | 0 | 6 | 0 |
| KING F.O. | 1937 | 3 | 0 | 0 | 0 | 0 | 0 | 0 | 0 | 3 | 0 |
| KING J. | 1975-77 | 12/2 | 0 | 1/1 | 0 | 1/2 | 0 | 0/2 | 0 | 14/7 | 0 |
| KING W.G. | 1905 | 1 | 0 | 0 | 0 | 0 | 0 | 0 | 0 | 1 | 0 |
| KINKLADZE G. | 1999-2002 | 60/33 | 7 | 2/1 | 0 | 3/1 | 1 | 0 | 0 | 65/35 | 8 |
| KINSEY G. | 1895-96 | 36 | 0 | 5 | 0 | 0 | 0 | 0 | 0 | 41 | 0 |
| KIRBY J. | 1929-37 | 173 | 0 | 18 | 0 | 0 | 0 | 0 | 0 | 191 | 0 |
| KITSON P. | 1991-94 | 105 | 36 | 5 | 1 | 7 | 3 | 13/1 | 9 | 130/1 | 49 |
| KNOWLES F.E. | 1921 | 3 | 1 | 0 | 0 | 0 | 0 | 0 | 0 | 3 | 1 |
| KNOX J.J. | 1886 | 0 | 0 | 2 | 1 | 0 | 0 | 0 | 0 | 2 | 1 |
| KONJIC M. | 2004-05 | 13/3 | 0 | 0 | 0 | 1 | 0 | 2 | 0 | 16/3 | 0 |
| KOZLUK R. | 1997-98 | 9/7 | 0 | 2/1 | 0 | 3 | 0 | 0 | 0 | 14/8 | 0 |
| KUHL M. | 1992-94 | 68 | 1 | 6 | 0 | 6 | 0 | 4 | 1 | 84 | 2 |
| LABARTHE TOME A.G. | 2003 | 0/3 | 0 | 0 | 0 | 1 | 0 | 0 | 0 | 1/3 | 0 |
| LAMB S. | 1905-06 | 30 | 1 | 3 | 0 | 0 | 0 | 0 | 0 | 33 | 1 |
| LAMPH T. | 1919-20 | 16 | 0 | 1 | 0 | 0 | 0 | 0 | 0 | 17 | 0 |
| LANE M.A.E. | 1924 | 0 | 0 | 1 | 0 | 0 | 0 | 0 | 0 | 1 | 0 |
| LANE S.B. | 1983 | 1 | 0 | 0 | 0 | 0 | 0 | 0 | 0 | 1 | 0 |
| LANGAN D.F. | 1976-79 | 143 | 1 | 6 | 0 | 6 | 0 | 0 | 0 | 155 | 1 |
| LANGLAND A.E. | 1889 | 2 | 0 | 0 | 0 | 0 | 0 | 0 | 0 | 2 | 0 |
| LATHAM A. | 1886-90 1901 | 48 | 1 | 8 | 0 | 0 | 0 | 0 | 0 | 56 | 1 |
| LAUNDERS B.T. | 1998 | 0/1 | 0 | 0 | 0 | 0 | 0 | 0 | 0 | 0/1 | 0 |
| LAURSEN J. | 1996-99 | 135/2 | 3 | 7 | 0 | 9 | 0 | 0 | 0 | 151/2 | 3 |
| LAW C.R. | 1952-53 | 33 | 2 | 0 | 0 | 0 | 0 | 0 | 0 | 33 | 2 |

| Player | Played | LEAGUE App | LEAGUE Gls | FA CUP App | FA CUP Gls | FL CUP App | FL CUP Gls | OTHERS App | OTHERS Gls | TOTAL App | TOTAL Gls |
|---|---|---|---|---|---|---|---|---|---|---|---|
| LAWRENCE G.H. | 1910-23 | 137 | 0 | 8 | 0 | 0 | 0 | 0 | 0 | 145 | 0 |
| LAWRENCE S.E. | 1887 | 0 | 0 | 4 | 0 | 0 | 0 | 0 | 0 | 4 | 0 |
| LEACH S. | 1897 | 1 | 0 | 0 | 0 | 0 | 0 | 0 | 0 | 1 | 0 |
| LECKIE C.T. | 1898-1904 | 126 | 1 | 13 | 0 | 0 | 0 | 0 | 0 | 139 | 1 |
| LEE F.H. | 1974-75 | 62 | 24 | 5/2 | 1 | 4 | 1 | 10 | 4 | 81/2 | 30 |
| LEE J. | 1950-53 | 93 | 54 | 6 | 2 | 0 | 0 | 0 | 0 | 99 | 56 |
| LEE R.M. | 2001-02 | 47/1 | 2 | 0 | 0 | 2 | 0 | 0 | 0 | 49/1 | 2 |
| LEES J. | 1888-89 | 10 | 2 | 0 | 0 | 0 | 0 | 0 | 0 | 10 | 2 |
| LEIGH A.S. | 1919 | 2 | 0 | 0 | 0 | 0 | 0 | 0 | 0 | 2 | 0 |
| LEIPER J. | 1892-99 | 157 | 0 | 20 | 0 | 0 | 0 | 1 | 0 | 178 | 0 |
| LEONARD H.D. | 1911-19 | 144 | 72 | 6 | 1 | 0 | 0 | 0 | 0 | 150 | 73 |
| LEONARD J. | 1897 | 1 | 1 | 2 | 1 | 0 | 0 | 0 | 0 | 3 | 2 |
| LEUTY L.H. | 1945-49 | 131 | 1 | 27 | 0 | 0 | 0 | 0 | 0 | 158 | 1 |
| LEWIS A.T. | 1971-72 | 2 | 0 | 0 | 0 | 0 | 0 | 1 | 0 | 3 | 0 |
| LEWIS M. | 1984-87 | 37/6 | 1 | 0/1 | 0 | 2 | 0 | 4 | 0 | 43/7 | 1 |
| LEWIS W.L. | 1931 | 8 | 3 | 0 | 0 | 0 | 0 | 0 | 0 | 8 | 3 |
| LIEVESLEY W. | 1920 | 1 | 0 | 0 | 0 | 0 | 0 | 0 | 0 | 1 | 0 |
| LILLIS M.A. | 1986-87 | 6/9 | 1 | 0/1 | 0 | 2/1 | 0 | 0 | 0 | 8/11 | 1 |
| LINACRE J.H. | 1898 | 2 | 0 | 0 | 0 | 0 | 0 | 0 | 0 | 2 | 0 |
| LISBIE K.A. | 2005 | 7 | 1 | 0 | 0 | 0 | 0 | 0 | 0 | 7 | 1 |
| LITTLE T. | 1892-93 | 16 | 1 | 1 | 1 | 0 | 0 | 0 | 0 | 17 | 2 |
| LLOYD A. | 1903 | 1 | 0 | 0 | 0 | 0 | 0 | 0 | 0 | 1 | 0 |
| LLOYD G.H. | 1901-02 | 10 | 1 | 2 | 0 | 0 | 0 | 0 | 0 | 12 | 1 |
| LONG J. | 1906-07 | 61 | 18 | 4 | 1 | 0 | 0 | 0 | 0 | 65 | 19 |
| LOVATT J. | 1981 | 2/2 | 0 | 0 | 0 | 0 | 0 | 0 | 0 | 2/2 | 0 |
| LOWELL E.J. | 1953 | 1 | 1 | 0 | 0 | 0 | 0 | 0 | 0 | 1 | 1 |
| LUNTLEY W. | 1885 | 0 | 0 | 3 | 0 | 0 | 0 | 0 | 0 | 3 | 0 |
| LYLE R.C. | 1910 | 7 | 0 | 0 | 0 | 0 | 0 | 0 | 0 | 7 | 0 |
| LYONS J. | 1919-22 | 80 | 31 | 6 | 2 | 0 | 0 | 0 | 0 | 86 | 33 |
| McALLE J.E. | 1981-83 | 51/7 | 1 | 3/1 | 1 | 4 | 0 | 0 | 0 | 58/8 | 2 |
| McALLISTER A. | 1904 | 24 | 0 | 0 | 0 | 0 | 0 | 0 | 0 | 24 | 0 |
| McANDREW R. | 1963 | 1 | 0 | 0 | 0 | 0 | 0 | 0 | 0 | 1 | 0 |
| McCAFFERY A. | 1978-79 | 31/6 | 4 | 0 | 0 | 4 | 0 | 0 | 0 | 35/6 | 4 |
| McCANN J. | 1962-63 | 55 | 2 | 3 | 0 | 0 | 0 | 0 | 0 | 58 | 2 |
| McCLAREN S. | 1985-87 | 23/2 | 0 | 0 | 0 | 5 | 1 | 2 | 0 | 30/2 | 1 |
| McCORD B.J. | 1987-89 | 3/2 | 0 | 3 | 0 | 1 | 0 | 0/1 | 1 | 7/3 | 1 |
| McCORMICK H. | 1946-47 | 7 | 0 | 0 | 0 | 0 | 0 | 0 | 0 | 7 | 0 |
| McCULLOCH D. | 1938 | 31 | 16 | 1 | 0 | 0 | 0 | 0 | 0 | 32 | 16 |
| MacDONALD W.J. | 1898-99 | 23 | 4 | 6 | 3 | 0 | 0 | 0 | 0 | 29 | 7 |
| McDONNELL M.H. | 1955-57 | 93 | 0 | 6 | 0 | 0 | 0 | 0 | 0 | 99 | 0 |
| McDOUGALL A.L. | 1928 | 2 | 0 | 0 | 0 | 0 | 0 | 0 | 0 | 2 | 0 |
| McFARLAND R.L. | 1967-80<br>1983 | 437/5 | 44 | 33 | 0 | 37 | 1 | 18 | 3 | 525/5 | 48 |
| McGILL J. | 1946-47 | 8 | 0 | 0 | 0 | 0 | 0 | 0 | 0 | 8 | 0 |
| McGOVERN J.P. | 1968-73 | 186/4 | 16 | 18 | 0 | 15 | 2 | 14 | 2 | 233/4 | 20 |
| McGRATH P. | 1996 | 23/1 | 0 | 2 | 0 | 0 | 0 | 0 | 0 | 25/1 | 0 |
| McINDOE M. | 2005 | 6/2 | 0 | 0 | 0 | 0 | 0 | 0 | 0 | 6/2 | 0 |
| McINTYRE J.M. | 1921-31 | 349 | 9 | 20 | 0 | 0 | 0 | 0 | 0 | 369 | 9 |
| MACKAY D.C. | 1968-70 | 122 | 5 | 7 | 0 | 16 | 2 | 0 | 0 | 145 | 7 |
| McKELLAR D. | 1978-79 | 41 | 0 | 2 | 0 | 0 | 0 | 0 | 0 | 43 | 0 |
| MACKEN A. | 1975-77 | 20/3 | 1 | 4/1 | 0 | 3/2 | 0 | 2/2 | 0 | 29/8 | 1 |
| McLACHLAN J. | 1890-92<br>1894 | 63 | 17 | 3 | 0 | 0 | 0 | 0 | 0 | 66 | 17 |
| McLACHLAN S. | 1938-52 | 58 | 1 | 5 | 1 | 0 | 0 | 0 | 0 | 63 | 2 |
| McLAREN H. | 1949-53 | 119 | 53 | 12 | 3 | 0 | 0 | 0 | 0 | 131 | 56 |
| MacLAREN R. | 1985-87 | 113/9 | 4 | 9 | 0 | 13 | 1 | 4 | 0 | 139/9 | 5 |
| McLAVERTY B. | 1920-27 | 115 | 1 | 2 | 0 | 0 | 0 | 0 | 0 | 117 | 1 |
| McLEAN T. | 1892 | 2 | 0 | 0 | 0 | 0 | 0 | 0 | 0 | 2 | 0 |
| McLEOD I.M. | 2002-03 | 24/15 | 4 | 0 | 0 | 1/1 | 0 | 0 | 0 | 25/16 | 4 |

| | | LEAGUE | | FA CUP | | FL CUP | | OTHERS | | TOTAL | |
|---|---|---|---|---|---|---|---|---|---|---|---|
| **Player** | **Played** | **App** | **Gls** | **App** | **Gls** | **App** | **Gls** | **App** | **Gls** | **App** | **Gls** |
| McMILLAN J.S. | 1890-95 | 116 | 45 | 9 | 4 | 0 | 0 | 1 | 1 | 126 | 50 |
| McMILLAN S.T. | 1914 | 1 | 0 | 0 | 0 | 0 | 0 | 0 | 0 | 1 | 0 |
| McMINN K.C. | 1987-92 | 108/15 | 9 | 6/1 | 1 | 11 | 3 | 12 | 1 | 137/16 | 14 |
| MACONNACHIE A. | 1897 | 23 | 9 | 3 | 0 | 0 | 0 | 0 | 0 | 26 | 9 |
| McQUEEN H. | 1895-1900 | 150 | 18 | 18 | 4 | 0 | 0 | 0 | 0 | 168 | 22 |
| McQUILLAN D. | 1952-55 | 18 | 1 | 0 | 0 | 0 | 0 | 0 | 0 | 18 | 1 |
| MAKIN C.G. | 2004 | 13 | 0 | 0 | 0 | 0 | 0 | 0 | 0 | 13 | 0 |
| MALLOCH G.C. | 1927-31 | 93 | 0 | 4 | 0 | 0 | 0 | 0 | 0 | 97 | 0 |
| MANEL | 2003 | 12/4 | 3 | 1 | 0 | 0 | 0 | 0 | 0 | 13/4 | 3 |
| MANN H.H. | 1928 | 4 | 0 | 2 | 0 | 0 | 0 | 0 | 0 | 6 | 0 |
| MARSHALL J. | 1888 | 16 | 0 | 0 | 0 | 0 | 0 | 0 | 0 | 16 | 0 |
| MARTIN B. | 1919 | 6 | 0 | 0 | 0 | 0 | 0 | 0 | 0 | 6 | 0 |
| MARTIN L. | 2000 | 7/2 | 0 | 2/1 | 0 | 0 | 0 | 0 | 0 | 9/3 | 0 |
| MARTIN R. | 1955-59 | 81 | 0 | 4 | 0 | 0 | 0 | 0 | 0 | 85 | 0 |
| MASKREY H.M. | 1902-09 | | | | | | | | | | |
| | 1920 | 202 | 0 | 20 | 0 | 0 | 0 | 0 | 0 | 222 | 0 |
| MASSON D.S. | 1977 | 23 | 1 | 3 | 2 | 0 | 0 | 0 | 0 | 26 | 3 |
| MATTHEWS R.D. | 1961-67 | 225 | 0 | 7 | 0 | 14 | 0 | 0 | 0 | 246 | 0 |
| MATTHEWS W. | 1912 | 1 | 0 | 0 | 0 | 0 | 0 | 0 | 0 | 1 | 0 |
| MAWENE Y. | 2000-03 | 54/1 | 1 | 4 | 0 | 2 | 0 | 0 | 0 | 60/1 | 1 |
| MAY H. | 1902 | 6 | 0 | 0 | 0 | 0 | 0 | 0 | 0 | 6 | 0 |
| MAY J. | 1898-1903 | 179 | 17 | 21 | 0 | 0 | 0 | 0 | 0 | 200 | 17 |
| MAYCROFT D. | 1884 | 0 | 0 | 1 | 0 | 0 | 0 | 0 | 0 | 1 | 0 |
| MAYS A.E. | 1949-59 | 272 | 21 | 9 | 0 | 0 | 0 | 0 | 0 | 281 | 21 |
| MEE G.W. | 1925-31 | 148 | 15 | 7 | 0 | 0 | 0 | 0 | 0 | 155 | 15 |
| MERCER J.T. | 1903-04 | 26 | 1 | 6 | 0 | 0 | 0 | 0 | 0 | 32 | 1 |
| METCALFE R. | 1966 | 1 | 0 | 0 | 0 | 0 | 0 | 0 | 0 | 1 | 0 |
| METHVEN J. | 1891-1906 | 458 | 0 | 52 | 0 | 0 | 0 | 1 | 0 | 511 | 0 |
| METHVEN J.Jnr | 1913 | 1 | 0 | 0 | 0 | 0 | 0 | 0 | 0 | 1 | 0 |
| MICKLEWHITE G. | 1984-92 | 223/17 | 31 | 8/3 | 4 | 23/3 | 2 | 8/3 | 6 | 262/26 | 43 |
| MIDDLETON F. | 1901-05 | 65 | 3 | 3 | 0 | 0 | 0 | 0 | 0 | 68 | 3 |
| MIDDLETON J. | 1977-79 | 73 | 0 | 3 | 0 | 4 | 0 | 0 | 0 | 80 | 0 |
| MIDDLETON R. | 1951-53 | 116 | 0 | 4 | 0 | 0 | 0 | 0 | 0 | 120 | 0 |
| MILARVIE R. | 1889 | 14 | 4 | 1 | 0 | 0 | 0 | 0 | 0 | 15 | 4 |
| MILLER D. | 1947 | 1 | 0 | 0 | 0 | 0 | 0 | 0 | 0 | 1 | 0 |
| MILLER J. | 1895-97 | 62 | 20 | 9 | 5 | 0 | 0 | 0 | 0 | 71 | 25 |
| MILLIN A. | 1955 | 1 | 0 | 0 | 0 | 0 | 0 | 0 | 0 | 1 | 0 |
| MILLS G.R. | 1982 | 18 | 2 | 3 | 0 | 2 | 0 | 0 | 0 | 23 | 2 |
| MILLS P.S. | 2002-05 | 40/18 | 0 | 5 | 0 | 1 | 0 | 0/1 | 0 | 46/19 | 0 |
| MILLS R.L. | 1994 | 16 | 7 | 0 | 0 | 0 | 0 | 0 | 0 | 16 | 7 |
| MILLS S. | 1891-92 | 45 | 7 | 2 | 0 | 0 | 0 | 0 | 0 | 47 | 7 |
| MINNEY G. | 1920 | 2 | 0 | 0 | 0 | 0 | 0 | 0 | 0 | 2 | 0 |
| MITCHELL H. | 1905 | 1 | 0 | 0 | 0 | 0 | 0 | 0 | 0 | 1 | 0 |
| MITCHELL J.D. | 1958-59 | 6 | 0 | 0 | 0 | 0 | 0 | 0 | 0 | 6 | 0 |
| MONEY R. | 1981 | 5 | 0 | 1 | 0 | 0 | 0 | 0 | 0 | 6 | 0 |
| MONKS I. | 1887-88 | 3 | 0 | 3 | 2 | 0 | 0 | 0 | 0 | 6 | 2 |
| MOONEY T.J. | 2002 | 7/1 | 0 | 0 | 0 | 0 | 0 | 0 | 0 | 7/1 | 0 |
| MOORE D.M. | 2005 | 14 | 1 | 0 | 0 | 0 | 0 | 0 | 0 | 14 | 1 |
| MOORE J. | 1904-05 | 5 | 0 | 0 | 0 | 0 | 0 | 0 | 0 | 5 | 0 |
| MOORE J. | 1913-25 | 203 | 75 | 15 | 7 | 0 | 0 | 0 | 0 | 218 | 82 |
| MOORE J.L. | 1957-63 | 144 | 3 | 7 | 0 | 5 | 0 | 0 | 0 | 156 | 3 |
| MOORE R. | 1919 | 1 | 0 | 0 | 0 | 0 | 0 | 0 | 0 | 1 | 0 |
| MOORE W.C. | 1906-08 | 11 | 0 | 0 | 0 | 0 | 0 | 0 | 0 | 11 | 0 |
| MORAN J. | 1954 | 2 | 0 | 0 | 0 | 0 | 0 | 0 | 0 | 2 | 0 |
| MORELAND V. | 1978-79 | 38/4 | 1 | 1 | 0 | 1/1 | 0 | 0 | 0 | 40/5 | 1 |
| MORLEY H.A. | 1884-88 | 4 | 0 | 6 | 0 | 0 | 0 | 0 | 0 | 10 | 0 |
| MORRIS C.R. | 1900-09 | 276 | 1 | 35 | 1 | 0 | 0 | 0 | 0 | 311 | 2 |
| MORRIS J. | 1948-52 | 130 | 44 | 10 | 3 | 0 | 0 | 0 | 0 | 140 | 47 |
| MORRIS L. | 1999-2003 | 62/29 | 17 | 2/2 | 0 | 1/4 | 1 | 0 | 0 | 65/35 | 18 |

| Player | Played | LEAGUE App | LEAGUE Gls | FA CUP App | FA CUP Gls | FL CUP App | FL CUP Gls | OTHERS App | OTHERS Gls | TOTAL App | TOTAL Gls |
|---|---|---|---|---|---|---|---|---|---|---|---|
| MORRISON A.C. | 1945-47 | 52 | 21 | 16 | 1 | 0 | 0 | 0 | 0 | 68 | 22 |
| MORTON W.H. | 1920-21 | 24 | 1 | 1 | 0 | 0 | 0 | 0 | 0 | 25 | 1 |
| MOSELEY G. | 1972-76 | 32 | 0 | 4 | 0 | 4 | 0 | 4 | 0 | 44 | 0 |
| MOZLEY B. | 1946-54 | 297 | 2 | 24 | 0 | 0 | 0 | 0 | 0 | 321 | 2 |
| MURPHY L. | 1921-27 | 221 | 46 | 14 | 3 | 0 | 0 | 0 | 0 | 235 | 49 |
| MURRAY A.D. | 1998-2002 | 25/31 | 0 | 4 | 0 | 3/1 | 0 | 0 | 0 | 32/32 | 0 |
| MURRAY W. | 1920 | 31 | 3 | 3 | 1 | 0 | 0 | 0 | 0 | 34 | 4 |
| MUSSON W.U. | 1945-53 | 246 | 0 | 34 | 0 | 0 | 0 | 0 | 0 | 280 | 0 |
| MYNARD L.D. | 1949-50 | 14 | 2 | 0 | 0 | 0 | 0 | 0 | 0 | 14 | 2 |
| NAPIER C.E. | 1935-37 | 80 | 24 | 8 | 2 | 0 | 0 | 0 | 0 | 88 | 26 |
| NASH R. | 1885-87 | 0 | 0 | 3 | 1 | 0 | 0 | 0 | 0 | 3 | 1 |
| NEAL R.M. | 1931 | 10 | 1 | 2 | 2 | 0 | 0 | 0 | 0 | 12 | 3 |
| NEEDHAM G.W. | 1919 | 5 | 0 | 0 | 0 | 0 | 0 | 0 | 0 | 5 | 0 |
| NEEDHAM T. | 1887-89 | 15 | 3 | 5 | 3 | 0 | 0 | 0 | 0 | 20 | 6 |
| NELSON E. | 1926 | 2 | 0 | 0 | 0 | 0 | 0 | 0 | 0 | 2 | 0 |
| NELSON J. | 1890 | 4 | 2 | 0 | 0 | 0 | 0 | 0 | 0 | 4 | 2 |
| NEVE E. | 1912-13 | 47 | 1 | 2 | 0 | 0 | 0 | 0 | 0 | 49 | 1 |
| NEWBERY P.J. | 1958-60 | 5 | 2 | 0 | 0 | 0 | 0 | 0 | 0 | 5 | 2 |
| NEWTON H.A. | 1973-76 | 111/6 | 5 | 15 | 1 | 10/1 | 0 | 13 | 0 | 149/7 | 6 |
| NICHOLAS J.T. | 1928-46 | 347 | 14 | 36 | 2 | 0 | 0 | 0 | 0 | 383 | 16 |
| NICHOLAS W.J. | 1905-10 | 130 | 0 | 13 | 0 | 0 | 0 | 0 | 0 | 143 | 0 |
| NICHOLLS H. | 1885 | 0 | 0 | 1 | 0 | 0 | 0 | 0 | 0 | 1 | 0 |
| NICHOLSON S.M. | 1992-95 | 73/1 | 1 | 4 | 1 | 4 | 0 | 5 | 0 | 86/1 | 2 |
| NIELSON N.F. | 1951-53 | 57 | 8 | 3 | 1 | 0 | 0 | 0 | 0 | 60 | 9 |
| NIMNI A. | 1999 | 2/2 | 1 | 1 | 0 | 0 | 0 | 0 | 0 | 3/2 | 1 |
| NISH D.J. | 1972-78 | 184/4 | 10 | 16 | 1 | 16 | 1 | 17 | 2 | 233/4 | 14 |
| NYATANGA L.J. | 2005 | 23/1 | 1 | 2 | 0 | 1 | 0 | 0 | 0 | 26/1 | 1 |
| OAKDEN H. | 1898 | 9 | 5 | 3 | 0 | 0 | 0 | 0 | 0 | 12 | 5 |
| OAKES A.M. | 2000-03 | 43 | 0 | 1 | 0 | 2 | 0 | 0 | 0 | 46 | 0 |
| O'BRIEN M.T. | 1926-27 | 3 | 0 | 2 | 0 | 0 | 0 | 0 | 0 | 5 | 0 |
| O'BRIEN R.C. | 1983 | 4 | 0 | 0 | 0 | 0 | 0 | 0 | 0 | 4 | 0 |
| O'HARE J. | 1967-73 | 247/1 | 65 | 17 | 3 | 28/2 | 8 | 13 | 5 | 305/3 | 81 |
| OLIVER J.A. | 1947-49 | 16 | 2 | 1 | 0 | 0 | 0 | 0 | 0 | 17 | 2 |
| OLIVER J.H.K. | 1949-57 | 184 | 1 | 9 | 0 | 0 | 0 | 0 | 0 | 193 | 1 |
| OLNEY B.A. | 1920-27 | 223 | 0 | 17 | 0 | 0 | 0 | 0 | 0 | 240 | 0 |
| O'NEIL B. | 2000-02 | 14/3 | 0 | 2 | 0 | 1/1 | 0 | 0 | 0 | 17/4 | 0 |
| O'RIORDAN D.J. | 1976-77 | 2/4 | 1 | 0 | 0 | 0/1 | 0 | 0 | 0 | 2/5 | 1 |
| ORMONDROYD I. | 1991 | 25 | 8 | 3 | 1 | 3 | 0 | 0 | 0 | 31 | 9 |
| O'ROURKE J. | 1900 | 5 | 0 | 0 | 0 | 0 | 0 | 0 | 0 | 5 | 0 |
| OSGOOD K. | 1979-81 | 61/8 | 10 | 2 | 0 | 3 | 0 | 0 | 0 | 66/8 | 10 |
| OSMAN L. | 2003 | 17 | 3 | 0 | 0 | 0 | 0 | 0 | 0 | 17 | 3 |
| OSMAN R.C.H. | 1953-54 | 2 | 0 | 0 | 0 | 0 | 0 | 0 | 0 | 2 | 0 |
| OXFORD K. | 1957-62 | 151 | 0 | 6 | 0 | 5 | 0 | 0 | 0 | 162 | 0 |
| PALMER C.A. | 1984-85 | 51 | 2 | 1 | 0 | 7 | 0 | 2 | 0 | 61 | 2 |
| PALMER D.F. | 1961 | 18 | 6 | 2 | 0 | 1 | 0 | 0 | 0 | 21 | 6 |
| PARKER P.A. | 1996 | 4 | 0 | 0 | 0 | 2 | 0 | 0 | 0 | 6 | 0 |
| PARKIN A.G. | 1949 | 9 | 0 | 0 | 0 | 0 | 0 | 0 | 0 | 9 | 0 |
| PARKIN F.W. | 1936 | 1 | 0 | 0 | 0 | 0 | 0 | 0 | 0 | 1 | 0 |
| PARNELL G.F. | 1903-04 | 9 | 0 | 0 | 0 | 0 | 0 | 0 | 0 | 9 | 0 |
| PARR J. | 1945-52 | 112 | 0 | 22 | 0 | 0 | 0 | 0 | 0 | 134 | 0 |
| PARRY A.J. | 1971-72 | 4/2 | 0 | 0 | 0 | 0 | 0 | 1 | 0 | 5/2 | 0 |
| PARRY J. | 1948-65 | 482/1 | 105 | 20 | 5 | 14 | 0 | 0 | 0 | 516/1 | 110 |
| PATERSON R. | 1897-99 | 19 | 0 | 2 | 0 | 0 | 0 | 0 | 0 | 21 | 0 |
| PATERSON W. | 1920-23 | 66 | 24 | 2 | 0 | 0 | 0 | 0 | 0 | 68 | 24 |
| PATON T.H. | 1904-05 | 35 | 4 | 3 | 0 | 0 | 0 | 0 | 0 | 38 | 4 |
| PATRICK R. | 1952-55 | 49 | 0 | 1 | 0 | 0 | 0 | 0 | 0 | 50 | 0 |
| PATTERSON M. | 1988-92 | 41/10 | 3 | 4 | 0 | 5/2 | 0 | 5/1 | 2 | 55/13 | 5 |
| PATTISON J.W. | 1921 | 15 | 2 | 0 | 0 | 0 | 0 | 0 | 0 | 15 | 2 |
| PAUL D.D. | 1953-55 | 2 | 0 | 0 | 0 | 0 | 0 | 0 | 0 | 2 | 0 |

| | | LEAGUE | | FA CUP | | FL CUP | | OTHERS | | TOTAL | |
|---|---|---|---|---|---|---|---|---|---|---|---|
| **Player** | **Played** | **App** | **Gls** | **App** | **Gls** | **App** | **Gls** | **App** | **Gls** | **App** | **Gls** |
| PAUL J. | 1894-97 | 28 | 9 | 1 | 0 | 0 | 0 | 1 | 0 | 30 | 9 |
| PAYNE F.E. | 1947 | 0 | 0 | 1 | 0 | 0 | 0 | 0 | 0 | 1 | 0 |
| PEART J.G. | 1919 | 9 | 1 | 0 | 0 | 0 | 0 | 0 | 0 | 9 | 1 |
| PEART R. | 1946 | 1 | 0 | 0 | 0 | 0 | 0 | 0 | 0 | 1 | 0 |
| PEMBRIDGE M.A | 1992-94 | 108/2 | 28 | 6 | 3 | 9 | 1 | 15 | 5 | 138/2 | 37 |
| PENNEY D.M. | 1985-88 | 6/13 | 0 | 1 | 1 | 2/3 | 1 | 1/3 | 1 | 10/19 | 3 |
| PESCHISOLIDO P.P. | 2003-05 | 35/42 | 17 | 2/1 | 3 | 2 | 0 | 2 | 0 | 41/43 | 20 |
| PHILBIN J. | 1934 | 1 | 0 | 0 | 0 | 0 | 0 | 0 | 0 | 1 | 0 |
| PHILLIPS J.L. | 1990 | 3 | 1 | 0 | 0 | 0 | 0 | 0 | 0 | 3 | 1 |
| PICKERING N. | 1988-91 | 35/10 | 3 | 3 | 0 | 7/1 | 0 | 3 | 0 | 48/11 | 3 |
| PITMAN R. | 1888-89 | 5 | 0 | 2 | 0 | 0 | 0 | 0 | 0 | 7 | 0 |
| PLACE C.A. | 1955 | 2 | 0 | 0 | 0 | 0 | 0 | 0 | 0 | 2 | 0 |
| PLACKETT H. | 1888 | 16 | 2 | 0 | 0 | 0 | 0 | 0 | 0 | 16 | 2 |
| PLACKETT L. | 1886-88 | 22 | 7 | 8 | 1 | 0 | 0 | 0 | 0 | 30 | 8 |
| PLACKETT S. | 1921-26 | 140 | 3 | 16 | 0 | 0 | 0 | 0 | 0 | 156 | 3 |
| PLUMMER C.A. | 1983 | 23/4 | 3 | 3/1 | 1 | 2 | 0 | 0 | 0 | 28/5 | 4 |
| POOLE K. | 2005 | 6 | 0 | 1 | 0 | 0 | 0 | 0 | 0 | 7 | 0 |
| POOM M. | 1996-2002 | 143/3 | 0 | 8 | 0 | 12 | 0 | 0 | 0 | 163/3 | 0 |
| POPPITT J. | 1946-49 | 16 | 0 | 0 | 0 | 0 | 0 | 0 | 0 | 16 | 0 |
| POWELL B.I. | 1979-81 | 86 | 7 | 2 | 1 | 4 | 0 | 0 | 0 | 92 | 8 |
| POWELL C.G.R. | 1995-97 | 89/2 | 1 | 5 | 1 | 5 | 0 | 0 | 0 | 99/2 | 2 |
| POWELL D.A. | 1995-2001 | 187/20 | 10 | 7/1 | 0 | 11/1 | 1 | 0 | 0 | 205/22 | 11 |
| POWELL K. | 1946 | 13 | 0 | 0 | 0 | 0 | 0 | 0 | 0 | 13 | 0 |
| POWELL S. | 1971-84 | 342/10 | 20 | 31/1 | 0 | 24 | 1 | 12 | 0 | 409/11 | 21 |
| POWELL T. | 1948-61 | 380 | 57 | 24 | 7 | 2 | 0 | 0 | 0 | 406 | 64 |
| PRATLEY R.G. | 1983-86 | 29/2 | 1 | 0/1 | 0 | 4 | 0 | 4 | 0 | 37/3 | 1 |
| PREECE D.W. | 1995 | 10/3 | 1 | 0 | 0 | 2 | 0 | 0 | 0 | 12/3 | 1 |
| PRIOR S.J. | 1998-99 | 48/6 | 1 | 4 | 0 | 5 | 0 | 0 | 0 | 57/6 | 1 |
| PUMFORD G.L. | 1924 | 2 | 0 | 0 | 0 | 0 | 0 | 0 | 0 | 2 | 0 |
| PYE J. | 1954-56 | 61 | 24 | 4 | 3 | 0 | 0 | 0 | 0 | 65 | 27 |
| PYNEGAR A. | 1904 | 1 | 0 | 0 | 0 | 0 | 0 | 0 | 0 | 1 | 0 |
| QUANTRILL A.E. | 1914-20 | 72 | 5 | 4 | 0 | 0 | 0 | 0 | 0 | 76 | 5 |
| QUY A.J. | 1994 | 0 | 0 | 0 | 0 | 0/1 | 0 | 0 | 0 | 0/1 | 0 |
| RAHMBERG M. | 1996 | 0/1 | 0 | 0 | 0 | 0 | 0 | 0 | 0 | 0/1 | 0 |
| RAISBECK W. | 1901 | 3 | 0 | 3 | 0 | 0 | 0 | 0 | 0 | 6 | 0 |
| RAMAGE A. | 1980-81 | 32/1 | 2 | 2 | 0 | 3 | 0 | 0 | 0 | 37/1 | 2 |
| RAMAGE C.D. | 1989-93 | 33/9 | 4 | 3/1 | 1 | 6/1 | 2 | 0/3 | 0 | 42/14 | 7 |
| RAMAGE P.M.F. | 1928-36 | 233 | 55 | 22 | 5 | 0 | 0 | 0 | 0 | 255 | 60 |
| RAMSELL E.A. | 1905 | 5 | 0 | 0 | 0 | 0 | 0 | 0 | 0 | 5 | 0 |
| RANCE C.S. | 1920-21 | 23 | 0 | 0 | 0 | 0 | 0 | 0 | 0 | 23 | 0 |
| RANDALL J. | 1930-34 | 52 | 4 | 0 | 0 | 0 | 0 | 0 | 0 | 52 | 4 |
| RANSFORD J. | 1906 | 15 | 3 | 2 | 1 | 0 | 0 | 0 | 0 | 17 | 4 |
| RASIAK G. | 2004-05 | 41 | 18 | 2 | 1 | 0/1 | 0 | 1 | 0 | 44/1 | 19 |
| RATCLIFFE E. | 1902-05 | 16 | 0 | 0 | 0 | 0 | 0 | 0 | 0 | 16 | 0 |
| RATCLIFFE K. | 1993 | 6 | 0 | 0 | 0 | 0 | 0 | 0 | 0 | 6 | 0 |
| RAVANELLI F. | 2001-02 | 46/4 | 14 | 1 | 1 | 2 | 1 | 0 | 0 | 49/4 | 16 |
| RAYBOULD S. | 1894 | 5 | 2 | 0 | 0 | 0 | 0 | 0 | 0 | 5 | 2 |
| READER R. | 1913 | 4 | 0 | 0 | 0 | 0 | 0 | 0 | 0 | 4 | 0 |
| REICH M. | 2003-04 | 36/14 | 7 | 2 | 0 | 1 | 0 | 1/1 | 0 | 40/15 | 7 |
| REID A.J. | 1980-82 | 27/3 | 1 | 1/1 | 0 | 2 | 0 | 0 | 0 | 30/4 | 1 |
| REID S.E. | 1931-35 | 16 | 0 | 0 | 0 | 0 | 0 | 0 | 0 | 16 | 0 |
| REVELL C. | 1950-51 | 22 | 2 | 0 | 0 | 0 | 0 | 0 | 0 | 22 | 2 |
| RHODES J.A. | 1964-70 | 5 | 0 | 0 | 0 | 1/1 | 0 | 0 | 0 | 6/1 | 0 |
| RICHARDS F. | 1898 | 2 | 0 | 0 | 0 | 0 | 0 | 0 | 0 | 2 | 0 |
| RICHARDS G.H. | 1901-13 | 284 | 33 | 25 | 4 | 0 | 0 | 0 | 0 | 309 | 37 |
| RICHARDS J.P. | 1982 | 10 | 2 | 0 | 0 | 0 | 0 | 0 | 0 | 10 | 2 |
| RICHARDS W. | 1979-81 | 16/3 | 0 | 3 | 0 | 0/1 | 0 | 0 | 0 | 19/4 | 0 |
| RICHARDSON J. | 1962-70 | 118 | 4 | 3 | 1 | 12 | 0 | 0 | 0 | 133 | 5 |
| RICHARDSON P.A. | 1984 | 7/7 | 0 | 1 | 0 | 0/2 | 0 | 0 | 0 | 8/9 | 0 |

| Player | Played | LEAGUE App | LEAGUE Gls | FA CUP App | FA CUP Gls | FL CUP App | FL CUP Gls | OTHERS App | OTHERS Gls | TOTAL App | TOTAL Gls |
|---|---|---|---|---|---|---|---|---|---|---|---|
| RICHMOND J.F. | 1957-62 | 6 | 0 | 0 | 0 | 0 | 0 | 0 | 0 | 6 | 0 |
| RIDDELL F. | 1908 | 3 | 0 | 0 | 0 | 0 | 0 | 0 | 0 | 3 | 0 |
| RIDDELL F.W. | 1907 | 3 | 1 | 0 | 0 | 0 | 0 | 0 | 0 | 3 | 1 |
| RIGGOTT C.M. | 1999-2002 | 87/4 | 5 | 2 | 1 | 7 | 1 | 0 | 0 | 96/4 | 7 |
| RIOCH B.D. | 1973-76 | | | | | | | | | | |
| | 1977-79 | 146/1 | 38 | 12 | 7 | 11 | 5 | 14 | 4 | 183/1 | 54 |
| RITCHIE A. | 1920-26 | 87 | 1 | 6 | 0 | 0 | 0 | 0 | 0 | 93 | 1 |
| RITCHIE D. | 1913 | 2 | 0 | 0 | 0 | 0 | 0 | 0 | 0 | 2 | 0 |
| RITCHIE P.S. | 2002 | 7 | 0 | 0 | 0 | 0 | 0 | 0 | 0 | 7 | 0 |
| RITCHIE W. | 1919 | 4 | 1 | 0 | 0 | 0 | 0 | 0 | 0 | 4 | 1 |
| ROBERTS E. | 1935 | 4 | 0 | 0 | 0 | 0 | 0 | 0 | 0 | 4 | 0 |
| ROBERTS W. | 1890 | 5 | 0 | 0 | 0 | 0 | 0 | 0 | 0 | 5 | 0 |
| ROBERTSON J.N. | 1983-84 | 72 | 3 | 5 | 0 | 6 | 1 | 2 | 0 | 85 | 4 |
| ROBINSON A. | 1909 | 1 | 0 | 0 | 0 | 0 | 0 | 0 | 0 | 1 | 0 |
| ROBINSON J.W. | 1891-96 | 163 | 0 | 16 | 0 | 0 | 0 | 1 | 0 | 180 | 0 |
| ROBINSON M.L.St C. | 1998-2002 | 3/9 | 1 | 0 | 0 | 0 | 0 | 0 | 0 | 3/9 | 1 |
| ROBINSON T.C. | 1927-29 | 9 | 0 | 2 | 0 | 0 | 0 | 0 | 0 | 11 | 0 |
| ROBINSON W. | 1909 | 3 | 0 | 0 | 0 | 0 | 0 | 0 | 0 | 3 | 0 |
| ROBSON J.C. | 1928-31 | 38 | 10 | 2 | 0 | 0 | 0 | 0 | 0 | 40 | 10 |
| ROBSON J.D. | 1967-72 | 170/1 | 3 | 12 | 1 | 19 | 0 | 9 | 1 | 210/1 | 5 |
| ROBSON J.W. | 1921 | 3 | 0 | 0 | 0 | 0 | 0 | 0 | 0 | 3 | 0 |
| ROBSON N. | 1930-32 | 35 | 6 | 0 | 0 | 0 | 0 | 0 | 0 | 35 | 6 |
| ROBSON W. | 1927-31 | 13 | 0 | 3 | 0 | 0 | 0 | 0 | 0 | 16 | 0 |
| ROBY D. | 1961-64 | 70 | 6 | 5 | 0 | 6 | 1 | 0 | 0 | 81 | 7 |
| ROSE C.H. | 1891-92 | 5 | 0 | 0 | 0 | 0 | 0 | 0 | 0 | 5 | 0 |
| ROSE W. | 1891-92 | 5 | 0 | 0 | 0 | 0 | 0 | 0 | 0 | 5 | 0 |
| ROULSTONE F. | 1888 | 1 | 0 | 0 | 0 | 0 | 0 | 0 | 0 | 1 | 0 |
| ROULSTONE W. | 1887-94 | 118 | 4 | 11 | 0 | 0 | 0 | 0 | 0 | 129 | 4 |
| ROUND S.J. | 1991-92 | 8/1 | 0 | 0 | 0 | 0 | 0 | 0 | 0 | 8/1 | 0 |
| ROWE G.W. | 1925 | 1 | 0 | 0 | 0 | 0 | 0 | 0 | 0 | 1 | 0 |
| ROWE V.N. | 1951 | 2 | 0 | 0 | 0 | 0 | 0 | 0 | 0 | 2 | 0 |
| ROWETT G. | 1995-97 | 101/4 | 2 | 5/2 | 0 | 8 | 2 | 0 | 0 | 114/6 | 4 |
| RUDDY T. | 1928-31 | 22 | 9 | 0 | 0 | 0 | 0 | 0 | 0 | 22 | 9 |
| RUSSELL J. | 1898 | 2 | 0 | 0 | 0 | 0 | 0 | 0 | 0 | 2 | 0 |
| RUTHERFORD J.B. | 1898 | 1 | 1 | 0 | 0 | 0 | 0 | 0 | 0 | 1 | 1 |
| RYAN G.J. | 1977-78 | 30 | 4 | 2 | 1 | 2 | 0 | 0 | 0 | 34 | 5 |
| RYAN R.A. | 1955-58 | 133 | 30 | 6 | 1 | 0 | 0 | 0 | 0 | 139 | 31 |
| SAGE M. | 1986-91 | 137/3 | 4 | 4 | 0 | 22/1 | 0 | 8 | 0 | 171/4 | 4 |
| SAUNDERS D.N. | 1988-90 | 106 | 42 | 6 | 0 | 12 | 10 | 7 | 5 | 131 | 57 |
| SAUNDERS S. | 1904-05 | 8 | 0 | 0 | 0 | 0 | 0 | 0 | 0 | 8 | 0 |
| SAVIN K.A. | 1950-55 | 65 | 0 | 1 | 0 | 0 | 0 | 0 | 0 | 66 | 0 |
| SAWYER T. | 1894 | 2 | 0 | 0 | 0 | 0 | 0 | 0 | 0 | 2 | 0 |
| SAXTON R. | 1964-67 | 94/2 | 1 | 3 | 0 | 9 | 0 | 0 | 0 | 106/2 | 1 |
| SCARBOROUGH B. | 1958-60 | 4 | 0 | 0 | 0 | 0 | 0 | 0 | 0 | 4 | 0 |
| SCATTERGOOD E.O. | 1907-14 | 182 | 3 | 10 | 0 | 0 | 0 | 0 | 0 | 192 | 3 |
| SCATTERGOOD K. | 1936-37 | 22 | 0 | 3 | 0 | 0 | 0 | 0 | 0 | 25 | 0 |
| SCHNOOR S. | 1998-2000 | 48/12 | 2 | 3 | 0 | 4/2 | 0 | 0 | 0 | 55/14 | 2 |
| SCOTT A.T. | 1927-33 | 27 | 0 | 5 | 0 | 0 | 0 | 0 | 0 | 32 | 0 |
| SCOTT K. | 1950 | 2 | 0 | 0 | 0 | 0 | 0 | 0 | 0 | 2 | 0 |
| SEAL C.E. | 1905 | 1 | 0 | 0 | 0 | 0 | 0 | 0 | 0 | 1 | 0 |
| SELVEY S. | 1888 | 1 | 0 | 0 | 0 | 0 | 0 | 0 | 0 | 1 | 0 |
| SELVEY W. | 1888 | 1 | 0 | 0 | 0 | 0 | 0 | 0 | 0 | 1 | 0 |
| SHANKS T. | 1898-1900 | 27 | 9 | 1 | 0 | 0 | 0 | 0 | 0 | 28 | 9 |
| HARMAN D.W. | 1950 | 2 | 0 | 0 | 0 | 0 | 0 | 0 | 0 | 2 | 0 |
| SHARPE I.G. | 1911-12 | 54 | 12 | 3 | 0 | 0 | 0 | 0 | 0 | 57 | 12 |
| SHEPHERD G. | 1919-20 | 2 | 0 | 0 | 0 | 0 | 0 | 0 | 0 | 2 | 0 |
| SHERIDAN F.M. | 1980-81 | 41/2 | 5 | 0 | 0 | 1 | 0 | 0 | 0 | 42/2 | 5 |
| SHILTON P.L. | 1987-91 | 175 | 0 | 10 | 0 | 18 | 0 | 8 | 0 | 211 | 0 |
| SHINER A.J. | 1920 | 1 | 0 | 0 | 0 | 0 | 0 | 0 | 0 | 1 | 0 |

| | | LEAGUE | | FA CUP | | FL CUP | | OTHERS | | TOTAL | |
|---|---|---|---|---|---|---|---|---|---|---|---|
| **Player** | **Played** | **App** | **Gls** | **App** | **Gls** | **App** | **Gls** | **App** | **Gls** | **App** | **Gls** |
| SHIRTCLIFFE E. | 1901 | 4 | 0 | 0 | 0 | 0 | 0 | 0 | 0 | 4 | 0 |
| SHORT J.C. | 1992-94 | 118 | 9 | 7 | 4 | 11 | 0 | 7 | 0 | 143 | 13 |
| SIMPSON P.D. | 1991-97 | 134/52 | 48 | 4/4 | 1 | 12/3 | 6 | 14/2 | 2 | 164/61 | 57 |
| SIMS J. | 1972 | 2/1 | 0 | 0 | 0 | 0 | 0 | 0/1 | 0 | 2/2 | 0 |
| SKIVINGTON G. | 1980-82 | 39/7 | 2 | 0 | 0 | 4 | 1 | 0 | 0 | 43/7 | 3 |
| SMITH A. | 1884-85 | 0 | 0 | 4 | 2 | 0 | 0 | 0 | 0 | 4 | 2 |
| SMITH F. | 1909 | 5 | 0 | 0 | 0 | 0 | 0 | 0 | 0 | 5 | 0 |
| SMITH F.E. | 1947 | 1 | 0 | 0 | 0 | 0 | 0 | 0 | 0 | 1 | 0 |
| SMITH H. | 1906 | 1 | 0 | 0 | 0 | 0 | 0 | 0 | 0 | 1 | 0 |
| SMITH J. | 1888-89 | 12 | 0 | 0 | 0 | 0 | 0 | 0 | 0 | 12 | 0 |
| SMITH J. | 1914 | 6 | 0 | 0 | 0 | 0 | 0 | 0 | 0 | 6 | 0 |
| SMITH J.W. | 1903-06 | 9 | 0 | 1 | 0 | 0 | 0 | 0 | 0 | 10 | 0 |
| SMITH M.J. | 1957-60 | 22 | 0 | 0 | 0 | 1 | 0 | 0 | 0 | 23 | 0 |
| SMITH S.J. | 1922 | 1 | 0 | 0 | 0 | 0 | 0 | 0 | 0 | 1 | 0 |
| SMITH T.W. | 2004-05 | 84/1 | 19 | 5 | 1 | 1 | 0 | 2 | 0 | 92/1 | 20 |
| SMITH V. | 1925-26 | 4 | 0 | 0 | 0 | 0 | 0 | 0 | 0 | 4 | 0 |
| SOAR T.A. | 1902 | 2 | 0 | 0 | 0 | 0 | 0 | 0 | 0 | 2 | 0 |
| SOLIS M. | 1996-97 | 3/8 | 0 | 0 | 0 | 1/2 | 0 | 0 | 0 | 4/10 | 0 |
| SPILSBURY B.W. | 1885-88 | 1 | 1 | 8 | 7 | 0 | 0 | 0 | 0 | 9 | 8 |
| SPRINGTHORPE J.A. | 1907 | 2 | 0 | 0 | 0 | 0 | 0 | 0 | 0 | 2 | 0 |
| SPOONER S.A. | 1978-81 | 7/1 | 0 | 0 | 0 | 0 | 0 | 0 | 0 | 7/1 | 0 |
| STALEY J. | 1891-1900 | 128 | 0 | 12 | 0 | 0 | 0 | 1 | 0 | 141 | 0 |
| STALLARD M. | 1991-95 | 19/8 | 2 | 2/2 | 0 | 2/1 | 2 | 3 | 2 | 26/11 | 6 |
| STAMPS J.D. | 1938-53 | 233 | 100 | 29 | 26 | 0 | 0 | 0 | 0 | 262 | 126 |
| STAPLETON F.A. | 1987 | 10 | 1 | 0 | 0 | 0 | 0 | 0 | 0 | 10 | 1 |
| STEEL W. | 1947-49 | 109 | 27 | 15 | 8 | 0 | 0 | 0 | 0 | 124 | 35 |
| STEEL W.G. | 1938 | 11 | 0 | 0 | 0 | 0 | 0 | 0 | 0 | 11 | 0 |
| STEELE E.G. | 1984-86 | 47 | 0 | 1 | 0 | 2 | 0 | 3 | 0 | 53 | 0 |
| STEPHENSON G.R. | 1961-62 | 11 | 1 | 1 | 0 | 2 | 0 | 0 | 0 | 14 | 1 |
| STEPHENSON G.T. | 1927-30 | 111 | 53 | 9 | 3 | 0 | 0 | 0 | 0 | 120 | 56 |
| STEVENSON J. | 1894-98 | 73 | 31 | 11 | 1 | 0 | 0 | 0 | 0 | 84 | 32 |
| STEWART A. | 1967-69 | 29/1 | 1 | 1 | 0 | 4 | 1 | 0 | 0 | 34/1 | 2 |
| STEWART F.H. | 1899 | 2 | 1 | 0 | 0 | 0 | 0 | 0 | 0 | 2 | 1 |
| STIMAC I. | 1995-98 | 84 | 3 | 7 | 0 | 2 | 0 | 0 | 0 | 93 | 3 |
| STOCKILL R.R. | 1934-38 | 66 | 29 | 3 | 1 | 0 | 0 | 0 | 0 | 69 | 30 |
| STOKOE J. | 1922 | 8 | 1 | 0 | 0 | 0 | 0 | 0 | 0 | 8 | 1 |
| STORER H. | 1920-28 | 257 | 60 | 17 | 3 | 0 | 0 | 0 | 0 | 274 | 63 |
| STORER W. | 1891-92 | 25 | 10 | 2 | 1 | 0 | 0 | 0 | 0 | 27 | 11 |
| STRAW R. | 1951-57 | 94 | 57 | 4 | 3 | 0 | 0 | 0 | 0 | 98 | 60 |
| STREETE F.A. | 1984-85 | 35 | 0 | 1 | 0 | 4 | 0 | 1 | 0 | 41 | 0 |
| STRUPAR B. | 1999-2002 | 32/9 | 16 | 0 | 0 | 2 | 0 | 0 | 0 | 34/9 | 16 |
| STURRIDGE D.C. | 1991-2000 | 142/48 | 53 | 8 | 2 | 9/4 | 4 | 2/1 | 0 | 161/53 | 59 |
| SUGG F.H. | 1884 | 0 | 0 | 1 | 0 | 0 | 0 | 0 | 0 | 1 | 0 |
| SUMMERS J.L. | 1935 | 2 | 0 | 0 | 0 | 0 | 0 | 0 | 0 | 2 | 0 |
| SUTTON S.J. | 1984 | | | | | | | | | | |
| | 1991-95 | 74/1 | 0 | 3 | 0 | 7 | 0 | 11 | 0 | 95/1 | 0 |
| SUTTON W.F. | 1994-95 | 4/3 | 0 | 1 | 0 | 0 | 0 | 0 | 0 | 5/3 | 0 |
| SVENSSON M. | 2003 | 9/1 | 3 | 0 | 0 | 0 | 0 | 0 | 0 | 9/1 | 3 |
| SWALLOW R. | 1958-63 | 118 | 21 | 4 | 1 | 6 | 0 | 0 | 0 | 128 | 22 |
| SWINDLEHURST D. | 1979-82 | 110 | 29 | 6 | 0 | 9 | 3 | 0 | 0 | 125 | 32 |
| SYLVESTER T. | 1908 | 2 | 0 | 0 | 0 | 0 | 0 | 0 | 0 | 2 | 0 |
| TAFT D. | 1948 | 6 | 1 | 3 | 1 | 0 | 0 | 0 | 0 | 9 | 2 |
| TALBOT J.C. | 2004 | 2 | 0 | 0 | 0 | 0 | 0 | 0 | 0 | 2 | 0 |
| TATE G.M. | 1955 | 1 | 1 | 0 | 0 | 0 | 0 | 0 | 0 | 1 | 1 |
| TAYLOR I.K. | 2003-04 | 67/14 | 14 | 3 | 0 | 1/1 | 1 | 1/1 | 0 | 72/16 | 15 |
| TAYLOR K. | 1984 | 22 | 2 | 0 | 0 | 4 | 0 | 1 | 1 | 27 | 3 |
| TAYLOR M.J. | 1989-96 | 97 | 0 | 5 | 0 | 7 | 0 | 11 | 0 | 120 | 0 |
| TAYLOR R.C. | 1921 | 2 | 0 | 0 | 0 | 0 | 0 | 0 | 0 | 2 | 0 |
| THIRLWELL P. | 2005 | 15/6 | 0 | 2 | 0 | 0 | 0 | 0 | 0 | 17/6 | 0 |

| | | LEAGUE | | FA CUP | | FL CUP | | OTHERS | | TOTAL | |
|---|---|---|---|---|---|---|---|---|---|---|---|
| Player | Played | App | Gls | App | Gls | App | Gls | App | Gls | App | Gls |
| THOMAS A.M. | 1982 | 0/1 | 0 | 0 | 0 | 0 | 0 | 0 | 0 | 0/1 | 0 |
| THOMAS E. | 1964-67 | 102/3 | 43 | 2 | 0 | 6 | 6 | 0 | 0 | 110/3 | 49 |
| THOMAS M.R. | 1985 | 9 | 0 | 0 | 0 | 0 | 0 | 0 | 0 | 9 | 0 |
| THOMAS R.J. | 1973-77 | 89 | 2 | 10 | 0 | 9 | 0 | 10 | 0 | 118 | 2 |
| THOME E.A. | 2005 | 3/1 | 0 | 0 | 0 | 0 | 0 | 0 | 0 | 3/1 | 0 |
| THOMPSON C.A. | 1948-49 | 16 | 3 | 0 | 0 | 0 | 0 | 0 | 0 | 16 | 3 |
| THOMPSON G.A. | 1908-10 | 46 | 5 | 9 | 1 | 0 | 0 | 0 | 0 | 55 | 6 |
| THOMPSON G.H. | 1920 | 4 | 0 | 0 | 0 | 0 | 0 | 0 | 0 | 4 | 0 |
| THOMPSON J. | 1897 | 1 | 0 | 0 | 0 | 0 | 0 | 0 | 0 | 1 | 0 |
| THOMPSON P. | 1958-61 | 52 | 19 | 2 | 2 | 1 | 1 | 0 | 0 | 55 | 22 |
| THOMS H.J. | 1922-27 | 179 | 4 | 16 | 0 | 0 | 0 | 0 | 0 | 195 | 4 |
| THORNEWELL G. | 1919-27 | 275 | 23 | 20 | 3 | 0 | 0 | 0 | 0 | 295 | 26 |
| TINKLER A. | 1909 | 2 | 0 | 0 | 0 | 0 | 0 | 0 | 0 | 2 | 0 |
| TODD C. | 1970-78 | 293 | 6 | 30 | 2 | 20 | 1 | 28 | 1 | 371 | 10 |
| TODD T.B. | 1955 | 4 | 3 | 1 | 0 | 0 | 0 | 0 | 0 | 5 | 3 |
| TOOTLE J. | 1924-25 | 7 | 0 | 0 | 0 | 0 | 0 | 0 | 0 | 7 | 0 |
| TOWIE T. | 1893 | 8 | 1 | 0 | 0 | 0 | 0 | 0 | 0 | 8 | 1 |
| TOWNSEND W. | 1945-52 | 79 | 0 | 14 | 0 | 0 | 0 | 0 | 0 | 93 | 0 |
| TRAVIS H. | 1936-38 | 12 | 4 | 0 | 0 | 0 | 0 | 0 | 0 | 12 | 4 |
| TREMELLING E.S. | 1905-07 | 2 | 0 | 0 | 0 | 0 | 0 | 0 | 0 | 2 | 0 |
| TROLLOPE P.J. | 1994-97 | 47/18 | 5 | 3/1 | 0 | 3/2 | 1 | 0 | 0 | 53/21 | 6 |
| TRUEMAN R. | 1908-09 | 16 | 0 | 3 | 1 | 0 | 0 | 0 | 0 | 19 | 1 |
| TUDGAY M. | 2002-05 | 53/39 | 17 | 4/1 | 1 | 2 | 0 | 0 | 0 | 59/40 | 18 |
| TURNER A.D. | 1902 | 21 | 1 | 0 | 0 | 0 | 0 | 0 | 0 | 21 | 1 |
| TURNER J.A. | 1896-97 | 51 | 2 | 10 | 0 | 0 | 0 | 0 | 0 | 61 | 2 |
| TWIGG G. | 2001-02 | 1/8 | 0 | 0 | 0 | 0 | 0 | 0 | 0 | 1/8 | 0 |
| UDALL W.E.G. | 1934-36 | 81 | 0 | 7 | 0 | 0 | 0 | 0 | 0 | 88 | 0 |
| UPTON F. | 1954-60<br>1965-66 | 259 | 17 | 8 | 1 | 5 | 0 | 0 | 0 | 272 | 18 |
| VALAKARI S.J. | 2000-03 | 34/12 | 3 | 0 | 0 | 5 | 0 | 0 | 0 | 39/12 | 3 |
| VAN DER LAAN R.P. | 1995-97 | 61/4 | 8 | 3/1 | 3 | 6/2 | 0 | 0 | 0 | 70/7 | 11 |
| VANN B.W. | 1906 | 3 | 0 | 0 | 0 | 0 | 0 | 0 | 0 | 3 | 0 |
| VARNEY H. | 1901-02 | 2 | 0 | 0 | 0 | 0 | 0 | 0 | 0 | 2 | 0 |
| VINCENT J.R. | 2003-04 | 22 | 2 | 0 | 0 | 1 | 0 | 0 | 0 | 23 | 2 |
| WALKER C. | 1948-54 | 25 | 0 | 0 | 0 | 0 | 0 | 0 | 0 | 25 | 0 |
| WALKER J.A. | 1889-90 | 11 | 0 | 2 | 0 | 0 | 0 | 0 | 0 | 13 | 0 |
| WALKER J.H. | 1911-19 | 84 | 4 | 4 | 0 | 0 | 0 | 0 | 0 | 88 | 4 |
| WALKER J.M. | 1967-73 | 35/7 | 3 | 0/1 | 0 | 8 | 0 | 2/2 | 2 | 45/10 | 5 |
| WALLACE J.M. | 1947 | 16 | 0 | 3 | 0 | 0 | 0 | 0 | 0 | 19 | 0 |
| WALLER P. | 1961-67 | 102/2 | 5 | 3 | 0 | 8 | 0 | 0 | 0 | 113/2 | 5 |
| WALLINGTON F.M. | 1985-86 | 67 | 0 | 8 | 0 | 11 | 0 | 3 | 0 | 89 | 0 |
| WALSH W. | 1946 | 1 | 0 | 0 | 0 | 0 | 0 | 0 | 0 | 1 | 0 |
| WALTON D.L. | 2003 | 3/2 | 0 | 0 | 0 | 0 | 0 | 0 | 0 | 3/2 | 0 |
| WALTON G. | 1905 | 1 | 0 | 0 | 0 | 0 | 0 | 0 | 0 | 1 | 0 |
| WALTON J. | 1921 | 7 | 0 | 1 | 0 | 0 | 0 | 0 | 0 | 8 | 0 |
| WANCHOPE P. | 1996-98 | 65/7 | 23 | 4 | 0 | 6/1 | 5 | 0 | 0 | 75/8 | 28 |
| WARD A.S. | 1995-97 | 32/8 | 10 | 2 | 1 | 1/1 | 0 | 0 | 0 | 35/9 | 11 |
| WARD C. | 1884 | 0 | 0 | 1 | 0 | 0 | 0 | 0 | 0 | 1 | 0 |
| WARD T.V. | 1937-50 | 238 | 4 | 22 | 1 | 0 | 0 | 0 | 0 | 260 | 5 |
| WARMBY H. | 1885-87 | 0 | 0 | 9 | 0 | 0 | 0 | 0 | 0 | 9 | 0 |
| WARREN A.R. | 1901 | 8 | 2 | 0 | 0 | 0 | 0 | 0 | 0 | 8 | 2 |
| WARREN B. | 1899-1907 | 242 | 19 | 27 | 14 | 0 | 0 | 0 | 0 | 269 | 33 |
| WARRINGTON J. | 1901-03 | 29 | 7 | 9 | 4 | 0 | 0 | 0 | 0 | 38 | 11 |
| WASSALL D.P.J. | 1992-95 | 90/8 | 0 | 4 | 0 | 9 | 0 | 11 | 0 | 114/8 | 0 |
| WATERHOUSE F. | 1919-20 | 26 | 0 | 2 | 0 | 0 | 0 | 0 | 0 | 28 | 0 |
| WATSON A.F. | 1990 | 5 | 0 | 0 | 0 | 0 | 0 | 0 | 0 | 5 | 0 |
| WATSON D.V. | 1983 | 34 | 1 | 3/2 | 0 | 2 | 0 | 0 | 0 | 39/2 | 1 |
| WAUGH R. | 1912-14 | 28 | 0 | 1 | 1 | 0 | 0 | 0 | 0 | 29 | 1 |
| WEBB D.J. | 1978-79 | 25/1 | 1 | 1 | 0 | 2 | 0 | 0 | 0 | 28/1 | 1 |

| | | LEAGUE | | FA CUP | | FL CUP | | OTHERS | | TOTAL | |
|---|---|---|---|---|---|---|---|---|---|---|---|
| Player | Played | App | Gls | App | Gls | App | Gls | App | Gls | App | Gls |
| WEBB G.H. | 1921 | 2 | 0 | 0 | 0 | 0 | 0 | 0 | 0 | 2 | 0 |
| WEBB J.A. | 1929-36 | 25 | 0 | 0 | 0 | 0 | 0 | 0 | 0 | 25 | 0 |
| WEBSTER R. | 1961-77 | 451/4 | 7 | 30 | 0 | 34 | 0 | 15/1 | 0 | 530/5 | 7 |
| WEBSTER S.P. | 1995 | 3 | 0 | 0 | 0 | 0 | 0 | 0 | 0 | 3 | 0 |
| WEBSTER T.C. | 1948-57 | 172 | 0 | 6 | 0 | 0 | 0 | 0 | 0 | 178 | 0 |
| WEST T. | 2000 | 18 | 0 | 1 | 0 | 1 | 0 | 0 | 0 | 20 | 0 |
| WHEATCROFT F.G. | 1903-04<br>1905<br>1907 | 25 | 8 | 0 | 0 | 0 | 0 | 0 | 0 | 25 | 8 |
| WHEATLEY S.P. | 1951-52 | 4 | 0 | 0 | 0 | 0 | 0 | 0 | 0 | 4 | 0 |
| WHEELER W. | 1910 | 1 | 0 | 0 | 0 | 0 | 0 | 0 | 0 | 1 | 0 |
| WHELAN N.D. | 2003 | 3/5 | 0 | 0 | 0 | 0 | 0 | 0 | 0 | 3/5 | 0 |
| WHITE A. | 1927-31 | 4 | 0 | 0 | 0 | 0 | 0 | 0 | 0 | 4 | 0 |
| WHITE W. | 1955 | 3 | 0 | 0 | 0 | 0 | 0 | 0 | 0 | 3 | 0 |
| WHITEHOUSE J.C. | 1923-28 | 186 | 82 | 14 | 4 | 0 | 0 | 0 | 0 | 200 | 86 |
| WHITTAKER W. | 1903 | 12 | 0 | 0 | 0 | 0 | 0 | 0 | 0 | 12 | 0 |
| WHITTINGHAM P.M. | 2005 | 11 | 0 | 0 | 0 | 0 | 0 | 0 | 0 | 11 | 0 |
| WHYMARK T.J. | 1979 | 2 | 0 | 0 | 0 | 0 | 0 | 0 | 0 | 2 | 0 |
| WICKS S.J. | 1978-79 | 24 | 0 | 0 | 0 | 0 | 0 | 0 | 0 | 24 | 0 |
| WIGHTMAN H. | 1919-27 | 180 | 9 | 9 | 0 | 0 | 0 | 0 | 0 | 189 | 9 |
| WIGNALL F. | 1968-71 | 29/16 | 15 | 3 | 1 | 4/2 | 0 | 3 | 1 | 39/18 | 17 |
| WILCOX G.E. | 1937-46 | 12 | 0 | 0 | 0 | 0 | 0 | 0 | 0 | 12 | 0 |
| WILEMAN S. | 1933-36 | 9 | 1 | 2 | 0 | 0 | 0 | 0 | 0 | 11 | 1 |
| WILKES H.T. | 1927-32 | 208 | 0 | 12 | 0 | 0 | 0 | 0 | 0 | 220 | 0 |
| WILKINS R.J.H. | 1949-53 | 30 | 11 | 0 | 0 | 0 | 0 | 0 | 0 | 30 | 11 |
| WILLEMS H.A.R. | 1995-97 | 41/18 | 13 | 4/2 | 2 | 2 | 1 | 0 | 0 | 47/20 | 16 |
| WILLIAMS D.G. | 1984-91 | 276/1 | 9 | 17 | 0 | 26/1 | 1 | 11 | 0 | 330/2 | 10 |
| WILLIAMS P.D. | 1989-94 | 153/7 | 26 | 8 | 3 | 10/2 | 2 | 14/1 | 2 | 185/10 | 33 |
| WILLIAMS P.J. | 1952 | 2 | 0 | 0 | 0 | 0 | 0 | 0 | 0 | 2 | 0 |
| WILLIAMSON A. | 1885-90 | 41 | 0 | 12 | 1 | 0 | 0 | 0 | 0 | 53 | 1 |
| WILLIAMSON M. | 1961-63 | 12 | 0 | 1 | 0 | 1 | 0 | 0 | 0 | 14 | 0 |
| WILSON A. | 1898 | 1 | 0 | 0 | 0 | 0 | 0 | 0 | 0 | 1 | 0 |
| WILSON A. | 1936 | 1 | 0 | 0 | 0 | 0 | 0 | 0 | 0 | 1 | 0 |
| WILSON C.K. | 1922 | 1 | 0 | 0 | 0 | 0 | 0 | 0 | 0 | 1 | 0 |
| WILSON I.W. | 1990 | 11 | 0 | 0 | 0 | 0 | 0 | 0 | 0 | 11 | 0 |
| WILSON K.J. | 1979-84 | 106/16 | 30 | 8 | 3 | 8/3 | 8 | 0 | 0 | 122/19 | 41 |
| WOMACK A.R. | 1957 | 2 | 0 | 0 | 0 | 0 | 0 | 0 | 0 | 2 | 0 |
| WOMBWELL R. | 1899-1901 | 85 | 17 | 10 | 1 | 0 | 0 | 0 | 0 | 95 | 18 |
| WOOD A.J.E. | 1905-06 | 60 | 2 | 6 | 1 | 0 | 0 | 0 | 0 | 66 | 3 |
| WOOD J. | 1905-06 | 37 | 7 | 3 | 0 | 0 | 0 | 0 | 0 | 40 | 7 |
| WOODHEAD D. | 1955-58 | 94 | 24 | 3 | 1 | 0 | 0 | 0 | 0 | 97 | 25 |
| WOODLEY V.R. | 1945-46 | 30 | 0 | 4 | 0 | 0 | 0 | 0 | 0 | 34 | 0 |
| WOOLLEY A. | 1894 | 6 | 3 | 0 | 0 | 0 | 0 | 0 | 0 | 6 | 3 |
| WRACK D. | 1994-95 | 4/22 | 1 | 0/2 | 0 | 0/3 | 0 | 0 | 0 | 4/27 | 1 |
| WRIGHT A.G. | 2005 | 7 | 0 | 0 | 0 | 0 | 0 | 0 | 0 | 7 | 0 |
| WRIGHT H.D. | 1910-11 | 15 | 2 | 1 | 0 | 0 | 0 | 0 | 0 | 16 | 2 |
| WRIGHT H.E. | 1937-38 | 25 | 0 | 1 | 0 | 0 | 0 | 0 | 0 | 26 | 0 |
| WRIGHT L.G. | 1888 | 4 | 1 | 0 | 0 | 0 | 0 | 0 | 0 | 4 | 1 |
| WRIGHT M. | 1987-90 | 144 | 10 | 5 | 0 | 15 | 0 | 7 | 0 | 171 | 10 |
| WRIGHT P.D.J. | 1967 | 12/1 | 0 | 0 | 0 | 0 | 0 | 0 | 0 | 12/1 | 0 |
| WYER P.W. | 1956 | 2 | 1 | 0 | 0 | 0 | 0 | 0 | 0 | 2 | 1 |
| YATES D.R. | 1994-97 | 65/3 | 3 | 3 | 0 | 3 | 0 | 0 | 0 | 71/3 | 3 |
| YORK C.H. | 1902-03 | 24 | 6 | 3 | 0 | 0 | 0 | 0 | 0 | 27 | 6 |
| YOUNG G.R. | 1953-65 | 253/1 | 5 | 6 | 0 | 9 | 0 | 0 | 0 | 268/1 | 5 |
| ZAVAGNO L. | 2001-03 | 48/4 | 3 | 2/1 | 0 | 0 | 0 | 0 | 0 | 50/5 | 3 |

5625278R00265

Printed in Great Britain
by Amazon.co.uk, Ltd.,
Marston Gate.